PRESIDENTIAL PROFILES
THE TRUMAN YEARS

Tracy S. Uebelhor

Facts On File
An imprint of Infobase Publishing

Presidential Profiles: The Truman Years

Copyright © 2006 by Tracy S. Uebelhor

Facts On File, Inc.
An imprint of Infobase Publishing
132 West 31st Street
New York NY 10001

Library of Congress Cataloging-in-Publication Data

Uebelhor, Tracy S.
   The Truman Years/Tracy Uebelhor.
      p. cm.—(Presidential profiles)
   Includes bibliographical references and index.
   ISBN 0-8160-5490-8 (alk. paper)
   1. Truman, Harry S., 1884–1972—Friends and associates. 2. Truman, Harry
      S., 1884–1972. Politicians—United States—Biography. 3. United States—
      Politics and government—1945–1953. 4. United States-History—1945—
      Biography. 5. United States—Biography. I. Title. II. Presidential profiles
      (Facts On File, Inc.)
   E747.U34 2005
   973.918/092/2 B22   2004063240

Text design by Mary Susan Ryan-Flynn
Cover design by Nora Wertz

Printed in the United States of America

VB Hermitage 10 9 8 7 6 5 4 3 2 1

This book is printed on acid-free paper.

CONTENTS

CONTRIBUTORS

Catherine A. Barnes
Columbia University

James Lewis Baughman
Columbia University

Jason Berger
University of Virginia

Scott R. Bernarde
University of Missouri

Mel L. Bernstine
New York University

David Billington

Rachel Burd
City University of New York

Susan B. Burns
Catholic University

Gregory Bush
Columbia University

John D'Emilio
Columbia Univeristy

Donna G. Ellaby
New School for Social Research

Diane A. Elliot
University of Michigan

Elliot Figman
University of Massachusetts

Jefferson Flanders
Harvard College

Stephen Flanders
Brown University

Beth Friend
State University of New York,
Stony Brook

Loren Goldner
University of California,
Berkeley

Rebecca S. Greene
Columbia University

Thomas L. Harrison
Columbia University

Clark S. Judge
Harvard University

Thomas M. Leonard
American University

Herbert M. Levine
Columbia University

Linda L. Moot
University of Pennsylvania

Margo Nash
Hunter College

Thomas O'Brien
New York University

Michael Quinn
State University of New York,
Binghamton

David M. Rosen
Rutgers University

Arthur E. Scherr
Columbia University

Glenn M. Speer
Rutgers University

Martin J. Swanson
University of Virginia

Todd F. Swanstrom
Washington University

Susan J. Tracy
University of Massachusetts

PREFACE

The Truman Years is a revised volume in Facts On File's Presidential Profiles series. It contains more than 400 biographies of individuals who contributed to American political discourse during the presidency of Harry S Truman. Many entries are about people who worked in the Truman administration. Others are about prominent congressional representatives and senators, justices of the Supreme Court, and influential state or local officials whose activities had a national impact. There are entries for people who never held office but nonetheless were politically significant. They include journalists and business, union, and civil rights leaders.

Each entry begins with the person's name, date of birth, and, if appropriate, date of death, followed by the title of the most significant office held or the occupation for which the individual was most famous during the Truman era. The biography contains a discussion of the individual's career, stressing activities during the years 1945 to 1953. There is also significant information about the individual's life before and, when appropriate, after the Truman period. Each biography indicates the person's major accomplishments as well as his or her influence on domestic or foreign affairs. A parenthetical reference notes if there is another biography for that person in a preceding or succeeding volume in the Presidential Profiles series.

Many of these entries are significantly revised versions of the biographies that appeared in the original edition. Virtually all have new information that carries the biography, as appropriate, up to the end of the person's life, the end of his or her career, or to the early 21st century. The release of many documents during the past 60 years and the publication of new secondary works on the Truman period provided new information or interpretations that have been included in many of the biographies.

The Truman Years contains several useful appendices. The chronology lists many important developments in politics, the cold war, and the Korean War, among other subjects. There is a list of members of Congress who served while Truman was president, as well as rosters of officials in cabinet departments and principal regulatory agencies, justices of the Supreme Court, and state governors. A selection of primary documents includes several of Truman's major speeches and a transcript of two of his news conferences. Also included is the Potsdam Declaration, George Kennan's long telegram, which spelled out the containment policy that guided American foreign policymakers to the end of the cold war, and a portion of NSC-68, the National Security Council report that recommended a large buildup in conventional arms to meet the Soviet threat. The final appendix is a selected bibliography.

The author owes a debt of gratitude to others who helped bring this volume to fruition. Owen Lancer, Facts On File editor-in-chief for history and political science, was supportive, kind, and patient. Dr. Robert H. Ferrell, the dean of Truman scholars, gave helpful suggestions on the introduction. My mother, Jo Ann Uebelhor, often gave encouragement. I hope readers will find *The Truman Years* a useful reference work on the events and people of an era that had a great impact on American and world history.

INTRODUCTION

The voice on the other end of the line sounded tense, Harry S Truman would later remember. The vice president was returning a telephone call from President Franklin D. Roosevelt's press secretary, Steve Early, just after entering Speaker of the House Sam T. Rayburn's hideaway on Capitol Hill. Early told the vice president to come to the White House through the front gate. Truman rushed back to his office to grab his hat and hurried off to the Executive Mansion. When he arrived there First Lady Eleanor Roosevelt informed him that the president had died. Somewhat dumbfounded by the news, Truman asked, "Is there anything I can do for you?" She responded, "Is there anything we can do for you? For you are the one in trouble now."

At first Truman was unsure of himself. He told Senator George D. Aiken, "I'm not big enough, I'm not big enough for this job." He asked reporters to pray for him and inquired whether a load of hay had ever fallen on them, saying that, when he was given the news of Roosevelt's passing, he felt like "the moon, the stars, and all the planets had fallen" on him. Senate Majority Leader Alben W. Barkley tried to buck him up by telling him, "Have confidence in yourself. If you do not, the people will lose confidence in you." Rayburn and former vice president John Nance Garner thought Truman would make a fine president. But others did not. The head of the Tennessee Valley Authority, David E. Lilienthal, exclaimed, "The country and the world don't deserve to be left this way." In Europe, Generals Dwight D. Eisenhower, Omar Bradley, and George S. Patton, Jr., discussed the situation. Bradley later wrote, "From a distance Truman did not appear at all qualified to fill Roosevelt's large shoes." Patton was acerbic in his dismissal: "It seems very unfortunate that in order to secure political preference, people are made Vice President who are never intended, neither by Party nor by the Lord to be Presidents." But the job was his.

The date Truman took the oath was April 12, 1945—nearly 80 years to the day when another wartime American president passed on before the strife was ended. Allied armies were pressing in on German forces in Europe, the Soviets from the east and the British and the Americans from the west. They would meet up within days on the Elbe River. Meanwhile Adolf Hitler awaited in his bunker some miracle to deliver him from his enemies. (Though mistaken, he thought the death of Roosevelt was that miracle.) On April 30, as Russian forces edged toward his underground hideaway, the führer would kill himself with a combination of gunshot and cyanide. Only a few days later Germany surrendered unconditionally.

Harry Truman in uniform as a member of the Missouri National Guard, 1907 *(Harry S. Truman Library)*

Meanwhile in the Pacific the war with Japan dragged on. The Okinawa campaign had become a bloodbath. Japanese soldiers and civilians fanatically resisted the Americans, and, when all else failed, they committed suicide rather than capitulate. Offshore, Japanese kamikaze bombers smashed into American vessels, sinking many and killing thousands of U.S. sailors. U.S. leaders worried that the bitter-end resistance of the Japanese as the Americans approached their home islands would lead to potentially heavy casualties among their forces as they invaded the last redoubt of Emperor Hirohito's army and navy. Truman made the awesome decision, based on predictions of rampant death, to deploy the most destructive weapon known to man at that time: the atomic bomb. A successful test of such a device in the New Mexico desert gave the president the confidence to use the two weapons at his disposal. On August 6 an American B-29 bomber, the *Enola Gay*, lifted off from its airfield in the Marianas headed toward the city of Hiroshima. The bomb detonated high above the metropolis, killing tens of thousands instantly; many more thousands would die of radioactive poisoning in the weeks and months to come. Three days later another bomb exploded over the city of Nagasaki. A few days after that, following a vague guarantee by U.S. authorities that the emperor would not have to abdicate, the Japanese surrendered.

After taking office Truman surrounded himself with familiar faces. He brought Representative Clinton P. Anderson and Senator Lewis B. Schwellenbach into the cabinet, as secretary of agriculture and secretary of labor, respectively. Anderson possessed a good grasp of farm policy, but Schwellenbach knew nothing of labor relations, and the president relied on an aide, John Steelman, to deal with the strikes that would become epidemic in 1945–46. He named an old political friend, Representative Fred M. Vinson, to be director of the Office of War Mobilization (OWM), and he soon made him secretary of the Treasury, replacing Henry Morgenthau, whom Truman held in low regard. Truman made Vinson chief justice in 1946 following the death of John Harlan Stone. To replace Vinson as OWM director and then as secretary of the Treasury, Truman hired a banker and friend from the president's time in the army reserve, John W. Snyder. Tom C. Clark, a Justice Department official who had assisted Truman's investiga-

tion of the defense program, became attorney general while a former aide, Charles S. Murphy, would become the president's point man with Congress. Former Senate aides James K. Vardaman and Harry Vaughan were appointed his naval and military aides. Vardaman quickly made a nuisance of himself, and he was elevated to the Federal Reserve Board—a position for which he was hardly qualified. Replacing him as naval aide was Clark Clifford, who would soon become White House counsel and a key figure in the administration. Vaughan would prove an embarrassment, but Truman stuck by him despite his behavior.

Liberals were seriously disappointed by Truman's selections. They seemed little men, not of the stature of Roosevelt's appointees. Worse, from their perspective, Truman retained very few of those officials who stood by the side of the great FDR. Truman himself thought very little of ideological liberals; he preferred pragmatic persons who would get things done and who understood politics. But he did keep some of Roosevelt's people. W. Averell Harriman was retained as ambassador to Moscow and he eventually became secretary of commerce. Curmudgeon Harold L. Ickes remained at the Department of the Interior, and an ailing Harry L. Hopkins stayed long enough to patch over a rough spot with Moscow in the early days of Truman's term. Henry A. Wallace, the darling of the liberals, would remain for a time as head of the Commerce Department, until he and the president parted ways over relations with the Soviet Union.

With the war won, the question arose: Would the United States win the peace both at home and abroad? Because of the need for reconversion of the domestic economy to peacetime pursuits, Truman tried to give guidance by proposing, in 1945, a twenty-one-point program that included a higher minimum wage, more federal public housing, among other social welfare proposals. Disappointed conservatives complained that Truman was proving to be as liberal as Roosevelt, and Congress would fail to approve much of his program.

Other issues also concerned the president. At home, wage and price controls had kept a lid on the economy for over three years. But now workers wanted higher wages as production slackened and the number of hours they worked declined. Workers at General Motors and oil refineries went off

Harry Truman in his army uniform during World War I, 1917 *(Harry S. Truman Library)*

the job in autumn 1945. Then, like a cascade, other unions followed: steelworkers, coal miners, railway trainmen, locomotive engineers, and more. At the height of the strike wave one million people had walked off the job. Truman seized the coal mines and the railroads to avert strikes. The shutdowns occurred anyway. Exasperated, Truman asked Congress to draft into the army those who were striking against the government. The move was aimed specifically at the striking railway workers, whose action had paralyzed the nation. During his address to Congress, Senate secretary Leslie Biffle handed him a note saying the strike had been settled. The assembled legislators roared in celebration, but Truman did not retract his proposal to draft the strikers. The House passed the bill by an overwhelming margin. In the Senate, however, conservative Robert A. Taft (R-Ohio) opposed the

action as unconstitutional, and some liberals also voiced objections. The bill went down to defeat as the railways began operating. Shortly after the rail strike ended, the coal walkout was settled. John L. Lewis, president of the United Mine Workers and a man whom Truman loathed at the time, won for his men a pay raise of 18-and-a-half cents an hour and a 5-cent royalty on every ton of coal mined to go to a welfare fund. The public had wholeheartedly cheered the president's action to break the railway strike, but labor leaders vowed revenge. The head of the Brotherhood of Railway Trainmen, A. F. Whitney, proclaimed he would empty the union's vaults in an effort to retire Truman if he ran in 1948 for a full term as president.

The public's approval of Truman would not last long. Whereas workers had wanted higher wages, businesses wanted price ceilings removed, both on principle and to boost profits. The administration had lifted caps on certain prices, such as for steel, to end the strikes, as businesses demanded compensation for wage hikes. In addition, during the last two years of the war Americans had saved 25 percent of their take-home pay, actions that amounted to a dam ready to burst in an economy still retooling for peacetime consumer goods. John Snyder at the Office of War Mobilization and Reconversion supported business in its desire to raise prices, whereas the director of the Office of Price Administration (OPA), Chester Bowles, a Roosevelt holdover and the sort of liberal Truman disliked, wanted to hold the line on prices. Congress passed a bill in 1946 that weakened the OPA dramatically. Rayburn told Truman he could not get a stronger bill through, and Snyder urged the president to sign the bill. Truman faced a problem. If he did not sign the bill, controls would end on June 30 and prices would skyrocket. If he did sign, the weakened condition of the OPA would ensure that inflation would occur anyway. The question was: would the people blame the president or Congress? Truman decided to veto the bill. Prices, of course, began to soar. Within a week food prices shot up 16 percent on average. Other prices also climbed rapidly. The increase in rents angered people the most. Congress pushed through a bill to re-create a feebler OPA. Truman decided to sign this bill.

Farmers and ranchers, however, refused to sell their goods under the price ceilings. Meat and other products became scarce; butcher shops closed and the black market revived. Democrats began to press the president to lift controls so shelves would be full again, and Rayburn fretted over "a damn beefsteak election." Truman withstood the pressure for a time, but in mid-October he capitulated and lifted the controls on meat. But it was too late. Republicans in the mid-term elections ran on the slogan "Had enough?" and they captured the House of Representatives and the Senate.

In foreign affairs, the immediate postwar years (1945–46) would witness a decline in relations between the United States and the USSR. Soviet forces occupied Eastern Europe and there was little the Western allies could do to counter their presence except to secure consent by the Soviets to hold elections in Poland after the war. The agreements were so loosely defined that they gave the Russians a virtual carte blanche in Eastern Europe, but, at first, most Americans did not read them that way. At Potsdam, Truman believed he could work with Soviet dictator Joseph Stalin, comparing him to political bosses at home; still, the Soviets did not bend in their objectives. Secretary of State James F. Byrnes's attempt to reach an agreement with the Soviets at the London Conference in autumn 1945 failed. In Moscow later that year, Byrnes tried to appease the Russians by bargaining over the composition of governments in Romania and Bulgaria. The Soviets agreed to allow token representatives of other parties within the governments of these nations and the United States granted them recognition. But Senator Arthur H. Vandenberg (R-Mich.) was outraged, and Truman was also annoyed because the secretary had not kept him up to date on the details of the negotiations.

Then, on February 9, 1946, Stalin gave a speech in which he affirmed that wars were inevitable in a capitalist-dominated world and would occur until communism triumphed. Americans looked upon the speech with grim foreboding. Harriman exclaimed that the Soviets were intent on expanding the borders of communism. One man who tried to sort things out for the administration was the chargé d'affaires in Moscow, George F. Kennan, who sent a lengthy cable to Washington in response to a query from the Treasury Department. The "long telegram," as it became known, set down the reasons for Soviet behavior. Kennan argued that Russian governments—czarist as well as Bolshevik—historically had needed enemies abroad to justify authoritarian rule at home. This mind-set made

negotiations pointless for the time being. The United States would have to contain the Soviets until internal pressures within their society brought about the changes that would make negotiations worthwhile.

Kennan's telegram accelerated a trend already occurring in the administration—a movement toward implementing a harsh line toward the Russians. Byrnes gave a tough speech on February 28 in New York, saying Americans could not permit "force or threat of force" to be employed "contrary to the purposes and principles" of the United Nations Charter. He talked about nations (obviously the Soviet Union) that occupied another country without that country's authorization and seized enemy property before a reparations settlement was agreed to. On March 5 former British prime minister Winston Churchill gave his Iron Curtain speech in Fulton, Missouri. Truman, who sat on the dais with Churchill, had approved the address in advance (although he did distance himself from it after some objected to it as too strident). When the Soviets remained in Iran, which had been occupied by the Allies during the war, beyond a scheduled withdrawal deadline of March 2, 1946, Byrnes sent increasingly harsh public notes to Moscow and moved to put the Iranian issue before the UN Security Council. Byrnes action irked Moscow, but the Soviets—after securing an oil concession from the Iranians—withdrew from the country. (The Iranians later reneged on the deal.)

Foreign policy caused a row at home in 1946 too. In September, Secretary of Commerce Wallace, increasingly worried about the course of American-Soviet relations, showed Truman a speech he was planning to give at a Soviet-American friendship rally in Madison Square Garden. Distracted by domestic problems, Truman read the speech, and failing to see it contradicted administration policy, gave it his approval. When asked about the pending speech at a press conference, the president said the address represented administration policy. However, the speech endorsed a Soviet sphere of influence over Eastern Europe, a policy that the administration emphatically did not endorse. After Wallace gave the speech, Byrnes told Truman either he or Wallace would have to go. The president tried for a time to keep both men in the administration, but, when he had to choose, he went with Byrnes. Now Wallace, finding himself outside the administration, would be a burr under its saddle for the next two years.

The administration continued its hard line in 1947. In January Byrnes, fearing for his health, stepped aside as secretary of state and was replaced by General George C. Marshall. Marshall, "the true organizer of victory," as Churchill called him, had earned a reputation as chief of staff of the U.S. Army for promoting men of the highest competence during the war, a feat that helped lead the United States to victory. Marshall became secretary of state at a time when the burdens of the world seemed to fall on America's shoulders. On February 21, 1947, Great Britain announced that it would end economic and military aid to Greece and Turkey in six weeks. The preeminence of British influence in the eastern Mediterranean was coming to a close, and the central question was: Would the United States take up the burden? The unpopular but pro-Western government in Greece was fighting a communist insurgency backed by Marxist-ruled Yugoslavia, Bulgaria, and Albania while the Soviet Union pressed Turkey for joint control of the Bosphorus and Dardanelles straits.

On February 27 Truman, Marshall, and Undersecretary of State Dean G. Acheson met with congressional leaders to discuss the crisis. Marshall asserted that if either Greece or Turkey fell behind the Iron Curtain, the rest of Europe, the Middle East, and Asia were endangered. Acheson, who believed that Marshall had not made the administration case with sufficient forcefulness, reiterated the secretary's warning, but he was much more strident and alarmist in his remarks. The foreign policy leader of the Republican Party in the Senate, Senator Vandenberg, told Truman, "Mr. President, if you will say that to the Congress and the country, I will support you and I believe that most of its members will do the same." Truman went before a joint session of Congress, and, although he did not mention the Soviet Union directly, it was clear to whom he was aiming his remarks. Admitting that the Greek government was not an ideal democracy, he contended that it could be improved and that the United States must help "free peoples who are resisting attempted subjugation by armed minorities or by outside pressures." The policy became known as the Truman Doctrine. Employing stark rhetoric, the president convinced enough Republicans—who wanted to cut spending and taxes—to approve $400 million in aid. Truman had stressed that economic and political aid should constitute the focus of U.S. efforts, and Acheson and Vandenberg emphasized to

the senators that the United States was not taking on a worldwide commitment, even though in the years to come the United States would move in that direction.

In 1947 the Truman administration took on a wider commitment beyond provision of Greek and Turkish aid. The war had devastated much of Europe and the winter of 1946–47 had been particularly bitter. Starvation loomed and, behind that, lurked the possibility of communist subjugation, if not from without then from within. In late May communists seized control of Hungary, making the issue all the more urgent. In June Marshall, in delivering comments after the commencement ceremony at Harvard University, called for a comprehensive aid program to Europe to be founded on cooperation among nations. The Marshall Plan, as Truman insisted it be called, aimed to put Western Europe on the road toward economic unification and material prosperity, which would lessen ancient national animosities. The hope was that the aid would help Western European countries to recover economically and, by so doing, to avoid the rise to power of local communist Parties. But to avoid the stigma of seeking to divide the Continent, Marshall offered aid to all of war-torn Europe, including the Soviet Union and its satellite states. The administration, however, placed such conditions on the offer that the Soviets rejected it. This made it easier for the Republican-controlled Congress to later vote for the implementing funds.

The administration also made the rehabilitation of Germany part of the aid program. Truman received a report from former president Herbert C. Hoover stating that the recovery of Europe's economy depended upon the restoration to economic health of Germany. This would require an economic union of the U.S., British, and French occupation zones in western Germany, which was completed by autumn 1947.

The Soviet Union did not allow its satellites to accept aid. Western European nations, on the other hand, grasped the lifeline Marshall provided with alacrity. They collectively asked for an impossible $29 billion spread over four years. The administration reduced that figure to $17.8 billion, but Republicans and many Democrats balked at such a price tag. Representatives and senators debated the Marshall Plan during the winter of 1947–48. Isolationists on the right objected to its costs and to the amount of commitment it would require. On the far left there were complaints that the program was designed to intentionally undermine cooperation with the Soviet Union. Still, congressmen who returned from visits to Europe came back with heart-rending stories of starvation and deprivation. Then in March 1948 Communists staged a coup in Czechoslovakia. A month later Congress passed the European Recovery Plan (as the Marshall Plan was officially called) with a 15-month appropriation of $6.8 billion. In all, between 1948 and 1952, when the program was terminated, $13.34 billion in aid went to Western Europe, assisting the region in engineering a remarkable economic comeback.

In June 1948, in the continuing effort to unite economically the western occupation zones of Germany, the United States, Britain, and France, introduced a new currency there. The Soviets condemned the move and shut down land and water access to the Western allies' zones in Berlin. Truman said the United States would stay in Berlin. But he decided against pushing an armed column down the autobahn through the Soviet zone in Germany to the city, as some officials were advising him. Instead, he initiated an airlift of food and fuel to the beleaguered city. He also dispatched three squadrons of B-29 bombers to England, although, this was something of a bluff as the planes were not fitted for atomic bombs.

Truman, however, did not want to rely on U.S. military might to deter the Soviets. He was determined to keep defense spending down and balance the budget. He wanted to rely chiefly on foreign aid, both economic and military, to fend off the Soviets. He was traditional in his belief in fiscal responsibility, thinking it was critical to balance the federal budget. Under Truman there were four years of surpluses and four of deficits.

Truman's main concern regarding the U.S. military was to achieve a unification of the services. In 1947 Congress passed the National Defense Act, which created the Office of the Secretary of Defense and the National Military Establishment, the National Security Council, and the Central Intelligence Agency. On the insistence of Secretary of the Navy James V. Forrestal, the defense secretary was merely to coordinate policy while the heads of the departments of the army, navy, and newly created air force, would have subcabinet rank with direct access to the president. Truman appointed Forrestal as the first defense secretary, and he quickly realized the deficiencies of the system he helped design. The

services continued their quarreling over an ever-shrinking defense budget and Forrestal did not have the power to stop the interservice conflicts. He then began to push for a stronger defense secretary and to reduce the power of the service secretaries to that of mere administrative positions without cabinet rank. The National Defense Act of 1949 achieved this goal while also mandating creation of the Department of Defense. Forrestal, who was suffering from exhaustion and who would later commit suicide, was replaced as defense secretary by Louis A. Johnson, who had been an assistant secretary of war during the Roosevelt administration and who had helped raise money for Truman's presidential campaign in 1948. Johnson, a bumptious character, sided with the air force in the division of budget funds, by supporting the building of the B-36 bomber and scrapping the navy's super carrier, which was already under construction. This action would lead to the "Revolt of the Admirals" when naval officers protested in claiming that the B-36 was an ineffective weapon. Chief of Naval Operations Louis E. Denfeld was ousted for his refusal to support the administration's policy.

On the domestic front, Truman had a difficult time dealing with the Republican 80th Congress, elected in 1946. The House of Representatives was headed by Joseph W. Martin, Jr., of Massachusetts, a man who excelled in backroom bargaining and political maneuvering. On the Senate side the effective leader of the Republicans on domestic issues was Robert A. Taft of Ohio. Intelligent and deeply partisan, Taft was a conservative on most issues, although he did support public housing and federal aid to education. On foreign affairs he was skeptical of foreign entanglements.

One of the Republicans celebrated causes in the 80th Congress was labor reform. The strikes of 1945–46 convinced Republicans and many other Americans that labor unions had become too powerful and had to be reined in. On the House side, the Labor Committee under Chairman Fred A. Hartley, Jr., of New Jersey pushed out a bill that clipped the wings of unions, including outlawing industrywide bargaining. On the Senate side, Taft, who chaired the Senate Labor Committee, produced a more moderate bill, which union leaders still denounced. The final bill allowed industrywide bargaining but gave the president the power to seek an injunction to postpone strikes in vital industries for an 80-day cooling-off period. It also listed unfair union practices that would now be illegal; banned union contributions to candidates for federal office; outlawed the closed shop, where potential employees had to be members of a union to be hired; and allowed states to prohibit union shops, where workers had to join a union after they were hired. Truman vetoed the measure as too extreme, but Congress overrode his veto. The president's action won back the union support he had lost following his actions in the wake of the rail strike. (Whitney would become a fervent supporter of Truman in 1948.)

The Republicans also wanted tax cuts. Truman feared that such cuts would be inflationary, and he disapproved that the proposed cuts would extend to those in the highest income brackets. He vetoed two tax-cutting bills in 1947 and, in 1948, proposed a $40 "cost of living" credit for each taxpayer and dependent. Congressional Republicans rejected the proposal and, in a compromise with Democrats, passed a tax reduction measure, which Truman vetoed and which Congress subsequently overrode. The law raised the exemption for taxpayers from $500 to $600 and allowed married couples to file joint returns and, in so doing, in effect to split their incomes. These and other modifications were estimated to reduce taxes by $4.8 billion.

Also in the aftermath of former Soviet agent Elizabeth Bentley's revelation of spying in the federal government, Republicans also pushed for an internal government security program to vet employees for loyalty risks. To offset this move, Truman somewhat reluctantly introduced a program to investigate civil servants for their political beliefs. Arguably such a program was justifiable given that after the war there were revelations of spying in Canada and accusations of such in the United States. But the program was administered in a rather unjust fashion. Civil servants who had no access to vital security information were investigated. Employees with liberal leanings on issues were immediately suspect, and individuals on occasion would be accused of being a communist, not for reasons that held any basis in truth, but rather because of personal animosity by the accuser. For instance, the accused were denied fundamental due process procedures, such as the right to cross-examine accusers. From a constitutional standpoint it could be and was argued that there is no right to governmental employment. But from a standpoint of basic justice, not to mention effectiveness, such safeguards would have made sense.

Civil rights constituted another domestic issue the president tackled at this time. Truman became the first president to speak to the National Association for the Advancement of Colored People in 1947, when he told the group that the federal government had to take the lead in protecting civil rights. In October Truman received a report titled *To Secure These Rights* from a committee he appointed to look into the issue. The document called for federal antilynching laws, abolition of the poll tax, voting rights legislation, a permanent Fair Employment Practices Committee, desegregation of the military, a civil rights division in the Justice Department, administration backing for civil rights suits in federal courts, and the founding of a Commission on Civil Rights. The president sent to Congress these civil rights proposals, but Southern Democrats and most Republicans would not countenance such recommendations. Faced with congressional rejection, Truman, on his own authority, desegregated the military, despite the objections of some senior officers. The Justice Department filed an amicus curiae brief in the case of *Shelly v. Kraemer*, which dealt with the question of whether restrictive housing covenants could be enforced in court. The Supreme Court would rule such covenants unconstitutional.

But the civil rights program cost Truman politically. Southern Democrats were in an uproar and only a minority of non-southern whites supported it. By early 1948, Truman's approval ratings were again declining. His political problems were compounded by the fact that Henry Wallace had, in late 1947, announced he would run for the presidency as the candidate of a newly formed Progressive Party. Wallace advocated a conciliatory foreign policy toward the Soviets as well as sweeping social welfare reform measures at home. Democrats of all persuasions began a drive to draft General Dwight D. Eisenhower, the hero of D day, for the Democratic presidential nomination. Eisenhower played coy for a time before making a (somewhat) Sherman-like statement against accepting the nomination.

The issue of a Jewish homeland constituted yet another political headache for the president. Palestine had been a British mandate since the end of World War I. But terrorist attacks against British authorities waged by those who wanted to establish a Jewish national state caused Great Britain to declare, in February 1947, that it would cede to the United Nations the authority to solve the vexing problem of rising Jewish-Arab tensions and that it

Harry S Truman being sworn in as the Jackson County, Missouri, presiding judge, 1931 *(Harry S. Truman Library)*

would relinquish its mandate. The UN General Assembly voted on November 29, 1947, for a partition of Palestine between Arabs and Jews. Arabs bitterly rejected the proposal and fighting soon broke out between the two peoples. The British government declared it would end its mandate on May 15, 1948.

Truman was caught in a difficult situation. The administration supported partition, in part for moral reasons, but also in part for political reasons. American Jews would be grateful to Truman for his support for the creation of a Jewish nation. But the State Department opposed the move, preferring a UN trusteeship over the area for fear of alienating oil-rich Arab nations. The UN Security Council also declared itself unwilling to accept partition as the solution. Marshall proposed a backup position to make Palestine a UN trusteeship in case partition proved impossible to carry out. When the administration announced this decision, Jewish leaders denounced it. White House Counsel Clark Clifford tried to convince Marshall that partition had to be accepted as the fighting in Palestine had made it, in

fact, a reality and thus the United States was duty bound to recognize the new Jewish state when it was declared. However, Marshall preferred to stay with the trusteeship idea and said to do otherwise would be blatantly political. He declared that he would break his personal vow of not voting, and if Truman recognized the Jewish state, he would vote against Truman in the upcoming election. A break between the president and the secretary of state would be disastrous to the administration's attempt to win support for the Marshall Plan and Truman retreated. In addition, he did not like disagreeing with Marshall, a man he revered above all others. But Clifford, working through Undersecretary of State Robert A. Lovett, managed to convince Marshall to acquiesce in the decision to extend de facto recognition to Israel when independence was declared on May 15 (May 14, Washington time).

Truman may have won the hearts and minds of most Jewish voters in 1948, but he still looked like a sure loser for the presidential election. The Republicans nominated moderate and internationalist governor Thomas E. Dewey of New York as their nominee, and the polls put Dewey in the lead after his nomination. The Democrats, dispirited, met in the same hall in Philadelphia where the Republicans had gathered two weeks earlier. The convention hall was sweltering hot, and a fight over the platform's civil rights plank occurred. Northern liberals pushed through a much stronger proposal than the southerners could stomach, with the result that the Mississippi and part of the Alabama delegations stormed out when it came time to nominate the presidential candidate. They and other southern dissidents would form the States' Rights Democratic Party (Dixiecrats) and nominate South Carolina governor J. Strom Thurmond as their presidential candidate.

To counter the dispirited sentiments of the Democratic delegates in Philadelphia, Truman gave a fiery acceptance speech that brought the delegates to cheers. In the speech the president basically laid out his campaign plan. Instead of running against Dewey he would run against the 80th Congress, which he deemed reactionary and which he said would take the country back to the boom and bust days of the 1920s, leading the country into another depression. He blasted the Republicans for cutting taxes for the rich, for the Taft-Hartley law, and for cutting funding for farm programs. Some of his attacks on the campaign trail were demagogic, claiming that the Republicans had stuck a pitchfork into the back of the farmer, for instance. He even made a comparison between the Republicans and Hitler, Mussolini, and Tojo. Meanwhile, guided by polls and afraid to alienate the different factions of the GOP, Dewey gave vague speeches filled with platitudes.

Still, most people believed Truman would lose. The last Gallup poll before the election, based on interviews taking between October 15 and 25, showed Dewey with a commanding lead. In the end, undecided voters surged to Truman in the last days of the campaign, and he pulled off what was considered a remarkable upset. Still, given that registered Democrats vastly outnumbered Republicans, it was Truman's election to lose, which he almost did. The president was able to stitch together Roosevelt's winning coalition of northern liberals, middle-income Americans, union and ethnic working-class voters, African Americans, plus enough southerners to win. Critically he won back farmers, who had drifted back to the Republican Party in the 1940s, by playing on their fears of cutbacks in farm programs. In traveling back to Washington from Independence, Missouri, where he voted, someone in St. Louis handed him a copy of the conservative *Chicago Tribune* with its famous premature headline "Dewey Defeats Truman." Standing on the rear platform of the presidential train, the *Ferdinand Magellan*, Truman grinned triumphantly as he held the paper up for the press and photographers to see.

After winning a second term Truman went before Congress in early 1949 and called for a "Fair Deal" for all Americans. His proposals were much the same as in 1945: a higher minimum wage, an extension of Social Security, more federal public housing, and national health insurance, among other requests. He also reiterated his demand made the year before for civil rights legislation. Congressmen were willing to build upon New Deal programs and raise the minimum wage, extend Social Security to groups heretofore not covered, and even fund more public housing. However, they were not willing to create large new programs like national health insurance, which never got of committee; nor were they willing to break the inevitable southern filibuster in the Senate to pass civil rights legislation.

In foreign affairs the administration continued the Berlin airlift until the Soviets agreed to end the blockade on the condition the West would hold a summit over the future of Germany. The conference made no headway in resolving differences between the West and the Russians, and soon West Germany declared itself a sovereign state, as did East Germany. Germany would remain divided for the next four decades.

Partly in response to the aggressive moves of the Soviets in 1948, Western European countries had formed a defensive alliance, the Western European Union. In 1949 the United States joined with these nations to form the North Atlantic Treaty Organization, another defensive alliance—the first such joined by Americans in peacetime. The United States also began to produce more atomic bombs in an effort to make its deterrent power more credible.

But then in September, the administration discovered that the Soviets had exploded an atomic device; the U.S. nuclear monopoly was over. A month later Chinese Communists won control of mainland China. Conservatives argued that the administration was responsible because it had not supported the pro-Western Chinese Nationalists strongly enough. A great deal of uncertainty and fear surrounded the aftermath of these events. In addition, scientist Klaus Fuchs, who had worked on the Manhattan Project, was arrested in Britain for passing atomic secrets to the Soviets. In early 1950 Alger Hiss, a former State Department official accused by former Communist Whittaker Chambers, was convicted of lying under oath that he was not a Communist agent. Julius and Ethel Rosenberg were arrested for passing atomic secrets to the Soviets. (Later it was shown through decrypts of messages from the Soviet embassy and consulates that Hiss and the Rosenbergs were in fact spies.) In February 1950 Senator Joseph R. McCarthy (R-Wisc.) claimed there was a Communist conspiracy at work in the State Department. He offered no credible proof, but, given ongoing events, many people were willing to believe him. A Senate investigation into his accusations showed them to be false, but the proceedings had degenerated into such a partisan brawl that many people did not see its findings as credible. McCarthy and like-minded members of Congress would bedevil the administration until Truman left office.

The Soviet atomic test and the fall of China also led Truman to order the development of the hydrogen bomb and a reevaluation of U.S. foreign policy. Defense and State Department officials worked together, despite the animosity shown by the new secretary of defense, Louis Johnson, toward the new secretary of state, Dean Acheson, who had replaced Marshall when he resigned in early 1949, and succeeded in producing National Security Council Paper 68, or simply NSC-68. In it the authors argued that the Soviets, now possessed of the initiative, were bent on a worldwide program of aggressive expansionism. To prevent such a dangerous event from occurring, these officials recommended a conventional military buildup. However, Truman, still very much concerned to keep the budget in balance, resisted calls to increase defense spending.

Truman's decision to keep defense outlays down would prove costly. On June 24, 1950, Acheson called the president, who was in Independence, and informed him that Communist North Korea had invaded pro-Western South Korea. A total of 150 North Korean tanks and 90,000 soldiers crossed the border on June 25, 1950 (Korean time). It was the gravest crisis yet of the cold war. Truman believed that Stalin had ordered the invasion in order to test U.S. resolve. Stalin had in fact approved the invasion going forward, but only on the pleading of North Korean dictator Kim Il Sung. A civil war between the North and the South had been going on since

the end of World War II. The two countries originated from the division of the peninsula at the 38th parallel into separate American and Soviet occupation zones. The Americans and the Soviets both departed by the end of the 1940s, but both sides left behind arms to their surrogates. The Soviets had left T-34 tanks, which were used to brush aside South Korean defenses in 1950. Critics of the administration claimed that, in a speech made in January 1950, Acheson had placed Korea outside of the U.S. "defense perimeter" and had thereby encouraged the North Koreans to attack. Acheson fudged the issue by saying the UN would react to any aggression against South Korea. But the next day Acheson admitted before the Senate Foreign Relations Committee that a Soviet veto in the UN Security Council would make military assistance to South Korea impossible. Thus Acheson was vulnerable to criticism for his remarks.

Acheson told Truman that he had requested the UN Security Council to call for an end to the invasion and the withdrawal of the North Korean army to positions north of the 38th parallel. By the next day Truman had returned to Washington and the UN had approved the U.S.-sponsored resolution. (The Russians had absented themselves from the forum, protesting the refusal of the United States to allow membership to be extended to Communist China, and therefore were not present to veto the resolution.) The UN vote failed to deter the North Koreans, who drove the forces of South Korea before them. The president held a meeting with top officials to determine what more could be done. All of his advisers thought the crisis required a strong reaction. A few believed Communist control of air bases in the South would increase the danger to Japan. But the main concern centered neither on South Korea nor on Japan; rather, it was feared that if the United States allowed the South to fall, it would be akin to the appeasement policy of the Western powers toward Nazi Germany in the 1930s, and would lead to like consequences, namely, it would encourage more aggression. Truman also decided that a massive buildup of the armed forces would better deter the Soviets.

Truman did not want South Korea to fall to the Communists, but neither did he want to commit American troops. However, by June 26, the situation was becoming desperate in South Korea. The president decided to commit American air and naval forces. He also increased aid to the French in

Indochina and to the Philippines, where government forces were fighting communist rebel insurgents. He sent the Seventh Fleet to the Formosa Straits to protect Chiang Kai-shek (Jiang Jieshi's) Taiwan from the mainland Communists. On June 27, the UN passed a resolution in support of sending air and naval forces to the peninsula. Yet the North continued its advances and Far Eastern commander, General of the Army Douglas MacArthur, urgently requested two U.S. divisions be sent from Japan to South Korea. Early on the morning of June 30 in Washington, Truman agreed. America would fight a land war in Asia, something U.S. leaders had diligently avoided before that time.

Truman probably made mistakes in his decision for war. For one, he refused to call the conflict a war. Senator William Knowland (R-Calif.) referred to the American reaction as a "police action." In a press conference Truman agreed to the terminology and insisted that the United States was not at war. He also failed to consult with Congress adequately. He did not ask for a declaration of war, which made it all too easy for critics to refer to the conflict as "Truman's War" when things went bad. His justification that, as constitutional commander in chief, he alone held the power to send troops into combat set a bad precedent, which would be exploited by Lyndon B. Johnson in launching American participation in the Vietnam War. In June 1950 Robert Taft did object to leaving Congress out of the equation, but most believed in the need for quick action. Even Taft supported intervention, and Congress endowed the president with war powers similar to the ones extended to Roosevelt during World War II.

The first troops sent to Korea were unprepared, whereas many of the North Korean soldiers had served in the Chinese civil war in the communist forces of Mao Zedong (Mao Tse-Tung). They continued to drive the UN forces—most of them American—and Republic of Korea soldiers southward. But the UN army was building up strength. It held air superiority and artillery fire and antitank weapons succeeded in slowing the Russian-built T-34s. By early August the North Koreans had suffered 58,000 casualties. An increasing number of Communist troops consisted of inexperienced conscripts and the North's supply lines were stretched to the breaking point. UN forces were able to hold on in the southeast corner of Korea, which became known as the Pusan perimeter, named for the port

city on which UN forces depended for supplies. The Americans realized by mid-August that they would not be driven off the peninsula. With the line stabilized, MacArthur began insisting upon approval of his plan to strike in the enemy's rear by mounting a surprise amphibious landing at the port of Inchon, about 30 miles west of Seoul. But it was risky. The coast here was swept by 32 feet high tides, and the assault would have to be perfectly timed to coincide with the highest of high tides, either on September 15, 27, or October 11. If a ship were sunk so as to block the harbor entrance, landing craft could become stuck when the tide receded. Naval officers doubted the operation would work.

Yet MacArthur had a reputation as a brilliant general, and officials in Washington were reluctant to challenge a field commander. So Truman approved the attack for September 15. It worked brilliantly. The Marines took Inchon and liberated Seoul 11 days later. Meanwhile the U.S. Eighth Army and South Korean troops pushed northward out from the Pusan perimeter. By October 1, UN forces were back at the old border, and the tide had turned.

Truman decided in late September to unify Korea under a pro-Western government headed by President Syngman Rhee. MacArthur advocated such a course, and his success at Inchon gave his word extra clout. But most U.S. officials were also eager to roll back the Communists and liberate North Korea. The administration, however, did not fully consider its decision. Communist China issued vaguely worded yet persistent threats that, should UN forces advance north, it would intervene. Again Truman barely consulted with Congress. There were other questions the administration should have asked, including how far north did MacArthur intend to go and the manner in which the two Koreas would be unified. But on they went, crossing the 38th parallel and driving the North Koreans rapidly before them.

Truman flew to Wake Island to confer with MacArthur in mid-October. Although the general had stated the United States should defend Taiwan, which was not official U.S. policy, MacArthur and the president agreed that the outlook was good in Korea. The general believed the war would be over by Christmas. Two weeks later, however, South Korean forces began capturing Chinese soldiers. Unfazed, MacArthur, on November 24, announced that the UN would launch the final assault of the war. A few days later the Chinese onslaught began.

MacArthur's offensive stopped short and a rout began. In his push to get up the peninsula, MacArthur had allowed a gap to develop within his forces and permitted his supply lines to be stretched too far. The general seemed to panic, saying, "We face an entirely new war." He blamed Washington for not supporting him enough, and he demanded that Chiang Kai-shek's army be allowed to fight in Korea, that Chinese cities be bombed, and that the Chinese coast be blockaded.

Now faced with "an entirely new war," Truman was also bedeviled with issues at home. He was the object of an assassination attempt when two Puerto Rican nationalists tried to shoot their way into Blair House, where the president was staying during the renovation of the White House. Police stopped them, with one assassin killed and the other wounded. The off-year elections proved to be a disaster for the Democrats. Using McCarthyism as a battering ram, Republicans defeated Majority Leader Scott W. Lucas of Illinois. Robert Taft beat his opponent in Ohio, which put him in a good position to run in the presidential race of 1952. In a heated Senate race in California, Richard M. Nixon beat Helen Gahagan Douglas, and McCarthy intervened in the Maryland Senate race to secure the defeat of Millard E. Tydings, who had led the investigation into the Wisconsin senator's accusations of Communists in the State Department. The Democratic majorities in the House and Senate were sharply pared and observers viewed the election results as marking was a repudiation of Truman's leadership.

After the Chinese assault at the end of November, Truman seemed beset by problems. In response to a reporter's question, the president remarked that the use of the atomic bomb had always been considered as a weapon in fighting the war, and the decision over use of such weapons rested with the commander in the field. An international uproar ensued, and a worried British prime minister, Clement Attlee, rushed to Washington for consultations. Press secretary Charles G. Ross issued a statement saying that only the president, not military officers, could order the use of the bomb. It soon became clear that while Truman would not order the use of atomic weaponry it was equally clear that the president was operating under a severe strain. Then, on December 5, his old friend Ross died of heart failure. Despite this tragedy, Truman went to see his daughter Margaret sing at Constitu-

tion Hall that evening. The next day he read a devastating review of Margaret's recital in the *Washington Post*. He dashed off an angry letter to critic Paul Hume, saying, "Some day I hope to meet you. When that happens you'll need a new nose, a lot of beefsteak for black eyes, and perhaps a supporter below." The letter, when it became public, produced an adverse reaction to the president's remarks, which were perceived to be intemperate.

With no end in sight for the rout in Korea, Truman declared a state of emergency on December 15. He asserted that a World War II–like regime of wage and price controls, coordinated defense production, and control of manpower, would have to be implemented.

As 1950 faded, the news from the front was all bad. Marines had to fight their way out from the Chosin Reservoir in northeastern Korea to the sea to be evacuated. The Army's Seventh Division was shot to pieces during its retreat as Communist forces dominated the hills abutting the roads in many areas. The commander of the Eighth Army, General Walton Walker, was killed in a jeep accident three days before Christmas.

Walker's replacement, General Matthew B. Ridgway, established a defensive line south of Seoul and halted the Chinese invaders. He went on the offensive in late January and retook Seoul on March 15. The administration decided to negotiate a settlement ending the war at approximately the old border. MacArthur found this unacceptable and demanded another drive north. Because of his earlier remarks calling for a wider war, the administration had ordered the general not to interfere with diplomatic issues without consulting the Pentagon. MacArthur blithely ignored the order. In mid-March he told a reporter that a defense line at or around the 38th parallel could not be held and that the forces that would be employed for that purpose would be better used for another drive to the Yalu River. A few days later, learning that the president would propose negotiations to end the conflict, MacArthur issued an ultimatum to the enemy commander to surrender to him. MacArthur's statement forced Truman to put aside his offer of negotiations for the time being. The Joint Chiefs of Staff reminded MacArthur of the administration's orders. Then in early April, House Minority Leader Joseph Martin read a response from the general to a speech the Massachusetts Republican had sent him calling for "a second Asiatic front" by

Chiang Kai-shek's Nationalists. MacArthur agreed and famously concluded, "There is no substitute for victory." After consulting with administration officials and politician friends, Truman relieved MacArthur of his command.

A firestorm accompanied Truman's decision to cashier the general. McCarthy said the president should be impeached. Senator William E. Jenner (R-Ind.) proclaimed that America was "in the hands of a secret inner coterie which is directed by agents of the Soviet Union." Senator Richard Nixon claimed, "The happiest group in the country will be the Communists and their stooges." Truman's action angered millions of Americans, who thought MacArthur a military genius and the president's limited war senseless. The general came back to a ticker tape parade in New York and gave his famous address to a joint session of Congress in which he recited an old barracks ballad: "Old soldiers never die. They just fade away." But the administration worked diligently to convince the American public of the fallacy of MacArthur's position. Republicans had insisted upon a congressional investigation into the general's dismissal, and the White House found it an excellent forum to educate Americans. Pentagon and State Department officials showed that MacArthur's advocacy of attacking China would, as Chairman of the Joint Chiefs general of the army Omar Bradley said, "involve us in the wrong war, at the wrong place, at the wrong time and with the wrong enemy."

Informal portrait of Senator Truman, 1940 *(Harry S. Truman Library)*

In the middle of all that, a debate—the "Great Debate" as it became known—sparked by the president's announcement he would send American troops to Europe to help defend America's NATO allies, was occurring in the Senate over the future course of American foreign policy. With the serious illness and then death of Senator Vandenberg in spring 1951, the bipartisan foreign policy that he helped forge with the Truman administration could not be sustained. Republicans, comprised of isolationists and Asia-firsters, and led by Robert Taft and Senator Kenneth S. Wherry of Nebraska, disparaged the administration's Europe-first strategy. The Senate passed a nonbinding resolution that the president might send U.S. troops to Europe to support NATO, but that the president should consult with Congress before sending the troops abroad. Truman indicated he would consult with Congress and added that the outcome of the debate showed America supported the North Atlantic Treaty.

Through 1951 and into 1952 the limited war ground on in Korea, to the frustration of the American people and the administration alike. Acheson asked the British in January 1952 if they would approve the U.S. blockading China and bombing military targets there. The new prime minister, Winston Churchill, would not agree to such action. The United States, however, would not assure the British that the atomic bomb would never be used in the war. Negotiations, which had begun between the UN and North Korea in 1951, had become stalemated on the issue of prisoner exchange. Truman would not send back to North Korea or China POWs who did not want to go. This issue would not be resolved and the war would not be ended until July 1953, after Truman left office.

Events proved no better for the president at home. Wartime inflation threatened to cause a strike in the steel industry in 1952. When negotiations broke down Truman seized the steel mills to make sure production continued. The Supreme Court, however, declared the seizure unconstitutional and workers subsequently walked off the job. However, the strike did not prove as disastrous as the administration had predicted and the dispute was settled with in a few weeks.

Truman also had to endure accusations of corruption leveled against the members of his Administration. There were accusations of influence peddling to acquire a mink coat and refrigerated freezers (which turned out to be defective). Military aide Harry Vaughan had been involved in the latter, admittedly minor, scandal. There were the 5 per-centers, lobbyists who charged 5 percent of the proceeds of the government contract or loans they secured. Though not illegal per se, it looked immoral to many Americans. There were accusations of graft in the Bureau of Internal Revenue and in the Reconstruction Finance Corporation. Truman's stubborn defense of subordinates like Vaughan made it appear that he was indifferent to corruption.

Probably the most bitter disappointment for the president was the loss by the Democrats of the White House in 1952. In the spring of 1950 Truman confided in his diary that he would not run for reelection. Throughout the year, with crises at home and abroad, he occasionally reconsidered his decision, but, in the end, he told aides twice in 1951 that he would step down in 1952. Who would run in his place? The president favored Chief Justice Fred Vinson, but Vinson turned Truman down. He then turned to General Dwight Eisenhower, but the commander of NATO said he would not run unless the people demanded it. Otherwise he remained silent. Then, in early 1952, the general announced he was a Republican and that he would accept that party's presidential nomination.

Truman considered others as candidates: Senator Richard B. Russell of Georgia and Senator Robert S. Kerr of Oklahoma, Vice President Alben Barkley, Averell Harriman. But all had liabilities. Truman would not countenance Senator C. Estes Kefauver of Tennessee, who was running in the primaries, because of a headline-grabbing investigation by a senatorial committee he chaired of organized crime and urban political machines (his snooping in Kansas City was especially galling). Finally, he fixed his sights on Governor Adlai E. Stevenson of Illinois. Stevenson proved indecisive, eventually saying he would not run, but that would accept a draft. Later he sounded even more categorical against a run for the White House. For a moment Truman reconsidered running himself but his advisers, and especially his wife Bess, argued against it. (The latter asserted her belief that neither she nor he could survive another term.)

With Stevenson inactive Truman then swung behind Barkley, but labor leaders would not accept the "Veep," considering him too old. Truman was at his wits' end. But then Stevenson made an electrifying welcoming speech to the delegates at the party

convention in Chicago. Stevenson allowed himself to be nominated. He won on the third ballot.

Meanwhile, a bitter contest for the Republican Party nomination that pitted internationalist Eisenhower against neo-isolationist Taft—who actually was more liberal than Eisenhower on some domestic issues—focused on a group of disputed delegates at the convention, also in Chicago. Eisenhower called for a "fair play" amendment in which disputed delegates could not vote on their own behalf. He won that vote, which paved the way to victory.

During the campaign Stevenson—much to the annoyance of Truman—distanced himself from the president. Then in an interview he tacitly agreed that there was a "mess in Washington." However, whatever irritation Truman felt toward Stevenson was dwarfed by his fury at Eisenhower, whom he believed had betrayed him by rejecting his offer of support for the Democratic nomination and who then proceeded to run as a Republican who blasted the president's record. Ike reconciled with Taft and denounced the doctrine of containment, favoring a policy that called for support for liberation from communist oppression instead. More galling from Truman's perspective was Eisenhower's endorsement of Joseph McCarthy and William Jenner, both of whom had made scurrilous attacks on George Marshall, the very man who had boosted Eisenhower's career. Eisenhower defended Marshall in Denver, but then he deleted a defense of his mentor in Milwaukee where he shared the stage with McCarthy. Bitter recriminations were exchanged on both sides. Truman at one point said Eisenhower had "surrendered his moral authority." The two grew to despise one another.

Truman campaigned hard to help Stevenson and defeat Eisenhower, but, most of all, to defend his record as president. However, the tide was against him and the Democrats, and Eisenhower clinched a victory when he said, "I will go to Korea" to size up the situation and come up with a solution to the war. Ike won in a landslide.

So the Truman era came to an end on January 20, 1953. The preceding eight years had been one of great triumph and bitter defeat for the 33rd president. World War II had ended with mushroom clouds over Japan. Reconversion had gone awry and the Republicans recaptured the Congress, the first time since the 1930s. The administration took dramatic action to resist communism in Iran and

Greece, promulgated the Truman Doctrine, launched the Marshall Plan that helped save Europe, and crafted a bipartisan foreign policy together with amenable Republicans. At home the administration found itself swept up in the postwar Red Scare. It established a Loyalty Review Board while the House Un-American Activities Committee hunted for Communists in Hollywood and Washington and Senator McCarthy would soon claim that the State Department was a den of subversives. In 1949 China fell to the Communists. On nuclear issues the Soviets managed to explode a test device. American scientists began serious work on a so-called H-bomb, or hydrogen bomb, and the Russians would follow, belatedly. The Korean War broke out with its subsequent ups and downs for diplomatic and military strategists. The administra-

tion witnessed the beginnings of the modern defense budget after the outbreak of the Korean War. In 1952 the Democrats lost the presidency for the first time in 20 years.

What, in long retrospect, can one say of the Truman presidency? It is becoming clear, with the perspective of a new century, that the successor to President Fanklin D. Roosevelt, so suddenly thrust into office in the crucial year 1945, was in many ways a success during his nearly eight years as his country's chief executive. His successes, to be sure, were almost all in foreign policy. But then that field of executive action was surely what mattered the most at the time of decision. The Missouri president hence did well by his country, helping set out its basic actions in the world for what proved another half century of policy.

Acheson, Dean G(ooderham)

(1893–1971) *secretary of state*

Born on April 11, 1893, in Middletown, Connecticut, the son of an Episcopal bishop of Connecticut, Dean Acheson grew up in comfortable New England surroundings. He attended the Groton School and graduated from Yale in 1915. After serving in the navy during World War I, he received a law degree from Harvard in 1918. Acheson served as secretary to Supreme Court Justice Louis D. Brandeis for the next two years and joined the prestigious law firm of Covington and Burling in 1921. Following the recommendation of FELIX FRANK-FURTER, the New Deal's unofficial talent scout, in March 1933 President Franklin D. Roosevelt appointed Acheson undersecretary of the Treasury. Six months later Acheson resigned in protest against what he considered the reckless and unconstitutional action by the president in reducing the gold content of the dollar. Acheson then resumed his legal practice. During 1939–40 he headed a committee to study the operation of the administrative bureaus of the federal government.

Acheson once again became active in public affairs with the outbreak of war in Europe. He worked to promote U.S. aid to Great Britain and collaborated with presidential aide BENJAMIN V. COHEN in drafting the constitutional justification for the 1940 destroyer-bases deal with the British. This brief impressed Roosevelt, who invited Acheson to rejoin the administration as assistant secretary of state for economic affairs.

Acheson served as assistant secretary from 1941 until 1944. Throughout the war he helped coordinate the lend-lease program. He was also liaison with Congress and contributed to the development of such postwar organizations as the United Nations Relief and Rehabilitation Agency (UNRRA), the World Bank, the International Monetary Fund, and the Food and Agriculture Organization. Acheson viewed these agencies as tools to rehabilitate Europe to insure stable pro-American governments and increased markets for surplus American industrial goods. He later lobbied for the UN charter in Congress.

In June 1945 President Harry S Truman appointed his old political rival, JAMES F. BYRNES, secretary of state. Byrnes asked Acheson to assume the post of undersecretary. During his year and a half in office, Byrnes was abroad a large portion of the time and therefore Acheson served as acting secretary. He was responsible for the administration of the department and for continuing the reforms introduced by EDWARD R. STETTINIUS, JR., to improve the functioning of the department's bureaucracy. Acheson introduced a clear, precise chain of command that ended with his office. When Byrnes was out of the country, Acheson briefed Truman daily on foreign affairs and developed a close relationship with the president. Acheson often found himself acting as mediator between Truman, always fearful that Byrnes sought to upstage him, and Byrnes, who was jealous of Truman for winning the vice presidency in 1944.

During the early postwar period Acheson was primarily concerned with the economic reconstruction of Western Europe. He testified before congressional committees in support of extension of aid to UNRRA and for the loan to Great Britain. Acheson even supported a recovery loan to the new government of Poland, already charged by many with being the puppet of the Soviet Union. He considered Poland's recovery crucial for the rehabilitation of Europe. Despite his support for UNRRA, Acheson was somewhat skeptical about the usefulness of the United Nations, seeing it as an example of 19th-century millenarianism with its belief in man's perfectibility. Such expectations would result inevitably in disappointment. Acheson, on the other hand, believed in power politics, plain and simple.

Acheson was also deeply involved with the development of U.S. policy on atomic weapons. A number of administration officials, led by Secretary of the Navy JAMES V. FORRESTAL, viewed the American nuclear monopoly as an important weapon which the United States could use to pressure concessions from the Soviet Union. Acheson disagreed, arguing in a memorandum to Truman in the fall of 1945 for international controls of atomic energy. He supported such nuclear scientists as LEO SZILARD, who warned that Russia would soon possess the bomb and that unless some control was established, a suicidal arms race would occur. Acheson joined HENRY L. STIMSON in advocating that procedures be established between the United States, Great Britain, and the Soviet Union for the exchange of information on nuclear weapons and the eventual international control of atomic material. Yet given congressional opposition, he concluded that sharing all information need not be done immediately. By October Truman insisted that the United States would not share industrial knowledge to make the bomb. In addition, Byrnes did not want to negotiate directly with the Soviets on the matter, but rather bring the issue before the UN, and that became the administration's approach to the problem.

In January 1946 Byrnes appointed Acheson to head a committee to compose a plan for the international control of atomic energy. Acheson and Tennessee Valley Authority head DAVID E. LILIENTHAL presented an idea of physicist J. ROBERT OPPENHEIMER, who had been in charge of the Manhattan project, to create an Atomic Development Authority that would control every aspect of atomic energy. The agency would make its resources available for peaceful uses, and control and license all nuclear activities. It would report any attempt to develop atomic weapons to the UN members who could take appropriate action. The report stipulated that the United States would end manufacture of nuclear devices at some point in the future and transfer atomic energy to the UN agency in stages. However, it stressed that there must be no immediate release of atomic knowledge.

Truman appointed BERNARD M. BARUCH, a politically influential and aggressively self-promoting financier, to present the plan. Acheson and Lilienthal were horrified. They believed the Soviets would look on the septuagenarian as someone who would put them at a disadvantage—the two were proven correct. Baruch altered the plan to include sanctions against violators that would not be subject to a UN Security Council veto. America would give up its atomic bombs (there were only three when Baruch presented the plan) only after it was assured no one else could make them. Acheson stated that such conditions would preclude Soviet acceptance. He also questioned the utility of sanctions—the only way to enforce the plan against a great power would be war, and he was skeptical that any nation would go to war to ensure compliance. Truman, however, backed up Baruch, and, subsequently, the Soviets rejected the plan in July. Truman later admitted to Acheson that he had made a mistake in appointing Baruch.

Early in Truman's administration, Acheson, although wanting to be resolute toward the Russians, also wanted to resolve differences between the two countries. He feared if they were not settled, Republicans might return America to isolationism through opposition to the Soviets. However, as a result of Soviet actions in Iran and Turkey and attempts to gain control of the eastern Mediterranean, he changed his position. By spring 1946 he had joined GEORGE F. KENNAN in warning that the Soviet Union was a power bent on world conquest, and he urged the United States to develop policies to resist Soviet expansion. He backed Kennan's recommendation for containment of the USSR and, over the remainder of the decade, helped develop programs implementing the plan. (Curiously, Kennan's Long Telegram explaining Soviet goals and his suggestions to thwart them did not impress Acheson.)

In 1947 Acheson played a major role in the formation of the Truman Doctrine. When administration officials met with congressional leaders, it was Acheson who convinced the congressmen and senators through highly charged rhetoric that the Soviet Union was on the verge of breaking through to Asia, Africa, and Europe if Greece fell to Communist insurgents. Freedom itself would be threatened. The chairman of the Senate Foreign Relations Committee, ARTHUR H. VANDENBERG (R-Mich.), said if the president spoke that way to Congress it would almost certainly support him. Acheson helped draft what an aghast Kennan thought was a bellicose speech. In the speech Truman proclaimed that the United States should support "free peoples everywhere" under threat from "armed minorities" or "outside pressures."

That spring Acheson also became involved in the formulation of the Marshall Plan of massive aid to war-torn Europe. In March 1947 he recommended a program of aid and coordinated studies on the feasibility of the project. Even before Secretary of State GEORGE C. MARSHALL unveiled the plan in his historic Harvard University address of June 1947, Acheson had already outlined the general philosophy of the proposal in a speech on May 8 in Cleveland, Mississippi. He announced that the United States must "push ahead with the reconstruction of those two great workshops of Europe and Asia—Germany and Japan." "Free people," he said, "desiring aid to preserve their institutions against totalitarian pressures would receive top priority for American reconstruction aid."

Acheson retired from government service in summer 1947. He resumed his legal practice but could not entirely avoid public affairs. He served as vice chairman of the Hoover Commission and lobbied on behalf of the Marshall Plan. In November 1948 President Truman asked Acheson to replace the ailing Marshall as secretary of state commencing the first of the year.

Acheson's appointment was applauded by many in the United States and Europe. *New York Times* correspondent James Reston wrote that the new secretary combined the best features of his four predecessors. Reston felt Acheson had the experience of Cordell Hull, the handsomeness of Edward Stettinius, the style of James Byrnes, and the mental discipline of George C. Marshall. The *Manchester Guardian* called him one of the most creative political minds of the time. Although the elegant, witty, urbane diplomat was distrusted by some members of Congress, most were impressed by his intellect and his determination to take a strong stand against the Soviet Union.

Despite their differences in backgrounds and personality, Acheson and Truman worked well together. Both men respected each other. Truman admired Acheson's intellect and dedication. Acheson, in turn, respected Truman's determination to make crucial decisions without hesitation. Both shared a desire to defend Western society from what

they thought was expansionist communism. This shared view enabled them to shape American diplomacy in close cooperation.

Acheson's experience in ending the Berlin Blockade convinced him that normal negotiations, involving concession, with the Soviets was pointless. The Russians relied on intimidation to obtain results, and only when the United States made it clear to them that this would not work would they adopt traditional diplomacy. As mentioned, Acheson viewed Soviet relations in terms of power politics. He opposed a Wilsonian emphasis on internationalism and appeals to abstract principles of right and wrong in the formation of policy. He believed that they were attempts to avoid the responsibility of exercising power. He accepted the inevitability of a bipolar world, at least within the foreseeable future. His major goals, therefore, were to contain communist expansion and to develop a strong military presence so that America could force the Soviet Union to negotiate on its own terms.

By the time Acheson assumed his post, some of the major aspects of the administration's containment policy had been developed. The Truman Doctrine had helped prevent a Communist takeover in Greece and the Marshall Plan had helped economically revitalize Europe, thwarting Communist attempts to use economic problems to gain a foothold in that area. Acheson, therefore, concentrated on maintaining a united Atlantic community and building a strong military alliance in Europe. The most pressing issue facing Acheson when taking office in 1949 was Senate ratification of the North Atlantic Treaty with Great Britain, France, and other Western European countries. In response to a question from a Republican senator during hearings regarding the treaty, Acheson asserted that the United States would not permanently station large numbers of troops in Europe. (He would later regret saying this when the administration asked for congressional support—eventually forthcoming— to send large numbers of U.S. troops to bolster NATO's defenses during the Korean War.) The treaty itself was readily ratified in July 1949.

Another problem facing the newly confirmed secretary was Germany. At first Acheson was noncommittal about the establishment of a West German state, even willing to contemplate Kennan's idea of the West and the USSR evacuating a reunified and demilitarized Germany. But he soon discovered the French and the British wanted to integrate West Germany into Western Europe. Acheson agreed that a West German government should be established, but that this should not preclude reunification. According to Acheson's biographer James Chace, to the secretary the question was whether reunification was practical or not. Opposition from the British and the French, however, made any immediate reunification impossible: the British feared the West would be forced into an indefensible position vis-à-vis the Soviets and the French feared a reunified Germany. He worked for the establishment of the German Federal Republic under the control of internationalists intent on Germany's participation in the Western alliance. Acheson also urged German entrance into the defense alliance and in 1950 took steps leading to the rearmament of that country.

In late 1949, in light of the fall of China to the Communists and the Soviet explosion of an atomic device, Truman commissioned a study of American foreign policy and defense capabilities. Acheson worked closely with the Department's Policy Planning Staff, headed by PAUL H. NITZE, in analyzing American foreign policy. The resulting document, NSC-68, reflected in part Acheson's evolution of thought on the Soviet threat. It was based on the premise that the Soviet Union was expansionist and would refuse to negotiate outstanding issues. Acheson stated later that the document was designed to force the upper echelons of government to realize the need to stop the nation's excessive reliance on atomic bombs and increase the size of the conventional military. The report cast the conflict between the United States and the USSR as one of good versus evil and advocated containing the Soviet Union along its entire border. This large-scale containment would need to be supported by adequate military force or it would be "no more than a policy of bluff." Yet NSC-68 only defined the threat to national interests, as the group thought interests themselves would be elastic over time. The cost of NSC-68 would be between $35 billion and $50 billion, sums far beyond Secretary of Defense LOUIS A. JOHNSON's desired $13.5 billion military budget. In the initially meeting over the document between Acheson's and Johnson's staff, the defense secretary berated Acheson for not giving him time to read it—actually he had given him a copy a week earlier—and stormed out of the office. Acheson became convinced that Johnson was mentally ill, but in the end Johnson endorsed NSC-68. State Department

officials George Kennan and CHARLES E. BOHLEN were skeptical about Paul Nitze's handiwork since the document ignored Soviet intentions and focused on capabilities. Both thought its description of Soviet aims simplistic and made it appear that war could not be avoided, although Bohlen would come to support increased military spending.

A reading of NSC-68 could lead one to think Acheson advocated meeting the Soviet threat throughout the world, yet he did not intend that. When given the report in April 1950, President Truman was initially reluctant to accept the report's recommendations, and he postponed any decision until he could find out the total cost. But with the outbreak of war in Korea, which the State Department felt might be a prelude to general Soviet expansion, he pushed for increased defense spending.

Acheson was often criticized both at home and abroad for being intransigent in his demands on negotiations and unrealistic in his policies. His opponents pointed out that his willingness to negotiate with the Soviets only after the freedom of Eastern Europe and the reunification of Germany made meaningful discussion on outstanding issues impossible. His foes observed that this demand called on the Soviets to capitulate, not negotiate. They pointed out that Acheson's hard-line position and emphasis on military superiority forced the Soviet Union to assume a similar stance, thus intensifying the cold war. Individuals such as Winston Churchill urged the opening of negotiations for fear of future war.

Acheson's diplomacy centered around the North Atlantic community, which he believed represented the peak of mankind's development. Asia was of secondary importance. He had little interest in the area and never felt confident of his understanding of the situation there. However, during his tenure, Acheson was forced to devote a large portion of his attention to the East.

Acheson became secretary of state the same day that Nationalist Chinese leader Generalissimo Chiang Kai-shek (Jiang Jieshi), in the midst of a civil war, resigned as president of the Republic of China—January 1, 1949. On February 7, 1949, Republican congressmen asked Acheson what would happen to the Chinese Nationalists, then being badly beaten by Mao Zedong's (Mao Tse-tung) Communists. Acheson said that the United States would have to wait "until the dust settles." This was reported in the press as his China policy, which Acheson denied, saying he merely confessed he could not predict the future, but the China Lobby, prominent supporters of Chiang, used this unfortunate remark as a launching pad to attack the administration's policy, eventually blaming it for the "loss" of China.

Shortly before Acheson became secretary of state a National Security Council paper said that the United States should prevent Red China from becoming a Soviet satellite. A short time later Acheson said the war was practically over, and that the Communists would eventually run most or all of China. Therefore, the United States should stop giving military aid to Chiang because his unpopularity would simply rally more Chinese to Mao's side and against America. The United States should reestablish regular economic activity among China, Japan, and the West, and try to keep Mao separated as much as possible from Moscow. Acheson thought Communist China could avoid becoming a Soviet satellite, just like Communist Yugoslavia had. Truman approved the policy in March 1949.

In pursuit of this goal Acheson stopped a bill to provide another $1.5 billion in loans to the Nationalists. However, to win support for European aid and NATO, Acheson agreed to continue spending funds previously allocated to the Nationalists past the original cutoff date of April 2, 1949. As the Communists advanced in China, Senator WILLIAM F. KNOWLAND (R-Calif.) and Representative WALTER H. JUDD (R-Minn.) demanded increased aid to Chiang, whom they argued was being ignored because of an emphasis on Europe. The partisan rancor that developed made it impossible for Acheson to recognize Mao's government in an effort to keep it from becoming a Soviet satellite. Acheson's policy was further undercut in late June 1949, when Mao said he would align with the Soviets. But the Chinese Communist leader passed word to the American ambassador that he hoped for good relations with the United States. In August 1949 Acheson released the State Department's *White Paper*, a defense of U.S. policy toward China since America's entry into World War II. The paper was long and inaccessible to the average person. Acheson's Letter of Transmittal, drafted by State Department official PHILIP JESSUP, was more accessible, but actually harmed the administration's position. Acheson blamed the Nationalists for the "loss" of China because of their ineptitude, corruption, and lack of popular support and explained how more U.S. aid would not have helped. It also said the Chinese Communists were subservient to Moscow. Acheson did not believe that but hoped, contradic-

torily, that it would appease the China Lobby and yet be little noticed. By saying that Mao was the mere tool of the Russians, Acheson had actually made recognition of Communist China much more difficult, because the China Lobby would use that argument against such a policy. The *White Paper* satisfied no one. Columnist Walter Lippman doubted Chinese Communists' subservience to Moscow, while the China Lobby and it allies in Congress, such as Representative Walter Judd, and senators William Knowland, STYLES BRIDGES (R-N.H.), KENNETH S. WHERRY (R-Neb.), and PAT A. MCCARRAN (D-Nev.), denounced it as a whitewash. But Acheson was adamant in his defense. In January 1950, in a speech before the National Press Club, he stated: "The Communists did not create this condition. They did not create this revolutionary spirit. They did not create a great force which moved out from under Chiang Kaishek. But they were shrewd and cunning to mount it, and to ride this thing into victory and into power."

Acheson still hoped to recognize Red China, but the China Lobby and the actions of the Chinese Communist government (e.g., the detention of the American consul Angus Ward for a year) made this increasingly difficult. Also, after being forced off the mainland, Chiang had managed to establish a presence on Taiwan, which the China Lobby argued presented an alternative to Communist China. Acheson recommended that the United States do nothing to prevent the Communists from seizing the island, as the fall of Taiwan to the Communists might make it easier to recognize Mao. Thus, in early January 1950, Truman announced the United States would do nothing to save Chiang on Taiwan.

For many Americans, China's fall to the Communists in December 1949 revealed the bankruptcy of the containment policy. They felt the Truman administration had failed to contain communism in the second largest nation in the world, which had been protected by the United States ever since the 19th century. Some conservatives refused to view the event as the result of poor diplomacy. In light of the continuing cold war and revelations of domestic subversion, they began to charge that there was a Communist conspiracy in the State Department to "sell out" China. The China Lobby pointed to China experts such as JOHN CARTER VINCENT as leaders of the allegedly pro-Communist contingent at the Far East desk. This sentiment was bolstered on January 25, 1950, when Acheson said that he had no intention of turning his "back on ALGER HISS."

Four days before, Hiss had been convicted of lying under oath in saying that he had not passed secret documents to the Soviets through WHITTAKER CHAMBERS. It was meant as a gesture of Christian charity—he referred reporters to Matthew 25:34 as constituting his attitude—but it was disastrous politically. Senators JOSEPH R. MCCARTHY (R-Wisc.) and RICHARD M. NIXON (R-Calif.) both denounced Acheson for his statement. Acheson's statement was poorly timed, coming during a period of great anxiety about the Communist threat: the Soviets now had the atomic bomb and the forces of Mao had forced Chiang's Nationalists out of mainland China. Yet little action was taken on the China Lobby's allegations until McCarthy, on February 9, 1950, announced he had a list of names of Communists in the State Department. McCarthy named people like JESSUP, JOHN S. SERVICE, and OWEN LATTIMORE as the culprits. (Lattimore had never been an employee of the department, just a consultant.) Acheson denounced McCarthy for reckless, false accusations. A Senate hearing led by Senator MILLARD E. TYDINGS (D-Md.) denounced McCarthy's charges as fabricated, but the committee did criticize Service for poor judgment in passing classified documents to the journal *Amerasia*, and Truman's Loyalty Review Board later dismissed him. Right-wing condemnation of Acheson crescendoed during the last three months of his time in office, and he became one of the most unpopular secretaries of state in the 20th century.

The conservative backlash prevented Acheson from pursuing his goal of opening normal relations with Communist China. Acheson decided to provide economic aid to the Taiwan government, but, as mentioned, he refused to tie the United States to defend the island, which the military deemed strategically worthless. During the Korean War, however, Acheson convinced the president to interpose the U.S. Seventh Fleet between Taiwan and the mainland to prevent attacks in either direction and thus spreading the war in Asia.

During the early 1950s Acheson extended containment to Asia. He championed military and economic aid to the French colonialists fighting the pro-Communist Viet Minh in Indochina. Although he acknowledged that nationalism was the chief rallying cry for individuals in developing nations, he feared the Communist connection with the movements. Acheson also wanted the French to participate fully in European military affairs. They could not possibly have done this without U.S. aid in Asia.

In January 1950 Acheson delivered a speech to the National Press Club in which he said America's "defensive perimeter" included the Aleutians, Japan, Okinawa, and the Philippines. He further said that South Korea, if attacked, would have to rely on its own defenses at first and then call on the United Nations for help. He said specifically, however, that the United States was responsible for South Korea and Japan. The widespread after-the-fact accusation from people like Senator ROBERT A. TAFT (R-Ohio), that the Press Club speech encouraged the North Koreans to invade the South is mistaken, according to historian Bruce Cumings. He noted that North Korean public statements immediately after Acheson's speech included South Korea as within America's defense perimeter. But more recent studies, based on archival research in the former Soviet Union, showed that Stalin was influenced by the speech to approve the invasion.

Then on June 24 (June 25 in Korea), the North Korean army poured across the 38th parallel, the border between North and South Korea. Acheson believed the Soviets had instigated the invasion, that it would have to be met by force, and that might mean American intervention. Although they had not instigated war, the Soviets had approved North Korean dictator Kim Il-Sung's plan to invade the South and supplied his army. Acheson, however, saw the Soviets as testing America's will to resist the march of communism, not just in Asia but in Europe as well, where there was still skepticism of American resolve to defend the Continent. Intervention in Korea, Acheson maintained, would, in the eyes of the NATO allies, serve as the final American atonement for its pre-1941 isolationist policy. Acheson told Truman that the United States should at first try to act through the UN to stop the invasion and, if that failed, Washington should act alone. The response should be concentrated against the North Koreans and the conflict should be a limited one, avoiding a general war with the Soviets. The United States went to the UN and won a major victory in gaining approval from the Security Council to extend assistance of the member nations to stop the North Koreans. (The Soviets were boycotting the council because the United States would not allow the Chinese Communists to take the seat of the Chinese Nationalists; hence, they were absent and unable to veto the resolution.) According to Chace, Acheson and Truman had extended America's vital interest to an area that had been of little importance to the country. By so doing they set a precedent that, in future, America might involve itself in areas that only slightly affected U.S. interests.

Acheson initially pressed for a congressional resolution approving Truman's action, but the president was dissuaded from doing so, ironically by Senate Majority Leader SCOTT W. LUCAS (D-Ill.). This may have been a mistake, as Republicans, who had initially supported the president, turned against his conduct of the war, noting that he carried full responsibility for America's entry into the conflict—dubbing it "Truman's war"—since he had no congressional authorization.

While trying to organize the resistance to the North Koreans, Acheson found himself undercut by Defense Secretary Johnson at home. Johnson asked W. AVERELL HARRIMAN to assist him in ousting Acheson, promising he would help him become secretary of state. Harriman reported this to Truman, who replaced Johnson with General George C. Marshall.

Once the United States intervened, the question of goals arose: simply restore South Korea to its old border or reunite the country? If reunification was the answer then what was needed was a military commander who would act cautiously and notify Washington when there was even a slight possibility of foreign intervention. General DOUGLAS MACARTHUR was simply not the man to act in this fashion. Acheson helped draw up the directive allowing MacArthur to cross the 38th parallel. The directive and other orders to MacArthur were ambiguous enough to allow the general to occupy all of North Korea with all UN troops, not just South Koreans. Premier Zhou Enlai warned that China would not tolerate any but South Korean forces to cross the parallel and would intervene if the armies of other nations did so, but Acheson did not take the warning seriously. He thought the administration risked much more in hesitation and timorousness than it did in invading the North. The trouble was that, in his race to the Yalu River, MacArthur began to employ American troops closer and closer to the border, which violated Acheson's political goal of not provoking China. Thus the Chinese did intervene as the Americans neared the Sino-Korean border, driving them back below the 38th parallel and catching Acheson and the administration off guard. MacArthur panicked, demanded more troops, and asked that he be allowed to expand the war to China, saying there was "no substitute for victory."

The situation in Korea improved in early 1951. General Matthew Ridgway, commander of the U.S. Eighth Army in Korea, stabilized the front and retook the 38th parallel. There he would stay, as Truman and Acheson were determined to keep the war limited and resisted the demand by MacArthur and leading Republicans to expand the war to China. Acheson indicated that he would rather settle for a compromise that would set the boundary along the old border. Acheson supported Truman's decision to relieve the obstreperous MacArthur, who kept making public statements contrary to administration policy. To Acheson civilian control of the military was of paramount importance. The secretary of state also used the Korean War to bolster U.S. defenses in Japan. Working with Republican JOHN FOSTER DULLES, Acheson negotiated peace and security treaties with that country.

With Soviet assistance, negotiations to end the Korean War began in July 1951, but Acheson failed to secure the peace in Korea through diplomatic channels. Although both sides privately acknowledged the inevitability of a divided Korea, they could not reach a compromise. Just as importantly, the secretary opposed the Communist demands for the forcible repatriation of prisoners of war, many of whom indicated they did not want to return to their northern homes.

At home, Acheson endured sniping from congressional Republicans, who voted overwhelmingly that he should be cashiered. After enduring hectoring from Senate Minority Leader WHERRY during an Appropriations Committee hearing in August 1950, Acheson tried to punch the senator, being stopped by another State Department official. Despite all the attacks, in the evenings he would usually go home and, with insouciance, have a drink.

During his years as secretary, Dean Acheson had difficulty communicating his cold war strategy to the American people. His intellect, aristocratic appearance, and contempt for those of lesser ability prompted many congressional leaders to distrust him. Acheson tried to ignore public opinion, calling his critics "primitives." He once said that he was thankful that there were no opinion polls at Valley Forge.

Acheson left office in a hail of criticism. In 1952 the Republican Party platform promised a new, bold foreign policy that would liberate Eastern Europe. Foster Dulles, the party's chief foreign policy spokesman, attacked Acheson's diplomacy for being amoral. The right continued to view the secretary and high administration officials as traitors. Yet in spite of attacks on him, his foreign policy accomplished what he intended. Western Europe remained politically and economically strong. It had also been reassured of U.S. military support if attacked. The secretary refused to make empty promises. He opposed the pledge to liberate Europe because the United States lacked the means short of war to accomplish this. In response to the charge that his foreign policy lacked morality, Acheson argued that he had combined morality with power to achieve results. He pointed to NATO, the Marshall Plan, and the Korean intervention as examples of noteworthy moral endeavors.

Acheson biographer David S. McClellan argues that his strategy vis-à-vis the Soviets was the proper one, given what the secretary saw as the obstinate position of the Russians. A patient containment policy would work until the Soviets changed their attitude that would make negotiations worthwhile. Moscow's turning away from Europe—where an attack could lead to total war—to an area (Korea) where containment had not yet been strengthened showed that the NATO-enforced European containment policy, which Acheson had so much to do in formulating, worked. Although Chace noted the insecurity of the Soviets, which the Americans exacerbated by their reaction to Soviet intransigence, undoubtedly was a cause of the cold war, he further indicated that recent access by the West to Soviet archives makes it fairly clear that Stalin still would have acted aggressively regardless of what the West did. Thus, Acheson was a chief architect of a strategy that held back the Soviets and prevented the cold war from becoming a world war.

Acheson welcomed retirement after 1953. Throughout the Eisenhower years he remained a vocal critic of administration foreign policy. He deplored Dulles's call for a moral crusade against communism and questioned the administration's reliance on nuclear weapons. During the 1960s he served as an adviser to both Presidents Kennedy and Johnson. In 1968 he was one of the men who advised Johnson to de-escalate the war in Vietnam. Acheson died on October 12, 1971, in Silver Springs, Maryland. (See *The Eisenhower Years, The Kennedy Years, The Johnson Years* Volumes)

—JB

Aiken, George D(avid)
(1892–1984) *member of the Senate*
Born on August 30, 1892 in Dummerston, Vermont, George D. Aiken grew up on a farm near Brattles-

boro, Vermont. Aiken developed an interest in agriculture at an early age. He was a pioneer in the commercial cultivation of wildflowers and became a recognized expert, publishing three books on the subject in the 1930s. He was elected to the Vermont House of Representatives as a Republican in 1930. Aiken moved up swiftly through Vermont politics to become governor in 1937. In 1940 he was elected to the U.S. Senate. Aiken had little trouble remaining in the upper house, winning reelection five times in a row, each time with more than 65 percent of the vote.

Aiken gained a reputation as an independent, often voting against the more conservative members of his party. He was one of four Republican cosponsors of "The Full Employment Act of 1945." Together with Robert F. LaFollette, Jr. (P-Wisc.), he sponsored the food allotment bill of 1946, a forerunner of the food stamp program. In 1947 he introduced a bill that would have authorized federal money to each state to raise below standard educational conditions—75 percent of the funds were designated to public school teachers' salaries. Aiken's bill would also have allocated money to private schools as well as public, but funds could not be used for private school teachers' salaries. He also cosponsored a bill to raise the minimum wage to 65 cents an hour. Aiken supported the building of the St. Lawrence Seaway, which would bring cheap feed grains and hydroelectricity to Vermont. He voted for the Taft-Hartley Act in June 1947 even though he opposed certain clauses in the bill.

Aiken was a critic of the emerging cold war between the United States and the Soviet Union. In July 1946 he warned, "Britain and Russia have been opposed to each other for 200 years. We should steer clear of this conflict and work instead to bring the two nations together." On the 1946 British loan, Aiken tried unsuccessfully to attach a condition to it stating that the British would have to lower trade barriers within one year of the start of the loan and before drawing over $1 billion of a $3.75 billion line of credit. However, he later supported the Truman Doctrine for the containment of communism in Western Europe. He voted for giving financial and military aid to Greece and Turkey in 1947 and supported the Marshall Plan in 1948. Aiken originally supported Truman's sending of troops to defend South Korea because North Korea had been the aggressor. After Chinese entry into the war in late 1950, Aiken rejected the position of other Republicans who wanted to widen the war, believing America would lose a wider land war in Asia. Yet he also blasted Truman's handling of the conflict and backed DWIGHT D. EISENHOWER for president in 1952 because he believed only he could end the war.

Aiken's views brought him into conflict with the conservative wing of the Republican Party, led by Senator ROBERT A. TAFT (R-Ohio). Shortly after the 1946 elections, the press widely reported that Taft had attempted to "purge" Aiken from positions of power within the Senate. By assuming the chairmanship of the Labor Committee, Taft was able to deny Aiken, who was next in line by seniority, that post. In February 1947 Aiken criticized those GOP leaders who assumed that the 1946 elections gave them a mandate for "an irresponsible slashing of expenditures and government employment and taxes on a straight across-the-board basis." He maintained that this jeopardized the party's chances for electing a president in 1948.

In consolation for the loss of the Labor Committee chairmanship, Aiken was made chairman of the new Committee on Expenditures in Executive Departments. In July 1947 he was appointed to the Commission on Organization of the Executive Branch of Government headed by former president HERBERT C. HOOVER. The commission made a number of recommendations in 1949 for a more efficient, vertical organization of the executive branch.

Although Aiken was many times labeled a liberal, in fact he was an old-fashioned progressive Republican. He inveighed against monopoly, but he also cast a wary eye on creating a too intrusive federal government. This is best seen in his approach to agricultural policy. In 1948, as chairman of the long-range farm policy subcommittee of the Agriculture and Forestry Committee, Aiken helped draw up a bill that called for phasing in a sliding scale for farm price supports, rather than the high, fixed supports that were then in existence. Aiken's bill met with stiff opposition, led by Senator RICHARD B. RUSSELL (D-Ga.). Aiken warned his fellow solons that if they continued to support farm prices at high, fixed levels "the time will not be far distant when the American people will rise up and say they will no longer have any farm price support program." The House, however, passed legislation sponsored by Clifford Hope (R-Kans.) for high, rigid supports. The result was a compromise, the Hope-Aiken Act, which continued high, fixed supports until 1950, when the Senate's sliding scale would be introduced.

Aiken was a major opponent of the Truman administration's farm policy, introduced in April 1949 by Secretary of Agriculture CHARLES F. BRANNAN. The Brannan Plan called for allowing farm prices to fall to low levels determined by supply and demand and making up the difference to farmers by direct cash payments. Aiken said the plan would lead to overproduction and increased government controls over agriculture. In June 1949 he warned, "When the farmers of America lose their freedom through the permanent application of government controls and penalties, there will be little hope left for maintaining democracy in America." The Brannan Plan was defeated, but the price support section of the Hope-Aiken Act was repealed. Instead high, rigid supports would continue through 1950, after which a sliding scale would be phased in. However, because of the increased demand for basic commodities during the Korean War, price supports were maintained at high, fixed levels throughout the conflict. It was not until the Agricultural Act of 1954 that a sliding scale was finally fixed into law, a law that Aiken helped put together.

In May 1952 Aiken charged that the Truman administration had manipulated farm prices during the 1948 presidential campaign, costing farmers a billion dollars. The purpose of this "dirty trick," he said, was to discredit the Hope-Aiken Act passed by the Republican-controlled Congress in 1948. A few days before the election in November 1952, he accused the Democrats of once again manipulating farm prices for political advantage.

In June 1950 Aiken joined Senator MARGARET CHASE SMITH (R-Maine) and five other Republican senators in signing a "Declaration of Conscience" denouncing the tactics of Senator JOSEPH R. MCCARTHY (R-Wisc.). The declaration criticized the Truman administration for "lack of effective leadership," but it also accused elements in the Republican Party of hoping to "[ride] the Republican Party to victory through the selfish political exploitation of fear, bigotry, ignorance and intolerance."

Aiken began to play a prominent role in foreign policy after he joined the Senate Foreign Relations Committee in 1954. He was an outspoken critic of the Vietnam War. The senator continued to wield influence over agricultural policy until his retirement in 1975 at the age of 82. Aiken left Washington to return to his farm in Vermont. He died on November 19, 1984, in Montpelier, Vermont. (See

The Eisenhower Years, The Kennedy Years, The Johnson Years, The Nixon/Ford Years Volumes)

—TFS

Allen, George E(dward)

(1896–1973) *director, Reconstruction Finance Corporation*

George E. Allen was born on February 29, 1896, in Booneville, Mississippi. He received a law degree from Cumberland University in 1917 and set up a practice in the small town of Okolona, Mississippi. Following service in the army during World War I, he returned to his law firm but soon left to manage some of Chicago's largest hotels. In 1929 he moved to Washington, D.C., where he became friendly with many New Deal politicians. As a result of the influence of Senator Pat Harrison (D-Miss.), Allen was appointed one of the three commissioners of the District of Columbia in 1933. He also served as an aide to Harry L. Hopkins, head of several government relief programs. He returned to private business in 1938 and became a director of several large manufacturing corporations.

Allen was a long-time personal aide to Senator Harry S Truman. While secretary of the Democratic National Committee in 1943, he helped lead the Truman for vice president campaign. After Truman assumed the presidency, Allen became a member of his informal "breakfast" cabinet. Allen was also fun to be around. He liked to play poker (the president's favorite game, which he dubbed "the art of probabilities"), told good jokes, and became akin to military aide Harry Vaughan, another mirthful fellow in Truman's inner circle. He acted as liaison between the White House and Congress, and, in September 1945, Truman asked Allen to survey the state of existing war agencies and suggest which ones should be liquidated.

Several months later the President appointed Allen director of the Reconstruction Finance Corporation (RFC), an agency formed during the Hoover Administration to give aid to banks, insurance companies, and railroads. After World War II it also took on the responsibility for disposing of government surplus. The appointment generated vocal opposition from a number of prominent liberals and conservatives, led by Senator ROBERT A. TAFT (R-Ohio). Interior Secretary Harold L. Ickes said Allen's was "the worst appointment so far made by President Truman, and that is adding fragrance to a skunk cabbage." These men and women saw it as a prime example of Truman's "cronyism." They maintained that Allen had received the post on the basis of friendship and not experience or ability, and they pointed to his parallel rise in business and influence in the White House. Many were dubious of a man who had seemed to ingratiate himself with powerful people for self-advancement. Some saw Allen as a court jester and took the appointment as a joke. Taft also raised the possibility of conflict of interest, since Allen said he could remain director of several businesses and still remain impartial. He said that he would resign from any directorship if any conflict should come up. The Senate Committee on Banking and Currency approved the appointment and the full Senate confirmed Allen, but, as Truman scandal expert Andrew J. Dunar noted, his appointment added to Truman's image as a creature of machine-style politics.

In October 1946 Allen led a team of members of the RFC, State, Treasury, Commerce, and War Departments in devising a program to make Germany economically self-sufficient, in studying its industrial potential and in reviewing American reparations policy. While in Germany he negotiated agreements granting loans to that nation to procure raw materials. Returning to the United States a month later, Allen participated in Anglo-American negotiations on unifying the British and American zones in Germany. He resigned in January 1947 after proposing an amendment to the RFC Act divesting the agency of powers granted during the war.

Allen played an important role in gaining Truman the Democratic presidential nomination in 1948. According to the *St. Louis Post Dispatch*, in July of that year Allen stopped a movement to draft General DWIGHT D. EISENHOWER by asking the general to issue a statement saying he would not run if nominated and not serve if elected. But the *Post Dispatch* overestimated Allen's role in Eisenhower's decision not to run in 1948. According to Eisenhower biographer Stephen E. Ambrose, the general merely told Allen he did not want to be bothered. It was a letter of Senator CLAUDE PEPPER (D-Fla.) saying that he would nominate Eisenhower at the Democratic Convention that finally forced the general to say he would not run. During the 1950s Allen became a business executive and wrote a book, entitled *Presidents Who Have Known Me*, as well as a number of articles in the *New York Times*.

In 1952 Allen produced his own television show, "Man of the Week." Allen died on April 23, 1973, in Palm Desert, California.

—RSG

Allen, George V(enable)
(1903–1970) ambassador, assistant secretary of state for public affairs

George V. Allen was born on November 3, 1903, in Durham, North Carolina. He received a B.A. from Duke University in 1924 and an M.A. in international affairs from Harvard in 1929. He worked as a teacher and reporter from 1924 to 1929 and entered the Foreign Service in 1930. During the decade he held posts in Kingston, Shanghai, Athens, and Cairo. In 1938 he joined the State Department's Near and Middle Eastern Division, eventually rising to head the division in 1944. Allen attended the Moscow, Cairo, and Potsdam conferences during World War II and was political and liaison officer at the San Francisco Conference in April 1945.

President Truman appointed Allen ambassador to Iran in April 1946. Iran was the focus of an early cold war struggle between the United States and the USSR. After the war Soviet troops had remained in the northern section of the country, giving support to a Communist uprising that led to the establishment of two socialist republics there. At the request of the United States, the troops were evacuated in March 1946, but only after Iran had signed an oil agreement with the USSR giving the Soviet Union controlling interest in a joint stock corporation.

Allen's major tasks were to prevent ratification of the oil treaty, aid in the removal of Communist elements in the nation, and ally Iran to the United States. He encouraged the buildup of the Iranian police force and increased U.S. aid to both the police and the army. Allen's presence and forcefulness convinced Leftist premier Ahmad Ghavam to dismiss Communist cabinet members. Allen developed a close relationship with Shah Mohammed Reza Pahlavi even to the point of playing tennis with him on a weekly basis. Allen also won an agreement that U.S. Army personnel would be the only foreign advisers to the Iranian army. During 1947 he spoke out vigorously against the proposed Iranian-Soviet oil treaty and encouraged resistance to Soviet penetration. He assured the Iranians that if they rejected the treaty, they could count on American support against the USSR. The Iranian parliament voted

down the agreement 102 to 2 in October 1947. Ghavam was forced to resign in December and was replaced by pro-Western Ibrahim Hakimi Al-Molk. The army then moved to eliminate the Communist governments in northern Iran.

In January 1948 Allen succeeded WILLIAM B. BENTON as assistant secretary of state for public affairs. During his tenure he consolidated Voice of America (VOA) programs under the department's supervision and, according to the *New York Times*, made the VOA a "full-fledged, hard-hitting propaganda machine." Allen was also active in exporting American culture, which had previously been the responsibility of the private sector.

Allen served as ambassador to Yugoslavia from October 1949 to March 1953. Although an anti-communist, he favored a conciliatory approach to Tito's Communist government. He encouraged trade with Yugoslavia and favored lifting restrictions on Americans wishing to travel to the country. Allen argued that the administration should encourage Yugoslavia's separatist tendencies with economic and military aid, and his suggestion became U.S. policy. He also contended successfully that America should not try to make Josip Tito align formally with the West, which might spark Soviet intervention.

From 1953 to 1955 Allen served as ambassador to India and Nepal. He became assistant secretary of state for Near Eastern, South Asian, and African affairs in 1955 and head of the U.S. Information Agency in 1958. Following his retirement from government service in 1960, he became president of the Tobacco Institute. President Lyndon B. Johnson appointed him head of the Foreign Service Institute in 1966. Allen retired in 1969 and died in Washington, D.C., on July 11, 1970. (See *The Eisenhower Years* Volume)

—AES

Allen, Leo E(lwood)
(1898–1973) member of the House of Representatives

Leo Allen was born on October 5, 1898, in Elizabeth, Illinois. Following service as an artillery sergeant in World War I, Allen obtained an A.B. from the University of Michigan in 1923. He taught in Illinois public high schools from 1922 to 1924 and then entered politics, winning election as clerk of the county circuit court at Galena, Illinois. He was elected as a Republican from the GOP-dominated

16th Congressional District in November 1932. In the House Allen established a record as a conservative isolationist, opposing lend-lease as well as the Selective Service Act. He was a foe of organized labor. Allen opposed government regulation of the economy and was an advocate of business interests.

During the Truman administration the representative continued his conservative voting pattern, supporting the Tart-Hartley Act of 1947 and the Internal Security Act of 1950. A states' rights advocate, he favored the Dirksen amendment calling for the state control of the U.S. Unemployment Service.

Following the Republican triumph in the 1946 congressional election, Allen became chairman of the House Rules Committee. He used his position to oppose much of the Truman administration's legislative program. He blocked appropriations for reclamation projects and voted against school lunch bills and guaranteed parity prices for farmers. Allen also delayed in committee a bill providing for public housing and slum clearance. His isolationism persisted into the cold war. He opposed aid to Greece and Turkey in 1947 and condemned the Marshall Plan in 1948. Allen even wished to eliminate Voice of America broadcasts to Eastern Europe to save money. He also opposed American participation in the World Health Organization.

During the postwar years Allen was known for his opposition to universal military training (UMT). He used his position as chairman of the Rules Committee in 1948 to block the UMT bill and opposed a revival of the draft. He ignored a request from House Armed Services Committee chairman Walter G. Andrews of New York to have hearings on the UMT bill. (American Legion National Commander James F. O'Neil, a UMT supporter, accused Allen of "political cowardice" for not allowing a vote on the bill.) After Truman again asked for UMT and a reinstitution of the draft in March 1948 in a special message, Allen denounced the president for requesting "world shaking legislation" and he said that there was "no more prospect" for a vote on UMT than had been the case previously. He did say he was willing to support the re-creation of Selective Service registration, but not the draft itself until an emergency required it. Allen proposed instead voluntary enlistments and bonuses for members of the Armed Forces. His bill, presented in May 1948, offered $1,000 bonuses to two-year enlistees and $1,500 for three-year men. Truman denounced the measure and attacked Allen in speeches during the

1948 presidential campaign. When the Armed Services Committee approved the bill providing for the draft, Allen delayed making a rule for its debate. After the Rules Committee voted to bring it to the floor, Allen urged its defeat, but failed.

Allen lost his chairmanship of the Rules Committee in 1949 but regained it following the Republican victory in the 1952 election. During the 1950s he formed part of the Southern Democratic–Republican coalition in the Rules Committee that prevented much social legislation from reaching the House floor. However, he broke with the Southern Democrats on the issue of civil rights. Allen declined to run for reelection in 1960. He died in Galena, Illinois, on January 19, 1973. (See *The Eisenhower Years* Volume)

—AES

Alsop, Joseph W(right)
(1910–1989) *journalist, author*

The son of parents with ties to the Roosevelt family, Joseph W. Alsop was born on October 11, 1910, in Avon, Connecticut, where he grew up. He attended the exclusive Groton School and graduated from Harvard College in 1932. Through family influence, he won a job as a reporter for the *New York Herald Tribune*. Despite his lack of experience, he soon developed into one of the paper's top feature writers. In 1936 he was sent to Washington to cover news in the capital. The following year he began a syndicated column, "The Capital Parade," which was distributed to almost 100 papers. During World War II Alsop joined General CLAIRE L. CHENNAULT's American Volunteer Group in China. His experience there left him a strong supporter of Generalissimo Chiang Kai-shek (Jiang Jieshi) and a staunch anticommunist.

Following the war Alsop joined with his brother Stewart on another syndicated column for the *Herald Tribune*, titled "Matter of Fact." The Alsops believed in the "rule of feet" and claimed that each article was based on interviews with four different sources. However, Joseph Alsop tended to be dogmatic and, according to a contemporary, he "seldom allowed facts to interfere with his prejudices," particularly his belief in U.S. supremacy. Alsop consistently took a strong stand against Soviet expansionism. He was one the first Americans in the Truman period to call for higher military spending. He also badgered U.S. officials to suppress Communist insurgencies. In November 1947, while in Prague, he wrote that "unless drastic countermeasures are taken, the iron curtain will clank down" on Czechoslovakia. The next year he turned his attention to Korea. In a column written with his brother, he railed against the National Security Council decision to evacuate the American zone in Korea. They warned that the effect would be to "throw all of Korea into the expanding Soviet Empire" and to weaken "the forces of resistance to Communist expansion throughout Asia," particularly in China. In 1950 Alsop maintained that the only way for the Western world to survive Soviet expansion was to increase its defenses.

Alsop consistently maintained that the true threat to the United States was external Soviet intrusion, not internal Communist subversion. He opposed McCarthyism and came to the defense of its victims. In May 1950 he sent a letter to Senator MILLARD E. TYDING's (D-Md.) office refuting the charge that OWEN LATTIMORE and JOHN S. SERVICE had supported the Communists in China. Alsop claimed that, based on his experience there, both men favored Chiang during the critical years 1942–44.

In October 1951 Alsop appeared before the Senate Internal Security Subcommittee to defend former vice president HENRY A. WALLACE and State Department official JOHN CARTER VINCENT against accusations that they had sympathised with the Chinese Communists during World War II. Again citing his own experience in wartime China, Alsop testified that both men had supported Chiang's campaign. Alsop went on to show that LOUIS A. BUDENZ, a former Communist, had lied to the panel in leveling charges against Wallace.

During the Eisenhower administration, Alsop took a gloomy view of world affairs. He viewed as desperate the situations in Korea, Indochina, and the Middle East. In 1954 Alsop joined his brother in denouncing the Atomic Energy Commission's refusal to reinstate J. ROBERT OPPENHEIMER's security clearance. During the 1960s Alsop strongly defended U.S. involvement in Southeast Asia. In 1973 he stopped writing his syndicated column and turned his attention to studies of Greek antiquities. Alsop died on August 28, 1989, in Washington, D.C. (See *The Eisenhower Years, The Kennedy Years, The Johnson Years* Volumes)

—EF

Anderson, Clinton P(resba)

(1895–1975) *secretary of agriculture, member of the Senate*

Born on October 23, 1895, in Centerville, South Dakota, Clinton P. Anderson was the son of a Swedish immigrant and fervent populist and grew up in the state he was born. Clinton's youth on a poor farm with a populist father and his bout with tuberculosis gave him an empathy for the downtrodden. He studied at Dakota Wesleyan University and in 1915 transferred to the University of Michigan. In 1916 his father broke his back, and Anderson had to return to South Dakota to help out the family. He went to work as a reporter for the *Mitchell* (S.Dak.) *Republican* in 1916. Rejected from service in World War I because he had tuberculosis, Anderson moved to New Mexico in 1917 to seek a cure. His health improved, and from 1918 to 1922, he worked as a journalist for the two Albuquerque newspapers, the *Herald* and the *Journal*. In 1925 he opened his own insurance agency.

Anderson was active in the Democratic Party and worked for Franklin D. Roosevelt's nomination in 1932. The governor of New Mexico appointed him state treasurer the following year. In 1935–36 he served as the administrator for the Federal Emergency Relief Administration and from 1936 to 1938 as chairman and executive director of the Unemployment Compensation Commission of New Mexico. In 1940 he won a seat in the U.S. House of Representatives, where he established a liberal record.

During the spring of 1945 Anderson served as chairman of a special committee investigating food shortages in the United States. The panel issued a strong indictment of bureaucratic mismanagement in government and criticized the War Food Administration's (WFA) "bare shelves policy," which was designed to cut back production to prevent a surplus after the war. President Truman, impressed with the committee's report, appointed Anderson secretary of agriculture in 1945. As a condition of his appointment, Anderson insisted that he be given control of the WFA activities. The president abolished the agency and turned its functions over to the Department of Agriculture.

Truman, who had little interest in agricultural policy, delegated responsibility for it to Anderson. The secretary quickly allied himself to the large, conservative farmers represented by the Farm Bureau Federation. Anderson was a vigorous opponent of rationing and agricultural subsidies paid to keep food prices low while maintaining farm income. The large farmers, particularly in the Midwest, demanded repeal of the subsidy because it left their future income vulnerable to the whim of Congress and accustomed consumers to low prices. In July 1945 Anderson remarked to the press that since consumers had the money, subsidies should be ended and prices raised.

Anderson's stand brought him into conflict with CHESTER BOWLES, head of the Office of Price Administration (OPA), who wanted to maintain subsidies and rationing to help the consumer and aid famine-stricken Europe. In November 1945 Bowles accepted Anderson's call for an end to meat rationing because of the difficulty of enforcement. The two men agreed to the gradual elimination of subsidies by June 1946 so long as there would be no net increase in the food price index. However, in January 1946, as inflation mounted, Truman announced the continuation of subsidies.

The secretary's desire to raise farm prices made him appear indifferent to the threat of famine in Europe and renewed inflation at home. Because of the relative prices of meat and grain, it was more profitable for farmers to sell their grain for fodder rather than bring it to the consumer market. In April 1946 Anderson proposed a 25-cent-per-bushel increase in the price of corn. Bowles called the proposal "dangerously inflationary," and it was rejected. By the third week in April, the United States was 512,000 tons behind its goal of shipments to Europe. On April 19, following Bowles's suggestion, the government offered large bonuses for corn and wheat. Still the grain stayed on the farm. On May 10 the government accepted Anderson's suggestion, announcing a 25-cent increase in the ceiling price of corn and a 15-cent increase in the ceiling on wheat. Grain flowed swiftly to market, and the United States met its commitment of six million tons by June. However, inflation also increased.

In spring 1946 a temporary meat shortage developed. On May 1 Anderson made a statement interpreted in the press as meaning that if supply remained tight, price controls should be lifted. In response farmers held cattle from market in order to get rid of the hated price controls.

With the expiration of the OPA at the end of June, controls went off food prices. The result was unprecedented inflation. Food prices went up 13.8 percent in one month. On September 1 the government put meat back under price control. Ander-

son took the extraordinary step of announcing his own price ceilings, but they were significantly above those planned by the OPA. Nevertheless there was a sudden drop in meat marketing, with 90 percent of retail butchers closed in Chicago. Truman, under pressure because of the upcoming elections, ended price ceilings on meat on October 14.

Anderson was successful in many of his initiatives. He helped see through Congress modification of agricultural credit policies, the Agriculture and Marketing Act of 1946, and wool legislation. He also succeeded in reducing cotton surpluses and encouraged technological advancement in farm work. The department under Anderson conserved wheat and reduced the amount of grain for feeding livestock, and he was able to stockpile enough food to meet the requirements of Truman's Nine Point Famine Relief Program. However, Anderson has received criticism from historians for not leading early enough an effort to feed a destitute Europe in 1945–46, for being too narrow- or partisan-minded in regard to tariff and wool policies, for not caring for consumer needs, and for failing to back the Bureau of Agricultural Economics.

Although Anderson was a vigorous supporter of farmers, he made enemies among agricultural producers with his attempts to reorganize the Department of Agriculture along commodity lines. In September 1946 he abolished the field service branch, which had been set up during the New Deal. Both the conservative Farm Bureau and the liberal Farmers Union opposed the reorganization, maintaining it would take power away from farmers and give it to processors. JAMES PATTON, president of the Farmers Union, warned Truman that the reorganization would "cause a widespread revolt among farmers with serious results . . . for the Democratic Party." Less than two weeks after Anderson issued the order, Truman announced its suspension.

The administration's clumsy and vacillating agricultural policy hurt the Democrats in the 1946 election. Consumers blamed meat shortages and inflation on the government. Although farm income was very high in 1946, the ineffectual attempts to control farm prices alienated most farmers. In the November 1946 congressional elections, not one Democratic candidate won in the predominantly rural districts in the Midwest. The Republicans captured both houses.

In 1947 Anderson became deeply involved in the growing debate over long-term agricultural policy. In order to prevent a ruinous collapse in prices such as that following World War I, Congress had passed the Steagall Amendment of 1942 requiring price supports for all farm commodities be maintained at 90 percent of parity until December 31, 1948. Anderson believed high, rigid prices supports only caused farmers to produce more, which lowered farm prices and led to calls for more government intrusion. Anderson recommended that rigid parity be abolished and replaced by a sliding scale of price supports so that prices could be dropped to discourage production where there was oversupply. He also suggested doing away with mandatory price supports for perishable commodities. He advised shifting the formula so that price supports would be lower for products for which there was relatively less demand than in the base period of 1910–14 and higher for those products, principally meats, fruits, and vegetables, for which there was relatively greater demand.

In May 1948 Anderson resigned to seek the seat of retiring senator Carl Hatch (D-N.Mex.). Anderson defeated his Republican opponent, PATRICK J. HURLEY, former ambassador to China, in the November election. His policies as secretary of agriculture were indirectly vindicated by Truman's upset victory that year. Iowa, Wisconsin, and Ohio, which had gone to the Republicans in 1944, went solidly for Truman.

As a member of the Agriculture Committee, Anderson continued to play a major role in the formation of farm policy. He quickly became embroiled in controversy over Secretary of Agriculture CHARLES F. BRANNAN's proposal calling for high, rigid price supports, but limiting them to only a portion of production, approximately the first $26,000 in sales, in order to benefit the small farmer. Anderson's successor had also recommended price supports of perishables in the form of direct cash payments to farmers rather than price support loans and purchases. This, he assumed, would encourage consumption by lowering prices to consumers. Anderson broke with the Truman administration on the Brannan Plan. He thought it would cost the government too much and would lead to overproduction. Instead, he reiterated his demand for flexible price supports.

When it became clear that the Brannan Plan did not have enough support for passage, Truman called Anderson to the White House and asked him to come up with a compromise bill. The resultant Agricultural Act of 1949 was a complicated com-

promise between those who favored high, rigid price supports and those who wanted flexible ones. The final version called for 90 percent supports through 1950 and the gradual introduction of a flexible system in 1951–52. Anderson included for the first time the cost of hired labor in the parity index.

As a member of the Senate Interior Committee, Anderson played an important role in the tidelands oil controversy over whether the states or the federal government should control offshore oil. Anderson, who backed the federal government's ownership, put together a compromise, the O'Mahoney-Anderson Resolution, which called for granting 37.5 percent of all revenues to the states. The bill was severely weakened on the Senate floor, and Anderson was only too glad to see it vetoed by Truman in May 1952.

Anderson also supported the administration's containment policy. Anderson was a typical postwar liberal politician who was liberal on domestic policy (except perhaps agricultural policy) and an internationalist on foreign policy.

Anderson became a member of the Joint Committee on Atomic Energy in 1951 and was made chairman in 1955. He played a major role in the U.S. atomic energy policy in the years that followed. He was involved in the U.S. space program and was a major proponent of medicare. Anderson retired from the Senate in 1972, and he died on November 11, 1975, in Albuquerque, New Mexico. (See *The Eisenhower Years, The Kennedy Years, The Johnson Years* Volumes)

—TFS

Armour, Norman
(1887–1982) *assistant secretary of state for Latin America affairs, ambassador*
Born in Brighton, England, on October 14, 1887, of American parents, Norman Armour received a bachelor's degree from Princeton in 1909, a law degree from Harvard in 1913, and a master's degree from Princeton in 1915. That year he entered the Foreign Service and was posted to Paris. From 1915 to 1919 Armour was stationed in Russia, where he was briefly imprisoned by the Bolshevik regime. In the 1920s and 1930s Armour served in various posts in Europe, Asia, and Latin America. He became ambassador to Chile in 1938. During World War II he served as ambassador to the fascist regimes in Argentina and Spain. In 1944 Armour was recalled

from Argentina and was named assistant secretary of state for Latin America affairs. Here Armour participated in establishing the United Nations. For a short time in 1945–46, he was ambassador to Spain, but withdrew when dictator Francisco Franco refused to adopt democratic reforms.

President Truman called Armour out of retirement in 1947 to become assistant secretary of state for political affairs. Known as the "ideal diplomat," he was responsible for coordinating the department's four geographical divisions, centralizing Foreign Service operations, and increasing the secretary of state's knowledge of Foreign Service officers.

Although Armour's principal responsibilities were administrative, he also played an active role as an adviser on Latin American policy. The diplomat urged greater U.S. economic aid to Central and South America in order to boost America's image there at a time when the State Department's focus was on Europe. Armour deplored U.S. indifference to the region, noting that Latin American's dissatisfaction with American assistance had led to a deterioration in relations with the United States. As a member of the delegation to the Ninth International Conference of the American States at Bogotá in 1948, he pressured Secretary of State GEORGE C. MARSHALL into assuring Latin American nations that the United States had not forgotten their problems.

Armour retired once again in July 1948 but was recalled in 1950 to become the ambassador to Venezuela, where the United States was carrying on delicate oil negotiations. He played an important part in developing contracts for foreign companies to extract oil in the eastern part of the country. He served until 1951, when he again left the diplomatic service. During the opening days of the Eisenhower administration, Armour joined other Foreign Service officers in protesting Senator JOSEPH R. MCCARTHY's (R-Wisc.) attack on the State Department. From 1954 to 1955 he was ambassador to Guatemala. Armour then went into retirement. He died on September 27, 1982, in New York City. (See *The Eisenhower Years* Volume)

—AES

Arvey, Jacob (Meyer)
(1895–1977) *chairman, Cook County Democratic Central Committee*

Born on November 3, 1895, in Chicago, Illinois, Jacob Arvey was the son of poor Jews. He worked as a delivery boy while attending John Marshall Law School at night. He began practicing in 1916 and two years later became assistant state attorney for Cook Company. In 1920 Arvey joined a law firm closely associated with Pat Nash and Ed Kelly, the leaders of the Democratic Party machine in Chicago. He soon became district leader and alderman of the predominantly Jewish 24th Ward. His ability to deliver votes and provide jobs for his constituents made him a major power in the machine by World War II. Arvey served in the army during World War II.

After he returned from the war then mayor Ed Kelly appointed him Cook County Democratic Central Committee chairman. The party had endured losses in the 1946 election, and the Republicans appeared ready to have one of their own elected mayor for the first time since the 1920s. The inept, corrupt leadership of Mayor Kelly and the electoral losses demoralized the party. Assuming that the organization could survive only if it changed its image, Arvey undertook a complete revitalization and reorientation of the machine. He viewed the traditional boss, whose power had rested on patronage and the distribution of charity, as an anachronism made obsolete by New Deal social programs. Instead, Arvey argued, the future of the machine must be tied to good, clean government pledged to prosperity and security for all.

During 1947 Arvey worked behind the scenes to maneuver Kelly out of another term. Instead the party sponsored Martin Kennelly, a businessman and civic leader, as its candidate. Running with the support of liberals and labor as well as traditional Democratic groups, "Honest Martin" Kennelly easily defeated Russell W. Root, the Republican candidate.

The victory made Arvey the most powerful Democrat in Illinois. In 1948 he guided the election of ADLAI E. STEVENSON as governor and PAUL H. DOUGLAS as senator. Although he clashed with Kennelly, whom he considered politically inept, Arvey worked well with the other reformers he had helped elect. Stevenson's progressivism gratified him because the governor linked the machine with good government and thus insured votes. Arvey acquired the image of an enlightened machine boss with his sponsorship of reform candidates like Kennelly, Stevenson, and Douglas. He strengthened the party in the city and state and used that power to swing Illinois to Truman in 1948. Unfortunately for Arvey, he supported a man for Cook County sheriff in 1950 who lost after it became known that he had become rich through illegal insider trading.

Arvey played an important role in persuading Stevenson to run for the Democratic presidential nomination in 1952. After Stevenson made it clear in early 1952 that he would not seek the presidency, his supporters asked Arvey to persuade the governor to change his mind. Arvey responded by promising not to apply pressure on Stevenson, but he unofficially announced that the governor would run if drafted by the convention. This proved to be a major incentive for the Stevenson forces to mobilize and successfully capture the nomination. Following the Democratic defeat in 1952, Richard J. Daley, an Arvey protégé, replaced his boss as party leader. Arvey then received a post within the Democratic National Committee, serving there until 1972, and remained an elder statesman in the Democratic Party. He continued to practice law and was active in Jewish affairs. Arvey died in Chicago on August 25, 1977.

—JB

Austin, Warren (Robinson)
(1877–1962) *ambassador*

Warren Austin was born on November 12, 1877, in Highgate, Vermont. He received a Ph.B. degree from the University of Vermont in 1899. Three years later he was admitted to the bar and began a career as a lawyer. In March 1931 Austin, a Republican, was elected to fill a Senate seat vacated by the death of Senator Frank L. Greene (R-Vt.). In the upper house Austin opposed many of Franklin D. Roosevelt's domestic policies. He was a leader in the fight against the Tennessee Valley Authority in 1935 and opposed Roosevelt's attempts to pack the Supreme Court in 1937. In contrast, Austin, who was a member of the Foreign Relations Committee, supported Roosevelt's foreign policy. Along with Senator ARTHUR H. VANDENBERG (R-Mich.), he was a major influence in infusing the Republican Party with a sense of internationalism and in gaining support for a bipartisan foreign policy. He was a strong supporter of an international organization to maintain the peace and, in conferences during World War II, pushed the Republican Party to back his position. During World War II Austin served two State Department advisory committees because of his internationalism and his support for a postwar international organization. He voted for the Ful-

bright Resolution of 1943 and the following year supported the Pepper Amendment committing the Senate more specifically to an "international authority" to maintain the peace. The liberal newspaper, *PM*, termed him an ultrainternationalist. However, because of his internationalism, he was removed as assistant minority leader by the Republican isolationist leadership, and not allowed to sit on the Foreign Relations Committee until late in the war.

At the end of the war, Austin was an adviser to the Inter-American Conference at Mexico City. He argued that American economic aid would be needed for postwar recovery and called for U.S. leadership in the UN. The president appointed

Warren H. Austin, 1951 *(Harry S. Truman Library, Abbie Rowe)*

Austin chief of the U.S. mission to the UN in June 1946 to bolster bipartisan support for the organization and enhance the prestige of the post by giving it to a national figure. In addition, Truman viewed the appointment as insurance against partisan attacks by a Congress that Secretary of State JAMES F. BYRNES assumed would be Republican-dominated. Due to a quirk in the Constitution, Austin was unable to assume the title until the current congressional session ended in January 1947.

Austin had great faith in the UN, more than Truman and his secretaries of state, with the possible exception of EDWARD R. STETTINIUS, JR. However, Austin had little influence over policymaking. Instead, he served as the administration's spokesman in the early battles of the cold war. He was an eloquent opponent of the Soviet Union's attempts to use the international organization as a propaganda forum. He continually ridiculed the USSR for professing to support peace while undertaking aggression. Austin was involved in the debates on the Berlin airlift, Palestine, and the Korean War.

Austin had his greatest difficulties at the UN over Palestine. The question concerned the fate of the area following the termination of the British mandate: should Palestine be continued as a trusteeship under the UN or should it be partitioned into Arab and Jewish states? Fearing the latter course would lead to war, both Truman and Austin advocated a trusteeship under the UN at least for a short term. Austin enunciated the position on March 19, 1948. On May 14 Truman, who had been notified that the provisional government of Israel would proclaim independence that midnight, announced de facto recognition of the government. Austin was telephoned the news while he was on the floor of the General Assembly. Instead of returning after the call, he drove home. DEAN RUSK, then director of the Office of UN Affairs and the one who telephoned Austin, later hypothesized that Austin ". . . thought it was better for the General Assembly to know very clearly that this was the act of the President in Washington and that the United States delegation had not been playing a double game with the other delegations."

The Communists, by refusing to abide by the UN resolution to withdraw from South Korea, converted him into an ardent cold warrior. He backed Truman's limited war in Korea, and his firing of General DOUGLAS MACARTHUR, despite being the highest-ranking Republican in the administration.

In spite of a heart ailment, which often prevented him from attending sessions, Austin continued in this post until the Eisenhower administration. Austin died on December 25, 1962, in Burlington, Vermont.

—MLB

B

Baillie, Hugh
(1890–1966) *president and general manager, United Press Association*

Hugh Baillie was born on October 23, 1890, in Brooklyn, New York, the son of a prominent political correspondent for the *New York World* and the *New York Tribune.* He attended the University of Southern California from 1907 to 1910 and then began a career in journalism. In 1915 he joined the United Press Associations (UP) and rose to become general news manager in 1922. In 1924 Baillie turned from the editorial to the business side of the organization with his appointment as sales manager. By 1935 he had become president of the organization. Periodically Baillie took off from his duties to report. He interviewed Adolf Hitler and Benito Mussolini in 1935 and Neville Chamberlain after the Munich Conference of 1938. In 1943 he covered the fighting in Sicily and the following year was wounded during the Belgian campaign.

During the postwar era Baillie became famous for interviews with world leaders. In 1945 he attempted to interview General Hideki Tojo when a U.S. officer came to arrest the former Japanese premier. Tojo tried to commit hara-kiri, but botched his attempt. The same year he chatted with Emperor Hirohito and was able to obtain written responses to written questions. The emperor said Japan now had a new orientation and would show itself equal to participation in the international community. Baillie traveled to Chungking, China, to interview Chiang Kai-shek (Jiang Jieshi). The generalissimo said the Japanese leaders who brought about the war should be punished after a fair trial and that humanitarian concerns should guide aid to Japan. Whether the Japanese emperor should be allowed to stay in power was something the Japanese people had to decide. Japan should have representative government, and he believed French Indochina and the Dutch East Indies should be granted much autonomy as a beginning step toward independence. He was optimistic that China would become unified and achieve internal peace.

Baillie obtained an exclusive interview with General DOUGLAS MACARTHUR, baiting him by showing him editorials criticizing him for being too lenient toward the Japanese. MacArthur talked with Baillie off the record, saying the army and navy had been made obsolete by the atomic bomb. Mounting criticism convinced MacArthur that he had to make the on-the-record interview that Baillie wanted. The general said the days of Japan as an international power were finished—she had been wrecked by the war. He noted, contrary to rumors, that the Japanese army and navy were to be abolished. When Baillie asked him whether the U.S. Army's presence constituted pacification or an invasion, the general asserted it was neither, but "the occupation of a conquered country by the forces which defeated it." Baillie found the general loquacious and a deliberate speaker, with a tendency toward imperious mispronunciations. He proclaimed he would judge war criminals and the guilty would be executed. He claimed he had no interest in politics and his proconsulship was his last assignment before he faded away.

The following year Baillie conducted an interview with Joseph Stalin in which the Soviet dictator stated that the USSR possessed no atomic weapons, desired U.S. economic assistance, and believed harmony between the two nations could continue if such "incendiaries" as Winston Churchill were ignored. The interview made headlines around the world. Baillie's extensive use of interviews increased the popularity of UP. In April 1947 he reported that UP had an unprecedented 2,689 clients.

Baillie campaigned for worldwide freedom of news dissemination. He emphasized, however, that freedom of the press as it was known in the United States was as yet impractical in some countries. In 1944 he detailed his demands: news sources and transmission facilities open to all and a minimum regulation of the flow of news. Two years later he requested that free international news exchange be adopted as UN policy. His pleas for an international agreement for reciprocity in the gathering and selling of the news went unheeded. At the Geneva Conference on Freedom of Information in 1948, France as well as the Soviet bloc countries opposed any agreement.

Baillie covered many of the important events of the Korean War. In September 1950 he wrote a dispatch describing the ceremony at which MacArthur returned Seoul to South Korean administration. After Chinese entry into the war, he conducted another exclusive interview with the general. MacArthur argued that the United States had to fight the Communists in Korea so war could be avoided in Europe. Baillie supported MacArthur's contention that U.S. bombing of Manchuria was necessary for victory and that the USSR would not intervene. Full of admiration for the sacrifices of American soldiers in Korea, he was disappointed at the apathy toward the conflict. In the summer of 1952 he instructed his reporters to revive interest in the war by means of photographs and first-person stories from troops under fire. Baillie insisted that Dwight D. Eisenhower take reporters with him on the trip to Korea he said he would undertake if he won the 1952 presidential election.

Baillie retired as president of UP in 1955 and became chairman of the board. At that time the agency had 1,518 clients abroad and 2,874 in the United States. He died of a heart attack on March 1, 1966, in La Jolla, California.

—AES

Baldwin, C(alvin) B(enham)

(1902–1975) *executive vice chairman, Progressive Citizens of America*

C. B. "Beanie" Baldwin was born on August 19, 1902, in Radford, Virginia. He attended the Virginia Polytechnic Institute from 1920 to 1923 and then worked for the Norfolk and Western Railroad. Baldwin opened his own electrical contracting company in 1929. In 1933 he became assistant to HENRY A. WALLACE, then secretary of agriculture. Seven years later Baldwin took over the Farm Security Administration (FSA). The FSA distributed low cost loans to small farmers and encouraged cooperatives. Critics of the agency charged that it was trying to "communize American agriculture" and was being used as a device to purchase the votes of the poor.

During his days in Washington Baldwin supported the most radical measures of the New Deal. He advocated legislation guaranteeing jobs for the poor, national health insurance, and increased federal housing. Baldwin favored a postwar world that would insure peace through a United Nations and continued Soviet-American collaboration. As a leading civil libertarian, he refused to sever his ties with his Communist friends and defended their right to work in government and participate in the political process. President Roosevelt removed Baldwin as head of the FSA in 1943 in part because of conservative pressure. The following year Baldwin became Sydney Hillman's assistant on the Congress of Industrial Organizations' Political Action Committee (PAC) and worked to bring out labor for Roosevelt in the election. In 1945 PAC founded the National Citizens Political Action Committee (NCPAC) to develop a liberal lobby that would include the middle class and intellectuals. The NCPAC invited all Americans, including Communists, to join. Baldwin became its executive vice chairman and its driving force.

During President Truman's first year in office, Baldwin and the NCPAC criticized the president for abandoning the New Deal and Roosevelt's policy of friendship with the Soviet Union. By spring 1946 Baldwin had already acknowledged that progressives would have to mount a third-party campaign for the presidency in 1948 because he saw Truman and the Democratic Party as indistinguishable from the Republicans. As writer Zachary Karabell has noted, Baldwin was seen by some observers as a leftist ideologue, but others saw him as a chameleon, supporting the ideology of whomever he was following.

In December 1946 the NCPAC and other liberal organizations merged to become the Progressive Citizens of America (PCA), with Baldwin as its executive vice chairman and chief political tactician. Throughout 1947 Baldwin wooed Henry Wallace to become the PCA's presidential candidate. Although Wallace rejected Baldwin's requests, he became the group's leading speaker, and Baldwin became one of his closest political advisers. After Wallace agreed to run for the nomination, Baldwin worked to get his name on state ballots and served as his campaign manager during the presidential campaign. Baldwin worried about the efforts of some party members to insert a denunciation of Stalinism in the platform, because he believed activist and singer PAUL B. ROBESON and others would object. Such language was blocked but to the frustration of many party members. Former New Dealer REXFORD G. TUGWELL was so upset that he thought of leaving the party. He confessed that he was "an uneasy member" of Wallace's party and that "the wrong people" had obtained control. Baldwin prodded Wallace to deny the Communists controlled the party and that he would not welcome anyone calling for revolution into his campaign. The announcement kept Tugwell from bolting. Although Wallace lost in 1948, Baldwin credited the campaign with moving Truman to the left. This, he believed, was victory enough in the campaign.

Wallace left the party in 1950, but Baldwin remained to be leader of the PCA until its dissolution in 1953. He died of cancer on May 12, 1975, in Bethesda, Maryland.

—JB

Baldwin, Raymond E(arl)

(1893–1986) *governor, member of the Senate*

Raymond E. Baldwin was born on August 31, 1893, in Rye, New York. After graduating from Wesleyan University in 1916, Baldwin served as an ensign in the navy during World War I. He obtained a law degree from Yale in 1921 and during the decade practiced with law firms in Connecticut. From 1927 to 1930 he was prosecutor for the town court of Stratford and from 1931 to 1933 a judge of the Stratford court. Baldwin was elected to the Connecticut House of Representatives in 1931 as a Republican. In 1938 he ran for governor on a platform promising a balanced budget, government aid to private enterprise, and low taxes. He won the election as a result of competition between Socialists and Democrats for the liberal vote. During his tenure he cut the budget, giving the state a million dollar surplus by 1940. He was defeated in the Democratic landslide of 1940. Baldwin won the governorship again in

1942 and 1944. He dealt with the state's postwar reconversion problems and developed a program to meet the crisis, including a state employment service and a job training program.

In 1946 Baldwin won a seat in the U.S. Senate by a record vote. During his one term in the upper house, he established a conservative record, voting for the Taft-Hartley Act and against an amendment giving the president standby rationing and wage-price control powers. Considering himself the spokesman of small business, he urged promotion of economic opportunity by state and local governments.

In 1949 Baldwin became embroiled in a controversy with Senator JOSEPH R. MCCARTHY (R–Wisc.) over the "Malmedy Massacre." During the Battle of the Bulge in December 1944, German SS troops slaughtered over 150 unarmed American and Belgian prisoners. A U.S. war crimes tribunal convicted the men of the massacre, sentencing many to death. In 1949 a Senate Armed Services subcommittee, chaired by Baldwin, investigated charges that the confessions were gained through torture. Although McCarthy was not a member of the panel. Baldwin gave him permission to attend meetings and cross-examine witnesses. The aims of the two men differed. Baldwin was concerned with clearing the army and allowing the prosecutors to present their sides. McCarthy, on the other hand, was anxious to discredit the army and win popularity among his German-American constituency. He claimed that the United States should not use techniques the Soviets used to obtain confessions. He was convinced the subcommittee wanted to whitewash the army prosecutors' conduct. Using tactics that would become famous, McCarthy bullied witnesses and misrepresented facts to win sympathy for the Nazis. Baldwin was hampered in containing the senator by the fact that one of the U.S. prosecutors in the case was one of his law partners. He, therefore, had to conduct himself cautiously to prevent charges of conflict of interest.

In May 1949, when the Armed Services Committee rejected McCarthy's request that the American prosecutors be subjected to lie detector tests during the investigation, he boycotted the hearings and denounced what he termed Baldwin's attempt to "whitewash a shameful episode" of American injustice. During July McCarthy called Baldwin "criminally responsible" in trying to protect his law firm. Baldwin was stunned by McCarthy's behavior, since he was such a genial man otherwise. A friend of McCarthy attributed this crusading attitude to the senator's romanticism. McCarthy himself, however, according to historian Thomas C. Reeves, was shaken by Baldwin's serene, even patronizing attitude toward his badgering, while other senators feared the Wisconsinite's wrath. The subcommittee maintained unity against McCarthy, and the full Armed Services Committee passed a resolution of confidence in Baldwin, condemning "the most unusual, unfair and utterly undeserved comments" against him. The committee adopted the Baldwin panel's report in October. It concluded that, despite irregularities, the trials had been fairly conducted, adding that the charges of mistreatment were part of a plot to "revive the German nationalistic spirit by discrediting the American Military Government" and to increase pro-Russian feeling in Germany. (Reeves noted the unlikelihood of this charge.)

Exhausted by the encounter with McCarthy, Baldwin decided to accept Connecticut governor CHESTER BOWLES's previous offer of a seat on the State Supreme Court of Errors. Baldwin resigned from the Senate in December 1949 to assume his duties. He rose to chief justice in 1959. He retired in August 1963 at the mandatory age of 70 and in 1965 was chairman of the Connecticut constitutional convention. Baldwin died on October 4, 1986, in Fairfield, Connecticut.

—AES

Baldwin, Roger Nash

(1884–1981) *director, American Civil Liberties Union*

Roger Nash Baldwin was born on January 21, 1884, in Wellesley, Massachusetts. The son of a prosperous leather merchant whose ancestors had sailed on the *Mayflower*, Baldwin was the product of a liberal Unitarian upbringing. He attended Harvard University, where he received a B.A. and an M.A. in anthropology and then moved to St. Louis to teach the first sociology course given at Washington University. In 1907 he was appointed chief probation officer of the city's juvenile court; the following year he became the first secretary of the National Probation Association, which he had helped to organize. Baldwin left the probation field in 1910 to become executive secretary of the St. Louis Civic League, a private organization dedicated to government reform. Exposure to the anarchist Emma Goldman and militant activists of the International

Workers of the World moved Baldwin's political beliefs to the left and deepened his commitment to radical individualism.

In 1917 Baldwin moved to New York and became secretary of the American Union against Militarism, a body created to keep the United States out of World War I. He refused to serve when he was drafted in 1918 and spent nine months in prison for his stand. During the war Baldwin helped to set up the National Civil Liberties Bureau to defend draft resisters and political dissidents. After the war he renamed the Bureau the American Civil Liberties Union (ACLU) and became its director. The ACLU had a broad mandate: the defense of all individual freedoms guaranteed by the Bill of Rights. Its statement of philosophy declared: "orderly social progress is promoted by unrestricted freedom of opinion."

During the 1920s and 1930s the ACLU battled for the rights of labor to assemble, form unions, and strike; fought the deportation of radical aliens; and participated in the defense of Sacco and Vanzetti. Baldwin contended that the Constitution shielded people you "feared as well as those you admire." The organization also led the fight against literary and film censorship; for instance, it successfully challenged the censoring of James Joyce's *Ulysses*. It was a prominent defender of freedom of speech. One of the most famous cases in which the ACLU played an important role was the Scopes "Monkey Trial" in 1925, in which the union tested a Tennessee statute banning the teaching of evolution. Over the years the ACLU was criticized for its constitutional purism, by the right for its defense of Communists, by the left for its representation of fascists and anti-Semites in free speech cases, and by patriotic zealots for its long battle in behalf of antistatist religious sects such as the Jehovah's Witnesses.

Zealous and energetic, Baldwin was the driving force behind the ACLU for 30 years. "Seldom has there been so complete an identification of an individual and an organization," said Dwight MacDonald in 1953. Baldwin's contribution to his organization was not as a theorist or litigator, but as an administrator, organizer, conciliator, planner, and guiding spirit. He was an articulate spokesman in defense of constitutional rights as well as a shrewd master of the internal politics involved in moving the ACLU in the direction he favored.

Baldwin evinced a broad range of political sympathies, joining and organizing scores of organizations dedicated to fighting injustice. In several of these Baldwin played the role of "fellow traveler," a prominent noncommunist sympathetic to Communist crusades. For a time Baldwin was also an enthusiastic partisan of the Soviet Union. He visited Russia and wrote articles and a book, *Liberty under the Soviets*, that condoned Soviet violations of civil liberties as a necessary step in the transition to socialism. In the late 1930s, particularly after the Nazi-Soviet pact of 1939, Baldwin repudiated his rhetorical tolerance of Stalin's dictatorship and opposed communism and any cooperation with Communists.

During World War II the ACLU continued to represent clients whose constitutional rights had been abridged, but many felt that its ardor in battling "national security" restrictions was not equal to that of its predecessor during World War I. After the war Baldwin and the ACLU opposed loyalty oaths for government employees, objected to Communists being refused entry into the United States, and criticized the McCarran Act as unconstitutional. It represented many employees who had been fired because their loyalty had been questioned. The union strongly opposed the 1948 indictments of 12 leading American Communists on charges of teaching and advocating the violent overthrow of the U.S. government.

In 1947, at the invitation of General DOUGLAS MACARTHUR, Baldwin visited Japan to inspect the state of civil liberties under the American occupation. Baldwin spent three months there, traveling and consulting, and laid the foundation for the Japanese Civil Liberties Union. "This is the greatest revolution I've seen," said Baldwin of postwar Japan, "and General MacArthur is leading it." Baldwin considered the general to be a sincere civil libertarian and wrote several magazine articles praising him and the reconstruction of the Japanese political system.

In 1950 Baldwin retired as director of the ACLU. At a testimonial dinner in his honor attended by hundreds of prominent liberals, he noted how the union had moved "from a position of suspected subversion to one of unexpected respectability." After his resignation Baldwin continued to serve as an active member of the ACLU's National Committee and acted as a liaison to the United Nations. In 1946 Baldwin had founded the International League for the Rights of Man—which later became the International League for Human Rights—an organiza-

tion dedicated to protecting civil liberties around the world, and, after his retirement, he dedicated much of his time to it. Baldwin died on August 26, 1981, in Ridgewood, New Jersey.

—TO

Ball, George W(ildman)

(1909–1994) *director, U.S. Strategic Bombing Survey; general counsel, French Supply Council*
George W. Ball was born on December 21, 1909, in Des Moines, Iowa. Following his graduation from Northwestern University Law School in 1933, Ball worked for the Farm Credit Administration and the Treasury Department. In 1933 he returned to Illinois and joined a Chicago law firm where ADLAI E. STEVENSON was one of his colleagues. At Stevenson's urging Ball reentered government service in 1942 in the Office of Lend-Lease Administration.

In 1944 Ball became a civilian member of the Air Force Evaluation Board, formed to study the effects of tactical air operations in the European theater. This role led to Ball's appointment as director of the United States Strategic Bombing Survey later that year. The 11-man civilian team was to determine the economic, social, and physical effects of the Allied bombing of Germany. Other members of the group included PAUL H. NITZE, JOHN KENNETH GALBRAITH, and—at Ball's invitation—Adlai Stevenson, as deputy director. During the closing months of the war, Ball and his associates followed the Allied troops in their advance through Europe. They interviewed members of the American and British high commands, surveyed bombing targets as they were captured, toured air installations, and interrogated Nazi prisoners, including Albert Speer, minister of economics and production. In *Life* magazine in December 1945, Ball discussed the group findings. The panel discovered that in some industries production had trebled immediately after bombing. Bombing, the article implied, had created a crisis of leadership among the Nazis that forced out incompetent managers in favor of more able men. It also served to unite the German people behind the government. His experience with the survey made him dubious of the effectiveness of the war's bombing campaign, which would feed his later skepticism of bombing North Vietnam during the Vietnam War. Ball believed that the most important contribution of Allied strategic bombing was that it forced the Luftwaffe out into the open, where Allied fighters could shoot down its planes. The attrition of the Luftwaffe allowed Allied forces to gain control of the skies of Normandy during the invasion, which helped lead to victory.

During his tenure with the Lend-Lease Administration Ball had come to know Jean Monnet. In September 1945 Monnet became chairman of the French Supply Council. He then asked Ball to be the council's general counsel in the United States. The council coordinated the economic restoration of France in the period immediately following the liberation. In his memoirs Ball explained that his job was to transform Monnet's ideas to "coherent exposition and, in the process, help him think." Monnet tended to jump around from problem to problem, twisting himself into knots; Ball's job was to untie him so the ideas became clear. After a French government had been established in 1946, the council's functions devolved to the French Planning Organization of which Monnet was also head. Through his work with these two groups, Ball participated in the development of the French Industrial Plan and in the subsequent negotiations for Marshall Plan trade credits and aid grants from the United States.

In May 1950 Robert Schuman, prompted by proposals that Monnet and his associates had developed, announced France's desire to place the coal- and steel-producing facilities of Germany and France under a single authority independent of either government and with the power to regulate these industries. Within days the Germans agreed. Ball spent most of the next year assisting in the detailed drafting of what came to be known as the Schuman Plan and in the negotiations that produced the European Coal and Steel Community Treaty. Of his work in this period he noted, "Since it was curious indeed for an American to be even marginally involved in such a uniquely European affair, I sought, so far as I could, to stay out of sight. Nevertheless, I knew all—or most—of what was going on. . . ." Ball's law firm, Cleary, Gottlieb, Steen and Ball, was named to represent the Coal and Steel Community in the United States. He remained the confidant and adviser of Monnet, who became the first president of the High Authority of the Coal and Steel Community.

In 1954 Ball helped found the Bilderberg Group, an organization of Western leaders who met every year to confer on policy after the war. Ball's urbane internationalism, however, did not sit well in the Red Scare of the 1950s. He denounced Senator

JOSEPH R. MCCARTHY (R-Wisc.) and came to loathe RICHARD M. NIXON (R-Calif.) for his heaping calumny on Secretary of State DEAN G. ACHESON.

Ball played a central part in Governor Adlai Stevenson's campaign for the presidency in 1952. Truman's political advisers approached him in January, asking him to act as a liaison between Truman and Stevenson, whom the president thought was the strongest possible Democratic candidate for the presidency that year. In January and again in March, at the White House's request, Ball arranged meetings between the governor and the president. On each occasion Truman asked Stevenson to run for president, but he declined. In February Ball, with Stevenson's knowledge, established a "Stevenson Information Center" in Washington. With Ball's assistance and encouragement articles concerning Stevenson soon appeared in *Look*, *Harpers*, and *The Saturday Evening Post*. Ball commissioned a fact sheet about Stevenson and distributed it to friendly newspaper editors around the country. The strategy, as he explained it to Stevenson in late February, was to "generate as much national publicity for you as possible," to create a swelling of support within the party so the governor would not "appear hand picked" by Truman. The plan suited Stevenson's temperament. Ball had suggested that Stevenson keep his own counsel about running until March, but the governor continued to deny that he was a candidate until the Democratic National Convention nominated him in July.

Ball was among those who planned the 1952 campaign against Eisenhower. He became executive director of the Volunteers for Stevenson, which coordinated the appeal to Republican and independent voters. After he completed organizing that section of the campaign in mid-September, he traveled with Stevenson. Ball wrote speeches and articles for the governor, taking aim at Eisenhower's running mate, Senator Nixon of California.

In 1956 and 1960 Ball once again helped plan and organize Stevenson's presidential bids. President John F. Kennedy, impressed with a report about economic and commercial policy that Ball had written for him, designated Ball undersecretary of state for economic affairs in January 1961. He became undersecretary of state, the second-ranking position in the State Department, in November. During the Johnson administration Ball was the first senior official to oppose large-scale troop commitments and intensive bombing raids against North

Vietnam. A quiet man who remained personally loyal to Johnson, Ball's determined opposition to the war in Vietnam became widely known only after publication of the *Pentagon Papers* in 1971. Ball died on May 26, 1994, in New York City. (See *The Kennedy Years, The Johnson Years* Volumes)

—CSJ

Ball, Joseph H(urst)

(1905–1993) *member of the Senate*

The son of a farmer, Ball was born on November 3, 1905, in Crookston, Minnesota. He attended Antioch College from 1923 to 1925 and the University of Minnesota from 1926 to 1927. In June 1927 he joined the *Minneapolis Journal* as a cub reporter. He left several months later to work as a freelance writer of fiction. In 1929 Ball joined the *St. Paul Pioneer Press*, becoming its reporter of state and local political news in 1934. He was known as a critic of Congress and the Roosevelt administration. During the 1930s he became a close friend of HAROLD STASSEN, who was elected governor of Minnesota in 1934. Following the death of isolationist Senator Ernest Lundeen (Farmer-Labor-Minn.) in a plane crash in 1940, Stassen appointed Ball his successor. The appointment was vigorously opposed by Republican isolationists who dominated Minnesota politics. In 1942 Ball won election on a platform that stressed international cooperation in a postwar world organization.

In the Senate, Ball became known for his opposition to unions as well as his support for an international organization. During World War II he urged legislation to support the open shop and sponsored a bill advocated by the National Association of Manufacturers to enforce a 20-day cooling off period before strikes in war industries could take place. The senator gained attention in 1943 when he submitted the Ball-Burton-Hatch-Hill Resolution, calling for the United States to initiate a United Nations with a peacekeeping force after the war. Ball supported Franklin D. Roosevelt in 1944 because he believed he was more committed to collective security than his Republican opponent, Governor THOMAS E. DEWEY.

Ball remained an opponent of organized labor throughout the postwar period. He was a defender of the Case labor disputes bill, which would have curbed union activities. He joined conservative Democrats and Republicans in a 7,500 word statement in June 1946 attacking PHILIP MURRAY, president of the Congress of Industrial Organizations, for opposing the measure. When coal miners struck in November Ball denounced the action as "more like an insurrection than a strike." In January 1947 he introduced a bill to outlaw the closed shop, union shop, and maintenance-of-membership contracts. He also offered a bill to prohibit industrywide collective bargaining by restricting negotiations to a single labor-market regional area.

An advocate of the Taft-Hartley Act, Ball helped Senator ROBERT A. TAFT (R-Ohio) draft the measure and sat on the conference committee formed to reconcile differences between the House and Senate versions of the bill. He defended the bill against a report by National Labor Relations Board chairman Paul Herzog attacking the measure as antiunion. Ball claimed that the report had been vetted by cabinet members, had distortions of fact, and claimed its basis was seemingly a memorandum of CIO counsel LEE PRESSMAN. Pressman was later forced to step down as counsel because of accusations that he had ties to Communists. He was appointed one of the Senate members of the Joint Labor-Management Relations Committee created by the act and, in 1947, was elected its chairman.

Ball was a foe of the European Recovery Program (ERP) designed to provide economic and military aid to halt communist aggression. He opposed unilateral U.S. action to defend Europe and instead joined other "revisionist" senators in urging collective action to meet aggression. In March 1948 he introduced an amendment to the ERP bill that would have set up an 11-nation Supreme Council separate from the UN Security Council but composed of UN members with a military force at its command to protect the peace. The panel would have required only seven votes to act. Senator ARTHUR H. VANDENBERG (R-Minn.) opposed the measure on the grounds that it would have committed the United States to war on the vote of foreign nations. Ball retorted that "the hour [was] late" for collective action. The Senate defeated the measure that month.

Ball lost his 1948 reelection bid to HUBERT H. HUMPHREY, who was running with the support of organized labor. After leaving the Senate Ball returned to journalism, editing *Joe Ball Washington Letter*. In 1953 he joined the States Marine Line and became its vice president in 1954. Ball died on December 18, 1993, in Chevy Chase, Maryland.

—AES

Barkley, Alben W(illiam)

(1877–1956) *member of the Senate, vice president of the United States*

The son of a poor Kentucky tobacco farmer, Alben W. Barkley was born in a log cabin in Wheel, Kentucky, on November 24, 1877. He worked as a janitor to pay his tuition at Morgan College. After graduating in 1897 he attended Emory College Law School but was forced to drop out after a short period because of a lack of funds. He returned to Kentucky to work as a law clerk and court reporter. This enabled him to save up enough money to study at the University of Virginia Law School. He was admitted to the bar in 1901. After holding a number of political positions in his home county, Barkley was elected in 1913 to the U.S. House as a Democrat. He enthusiastically supported Woodrow Wilson's progressive legislation and considered Wilson the greatest president he had known. In the 1920s he belonged to the progressive rural faction in the House. In 1923 Barkley waged an unsuccessful populist campaign for Kentucky's governorship. Three years later he won a Senate seat.

Barkley was one of the most consistently liberal southerners in the Senate. He supported Roosevelt's New Deal and was a leader in the fight for the Rural Electrification Administration, the Agricultural Adjustment Administration, and the Farm Security Administration. With Roosevelt's assistance he became Senate majority leader in 1937. Barkley worked with Roosevelt to obtain Senate support for such foreign policies as lend-lease, and, during the war he backed legislation committing the United States to enter the United Nations. In 1944 Barkley clashed with Roosevelt over a tax bill veto message and resigned as majority leader. He was reelected immediately. The clash was one of the factors leading to Roosevelt's passing Barkley over as a candidate for vice president in favor of Harry Truman.

When Truman became president in 1945, his friend from the Senate, Barkley, was one of his closest confidants and legislative strategists. He supported a large portion of the president's domestic program. Barkley fought to continue price controls, opposed Republican efforts to restrict union power, and supported increases in the minimum wage, unemployment insurance, and social security benefits. On civil rights he broke with his fellow southerners in sponsoring the futile efforts to impose cloture on the filibusters against the poll tax and the federal Fair Employment Practices Commission

bill. In 1947, when the Republican Party took control of both houses, Barkley became Senate minority leader. Over the next two years he waged a hopeless campaign for the passage of Truman's legislative program. Barkley supported the president on the Taft-Hartley veto and aided in the approval of funds for the Truman Doctrine and the Marshall Plan.

By the late 1940s the jovial, outgoing Barkley had become a symbol of the Democratic Party. He delivered the keynote address at the 1948 Democratic National Convention. Known for his oratorical skills, he exhorted the party to continue to work for liberalism at home and an internationalist foreign policy. He blasted the Republican Party for its opposition both to Roosevelt's and Truman's policies. Barkley refused to join the Dixiecrat revolt because of his loyalty to the party and his moderate stand on civil rights. During the convention he did not know he was Truman's second choice for the vice presidency. When Supreme Court Justice WILLIAM O. DOUGLAS turned down the president, Truman offered Barkley the nomination. During the campaign Barkley toured the nation joining Truman in attacking the Republican Party for opposing liberal legislation. According to historian Harold I. Gullan, Barkley proved important in the 1948 campaign. His extensive tours in the South helped hold much of that region for Truman in the face of the Dixiecrats' challenge. He was also effective in winning over the Midwest states that had gone for Republican governor THOMAS E. DEWEY in 1944. He flew 150,000 miles and made more than 250 speeches in all the states but 12.

Upon taking office Barkley promised that he would not be satisfied with being a mere "gavel pounder." Before he became vice president he told a joke to a friend that there was a man who had two sons: "one went to sea and the other was elected vice president, and the father never heard of either of them again." He stopped telling the joke after he became vice president and found that his defined role was in fact to preside over the Senate. Yet he seemed to take it in stride and told people that his grandson had suggested he put two "e"s between the initials V.P. The nickname caught on, and Barkley was affectionately referred to as the "Veep." Nevertheless Barkley did have a significant role in the Truman administration. He toured the nation delighting crowds with his homespun wit and inspiring party workers with his enthusiasm. He appealed for support for the Fair Deal and used his influence in the Senate to push legislation. He backed NATO, the U.S. intervention in the Korean War, and the dismissal of General DOUGLAS MACARTHUR. He frequently attacked Senator JOSEPH R. MCCARTHY (R-Wisc.) and defended the administration's Korean policy.

In 1952 Barkley indicated his availability for the Democratic presidential nomination. Truman promised to support him if ADLAI E. STEVENSON chose not to run. Many liberals, who admired Barkley for his civil rights stand, encouraged him. However, Barkley was hurt because of his age, 76. His chances were destroyed when a group of labor leaders turned him down because of his advanced years. After removing his name from the running, Barkley addressed the convention on July 23, affirming his loyalty to the party. The delegates greeted the revered old party leader with an even more thunderous reception than Stevenson obtained. Barkley campaigned hard for Stevenson.

After leaving office, Barkley worked as a commentator on a local television program entitled, "Meet the Veep." In 1954 he decided to return to politics, running a vigorous campaign for the Senate. He defeated the incumbent, John Sherman Cooper (D-Ky.) He was stricken with a fatal heart attack while speaking to college students in Lexington, Virginia, on April 30, 1956.

—JB

Barnard, Chester I(rving)

(1886–1961) *president, New Jersey Bell Telephone Company*

Born into a poor New England family, Chester I. Barnard attended Harvard on a scholarship for three years. (He also helped pay for his school though tuning pianos and managing a dance band.) However, he left college in 1909 to enter the business world. He joined American Telephone and Telegraph Company that year as a clerk. Barnard became assistant vice president and general manager of Bell Telephone Company of Pennsylvania in 1923 and rose to the presidency of the New Jersey Bell Telephone Company in 1927. Regarded as an expert on telephone commercial methods and the economies of telephone rates, he also gained a reputation as a keen student of business organization. According to Fritz Roethlisberger, a human relations expert, Barnard was the only executive who

could not only manage a business well but also talk intelligently about what he was doing. Bernard's writings made important contributions to the model of formal organization, status, and behavior in organization theory. For instance, *In the Function of the Executive* (1938), his study of organizations, Barnard found that past studies had focused too much on church and state. Most researchers examined societal friction and reform, and hardly discussed organization as the way by which societal action is done. Barnard also believed that in order to avoid societal failing one had to develop cooperation within an organization. In a widely acclaimed series of essays, *Organization and Management* (1948), Barnard gave his opinions on leadership training, organization status systems, and personnel relations. During the 1930s Barnard advised various government agencies. He helped organize New Jersey's Emergency Relief Administration in 1931 and served in the reorganized agency in 1935. Six years later he was appointed special assistant to the secretary of the Treasury on special assignment. Barnard was elected president of the United Service Organizations, Inc. (USO) in 1942 and served there until the end of the war.

During the Truman administration Barnard was a consultant to the U.S. representative on the United Nations Atomic Energy Commission. At that post he helped write the Acheson-Lilienthal Report on Atomic Energy, designed to be a working blueprint for atomic control. The paper, released in March 1946, was drawn up by Barnard, J. ROBERT OPPENHEIMER, and other experts. It called for control of atomic energy through an international agency that would have a monopoly on the world's uranium supply, limit the substance to peaceful industrial uses, and forbid its allocation in construction of explosive devices. The report stipulated that U.S. manufacture of nuclear bombs would cease and that the transfer of atomic information to the international authority would be done in stages. However, it stressed that there must be no immediate release of atomic knowledge. The paper provided the basis for the Baruch Plan submitted to the UN in June.

Barnard was a member of the Eberstadt Survey Committee, part of the Hoover Commission to Reorganize the Government's executive branch, which was concerned with the organization of the military services. The group uncovered serious waste and inefficiency in the military establishment and pointed out six areas in which improvement was necessary. It suggested that: central military authority be strengthened; budgets be overhauled and improved; policies be coordinated between various branches of the armed forces; scientific research be closely related to strategic planning; plans be expedited for complete civilian mobilization in case of war; and, adequate provisions be made for unconventional warfare. It rejected Barnard's proposal for the creation of a general staff and a single chief of staff.

From 1948 to 1952 Barnard served as president of the Rockefeller Foundation. Appointed to the New York City Board of Health by Mayor Robert Wagner in 1957, Barnard established a new health code for the city that took effect two years later. Barnard died of a heart attack on June 7, 1961, in New York City.

—AES

Baruch, Bernard M(annes)

(1870–1965) *financier; representative, United Nations Atomic Energy Commission*

Baruch was born August 19, 1870, in Camden, South Carolina, the son of a German-Jewish doctor and a descendant on his mother's side of one of South Carolina's oldest Portuguese-Jewish families. He graduated from the City College of New York in 1889 and then found employment on Wall Street as an office boy in the brokerage house of A.A. Housman and Company Baruch moved up in the company to first become a broker and then a partner. Known as one of the youngest financial wizards on Wall Street, Baruch was a millionaire by the age of 30. In 1903 he left his company to set up his own business in the field of industrial development.

Baruch was a strong supporter of Woodrow Wilson, whom he became convinced was one of the greatest men of his era. In 1916 Wilson appointed him to a number of regulatory agencies that handled the preparedness program for possible U.S. entry into World War I. Impressed with Baruch's ability as an administrator and financier, Wilson named him chairman of the War Industries Board in 1918. Baruch had near dictatorial powers in mobilizing the nation during the war and became known as the second most powerful man in the nation.

The financier was a major contributor to the Democratic Party during the 1920s. He also secretly advised Republican presidents on economic policy.

Following his 1932 victory, Franklin D. Roosevelt offered Baruch the post of secretary of the Treasury. Baruch turned him down preferring to be an unofficial adviser on the economy and politics, a role he held until the president's death in 1945. Baruch became known as the Park Bench Statesman after he told reporters his only office was a park bench across the street from the White House. In 1944 DAVID E. LILIENTHAL described the way Baruch worked. "He likes to have his finger in all the pies, working by remote control, so that if things go wrong he doesn't have to take responsibility. And [he is] about the vainest old man I have ever seen."

During World War II Baruch served on several presidential committees formed to deal with economic problems. He was also adviser to JAMES F. BYRNES, director of the Office of Defense Mobilization. In spring 1946 Truman appointed Baruch representative to the UN Atomic Energy Commission, then discussing the international control of nuclear energy. The recommendations for a U.S. proposal to the committee had been worked out by a panel headed by Lilienthal and DEAN G. ACHESON. In an effort to make the plan more acceptable to Congress, the respected financier was asked to present it.

The report called for the establishment of an international atomic development agency to survey nuclear raw materials and to assume control of dangerous fissionable materials and production plants. The agency would make its resources available for peaceful use, and control, inspect, and license all nuclear activities. It would report any attempt to build atomic weapons to the UN, whose members could take appropriate action. The report stipulated that the United States would end the manufacture of nuclear devices at some point in the future and transfer atomic knowledge to the UN agency in stages. However, it stressed that there must be no immediate release of atomic knowledge.

To the surprise of government officials, Baruch demanded the right to change the proposal. He feared that since the agency would derive its authority from the Security Council, members of that body, specifically the Soviet Union, would veto its action. Baruch demanded that members be prohibited from using the veto when considering atomic energy and that penalties be fixed for illegal possession or use of atomic bombs and other materials. The report's defenders argued that Baruch's proposals were unnecessary because a veto would be a

presumption of guilt. They also stressed that the Soviet Union would never agree to his plan. Baruch threatened to resign if he did not get his way, and Truman, who later charged that the financier's main concern was to see that he received sufficient public recognition, accepted his changes.

On June 14, 1946, Baruch presented the report to the UN. The Soviet Union condemned it as an attempt to undermine the Security Council and demanded the immediate destruction of all nuclear weapons. In December 1946 the UN Atomic Energy Commission voted unanimously to recommend the Security Council adopt the Baruch Plan. The Soviet Union and Poland abstained. When the Security Council took up the proposal, the Soviets vetoed it. The Baruch Plan, with its demand for international inspection, remained the basis for the U.S. position on nuclear disarmament into the 1960s.

Baruch supported Truman's presidential bid in 1948 and helped him plan campaign strategy. In June 1948 he advised Truman to call the Republican-controlled 80th Congress into special session to make the Republican Party's platform promises into law. Baruch reasoned that the Republicans would fail, thereby giving Truman an issue with which to embarrass the party in the fall campaign. Truman agreed and this tactic helped him achieve his victory in November.

Baruch's relations with the president were often stormy. The two men clashed on fiscal policy. The conservative financier opposed the deficit spending of the Fair Deal and urged a balanced budget and diminished national debt. When some cabinet members recommended obtaining Baruch's support for the Greek-Turkish aid bill, Truman refused: "I'm just *not* going to do it. I am not going to spend hours and hours on that old goat, come what may. If you take his advice, then you have him on your hands for hours and hours, and it is *his* policy." In September 1948 the break between the two men became sharp. That month Baruch was asked to serve on the Democratic National Finance Committee. He turned the request down because he never served on fundraising committees. Truman sent him a harshly written reprimand for his refusal, the contents of which were leaked to the press. Columnist Westbrook Pegler increased the rift by publishing parts of an off-the-record conversation he had had with Baruch. In it the elder statesman made a number of insulting remarks about the president, calling him "rude and uncouth."

Baruch had a minimal advisory role in Truman's second administration. Truman rejected recommendations for a balanced budget and, at first, wage and price controls during the Korean War. In 1952 Baruch, a lifelong Democrat, voted for DWIGHT D. EISENHOWER, the Republican presidential candidate, rather than ADLAI E. STEVENSON. During the 1950s Baruch broke with the Democratic Party over fiscal policy. Although he remained an adviser to Democratic and Republican presidents for the rest of his life, increasingly politicians ignored the aging "Advisor to the Presidents" as they turned to Keynesian economics and away from the fiscal and monetary discipline he advocated. He predicted Japan, Germany, or other countries with low standards of living would win more market share in the international economy if America continued to be profligate. He died of a heart attack on June 20, 1965, in New York City.

—JB

Beirne, Joseph A(nthony)
(1911–1974) *president, Communications Workers of America*

The son of Irish immigrants, Joseph Beirne was born on February 16, 1911, in Jersey City, New Jersey. He was a stockboy, drill-press operator, and department store clerk before he began working for Western Electric Company in 1928. During the 1930s he became a leader of its employees' association. He and his wife began organizing for the independent National Federation of Telephone Worke (NFTW) in the later part of the decade. In 1943 was elected president.

In March 1946 the telephone industry be involved in a dispute over wage increases. A ened national walkout was averted a h before the deadline when Bell System increases for 150,000 employees. Throu talks Beirne insisted that the compani industrywide negotiations. The bar rounding the dispute marked the American Telephone and Telegra (AT&T) resistance to systemwide November of that year the Comr ers of America (CWA) was forr NFTW, and Beirne was elect dent. The new union represe and consolidated the federa unions.

In 1947 talks between the union and its affiliates and AT&T and its affiliates reached an impasse, and Beirne in late March reported the policy committee of the union had voted 15 to 1 for a possible strike. The union demanded a $12 a week wage increase, the union shop, and increased pensions. Beirne in early April said he would consider arbitration, but to no avail and later that month 340,000 communications workers went out on strike. Beirne cited the wage increases granted to workers in other major industries as a justification for the walkout. As with the 1946 bargaining he insisted on a nationwide settlement, but AT&T held out for negotiations and arbitration conducted locally. Beirne believed that arbitration on a local basis would create a "hodgepodge of wages and working conditions around the country." The strike, which lasted six weeks, was bitter and included injuries, arrests, cut phone cables and a threat by the federal government to seize the telephone lines. Beirne's hopes for an industrywide settlement were not realized. More than 20 individual settlements were negotiated, many for less than the wage increase the union had demanded.

In 1949 Beirne used Senate hearings on the Taft-Hartley Act as a forum for his attack on AT&T's policy of separate bargaining between the telephone unions and the individual operating companies. He spoke in favor of an amendment to the bill which would have compelled national bargaining in industries which had countrywide operations.

In May 1947 PHILLIP MURRAY, president of the Congress of Industrial Organizations (CIO), called for an industrial union of telephone workers. Beirne opposed his union's joining the CIO at this point. However, two years later he favored the move, fearing his union would lose many workers to the CIO if it did not vote to affiliate. Beirne was elected president of the CWA in June of that year and soon became a CIO vice president. After the AFL-CIO merger in 1955, he became a vice president of that organization.

Beirne opposed communism and waged a battle against its spread at home and abroad. In the early 1950s he led the effort to rid the CIO of communist-dominated unions. During the decade CWA developed training in unionism for Latin American communication workers. Beirne defended anticommunist activities in Latin America carried out by the AFL-CIO through the American Institute for Free Labor Development (AIFLD), an

organization he had urged the AFL-CIO to establish in 1960.

In the 1960s Beirne waged a bitter fight with James Hoffa and the Teamsters Union, which began raiding the CWA. Beirne broke with GEORGE MEANY and during the 1972 presidential campaign became secretary-treasurer of a national labor committee supporting Senator George McGovern (D-S.D.). Beirne remained president of CWA until his death from cancer on September 2, 1974, in Washington, D.C. (See *The Eisenhower Years, The Kennedy Years, The Johnson Years, The Nixon/Ford Years* Volumes)

—EF

Benson, Elmer A(ustin)
(1895–1985) *chairman, National Citizens Political Action Committee; chairman, Progressive Party*

Elmer Benson was born on September 22, 1895, in Appleton, Minnesota. After earning an LL.B. from St. Paul College of Law in 1918, he returned to the town of his birth, where he worked as a bank cashier and part owner of a clothing business. He became active in the Farmer-Labor Party, which had been formed in 1918 by the state Federation of Labor and the Non-Partisan League, a radical farmers' movement. With a following among poor Scandinavian farmers and urban blue-collar workers, the party dominated left-of-center politics in Minnesota. It succeeded in taking over state government in 1932 with the election of Floyd Olson as governor. The following year Olson appointed Benson state commissioner of banks and securities and two years later selected him to fill the unexpired term of Senator Thomas D. Scholl (R-Minn.).

In 1936, following Olson's death in office, Benson ran for governor. He won by the largest plurality in the history of the state. Unlike his charismatic predecessor, Benson was a lackluster figure who commanded no significant personal following. As a result, he depended on the support of a small, but well-organized communist group and, in turn, promoted its members to positions of influence in Farmer-Labor circles. In addition, Benson tied his party more closely to the Roosevelt administration and the New Deal, thereby weakening it as an independent political force. In 1938 he was defeated for reelection by his Republican opponent, HAROLD E. STASSEN, who drew attention to Benson's Communist ties. The loss of the governorship inaugurated

a decade of GOP domination in Minnesota, during which the Farmer-Labor Party under Benson's leadership declined. In 1944 Benson helped arrange a merger between the Farmer-Labor Party and Minnesota's Democratic organization. Until then the latter had been an almost negligible political force. It was dominated by local federal officials and professors at the state university, with a small following among Irish Catholics living in St. Paul and Duluth.

During the postwar years Benson was visible on the national scene as an opponent of the growing international polarization between the United States and the Soviet Union. Elected chairman of the National Citizens' Political Action Committee (NCPAC) in 1945, he and C. B. "BEANIE" BALDWIN, director of the NCPAC, sought to organize New Dealers around a policy of maintaining the wartime "Big Three unity." In December 1946 Benson urged HENRY A. WALLACE to run against President Truman in the 1948 presidential elections. He became a vice chairman of the Progressive Citizens of America (PCA), which began to promote an independent Wallace campaign. During the following year, as liberals divided between the Communist-influenced PCA and the anticommunist Americans for Democratic Action, Benson toured the country denouncing the Marshall Plan and the Greek-Turkish aid program as means of bolstering right-wing governments abroad and preparing for war with the USSR. In January 1948 the PCA was dissolved and replaced by the National Wallace for President Committee. Benson was named chairman of the organization and served, along with Baldwin, New Dealer REXFORD TUGWELL, sculptor Jo Davidson, and singer PAUL ROBESON, as one of the candidate's respected advisers. Benson, according to writer Zachary Karabell, provided the connection between Wallace's Party and the Old Progressivism of the Midwest.

Although the panel planned to run Wallace as a third-party candidate in most states, it hoped to put his name on the Minnesota ballot under the Democratic–Farmer-Labor line. Benson's faction dominated the party's state executive committee, which traditionally approved delegates to the state convention where the presidential electors were chosen. The Wallace effort countered opposition in Minnesota from anticommunist liberals led by Minneapolis mayor HUBERT H. HUMPHREY. In February the Humphrey group forced the meeting of the Democratic–Farmer Labor State Central Committee, made up of old-line Democrats, which

took control of all arrangements for the state convention scheduled for June.

During the following month a battle between the factions raged through every level of the party. Only a few precinct caucuses elected Wallace delegates, and in June the Humphrey-dominated credentials committee refused to seat them. Still claiming that it represented the official party, Benson's group convened a rump convention, which organized itself as the Progressive Democratic–Farmer-Labor League. In October, after the Wallaceites had lost every major contest in the Minnesota popular primary, the league nominated its own candidates for several state offices. However, it did not enter a third candidate in the Senate race between Humphrey and incumbent Republican JOSEPH H. BALL.

In July Benson presided at the Progressive Party Convention in Philadelphia and was elected party chairman. At the polls in November Progressive candidates received fewer votes than most party leaders had expected. Benson attributed the party's lack of popularity to its identification with communist ideology. In 1950 he joined Wallace and Baldwin in demanding a statement in the party platform criticizing the USSR. Yet Benson was critical of Wallace for his support for the administration at the outbreak of the Korean War. Benson served as chairman through the second Progressive presidential campaign in 1952, by which time the communists had withdrawn from the organization. The party dissolved shortly afterward. Although Benson was involved in various left-wing causes over the years, he disappeared almost entirely from prominence. Benson died on March 13, 1985, in Minneapolis, Minnesota.

—TLH

Bentley, Elizabeth T(errill)
(1908–1963) *Communist Party member*

Elizabeth Bentley was born in 1908 in New Milford, Connecticut, and was the daughter of middle-class Republican parents. She graduated from Vassar College in 1930 and received a master's degree in languages from Columbia University in 1933. She then studied at the University of Florence. While in Italy she was "revolted" by the fascist rule and upon returning to the United States joined the U.S. Communist Party in 1935.

Three years later Bentley was introduced to Jacob Golos; the two quickly became lovers. Golos managed a Comintern-owned business, World

Tourist, which arranged trips to the USSR for communists and fellow travelers. The Justice Department launched an investigation of Golos and his company, and he was arrested and tried for spying and breaking U.S. neutrality laws. (He had helped volunteers go to Spain to fight in the communist-controlled International Brigades.) Golos plea-bargained and was fined $1,000 and put on probation for a time. He had been ordered to plea guilty to a lesser charge in exchange for other communist organizations being left alone, and he resented having to do that.

Golos trained Bentley to be an agent, and she was highly prized because she was non-Jewish in a time when there was still much anti-Semitism in American government. She served as courier.

Soon trouble began to arise between Golos and Soviet agents he was in contact with, whom he thought were lazy, careless amateurs. Golos became infuriated when the Soviets ordered him to turn over contact of his American sources to them; they even purloined Bentley, whom Golos warned "to be firm" in working with the Soviets. A deeply disgruntled Golos died in November 1943, and the Russians began to focus more on Bentley, who knew more about Golos's operation than they did. Because the FBI had been watching him more and more as time went on, he gave Bentley the responsibility to deal with Treasury employee Nathan Gregory Silvermaster's spy ring in the government, as well as other sources in Washington. After Golos's death, Bentley refused to introduce Russian agent Itzhak Akhmerov to Silvermaster, saying he and others among Golos's sources feared direct contact with the Soviets. Bentley fought for several months their attempts to control Golos's operation, but the Soviets put pressure on American Communist Party chief Earl Browder, who ordered Bentley in June 1944 that Silvermaster would from now on see Akhmerov directly. Browder, however, saw that his power would fall with Bentley's so he had her contact other Communists in the government, including Victor Perlo, a member of the War Production Board, and others. Bentley's meetings with these people led to complaints from the Soviet foreign intelligence agency (NKGB) stations in New York and Washington that she intruded too much. Akhmerov liked Bentley, but noted she was protective of her spy ring contacts. She became increasingly alienated from the Russians. For a time Akhmerov thought Bentley needed a husband and

tried to arrange one. By now other Americans working for the Soviets were notifying the Russians of Bentley's carelessness, and how this threatened operations.

Bentley began to have a relationship with Peter Heller, who claimed to be a U.S. spy (he was not). The Soviets, increasingly worried about Bentley, began planning for her to leave the country—involuntarily, if necessary. In a meeting in late September 1945 with Soviet operative Anatoly Gorsky, a drunken Bentley demanded financial assistance for her company, U.S. Shipping Corporation. If she did not receive it she would discontinue meeting with the Russians and even threatened to testify to the House Un-American Activities Committee. She said the Soviets "were gangsters and care only about Russia" and the American Communist Party was "a gang of foreigners." Gorsky wired back to Moscow that the only way to deal with Bentley at this point was to kill her. The NKGB rejected that advice and told him to calm her down and offer her money to help her company.

Gorsky met with her again in November, and she was much calmer, but, unbeknownst to Gorsky, she was now cooperating with the U.S. government. Bentley contacted FBI agents in August and began serving as a double agent. The Soviets soon received word of her defection from Harold "Kim" Philby, who was a British intelligence official, but also a double agent. In response to her defection the NKGB in November 1945 ordered its U.S. station chiefs to break off contact with sources known to Bentley, and Russian agents who worked with Bentley were recalled to the USSR. Gorsky urged the "liquidation" of Bentley, but he did not know how it could be done, and the NKGB was trying to find Bentley as late as 1955.

Bentley attributed her disenchantment with communism to "a good old New England conscience." However, in her autobiography, she said that the change was prompted by "gangster-type" Soviet agents taking over her sources of information. In July 1948 she testified before two congressional committees investigating domestic subversion. She told them that she had received secret military, diplomatic and economic information through top government sources in Washington. Among those she named as contacts were Lauchlin Currie, President Roosevelt's aide during World War II, WILLIAM W. REMINGTON, a Commerce Department official, and HARRY DEXTER WHITE, a former assistant secretary of the Treasury. Bentley also described two spy networks headed by Nathan Gregory Silvermaster, a former government employee, and Victor Perlo, a member of the War Production Board during World War II.

All those implicated denied the charges. Silvermaster called Bentley "a neurotic liar" and described her accusations as "false and fantastic." Remington was later convicted of perjury for lying about his past Communist Party membership. Bentley's charges against White eventually involved the White House. Truman called the anticommunist hearing a "red herring" designed to distract attention from the failings of the Republican-controlled Congress. However, investigators charged that the president had promoted White to a post at the International Monetary Fund (IMF) despite reports, based on Bentley's testimony, that implicated White in spying. Truman maintained that he had made White a member of the executive board of the IMF so that the FBI could continue its probe without attracting attention. J. EDGAR HOOVER denied this, White died before an investigation could be made. But later evidence proved White had been involved with a Communist cell. ALGER HISS, another accused by Bentley, and WHITTAKER CHAMBERS, also was convicted of perjury. Bentley testified at the trial of JULIUS and ETHEL ROSENBERG and Martin Sobell, who were accused of selling U.S. atomic secrets to the Soviet Union. The three were found guilty in March 1951. However, according to her biographer, Kathryn S. Olmsted, Bentley began fabricating information on spying to prolong her career as an informer.

In 1948 Bentley was converted to Catholicism by Monsignor Fulton J. Sheen. Her godfather was LOUIS F. BUDENZ, former editor of the *Communist Daily Worker*. She published her autobiography, *Out of Bondage*, in 1951. During the 1950s Bentley worked intermittently as a teacher and lectured on communism. Her last years were spent in obscurity as an instructor at a girls' correctional institution in Connecticut. She died after surgery for an abdominal tumor on December 3, 1963, in New Haven, Connecticut.

Bentley's role in Soviet spying operations and what the Russians thought of her work became clearer in the 1990s with the release of the Venona transcripts. Venona was the code name of an American military intelligence operation to decipher coded messages from the Soviet embassy and consulates in America to Moscow.

—RB

Benton, William B(urnett)

(1900–1973) *assistant secretary of state for public affairs, member of the Senate*

Born on April 1, 1900, in Minneapolis, Minnesota, William B. Benton was the son of a Congregationalist clergyman. He graduated from Yale in 1921. Although awarded a Rhodes Scholarship, he accepted a position as an advertising copywriter. Benton eventually rose to become assistant general manager of Albert Lasker's Lord and Thomas Agency in Chicago before leaving in 1929 to join CHESTER BOWLES in founding the firm of Benton and Bowles. The agency prospered, even in the Great Depression, as it pioneered in such fields as the sponsorship of soap operas and consumer product surveys. Benton was also credited with introducing the studio audience as well as commercials with sound effects.

In 1936 Benton became vice president of the University of Chicago, where he helped pioneer educational radio and motion pictures. His radio program, "The University of Chicago Round Table," won several awards as an adult education show. In 1943, at Benton's suggestion, the university acquired the *Encyclopaedia Britannica*. Benton provided the necessary capital for the acquisition and became board chairman of Britannica's American, English, and Canadian companies.

Benton entered public service in 1939 as an adviser to NELSON A. ROCKEFELLER, then coordinator of Inter-American Affairs. In 1942 he became vice chairman of the Committee on Economic Development, a nonprofit organization which he helped found. In the summer of 1943 he made a study of Anglo-American economic policy, outlining major areas of potential conflict between the United States and Britain. His incisive comments proved to be one of the major factors leading to his appointment as assistant secretary of state for public affairs in September 1945. During his two year tenure Benton organized the Voice of America broadcasts, placing emphasis on the use of radio, motion pictures, and information centers to communicate the "news untainted by special pleading or propaganda" to those abroad. He also advocated the formation of a government information service. Benton convinced Secretary of State JAMES F. BYRNES to establish a separate intelligence section at State. In what he considered his most important act as assistant secretary, Benton prevented the American Society of Newspaper Editors from condemning his informational and education program by instead establishing an investigation committee that issued a favorable and influential report of his program. In addition, Benton was active in the establishment of the United Nations Educational, Scientific and Cultural Organization (UNESCO).

In 1949 Bowles, then Democratic governor of Connecticut, appointed Benton to fill a Senate seat vacated by the retirement of RAYMOND E. BALDWIN. The following year Benton won election against Republican Prescott Bush for the remainder of the term after a campaign in which Senator JOSEPH R. MCCARTHY's (R-Wisc.) anticommunist crusade was a major issue.

Benton was a member of a small group of liberals who strongly supported the Fair Deal. In his maiden Senate speech in March 1950, Benton called for a "Marshall Plan of Ideas" for the promotion of democracy and worldwide freedom of information, among other things. Hearings were held on the idea, but no action resulted from them. Benton saw only one of his bills enacted: a law that stated that when the Mutual Security Administration bought materials outside the United States, it should prefer businesses where the union leadership was noncommunist. It was known as the "Benton Amendment." He backed the establishment of a Fair Employment Practices Commission and proposals to strengthen anticorruption laws. Benton opposed the McCarran Internal Security Act, which he saw as restricting civil liberties. He voted for the legislation, however, after Senate Democratic leader SCOTT W. LUCAS (D-Ill.) decided to support the measure. He unsuccessfully fought against the enactment of the McCarran-Walter bill, which he regarded as restricting immigration of Eastern and Southern Europeans to America. Benton supported Senator HERBERT H. LEHMAN's (D-N.Y.) attempts to amend Senate Rule XXII to permit cloture more easily, and he joined Senator C. ESTES KEFAUVER (D-Tenn.) in an attempt to establish firm rules for congressional investigations.

During his short tenure in the Senate, Benton gained national attention as a vigorous opponent of McCarthy. He defended PHILIP JESSUP and ANNA ROSENBERG against the Republican's charges that they were procommunist. He vigorously supported Secretary of State DEAN G. ACHESON, whom McCarthy frequently attacked. In early 1951 Benton reproached the Republican Committee on Committees for appointing McCarthy to the subcommittee charged with handling the State Department's bud-

get. He regarded the appointment as an opportunity for McCarthy to serve as "his own kangaroo court" for a department of which he was "an implacable and . . . irresponsible enemy." He summarized McCarthy's method with the slogan, "If you can't make one libel stick, try another and then try another." Committee members defended McCarthy's appointment, however, as a normal result of the seniority system.

As a member of the Rules Committee, Benton received an advance copy of the Maryland investigation by the Rules Subcommittee on Privileges and Elections, headed by Guy M. Gillette (D-Iowa). The investigation was a probe of McCarthy's role in that state's 1950 senatorial campaign. Senator MILLARD E. TYDINGS (D-Md.), an early vocal opponent of McCarthy, had been defeated by JOHN M. BUTLER (R-Md.) based on what Tydings regarded as a "smear campaign" launched by the Wisconsin Republican. Tydings denounced the "malicious and false attacks" on him and subsequently lodged a complaint in the Senate, which brought about a probe. The Maryland Report reprimanded McCarthy for his conduct during the campaign without discussing the matter deeply. In August 1951 Benton, on the basis of the report, introduced a resolution in the Rules Committee to examine the conduct of McCarthy with a view to expelling him from the Senate. Having previously labeled the Wisconsin Republican, "a very talented propagandist of the Soviet type," Benton suggested that McCarthy's only honorable recourse lay in voluntary resignation; failing that, he should withdraw from Senate business until his fate was decided.

During the first week in which the resolution was presented, not one senator rose to support it. Benton did not expect to win the necessary two-thirds vote needed for expulsion. He hoped instead to underscore the conclusions of the Maryland Report, to focus attention directly on McCarthy himself, and "to encourage the voters of Wisconsin to expel him in 1952," when McCarthy sought reelection. When hearings were eventually held on Benton's resolution, he presented a lengthy 10-point indictment of McCarthy. Benton charged him with having "practiced deception" on his colleagues in the Senate and having propagated "deliberate falsehood" in the Maryland campaign. The Connecticut senator pointed to McCarthy's much-publicized willingness to provide a list of communists in government that he did not, in fact, possess. Benton cited McCarthy's unethical conduct in his acceptance of a $10,000 fee for an article endorsing private housing paid for by the Lustron Corporation, a private housing concern. In addition, he denounced McCarthy's attacks on General GEORGE C. MARSHALL, stating that if the Wisconsin Republican believed his slanderous remarks, then the Senate should consider McCarthy's expulsion based on mental incompetence. In response to public hearings on the Benton Resolution, McCarthy concluded that the senator was "an odd mental midget who only would be dangerous if he were more intelligent," and he subsequently filed a $2 million libel suit.

Hearings on the Benton Resolution ultimately contributed to McCarthy's censure in 1954. By that time William Benton had left the Senate, having been defeated at the polls in 1952. At the time McCarthy's enmity was generally credited with having helped in the defeat, but historians later suggested that the Eisenhower landslide was more important in undermining Benton's reelection. Out of office, he campaigned for ADLAI E. STEVENSON in 1956 and again in 1960. In 1958 Benton ran unsuccessfully for the Democratic senatorial nomination from Connecticut. From 1965 until 1968 he was chief U.S. member of the UNESCO executive board with rank of ambassador. In 1972 he served on the platform committee at the Democratic National Convention. Benton died on March 18, 1973, in New York City. (See *The Eisenhower Years* Volume)

—DGE

Berle, Adolf A(ugustus), Jr.

(1895–1971) *ambassador; chairman, New York State Liberal Party*

The son of a liberal Congregationalist minister, Berle was born on January 29, 1895. He received an education at home and graduated from Harvard at the age of 18. By 1916, at age 21, he had received his LL.B. cum laude from Harvard and joined the law office of Louis D. Brandeis. He served in army intelligence in World War I and attended the Versailles Peace Conference. Unhappy with the terms of the Treaty of Versailles, he resigned the commission and went to New York to practice law. In addition to his legal practice, Berle taught at several universities during the 1920s and early 1930s. He was most prominently associated with Columbia. In 1932 he and Gardiner Means published *The Modern Corporation and Private Property*. This influential work was used as a text throughout the decade. Berle was one of Franklin D. Roosevelt's "brain trusters," advising him on economic issues during his first presidential race and preparing much of the early New Deal legislation. From 1933 to 1938 he served as New York City chamberlain under Fiorello LaGuardia. He was assistant secretary of state for Latin American affairs from 1938 to 1945, when he became ambassador to Brazil, where he quietly backed Democratic reform. He left that post at the end of 1946.

Although he had little influence on the conduct of foreign affairs, Berle attempted to promote his ideas of hemispheric solidarity and neutrality, believing that the Western Hemisphere's interests would best be served through a process of economic unification of nations in continental common markets. His influence was dominant in helping to shape Roosevelt's Good Neighbor Policy of inter-American dependence. Berle's goal of an inter-American system, expanding the Monroe Doctrine of 1823 to a hemispheric agreement in which each American republic guaranteed the integrity of the others against attack, was finally achieved at the Rio Conference in 1947.

Berle returned to his law practice and teaching in 1946. The following year he was elected chairman of the newly formed New York State Liberal Party, which had broken away from the communist-dominated American Labor Party. In articles and editorials for the Liberal Party's publication, Berle outlined the organization's philosophy. He viewed the party as a grassroots movement to deal with the economic expansion anticipated during the postwar years that neither the Democratic Party nor Republican Party was equipped to handle. Berle distinguished his group from the American Communists, whom he accused of serving foreign interests. "A liberal does not want to make a dictatorship of the proletariat. He wants to abolish the concept of a proletariat." Until his retirement in 1955 Berle served as spokesman and policymaker for the Liberal Party, providing pressure on Democrats to move toward the party's economic and humanitarian policies.

In 1939, when he was assistant secretary of state, Berle also served as Roosevelt's intelligence liaison. In that year he met with a former American intelligence operative for the Soviets, WHITTAKER CHAMBERS. Chambers told Berle of communist subversives, and Berle outlined the conversation under the heading "Underground Espionage

Agent." Berle told Chambers that he had to move cautiously so as not to undermine confidence in the government. He noted in his diary that some steps had to be taken but revealed his skepticism. Yet he did ask the FBI to follow up on Chambers's story in 1940 and 1941. Berle also talked to Roosevelt's appointment secretary, Marvin McIntyre, but nothing came from that meeting. Only in 1942 did FBI agents talk to Chambers, and then only at the suggestion of journalists. To Chambers's surprise, they did not seem aware of his revelations to Berle. He called Berle, who assured him it was okay to talk to the agents. However, Chambers was suspicious and hedged in his interview, so much so that the agents came away dismissive of his claims. It was not until 1943 that the bureau asked Berle for his notes, and it was not until the winter of 1945 that an agent came to talk to Chambers again; more agents returned to Chambers's home in May and July. But Chambers was more reticent then when he met with Berle, since nothing had come of that meeting, and Chambers was afraid to disclose the illegal activities he had been involved in.

Berle did testify at the House Un-American Activities Committee's hearings over ALGER HISS about his meeting with Chambers. He said Chambers had told him of a Marxist "study group" in the government, not that there was a Soviet spy ring there. Berle did say he subsequently improved security at the State Department, which, according to him, had "kept things pretty clear" there for years. According to Chambers's biographer, Sam Tanenhaus, Berle did not reveal all he knew because he believed surveillance was a better way to deal with spies than prosecution. John Earl Haynes and Harvey Klehr speculate that if the government had followed up on Chambers's story sooner, it could have avoided damage to U.S. national security and that much of the foundation for the postwar controversy over subversion could have been eliminated. Berle's notes ended up being entered as evidence in the second perjury trial of Hiss.

During the 1950s Berle continued to pursue Latin American diplomacy as a private citizen, maintaining his contacts with Latin American intellectuals and politicians, supporting democratic movements, and fighting the incursions of Communist governments in the Western Hemisphere. Continuing his study of the modern corporation begun in the 1930s, he wrote several books, including *The Twentieth Century Capitalist Revolution*

(1954), in which he further explored the nature of the American economic structure. He worked on the assumption that to assure growth American industry would continue to be dominated by corporations able to produce at minimum costs. Berle sought means of controlling possible abuses of the power concentrated in the hands of corporate management, which he termed a "nonstatist civil service." He stressed the need for making managers aware of the corporation's responsibilities toward society and for exercising their powers in accordance with "the public consensus."

During 1961 Berle served as chairman of the Interdepartmental Task Force on Latin America, whose recommendations formed the basis for the Alliance for Progress. Berle remained active in New York City politics and as a government adviser during the 1960s while still continuing to write on Latin America and economics. Berle died on February 17, 1971, in New York City. (See *The Kennedy Years* Volume)

—DAE

Bethe, Hans A(lbrecht)
(1906–2005) *physicist*

The son of a distinguished German physiologist, Hans A. Bethe was born on July 2, 1906, in Strasburg, Germany, now Strasbourg, France. He was educated in Germany, where he received his doctorate from the University of Munich in 1928. He taught at various German universities until forced, because of part-Jewish ancestry, to flee to England in 1933. In 1935 he came to the United States, where he joined the physics department at Cornell University. As early as 1937 he published discoveries about the carbon cycle, the source of celestial energy, which later became the theoretical basis for the development of the hydrogen or fusion bomb. From 1943 to 1946 Bethe worked under J. ROBERT OPPENHEIMER as head of the theoretical division of the Manhattan District Project. In 1945 the project achieved its primary goal, the development of an atomic or fission bomb, having abandoned work on the idea of a fusion bomb because of technical problems.

During World War II Bethe did not question the necessity of the nuclear research in which he was engaged. After the use of the atomic bomb against Japan, however, he became one of a number of scientists who publicly expressed concern over the dangers of escalating atomic weapons development. From 1946 to 1950 Bethe was a cofounder and member of the Emergency Committee of Atomic Scientists, chaired by ALBERT EINSTEIN. This organization sought to enlighten the public on the dangers of atomic warfare and to establish international controls over atomic power.

In 1946 the Soviet Union rejected the Baruch Plan for the international control of nuclear power through a pooling of technological resources and an inspections system. Bethe then became a leading spokesman, along with Oppenheimer, for "finite containment" of Russian expansion. Members of the "infinite containment" school of thought, led by physicist EDWARD TELLER, felt that the Soviet threat could be countered only by the development of more powerful and destructive nuclear arms. However, scientists advocating finite containment believed that, although the United States must maintain an arsenal of atomic weapons as a deterrent to Soviet expansionism, it would be to America's military and moral advantage to limit the nuclear arms race by international agreement. They hoped to avoid the devastation of total war through an emphasis on the development of smaller tactical nuclear weapons and conventional armaments.

After the explosion of the first Soviet atomic device in 1949, Teller tried to convince Bethe to return to Los Alamos to work on a hydrogen weapon. Bethe was unsure what to do at first. He and Teller met Oppenheimer, but he too was undecided and could not help Bethe make his own decision. Bethe then went to a meeting of the Emergency Committee of Atomic Scientists. He conversed with a friend, theoretical physicist Victor Weisskopf, who noted that one H-bomb would destroy New York City and what that would mean. Even if the United States were to win such a war, they would lose the world they wanted to save. The conversation convinced Bethe to oppose the Super, and he told Teller he would not go back to Los Alamos to work on it. In a fateful meeting of the General Advisory Committee of the Atomic Energy Commission in October 1949, Bethe pointed to the technical problems that would have to be solved for a hydrogen bomb to work. He also talked to some of the committee members about his and Weisskopf's horrific vision of a post–nuclear war world. The committee recommended against making the hydrogen bomb. President Harry S Truman's decision to proceed with the project, despite the opposition from the Atomic Energy Commission's (AEC) General Advi-

sory Committee, impelled Bethe and a group of physicists to state, "We believe that no nation has the right to use such a bomb, no matter how righteous its cause." With the outbreak of the Korean War, Bethe returned to research at Los Alamos, hoping to prove through his theoretical work the impossibility of actually producing a hydrogen bomb. However, in part through Bethe's work, the technological obstacles to the production of the H-bomb were overcome by June 1951, and he came to regard the hydrogen bomb as "inevitable." The first experimental device was exploded in November 1952.

During the early years of the Eisenhower administration, Bethe became a leading defender of Oppenheimer, who had been suspended from his post as consultant to the AEC partly for his failure to endorse a crash development program for the hydrogen bomb. Bethe served as presidential adviser in both the Eisenhower and Kennedy administrations, first as a member of the President's Scientific Advisory Committee and later as the chairman of a panel to study the possible effects of a nuclear test ban agreement. He continued to be a spokesman for finite containment, arguing before the Senate Disarmament Subcommittee in 1959 in favor of a suspension of nuclear testing to facilitate a controlled disarmament agreement with the Soviets.

During the course of his career, Bethe won many scientific honors, including the Max Planck Medal, West Germany's highest scientific honor, for his research on celestial energy. He received the AEC's Enrico Fermi Award in 1961 and was awarded the Nobel Prize in 1967. Bethe continued to teach at Cornell until he retired in 1975. Hans Bethe died on March 6, 2005, in Ithaca, New York. (See *The Eisenhower Years, The Kennedy Years* Volumes)

—DAE

Biddle, Francis B(everley)
(1886–1968) *member, International Military Tribunal; national chairman, Americans for Democratic Action*

Francis B. Biddle was born on May 9, 1886, in Paris, France, into a patrician Philadelphia family. He received a B.A. in 1909 and a law degree from Harvard in 1911. He then began a successful legal practice in Philadelphia. Originally a Republican, Biddle switched his loyalties to the Democratic Party during the Great Depression and became an ardent New Dealer. He served as chairman of the National

Labor Board from 1934 to 1935, chief counsel to a joint congressional committee investigating the Tennessee Valley Authority in 1938, judge on the U.S. Third Circuit Court from 1939 to 1940, and U.S. Solicitor General from 1940 to 1941.

Biddle was named U.S. Attorney General in September 1941. While in that post he supervised relocation and interment of Japanese and Japanese Americans. The FBI had so convinced him Communists were a danger to the United States, that he refused to end a deportation case against long-shoremen union leader and alleged Communist HARRY BRIDGES, despite his cooperation on the docks in the loading of supplies for the fighting men during the war. (It was later proved that Bridges was at one point a Communist.) And Biddle agreed to list the Communist Party, as well as the German-American Bund, as subversive organizations. But he did later regret his action in interning the Isei and the Nisei, and generally he established a liberal record guarding against government infringements on civil liberties during the war. For instance, Biddle shut down a program of J. EDGAR HOOVER's, which had not been authorized, to list people the FBI chief considered politically suspect who would be detained during an emergency. (Hoover continued this program, but under a different name without informing Biddle.) Biddle reported to Congress that a mandated investigation of civil servants that the House Un-American Activities Committee had considered Communist loyalty risks had led to the investigation of people who clearly were not disloyal. He made the FBI cut down to 20 pages and remove the names in a proffered five-volume report to Congress listing alleged subversives. And, with the exception of the Bund and the Communist Party, he was skeptical of the idea of a subversives' list. As Ellen Schrecker has pointed out, Hoover's Communists were, in Biddle's eyes, liberals. When Harry S Truman became president, he and Biddle hardly knew each other. Truman later wrote in an assessment of the cabinet he inherited from Roosevelt a rather cryptic remark about Biddle: "make your own analysis." Desiring a cabinet of his own making, Truman asked Biddle to resign.

In September 1945, the president selected Biddle to be a member of the International Military Tribunal established to try Nazi leaders for war crimes. The trials began in Nuremburg, Germany, in November 1945. Biddle, along with judges from Britain, France, and the Soviet Union, heard evidence over the next nine months against 22 defendants. The judges began drafting their final statement late in June 1946. Biddle was largely responsible for the declaration of law in the document. The tribunal's judgment, handed down on October 1, 1946, found 19 of the 22 defendants guilty, held four Nazi organizations to be criminal, and set forth principles of international law. It affirmed that a nation lacked authority to resort to war except in self-defense or as permitted by international procedure. It also held that the individual was responsible for actions considered illegal under international law. On his return to the United States, Biddle submitted a report to the president which noted that the Nuremberg judgment had formulated judicially for the first time the proposition that aggressive war was a crime and should be treated as such. He resigned his post on November 9, 1946.

In January 1947 Truman nominated Biddle as the U.S. representative to the United Nations Economic and Social Council. Several Senate Republicans opposed his appointment because of his close ties to the New Deal, and the Senate Foreign Relations Committee held up action on the nomination for over five months. Finally, at Biddle's request, Truman withdrew the nomination in July.

On April 2, 1950, Biddle was elected national chairman of Americans for Democratic Action (ADA), a liberal anticommunist organization founded in 1947. During his three years as head of ADA, the group backed civil rights legislation, Truman's Fair Deal proposals, and the U.S. role in Korea. It opposed aid to the Franco regime in Spain and urged reform of the federal loyalty program to prevent abuses. The ADA fought the Internal Security Act of 1950 and came out for repeal of the Smith Act in December 1951. About the same time Biddle published *The Fear of Freedom* in which he spoke out against anticommunist hysteria and attacked the House Un-American Activities Committee, the censorship of textbooks, the institution of loyalty oaths for educators, and the dismissal of nonconforming teachers. He condemned the tactics of Senator JOSEPH R. MCCARTHY (R-Wisc.) during the early 1950s. Yet he opposed the ADA issuing a statement against the *Dennis* decision, fearing it would lead many people to leave the organization. Biddle worked with several other ADA leaders to help ADLAI E. STEVENSON gain the 1952 Democratic presidential nomination.

Biddle stepped down as ADA chairman in May 1953. During the 1950s and 1960s he wrote and lectured, served as an adviser to the American Civil Liberties Union, and was a member of a committee named to plan a national memorial to Franklin D. Roosevelt. Biddle died in Hyannis, Massachusetts, on October 4, 1968.

—CAB

Bilbo, Theodore G(ilmore)

(1877–1947) *member of the Senate*

Born on October 13, 1877, in Poplarville, Mississippi, Theodore G. Bilbo became a part-time Baptist preacher at 19 and later attended the University of Nashville and Vanderbilt University. He entered Mississippi politics in his twenties as a protégé of James K. Vardaman, a charismatic demagogue who was known to his followers as the "Great White Chief." Vardaman's election to the governorship in 1904 ended the era in which state government had been dominated by the aristocratic planter families of the delta region. In 1907 Bilbo won a seat in the Mississippi Senate as a Democrat. Like Vardaman, he had campaigned as an enemy of the rich and educated and as a violent advocate of white supremacy. He perfected a style of oratory, combining profanity with biblical allusions, that appealed strongly to the poor tenant farmers and sharecroppers of Mississippi's hill country.

Bilbo first achieved notoriety three years later, when he admitted accepting a bribe. The Mississippi Senate declared him "unfit to sit with honest, upright men in a respectable legislative body." Nevertheless, Bilbo's backwoods supporters elected him lieutenant governor in 1911 and governor in 1915. Unable to succeed himself, he ran unsuccessfully for the U.S. House in 1920. Eight years later Bilbo was again elected to the governorship after a campaign in which he condemned his opponent for having called out state troopers to prevent a black from being lynched.

In 1934 Bilbo won a U.S. Senate seat. He supported the New Deal but also crusaded against antilynching legislation and proposed to solve unemployment by deporting blacks to Africa. During World War II, when equality in the hiring of blacks was considered necessary to overcome the manpower shortage, Bilbo opposed the Fair Employment Practices Act. Repeatedly his prolonged filibusters against the measure impeded other important legislation.

Bilbo at first welcomed the ascension of Truman to the presidency, but he soon found he strongly disagreed with many of his policies. He rejected universal military training, the loan to Great Britain, higher unemployment compensation, the Full Employment bill, and a higher minimum wage. On the last point the senator feared that a higher minimum wage would indirectly lead to higher wages for uncovered farm workers. Bilbo's shift from economic liberalism to conservatism may have resulted from his animosity toward the growth of the Congress of Industrial Organizations, which fought against discrimination and would target Bilbo in 1946 for being such a flagrant bigot. His conversion also may have reflected the anger of southern farmers to government wartime price controls on crops. Also wartime prosperity had helped many of Bilbo's constituents out of poverty, lessening the economic hatreds that Bilbo had exploited before the war. In 1945 the senator launched his two-day filibuster of an appropriations bill in order to eliminate the Fair Employment Practices Commission (FEPC). He managed to get its funding cut in half.

In September 1945 President Truman asked Congress to reconstitute the FEPC on a permanent basis. When a bill to establish the panel was brought before the Senate early the following year, southerners responded with a filibuster lasting three weeks. Bilbo insisted that the FEPC was "nothing but a plot to put [blacks] to work next to your daughters . . ." and called its supporters "Quislings of the white race." Finally, the Senate leadership was forced to remove the item from the agenda.

Threatened by new civil rights initiatives from Washington, Bilbo's former opponents among Mississippi's conservative elite rallied in support of his reelection in 1946. Unlike prior elections in which he stressed economic concerns, Bilbo in 1946 would focus almost exclusively on race baiting. Prior to the voting Bilbo issued inflammatory statements aimed at discouraging Mississippi blacks from exercising their right—recently upheld by the Supreme Court—to participate in the primaries. In an apparent invitation to terrorism, which received nationwide publicity, he declared, "I call on every redblooded white man to use any means to keep [blacks] away from the polls. If you don't understand what that means you are just plain dumb." Northerners with Italian or Jewish surnames who wrote letters of protest to Bilbo received replies filled with ethnic epithets.

The senator won the primary, which in solidly Democratic Mississippi was tantamount to reelection.

In the aftermath of the election, the Senate held two investigations of Bilbo. One was of his tactics to intimidate blacks from going to the polls. The investigating committee's Democratic majority—composed mostly of southerners—quickly cleared the senator, but later the Justice Department would launch its own investigation.

The second congressional investigation looked into charges of bribery and influence peddling by Bilbo on behalf of Mississippi defense contractors. It was alleged that, in return, businessmen had provided cash to him and free construction at his "Dream House" in Poplarville, Mississippi. In response to one accusation of ill-gotten gain, the senator said, "Well, I didn't get a damn cent of it." The committee declared that evidence that it had received "clearly indicated that Senator Bilbo improperly used his high office . . . for his personal gain." As a result, at the initiative of Senator ROBERT A. TAFT (R-Ohio), the Senate's Republican leadership recommended that when the chamber convened in January 1947, Bilbo be barred at the door and thus prevented from taking the oath of office. When the Senate met, southern supporters of Bilbo began a filibuster that deadlocked the body and prevented any senator from being sworn in.

Sensing that southerners would not be able to win this filibuster, Bilbo offered to leave Washington for New Orleans for an operation for oral cancer, if they would allow him to continue receiving his Senate salary. Republicans and Democrats agreed to this compromise, and Bilbo's credentials were tabled until such time as he returned, which he never did, dying in New Orleans on August 21, 1947.

—TLH

Black, Eugene R(obert)

(1898–1947) *president, International Bank for Reconstruction and Development*

Eugene R. Black was born on May 1, 1898, in Atlanta, Georgia. He was raised in an Atlanta family with banking interests—his father was president of the Atlanta Trust Company and a governor of the Federal Reserve Board. After graduating from the University of Georgia and serving as an ensign in the navy during World War I, Black began his career with a New York investment house in 1918. He achieved a reputation in investment banking

through salesmanship and expertise in the bond market. In 1933 he became a vice president with Chase National Bank. Three years later he was appointed undersecretary of the Treasury, where it was hoped he could help finance the soldiers' bonus. A few months later, however, he turned down the appointment because of the financial sacrifice involved. During and after World War II Black became increasingly active in the international operations of Chase.

The International Bank for Reconstruction and Development (World Bank) was established by 44 nations at the Bretton Woods Conference of 1944. It began operations in June 1946 but encountered a lack of investor confidence because of its liberal lending policies. In late December 1946 JOHN J. MCCLOY was offered the job of president of the World Bank. McCloy sought the advice of Black as to what to do. Black had just been to a devastated Europe and thought the World Bank was necessary in such a time. He told McCloy that real power at the bank rested with the U.S. executive director, and that he should accept such a job only if he was given the right to choose the director. Therefore, that was one of the conditions McCloy set; another was that Black would be the executive director. The other directors grudgingly accepted his terms. Truman appointed Black and McCloy accepted the job in February 1947. Black's reputation in financial circles restored investor confidence, and, within a few months, the bank floated a $250 million bond sale in the U.S. market. In 1947 the bank loaned $497 million to four European countries: France, the Netherlands, Denmark, and Luxembourg. The loans maintained the flow of essential imports into those war-torn economies.

Following the adoption of the Marshall Plan in April 1948, the focus of the World Bank shifted from the reconstruction of Europe to building the economies of the developing nations. Black, who succeeded McCloy as the third president of the World Bank in 1949, saw the "revolution of rising expectations" in that area of the world as a great challenge to the West. Western nations, he felt, should help the poor countries develop while striving to reserve the checks and balances of free institutions. But Black was critical of bilateral foreign aid because of its susceptibility to political influence. Instead he favored international agencies, like the World Bank, making loans on the basis of their contribution to development without political conditions. Black believed this was the best way to fight communism. By raising the standard of living in developing areas, the West could help eradicate what he called the "natural breeding ground" of communism.

Under Black's leadership the World Bank concentrated on the services that stimulated growth. Two-thirds of the development lending was for power and transportation projects, such as electric utilities and highways. Black was an advocate of loans for the Aswan Dam project in Egypt, which was eventually financed by the Soviet Union. Under Black the World Bank also emphasized technical assistance, and he began a series of economic surveys to recommend development programs to particular countries. Beginning with the first mission to Colombia in 1949, more than 20 surveys were completed during Black's presidency.

After retiring from the World Bank in 1962, Black remained active in business and politics. He was on the board of directors of Chase Manhattan Bank, International Telephone and Telegraph, as well as other corporations. In 1965, as criticism of U.S. involvement in Vietnam mounted, President Johnson chose Black to head a development program for Southeast Asia. Black died on February 20, 1992, in Southampton, New York. (See *The Eisenhower Years, The Kennedy Years, The Johnson Years* Volumes)

—TFS

Black, Hugo L(afayette)
(1886–1971) *associate justice, U.S. Supreme Court*

Hugo Black was born on February 27, 1886, in Harlan, Alabama. In 1906 he graduated from the University of Alabama Law School and practiced privately in Birmingham, where he was elected to several local offices. For a brief period, from 1923 to 1925, he was a member of the Ku Klux Klan. First elected to the U.S. Senate in 1926, Black was re-elected in 1932 and in his second term proved to be a strong supporter of the New Deal. President Franklin Roosevelt chose Black as his first Supreme Court nominee in August 1937. The next month a Pittsburgh newspaper published evidence of Black's former Klan membership. In an October 1 radio address, Black acknowledged his past tie to the organization but said he had long since resigned and had had no further dealings with the Klan.

On the bench Black soon displayed an iconoclastic streak. During his first term, for example, he asserted that, contrary to long-established precedent, he did not believe the "person" protected by the 14th Amendment included corporations. He voted to sustain New Deal legislation and opposed the view that courts should determine for themselves the "reasonableness" of economic and social legislation. Justice Black gave wide scope to the federal government's power to regulate commerce, but unlike some other Roosevelt Court appointees, he also accorded the states considerable power over commerce. Black had strong antimonopoly views, and, throughout his years on the bench, he supported the rigorous application and enforcement of antitrust laws.

Although it took the justice some time to develop his philosophy on individual rights, he began taking strong libertarian stands early in his judicial career. In 1942, for example, Black argued in a dissent in *Betts v. Brady* that the right to counsel should be guaranteed to all state as well as federal defendants accused of serious crimes. Two years later, in *Korematsu v. U.S.*, however, in what may have been his most heavily criticized opinion, Black spoke for the Court to sustain the government's wartime evacuation and relocation of Japanese Americans.

In a June 1947 case, *Adamson v. California*, Justice Black gave his first full expression to a view that became one of the foundations of his judicial philosophy. When a five-man majority ruled that the Fifth Amendment's privilege against self-incrimination applied only to the federal government and not the states, Black in dissent argued that the 14th Amendment was intended to extend to the states all the liberties in the Bill of Rights, including the Fifth Amendment's. Black had made an in-depth study of the legislative history of the amendment. But as his biographer Roger K. Newman has noted, Black had not studied the entire historical atmosphere of the time. Black never won a Court majority for this "total incorporation" approach, but, in later years, the Court applied most of the Bill of Rights to the states on a case-by-case basis.

Black gave great expression to his theory of the First Amendment during the Truman era as an increasing number of loyalty-security cases came before the Court. The justice considered the guarantees of free speech and thought the most fundamental of rights, the ones essential to the maintenance of all other liberties. He also contended that these guarantees were absolutes; the government might regulate the time and place of an individual's speech, but it could never, Black insisted, control its content. The justice, who referred to himself as a "backward country fellow," believed the words of the Amendment—that "Congress shall make no laws . . . abridging the freedom of speech, or of the press"—meant what it said: Congress shall make *no* law. In oral arguments, when a litigant disagreed with his stance, usually beginning, "But, Mr. Justice," Black would softly interrupt, "But nothing." He would then pull out of his pocket a 10-cent copy of the Constitution and ask the counsel to read it. When he would reach the words "no law," Black would say "thank you" and indicated that an absolutist interpretation was required by such language. He regularly voted to overturn the various restrictions and penalties imposed on Communists because he regarded them as infringements on freedom of belief and expression. For example, Black dissented in *American Communication Association v. Douds* in May 1950. The question in this case was whether the anticommunist oath required of union officers under the Taft-Hartley Act was unconstitutional. The majority noted that it was a reasonable expectation that the Communist Party would launch political strikes to disrupt commerce, and that Congress had the right to prevent such disruption under the commerce clause. Since the Communist Party presented a "clear and present danger" their political rights under the First Amendment could be restricted. Black dissented, saying the First Amendment was added to ensure that the Constitution's enumerated powers would not be used by Congress to abridge a person's beliefs or speech. He again objected in June 1951 in *Dennis v. U.S.* when a majority sustained the conviction of 11 Communist Party leaders under the Smith Act. He argued that the act's prohibition of a conspiracy to teach and advocate overthrow of the government was unconstitutional. Black also opposed in February 1947 the Hatch Act's ban on political activity by government employees as a violation of the First Amendment. He dissented in *Beauharnais v. Illinois* when the Court upheld a state law against group libel in April 1952.

The Vinson Court decided a series of cases brought under the First Amendment clause barring government establishment of religion. In the initial February 1947 case, *Everson v. Board of Education of Ewing Township*, challenging state payments for the transportation of children to parochial schools, Black spoke for the majority. He set forth the prin-

ciple that the amendment prohibited state and federal governments from passing laws "which aid one religion, aid all religions, or prefer one religion over another." But he then upheld the state payments in this instance on the ground that they constituted a social welfare measure and not aid to religion. Black for the majority averred that the First Amendment requires states to maintain neutrality in regard to religion or nonbelief; the government does not have to be their adversary. In March of the next year in *Illinois ex rel. McCollum v. Board of Education*, however, Black again wrote for the majority to overturn a program of released-time, religious instruction conducted in public schools. Four years later, in *Zorach v. Clausen*, he dissented when the Court upheld another released time program in which the classes were held outside the public school building.

In criminal cases Black maintained his position in favor of enlarging the right to counsel and he took a strong stand against convictions based on coerced confessions. In contrast to his expansive view of most criminal rights, Black had a restrictive approach to the Fourth Amendment. In May 1947, for example, he was part of a five-man majority that considerably widened the scope of a search law enforcement officials might make incident to a valid arrest.

Black tended to be liberal in other cases as well. On questions of racial discrimination, Black supported the Vinson Court's trend expanding the constitutional rights of minorities. He wrote the opinion in a June 1948 decision invalidating a California law that barred Japanese aliens from commercial fishing. When the majority ruled in June 1946 in *Colgrove v. Green* that legislative apportionment was a political question that the judiciary could not consider, Black vigorously dissented. Sixteen years later the Court overturned this precedent and adopted Black's position. In June 1952 Black wrote the leading opinion in *Youngstown, Sheet & Tube Co. v. Sawyer*, when the Court invalidated Truman's seizure of the steel industry.

On June 10, 1946, Justice ROBERT H. JACKSON, who was on leave from the Court at the Nuremberg war crimes tribunals, issued a statement attacking Black for having participated in the decision of a May 1945 case, which was argued by his former law partner. The case, *Jewell Ridge Coal Corporation v. Local No. 6167, United Mine Workers of America*, involved portal-to-portal pay for mineworkers. The War Labor Board had approved contracts endorsing the employee's stand not to pay for the time miners were transported from the surface to a below-surface worksite. A local of the United Mine Workers sued under the Fair Labor Standards Act to receive the pay. One of the lawyers for the union, Crompton Harris, had 17 years earlier been Black's law partner. Jackson insisted that Black recuse himself from the case, but he refused, and his vote won the case for the union. Jackson remained convinced Black had acted improperly. This remained private for a year, when, in 1946, Chief Justice HARLAN FISKE STONE died. Truman appointed Treasury secretary and political friend FREDERICK M. VINSON chief justice. On leave serving as a prosecutor at the Nuremberg war crime trials, Jackson revealed the controversy over the mineworker case. One reason Jackson disclosed the controversy was his belief in Felix Frankfurter's private revelation that Black had influenced Truman not to appoint Jackson chief justice. Black had passed word to the president that he would resign if Jackson were promoted. (President Franklin Roosevelt had apparently intimated to Jackson he would nominate him for the top spot on the Court.) When the controversy became public, Truman said that the "Supreme Court has really made a mess of itself." Black never responded publicly to Jackson's statement, which was in part a product of the many ideological and personal differences among the members of the Court. Black's defenders, however, pointed out that the partnership in question had ended over 17 years earlier when Black entered the Senate and that other justices had heard cases argued by former professional associates.

Through much of the 1940s, Black was regarded as the leader of a four-man liberal bloc on the Court. Personnel changes in 1949, however, reduced the "liberal wing" to Black and Justice WILLIAM O. DOUGLAS. For most of the Vinson Court years, Black found himself in the minority on many civil liberties and criminal rights issues. Nonetheless, he adhered to his principles and, later, when the Court took a libertarian and activist turn under Chief Justice EARL WARREN, it adopted many of Black's views on the First Amendment, defendants' rights, and reapportionment. As a result, Black made a profound impact on constitutional law. He has been ranked as one of the foremost justices in the Court's history. A man of great intelligence, energy, and hard work. Black was best known for his devotion to the individual liberties guaranteed in the Bill of Rights and for his contribution to the nationalization and stricter enforcement of most of those rights. Black died on September 25, 1971, in Bethesda, Maryland. (See *The Eisenhower Years*, *The Kennedy Years*, *The Johnson Years*, *The Nixon/Ford Years* Volumes)

—CAB

Bloom, Sol
(1870–1949) *member of the House of Representatives*

The son of poor Polish-Jewish immigrants, Sol Bloom was born on March 9, 1870, in Pekin, Illinois. He had little education, and, as a child in Peoria, Illinois, he sold newspapers to help his father feed the family. In 1878 the Bloom family moved to San Francisco, where Sol found a job in a brush factory. At the age of 13 he obtained a bookkeeper's job. He was interested in the theater and, by age 19, had already managed a ticket office, acted in and produced plays, and even built and owned a theater. In 1893 Bloom moved to Chicago to become an impresario for the world's fair. He invited exotic dance companies from all over the world. He thought his most lasting contribution to the fair was the premiere of the "Hootchy Kootchy" dance. Following his success at the exposition, he opened a chain of sheet music stores, ran a copyright business, and promoted boxing matches. In 1910 Bloom, by this time a wealthy man, moved to New York to enter the theater and real estate business. He decided to retire in 1920 to devote his life to public service. With the backing of Tammany Hall, he won a seat in the U.S. House of Representatives in 1923. During the 1920s Bloom devoted his attentions to representing entertainment interests on Capitol Hill.

Bloom was a supporter of the New Deal. In 1939 he took over the chairmanship of the Foreign Affairs Committee and helped push through the House some of the Roosevelt administration's most important foreign policy legislation. This included measures granting funds for the draft and lend-lease. During World War II Bloom served as one of Roosevelt's congressional advisers. He contributed to the planning and the congressional approval of the United Nations Relief and Rehabilitation Agency (UNRRA) and was praised by Secretary of State EDWARD R. STETTINIUS, JR., who valued his contribution to U.S. diplomacy, measuring public opinion, and helping the Congress understand the president's difficulties in foreign affairs. Just before his death Roosevelt appointed Bloom a delegate to

the San Francisco conference held in the spring of
1945. In his autobiography, Bloom believed that the
most important task at San Francisco was to build
confidence among the small countries that the large
countries wanted their participation, otherwise
nothing of significance would have happened. He
also insisted that delegates act on behalf of their
people, rather than their governments. In 1946
Bloom represented the United States at the second
meeting of the UN in London, where he helped
persuade the delegates to continue funding the
UNRRA. Bloom served on the American delegation
to the Rio Conference of August 1947 in which the
United States and the Latin American states formed
an alliance.

Bloom was particularly concerned with the fate
of European Jews. In the late 1930s and during the
war, he unsuccessfully fought for the United States
to receive more refugees. When Jews were attacked
in Poland in 1946, Bloom demanded that the
United Nations protect them, pointing to the guarantee of equal rights in the UN Charter. Bloom
criticized the Displaced Persons Act of 1948, which
admitted more than 200,000 displaced persons who
had entered the Western zone before December
1945. The representative declared this inadequate
and argued that it discriminated against Jews, many
of whom left Poland in 1946. Because of the United
States's stringent immigration laws, Bloom came to
believe that Palestine should be the refuge for the
victims of the Holocaust. At the San Francisco Conference he sat in on the Trusteeship Committee,
where he worked for passage of Article 80 that
promised to safeguard Jewish rights in Palestine.
When Congress took up the charter, Bloom
defended the Palestine Resolution in the House and
the Senate. Bloom supported the partition plan proposed by the UN, which would split Palestine
between Arab and Jew. He conferred with many of
the UN delegates to convince them to vote for the
creation of the state of Israel. Just before Israel proclaimed itself a nation on May 14, 1948, Bloom conferred with Truman to try to persuade him that the
United States should immediately recognize the
Jewish state. In addition to his interest in Israel,
Bloom supported independence for India.

In early 1947 CHARLES A. EATON (R-N.J.) took
over the chairmanship of the Foreign Affairs Committee. Bloom worked with him to win committee
approval for the funding of the Truman Doctrine
and the Marshall Plan. Following the Democratic

victory of 1948, the 78-year-old Bloom regained
chairmanship of his committee. He died of a heart
attack on March 8, 1949, in Washington, D.C.

—JB

Blue, Robert D(onald)
(1898–1989) *governor*

Robert D. Blue was born on September 24, 1898, in
Eagle Grove, Iowa. Blue attended Capital City
Commercial College in 1917 and Iowa State College at Ames in 1918. He received an LL.B from
Drake University in 1922 and practiced law with
the firm of Hobbet, Blue, and Blue in Eagle Grove,
Iowa. From 1924 to 1931 he was attorney for
Wright Company and in 1932 was Eagle Grove city
attorney. Blue won election as a Republican to the
Iowa House of Representatives in 1934, where he
served four terms. He was floor leader from 1937 to
1941 and speaker from 1941 to 1943. Blue was
elected lieutenant governor in 1943 and governor
the following year.

During his two terms in office, Blue advocated
reforms, sponsoring a property assessment law that
made valuation standards uniform across the state
and proposing the extension of the state hospital
program. The governor inaugurated what he called
"the largest construction program in our history"
for Iowa schools and increased state aid to them
from $421,000 in 1944 to $13 million in 1947.
Many of his proposals were opposed by businessmen who felt burdened by the higher taxes they
required.

A supporter of states' rights, Blue told a Republican National Committee meeting at Chicago in
December 1945 that the federal government was
socialistic and totalitarian and was wasteful compared to state governments. "While state governments are carefully husbanding the tax-dollar and
prudently creating surpluses, the federal government is throwing more out of the back door than
the taxpayer can bring in the front door," he
declared. He decried the federal "alphabetical agencies" and attacked the Office of Price Administration for its wage-price control policies. He was
among 26 governors who signed a statement urging
a balanced budget in April 1946.

Blue came under strong criticism from organized labor. In April 1947 he signed a bill abolishing
the closed and union shops. Responding to organized protests against the action, the governor

defended the legislation, saying it was "not unfriendly to union labor." During the Congress of Industrial Organizations United Packing House Workers meat strike in 1948, he sent the National Guard to Waterloo, after a striker was shot and killed by a strikebreaker.

In June 1948 a coalition of farmers and union members defeated Blue's attempt to secure nomination. He retired to Eagle Grove, where he became head of a small bank. He died on December 14, 1989, in Fort Dodge, Iowa.

—AES

Bohlen, Charles E(ustis)

(1904–1974) *special assistant to the secretary of state; counselor, State Department; minister to France*

Charles E. Bohlen was born on August 30, 1904, in Clayton, New York, the son of a rich sportsman and a descendant of the first U.S. ambassador to France. He graduated from Harvard in 1927 and joined the Foreign Service two years later. After service as a vice consul in Prague, he was assigned to Paris in 1931, where he took intensive courses in Russian language and culture in preparation for a specialization in Soviet affairs. Ambassador WILLIAM C. BULLITT requested Bohlen be assigned to the first mission to the Soviet Union in 1934. Bohlen was posted to Tokyo in 1940. Upon his return to the United States in 1942, he became acting chief of the Division of Eastern European Affairs. During World War II Bohlen was the State Department's chief Russian translator, an expert on Soviet affairs, and head liaison between the State Department and the White House. He accompanied President Roosevelt to the Tehran and Yalta conferences in 1943 and 1945, helped write the "Declaration of Liberated Europe" in the latter conference, and served as liaison between the State Department and the White House.

Bohlen, along with Ambassador to the Soviet Union W. AVERELL HARRIMAN, was an early proponent of a firm policy toward the USSR. His years in Moscow had taught him to mistrust the Soviets and to doubt the value of continuing the wartime alliance. Bohlen believed that Soviet policy was based on its ideological conviction that capitalism must be destroyed. Therefore, he maintained, cooperation with Russia was impossible. Influenced by White House optimism during the war, however,

Bohlen became less critical of the Soviets and defended the Yalta Accords, despite his reservations on the Far East and United Nations agreements. Although critical of the Soviets, Bohlen argued that the United States should accept a Soviet "open" sphere of influence in Eastern Europe—"the Bohlen plan of trying diplomacy first" as ARTHUR M. SCHLESINGER, JR., called it. He thought the United States had to be firm on the issue while maintaining friendly relations with the Soviet Union. Shortly after Truman became president Bohlen recommended sending Roosevelt's aide HARRY L. HOPKINS to Moscow to try to repair the rift in the wartime alliance resulting from disagreements over the Yalta Accords. Bohlen accompanied Hopkins on the trip and served as translator during the inconclusive talks held with Stalin. He later was translator for President Truman at Potsdam. By early 1946 he shifted to the more hard-line policy toward the Soviets advocated by George F. Kennan.

During the first years of the Truman administration, Bohlen was an adviser to Secretaries of State JAMES F. BYRNES and GEORGE C. MARSHALL. He was appointed the department's counselor in 1947. He played a role in the formation of the administration's containment policy toward the Soviet Union, helping frame the Truman Doctrine and drafting Marshall's address announcing a massive economic aid program for Europe. During 1948 he also participated in policy discussions on Berlin, as he headed the State Department's committee that oversaw the Berlin blockade and airlift.

In the summer of 1949 Secretary of State DEAN G. ACHESON appointed Bohlen minister to France, the second-ranking position in the embassy. After the North Korean invasion of the South the following year, Bohlen returned home to advise Acheson on the Soviet role in the war. Bohlen concluded that Stalin's goals were limited to the Korean Peninsula and the attack was not a prelude to more Soviet military operations around the world. The administration rejected his position as it hastened to strengthen the North Atlantic Treaty Organization in anticipation of a Soviet move on the West. Two weeks after the invasion began Bohlen changed his mind and said a general war was possible or that the Soviets could blockade Berlin again. Bohlen also opposed American troops crossing the 38th parallel to invade North Korea on the grounds that it would goad the Communist Chinese into the war.

President Eisenhower appointed Bohlen ambassador to the Soviet Union in 1953. The nomination unleashed the fury of the Republican right, led by Senator JOSEPH R. MCCARTHY (R-Wisc.), who charged Bohlen with the responsibility for the "sellout at Yalta." After a grueling confirmation debate, the Senate approved Eisenhower's request. Senate Republican leader Robert A. Taft, however, warned against any more controversial appointments, saying, "No more Bohlens." In Moscow Bohlen served merely as a source of information for the administration. Although the ambassador did make policy recommendations, Secretary of State JOHN FOSTER DULLES rarely followed them. In 1957 Bohlen was transferred to the Philippines as ambassador. He served there until 1959, when Secretary of State CHRISTIAN A. HERTER appointed him special assistant on Soviet affairs. In 1962 President John F. Kennedy made Bohlen ambassador to France. He remained in Paris until the end of 1967, when he became undersecretary of state for political affairs. Bohlen retired in January 1969 and died on January 1, 1974, in Washington, D.C. (See *The Eisenhower Years, The Kennedy Years, The Johnson Years* Volumes)

—JB

Bolton, Frances (Payne)

(1885–1977) *member of the House of Representatives*

Born on March 29, 1885, in Cleveland, Ohio, to one of the state's wealthiest families, Frances Bingham married Chester E. Bolton, a steel executive, in 1907. She then devoted her time to philanthropies and politics. In 1904, Bingham volunteered to assist nurses who helped Cleveland's poor. What she saw during this time made her a lifelong supporter of nurses. She convinced the secretary of war to establish an army school of nursing during World War I. In 1923 she endowed the school of nursing at Western Reserve University (now Case Western Reserve University), which bears her name. During 1936 Bolton participated in her husband's successful campaign for the U.S. House of Representatives and, upon his death four years later, succeeded to his suburban Cleveland seat. Bolton opposed the Selective Service Act and, as a member of the House Foreign Affairs Committee, voted against lend-lease. However, after Pearl Harbor, she supported the war effort. During World War II she called for the desegregation, both by race and sex, of military nursing units. Under her guidance in 1943, Congress approved the Bolton bill, which provided funds to assist nursing students and schools and established the Cadet Nurse Corps.

A member of the Republican Party's conservative wing, Bolton voted for the Taft-Hartley Act and the Submerged Lands Act, as well as cuts in federal spending. She did vote apart from the GOP mainstream on public housing and opposed outlawing union and closed shops, although in the end she voted for Taft-Hartley. She traveled abroad, including to the Soviet Union in 1947, to discuss nursing issues on an international scale. She was the first woman to conduct a congressional study outside the United States. In 1951 she sponsored a long-range bill for nursing education that would have cost the government $47 million in its first year. The measure was defeated. In 1952, Bolton's son, Oliver Payne Bolton, became a U.S. representative from Ohio's 11th Congressional District—the first time a mother and a son had served at the same time in Congress.

A strong anticommunist, Bolton called for "the abandonment of any semblance of appeasement" toward the Soviet Union in 1946. Four years later she spoke in favor of sending U.S. troops to Korea. The representative voted for the domestic anticommunist legislation of the period, including the Mundt-Nixon bill of 1948 and the Internal Security Act of 1950.

Bolton was a vocal advocate of the conscription of women. She argued that military preparedness was vitally important and that women should continue to play the prominent role in defense that they had done during World War II. Bolton saw no threat to the institutions of marriage and family and argued that women's military involvement would only develop their character, enhancing their role in the family.

As a member of the House Foreign Affairs Committee, Bolton was a frequent defender of the UN and particularly of UNICEF. Bolton was appointed as a congressional delegate to the UN by President DWIGHT D. EISENHOWER. She also advocated independence for African colonies. During the Johnson administration Bolton, then ranking member of the Foreign Affairs Committee, criticized foreign aid and Vietnam policies. However, she supported the president on all important votes. She continued her campaign for women's rights, working to include bans against sex discrimination in civil rights proposals. Bolton remained popular in her district until 1968. At the age of 83 she lost her seat as the result of redistricting. She died on March 9, 1977, in Lyndhurst, Ohio. (See *The Eisenhower Years*, *The Johnson Years* Volumes)

—MN

Bowles, Chester

(1901–1986) *director, Office of Price Administration; governor; ambassador*

Chester Bowles was born on April 5, 1901, in Springfield, Massachusetts. His grandfather was a prominent newspaper publisher, his father a prosperous owner of a New England paper mill. After attending a number of prestigous schools, Bowles accepted a copywriters position in a New York advertising agency. In 1929 he and a friend, WILLIAM B. BENTON, founded their own agency, Benton and Bowles. Their business prospered during the depression, pioneering a number of sophisticated advertising techniques for radio.

A liberal Democrat, Bowles supported Franklin D. Roosevelt's domestic programs. Fearing that a drift toward war would set back reform at home, he opposed the president's foreign policies and joined the isolationist organization, American First. After U.S. entry into World War II, Connecticut governor Robert A. Hurley appointed Bowles administrator of rationing. In 1943 he became state director of the federal Office of Price Administration (OPA). Bowles's performance in Connecticut impressed Roosevelt, who appointed him director of the federal Office of Price Administration in 1943. The new director soon emerged as a leading liberal within the administration. Torn between business desire to raise prices and consumer demand for continued regulation, Bowles championed the consumer, and he established public and congressional support for wartime controls.

When he became president, Truman asked Bowles to remain at his post to aid the conversion to a peacetime economy. During the summer and fall of 1945, fearing an inflation similar to that after World War I, Bowles attempted to pursue a policy of increasing the production of consumer goods by returning men to the labor pool while retaining reasonably stable levels of prices and wages. He negotiated an informal agreement between labor and industry to increase wages up to 10 percent while holding prices on goods, and he began a gradual lifting of rationing and price controls.

His plan for gradual removal of restraints was supported by Truman and reluctantly by John W.

Synder, head of the office of War Mobilization and Reconversion. Secretary of Agriculture Clinton B. Anderson, however demanded immediate deregulation. During the fall Bowles fought with Anderson, who wished to increase farm prices and had suggested that farmers keep their grain off the market to raise commodity prices. Bowles opposed the secretary's actions because he thought they would increase prices and thus fan inflation. It would also prevent grain shipments to famine-threatened Europe. Nevertheless, the administration acquiesced to the farmers' demands.

In February 1946 Bowles clashed with Snyder over demands from the steel industry for price increases. When Snyder granted them an increase nearly three times that recommended by Bowles, the director resigned. Several days later Bowles agreed to serve as director of economic stabilization with the power to set policies on wages, prices, rents, rationing, and production. Despite his seemingly greater power, Bowles's influence in the administration decreased during his tenure. He clashed with organized labor over wage increases and with farmers over agriculture prices. In 1946 Bowles resigned in protest to Congress's crippling the president's anti-inflation program, which called for the continuation of price controls. In 1946 he attempted unsuccessfully to win the Democratic nomination for governor of Connecticut.

Out of office Bowles joined other liberals in searching for a way to move Truman to the left. Bowles enthusiastically supported the formation of the Americans for Democratic Action (ADA) in January 1947. He delivered the major address at its organizational dinner, denouncing Republican reaction at home and Russian totalitarianism abroad. He also maintained close ties with the Progressive Citizens of America (PCA), led by HENRY A. WALLACE. Bowles supported Wallace's calls for cooperation with the Soviet Union and for domestic reform. Yet, during the spring of 1947 he moved closer to the ADA as a result of the communist coup in Czechoslovakia, which Wallace and the PCA refused to condemn.

As chairman of the ADA's Committee for Economic Stability, Bowles continued his criticism of the Truman administration's economic policy. He was angered that Truman had failed to find a substitute for the disbanded OPA and seemed incapable of dealing with the question of inflation. In April 1947 Bowles met with Truman to suggest the creation of a price board, manned by businessmen, to make voluntary recommendations for controls. The following month Bowles's committee unveiled its own economic program, which included voluntary price reductions, housing assistance, farm subsidies, higher unemployment benefits, and an increase in the minimum wage. Many of these proposals soon became administration policies.

In 1948 Bowles was a delegate to the Democratic National Convention. Because he was running for governor of Connecticut that year, he fought Truman's nomination, believing that Truman on the ticket would hurt his own election bid. Instead he backed a drive to draft Supreme Court Justice WILLIAM O. DOUGLAS. When that failed Bowles supported Truman. He was elected for a two-year term in November over incumbent James C. Shannon.

During his short term in office, Bowles established a massive housing program for low and lower-middle-income families. At his insistence the General Assembly passed several civil rights laws guaranteeing equality in housing, employment, and public facilities. He was the first Connecticut governor to establish a state commission on civil rights. He also raised welfare rates and established emergency teacher-training programs. However, he failed to win approval for state-financed medical insurance programs. In 1950 Bowles ran for reelection but was defeated by John Davis Lodge by a margin of less than 1 percent. Lodge had depicted Bowles as a radical.

Following his defeat Bowles lobbied for a diplomatic post, reflecting his long interest in foreign affairs. Truman offered him his choice of several ambassadorships. Bowles decided to go to India. He developed close personal ties with Prime Minister Jawaharlal Nehru and worked with the Indians on the implementation of U.S. foreign assistance programs. Bowles was particularly impressed with the socialist direction of the Indian government and defended it against conservative critics in the United States who labeled it communistic. After a difficult confirmation fight, Bowles became the third U.S. ambassador to India. Republicans worried that Bowles would demand much congressional funds for the newly independent country. And this is what the ambassador did, demanding $250 million per year in U.S. aid to India. Bowles saw the victory of democracy in the rest of Asia contingent on India's economic success. He feared too little aid would cause India to drift toward communism. Although he did win some aid for India, Bowles never secured the huge outlays he requested.

Bowles resigned in 1953 at the beginning of the Eisenhower administration. During the 1950s he embarked on a career of writing and lecturing. His first book, *Ambassador's Report* (1953), chronicled his service in India and pleaded for American understanding of Nehru's neutralist policies. *Ambassador's Report* made the bestseller list for five months and sold 35,000 copies. In subsequent books Bowles argued for a liberal approach to foreign policy that would stress economic aid to the non-Western world. From 1959 to 1961 Bowles served as a representative from Connecticut in the U.S. House. President John F. Kennedy appointed him undersecretary of state in January 1961. Bowles was forced to resign in November in a dispute over policy toward the Soviet Union. To placate the liberals Kennedy first appointed him a special adviser and then ambassador to India. Bowles remained in New Delhi until the end of the Johnson administration. Bowles died in Essex, Connecticut, on May 25, 1986. (See *The Eisenhower Years, The Kennedy Years, The Johnson Years* Volumes)

—JB

Bowron, Fletcher
(1887–1968) *mayor*

Bowron was born on August 13, 1887, in Poway, California. He was a descendant of colonial settlers, and he grew up on a fruit ranch in San Diego County, California. He entered the University of California at Berkeley in 1907 and studied law at the University of Southern California in 1909. He left after two years without obtaining a degree. From 1911 to 1917 Bowron worked as a reporter in San Francisco and Los Angeles. He was admitted to the bar in 1917. Following service in the army during World War I, Bowron entered law practice in Los Angeles. He became deputy state corporate commissioner in 1923 and a judge of the Los Angeles Company Superior Court three years later. During his 12 years on the bench, Bowron opposed municipal corruption under Mayor Frank L. Shaw. In 1938 an election was held for Shaw's recall. Drafted as a candidate on a fusion ballot, Bowron won the race by a two-to-one margin. He held office from 1938 to 1953, longer than other man up to that time.

During Bowron's tenure the city grew tremendously: the population increased by 650,000. To service the needs of the city, the mayor initiated construction of an airport and an elaborate freeway system. He also negotiated an agreement with the

Federal Housing Authority to spend $100 million in federal funds for the construction of 10,000 housing units.

Bowron assumed the position of unofficial leader of the nation's mayors in their confrontations with Washington. As president of the American Municipal Association, which represented 9,500 cities in 40 states, he sought federal compensation for the loss of tax revenue on city property owned by the national government. In an article titled "How Uncle Sam Mooches on Your City," published in 1946, he maintained that city taxes were high because the federal government preempted sources of revenue. In 1947 Bowron had to deal with a threatened secession of the Port of San Pedro, whose leaders claimed the port was not receiving its fair share of improvements. Bowron blamed Communists and CIO unions, in particular the International Longshoremen's Union, for the movement.

As mayor, Bowron was concerned with the elimination of organized crime from municipal government, particularly the police department. He was hampered in his efforts by the lack of power to dismiss civil servants. Nevertheless, in his first seven months in office, he secured the resignation of 23 police officials. By 1949 a representative of the International Association of Police Chiefs described the Los Angeles department as "outstanding" among large cities. In March Governor EARL WARREN's special civic study commission on organized crime announced that Warren and Bowron were the men slot machine kingpins thought most dangerous to their interests. The panel also supported Bowron's assertion that organized crime was exerting pressure to make Los Angeles a "wide-open town." In response Bowron recommended laws making transportation of money to aid political campaigns for the purpose of establishing illicit operations a federal offense.

Bowron's popularity declined during his fourth term. In 1949 Assistant Police Chief Joseph J. Reed and former police chief Clement B. Horrall were accused of lying under oath before a grand jury investigation regarding the interactions—including bribery—of police officers with the operator of a Hollywood bordello, Brenda Allen. Bowron said, "I would be willing to testify as a character witness at their trial." There was discontent when the perjury charges were dropped. Bowron's supporters claimed the grand jury investigation was a plot by Democrats to recall the mayor. The Los Angeles Citizens Committee, moving his recall, claimed he was responsi-

ble for high taxes and police corruption. In January 130,000 signatures appeared on a petition for his removal. The city council voted to hold an election. Seven candidates sought Bowron's job, but he won by a three-to-two margin in November, receiving 388,000 votes to 245,000 for his opponents. He suspected that the underworld had promoted the movement for his recall, and his supporters charged that organized crime and pro-communist elements had been behind the attempt.

In 1953 Bowron, a Republican, lost his reelection bid to Republican representative Norris Poulson, an opponent of public housing. Four years later he was appointed judge of the Los Angeles Superior Court, a post he held until 1962. Bowron died of a heart attack on September 11, 1968, in Los Angeles.

—AES

Boyd, James
(1904–1987)   *director, Bureau of Mines*

The son of an Australian mining engineer, Boyd was born in Kanowa, Australia, on December 20, 1904. Boyd received schooling in England. His parents emigrated to the United States after World War I, and Boyd followed in 1922, becoming an American citizen three years later. He studied engineering at the California Institute of Technology and did prospecting in the West before entering the Colorado School of Mines in 1929. He earned a doctorate in geophysics from that institution in 1934. Boyd taught there from 1934 to 1941 and also did consulting work for mining and engineering companies. He served in the Army during World War II. After the war he was responsible for the rehabilitation of German industry in the American zone. He reported in October 1945 that 75 percent of Germany's industry was intact or reparable, but because of low Ruhr coal production and damaged transportation services it would take five years for Germany to recover to approximately the standard of living desired by the Allies. His aim was to change the German economy from one producing arms and heavy industry to that of an agrarian state designed to produce consumer goods. He did not know, however, to what extent that goal could be reconciled with another one, that of a self-sufficient Germany. Returning to civilian life in 1946, Boyd became dean of the faculty of the Colorado School of Mines.

Early in March 1947 President Truman nominated Boyd to become director of the Bureau of

Mines. JOHN L. LEWIS, head of the United Mine Workers Union, denounced the appointment as politically motivated and called Boyd "incompetent" and "ignorant" about safety conditions in the mines. Lewis threatened to call a nationwide coal strike if the nomination was approved. A few days later, 11 men were killed in the Centralia mining disaster, the worst mining accident in the nation's history. Concern over the disaster led the Senate to postpone confirmation of Boyd indefinitely. Truman, nonetheless, appointed Boyd acting director of the bureau in August 1947, a position which he held without pay for over a year. In May 1948 the Republicans, who controlled the Senate, decided to put Boyd's and others' confirmations on hold until after the presidential election, which they believed would be won by a member of their party. Truman made another recess appointment for Boyd. After Governor THOMAS E. DEWEY lost to Truman, the president nominated Boyd again. In March 1949, when it appeared that the Senate was preparing to approve Boyd's nomination, Lewis called a strike as he had threatened. This time, however, the Senate was undeterred. On March 22, 1949, Boyd finally became director of the Bureau of the Mines.

Despite Lewis's charges, Boyd's tenure with the bureau witnessed improvements in mine safety. Inspections of the nation's mines increased, and, in 1948, there were fewer mining casualties than in any previous year. The 1951 annual report of the Bureau of Mines indicated that accidents in the coal mines had continued to decline, although Boyd admitted that major advances in safety were still necessary.

Mine safety was only one of Boyd's concerns. He was also responsible for advancing scientific research in mineralogy. Under Boyd the bureau brought titanium to the point of commercial production. Boyd also established the first demonstration plants for obtaining oil from coal and oil shale. During the Korean War Boyd headed the newly created Defense Minerals Administration with responsibility to expand the supply of essential minerals for war production.

Boyd resigned from the Bureau of Mines in October 1951 to become an executive for the Kennecott Copper Corporation. He remained with Kennecott until 1960, when he became president of the Copper Range Company. Boyd also served on the board of directors of other mining companies. He served on the committee on mineral research of the National Science Foundation from 1952 to 1957, and, in 1971, he became chairman of an Inte-

rior Department advisory committee on mine safety. In 1969 he became president of the American Institute of Mining Engineers. He died in 1987.

—DAE

Boyle, William, M(arshall), Jr.
(1902–1961) *chairman, Democratic National Committee*

William M. Boyle, Jr., was born on February 3, 1902, in Leavenworth, Kansas. After his family moved to Kansas City, Missouri, Boyle organized a Young Democrats' club at age 16. His service caught the attention of Kansas City Democratic leader Tom Pendergast and Boyle advanced to ward leader while making the acquaintance of Harry S Truman. After attending Kansas City Junior College, he studied law at Georgetown University. Boyle received an LL.B. from Kansas City in 1926.

Until 1939 Boyle practiced law and continued working as a ward leader for the Pendergast machine. He supported Truman in his 1934 race for the U.S. Senate. Boyle was named police director of Kansas City in 1939, after an investigation revealed no evidence of his involvement in the income tax scandals that had toppled the Pendergast machine.

In 1941 Truman brought Boyle to Washington as assistant counsel for his War Investigating Committee. The following year Boyle became Truman's personal secretary. In 1944 Boyle joined the Democratic National Committee, where he helped manage Truman's campaign for the vice presidency. After Truman's election Boyle opened a law office in Washington.

In 1948 Truman called on Boyle to help manage his presidential campaign. Hoping to overcome the president's image as a loser, Boyle advised a whistle-stop campaign concentrating on local issues. In a crucial move Boyle persuaded the candidate to campaign in the farm sections of Ohio and Illinois. Truman carried these states in November. Their electoral votes played an important part in winning him the presidency.

In February 1949 Truman chose Boyle as executive vice chairman of the Democratic National Committee. Boyle was put in charge of the administrative operations at headquarters. At the time of the appointment, journalists noted the potential dangers in appointing a lawyer in private practice to a post in which he was able to disperse positions to his clients. Boyle, however, discounted any conflict of interest. He intended to serve without pay, but, following criticism about possible conflict of interest, he accepted a salary and announced the closing of his practice. Six months later he was elected Democratic national chairman. In February 1950 the Investigations Subcommittee of the Senate Banking and Currency committee, chaired by Senator J. WILLIAM FULBRIGHT (D-Ark.) opened a probe of favoritism affecting loan decisions of the Reconstruction Finance Corporation (RFC). Rex C. Jacobs testified that he suggested to Kaiser-Frazer president Edgar Kaiser that he should ask Doyle's law firm to take over his company's RFC affairs. One year later the Fulbright panel issued its report charging Boyle and others—including White House aide Donald Dawson—with exerting pressure on the RFC to grant loans to particular companies. Truman called the report "asinine" and said it contained no basis for the charges against Boyle.

Following further allegations in the press, the Investigations Subcommittee of the Senate Committee on Expenditures, chaired by Senator CLYDE R. HOEY (D-N.C.), opened hearings in September 1951 on charges that Boyle had used political pressure to influence an RFC loan to the American Lithofold Corporation. Boyle was charged with maintaining a relationship with American Lithofold, his former law client, while Democratic national chairman and using his influence to obtain a $565,000 loan for an $8,000 fee. Boyle admitted accepting $500 a month from the company for an undisclosed period, but said he had quit before taking over the chairman's job. He denied pressing for the loan, which had been refused twice before being granted one month after he became national chairman.

Following the Hoey panel's hearings in October 1951, Boyle resigned as national chairman giving ill health as his reason. Truman stated he had not asked for Boyle's resignation and regretted his quitting. The subcommittee released its report in January 1952. It stated that Boyle had done nothing "illegal or immoral" but that his "conduct was not such that it would dispel the appearance of wrongdoing." Boyle died in his sleep on August 31, 1961, in Washington, D.C.

—MJS

Braden, Spruille

(1894–1978) *assistant secretary of state for American Republics Affairs*

Spruille Braden was born on March 13, 1894, in Elkhorn, Montana. He was the son of an engineer who played a role in the development of the Anaconda Copper Company's Chilean properties. Braden received a Ph.B. in mining engineering from Yale University in 1914. He then engaged in engineering and construction in Latin America and served as an economic adviser to several South American governments. He served as the American delegate to several Latin American conferences. From 1938 to 1942 he was minister to Colombia and from 1942 to 1945 minister to Cuba. President Roosevelt appointed Braden ambassador to Argentina in 1945. During four months at the post, he worked for the overthrow of the fascist regime of Juan Perón. In his Braden memorandum, of April 1945, the diplomat argued dictatorships were incubators for communism and in Latin America policy should treat authoritarian leaders with "aloof formality" and only recognize governments that reflected the will of the people.

In August 1945 Braden was nominated to succeed NELSON A. ROCKEFELLER as assistant secretary of state for American republics affairs; he was not confirmed by the Senate until October. The Senate Foreign Relations Committee opposed him as an "interventionist" who had stirred up trouble between the United States and Perón, a needed ally against communism. Perón had accused him of inspiring an abortive revolt that took place after his recall, and Braden was held responsible for the State Department's cancellation of a projected Inter-American Conference on Peace and Security for Hemispheric Defense, which would have included Argentina.

As assistant secretary, Braden continued his campaign against Perón. In an unsuccessful effort to thwart Perón's reelection attempt in 1946, he published a massive documentary collection from German archives (the so-called Blue Book) revealing that Argentina had served as a haven for Nazi submarines and subversives during the war. He tried to have Ambassador George Messersmith, a Peron supporter, recalled, but Truman refused his request.

Braden was an advocate of economic rather than military assistance to Latin American nations. He maintained that this policy would prevent an arms race in the hemisphere and promote the development of the region. However, the Truman administration refused his advice and, during the spring of 1947, drafted a bill for $1 billion in arms sales to the region. In response, Braden resigned.

Braden returned to his business career and served as a U.S. delegate at international conferences.

During the 1950s he criticized the Eisenhower administration's foreign aid program. An anticommunist, in 1961 Braden was reportedly an organizer of the John Birch Society. Braden died on January 10, 1978, in Los Angeles, California. (See *The Eisenhower Years* Volume)

—AES

Bradley, Omar (Nelson)

(1893–1981) *veterans' affairs administrator; army chief of staff; chairman, Joint Chiefs of Staff*
Omar Bradley was born on February 12, 1893, in Clark, Missouri. He graduated from the U.S. Military Academy at West Point in 1915 and began a career in the infantry. In 1920 he returned to West Point, where he served as an instructor in mathematics for four years. He graduated from the Infantry School in 1925, the Command and General Staff School in 1929, and the Army War College in 1934. He was an instructor at the Infantry School from 1929 to 1933 and at West Point from 1934 to 1938. He was called to Washington in 1938 to serve on the War Department General Staff; three years later, he was appointed commandant of the Infantry School.

During World War II Bradley commanded U.S. forces in North Africa and Italy. General DWIGHT D. EISENHOWER chose him to lead the American contingent in the Normandy invasion. His troops liberated Paris in August 1944 and even-

A signed commemorative photograph of (*left to right*) Hoyt Vandenburg, Louis Denfeld, and Omar Bradley (*Harry S. Truman Library*)

tually drove through central Germany to establish the first Allied contact with Soviet troops. Known as the "soldier's soldier," the mild-mannered Bradley maintained a plain, homespun image, essentially one of rural America. His manner was without pretense or flamboyance, yet he was a confident professional and one of the most competent field commanders in American history. By war's end he was in command of over one million soldiers, the largest ground army ever commanded by an American general.

Shortly after V-E day President Truman named Bradley administrator of veterans' affairs, a post he held for two years. The VA was in poor shape, and demobilization would make 43 percent of the American male population veterans. Bradley managed the reorganization of the government's largest independent agency during his two years there, which made it better able to handle the postwar veterans' boom. Bradley was named army chief of staff in 1948, and, after Dwight D. Eisenhower rejected the new position of chairman of the Joint Chiefs of Staff, Truman appointed Bradley, who then assumed the position in August 1949. As chairman, Bradley advocated the strengthening of the North Atlantic Treaty Organization (NATO) and the integration of West Germany into defense efforts. Testifying in Senate hearings on the North Atlantic Treaty in 1949, he declared that a large American troop commitment to Europe was imperative in maintaining Allied cohesion and indicating to the Europeans that the United States would not abandon them in case of Soviet aggression. Bradley served as the first chairman of the Military Committee of NATO, which consisted of the military chiefs of the member nations.

Bradley was a proponent of a strong conventional army, defending it against claims that it was outdated. The general believed that despite such modern methods of warfare as air power and nuclear weapons, victory in any war with the Soviet Union would ultimately depend on large-scale land operations. Bradley supported building the superbomb, but thought its effect would largely be psychological. He minimized the importance of the navy, stating that because of the atom bomb, surface fleets were "a thing of the past." Bradley supported the "economy" defense budgets of 1949 and 1950. He maintained that the nation could afford only limited spending for the defense in peace time. However, with the coming of the Korean War, he advocated higher defense spending.

After the outbreak of the Korean War, Truman briefly considered sending Bradley to replace General DOUGLAS MACARTHUR, but he decided to keep Bradley as chairman and, in September, promoted him to the rank of general of the army. Bradley thought MacArthur a genius, but also insufferably arrogant. He constantly cautioned MacArthur on his conduct of the war, but MacArthur largely ignored him. He was horrified by the UN commander's outspoken criticism of the way the administration was handling the war. In April 1951 President Truman recalled MacArthur as the UN military commander in the Far East. Speaking in opposition to the president, MacArthur had advocated an economic and naval blockade of Communist China as well as American bombing of Manchuria and the use of Nationalist Chinese troops on Formosa against the Communists. Although he did not think MacArthur had technically been insubordinate, Bradley supported Truman's decision to relieve him of his command. He criticized MacArthur's recommendations, saying that they would unnecessarily increase the risk of global war. He pointed out that stepped up activity against China would require a large-scale commitment of American troops to get decisive results. Bradley depicted the Korean fighting as just one phase in the continuing battle between the United States and the Soviet Union. He said that MacArthur's policy would have "stripped" much American strength from other areas where it was needed without lessening any danger of Soviet intervention. The general summed up his views by saying that MacArthur's proposal would put "the U.S. in the wrong war, at the wrong place, at the wrong time and with the wrong enemy." Bradley stated that the Joint Chiefs of Staff also approved MacArthur's recall because they felt the general's actions tended "to jeopardize the civilian control over the military authorities."

In May 1953 he retired as chairman of the Joint Chiefs and from the army to become chairman of the board of the Bulova Research and Development Laboratories of the Bulova Watch Company. Following his retirement Bradley periodically appeared on Capitol Hill to testify before various congressional committees on defense matters. In 1955 President Eisenhower named him head of the Commission on Veterans' Pensions. Ten years later President Johnson appointed him to a panel to study federal employees' raises. He was a strong advocate of the Johnson administration's Vietnam policy, speaking out in favor of the war. He was a senior adviser for the

Oscar-winning film *Patton*. Bradley nearly died from a blood clot in the lung in 1973, and he passed away in New York City on April 8, 1981.

In recent years it has been revealed that Bradley apparently made a critical decision in regard to military intelligence. Fearful of news leaks from the White House, Bradley did not inform Truman about the Venona Project, in which military intelligence was decoding messages from the Soviet embassy and consulates to Moscow about its spying operations in the United States. This proved important because Truman did not know that many of the revelations of ELIZABETH BENTLEY and WHITTAKER CHAMBERS were true as confirmed by Venona. Truman received reports from FBI chief J. EDGAR HOOVER about Soviet spying, but the president distrusted him, believing he exaggerated such reports for political ends. According to John Earl Haynes and Harvey Klehr, if Truman had known these reports were based on solid intelligence, people in his administration might not have tried to indict Chambers for perjury and discredit Bentley.

—GMS

Brannan, Charles F(ranklin)
(1903–1992) *secretary of agriculture*

Charles F. Brannan was born on August 23, 1903, and raised in Denver, Colorado, by a Quaker family. His father was an electrical engineer. Brannan received his LL.B. from the University of Colorado in 1929. From 1929 to 1935 he practiced in Denver, specializing in irrigation and mining law. Brannan was an ardent supporter of the New Deal from its beginning. In 1935 he joined the Department of Agriculture as assistant regional attorney in the Resettlement Administration, where he relocated destitute farmers caught in the "dust bowl." In 1937 he was promoted to regional attorney in the office of the solicitor of the Department of Agriculture where he helped farmers with cooperative projects. He joined the Farm Security Administration in 1941. Brannan administered loans for water facilities and arranged credit for needy families in Colorado, Wyoming, and Montana.

In June 1944 President Roosevelt appointed Brannan assistant secretary of agriculture. Secretary of Agriculture CLINTON P. ANDERSON put him in charge of the subcommittee on long-range planning of the Policy and Program Committee at the end of 1946. When Anderson resigned as secretary

in May 1948, he recommended Brannan as his successor. JAMES PATTON, a close friend of Brannan and president of the liberal Farmers Union, also lobbied for his appointment. Truman followed their advice, and Brannan became the new secretary of agriculture in May 1948.

Brannan quickly emerged as an aggressive campaigner for Truman in 1948. Grain prices fell in the summer and fall of 1948 and most polls conceded the farm vote to Truman's opponent. THOMAS E. DEWEY. On September 2 HAROLD E. STASSEN visited Dewey and made a statement charging that the Department of Agriculture had deliberately increased food prices by making unnecessary grain purchases for export. The next day Brannan called a press conference and accused Stassen and Dewey of attacking the price support system. He pointed out that the Republican-controlled 80th Congress had undercut the system by failing to provide adequate storage facilities. With a record corn crop in 1948, corn prices had fallen below support prices, but without storage facilities many farmers had been unable to take advantage of price supports. Brannan succeeded in making the issue a major component of Truman's campaign. In more than 80 speeches that fall, he hammered away at the alleged Republican sabotage of price supports and played up fears of a new farm depression. Farmers were receptive as corn prices plummeted from $1.78 in September to as low as $1.00 a bushel in some markets on election day. Some of Truman's biggest upsets were in the farmbelt; he won Iowa, Wisconsin, and Ohio—states that the Roosevelt ticket had lost in 1944. Brannan's campaigning made him a major figure in the administration. Truman brought him into the inner circle of advisers, and he helped formulate the Fair Deal.

In 1949 Brannan presented the administration's controversial farm program. The proposal, known as the Brannan Plan, was a major departure from previous agricultural policies. It was designed to maintain farm income at record wartime levels while letting supply and demand determine the market price of commodities. The plan would give an incentive to produce fewer grain crops and raise more livestock. This was designed to reduce the surfeit of grains and lower the price of meat and dairy products. Working with Roosevelt's program of restricting production and marketing to maintain prices, Brannan proposed direct payments to farmers when prices fell below support levels. He recommended guaranteeing farmers a secure income based on the average cash receipts for the first 10 of the last 12 years (the old parity base of 1909–14 would be scrapped). This had the effect of guaranteeing high, rigid price supports at from 90 percent to 100 percent of parity. Brannan recommended extending income protection to producers of 75 percent of the nation's farm commodities, as contrasted with 25 percent under the existing legislation. He hoped to do this by extending support to perishables such as milk and eggs. The Brannan system's low market prices would encourage consumption while the payments would guarantee farm income. Finally Brannan proposed limiting the receipt of benefits to approximately the first $26,000 worth of crops in order to protect what he called "the family-sized farm."

In his defense of the plan, Brannan repeatedly stressed that depressions are "farm-led and farm-fed." Guaranteeing farm income, he asserted, would help stabilize the economy. He also stressed that if prices of commodities such as meat and milk were allowed to sink to their natural market levels, consumption would increase and nutrition would improve, especially for the poor. Brannan's friend, James Patton, and the Farmers Union came out strongly in support of the plan. So did the Congress of Industrial Organizations (CIO), which thought the plan would lower prices for the working man. Liberals applauded it both as a means of solving the surplus problem and as a potential breakthrough in politics. Agricultural columnist Angus MacDonald wrote, "If Brannan is right, the political miracle of 1948 will become a habit as farmers, labor and consumers find common political goals."

Gradually, a powerful coalition led by conservatives combined to defeat the plan. The opposition was led by the conservative American Farm Bureau Federation whose president, ALLAN B. KLINE, identified the Brannan Plan with the "left wing." He called it "a statement of political economic philosophy—not a farm program." The National Grange, the National Association of Manufacturers, and the Chamber of Commerce also lined up in opposition. Congressional Republicans attacked the plan as too costly. Direct government payments were denounced for their "socialistic tendencies." Republicans worried the plan would ally farmers and urban workers within the Democratic Party. Senator GEORGE D. AIKEN (R-Vt.) also called it an attempt to "regiment" American agriculture because the proposal

gave the secretary of agriculture greater powers to limit production if surpluses rose.

In July 1949 the House Agriculture Committee recommended the Brannan-Pace bill, which included a trial run for production payments on three commodities of the secretary's choosing. Representative ALBERT GORE (D-Tenn.) offered a counterproposal calling for 90 percent of parity for the basic storables and 60 percent to 90 percent for the perishables. Southern Democrats swung into opposition against the Brannan Plan. Large cotton planters opposed the $26,000 cutoff. Others viewed with suspicion any proposal with strong labor backing. Many farmers objected to the direct cash payments as government "hand-outs." Speaker SAM T. RAYBURN (D-Tex.) made a last minute appeal to fellow Democrats. However, the coalition of Southern Democrats and Republicans adopted the Gore substitute 239 to 170, thereby killing the Brannan Plan in the House.

In the Senate, now senator Anderson led the fight against the proposal. He advocated a plan calling for a sliding scale of 75 to 90 percent of parity. The Senate Agriculture Committee unanimously rejected the Brannan Plan and endorsed the Anderson bill. The 1949 Agricultural Act (Gore-Anderson Act) represented a defeat for the Brannan Plan and a compromise on the sliding scale, which was to be gradually introduced starting in 1951.

Undeterred by the defeat, Brannan continued to speak out in favor of his proposal. In response, Aiken accused him of using taxpayers' money to support his own political cause. Critics of the Brannan Plan frequently charged that department funds were being used for propaganda purposes. Aiken's charges were investigated by the House Select Committee on Lobbying Activities. Its Democratic majority concluded in October 1950 that Brannan had done no wrong.

The Korean War led to crop shortages and rising agricultural prices. Brannan's influence fell during the war, and he believed he was losing control of agriculture policy to officials concerned with fighting inflation. Truman was concerned with the war and paid little attention to Brannan's advice. In September 1950 Brannan imposed strict export controls on cotton in order to assure domestic supplies and keep prices down. However, he was soon forced to back off because of the pressure from the southern cotton bloc in Congress. In May 1951 Brannan supported the 10 percent rollback in beef prices initiated by the Office of Price Stabilization. During that year he kept price supports at 90 percent of parity to encourage production for wartime needs even though the 1949 Agricultural Act gave him a permissible level of 80 to 90 percent. Since demand was high, the government had to make few purchases to maintain parity price levels. In 1951 production controls were removed from all basics except peanuts and tobacco. Brannan maintained price supports at 90 percent for basic commodities through 1952.

Brannan was a vigorous supporter of the family farm. In January 1951 he helped boost the Farm Family Policy Review designed to encourage a grassroots movement on behalf of the family farm. In part this was to regain influence within the administration. However, the Farm Bureau vigorously attacked the new program charging that accused Communist ALGER HISS had helped formulate it. The grassroots meetings called by the department met with mixed success, and Brannan's crusade for the family farm stalled.

Brannan campaigned vigorously in the 1952 election, touring 14 states emphasizing his party's achievements for the farmer. After Eisenhower's victory he retired to practice law in Denver, where he became general counsel to the Farmers Union. Brannan continued to speak out on agricultural issues. In 1962 Secretary of Agriculture Orville Freeman appointed him to a committee to study the effectiveness of the farmer committees that administered farm programs. In 1973 Brannan had the satisfaction of seeing his proposals on farm income and production payments enacted into law. Brannan died on July 2, 1992, in Denver, Colorado.

—TFS

Brewster, (Ralph) Owen

(1888–1961) *member of the Senate*

A descendant of William Brewster, who came over on the *Mayflower*, Owen Brewster was born on February 22, 1888, in Dexter, Maine. He attended Bowdoin College, where he graduated in 1909. He received a law degree from Harvard in 1913 and began practice in Portland, Maine. He was elected to the Maine House of Representatives as a Republican in 1916. With the exception of a year's service in the army during World War I, he remained in the lower house until 1923, when he became state senator. He was elected governor of Maine in 1925. Brewster supported Prohibition and created the

Maine Development Commission to promote tourism and industry in the state. He was elected to the U.S. House of Representatives in 1934 and the Senate six years later.

Brewster became a critic of the Roosevelt and Truman administrations. As a member of the Joint Congressional Committee Investigating the Pearl Harbor Attack, he subscribed to the minority report blaming President Roosevelt for the disaster. In January 1946 he demanded that Prime Minister Winston Churchill testify at the hearings as to whether Great Britain and the United States had cooperated in the Far East before the incident. Brewster became chairman of the Special Senate Committee to Investigate the National Defense Program in January 1947. He used this post as a forum to attack Democrats, delving into the Roosevelt administration's allegedly inefficient handling of the war. Brewster cited as evidence the president's failure to create a national war resources board, recommended by EDWARD R. STETTINIUS, JR., in 1938, in the event of conflict, and the disposition of a $648 million emergency fund set up for the late president.

A supporter of a Jewish state in Palestine, Brewster was a critic of Arab nations. He opposed British collaboration with Arab governments and plans for a federation between Jews and Arabs in Palestine. In May 1946 the senator attacked British assistance to Saudi king Ibn Saud, deriding him as a British puppet. Brewster urged formation of a Zionist state. Despite Saudi protests to the State Department, Brewster continued his criticism. He again attacked the Arabs and the British when he discovered that Great Britain had used lend-lease funds to bolster Saudi Arabian oil concessions and that American oil companies had given exorbitant royalties to Ibn Saud. As adviser to the Political Action Committee for Palestine, he denounced the U.S. arms embargo on Israel in February 1948.

In November 1947 Brewster inquired into the activities of the Arabian-American Oil Company in the Middle East, requesting the Justice Department to investigate its ownership by Standard Oil, Texaco, and Socony-Vacuum. He charged that the United States had given away $80 million in unreceived oil payments to this company and that by overcharging the United States it had gained $5 million profits on $18 million in sales in 1946. He denounced those American oil companies that incorporated abroad, evading payment on $117 million in untaxed profits. Brewster urged the Attorney

General to investigate how the corporations were disposing of oil, hinting that national interests were suffering.

Brewster favored military initiatives during the Korean conflict. In July 1950 the senator urged that General DOUGLAS MACARTHUR be permitted to use the atomic bomb against North Korea at his, not Truman's, discretion. Brewster believed MacArthur should invade China if attacked by Chinese troops. In an effort to achieve a bipartisan foreign policy, the Democrats agreed to allow Brewster to have a seat on the Foreign Relations Committee on May 1951. He used this opportunity to assail Secretary of State DEAN G. ACHESON during hearings on MacArthur's dismissal, charging that the secretary's account of the fall of China in 1949 was an example of "deceit." He signed the minority report that denounced the Roosevelt and Truman administrations for the "most desolate failure in the history of our foreign policy" by their pursuit of an inept program of a weak defense and appeasement of communism since the Yalta Conference in 1945.

Brewster was a leading supporter of Senator JOSEPH R. MCCARTHY's (R-Wisc.) anticommunist crusade and backed the senator's investigation of the State Department in 1950. That year he contributed $1,000 to the Senate campaign of John Marshall Butler, who was running against Senator MILLARD E. TYDINGS (D-Md.), an opponent of McCarthy.

During 1952 Brewster was implicated in questionable or illegal activities. He admitted to the House Ways and Means Committee that he had, through an intermediary under investigation, given $10,000 to RICHARD M. NIXON's 1950 Senate primary campaign, although it was against the rules of the Republican Senate Campaign Committee of which he was chairman. During a state legislative hearing both he and Maine governor F. G. Payne were implicated in graft and influence-peddling in the state liquor monopoly.

Brewster, a supporter of Robert A. Taft (R-Ohio), was defeated in the Republican primary of 1952 by Payne who backed DWIGHT D. EISENHOWER. In 1954 McCarthy suggested Brewster as chief counsel to the Senate Government Operations Committee, but the appointment was defeated because of Democratic opposition. Brewster died on December 25, 1961, in Brookline, Massachusetts.

—AES

Bricker, John W(illiam)

(1893–1986) *governor, member of the Senate*

Born on September 6, 1893, in Madison County, Ohio, and raised in rural Ohio, John W. Bricker graduated from Ohio State University in 1916 and received his law degree from that institution in 1920. During World War I he served as a first lieutenant in the army. From 1920 to 1928 he was solicitor for Grandview Heights, Ohio, and assistant attorney general. Bricker served as a member of the state public utilities commission from 1929 to 1932. He was elected Ohio's attorney general in 1932 and held this position until 1937, when he lost a bid for reelection. In 1938 he was elected governor of Ohio on the Republican ticket. He was twice reelected to the governorship.

An outspoken foe of the New Deal, Bricker was selected as candidate for vice president by the Republican National Convention in 1944. Two years later he ran for senator, describing himself in his campaign as a "middle of the roader." His platform emphasized the importance of legislation to curtail labor activities. He also advocated the restriction of the powers of the executive branch of government. He won the general election by approximately 300,000 votes.

When he took his seat in 1947, Bricker joined the conservative "Old Guard" wing of the Republican Party. He backed the Republican-controlled Congress in its concern to "clear away the rubble of the New Deal and the war," opposing social legislation and supporting the reduction of federal spending and taxes. Bricker criticized federal subsidization of public housing, voting against the Taft-Ellender-Wagner Act of 1949, which allocated funds for urban redevelopment and public housing. As to the sponsorship of the measure by his Ohio comrade, Robert A. Taft, Bricker huffed, "I hear that the Socialists have gotten to Bob Taft." In a cynical move, Bricker attempted to shoot down the housing bill by trying to attach an amendment that would have made discrimination in public housing illegal. He was trying to strip away Southern Democratic support from the bill. The maneuver failed when liberals, with a great deal of agonizing, voted against the rider to save the overall bill. He also supported the reduction of individual income tax rates and fought the Revenue Act of 1951, which sought to raise taxes. An ardent foe of price controls, he sponsored a successful amendment in 1949 limiting the president's authority to impose general regulations.

According to Bricker biographer Richard O. Davies, Bricker's ultraconservative views on issues isolated him on the GOP far right.

Bricker maintained a staunch anticommunist stance throughout his years in the Senate. He opposed confirmation of DAVID E. LILIENTHAL as chairman of the Atomic Energy Commission because of the liberal's allegedly extreme left-wing views. He supported the 1948 Mundt-Nixon bill, which required the registration of all communist and communist-front organizations, and in 1950 he voted for the Internal Security Act, which incorporated provisions from the earlier measure.

As Davies noted, conservative Republicans faced a dilemma in regard to cold war foreign policy: they could revert to their prewar noninterventionism, and not do anything about communism abroad, or resist communism internationally, but then become entangled in the political affairs of other countries. Bricker, despite his fervent anticommunism, chose a noninterventionist approach. Bricker denied he was a postwar "isolationist." Bricker liked a unilateral foreign policy, was suspicious of collective security, and saw the threat to America in a large budget deficit, rather than communist activities abroad. He argued that the United States could beat communism by maintaining its economic strength at home through a free market and by avoiding unnecessary commitments abroad. In 1947 Bricker opposed passage of a bill allocating financial assistance to Greece and Turkey. Although he voted for the Marshall Plan in 1948, he favored cutting its appropriations by 10 percent. One year later he voted against the Mutual Defense Assistance Act that authorized military aid to the North Atlantic Treaty Organization and countries concerned with the threat of communism. He was an opponent of the Foreign Economic Assistance Act of 1950, which established aid to underdeveloped countries. In 1951 he endorsed the imposition of embargoes on Soviet trade to all countries receiving U.S. aid.

Bricker strongly criticized American concessions at the Yalta Conference as a sell-out of democratic principles and considered Roosevelt's compromise directly responsible for Soviet occupation of Eastern Europe. He attributed the agreement to the growth of executive powers and the failure to include Congress in postwar negotiations. In reaction to these events, Bricker urged the restriction of presidential treaty-making powers. In 1951 mounting criticism of Truman's decision to send U.S. forces into Korea prompted Bricker to sponsor a motion to curtail the Administration's postwar foreign policy. The article required the president to consult the Senate Foreign Relations Committee, the House Foreign Affairs Committee, and the Senate and House Armed Services committees before sending troops abroad.

Bricker's advocacy of restraint on presidential treaty-making gained momentum, and in 1952 his proposal received the endorsement of the Republican Party platform. He subsequently introduced another version of his article in 1953, which sparked an intensive debate. The controversy over the Bricker Amendment extended into 1954, when the Senate defeated a similar measure by a one-vote margin.

In 1958 Bricker was defeated for reelection by Democrat Stephen M. Young. His support of pro-business, antilabor legislation was generally credited with causing his defeat. Bricker retired from public service and entered private practice in Columbus, Ohio. He died there on March 22, 1986. (See *The Eisenhower Years* Volume)

—DGE

Bridges, Harry (Alfred) (Renton)
(1910–1990) *president, International Longshoremen's and Warehousemen's Union*

The son of a prosperous realtor, Bridges was born in a comfortable suburb of Melbourne, Australia, on July 18, 1910. He dropped out of school at 16 to become a merchant seaman. In 1920 Bridges disembarked at San Francisco after a quarrel with his ship's captain and found work on American vessels sailing along the Pacific coast. During this period he joined the sailors union and was briefly a member of the radical Industrial Workers of the World. In 1922 he settled in San Francisco and became a longshoreman.

Shrewd, pugnacious, and highly respected by his fellow workers, Bridges emerged in the early 1930s as a leading spokesman for the growing discontent on the San Francisco waterfront. With the aid of a small nucleus of communist organizers, he took over a recently formed local of the International Longshoremen's Association (ILA) in 1934. The union demanded an end to the notorious "shape-up" hiring system, which encouraged job selling and favoritism. Under Bridges's leadership a strike committee was formed in May, and the work stoppage quickly spread along the coast. After the police intervened and killed two pickets in San Francisco, a general strike involving the entire city was launched in July. The union finally won recognition, and Bridges was catapulted into national fame. The principal achievement of the 1934 strike was the establishment of union-run hiring halls that equalized work and earnings among longshoremen and effectively took the power to hire out of the hands of the employers. As a result, the longshoremen came to view their union, not the companies, as the focus of their work lives. They developed strongly personal attachments to the organization and to Bridges himself.

In 1937 Bridges led the Pacific District of the ILA out of the American Federation of Labor (AFL) and into the new International Longshoremen's and Warehousemen's Union (ILWU) affiliated with the Congress of Industrial Organizations emerged as one of the most prominent spokesmen for the communist wing of the CIO, which became increasingly important during the late 1930s. Bridges's relations with the Communists became a source of persistent public controversy and judicial action. Having failed to take out citizenship papers since establishing residency in the United States, he was brought before immigration hearings in 1938 and 1941 in an effort by the government to deport him on the grounds that he was a communist. Attorney General ROBERT H. JACKSON in 1940 ordered the FBI to begin investigating Bridges. Sixteen years later Bridges's file at the bureau was 38,000 pages long. After Attorney General FRANCIS BIDDLE ordered him deported in 1942, Bridges's lawyers appealed to the Supreme Court, which ruled in his favor in 1945.

The ILWU's public policy statements were closely aligned with the positions of the Communist Party throughout the 1930s and 1940s. Although he openly backed the Communist Party, Bridges always claimed not to be a Communist himself, but evidence surfaced in 1992 from opened files of the Communist International that Bridges had been elected to the Communist Party's national central committee in 1936. Up until 1939 Bridges supported Franklin D. Roosevelt's foreign policy, but he suddenly reversed himself following the Hitler-Stalin Pact in that year and attacked the administration for giving aid to the Allies. When Germany invaded the USSR in June 1941, however, the ILWU became vehemently pro-war. After Pearl Harbor Bridges joined the rest of the CIO in a no-strike pledge for the duration of the conflict.

Bridges set up the Pacific Coast Maritime Industry Board, through which the union cooperated with the shipowners to speed up cargo handling. He also urged greater wartime cooperation with the government and the military than the CIO national leadership was willing to grant. The ILWU supported the army and navy call in 1944 for compulsory service legislation even when CIO president PHILIP MURRAY condemned it as destructive of civil liberties. Bridges's union also helped break a CIO authorized strike against Montgomery Ward.

Bridges attempted to maintain his new partnership with industry after the war, and in line with the Communist position at the time, he urged that the CIO no-strike pledge be extended into the reconversion period. With the collapse of the wartime alliance between the United States and the Soviet Union, however, he abruptly shifted to a more militant stance. Seeking to extend his influence throughout the maritime industry, he organized in 1946 a conference of longshoremen and shipping unions, which he hoped would lead to a single national federation of maritime organizations under his leadership. The unity move collapsed after a few months, however, because of conflicts between Bridges and JOSEPH E. CURRAN, the head of the National Maritime Union, who was then in the process of breaking away from his Communist backers.

Negotiations for a new longshoremen's contract opened in 1947 shortly after congressional passage of the Taft-Hartley Act, which was aimed, in part, at outlawing the union hiring hall in the maritime industry. Hoping to take advantage of Bridges's growing unpopularity, the shipowners declared that they would not bargain with Communists and notified the union that any new agreement could not include the hiring hall. The strike began in June 1948 after an unsuccessful injunction imposed under the Taft-Hartley Act. It lasted 95 days and ended in a dramatic victory of the union. The hard-line anti-Bridges group was ousted from the leadership of the waterfront employers' association and replaced by men who were willing to cooperate with the ILWU. The following year the union also won a major strike in Hawaii, which had paralyzed the islands for six months. After World War II the ILWU had succeeded in recruiting Hawaiian sugar and pineapple plantation workers as well as longshoremen and, as a result, had become an important force in the territory's political and economic life.

Bridges's outspoken denunciations of the Truman administration's foreign policy in the late 1940s and his frank endorsement of Soviet aims provoked renewed demands for his prosecution and deportation. A month after the 1948 strike ended, Bridges was indicted for allegedly having committed perjury three years earlier when, while applying for citizenship, he had sworn that he was not a Communist. Although convicted, he was cleared in 1953 by the Supreme Court, which ruled that the statute of limitations had expired before the trial.

Meanwhile, a growing rift emerged between Bridges and the national CIO leadership, which was moving toward an anticommunist purge. In retaliation for Bridges's opposition to the Marshall Plan and support for the third-party candidacy of HENRY A. WALLACE, Murray ousted him from the post of Northern California regional director and, it was rumored, even collaborated with the Justice Department in his 1948 prosecution. In 1950 formal charges were brought against the ILWU at the CIO convention. The union was expelled in August on the basis of a trial committee's findings that Bridges, whether or not he had ever actually been a member of the Communist Party, had participated in party faction meetings where he had received instructions from Communist leaders. The CIO maintained that since the 1930s the policies of the ILWU had been "consistently directed toward the achievement of the program and purposes of the Communist Party rather than the objectives and policies set forth in the CIO constitution.

Contrary to the expectations of most observers, Bridges's power was not weakened by the ILWU's ouster from the CIO. Bridges had earlier dropped his refusal to cooperate with the provisions of the Taft-Hartley Act and had signed the noncommunist affidavit in order to use the services of the National Labor Relations Board. Consequently, the ILWU successfully resisted raiding efforts by other unions. In 1950 all but one ILWU local pledged all-out support to the Korean War effort, despite Bridges's declared opposition to U.S. intervention in the conflict. Shortly afterward the union's policy committee voted to end connections with the Communist-controlled World Federation of Trade Unions and its maritime affiliate, of which Bridges was honorary president. Despite the longshoremen's repudiation of Bridges's politics, they never made an organized challenge to his personal domination of the union. This was perhaps because Bridges allowed much par-

ticipation in union decisions by the rank and file. For instance, local delegates came together periodically in the longshoremen's caucus to make decisions on contract issues. Bridges had a rule that 15 percent of the union's members could petition for the removal of any official, including him. Referendums were held of the entire union on most major decisions.

The isolation of the ILWU during the 1950s induced Bridges to adopt a friendlier attitude to the employers. After 1948 a period of labor peace on the West Coast waterfront began that lasted for the next 23 years. In 1960 the shipowners obtained ILWU approval of a Mechanization and Modernization agreement under which the union surrendered its claims to job control and security in return for cash bonuses for retiring longshoremen. Bridges himself sought respectability as a registered Republican. He retired as head of the ILWU in 1977. Bridges died on March 30, 1990, in San Francisco, California. (See *The Eisenhower Years, The Kennedy Years, The Johnson Years , The Nixon/Ford Years* Volumes)

—TLH

Bridges, (Henry) Styles
(1898–1961) *member of the Senate*

Born the son of a farmer on September 9, 1898, in West Pembroke, Maine, Bridges graduated from the University of Maine with a degree in agriculture in 1918. During the 1920s he was an agricultural adviser and a writer in New Hampshire. Bridges served on the State Public Service Commission from 1930 to 1934, when he was elected governor. He was the youngest man in the state's history to hold the post. The governor was a serious contender for the Republican vice presidential nomination in 1936 until it was humorously suggested that Democrats could use the slogan "Landon-Bridges falling down." Bridges won a Senate seat in 1936, where he compiled a conservative record as an opponent of most New Deal legislation. However, he did support Roosevelt's foreign policy. In 1940 Bridges ran unsuccessfully for the Republican presidential nomination.

When Harry Truman became president in April 1945, Bridges was one of the most powerful Republicans in the Senate, ranked below Senator ROBERT A. TAFT (R-Ohio) and Senator ARTHUR H. VANDENBERG (R-Mich.). As chairman of the Appropriations Committee during the 80th Congress and minority leader in 1952, he was a leading opponent of Truman's domestic program. He voted for the Case labor dispute bill and the Taft-Hartley Act and opposed portal-to-portal pay for miners. He supported the Republican tax cut proposals of 1947 and 1948, which granted relief primarily to upper-income individuals. As chairman of the Joint Committee on the Legislative Budget, he was a vigorous advocate of large cuts in spending. The senator was committed to a "pay as you go policy" and said Truman's fiscal policy was "squandermania," and a "blueprint for waste." In all Bridges engineered a $6 billion reduction in Truman's 1947 budget. The senator condemned Truman's proposed 1949 National Health Insurance Program as a move toward socialized medicine. In 1950 he inveighed against federal aid to education as a plot to brainwash students.

In 1946 Bridges became involved in settling a United Mine Workers' strike. The dispute involved the retired mine workers' pension. UMW president JOHN L. LEWIS wanted higher payments: the operators resisted. Bridges was asked to mediate and ruled in favor of the miners. Subsequently in 1948, Lewis, who liked Bridges's straightforward manner, asked the senator to become the "neutral" member of a three-man panel formed to oversee the UMW pension fund. He assumed the post in the midst of a miners strike called to force the mine owners to come to an agreement on the specifics of welfare benefits. On April 12 Bridges engineered a compromise, accepted by all parties, that gave in to the union on the issue of eligibility but was far less generous on benefits than the UMW desired. The following year Bridges was embarrassed when it was revealed that he had received $35,000 as a welfare fund trustee. He denied that this made him pro-union and asserted that the fees were spent on legal counsel for his job. He left his post in November 1949. Bridges was involved in another scandal when it was revealed in hearings before Representative CECIL R. KING's Ways and Means subcommittee that the senator, on the prompting of shady lobbyist HARRY W. GRUNEWALD, had intervened with the Bureau of Internal Revenue's chief counsel CHARLES A. OLIPHANT on behalf of Baltimore liquor dealer Harvey Klein, who owed $17 million in back taxes. Bridges felt exonerated when he was not mentioned in the subcommittee's final report, but once again his ethics had become the subject of doubt.

Bridges was primarily known as a vocal critic of President Truman's foreign policy. The senator

viewed communism as a monolithic movement, directed by Moscow, to take over the world. He, therefore, opposed giving any aid to Communist countries, including Yugoslavia, and after World War II demanded all lend-lease aid to the Soviet Union be stopped. He considered U.S. diplomatic recognition of the Soviet government to be a tragic mistake because it allowed Soviet spies to cross U.S. borders. In 1951 he called for severing diplomatic ties with all Communist governments.

Bridges was particularly concerned with policy toward China. In 1945 he charged that the administration was dragging its feet on a $120 million military aid program to China and was planning to abandon China to the Communists. He encouraged PATRICK J. HURLEY, former ambassador to China, to continue his charges that a number of American Foreign Service officers were working to defeat the Nationalists. Bridges and others on the Appropriations Committee in March 1949 supported a bill to send $1.5 billion to aid Chiang Kai-shek's (Jiang Jieshi) Nationalists. Secretary of State DEAN G. ACHESON said such aid would be wasted, as Chiang's army was beyond salvation. The fall of China to Mao Zedong's (Mao Tse-Tung) Communists affected him deeply. "China," he said, "asked for a sword and we gave her a dull paring knife." When the State Department issued its "White Paper" defending its China policy, Bridges responded, "It is clear to me that the Chinese war was lost in Washington and not in China." Bridges joined Senator JOSEPH R. MCCARTHY's (R-Wisc.) campaign for the ouster of Acheson for "the loss of China." In an effort to revive bipartisan foreign policy, Truman invited Bridges to White House briefings and discussions after he became Senate minority leader. However, the New Hampshire Republican continued to attack the administration.

After the outbreak of the Korean War, Bridges gave a speech outlining what he called "a blueprint for victory." He said that the United States must face up to the fact that it was locked into an all-out war with communism. In order to meet the challenge, the administration had to place ceilings on wages and prices, support a Nationalist invasion of mainland China, throw all Communist nations out of the United Nations, and create an "American Foreign Legion of Anti-Communists." Bridges insisted that General DOUGLAS MACARTHUR should be given the authority to fight in Korea by any means he saw fit. He called MacArthur's dismissal in April 1951 a tragedy.

Bridges supported McCarthy's demand for an investigation of subversives in the State Department. He claimed that the department had "fallen to a condition of degeneration unparalleled in the nation's history." "Stalin is not a superman," the senator claimed, "He had to have help from inside our ranks." Truman requested that Bridges desist in his charges. When the senator refused, the president linked Bridges with his other Republican critics, calling them "the greatest asset the Kremlin has." Yet Bridges was not a blind supporter of McCarthy. Bridges and Senate Minority Leader KENNETH S. WHERRY (R-Neb.) went to McCarthy's apartment after one speech in which he proclaimed the government was honeycombed with subversives. They demanded he give them the list of Communists. An inebriated McCarthy refused.

As was his habit, Bridges refused to endorse either Taft or General DWIGHT D. EISENHOWER before the nominee was chosen. Once Republicans nominated Ike, Bridges vigorously campaigned for him. During Eisenhower's two terms, Bridges urged the president to follow policies dictated by the party's conservative wing. He remained a public supporter of McCarthy, opposing his censure in 1954. Bridges died of a heart attack on November 26, 1961, in Concord, New Hampshire. (See *The Eisenhower Years, The Kennedy Years* Volumes)

—JB

Browder, Earl (Russell)
(1891–1973) *Communist Party leader*

Born on May 20, 1891, in Wichita, Kansas, Earl Browder was one of 10 brothers and sisters of an old stock American family. Browder quit school after the third grade to help support his family. By 21 he had held many jobs including errand boy, bookkeeper, and accountant. Browder was introduced to radicalism by his father, who drew him into the Socialist Party. He left the Socialists in 1912 and became associated with the Syndicalist League of North America, led by WILLIAM Z. FOSTER. In 1917 he served a three-year sentence for draft refusal. The October Revolution in Russia influenced Browder greatly, so that upon his release from prison in 1920 he abandoned his wife and child and went to New York City to join the Communist Party USA (CPUSA) as one of its earliest members. He joined Foster as a Trade Union Educational League (TUEL) delegate and went to Moscow in

1921 to attend the opening convention of the Red International of Trade Unions (Profintern), where he met Lenin. During 1925 Browder served as general-secretary of the American Communist Party and in 1926 returned to Moscow to attend a trade union conference. Here he decided to hitch his wagon to Joseph Stalin's star, and for the next quarter century would call for Stalinism and domestic reform at the same time. He was sent to China as Profintern representative to help the Pan-Pacific Trade Union Secretariat. During his nearly three year stay in the East, Browder edited the underground *Pan-Pacific Worker.* He returned to the United States in 1929.

The expulsion of the Trotskyites and Lovestoneites in the 1920s led to the CPUSA being led by a troika of Foster, Browder, and William W. Weinstone. Foster's health problems and Weinstone's laziness helped pave the way for Browder's ascendancy to a re-created general secretaryship in 1934. In 1935 he went to Moscow to attend the Seventh World Congress of the Communist International. He championed the new line introduced at the Congress in his famous slogan, "Communism is Twentieth Century Americanism." The Nazi-Soviet nonaggression pact deeply troubled him. Until the German invasion of the Soviet Union in May 1941, he assailed the growing hostilities as a "second imperialist war" and called for America to remain out of the war. After American entry into the conflict, he was the most vehement supporter of the war effort. He was convicted of passport violation and sentenced to prison in 1940 but was pardoned by President Roosevelt in May 1942.

Browder obtained high contacts in 1942–43, conferring with Undersecretary of State Sumner Welles three times on foreign policy, while corresponding with him often. After Franklin Roosevelt, Winston Churchill, and Stalin met at Tehran, Browder believed that if capitalism and communism could live harmoniously together in the world, why could they not in America? He proposed the Tehran Thesis: he called for collaboration between bourgeoisie and proletariat to increase foreign sales dramatically and double the American adult wage earners' purchasing power. It was a rather incoherent program to which neither communists nor capitalists paid attention.

In 1944 Browder called for the transformation of the Party into the Communist Political Association (CPA). The new organization was to abandon its function as a political party and would not raise the issue of socialism in the postwar period "in such a form and manner as to weaken national unity." For this action Browder was severely attacked by a leading French Communist. In June Browder was repudiated for "opportunist errors," at a CPA executive meeting. When the Communist Party was reconstituted in July under Foster's leadership and adopted a new, more militant line, Browder charged these developments were a turn toward "bohemian anarchism." Nonetheless, by August he was barred from doing any further party work unless he came to terms with his past mistakes.

In September 1945 Browder was ordered to testify before the House Un-American Activities Committee. But he refused to answer any question concerning his ouster from his CPA leadership position. He was formally expelled from the party in February 1946. To seek redress, Browder traveled to Moscow in May where he met with Soviet foreign minister V. M. Molotov. Upon his return to the United States, he served as a distributor for Soviet scientific literature; he held that position until mid-1949.

In July 1948 Browder applied for readmission to the party only to be rejected at its August convention. Following the indictment of 12 party leaders for Smith Act violations in July, he was attacked by some in the party as a "lackey" of Truman. He rejected various rumors that he was going to testify against the party at the Smith Act trials.

Between 1948 and 1950 Browder privately published a series of pamphlets addressed to his former comrades seeking to show them that he was still Marxist and essential to the party. During this same period he worked for MICHAEL QUILL, president of the Transport Worker's Union. In April 1950, as McCarthyism intensified, he testified before a Senate Foreign Relations subcommittee investigating Communist infiltration of the State Department. As a result of Browder's refusal to answer questions about communism or the party, he was cited for contempt. In November a federal grand jury indicted him for contempt of Congress; he went to jail in December when he was unable to post the $1,500 cash bond. Browder was acquitted the following year after a federal judge ruled that he was within his rights in refusing to answer irrelevant questions posed by the Senate committee.

Browder's final break with communism came in 1952. He spent the last 20 years of his life as, in the words of one observer, "a virtually forgotten man." On his 80th birthday in 1971, he no longer considered himself a Marxist. He lived the last years of his life with one of his three sons in Princeton, New Jersey, where he died on June 27, 1973.

With the opening of Russian and American records, such as the Venona transcripts, in the late 20th century, it became clear that Browder had oversight of some Soviet spy operations and knew of others, that during World War II he had worked closely with the NKVD, and that he had provided for the Soviets members of the CPUSA to carry out espionage.

—DMR

Brown, Clarence J.
(1895–1965) *member of the House of Representatives*

A descendant of early Ohio settlers, Clarence J. Brown was born on July 14, 1895, in Blanchester, Ohio. He studied law from 1913 to 1915. Instead of practicing, he became a publisher, forming the Brown Publishing Company in 1917. By 1947 the company owned five southwestern Ohio newspapers as well as printing shops in three Ohio cities. In 1918 Brown was elected Republican lieutenant governor of Ohio, becoming the youngest man in the state's history to hold that office. He became secretary of state in 1926 and served until 1932. Brown made unsuccessful bids for governor in 1932 and 1934. He served as manager for Frank Knox's vice presidential campaign in 1936.

In 1938 Brown won a seat in the U.S. House of Representatives, where he compiled a conservative record as an isolationist and opponent of Franklin D. Roosevelt's domestic program. He opposed much of Truman's Fair Deal. A vigorous foe of organized labor, Brown in 1946 supported the Case labor disputes bill, designed to curb labor's right to organize, and the following year he voted for the Taft-Hartley Act. He was a strong anticommunist, voting for an amendment to establish the House Un-American Activities Committee on a permanent basis in 1945 and supporting the Internal Security Act of 1950. Brown advocated decreased federal spending in both domestic and foreign programs. However, in 1946 he strongly supported a national mental health bill that provided $14.5 million in federal aid for research on mental illness. "We spend as much money every year to guard against cattle going wild from eating loco weed as this bill would cost," he bluntly told his opponents. Brown was also an ardent critic of Truman's foreign policy. Brown did support civil rights. He voted to abolish the poll tax and sponsored an amendment to the failed nurse draft bill to bar racial and religious discrimination in the recruitment of nurses. On the lighter side, Brown liked to fish and ride horses. An amiable and ample man, he was also the 1947 smelt-eating champion of the lower house of Congress.

The representative and Senator HENRY CABOT LODGE (R-Mass.) cosponsored a bill creating the Commission on the Organization of the Executive Branch of Government (Hoover Commission) in 1947. Brown also served on the panel. The task of the Committee was to look into ways the executive branch could become more efficient. Brown rejected several of the commission's centralizing proposals, among them one to create a transportation service and another to institute a united medical administration. Brown also served on the second Hoover Commission of 1953.

A leading party organizer, Brown gained a reputation for his blunt attacks on Democrats. As Republican campaign director in the election of 1946, he condemned the Democratic Party as cryptosocialist and charged that the Congress of Industrial Organizations' Political Action Committee was "a conduit of Communism." In August 1946 he attacked Truman's budget proposals as a misleading "ingannation," [sic] a word he coined for the occasion. When Truman belatedly removed price controls on meat two months later, Brown jeered, "It demonstrates Mr. Truman's ability to do the right thing too late." He became a member of the GOP House Steering Committee in 1943, and helped plan policy initiatives for the Republican 80th Congress. In the vote for majority leader of the 80th Congress, which was seen as foreshadowing the 1948 presidential nomination contest between New York governor THOMAS E. DEWEY and Ohio senator ROBERT A. TAFT, Brown was talked about as a possible rival of Charles A. Halleck of Indiana. Brown said he was not a candidate, but would serve if elected; he was not.

Brown managed Taft's and Ohio governor John Bricker's failed attempts to win the 1940 and 1944 Republican presidential nominations, respectively. In 1948 Brown again supported Senator Taft for the nomination. He served as Taft's campaign manager and was one of the senator's major strategists. Nevertheless, he was too busy in Congress to devote all his time to Taft's campaign and even refused to write or sponsor a campaign biography for his candidate. Brown opposed an alliance with moderate Republicans and rejected a suggestion by HAROLD E. STASSEN's supporters that they form a coalition against Governor Thomas E. Dewey. When Taft supporters sought to create a new image for him, Brown demurred, saying, "I don't think we should try to sell him as a liberal." As a proponent of public housing, Taft urged Brown, who was a member of the House Rules Committee, to push Truman's proposals through the panel in order to help his chances with liberals, but Brown adamantly refused. His stand contributed to Taft's loss of the presidential nomination in 1948.

As a ranking member of the Rules Committee in the 1950s and 1960s, Brown had an important influence on legislation. During the Eisenhower administration he helped block housing, school aid, and minimum wage bills but supported civil rights measures. He was one of the leading opponents of President John F. Kennedy's liberal domestic program. Brown died of uremic poisoning in Washington, D.C., on August 23, 1965. (See *The Eisenhower Years, The Kennedy Years* Volumes)

—AES

Brown, Irving J(oseph)

(1911–1989) *European representative, American Federation of Labor*

The son of a Teamsters official, Irving Brown was born on November 20, 1911, in New York, New York. He earned a B.A. in economics from New York University and attended Columbia University for two years. During the 1930s he was a union organizer in the auto and metal industries and a member of a small anti-Stalin communist group headed by former Communist Party leader JAY LOVESTONE. In 1937 and 1938 Brown and a number of other "Lovestoneites" were embroiled in a bitter conflict dividing the United Automobile Workers (UAW). With the support of International Ladies Garment Workers Union leader DAVID DUBINSKY and American Federation of Labor (AFL) president WILLIAM GREEN, they persuaded a few UAW locals to break away from the Congress of Industrial Organizations (CIO) and led them back into the AFL in 1939. Brown was subsequently hired by Green as a national organizer for the federation.

During World War II Lovestone and his followers became influential foreign policy advisers to the AFL leadership. After serving as a labor representative on the War Production Board, Brown was appointed director of the labor and management division of the Foreign Economic Administration (FEA) in 1945. Meanwhile Lovestone had begun organizing an AFL overseas apparatus, staffed by his entourage, with the aim of preventing communists from entrenching themselves in postwar Germany and of undermining Communist Party domination of French and Italian unions. Six months after taking the post, Brown resigned from the FEA. In 1946 he became the AFL's permanent European representative.

Reporting to Lovestone at the headquarters of the AFL-sponsored Free Trade Union Committee (FTUC) in New York, Brown traveled throughout Western Europe, intervening in the affairs of unions, dispensing money, equipment, and advice, and coordinating the FTUC's network of American operatives. In Germany he lobbied the American military government to permit the organizing of national unions and saw to it that they were headed by anticommunists. In Greece he gave assistance to Fotis Makris, a monarchist labor leader who worked closely with the conservative Greek government after Communists were purged from the unions in 1946.

Brown's activity was centered in France. Emerging from the resistance movement as a political force, the Communists had achieved predominance in the Confédération Générale du Travail (CGT), the country's major labor body. After a period of collaboration with the government in 1945–47, the Communists, Brown believed, had transformed their union cadres into paramilitary units, geared to obstruct reconstruction, sabotage delivery of U.S. arms, and act as partisan forces in the event of a Soviet invasion. Consequently he urged his French labor contacts to split from the CGT as quickly as possible and set up a rival union federation. At Brown's direction the AFL poured aid, in the form of office supplies and funds, into the anticommunist Force Ouvrière (FO) faction of the CGT. In 1948, unions withdrew from the CGT and regrouped as the CGT-FO. By this time, moreover, AFL objectives had merged with U.S. foreign policy. With the beginning of the cold war, the Truman administration became interested in counteracting Communist labor support in France and other European countries. As a result the Central Intelligence Agency (CIA) and other agencies subsidized Brown's operations.

While attempting to fragment Communist strength in France, Brown strove to break up the World Federation of Trade Unions (WFTU), an international venture sponsored by British and Soviet unions and the American CIO, which the AFL had boycotted since its formation in 1945. In 1947 Brown began laying the basis for a new international labor center with a series of conferences involving unions from countries receiving Marshall Plan aid. These efforts culminated in 1949 when, after the CIO and British Trade Union Council withdrew from the WFTU, delegates from labor groups in 50 countries attended the founding conference of the International Confederation of Free Trade Unions (ICFTU).

During the late 1940s increasing controversy surrounded Brown's operations. In response to the refusal of Communist maritime unions to unload American arms in Marseilles and other French ports in 1949, Brown organized the Mediterranean Committee, headed by Pierre Ferri-Pisani, a dockworker leader with underworld connections. Although ostensibly an arm of the ICFTU, the committee was generally regarded as a strong-arm squad, paid by the CIA to protect longshoremen who worked in defiance of the CGT. Brown's role in this episode was celebrated by the American press but provoked some criticism within U.S. labor circles. Many CIO leaders were troubled by Brown's CIA connections and suspected that his activities had more to do with espionage and the collection of hard intelligence than with the promotion of trade unionism.

Brown was part of the effort in 1950 to steer the new Congress of Cultural Freedom into anticommunist direction and became a member of its executive committee. Ironically, despite his effectiveness in fighting communism, Brown was redbaited by columnist Westbrook Pegler.

During the 1950s Brown continued to represent the AFL in Europe. In 1962 he was named ICFTU representative to the United Nations. Three years later he was appointed director of the AFL-CIO African-American Labor Center. Brown died on February 10, 1989, in Paris, France.

—TLH

Bruce, David K(irkpatrick) E(ste)

(1898–1977) *assistant secretary of commerce, ambassador to France, undersecretary of state*
The descendant of a politically prominent Maryland family, David K. E. Bruce was born on Febru-

ary 12, 1898, in Baltimore. He studied at Princeton but left to enlist in the army during World War I. He worked briefly as a diplomatic courier in Europe after the war. When he returned to the United States, he attended law school and received an LL.B. from the University of Maryland in 1921. Three years later he was elected to the Maryland House of Delegates. From 1925 to 1927 he served as vice consul in Rome but quit to become an investment banker. His marriage to heiress, Ailsa Mellon, daughter of Andrew Mellon, introduced him to the upper echelons of finance. At one point he served on the board of directors of 25 companies. During the mid-1930s, however, he spent his time as a gentleman farmer and wrote a book on early American history, *Revolution to Reconstruction* (1939). Bruce represented the U.S. Red Cross in Britain in 1940. A year later he helped William J. Donovan organize the Office of Strategic Services (OSS) and headed its European theater of operations from 1943 to 1945.

In 1947 Bruce became assistant secretary of commerce under W. AVERELL HARRIMAN, a longtime friend and business associate. His primary responsibility was supervising the Bureau of Foreign and Domestic Commerce. Hopes to work on the Marshall Plan in Europe had led Bruce back to government service in the first place, and within a year he was recruited to head the Economic Cooperation Administration's (ECA) mission to France. At the time of Bruce's arrival, France was in economic and political turmoil, which gave Bruce, with the aid money he distributed, leverage over government. The government feared that the impoverished condition of many workers would leave them vulnerable to Communist influence. Bruce studied an investment plan conceived by Jean Monnet, which called for the revitalization of the French coal and steel industry and repair of railroad equipment. He recommended that ECA counterpart funds be made for Monnet's program in return for specific governmental commitments to economic stabilization measures. The release of further counterpart funds was contingent on these efforts. Under this plan France's 1949 productivity exceeded its 1938 level. Bruce returned to Washington in 1949 and testified before the Senate Foreign Relations Committee for continuing financial aid to France.

In April President Truman appointed Bruce ambassador to France. He impressed that nation with his intelligence and knowledge of French literature and customs. During his tenure he per-

suaded French officials to pursue foreign policy goals favored by the United States. A *Washington Post* editorial called him "an evangelist, in his quiet and persuasive way, for the Marshall Plan," who "won the liking and the trust of labor leaders and shopkeepers as well as politicians." According to Michael J. Hogan, as ambassador to France, Bruce thought the interdependence of Britain and the Continent's economies made integration impossible without British participation. Also from his perch in Paris, Bruce saw the West Germans attempting to gain advantage in an integrated Western European market during the negotiations over the Schuman Plan. Bruce supported the establishment of the European Defense Community.

In 1952 Bruce returned to the United States to serve as undersecretary of state, where he continued his support for the Schuman Plan and the EDC. He also became an alternate governor of the International Monetary Fund and a governor of the International Bank for Reconstruction and Development. He left the State Department at the beginning of the Eisenhower administration. An early supporter of European unity, Bruce was appointed ambassador in 1953 to help coordinate the establishment of the EDC. He was unable to convince the French to join, and the EDC failed.

Bruce served as the ambassador to Germany from 1957 to 1959 and was ambassador to Great Britain during the Kennedy administration. He retired from the Foreign Service in 1969 to serve as a parttime State Department consultant. A year later he became a U.S. representative to the Vietnam peace talks in Paris. In 1973 he went to Peking as the liaison officer to the People's Republic of China. Bruce represented the United States on the North Atlantic Treaty Organization Council from 1974 until his retirement in 1976. He died of a heart attack on December 4, 1977, in Washington, D.C. (See *The Eisenhower Years, The Kennedy Years, The Johnson Years, The Nixon/Ford Years* Volumes)

—RB

Budenz, Louis F(rancis)

(1891–1972) *ex-Communist Party member and informer*

Louis Budenz was born on July 17, 1891, in Indianapolis, Indiana. Raised in a strict Catholic family, he attended parochial schools through college. He received his law degree from Indianapolis Law

School in 1912 and was accepted to the Indiana bar the following year. Budenz practiced law for only a short time; later that year he became associate editor of the *The Carpenter*, the official newsletter of the carpenter's union. In the 1920s he took over as editor of *Labor Age*, a socialist magazine, and became increasingly involved in the labor movement. During the decade he was arrested 21 times on picket lines. Budenz was elected secretary of the Conference of Progressive Labor Action in 1932 and later joined the American Workers' Party. He left that organization during 1934 in a dispute over its merger with the Trotskyites. Budenz joined the Communist Party in 1935 and worked intermittently for the *Daily Worker*, the party newspaper. He also served on the party's national committee until EARL BROWDER, who headed the organization, asked him to leave in order to disassociate the *Daily Worker* from the party in the eyes of the public. He later became the paper's labor editor and was appointed managing editor in 1941.

Although Budenz had been excommunicated from the Roman Catholic Church, in 1943 he came back to the Catholic Church and tried for two years to be both a Catholic and a Communist. He found that he could not and chose the former. He reportedly was disillusioned with its subservience to the Soviet Union and became convinced that Russian communism was based on the enslavement of its people. Budenz wrote in August 1945 to Monsignor Fulton J. Sheen, with whom he had had contact during the Popular Front years. He had his common law wife Margaret Rogers and their four children baptized, and Sheen married the two. He became a professor of economics and journalism at Notre Dame. Budenz then began a "year of silence"; he made no public statements until October 10, 1946, when, in a radio broadcast, Budenz announced his resignation from the party and denounced communism. He did, however, have private contacts with the FBI concerning party activities.

During the postwar period Budenz spent approximately 3,000 hours testifying before various congressional committees investigating Communist activities in the United States. In late 1946 Budenz identified Gerhardt Eisler, an Austrian-born immigrant, as "the number one Communist spy in the U.S." Eisler was arrested the following year and was charged with conspiracy to overthrow the U.S. government. Later convicted for contempt of Congress and released on bail, he left the country illegally.

Budenz testified that the leader of the American Communist Party's underground operation, Josef Peters, had informed him in 1935 of conspiratorial activities. During the next few years Budenz was in contact with Jacob Golos, a Communist International agent and Soviet intelligence officer who wanted to infiltrate the ranks of American Trotskyites. Budenz introduced to the Soviets a friend, Ruby Weil, and they used Weil to get access to the Mexican home of Leon Trotsky, whom they had assassinated in 1940.

Budenz was billed as the "star witness" during the 1948 Senate Internal Security Subcommittee hearings on Communist infiltration in the federal government. He stated that "possibly thousands" were involved, a number of whom held "fairly important jobs." Later that year, during the House Un-American Activities Committee investigation of ALGER HISS, Budenz testified that he considered Hiss "under [Communist Party] discipline." In April 1950 Budenz appeared before the Tydings Committee to accuse OWEN LATTIMORE, an expert on Far Eastern affairs and an occasional State Department adviser, of being a Communist. Lattimore had been cited by Senator JOSEPH R. MCCARTHY (R-Wisc.) as a "Soviet agent" who had led "several pro-Russian student uprisings in China." The Tydings Committee exonerated Lattimore, qualifying much of Budenz's testimony as "hearsay." Budenz was again called to testify against Lattimore during the 1951–52 Senate Internal Security Subcommittee investigation of the Institute of Pacific Relations, with which Lattimore occasionally worked. Charges of hearsay leveled at Budenz's statements during the first hearings were discounted, and the panel found Lattimore "a conscious, articulate instrument of the Soviet conspiracy." The charge was never proved, and a later Justice Department indictment for perjury was dismissed.

Budenz's testimony elicited severe criticism from the left and other former Communists. Dr. Bella V. Dodd, a Communist Party National Committee member until her expulsion in 1949, testified that Budenz was "an ineffective man" who exaggerated his party activities for his own gratification. During the Tydings hearings Dodd denounced Budenz, and Browder denied knowing Lattimore, contradicting most of Budenz's testimony. No one listed by Budenz as a Communist was ever convicted of spying. However, the opening of Soviet archives in the early 1990s revealed that Budenz had been truthful about the American Communist underground and its ties to Russian intelligence.

Budenz taught economics at Fordham University from 1946 to 1956, when he left teaching to write. He published four books and numerous articles. He was completing his second autobiographical book when he died on April 28, 1972, in Newport, Rhode Island.

—RB

Bullitt, William (Christian)
(1891–1967) *diplomat*

William Bullitt was born on January 15, 1891, in Philadelphia, Pennsylvania. A product of one of the city's oldest and wealthiest families, he graduated from Yale in 1913 and then dropped out of Harvard Law School to pursue a career in journalism. He started as a $10-a-week reporter for the Philadelphia *Public Ledger*, first covering local stories. In 1916 he became a war correspondent and was then made head of the paper's Washington bureau. When the United States entered World War I, Bullitt was placed in charge of the State Department Bureau of Central European Affairs. Woodrow Wilson selected the young journalist to accompany him to the Versailles Peace Conference as chief of the delegation's Division of Current Intelligence Summaries. His work in Paris was interrupted when Wilson secretly sent him to Russia to try to negotiate a truce between the Bolsheviks and the White Russians. Bullitt succeeded in his task. He returned to Paris recommending that the United States recognize the Communist government. However, the truce broke down, and Washington refused Bullitt's suggestion.

Bullitt broke with the administration over the Treaty of Versailles. He believed it contained the seeds of future world conflicts. In testimony before the Senate Foreign Relations Committee, he attacked the treaty and divulged secret information on its negotiation. He then went into self-imposed exile in Paris, where he wrote a novel.

During the Roosevelt administration Bullitt, a longtime friend of the president, arranged details of the American recognition of the USSR. In November 1933 he became the first U.S. ambassador to the Soviet Union. Although the Soviets initially welcomed him, Bullitt's relations with the Kremlin eventually chilled. He openly denounced Soviet suppression of civil and religious liberties. In

Moscow during a period when xenophobic feelings were increasing, Bullitt was virtually isolated in his embassy. Roosevelt transferred him to Paris in 1936, where he served until the French government fell to the Germans in 1940. When war broke out in 1939, Bullitt recommended that the United States give the Allies all-out aid short of troops. From 1940 to 1944 he served as Roosevelt's special adviser on foreign policy, particularly on Soviet affairs. The former ambassador was one of the few specialists in Washington who questioned the possibility of U.S.-USSR cooperation. He was forced to resign in 1944 as a result of a number of personal feuds he had with other members of the administration. He went back to France where he became an officer in the Free French Forces and helped in the liberation of Paris. Bullitt then returned to a career in journalism.

During the postwar period Bullitt was one of the most popular conservative critics of the Roosevelt and Truman administrations' Soviet policies. In articles appearing in *Life* and *Time* magazines, and in a book, *The Great Globe Itself* (1946), he denounced the Democrats for trying to accommodate the Russians. Bullitt charged that Roosevelt had "sold out" Eastern Europe at the Teheran and Yalta conferences. In addition, he said, the president, based on faulty advice from General GEORGE C. MARSHALL, had given Stalin all of Manchuria in return for the Russian entry into the war against Japan. Bullitt claimed that this deal was not necessary because Tokyo was on the verge of surrendering.

Bullitt was also a vigorous critic of the administration's China policies. As a leading publicist of the "China Lobby," he described what he felt was the U.S. betrayal of its Nationalist Chinese allies. He pointed to Marshall as the central figure in the fall of China. He claimed that Marshall's erroneous advice had convinced Roosevelt to turn over Manchuria to Stalin. The temporary truce Marshall negotiated between Chiang Kai-shek (Jiang Jieshi) and Mao Zedong (Mao Tse-tung), Bullitt said, enabled the Communists to consolidate their position. Bullitt accused Marshall of being under the influence of the pro–Communist China experts in the State Department and suggested that the General should have traveled to the Nationalist camp to provide it with military advice to win the war. He also claimed the Soviets were using the Red Chinese as their instruments in the Far East. He recommended that the United States provide Chiang military and economic assistance to win the war and suggested Truman transfer General DOUGLAS MACARTHUR from Tokyo to China to coordinate the effort. Rather than following this policy, the administration, according to Bullitt, callously curtailed aid to the Nationalists. In 1947 Bullitt went to French Indochina on the invitation of the French and subsequently argued that Vietnamese emperor Bao Dai should serve as the anticommunist ruler to lead Vietnam on behalf of France. In an article for *Life*, he noted that most Vietnamese were not communists, but wanted independence. Millions followed Ho Chi Minh, even though they disagreed with him politically. But a victory by Ho would only replace French control with that of Stalin.

From 1950 to 1953 Bullitt wrote a number of articles on the Korean War for the *Reader's Digest*. Believing that Western civilization depended on the United States's escalation of the conflict, he was angered that the administration refused to pursue a policy of total victory. In one coordinated attack, he maintained, the United States and its allies could frustrate Stalin's dream of controlling all of China and Southeast Asia. The former ambassador joined many conservatives in advocating "unleashing" Chiang. He found it inconceivable that the United States refused to use the 600,000 Nationalist Chinese troops on Taiwan to invade the mainland. He felt their reconquest would have relieved the American troops in Korea. Bullitt promised that the Chinese people would greet the troops as liberators. The army could then move to Southeast Asia to defeat the Communists fighting the French colonialists. He recommended American air strikes in Manchuria as well.

A longtime Democrat, Bullitt left the party for the Republicans in 1948. He was told if Governor Thomas E. Dewey won the election, he would become undersecretary of state. During the 1952 presidential campaign Bullitt served as an adviser to senators ROBERT A. TAFT (R-Ohio) and RICHARD NIXON (R-Calif.). He continued to write on foreign policy during the 1950s. Bullitt died of leukemia on February 16, 1967, in Paris, France.

—JB

Bunche, Ralph J(ohnson)
(1904–1971) *chief United Nations mediator in Palestine*

The son of a barber and a musician, Ralph J. Bunche was born on August 7, 1904, in Detroit, Michigan. Orphaned at the age of 13, he was left in the care of

Ralph Bunche, 1951 *(Library of Congress, Prints and Photographs Division, Carl Van Vechten Collection)*

his maternal grandmother in Los Angeles. As an undergraduate at the University of California at Los Angeles, Bunche developed an interest in the field of race relations. He graduated Phi Beta Kappa in 1927. Bunche received a Ph.D. in government and international relations from Harvard in 1934 and won the university's Tappan Prize for the best essay in the social sciences. From 1938 to 1940 he served as chief aide to Gunnar Myrdal, the celebrated Swedish sociologist who was studying the conditions of blacks in America.

Bunche was afraid a Nazi conquest of Europe would lead to fascism in the United States, which would be disastrous for African Americans. In 1941 he became a senior analyst for the Office of the Coordinator of Information (later the Office of Strategic Services). His proposal for the agency to look into the problems of postwar decolonization was rejected, and in 1944 he left for the State

Department's Division of Dependent Area Affairs, where he specialized in colonial problems. By the mid-1940s he was involved in planning the United Nations. Bunche advised the American delegation at the Dumbarton Oaks and San Francisco conferences regarding the establishment of the United Nations. The president appointed Bunche to the U.S. delegation to the preparatory mission of the UN in 1945 and the first meeting of the UN General Assembly in 1946 in recognition of his abilities in formulating policies on colonies and trusteeships. In April of that year he was temporary director of trusteeships of the UN Secretariat. In May 1946, at the request of Secretary-General Trygve Lie, Bunche joined the United Nations as temporary director of the Trusteeship Division. The following year he retired from the State Department to become a permanent member of the UN Secretariat.

On June 12, 1947, Bunche flew to Palestine as the representative of the Secretariat to the Special UN Commission on Palestine (UNSCOP). The panel had been formed to examine the problems in the area and return to the General Assembly in September with recommendations. It was faced with conflicting claims by Jews, who looked to the area as a homeland, and Arabs, who claimed Palestine was their territory and feared it would be overrun by Jews fleeing Europe. The problem was further complicated by the attitude of the British, who had been given a League of Nations mandate to govern Palestine. Britain was attempting to limit and eventually halt Jewish immigration to the area. During the summer Bunche met with representatives from all sides to clarify the central issues in the dispute. In August he formulated the commission's proposals for the General Assembly, including recommendations for the partition of Palestine. Ironically Bunche wrote the commission's majority report, which called for partitioning Palestine between Arabs and Jews, and the minority report, which recommended the establishment of a federal state. On November 29, 1947, the General Assembly voted in favor of partition. The following month Lie appointed Bunche secretary to the Palestine Implementation Commission (PIC), formed to carry out the decision. In January 1948 the commission, influenced by Bunche, reached an informal decision to ask the Security Council for an international armed force to carry out the partition plan.

Following the declaration of the state of Israel in May and the resultant Arab-Israeli war, Bunche was chosen chief representative of the secretary-general in Palestine. In this capacity he acted as assistant to Count Folke Bernadotte, whom the UN had chosen to mediate the dispute. Together the two men established a truce between the warring parties, increased the force of UN observers to uphold the cease-fire, and began negotiations between Arabs and Israelis. In early September Bunche and Bernadotte drafted a report that called for a united Arab and Jewish state in Palestine, free immigration for two years, the return of the Negev and Jerusalem to the Arabs, and the ceding of western Galilee to the Jews.

On September 17 Bernadotte was assassinated in Jerusalem, and Bunche became acting mediator. During October he appeared before the Political Committee of the UN General Assembly to back the Bernadotte report. On the same day that Bunche presented his views, the Israelis broke the cease-fire and quickly occupied all of the Negev, except the Gaza Strip. During November Bunche developed an armistice plan that involved a large neutral zone between the armies in the Negev, followed by a reduction of forces and a return to peacetime conditions. He pushed the plan through the Security Council and, in December, arranged for Israel to negotiate separately with each of the Arab nations. During the first half of 1949, Bunche presided over tense deliberations, the first important peace talks the UN had attempted.

Throughout the arduous talks, the calm, soft-spoken Bunche used his diplomatic skills to break down severe resistance to compromise. Often working 18 to 20 hours a day, he helped set the agenda, facilitate meetings between rival parties, and draft reports of agreements reached. By July all parties had signed an armistice agreement. For his efforts in negotiating the Middle East peace, Bunche was awarded the 1950 Nobel Peace Prize, the first African American to be so honored.

In 1949 he had rejected the appointment of assistant secretary of state to avoid the segregation existing in Washington at that time. During the 1950s and 1960s Bunche directed peacekeeping efforts in the Suez, the Congo, and Cyprus. He served as UN Secretary-General Dag Hammarskjöld's chief troubleshooter and became principal adviser to U Thant. Bunche was also active in the American civil rights movement and spoke at the 1963 March on Washington. He died on December 9, 1971, in New York City. (See *The Eisenhower Years*, *The Kennedy Years*, *The Johnson Years* Volumes)

—EF

Bunting, Earl

(1893–?) *president, National Association of Manufacturers*

Earl Bunting, the son of a country storekeeper and farmer, was born on July 29, 1893, in Berryville, Illinois. Raised in that state, he moved to Oregon as a young man and worked as a surveyor's stake boy while studying engineering and business administration. In 1922 he started his own business, Earl Bunting and Associates, industrial engineers and marketing consultants. In 1938 he was made a director of O'Sullivan Rubber Company of Virginia. Three years later he rose to president of this firm. During the later 1930s and 1940s Bunting was named director of other companies. He served on the Rubber Advisory Committee of the War Production Board during World War II. Bunting was also chairman of the marketing research committee of the National Association of Manufacturers (NAM) of which he became a director in 1945.

At the December 1946 convention Bunting succeeded Robert R. Wason as president of NAM, which represented 16,500 companies. Bunting took responsibility for presenting to the public NAM's new labor policy, passed over minority opposition at the convention. NAM, which was often labeled reactionary, came out in 1946 in support of collective bargaining. Bunting said that future labor policy must be formulated in a spirit of cooperation, looking out for the best interests of all. However the organization remained conservative on most issues of importance to organized labor. Although NAM did not come out for repeal of the Wagner Act, it did call for changes in the labor laws. These included prohibiting sympathy strikes, strikes against the government, secondary boycotts, and the closed shop. Bunting supported the Taft-Hartley Act, which he said was "the answer of an outraged public's demand for an end to practices which have made faceless cattle out of millions of free American workers." NAM also called for a 20 percent across-the-board income tax cut, and it urged the reduction of federal spending with the goal of a budget of not more than $20 billion—half the then current budget—with the use of $2.5 billion a year to retire the national debt.

Bunting crisscrossed the country in 1947 presenting NAM's point of view. He called for the elimination of all wartime controls and emergency powers not necessary for national security. He said there was little chance of an end to price increases if the 15 cent an hour steel industry wage increase was used as a yardstick. In April he criticized the Federal Trade Commission (FTC) for asserting that there was a loophole in the antitrust laws because companies could not be prevented from buying the assets of competitors. Bunting called the charge "sheer nonsense" and said the FTC had "fallen under the influence of left wingers and antibusiness crusaders." In August he called for a $6 billion tax cut to aid the accumulation of venture capital, asserting that the move would create jobs. He countered critics who claimed that the profit rate of business was too high, citing higher rates in the five past years. In November he presented NAM's recommendation to President Truman on aid to Europe. He urged that 11 "conditions" be met before the aid was given. These included the requirement that the assistance be given to private enterprises instead of to governments, that the recipient countries not undertake further nationalization projects, and that they not discriminate against American businesses.

As was customary, Bunting was elected chairman of the board of NAM for 1948. After this he served as managing director of NAM for 10 years. Bunting continued as a spokesman for NAM policies. In November 1949 he appeared before a House Judiciary subcommittee investigating monopolies. He testified that unions should also be subject to antitrust laws. Bunting argued that industrywide bargaining was a monopolistic practice in restraint of fair trade. He also maintained that no "artificial limitations" should be placed on business size because that would make businesses less efficient. After leaving NAM he became an industrial consultant.

—TFS

Burton, Harold H(itz)

(1888–1964) *associate justice, U.S. Supreme Court*

Born on June 22, 1888, in Jamaica Plain, Massachusetts, Harold H. Burton graduated from Harvard Law School in 1912 and practiced in Ohio, Utah, and Idaho before finally settling in Cleveland after World War I. He became a member of the state House of Representatives as well as director of law in Cleveland in 1929. Burton was elected mayor of the city in 1935 and was twice returned to that post. In 1940 he won election to the U.S. Senate over the opposition of state party leaders. A middle-of-the-roader on domestic issues, Burton cosponsored a hospital construction bill under which the federal government ultimately contributed millions toward the building of health facilities. However, he also proposed legislation placing various restraints on labor unions. The Ohioan was an internationalist in foreign policy who encouraged U.S. participation in a postwar international organization. He worked with Harry S Truman on the Senate committee that investigated profiteering and fraud in government war contracts. President Truman chose Burton as his first Supreme Court appointee in September 1945, and the Senate quickly confirmed his nomination. The first Republican named to the high court since the Hoover administration, Burton took his seat on October 1, 1945.

As a justice, Burton normally followed a policy of judicial restraint and supported the government in individual rights cases. For instance, in *Duncan v. Kahanamoku* (1946) the majority decided that a military trial of civilians in Hawaii held in the aftermath of the attack on Pearl Harbor, while civilian courts were open, was unconstitutional. Burton dissented saying the situation after that the attack was uncertain, that the fear of sabotage and invasion seemed a real possibility, and that the executive branch in such instances should be given the benefit of the doubt in declaring martial law. Burton also generally voted to sustain both federal and state loyalty programs. In the two most significant loyalty-security cases of the Truman era, he joined the majority in *American Communications Association v. Douds* (1950) to uphold the noncommunist affidavit provision of the Taft-Hartley Act, and the conviction of 11 American Communist Party leaders under the Smith Act in *Dennis v. the U.S.* (1951). Burton sometimes voted with his more liberal colleagues in security cases but generally for statutory or procedural, not constitutional, reasons. In *Joint Antifascist Refugee Committee v. McGrath*, a 1951 case involving the constitutionality of the federal loyalty program, Burton delivered his most libertarian decision of the last three Vinson terms. The decision curtailed the power of the Attorney General to put organizations on his list of subversive groups. The Attorney General may make such a list, but, if challenged, he must go to trial and justify any particular group being listed. Burton also said it was unnecessary to determine the constitutionality of the Attorney General's ability to put groups on a list because Executive Order 9835 did not call for the Attorney General to act capriciously or arbitrarily. Burton also dissented

in March 1952, when the majority decided that alien Communists facing deportation could be held without bail if the Attorney General considered this necessary to national security. In June 1953 Burton wrote the majority opinion for *Bridges v. the U.S.*, setting aside the perjury conviction of radical labor leader HARRY A. BRIDGES because the statute of limitations had run out before his indictment.

Burton displayed a conservative bent in other civil liberties cases. He dissented in January 1946 when the Court in *Marsh v. Alabama* upheld the right of Jehovah's Witnesses to distribute their literature in a company town and again in June 1948 in *Saia v. New York* when the majority overturned a local ordinance banning the use of sound trucks without a police permit. In criminal cases Burton usually voted against defendants who claimed their rights had been violated. Burton trusted the police and thought they should be given the benefit of the doubt most times in preserving order. In *Bute v. Illinois* (1948), he declared the right to council was not a general constitutional prerequisite to a fair trial. However, he dissented from an unprecedented January 1947 decision in *Louisiana ex rel. Francis v. Resweber*, in which the majority ruled that Louisiana could try again to execute a man who had survived a first execution attempt because the electric chair had malfunctioned. Burton said another execution attempt would violate the double jeopardy provision of the Fifth Amendment, and the cruel and unusual punishment ban of the Eighth Amendment.

In *Morgan v. Virginia* (1946), Burton in his first civil rights case dissented from the majority's opinion that Virginia's mandated segregation in interstate and intrastate commerce was unconstitutional. Burton argued that the appellant had not shown a significant "burden upon the national interest in interstate commerce as to outweigh whatever state or local benefits are attributable to the statute and which would be lost by its invalidation. The Court should allow for diversity on the issue according to the conditions in different parts of the nation." Thereafter, however, he joined in a Court trend expanding the constitutional rights of blacks. In June 1950 Burton wrote the opinion of the Court in a case holding racial segregation in railroad dining cars illegal under the Interstate Commerce Act.

In Fair Labor Standard Act cases, Burton was opposed to extending the coverage of the law. Burton wrote several important antitrust opinions, and he believed enforcement of antitrust laws should be aimed at encouraging big business. He affirmed that the economic impact of an alleged trust should determine the Court's decision and the Court should avoid acting against business for its own sake. Although he tended to oppose increased government authority in antitrust cases, in *American Tobacco Company et al. v. the U.S.* (1946), Burton ruled against three major tobacco companies in which he established the precedent that a combination or conspiracy creating the power to exclude competition or raise prices violated the Sherman Antitrust Act, even if the power had never been exercised. In *Youngstown Sheet and Tube Co. v. Sawyer* (1952), the steel seizure case, Burton voted against the Truman administration, concurring separately with Hugo Black's majority opinion. Burton said there was no statutory procedure for seizure of private industries.

During the years presided over by Chief Justice FRED M. VINSON Burton was usually aligned with Truman's other judicial appointees. From 1949 to 1953 this group, joined by Justice STANLEY F. REED, dominated the Court. Under Chief Justice EARL WARREN, Burton adhered to a pattern of mostly conservative but occasionally liberal votes in loyalty-security cases. However, he was now more often among the dissenters, as alignments among the justices and voting trends began to change in civil liberties cases. Burton joined in the celebrated *Brown* decision of May 1954, which held racial segregation in public schools unconstitutional. He retired from the Supreme Court in October 1958 because of ill health. Burton died on October 28, 1964, in Washington, D.C.

Although basically conservative in his orientation, Harold Burton was considered by both fellow justices and outside observers to have a particularly "judicial" temperament because of his effort to remain dispassionate and approach issues with an open mind. He was an independent and very hardworking jurist. Despite the fact that the quality of his opinions steadily improved, he was regarded at the end of his tenure as an average jurist who was not a great scholar or leader on the bench. Burton made a special contribution to the Court, however, particularly during the Truman period, by acting as a unifying influence at a time when the Court was deeply and sometimes bitterly divided. Yet he was quite willing to disagree with the other justices and his clerks when necessary. The justice's "personality, including his calm, quiet, earnest manner, his moderation, and his tendency to find narrow grounds for decisions,"

according to historian Richard Kirkendall, "enabled him to become one of the most effective promoters of cooperation among men who frequently disagreed with one another on fundamental issues." (See *The Eisenhower Years* Volume)

—CAB

Bush, Vannevar

(1908–1974) *chairman, Carnegie Institution of Washington; chairman, Office of Scientific Research and Development*

Vannevar Bush, the son of a Universalist minister, was born on March 11, 1890, in Everett, Massachusetts. He earned both his B.S. and M.S. degrees from Tufts College in 1913. He taught there while working toward his doctorate in engineering in a joint program at Harvard and the Massachusetts Institute of Technology (MIT). He received his Ph.D. in 1916 and then worked in a navy antisubmarine laboratory before joining the MIT faculty in 1919. While Bush pursued his academic career, becoming the institute's vice president and dean of its engineering school in 1932, he also found time to establish several successful manufacturing firms. A prolific inventor, he patented hundreds of designs. His greatest contribution was the differential analyzer, a forerunner of the computer.

In 1939 Bush left MIT to become president of the Carnegie Institution of Washington, a large basic research organization. In 1940 Bush, fearing that the United States was technologically unprepared for war, asked and received President Franklin D. Roosevelt's permission to form the National Defense Research Committee (NRDC). The panel was designed to mobilize scientists in the service of the government. In 1941 Dr. Bush took over the chairmanship of the Office of Scientific Research and Development (OSRD), created to include both the NDRC, then headed by Dr. JAMES B. CONANT, and the Committee on Medical Research.

While Bush made no technical contributions during the war, his administrative expertise facilitated a unique collaboration between military men and civilian scientists and engineers. The most dramatic result of this collaboration was the creation of the atomic bomb. Bush created Section S1 of the NDRC to coordinate nuclear research, and he served as chairman of the Military Policy Committee, which supervised the construction of the first atomic bomb by the Manhattan District Project.

Office scientists and engineers also developed radar and the proximity fuse and advanced military medicine, among other accomplishments.

In 1945 President Harry S Truman appointed Bush to the Interim Committee to help formulate atomic policy. The committee recommended that the first atomic bomb be used against a dual civilian-military Japanese target without prior warning. Bush later stated that at the time he felt that this use of the weapon would ultimately save lives by precluding an invasion of Japan and that it might even be a step toward ending all wars. Although he supported the 1945 May-Johnson bill, which sought to keep atomic energy under military aegis after the war, he came to advocate the international control of atomic energy. In November 1945 he drew up the Truman-Atlee-King Declaration, which called for an open exchange of scientific information and the elimination of atomic weapons. These proposals were incorporated into the Baruch Plan, presented to the UN in 1946 but subsequently rejected by the Russians.

Bush's government involvement lessened after the war. However, he had made clear his views on the need for continued federal support of basic scientific research in an OSRD report, "Science the Endless Frontier," produced at President Roosevelt's request in 1945. Bush felt that, even in peacetime, channels must be maintained "by which the freedom and initiative always present in academic circles and in well-managed industry can be joined with the military." Bush advocated establishing a National Research Foundation—later renamed the National Science Foundation—to assist basic research. He also called for government support of basic and applied research in health and national security. He urged financial aid be granted to college science students. The report called for a National Science Board to be made up of qualified individuals who would name and supervise the foundation's director. The report de-emphasized any role the foundation might have in giving counsel to the Congress and the president.

President Truman released the report, but his director of the Bureau of the Budget, HAROLD D. SMITH, objected to the way the foundation would be organized, which he thought would be inefficient and did not allow for enough accountability. The administration offered its own bill to Congress that conflicted with legislation based on Bush's report.

Truman vetoed the bill that came out of the Republican-controlled 80th Congress, insisting that

the director be appointed by the president and responsible to him, not the board. The Democratic 81st Congress passed such legislation and Truman signed it in 1950. The provisions for national defense and medical programs had been excised. The NSF had a tiny budget to start and it could not compete with the research the military and the National Institutes of Health were conducting. (It was not until after the Soviet launched *Sputnik* in 1957 that the NSF budget begin to grow and exert the effect Bush had originally proposed.) During the Truman administration Bush served as chairman of the Research and Development Board and as a member of a special State Department Advisory Committee on Disarmament, but he never again wielded the influence he had exerted during World War II. When, in hopes of limiting the arms race, he tried to induce the U.S. government to negotiate with the Russians before testing the first hydrogen bomb in 1952, his advice was declined.

During the early 1950s Bush was a vocal critic of abuses in security investigations. He deplored the suspension of J. ROBERT OPPENHEIMER's security clearance in late 1953. In 1951 Bush became chairman of the MIT Corporation and in 1959 its honorary chairman. He continued to write and lecture on national defense through the 1960s. In 1974 Bush suffered a stroke and died of pneumonia shortly afterward on June 28 of the same year in Belmont, Massachusetts. (See *The Eisenhower Years* Volume)

—DAE

Butler, Hugh (Alfred)
(1878–1954) *member of the Senate*

Hugh Butler was born on February 28, 1878, in Missouri Valley, Iowa. He grew up in Cambridge, Nebraska, where his father worked in a flour mill. Upon graduation from Doane College in 1900, he joined a railroad construction crew and eventually attained the position of construction engineer. In 1908 he bought a grain elevator and flour mill. Over the next few decades he built it into one of the largest and most prosperous grain firms in the Midwest. Butler also developed a successful ranch of 1,800 acres, which permitted him to campaign as a farmer in his subsequent political career. He was active in Republican Party circles in the 1930s, becoming chairman of the Douglas County Republican Central Committee in 1934 and Republican national committeeman from Nebraska in 1936. He won election to the U.S. Senate in 1940. He won reelection easily in 1946 and 1952, crushing in the primaries moderate Republican governors DWIGHT P. GRISWOLD and F. Valdemar "Val" Perterson, respectively. Democrats put up only feeble opposition in both elections. He kept in close contact with Republicans throughout Nebraska and by such attention kept control of the state party machinery. He also maintained a system of keeping close connections to his constituents, and was able to send condolences or congratulations as the situation demanded.

Throughout his Senate career Butler was a staunch member of the Republican "Old Guard." He defended the farm and cattle interests, denounced internationalism and foreign aid, opposed all manifestations of New Deal and Fair Deal liberalism, and extolled free enterprise.

A strong anticommunist but an even stronger isolationist, Butler was one of a small band of conservative senators who refused to join the bipartisan movement in support of the Truman administration's foreign policy. He opposed the postwar loan to Great Britain, the Greek-Turkish aid program, and the Marshall Plan. In 1949 Butler was one of seven senators to vote against a bill authorizing $5.5 billion for the European Recovery Program. In that year he fought to weaken the North Atlantic Treaty and supported an amendment declaring that congress was under no obligation to declare war if another Atlantic treaty country were attacked. The amendment was defeated, 87 to 8. Butler consistently opposed appropriations for foreign aid. He did, however, cast a reluctant vote in favor of U.S. membership in the United Nations.

Butler often made harsh attacks on New Dealers prominent in the Truman administration. He opposed Senate confirmation of DAVID E. LILIEN-THAL as chairman of the Atomic Energy Commission, contending that Lilienthal was a "dictator." Butler voiced a widespread Republican hostility toward Secretary of State DEAN G. ACHESON: "I watch his smart-aleck manner and his British clothes and that New Dealism, everlasting New Dealism in everything he says and does, and I want to shout 'get out, get out. You stand for everything that has been wrong with the United States for years.' " In July 1949 he demanded an investigation of ex-government officials who collected "fat legal fees" representing private firms in dealing with government agencies for which they formerly worked.

Among such "influence men" singled out by Butler were New Dealers JAMES M. LANDIS, Thurman Arnold, PAUL A. PORTER, and Abe Fortas.

As senior member of the Finance Committee, Butler criticized the free trade policy of the Truman administration and consistently sought to block renewal of the reciprocal trade agreements. He attacked the program as "a gigantic hoax on the American people." Butler was an outspoken foe of the Truman domestic policy on all fronts, opposing price controls, federal aid to education, public housing, and backing substantial budget cuts year after year. In an 88 to 2 Senate vote to expand social security coverage and increase benefits in June 1950, Butler was one of the two opposing votes. He favored the Taft-Hartley Act to restore balance in management-labor relations.

As chairman of the Committee on Public Lands in the 80th Congress, Butler managed to postpone action on the issue of statehood for Hawaii and Alaska. In 1949 Butler charged that union leader HARRY A. BRIDGES "[was] the unseen Communist dictator of the territory of Hawaii" and urged that "statehood be deferred until Communism in Hawaii is under control." In 1952, after a trip to the area convinced him that the Hawaiians had communism under control, Butler came out in support of statehood. That year the Senate approved a Hawaiian statehood bill for the first time.

Butler supported Senator ROBERT A. TAFT (R-Ohio) for the GOP presidential nomination in 1948 and 1952. The victory of other Republicans at the conventions (THOMAS E. DEWEY in 1948 and DWIGHT D. EISENHOWER in 1952) disappointed him, but he did support them against the Democrats in the general elections. Butler died of a stroke on July 1, 1954, in Bethesda, Maryland.

—TO

Butler, John Marshall
(1897–1978) *member of the Senate*

John Marshall Butler was born on July 21, 1897, in Baltimore, Maryland. He attended Johns Hopkins University from 1919 to 1921 and then went to work in his father's real estate business. He received an LL.B from the University of Maryland in 1926 and over the next 20 years practiced law with the firm of Venable, Baetyer, and Howard. From 1947 to 1949, Butler served on the City Service Commission of Baltimore.

With the support of the state's Republican bosses, Butler ran for the U.S. Senate in 1950 against the 27-year incumbent, Democrat MILLARD E. TYDINGS, a foe of Senator JOSEPH R. MCCARTHY (R-Wisc.). The Wisconsin senator and his staff supervised his campaign. McCarthy made speeches on behalf of Butler and secured contributions from Republicans. The campaign achieved notoriety for the use of fraudulent techniques by Butler's managers. In one of the most famous incidents of the race, McCarthy forces issued a photograph of Tydings in apparent earnest conversation with American Communist Party leader EARL BROWDER. It was labeled a composite, but not many voters noticed the disclaimer. Butler won the election by an impressive margin of 43,000 votes.

Enraged by his defeat, Tydings in April 1951 petitioned the Senate to disqualify Butler, whom he maintained had violated state and federal election laws concerning excessive and unreported expenditures. Butler did not deny the charge, saying he "did not personally disburse any campaign funds." A special Senate elections subcommittee was created to investigate Tydings's accusations. After four months of hearings, it reported that Butler had used "despicable methods in unseating Tydings" and condemned McCarthy's intervention in the election. However, it did not recommend expulsion. In Maryland courts Butler's manager, John M. Jonkel, was fined $5,000 for violating the state's corrupt practices act and pleaded guilty to improper accounting of contributions. The Butler campaign provided the impetus for Senator WILLIAM B. BENTON's (D-Conn.) resolution, introduced in August 1951, proposing an inquiry into McCarthy's possible expulsion.

Butler compiled a conservative record in the Senate, voting to reduce the number of government agencies and employees. He supported cuts in soil reclamation and conservation allocations and decreases in foreign aid. Butler backed attempts to return offshore oil lands to the states. In 1951 he opposed granting the president authority under the North Atlantic treaty to send troops abroad without congressional consent. Two years later he voted for the Bricker Amendment.

In November 1952 Butler urged the incoming Eisenhower administration to rid the federal bureaucracy of "crypto-Socialists" who preferred organized labor to big business. Seeking to thwart communism in the United States, he introduced a bill the following year to forbid the representation of "Communist-dominated" unions before the National Labor Relations Board, giving the Subversive Activities Control Board authority to designate such unions. He headed a probe of Communist infiltration in labor unions in November 1953. Butler voted against McCarthy's censure by the Senate in 1954. He retired from the Senate in 1963. Butler died of a heart attack on March 16, 1978, in North Carolina.
—AES

Byrd, Harry F(lood)
(1887–1966) *member of the Senate*

Born on June 10, 1887, in Martinsburg, West Virginia, Harry F. Byrd was the scion of a Virginia line dating back to 1674. His father was a lawyer, newspaper publisher, and, at one time, speaker of the Virginia House of Delegates. Byrd left school at the age of 15 to restore his father's paper, the *Winchester* (Va.) *Star*, to solvency. He established his own newspaper at the age of 20 in Martinsburg, West Virginia, and in 1923 acquired the *Harrisonburg* (Va.) *NewsRecord*. Byrd also became involved in apple growing. His chain of orchards in the Shenandoah Valley grew to one of the largest in the world.

Byrd entered the Virginia State Senate in 1915 and within a decade was the dominant figure in Virginia politics. He remained so for the next 40 years. A master political technician, Byrd built a durable personal fiefdom out of the existing Democratic Party machine, which was based on farmers, rural businessmen, and county courthouse cliques. He won prominence by his key role in the defeat of a bond issue for roads in 1923. The "pay-as-you-go" principle of government finance became the trademark of Byrd's political career. He served as Virginia's governor from 1926 to 1930, and his frugal regime was considered innovative and successful. Appointed to the Senate in 1933 at the urging of President Franklin D. Roosevelt, Byrd ironically became one of the most bitter opponents of the New Deal. With his installment as chairman of the newly created Joint Committee on Reduction of Nonessential Federal Expenditures in 1941, he attained a forum for his relentless sallies against unbalanced budgets and social welfare programs.

When Truman first ascended to the presidency in April 1945, Byrd supported him, but he turned against him when he introduced his liberal and expensive 21-point domestic program later in the year. After that Byrd actively attempted to obstruct passage of the president's Fair Deal program.

Republicans found Byrd's staunch advocacy of government retrenchment so congenial that they allowed him to retain his chairmanship of the Joint Committee when they took control of the 80th Congress in 1947. He and fellow southern conservatives joined with the Republicans to produce a solid majority in the Senate favoring substantial cuts in Truman's budget. Besides voting down the line in favor of reduced appropriations, Byrd periodically issued calls for mass dismissals of government employees to achieve fiscal economy. In December 1949, for example, he suggested discharging about 250,000 on the federal payroll.

Pro-business and antiunion, Byrd opposed attempts to regulate business while he enthusiastically backed government curbs on labor such as the Case labor disputes bill and the Taft-Hartley Act, which he helped formulate. In April 1946 he voted against a proposal to increase the minimum wage.

Byrd voted against Truman's nomination of DAVID E. LILIENTHAL as chairman of the Atomic Energy Commission in 1947 and opposed a federal aid to education bill the following year. He was a leader of southern efforts to block any civil rights legislation. Byrd first opposed the Republican sweeping tax cut in 1947 on the grounds that budget slashing should precede tax reduction. After Congress failed to enact this tax cut over Truman's June veto, Byrd switched to support a second version, which would take effect in January 1948 and thereby reduce the revenue loss for 1947. His shift was important, since he carried with him the votes of most of the Virginia House delegation and that of his colleague, Senator A. WILLIS ROBERTSON (D-Va.). However, the Senate failed to override Truman's second veto in July. A third attempt at a tax cut succeeded in 1948 when Congress overrode Truman's veto.

Although he approved U.S. participation in the International Monetary Fund and the World Bank, and ratification of the United Nations Charter and the North Atlantic Security Pact, Byrd's unyielding frugality placed him in opposition to the implementation of much of Truman's foreign policy. He opposed the loan to Great Britain, the Greek-Turkish aid program, the Marshall Plan, and the Point Four program. Byrd preferred a Fortress America approach to foreign policy: building America's own defenses rather than spending money on foreign aid, saying that America could not become "Santa Claus" to the world. However, according to Ronald

L. Heinermann, he later came to regret opposing the Marshall Plan when it proved a success.

A vivid demonstration of Byrd's power in the Senate came in 1950 when freshman Senator HUBERT H. HUMPHREY (D-Minn.) attacked the utility of Byrd's Joint Committee on the Reduction of Nonessential Federal Expenditures. Humphrey argued that the committee squandered government funds, needlessly duplicated the work of the Senate Committee on Executive Expenditures, and made little constructive contribution with its periodic calls for vague, sweeping firings and budget cuts. The next day, senator after senator rose to castigate Humphrey for criticizing Byrd; none defended the Minnesota liberal.

Later in the year the Senate again paid heed to Byrd's stature when it rejected, by a vote of 59 to 14, the appointment of Martin A. Hutchinson to the Federal Trade Commission. Byrd led the fight against confirmation. Hutchinson had been Byrd's opponent in the 1946 Democratic primary in Virginia.

The ideological antagonism between Byrd and President Truman transcended their common party label. Although he remained aloof from the Dixiecrat States' Rights Party in the 1948 presidential election, Byrd also declined to support Truman and predicted his defeat. In May 1949 Truman complained in a speech that "there were too many Byrds in Congress." He also called the senator "Mr. Demopublican." In November 1951 *U.S. News and World Report* announced that Byrd was "calling for advance organization to prevent a Truman third term." Byrd proposed that the South present an anti-Truman front so formidable that the president would decide not to run.

Refusing to back the 1952 Democratic presidential nominee ADLAI E. STEVENSON—maintaining the so-called Golden Silence—Byrd concentrated on his own reelection. Virginia's 12 electoral votes went to DWIGHT D. EISENHOWER. During the 1950s and 1960s Byrd maintained his unbudging opposition to deficit spending, social welfare programs, big government, and foreign aid. He stood in the forefront of southern resistance to civil rights proposals and mobilized support for the 1956 Southern Manifesto, a rhetorical defiance of the Supreme Court's 1954 decision outlawing school segregation. A national symbol of fiscal conservatism and states' rights resistance to the federal government, Byrd received demonstrations of support in the presidential elections of 1956 and 1960, although he was not a declared candidate.

Byrd retired from the Senate in November 1965 and was succeeded by his son Harry F. Byrd, Jr. He died of a brain tumor on October 20, 1966, in Berryville, Virginia. (See *The Eisenhower Years, The Kennedy Years, The Johnson Years* Volumes)

—TO

Byrnes, James F(rancis)
(1879–1972) *secretary of state, governor*

Byrnes was born on May 2, 1879, in Charleston, South Carolina. The son of Irish immigrants, he was apprenticed as a law clerk at 14 and worked as a court stenographer at 21. In 1903 he was admitted to the South Carolina bar and purchased the *Aiken* (S.C.) *Journal and Review*, which he edited for four years. Byrnes ran successfully for solicitor of the second judicial court in 1908. Two years later he won a seat in the U.S. House as a Democrat, where he served until 1925. He was elected to the U.S. Senate in 1930. During the early New Deal Byrnes emerged as one of Franklin D. Roosevelt's chief legislative tacticians. An innately optimistic man with the talent for finding compromises, he helped gain southern support for key New Deal measures, despite his reservations about increasing the power of the federal government. As Roosevelt's recovery program became more radical, Byrnes joined the Democratic opposition to the New Deal. However, he continued to support Roosevelt's foreign policy, vigorously pushing for repeal of the Neutrality Act and the passage of lend-lease. In 1941 Roosevelt named Byrnes to the Supreme Court.

Sixteen months later Byrnes resigned to head the Office of Economic Stabilization, the wartime agency charged with keeping a lid on inflation. In 1943 Byrnes became director of the Office of War Mobilization. Known as the "assistant president on the home front," he supervised the production of war and consumer goods, thus releasing Roosevelt to devote his attention to fighting the war and planning for peace. Government officials, the press, and the public all praised Byrnes for his administrative ability. His reputation as a compromiser enabled him to work closely with Congress and the confused bureaucracy Roosevelt had established to run the war effort. As the election of 1944 drew closer, it seemed certain that Roosevelt would not choose Vice President HENRY A. WALLACE to run again, and Byrnes became one of the front runners for the second spot. When Roosevelt chose Harry Truman, Byrnes felt cheated.

Byrnes accompanied Roosevelt to the Yalta Conference in April 1944 and played a major role in getting Congress to accept the agreements reached there. Before the conference ended Byrnes returned to the United States and, in a series of conferences with congressional leaders, explained and justified the "Declaration of Liberated Europe," which reaffirmed the principles of the Atlantic Charter and called for the formation of provisional governments in Eastern Europe representing all parties. The declaration also pledged the establishment of free elections. Reaction from the press and Congress was initially favorable.

After Truman ascended to the presidency, he asked Byrnes to sit on a committee to determine what to do with the atomic bomb. Byrnes biographer David Robertson argued that he became convinced that the Japanese would offer fanatical resistance to a U.S. invasion because of his knowledge of the same type of resistance of Confederate soldiers toward the end of the Civil War. Thus, he favored using the bomb without warning on the Japanese so as to avoid American casualties in an invasion of the home islands. Also according to Robertson, Byrnes realized it would be politically disastrous if the administration allowed American soldiers to be killed when this superweapon was available. The committee agreed with Byrnes that the bomb should be used. After the bombings Byrnes argued against accepting Japanese conditions to keep the emperor, but yielded to others in the administration and drafted a reply to the Japanese saying the emperor would be subject to Supreme Commander of Allied Forces DOUGLAS MACARTHUR.

Following the retirement of EDWARD R. STETTINIUS, JR., in July 1945, Truman appointed Byrnes secretary of state. Truman realized that because of the presidential succession law, Byrnes would be next in line for the presidency. Since Byrnes had had extensive administrative experience and knew Congress well, he was a wise choice for that position. Another reason was that Byrnes was at Yalta and allegedly knew well the agreements reached there. Truman also later acknowledged that he had chosen Byrnes out of guilt over his receiving the vice presidential nomination in 1944.

From the beginning of his tenure, Byrnes had difficulty working with Truman. Intent on being a strong secretary of state and used to having virtual autonomy from the president, Byrnes often acted as an independent agent. He refused to keep Truman informed of events on a regular basis. The secretary persisted in calling the president Harry, even in the presence of other people. To many in the Truman White House, this reeked of contempt. Byrnes also failed to establish a close working relationship with the State Department. His reluctance to consult subordinates, frequent absences at international conferences, and poor administrative ability in this office undermined morale in the department.

Byrnes and Truman initially approached foreign policy with two objectives in mind—to maintain the wartime alliance and restrain the Soviet Union in Eastern Europe. They both saw Soviet leaders not as ideologues anxious to assert a philosophy but as fellow politicians willing to compromise. They pushed for a postwar settlement that would result in the revitalization of Germany, the withdrawal of Soviet troops from occupied lands, and the establishment of representative government in Eastern Europe.

Byrnes accompanied Truman to the Potsdam Conference called, among other reasons, to establish a reparation policy for Germany and to discuss a settlement of the Eastern European question. Determined not to permit German restoration to become a burden on the United States, Byrnes negotiated a reparation settlement that permitted the taking of reparations only after imports essential to maintain the German economy had been paid for. The final agreement permitted the occupying powers to take what they wanted from their own sections. Great Britain and the United States granted the Soviet Union from their zones 10 percent of "such industrial capital equipment as is unnecessary for the German peace economy." The Soviet Union was also given an additional 15 percent in return for food and other commodities from its zone. In return for this agreement, however, Truman and Byrnes had to transfer part of Eastern Germany to Poland. Efforts to secure Stalin's stronger commitment to the Declaration of Liberated Europe also failed.

The reparations agreement helped solidify a divided Germany. Many leading Americans at the conference came away ambivalent about future cooperation with the Soviet Union. Byrnes, however, maintained that the agreement reflected the realities of the situation in Eastern Europe and felt confident about future negotiations. This assurance was reinforced by America's successful use of the atomic bomb against Japan. America's monopoly on the weapon would, Byrnes asserted, "make Russia more manageable in Europe." The secretary did not intend to use the bomb as a threat. But he did hope to hinge an agreement on nuclear disarmament on Soviet concessions in Eastern Europe.

The London Conference of Foreign Ministers, held in September, surprised and disappointed Byrnes. The Russians demanded U.S. recognition of Soviet imposed governments in Romania and Bulgaria. Byrnes, in turn, reiterated U.S. willingness to see governments friendly to Moscow in the area, but maintained that they must be democratically elected. Also the Soviets insisted that only the Big Three—Great Britain, the United States, and the Soviet Union—should negotiate peace treaties with Bulgaria and Romania, excluding France and China. The two parties remained deadlocked. U.S. atomic power, upon which Byrnes had placed so much reliance, proved an ineffective bargaining device. The Soviets seemed to almost go out of their way to ignore it. In addition, Truman undermined Byrnes's position when, on October 3, he implied that the United States was committed to international control. Upon his return to the United States Byrnes warned, "we are facing a new Russia, totally different than the Russia we dealt with a year ago. . . . Now that the war was over they [are] taking an aggressive attitude and stand on political and territorial questions that [is] indefensible." Although Byrnes subsequently told other cabinet members that the Soviets had broken the Yalta agreements, he still recognized what he considered legitimate Soviet security needs.

During the fall Byrnes was unwillingly drawn into the growing debate on international control of atomic energy. Believing that the U.S. monopoly on the atomic bomb would make Russia easier to deal with, he opposed discussing this subject until the European peace treaties had been signed. After Truman committed himself to eventual international control in October, Byrnes managed to delay discussion for a time. Nevertheless, by November he had been pushed into beginning discussions in preparation for impending talks with the British and Canadians. The U.S. proposal, drawn up over a weekend by VANNEVAR BUSH, called for the establishment of a UN Commission that would work for the control of atomic energy to ensure its peaceful use, the elimination of nuclear weapons, and the establishment of effective safeguards to protect complying nations against violations. The accord was approved in November.

That month Byrnes pressed for another meeting with the Soviets to solve the Romanian and Bulgarian questions. Having put aside his reservations about the Soviet Union, he hoped that he could reach a compromise with the Russians on the issue. In Moscow Byrnes won Soviet acceptance of the American atomic energy plan. (Later modifications to the plan by Bernard Baruch scuttled the agreement.) In addition, the Russians agreed to allow two local opposition figures to be members in the Communist governments in Bulgaria and Romania. The Americans and the British in exchange would recognize the two Balkan countries. This permitted the negotiations on peace treaties with the Eastern European nations to be continued. In return, the United States made token concessions on Japan, permitting the Russians to play a role in the occupation without jeopardizing American authority.

Although the press initially reacted favorably to the agreements, Byrnes's compromises met with a storm of protests. Powerful congressional Republicans who had long resented Byrnes's failure to consult them on foreign policy and had feared his tendency to compromise, lashed out at the accord. Senator ARTHUR H. VANDENBERG (R-Mich.) termed it "one more typical American 'give away'." The president, too, was angered by the agreement and the manner in which it was concluded. Byrnes, he said, had "lost his nerve at Moscow." His anger was fanned by the secretary's refusal to keep him informed during the conference and by Byrnes's public presentation of the results before reporting to the president. However, according to Robertson, Truman probably did not give Byrnes the dressing down the president later claimed he did.

In response to congressional pressure, changing public opinion, and the recommendations of such Soviet experts as GEORGE F. KENNAN and White House aide CLARK CLIFFORD, the administration moved toward a policy of confrontation with the Soviet Union. Rather than compromise, Byrnes proposed "patience with firmness." The secretary first formally expressed this hardened policy in February 1946 during a speech to the Overseas Press Club. He denounced the Soviets for stationing troops in Eastern Europe, refusing to negotiate peace treaties, and seizing enemy property before reparation agreements were made. Byrnes concluded, "If we are to be a great power we must act as a great power, not only in order to ensure our own security but in order to preserve the peace of the world."

The manner in which Byrnes handled the Iranian crisis the following month confirmed the administration's new policies. The Big Three had occupied Iran during the war to prevent its oil from falling into the hands of the Axis. The British and the Americans pulled out as the prearranged withdrawal deadline approached after the war. The Soviets did not, however, and, instead, began to assist the Tudeh Party in its effort to win autonomy for the Iranian province of Azerbaijan. When the early March 1946 deadline for Soviet withdrawal of troops from Iran passed, Byrnes demanded an immediate withdrawal. When Byrnes heard that Soviet troops were headed toward Tehran, he said, "Now we'll give it to them with both barrels." Throughout March the United States kept pressure on the USSR through diplomatic channels and at the UN. When the Soviet Union asked that the question be withdrawn from Security Council debate in return for a promise to withdraw troops within five or six weeks, Byrnes refused. The Iranians announced they would consider granting oil concessions to the Soviets and to honor Azerbaijan autonomy. On May 6 the Soviets reversed their advance toward Tehran and withdrew their troops from Iran. Late in 1946, the Iranian government reneged on the agreement and sent troops to reoccupy Azerbaijan.

The secretary continued his hard-line policy throughout the summer. While at the Paris Peace Conference Byrnes, according to one observer, "gave the impression of a clever politician determined not to give an inch." During the conference Byrnes attempted to push for a four-power accord guaranteeing the disarmament of Germany as a means of testing the Soviet objectives in the area. The Soviets rejected the proposal. Byrnes, convinced that Russia would not live up to the Potsdam agreements on the eventual unification of that nation, moved toward the establishment of a divided Germany as an alternative to a Russian-dominated state. In an important reversal of the American position, which had stressed unification, Byrnes announced in September 1946, "If complete unification cannot be secured, we shall do everything in our power to secure maximum possible unification." He warned, "We do not want Germany to become a satellite of any power. Therefore, as long as there is an occupation army in Germany, American armed forces will be part of that occupation army."

On the question of subversives in the State Department, Byrnes always respected the legal rights of accused employees. During the investigation of the Amerasia incident, he refused to criticize JOHN S. SERVICE who had passed documents to a journal on Asian-American relations. After a bipartisan congressional committee and a grand jury cleared Service, Byrnes wrote a public letter proclaiming Service's vindication. This upset conservatives who saw Service as a subversive, and Byrnes's enemies in the administration, such as Admiral WILLIAM D. LEAHY and Clifford, used the subversive issue to argue to Truman that the secretary was soft on communism.

Discouraged by continued criticism that he was an appeaser, Byrnes left the State Department in January 1947. The year and a half he served proved to be a difficult period in his life. The vicious response to the Moscow compromise hurt him, and his constant traveling isolated him from policy formulation. In addition, Byrnes, a segregationist and an economic conservative, did not want to continue to be associated with an administration he considered pro–civil rights and too liberal. Byrnes remained in Washington practicing law and occasionally delivering speeches condemning the administration's domestic policies. In June 1949, Byrnes proclaimed, "We are going down the road to statism," which was an obvious reference to Truman's domestic program. The president shot a letter to Byrnes saying, "Et tu, Brute?" Byrnes, somewhat taken aback, wrote back that he was no Brutus, and that Truman was no Caesar. The two never again communicated with one another.

In 1950 Byrnes, then 70 years old, won the governorship of South Carolina on a states' rights platform. While in office he pushed through the legislature a program of moderate reform, upgrading state mental health facilities and passing legislation aimed at stopping the Ku Klux Klan. Believing that the federal government would attempt to integrate South Carolina's schools, Byrnes set up a major program to preserve segregation. He pushed through the state legislature a bill to equalize funding for African-American schools so as to adhere to the "separate but equal" requirement of the *Plessy v. Ferguson* precedent. In 1951 the NAACP challenged the state's segregated school system in *Briggs v. Elliot*. Byrnes hired famed lawyer JOHN W. DAVIS to defend the state's segregationist policies before the Supreme Court. The high court later combined the *Briggs* case with several others in *Brown v. Board of Education*. In 1954, when the Court ruled in *Brown* that segregation was illegal, Byrnes led the fight against the decision. Trying to end the South's loyalty to the Democratic Party, which he saw as becoming too liberal, Byrnes threw his support behind Republican presidential candidate DWIGHT D. EISENHOWER in 1952, helping the general to win four of the 11 states of the old Confederacy. Unable to succeed himself, he retired in 1955. Byrnes died on April 9, 1972, in Columbia, South Carolina. (See *The Eisenhower Years* Volume)

—JB

C

Caldwell, Millard F(illmore), Jr.

(1897–1984) *governor; administrator, Federal Civil Defense Administration*

The son of an attorney and cotton planter, Millard F. Caldwell was born on February 6, 1897, in Knoxville, Tennessee. He studied at the University of Mississippi from 1917 to 1918. Following service in the army during World War I, he attended the University of Virginia. Caldwell was admitted to the Tennessee bar in 1922 but, instead of practicing law, became a cotton planter in Mississippi. From 1925 until 1933 he had a law practice in the small town of Milton, Florida. Elected attorney of Santa Rosa County on the Democratic ticket in 1926, he served in this post until 1933. He was also city attorney of Milton from 1926 to 1930. Caldwell won election to the state legislature in 1928 and four years later was elected to the U.S. House. There he supported the New Deal and urged increased preparation for defense. He returned to his law practice in 1941.

Caldwell won election as governor of Florida in 1944. During his tenure he instituted a series of reforms. He increased taxes on luxuries as a means of raising educational and welfare funds by $6 million. Concentrating on advertising to promote tourism, he proposed an annual $500,000 appropriation for that purpose. He advocated increased housing construction, improved highways, and conservation measures.

Caldwell was interested in improving southern educational standards at the college and graduate-school level. In a speech to the Florida Chamber of Commerce in 1946, he derided the state's poor record in educational achievement and warned it was "downright poor business judgment" that it persisted in this manner. At the Southern Governors' Conference in December 1946, Caldwell advocated a regional college program by which the southern states would pool their resources to provide outstanding graduate and professional schools that they could not individually afford. He was elected chairman of the Conference's Committee on Regional Education in February 1948.

Caldwell favored the creation of high educational standards within the segregated system, believing that blacks "could be trained within the framework of the South and know how to do the job for the South." Nevertheless, he said the southern states would not seek federal aid for their regional university program in order to preserve segregation. In June 1949 the Southern Regional Education Program was organized in Daytona Beach, Florida. The states agreed to pool educational costs and facilitate construction of new universities. Caldwell was chosen chairman of the program's board of control.

As president of the Council of State Governments in 1946 and chairman of the Southern Governor' Conference in 1946–47, Caldwell represented the states in Washington. He urged the federal government to continue rent control, improve education and welfare programs, and return offshore oil reserves to the states. Caldwell retired at the end of his term.

President Truman appointed Caldwell administrator of the newly created Federal Civil Defense Administration in December 1950. He was to review civil defense activities in government agencies and coordinate them with states and neighboring countries. Caldwell vigorously sought congressional approval of Truman's request for $535 million for civil defense in August 1951. Caldwell soon ran into trouble with the apathy toward civil defense, which made the Congress unsympathetic to spending large amounts on it. He sought congressional approval of Truman's request for $535 million for civil defense in August 1951, but the House Appropriations Committee reduced his request to $65 million, claiming he did not have a "realistic" plan for civil defense. Caldwell disagreed, saying the problem was that the average person "was not quite willing to volunteer his services and do anything about it," and that no city in the country "has even approached the point where it could withstand an atomic attack now." The administrator warned that the USSR possessed more powerful bombs than the United States had dropped on Japan and estimated that a million casualties could result from six atomic bombs dropped on major U.S. cities. Caldwell's efforts had little effect on Congress, which approved $75 million for civil defense. He resigned his post in November 1952 and at the end of his tenure Caldwell appeared more satisfied with the public's response to civil defense.

In the 1956 Florida Democratic presidential primary, Caldwell gave his support to ADLAI E. STEVENSON, whom he regarded as a less ardent integrationist than his opponent ESTES KEFAUVER. Partly as a result of Caldwell's efforts, Stevenson defeated Kefauver in the primary. Caldwell served as chairman of the Florida Commission on Constitutional Government from 1957 to 1966 and became a judge of the Florida Supreme Court in 1962. He was appointed chief justice in 1967. Caldwell died on October 23, 1984, in Tallahassee, Florida.

—AES

Cannon, Clarence

(1879–1964) *member of the House of Representatives*

Cannon was born in Elsberry, Missouri, on April 11, 1879. He was raised in Missouri, where he received B.A. and M.A. degrees from William Jewell College. While teaching history at Stephens College, he studied law at the University of Missouri, obtaining his degree in 1908. After practicing for a few years, he became confidential secretary to Champ Clark, the Speaker of the House of Representatives. He developed into what many regarded as the greatest living authority on House procedure and was credited with greatly reducing the time spent debating parliamentary questions. He published numerous books and articles for encyclopedias on the topic.

From 1920 on, he served as parliamentarian of the Democratic National Convention.

This knowledge served him in good stead when he was elected to the House in 1922 as a Democrat. He developed a reputation as a stubborn, effective legislative strategist. Often known as "The Little Bantam," Cannon occasionally resorted to physical violence to get his argument across. In 1945, for example, he scuffled with Representative JOHN TABER (R-N.Y.) during an argument over expense accounts for House members. Taber suffered a split lip. Five years later Cannon almost had a brawl with the chairman of the Senate Appropriations Committee, 81-year-old KENNETH D. MCKELLAR (D-Tenn.) They argued over an omnibus spending bill. At one point, McKellar shouted that Cannon was "blind," "stupid," and "pig-headed." Cannon lunged at McKellar, who grabbed his heavy silver-headed cane, which he also used as a gavel, and prepared to hit Cannon. Other committee members separated the two congressional warriors. Nevertheless, Cannon was known less for his physical outbursts than for his sarcasm and ruthlessness in dealing with his enemies. When Democrats reclaimed control of Congress in 1949, Cannon groused about representatives who had voted for tax cuts in the previous Congress, only to vote for more spending in the current session, and compared them to Senator Claghorn, a character on the Fred Allen show who voted for all spending bills and against any tax hike.

In 1941 Cannon was made chairman of the powerful Appropriations Committee. He remained at that post continuously until his death, except for the years when the Republicans controlled the House (1947–49, 1953–55). As chairman, Cannon enhanced his power by shifting subcommittees and sitting in and voting on each. He also presided over the one panel dealing with funds for public works projects.

In 1942 General GEORGE C. MARSHALL and Secretary of War HENRY L. STIMSON asked for appropriations for a "secret weapon." Cannon hid the request in appropriation bills for the war effort, since the military wanted to keep it a secret. Cannon did this for two budget cycles, but he did it rather reluctantly, since the committee had always known before what their appropriations were going toward. Finally he demanded more information, as no secret weapon had been forthcoming. The military allowed Cannon and four other members of the committee to visit the facility at Oak Ridge, Tennessee, which was helping in the production of the atomic bomb. Military officials assured the committee members that the weapon was near conclusion. Convinced, Cannon moved the money through the committee and Congress and waited nervously to see if the weapon would be a success or a failure. He was relieved when he heard the atomic bomb had worked when used on Hiroshima.

Cannon became an effective battler for economy in government. In 1944 and 1945, as World War II drew to a close, he fought hard to recapture the unexpended war appropriations, estimated at $130 billion. Cannon on the floor of the House proclaimed "we have been on a spending spree such as the world has never known, for 15 years we have been running the government on IOUs. . . . In the end, disaster must overtake any Nation that fails to pay its way." Cannon and Republican John Taber of New York—the two switched as chairman and ranking minority member of Appropriations depending on which party was in power—were able to reduce the budget from $76 billion in fiscal 1946 to $47 billion in fiscal 1950. However, the Korean War drove the budget up again to $94 billion by fiscal 1953. Cannon joined with Senator HARRY F. BYRD (D-Va.) to produce for the 1951 fiscal year an omnibus appropriations bill, the first since 1789, in an effort to limit the effectiveness of lobbyists in having representatives and senators treat individual appropriations bills as Christmas trees. Such a consolidated appropriations bill, in Cannon's opinion, would make it easier to see how drastically federal spending was increasing and to predict whether there would be a deficit, which he said would make it easier to control outlays. He did not succeed in any future Congress to effect the same deal. Determined opposition from CARL T. HAYDEN (D-Ariz.), Speaker SAM T. RAYBURN (D-Tex.), and even members of Cannon's own Appropriations Committee prevented it.

Although his power was independent of the White House, Cannon generally supported the policies of Roosevelt and Truman. During the Truman administration he supported welfare appropriations for the blind, dependent children, and the unemployed, and he backed old-age pensions. In 1946 he defended the Office of Price Administration against attempts to cut its appropriations. He supported collective bargaining and, in 1947, voted against the Taft-Hartley Act. The same year Cannon, now ranking minority member on Appropriations, Chairman John Taber, and two other

committee members toured war-torn Europe to estimate the cost of the administration's proposed Marshall Plan. Cannon came back arguing forcefully for quick passage of Truman's European Recovery Program. He said the law would help the Europeans pull themselves out of the mire and would prevent the Communists from taking over the Continent. He helped guide the bill through Congress, although he made several substantial cuts.

Cannon's drive for economy in government gave way as the cold war intensified. In 1949 the House approved a record peacetime military outlay of almost $16 billion. Cannon's committee added $786 million above what had been proposed for the air force. He gave an impassioned speech in the House defending the spending as necessary to prevent World War III. He said that land-based planes would enable the United States to drop atomic bombs on every major center in Russia within one week after war began. Cannon also suggested that the United States equip its allies in Europe to do the actual fighting, "not our boys." Many criticized this speech, including the Soviet newspaper *Izvestia*.

Cannon opposed the Internal Security Act, which was passed over Truman's veto in September 1950. Together with Senator HERBERT H. LEHMAN (D-N.Y.), he proposed an unsuccessful substitution. The new bill would have eliminated the provision requiring Communists and their front organizations to register with the government, but it would have strengthened provisions for dealing with sabotage and espionage. It would have protected the FBI from revealing confidential sources and authorized the heads of government agencies to dismiss employees without delay when actual security was in danger.

Cannon continued to press for economy in government during the 1950s and early 1960s. In 1962 he and Senate Appropriations Committee chairman Hayden delayed final consideration of appropriations bills for over three months in a dispute over procedure. Cannon died on May 12, 1964, in Washington, D.C. (See *The Kennedy Years* Volume)

—TFS

Capehart, Homer E(arl)

(1897–1979) *member of the Senate*

Born in Highbanks, Indiana, on June 6, 1897, Homer E. Capehart was the son of a tenant farmer.

He enlisted in the army in 1917, and, after his discharge in 1919, he began a career as a successful salesman of farm equipment for several companies in the Midwest. In 1927 he founded the Capehart Automatic Phonograph Company to manufacture and sell jukeboxes. Although initially successful, the company succumbed to the Great Depression. From 1933 to 1940 Capehart served as vice president for the Rudolph Wurlitzer Corporation in Ohio. He subsequently established another company, the Packard Manufacturing Company, that made equipment for the jukebox industry.

Capehart became prominent in the GOP when he organized the "Capehart Cornfield Conference" on his farm in southern Indiana, which launched the Republican Party's 1938 congressional campaign. The meeting brought together state and national Republican leaders. According to Capehart biographer William B. Pickett, the conference marked the start of a shift in America toward anti–New Deal politics. Six years later he defeated popular Democratic governor Henry F. Shricker for the U.S. Senate.

A fiscal conservative, Capehart spoke out against government expenditures and deficit spending. He advocated a balanced budget and a reduction of the national debt to stabilize the economy. In 1946 he said that this could be done by cutting at least 700,000 federal jobs and ending all subsidies. Capehart supported removal of all price controls, but, in 1947, when controls were lifted and inflation was rampant, he recommended a price freeze as a means of bringing order to "economic chaos." In the midst of the 1946 railroad strike, he urged legislation giving strikers a choice of returning to work or losing their rights under existing labor laws. In 1947 Capehart supported the Taft-Hartley Act, which restricted union's strike activities. Capehart opposed Truman's Fair Deal, voting against such laws as the Employment Act of 1946.

Capehart's fiscal conservatism was also evidenced in his foreign policy views. In 1945 he spoke against the use of lend-lease material for postwar reconstruction. The Senate rejected his proposed amendment to the 1946 British loan, which would have reduced the amount from $3.75 to $1.5 billion and restricted its use to the British trade deficit with the United States. In May 1946 he opposed Secretary of State JAMES F. BYRNES's suggestion for a four-power, 25-year treaty to keep Germany demilitarized, maintaining it was too expensive. Although

Capehart supported the 1947 Greek-Turkish aid bill, he advocated a nongovernmental industrial reconstruction board as the most efficient way to direct European postwar recovery. He spoke against potential government red tape and the high cost of the Marshall Plan in 1948. He was initially against the idea of collective security.

Capehart's successful campaign for reelection in 1950 was marked by his criticisms of Truman's welfare state and "bungled" foreign policy. With Republican senators JOSEPH R. MCCARTHY (R-Wisc.) and WILLIAM E. JENNER (R-Ind.), he condemned the Truman administration for allegedly allowing subversives into and to remain in the government. Until 1962 he continually opposed government social legislation, and he remained an ardent anticommunist. Capehart was upset in his bid for a third term in 1962 by 34-year-old state legislator Birch E. Bayh. Capehart died in Indianapolis, Indiana, on September 3, 1979. (See *The Eisenhower Years, The Kennedy Years* Volumes)

—TML

Carey, James B(arron)
(1911–1973) *president, International Union of Electrical, Radio, and Machine Workers*

James B. Carey was born August 12, 1911, in Philadelphia, Pennsylvania. He liked to brag that at age 10 he led his schoolmates in a strike against excessive homework. Thirteen years later, dismayed by growing unemployment in Philadelphia and by automation in the Philco Radio Corp., where he worked, Carey led a successful strike. Later that year the 23-year-old Carey was elected head of the Radio and Allied Trades National Labor Council, newly formed by the American Federation of Labor (AFL) and independent unions. Because he disagreed with the AFL policy of assigning workers in the mass production industries to the federation's craft unions, Carey and others formed the United Electrical Radio and Machine Workers of America (UE) in 1936 as an independent industrial union. Carey was elected president and six months later led the 30,000 member union into the Committee for Industrial Organizations (CIO). In 1938 he was elected CIO national secretary, and in 1942 he became general secretary–treasurer.

Within his union Carey, a liberal anticommunist, faced growing opposition from a coalition of moderate and Communist local union leaders.

According to Ronald W. Schatz, Carey was influenced by the encyclicals of Pope Leo XIII and Pius XI in regard to labor and the reformist attitude of the Democratic Party, which put him at odds with unionists influenced by Marxist ideology. In a battle over American foreign policy and the role of Communists in the internal workings of the union, Carey was defeated for reelection in 1941 by ALBERT J. FITZGERALD. Carey formed an opposition caucus but was unable to regain control of the UE. The right-wing unionists under Carey challenged the left-wing leadership at the UE's 1946 convention in Milwaukee. The right-wing candidate and resolutions were defeated by 8 to 1 margins. The left won again in 1947 and 1948. In 1949, the possibility that right-wingers could overturn the left appeared good; however, they lost. The anticommunists said their candidate for president would have won if not for the left's ballot box stuffing—something the left denied. The left noted that leftist Canadian unionists had not been allowed in the country by the government, who claimed they were Communists. The right could not expect to come so close to winning again, as its locals were being raided by other unions. Raiding and the right's challenges were making the UE impossible to lead for the left.

The UE executive board demanded that CIO head PHILIP MURRAY stop its affiliates from raiding; if he did not the union would leave the CIO. Murray guaranteed them nothing and at the November CIO convention in Cleveland, the anticommunist majority voted to end the Communist presence in the organization, and expelled the UE—as well as other unions—for alleged Communist influence. Carey, who controlled some of the largest UE locals, was presented with a charter to form a new union, which eventually became the International Union of Electrical, Radio, and Machine Workers (IUE). President Truman sent a letter to the convention urging support for Carey and his union.

A long period of jurisdictional warfare between the UE, the IUE, and several AFL craft unions followed the CIO action. In November 1949, after restraining orders had been served on him, Carey urged the officers of the IUE to defy any court injunctions that interfered with their organizing efforts. Carey advocated a militant program that demanded wage increases, employer-financed pensions, and social insurance as an inducement to workers to join the union. During the next six months the IUE won 80 percent of the National Labor Relations Board supervised elections for employee representatives. In June 1950 Carey charged certain segments of the electrical manufacturing industry with aiding the UE in an effort to divide and conquer.

Carey consistently resisted UE efforts to cooperate during this period. Preceding the 1952 negotiations with General Electric Company (GE) and Westinghouse Company, the UE asked 16 unions, including the IUE, to work together for wage increases. Carey rejected this offer, claiming the UE had "nothing to offer us or the workers of our industry except weakness, moral corruption and political perversion." Following an agreement between the UE and GE in September, Carey accused the rival union of entering into a "collusive arrangement" with GE. He labeled this deal a stumbling block in the bargaining between his union and the company.

The expulsion of Communist-dominated CIO unions was a boon to the Truman administration. It allowed CIO leaders to join the AFL–State Department coalition in foreign affairs. Carey, who was the main CIO delegate to the World Federation of Trade Unions (WFTU), walked out of the group's meeting in January 1949. He believed the WFTU was Communist-controlled and "had therefore become bankrupt." In May the CIO Executive Board voted to withdraw from the WFTU. Carey's walkout and joint AFL-CIO negotiation eventually led to the creation of the anticommunist International Confederation of Free Labor Unions.

In the last years in office, Carey grew increasingly rigid and ineffective in his dealings with employers and union leaders. In the fall of 1960, on short notice, Carey called a strike against GE, which proved to be a dismal failure. In 1965 Paul Jennings defeated him for the presidency of his union. Carey died on September 1, 1973, in Silver Spring, Maryland. (See *The Kennedy Years* Volume)

—EF

Case, Francis H(igbee)

(1896–1962) *member of the House of Representatives, member of the Senate*

The son of a Methodist minister, Francis Case was born in Everly, Iowa, on December 9, 1896, and moved with his family to South Dakota. He graduated from Dakota Wesleyan University in 1918 and served as a private in the Marines during World

War I. Case received an M.A. in journalism from Northwestern University in 1920. From 1920 to 1922 he was assistant editor of the Epworth *Herald*, published in Chicago by the Northern Methodist Church. During the remainder of the decade he was editor of the *Rapid City* (S.Dak.) *Daily Journal* and editor and publisher of the *Hot Springs Star* and *Custer* (S.Dak.) *Chronicle*. In 1936 Case, a Republican, won election to the House of Representatives from a rural district, one-eighth of whose inhabitants were Indians.

In the lower house, Case faithfully represented the demands of his conservative constituency during the Roosevelt and Truman administrations. He opposed most labor and social welfare legislation and supported the anticommunist measures of the postwar period. He sponsored various bills for water conservation and weather research. His "Case Resolution" of 1940 eventuated in Congress passing the Missouri River Flood Control Act of 1944. Anxious to keep down government spending, in 1942 Case proposed that all military contracts contain a 6 percent profit ceiling. He supported the production of atomic weaponry to deter Communist aggression. He supported the 1946 British loan and the 1947 Greek-Turkish aid bill. But he voted against the Marshall Plan, believing it too open-ended. He also did not support aid to Chiang Kai-shek (Jiang Jieshi), saying the Chinese people did not support him.

The obscure congressman gained national attention in 1946, when he submitted his labor disputes bill. The measure was prompted by a wave of strikes in 1945–46, the intransigence of large unions in labor disputes both with management and with the government, and John L. Lewis's defiance of government wishes. The bill, which Case wrote in conjunction with three conservative members of the Rules Committee, HOWARD W. SMITH (D-Va.), EUGENE E. COX (D-Ga.), and CHARLES A. HALLECK (R-Ind.), was designed to "provide additional facilities for the mediation of labor disputes." It passed the House by a margin of 258 to 155 and the Senate by 49 to 29. As it emerged from Congress, the measure provided for the creation of a five-member labor-management mediation board and prohibited strikes or lockouts until 60 days after a mediation conference request had lapsed. The bill provided harsh punishments for labor violations of the act and, in effect, repealed the Norris-LaGuardia Anti-Injunction Act of 1932. The Case bill empowered federal district courts to issue injunctions against

striking unions, as well as enforce contracts by civil suits, collecting damages from union assets. Secondary boycotts, jurisdictional strikes, and conspiracy with employers to fix prices were also prohibited. Truman vetoed the controversial bill in June 1946; Congress sustained the veto by five votes. However, many of its provisions later appeared in the Taft-Hartley Act of 1947.

Case returned to obscurity after 1946. Appointed a member of the House Un-American Activities Committee in 1949, he supported RICHARD M. NIXON's (R-Calif.) investigation of ALGER HISS. Case beat the Republican incumbent senator, Chan Gurney, in the 1950 primary and dispatched his Democratic opponent in the general election with ease. He continued his anticommunist crusade as a senator. A friend of Senator JOSEPH R. MCCARTHY (R-Wisc.), he was the only member of the Watkins Committee in 1954 who opposed the censure of the Wisconsin Republican. Case tried to defeat the move with an unsuccessful proposal, rejected even by McCarthy, that the senator apologize for his discourtesy to the Senate.

As a member of the upper house, Case became known as the "amendingest senator" and "Senator Comma" for his painstaking review of bills. As a member of the Public Works Subcommittee on Roads and Highways, Case played a role in putting together the Federal Highway Act of 1956.

During his reelection campaign in 1956, Case openly denounced a $2,500 "contribution" to his campaign fund by oil corporations seeking to win his vote for a pending natural gas bill. His charges led to investigations both by the FBI and a special Senate committee, resulting in three indictments and the president's veto of the bill. Case was in the Senate when he was stricken with a heart attack and died on June 22, 1962, in Bethesda, Maryland.

—AES

Caudle, T(heron) Lamar

(1904–1969) *assistant attorney general, Criminal Division, Tax Division*

Caudle was born on July 22, 1904, in Wadesboro, North Carolina. He later received a law degree from Wake Forest College in 1926 and joined his father's firm in Wadesboro. In 1931 he was appointed prosecuting attorney for Anson Company, North Carolina. President Roosevelt named Caudle U.S. attorney for the western district of the state in 1940. He came to Washington in 1945, when President Truman made him an assistant attorney general in charge of the Criminal Division of the Justice Department. With the post Caudle assumed responsibility for the direction of all criminal prosecution in the federal courts. Two years later he became head of the Tax Division.

In fall 1951 a House Ways and Means subcommittee probing reports of irregularities in tax collection and in prosecution of tax fraud called Caudle to testify. During his October appearance Caudle admitted that two wine merchants with financial difficulties had paid most of his expenses on a trip to Italy in 1950. Attorney General J. HOWARD MCGRATH quickly announced that he did not consider the trip improper. On November 1, General Services administrator JESS LARSON confirmed that he and Caudle had briefly been involved in Oklahoma oil speculation in 1950. The next day the subcommittee announced it would investigate Caudle's tax returns. The panel was also interested in why the Justice Department had dropped tax fraud cases that Bureau of Internal Revenue (BIR) tax agents asked be prosecuted.

On November 14 Caudle denied having interceded with Assistant Attorney General John Mitchell to stop prosecution for tax fraud of officials in an Alabama tobacco company. Mitchell later testified that Caudle had pressured him on the matter. Mitchell told the committee that Caudle gave him no more assignments after he had obtained indictments against the company. Truman, already worried about the political impact of the investigation, asked Caudle to resign on November 16. Caudle, who became known during the tax investigation for his florid, theatrical way of speaking—he punched up his testimony with such phrases as "Lord God Almighty" and "Lord have mercy"—told reporters that his heart was broken. "I have been an honest, loyal public servant," he said.

Later in November Caudle told the subcommittee that his wife had purchased mink coats for herself and the wives of other government officials at cut-rate prices through the "connections" of a New York tax lawyer. Caudle also admitted having accepted gifts from people under investigation. He testified that in 1947 he and BIR counsel CHARLES A. OLIPHANT had accepted a free plane ride to Key West for deep sea fishing from a North Carolina executive under tax fraud investigation. Caudle further stated that in 1949 he interceded with Oliphant to have two tax liens estimated at between $44,000

and $200,000 removed from the executive's property. Later testimony revealed Caudle had taken several free airplane rides and that Supreme Court justice TOM C. CLARK, then Attorney General, had joined him on several occasions. Caudle asserted that McGrath had approved his acceptance of a $5,000 commission he received from the sale of an airplane to a person he knew was working to clear two men under indictment for tax evasion. This was at a time when Caudle handled tax fraud prosecutions and had already postponed the trial twice. Although Caudle had told McGrath that the airplane buyer was a friend of the indicted men, he did not tell him he was their investigator.

In early December allegations of "shakedowns" and bribes involving Caudle and BIR officials surfaced. Abraham Teitelbaum, a Chicago lawyer, who had once been a counsel for Al Capone, claimed that Frank Nathan and Bert K. Laster had tried to extort $500,000 from him in 1950. The two men warned Teitelbaum that if he did not pay he would have "trouble" in a tax fraud case. They claimed to be connected with a Washington clique that included Caudle, Oliphant, Larson, and two ex-commissioners of the BIR, GEORGE J. SCHOENEMAN and Joseph D. Nunan, Jr. After Teitelbaum spurned Nathan and Naster's attempt at extortion he found that his case had been sent to the Justice Department for prosecution. All seven men Teitelbaum named denied the story. In testimony, Caudle acknowledged having many conversations with Nathan, but he denied ever discussing the Teitelbaum case, Caudle further admitted he was aware Nathan had once been prosecuted for a federal offense and was considered by many to be a "fixer."

Republicans, seizing upon Caudle's case and other disclosures about tax scandals, charged that corruption was widespread in the Truman administration. On December 10 subcommittee chairman Representative CECIL R. KING (D-Calif.) accused Caudle of betraying public trust. The next day, McGrath defended Caudle as honest. He said he disapproved of Caudle's "indiscretions" but added, "If ever a man had a right to depend or believe in a man, I felt I had a right to believe in Lamar Caudle." In mid-December columnist DREW PEARSON claimed that about 60 percent of tax fraud cases investigated and recommended for prosecution were "quashed" by Caudle, Oliphant, or U.S. Attorney's offices throughout the country. Truman told reporters on December 13 that he was planning quick, drastic action to clean up the scandals.

In January 1952 Caudle paid the government approximately $1,000 to settle his 1950 income taxes. Later that month Senate Crime Committee investigators charged Caudle had delayed prosecution of a Washington gambler for two years after BIR agents recommended criminal action. In September 1952 Caudle told a House Judiciary special subcommittee investigating the Justice Department that some government officials and members of Congress put "more than normal" pressure on him to influence his decisions in tax cases. He said that then Attorney General Clark had forced him to kill several important cases. Clark refused to testify. At the end of Caudle's testimony, subcommittee chairman Representative Frank Chelf (D-Ky.) defended Caudle, maintaining he had been made a "scapegoat" for higher Justice Department officials. Chelf termed him honest but "indiscreet in his associations and a pliant conformer to the peculiar moral climate of Washington."

In December 1955 Caudle and MATTHEW J. CONNELLY, Truman's appointments secretary, were indicted on charges of conspiracy to defraud the government. The government claimed they had conspired to sidetrack criminal prosecution for tax fraud of Irving Sachs, a St. Louis shoe manufacturer. They were also indicted for bribery and perjury. Both men were convicted in June 1956. After an unsuccessful appeal, Caudle served six months of a two-year term in federal prison in Tallahassee, Florida. He was paroled in 1961. President Johnson pardoned him in 1965.

Caudle returned to Wadesboro to practice law after his pardon. He died there on April 1, 1969.

—JF

Celler, Emanuel
(1888–1981) *member of the House of Representatives*

Emanuel Celler was born on May 6, 1888, in Brooklyn, New York. After receiving a bachelor's degree from Columbia in 1910 and a law degree from that institution two years later, Celler practiced law in New York City. In 1922 he ran for the U.S. House from New York's 10th Congressional District, a predominantly middle-class Jewish section of Brooklyn. Stressing "the evil of Prohibition and the virtues of the League of Nations," he upset

the incumbent Republican. Celler represented Brooklyn in Congress for the next half century. A vigorous supporter of the New Deal, he established a liberal record by fighting to liberalize immigration laws, strengthen civil rights legislation, and regulate monopolies. He did, however, oppose Roosevelt's court-packing plan.

Celler continued his liberal voting pattern in postwar years. Celler was an ardent supporter of the Fair Deal; for example, he voted for the Full Employment Act and to end the poll tax. He opposed military and economic aid to China and Franco's Spain. He also voted against the Truman Doctrine, which pledged economic and military aid to Greece and Turkey and resistance to Soviet aggression elsewhere in Europe. However, he supported the Marshall Plan and the establishment of the North Atlantic Treaty Organization. Celler opposed the Taft-Hartley Act of 1947 and voted to sustain President Truman's unsuccessful veto of the measure.

Celler's concern for immigration coincided with two other causes he championed: independence for India and the establishment of a Jewish state in Palestine. He sponsored a bill in July 1946 that would, for the first time, authorize admission of Indians to the United States. Of Jewish background, Celler was a staunch Zionist by the age of 25. He vigorously attacked the British White Paper of 1939, which limited Jewish immigration to Palestine to 15,000 per year "at the height of their tragic need." Celler opposed postwar aid to Britain, later admitting that it was probably due to "my emotionally violent reaction to British foreign policy in Palestine, in India and in Ireland." In June 1948 he steered a displaced persons bill through Congress, which made it possible for more European refugees to enter the United States.

Celler was one of the Congress's strongest opponents of the postwar anticommunist crusade. He opposed the Mundt-Nixon bill and voted to sustain Truman's veto of the McCarran Internal Security Act in 1950. In 1945 he unsuccessfully opposed a measure that converted the Special House Un-American Activities Committee into a regular standing committee. He more than once voted against appropriations for the panel. Celler mocked the excesses of anticommunist crusade in speeches: "Is it un-American to get up on the *left* side of the bed in the morning?" He argued strenuously, but unsuccessfully, at the Democratic National Convention of 1952 to have an anti-McCarthyism plank included in the party platform. Celler did, however, see a Communist threat to American institutions. In 1954 he voted for a bill banning the Communist Party.

When the Democrats took control of the House in 1949, Celler became chairman of the powerful Judiciary Committee. In July he established a special subcommittee to investigate antitrust violations. The probes conducted by this panel from 1949 to 1952 gave Celler a national reputation as an opponent of big business. At the general hearings the panel investigated concentration in steel, newsprint, and aluminum. Hearings focused on the malevolent effects of concentration, pointing out that small businesses were being driven out of the marketplace. Celler was cosponsor of the Celler-Kefauver Anti-Merger Act of 1950, which plugged a major loophole in the 1914 Clayton Antitrust Act. The early statute had prohibited the acquisition of stock when the effect "may substantially lessen the competition." The 1950 measure prohibited the acquisition of assets that could substantially lessen competition.

In 1951 Celler's subcommittee conducted hearings on whether professional baseball's reserve clause violated antitrust laws. The clause bound a player to one team, unless he was traded or sold. Celler, while critical of the reserve clause, opposed any specific legislation to regulate baseball.

Celler continued to work in the House for the next two decades in support of immigration, civil rights, and antitrust laws. He helped draft and pass through Congress the Civil Rights Act of 1957 and that of 1960, and he helped put through the House the 1964 Civil Rights Act. Celler played a significant role in the Immigration Act of 1965 (the Hart-Celler Act), which ended discrimination in favor of immigrants from Northern and Western Europe. He was forced into retirement, at the age of 84, by his defeat in the 1972 Democratic primary. Celler went back to New York to resume the practice of law. He died in Brooklyn on January 15, 1981. (See *The Eisenhower Years, The Kennedy Years, The Johnson Years, The Nixon/Ford Years* Volumes)

—TFS

Chambers, Whittaker
(1901–1961) *journalist*

Born on April 1, 1901, in Philadelphia, Pennsylvania, Whittaker Chambers grew up on Long Island, New York. His father was a commercial artist and his mother had been an actress. After a desultory academic career at Columbia University, which he left without graduating, Chambers joined the Communist Party in 1925. He wrote for the *Daily Worker* until 1929 and then edited and wrote short stories for the radical *New Masses*. In 1932 Chambers entered the Communist underground as a secret party agent, a role that came to include the transmittal of secret U.S. government documents from his accomplices in the government to agents of the Soviet Union.

By 1937 Chambers had become disaffected by Marxist ideology and Communist discipline. According to his autobiography, his renunciation of communism began in 1937; his desertion of the Communist Party occurred in April 1938. Chambers then became an editor of *Time* and *Life*. He embraced Quakerism and became a fervent anticommunist.

Chambers informed State Department official ADOLF A. BERLE in 1939 about the Communist network. Berle told the president, but he refused to believe it. In 1942 Chambers informed the FBI, but again nothing happened. In May 1945 Chambers once again "named names" but did not disclose illegal activities, as nothing had come out of the previous meetings. Some of the officials he named as Communists were high up in the administration, and Chambers feared personal ruin if he attempted to bring them down and failed. The Justice Department's apparent lackadaisical investigation in the Amerasia case in the summer of 1945 convinced him to stay quiet. But after courier ELIZABETH BENTLEY revealed the Communist network inside the government, the House Un-American Activities Committee (HUAC) subpoenaed Chambers to corroborate her story.

In his first hearing with HUAC on August 3, 1948, Chambers lied that he did not know of any spying. He did not hesitate to name the people he was sure were Communists, but was more reticent than other witnesses, such as Bentley. Sam Tanenhaus speculated this might have added to his credibility to the committee. He did corroborate Bentley's testimony that HARRY DEXTER WHITE was friendly with the Communist underground. Chambers named other former government members, but by far the most notable was ALGER HISS, a former State Department official who had accompanied the American delegation to the Yalta Conference, played a major role in the creation of the United Nations, and was currently serving as president of the Carnegie Endowment for International Peace. Chambers's accusation against Hiss was the first act of a tempestuous political and legal drama that continued for decades.

On August 5 Hiss appeared before the committee and emphatically denied Chambers's charges. He declared that he had never belonged to the Communist Party or any Communist-front organization, or adhered to the tenets of communism. He stated that he had never known anyone named Whittaker Chambers.

Most of the committee members were inclined to believe the erudite Hiss rather than the dumpy Chambers, but Representative RICHARD M. NIXON of California remained suspicious of Hiss. Nixon knew about accusations against Hiss a year before the latter's testimony before HUAC, despite later claims that Chambers's testimony was the first time he had heard Hiss's name. On August 17, he brought Hiss face to face with Chambers at a special HUAC session held at the Hotel Commodore in New York, Hiss acknowledged that Chambers resembled a "George Crosley" he had been acquainted with in 1934–36, a freelance journalist who had subleased Hiss's apartment for a time and borrowed money from Hiss without repaying. Chambers admitted that Hiss had not known him by his real name, but he maintained that his pseudonym was "Carl," not "George Crosley." Chambers agreed to take a lie detector test, but Hiss declined.

On August 25 the two men appeared before HUAC in a dramatic televised confrontation and gave radically conflicting accounts of their relationship. Among the welter of contradictory testimony produced during the 10-hour session was Chambers's characterization of Hiss as "a dedicated and rather romantic Communist in 1934–35"; Hiss denied ever being a Communist. Chambers said they were introduced by the head of the Communist underground in Washington; Hiss said that Chambers came to him as "George Crosley" writing a series of articles on subjects being investigated by the Nye Committee. Chambers alleged that the money Hiss gave him was party dues; Hiss maintained it was merely a loan. Chambers described their last meeting as having occurred in 1938, when he unsuccessfully tried to persuade Hiss to leave the party with him. Hiss claimed he last saw "Crosley" in 1935. Chambers accused Hiss of lying, while Hiss disparaged Chambers as "a self-confessed liar, spy and traitor." In response to Hiss's challenge to repeat his charges outside the committee and its umbrella of immunity, Chambers declared on an

August 27 "Meet the Press" broadcast that "Alger Hiss was a Communist and may still be one." One month later Hiss filed a suit for slander against Chambers, claiming damages of $75,000.

In October Chambers testified before a New York grand jury that he had no direct knowledge of Soviet espionage in America. He was still afraid to disclose Hiss's spying for fear that even then the Truman administration would not be interested in investigating Hiss and was more concerned with crushing anticommunists. Chambers also had had a long-standing fear he would be prosecuted for espionage if he implicated Hiss. (As it turned out the statute of limitations had expired on his spying activity, but he could have been charged with perjury for lying to the grand jury and HUAC.) After the election Chambers was glum and sensed Truman's Justice Department would exact retribution. In November, however, during the pretrial discovery process of the slander suit, Chambers for the first time charged that he and Hiss had engaged not merely in the promotion of Communist influence in the New Deal but in espionage for the Soviet Union. As evidence Chambers produced a cache of classified State Department documents from 1938 that he said Hiss had delivered to him. There were four memorandums in Hiss's handwriting and 65 pages of retyped State Department papers that had gone through Hiss's office. Chambers later maintained that he had denied any knowledge of espionage until then in order to protect Hiss, but finally decided to produce the evidence of spying in order to convince the world that he was telling the truth about the Communist conspiracy. He claimed that his original purpose in saving the 1938 documents was because of his fear of assassination by Communist agents following his defection from the party. Chambers said he had planned to use the State Department material as a "life preserver," as proof of the spy ring he threatened to expose if any harm befell him.

The new information in the Hiss-Chambers case did not become publicized until December when, in response to a HUAC subpoena, Chambers dramatically handed over to committee investigators additional material in the form of five rolls of microfilm, which he had hidden in a hollowed-out pumpkin the day before. The microfilm, two rolls of which contained classified State Department documents initialed by Hiss, became known as the "Pumpkin Papers." Chambers's latest disclosures were a stunning development in a case that now received daily sensational coverage in the press. A moment of confusion occurred when a technician mistakenly claimed the film had been manufactured in 1945. Nixon angrily phoned Chambers and demanded he explain himself. Chambers was flummoxed, and collected tins of rat poison before finding out the technician had made a mistake—the film had been made in 1937.

For a week Chambers and Hiss told their respective stories to a New York grand jury. On December 15 the grand jury indicted Hiss on two counts of perjury, alleging that he lied when he said he had not seen Chambers after January 1, 1937, and when he denied passing government documents to Chambers. (The charge was perjury because the statute of limitations had run out on espionage.) Hiss pleaded not guilty.

At Hiss's two 1949 trials Chambers was the star witness; the central issue was whether his story or Hiss's was true. His documents were the state's main exhibits. Hiss's lawyers waged a violent attack on Chambers's credibility. Lloyd Paul Stryker, Hiss's lawyer at the first trial, excoriated Chambers as "a thief, a liar, a blasphemer, and a moral leper." Chambers's numerous lies in the past were emphasized, most tellingly his false testimony before the October 1948 grand jury. The prosecution, on the other hand, stressed Chambers's extensive recall of the details of Hiss's life as proof, together with the documents, that Hiss lied about their relationship. The fact that many of the documents had been typed on Hiss's typewriter, a Woodstock model, and that others contained his initials or were in his handwriting, was compelling corroborative evidence.

The defense introduced at the second trial testimony by two psychiatrists who characterized Chambers as a "psychopathic personality." Neither had ever directly examined Chambers, however, and the prosecution effectively undermined their testimony. The personal contrast between Chambers and Hiss was nonetheless vivid. The portly Chambers had a rumpled appearance, an unstable past, a fretful disposition, and a melodramatic manner. Hiss was handsome, upright, and composed; his career was an unbroken chain of advancement and respectability. Two Supreme Court justices were among the eminent witnesses attesting to his character.

The first Hiss trial ended in a hung jury, eight to four, on July 8, 1949. The jury in the second trial found Hiss guilty of perjury on January 21, 1950. He served 44 months in prison from 1951 to 1954. In later years he continually insisted that he was inno-

cent, that Chambers was a man of unsound mind who had accomplished "forgery by typewriter." Chambers was equally emphatic about Hiss's guilt. In 1959 he wrote that Hiss had not paid his penalty for perjury "except in the shallowest legalistic sense." "There is only one main debt," Chambers said, "and only one possible payment of it, as I see it, in his case. It is to speak the truth." Perhaps most significantly, in speaking the truth, he had shown how connected the Communist Party USA was with Soviet intelligence operations in America.

For the rest of his life, Chambers was identified by his role in the Hiss case. He left his $30,000-a-year job for *Time* in December 1948. In 1952 he published his autobiography, *Witness*, a pessimistic rumination on the melancholy prospect for religion and Western values in the battle against communism and secular liberalism. To many on the right Chambers was a hero for his renunciation of communism and was hailed as a profound conservative thinker. He wrote for the *National Review* from August 1957 to December 1958. To believers in Alger Hiss, Chambers was a renegade and a scoundrel. Liberal intellectuals dismissed his apocalyptic anticommunism as absolutist bombast.

Chambers enrolled as an undergraduate at Western Maryland College in 1959. He was still a student when he died of a heart attack on July 9, 1961, in Westminster, Maryland. In 1978 historian Allen Weinstein, after examining FBI documents, Hiss's defense files, and letters written by Chambers around the time of his break with communism, concluded in his massive study of the Hiss-Chambers case that Chambers had been telling the truth in his accusations against Alger Hiss. Then in the 1990s the National Security Agency began to release transcripts of a decoded Soviet transmission from their embassy and consulates in America. These Venona decrypts showed that Hiss was in fact a spy for Soviet military intelligence. (See *The Eisenhower Years* Volume)

—TO

Chapman, Oscar L(ittleton)

(1896–1978) *assistant secretary of the interior, undersecretary of the interior, secretary of the interior*

The son of a poor farmer, Oscar L. Chapman was born on October 22, 1896, in Omega, Virginia. Chapman, even as a youth in conservative Virginia, was a liberal. For instance, when he was a boy he gave to his school a picture of Abraham Lincoln, anathema in the home state of Robert E. Lee. For this he was temporarily suspended. He joined the navy following his graduation from Randolph-Macon Academy in 1918. During his naval service Chapman contracted tuberculosis and was sent to Denver, Colorado, for treatment. He remained there after his discharge, studying nights at the University of Denver Law School. During the day he worked as a probation officer for Judge Ben Lindsay, who headed the city's famous juvenile court. From 1922 to 1927 Chapman handled over 10,000 cases. He obtained his law degree from the Westminster Law School in 1929 and then became partners with Edward P. Costigan, a leading Colorado Democrat. During the 1920s Chapman became active in Democratic politics. He helped found the Spanish-American League to combat exploitation of Mexican workers and worked to improve child welfare in the state. In 1930 he managed his associate's successful run for the U.S. Senate; two years later he directed Alva Adams's senatorial campaign.

In gratitude for his aid, Costigan recommended Chapman for a position in the Roosevelt administration. Chapman chose the Interior Department because of his interest in minority groups. Working in the shadow of HAROLD L. ICKES, he helped direct department policy toward supporting conservation, working to provide for poor farmers' easy access to land, and resisting the efforts of leading corporations to exploit natural resource reserves held by the federal government. Chapman was a forceful advocate of Indian rights and a leading opponent of segregation. One of Roosevelt's leading tacticians, he managed the presidential reelection campaign in 1940 and served as the Western coordinator for Roosevelt's 1944 presidential bid. Within the Democratic Party Chapman belonged to the liberal faction headed by HENRY A. WALLACE.

Truman allegedly offered Chapman Ickes's job when the temperamental secretary stepped down in February 1946, but Chapman turned it down. However, Chapman did consent to serve as acting secretary, until Truman found a replacement, and continue as assistant secretary. In a rather unusual situation Chapman was fulfilling the role of four men, as the undersecretary and another assistant secretary also left, and he was forced to sign off on all departmental documents. He was also one of the few New Dealers to remain in high appointive office

Oscar Chapman *(Harry S. Truman Library, Abbie Rowe)*

during the Truman administration. Truman appointed JULIUS A. KRUG the new secretary of the interior in 1946 with Chapman as his undersecretary. Chapman continued to perform the same duties he had under Ickes. His major interest was in the continuation of the land use reclamation projects that provided free water for farm families in arid regions. Chapman successfully resisted the efforts of Senator Sheridan Downey (D-Calif.), a representative of large agricultural interests, to end the program. He also testified in support of building the St. Lawrence Seaway and backed Hawaiian statehood, and he argued for the compensation of Japanese-Americans interned during the war. Krug, however, soon lost interest in the post, and Chapman became de facto secretary by early 1947. Chapman did little to stop the dismantling of many of the policies that he and Ickes had established. The department began to emphasize assimilation again over cultural rejuvenation for the Amerindians. There was a shift toward appeasing business interests in conservation policy.

Chapman played an important role in Truman's 1948 reelection campaign. After receiving a call from the president of the University of California at Berkeley that the college wanted to give Truman an honorary degree, Chapman organized Truman's spring 1948 "nonpolitical" tour of the West, which went well after some early missteps. He also helped put together the autumn "whistle stop" election campaign, saying that he had "traveled 26,000 miles for President Truman in my suitcase." When the president's Labor Day speech was in danger of not being broadcast because of insufficient funds, Chapman, just days before the speech, was able to have Oklahoma governor Roy Turner raise the needed $50,000. The rest of the campaign, too, was, of course, a great success. He served as the president's leading advance man, traveling ahead of the presidential train to drum up support for Truman. It was Chapman's efforts that led to the large crowds that greeted Truman in his historic spring and fall tours.

Following the election Truman grew disappointed with Chapman's boss, who had refused to campaign for him. In addition, Ickes spread a rumor around Washington that Krug neglected his duties, showed little interest in conservation and was apathetic to the plight of Native Americans. Following Krug's resignation in November 1949, Truman appointed Chapman secretary of the interior. Liberals, led by the *Nation* and the *New Republic* hailed this appointment as a renewed commitment to the policies of Ickes. Chapman possessed great power as secretary. He headed the reclamation projects, the Bureau of Indian Affairs, the National Park Service, and the Office of Territories. He made the final determination of how much land in the West should be set aside for mining and agricultural use. During the Korean War he had the authority to ration the nation's leading natural resources.

Chapman's performance as secretary was marred by his inability to deal with powerful special interests. Industry and the power companies pressured him to open up more natural resources for commercial use and more rivers for power facilities under private control. Environmentalists urged him to resist such arguments. Public power advocates lobbied for the government ownership of the future plants built on the western river networks. During the Korean War oil companies requested the right to explore for more oil. Chapman failed to satisfy any of these interests. Rather than making decisions he appeared to temporize. Nevertheless, an overall assessment of Chapman's performance in office indicated that he tended to favor environmentalists and public power advocates over their adversaries.

Chapman advised ADLAI E. STEVENSON in the 1952 campaign. He then founded a Washington law firm that specialized in energy and trade law. Ill health forced him to retire in the summer of 1977. Chapman died on February 8, 1978, in Washington, D.C., after a long illness.

—JB

Chavez, Dennis
(1888–1962) *member of the Senate*

Dennis Chavez was born on April 8, 1888, in Los Chavez, New Mexico. A descendant of Spanish colonial governors, he dropped out of school at the age of 13 to help support his family. In 1916 he served as a Spanish interpreter for Senator A. A. Jones (D-N.Mex.) and was rewarded with a job as a Senate clerk. Upon passing a special entrance examination, he was admitted to Georgetown University Law School. He obtained his degree in 1920 and subsequently established a practice in Albuquerque, New Mexico. During the 1920s Chavez served in the New Mexico House of Representatives and in 1930 won a seat in the U.S. House. He lost the race for U.S. Senate in 1934 but was appointed to the seat following the death of the incumbent. He won election to a complete term in 1936.

Chavez established a liberal reputation as a supporter of New and Fair Deal programs. Although he urged neutrality before Pearl Harbor, he did vote for lend-lease and supported Roosevelt's war policies following the attack. During his career Chavez served on the Labor, Indian Affairs, Irrigation and Reclamation, Territories and Insular Affairs, Public Work, and Appropriations Committees, and on the important Appropriations Defense Subcommittee. He often voted for civil rights legislation and for measures granting equal rights to women. During the postwar period Chavez backed the president's plans for the containment of the Soviet Union, including the Truman Doctrine and the Marshall Plan. The only Spanish-surnamed senator, he pressed for recognition of Franco's Spain, urged increased aid to Latin America, and sought to improve conditions in Puerto Rico. (He was known as "Puerto Rico's senator.")

Chavez was the leader for the fight for a permanent Fair Employment Practices Commission (FEPC). As head of the Education and Labor Committee's subcommittee on the FEPC, he pushed the bill through committee in May 1945. At the same time Chavez led the fight against the filibuster staged to prevent restoration of funds to the temporary commission. He was able only to gain a compromise, giving the agency half the amount originally recommended. Chavez succeeded in bringing his bill for a permanent FEPC to the floor in January 1946. The measure prevented discrimination by an employer or union on the basis of race, creed, or color. It called for a five-person panel, appointed by the president, to carry out the bill's provisions. Southern senators again led a filibuster against the proposal. Attempts at cloture were unsuccessful, and the measure died.

That same year Chavez fought a bill that would have facilitated the recruitment of Mexican farm laborers, claiming it would have reinstated a form of slavery. An amendment suggested by Chavez, giving U.S. farm workers priority in government benefits, was rejected. A year later he helped write a bill that increased unemployment and sickness benefits for railroad workers. This measure was passed over strenuous opposition from members of the railroad industry. Chavez denounced the Second Red Scare as "a period when we quietly shackled men's minds."

During the Eisenhower administration Chavez gained prominence as an opponent of the president's national defense policies. He died of cancer on November 18, 1962, in Washington, D.C. (See *The Eisenhower Years* Volume)

—RB

Chennault, Claire L(ee)
(1890–1958) *army officer, airline executive*

Claire L. Chennault was born on September 6, 1890, in Commerce, Texas. The son of a modest Louisiana cotton planter, he worked his way through Louisiana State Normal College and became a high school teacher. He enlisted in the army during World War I and served in the Aviation Section. After the war he became a noted flight instructor. Chennault was an innovator in the tactics of modern air warfare, such as flying in formation rather than singly, and was one of the first to experiment with paratroop landings. After an army medical board recommended his discharge—he was hard of hearing and had bronchitis—Chennault left the army in 1937.

In July 1937 he was persuaded to help China rebuild its air force, which the invading Japanese had decimated. Plagued by a lack of equipment,

Chennault managed to send some U.S. planes to China after lend-lease began in 1941. He created a volunteer force of American pilots and mechanics called the "Flying Tigers," which was consistently victorious against superior Japanese forces. It destroyed 20 Japanese planes for every one it lost. In 1942 Chennault's forces were incorporated into the U.S. Army. He was promoted to major general and became chief of U.S. Army Air Forces in China. Chennault also served as chief of staff of the Chinese air force. He became a close friend of Generalissimo Chiang Kai-shek (Jiang Jieshi).

Despite his success, Army Chief of Staff, GEORGE C. MARSHALL and Army Air Forces Chief of Staff Henry "Hap" Arnold refused to promote Chennault to lieutenant general because they thought he was too close to the Nationalist Chinese. When his major backer, President Roosevelt, died in April 1945, the chiefs began to curtail his authority. A bitter Chennault requested retirement in July 1945 after General George Stratemeyer superseded him in command, and he returned to America a month later. His resignation caused great controversy when it was rumored that he was "eased out" by pressure from the Chinese Communists. Undersecretary of War ROBERT P. PATTERSON denied this before the Senate Military Affairs Committee. After his resignation Chennault spoke out strongly against those who criticized the Chinese Nationalists. He called Chiang Kai-shek "one of the world's greatest men" and said Chiang was not a dictator but democratic minded. In late 1945 Chennault charged that the U.S. policy of aid to Chiang was being "nullified by a few individuals in the State and War Departments."

During the late 1940s he became a prime spokesman for the "China Lobby," which advocated increased American military assistance to Chiang. He wrote frequently for the *Reader's Digest*, HENRY R. LUCE publications, and Scripps-Howard newspapers, damning Truman administration policy in China. In his memoirs, published in 1949, he accused General Joseph Stilwell of plotting to sweep out the best Chinese Nationalist leaders. That same year he recommended to the Senate Armed Services Committee a "minimum program" of $700 million a year in military aid to stop the Communists. He saw the Chinese Communists as an arm of Russian aggression and predicted that, if China fell, Indochina, Malaya, Siam, Burma, and Indonesia would also fall. After the Korean War began he recommended to the Senate Armed Services Committee that Chinese Nationalist forces be used to fight communism in Asia.

In early 1946 Chennault returned to China to look into establishing a commercial airline there. With Whiting Willauer, he obtained a contract from the Nationalist government to transport supplies into the interior, and their CNRRA Air Transport began operations in late 1947. The next year Chennault and Willauer formed a commercial airline to take over from the relief operation, and their Civil Air Transport (CAT) was soon embroiled in the Chinese civil war. CAT began contract operations for the Central Intelligence Agency in 1949, as the agency was trying to form an anticommunist resistance in western China. In 1950 the CIA secretly bought CAT, and Chennault led the first CIA air proprietary. (He had long wanted to form such a volunteer air force to combat the Communists.) During his tenure as leader the airline dropped supplies and agents in to China, backed anticommunist forces in Burma, and helped supply the French at Dien Bien Phu by providing pilots for the missions. (CAT eventually became Air America and played a role in CIA operations in the Vietnam War.)

The CIA tightened its control of CAT in 1955 because of concerns over financial losses, and Chennault became a figurehead chairman of the board. Two days before the end of his life, the Eisenhower administration announced Chennault's promotion to lieutenant general; he complained that it should have come 10 years earlier. Chennault died July 27, 1958, in New Orleans, Louisiana.

—TFS

Clark, Mark (Wayne)

(1896–1984) *commander, U.S. Occupation Forces in Austria, and American High Commissioner in Austria; commander, Sixth Army; commander, Army Field Forces; United Nations supreme commander in Korea*

Mark Clark, the son of an army colonel, was born on May 1, 1896, at Madison Barracks, New York, a military post. He graduated from West Point in 1917, two weeks after the United States entered World War I. He served in France as a captain and was wounded in action in the Vosges. After the war Clark attended the army's most prestigious schools—Infantry, General Staff and War College—and also served as an instructor of the Indiana National Guard.

When World War II began, Clark, a lieutenant colonel, had a reputation as a good infantryman who knew how to train others. The job of training men to fight, he said, was essentially "training them to kill without getting killed." He believed troops should be able to do this in any way, anywhere, and he established training centers that simulated real battle conditions. In summer 1942 Clark, then a major general, went to England as General DWIGHT D. EISENHOWER's subordinate to command all U.S. ground forces in the European theater. Later that year he helped plan the Allied invasion of North Africa. After serving as Eisenhower's second in command in North Africa, Clark took command of the Fifth Army in Italy.

Clark was an important figure in the early cold war. The Fifteenth Army Group, which he commanded, almost came to blows with Yugoslavian leader Josip Tito's partisans when the latter attempted to seize territories along the Italian and Austrian borders (Venezia Giulia, Trieste, and Carinthia). In 1945 Clark was appointed U.S. occupation commander and American high commissioner in Austria. When Clark arrived in Vienna he found the Russians in full control: transporting Austrian factory equipment and natural resources back to the Soviet Union; feeding the Viennese less than 1,000 calories of food a day; flooding the country with worthless occupation marks; and, attempting to control the Austrian economy.

Through tough, clever negotiating and diplomatic maneuvers, Clark was able to earn the Russians' respect and reduce Soviet dominance in Austria. Clark, respectfully called the "American Eagle" by the Russians, increased Austrian food rations with Soviet cooperation; curbed inflation by barring Russia's access to Austrian currency reserves; reduced exorbitant Russian occupation cost levies by more than half; and slowed the Russian removal of Austrian industrial and natural resources. To gain concessions from the Soviets, Clark learned to use to his advantage the Russians' sensitivity to adverse publicity and negative world opinion. When they became too adamant during negotiations, Clark would notify the press. He also served as a deputy to the foreign ministers in their London and Moscow meetings and was the main negotiator in the early going of drafting an Austrian peace treaty.

Clark left Austria in May 1947 and, in June, became commander of the Sixth Army at the Presidio in San Francisco. In October 1949 he became head of Army Field Forces. In 1951 President Truman nominated him as America's first ambassador to the Vatican. However, he asked that his name be withdrawn from consideration when Protestant groups opposed U.S. recognition of that state.

In 1952 Clark succeeded General MATTHEW B. RIDGWAY as United Nations Supreme Commander in Korea and as commander of all U.S. forces in the Far East. Appraising the stalled peace talks at Panmunjom, Clark, who favored decisive victory over the North Koreans, said, "The more you deal with these fellows [the Communists], whether at Vienna, London, Moscow or Panmunjom, the more you realize that their goal is the same simple, unchanging one of world domination. My experience has been that when you meet them with a show of force and with determination, they stop, look, and listen."

The situation in Korea reminded Clark of the Italian campaign during World War II, as his troops were bogged down along the 38th parallel. He increased the bombing raids on North Korea to regain the initiative. Negotiations were stalled over the issue of prisoner of war repatriation. Clark was finally able to sign an armistice on July 27, 1953, and commented later that he had had the dubious distinction of being the first American army commander to conclude a truce without winning the war. Clark believed more resources and the use of atomic weaponry would have defeated the communists.

After the Korean armistice was signed in 1953, Clark retired from the army as a four-star general. From 1954 to 1966 he served as president of The Citadel and later became head of the American Battle Monuments Commission. He was a hawk during the Vietnam War and supported President Nixon's bombing of North Vietnam. He died April 17, 1984, in Charleston, South Carolina. (See *The Eisenhower Years* Volume)

—SRB

Clark, Tom C(ampbell)
(1899–1977) *U.S. Attorney General; associate justice, U.S. Supreme Court*

Tom C. Clark was born on September 23, 1899, in Dallas. He received a bachelor's degree in 1921 and a law degree in 1922 from the University of Texas. He then entered private practice in Dallas. Active in local Democratic politics and a protégé of Senator Tom Connally (D-Tex.) and Representative Sam T. Rayburn (D-Tex.), Clark served as civil district

attorney of Dallas Company from 1927 to 1932. He was named to a Justice Department post in 1937. Over the next six years Clark worked primarily in the Antitrust Division. He coordinated the program under which Japanese-Americans were evacuated from the West Coast and interned during World War II and also led a special unit that investigated war frauds. Clark was appointed head of the department's Antitrust Division in March 1943 and, five months later, was placed in charge of the criminal division.

Clark's war frauds unit cooperated with the Senate committee chaired by Harry S Truman that investigated the defense effort. The Texan supported Truman for the vice presidential nomination at the 1944 Democratic National Convention. On May 23, 1945, President Truman selected Clark as his Attorney General. Attorney General FRANCIS B. BIDDLE was aghast that Truman would replace him with Assistant Attorney General Clark, whom he had been planning to fire for his tendency to allow political considerations to determine prosecutorial decisions. According to Alonzo Hamby, Truman probably thought partisanship a good thing, and Clark had been the only Justice Department official willing to give Senator Truman patronage appointments. Clark also was supported by Speaker of the House Sam Rayburn. Clark was sworn in late the next month. He proved to be energetic and resourceful in his new post and was a Truman loyalist who became a close presidential adviser on domestic issues. Clark started 160 antitrust cases while attorney general and personally argued a major suit against Paramount Pictures in the Supreme Court. He expanded the Justice Department's role in civil rights by filing an *amicus curiae* brief in a case challenging racially restrictive housing covenants. In May 1948 the Supreme Court adopted the government's position that the covenants were not enforceable in federal or state courts. Clark, along with minority affairs aide David Niles recommended an investigation on civil rights in America. Truman appointed a committee in early 1947 to do that, and it issued the report *To Secure These Rights*, advocating major reforms. Clark also initiated, in 1946, the litigation that led to the conviction of JOHN L. LEWIS and the United Mine Workers for contempt of court for having disregarded an antistrike injunction issued at a time when the government had seized the mines. The attorney general argued the case himself when it was appealed to the

U.S. Attorney General Tom C. Clark *(Harry S. Truman Library)*

Supreme Court. The justices upheld the government in a March 1947 decision.

Clark also played a key role in the development of the Truman administration's loyalty program. He urged the president to appoint a committee to review existing loyalty procedures for federal workers. The Temporary Commission on Employee Loyalty was named in November 1946. Clark sent a memorandum to its members to view the problem in which even one disloyal federal employee was a serious threat to national security. Hamby has argued such disproportionate concern caused the commission to call for exhaustive loyalty investigations of even the most inconsequential federal employees. When a new loyalty program, based on its recommendations, was established in March 1947, Clark successfully argued that the FBI should be chosen as the investigative unit for the program.

Clark also won presidential approval of the use of wiretaps by the FBI in national security cases. In 1948 and 1949 he recommended legislation to make

unauthorized disclosure of national defense information a crime, to require Communist Party members to register as foreign agents, and to remove the statute of limitations in espionage cases. He drew up the first attorney general's list of subversive political organizations in 1947 and the next year started proceedings against the leaders of the U.S. Communist Party for violation of the Smith Act. Clark made frequent public statements on the dangers of communism and the threat of internal subversion. He encouraged the adoption of loyalty standards by nongovernmental organizations and, in the 1948 presidential campaign, defended Truman against charges that he was "soft on communism."

Clark's anticommunist efforts were the most controversial aspect of his years as attorney general. He defended his actions as necessary steps to prevent subversion. His supporters argued that the Truman administration's loyalty program, unlike later anticommunist probes, recognized certain constitutional limitations on antisubversive endeavors. Clark himself declared in 1947, "Those who deny freedom to others cannot long retain it for themselves—and under a just God they do not deserve it." J. EDGAR HOOVER and the FBI's alarmist view of the danger of domestic subversion was not shared by Truman and Clark. Clark later recalled when he took over the Justice Department in 1945 that there was a dramatic increase in reports that he received from Hoover discussing alleged Communist infiltration. Many times they were somewhat vague; others were simply not credible. He soon had an aide screen them for him. Truman and Clark might have been able to set up a program that was less disruptive if that had known about the Venona program that was decoding messages from the Soviet embassy to Moscow about its spying operation in the United States. But Hoover did not tell them about it. Clark's critics charged, however, that even the Truman program too often disregarded civil liberties and that the attorney general exaggerated the danger of subversion. Clark's anticommunist statements and actions, critics asserted, helped legitimize inquiries into individual political beliefs and helped create the atmosphere that made McCarthyism possible.

On July 28, 1949, Truman announced Clark's nomination to the Supreme Court. Despite criticism from some liberals who alleged that he was antilabor and anti–civil liberties, Clark's appointment was confirmed by the Senate on August 18 by a 73 to 8 vote. Justice Clark was scrupulous about disqualifying himself from cases that had been handled by the Justice Department while he was Attorney General. As a result, he did not participate in many important cases during his early years on the bench. When he did join in decisions, Clark regularly voted in accord with Chief Justice FRED M. VINSON, another Truman appointee. He showed little independence and innovation, dissenting only 15 times in the four terms from 1949 to 1952. His accession to the Court helped create a five-man conservative bloc, led by Vinson, that generally supported the government in loyalty-security and criminal cases against individual rights claims.

Justice Clark, for example, wrote for a five-man majority in June 1951 in *Garner v. Board of Public Works of Los Angeles* to uphold a Los Angeles ordinance requiring city employees to swear that they were not members of the Communist Party and had not advocated overthrow of the government. In March 1952 in *Adler v. Board of Education* he voted to sustain a New York State law that barred members of subversive organizations from teaching in public schools. Later the same month he voted to approve the holding of alien Communists facing deportation without bail if the Attorney General considered them security risks.

Clark was not insensitive to all civil liberties claims. In a unanimous May 1952 case, *Burstyn v. Wilson*, he wrote the opinion of the Court holding that movies were entitled to protection under the First Amendment and overturning a state ban on the Italian film, *The Miracle*, because it was allegedly sacrilegious. He also spoke for the Court in December 1952 when in *Wieman v. Updegraff* it held an Oklahoma law requiring loyalty oaths from state employees unconstitutional. Unlike the Los Angeles law he had upheld, the Oklahoma program made no distinction between innocent and knowing membership in a subversive organization. Clark also joined the majority in two June 1950 decisions that eliminated racial segregation at the University of Texas law school (*Sweatt v. Painter*) and at the graduate school of the University of Oklahoma (*McLaurin v. Oklahoma State Regents*).

The one major exception to Clark's alignment with Vinson and to his progovernment tendency in this period came in the June 1952 steel seizure decision. There Clark agreed with Vinson that the president could act on his own to resolve national emergencies in the absence of any congressional authorization. But here, he concluded, Congress had passed laws establishing procedures to deal with a threatened steel strike, and in such a case, the president was obliged to follow the methods prescribed in the law. Since Truman had not, Clark wrote in a concurring opinion, the steel seizure was invalid. This action caused the president to declaim Clark's appointment to the high bench as his worst mistake, although they apparently patched things up as Clark had a long visit with Truman shortly before his death. Clark concurred in the result but not the reasoning of the majority's decision to declare the seizure unconstitutional. Clark disagreed with Hugo Black's opinion because presidential power to act in times of national crisis was subject to curtailments enacted by Congress, such as those put in place by Taft-Hartley, Selective Service, and Defense Production acts.

On the Warren Court, Clark demonstrated greater self-confidence as a jurist and gradually took on a more independent role. He remained a conservative in most loyalty-security cases but became more moderate on other issues such as criminal rights. He retired from the Court in June 1967, after his son Ramsey was named attorney general. By that date Justice Clark was rated by scholars as a careful legal craftsman who grew significantly during his 18 years on the bench in his command of constitutional issues and his contributions to the law. Clark died on June 13, 1977, in New York City. (See *The Eisenhower Years*, *The Kennedy Years*, *The Johnson Years* Volumes)

—CAB

Clay, Lucius D(ubignon)

(1897–1978) *deputy military governor of Germany (U.S. zone), military governor of Germany (U.S. zone)*

Great grandnephew of Henry Clay and son of a U.S. senator, Lucius D. Clay was born on April 23, 1897, in Marietta, Georgia. He followed a military career, graduating from West Point in 1918, and was an army engineer during the next two decades. During the Great Depression he helped Harry L. Hopkins establish the Works Project Administration. He excelled as an administrator in the period of a variety of posts. During World War II he coordinated the production and procurement of army supplies as director of materiel. In 1944 he became deputy director for war programs and general administrator in the Office of War Mobilization and Reconversion (OWMR). In that position he became known as the "third most powerful" man in the country after Roosevelt and OWMR director JAMES F. BYRNES.

In March 1945 Clay was appointed deputy to General of the Army DWIGHT D. EISENHOWER, supreme commander of the Allied expeditionary force, with the understanding that upon Germany's surrender he would be placed in charge of American occupation under Eisenhower, who would be military governor of Germany and European theater commander. Clay's designation came as a surprise to members of Eisenhower's staff who had expected that the occupation would be directed through them. Clay and his supporters in the State Department and War Department wanted a separate group running occupation operations in Germany. Clay believed that dividing the occupation management from purely military affairs in Europe would facilitate the ultimate transition from military to civilian government by allowing the easier development of native agencies to parallel those of the foreign forces. Shortly after he reported to Eisenhower's headquarters in April 1945, Clay won the general's acquiescence to his intended role, although Eisenhower's staff, in particular the chief of staff, General WALTER BEDELL SMITH, resisted Clay's arrangement and his direct access to the commander in chief. (Such problems would continue under Eisenhower's successor as military governor and European theater commander, Joseph T. McNarney, who assumed these positions in November 1945. The staff situation was not resolved until March 1947, when Clay was appointed military governor and U.S. commander in chief, Europe.)

Clay played an increasingly central role in the occupation from the surrender of Germany onward. In late June Clay negotiated with the Soviet Union, France, and Great Britain procedures for dividing and then supplying Berlin. Clay also oversaw the subsequent reestablishment of vital services to the American zone of the city and the installation of military control in the U.S. zone.

As the war drew to a close, Clay emerged as a leading advocate of a lenient policy toward the vanquished enemy. Along with Secretary of War HENRY L. STIMSON and Assistant Secretary JOHN J. MCCLOY, he became increasingly concerned about the danger that the Soviet Union presented to postwar Europe. They therefore favored the establishment of an economically and politically strong

Germany as soon as possible as a citadel against Soviet expansion. In May 1945 Clay protested Joint Chiefs of Staff order 1067/6 which reflected the harsh position advocated by Secretary of the Treasury HENRY MORGENTHAU, JR. The directive precluded the occupation from becoming involved in the rehabilitation and maintenance of the German economy except to maximize agriculture. Only the production of light consumer goods was to be encouraged. Clay asserted that the directive had failed to deal with the economic realities of the situation. Germany, he maintained, would have to revive its industrial production immediately for it would starve unless it could produce for export. As the cold war developed through the balance of 1945 and into 1946, Clay gained allies for his position. By the time he assumed full responsibility of the occupation, the administration supported a resurgent Germany as a barrier to the Soviet Union.

In spring 1946 Clay, with the approval of Washington, halted the dismantling of German industrial plants and suspended the payments of reparations from the U.S. zone to the Soviet Union. In explaining the action he maintained that all the more punitive policies prescribed at the wartime conferences had been adopted with an economically integrated Germany assumed. The German economy in the American zone at least could not support those measures without being tied to the rest of Germany, a course blocked by the Soviets. Clay argued that because the zones were not sufficiently strong to carry the burden in isolation, the occupying powers would have to absorb any balance of payments deficit that reparations would generate. The United States would find itself financing its zone's payments to the USSR.

During the same period Clay took steps to turn de-nazification over to the fledgling German government in an effort to slow down the task. Clay and his superiors shared a desire to root out Nazism. By the end of his tenure more Nazis had been brought to trial in the American zone than any other, although the U.S. zone lagged behind the Soviet in numbers removed or excluded from prominent positions. However, Clay and his superiors viewed extensive de-nazification as an impediment to Germany economic recovery. Too large a portion of the German population had been involved in the Nazi party to permit a purge without serious economic consequences. As German regeneration became a larger U.S. objective, de-nazification became a less attractive goal.

Clay also viewed decartelization as increasingly unimportant. After the establishment of a federal banking system similar to the United States and the dissolution of the I. G. Farbenindustrie, an important industrial firm, Clay resisted the division of large German corporations. He was eventually criticized by the Department of the Army for his conduct, but he maintained that extensive decartelization was a threat to German recovery.

The American military commander saw the creation of the German state as occurring in two stages: the development of local government and the economic reunification of the British, French, and American zones. He moved quickly to meet his first goal. Elections were held during the first half of 1946. By December each of the states in the American zone had ratified constitutions and elected state parliaments. During spring 1946 Clay pushed for the unification of the French, British, and American zones. The French demurred, fearing an industrialized, strong Germany, but, during the next year and a half, extensive administrative and economic unification was achieved in the British and American zones. The most important step toward economic unification was the introduction of a common currency in 1948. This action had been planned for several years. The French at first resisted but acquiesced when Clay, after extensive negotiations and some compromise, threatened to go forward without them. The new currency was introduced to the Western zones on June 20 and to the Western zones of Berlin three days later. It was this last action and the clear indication it gave that the Western powers intended to go forward with the creation of a West German state with the inclusion of West Berlin that prompted the Soviets to blockade Berlin on June 24.

It was the tensest moment yet in the cold war. Clay himself had inadvertently generated a panic two months earlier with his "war warning" to the army's director of intelligence, Lieutenant General Stephen J. Chamberlain, on March 5, 1948. Clay had been sending messages to Washington that indicated no alarm, including one to Senator HENRY CABOT LODGE (R-Mass.) on the same day as he sent the cable to Chamberlain, which said:

> For many months, based on logical analysis, I have felt and held that war was unlikely for at least ten years. With the past few weeks, I

have felt a subtle change in Soviet attitude which I cannot define but which now gives me a feeling that it may come with dramatic suddenness.

Clay admitted later that he had sent it to Chamberlain to get the Congress to reestablish the draft, and that it would have only been read in executive session of congressional committees. If he had known it would become public, he would not have sent it. But word did leak out, and it and the recent Communist coup in Czechoslovakia set off a hysteria that Europe was on the verge of war. Now Clay was faced with a very real crisis. The Soviets had made clear for some time that they would cut off Berlin should the new currency be introduced there. As soon as they acted, Clay called for the city to be supplied by air. Over the next year he became a leading advocate of waiting out the Soviets. He resisted suggestions from Washington that he slow the pace of currency reform or negotiate the issue, believing that U.S. prestige was at stake. He did not think that the Soviets wanted war over Berlin, and he tended to discount the strength of their threat. In July he suggested sending out an armed convoy from the city to challenge the Soviets. He contended, "If we move out of Berlin, we have lost everything we are fighting for." While Washington turned down this suggestion, it backed Clay's plan for an airlift to the beleaguered city (Operation Vittles). At the height of the airlift, planes ferried 13,000 tons of supplies to the city a day. The blockade was lifted on May 12, 1949, as a consequence of negotiations at the United Nations, talks that were kept secret from Clay. Clay declined to meet the first train to arrive in Berlin.

While the blockade was in force, Clay was involved in the negotiations to establish a German constitution. The Allies differed on the type of government to be granted Germany. The French proposed a weak central government, the British a strong one. In January 1949 Clay succeeded in getting the two nations to accept the American plan for a moderately strong federal government with limited taxing power. Clay also convinced both major German parties to accept the plan. The military governors approved the final draft of the constitution in Berlin on the day the blockade was lifted.

The approval of the new constitution ended the military's phase of the occupation. On May 15, 1949, Clay left Germany and was replaced by John McCloy, the civilian high commissioner for Germany. Clay retired on returning home. A year later he became chairman and chief executive officer of the Continental Can Company. He played an active role in the effort to persuade Eisenhower to seek the presidency in 1952 and served as a liaison between the general and the professional politicians campaigning for him throughout the United States. Clay was a close adviser to the president for the next eight years, becoming, among other things, one of the principal architects of the interstate highway program. When John F. Kennedy became president, he served as an adviser on U.S. foreign policy, particularly on Berlin. During the 1960s he was a supporter of Lyndon Johnson's Vietnam policy. Clay retired as chairman of the Continental Can Company in 1970. He died of emphysema on April 16, 1978, in Chatham, Massachusetts. (See *The Eisenhower Years, The Kennedy Years* Volumes)

—CSJ

Clayton, William L(ockhart)

(1880–1967) *assistant secretary of state for economic affairs, undersecretary of state for economic affairs*

William L. Clayton was born on February 7, 1880, in Tupelo, Mississippi, and grew up in poverty in rural Mississippi. He quit school to work as a clerk in a local court and became stenographer to a St. Louis cotton broker at age 16. In 1904 he formed his own firm, Anderson, Clayton & Company, which eventually became the world's largest cotton brokerage house. During the 1930s he became an outspoken supporter of free trade, believing it was necessary for the economic health of the South. In 1940 he joined the office of the Coordinator of Inter-American Affairs and later worked in the Federal Loan Administration. Clayton was named assistant secretary of commerce in charge of the Reconstruction Finance Corporation's foreign activities and was vice president of the Export-Import Bank. During 1944 he was war surplus administrator. Roosevelt appointed Clayton assistant secretary of state for economic affairs in December 1944. In August 1946 he was elevated to the rank of undersecretary of state for economic affairs.

Clayton sat on the S-1 committee, which advised Truman on whether to use the atomic bomb. Clayton wanted the panel's scientific advisers to present as many options as possible. He inquired whether the bomb could be dropped in some unin-habited area to overawe the Japanese. The scientists indicated that production of the bombs was slow and even if a display test succeeded technically, it might not persuade the Japanese to surrender. This would adversely affect their ability to bomb a real target because it took so much time to build an atomic bomb. Worse, such a test might fail. Then there was the question of how the atomic bomb would affect relations with the Soviets. Clayton doubted that the bomb could be used as leverage against the Russians, but he was also skeptical that any international cooperation on the control of atomic energy could be effected.

Clayton was a major force in the development of the Truman administration's foreign economic policy. Anxious to prevent a worldwide depression such as that which occurred after World War I, he recommended that the United States offer Western allies loans and grants to help rebuild their economies. In return, the nations would have to agree to eliminate trade barriers, thus expanding U.S. markets. Clayton also assumed that economic prosperity would prevent the expansion of communism.

In pursuit of his goal of worldwide prosperity, Clayton successfully fought the plan of Secretary of the Treasury HENRY MORGENTHAU, JR., to transform Germany into an agrarian nation. He asserted that for Europe to recover from the war it would need the industrial might of Germany. What the allies needed to do was not to dismantle German factories but to turn them to peaceful uses.

In 1945 and 1946 Clayton strongly urged a reluctant Congress to continue aid to the United Nations Relief and Rehabilitation Agency. When lend-lease aid to Great Britain ended after the war, Clayton arranged a $3.75 billion loan. His task had been to negotiate with Britain's Lord Maynard Keynes for eliminating imperial preference, restoring sterling convertibility, and establishing a postwar international economic order with British approval of the Bretton Woods agreement. Clayton secured, in exchange for the loan, a weak, but nonetheless significant, reiteration of British promises to open up trade, a delayed but firm promise for sterling convertibility, and a strong promise for quick approval of Bretton Woods. Clayton's great hope for increased access to Commonwealth markets, however, was never fully realized. Congress approved the loan in 1946, but Clayton found he had had to rely increasingly on pointing to the Soviet threat to win votes. He also argued the loan was necessary for humanitarian reasons and a strong American economy.

On March 5, 1947, Clayton drafted a memorandum pondering Britain's decline, Soviet expansionism, and the U.S. role in European recovery. Britain was losing its traditional hegemonic place in the world. Either the Soviets or the Americans would take its place. If the Russians did so there would be a war within a decade. If the United States took charge war could be averted. Therefore, America should assume world leadership, but Americans would not do so unless they were shocked into doing so by the secretary of state telling them the truth. He painted a bleak picture of Communists extending their grip over Greece and Turkey and then to the rest of Europe, the Middle East, and Africa. He argued that the United States must assist with financial, technical, and administrative aid countries whose independence was threatened by internal and external forces. Further, he said the Congress should give the administration $5 billion to assist such nations and create a council of national defense to distribute the funds. If the United States did not do this the fate of these countries would become so hopeless that it would lead to a third world war. He thought the United States could afford whatever financial burden would be required to fend off the threat. Clayton used the memorandum in his discussion with other members of the State Department and probably even with Truman. In late April, Secretary of State GEORGE C. MARSHALL told GEORGE F. KENNAN to take charge of a new policy planning staff to begin work on a proposal for U.S. aid to Europe. In April and May, Clayton was in Europe to direct U.S. efforts at trade liberalization in Europe and to represent the United States before the UN's Economic Commission for Europe. He saw the desperate plight of France and Italy, which were on the verge of anarchy, and yet the administration seemed insensitive to the situation in Europe. On May 27 Clayton gave Marshall a second memorandum on how he thought the United States should proceed in regard to aid to Europe. This memo, along with a report from the head of the Policy Planning Staff, Kennan, greatly influenced Marshall's June speech at Harvard calling for an aid package to Europe. In his memo Clayton recommended $6–7 billion in aid each year over a three-year period to prevent Europe's economic disintegration and to stop the Communists. Such aid would also boost America's export trade and should be used to build a unified European economy.

After Marshall made his speech, Clayton attempted in the summer of 1947 to cajole the British to lower trade barriers and begin monetary reform, persuade the French to approve reindustrialization of Germany, and get Congress to provide enough interim funds to stave off collapse in certain nations. Clayton told British officials it was up to the Europeans to take the initiative in planning how the aid plan should be structured. He indicated to British foreign minister Ernest Bevin that if the Soviets refused to join the program, the United States would proceed to support Britain, France, and other countries willing to cooperate. As Bevin predicted, the Soviets refused to cooperate.

Perhaps most important, Clayton, in his discussions with the Europeans, showed a flexibility even on long-held positions, such as multilateral free trade, to give the Europeans a chance to open markets bilaterally to spur recovery. His main problem centered on Britain's refusal to abandon imperial preference at the Geneva General Agreement on Tariffs and Trade negotiations. Clayton warned the British that their obstinacy not only jeopardized the GATT talks but also the Marshall Plan. Finally, in September, he reached an agreement in which the British slightly reduced imperial preference while the Americans offered to lower their tariffs further than originally proposed. GATT was now a reality. In addition, Marshall announced the administration's willingness to accept the Europeans' plan requesting $29 million in aid, with the stipulation that the United States would cut down the amount. With Clayton's dream of wider free trade realized, he resigned from the government in October 1947. He did, however, assist in negotiating the charter of the International Trade Organization (only to see it rejected by Congress) and lobby for passage of the European Recovery Act. Clayton's biographer Gregory A. Fossedal insists that Clayton's most important role was directing the attention of Secretary of State George C. Marshall to the dire fate of Europe, and that many people helped in the formulation of the Marshall Plan.

Clayton returned to his business in 1948. He retired from administrative duties in 1951 but remained a director until his death on February 8, 1967, in Houston, Texas, at the age of 87.

—JB

Clifford, Clark (McAdams)

(1906–1998) *special counsel to the president*

Clark Clifford, the son of a railroad official, was born on December 25, 1906, in Fort Scott, Kansas, and was raised in St. Louis, Missouri. He received a law degree from Washington University in 1928 and entered practice with the firm of Holland, Lashly, and Donnell. Initially handling the defense of indigent persons, Clifford gained a reputation as a successful trial attorney specializing in corporation and labor law. He was commissioned a lieutenant in the naval reserve in 1944, and he became assistant to President Truman's naval aide, JAMES K. VARDAMAN, the following year. In 1946 Clifford replaced Vardaman. Aside from his military responsibilities, he assisted Truman's leading speech writer and special counsel, Samuel Rosenman. The young man impressed Rosenman and Truman with his speech writing ability and, more importantly, with his shrewd political common sense. After Rosenman retired in February 1946, Clifford undertook some of the president's legal work. He prepared an important study on universal military training and helped establish the National Intelligence Agency and the Central Intelligence Group, the forerunner

Clark M. Clifford *(Harry S. Truman Library)*

of the Central Intelligence Agency. In June Clifford succeeded Rosenman as special counsel.

Although possessing little political experience Clifford became one of Truman's most trusted advisers, playing critical roles in the development of the administration's foreign and domestic programs. Known as the "Golden Boy" of the administration, Clifford attempted to avoid publicity. He rarely gave interviews and never delivered speeches, preferring, instead, to lobby within the White House for his positions. His influence was such that he was considered one of the most powerful men in Washington.

Clifford's power was based primarily on his strong personal friendship with Truman. The president was comfortable with him. Truman admired his charm and self-assurance and appreciated the encouragement, reassurance, and counsel the young man could give him. Just as importantly, Clifford spoke Truman's political language. He was a political pragmatist whose outwardly cordial manner concealed a tough inner resolve. He reinforced Truman's penchant for action, urging the president to stand fast and fight rather than go slow and compromise.

During 1946 Clifford helped shape Truman's response to the wave of strikes that gripped the nation. In editing Truman's speeches, which often contained hysterical outbursts against union leaders, Clifford was careful to stress that the president was a friend of labor. Nevertheless, he condemned what he thought was union irresponsibility and urged Truman to take a strong stand against strikes that threatened the national interest. Clifford was particularly insistent that Truman stand up to JOHN L. LEWIS, head of the United Mine Workers, who had gone on strike repeatedly during the postwar period. He assured Truman that if the president got into an open fight with Lewis and won, Truman's political popularity would rise. During the fall of 1946 Clifford planned the strategy that led to a contempt citation against the union leader, who had threatened to pull his workers out of the mines in defiance of an injunction barring a strike.

Clifford was a major force in molding what came to be known as the containment policy against the Soviet Union. In the summer of 1946, increasingly exasperated with what he saw as Soviet intransigence, Truman asked Clifford to write up a record of violations by the Soviets of international agreements. Clifford, working with GEORGE M. ELSEY, decided instead to call for the opinions of senior officials regarding the Soviet Union to see if a consensus existed on the matter. Clifford later claimed that he acted the role that National Security Advisors would play in a later day.

Clifford and Elsey prepared the report, which they titled "American Relations with the Soviet Union." When they submitted it in September, the president saw it as so explosive that he locked all 20 copies in the White House safe without distributing them. Clifford based the memorandum on their belief that "the key to an understanding of current Soviet foreign policy is the realization that Soviet leaders adhere to the Marxian theory of ultimate destruction of capitalist states by Communist states." The report argued that a new strategy was needed against the Soviets. It also revealed that a consensus had formed on Soviet-American relations in the administration. Clifford and Elsey further contended that the Soviets might try to expand their borders through war, and that the United States should have the armed forces to deter such a course of action. "The language of military power," they said, "is the only language which [sic] disciples of power politics understand. The United States must use that language in order that Soviet leaders will realize that our government is determined to uphold the interests of its citizens and the rights of small nations. . . ." At the same time, the United States should show the Russians through a variety of venues that it preferred "peaceable coexistence" with the Communist world. The United States should be prepared for the possibility that the Soviet Union would not cooperate in the solution of international problems, and until they did "the United States should enter no proposal for disarmament or limitation of armament." The United States should be prepared to ally itself with other Western nations to build our own sphere of influence, while recognizing the Soviet sphere. Washington should assist countries threatened by Soviet expansionism, particularly through economic aid, while reserving military help as a last resort. Clifford argued in his memoirs that the report caused the president to abandon any thought of a long-term, low-interest loan to the Russians. Although locked away in the White House safe, the Clifford-Elsey report laid the groundwork for the Truman Doctrine, the Marshall Plan, NATO, and the Point Four program.

Historian Melvyn Leffler contended that Clifford and Elsey relied heavily on information from the military and argued that the two exaggerated Soviet strength, and that the report was not an objective study but rather a justification for what the Americans had already done and would do in the future.

In 1947 Clifford reiterated and elaborated on the report's ideas in his draft of Truman's speech requesting aid to Greece and Turkey. He found the State Department's version of the address too bogged down in economics. Believing that the speech should be "the opening gun in a campaign to bring people up to [the] realization [that] war was not over by any means," he redrafted it. Clifford played on the emotions of Congress and the people by stressing the danger to the Western world if Greece and Turkey fell to the Communists and promising U.S. aid against Communist aggression. The president's address proved a success, and the Truman Doctrine, as it became known, proved one of the foundations of the administration's foreign policy.

Clifford was also credited with playing a major role in reversing the administration's policy on Palestine. On February 21, 1948, Truman received a communication aboard the presidential yacht *Williamsburg* in the Caribbean from the State Department that gave the gist of a speech to be given by UN ambassador WARREN AUSTIN to the Security Council. Austin was to argue that the council did not have any authority to enforce partition in Palestine and suggesting if partition was no longer possible then the United States might have to support a trusteeship for the area. Truman agreed as long as it was clear that the United States still stood behind eventual partition.

Truman met with Secretary of State Marshall and Undersecretary ROBERT A. LOVETT on March 8. They told the president that the UN Security Council was not prepared to accept the General Assembly's partition resolution. They proposed the trusteeship position and presented him with a draft for Austin to deliver. Apparently thinking trusteeship as only a postponement rather than the denial of Jewish statehood, Truman agreed.

Truman met Zionist leader Chaim Weizmann on March 18, 1945. Weizmann probably left thinking the president would recognize a new Jewish state. The next day Austin made his speech proposing trusteeship. Truman apparently did not understand that trusteeship would probably end the move toward partition. But the trusteeship soon proved unworkable. Weizmann claimed de facto partition had already taken place in Palestine, and a trusteeship would have meant a substantial U.S. military contribution that it could not afford with the ongoing crisis in Europe.

On May 12, 1948, Truman, Marshall, Lovett, Clifford, and others met at the White House to discuss the matter. Clifford presented the case to support partition. The White House aide pointed out that Palestine was already divided between Jewish and Arab sections, and thus a single trusteeship would not work, and that the administration should return to the president's original position on partition. He proposed the president the next day announce his intention to recognize the Jewish state. The United States had a moral obligation to help the Jewish people after the Holocaust and centuries of persecution. The United States should also have a democratic ally in that part of the world.

Marshall exploded that he did not know why Clifford was even there—he was a domestic adviser, and this was foreign policy. Truman said that he was there because he asked him to be. Marshall continued that the only reason Clifford was there was politics involved (meaning an attempt to win the Jewish vote in the presidential election), and that if he were to violate his policy of not voting he would vote against Truman if he followed Clifford's policy.

After that outburst, Truman adjourned the meeting fairly quickly and tried to assuage the general. Clifford later insisted that domestic politics were not involved in his pushing for recognition, but that is rather unlikely given Clifford's role as Truman's political adviser, who occasionally delved into national security issues at the direction of the president, for there not to be a connection.

Robert Lovett met with Clifford after the disastrous meeting and asked him if the president would modify his position. Clifford claimed the president would not back down—which was hardly the case—and Marshall should concede. Clifford continued this bluff and contended that the president was adamant when Lovett suggested the next day that recognition of Israel be put off for a time. When Lovett suggested recognizing Israel on a de facto basis rather than a de jure one, Clifford proved willing to compromise on this point—again without checking with the president. Clifford realized Marshall would not change his position, but he asked that the general not come out in opposition. Lovett said he would do what he could do. Lovett finally was able to convince Marshall to agree not to oppose openly Truman's recognition. Within a few minutes after Israel's declaration of independence, the administration extended to it de facto recognition.

In a memorandum after recognition, Lovett claimed that domestic politics had determined the administration's course. Clifford denied this, but he did admit during one of their meetings that they did discuss the presidential election; still Clifford claimed (rather lamely) that he had not linked the two subjects in the conversation.

During 1947 and 1948 Clifford served as the chief liberal spokesman in the administration. Truman was often irritated by liberals whom he considered arrogant, self-righteous idealists tied too closely to Franklin D. Roosevelt and HENRY A. WALLACE. However, he worked well with Clifford, who combined pleas for a continuation of New Deal programs with the promise that it would obtain votes for the president.

Clifford did not originally write the famed 43-page memorandum of November 1947 explaining how Truman could win in 1948—James Rowe did. But Truman looked upon Rowe with disfavor because he was an associate of Tommy Corcoran, whom the president despised. Without reading it, Truman had Clifford vet it for him. Clifford rewrote the memorandum and presented as his own to avoid the president dismissing it as something Rowe had written. Analyzing the composition of the Democratic Party, Clifford found it an unhappy alliance of Southern conservatives, liberal unions, and Western progressives. Success required the ability "to lead these three misfit groups to the polls. . . ." The Southerners, Clifford argued, were a guaranteed part of the coalition. (He proved wrong on that assumption.) Truman, therefore, should focus his attention on the West and on the unions. He could retain the support of the West by supporting a continuation of New Deal agricultural and reclamation programs. Truman's problem, Clifford suggested, was Wallace's attraction to the liberals. For Truman to win that vote he must discredit Wallace by linking him with Communists and, more importantly, offering a broad program of liberal social legislation. Clifford realized that because the Republicans controlled Congress much of the program would fail. However he thought that Truman could then use the failure against the Republicans in the general election.

Clifford also made a number of tactical suggestions to improve Truman's image. The president's enemies had circulated false rumors, Clifford wrote, that "everything good about administration foreign policy is Marshall; everything bad is Truman." Clifford recommended that Truman counter this by tying himself more publicly with foreign policy and pushing the secretary into the background. He also recommended that Truman take advantage of the office of the presidency to obtain more publicity by taking more trips and giving more speeches, emulating Franklin Roosevelt's famed election year "inspection tours." This suggestion evolved into the legendary whistle-stop campaign of 1948. Clifford and other advisers convinced the president to speak extemporaneously more often, as his ability to read a speech was poor.

Clifford's memorandum helped determine Truman's strategy in 1948. The president's January State of the Union Address was a ringing call for a liberal program that included proposals for comprehensive health insurance, expansion of social security and unemployment benefits, federal aid to housing and education, an increase in the minimum wage, a continuation of federal price supports for farmers, and a far-reaching civil rights program to end segregation in the South.

In June Truman, accompanied by Clifford, toured the Midwest and West damning the "do-nothing 80th Congress." Following Truman's nomination at the Democratic National Convention, Clifford helped draft the president's acceptance speech in which he repeated his charges made on the tour and astonished all by promising to call Congress into session, challenging it to pass measures recommended in the Republican platform. Clifford then accompanied Truman on his successful fall speaking tour. The election resulted in a surprising victory for the president, which some observers credited to Clifford's strategy.

Clifford left government in 1950 to return to his private law practice. His departure upset liberals. The *Nation* wrote, "Clifford has been the mainstay of the Fair Deal, the author of its best presidential speeches, and the originator of its most important strategies." The *New Republic* agreed, "Clifford's retirement as special counsel further weakens our side in the White House. . . . Clifford knows the score. In many ways he was the strongest liberal influence in the presidential entourage."

During the 1950s Clifford became one of the capital's most influential and wealthiest lawyers, using his legal and political knowledge to aid some of America's largest corporations in their dealings with government. He served as a presidential adviser on foreign intelligence during the Kennedy and Johnson administrations. In 1968 President Johnson appointed him secretary of defense. As a trusted friend of the president, Clifford urged the de-escalation of the Vietnam war. Clifford left office in January 1969 and returned to his law practice.

In 1981 Clifford, acting on behalf of Arab investors, won approval from the Federal Reserve Board for their acquisition of an American bank that became known as First American Bankshares, which soon became the largest bank in Washington. It was revealed in 1991 that the Arab investors were, in fact, fronting for the Bank of Credit and Commerce International, a notorious offshore bank that had been banned from the United States since 1971. Clifford had assured the Federal Reserve that First American Bankshares would in no way be controlled by BCCI. In 1991 the BCCI was accused of fraud and money-laundering, and Clifford was indicted for fraud, conspiracy, and bribe taking. Clifford claimed that he had been duped, but, given his years of experience in Washington representing clients, this was difficult to believe. Clifford's indictment was set aside because of his advancing age and declining health, and when his partner, Robert Altman, was acquitted for similar charges, he claimed vindication. However, he and Altman were forced to pay $5 million to settle the Federal Reserve's civil suit against them, and Clifford's sterling reputation was damaged. He died on October 10, 1998, in Bethesda, Maryland. (See *The Kennedy Years, The Johnson Years* Volumes)

—JB

Cohen, Benjamin (Victor)
(1894–1983) *counselor, State Department*

The son of a prosperous ore dealer, Cohen was born on September 23, 1894, in Muncie, Indiana. He graduated from the University of Chicago in 1914 at the age or 15 and earned a law degree from the same institution the following year. In 1916 he obtained a doctorate in law from Harvard, where he was a student of FELIX FRANKFURTER. Cohen developed a lucrative law practice in New York, specializing in corporate reorganization. His clients included some of the largest companies in the nation. He also offered legal advice to the Amalgamated Clothing Workers Union and the National Consumers League. A Zionist, he assisted in the negotiations creating the Palestine Mandate at the Paris Peace Conference of 1919.

During the 1930s Frankfurter brought Cohen to Washington to help develop New Deal legislation. His specialty was drafting the bills presented to Congress. Cohen contributed to the framing of the Securities Act of 1933, the Securities and Exchange Act of 1934, the Utility Holding Act of 1935, and the Fair Labor Standard Act of 1938. His activities earned him the reputation of being one of the most liberal members of the administration.

Cohen left government in 1940 when Roosevelt did not appoint him general counsel for the State Department. He returned, however, the following year to serve as economic counselor in the American embassy at London, where he participated in lend-lease negotiations. In 1942 he became counsel to JAMES F. BYRNES, director of war mobilization. As a result of the contacts he had made in Congress during the New Deal and his post as Byrnes's assistant, Cohen wielded great power in Washington. He further developed a close relationship with Congress, which proved to be valuable for Byrnes and the president. A shy, reticent man, Cohen shunned publicity, preferring to work privately. He rarely delivered speeches and consented infrequently to interviews. Few people outside government were aware of his work.

When Brynes became secretary of state in the summer of 1945, he invited Cohen to be counselor to the State Department. At that post he coordinated policy and served as Byrnes's chief adviser. Cohen accompanied the secretary to all major postwar conferences as well as numerous foreign minister's meetings in 1945 and 1946. He concerned himself mostly with United Nations affairs. From 1948 to 1952 Cohen served on the U.S. delegation to the United Nations. Sitting on the ad hoc Political Committee, he debated the Soviets and their allies on human rights.

In 1952 Truman named Cohen to represent the United States on the United National Disarmament Commission. Cohen defended the American-British-French proposal calling for disclosure of weapons, adequate inspection, and international control of armaments. He charged the Soviet Union with using the commission as another forum for the cold war because it had criticized the Western proposal but failed to suggest an alternative. Instead, Cohen maintained, the Russians had introduced a "phantom" plan, one so vague it never really existed.

Following his resignation as State Department counselor, Cohen returned to his law practice. He continued his legal work until the 1970s, when ill health forced him to curtail his activities. During the 1950s, 1960s, and 1970s, Cohen served as one of the leading elder statesmen of the Democratic Party. Cohen died on August 15, 1983, in Washington, D.C.

—JB

Collins, J(oseph) Lawton
(1896–1987) *army chief of staff*

J. Lawton Collins was born on May 1, 1896, in New Orleans, Louisiana. His father was an Irish immigrant who, at the age of 16, joined the Union army. Young Collins attended Louisiana State University for one year before entering the U.S. Military Academy at West Point in 1913. After graduating in 1917 he began a career as an infantry officer. During 1919 he commanded a battalion in occupied Germany. Collins served in various military capacities in the 1920s and 1930s. At the outbreak of World War II, he was an instructor at the Army War College. Beginning with his first assignment as chief of staff of the Seventh Corps in January 1941, Collins achieved notable military victories, particularly in the European theater. In June 1945 he was made permanent brigadier general, and, in January 1948, he was promoted to the rank of permanent major general.

From August to December 1945 Collins acted as deputy commanding general and chief of staff of the Army Ground Forces. He was then appointed director of information in the War Department. Collins was responsible for guiding the army's budget requests through Congress and directing public relations. He was named deputy chief of staff of the army in September 1947 under Chief of Staff DWIGHT D. EISENHOWER and vice chief of staff in November 1948 under Chief of Staff OMAR BRADLEY. Collins became army chief of staff himself in August 1949 when Bradley was promoted to chairman of the Joint Chiefs of Staff (JCS). Collins's duties included command of all components of the army and of the supply and service establishments. He was responsible to the secretary of the army for preparing them for war and for their use in combat. Collins oversaw the Army's integration into NATO forces, and Truman's desegregation of the Army.

Collins was a strong advocate of the development of nuclear weapons. In June 1950 he warned that the United States "was approaching practical limits in the development of conventional antiaircraft weapons" and "must look for more promising ones," such as rockets and guided missiles. The following year he urged a major expansion of the atomic weapons program. Collins assumed that this would eventually free U.S. divisions in Europe for action elsewhere.

As army chief of staff, Collins was deeply involved in explaining and justifying the administration's Korean policy. Collins backed sending combat troops to Korea and was in charge of trying to keep UN commander DOUGLAS MACARTHUR to the limited war strategy. MacArthur wanted the resources to win a total victory. To obtain that he also wanted to attack China. Collins and the other military chiefs contended that America had to maintain troop strength and strategic resources, particularly in NATO. MacArthur, in a letter to House Minority Leader JOSEPH MARTIN, publicly condemned Truman's backing of the Joint Chief of Staff's position. Collins and the other member of the JCS supported the president's decision to relieve MacArthur. In May 1951 a joint committee of Senate Armed Services and Foreign Relations committee members called him to testify on the dismissal of General MacArthur. He told the panel that MacArthur had sent U.S. troops to the Manchurian frontier in 1950 in violation of a "clear directive" to let the South Koreans go all the way to the border. Collins said the chiefs of staff had decided that MacArthur should be removed from command for fear he would commit "more serious" violations of policy. In June Collins testified before a House Appropriations Committee that the Korean War could drag on for 10 years because defense requirements in other places would prevent a knockout of the Communists in Korea. Later that year Collins assured the South Korean government that U.S. forces would not leave the nation after an armistice was reached until the South Korean army was strong enough to withstand another attack.

From 1954 to 1955 Collins served as special representative to Vietnam. He retired from the army in 1954. Collins served as director of Charles Phizer & Company, Inc. until 1969 and as vice president of Phizer International subsidiaries until 1972. He died on September 12, 1987, in Washington, D.C. (See *The Eisenhower Years* Volume)

—MLB

Conant, James B(ryant)

(1893–1978) *chairman, National Defense Research Committee; member, General Advisory Committee to the Atomic Energy Commission*
James B. Conant was born on March 26, 1893, in Dorchester, Massachusetts. He graduated from Har-

vard with high honors in 1913 and received his doctorate in chemistry there in 1916. During World War I he held the rank of major in the Chemical Warfare Service, supervising the production of poisonous gases. Returning to Harvard after the war, Conant won recognition for his research in organic chemistry, winning several awards for his efforts, and gained increasing influence as an educator. In 1933 he became president of Harvard, a post he retained until 1953. Conant's curriculum innovations and administrative reforms led him to national prominence.

When World War II broke out in Europe, Conant became an outspoken interventionist, calling for universal conscription and all-out aid to England. In 1940 he was asked by Dr. VANNEVAR BUSH to serve on the National Defense Research Committee (NDRC) to investigate how American scientists could assist in the defense effort. As chairman of the NDRC, which in 1941 became part of the Office of Scientific Research and Development headed by Bush, Conant was assigned the task of organizing chemists into research groups to help the army and navy. The practice instituted by Bush and Conant of drawing up contracts with universities and industrial laboratories revolutionized the relationship of universities and private scientists to the federal government. For the first time scientists were mobilized for defense efforts in their own laboratories, giving the government access to the full range of advanced technology. In 1941 Conant was sent to Britain to aid in establishing an NRDC office there to coordinate an exchange of information between British and American scientists. On his return Conant suggested that the United States, still technically neutral, recruit specially trained army officers who would be sent to England as "observers," instructed to assist the British in all areas but combat.

Conant was a believer in "total war," in which the entire country would be mobilized. After American entry into the war, Conant arranged the priorities for spending $350–500 million in arms research. President Roosevelt, on the recommendations of Bush, Conant, and other top advisers, decided to proceed with the secret construction in Chicago of a uranium pile. This was the first phase of the Manhattan District Project, which led to the creation of the fission or atomic bomb. Dr. Conant was given primary administrative responsibility for the uranium research, and, with his many university and scientific contacts, he could gather the financial resources—through setting up government weapons contracts directly with universities—and the technical and scientific know-how to build the atomic bomb. He was present at the explosion of the first atomic bomb in the New Mexico desert in July 1945.

As a member of the Interim Committee, organized in 1945 to advise President Truman on atomic energy policy, Conant was one of those who voted to use the bomb in a surprise attack on Japan. He also helped choose the target in Japan; he believed a factory adjacent to workers' homes should be the place—Hiroshima was perfect. He came to this decision despite the protests of many of the scientists who had worked to develop the bomb. Conant later wrote that he had never had any misgivings; he wished that the bomb could have been used months sooner to end the war. As a drafter of the May-Johnson bill, which would have allowed the military to retain control of atomic energy after the war, Conant further incurred the distrust of many younger scientists who lobbied against the measure. This distrust was in part responsible for his failure in 1950 to win election as president of the National Academy of Sciences.

After the war Conant returned to Harvard while continuing to act as a government adviser on scientific matters, especially those relating to atomic energy. He was among those scientists who saw a free exchange of scientific information and international control of atomic energy as the only way to secure peace. Although a member of the U.S. delegation to the Four Power Conference in Moscow in 1945, Conant had no chance to bring up his carefully prepared proposals. In 1946 he served on the Acheson-Lilienthal Committee, helping to draw up proposals for an international atomic energy authority that were later presented to the United Nations as the Baruch Plan. When the Soviets rejected the plan, Conant advocated a strengthening of the Western allies' ground forces in Europe. He felt that the United States must establish a means of countering Soviet aggression without recourse to atomic weapons before "negotiations with the Soviet Union could begin to take a realistic turn."

As a member of the General Advisory Committee to the Atomic Energy Commission from 1947 to 1952, Conant strongly opposed the development of the hydrogen bomb. He was never convinced that any benefits would accrue from the use of atomic energy even for peaceful purposes, believing that its awesome potential for destruction out-

weighed any possible gains. As early as 1951 he warned about the problem of nuclear waste disposal, suggesting that solar energy be developed as a future power source. Conant and Vannevar Bush supported the internationalization of atomic power and argued that an arms race must not occur.

In the postwar era Conant concerned himself with the place of education in society. He contended that an intellectual elite should lead a people that was informed and trained. As students and money poured into Harvard as a result of the G.I. Bill, the university began to reflect Conant's ideas. He argued on the behalf of a widespread adoption of the social science focus of Harvard's Graduate School of Education as the best way to find future leaders.

In the late 1940s Conant warned against the "divisiveness" engendered by nonpublic schools. This was largely seen as an attack on Catholic parochial schools. Conant's supporters insisted that Conant only wanted to prevent the weakening of public schools.

During the early 1950s Conant was critical of the anticommunist investigations in schools and government, and he opposed a proposed loyalty oath for the Harvard faculty. In 1954 he defended J. ROBERT OPPENHEIMER, former chairman of the General Advisory Committee to the Atomic Energy Commission, whose initial opposition to the hydrogen bomb had been cited by government interrogators as proof of his alleged Soviet sympathies.

From 1953 to 1955 Conant served as high commissioner for Germany, helping to prepare West Germany for independent status. In 1955 he became ambassador to the newly formed Federal Republic of Germany. He resigned this post in 1957 to devote himself to educational projects. Conant continued to write and lecture on education and foreign policy through the 1960s. He supported the Johnson administration's conduct of the Vietnam War. He died on February 11, 1978, in Hanover, New Hampshire. (See *The Eisenhower Years* Volume)

—DAE

Condon, Edward U(hler)

(1902–1974) *director, National Bureau of Standards*

Condon, the son of a civil engineer, was born on March 2, 1902, in Alamogordo, New Mexico, the town near the site of the first atomic bomb explosion. He received his bachelor's degree from the

University of California at Berkeley and formulated James Franck's theory of molecular transitions, writing this into a dissertation on a weekend. Berkeley refused to accept a "weekend dissertation" and it was not until 1926 that he was awarded his Ph.D. After an unsatisfactory year of study at Göttingen and Munich universities, Condon returned to the United States in 1927 to work for Bell Telephone Laboratories. He taught at Columbia and Princeton from 1928 to 1937. His research laid the groundwork for modern nuclear theory and influenced research in atomic energy. Condon then joined the Westinghouse Electric Company as associate director of research, where he remained until 1945. During World War II he made significant technical contributions to the development of microwave radar and the atomic bomb. He helped in devising the process to isolate the uranium used in the first bombs and assisted J. ROBERT OPPENHEIMER in organizing the Manhattan District Project. In November 1945 President Truman appointed him director of the National Bureau of Standards.

The politically liberal and Quaker Condon joined with other leading American scientists in the late 1940s in opposing the military's attempt to control the nation's atomic energy program. They feared atomic research controlled by the military would center on weapons development rather than on peaceful or industrial use. During 1946 Condon served as technical adviser to the Senate Special Committee on Atomic Energy. The panel had been formed to help resolve the controversy over civilian versus military control of atomic energy development. Condon helped formulate the committee's proposal for a civilian controlled Atomic Energy Commission with a liaison to the military. This measure, the McMahon-Johnson Act, was signed into law in August 1946. As head of the Bureau of Standards, Condon advanced the use of applied mathematics for the government and started work on electronic computers.

Condon believed that atomic energy should be explored on an international level by the United Nations. He called for continued cooperation between scientists around the world. While not advocating the disclosure of atomic secrets, Condon claimed foreign scientists would quickly acquire the knowledge and therefore no sound policy could be based solely on security. In March 1946 Condon lashed out at restrictions on travel abroad for scientists and what he viewed as ignorant military censorship of the exchange of knowledge. Condon, a member of the American-Soviet Science Society, suggested Russian scientists be welcomed into American laboratories. His outspoken support of a civilian-run Atomic Energy Commission (AEC), East-West scientific cooperation, and his friendship with Progressive Party members and suspected Communists made him a target for conservatives in Congress.

On March 1, 1948, Representative J. PARNELL THOMAS (R-N.J.), chairman of the House Un-American Activities Committee (HUAC), released a brief report characterizing Condon as "one of the weakest links in America's atomic security." The report, which the *New York Times* called a "masterpiece of innuendo," noted that Progressive Party leader HENRY A. WALLACE had recommended Condon for the directorship of the Bureau of Standards and that Condon's wife was of Czechoslovakian origin. HUAC also charged that Condon had been "associating" with unnamed American Communist Party members as well as an alleged Soviet spy. Thomas called for Condon's ouster on grounds of questionable loyalty. The panel did not comply with Condon's request for an open hearing on the charges. The Truman administration quickly came to his defense and the Commerce Department's loyalty board cleared him of any misconduct.

In April Truman defied the congressional resolution and refused to release material from Condon's loyalty file. The AEC, after a complete review of Condon's file, including FBI reports, gave him a full security clearance three months later. On the campaign trail Truman continued his defense of Condon, warning in September 1948 that scientific research vital for national security might be made impossible by "the creation of an atmosphere in which no man feels safe against the public airing of unfounded rumors, gossip and vilification." HUAC member RICHARD M. NIXON (R-Calif.) said the committee had treated Condon unfairly by releasing its report before questioning him.

In 1951 Representative Richard B. Vail (R-Ill.) reopened the question of Condon's loyalty. When Condon resigned from the Bureau of Standards in August, citing financial difficulties, members of HUAC termed it a resignation "under fire." That month Condon became director of research at Corning Glass Works. In September 1952 Condon was subpoenaed to appear before HUAC to answer questions about past associations during the war years with suspected Communists at Berkeley's Radiation Laboratory. Condon denied he had been a Communist or had had any knowledge of espionage activities. HUAC's annual report classified him as a security risk.

Condon left Corning Glass in December 1954 after the navy revoked his security clearance at Vice President Nixon's urging. Stating that his health and efficiency had been impaired by the long struggle over his loyalty, he returned to academic life. He first assumed a position at Washington University and in 1963 moved to the University of Colorado at Boulder. Condon died in Boulder, Colorado, on March 26, 1974.

—JF

Connally, Thomas (Terry)
(1877–1963) *member of the Senate*

Born on a Texas farm in McLellan County, Texas, on August 19, 1877, Tom Connally graduated from Baylor University in 1896 and obtained a law degree from the University of Texas two years later. Connally served in the army during the Spanish-American War and then returned to hold elective offices as a Democrat in both houses of the Texas state legislature. Elected in 1916 to the U.S. House of Representatives, he voted for entry into World War I the next year and resigned to serve again in the army. Following the war Connally returned to the House, where he obtained a seat on the Foreign Affairs Committee and began a lifelong interest in diplomacy. A supporter of Woodrow Wilson, Connally campaigned for U.S. involvement in the League of Nations and the World Court. During the 1920s he represented the United States at a number of international conferences.

In 1928 Connally won the Democratic senatorial primary (tantamount to election) against Carle E. Mayfield, who had the backing of the Ku Klux Klan. As a good Wilsonian and a cotton state legislator, he opposed the Hawley-Smoot Tariff. He also voted against Hoover's national sales tax proposal. He argued for better relations with Latin America and Caribbean nations. He supported much of the New Deal in Franklin Roosevelt's initial term, but he voted against the National Industrial Recovery Act in 1933. Connally broke with FDR on the court-packing plan of 1937 and as a member of the Judiciary Committee helped to defeat it. In the late 1930s and 1940s he led filibusters against civil rights measures, such as legislation to outlaw lynching and to end the poll tax, and

supported bills to control organized labor. He helped write the Smith-Connally Act of 1943 expanding the president's power to seize strike-bound war plants. Connally was a strong supporter of Roosevelt's foreign policy. He favored repeal of the arms embargo and supported lend-lease. As chairman of the Foreign Relations Committee after 1941, he helped write the U.S. declaration of war against the Axis countries. Connally was a strong supporter of the United Nations and, in 1945, was vice chairman of the U.S. delegation to the San Francisco Conference.

After Truman became president, Connally was a frequent adviser on foreign policy and continued to represent the United States at important international conferences. With the ranking Republican senator on the Foreign Relations Committee, ARTHUR H. VANDENBERG (R-Mich.), he worked to push Truman's foreign policy through the Senate. Connally led the fight for ratification of the UN Charter in 1945, dramatically denouncing proposed amendments that would have crippled it. The charter passed the Senate by a vote of 90 to 2. He was also that year vice chairman of the U.S. delegation to the San Francisco Conference on the UN. He served as a member of the American delegation in the 1946 London Conference on the UN, and was at the initial meeting of the UN General Assembly. However, the following year he submitted a successful measure, known as the Connally Amendment, restricting the jurisdiction of the World Court involving the United States to those cases the Senate decided the court was competent to judge. He also counseled Secretary of State JAMES F. BYRNES during the early meetings of the Council of Foreign Ministers.

When the Republicans took control of Congress in 1947, Vandenberg became chairman of the committee. The two men continued to work together to gain ratification of Truman's policies of containment toward the USSR. Both joined in the administration's deliberations on aid to Greece and Turkey, which resulted in the formulation of the Truman Doctrine. Connally defended the measure before the Senate and helped to allay fears that the doctrine would be an open-ended commitment to U.S. intervention by providing Undersecretary of State DEAN G. ACHESON a forum to deny the charge. The following year Connally worked with Vandenberg to gain approval of the Marshall Plan.

In January 1949 Connally resumed the chairmanship. He remained a strong supporter of Truman's diplomacy and was a vigorous champion of the Senate's prerogatives in foreign affairs. Connally expressed reservations about the North Atlantic Treaty, opposing "the inclusion in the North Atlantic Pact of any clause or provision requiring the United States automatically to go to war, if any one of the signatories should be attacked." Only Congress, he pointed out, could declare war. When assured that this prerogative was protected in the final treaty, Connally supported it and backed the aid package for the alliance. He worked against Republican senator ROBERT A. TAFT's (R-Ohio) attempts to interfere with presidential prerogatives in deploying the military.

When North Korea invaded South Korea in June 1950, Connally participated in policy deliberations on U.S. action. Initially the Texas senator defended the administration's decision to send only arms to the South rather than intervene, as members of the Republican right demanded. However, when Truman decided to commit troops, Connally enthusiastically supported his policy and defended his constitutional power to do so. During the latter part of 1950 he led the fight to bottle up the Kem Resolution. The measure was a partisan attack by conservative Republicans who claimed that Truman had not consulted them on foreign policy. It called on the president to give Congress a detailed report of his talks on Korea with Western leaders and submit in treaty form any agreements reached.

Although a loyal supporter of Truman's foreign affairs, Connally opposed the administration on domestic issues. He voted for such antiunion measures as the Taft-Hartley Act and the Portal-to-Portal Pay Act. Connally continued his opposition to antilynching and anti–poll tax measures as violations of states' rights. Nevertheless, he refused to join the Dixiecrat revolt of 1948.

Connally decided not to seek reelection in 1952, mainly because Texas oil men wanted a stronger supporter of their interests in Congress. Connally was apparently made to believe he could not beat Texas attorney general Price Daniel in the primaries, so he stepped aside. Connally remained in Washington and practiced law. He died there on October 28, 1963, after a long illness.

—JB

Connelly, Matthew J(oseph)

(1907–1976) *appointments secretary to the president*

The son of a janitor, Matthew J. Connelly was born on November 19, 1907, in Clinton, Massachusetts. He graduated from Fordham College in 1930 and

worked in the securities business for the next three years. After a year with a federal agency in Boston, Connelly moved to Washington and was employed by the Works Progress Administration until 1938. The following year he started working as an investigator for congressional committees. He became friends with Senator Harry S Truman (D-Mo.) who appointed Connelly chief investigator for the Special Committee to Investigate the National Defense Program from 1941 to 1944.

Truman retained the easygoing Connelly as his executive secretary when he was elected vice president in 1944. Upon his accession to the presidency, Truman named Connelly his appointments secretary. At this point the astute, discreet Connelly controlled access to the president. He learned the inner workings of the White House and became a Truman confidant. Connelly, whom journalist Paul Anderson described as a "cool, behind-the-scenes operator," was a member of the White House "brain trust" that directed Truman's whistle-stop campaign of 1948. Connelly had also worked on the June 1948 "nonpolitical" trip to the West, in which Truman tried to publicize himself and his policies, along the lines of Roosevelt's "inspection tours" of World War II. Following the election, Truman put Connelly in charge of a congressional relations team.

In August 1949 the Senate Permanent Investigations Subcommittee, chaired by Senator CLYDE R. HOEY (D-N.C.), named Connelly as one of four people in government, including Mrs. Truman, who had accepted the gift of a freezer from a manufacturer seeking wartime-scarce sheet metal in 1945. The January 1950 Hoey Committee report did not accuse Connelly. At the close of the Truman administration in January 1953, the former secretary went into the public relations business in New York.

In December 1955 a federal grand jury indicted Connelly, Truman's former assistant attorney general T. LAMAR CAUDLE, and lawyer H. J. Schwimmer for conspiracy to defraud the government. In addition to conspiracy, the grand jury charged Connelly with bribery and perjury. These charges arose from a 1951 tax case in which shoe manufacturer Irving Sachs pleaded guilty to charges of income tax evasion. Sachs was then fined $40,000. He was spared a prison term on the grounds of ill health. The 1955 grand jury asserted that Schwimmer, Sachs's attorney, had bribed Connelly and Caudle to stop prosecution, and although the government officials were unable to end legal proceedings, they had prevented Sachs's imprisonment.

Connelly asserted his innocence and charged that the Republican administration had timed his indictment to coincide with the 1956 election. In June 1956 a federal court in St. Louis found the former Truman aide guilty of tax fraud conspiracy along with Caudle and Schwimmer. The court revealed that Connelly had received an oil royalty worth $7,500 and gifts of clothing from Schwimmer for his part in the fix. After unsuccessfully appealing his conviction, Connelly entered the federal prison at Danbury, Connecticut, in May 1960. He was released six months later and returned to his public relations business in New York. In November 1962 President John F. Kennedy pardoned Connelly allegedly at Truman's request. Connelly died on July 10, 1976, in Oak Park, Illinois.

Cooper, (Leon) Jere

(1893–1957) *member of the House of Representatives*

Born on July 20, 1893, on a farm in Dyer County, Tennessee, Jere Cooper grew up in Dyersburg, the county seat, where his father was employed in a cotton-oil mill. He took private elocution lessons in high school and won an oratorical contest sponsored by the United Daughters of the Confederacy. He attended Cumberland University, a one-year law school, and was admitted to the Tennessee bar at the age of 22. Following service overseas during World War I, Cooper returned to Dyersburg, became active in the American Legion, and served as city attorney from 1920 to 1928. In that year he won election to the House of Representatives over four Democratic rivals.

Cooper supported New Deal legislation. He wielded his influence during the Roosevelt era as a member of the Ways and Means Committee, particularly after he assumed chairmanship of its special tax subcommittee in 1939. Committee chairman ROBERT L. DOUGHTON (D-N.C.), who stayed in the post until he retired in 1953 at age 89, came to rely on Cooper for his diligence and expertise. Cooper played a major role in the creation of a mass tax system during World War II and was labeled the "Committee's best tax brain" by *Time* magazine in 1943. As a House leader and skilled parliamentarian, he was frequently called upon by Speaker SAM T. RAYBURN (D-Tex.) to mobilize Democratic majorities and defuse troublesome situations.

In 1945 Cooper was named vice chairman of the Congressional Pearl Harbor Investigating Committee inquiring into the responsibility for the 1941 disaster. The committee's majority report, released in July 1946 and signed by Cooper, concluded that President Roosevelt and his cabinet did not "incite" or "cajole" Japan into the attack. Praising them for their efforts to avert war, the report said that "ultimate responsibility" for an "unprovoked act of aggression" lay with Japan. The committee criticized Washington officials for not giving sufficient consideration to reports that Japan was preparing an attack and blamed the army and navy for America's state of unreadiness.

A proponent of a liberal trade policy, Cooper consistently defended the reciprocal trade agreements negotiated by Roosevelt's secretary of state, Cordell Hull, and during the Truman years fought Republican attempts to weaken the treaties and enact protectionist amendments. He was unsuccessful in the Republican-controlled 80th Congress. In 1948 the Republicans managed to pass a one-year extension of the Trade Agreements Act (instead of the three-year extension desired by the Democrats) along with increased authority for Congress to make tariffs higher than those erected by the president. In 1949, however, the Democratic 81st Congress reversed these acts.

In 1947 Cooper opposed the Republican tax cut, and still opposed it in 1948 when Republicans reduced the cut to win over Democrats and pass the bill over the president's veto. He supported raising the minimum wage from 40 cents to 70 cents an hour in 1949. He voted in favor of the Taft-Hartley Act as well as the Case labor disputes bill to create a board empowered to seek injunctions to halt strikes or lockouts. In 1948 he supported the Mundt-Nixon bill to require Communist and Communist-front organizations to register with the government, and in 1950 he endorsed the Internal Security Act. Cooper opposed all civil rights laws, backed rigid farm price supports, and voted in favor of the National Housing Act of 1949. He was more consistent in supporting foreign policy initiatives of the Truman administration, backing Greek-Turkish aid in 1947, the Marshall Plan and extension of the draft in 1948, and the Korea Aid Act in 1950. In 1948, however, he opposed an administration-backed measure to allow 200,000 displaced persons to enter the United States.

During the Eisenhower years Cooper led House Democratic opposition to Republican tax policy. In 1954 and 1955 he was the spokesman for the alternative tax reduction plan put forth by the Democrats that failed to pass Congress. He continually worked on behalf of extensions of the reciprocal trade agreements and higher appropriations for the Tennessee Valley Authority. He served as chairman of the Ways and Means Committee from January 1955 until his death from a heart attack on December 18, 1957, in Bethesda, Maryland. (See *The Eisenhower Years* Volume)

—TO

Coplon, Judith

(1921–) *convicted spy*

Judith Coplon was born in 1921 in New York City. She was the daughter of a toy manufacturer and grew up in Brooklyn. She attended Barnard College on a partial scholarship, majoring in history and serving as managing editor of the college newspaper. She was also involved with a Communist study group. After graduating cum laude in 1943 she went to work in New York in the Justice Department's Economic Warfare Section as an "economic journalist." In 1945 she was transferred to the Justice Department's Foreign Registration Office in Washington, where her job involved analyzing records of foreign agents registering for activities in the United States. In May 1948 Coplon received a promotion and a commendation from the Attorney General for political analysis. With a good job and promise of advancement, she began to study for her master's degree at American University.

However, Coplon was not what she seemed. Venona decrypts and a KGB document show that a Communist friend of Coplon, Flora Wovschin—already working for the KGB—reported she could be recruited, and after some delay she signed on in January 1945. The KGB officer who spoke with her, Vladimir Pravdin, said in his report that she was a "serious person who is politically well developed and there is no doubt of her sincere desire to help us. She had no doubts about whom she is working for." Her value had increased in the interim as she had been transferred to the Foreign Agents Registration section of the Justice Department. She started spying, doing a good job, and even studied Russian to gain access to FBI material covering the bureau's counterintelligence operations against suspected Soviet agents. Her work with these documents allowed her to tip off the KGB to warn sources to stop spying

and to break off contact with Soviet agents. This meant that by the time the FBI began watching suspects they had been forewarned and such surveillance did not succeed in producing much evidence.

In December 1948, when one of Coplon's associates accused her of slanting her reports in favor of the Soviet Union, a loyalty check was initiated and several suspicious connections uncovered. The FBI put Coplon under surveillance, following her on trips to New York to visit her parents. On January 14, 1949, agents followed her to a rendezvous with a man later identified as Valentin Gubitchev, a 32-year-old Soviet engineer employed by the United Nations. On her return to work in Washington, Coplon was transferred without explanation to another department where she had no access to the top secret documents concerning foreign agents. However, she often returned to her old office and asked to use the files.

When, in early March 1949, Coplon requested access to top secret files, she was given a decoy letter prepared by FBI chief J. EDGAR HOOVER. The message containing false information about several double agents and about the "geophone," supposedly a device for measuring atomic blast pressures. FBI agents again followed her to New York, trailing her and Gubitchev for several hours as they rode separate buses and subways around the city. When the two made contact, they were arrested. Hoover's letter along with abstracts of other Justice Department documents was found inside a magazine in Coplon's purse. The two were arraigned on March 5, and Coplon was indicted a week later in both New York and Washington for stealing government papers and for passing them to a foreign agent with intent to harm the United States.

During her trials Coplon maintained her innocence, testifying that she had fallen in love with Gubitchev and that their clandestine meetings had been arranged to outwit Gubitchev's wife. Despite Coplon's statements, the evidence against her was strong. She was convicted on June 30, 1949, in federal district court in Washington of stealing secret papers from the FBI and the Justice Department and sentenced to 40 months to 10 years in prison. On March 7, 1950, she was convicted in New York of passing those papers to Gubitchev with intent to harm the United States and sentenced to an additional 15 years. Gubitchev, who also received a 15-year sentence, was deported upon waiving his right to appeal.

During her trials and appeals Coplon remained free on bail. In May 1950 she married Albert

Socolov, one of the lawyers on her case. At the end of the year Coplon's New York conviction was reversed in the Appeals Court—in an opinion written by Judge Learned Hand—on the grounds that FBI agents had arrested her without a warrant and that the FBI had wiretapped her phone conversations since January. Wiretaps were illegal, and the prosecution had to prove that any evidence used to convict her had not been derived from the taps. The trial judge did not turn over to the defense some of the wiretap records on the grounds it might harm national security. Instead, he reviewed them himself and concluded that the taps had not tainted the evidence. Hand said this violated her Sixth Amendment rights. Hand noted that she was obviously guilty and did not dismiss the indictments, saying that the FBI might be able to produce evidence in a future trial showing that Coplon planned to escape before a warrant could be issued or the Justice Department might be willing to turn over to the defense all the wiretap records. Coplon, however, was not retried in New York, and the indictments were dismissed in 1967. The Washington conviction for stealing documents was upheld on appeal, but the wiretaps in the District of Columbia had included conversation with her lawyer before and during the trial. The D.C. Court of Appeals decided that this had also deprived her of her Sixth Amendment rights and approved a hearing on the wiretap complaint. After the Supreme Court denied a Justice Department request to review both decisions, the government put Coplon's case in abeyance pending legislative action on the admission of wiretap evidence in espionage cases. Congressional failure to enact such laws left the case unsettled. Of course the FBI could not reveal the Venona decrypts that proved her guilt because it would have exposed the decryption project.

—DAE

Cox, E(dward) Eugene

(1880–1952) *member of the House of Representatives*

E. Edward Cox was born on April 3, 1880, in Mitchell County, Georgia. After receiving a law degree from Mercer University in 1902, Cox opened a legal practice in the small town of Camilla, Georgia. From 1912 to 1916 he served as a judge of the Superior Court of the Albany, Georgia, circuit. He ran unsuccessfully for the U.S. House of Representatives as a

Democrat in 1916 but was elected from southeastern Georgia's Second Congressional District in 1924. Cox was an opponent of New Deal legislation. An influential member of the House Rules Committee, he attempted to block passage of Works Projects Administration appropriations and the Fair Labor Standards Act. He denounced strikes in defense industries in 1940 and 1941, demanding compulsory arbitration of labor-management disputes. After Pearl Harbor Cox urged the scuttling of all progressive legislation in the interest of wartime unity.

Cox supported the Truman administration's containment policies, warning in 1946 that the Soviet Union sought "to communize the world." He was a leading backer of increased funds for the Voice of America, which he thought necessary in the fight against communist penetration of Eastern Europe. Cox voted for U.S. aid to Greece and Turkey in 1947 and supported the Marshall Plan in 1948. He urged that Spain be included in the European Recovery Program despite its authoritarian government, denouncing an effort to exclude Franco as a "shameful and cowardly surrender to leftists." Cox supported a lenient policy toward Germany because "we now desperately need these people in a common effort to stop the aggressions of Russia." In 1948 he advocated extending military assistance to that nation.

As a leading member of the Rules Committee, Cox used his power to oppose Fair Deal legislation. He fought efforts to improve the condition of organized labor and supported the Case labor disputes bill and Taft-Hartley Act. He was one of the few Democrats to favor Republican proposals to reduce taxes. Cox was an ardent foe of civil rights legislation, denouncing such measures as "Communistic." He opposed proposals to abolish the poll tax in 1945 as an unconstitutional "expression of venomous, ignorant, unreasonable hostility." In 1948 he asserted that "Harlem is wielding more influence with the administration than the entire white South." After the 1948 presidential election, Americans for Democratic Action unsuccessfully pushed for Cox's ouster from the Rules Committee for his opposition to liberal legislation.

The volatile Cox occasionally descended to violence to assert his position. In June 1949 he engaged in a fight with Rules Committee chairman ADOLPH F. SABATH when the latter refused him 10 minutes to speak against the Truman administration's public housing bill. The outcome was a peaceful reconciliation in which Sabath granted him seven minutes to denounce the measure. He launched into a tirade against the bill as a "socialist scheme" that would lead to a bureaucratic invasion of privacy and urged, instead, increased aid to private industry to build housing. Another time Cox tried to make a point on the House floor by pulling the hair of Representative Will Rogers, Jr., son of the humorist. Yet he also could talk in a way that the *New York Times* recorded as akin to "a Ciceronian oration." Cox was a prominent opponent of attempts to limit the power of the Rules Committee. Until 1949 the panel could control the flow of legislation to the House floor by reporting or refusing to report the rules governing the terms of debate and the offering of amendments. That year the chamber passed the "21-day rule" permitting committees under certain conditions to bypass the Rules Committee and bring their bills directly to the floor. Shortly after passage Cox moved that the committee be restored to its former power. Over Sabath's opposition he brought the bill to the floor in January 1950. Truman administration forces were able to defeat the measure, but Cox was successful the following year.

Cox was a foe of those he saw as subversive. He supported the House Committee on Un-American Activities in its investigation of alleged subversives. When 54 people were cited for contempt for refusing to answer questions of HUAC, Cox talked scornfully of representatives who voted for the first contempt citation, but who had previously opposed HUAC "for its effort to chase out of the country and out of responsible positions in government the agents of the Russians." He continued that he "was amused yesterday to observe the stampede in the ranks of Reds, pinkos, and leftists" of Congress to vote for the contempt citation for an official of the United Electrical Workers Union, Julius Emspak. During 1952 Cox led an investigation of possible support of subversive activities by the nation's educational and philanthropic foundations. After study he concluded that several organizations had unwittingly aided Communists. Cox died of a heart attack on December 24, 1952, in Washington, D.C., in the midst of his investigation.

—AES

Crump, Edward H(ull)
(1874–1954) *chairman, Democratic Party, Memphis, Tennessee*

Edward H. Crump was born on a Mississippi farm in Holly Springs, just outside Memphis, on October 2, 1874. Following an apprenticeship as a printer, he

moved to that city in 1892 to accept a job as a bookkeeper for a harness concern. Eight years later he bought the company. Crump later invested in banking, mortgage loans, and real estate businesses, and, in 1920, set up E.H. Crump Company, an investment, mortgage loan, insurance, and real estate business. In 1901 he received his first political job—election officer for one of the city wards. Four years later he defeated the reigning machine and began consolidating his own power. Crump served as mayor of Memphis from 1910 to 1915, when he was ousted from office for refusing to enforce the Prohibition laws.

The defeat did not hurt Crump. By 1922 he had constructed a political machine that was to dominate Memphis and the state for 30 years. The Crump machine provided Memphis with efficient government. Crump promoted popular civic projects such as parks, hospitals, new schools, and harbor improvements. He kept tax rates and property assessments low and built a city-owned utilities system that provided increased electrical power to the city at minimal rates. A supporter of much of the New Deal, he backed the development of city-owned utilities. The police were efficient but sometimes brutal. The city was often honored for its municipal achievements. Crump occasionally held elective office during this period: county treasurer from 1917 to 1923 and U.S. representative from 1931 to 1935. In 1939 he won election as mayor but resigned shortly thereafter, giving his post to one of his followers.

The boss's power did not rely either on the elective offices he held or on the traditional technique of stuffing ballot boxes. His machine was based on patronage. Unprotected by civil service, municipal workers voted as Crump wished in return for their jobs. Senator KENNETH D. MCKELLAR (D-Tenn.) was long indebted to the boss for his position. In return he gave Crump control of federal patronage. Because he controlled the state legislature, Crump was able to trade support for bills in return for loyalty to the machine. Still another factor in his strength was the poll tax. Originally adopted to disenfranchise blacks, by the mid-20th century it was used to keep the white vote to a level controllable by political leaders. The Crump machine did not permit any opposition; reformers were constantly defeated. Those who opposed it would find their businesses harassed by overzealous city officials determined to enforce the law. If this did not work, the machine used strong-arm tactics.

Crump's support of the national Democratic Party did not survive the war. He was particularly displeased with Truman's stand on civil rights. Crump was not a strident racist. In fact, blacks were an important component of his machine. However, he believed in segregation and opposed all attempts to begin integration. The president, he said, had made a "coldblooded effort to outdo HENRY WALLACE and Governor [THOMAS E.] DEWEY . . . for the Negro vote, he has endeavored to reduce the South to a country of crawling cowards." In March 1948 he lashed out at ELEANOR ROOSEVELT for her "frogging around with her Communist associates in America." She was, Crump asserted, "practically Truman's mentor. The time has come for a showdown in the South." Crump also accused Congress of Industrial Organizations organizers of communism.

The showdown came in the state's 1948 senatorial primary. Liberals backed Republican ESTES KEFAUVER (D-Tenn.), who had supported the New Deal and opposed the poll tax. Crump dumped the incumbent, Senator Thomas Stewart (D-Tenn.), and replaced him with John A. Mitchell, a veteran who could gain the support of former soldiers. Stewart, however, decided to remain in the race. Crump ran Mitchell's campaign on the issue of Kefauver's alleged Communist sympathies. He pointed to similarities between Kefauver's record and that of leftist VITO MARCANTONIO. In addition, Crump maintained, he had voted against the House Un-American Activities Committee and had spoken before left-wing organizations. Crump unwittingly gave Kefauver a campaign slogan when he compared him to a raccoon. Kefauver replied that he might be a raccoon, but he was not Crump's raccoon, and he took to wearing what became his signature coonskin cap. Kefauver won the primary largely because of the vote split between Mitchell and Stewart.

Although this election was interpreted as a major defeat for the machine, Crump soon recovered, and, until his death in 1954, his candidates continued to win elections. The boss eventually made peace with Kefauver. However, he did not reconcile himself with Truman. In 1948 he supported the Dixiecrat candidate for president, J. STROM THURMOND. Crump died of a heart ailment on October 16, 1954, in Memphis Tennessee.

—JB

Curran, Joseph E(dwin)

(1906–1981) *president, National Maritime Union*

Born March 1, 1906, in New York City, Joseph E. Curran was the son of Irish-American parents and became a seaman at 16. He joined the independent Marine Workers Industrial Union in 1930 and, after it disbanded in the mid-1930s, became a member of the AFL's International Seamen's Union (ISU). He led an unsuccessful wildcat strike of the crew of the S.S. *California* that same year. In 1936 he refused the settlement negotiated between the ISU and the maritime companies and lead 35,000 ISU members out of the union to form the National Maritime Union. The new union joined the Congress of Industrial Organizations (CIO), at that time more leftist than its rival, the AFL.

In 1937 Curran was elected as the first NMU president. Between 1938 and 1946 he worked closely with Communist Party members in leading the new union, and although he claimed he never joined the party—experts disagree on this point—almost all the other top NMU officials were members of the party. In 1940 Curran usually followed the party line, such as opposing Roosevelt's defense policy and lend-lease until the Soviet Union was attacked in June 1941. Once the United States and the Soviet Union were allied, Curran agreed to a no-strike pledge and served on the War Manpower Commission. Curran ran unsuccessfully for Congress on the American Labor Party Ticket in 1940.

In early 1946 seven leading CIO seafarer's and longshoremen's unions formed a "united front" Committee for Maritime Unity (CMU) to bolster contractual negotiations. It was co-chaired by Curran and HARRY A. BRIDGES, president of the International Longshoremen's and Warehousemen's Union. The CMU's actions culminated in a general strike on the nation's waterfronts during the summer of 1946. In addition to serving as CMU cochairman, Curran was also president of the Greater New York Industrial Union Council (CIO) and official of the World Trade Union Federation. In November 1946 he became a CIO vice president. After the war he served as a representative to several international labor conferences, and he was a member of the first U.S. labor delegation to the Soviet Union since 1927.

In December 1946 Curran broke with the CMU, claiming that Bridges had prolonged the strike because of Communist policies aimed at creating a national maritime crisis; he also charged that the CMU was run by Communists. Curran further argued that the NMU's financial support of the CMU was draining the union. In addition, he feared that the strike's success would serve to extend Bridges's influence into the East Coast waterfront, a challenge he did not want to face. Curran's break with the CMU set the stage for a bitter political struggle within the NMU.

In early 1947 Curran began his campaign to expel Communists from the union. He started by attacking a number of vice presidents, who were acknowledged party members, for disrupting the union, falsifying election ballots, and staffing the organization with fellow Communists. Not surprisingly, a number of these vice presidents had opposed his break with the CMU. Curran charged that, although there were only some 500 Communists among the union's 70,000 members, they controlled 107 of the 150 elected offices.

Curran's growing anticommunist stand coincided with a move within the CIO to expel Communists. At the CIO's November 1946 convention the delegates unanimously adopted a resolution rejecting any interference from the Communist Party or any other party. In March 1947 the CIO Executive Board established a special subcommittee, headed by Curran, to bar Communists from all CIO seafaring unions. Five months later Congress passed the Taft-Hartley Act, which, in part, required union leaders to sign noncommunist affidavits in order to receive certification from the National Labor Relations Board. In September Curran, along with CIO president PHILIP MURRAY and nine other CIO leaders, refused to sign the pledge because it violated their constitutional rights. During the spring 1948 union election campaign, Curran supporters wore buttons proclaiming, "Vote Rank-and-File Slate—Smash Communist Control in NMU." They won the election by nearly a three-to-one majority, securing all 32 seats on the NMU National Council and greater control over the New York port, the Communist stronghold.

Curran moved decisively to rid the union of Communists and consolidate his control over the New York port in 1949. At the September convention, the union adopted a resolution backed by Curran barring Communists from joining the union. The right-wing forces behind him triumphed on almost every issue, including one

expelling 40 "left-wing disruptives." Among those dismissed were the union's former national secretary, a key vice president, and the head of the New York port. Following the convention Curran appointed a trusted vice president to administer the New York port.

The officer immediately dismissed the elected port agent and 14 other local representatives. This action precipitated a four-month period of violent confrontation between Curran supporters and opponents. By year's end Curran had forced the leftists out and secured control of the New York port. At the 1949 CIO national convention, Curran and WALTER P. REUTHER led a purge of pro-Communist unions and Executive Board members. During this period he was also active in a move to withdraw the CIO from the Communist-dominated World Federation of Trade Unions.

Following HENRY A. WALLACE's announcement to run for president on a third-party ticket in January 1948, the CIO Executive Board voted 33 to 11 against support of a third party; Curran was one of those who voted in the minority. The NMU suffered a major setback in early 1950 when the Supreme Court ruled that the union's hiring halls were discriminating against nonunion seamen and violating the Taft-Hartley Act. Curran assailed the decision, saying that the ruling would give Communists "a field day." During the 1950s Curran saw the reestablishment of hiring halls, repeal of the Taft-Hartley Act, the 40-hour workweek for seamen, and the establishment of an employer-financed health and welfare plan as the principal goals of the union. In July 1950 Curran was reelected NMU president by a six-to-one majority.

Following the expulsion of the marine cooks and stewards union from the CIO in early 1951, Curran led an unsuccessful attempt to recruit the union's 7,000 members into the NMU. During the summer of 1951 Curran led a successful NMU work stoppage against East and Gulf Coast maritime companies over wages, hours, and benefits issues. President Truman did not invoke the Taft-Hartley Act to stop the stoppage because the union promised not to tie up defense, foreign aid, and other essential cargoes.

Following NMU affiliation with the AFL-CIO in 1955, Curran became one of its vice presidents and a member of the executive committee, where he frequently wrangled with organization president

GEORGE MEANY. The issues included the organization's policy of endorsing presidential candidates and the expulsion of the Teamsters from the AFL-CIO. In the late 1960s Curran faced growing opposition to his leadership. He retired as president in 1973. He successfully fended off a challenge by NMU dissidents to his million-dollar pension and died in Boca Raton, Florida, on August 14, 1981. (See *The Eisenhower Years, The Kennedy Years, The Johnson Years, The Nixon/Ford Years* Volumes)

—DMR

D

Davidson, C(row) Girard

(1910–1996) *assistant secretary of the interior*

C. Girard "Jebby" Davidson was born on July 28, 1910, in Lafayette, Louisiana. Raised in that state, he received his A.B. from Southwestern Louisiana Institute in 1930 and his LL.B. from Tulane University in 1933. After winning admission to the Louisiana bar in 1933, he pursued graduate studies for a year as a Sterling Fellow at Yale University. An ardent New Dealer, young Davidson served as attorney for the Tennessee Valley Authority (TVA) in Knoxville from 1934 to 1937. He spent nine months in 1939 as an attorney with the U.S. Housing Authority before moving to Oregon where, from 1943 to 1946, he served as general counsel for the Bonneville Power Administration. In this post Davidson worked toward his goal of public utilities ownership, often encouraging sympathetic journalists to prod the power administration into a more vigorous advocacy of public ownership.

Appointed assistant secretary of the interior in 1946, Davidson gained a reputation among his colleagues and the press as a zealous reformer. Constantly prodding his superiors toward more liberal policies, he pleaded for President Truman to attack the conservative programs of the 80th Congress, arguing, for instance, that the president should veto the Taft-Hartley bill. Through his friend CLARK CLIFFORD, Truman's chief aide and a major presidential speech writer, many of his views made their way into Truman's speeches. Davidson was a member of what Clifford called the "Monday-Night Group," which had about six "core members" that met every two weeks starting in the winter of 1946–47. Besides urging the veto of Taft-Hartley, the group urged Truman to recognize Israel, among other things.

In December 1946 Davidson told the American Society of Mechanical Engineers that they should work to stop the wasting of natural gas, such as through flaring. He suggested an industry advisory group should be employed as the best way to foster government and industry cooperation. He advised something had to be done as there was only a 30-year supply in the domestic reserves of natural gas. Davidson also said engineers should help create and develop petroleum substitutes as there was estimated to be only a 12-year supply of reserve at the 1944 rate of extraction.

In a September 1948 letter Davidson attacked Secretary of Commerce CHARLES SAWYER for siding with the Steel Products Advisory Committee in denying additional steel needed for drill pipes and tubing in the petroleum industry. When, in his 1949 State of the Union message, President Truman urged government aid to expand the steel industry, including government construction of new plants if necessary, he was echoing a plan Davidson had advocated almost two months earlier. While most of the Interior Department favored privately owned utilities, Davidson fought for the establishment of regional power authorities similar to the TVA to provide cheap power and combat severe postwar power shortages. Members of Congress from the Northwest who were pushing for these regional power authorities in the Missouri and Columbia River valleys relied on Davidson to be their advocate in the executive branch. In January 1949 President Truman also endorsed the TVA method.

In April 1949 Davidson called for increased electrical power output and lower rates, saying they were necessary for continued prosperity. He contended that, to keep the economy in good shape, the total capacity of the country's power system had to be doubled in 10 years. Also, electricity rates would have to be reduced from 3 to 5 cents a kilowatt hour to 1.5 cents so Americans could afford to buy and use electrical appliances to achieve a higher standard of living.

In 1950 Davidson resigned his Interior Department post to return to private law practice and to pursue a political career in Oregon. From 1956 to 1963 he was a member of the Democratic National Committee from Oregon and from 1960 to 1963 served as chairman of the Democratic Committee on Natural Resources. Davidson died on September 20, 1996, in Portland, Oregon.

—DAE

Davies, John P(atton), Jr.

(1908–1999) *State Department officer*

The son of a Baptist missionary, John Patton Davies was born on April 6, 1908, in Kiating, China; he spent his early years in China. Before receiving his bachelor's degree from Columbia in 1931, he studied at the University of Wisconsin and Yenching University. Davies joined the Foreign Service after graduation and soon returned to China as a consul. During the 1940s he served as an adviser to both Joseph Stillwell, the American military attache, and PATRICK J. HURLEY, the U.S. ambassador. During that period Davies issued frequent reports and policy recommendations on the Chinese civil war. The diplomat was a dispassionate observer who viewed foreign relations in terms of realpolitik rather than morality. He expressed little hope that the Nationalists, led by Chiang Kai-shek (Jiang Jieshi), could win the war because of corruption in the regime and the generalissimo's own inability to rally his people. Yet he did not see the Communists as the moral force of the future either, assuming that, once in power, they too would become corrupt. Davies viewed the civil war as a conflict foreigners could not understand and a struggle in which the United States should not become deeply involved. In a memo to Stillwell written in January 1944, Davies outlined his recommendations for future American goals in the Far East. He urged a military and political mission to the Chinese Communists to prevent them from moving closer to Moscow. Later he found that he underestimated the Communists' pro-Soviet inclinations and what he saw as a Communist belief in democracy was, rather, merely a reflection of their popularity.

That November Davis worked with Hurley in an attempt to create a truce between Mao Zedong (Mao Tse-tung) and Chiang. Davies recommended that the United States not abandon Chiang but continue to recognize his government and give it nominal support until a coalition could be created. However, if China went Communist, as he assumed it would, the United States must be prepared to work with Mao to prevent a Sino-Soviet alliance.

Hurley interpreted this position to be pro-Communist. As additional proof he cited a memo by Davies recommending that if Chiang did not cooperate with the United States to defeat the Japanese, the United States should aid "whatever Chinese forces we believe can contribute most to the war against Japan." The ambassador inferred that Davies advocated the U.S. support of the Communists. Following his resignation in November 1945, Hurley became a spokesman for the "China Lobby," a loose coalition of businessmen, religious leaders, and politicians who believed that a pro-Communist conspiracy in government was sabotaging policies helpful to Chiang. Hurley cited Davies as one of these disloyal Americans.

The China Lobby began an extensive campaign to pressure the government to rid itself of Davies. However, until the beginning of the Eisenhower administration, the pro-Chiang forces failed. From 1947 to 1951 Davies served on the prestigious State Department Policy Planning Staff. He then joined the U.S. High Commission in Germany and was director of political affairs at the U.S. mission in Bonn from 1951 to 1953. Despite the complaints of the China Lobby, Davies advocated a forceful anticommunist foreign policy. He declared the pro-Soviet attitude of Chinese Communists as reprehensible and, in 1950, contended the United States should use its superiority in atomic bombs to provoke a showdown with the Soviets. Soon after the Korean War began, Davis warned of the increasing likelihood of Chinese intervention. He urged the Truman administration to tell the Chinese government that, if it did intervene, the United States would launch a bombing campaign against China. Davies also assisted in arranging unofficial Soviet-American talks that led to peace negotiations in Korea. Nevertheless, between 1948 and 1953 Davies underwent eight security investigations. Each cleared him, but the continued probes heightened implications of his guilt. His most difficult investigation was conducted in 1951 by the Senate Internal

Security Subcommittee. Following the fall of China to the Communists, Davies had served on a tripartite committee, composed of members of the State and Defense departments and the Central Intelligence Agency (CIA), to develop clandestine ways of keeping abreast of developments in China. Lyle H. Munson, the CIA liaison, asked Davies for a list of individuals acquainted with the Communist leadership who could provide information to the intelligence agency. Davies recommended a number of experts who shared many of his earlier views on the course of the civil war. Munson leaked the names to Alfred Kohlberg, a top China Lobby official, who then gave them to Senator JOSEPH R. MCCARTHY (R-Wisc.). McCarthy offered the list as evidence that Davies had tried to infiltrate the government with individuals considered Communists. The subcommittee examined the charges and cleared the diplomat.

Secretary of State JOHN FOSTER DULLES dismissed Davies in 1954 for failing to meet the standards of a Foreign Service official. His action came after a ninth investigation by the State Department Loyalty Board, which ruled Davies disloyal based, in part, on earlier testimony by Hurley. Following his dismissal, Davies opened a furniture business in Lima, Peru, where he had been stationed. In 1964 he returned to Washington to request a review of his case. His name was cleared in 1968. Davies died on December 23, 1999, in Asheville, North Carolina. (See *The Eisenhower Years* Volume)

—JB

Davis, Chester C(harles)

(1887–1975) *presidential adviser*

Chester C. Davis was born on November 17, 1887, in Linden, Iowa, and was the son of a tenant farmer. He graduated from Grinnell College in 1911 and served as managing editor of the *Montana Farmer* from 1911 to 1917. Davis became state commissioner of agriculture and labor in 1921, director of grain marketing for the Illinois Agricultural Association in 1925, and executive vice president for the Maizewood Products Corporation in 1929. Four years later he was appointed administrator of the Agricultural Adjustment Administration. There he supported Franklin D. Roosevelt's efforts to deal with agricultural surpluses and low farm income by limiting planting. Davis was a member of the Federal Reserve Board of Governors from 1936 to 1941

and headed the National Defense Commission's agricultural division from 1940 to 1941. He then resigned to accept the presidency of the Federal Reserve Bank of St. Louis. He served at that post for 10 years. In April 1943 Roosevelt called him back to Washington to become War Food Program administrator. Davis resigned three months later, charging that the administration had failed to grant him real authority over food prices and had become subservient to the wishes of the unions.

During the postwar period Davis became prominent in efforts to rebuild Western Europe. He looked toward foreign aid, especially American agricultural exports, as the keystone to European recovery as well as to increasing U.S. prosperity and world stability. In 1946 he headed the president's Famine Emergency Committee, formed to make food available to Europe. The following year he was appointed a member of the president's Committee on Foreign Aid, European Recovery, and American Aid and was named chairman of its Food Resources Subcommittee. The committee report urged that Europe be given assistance for strategic reasons as well as to meet humanitarian needs. The panel stressed that such action would benefit the U.S. economy by eventually restoring the balance of payments and lessening the danger of inflation. Davis's own subcommittee asserted that food was the prime requisite for European recovery. Surveying the needs abroad and at home, the committee advocated grain rationing and broader presidential powers over U.S. agricultural production and distribution. It concluded that the European food shortage was "a source of insecurity not only to the food deficient countries, but also through its effects on political stability throughout the world to ourselves. . . ." The dissolution of the committee in 1946 was the last advisory post for Davis in Washington.

Davis returned to his business in St. Louis and became associate director of the Ford Foundation in 1951, where he helped formulate and implement the foundation's plans for India and Pakistan. He retired in 1953 to resume his business career. Davis died on September 25, 1975, in Winston-Salem, North Carolina.

—AES

Davis, Elmer H(olmes)

(1890–1958) *news commentator*

Born on January 13, 1890, in Aurora, Indiana, Elmer H. Davis was the son of a small town banker.

He earned a bachelor's degree from Franklin College in 1910 and a master's degree the following year. He then went to Oxford on a Rhodes Scholarship. From 1914 to 1924 Davis worked for the *New York Times* as a sports writer, political analyst, foreign correspondent, and editorial writer. For political convention analysis he invented the Hoosier political commentator Godfrey G. Gloom from Amity, Indiana. During the 1920s and 1930s he pursued a successful literary career as a writer of romantic novels, short stories, and historical essays.

Davis began a career as a radio commentator in 1939, when CBS invited him to fill in for H. V. Kaltenborn, who was in Europe. His candid, witty style made him extremely popular and, by 1941, he had an audience of 12.5 million listeners daily. President Roosevelt—who referred to Davis as the man "with the funny voice, Elmer-Elmer Something"—appointed him director of the Office of War Information (OWI) in 1942, where he was in charge of coordinating government war news and propaganda. Davis insisted on freedom of information even in wartime and clashed with the president over the issue. In the last months of the war in Europe, Davis helped coordinate the work of the OWI and the Psychological Warfare Branch in Germany.

Davis returned to radio broadcasting as a commentator for ABC in 1945. A liberal anticommunist, he supported much of the Truman administration's foreign and domestic program. He reluctantly backed Truman's request for aid to Greece and Turkey, hoping that the rightist Greek government could be reformed by its means. Davis warned against appeasement of Communists, maintaining that despite ideological differences communism and fascism practiced the same methods. Following the outbreak of the Korean conflict in 1950, he told his audience, "This is where we came in, say, about 1938, when the pattern of totalitarian aggression had been clear." He praised Syngman Rhee's aggressive anticommunism and supported unconditional Communist surrender in Korea and the unification of the North and South by UN forces.

The commentator took a decisive stand against the domestic anticommunist crusade of the late 1940s and early 1950s. He opposed outlawing the Communist Party in March 1947, when it was urged by Secretary of Labor LEWIS B. SCHWELLENBACH. In his view the Constitution was "too good a barn to burn down just to get rid of a few rats." Davis denounced the tactics of Senator JOSEPH R.

MCCARTHY (R-Wisc.) and warned his listeners that the most dangerous menace to American freedom was not the Soviet Union but the demagogic techniques of the Wisconsin senator and his followers who attacked freedom of speech. Davis compared McCarthy's techniques to those of Hitler and Stalin, and he warned his radio audience that McCarthyite victories in the 1950 elections were endangering American liberties. He defended OWEN LATTIMORE, a noted Far Eastern scholar and former OWI overseas employee, against McCarthy's allegations that Lattimore was a Communist. In an article in the *New Leader*, Davis said that Lattimore must not be abandoned since that would "mean that the anticommunist left must keep its mouth shut, leave the field to McCarthy, and regard everyone whom he accuses as guilty until he proves his innocence." When he contended that Americans "had better wait and see if the evidence justified conviction," one angry audience member penned a letter saying, "We cannot wait for convictions; what we want is confessions." Davis wrote that he did not like talking about McCarthy, but to not do so "would be as if people refused to mention the anopheles mosquito in a malarial country. (There is a quinine that can neutral his venom; it is called courage. It does not seem to be widely distributed in the upper ranks of the government.)"

In October 1953 Davis retired from his nightly news broadcast because of poor health, but the following year he began a weekly TV news commentary program. During the 1950s he published two books, *But We Are Born Free* (1954), a series of revised letters and articles attacking McCarthy, and *Two Minutes to Midnight* (1955), which outlined his opposition to JOHN FOSTER DULLES's policy of massive retaliation. Davis died on May 18, 1958, in Washington, D.C.

—AES

Davis, John W(illiam)
(1873–1955) *attorney*

Born the son of a leading West Virginia lawyer on April 13, 1873, in Clarksburg, West Virginia, John W. Davis received a law degree from Washington and Lee University in 1895 and then entered his father's firm. He served a term in the West Virginia House of Delegates in 1899 and one in the U.S. House of Representatives beginning in 1911. Woodrow Wilson appointed him Solicitor General in 1913. During his five years at that post, Davis argued 67 cases before the Supreme Court—defending much of Wilson's progressive legislation—and won 48; Justice Oliver Wendell Holmes said of him, "Of all the persons who appeared before the Court in my time, there was never anybody more clear, more concise, or more logical than John W. Davis." He eventually earned a reputation as one of America's greatest Solicitor Generals. Davis was named ambassador to Great Britain in 1918 and served as adviser to Wilson at Versailles. In 1921 he joined the Wall Street law firm of Stetson, Jennings, and Russell. A man who considered himself a Jeffersonian-Republican, Davis achieved a nationwide reputation as a corporate counsel who argued against expansion of government power into the commercial sector. In 1924 he ran unsuccessfully for the presidency against the Republican incumbent, Calvin Coolidge.

Davis supported Franklin D. Roosevelt for president in 1932, but he quickly became disillusioned with the expansion of federal government under the New Deal. He argued against much of the president's legislative program in the courts, including the National Labor Relations Act. He helped establish the ultraconservative Liberty League. A strong civil libertarian, he battled for the rights of conscientious objecters during World War II.

Davis continued his struggle against government interference in civil liberties and business during the Truman administration. As vice president of the Carnegie Endowment for International Peace, he supported its president ALGER HISS during a House Un-American Activities Committee investigation into his loyalty. He gave Hiss legal advice during the probe and appeared as a character witness before the panel. When Hiss asked to resign from the endowment, the board of directors, led by Davis, rejected his plea, giving him a leave without pay instead. Although he backed the United Nations and President Harry S Truman's containment policy, he condemned his Fair Deal.

During 1952 Davis served as counsel for the steel industry during its court fight against Truman's seizure of the steel mills. The president had ordered Secretary of Commerce CHARLES SAWYER to seize the mills following a breakdown in labor negotiations, which threatened a strike. Truman justified his action on the grounds that a strike could jeopardize national security by stopping production of materials needed for the war in Korea. On April 11,

1952, Davis sought an injunction against the action. Federal District judge DAVID A. PINE granted it on the grounds that Truman's action was unconstitutional because he could have invoked the Taft-Hartley Act. Pine then ordered the government to return the properties to the industry. As a result, the United Steelworkers went on strike. The government then asked the Court of Appeals for a stay, which was subsequently granted, and the strike was called off. The industry appealed to the Supreme Court.

While industry lawyers constructed the written brief, Davis handled the oral argument before the Court. The lawyer pointed out that the government had conceded that Truman had acted under no statutory authority. Congress, he maintained, had passed the Taft-Hartley Act specifically to deal with emergencies such as that faced by the steel industry. It had deliberately not included a seizure provision under the statute. The implementation of the Taft-Hartley Act was not mandatory, but in trying to seize the mills, Davis maintained that the president had attempted to make legislation, thus violating the separation of powers doctrine of the Constitution. Davis argued that Truman's action was unprecedented and "a reassertion of the kingly prerogative, the struggle against which illumines all the pages of Anglo-Saxon history." Representing the government, Solicitor General PHILIP B. PERLMAN asserted that the crisis of war was so great that Truman had no choice but to resort to seizure. The Court sided with Davis and the steel industry, arguing that the president's conduct amounted to an unconstitutional usurpation of the lawmaking power.

During the 1950s Davis defended South Carolina's segregated school system in a series of cases that became known as *Brown v. Board of Education*. He also served as legal counsel to J. ROBERT OPPENHEIMER during the government's investigation of his loyalty. During his legal career, which spanned over half a century, Davis appeared before the Supreme Court more than any other attorney. Davis firmly believed in stare decisis, states' rights, and a strict constructionism when it came to the Constitution. He adamantly contended that property and human rights could not be separated. He was commonly considered one of the great advocates of his age. Davis died on March 24, 1955, in Charleston, South Carolina. (See *The Eisenhower Years* Volume)

—RSG

Dawson, Donald S(helton)

(1908–   ) *administrative assistant to the president*

Donald Dawson was born on August 3, 1908, in El Dorado Springs, Missouri. He received his B.A. degree from the University of Missouri in 1930. After graduation he moved to Washington, D.C., and worked in the credit section of the Reconstruction Finance Corporation (RFC) while attending George Washington University Law School. Dawson received his LL.B. degree in 1938. Between 1933 and 1939 he rose through the ranks to the position of loan liquidation examiner. From 1939 to 1941, he worked for the Federal Loan Administration. Returning to the RFC in 1941, Dawson was promoted to personnel director. He also served with the ground safety division of the air force during World War II. President Truman chose Dawson as his personnel director in charge of patronage recommendations in August 1947. Dawson initiated FBI field investigations of all proposed presidential appointments. Also, he revised the Classification Act in 1949, which set federal employees' compensation and grades. Dawson helped formulate RFC policy because of his experience and his position in the White House.

Following World War II the RFC flourished as an easy-credit government agency and increasingly extended loans to speculative ventures such as oil wells and resort hotels. The financial collapse of the RFC-backed businesses between 1947 and 1950 prompted headlines accusing the Truman administration of mismanagement, favoritism, and the application of pressure to the agency. The accusation charged that Dawson used his influence to obtain appointments and promotions at the RFC and conspired with a group of lawyers and influence peddlers in Washington, who, in return for fees and lengthy employment, would make the case of borrowers to the RFC. These debtors were then expected to contribute to the Democrats.

In February 1950 a Senate banking and currency subcommittee, headed by Senator J. WILLIAM FULBRIGHT (D-Ark.), quietly opened an investigation of the RFC. Not long after the investigation began, Dawson convinced Truman that Fulbright was gunning for him—which was not far from the truth for Fulbright saw the president as a burden to the Democratic Party and wanted to prevent his renomination in 1952. Dawson then arranged for the appointment of three pliable directors to the RFC. Fulbright stopped their confirmation, and

then arranged a meeting with the president to discuss reorganizing the RFC. According to Fulbright it was a friendly meeting, but two weeks later, Truman resubmitted the three unacceptable nominees. Dawson attempted to end funding of Fulbright's subcommittee, working through Senator Burnett Maybank (D-S.C.), chairman of the Banking and Currency Committee and a supporter of the administration. It came to nothing, but Fulbright was tired of playing games and released an interim report in February 1951 titled "Favoritism and Influence" without giving an advance copy to Truman. It accused the RFC of mismanagement and blasted Dawson for being part of an influence-peddling ring having sway over some RFC directors. The relationship between Dawson and directors Walter L. Dunham and William E. Willett was especially criticized. It specifically accused RFC director Dunham, a Truman appointee, of being completely subordinate to Dawson for fear of being fired. Two other directors said Willett did whatever Dawson told him to do. The committee also accused the administration of turning a blind eye toward the scandal. Truman erupted, calling the report "asinine," and maintained that the charges were directed against him. Fulbright responded by opening public hearings with sworn testimony in late February 1951.

Testifying the following month, Dunham said he felt "used" by Dawson. He stated he had promised the Truman aide to "work in harmony with the Democratic Party" but denied Dawson had ever tried to influence his decisions at the RFC. Some people in the administration urged Truman to oust Dawson, but the president would not turn his back on his friend. Truman also assured reporters he did not intend to fire Dawson.

Probably on Dawson's suggestion Truman collected letters from representatives and senators trying to influence the RFC's decisions, including letters written by Fulbright and other members of the committee. He let one of the members of the panel, CHARLES W. TOBEY (R-N.H.), know that he might reveal that the members of the committee were the "real crooks and influence peddlers." Truman did not release the letters, but he had called into question the integrity of some of the members of Congress. (Tobey would later charge White House aide DAVID K. NILES and former senator Burton K. Wheeler with trying to influence him to "go easy" on Dawson.) Despite all the acrimony, Truman did support a Fulbright-sponsored reorganization plan for the RFC that replaced the five-member board of directors with a single administrator.

Dawson himself appeared before the subcommittee in May. He denied ever trying to influence the RFC but stated that all appointments to the agency were first cleared by the Democratic National Committee. Dawson admitted accepting free vacations at Miami Beach's Saxony Hotel, which had received a $1.5 million RFC loan, and admitted vacationing at the estate of Rex Jacobs whose company had received a $3 million loan. He denied any impropriety and pointed out that several senators had accepted free vacations at the Saxony.

Following Dawson's testimony, Truman called a press conference and reiterated support for his aide. In fact Fulbright, in his closing statement, told Dawson that the hearings had not been directed at him, but at the RFC, and that he had only been the "necessary background" to the hearings. Dawson was quite bitter about the hearings and accused the committee of "intellectual McCarthyism." No perjury charges were brought against the presidential aide. The committee's report, released in August 1951 and approved by a majority of the full Senate Banking and Currency Committee, substantiated Fulbright's accusations that pressures were at work in the RFC. The agency was abolished during the Eisenhower administration. Dawson continued to serve as Truman's patronage chief until the end of the administration. He was the last to leave the White House with Truman following the inauguration of President Dwight D. Eisenhower. He then established a law practice in Washington.

—MJS

Dawson, William L(evi)
(1886–1970) *member of the House of Representatives*

William L. Dawson was born on April 26, 1886, in Albany, Georgia. He graduated magna cum laude from Fisk University in 1909, and moved to Chicago in 1912. There he attended Kent College Law School. He left law school to serve in the military in World War I, where he was injured. He came back from the war to Chicago and finished his law degree at Northwestern University Law School and won admission to the Illinois bar in 1920. A Republican, Dawson ran unsuccessfully for the House of Representatives in 1928. Four years

later he won the race for alderman from Chicago's South Side and served until 1939. In 1938 he ran for Congress as an anti–New Deal Republican and lost. In 1939 he became a Democrat, in part, because his African-American constituents had left the Republican Party for the Democratic Party of Franklin D. Roosevelt. In 1942 he won a seat in the U.S. House of Representatives and was the only African-American representative at that time.

During the 1940s Dawson used his position to build a powerful political machine, which controlled the city's black ghetto. In exchange for votes Dawson delivered low-paying patronage jobs and small favors, such as help with welfare or legal problems. According to journalist Mike Royko, Dawson also protected organized crimes in the wards.

Dawson rose gradually both within the party and within Congress. In 1944 he was named to the Democratic National Committee. The party leadership chose Dawson to head the Negro Division of the Democratic Committee in 1948, and in 1950 he became a vice chairman of the party. In January 1949 Dawson became the first black to head a standing committee in Congress when he assumed chairmanship of the Expenditures (later Government Operations) Committee. JOHN W. MCCORMACK (D-Mass.) waived his seniority to give Dawson the chairmanship. He supported President Harry S Truman's anticommunist foreign policy.

Dawson did not frequently sponsor bills or give speeches. During the early years of his career, his voting participation was low, 38 percent in 1947–48. Instead, he preferred to wield his influence behind the scenes. Dawson was, however, a vocal spokesman for civil rights. In 1943 he took a leading role in the fight against the poll tax. In 1944 he cosponsored the unsuccessful Scanlon-Dawson bill to create a permanent Fair Employment Practices Commission with powers to enforce a ban on racial discrimination in employment, and he railed against discrimination in defense plants. In April 1951 he gave an impassioned speech before the House against a proposal for segregation in the armed services. He told how he was permanently maimed because he had received inferior treatment in a segregated unit during World War I. He appealed to patriotism to unite blacks and whites and pointed out that the greatest propaganda instrument used by the Soviet Union was the treatment of blacks in the United States. The measure was defeated. That same year he and Adam Clayton Powell, Jr. (D-N.Y.), led a successful fight against a proposal to build a separate black veterans' hospital.

Dawson thought the best way for blacks to advance was to work faithfully within the Democratic Party, using that tactic to gain footing to bargain with whites from a position of strength. Consequently, he often placed loyalty to party ahead of support for civil rights. At the 1952 Democratic National Convention, Dawson spoke against attempts to strengthen the civil rights platform and blocked a minority report by liberals. Powell called him the "Uncle Tom" of the convention. Dawson defended himself by saying, "The [platform] committee's job was to work out a good plank that would be effective and hold our great party together. My job was not to disrupt and split the party." The influential black leader helped choose Senator JOHN J. SPARKMAN (D-Ala.) as the running mate of ADLAI E. STEVENSON in 1952.

During the 1950s and 1960s Dawson became more and more alienated from the civil rights movement. He aroused Powell's wrath again in 1956 when he opposed an amendment that would have denied federal funds to segregated schools. Nevertheless, by margins of more than two to one, Dawson turned back attempts by insurgent blacks to unseat him. He decided not to seek reelection in 1970. On November 9 of that year he died of cancer in Chicago. (See *The Eisenhower Years, The Kennedy Years, The Johnson Years* Volumes)

—TFS

Denfeld, Louis E(mil)

(1891–1972) chief of naval operations

Louis E. Denfeld was born on April 13, 1891, in Westboro, Massachusetts. He graduated from the U.S. Naval Academy in 1912. The first few years of his career were spent on battleships, but most of his career was devoted to personnel work. He served as aide to Admiral WILLIAM D. LEAHY during the late 1930s and was chief of staff and aide to the commander of the Atlantic Fleet Support Force during the early 1940s. In 1942 he became assistant to the chief of the Bureau of Navigation. From March to September 1945 Denfeld was on ship duty as a rear admiral, commanding a battleship support unit operating in the Pacific under Admiral William F. Halsey. He was chief of the Bureau of Naval Personnel during 1945 and deputy for personnel to the Chief of Naval Operations from 1945 to 1946. In

this capacity Denfeld was responsible for demobilization and the development of the postwar navy. In February 1947 Denfeld, by then a full admiral, assumed command of the Pacific fleet. In July, soon after the United Nations agreement for U.S. trusteeship of the Pacific islands formerly under Japanese mandate was formalized, Denfeld became high commissioner.

President Truman appointed Denfeld chief of naval operations in December 1947. During his first two years at the post the admiral was a figure in the debate over the role of the navy in a unified defense system. Denfeld disagreed with the idea that wars would be fought with strategic nuclear weapons and that, therefore, strategic bombing should be made the keystone of American striking power. In conjunction with Secretary of Defense JAMES V. FORRESTAL, he recommended a balanced land-sea-air service. Nevertheless, Congress and the administration supported a strong air force and cut navy appropriations in the 1950 fiscal budget. In April 1949 Secretary of Defense LOUIS A. JOHNSON stopped production of the supercarrier *United States*.

The dispute between the services came to a climax during the autumn of 1949, after Denfeld was renominated to another two-year term. In desperation the navy used the hearings on the air force's proposed B-36 bomber to reiterate its position. As historian Jeffrey C. Barlow has noted, Denfeld could not decide how he would testify—one aide told him to battle for naval aviation; another urged caution for fear the CNO would be terminated. During his testimony in October Denfeld stated that the navy was being weakened by decisions from the Joint Chiefs of Staff that he claimed were "uniformed and arbitrary." He thought that the army and air force were seeking to destroy the navy's air arm and warned that, "a navy stripped of its offensive power means a nation stripped of its offensive power." He accused Johnson of violating "the spirit and concept" of the Unification Act in his decisions on the navy. He criticized his decision to cancel the carrier and his order to cut the navy's budget. Denfeld's testimony angered Johnson, Secretary of the Navy FRANCIS P. MATTHEWS, and Chairman of the Joint Chiefs of Staff general OMAR BRADLEY. Bradley denounced the navy's high command in his own testimony. But Denfeld and the other naval officers, as Barlow has indicated, were following the mandated request of the House Armed Services Committee for their honest opinion.

On October 25, Matthews told Truman, "Either Denfeld goes or I do." He believed that Denfeld was "utterly impossible to work with" because of the latter's disagreements with administration policy. Truman removed the admiral at the end of the month.

The president's action unleased a new controversy. Several members of Congress, led by Representative CARL VINSON (D-Ga.), called the dismissal a "purge" and "dictatorship," and they demanded Matthew's resignation. Others termed the action necessary for the success of unification. Denfeld's reaction was expressed when he said, "For 31 years I have been sticking to my guns, and if they want to kick me out, I'm still sticking to my guns." In December 1949 Denfeld rejected an appointment as naval commander in the Eastern Atlantic and Mediterranean. He felt that after being fired as chief of naval operations the nations with which he would have to deal "would not have the necessary respect for and confidence in me."

In January 1950 Senator JOSEPH R. MCCARTHY (R-Wisc.) held up confirmation of Denfeld's successor on charges that the admiral's removal had been illegal. McCarthy contended that Matthews had no power to remove Denfeld after the latter had received a commission, signed by both Matthews and Truman, renewing his appointment, and he proposed that Matthews be impeached by the Senate.

In March 1950 Denfeld retired from the navy and ran unsuccessfully for the Republican nomination for governor of Massachusetts. Denfeld then became a consultant for the Sun Oil Company. He died on March 29, 1972, in Westboro, Massachusetts.

—MLB

Denham, Robert N(ewton)
(1885–1954) *general counsel, National Labor Relations Board*

Robert Denham, the son of Scots immigrants, was born on October 23, 1885, in St. Louis, Missouri. In St. Louis he apprenticed as a machinist during his high school years. He received an LL.B. from the University of Missouri Law School in 1907 and an LL.M. from the University of Michigan in 1908. Forced by ill health to spend two years in Texas, Denham worked as a cowpuncher and served as a county attorney. From 1910 to 1917 he practiced law in Washington State. As a second lieutenant in World War I, he supervised production of aircraft material in Oregon. After his discharge in 1919 he served for two years as a civilian on special duty for the secretary of war.

During the 1920s and early 1930s Denham practiced law, specializing in reorganizing financial institutions. He also engaged in business ventures. In 1933 Denham went to Washington, D.C., where he worked for a year as a special counsel to the comptroller of the currency, helping to reorganize closed banks. He then practiced law in Washington until his selection in 1938 as a trial examiner for the National Labor Relations Board (NLRB), operating under the Wagner Act.

As a trial examiner for the NLRB, Denham traveled all over the country to hear cases involving charges of unfair labor practices. His rulings served as recommendations that could be appealed to the NLRB in Washington and beyond that to the U.S. Circuit Court and Supreme Court. During his nine years as trial examiner, Denham gained a reputation for supporting the claims of management in opposition to the pro-labor views of the NLRB. While many of Denham's antiunion decisions were overruled by the board or the courts, he was responsible for several decisions, including one that said a man fired for union activity must be reinstated but could not claim back pay unless he had applied for work at the U.S. Employment Service. In another ruling, Denham upheld the right of employers to discourage their workers from joining unions. In 1947, when Congress began deliberating the Taft-Hartley bill, Denham submitted a report on what he viewed as Wagner Act abuses to Senator FORREST C. DONNELL (R-Maine), a member of the Senate Labor Committee and Denham's longtime friend. A number of Denham's ideas were written into the measure.

In 1947 President Truman appointed Denham general counsel to the NLRB, a post created under the Taft-Hartley Act. He was to be in charge of the trial examiners, representation cases, and applications for discretionary injunctions. According to R. Alton Lee, the NLRB realized that, since the general counsel had the responsibility to prosecute, he would have to have power over the officials of the board's prosecutor's department. There are two accounts of how Denham got the job. One is that he had to be convinced to take it and not until things were operating smoothly. The other is that he lobbied for the job. According to Lee, Denham's actions as general counsel made it more likely he lobbied for it. The administration appointed Denham, a Republican, so as to ward off criticism that it was evading enforcing the law. Truman told Denham that, although he did not like Taft-Hartley, it was now the law, and he expected it to be enforced. Denham's approach to labor relations was markedly different from that of the administration's. He thought the New Deal NLRB had been too sympathetic to labor and too inclined to side with the unions regardless of what they did. Once appointed Denham extolled Taft-Hartley as "balanced regulating legislation," and excoriated the Wagner Act as one-sided. He also openly criticized the board for its attachment to the original act and its hope that the Taft-Hartley amendments would be repealed.

As an independent prosecutor, Denham was responsible for administering and interpreting the new labor law. He took over many of the powers formerly assigned to the NLRB, including the decision as to what cases should come before the board, the obtaining of injunctions against strikers, and the administration of all regional offices. Denham's pro-management interpretation of the Taft-Hartley Act and exercise of power brought him into conflict not only with the unions, who called for his ouster, but also with the members of the NLRB, who sought to limit his authority. With unions threatening to boycott the NLRB, the board repeatedly overturned Denham's decisions, particularly in cases involving injunctions against union practices. In 1947 Denham insisted on the filing of noncommunist affidavits by officers of national labor organizations before local unions would be allowed to file complaints with the NLRB. The board decided that Denham had misinterpreted the law and overruled him. They also overruled Denham's demand that the board hear every unfair practice complaint he filed and forbade him to hire or fire regional NLRB officers without board approval.

In March 1950 President Truman, attempting to establish "direct lines of authority" in the administration of the Taft-Hartley Act, sent Congress a plan for the reorganization of the NLRB, which would have abolished Denham's post. The Senate rejected this plan. On September 15 Denham resigned at the president's request. Truman blamed the situation leading to Denham's ouster on the

"confusions and conflict" between the General Counsel and the NLRB that had arisen from the "administratively unworkable arrangement" created by the Taft-Hartley Act. Denham returned to private practice in Washington and died of a heart attack on June 18, 1954, in St. Louis, Missouri.

—DAE

Dever, Paul A(ndrew)
(1903–1958) *governor*

Paul Dever was born on January 15, 1903, in Boston, Massachusetts. An Irish Catholic, he came from a family active in Boston politics. Although admitted to Harvard University, he did not attend because his family could not afford the tuition. Instead, he worked his way through Northeastern and Boston universities. After obtaining his degree in 1926, Dever began practicing law in Boston. He was defeated when he ran for the state Senate in 1926, but two years later became the first Democratic member of the General Court to be elected from Cambridge. Reelected in 1930 and 1932, Dever won popularity for his espousal of labor and welfare legislation. In 1934 he won the race for attorney general of Massachusetts, becoming the youngest man to hold that office to date. He was reelected in 1936 and 1938.

Dever ran for governor in 1940, losing narrowly to LEVERETT B. SALTONSTALL. He returned to his law practice and lectured at Boston University from 1941 to 1942. He served in the U.S. Naval Reserve during World War II. In 1946, he waged an unsuccessful campaign for lieutenant governor.

In 1948 Dever again ran for governor. He was helped in winning the primary in September 1948 when former governor MAURICE J. TOBIN abandoned the race when President Truman appointed him secretary of labor. Aided by a strong Democratic political organization, he concentrated his attack on the deteriorating condition of Massachusetts highways under the Republican administration, deriding them as "washboard roads." He pledged to maintain the 10-cent bus and subway fare in the state's Metropolitan Transit Authority (MTA) against Republican predictions that it would have to be raised to 15 cents. Dever avoided the more sensitive issues, such as state referendums on the closed shop and state birth control information centers. Instead, he avowed his support of a "consumer's counsel" to participate in state investigations. He campaigned for increased aid to state hospitals and mental institutions and backed an amendment to the state constitution providing for a graduated income tax. He urged pay raises for state employees and opposed sales tax proposals. Dever beat the incumbent Robert F. Bradford by a margin of 300,000 votes, carrying a Democratic lower house with him in a contest that witnessed the greatest voter participation in Massachusetts to that date.

As governor, Dever pushed for more federal aid to New England to alleviate the effects of the postwar recession. He attempted to redeem his campaign promise to preserve Boston's 10-cent fare by calling for the MTA to be exempt from taxes, for it to be designated as a public highway eligible for $1.9 million in state assistance, and for any operational deficit to be paid for out of the state's general fund. The legislature, however, would only exempt the MTA from certain taxes, and fares had to be increased in August 1949 and January 1950.

An anticommunist, he signed a bill in August 1949, barring Communists from holding government jobs and requiring loyalty oaths from applicants. He proclaimed November 27 Herbert A. Philbrick Day in 1951 to honor a former-FBI agent from Boston who had infiltrated the American Communist Party and spied on it for nine years.

Dever won reelection to the governorship in 1950. His popularity declined in May 1952, when he requested authorization from the legislature to seize the Eastern Massachusetts Street Railway, which served 75 Massachusetts cities. The American Federation of Labor's carmen's union had launched a strike against the system in March.

Dever delivered the keynote address at the 1952 Democratic National Convention. He fervently denounced Republican "dinosaurs of political thought" who believed that "the present global struggle can be ended victoriously with lower taxes, fewer soldiers and no allies." A victim of the Eisenhower landslide of that year, he lost his bid for reelection to CHRISTIAN A. HERTER by a narrow margin of less than 200,000 votes out of a total of 3.5 million cast. Dever remained active in state politics after his defeat. He died of a heart attack on April 11, 1958, in Cambridge, Massachusetts.

—AES

Dewey, Thomas E(dmund)
(1902–1971) *governor, Republican Party presidential candidate*

Born on March 24, 1902, in Owosso, Michigan, Thomas E. Dewey grew up in this central Michigan town, where his father was postmaster and published the Republican newspaper. After earning his B.A. in 1923 at the University of Michigan, Dewey enrolled at Columbia Law School in New York City. Although he seriously contemplated a career in opera (he possessed a resonant baritone that served him well in politics), Dewey completed his legal studies in 1925. Practicing law for the next decade (except for five weeks as acting U.S. attorney for the southern district of New York), Dewey established an impressive record as a trial attorney. In 1935 Governor Herbert H. Lehman named him special prosecutor to investigate racketeering and vice in New York. Two years later Dewey won election on the Republican ticket as district attorney for New York County. He earned a national reputation as a crime fighter. In 1938 he narrowly lost to Democrat Lehman in the New York gubernatorial election. His strong showing, however, made him the early favorite, despite his youth, for the 1940 Republican presidential nomination. He lost to Wendell L. Wilkie. Two years later, when Wilkie declined Republican leaders' offers of the New York gubernatorial nomination, Dewey ran again, this time winning handily and thus becoming the first Republican governor of New York in 20 years. He easily won reelection in 1946 and 1950.

As governor, Dewey proved an efficient administrator and advocate of some social reforms. He oversaw a long delayed reapportionment of congressional and legislative districts, and aided the state's private and public universities. For instance, he had three military bases converted into colleges for discharged soldiers and initiated the creation of the State University of New York. Dewey backed a bill (Ives-Quinn) setting up the Fair Employment Practices Commission, which made employment discrimination by race and religion a misdemeanor, subject to a $500 fine or one year in jail. The bill passed and Representative Adam Clayton Powell of Harlem called it the most important advance for African Americans since the Fourteenth and Fifteenth Amendments. Similar laws followed in ending discrimination in education and public housing. In a postwar period filled with labor strife, he successfully ended a strike by 15,000 building service

Governor Thomas Dewey talking to reporters, 1951 *(Harry S. Truman Library, Abbie Rowe)*

employees, which brought him national attention. He liberalized the state unemployment insurance law and committed New York to an ambitious public housing and highway expansion program. Writing in 1949, the journalist Robert G. Spivak considered Dewey's gubernatorial tenure relatively "cautious" and "unimaginative" but also found that Dewey was "intelligent, has administrative ability, and lives on his salary—three qualities rare in a New York politician."

Despite an initial reluctance to run against Franklin D. Roosevelt, Dewey campaigned for and won the Republican presidential nomination in 1944. In contesting Roosevelt in the midst of World War II, he faced and never overcame great odds. At first Dewey conducted a unity-oriented campaign,

but Roosevelt and his supporters eventually provoked him into intense personal attacks on the administration. He lost, receiving 44.5 percent of the popular vote to Roosevelt's 52.8 percent.

Despite his 1944 defeat Dewey remained a prospect for 1948. His overwhelming 1946 gubernatorial race victory, winning with 58.6 percent of the vote, caused Walter Lippmann to declare the governor the most likely opponent to Truman in the next election. He consistently commanded the largest share of GOP voter support in the Gallup polls, and Democratic strategists expected him to be the Republican nominee. Dewey strengthened his identification with the GOP's Eastern, internationalist wing by his early support of the Truman administration's pleas for a bipartisan foreign policy. He loaned Truman his foreign policy adviser, JOHN FOSTER DULLES, for diplomatic services and endorsed the president's containment policies. In March 1947 Dewey backed the Greek-Turkish aid bill; later in that year, he spoke for the Marshall Plan. The extent and rapidity with which Dewey embraced these actions reinforced suspicions of him by the GOP's conservative, nationalist wing led by Senator ROBERT A. TAFT (R-Ohio). Only Dewey's repeated pleas in 1947 and 1948 for greater U.S. aid to Nationalist China and attention to Asia generally—his call for a "two-ocean foreign policy"—distanced him from the Truman foreign policy.

Despite Dewey's identification with Democratic diplomacy, his opponents' ineffectiveness assured him his nomination for president in 1948. HAROLD E. STASSEN jeopardized Dewey's chances when he upset the governor in the Wisconsin and Nebraska primaries. Dewey had confidently anticipated winning and had hence failed to campaign as extensively as the seemingly tireless Stassen. In the May Oregon primary, however, Dewey matched Stassen's speechmaking labors and performed well in a radio debate over the question of outlawing the American Communist Party. Dewey had earlier asserted, "You can't shoot an idea with a gun," and in the debate criticized Stassen's support for the ban as antithetical to a democratic society. Dewey went so far as to have his campaign pour money into betting halls to reverse the pro-Stassen odds. Dewey won the primary and crushed Stassen's hopes for the nomination. At the June Republican National Convention, Stassen refused to throw his delegate support to Taft, Dewey's major rival, and Taft declined to withdraw in favor of a compromise candidate, Senator ARTHUR H. VANDENBERG (R-Mich.). Because of his foes' disunity—and his own unexpected strong first and second ballot strength—Dewey secured the nomination on the third tally. He then chose the popular governor of California, EARL WARREN, as his running mate.

Three factors shaped his noncommittal campaign. First, the polls gave him a commanding lead that made a highly partisan strategy unnecessary if not hazardous. Experts nearly unanimously foresaw Dewey's election, predicating their view on the Republicans' vast gains in the 1946 elections, President Truman's low popularity and apparent ineffectiveness as a political leader, and the nominations of separate presidential tickets by Democratic splinter groups. Second, the Republican Party was divided between the conservative midwestern bloc and the more liberal Eastern internationalists. Dewey privately disapproved of the 80th Congress, led by the Midwestern Republicans, both for certain legislation enacted and for failure to legislate in other areas. However, he could not afford to alienate that important segment of the party. Finally, Dewey determined, after the outset of the Berlin airlift and consultations with Vandenberg and Dulles in August, to avoid discussing foreign policy. Instead, the GOP nominee promoted national unity amid rising cold war tensions with the Soviet Union.

Dewey's public personality perfectly suited his 1948 strategy. His campaign itineraries ran like clockwork; cartoonists likened him to an adding machine. Although a skilled orator, he rarely appealed to emotions. Such common Dewey phrases as "Your future is still ahead of you," caused detractors to dub him "the boy orator of the platitude." He "behaved more like an incumbent than a challenger," Joseph Goulden later observed. Dewey did not begin campaigning until one week after Labor Day; Truman gave twice as many speeches as the GOP nominee. Capable of warmth and humor in private, Dewey nevertheless adhered to an older perception of dignified statesmanship; he was oblivious to the newer, personalized political style of Roosevelt or Truman. "Short, immaculately groomed, neatly moustached," historian James Patterson wrote, "Dewey appeared prim, stiff, meticulous and impersonal." Dewey did not help his image as being cold and aloof in an incident in Illinois. The campaign train started backing into a crowd and he was heard to say, "That's the first lunatic I've had for an engineer. He probably should be shot at sunrise." Truman gleefully exploited this widely reported gaffe.

Dewey never attacked Truman by name. Only occasionally did he discuss specifics. In September the GOP nominee suggested that his administration would remove Communists from government "just as fast as a Republican president can be elected." But he resisted recommendations from Republican National Committee chairman HUGH D. SCOTT and others that he emphasize the issue of domestic subversion. Attempting to undercut Truman's support among Jewish voters, in October Dewey issued a strong statement of sympathy for the state of Israel. His action had the unintended effect of compelling Truman to assume an even more vigorous position. Briefly in mid-October Dewey worried that the president, who had edged up in the Gallup poll, might overtake him. Disquieting news of GOP overconfidence caused Dewey to experiment in Pennsylvania at hitting Truman hard on labor relations. His staff was aghast and successfully convinced him to go back to the platitudes. Toward the end of the campaign the governor began slipping in the polls and became worried, but said it was too late to change campaign strategy. When Truman all but accused Dewey of being a front man for fascists, he wanted to lash out at the president, but a poll of his advisers convinced him not to. Dewey took a week's vacation. On October 30 he decried Truman's "desperate tactics" and soon awaited confirmation of the expert consensus.

On November 2 voters reelected Truman, who received 49.5 percent of the popular vote to Dewey's 45.1 percent. Dewey blamed the low turnout, even though the percentage of eligible voters participating roughly equaled that for 1944, when Dewey had lost by a similar margin. Furthermore, political analyst Samuel Lubell claimed that a larger turnout would have resulted in a greater Truman margin. According to historian Harold I. Gulman, the real upset would have been if Dewey had won—given that Democrats outnumbered Republicans—and he nearly pulled it off. The public, Lubell reported, feared a Republican administration might usher in another depression. (Truman had played on these anxieties, and Dewey had failed to allay them.) Many observers, including Dewey, uncovered strong resentment among normally Republican farmers for low corn prices, which in November 1948 had fallen to their lowest levels in a decade. Truman had attributed the farmers' plight to the legislation of the 80th Congress, which he, ironically, had signed without protest. Truman ran surprisingly well in the corn belt areas.

Then, too, pollsters had exaggerated support for the Democratic splinter party candidates, HENRY A. WALLACE and J. STROM THURMOND. These candidates cost Truman support in the East and South, respectively, but not enough to elect Dewey. Political reporters had underestimated Truman, who waged a "bold, aggressive" campaign. The president enjoyed effective and unheralded financial and voluntary support from major unions, as well as among Jewish and black voters. The massive Republican gains of 1946, upon which many had projected 1948 returns, may have been an aberration caused by a low turnout then, and the problems of labor, unrest, and inflation of that year were resolved amid prosperity in 1948. Gallup polls in 1947 and January 1948 had shown Truman leading Dewey with Wallace in the race. By failing to defend the 80th Congress, Dewey, in effect, gave the president a free hand with an issue that he made the major one of the campaign. *The New Republic* and Truman himself contended that the president won largely because he had somehow kept assembled the New Deal coalition of city dwellers, union members, the lower classes, minority groups, and the bulk of the South.

In the long run Dewey's defeat may have created baneful influences in the Republican Party and the nation itself. Because they were stung by Truman's reckless demagoguery and because his triumph kept the GOP out of the White House for an additional four years, many important party leaders felt confused and embittered, and took up what some historians considered a harsh and destructive partisanship. In desperation, some historians have maintained, Republicans like Taft came to tolerate for the first time the most unprincipled anticommunism characterized by Senator JOSEPH R. MCCARTHY (R-Wisc.) on the grounds that the party would gain voter approval.

Between 1949 and 1952 Dewey continued to be in public view while privately playing president-maker. As before, he supported key components of the administration's foreign policy; he endorsed the North Atlantic Treaty Organization and its extension into the Mediterranean and backed U.S. intervention into Korea. Shortly after he lost in 1948, Dewey began to press General Dwight D. Eisenhower to run for governor of New York in 1950, then the presidency in 1952. Eisenhower shared Dewey's views on foreign policy and enjoyed many of the same contacts with the New York financial, journalistic, and legal community. Dewey told the general that only he could preserve democracy, but Ike only agreed to consider entering politics. Dewey publicly backed the general in October 1950. He loaned key advisers, including his 1944 and 1948 campaign manager, Herbert Brownell, to the Draft Eisenhower Committee. He also began to line up New York delegates to the 1952 GOP convention for him. He used strong-arm tactics against some recalcitrant delegates by threatening them with a loss of patronage. But for the superbly run Eisenhower campaign, Republicans probably would have nominated Taft; Dewey in turn earned the undying hatred of Taft supporters for his opposition to the Ohioan's candidacy. As a sop to the Taft wing, Dewey helped secure the vice presidential nomination for Senator RICHARD M. NIXON of California. In mid-April 1952 Dewey had seen Nixon speak and immediately had seen him as a vice presidential prospect.

When Nixon became embroiled in the "slush fund" controversy, Dewey told Nixon that he did not think Eisenhower should make the decision, and that the senator should go on television and ask the American people to decide. Nixon replied that such a program was already being planned. Shortly before the speech Nixon claimed Dewey told him over the phone that Ike's advisers wanted him to resign his candidacy on the air. The governor said he did not agree with this suggestion, but that it was his job to pass along the news. Dewey evaded when asked what Eisenhower thought. Then he bizarrely told Nixon he should resign his Senate seat and vindicate himself in a special election. When Dewey asked him what he would do, Nixon said he did not know and added they could watch the show to find out. He huffed, "And tell them I know something about politics too," and hung up. Dewey's biographer Richard Norton Smith, however, argued that the governor, after some hesitation, rallied to the candidate's side. The Eisenhower-Nixon slate won in November.

Dewey did not run for a fourth term as governor in 1954 and declined to serve in the Eisenhower administration. Many of his former aides and advisers, including Dulles, Brownell, Leonard Hall, William P. Rogers, Gabriel Hauge, and James C. Haggerty did, however, hold key positions in the Eisenhower presidency. Dewey occasionally advised the president; but the New York Republican refrained from an active political role in favor of a successful Wall Street law practice. Dewey addressed the 1956, 1960, 1964, and 1968 Republican National Conventions and served on the Republican Coordinating Committee, a special leadership panel operating between 1965 and 1968. Nixon, elected president in 1968, immediately offered Dewey appointment as secretary of state or chief justice, but the former governor rejected both assignments. After being feted by Nixon at the Florida White House and playing 18 holes of golf, Dewey suffered a heart attack and died on March 16, 1971, in Bar Harbor, Florida.

—JLB

Dingell, John D(avid)
(1894–1955) *member of the House of Representatives*

The son of a Polish-American blacksmith, John D. Dingell was born on February 2, 1894, in Detroit, Michigan. He attended parochial school and public high school in Detroit. He worked as a compositor and reporter for the *Detroit Free Press* from 1913 to 1916, when he moved to Colorado for health reasons. In the 1920s he was active in Democratic politics, served as campaign manager for Colorado governor William Sweet, and helped organize the Colorado Springs Labor College. From 1925 to 1930 Dingell was a construction engineer in the laying of a natural gas pipeline from Texas to Colorado. He returned to Detroit in 1930 and worked as a wholesale dealer in beef and pork products until his election to the U.S. House in 1932 from a newly created Detroit district.

A liberal, Dingell backed New Deal measures, particularly social welfare and labor legislation. He was one of the authors of Section 7a of the National Industrial Recovery Act, which stated that employees should be free to bargain collectively with employers. He was a supporter of the Wagner Act, which incorporated this principle in 1935. Dingell also cosponsored the Social Security Act.

In the 1940s Dingell advocated for an expansion of the welfare state. Along with Senator ROBERT WAGNER (D-N.Y.) and Senator JAMES E. MURRAY (D-Mont.) he introduced a sweeping measure in 1943 to extend Social Security coverage to 15 million additional citizens, raise old age and disability benefits, expand unemployment compensation, and, most controversial, institute a national health insurance program. Known as the Wagner-Murray-Dingell bill, the plan was to be financed by raising the employee payroll tax and employer contributions. The measure won the endorsement of labor groups but was doomed by the opposition of the American Medical Association (AMA), which denounced its medical care provisions as "creeping socialism." AMA spokesman Dr. Morris Fishbein called the proposal "perhaps the most virulent scheme ever to be conjured out of the mind of man."

The Wagner-Murray-Dingell bill died in committee. Dingell reintroduced the measure in 1945 and in each subsequent Congress. It suffered the same fate each time despite the blessing of President Truman. A bill sponsored by Dingell in 1947 to increase social security benefits by 50 percent never reached a vote.

In 1949 he criticized an American Medical Association–sponsored voluntary health insurance plan as "a cheap imitation of the real thing and a plan to perpetuate pauperism of the sick and helpless."

Dingell dismissed a compromise health insurance measure of Senator PAUL H. DOUGLAS (D–Ill.) for the federal government to cover only catastrophic illnesses. Dingell urged Truman to speak out against an October 1950 AMA publicity blitz against national health insurance. The president had spoken out against opponents earlier in 1950, but he did not respond to the October campaign of the association against the bill. In 1952 Dingell introduced an administration proposal for hospital insurance for the old—a precursor of Medicare—but it came to nothing.

Dingell was one of the Ways and Means Committee's strongest advocates of progressive taxation, arguing in general against reliance on excise taxes for revenue and in favor of higher taxes on corporate profits and high incomes. He fought unsuccessfully in 1943 against the Ruml Plan forgiving a large portion of income taxes for 1942.

Similarly, Dingell was a vocal opponent during the 80th Congress of the Republican across-the-board tax reduction of approximately 20 percent. He joined other Democrats in denouncing the measure as inflationary and inequitable, giving relief to the wealthy but providing only nominal cuts for lower income people. Congress passed the tax cut twice in 1947, but both times Truman vetoed it.

Early in 1948 Dingell introduced the administration's tax proposal, which would have removed over 10 million low-income citizens from the tax rolls, given each taxpayer a $40 tax credit and raised taxes on corporations. The Dingell bill failed to pass, and once again the Republican measure, altered somewhat along more progressive lines, won a large House majority. On this occasion Congress overrode Truman's veto of the sweeping tax cut, with Dingell remaining in the pro-administration minority.

Dingell usually lined up in the liberal minority on major votes. He voted against the Taft-Hartley Act of 1947, the Mundt-Nixon bill of 1948, and the continuation of the House Un-American Activities Committee. He backed proposals to outlaw the poll tax. Dingell supported the major foreign policy initiatives of the Truman administration such as the 1946 British loan, Greek-Turkish aid, and the Marshall Plan. He labored on the Ways and Means Committee to preserve the administration's recip-

rocal trade agreements from Republican protectionist amendments. For two decades he called for the construction of the St. Lawrence Seaway. It was completed a few years after his death on September 19, 1955, in Washington, D.C.

—TO

Dirksen, Everett M(cKinley)
(1895–1969) *member of the House of Representatives, member of the Senate*

The son of German immigrants, Everett M. Dirksen was born on January 4, 1895, in the small town of Pekin, in central Illinois. After his father died, he worked on the family farm and sold produce on the way to school. In 1914 he entered the University of Minnesota at Minneapolis but left his studies to serve in the Army Balloon Corps during World War I. After his return to Pekin in 1919, Dirksen worked first as a general manager of a dredging company and then joined his family's wholesale bakery business. In 1932 he was elected to the House of Representatives as a Republican. During his campaign Dirksen was careful to disassociate himself from the Republican Party and President Herbert Hoover, blamed by many for the Great Depression.

Refusing to oppose the New Deal solely for partisan reasons, Dirksen provided support for such key legislation as the National Recovery Act, the Social Security Act, and the Agricultural Adjustment Act. However, he differed with Roosevelt on monetary and fiscal policy. During this period he gained the attention of the Eastern press as a progressive Republican and able orator. At first a determined and strident isolationist, Dirksen voted against repealing the arms embargo in 1939 and opposed the draft and lend-lease in 1940. However, in 1941, just weeks before Pearl Harbor, he renounced isolationism and called for bipartisan support of Roosevelt's foreign policy. Throughout World War II Dirksen pushed his newfound internationalist views. In 1944 he made an unsuccessful bid for the Republican presidential nomination.

After Truman ascended to the presidency, Dirksen in June 1945 sent the president a private message recommending using lend-lease aid as leverage against the Soviets in Eastern Europe. In the autumn of 1945 a prescient Dirksen worked with fellow representative CLARE BOOTH LUCE (R-Conn.) to produce a bill committing aid to rebuild Europe, but it failed to pass Congress. When

Republicans won control of Congress in 1946, Dirksen, like ARTHUR H. VANDENBERG (R-Mich.) in the Senate, helped build a bipartisan foreign policy. He backed U.S. membership in the United Nations, the Bretton Woods agreement, aid to Greece and Turkey, and the Marshall Plan. However, he did not support a $3.75 billion loan to Great Britain because of the Labour government's announced intent to nationalize industry and its opposition to the formation of a Jewish state in Palestine.

Dirksen supported Truman less on domestic policy. He voted for the Case labor disputes bill of 1946 and the Taft-Hartley Act of 1947, which unions opposed, and he voted many times to reduce the president's domestic budget. But he voted for the Employment Act of 1946, the Atomic Energy Act, and the Veterans Emergency Housing Act. Dirksen also backed civil rights measures, such as bills to eliminate the poll tax and segregation in federally aided schools. He unsuccessfully ran for majority leader in 1947, conceding the position to CHARLES A. HALLECK of Indiana.

Dirksen began to suffer from eye trouble in 1946. A year later doctors diagnosed his problem as cancer of the retina and recommended the removal of his left eye. After much prayer Dirksen declined, but he decided not to run for reelection. Later his eye began to recover, but it was too late to file for reelection, so he helped with the presidential campaign of Governor THOMAS E. DEWEY of New York. But Dewey's passive campaign style dismayed him, and he was not surprised when Dewey lost to Truman.

Dirksen decided in 1949 to run for the Senate against a friend from the American Legion, SCOTT W. LUCAS. It seemed a daunting task—Lucas was popular in the state and majority leader—but Dirksen had become concerned with Truman's Fair Deal, which he saw as too costly and concentrating too much power in Washington and the president. He opposed national health insurance and the Brannan Plan for centralized management of agricultural policy. Dirksen had assisted in pushing the Marshall Plan through the House, but had not seen it as a permanent program. He now said the plan was a "mistake," arguing, "We haven't gotten our money's worth. . . . It's a bottomless pit." He was disturbed by Truman's ambitious Point Four Plan of aid to developing countries, and preferred to see the private sector utilized to bring prosperity to these newly independent nations, which, by so doing, would stop communism. Some, however, saw

Dirksen as shifting from an internationalist to an isolationist position, and his biographer Neil Mac-Neil claimed this was done to gain the approval of conservative Illinois Republicans, including Colonel Robert R. McCormick, publisher of the *Chicago Tribune*. After the Korean War broke out, he increased his attacks on Truman, saying, like Senator JOSEPH R. MCCARTHY (R-Wisc.), that the Democrats were soft on communism. Dirksen came under criticism for his alleged shift. "The case of Representative Dirksen is not essentially significant" columnists Stewart and JOSEPH W. ALSOP wrote, "unless the essential squalor of political human nature happens to excite your morbid interests." In October 1950 the *Chicago Sun Times* attacked Dirksen for equivocation on the issues, claiming that as a representative he had changed his position 31 times on military preparedness, 62 times on foreign policy, and 70 times on farm policy.

Lucas, however, had his own problems. As majority leader he felt obliged to support Truman's domestic and foreign programs, even though he disagreed with some of them. Dirksen hung unpopular Fair Deal policies and the Korean War around Lucas's neck like a millstone. What perhaps dragged Lucas down to defeat was the revelation of a scandal involving the Democratic candidate for Cook County sheriff, Chicago police captain Daniel "Tubbo" Gilbert. Word leaked from the organized crime committee of ESTES KEFAUVER—whom Lucas had pleaded with not to come to Chicago—that Gilbert had assets of over $300,000 on a salary of $9,000. The "richest cop in the world" testified innocently that he won his wealth through illegal gambling. The Gilbert affair helped Republicans throughout the state, including Dirksen, who beat Lucas by nearly 300,000 votes.

Once in the Senate Dirksen proved to be a staunch supporter of Senator ROBERT A. TAFT (R-Ohio) and joined the conservative GOP bloc in the upper house. He fought to cut the Mutual Security foreign aid bill in 1951 and questioned why the United States should spend money on France, where there had been a large number of votes for the Communists in the last election, and Great Britain, where there was an anti-American peace movement. Dirksen continued to blast Truman's handling of the Korean War. "In heaven's name," he said, "let us not slaughter any more youngsters over there when it looks as if they are going to run us out of there anyway." He termed the Democrats a "war party" and criticized the mounting war casualties. He joined with other Republican senators in opposing Truman's recall of General DOUGLAS MACARTHUR from Korea. In 1951 the American Federation of Labor made him assistant to "Coach Taft" on its fictional "All-American team of reactionary senators." Yet Dirksen considered himself a "moderationalist." He did not want to rip out the New Deal by its roots nor return to the ardent isolationism of the prewar era.

Dirksen became a key figure in Taft's drive to capture the 1952 presidential nomination. In November 1951 he announced he would work with Taft to collect convention delegates in the Midwest. Throughout the spring and early summer of 1952, Dirksen stumped for Taft, often challenging Taft's main rival, DWIGHT D. EISENHOWER to clarify his stands on the issues. Dirksen claimed Eisenhower represented the "me-too" liberal Wilkie-Dewey wing of the GOP. That group, he said, had doomed the Republican Party to failure by imitating the Democrats on the major issues. Dirksen still nurtured the hope that Taft would choose him as a running mate if he gained the nomination.

At the National Convention held in Chicago in June, Taft counted on Dirksen's eloquence to help his cause. The critical issue was whether to seat a pro-Taft delegation or a pro-Eisenhower one from Georgia. Taft asked Dirksen to speak on his behalf. Instead of preparing a speech, the Illinoisan took a nap, and then disastrously improvised a speech at the podium. In a rather raucous atmosphere, Dirksen pointed to Dewey, an Eisenhower supporter, and said, "We followed you before and you took us down the path of defeat." A near-riot erupted, with fistfights, catcalls, and shouts of encouragement. (Dirksen later claimed he had become infuriated when he saw a cocky Dewey strutting across the floor holding a beer.) Subsequently, the convention voted to seat the Eisenhower delegates. Dirksen gave a more measured nominating speech the next evening, but Taft went down to defeat. Taft recommended Dirksen as Eisenhower's running mate, but the anger among many of the delegates made this impossible. Governor William S. Beardsley of Iowa said that "after what Dirksen said the other night, the people of Iowa wouldn't use him to wipe their feet on." Dirksen did play an important role in reconciling a bitter Taft with Eisenhower, thus helping the latter's successful campaign.

During Eisenhower's first administration, Dirksen lent presidential policies only lukewarm support. He was one of the few senators to support McCarthy through the Army-McCarthy hearings and the censure proceedings. After 1955, however, he moved to embrace administration positions on foreign policy and civil rights. In 1959 he became minority leader and coupled a political shift to the center with attempts to build party unity in Congress.

As minority leader during the 1960s, Dirksen became a nationally known symbol of the GOP. His unruly hair, rumpled clothing, and old-fashioned theatrical oratory made him stand out in the public mind. He supported Democratic civil rights and foreign policy proposals during the Kennedy and Johnson administrations. During the late 1960s Dirksen's stature as a party leader declined. On September 7, 1969, in Washington, D.C., he died of heart failure after surgery for lung cancer. (See *The Eisenhower Years, The Johnson Years, The Kennedy Years, The Nixon/Ford Years* Volumes)

—JF

DiSalle, Michael V(incent)

(1908–1981) *mayor, director of price stabilization*

The son of Italian immigrants, Michael V. DiSalle was born on January 6, 1908, in New York City. He moved to Toledo, Ohio, when he was three years old. After receiving a law degree in 1931 from Georgetown University, he returned to Toledo where he set up a law practice and became active in politics. In 1937 he served in the Ohio House of Representatives, and, from 1939 to 1941, he was assistant city law director of Toledo. The following year he was elected to the Toledo City Council. He received nationwide attention in 1945 as the originator of the "Toledo Plan," which utilized a citizen's committee (the Toledo Labor-Management Committee) to arbitrate labor disputes. In 1947 the City Council appointed DiSalle mayor. As mayor he put into effect a 1 percent business and income tax, which allowed the city to eliminate its debt, making Toledo one of the few debt-free cities in the United States. Toledoans admired DiSalle for his amiability and capacity for hard work.

In December 1950 President Truman appointed DiSalle director of price stabilization as part of a "triumvirate" to handle wage and price controls during the Korean War. According to the *New York Times*, his chief qualifications for the office appeared to have been his "legal training, a sense of humor and a faculty for getting along with people." DiSalle soon became involved in a public dispute with his boss, ALAN VALENTINE, head of the Economic Stabilization Agency (ESA). During his confirmation hearing DiSalle had testified in support of trying voluntary price controls before imposing compulsory limits. However, in response to increased inflation, he came out for an immediate 30-day freeze on prices of all necessities in January 1951. Valentine favored selective controls and a greater reliance on voluntary methods. CHARLES E. WILSON, the director of defense mobilization, eventually intervened on behalf of DiSalle, and Valentine resigned. On January 26, 1951, DiSalle and wage control czar Cyrus Ching announced the administration's general freeze on wages and prices. Throughout the rest of his term he fought steadily against attempts to weaken the program. DiSalle, however, simply did not have the staff to enforce controls. He was further dismayed when control enforcement powers were transferred to the Justice Department, because he believed the investigating body should prosecute violators.

In February 1952 DiSalle decided to run for the U.S. Senate from Ohio. He won the Democratic nomination but lost to the Republican incumbent, JOHN W. BRICKER (R-Ohio). Shortly after the election DiSalle was called back to Washington as a special consultant to the ESA. His return was designed to end reports that the administration was about to abandon controls. He recommended that controls be kept on at least until January 20, 1953, when the Eisenhower administration would take over. DiSalle served as head of the ESA during the last weeks of the Truman administration. He returned to private law practice in 1953.

DiSalle was elected governor of Ohio in 1958 and played a major role in helping John F. Kennedy win the Democratic nomination for the presidency two years later. He was defeated for reelection in 1962. DiSalle went back to practicing law and remained active in Democratic politics, but he did not run again for elective office. He attempted to win the Democratic presidential nomination for Senator Edward Kennedy at the 1968 convention and was honorary chairman for Kennedy's 1980 bid for the nomination. DiSalle died in Italy on September 15, 1981. (See *The Eisenhower Years, The Kennedy Years* Volumes)

—TFS

Donaldson, Jesse M(onroe)
(1885–1970) *Postmaster General*
Jesse M. Donaldson was born on August 17, 1885, in Shelbyville, Illinois. He began his career as a country schoolteacher in Illinois. The son of a local postmaster, he became enthusiastic about the postal service and took a cut in pay in order to become a mail carrier in 1908. Donaldson displayed energy at the job, taking business courses at night and passing competitive examinations that made him a postal inspector in Kansas City from 1915 to 1932. After a year as an inspector in Chattanooga, Tenn., he was transferred to Washington as deputy second assistant postmaster general. He became first assistant Postmaster General in 1945. During 1946, as Postmaster General ROBERT E. HANNEGAN became unenthusiastic about his job, Donaldson sat in for him at cabinet meetings.

Truman appointed Donaldson Postmaster General in 1947 upon Hannegan's resignation. The appointment, which came as a surprise to Donaldson, was unprecedented. Traditionally, this cabinet post had gone to a political leader of the president's party. Donaldson was the first career civil servant to hold the office.

During his first year the enthusiastic Donaldson pressed forward with plans for postal expansion and modernization. He spearheaded the use of improved stainless steel railway mail cars. He pushed for the use of air parcel post, raised the wages of Hawaiian postal workers, and urged increased mechanization as well as an expanded range of services.

By 1949 Donaldson's reforms were threatened by increased department deficits. In an attempt to offset the $551 million deficit of that year, he lobbied unsuccessfully for further congressional funding. When, in 1950, Truman ordered a reduction in the postal deficit and the House Appropriations Committee recommended a $25 million cut for the coming fiscal year, Donaldson instituted a "shock treatment." He ordered drastic cuts in mail service and indicated the probable furloughing or firing of 10,000 postal workers. Congress still refused to act, and a storm of protests rose from the government and labor. The Senate Post Office Committee voted to have Donaldson rescind the order. The National Association of Letter Carriers termed the order "a rape of postal service" and called for Donaldson's ouster. Nevertheless, Donaldson remained in office until the Eisenhower administration.

Although prices rose and deliveries were cut, Donaldson was credited with creating or extending facets of the service: the domestic air parcel post, the stamp-vending machine, the highway post office system, the research and development group, the international air parcel service, and the expansion of motor vehicles available for use. Donaldson died on March 25, 1970, in Kansas City, Missouri.

Donnell, Forrest C.

(1884–1980) *member of the Senate*

The son of a storekeeper, Forrest C. Donnell was born on August 20, 1884, in Quitman, Missouri. He graduated from the University of Missouri in 1904 and received an LL.B. from that institution three years later. Over the next three decades he practiced law in St. Louis and was active in Republican politics. In 1940 he narrowly won election as governor, the only Republican to gain state office in Missouri that year. Four years later he was elected to the Senate by a plurality of less than 2,000 votes.

Donnell, who was a stickler for detail and carried a dictionary almost everywhere he went, established a conservative record in the upper house, opposing aid to education and supporting measures to curb unions. In 1946 he proposed amendments to strengthen the Case labor disputes bill and in 1947 to toughen the Taft-Hartley Act. During the liberal attack on the Taft-Hartley Act in 1949, he cosponsored the Taft-Smith-Donnell labor bill, which would have preserved most of the original act.

Donnell was a strong critic of American involvement in Europe. He reluctantly voted for the Marshall Plan in 1948 but opposed the North Atlantic Treaty in 1949. Donnell interpreted the agreement as a "moral commitment" on the part of the United States to participate in European wars. He offered an unsuccessful amendment to the treaty that would have required a two-thirds vote of the Senate to approve a presidential commitment of troops to the North Atlantic Treaty Organization.

As a member of the Labor and Public Welfare Committee, Donnell became deeply involved in the debate over national health care. In 1947 he offered a bill to counter a proposal for national health insurance made by Senator JAMES E. MURRAY (D-Mont.). The Taft-Donnell health bill, as it was known, provided for equal contributions by state and federal governments to the medical costs of those unable to pay. No action was taken on the measure. Two years later Donnell introduced a revised version. Intended as a rival to the president's program, the measure authorized $1.5 billion in grants over a five-year

period. The states would bear part of the cost of their health plans themselves but would get federal assistance on a sliding scale ranging from one-third to three-fourths of the cost according to need. Liberals denounced the bill as a "subterfuge" and a "charity system."

During his 1950 reelection campaign Donnell became embroiled in the issue of McCarthyism. Although associated with the Republican right wing, Donnell had not been connected with Senator JOSEPH R. MCCARTHY (R-Wisc.), who was unpopular in Missouri. Nevertheless, in October 1950, McCarthy campaigned for him, denouncing Donnell's opponents as "Commiecrats." Donnell refused to take up the issue of subversion in government, honestly admitting that he had no evidence to substantiate McCarthy's claims. On the other hand, his Democratic opponent, Thomas Hennings, stressed the issue, attacking McCarthy. Donnell's failure to confront McCarthyism cost him the race: Hennings won by a wide margin. He was the only Republican senator defeated in 1950. After leaving the Senate Donnell returned to his law practice. Donnell died on March 3, 1980, in St. Louis, Missouri.

—AES

Doughton, Robert L(ee)

(1863–1954) *member of the House of Representatives*

The son of a Confederate captain, Robert L. Doughton was born on November 7, 1863, in Laurel Springs, North Carolina, and grew up on a farm. He attended a local high school his father had helped establish. Over the years Doughton prospered as a farmer, storekeeper, livestock trader, and, after 1911, president of a small country bank. He served on the state board of agriculture from 1903 to 1909 and in the state Senate from 1908 to 1910. In that year he won election to the U.S. House of Representatives over the Republican incumbent. Doughton's district stretched from the mountainous region near the Tennessee border, where Republicans were numerous, to the tobacco-growing Piedmont area.

Doughton was a conscientious legislator, moving gradually into the ranks of the House Democratic leadership. He first became conspicuous in 1932, when he led a successful campaign against a national sales tax requested by the Hoover administration. The following year Doughton became chairman of the Ways and Means Committee. With the exception of the 1947–49 congressional session, he remained in that powerful post until 1953. Coming into power at the birth of the New Deal, Doughton presided over the shaping of the modern American tax system. His tenure coincided with the fiscal revolution whereby the income tax was greatly increased, graduated, and broadened in order to finance the welfare state and World War II.

A generally reliable supporter of the Roosevelt administration, Doughton often voted for New Deal measures more out of party loyalty than enthusiasm. He sponsored the Social Security Act of 1935 and was a champion of Secretary of State Cordell Hull's reciprocal trade agreements. On tax matters Doughton mediated between the Roosevelt administration, desirous of increased revenue, and reluctant members of Congress, sensitive to the resistance of constituents and business interests to higher taxes. The usual result was a compromise designed by Doughton and a handful of others that produced the desired revenue in a package containing exemptions and preferences for favored groups.

Doughton made popular his homespun maxim that the aim of taxation was "to get the most feathers you can with the fewest squawks from the goose." In commenting on an administration request for a $10 billion tax cut in 1943, he said, "You can shear a sheep every year but you can't skin him but once." The resulting $2 billion measure was vetoed by President Roosevelt for being loaded with provisions "not for the needy but the greedy." Doughton voted to overturn the veto, the first time in American history a tax bill was passed over a president's veto. Doughton was an architect of the tax withholding system instituted in 1943 and strongly opposed the Ruml Plan to forgive personal income taxes for the previous year. Nicknamed "Muley Bob" for his alleged stubbornness, Doughton, according to Jordan Schwarz, still possessed "a flexibility that enabled him to move onto the winning side of most issues."

After World War II Doughton's committee acted favorably on a request by the Truman administration for a $5 billion tax reduction. Instead of ending the excess profits tax outright, the committee, at Doughton's urging, voted to continue the levy until January 1, 1947, at a reduced net rate of 60 percent. Doughton believed that immediate repeal would be a boon to some corporations but mean nothing to most. Nevertheless, when the Senate voted outright repeal, he and the other House conferees accepted the Senate's version.

In the 80th Congress Doughton followed a shifting course in the battle over the Republican-proposed 20 percent personal income tax cut. Speaking as the ranking minority member, rather than chairman, of the Ways and Means Committee, Doughton criticized the bill as "a hurriedly conceived, untimely, discriminatory, and unsound patchwork of political expediency." The measure passed the House, 273 to 137, in March 1947. It provided for a tax cut of 20 percent for taxpayers earning between $1,000 and $2,000, with different-sized reductions for those in the other income brackets. The Senate passed the cut with a slightly more progressive slant. Doughton signed the conference report, which decreased the reduction for those earning between $136,720 and $302,400 from 20 percent to 15 percent. President Truman vetoed the bill, charging that the cut was inflationary and inequitable because it granted savings of less than $30 to a taxpayer in the $2,000 bracket and almost $5,000 to one in the $50,000 bracket. In another shift Doughton voted to sustain Truman's veto. His switch was crucial, since the House failed to override the veto by only two votes.

The Republican chairman of the Ways and Means Committee, Representative HAROLD KNUTSON (R-Minn.), immediately reintroduced the tax cut bill, slightly revised to take effect on January 1, 1948, and thus reduce the revenue loss for fiscal 1948. Doughton backed this version and influenced other Democrats to support the bill, which passed, 302 to 112, in July. The Senate approved the cut, and Truman again vetoed it. This time the House, with Doughton in the majority, voted to override the veto, but the Senate fell short of the required two-thirds by five votes.

Early in 1948 Truman proposed his own tax cut program tailored toward lower bracket taxpayers. The Truman plan included a $40 tax credit for each taxpayer and an excess profits tax to make up for lost revenue. Doughton, who was not consulted during the preparation of the administration's tax program, voiced his opposition. He stated that he could not support any tax revision that did not include tax relief "all along the line" and a provision allowing "income splitting" for married couples filing joint returns. Doughton voted against the Truman plan, introduced by Representative JOHN D. DINGELL (D-Mich.), as well as a substitute introduced by Minority Leader representative SAM T. RAYBURN (D-Tex.). With Doughton's influential backing, the Republican across-the-board tax cut, which now included provisions for income-splitting, raising the personal exemption from $500 to $600 and giving an additional $600 exemption to the blind and persons over 65, passed by a vote of 297 to 120. In March the Senate passed a reduced tax cut, which Doughton and the House approved. Truman again vetoed the bill, but this time both houses produced the needed majorities, and the revenue bill of 1948 became law in April.

A supporter of a liberal trade policy, Doughton fought against efforts by protectionist Republicans to weaken or kill the administration's reciprocal trade program. In the 1948 trade law battle, he introduced a key motion to approve a three-year extension of the Trade Agreements Act instead of the one-year extension pushed by Republicans through the Ways and Means Committee. The House rejected Doughton's motion, 211 to 166. With the return of Democratic majorities to Congress in 1949, however, Doughton and the Democrats reversed the Republican changes in the trade program.

Although a generally reliable supporter of Truman's foreign policy initiatives, Doughton himself expressed some skepticism on containment, saying he did "not believe we can stop the march of communism by the expenditure of any amount of money." He leaned in a conservative direction on domestic issues. He often spoke of the need for cutting government expenditures, particularly when he considered tax increase proposals. Doughton played a key role in the financing of the Korean War, helping to shape a new excess profits tax to produce revenue and bottling up proposals for a national sales tax within his Committee, saying in regard to such proposals:

> Witnesses . . . while all for preparedness, would preface their statements by saying that while those who they represented or spoke for wanted to do their full part in producing the revenue necessary to finance emergency expenditures, they usually, with few exceptions, claimed that any additional revenue should be raised from some other source. We were not given much help as far as the other sources were concerned, except a few I believe did recommend a general sales tax.

After 42 years in the House, Doughton retired in 1953. He died at the age of 90 on October 1, 1954, in Laurel Springs, North Carolina.

—TO

Douglas, Helen (Mary) G(ahagan)
(1900–1980) *member of the House of Representatives*

Helen Gahagan was born on November 25, 1900, in Boonton, New Jersey. Brought up as a Republican in Brooklyn, New York, she studied theater from 1920 to 1922. During the 1920s and 1930s she became a famous theater actress and internationally acclaimed opera singer.

In 1939 she became active in politics. An ardent New Deal supporter, she joined the Works Projects Administration's national advisory committee, the state advisory committee of the National Youth Administration, and the Farm Security Administration. In 1940 she became a Democratic national committeewoman from California and in 1941 was chosen vice chairman of the Democratic State Central Committee. Although a nonresident, Douglas ran for Congress from the 14th district in 1944. Supported by the Congress of Industrial Organizations and the International Ladies' Garment Workers Union, she urged protection for organized labor, small business, and the farmer, and equal rights for minorities. Regarded as the "Democrats' answer to CLARE BOOTHE LUCE," she was elected in November.

As a representative, Douglas supported New and Fair Deal legislation. She backed federal housing and tax relief to low income groups. She condemned President Truman's loyalty board program as reminiscent of Soviet totalitarianism. She cosponsored the McMahon-Douglas bill, under which atomic patents and power would be controlled by civilians. She believed that to show the world the United States' peaceful intentions, civilians must control nuclear energy. Although her husband joined the Americans for Democratic Action, she preferred to remain independent.

A member of the House Foreign Affairs Committee, Douglas was reluctant to see the United States get involved in the cold war. She opposed the Truman Doctrine of aid to Greece and Turkey, fearing that it would provoke war with the USSR, and favored the administration of aid under UN auspices. Douglas supported the Marshall Plan, however, as part of the fight for "a free Europe, a democratic world, and peace." Although she was an early supporter of HENRY A. WALLACE's crusade for rapprochement with the USSR, Douglas opposed his third-party presidential attempt. She feared that the Progressive Party was Communist-dominated and that a third party might lead to a Republican victory in the 1948 election.

Douglas was a strong anticommunist who denounced the Soviet takeover of Czechoslovakia and warmly supported the North Atlantic Treaty of 1949. She opposed the domestic anticommunist crusade, urging that civil liberties be preserved despite the public's fear of Communist subversion. In November 1947 she introduced a bill that gave defense rights to witnesses before congressional committees and persons about whom committees had made "deterimental" statements. She voted against the McCarran Act and opposed the House Un-American Activities Committee. The California State Senate Committee on Un-American Activities listed her as a Communist fellow traveler in a report in June 1949.

Seeking to win the Democratic nomination for U.S. senator, Douglas challenged the conservative incumbent, Senator Sheridan Downey (D-Calif.) in the 1950 primary. She later said she challenged the incumbent because he wanted to change the 1902 Reclamation Act, which limited inexpensive federal irrigation water to small farmers. She attacked him for favoritism to special interests; he, in turn called her an "extremist." Downey resigned from the race due to illness, and Douglas then concentrated her attack on his replacement, newspaper editor Manchester Boddy. Focusing on the issue of domestic communism, Boddy dubbed Douglas a "red-hot" and accused her of pro-Communist sympathies. His campaign was aided by Downey, who charged her with supporting Labor Party leader VITO MARCANTONIO (ALP-N.Y.) in Congress. Many other conservative Democrats campaigned against her, linking her with Marcantonio. She won the primary by a plurality of votes, but her candidacy alienated conservative Democrats.

Douglas ran against RICHARD M. NIXON in the general election. He denounced the Democrats as purveyors of "the same old Socialist baloney, any way you slice it." Both Douglas and Nixon claimed to be vigorous anticommunists. Nixon, copying the campaign techniques by which conservative Democrat GEORGE A. SMATHERS had defeated liberal senator CLAUDE PEPPER (D-Fla.) in the Florida primary, called Douglas the "Pink Lady." Douglas fired back, calling Nixon "tricky Dick," and accused him of emulating Hitler and Stalin in using the "big lie." Although Douglas accused Nixon of voting with Marcantonio on significant issues, such as voting against assistance to Korea and for foreign aid cuts, his supporters said that he had voted against aid to South Korea because the bill excluded Taiwan and they

claimed that she had voted with Marcantonio 354 times. They printed their findings in a leaflet widely distributed throughout the state and printed on bright pink paper (the "pink sheet"). Irwin Gellman noted that both had attacked the other, but underneath the charges and countercharges lay true ideological differences on the issues, and Nixon was more in step with the conservative tendencies of California. Nixon won the election by over 680,000 votes.

Her political career ended, Douglas returned to the theater. She died on June 28, 1980, in New York City.

—AES

Douglas, Paul H(oward)
(1892–1976) *member of the Senate*

Born on March 26, 1892, in Salem, Massachusetts, Douglas was reared in northern Maine. He worked his way through Bowdoin College, graduating in 1913. He obtained an M.A. and a Ph.D. in economics from Columbia University and taught economics at a number of colleges before joining the prestigious University of Chicago faculty in 1920. Douglas won professional renown for his scholarly works, the most notable of which were *Wages of the Family* (1925), *Real Wages in the United States, 1890–1926* (1930), and *Theory of Wages* (1934). He entered the political arena in 1929, when he undertook an investigation of Chicago utilities magnate Samuel Insull, then at the peak of his power. Persistent in the face of harsh opposition from the financial and political establishment, Douglas displayed the doggedly independent liberalism that became his trademark as a political figure.

During the depression Douglas served on a variety of government commissions and committees. In 1930 he was a secretary to the Pennsylvania Commission on Unemployment and the New York Committee to Stabilize Employment. From 1931 to 1933 he was a member of the Illinois Housing Commission. He helped formulate the state's Utilities Act of 1933, Old Age Pension Act of 1935, and Unemployment Insurance Act of 1937. He also participated in the drafting of the national Social Security Act of 1935.

In 1938 Douglas won election as a Chicago alderman with the support of the Democratic machine as well as intellectuals and upper-middle-class reformers from the Hyde Park area. In office he alienated the regular organization with his exposures of graft and corruption and lost the 1942 Democratic nomination for U.S. senator to a machine-backed candidate. Immediately following his defeat Douglas enlisted in the marine corps as a private, despite his age, 50, and his Quaker faith. (He had been a pacifist at the time of World War I.) He was assigned to the Pacific and was wounded at Okinawa.

Douglas spent 14 months recuperating in military hospitals, leaving in November 1946 with a disabled left arm. Returning to his professorship at the University of Chicago, he again ran for the Senate in 1948 on a platform advocating a federal housing program, inflation and monopoly controls, federal aid to education, repeal of the Taft-Hartley Act, and support of President Truman's foreign policy. The left-wing Progressive Party opposed Douglas because of his vigorous anticommunism. He defeated the Republican incumbent, C. Wayland Brooks (R-Ill.) by 400,000 votes in November.

Paul Douglas came to the Senate in 1949 determined to fight for liberalism, but also just as determined to maintain his independence. "I began my senatorial career," Douglas said in his autobiography, "by becoming involved in no fewer than five struggles: to change Rule XXII, to provide good housing, to repeal or modify the Taft-Hartley Act, to preserve and protect legitimate competition, and to wage my own war on the pork barrel of the rivers and harbors bill." Douglas and other liberals worked to reform Rule XXII, the rule allowing filibusters, that Southerners had used to block civil rights measures. The rule said that filibusters could only be broken if two-thirds of senators present voted to stop it. Douglas and other liberals backed a Truman administration proposal to allow a simple majority to stop filibusters. Douglas made his first speech in the Senate condemning the coalition of Republicans and Southern Democrats who were preventing a change in the Rule, and spelled out how the filibuster damaged representative democracy. He noted that senators representing only 8 percent of the population could thwart the will of those representing over 90 percent of Americans. The efforts of Douglas and pro–civil rights senators to amend the rule and make it easier to end a filibuster were defeated again and again during the 1950s.

The battle to repeal the Taft-Hartley Act was also unsuccessful. Douglas argued in favor of swift passage of a series of amendments instead of outright repeal, but labor groups as well as the Truman administration wanted thorough repeal. His bill failed in 1949 by a 50 to 40 vote.

From his seat on the Banking and Currency Committee, Douglas helped shape the National Housing Act of 1949. He managed the floor debate for Title I of the law, which subsidized slum clearance. He hung pictures of slums around the Senate Chamber to emphasize his points. He took a delegation of senators to Washington, D.C.'s, worst slums, one just down the street from the Senate Office Building. Title I passed easily. When the public housing parts came to a vote, Douglas played an important strategic role by arguing against a Republican-sponsored amendment to mandate racial integration of projects. The amendment was designed to sabotage the bill by detaching its Southern supporters. Douglas and other civil rights proponents stood firm against it, the amendment was defeated, and the housing bill passed.

Parallel to Douglas's espousal of social welfare liberalism was his advocacy of greater economy in government, particularly in the area of public works, or "pork barrel," projects. This stance earned him the hostility of many of his colleagues. Douglas opposed what had become an annual event: Chairman of the Appropriations Committee senator KENNETH D. MCKELLAR's (D-Tenn.), doling out of harbors and rivers public works projects, most of which was pork barrel, to his allies. When it was pointed out to Douglas that Illinois benefited from this bill, Douglas said senators should consider the national, not parochial, interests. He was defeated in his efforts. In April 1950 he strenuously, and unsuccessfully, objected to $840 million worth of navigation and flood control projects in a $1.84 billion public works authorization bill. The measure was approved by the Senate 53 to 19. He also advocated reducing government spending by cutting waste and inefficiency. He argued in 1949 that $3 billion could be cut from Truman's $42.2 billion budget. Douglas believed the budget could be balanced through such spending cuts and not through tax increases. Such a stand did not make him popular with the administration. For the most part his campaign to prune public works expenditures was a quixotic crusade.

Equally frustrated was his long battle on behalf of tax reform. In the summer of 1950 Douglas and a handful of maverick liberal senators spent several days vainly attempting to remove special tax provisions favoring corporations and wealthy individuals.

They supported a limitation of the capital gains exemption, an ending of special treatment for family partnerships, and a reduction in the $27^1/_2$ percent depletion allowance for oil and gas income. Douglas and his cohorts not only failed to dent the oil depletion allowance but also were unable to thwart the extension of the depletion principle to such products as sand and gravel, oyster and clam shells. In 1951 the liberals' effort to cut the oil depletion allowance to 15 percent was overwhelmingly defeated, 71 to 9.

Douglas also confronted the petroleum industry in 1950 in a struggle over the regulation of natural gas prices. The focus of the dispute was Senator ROBERT S. KERR's (D-Okla.) bill to exempt natural gas producers from price regulation by the Federal Power Commission. For three days in March Douglas held the Senate floor, marshaling detailed and emotional arguments against the measure. His main point was that the concentration in the industry, combined with the vulnerability of gas consumers, made price competition a myth. Freedom from regulation would mean an intolerable increase in gas prices and put "the high prices paid by the consumer of the North, not into the pockets of the people of the Southwest, but into the pockets of the big oil and gas groups." Douglas's powerful attack on the bill, punctuated by clashes with the knowledgeable and acerbic Kerr, had a significant impact on the Senate. Instead of the smooth passage predicted early by the bill's proponents, it won by a margin of only seven votes. Its opponents continued to fight it vociferously, with Douglas denouncing it on the radio every night and calling on President Truman to veto it. Influenced by the public clamor aroused by the Kerr bill, Truman did veto it. His message deplored the possibility of "unreasonable and excessive prices, which would give large windfall profits to gas producers at the expense of consumers."

On other social welfare issues, Douglas also hewed an independent path. He rejected the administration-backed Murray-Dingell bill for national health insurance. He wanted some form of national health insurance, but he felt that the bill tried to cover too much, too soon. He argued for more limited program that covered only catastrophic illness and made the families pay a deductible. He was afraid nothing would happen because of the overwhelming opposition to the Murray-Dingell bill. However, the American Med-

ical Association opposed his bill, too, and neither was passed. Douglas supported federal aid to education, but failed to pass legislation during the Truman years because of Roman Catholic insistence on funding for parochial schools opposed by the National Education Association and many Protestant churches. Douglas helped put together a compromise by which federal funds would be used to pay teaching expenses at public schools, but not private schools, while separate funding would help private schools for non-teaching expenses such as transportation. It passed the Senate, but not the House of Representatives.

However, Douglas succumbed to the anticommunist atmosphere of the time. Douglas supported the Kilgore bill—a bill for rounding-up subversives during a national emergency. Liberals offered it as a substitute to the McCarran bill, which called for the registration of Communist and Communist-front groups. The bill failed to pass, but then was attached to the McCarran bill. Douglas reluctantly voted for the McCarran bill, but he soon regretted it. Truman vetoed the bill, and for atonement Douglas and a few other liberals launched a 32-hour filibuster to help sustain it. They failed, and the veto was overridden.

As a vigorous foe of Communist expansion overseas, Douglas was a consistent supporter of the Truman administration's containment policy in foreign affairs. He strongly backed the North Atlantic Treaty and Truman's dispatch of American troops to repel the North Korean invasion of South Korea in 1950. As the conflict became a stalemate, Douglas suggested the use of the atomic bomb against Communist Chinese forces.

Despite his support of the president's foreign policy and their general harmony over domestic matters, Douglas and Truman had an antagonistic personal relationship. Outspoken in defense of his political principles, Douglas did not shrink from criticizing the president on occasion, while Truman was suspicious and derisive of idealistic liberals like the Illinois senator. They divided bitterly over the filling of two vacancies on the federal bench for northern Illinois. Truman rejected Douglas's choices for the positions and, in July 1951, nominated instead two individuals more favorable to the Cook County Democratic organization. Douglas successfully appealed to the Senate to reject the nominees. Truman refused to nominate Douglas's candidates, and the positions remained vacant until the Eisenhower administration. Although Truman did not care for him, early in 1950 *Time* magazine named Douglas one of the 10 "most valuable" senators. Yet Douglas was high-strung. Once, in response to criticism on the floor, he screamed and ran crying from the chamber.

Throughout the 1950s and 1960s Douglas continued to steer his stubbornly independent course in the Senate. He promoted stimulative economics during the Eisenhower years, castigated tax loopholes, endorsed social reform legislation, and never wavered from his firm anticommunist views in foreign relations. In 1966 Douglas lost his Senate seat to Republican Charles Percy. He died on September 24, 1976, in Washington, D.C. (See *The Eisenhower Years, The Kennedy Years, The Johnson Years* Volumes)
—TO

Douglas, William O(rville)

(1898–1980) *associate justice, U.S. Supreme Court*

Born on October 16, 1898, in Maine, Minnesota, Douglas grew up in an impoverished family in Yakima, Washington, and attended Whitman College on a scholarship. He worked his way through Columbia Law School, graduating second in his class in 1925. After a brief period in private practice, Douglas taught from 1927 to 1934 at Columbia and then Yale law schools, where he developed a reputation for his work on corporate law and bankruptcy. From 1934 to 1936 he directed a study of protective and reorganization committees for the Securities and Exchange Commission (SEC). As a member of the SEC in 1936 and its chairman from 1937 to 1939, Douglas secured a reorganization of the stock exchange, promoted securities reforms and helped establish the basic guidelines of federal securities regulations. Part of the New Deal inner circle, Douglas was Franklin Roosevelt's fourth Supreme Court appointee, nominated in March 1939 and easily confirmed the next month. At the time he took his seat, Douglas was the youngest man to fill that position in 125 years.

When named to the Court, Douglas was viewed as a financial and corporate law expert. Over the years he wrote important opinions in areas such as rate making by public utilities, bankruptcy, patents and securities. He supported New Deal measures expanding government power over the economy and favored rigorous enforcement of antitrust laws. In June 1948, for example, Douglas

vigorously dissented when the Court sanctioned the purchase of Columbia Steel Company, the largest independent steel fabricator on the West Coast, by U.S. Steel. The next June he objected to a majority ruling that he believed would lead oil companies to supplant independent service station operators with their own stations. In the same month Douglas criticized the long-established rule that the 14th Amendment applied to corporations. He also wrote the majority opinions in two June 1950 cases involving offshore oil deposits. Douglas ruled that the federal government had "paramount rights" to the disputed areas off the Texas and Louisiana coasts.

Despite his record in business law, Justice Douglas ultimately became best known as one of the foremost exponents of individual freedom on the Court. His civil libertarianism developed significantly in the years after World War II as he came to the conclusion that First Amendment freedoms were the cornerstone of a democratic society. Douglas insisted that government infringement on these rights was justified only when they seriously imperiled an important government interest. Under this "clear and present danger" standard, the Justice rarely found government interference with First Amendment rights permissible.

In *Saia v. New York* (1948) Douglas, speaking for a five to four majority, struck down a city ordinance that gave the chief of police discretionary authority to license sound trucks, saying it was an unconstitutional "prior restraint" of speech. In *Kovacs v. Cooper* (1949) Hugo Black and Douglas in the minority declared a Trenton, New Jersey, ordinance banning sound trucks emitting "loud and raucous noises" was too broadly drawn. In *Terminiello v. Chicago* (1949), speaking again for a five to four majority, Douglas overturned the disorderly conduct conviction of a speaker whose anti-Semitic utterances had nearly caused a riot. In the controversial opinion he declared that free speech must be guaranteed even to a speaker who "stirs the public to anger, invites dispute, brings about . . . unrest or creates a disturbance." In *Feiner v. New York* (1951) Black and Douglas believed the police should have arrested the man who threatened violence against a speaker. The Justice dissented in *Dennis v. U.S.* (1951) when the Court upheld the conviction of American Communist Party leaders for violation of the Smith Act. In what some consider his best single opinion, Douglas pointed out that the defendants were not charged with conspiring to overthrow the government or with any overt acts of subversion, but only with conspiring to form groups that would teach and advocate overthrow of the government. In a careful application of the clear and present danger test, Douglas found no evidence of any imminent peril to the government in such activity that justified the denial of free speech rights.

Justice Douglas also opposed the deportation of aliens solely because they had once been members of the Communist Party and objected to loyalty oaths. In a vivid dissent in *Adler v. Board of Education* (1952) he attacked a New York State statute, the Feinberg Law, which barred members of subversive organizations from teaching in public schools, as a destroyer of free thought and expression in the classroom. Douglas contended, "The law inevitably turns the schools system into a spying project." In a case involving Truman's government employee loyalty program, *Bailey v. Richardson* (1951), Douglas insisted that loyalty board reviews of civil servants needed the attributes of a fair trial, such as allowing the accused to confront his accusers. The associate justice also criticized the list of subversive groups compiled by the U.S. Attorney General, saying it subverted procedural and First Amendment rights. During the 1950s Douglas's views on the First Amendment became even more liberal. He abandoned the clear and present danger rule and took the more absolutist position that the First Amendment barred all government regulation of expression unless it was tied to illegal action.

Douglas took a relatively moderate position in church-state cases during the Truman era. He voted in *Everson v. Board of Education of Ewing Township* (1947) to uphold state payments for the transportation of children to parochial schools. In *Illinois ex rel. McCollum v. Board of Education* (1948) he joined in a decision that overturned a program of released-time for religious instruction in public schools. However, four years later in *Zorach v. Clausen* he wrote the majority opinion in a case sustaining a similar program in New York City. Because the religious instruction in New York did not take place in the schools or at public expense, Douglas held it was permissible. He declared that the First Amendment required only government neutrality, not government hostility, toward religion. As his views evolved, however, Douglas later came to demand as complete a separation of church and state as possible and to disavow his earlier acceptance of any state aid to parochial education.

In criminal cases Douglas generally gave a broad interpretation to the guarantees afforded in the Bill of Rights. Like Justice HUGO L. BLACK, the colleague with whom he was most closely aligned on civil liberties questions, Douglas believed these guarantees should extend to state as well as federal defendants. He favored extending the right to counsel to all accused of crime and took a strong stand against denials of the privilege against self-incrimination. Douglas pursued a liberal course on Fourth Amendment issues in the late 1940s, in *Wolf v. Colorado* (1949) he voted to extend the amendment's ban to the states on unreasonable searches and seizures. He dissented when the Court at the same time held that state courts might still use illegally seized evidence. In *Haley v. Ohio* (1948) Douglas invalidated the confession of a 15-year-old boy who had been exhausted by police interrogation for five straight hours.

In February 1946 Douglas turned down President Truman's offer to name him secretary of the interior. In all three presidential elections of the 1940s, Douglas was mentioned as a potential candidate. In 1946 some friends started a presidential campaign for the justice. He said he was not a candidate in early July, but was then asked by Truman to run with him as the Democratic vice presidential nominee. After several days of considering the proposal, Douglas once again turned down the president. Douglas had left the door open to a draft for the top job when he said he was not a candidate, but this did not happen. In 1951 the associate justice wrote a letter to the president saying he would stay on the Court for the rest of his life, and the statement was later made public. Despite this, Douglas continued to speak out on public issues.

Douglas remained on the Court for more than 36 years, making him the longest tenured justice in history. But the Court was never a full-time job for him. A quick worker, Douglas had time for other interests after finishing his judicial tasks, and his many outside activities made him a unique figure on the Court. He became an avid outdoorsman after first taking up hiking in his youth to overcome the effects of polio. His enthusiasm for backpacking and mountaineering persisted even after a horseback riding accident in October 1949 left him seriously injured and kept him away from the Court through March 1950. Douglas traveled widely. He was a naturalist and conservationist who wrote 20 books on his travels, the environment, and international affairs. Never afraid of controversy, Douglas often spoke out on public questions, recommending in

1951, for example, that the United States recognize Communist China.

Even as a justice, Douglas was often controversial. To critics he was a willful, result-oriented judge who showed little regard for history or precedent and whose opinions were distressingly short on legal analysis and exposition. Douglas's defenders, however, have praised his growth while on the bench, the exceptional range of his judicial interests, and his willingness to face new problems with a fresh outlook. Despite both belonging on the libertarian wing of the Court, by the middle to late 1940s, Douglas had developed a judicial philosophy different from Black's. According to his biographer James F. Simon, Douglas spoke in clear-cut terms and his constitutional interpretation tied together personal and economic freedom. He did not like consolidated power, whether of the political or economic variety. Black was a theoretician; Douglas, a pragmatist; and Douglas, unlike Black, did not feel bound by *stare decisis*. Adaptability, according to Douglas, was what allowed the law to survive. Over the years Douglas became more liberal in his views, always moving in the direction of giving greater scope to constitutional liberties. During most of the Truman and Eisenhower eras he expressed many of his views in dissent, but in the 1960s a liberal Court majority adopted positions he had espoused in areas such as criminal rights, citizenship, and reapportionment. By the time of his retirement in November 1975, Douglas was something of an institution, recognized for his deep commitment to individual freedom. Douglas died on January 19, 1980, in Washington, D.C. (See *The Eisenhower Years, The Kennedy Years, The Johnson Years, The Nixon/Ford Years* Volumes)

—CAB

Driscoll, Alfred E(astlack)
(1902–1975) *governor*

Alfred Driscoll was born on October 25, 1902, in Pittsburgh, Pennsylvania. He received a bachelor's degree from Williams College in 1925 and a law degree from Harvard three years later. He entered practice in New Jersey and became active in Republican politics. Driscoll served on the Haddenfield, New Jersey, Board of Education from 1929 to 1937. The following year he won election to the state Senate, where he established a liberal reputation, sponsoring legislation aiding tenants and blacks. In 1941

he was appointed state alcoholic beverage control commissioner. His administration was so fair that both the Women's Christian Temperance Union and the Retail Beverage Association passed resolutions praising him. Driscoll's outstanding record brought him the 1946 Republican gubernatorial nomination. He went on to win the general election by the greatest plurality in a gubernatorial race to that date.

As governor, Driscoll established a liberal record. During his tenure he developed a $50 million veterans emergency housing program, increased salaries of state employees by 33 percent, inaugurated a $25 million building program for state institutions, and pushed through the legislature measures authorizing temporary disability benefits. Driscoll reduced the number of state employees and increased efficiency, saving taxpayers about $2 million a year. He also undertook an extensive road building program, including the construction of the New Jersey Turnpike. Not all of Driscoll's efforts were successful. His $100 million slum clearance program failed as did his efforts against organized crime.

Driscoll's major contribution was the revision of the state's 100-year-old constitution. The new charter, adopted in 1947, contained a bill of rights, a provision specifying collective bargaining as a means of ending labor disputes, and an equal rights clause under which segregation was ended in schools and the state militia. The governor was given increased power to appoint officials and was permitted to serve two terms. In the charter revision, Driscoll called for an end to the restriction on governors succeeding themselves and wanted to increase the term of governors from three to four years. The charter allowed a governor to succeed himself once, while his term was increased from three to four years. Elections were to be held in off years so as to focus on state rather than national issues. The constitution also reorganized the archaic court system.

A liberal Republican, Driscoll supported Governor THOMAS E. DEWEY for the presidential nomination in 1948. The following year he won reelection in a race that pitted him against state senator Elmer H. Wine, the candidate of Democratic boss FRANK HAGUE. The election effectively destroyed Hague's power. Despite his liberal reputation, Driscoll, in the face of a strike by telephone workers, supported a bill pushed through the legislature instituting fines of $250 to $500 a day and up to 30 days of jail time for those striking against a state-seized company.

During his second term Driscoll gradually lost the support of the conservative wing of the party because of his failure to employ patronage and support leading national candidates. In March 1952 Senator ROBERT A. TAFT (R-Ohio) quit the New Jersey presidential primary after Driscoll endorsed General DWIGHT D. EISENHOWER. Taft claimed that Driscoll had broken his pledge of neutrality, but the governor denied this charge, contending that Taft was using it as an excuse for him to withdraw from the campaign.

In 1953 Driscoll was accused of attempting to stop an investigation of corruption in the Republican Party and of accepting bribes from underworld figures. He denied the charges and no action was taken. Following his retirement in 1954, Driscoll became president of Warner-Hudnut Drug Corporation. He served as chairman of the New Jersey Turnpike Authority and member of the New Jersey Tax Policy Commission from 1969 to 1975. On March 9, 1975, Driscoll died in Haddonfield, New Jersey, where he had lived since his childhood.

—AES

Dubinsky, David

(1892–1982)   *president, International Ladies Garment Workers Union*

David Dubinsky was born on February 22, 1892, in Brest-Litovsk, Russia. He led his first strike at age 15 while working as a baker in Lódź, Russia (now in Poland). Arrested later as a labor agitator, he was exiled to Siberia but managed to escape en route, and he immigrated to the United States in 1911. In New York City Dubinsky learned the cloakcutting trade, joined the International Ladies Garment Workers Union (ILGWU) and was active in the Socialist Party. During the early years of his union membership, Dubinsky fought for the abolition of the seniority principle in favor of equal division of work during the slack periods.

In 1922 Dubinsky became a member of the union's executive board. He tightly controlled the cutters' local and waged a successful 10-year battle with the Communists. Assuming the duties of acting president in 1927, he was elected ILGWU president in 1932. The Great Depression caused a grave reduction in ILGWU power and membership, and the union was virtually bankrupt. He became a vice president of the American Federation of Labor (AFL) in 1935. In 1935 Dubinsky joined JOHN L.

LEWIS and other industrial union advocates to form the Committee for Industrial Organization (CIO). Although Dubinsky strongly supported its organizing drives, he opposed the establishment of the CIO on a permanent basis as a separate organization and his relations with Lewis deteriorated. The ILGWU rejoined the AFL in 1940, and Dubinsky attacked Lewis for endorsing Republican Wendell Wilkie for president in 1940.

An ardent supporter of President Franklin D. Roosevelt, Dubinsky joined Sidney Hillman, Alex Rose, and others in forming the American Labor Party (ALP) to support the New Deal. Because of growing Communist strength in the ALP, Dubinsky, Hillman, and Rose left in 1944 to form the Liberal Party. He helped found Americans for Democratic Action in 1947 and was elected to its board in March of that year. During this time the ILGWU grew to 425,000 members by 1950, representing over 85 percent of the American and Canadian women's garment workers. After the war the AFL readmitted Dubinsky to its executive board.

Dubinsky believed that a union existed to serve its members, and by 1949 the ILGWU's welfare programs were among the most extensive of any union in the country. It had established its own health centers, radio stations, a major cooperative housing project in New York's Lower East Side, and extensive recreational facilities. During the 1950s other important gains were made. In 1952 the eligibility requirements for welfare benefits were standardized. This was crucial in an industry in which employers could easily relocate their business to union-free areas, forcing workers to move in search of employment. In that same year all the pension funds in the Eastern region were consolidated. By December 1964 the union had a single fund covering 400,000 members throughout the United States Dubinsky led a successful battle at the 1950 union convention for a plank asking for a provision in all future contracts for employer contributions to a severance fund. By 1960 it was established nationwide.

Dubinsky felt that the union was part of a larger community and must contribute to it. The ILGWU pioneered in adult-education programs and gave millions of dollars in gifts to philanthropic and labor causes. His belief in his union's wider responsibility extended into the international arena as well. In 1944, with considerable ILGWU support, the AFL established the Free Trade Union Committee (FTUC) as a permanent arm of the Federation.

Dubinsky believed that democracy could revive in the countries overrun by fascism only if its trade unions were kept free and independent. After the war he used the (FTUC) to fight against a Communist takeover of the German unions. In Italy he supported a coalition that went on to narrowly defeat the Communists in the postwar elections. He also facilitated the merger of many Catholic and socialist trade unions. At the 1946 AFL convention he argued for the creation of an International Labor Relations Department, which helped in fighting the cold war. He said in 1950 that his union had for some time "been fighting that war, both cold and hot, against the Communist attempt to grab American trade unions and use them for forcing on the American people a Moscow-type of dictatorship. . . . Unless the free labor movement is in the forefront of the fight, the cold war can never be won by the democracies." During the cold war the ILGWU gave millions of dollars to anticommunist unions around the world, including French and Italian clothing worker unions and the Israeli labor federation, Histadrut.

In 1947 Dubinsky fought for AFL support for the Marshall Plan, which he believed represented the best hope for the democratic reconstruction of Europe. The following year, at a time when a rift developed between Soviet premier Joseph Stalin and Yugoslavia's Marshal Tito, he helped persuade U.S. officials and the AFL Executive Council to assist Tito. Dubinsky believed such aid would restrict Soviet expansionism. During the postwar years Dubinsky also fought against Central Intelligence Agency (CIA) interference with foreign labor forces. He believed the CIA's involvement blocked communication between U.S. free labor and its foreign counterpart.

Through the ILGWU and the Liberal Party, Dubinsky supported Truman while the AFL stayed officially neutral. Dubinsky believed Truman's reelection was the surest way to repeal the Taft-Hartley Act. Because that law prohibited unions from spending their own funds for political purposes, he organized a campaign for voluntary contributions from garment workers throughout New York.

Dubinsky also sought to pressure the ILGWU and the AFL to deal forcefully with the criminal elements in member unions and in the garment industry. After World War II he tried, somewhat unsuccessfully, to reform a trucking local that was deeply penetrated by organized crime. In 1952 the

Executive Committee of the AFL appointed Dubinsky to its antiracketeering committee, where he played an active role in trying to safeguard union funds from corrupt union officials. That year he successfully initiated the AFL's expulsion of the racketeer-infested International Longshoremen's Association. Five years later he recommended the expulsion of the Teamsters' Union.

In the 1960s Dubinsky remained active in Liberal Party politics and aided John V. Lindsay's mayoral campaigns in 1965 and 1969. He retired as ILGWU president in 1966. He died in New York City on September 17, 1982. (See *The Eisenhower Years*, *The Kennedy Years* Volumes)

—EF

Dulles, Allen W(elsh)
(1893–1969) *deputy director, Central Intelligence Agency*

Allen W. Dulles was born on April 7, 1893, in Watertown, New York. He came from a family in which service to the government was a tradition. His father, a Presbyterian minister, was the nephew of John Welsh, envoy to Britain during the Hayes administration. Dulles's maternal grandfather, John W. Foster, was secretary of state under President Benjamin Harrison. Robert Lansing, an uncle by marriage, held the same post in the Wilson administration.

Dulles attended private schools in upstate New York and Paris. He received his B.A. degree from Princeton in 1914. After travel to the Far East, where he taught English in India and China, he returned to Princeton and earned his M.A. degree in 1916. The same year he began a decade of service in the diplomatic corps, then under the direction of his uncle, Robert Lansing. Dulles was assigned first as third secretary to the American embassy in Vienna. When war broke out between the United States and Germany, he was transferred to the American legation at Berne, in neutral Switzerland. There he was placed in charge of intelligence for the legation. In that position he gathered information on what was going on behind the front in southeastern Europe. For instance, one of his jobs was to make contact with anticommunists in the Balkans and the collapsing Austro-Hungarian Empire.

Delegated to the Paris Peace Conference in 1919, Dulles helped draw the frontiers of Czechoslovakia and worked on the peace settlement in Central Europe. He attended the conference as assistant head of the Department of Current Political and Economic Correspondence, where he supported German-American rapprochement as an answer to the problems created for the West by the Bolshevik Revolution of 1917.

When the conference closed Dulles was appointed to the first postwar U.S. mission in Berlin. After a tour of duty in Istanbul, he came back to Washington in 1922, where he served four years as chief of the Near Eastern Division at the State Department. He began the study of law and in 1926 received his LL.B. degree from George Washington University. That year he resigned from the diplomatic corps and joined the New York International law firm of Sullivan and Cromwell, in which his brother JOHN FOSTER DULLES was senior partner.

His law practice was interrupted for periods of government service in the late 1920s and early 1930s as legal adviser to the American delegations at the League of Nations conferences on arms limitations. In 1938 he was defeated as a Republican candidate for Congress. During the decade before World War II, Dulles, in connection with his international legal work, came to know the political and industrial elite of Europe and, in particular, of Germany. He also became director of the J. Henry Schroder Banking Corporation, which had ties with Nazi businessmen, for which Dulles was later criticized.

General William J. Donovan drew on this knowledge when he picked Dulles as chief of the Office of Strategic Services (OSS) in Berne during World War II. Dulles was credited with several major successes for the wartime intelligence service. By 1943 he had penetrated the German Abwehr, Hitler's intelligence arm. One of Dulles's agents, "George," turned over to him 2,000 microfilmed copies of Germany military documents. Dulles also received information about Peenemünde, the research center of the German V-rocket project, which the Allies bombed, setting work back for a critical six months. In 1945, in "Operation Sunrise," he helped negotiate the surrender of German troops in northern Italy. Controversy surrounded the operation as Soviet dictator Joseph Stalin complained to President Franklin Roosevelt that Dulles, and thus the United States, had excluded the Soviets from the negotiations. Some historians claimed this incident marked the beginning of the cold war. After the collapse of Germany, Dulles headed the OSS mission in Berlin. At the time he was among those who believed that the wartime friendship between the

Allen Dulles with President Truman *(Harry S. Truman Library)*

Western Allies and the Soviet Union could be kept alive by a common effort to solve the question of Germany. But in the months that Dulles spent in Germany, he saw the "one-world" conception of a postwar relationship with the Russians fall apart. His experiences with the Soviet forces in occupied Germany made him a skeptic of postwar Russian intentions.

With the defeat of Japan, Dulles returned to New York and the practice of law. In an address before the Foreign Policy Association in early 1946, he advocated that Germany be "de-Prussianized" and "de-Bismarkized" but allowed as much self-government as possible. Speaking later that year at the National Foreign Trade Convention, he stressed the need for a solvent Germany. Again, Dulles began to perceive that a restored Germany with ties to the West was important to resistant an increasingly aggressive Soviet foreign policy.

General Donovan in November 1944 had given to President Roosevelt a blueprint for the establishment after the war of a permanent central intelligence organization. Donovan, Dulles, and other OSS officers maintained that world leadership had passed from Great Britain to the United States and that an American intelligence service was needed to pick up where the British Special Intelligence Service left off. President Truman, however, disbanded the OSS in September 1945. Dulles kept in touch with many of the OSS veterans, a number of whom remained on during this period in the various intelligence units, which functioned under the aegis of the State and War departments.

Shortly after he had abolished OSS, Truman found that the conflicting intelligence reports transmitted to the White House left senior policy makers confused and uninformed. At the same time, with the Soviet Union tightening its control of Eastern Europe, the need to know Russian intentions became more urgent. In January 1946 Truman issued an executive order setting up a National Intelligence Authority and, under it, a Central Intelligence Group (CIG). The CIG was responsible for the coordination and evaluation of intelligence from the various departmental intelligence services. Because the budget and personnel of the CIG were under the control of the Army, Navy, and State departments, Dulles and others argued that it could not function independently and effectively. After a year of experiment and debate Congress passed the National Security Act of 1947. The act legislated the unification of the defense establishment, abolished the CIG, and reconstituted it as the Central Intelligence Agency (CIA), under the supervision of the newly formed National Security Council (NSC).

Dulles was among those who testified before Congress as to the kind of organization the CIA should be. He urged that the CIA should control its own personnel and have its own budget. He proposed that its director should have complete authority to pick his own assistants. According to Dulles, the agency should have supervision over intelligence operations and access to all intelligence relating to foreign countries. It should be the "recognized agency" for dealing with the central intelligence agencies of other nations. Dulles called for "official secrets" legislation to protect and punish CIA personnel who breached security.

Dulles wanted the CIA headed by a civilian, if possible, and he opposed making it "merely a coordinating agency for the military intelligence services." But at the same time he did not see the agency as a policy-making body. "The Central Intelligence Agency should have nothing to do with policy," Dulles said. "It should try to get at the hard facts on which others must determine policy." In a memorandum prepared for the Senate Armed Services Committee, he proposed a special advisory group, including representatives of the president, the secretary of state, and the secretary of defense, to "assume the responsibility for advising and counseling the Director of Intelligence and assure the proper liaison between the Agency and these two Departments and the Executive." Dulles's supervisory body became the NSC.

A young lawyer who had served in the OSS, Lawrence Houston, drew up the legislation for that part of the act concerning the CIA, working with the help of Dulles and another OSS veteran, John Warner. They incorporated large parts of the blueprint General Donovan had submitted to Roosevelt in 1944. The new agency had three duties: to advise the NSC on intelligence, to correlate and evaluate intelligence related to national security, and to perform "such other functions and duties related to intelligence affecting the national security" as directed by the NSC. The agency had "no police, subpoena, law-enforcement powers, or internal-security functions."

By the time of passage of the NSA in 1947 there was a growing bipartisan concern in Washington that the Soviet Union was seeking to take advantage of Europe's World War II devastation. Two weeks after Secretary of State GEORGE C. MARSHALL called for a concerted recovery plan for Europe at Harvard in June, Dulles told Brown University that a "world crisis loomed threateningly ahead" but that U.S. economic aid could keep Europe from becoming Communist. As Allen Dulles's biographer Peter Grose has pointed out, Allen did not believe the Soviets posed a military threat; more important was Russia's political and ideological aggression. What was needed was a policy promoting what Dulles initially called "insulation." (Dulles readily adopted George Kennan's term, "containment.") Presciently, Dulles told a Senate committee in April 1947 that the objects of intelligence work now was not only military, but also

scientific—in the field of atomic energy, guided missiles, supersonic aircraft and the like. They are political and social. We must deal with the problem of conflicting ideologies as democracy faces communism, not only in relations between Soviet Russia and the countries of the west, but in the internal political conflicts within the countries of Europe, Asia and South America.

He was appointed one of three consultants to the Herter Commission, which visited Europe on a fact-finding mission before making recommendations to Congress on European aid. Later Dulles served as a member of the Committee on the Marshall Plan to Aid European Recovery. In 1948 he accompanied the Republican presidential candidate THOMAS E. DEWEY on his campaign as his foreign policy adviser. Participating in a radio forum in May of that year, he stated that two of the measures necessary to world peace were the continuation of the Marshall Plan for four years and the supplying of friendly nations with arms for defense.

In the wake of the 1948 Communist takeover in Czechoslovakia, Secretary of Defense JAMES V. FOR-RESTAL became alarmed that the Communists might win the Italian elections. In an effort to influence the outcome, he started a campaign among Wall Street colleagues to raise enough money to finance a private clandestine operation. Dulles felt the problem could not be dealt with effectively in private hands. He urged strongly that the government establish a covert organization to carry out a variety of special operations. The NSC in the summer of 1948 issued a paper authorizing such special operations be kept secret and that they be plausibly deniable by the government.

Alarmed over a global Soviet threat, senior U.S. officials saw covert action as an alternative to the traditional options of diplomacy and war. A decision was reached to create an organization within the CIA to conduct covert operations. The new branch was called the Office of Policy Coordination (OPC). Dulles had been consulted as to whom should be appointed to head OPC and his candidate, his old OSS assistant FRANK G. WISNER, was chosen. Although OPC was a CIA component, policy guidance came to Wisner from the State and Defense departments. From its inception the CIA had been involved in the covert collection of intelligence. OPC added to this the counterpart capability for clandestine activities abroad.

Although independent and with its own budget, the early CIA preserved the personnel and structure of the CIG. The CIA inherited likewise its predecessor's troubles in its attempts to direct interagency coordination for national intelligence estimates. The efforts were hampered by organizational problems and by the agency's difficulties in asserting its position relative to the other better established departments.

These difficulties led Truman to ask Dulles in 1948 to head a committee of three charged with reporting on the effectiveness of the CIA as organized under the 1947 act and on the relationship of CIA activities to those of other intelligence organs of the government. While the other members concentrated on counterespionage and administrative restructuring, Dulles went into the problems of clandestine collection of intelligence and covert operations. Their report (NSC50) recommended many changes in the organization of the CIA, especially in the intelligence estimative process. The report was submitted to Truman upon his reelection.

In October 1950 General WALTER BEDELL SMITH took over as director of central intelligence (DCI) from Admiral ROSCOE H. HILLENKOETTER, the first head of the CIA. At the time the president appointed Smith, Truman handed him the 1948 report that Dulles had helped to write, which had been largely ignored up to that point. Smith asked Dulles to implement his recommended reorganization of the CIA. Dulles originally went to Washington as a consultant for six weeks; he remained there with the CIA for 11 years.

One of the major recommendations Dulles had made in the report was that OPC should be brought under CIA control. Shortly after taking charge of the CIA, Smith announced that OPC would be fully integrated into the agency. It was placed under the jurisdiction of Dulles, who was made deputy director of plans. In this post he was in command of the agency's covert activities. Wisner was made a component chief and reported to Dulles.

In November 1951 Dulles became deputy director of the CIA, and Wisner took his place as head of plans. Both men in the early 1950s believed that the liberation of Eastern Europe, where the Russian armies would be rolled back beyond the Soviet frontiers, was possible. Many of the covert operations initiated at the time were designed with the liberation of the Soviet Union's Eastern satellites in mind. In 1952, in violation of its charter prohibiting domestic security actions, the CIA undertook a program to intercept, screen, and open mail passing between the United States and select foreign countries. The program lasted for 21 years.

By 1953 Smith and Dulles had given the agency the basic structure and scale it would retain for the next 20 years. From 1950 to 1952 there had been operational conflicts between OPC and the Office of Special Operations (OSO), the agency's clandestine collection component. In August 1952 the two were merged into the Directorate for Plans (DDP). The distinctions between the OPC "operators" and the OSO "collectors" quickly ceased. Eventually all clandestine activities, including counterespionage and political or psychological warfare, were brought under one management.

The Directorate for Intelligence (DDI) carried on the evaluation of intelligence and preparation of intelligence estimates. Continuing the tendency begun in the CIG, the production of new intelligence rather than the coordination of existing intelligence dominated the DDI. To consolidate the management functions of the burgeoning organization, the Directorate for Administration (DDA) was formed. From the outset, much of the DDA's effort supported field activities—one-quarter of its total personnel was assigned to logistical support for overseas operations. By 1952 the DDP accounted for three-quarters of the agency's total budget and three-fifths of its manpower.

With the inauguration of President Eisenhower in 1953, Allen Dulles rose to DCI. Dulles was the first civilian head of the CIA. His personal style quickly became the public's image of the agency and its formal standard of behavior. Charming, urbane, educated in the Ivy League like many early CIA officials, and armed with his pipe and wit, Dulles was able to impress upon his listeners in public and government circles the need for secrecy in CIA operations. He used this argument to forestall an investigation by Senator JOSEPH R. MCCARTHY (R-Wisc.) into the CIA and William P. Bundy, an agency employee at the time.

Dulles's marked orientation toward clandestine operations and cold war tensions combined to emphasize the agency's operational capability during his tenure. Clandestine activities came to equal intelligence analysis as a CIA goal.

The close working relationship between Dulles and his brother, who became secretary of state, had a further role in shaping the scope and direction of the CIA. The agency gradually became centrally involved in establishing and executing U.S. foreign policy. During the Eisenhower years both men came to see that foreign policy more as a modified con-

tinuation of the Truman administration's containment strategy rather than a strategy of liberation. This containment policy was backed up by airborne American nuclear deterrence and by clandestine CIA actions.

Dulles continued as DCI under President Kennedy. In April 1961 the CIA-backed Bay of Pigs invasion of Cuba ended in failure. Dulles resigned in September. In 1964 he served on the Warren Commission investigation of the Kennedy assassination. Dulles died in Washington, D.C., on January 30, 1969. (See *The Eisenhower Years* Volume)

—SF

Dulles, John Foster
(1888–1959) *member of the Senate; ambassador, Japanese Peace Treaty Conference*

John Foster Dulles was born on February 25, 1888, in Washington, D.C. He was descended from a long line of ministers and diplomats. His paternal grandfather was a missionary in China and his father a Presbyterian minister who taught philosophy at Auburn Theological Seminary. His maternal grandfather was Benjamin Harrison's secretary of state and his uncle, Robert Lansing, held the same post under Woodrow Wilson. Following graduation from Princeton University in 1908 and a year of study at the Sorbonne—where he studied with philosopher and future Nobel Prize winner Henri Bergson—Dulles decided to become a lawyer. He earned his degree in 1911 from George Washington University and then joined the prestigious New York firm of Sullivan and Cromwell. He served as special agent for the State Department in 1917, working to negotiate a treaty with Latin American countries to defend the Panama Canal, and, after U.S. entry in World War I, he worked in the army intelligence service and on the War Board of Trade. Dulles was a member of the Reparations Commission at the Versailles Peace Conference. He returned from Paris to become an executive partner in his law firm, where he established a reputation as a specialist in international law. He was active in various organizations concerned with diplomacy, such as the Council on Foreign Relations and the Carnegie Endowment for International Peace.

Dulles lectured and wrote on foreign policy throughout the 1930s. In 1939 he published *War, Peace and Change* in which he blamed the Treaty of

Versailles for the rise of fascism. Because the victorious allies had insisted on maintaining the status quo to protect their interests, Dulles maintained, they had forced Germany to adopt violent means to achieve its goals. Dulles suggested the creation of "international mechanisms" to legitimize change. Dulles was not as active as other internationalists in calling for Britain and France to arm against Germany in the 1930s. This led to unfounded allegations that he was sympathetic to Nazi Germany. In reality, he thought the European democracies attempt to maintain the status quo was what led to the rise of fascism in the first place. What interested him the most as it became apparent the United States would join the war, was postwar planning so as to avoid another Treaty of Versailles fiasco.

In 1940 he assumed the chairmanship of the Federal Council of Churches' Commission on a Just and Durable Peace, where he worked to create a successor to the League of Nations without its weaknesses. The committee's plan was outlined in "the Six Pillars of Peace" (1943), which was similar to Woodrow Wilson's Fourteen Points, in which Dulles called for the creation of a future United Nations whose authority would be based on moral law. This institution and others like it would ensure cooperation among nations, free trade, and interdependency, in which the great powers would limit arms and call for basic human freedoms throughout the world. Dulles's work impressed both President Franklin D. Roosevelt and New York governor THOMAS E. DEWEY, one of the leaders of the internationalist wing of the Republican Party. Dulles served as Dewey's foreign policy adviser during the 1944 presidential campaign and aided the Roosevelt administration in formulating peace goals that included the establishment of the United Nations. In early 1945 Roosevelt appointed Dulles one of the delegates to the first UN conference in San Francisco.

When Harry Truman became president in April 1945, he hoped to continue a bipartisan foreign policy and asked Dulles to remain as an adviser. From 1945 to 1952 the Republican served as a delegate to the United Nations, adviser to the secretary of state at the meetings of the Council of Foreign Ministers, and negotiator of the Japanese peace treaty. Like many Americans, Dulles was optimistic about Soviet-American cooperation during the immediate postwar period. However, his first encounter with the Soviets at the 1945 London Foreign Ministers Conference proved to be a disturbing experience. He found the Soviets belligerent and anxious to divide the Western allies. Dulles praised Secretary JAMES F. BYRNES for refusing to compromise with his Russian counterparts. In Dulles's view, he had restored "morality and principle" to American diplomacy, which Roosevelt had been forced to sacrifice in favor of military expediency.

Anxious to understand Soviet policy, Dulles began a study of communism, in particular, Stalin's *Problems of Leninism.* Dulles's biographer, Townsend Hoopes, wrote that he "memorized the book as thoroughly as he had the Bible." What he saw as Stalin's paranoiac view of the world and plan for Soviet expansion frightened Dulles. In two *Life* magazine articles in June of 1946, Dulles outlined the Soviet Union's goals and recommended action to meet the threat. He advocated military preparedness and the marshalling of American moral strength to ideologically combat the Soviet Union. The United States would have to prove to the world that the American system worked spiritually as well as materially. Dulles later supported Truman's policies for containing the Soviet Union, including the Truman Doctrine.

Dulles served as Dewey's foreign policy adviser during the 1948 election campaign. He recommended that the candidate ignore foreign policy in his attacks on Truman. Besides supporting the policies, Dulles believed that Dewey would win the election and that he would need to maintain a bipartisan consensus on foreign policy. The press was so sure of Dewey's victory that it proclaimed Dulles the next secretary of state. Dulles even began discussing with GEORGE C. MARSHALL the steps necessary for the transition. Truman's reelection temporarily crushed Dulles's hope of becoming secretary of state.

In July 1949 Dewey appointed Dulles to fill a Senate seat made vacant by the resignation of ROBERT F. WAGNER, Sr. Dulles's maiden speech on the Senate floor was in support of the North Atlantic Treaty. He also voted for the appropriation bills for the Marshall Plan and the North Atlantic Treaty Organization. However, Dulles broke with the administration by supporting continued aid to the Nationalist Chinese. In 1950 he ran for the Senate seat against the popular former governor of New York, HERBERT H. LEHMAN. He offended conservatives in the campaign by refusing to attack the Truman administration's foreign policy and lost the support of liberals by deploring the New and Fair Deals as too liberal. Dulles charged that Lehman was accepting Communist support, while Lehman accused him of being anti-Catholic and anti-Semitic. Lehman defeated Dulles by 200,000 votes in a vicious campaign.

Following his defeat, Dulles wrote *War or Peace.* In it he questioned the administration's foreign policy for the first time. Containment, he maintained, had prevented the Soviet Union from expanding into Western Europe, but it had failed to liberalize Eastern Europe or scare China. Viewing the struggle in terms of morality, he called for a crusade that would defeat Soviet communism throughout the world. He rejected war as the means of accomplishing his goal; indeed, he feared overmilitarization in America. Instead he called for a "moral offensive" without defining his terms.

During 1950 and 1951 Dulles negotiated the U.S. peace treaty with Japan. He approached his task with two major goals in mind. He would not demand that the Japanese pay heavy reparations and he would align Japan with the United States to provide a barrier against Soviet expansion in Asia. Dulles was not the architect of the Japanese peace treaty. Instead he negotiated, modified, and carried out an earlier proposal. The treaty was based on a National Security Council paper issued in 1948. The council had recommended that Japan be permitted to create a 150,000 man national police force and be granted wider discretion in determining the pace of occupation-dictated reforms. It also proposed efforts to strengthen the economy. The treaty with Japan was signed in September 1951. At the same time Dulles also concluded a bilateral U.S.-Japanese security pact providing for continued American forces in Japan. His efforts won him great respect from all wings of the Republican Party and made him its chief authority on foreign affairs.

Dulles helped draw up the foreign policy plank in the 1952 Republican platform, which called for the liberation of Eastern Europe. He campaigned vigorously for the Eisenhower ticket. The general, however, clarified Dulles's advocacy of liberation of Eastern Europe to mean only peaceful means.

Eisenhower apparently considered JOHN J. MCCLOY as his first secretary of state, but party regulars noted that McCloy was unacceptable to Taft Republicans because he was seen as too close to the Rockefeller interests and had served under President Roosevelt in the War Department. Dulles had similar internationalist credentials, but at least he had not served under Roosevelt. One account, according to McCloy biographer Kai Bird, has Eisenhower agreeing to appoint Dulles as secretary, then after a year move him to the White House to be a foreign policy adviser, while McCloy would be named secretary. Dulles, however, explained to McCloy that he would merely administer the department while he, Dulles, would advise the president. This misrepresented what Ike had in mind, but McCloy did not realize this at the time and turned the offer down. Only later did he learn that Dulles had misled him.

Dulles served as Eisenhower's secretary of state from 1953 to 1959. During that period he and Eisenhower molded a foreign policy that reflected a moralistic view of the cold war. Early in the administration Dulles was forced to give up the idea of liberating Eastern Europe from communism. Instead, he developed a plan for containing communism through the use of a system of multinational military alliances and the threat of massive nuclear retaliation. Dulles died of cancer on May 24, 1959, in Washington, D.C.

Dulles biographer Ronald W. Pruessen has argued that by the time he became secretary of state, Dulles was a man of considerable breadth and depth, that he had an excellent aptitude for digging out the economic roots of international strife, and that he could at times integrate various global issues that confronted him. Yet he had trouble articulating solutions to these international problems. He tended to reduce issues to economic questions with economic answers, such as lowering the tariff and establishing stable currency exchangeability. He thought such proposals would not only resolve international conflict but internal ones as well. He considered Africa and Asia only inasmuch as their resources could ease tensions in Western Europe and Japan. Also according to Pruessen, Dulles's narrow answers to international conflicts of his time revealed a conservative mind-set, even though Dulles saw himself as a reformer, and he was much more in tune with the status quo then he would admit. He often concluded that international reforms that would benefit the United States would also benefit the rest of the world. He endowed his solutions with a substantial amount of religiosity and firmly believed America had a special role to play in the fight against the Soviet Union. (See *The Eisenhower Years* Volume)

—JB

Durham, Carl (Thomas)

(1892–1974) *member of the House of Representatives*

Carl Durham was born on August 28, 1892, in White Cross, North Carolina. He graduated from the University of North Carolina at Chapel Hill, where he majored in chemistry. After serving as a pharmacist's mate in the navy during World War I, he returned to Chapel Hill and set up his own drugstore. He became involved in local politics, serving as a member of the Chapel Hill City Council from 1924 to 1932 and the County Board of Commissioners from 1933 to 1938. In that year he was elected to the first of 11 terms in the U.S. House of Representatives.

A member of the Military Affairs Committee, Durham emerged in the Truman years as an architect of congressional policy in the new field of atomic energy. In 1945–46 he fought a proposal to leave the Atomic Energy Commission (AEC) under military control. Durham's battle to make the new agency a civilian establishment was lost in the House, but the issue was finally settled in his favor by the House-Senate conference committee, on which he served. Durham became a member of the Joint Committee on Atomic Energy, created in 1946. During most of the Truman and Eisenhower years he served either as chairman or vice chairman of the committee and exercised a strong influence on the course of atomic policy.

Durham's advocacy was an important influence on President Truman's decision to develop the hydrogen bomb. In 1951 he sponsored a House resolution calling for a six-fold expansion in the program to produce atomic bombs, increasing the atomic budget from one billion dollars to six billion dollars. Durham looked forward to making the cost of an atomic weapon "cheaper than the cost of a single tank." In 1954 he argued for a "crash program" to develop intercontinental bombers equipped with nuclear missiles.

Durham was an active supporter of other defense innovations. In 1949 he won House approval for a bill authorizing $161 million to set up a radar network around the United States and Canada. He also sponsored a measure in 1950 creating the Federal Civil Defense Administration. Durham was a strong proponent of the development of atomic energy for peaceful purposes. In 1955 he secured passage of an amendment adding $25 million to the AEC's funds to support peaceful nuclear reactor research. In the debate over private versus governmental development of atomic power for industrial purposes, Durham generally favored the government.

Durham was a faithful supporter of the Truman administration's foreign policy. He voted in favor of the loan to Great Britain in 1946, Greek-Turkish aid in 1947, and the Korea-Formosa economic aid bill in 1950. He voted against congressional moves to slash foreign aid appropriations and periodically backed extensions of the military draft.

A few weeks after the start of the Korean War, Durham contended that if the Soviets were using its satellites to weaken the United States, then America should attack the Soviet Union: "If it becomes clear beyond all doubt that that is the Russian policy, then I say that we have no alternative but to go to war with Russia in which event, we must pick the time and place."

Durham was less inclined to support the administration in the domestic area. He voted to override presidential vetoes of the Taft-Hartley bill in 1947 and an income tax reduction measure in 1948. In 1950 he voted in favor of a Republican amendment to reduce total appropriations by $600 million. He opposed the public housing program of 1949 and voted to cut funds for the Tennessee Valley Authority by $14 million in 1952. Durham also voted against all civil rights legislation. However, he backed measures to increase social security benefits and the minimum wage, and he favored rigid price supports for farm products. Durham retired from the House in 1961. He died on April 29, 1974, in Durham, North Carolina, at the age of 81.

—TO

Eastland, James O(liver)
(1904–1986) *member of the Senate*

James O. Eastland was born on November 28, 1904, in Doddsville, Mississippi, into a well-to-do, politically influential family. After attending Vanderbilt University and the University of Mississippi, he began a legal practice in Sunflower County, in the Mississippi Delta region. From 1928 to 1932 he served as a representative in the Mississippi state legislature, where he often backed Governor Theodore G. Bilbo, and then practiced law and ran the family's 5,400-acre cotton plantation. In 1941 Eastland was appointed to a temporary 90-day term in the U.S. Senate. He won the seat outright in the 1942 election.

During the Truman administration Eastland compiled a conservative record as an opponent of social welfare legislation and organized labor. He was also a supporter of anticommunist measures. Eastland voted for the Case labor disputes bill of 1946 and the Taft-Hartley Act of 1947. In 1948 he favored the elimination of the public housing sections of the Taft-Wagner-Ellender housing bill. Along with KENNETH S. WHERRY (R-Neb.), Eastland worked to amend the Espionage Act of 1947 to prevent American businesses from selling radar and other electronic devices to foreign countries. A strong supporter of states' rights, he backed attempts to give states title to tideland oil. Hailing from a cotton state and owning a plantation himself, and from his perch on the Agricultural Committee, he defended farm price supports. He himself collected over $100,000 a year in subsidies.

Eastland supported the administration's foreign policy, voting for the British loan in 1946, the Greek-Turkish aid bill in 1947, the Marshall Plan in 1948, and the North Atlantic Treaty in 1949. In 1947 he charged that HENRY A. WALLACE was in accord with Communists for his demands for reconciliation with the Soviet Union. After making a trip to Europe in 1945, he pleaded for the redevelopment of Germany to prevent that nation from being "driven into the hands of the Communists and stop the U.S. loss of a strategic location and an important market."

A vigorous opponent of civil rights, Eastland voted against antilynching and anti–poll tax legislation. In 1945 he opposed the extension of the Fair Employment Practices Commission, alleging that its efforts to improve the status of blacks were associated with communism. Following the Supreme Court's ruling in 1947 that Oklahoma had to provide legal training for blacks, Eastland asserted that the Court was "not judicially honest." In January 1948 Eastland advocated that southern Democrats withhold their electoral votes from the party in the upcoming presidential election in order to force the election into the House of Representatives, where he believed a southerner would emerge as president. Following the adoption of a strong civil rights platform by the Democratic Party at its 1948 National Convention, Eastland joined other southerners at the States Rights Convention in Birmingham, Alabama, that July. He supported South Carolina's governor J. STROM THURMOND for president. Eastland ran unopposed for reelection that November.

Eastland returned to the Senate in January 1949 for another six-year term. Eastland won appointment to the Senate Judiciary Committee's Internal Security Subcommittee, which he chaired beginning in 1955. He was ever on the hunt for Communist subversives, which he saw influencing unions, liberals, civil rights organizations, the Supreme Court, and journalists. When the High Court desegregated public schools in *Brown v. Board of Education*, Eastland claimed it had been "brainwashed" by Communists. Named chairman of the Senate Judiciary Committee in 1956, he continued to oppose civil rights legislation. Eastland was an outspoken critic of the Kennedy-Johnson social and civil rights programs in the 1960s, and he did not endorse Johnson in 1964. A vigorous anticommunist, he supported Johnson's Vietnam policy and voted against the Cooper-Church amendment to limit American military involvement in Cambodia in June 1970. In 1972 he backed RICHARD M. NIXON for reelection and defended him during the Watergate scandal. Eastland died in Greenwood, Mississippi, on February 19, 1986. (See *The Eisenhower Years, The Kennedy Years, The Johnson Years, The Nixon/Ford Years* Volumes)

—TML

Eaton, Charles A(ubrey)

(1868–1953) *member of the House of Representatives*

Charles A. Eaton was born on March 29, 1868, in Cumberland County, Nova Scotia. Raised in the province, he attended the Newton Theological Institute, a Baptist divinity school in Massachusetts. He was ordained in 1893 and for the next 26 years served congregations in Toronto, Cleveland, and New York. Eaton also became a specialist in labor relations, publishing numerous articles on the subject in magazines and newspapers in the United States and Canada. He left the church in 1919 to edit a national magazine for a year and then to head the industrial relations department of the National Lamp Works of General Electric. In 1925 he won a seat to the House of Representatives as a Republican.

A conservative, Eaton opposed New Deal and Fair Deal legislation. However, unlike many Republicans, he supported Roosevelt's and Truman's foreign policies. As the ranking Republican member of the Foreign Affairs Committee, he worked closely with committee chairman SOL BLOOM (D-N.Y.) to win approval of funds for the draft, lend-lease, and the United Nations Relief and Rehabilitation Agency (UNRRA). Eaton participated in high-level meetings between Roosevelt and congressional leaders concerning war strategy and the planning of the United Nations. He served on the American delegation to the San Francisco Conference held in the spring of 1945, where he was delegated to negotiate the "general provisions" of the Dumbarton Oaks proposals, and the London Conference of 1946. In early 1947, with the Republican Party in control of both houses of Congress, Eaton succeeded Bloom as chairman of the Foreign Affairs Committee.

Eaton's actions on the committee were determined by two major beliefs. Eaton thought that the United States was compelled to replace Great Britain as the stabilizing force in the world. A strong anticommunist, he saw the Soviet Union as a force "which [had] no morals, which [had] the cleverness of the devil himself and which proposed to break down all resistance by international penetration and finally achieve world mastery. The contribution of that force to the present world confusion [was] almost universal." Therefore, he supported passage of legislation implementing the president's policy of containment toward the USSR.

Following extensive collaboration with the State Department and the White House, Eaton introduced the bill implementing the Truman Doctrine. The measure called for the allocation of $400 million in economic and military aid to Turkey and Greece. Under the plan, the president could send government employees to the two countries and assign a limited number of military personnel to advise the nations. Greece and Turkey would have to acquiesce to U.S. supervision of the expenditure. Aside from these stipulations, Truman was given the authority to draw up all rules for the administration of the measure. He was also given the general power to commit American forces in defense of the government's fighting Communist aggression. Critics complained that the Truman Doctrine undercut the United Nations, might provoke a clash with the USSR, and would dangerously expand the power of the presidency. Eaton marshaled support for the measure both in hearings and on the House floor and collaborated with Senator ARTHUR H. VANDENBERG (R-Mich.) to prepare the final version of the act which Truman signed.

Also in 1947 Eaton introduced a bill to provide $350 million in relief to Greece, Italy, Poland, Hungary, Austria, and China, to prevent starvation. But in the House Foreign Affairs Committee the proposal met with stiff resistance from Midwestern Republicans, led by John M. Vorys of Ohio. Vorys wanted to reduce the authorization to $200 million in what appeared to be a postwar reassertion of midwestern isolationism. The amount was not reduced.

Another deadlock was ended when restrictions were written into the bill to prevent Poland and Hungary from using aid money to fund propagation of communism. Further attempts to cut funding on the House floor also failed, and it was passed by Congress and signed by the president.

The following year Eaton helped shape the bill implementing the Marshall Plan. Eaton assumed that the House would be more likely to pass an omnibus aid bill rather than another in a series of measures designed to assist specific areas. Against the advice of the State Department, he attached additional aid for China, Turkey, and Greece and relief for hungry children throughout the world to the original proposal. Congress passed the Marshall Plan legislation on April 3. For his role in the passage of the Truman Doctrine and Marshall Plan measures, Eaton earned the praise of the president, the press, and many Democrats.

Eaton once again became the ranking minority member of the Foreign Affairs Committee when the Democrats took power in 1949. He participated in conferences with Truman during the Korean War. Eaton retired in 1953 and died that year on January 23 in Washington, D.C.

—JB

Eccles, Marriner S(toddard)

(1890–1977) *chairman and member, Board of Governors, Federal Reserve System*

Eccles was born on September 9, 1890, in Logan, Utah. One of 21 children of a polygamous Mormon family, he quit high school, on his father's urging, half way through his senior year. His father died when Eccles was 22, and he became guardian of the family's sizable enterprises. Within 16 years Eccles had developed this base into one of the largest fortunes in the western United States. He was president of several banks, as well as hotels and construction and sugar companies.

Although a Republican, Eccles supported Franklin D. Roosevelt in 1932. Under the influence of the writings of William Foster and Wadill Catchings, Eccles became convinced that underconsumption had caused the Great Depression. The actions that were needed to lift the nation from the depression were massive federal spending to exceed revenues, a minimum wage, and federal regulation of agriculture. Although during the depression he favored a loose monetary policy, he preferred fiscal

policy to the open-market operation of selling bonds. Eccles also contended the Federal Reserve should have more control over banking. Early in 1933 he expounded these views before a congressional committee and was soon named an assistant secretary of the Treasury with responsibility for credit and monetary matters. While at this post he became one of the principle authors of the Banking Act of 1935, which restructured the Federal Reserve System. In 1936 Roosevelt named Eccles chairman of the Federal Reserve Board. He remained a close economic adviser to the president and a strong advocate of deficit spending and large welfare programs. His Mormonism had imparted to Eccles a certain amount of collectivist thinking, which he joined with his capitalist genius.

When the United States entered World War II, Eccles led the Federal Reserve into an agreement with the Treasury to help finance the war. Eccles and his colleagues agreed to support, until peace, the interest rates on both short- and long-term government bonds at their then very low level. This policy, which helped to finance a $20 billion increase in the federal debt, drew criticism from some quarters during the war. The Federal Reserve became known to its detractors as the "engine of inflation." In 1944 as the war ended, Eccles was among the U.S. delegates to the Bretton Woods Conference, where he became an early and important supporter of the concept of the International Monetary Fund (IMF).

After Roosevelt's death Truman asked Eccles to remain board chairman. In May 1945 Eccles was a member of the delegation that negotiated with the British an agreement to cancel that nation's lend-lease obligations, turn over to London American military equipment stockpiled in Britain, and lend Britain 6 billion dollars without interest for the first six years and 2 percent interest thereafter. Without the loan, Eccles believed, the British economy would have been paralyzed following the war and Britain would have been unable to participate in the IMF.

Eccles anticipated that once the war was over inflation would be the nation's major economic problem. Most economists at the time expected a short period of inflation followed by another depression. Eccles foresaw collapse only if inflation became uncontrollable. He argued that by retaining wartime economic controls and taxes, consumption could be held in check while production was adjusted to meet civilian demands. A shortage of labor and materials, not demand and capital, was the critical weakness he perceived in the American economy at the time. Eccles also advocated large budget surpluses and a tighter monetary policy to dampen inflation.

The administration ignored Eccles. The excess profit tax was dropped with the Tax Act of 1945, and Truman began relaxing economic controls days after the Japanese surrendered. Nevertheless, for reasons of their own, Truman and Secretary of the Treasury JOHN W. SNYDER, Truman's chief budgetary adviser, chose to have budget surpluses.

In the fall of 1947 Eccles drew up the Federal Reserve's proposals to Congress on the problem of inflation. He was still bound by the board's wartime agreement. But with the war won and the government's critical need for money ended, the agreement served no function that Eccles considered useful. It merely gave holders a strong incentive to sell their government securities and turn to more lucrative but inflationary investments. Eccles and his associates had begun several months before attempting to free themselves from this obligation. Despite opposition from the Treasury Department, they had ended support of several relatively insignificant short-term instruments. Now they proposed that the system receive power to require that banks invest a portion of their assets in government securities, freeing these securities from money market pressures. Snyder opposed the plan in testimony in Congress. In response to questioning he called it unworkable. The press made much of these differences, and Eccles's proposal never left committee.

During the last week of January 1948, Eccles received word that he would not be reappointed when his term as chairman expired on February 1. Truman refused to give a reason for the change. Eccles, however, believed that it was prompted by his decision to investigate the expansion of the Bank of America whose officers were close friends of John Snyder. According to Donald F. Kehl, however, it was Eccles's push for a tighter monetary policy after the war that probably led to his troubles with Truman. The president had favored a loose policy ever since his haberdashery failed in the early 1920s, from what he thought was President Warren G. Harding's tight monetary policy. Although ousted as chairman, Eccles decided not to resign his seat as a member of the Federal Reserve Board and remained a central figure in the conflict between the Federal Reserve and the Treasury.

This struggle came to a head in January 1951. Six months earlier inflation had resumed as the country emerged from the 1949–50 recession and entered the Korean War. On January 9, 1951, Snyder, without consulting the Reserve Board, announced the system would move to maintain the $2^1/_2$ percent yield on federal long-term bonds. Fourteen days later Eccles, speaking for the board, told a congressional committee that it did not support the low rate because it would fan inflation.

On January 31 Truman called members of the board to the White House to resolve the dispute. The meeting, according to a memorandum written by the board, proved inconclusive. Yet, the next day the White House and Treasury reported to the press that the governors and the Open Market Committee had agreed to continue the wartime support of long-term rates. Reporters called Eccles to confirm the account, and he, without approval of the board, said the stories were untrue.

On February 2 the White House released a letter from Truman to the chairman of the Federal Reserve stating that the Reserve had agreed to support the Treasury for the duration of the Korean conflict. Eccles responded by releasing a statement with the board's memo concerning the meeting of January 31. His revelation of White House duplicity coalesced public and congressional support behind the Federal Reserve. In late February the Treasury and the Federal Reserve, with Eccles directing its bargaining, reached an agreement that freed the Reserve of all commitments to the Treasury.

In July Eccles resigned from the board. Truman gave him a cold farewell. The following year Eccles sought the Republican nomination for senator from Utah. His association with Roosevelt and his inept campaign hurt him. So, too, did the fact that he was opposing an incumbent. He returned to his control of his family's holdings and continued active in public affairs. In 1952 he spoke against American involvement in Indochina, advocated recognition of Communist China, and warned against the dangers of overpopulation. Eccles died on December 18, 1977, in Salt Lake City, Utah.

—CSJ

Einstein, Albert
(1879–1955) *physicist*

Einstein, the son of nonreligious German Jewish parents, was born on March 14, 1879, in Ulm, Germany. He taught himself mathematics and physics at an early age. Never an outstanding student, his intellectual independence and creativity soon brought him into conflict with the strict regimentation of the German Catholic schools to which his parents sent him. While attending the Zurich Federal Institute of Technology from 1896 to 1900, he applied for and received Swiss citizenship. Upon graduation from the institute, Einstein, unable to secure a university position, took a job at the Swiss Patent Office, pursuing scientific studies in his spare time. In 1905 he published his revolutionary theory of relativity, showing that space and time, once thought to be absolutes, were actually relative to the observer. Einstein's conclusion that matter is really concentrated energy, a most important consequence of relativity, led directly to the development of the atomic bomb.

Einstein received his doctorate from the University of Zurich in 1909 and then taught in Zurich, Prague, and Leiden. He became director of the Kaiser Wilhelm Institute of Sciences in Berlin in 1913. In 1921 he received the Nobel Prize for his work in atomic physics. The suffering of European Jews after World War I led Einstein to become an active Zionist, traveling extensively during the 1920s to raise money for the Jewish settlement in Palestine. In 1933 he fled Nazi Germany and accepted a professorship at Princeton's Institute for Advanced Study.

Appalled by Nazi tyranny and the rearming of Germany, Einstein reversed his pacifist view in 1933, warning European countries to arm against Hitler's threat. In 1939 scientists proved the possibility of releasing the atom's energy through nuclear chain reaction. Acting on the belief that the Germans were close to developing an atomic bomb, Einstein addressed a letter to President Franklin D. Roosevelt describing the destructive potential of the new weapon and urging an accelerated research program so that the United States would be the first nation with the bomb. This letter spurred Roosevelt's decision to institute a crash program for the manufacture of the weapon. Einstein himself was not involved in building the bomb—authorities considered him a security risk.

With the creation of the first bomb in 1945, Einstein, along with many of the scientists working on the project, began to fear that the United States would use the bomb offensively against Japan, thus initiating an atomic arms race. Hoping to preclude the bomb's use, Einstein signed a letter to Roosevelt,

warning that any momentary military advantage the bomb might give the United States would be offset by grave political and strategic disadvantages. Roosevelt died before receiving the letter. The Truman administration disregarded the warning and dropped atomic bombs on Hiroshima and Nagasaki. In 1947 he said, "Had I known that the Germans would not succeed in developing the atom bomb, I would not have supported its construction."

After the war Einstein, troubled by his role in helping to unleash the bomb, became a passionate spokesman for the "control" school of thought, those scientists who felt that the only hope for peace was to place all control of nuclear power in a supranational government. In 1945 he organized the Emergency Committee of Atomic Scientists to educate the public about the possibilities and dangers of atomic power. In numerous speeches, broadcasts, and letters, he warned against the physical danger and cultural repression that would result from an arms race. He deplored the United States's postwar policy of nuclear rearmament, warning, "We must realize that we cannot simultaneously plan for war and peace." In 1948 he joined in a denunciation of universal military training and in 1950 signed a protest against the penetration of the Military Establishment into the civilian educational system. He opposed the production of the hydrogen bomb, stating in 1950 that the arms race was the worst method to prevent conflict and advocating the Ghandian tactic of "nonparticipation in what you believe is evil."

During the late 1940s and early 1950s Einstein was a vocal opponent of what he viewed as the increasingly nationalistic mood in American society. He spoke out against the anticommunist crusade of the early 1950s, urging clemency for JULIUS and ETHEL ROSENBERG, who were convicted of atomic espionage, and supporting J. Robert Oppenheimer against charges that he was a security risk. He also congratulated men who would not fight in the Korean War. Because of his many public efforts to effect a reconciliation between the United States and the Soviet Union, Einstein himself was accused of Communist leanings.

In 1953 Einstein completed his last great piece of scientific work, the Unified Field Theory, which related his work in quantum mechanics to the theory of relativity. In the year of his death, 1955, he and Bertrand Russell made a world appeal against the dangers of thermonuclear war. This statement, signed by six other Nobel Prize winners, led to the Pugwash Conference of 1957, a movement to utilize the internationalism of science as a force for peace.

There are remaining questions as to whether Einstein helped the Soviets in their atomic bomb research. Herbert Romerstein and Eric Breindel try to make the case that Einstein offered nuclear secrets to the Soviets, but their case is circumstantial and gives no clear indication that Einstein assisted the Soviets. In addition, writer Fred Jerome has shown that J. Edgar Hoover—who collected information on Einstein to discredit him—never found anything credible to back up any espionage charges. Jerome also refuted Romerstein and Breindel's accusations. Einstein died in Princeton, New Jersey, on April 18, 1955.

—DAE

Eisenhower, Dwight D(avid)
(1890–1969)   *army chief of staff; president, Columbia University; supreme commander, Allied Forces Europe*

Dwight D. "Ike" Eisenhower was born on October 14, 1890, in Dennison, Texas. He was the third of seven sons born into a family of Swiss-German descent and grew up in the midwestern prairie town of Abilene, Kansas, where his father worked in a local creamery. In 1915 Eisenhower graduated from West Point. During World War I he was a tank instructor and remained in the army after the armistice. From 1929 to 1933 Eisenhower served in the War Department and came into contact with U.S. Army Chief of Staff DOUGLAS MACARTHUR. In 1935 he accompanied MacArthur to the Philippines, where he served as an assistant military adviser for four years.

Following a rapid series of promotions after American entry into World War II, Eisenhower was given command of the U.S. forces in Western Europe. He oversaw the successful Allied invasions of North Africa in 1942 and of Sicily and Italy in 1943. In 1944, as supreme commander of Allied forces, Eisenhower supervised the Normandy invasion. Between July and November 1945 he directed the occupation forces in Europe. The chief goal was to install democracy in Germany. He remarked that if in 50 years, "the Germans are together and democratic and part of the free world, we have succeeded." Eisenhower insisted on de-nazification, which eventually led him to relieve General George

S. Patton, who thought cooperation with even former Nazis necessary to stop the Russians. However, Eisenhower abandoned the idea of German pastoralization, which he had backed during the war, due mostly to the influence of his chief deputy, General LUCIUS D. CLAY, and Eisenhower's own growing mistrust of the Soviets. Yet he was slower to grow wary of the Russians than others in the Truman administration. For instance, he did not think the atomic bomb should be used against Japan for fear it would make the Soviets question America's intentions. Despite the advice of Winston Churchill, he also agreed to a quick withdrawal of U.S. troops from the Russian zone in Germany.

Then in November he was recalled to the United States to replace retiring GEORGE C. MARSHALL as army chief of staff. Eisenhower did not relish returning to a desk in Washington, and, in fact, he left daily administration to his staff as he made speeches in support of continuing the draft, armed services' unification, and universal military training. Although he emphasized the importance of air power and the creation of new scientific methods of warfare, he favored the preparedness of surface forces as well, refusing to consider the atomic bomb as America's sole defense against Soviet aggression. Ike grew to dislike the job as Truman continued to refer to Marshall for strategic counsel. Eisenhower also did not care for Truman's partisanship.

During the immediate postwar years Eisenhower supported continuing close relations with the Soviet Union. However, as the cold war developed, Eisenhower adopted a harder line. He supported Truman's policies of containment and increased military and economic aid to European nations to resist Communist penetration.

In February 1948 Eisenhower resigned as army chief of staff to become president of Columbia University. The university's Board of Trustees had sought him out with the hope that his name and prestige would contribute to fund-raising efforts. In accepting this position Eisenhower made clear his belief that education was the best way to achieve peace, and, in a speech in Boston University, he invited educators to "put people in my profession out of a job." He established at Columbia the American Assembly, in which various societal leaders talked policy from a conservative perspective (which Columbia's liberal faculty held in disdain.) At Columbia he wrote *Crusade in Europe*, his account of that continent's liberation (it became a best seller), and Ike's mere presence at Columbia brought in sizable donations to the university. Eisenhower began to accumulate a coterie of rich friends. Their political views—internationalist abroad and conservative at home—meshed well with his. Eisenhower also served at this time as an informal chairman of the Joint Chiefs of Staff, trying to gain the navy's acceptance of unification and advocating more money for defense.

Uncomfortable in the academic world and disillusioned with large bureaucratic tasks that hindered close contact with students, Eisenhower resigned his appointment in 1951 to assume command of the Armed Forces of the North Atlantic Treaty Organization (NATO). In testimony before the Armed Services and Foreign Relations committees in 1951, he suggested that the United States should take the leadership of NATO in the absence of any other acceptable leader. He supported increasing U.S. troop commitments in Europe but maintained that the Europeans would have to supply the bulk of the land forces. The general believed that if America was to retain its freedom, Western Europe had to be defended against "Communist imperialism." But he felt that the United States's chief purpose should be the contribution of munitions and equipment to help the Europeans build their own economy and defense. He advocated the political unification of Europe as a means of strengthening its security against Soviet aggression.

Eisenhower's name was frequently mentioned as a possible presidential candidate during the late 1940s. In January 1948 a Draft Eisenhower League was formed with plans to enter Eisenhower's name in several presidential primaries. Liberal Democrats, such as members of the Americans for Democratic Action and Senator CLAUDE PEPPER of Florida, appeared especially desperate to draft Eisenhower in 1948, given their belief that Truman was a sure loser. At an earlier point Truman had been willing to step aside for Ike, but by 1948 Truman was determined to win vindication. Publicly Ike proclaimed he had no interest in running for office, but privately he had intimated to his wartime chief of staff, WALTER BEDELL SMITH, in the autumn of 1947 that to refuse an "unmistakable call" of a draft would be a dereliction of duty. Eisenhower also confided to attorney Edwin Clark in July 1948 in his interest in the presidency. However, Eisenhower believed Republican THOMAS E. DEWEY would win, and, refused offers by Democrats to run on their ticket. After Dewey

lost, representatives of the liberal interventionist wing of the Republican Party tried to persuade Eisenhower to run with the hope that with the general as their candidate they could prevent the nomination in 1952 of the favorite of the midwestern nationalists, Senator ROBERT A. TAFT of Ohio. Eisenhower supported their stand for bipartisan foreign policy with full American participation in European affairs and their conception of a strong American economy unencumbered by government interference.

As historian William B. Pickett has shown, Eisenhower worked quietly with certain Republicans to win the nomination, while he acted like he would only accept a draft in public. He consented to have his name put on the ballot in some primaries, although he remained publicly uncommitted so that he could continue his work with NATO. However, because of support for Taft among party regulars, Eisenhower resigned from the army early in the summer of 1952 to campaign actively. In a hard-fought race and convention, Republicans decided to go with the general on the first ballot.

Throughout his campaign against his Democratic opponent, ADLAI E. STEVENSON, Eisenhower concentrated on three issues: the Korean War, government corruption, and Communist subversion. He supported U.S. participation in the United Nations and NATO, and he favored continued aid to foreign countries. He also pledged that, if elected, he would go to Korea to try to bring that conflict to an end. Eisenhower triumphed in November with a landslide victory over Stevenson.

Eisenhower viewed his presidency as a period of consolidation and unification after the dramatic reforms of the New Deal. Although he attempted to limit government intervention in many areas, he did not favor large cuts in social services, and his presidency served to further the acceptance of the welfare state. He saw himself above partisan politics, and his cabinet consisted of men who shared his belief in the need to limit government action and maintain a free economy.

In foreign affairs Eisenhower ended the Korean War and prevented outright American participation in other conflicts. Along with his secretary of state, JOHN FOSTER DULLES, he molded a foreign policy that served to solidify the cold war with his conception of the world as divided in a moral struggle between freedom and communism. Despite his career as an army officer, Eisenhower attempted to reduce defense expenditures and advocated the "New Look" military budgets, which limited conventional army and navy systems in favor of modern, strategic warfare, including missiles and nuclear weapons. In his farewell address in January 1961, Eisenhower warned of the danger of a "military-industrial complex" as a threat to the very nature of a democratic society.

Retiring to his farm near Gettysburg, Pennsylvania, Eisenhower remained a popular figure in the Republican Party and throughout the country. Despite previous criticisms by historians and intellectuals, by the end of the 1960s, scholars viewed him as a man of peace who had given unifying leadership to a divided nation. Later studies by Stephen E. Ambrose and Fred I. Greenstein have shown that Eisenhower was a shrewd behind-the-scenes operator in pursuit of his policy goals. He died on March 28, 1969, in Washington, D.C., after a heart attack. (See *The Eisenhower Years, The Kennedy Years, The Johnson Years* Volumes)

—GMS

Ellender, Allen J(oseph)

(1890–1972) *member of the Senate*

Allen J. Ellender was born on September 24, 1890, in Montegut, Louisiana, to Wallace and Victoria Ellender. Allen's father was a sugar farmer. The future senator attended St. Aloysius High School and graduated in 1909. After receiving his LL.B. from Tulane University in 1913, Ellender practiced law in Houma, Louisiana, for the next two years. He simultaneously pursued careers as a farmer and politician, serving as district attorney of Terrebonne Parish in 1915 and then as Democratic member of the Louisiana House of Representatives from 1924 to 1926. Although Ellender initially disagreed with Huey Long's politics, he eventually formed an alliance with the Louisiana boss in 1929 and defended him at his Senate impeachment. When Long was assassinated in 1935, the machine chose Ellender to replace him in the U.S. Senate.

In the Senate Ellender, like many southerners, supported early New Deal legislation while opposing the president's efforts on civil rights. He backed Roosevelt's foreign policy, including lend-lease, but was concerned that the Soviet Union and England pay back their share in oil, tin, rubber, and iron lest the cost of the program severely increase the national debt.

During the Truman administration Ellender supported the president's containment policies toward the Soviet Union and U.S. involvement in the United Nations. Disagreeing with Truman's declaration at Potsdam that the United States did not want any territorial or monetary rewards from World War II, Ellender advocated American control of military bases throughout the world. After a 42-day tour of China in 1946, he asserted that the situation there was hopeless and the United States should withdraw its marines from the country after the Japanese had been repatriated. Ellender voted in favor of aid to Greece and Turkey and the Marshall Plan, but he was concerned with the latter's expense, and voted against further funds once a European recovery set in in the late 1940s. He also opposed the St. Lawrence Seaway project, seeing it as a threat to the port of New Orleans. He did support Truman's decision to cashier General DOUGLAS MACARTHUR in 1951.

Ellender remained a moderate in domestic affairs. He opposed civil rights measures and voted against the appointment of an African-American as governor of the Virgin Islands. Also typical of a southern senator of that time, Ellender opposed federal antilynching legislation, elimination of the poll tax, and a permanent Fair Employment Practices Commission, but he refused to join the Dixiecrat revolt of 1948. Ellender voted against raising the minimum wage from 40 cents an hour to 75 cents an hour and an unemployment compensation bill providing 25 dollars a week for 26 weeks. He supported the Case labor disputes bill, which would have established a labor mediation board and 60-day cooling off period before strikes could begin. He also voted in favor of the Taft-Hartley Act. He stood against the Wagner-Murray-Dingell compulsory medical insurance bill because it denied patients and doctors choice. He did vote for the Hill-Burton Act of 1946, which subsidized hospital construction, and in 1949 offered amendments to that law. His proposals, enacted that year, extended the life of the program and permitted increases in the federal share of construction costs. He cosponsored a bill with RICHARD B. RUSSELL providing for the use of surplus farm commodities to fund a school free lunch program, which became law in 1946. Ellender sponsored with Robert Taft federal aid to education, but their bill died in the House. He was a strong advocate of agricultural subsidies, especially for sugar, which was a major crop in Louisiana.

Ellender was primarily noted as a supporter of public housing. As a member of the Banking and Currency Committee's Housing and Urban Redevelopment Subcommittee, he helped write a report in 1945 assessing the nations' housing needs. It warned that 1.25 million homes a year would be needed over the next 10 years, primarily for low-income families. That August Ellender joined Senator ROBERT F. WAGNER (D-N.Y.) and Senator ROBERT A. TAFT (R-Ohio) in sponsoring a bill liberalizing the terms of Federal Housing Authority (FHA) mortgages and establishing a program of FHA "Yield Insurance" for investors in large-scale rental housing. It also provided for building of 500,000 units of public housing, aiding farm housing, and inaugurating research into costs and housing problems. The Senate passed the bill in 1946; however, it was killed in the House by powerful lobbying efforts. The Senate passed a similar measure in 1948, but again, it failed to get out of committee in the House. In 1949 Congress finally succeeded in passing a measure incorporating features of the earlier proposal after bitter debate.

Opponents of the omnibus housing bill, including real estate, business and trade groups, termed it socialist, bureaucratic, and contrary to democratic government. Ellender, backed by labor, liberals, consumer groups, and welfare organizations, defended the measure. He maintained that private industry could not meet these demands. He added, "The most realistic way to defeat communism, fascism and in fact any other 'ism' is to make democracy work— make it a living, breathing, institution responsive to the needs of our people, by placing within their reach the basic necessities of a happy life."

During the 1950s and 1960s, as chairman of the Agriculture and Forestry Committee, Ellender played a major role in shaping farm policy. Although a staunch conservative on most domestic issues, he was a leading advocate of closer relations with the USSR and a critic of defense spending. At his death on July 27, 1972, in Bethesda, Maryland, Ellender was president pro tempore of the Senate. (See *The Eisenhower Years, The Kennedy Years, The Johnson Years, The Nixon/Ford Years* Volumes)

—RSG

Elsey, George M(cKee)

(1918–   ) *special counsel to the president, administrative assistant to the president*

George M. Elsey was born on February 5, 1918, in Palo Alto, California. He graduated from Princeton in 1939. After receiving an M.A. in American history form Harvard in 1940, he served on active duty with the U.S. Naval Reserve. During World War II he was assigned, along with CLARK CLIFFORD, to the White House map room, where he was President Truman's assistant naval aide. In 1946, when Clifford became special counsel to the president, Elsey's duties expanded to those of civilian administrative assistant and speech writer. Known as a self-contained man who tackled problems with "balance and incisiveness," Elsey left his stamp on many presidential communications through his judicious editorial comments on the materials submitted to Truman for inclusion in speeches and legislative programs.

In the summer of 1946 Truman asked Elsey and Clark Clifford to write up a list of Soviet violations of agreements with the United States. The secret report, "American Relations with the Soviet Union," was given to Truman in September and went far beyond the president's request, providing a comprehensive analysis of Soviet policy. Elsey and Clifford based their report on their contention that "the key to an understanding of current Soviet foreign policy is the realization that Soviet leaders adhere to the Marxian theory of ultimate destruction of capitalist states by Communist states." The memorandum documented how the Soviets had pursued an expansionist policy and violated or interpreted to suit their own aims in the Teheran, Yalta, and Potsdam agreements, had delayed peace settlements to maintain their army's control of Eastern Europe, and were promoting communism in Turkey, Greece, and China. Elsey and Clifford reported that the Soviets were developing their own nuclear weapons and were directing espionage and subversive movements in the United States in preparation for war. They urged that the situation necessitated a new strategy against the Russians and showed that a consensus had formed on Soviet-American relations in the administration. They argued that the United States should have the military forces to deter any Soviet attempt to expand its borders through aggression. The United States also must continue to develop more sophisticated atomic weaponry and techniques of biological warfare as deterrents. "The language of military power," they said, "is the only language which [sic] disciples of power politics understand. The United States must use that language in order that Soviet leaders will realize that our government is determined to uphold the interests of its citizens and the rights of small nations. . . ." Simultaneously, America should make it known to the Soviets that the United States wanted "peaceable coexistence" with them, but the administration should be prepared for the possibility of the Soviets not cooperating to solve problems, and until they did "the United States should enter no proposal for disarmament or limitation of armament." The United States should be ready to ally itself with other countries in the West to create their own sphere of influence, while recognizing the Soviet sphere. America should help nations, through economic aid, that were threatened by the Soviets, while reserving military assistance as a last resort.

Elsey's report foreshadowed the Marshall Plan's strategy of U.S. aid to threatened democratic nations. It was designed to change the views of other members of the administration who tended to favor disarmament and a softer policy toward the Soviets. Fearing that the report was too explosive, however, Truman decided not to distribute it among his staff members.

Historian Melvyn Leffler has argued that Clifford and Elsey were dependent on information from the armed services and that the two overstated the strength of the Soviets. He further contended that the report was not objective, but rationalized what the administration had done and would do.

In March 1947 Elsey worked with Clifford on the final draft of the speech that set forth the Truman Doctrine. Delivered by the president on March 12, 1947, it called for aid to Turkey and Greece in resisting Communist intervention. Although Elsey personally saw no justification for the strength of the anticommunist rhetoric in the draft he and Clifford had received from the State Department, the final draft retained the State Department's strong phrasing. It called for the United States "to support free peoples who are resisting attempted subjugation by armed [internal] minorities or by outside pressures."

In 1953 Elsey joined the American Red Cross, serving from 1958 to 1961 as its vice president. During the 1960s he worked as assistant to the presidents of several large corporations, including Pullman, Incorporated, in addition to serving on such public welfare committees as the American Food for Peace Council. In 1970 he returned to the Red Cross to serve as its president. During the early 1970s he fought President Richard M. Nixon's concept of state disaster responsibility, believing that only the national government had the fiscal, manpower, and structural ability to provide a consistent standard of disaster relief.

—DAE

Ethridge, Mark F(oster)
(1896–1981) *newspaper publisher*

One of nine children of a lawyer, Mark F. Ethridge was born on April 22, 1896, in Meridian, Mississippi. He was a reporter for the local newspaper before he graduated from high school. Following a year at the University of Mississippi, he became a reporter on the progressive *Macon* (Ga.) *Telegraph*. He served in the navy during World War I and during the 1920s and early 1930s held a number of editorial and managerial positions on such papers as the *New York Sun* and the *Washington Post*. His credentials impressed Barry Bingham, whose father owned the *Louisville* (Ky.) *Courier-Journal* and *Times*. In 1936 the elder Bingham invited Ethridge to be the vice president and general manager of the two papers. Eight years later he became the publisher.

Under Ethridge's direction the *Courier-Journal* emerged as one of the most liberal papers in the South. It supported the New Deal and, during the Roosevelt and Truman administrations, called for racial justice in the region. The paper opposed the poll tax and white primaries as a "complete denial of the democratic process and a complete humiliation of all people who profess any faith in democracy." Ethridge favored economic opportunity for blacks but believed that integration should result from education, not legal duress. He served as chairman of Roosevelt's Fair Employment Practices Commission in 1941 and wrote reports that resulted in an executive order abolishing segregation in government agencies.

In the fall of 1945 Secretary of State JAMES F. BYRNES appointed Ethridge his special representative to observe the general elections in Bulgaria and Romania. He was selected because of his training in journalism and ability "to get at the factual root of any given situation." While on his mission Ethridge also visited Moscow and held meetings with Andrei Vyshinsky, deputy commissar for foreign affairs.

Ethridge submitted his report to Byrnes on December 8. He found that neither the Bulgarian nor the Romanian governments was broadly representative of the people. Instead, these nations were dominated by authoritarian regimes. Ethridge doubted whether the Bulgarian election was a fair one and predicted future ones in the area could not be democratic. He said that the Soviets' "constant and vigorous intrusion . . . into the internal affairs of these countries is so obvious to the impartial observer, that Soviet denial of its existence can only be regarded as a reflection of party line." Any concession the United States would make to the Soviet Union in the future, he warned, would invite further aggression. Ethridge predicted Greece and Turkey would be the next area of contention between the big powers.

Ethridge believed peaceable coexistence between the Soviets and the United States was still possible. Because of this sentiment, according to historian Hugh Thomas, Ethridge's report carried more weight and affected both Washington and the Council of Foreign Ministers in Moscow. He was able to persuade the State Department to send him to Moscow to discuss what he saw with Vyshinsky. In the aftermath of this conversation, the Soviets tried to gain more support for their policies in Bulgaria by inviting noncommunist politicians into the government. They, however, demanded new elections for the National Assembly and the removal of Communist interior minister Anton Yugov from office. The Soviets rejected these demands.

In December 1946 the United Nations created a commission to investigate Greek charges that its neighbors aided the Communists in its civil war. President Truman appointed Ethridge to be the American representative to the body. Ethridge believed the fall of Greece to the Communists would lead to their triumph in France and Italy as well as the Near East. While the investigation was in process, Ethridge pressed Washington to aid the embattled Greek government. His cables predicting the immediate fall of the pro-Western government played an important role in persuading Truman to ask Congress for immediate economic and military assistance to Athens. When it became known that the Americans were going to come to the aid of Greece, the Soviet delegate on the UN commission, Alexander Lavrishchev, asked Ethridge the meaning of the administration's decision, the latter responded, "It means that you can't do it." The Russian grinned and said, "I quite understand, Mr. Ethridge." In May 1947 the UN commission reported Albania, Bulgaria, and Yugoslavia were assisting the guerrillas. (Ethridge had tipped off the administration on what the report would say.) Ethridge completed his UN duty in June 1947 and returned to his newspaper.

During the remainder of the Truman administration, Ethridge served on several governmental panels and was U.S. representative to the UN Conciliation Committee for Palestine. Ethridge contin-

ued to be a voice for moderation on the civil rights issue during the 1950s. In 1956, for example, he condemned resistance to resist the Supreme Court's decision outlawing segregation in public schools. Ethridge left the *Courier-Journal* in 1962 to become vice president and editor of New York's Long Island *Newsday*. He retired in 1963. After retirement he taught journalism at the University of North Carolina until 1968. He died on April 5, 1981, in Moncure, North Carolina.

—JB

Ewing, Oscar R(oss)
(1889–1980) *administrator, Federal Security Agency*

Oscar R. Ewing, a descendant of colonial Scots settlers, was born on March 8, 1889, in Greensburg, Indiana. He graduated from Indiana University in 1906 and from Harvard Law School in 1913, where he edited the *Harvard Law Review*. After service in the army during World War I, he joined the firm of Hughes, Sherman, and Dwight, headed by Charles Evans Hughes. When the firm dissolved in 1937, Ewing formed Hughes, Hubbard, and Ewing with Charles Evans Hughes, Jr., who was at one time U.S. Solicitor General. Ewing became active in Democratic Party politics, and by the 1940s he was frequently mentioned as a candidate for high office. In 1942 he became special assistant to the Attorney General in prosecuting William Dudley Pelley for sedition. After the war he helped the Attorney General in the trial of Douglas Chandler and Robert Best, both accused of broadcasting for the Nazis.

Shortly after the Democratic defeat in the elections of 1946, Ewing, then acting chairman of the Democratic National Committee, proposed the establishment of a liberal advisory group to counter the influence of conservatives in the White House. Among those on the panel were CLARK CLIFFORD, LEON H. KEYSERLING, and DAVID A. MORSE. The group met once a week in Ewing's Wardman Park Hotel apartment. These men mapped out strategy for the 1948 campaign and developed much of the contents and tactics of the Fair Deal.

Ewing, whom one popular magazine termed "Mr. Welfare State Himself," was appointed administrator of the Federal Security Agency (FSA) in August 1947. The Senate confirmed the appointment in December. The FSA was composed of several independent agencies formed to promote the health, education, and economic security of the nation. Ewing was to revitalize the agency and to prepare it for cabinet status. With this goal in mind he improved cooperation between state and federal agencies, and attempted to integrate services and increase social research. During his tenure he ended the exclusion of black doctors from white hospitals in Washington and urged increased scholarships for medical students. Charging that many U.S. children were receiving inadequate medical, educational, and welfare services, he established a committee in 1948 to coordinate the work of federal agencies dealing with children.

Ewing's main concern as FSA head was the adoption of comprehensive national health insurance paid for through Social Security. Under Ewing's advice, Truman called a National Health Assembly for May 1948. The conference made several recommendations but did not express approval of national health insurance. Despite this, in his September 1948 report on the conference, *The Nation's Health—A Ten Year Program* (1948), Ewing contended, "I have re-examined the whole matter as objectively as possible . . . and I still find myself compelled to recommend" comprehensive national health insurance.

Truman endorsed this view in the 1948 campaign, and made it a part of his 1949 Fair Deal program. The plan called for a comprehensive prepaid health insurance program financed through a raise in social security payments. It covered medical, nursing, hospital, laboratory, and dental services.

Recipients would choose their own physicians and health care facilities. The American Medical Association counterattacked with the most costly lobbying blitz up to that time to defeat the proposal. The AMA called Truman and Ewing's plan "socialized medicine" and exploited the anticommunist fervor of the time to defeat it—it was bottled up in committee in Congress. Ewing's vigorous advocacy of federally financed health insurance created a backlash, and Congress rejected his plan for the creation of a cabinet-level Department of Health, Education and Welfare. He left his post at the end of the Truman administration. Ewing's brush with death from the AMA ruined him politically for years, and any hope of running for president or New York governor was dashed. Still Ewing did seem to scare the AMA into accepting private health insurance, which it had opposed before, in order to ward off government-provided health care.

Ewing played a leading role during the 1960 Democratic presidential primaries. As vice chairman of the HUBERT H. HUMPHREY for President Committee, Ewing helped plan the campaign strategy for the West Virginia Democratic presidential primary race against John F. Kennedy. He later joined the LYNDON B. JOHNSON National Committee. From 1963 to 1967 Ewing was chairman of Research Triangle Regional Planning Commission. Ewing died on January 8, 1980, in Chapel Hill, North Carolina.

—RSG

Fairbank, John K(ing)

(1907–1991) *State Department adviser*

John K. Fairbank was born on May 24, 1907. He received his bachelor's degree from Harvard University, summa cum laude, in 1929. A Rhodes scholar, he went to China in 1932, studying and lecturing for three years at Tsinghua University in Peking, where his major interest was the impact of Western imperialism on Chinese society. He received his Ph.D. from Oxford in 1936 and joined the Harvard faculty that same year.

In 1941 Fairbank was granted a leave of absence from Harvard to serve in the Washington office of the Coordinator of Information and with the Office of Strategic Services. He went to China in 1942 as a special assistant to the U.S. ambassador. In his memoir *Chinabound* (1982), Fairbank said he became convinced that, due to conditions in China, revolution was virtually inevitable. During 1944 Fairbank worked with the Office of War Information, where he also acted occasionally as the deputy director in charge of Far Eastern operations. The following year he returned to China as the director of the United States Information Service. In 1946 he resumed his position at Harvard.

In his 1948 book *The United States and China*—described at the time as "the best one volume history of China"—Fairbank attempted to analyze China in terms of its cultural and historical background. He emphasized China as a society different from the West, one of authoritarian traditions that did not easily lend itself to the development of liberal capitalism. His book was praised as a scholarly work, although some critics disagreed with Fairbank's criticism of Chiang Kai-shek's (Jiang Jieshi) government. Fairbank accused Chiang of presiding over a corrupt regime of "carpet-bagging generals and politicians" with as "shameful a record of official looting as modern history has displayed." He also criticized Chiang's government for its use of force against intellectuals and demonstrating students, its ineffective administration, and for the generalissimo's failure to develop any sort of rural reconstruction program.

The following year Fairbank argued, in *The Next Step in Asia*, that the United States had to accept the fact that the Communists had defeated the Nationalists in China. He urged the United States to take a more practical approach and support that inevitable changes with American aid and technology. In a *Harvard Crimson* article in 1950 Fairbank called for the recognition of Communist China, which, in his view, was not an act of moral approval but only a realistic step in which the United States could "deal with the Communists but be under no compulsion to accept their terms."

After Communist China's entry into the Korean War, Fairbank spoke out against extending the conflict to China. He pointed out that there was a lack of installations in China worth bombing, and he maintained that an attack would only serve to spur the Chinese war effort. Fairbank said it would be a "fallacy" to think that the application of force would result in defeating the Communists.

In 1951 and 1952 the Senate Permanent Investigations Subcommittee probed charges that Fairbank was a Communist. Fairbank testified before the panel in March 1952, repeating under oath his previous denials that he had ever been a member of the party. He criticized what he termed the "totalitarian" methods used by the group. He did admit that he had once supported an effort to bring about an amalgamation of Communists and Nationalists in the Chinese government, but he pointed out that this policy had been advocated by GEORGE C. MARSHALL and other Chinese experts. Fairbank was able to save his career through his testimony that gained a favorable impression before the Senate Internal Security Subcommittee (McCarran Committee).

Although Fairbank was ultimately cleared of the charges, he was for a time refused a passport. During the 1950s and 1960s he continued his academic career. In the mid-1960s he emerged from obscurity with the renewal of public discussion of America's China policy. He presented the view that there was continuity in Chinese leadership and opposed the vision of a distinct Communist dictatorship. Fairbank died on September 14, 1991, in Cambridge, Massachusetts.

—GMS

Fairless, Benjamin F(ranklin)

(1890–1962) *chairman of the board, United States Steel Corporation; president, American Iron and Steel Institute*

Benjamin Williams was born on May 3, 1890, in Pigeon Run, Ohio. He was the son of an impoverished Welsh immigrant coal miner. Because educational opportunities were poor where his parents had settled and because of an injury to his mother, they sent him to live with an aunt and uncle, Sarah and Jacob Fairless. The couple legally adopted him, and he took their name. Fairless worked as an attendant in a mental hospital during summers to help pay his way through Ohio Northern University. Following his graduation in 1913, he went to work as a surveyor for the Wheeling and Lake Erie Railroad. Soon after he joined the Central Steel Company as a civil engineer. By 1928 he had become president and general manager. When the company and several others merged to form the Republic Steel Corporation in 1930, he was appointed executive vice president. In 1935 he became president of Carnegie-Illinois Steel Corporation, newly formed from units of U.S. Steel. He became president of the parent company in January 1938. During World War II Fairless served on various advisory panels, among them the Iron and Steel Advisory Committee and the War Production Board. In the postwar years he defended U.S. Steel against critics of large businesses. He once labeled them "Calamity Johns suffering from a midget complex."

During 1949 Fairless became involved in a bitter struggle with PHILIP MURRAY, head of the Steelworkers of America. In July negotiations broke down between the union and U.S. Steel after Fairless rejected the union's demand for a wage increase and a company-funded pension plan. President Truman quickly named a three-member panel to consider the union demands under a 60-day strike truce. Fairless agreed to the truce after obtaining Truman's assurance that the board's recommendations would not be binding on either party. In September the president's panel denied the union's demand for a wage increase but recommended that the company initiate employer-funded pension and welfare programs. Fairless labeled the principle behind such programs "revolutionary doctrine." He rejected Murray's call for further bargaining contingent on acceptance of the board's recommendations as contradictory to Truman's assurances that the board's findings would not be binding. On October 1, after federal mediation efforts collapsed, Murray called a national steel strike. The walkout lasted 42 days and involved 500,000 workers. The steel companies and the union reached an agreement on November 11. The new contract required U.S. Steel to finance a pension program and to share the cost of a social insurance plan with its employees.

Fairless again clashed with the union and the government in 1952. This time the dispute led to a 53-day strike, which crippled the industry. In March 1952 the Wage Stabilization Board, which had been holding hearings on union demands, recommended a wage increase of 26.4 cents an hour over 18 months and proposed a union shop. In a radio address delivered on April 6 Fairless rejected the wage increase as inflationary. He maintained the proposal for a union shop was as "contrary to every concept of American liberty that we have cherished." On April 8 President Truman, in the face of a nationwide walkout by steelworkers, directed the secretary of commerce to seize the steel mills and keep them operating. Later that month Federal District Court judge DAVID A. PINE ruled that the seizure was unconstitutional and ordered the return of the mills to private ownership. In June the U.S. Supreme Court upheld Pine's decision and the union went out on strike. Throughout this period, union and company officials tried unsuccessfully to reach an agreement.

On July 24 Truman summoned Fairless and Murray to the White House. After a stern warning from the president to settle, "or else," Fairless and Murray agreed to a contract. The agreement, which was substantially the same wage and price terms as the company had offered in March, called for a wage increase of 16 cents an hour, a fringe benefit program and a compromise form of the union shop. The government, in turn, allowed the steel companies to charge $5.20 more per ton of steel. Fairless blamed the lengthy strike on the union's demand for compulsory union membership.

In the aftermath of the acrimonious 1952 strike, Fairless decided a change was in order. He had had poor relations with United Steelworkers of America president Phillip Murray. When he died in November 1952, Fairless attempted a rapprochement with his successor, David J. MacDonald. The two visited steel plants together, and the "Ben and Dave" tour, after which there were no more strikes against U.S. Steel while Fairless was chairman.

Throughout the 1950s Fairless often represented the steel industry at government hearings. In 1954 he was named to head the Citizens Advisers on Mutual Securities Program whose job it was to study U.S. foreign aid problems. In May 1955 Fairless left his positions at U.S. Steel. He was named president of the American Iron and Steel Institute that same year and held the position until his death. Fairless died on January 1, 1962, in Ligonier, Pennsylvania. (See *The Eisenhower Years* Volume)

—EF

Ferguson, Homer
(1889–1982) *member of the Senate*

Homer Ferguson was born on February 25, 1889, in Harrison, Pennsylvania. He received his degree from the University of Michigan in 1913 and practiced law in Detroit until 1929, when he was appointed a circuit judge. He was elected to a full term in 1930 and reelected again in 1935 and 1941. Ferguson achieved fame investigating official corruption in Wayne County. As a result of his probe, a former mayor of Detroit, a county prosecutor, several police officials, and many underworld figures were sent to jail. In 1942 Ferguson ran for the Senate as a Republican and narrowly defeated the incumbent Democrat, Prentiss M. Brown.

In the Senate Ferguson proved himself a loyal party man. He opposed most New Deal and Fair Deal domestic programs. He generally supported attempts to cut the domestic expenditures of the

federal government and to limit the growing power and independence of the executive branch. In foreign affairs he followed the lead of his senior colleague from Michigan, Republican senator ARTHUR H. VANDENBERG, and supported an internationalist foreign policy. He voted for aid to Greece and Turkey in 1947, for the Marshall Plan in 1948, and for the North Atlantic Treaty in 1949.

Ferguson earned a reputation as a tireless investigator. In 1943 he was given a seat on the Senate Special Committee to Investigate the National Defense Program, better known as the Truman Committee for its chairman, Harry S Truman. Ferguson was also a member of the Joint Committee to Investigate Pearl Harbor, which Congress authorized in August 1945 after the release of an army and navy report on the Pearl Harbor attack. When the panel's hearings began in November, Ferguson pushed hard to have the committee examine the role of President Roosevelt in the events leading up to the attack. He grilled U.S. Army Chief of Staff general GEORGE C. MARSHALL for over five days. On July 20, 1946, the committee's majority released a report exonerating Roosevelt and other administration officials, while laying the blame for the disaster on errors in judgment by military officers. However, Ferguson, along with Senator OWEN BREWSTER (R-Maine), issued a minority report accusing Roosevelt of "failure to perform the responsibilities indispensable to the defense of Pearl Harbor," and placing principal blame for the disaster on Roosevelt, Secretary of War HENRY L. STIMSON, Secretary of the Navy Frank Knox, and Marshall, in addition to the field commanders.

In succeeding years Ferguson led investigations into the activities of the executive branch of government. During August 1947, as chairman of a subcommittee of the Senate War Investigations Committee, he conducted highly publicized hearings into the wartime defense contracts of Howard Hughes. The following year he was chosen to head a subcommittee with the power to probe the activities of the executive branch. A vigorous anticommunist, Ferguson used his position to focus on domestic subversion. In August 1948 he began an inquiry into allegations that persons accused of disloyalty were being kept in federal jobs. When President Truman withheld from the committee Loyalty Review Board files on WILLIAM W. REMINGTON, Ferguson announced that impeachment proceedings might be necessary. Over the next two years he continued to investigate the workings of the loyalty program and frequently charged the administration with inefficiency and lax enforcement.

Ferguson supported several legislative proposals to deal with internal subversion. He introduced a subversive activities control bill in 1949, and the following year he sponsored with Senator KARL E. MUNDT (R-S.Dak.) a bill requiring the registration of all members of the Communist Party. A version of the proposal was incorporated in the Internal Security Act of 1950, passed by both houses of Congress in September. After President Truman vetoed it, Ferguson voted with the majority to override the veto. As Senator JOSEPH R. MCCARTHY (R-Wisc.) took the lead in the domestic anticommunist crusade, Ferguson's role became less significant, but he continued to support McCarthy's efforts.

After Eisenhower's election in 1952 Ferguson became part of the Republican congressional leadership. He began to distance himself from McCarthy, and voted to condemn him for misconduct in 1954. He was narrowly defeated for reelection in 1954 by Patrick V. McNamara. In 1955 Ferguson was named ambassador to the Philippines. The following year he was appointed an associate justice on the U.S. Court of Military Appeals in Washington D.C., and in 1971 he became a senior judge on the court. He retired in 1976 and died at Grosse Pointe, Michigan, on December 17, 1982. (See *The Eisenhower Years* Volume)

—JD

Fermi, Enrico
(1901–1954) *physicist*
Enrico Fermi was born on September 29, 1901, in Rome, Italy. He grew up there, the son of a railroad administrator and former schoolteacher. He received his Ph.D. in physics magna cum laude from Pisa in 1922 and was awarded a scholarship to study at Göttingen with the internationally famous physicist Max Born. Receiving little encouragement there, Fermi returned after seven months to teach at the University of Rome. In 1925 he made his first major contribution to theoretical physics, publishing a theory of monatomic gases that led to his widely used statistical model of the atom. In 1926 Fermi won the newly created chair of theoretical physics at the University of Rome and began to gather a research team of brilliant young physicists. In 1934 this group attempted to duplicate the

Curies' production of artificial radioactivity by bombarding the nuclei of various elements with slow-moving neutrons. During this series of experiments, Fermi actually succeeded in splitting the uranium nucleus, though at the time he believed this impossible and theorized that new transuranic elements had been created.

With the enactment of anti-Semitic legislation in 1938, Fermi, whose wife was Jewish, left Italy. After traveling to Sweden to receive a Nobel Prize, Fermi settled in the United States, where he accepted Columbia University's offer of a professorship. With the outbreak of war in Europe in 1939, the European physicists working in the United States, fearing that the Germans might be developing an atomic bomb, chose Fermi to warn the government. However, Fermi was never able to gain access to high officials. Not until December 1941 did Washington decide to accelerate the atomic research program, creating the Manhattan District Project.

The research efforts were at first concentrated at the University of Chicago Metallurgical Laboratory. There Fermi and his team of scientists constructed a primitive uranium reactor and succeeded in producing, in December 1942, the first self-sustaining controlled nuclear reaction. In 1944 Fermi became associate director of the Los Alamos, New Mexico, laboratory, where the actual construction of the atomic bomb was in progress under the direction of J. ROBERT OPPENHEIMER. The following year Fermi observed the first atomic explosion.

As one of the four-man scientific panel to advise President Harry S Truman's Interim Committee, Fermi was responsible in the summer of 1945 for making recommendations on wartime and long-range nuclear policy. While many of the nuclear scientists opposed use of the atomic bomb on Japan, Fermi and other panel members recommended that the bomb be used to end the war quickly and save lives. However, they stressed that, as scientists, they had "no claim to special competence in solving the political, social and military problems" raised by atomic power. In addition the panel recommended that the government appropriate $1 billion a year for continuing atomic studies.

After World War II Fermi accepted a professorship at the newly formed Institute for Nuclear Studies at the University of Chicago. Favoring an end to secrecy in atomic research and an international agreement that would allow for free exploration of the peaceful uses of atomic energy, Fermi supported the 1945 May-Johnson bill. The measure called for the creation of an atomic energy authority controlled by the military. Most scientists opposed the measure, and it was eventually replaced by the Atomic Energy Act of 1946, which created a civilian Atomic Energy Commission (AEC). The AEC was to be advised by a Military Liaison Committee and a group of scientists in a General Advisory Committee (GAC).

From 1947 to 1950 Fermi served on the GAC under Oppenheimer's chairmanship. Along with other members of the board, he believed that the United States should maintain its nuclear weapons as a deterrent force but should avoid involving other nations in a deadly arms race. Then there was the question of whether to build a hydrogen bomb. Fermi had told superbomb advocate EDWARD TELLER before "a critical October 1949 meeting" that he was not interested in the superbomb. Fermi had been skeptical of making such a bomb, and in the meeting, JAMES B. CONANT's ethical argument against the bomb swayed Fermi to come out firmly

against the thermonuclear device. Fermi and physicist Isidor Rabi tried to forge a practical modus vivendi: the United States should forego building an H-bomb if other countries also refrained from doing so. The two put their faith in being able to detect another nation's attempt to test a super, just as the United States had detected the Soviet atomic bomb test. Fermi stated in a memorandum attached to the majority report that he believed it "wrong on fundamental ethical principles to initiate the development of such a weapon." The following year Truman ordered an all-out effort to develop a hydrogen bomb. When, in 1951, Teller proposed a device that would make the new bomb possible, Fermi along with other GAC scientists took an active part in the calculations to corroborate Teller's theory.

Fermi returned to the University of Chicago full time at the expiration of his GAC term in August 1950. He produced theories on the origin of cosmic rays and the polarization of proton beams before his premature death on November 30, 1954, in Chicago, Illinois. Fermi was posthumously awarded a Congressional Medal of Merit. An act of Congress established the AEC's Enrico Fermi Award and named Fermi as its first recipient.

In 1982, in an effort to get back into the good graces of the Kremlin, Pavel Sudoplatov, Soviet chief of atomic bomb espionage, reminded Soviet leader and former KGB chief Yuri Andropov that he had obtained classified information from Fermi, Klaus Fuchs, J. Robert Oppenheimer, and others in the Manhattan Project. Authors Herbert Romerstein and Eric Breindel contend it would have been dangerous to lie to Andropov, who could have easily checked Sudoplatov's claims. However, no corroborating evidence has been found to support this allegation, and it seems rather unlikely that it is true given that Fermi did not support the Baruch Plan because he did not trust the Russians.

—DAE

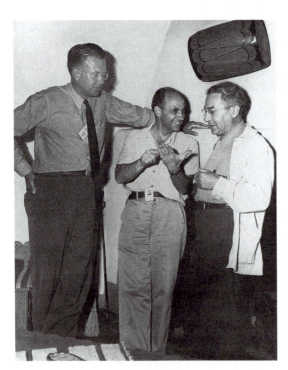

(left to right) E. O. Lawrence, Enrico Fermi, and I. I. Rabi, Alamogordo, New Mexico, 1945 *(Harry S. Truman Library, I Lansing Lamont)*

Field, Marshall, III

(1893–1956) *businessman*

Marshall Field III was born on September 28, 1893, in Chicago, Illinois. He was the grandson of the founder of the Chicago department store, Marshall Field and Company, and heir to a large personal fortune. After Field's father died of a self-inflicted gunshot wound in 1906, the Field children were taken by their mother to England, where Marshall attended Eton and then studied history and economics at Trinity College, Cambridge. He returned to the United States at the age of 21 to help administer the family estate. Field served in the army during World War I. For a short time after the war he worked for Chicago's Bureau of Justice, helping get jobs for former servicemen and organizing community centers. In 1921, after starting his own investment banking firm, he moved his family to New York and built Caumsett, an elegant Long Island country estate run by a staff of 85 servants. There he led the life of a country gentleman while managing his investment firm and serving as director of a dozen corporations. At that time Field was worth over $90 million.

In 1934 Field, increasingly dissatisfied with his pattern of life, went into psychoanalysis and emerged with new interests and social values. He gave up his investment firm and became an ardent New Dealer and supporter of liberal causes. In 1940 he set up the Field Foundation, which continued through the 1950s to channel money into the areas of child welfare and race relations. That same year Field embarked on his first publishing venture, becoming the major investor and later sole owner of RALPH M. INGERSOLL's experimental liberal newspaper, *PM*. The new daily paper was to have an unconventional format, top-quality writing, and no advertising. Field agreed with *PM*'s editorial policies and spent much time in its office, though he exercised no editorial control. Unable to live up to its initial promise, *PM* failed to gain a wide readership and was forced to cease publication in June 1948.

Starting on December 4, 1941, Field began publishing the *Chicago Daily Sun*, a morning newspaper intended to compete with the conservative, isolationist *Chicago Tribune*. The *Tribune*'s publisher, Robert R. McCormick, attempted to deny access to the Associated Press wire service to the *Sun*, but the Supreme Court in 1945 ruled in favor of Field, holding that the AP's restrictive membership provision violated antitrust laws. Intimately involved in running the new paper, Field directed the editorial page himself and even wrote an occasional editorial. During World War II the *Sun* supported and publicized President Roosevelt's decisions and reflected Field's moral conviction that men must fight disease, injustice, and ignorance. In 1945 Field published a small book, *Freedom Is More Than a Word*,

defending free thought and free speech in democracy and calling for the kind of "real competition" in the communications media that would provide for representation of a wide range of views.

Field questioned Truman's ability to carry through the great projects of the New Deal. When the Republicans took both houses of Congress in the 1946 elections, Field published a signed front-page editorial in the *Sun* proposing that Truman resign in favor of a Republican and thus give the Democrats a chance to recoup in the next election. Field's editorial aroused the wrath of many high-ranking Democrats. In March 1947 he opposed the Truman Doctrine, which called for unilateral military and economic aid to Communist-threatened Greece and Turkey. Field argued that by ignoring the United Nations and undercutting the nation's multilateral alliances, the United States would exacerbate the cold war. He warned of the danger of trying to smother communism by force, writing that the president's policy failed "to distinguish between containing Russia and containing Communism." Almost alone in its stand, the *Sun* was violently attacked for its "Red sympathies."

In 1947 Field purchased another Chicago paper, the *Daily Times*, in order to secure its printing plant. For a short time after the purchase, Field published two papers, a morning and an evening tabloid, but by March 1948 he had merged them into one all-day paper, the *Sun Times*. After the merger he became less involved in running the paper, turning over its daily operation to his son, Marshall Field IV, in 1950. Following his retirement, the editorial policy of the *Sun Times* became increasingly conservative. Although the paper had supported Truman's reelection in 1948, it came out strongly for DWIGHT D. EISENHOWER in 1952, to Field's disappointment.

By the early 1950s Field's business empire included the Field Estate, which dealt in real estate, stocks and bonds; Field Enterprises, comprising the *Sun Times*, four radio stations, *World Book Encyclopedia*, the Sunday supplement *Parade*, and partial interest in Simon and Schuster, Inc., and Pocket Books; and the philanthropic Field Foundation. In 1951 Field returned to New York to live. He remained active in many other civic and educational organizations until his death on November 8, 1956, in New York City.

—DAE

Finletter, Thomas K(night)

(1893–1980) *chairman, Temporary Air Policy Commission; chief, Economic Administration Mission in England; secretary of the air force*

The son of a prominent judge, Thomas K. Finletter was born on November 11, 1893, in Philadelphia, Pennsylvania. He graduated from the University of Pennsylvania in 1915 and served as a captain in the army during World War I. After obtaining a law degree from the University of Pennsylvania Law School in 1920, Finletter practiced with the New York firm of Cravath and Henderson and joined the prestigious firm of Coudert Brothers in 1926. Finletter took a leave of absence in 1941 to serve as special assistant to Secretary of State Cordell Hull. Two years later Hull appointed him executive director of the Office of Foreign Economic Coordination, charged with supervising economic planning in Allied controlled areas. He also worked as a consultant to the committee to establish the foundation for the United Nations and was an aide to ADLAI E. STEVENSON at the San Francisco Conference.

In July 1947 Truman appointed Finletter to head the Temporary Air Policy Commission (the Finletter Commission), formed to survey national aviation policies and problems in relation to security needs. He ignored the mandate of the commission for a force that was balanced, and the Joint Chiefs of Staff's counsel for a gradual strengthening of land- and carrier-based aviation through 1952. The panel's 1948 report, *Survival in the Air Age*, which was largely written by Finletter, warned that the nation could no longer rely on armies and navies in the nuclear age. It predicted that by 1952 the Soviet Union would achieve nuclear and air parity with the United States. To meet the challenge, the report said, the United States had to increase the air force to 95 wings at a cost of $18 billion. President Truman, the press, and leading defense analysts praised the report. During the late 1940s it became the basis for the air force's continued requests for budget increases.

In May 1948 Finletter became chief of the Economic Administration Mission in London. During his tenure he directed the spending of $1.2 billion to aid the foundering British economy. Finletter did his job with such care and courtesy that Sir Stafford Cripps said there was a "Finletter cult" in the British Treasury that was "prepared to do anything he asked." Finletter did express concerns in this post toward the administration idea of encouraging a European union, believing it might cause there a "new isolationism" or a European "Third Force" between the United States and the USSR. Finletter resigned his post in June 1949 to resume his law practice.

Finletter returned to government in April 1950 as secretary of the air force. By the time he had assumed the post, the bitter rivalry between the services over their role in defense had already peaked, and relations between the army, navy, and air force had improved. Finletter consolidated the peace by maintaining good personal relations with the other service secretaries and pursuing the "joint task concept" by which the secretary of defense judged what needed to be done for defense in terms of a combined effort of all services. Despite his support for a coordinated defense, Finletter emerged as the administration's leading advocate of air power as a first deterrent. He pushed the idea that strategic bombers should have priority in military planning by arguing that the American ability to deliver nuclear weapons was its greatest force for peace.

During the 1950s Finletter served as a foreign policy and defense adviser to Adlai Stevenson and the Democratic Party. He was a major critic of the Eisenhower administration's defense policies, arguing that they had lost the United States its nuclear superiority. In 1956 Finletter headed the New York State Stevenson for President Committee. Four years later he helped organize the draft Stevenson movement. He was active in New York State Democratic politics and in 1958 ran unsuccessfully for the Democratic senatorial nomination. Finletter served as ambassador to the North Atlantic Treaty Organization from 1961 to 1965. He returned to the practice of law until he retired in 1970. He died in New York City on April 24, 1980. (See *The Eisenhower Years* Volume)

—JB

Fitzgerald, Albert J.

(1906–1982) *president, United Electrical, Radio, and Machine Workers of America*

The son of Irish immigrants, Albert J. Fitzgerald was born in 1906 in Lynn, Massachusetts, where he grew up. After graduating from high school he went to work as a lathe-turner for General Electric Company. Fitzgerald was a charter member of the union, formed in 1933, that later affiliated with the United

Electrical, Radio and Machine Workers of America (UE). He gradually moved up to become president of the Lynn local. In 1941 the UE national convention divided on the issue of whether locals had the power to bar Communists from union office. Fitzgerald, who opposed any discrimination against union members on the basis of political beliefs, ousted the incumbent president, JAMES B. CAREY, on this issue.

After deferring wage increases during World War II, the union struck for a major raise in 1946. In the midst of the strike, in February 1946, Fitzgerald told the Senate Education and Labor Committee that workers wanted to recover the high incomes—due to overtime—they had had during the war. General Electric president Charles E. Wilson agreed it would be desirable for that to happen, but only higher productivity would justify the wage hikes the union wanted. In March the UE won an 18.5-cent-per-hour increase. The strike against Westinghouse lasted 119 days before both sides accepted a compromise 19-cents per hour. By September 1946 the UE represented 600,000 workers in collective bargaining agreements in the United States and Canada. Opposed to the Taft-Hartley Act's provision that union officials sign a noncommunist affidavit, Fitzgerald, along with officers of other unions, refused to comply with the law. As a result the UE could not appear on ballots for any union elections held by the National Labor Relations Board (NLRB).

In January 1948 Fitzgerald resigned from the Political Action Committee of the Congress of Industrial Organizations (CIO) when it went on record as being opposed to the third-party candidacy of HENRY A. WALLACE. Fitzgerald was named chairman of the National Labor Committee for Wallace and Taylor and helped found the Massachusetts Progressive Party. However, at the UE convention in September 1948, he opposed the union formally endorsing any candidate in the election, a stand adopted by the union. At the meeting Fitzgerald also came out "unalterably opposed" to Truman's Economic Recovery Plan, saying it was run by industrialists and bankers and not in the interest of workers.

In retaliation for the UE's leftist political stand, CIO unions began raiding UE shops. The other CIO unions gradually signed the noncommunist affidavits, making it easy for them to oust the UE because it could not appear on the NLRB election ballot.

In 1949 Fitzgerald defeated a strong challenge from rightists in the union. Faced with threats of expulsion by the CIO unless it stopped following pro-Communist policies, the UE countered with an ultimatum to the federation. The union threatened to withhold its per capita dues from the CIO unless the organization ordered the locals that quit the UE to return and disciplined officers of unions that raided the UE. If CIO leaders ignored the demands, Fitzgerald said, "then the hell with them." The convention also voted to instruct its officers to sign the noncommunist affidavits required for use of the NLRB.

The UE did not send any delegates to the November 1949 CIO convention—despite the advice of the Communist Party to stay in the CIO and fight the anticommunists. Consequently, the CIO expelled the UE for being "Communist dominated" and, with the aid of the electrical companies, helped form the International Union of Electrical, Radio and Machine Workers (IUE) with Carey as its president.

Under Truman's Loyalty Order of 1947, which applied to companies with government contracts, alleged Communist members of the UE were fired. The UE was also investigated by the House Un-American Activities Committee, which, in December 1948, listed Fitzgerald as a Communist.

Fitzgerald continued as president of the UE through the 1950s, 1960s, and 1970s. UE membership declined to 90,000 by 1955 but rose again to 165,000 by 1966. During 1969–70 Fitzgerald led the UE in a successful strike involving 150,000 workers against General Electric. Fitzgerald resigned as UE president in 1978 and died on May 1, 1982, in Boston, Massachusetts.

—TFS

Flanders, Ralph E(dward)
(1880–1970) *member of the Senate*

Ralph E. Flanders was born on September 28, 1880, in Barnet, Vermont. He was raised in poverty and received only seven years of formal education. He took a correspondence course in engineering and went on to become a working engineer and an author of articles on machine designing. For five years he was associate editor of the periodical *Machinery* and published two books on gears. Following World War I Flanders lectured and wrote on the causes of economic dislocation. In 1933 he was appointed to the newly formed Federal Business

Advisory and Planning Council, where he vociferously opposed New Deal programs. That year he also succeeded his father-in-law as president of the Jones and Lamson Machine Company. In 1940 he lost the Vermont Republican senatorial primary to GEORGE D. AIKEN. Four years later he became president of the Federal Reserve Bank of Boston. During World War II Flanders served in the Office of Price Administration and on the Economic Stabilization Board and the War Production Board.

In 1946 Vermont governor Redfield Proctor appointed Flanders to fill the unexpired term of Senator WARREN AUSTIN (R-Vt.). He won a full term that same year with the aid of labor. Flanders quickly became identified with the Republican's liberal wing and soon was one of his party's chief policy makers on price legislation. In 1947 he chaired a subcommittee that investigated consumer prices in 14 Eastern cities. The panel recommended that President Truman find ways to limit speculation on the nation's large grain exchanges as a means of combatting inflation.

He also became a Republican "Young Turk" after entering office. These junior senators wanted a larger role in the Senate. He told the conservative Republican leader Senator ROBERT A. TAFT (R-Ohio), "I wish the whole party leadership were more positively interested in people."

In the late 1940s Flanders backed liberal domestic policies, including a bill that called on the federal government to take responsibility for correcting substandard housing. In 1949 he joined a group of independent Republicans sponsoring a health care bill which recommended federal subsidies to voluntary health insurance programs. Under the bill's provisions, the insurance agencies would charge a percentage of their subscriber's income, rather than a flat fee. However, he did anger his labor supporters by voting for the Taft-Hartley Act.

Flanders backed the Truman Doctrine, the Marshall Plan, and the Selective Service Act of 1948. However, he saw the Soviet Union as more of an economic threat than a potential military opponent. Consequently, in October 1948, when he perceived a shift in the Marshall Plan from supporting European economic recovery to rearming Europe, Flanders predicted the changed emphasis would eventually fulfill the Soviet Union's aim of weakening the United States economically. That year he supported a limited military budget, and in 1949 he opposed the North Atlantic Treaty Organization and argued for revising the veto power in the UN Security Council, which had been abused by the Soviets. In April 1949 he proposed that America launch a propaganda program that attacked the "predatory imperialism" of the Soviet Union, not communism as such. He suggested that the United States use guided missiles and remote-controlled planes to deliver the message to the Soviet people. Flanders's approach to combating communism in Korea was not as pacific. In December 1950 he spoke in favor of using the atomic bomb against Chinese forces in Korea if the United Nations Assembly ordered and approved its employment.

Flanders's attitude toward Senator JOSEPH R. MCCARTHY (R-Wisc.) was, for a long period, ambivalent. Until the spring of 1954 he felt the best way to neutralize McCarthy was by implementing alternatives to the misguided policies of the Democratic Party. Although he concurred with conservative Republicans that the New Deal programs leaned too far to the left, he still remained wary of McCarthy. In 1950 he told his constituents that he was not sure how well-founded McCarthy's allegations were; he guessed that 90 percent were "baseless," but the other 10 percent troubled him. During the 1950 Tydings Committee investigations of Secretary of State DEAN G. ACHESON, Flanders did not join others in attacking the secretary as soft on communism. However, in 1951, when the senator's old friend, WILLIAM B. BENTON (D-Conn.) recommended a Senate investigation of McCarthy's activities with a view toward expulsion, Flanders criticized the effort. He believed it brought McCarthy attention at a time when he was fading from public view. Three years later Flanders launched his first direct attack on McCarthy, which soon led to his motion for censure.

Flanders backed Dwight D. Eisenhower for president in 1952, even though the senator was a friend of Taft, Eisenhower's opponent for the Republican nomination. He wrote Eisenhower that he was ill at ease with "lifelong Republicans." Flanders himself was easily reelected in 1952.

During the Eisenhower administration, Flanders continued to advocate liberal policies. In 1958 he chose not to run for reelection and took up pig farming in Vermont. Flanders died on February 19, 1970, in Springfield, Vermont. (See *The Eisenhower Years* Volume)

—EF

Flynn, Elizabeth G(urley)
(1890–1964) *Communist Party official*

Elizabeth Gurley Flynn was born on August 7, 1890, in Concord, New Hampshire. A descendant of Irish revolutionaries, Flynn became active in socialist affairs when still a child. In 1906 she joined the Industrial Workers of the World and the following year left high school to work full time for the organization. During the next decade she participated in several historic strikes, including the textile strike in Lawrence, Massachusetts, in 1912, the silk strike in Paterson, New Jersey, in 1913; and the Mesabi Range iron strike in Minnesota in 1916. She helped found the American Civil Liberties Union in 1920 and worked for the defense of Bartolemeo Vanzetti and Nicola Sacco during the 1920s. Flynn joined the Communist Party in 1937. She subsequently wrote a weekly column for the party's newspaper, *The Daily Worker*, for 24 years, and, in the 1940s, she was a member of the party's National Committee. She was expelled from the ACLU for being a Communist in 1940, which historian Ellen Schrecker has argued foreshadowed the second Red Scare's dependence on guilt by association.

In 1948 the government indicted 11 members of the National Committee for violation of the Smith Act, which made it a crime to advocate the violent overthrow of the U.S. government. Flynn was the only member of the group not indicted. In an interview in the *New York Times*, she said she was "somewhat miffed that she was not included in the indictment." Flynn worked for the defense of the officials throughout their trial, attempting to stir popular and financial support. Their convictions were sustained by the Supreme Court in 1951 and Flynn, along with Pettis Perry and WILLIAM Z. FOSTER, took over party leadership. With the death of Ella Reeve (Mother) Bloor that same year, she became the leading female Communist in the United States.

Flynn led the resistance to the Internal Security Act of 1950, which required all Communist-action or front groups to register with the U.S. Attorney General. She was one of 135 plaintiffs who signed a suit to declare the act unconstitutional. In September 1951 Flynn was among the 21 party members indicted for criminal conspiracy under the Smith Act. Only 17 went to trial. More than 200 lawyers refused pleas to defend them. She headed the Self-Defense Committee of the 17 Victims and served 30 days on contempt of court charges in 1952. During

Elizabeth Gurley Flynn, 1915 *(Library of Congress, Prints and Photographs Division, George Grantham Bain Collection)*

the monthlong trial she defended herself forcefully and fluently, but she and her codefendants were forced to rest their cases soon after because of a lack of funds. She was among the 13 who were finally convicted in 1953. Flynn served slightly more than two years of her three-year sentence beginning in January 1955. She was elected national chairman of the Communist Party in March 1961 and died on September 5, 1964, in Moscow while touring the Soviet Union.

—RB

Ford, Henry, II
(1917–1987) *president, Ford Motor Company*

Henry Ford II was born on September 4, 1917, in Detroit, Michigan. He was the grandson of the auto manufacturer and the son of Ford Motor Company president Edsel Ford. A sociology major at Yale, he left the university in June 1940 before he had earned enough credits to graduate. In 1941 he enlisted in the navy. Ford was on active duty during World War II, but Secretary of the Navy Frank Knox worried that the senior Henry Ford, who had taken over the company again after his son Edsel died in 1943, could not manage the company during the wartime emergency. This was critical as Ford was an important part of war production. Henry I had not established modern accounting methods, and Ford was losing $9 million each month. The company appeared on the edge of collapse. Knox discharged Henry II in August 1943 so that he could return to the company. He began a management apprenticeship under his grandfather, and he became vice president of the company in December 1943. Henry II began to take control from Henry I and introduced to the company more up-to-date management methods and an international vision. He was named president of the company in 1945 at the age of 28.

Ford took over a company beset by problems. Upheavals in top personnel and the firm's lack of salesmindedness during his father's tenure had caused Ford Motor to fall behind General Motors (GM) and Chrysler. Ford's goal was "to put the company back into first place in production and sales." He initiated a program of reorganization and enlisted the aid of a group of 10 young men from the Office of Statistical Control in the air force to analyze the company's problems. The group, which included Robert S. McNamara, was dubbed the "Whiz Kids."

By April 1946 Ford was set on remodeling the company along the decentralized lines of GM. Under that system each of the company's operations functioned as an integral unit complete in itself. He hired Ernest R. Breech, president of the Bendix Aviation Corporation, to become general director of operations and supervise the reorganization. Ford's plan included the GM practice of definite allotment of responsibility. By September proposals for an organizational structure based on "decentralized operation and centralized control" were unveiled. To reduce corporate losses Ford began to concentrate on automobile production; numerous nonproductive properties that had drained the company of resources were sold off. These included a Brazilian rubber plantation, a soybean processing factory, much of the senior Ford's farmland, and large tracts of mineral lands. In addition, Ford worked with Breech to create a more humane working environment within the company. He believed that Ford Motor could not "build [its] products as cheaply as it could build them if [it] had good human relations." In November 1946 steps were taken to eliminate the old "driver" attitude under which fear was the foundation on which the company rested.

Ford's more liberal attitude was reflected in his relationship with unions. Unlike his grandfather, who bitterly opposed unionism, he developed a more flexible stance toward the demands of the United Automobile Workers (UAW). In January 1946, speaking before the Society of Automotive Engineers, he called for cooperation between labor and management in solving common problems. Later that month an agreement was reached with the UAW that called for wage increases averaging 15 percent above 1945 levels. The final agreement also provided for union responsibility for illegal work stoppages. Relations between the union and management steadily improved. The contract negotiated in September 1949 provided for a pension plan for hourly employees, the first of its kind in the automotive industry. In addition, the company dropped the security clause of the preceding contract.

Ford's revitalization of the company succeeded. A new Ford model was unveiled in June 1949. The first half of 1950 represented the best period the company had known since 1929. Production rose and new plans for expansion were being developed when the Korean War erupted. During the conflict automobile production slowed down in favor of the manufacture of war goods. By 1951 the Ford Motor Company had accepted nearly a billion dollars worth of war contracts.

After government restrictions on auto productions were lifted following the war, Ford began a campaign to overtake GM in production and sales. New models, including the unsuccessful Edsel, were introduced during the 1950s, but Ford never achieved first place among the top three auto makers.

Under Henry II's guidance the Ford Foundation became the largest philanthropy in the world. Ford resigned as president in 1950, but he continued as the chairman of the board of trustees. The same year the foundation shifted its attention from exclusively local Michigan issues to national and international affairs. Over the years, as he became less involved in the affairs of the foundation, under McGeorge Bundy it began to take sides in civil rights issues and to fund political groups, whereas Ford thought the money should go to minority education and vocational training. He grew increasing aggravated at what he saw as its radical programs and resigned from the board of trustees in 1977.

Ford was a prominent backer of antipoverty programs during the 1960s. He served on the president's Advisory Committee on Labor-Management Policy in the early part of the decade. In 1964 Ford, a Republican, supported Lyndon B. Johnson's presidential candidacy. Henry II died in Detroit on September 29, 1987, from Legionnaires' disease. (See *The Eisenhower Years, The Kennedy Years, The Johnson Years, The Nixon/Ford Years* Volumes)

—EF

Forrestal, James V(incent)

(1892–1949) *secretary of the navy, secretary of defense*

Born on February 15, 1892, in Beacon, New York, James Forrestal was the son of an Irish building contractor who was active in New York State politics. In 1912 he entered Dartmouth College and a year later transferred to Princeton, where he was active in student affairs and became editor of the *Daily Princetonian.* Voted most likely to succeed, he was forced to leave school six weeks before graduation because of a lack of funds. Forrestal held a number of jobs in New York City before becoming a bond salesman for the banking firm of William A. Read and Company (later Dillon, Read, and Company). Following service as an aviator during World War I, Forrestal returned to Dillon, Read, where he rose to become vice president in 1926 and president in 1938.

During the 1930s Forrestal was one of the few Wall Street executives who supported the Roosevelt administration's efforts to regulate the stock market, and he helped draft the Securities and Exchange Act of 1933. Roosevelt, anxious to renew his ties with business to increase industrial production of war materials, appointed Forrestal his administrative assistant in June 1940. The financier took a $170,000 cut in pay to accept this post. Two months later Roosevelt made him undersecretary of the navy. During World War II he supervised the production and deployment of naval craft and organized the Office of Procurement and Material in the Navy Department. When Secretary of the Navy Franklin Knox died in May 1944, Forrestal succeeded him. By the end of the war, the intense,

humorless Forrestal had gained a reputation as an excellent administrator totally dedicated to his position. When Harry Truman succeeded to the presidency, Forrestal was asked to remain at his post, where he advised the president on foreign and defense policy.

A vigorous anticommunist, Forrestal was one of the first of the presidential advisers to urge the abandonment of cooperation with the Soviet Union. He warned both Roosevelt and Truman that the Russians would not live up to their wartime agreements granting representative government in Eastern Europe. Forrestal was convinced that the Kremlin would exploit the postwar anarchy and expand into Europe, Asia, and the Middle East. For this reason, he argued that the United States should not demobilize but rather remain ready to resist aggression. "Peace without power to enforce it must remain an empty dream," he said. Forrestal opposed sharing the scientific secrets—the administration never considered sharing the technological knowledge—of the atomic bomb with the Soviets.

During the early postwar period Truman resisted Forrestal's advice. He hoped to reach some agreement with the Soviet Union over Eastern Europe and wanted to accommodate domestic desires for a quick reconversion to peace. Nevertheless, Forrestal continued to do everything within his power to maintain military readiness and show an American military presence abroad. In early 1946, Forrestal, under the advice of Vice Admiral Forrest Sherman, sent to Turkey the body of the late Turkish ambassador, Mehmed Ertegun, on the battleship USS *Missouri.* Turkey was under pressure from the Soviets to share control of the defense of the Dardanelles, and sending the warship was a sign of support. Forrestal used the incident to start a significant naval buildup in the Mediterranean. On the home front he opened a drive to recruit officers and urged pay increases for the armed forces. He also advocated the development of a permanent core of civil servants modeled after the British system.

Forrestal supported a revived, rehabilitated Germany and Japan to serve as checks on the Soviet Union. The secretary questioned the administration's efforts to negotiate a truce in China between the Communists and Nationalists, maintaining that General GEORGE C. MARSHALL, who headed the mission, did not understand the Communist menace. Forrestal recommended that the United States increase its aid to the pro-Chiang forces to win the civil war and thus remove the Soviet Union from Asia.

During the spring of 1946, as negotiations with the Soviets broke down and public opinion became more anticommunist, the administration took a firmer stand toward the Soviet Union. Forrestal applauded the move and supported GEORGE F. KENNAN's recommendation for a policy of containment of Communist expansion. Kennan's Long Telegram had influenced Forrestal, and W. AVERELL HARRIMAN thought Forrestal's reaction had the most impact on America's view of the Soviet Union. Forrestal had Kennan write the X article for *Foreign Affairs*, which advocated containment. Forrestal recommended to Secretary of State George Marshall that Kennan head the new State Department Policy Planning Staff. When the British withdrew military and economic aid from Greece and Turkey in 1947, the secretary urged the United States to take over assistance. He recommended a complete mobilization of the American people to defeat the Communists and urged a program of massive economic aid to rebuild the shattered economies of Europe. Forrestal supported the Marshall Plan and early attempts to form a defense alliance in Western Europe.

The secretary was so concerned about the Communist threat that he questioned the loyalty of the domestic Communist and noncommunist left. Forrestal believed that not only Communists threatened capitalism but so did New Dealers and British Labour Party leaders, who he thought were undermining private property and the free market. (He would eventually learn that Socialists were some of the fiercest enemies of communism.) At one point, for example, he ordered an aide to analyze the stands the *Nation* and the *New Republic* had taken on the issues of preparedness prior to World War II. The memo presented to him confirmed to his satisfaction that the magazines had been disloyal then, as he thought they were during the early cold war. Forrestal's office also served as an unofficial government repository for material on American Communists. He subscribed to far-right magazines and received countless unsolicited material documenting the Communist conspiracy to take over America. The FBI and army and navy intelligence all kept Forrestal informed of the activities of the Communist Party.

Forrestal was a vigorous foe of Secretary of Commerce HENRY A. WALLACE, who urged conciliation with the Soviets. In the summer and fall of 1946, when Wallace publicly criticized the adminis-

tration's foreign policy, Forrestal pressed for his removal from the cabinet. Following Wallace's controversial Madison Square Garden speech criticizing Truman, Forrestal personally attacked his adversary. He was gratified when Truman fired Wallace. He then searched for ways to muzzle the former cabinet member. Forrestal inquired whether Wallace could be denied a passport to prevent him from traveling abroad to criticize the administration's foreign policies. Forrestal also assigned an aide to investigate whether Wallace could be prosecuted under the Logan Act, which prohibited Americans from acting as agents of a foreign government. His aide suggested that the government did not have the evidence to do so.

As secretary of the navy, Forrestal became embroiled in the controversy over integrating the military services into one cabinet agency headed by a civilian. Presidents Roosevelt and Truman, the War Department, and leading members of Congress supported the creation of a Department of Defense. Forrestal, however, opposed the consolidation for fear that the navy's role in the future defense would be reduced. He also argued that having three cabinet-level secretaries of the navy, army, and, in the future, air force, would serve as a system of checks and balances in the formulation of defense policy. To concentrate all power in the hands of one man would create, in Forrestal's words, "a centralization of errors." He believed that no man possessed the capacity to administer the total defense needs of the nation. He asserted that his experience on Wall Street had shown him that consolidation of several companies adversely affects the initiative and vitality of previously independent businesses. He said, "You will recall that one architect of railroad consolidation, I believe it was James J. Hill, finally decided no one man could run more than 10,000 miles of railroad." Forrestal proposed an alternative plan, drafted by former Munitions Board chairman Ferdinand Eberstadt, which would establish security council consisting of the military secretaries and chiefs and the secretary of state with the president serving as chairman. Forrestal argued that there was a need for group deliberation in Washington as distinguished from the need for unified command in the field.

During 1946 Forrestal lobbied against a national security bill, which centralized powers in the hands of a secretary of defense. When it became apparent that the measure would pass, he tried to protect the power of the branch secretaries at the expense of the new defense chief. Forrestal was successful in obtaining for the future secretaries of the navy, army, and air force subcabinet rank. More important, he succeeded in giving them their own delegated administrative and policy duties. The secretary of national defense would coordinate, but not administer, policy.

Truman signed the National Security Act on July 26, 1947, and appointed Forrestal the nation's first secretary of defense. The press and most politicians praised the appointment. The appointment was shrewd because now Forrestal would now have to guide the military in an office he had worked to weaken. Thus Forrestal's effectiveness was limited. Because he successfully preserved the power of the branch secretaries, these men did not feel the need to follow his policy recommendations and often clashed openly with the secretary. Forrestal's checks and balances argument worked against him because the secretaries, especially Secretary of the Air Force STUART SYMINGTON, often went over his head to present their views to the president and to Congress. Forrestal's argument that no man possessed the capability to oversee the defense of the nation was often used against him. As a result he lobbied for a more centralized department administered by a powerful secretary of defense. This organization was approved in the spring of 1949.

As secretary of defense Forrestal was a major proponent of a balanced defense establishment in which each service contributed equally to the national security. He opposed efforts, led by Symington—who became increasingly insubordinate—to increase the air force at the expense of the army and navy. Nevertheless, Symington's position that the air force would be America's prime deterrent in a nuclear age impressed the administration and Congress, which voted for the increases. Forrestal also lost his battle over the Defense Department budget. Deeply committed to a strong military establishment to resist Soviet aggression, he requested an $18.5 billion defense budget for 1949. Truman reduced it to $15 billion. As a result of the cuts Forrestal developed doubts about the U.S. ability to resist a Soviet attack, which he was more inclined to believe was coming. This put him in conflict with the president and Secretary Marshall, who thought the Soviets wanted to avoid war. These fears in turn, affected his mental stability, and he

began to expect an imminent war, which the United States would lose.

During 1948 Forrestal thought of running as Truman's vice president or of entering the contest for governor or senator from New York. However, he could generate little support. His strong anticommunist views and his conduct toward Wallace alienated liberals. In addition, he won the enmity of Jews because of his opposition to the state of Israel. Forrestal had urged Truman not to recognize the new nation for fear of alienating the Arabs with their vast oil holdings, and thus giving the Soviet Union a possible foothold in the Middle East. In addition many felt he lacked the political experience to run for high elective office. According to Forrestal biographers Townsend Hoopes and Douglas Brinkley, Forrestal desperately wanted to remain in government because public service had become his life. In his desperation he may have talked to Republican presidential candidate Governor THOMAS E. DEWEY about staying in the office in case the governor was elected president, which looked likely throughout most of the 1948 campaign.

Following his victory in the 1948 presidential race, Truman decided to replace Forrestal with someone more congenial to his defense policies. More important, Forrestal was showing signs of a potential nervous breakdown. At times during meetings Forrestal was easily distracted from the topic. He suffered from forgetfulness, memory slips, and mistakes in identity. He had been worn down by interservice rivalries—especially between the air force and the navy—and his increasing fear that America was insufficiently prepared for war. He was under increasing attack by columnist DREW PEARSON, who was determined to drive him from public life because of his conservatism. Forrestal also began to believe Zionists and Communists were following him, and that his house was bugged. Reluctantly he resigned as of March 28, 1949. On that day Truman presented him with the Distinguished Service Medal. Forrestal then went to Florida for a rest but suffered a nervous breakdown on April 2. He was admitted for psychiatric observation at the Bethesda Naval Hospital in Maryland. His recovery impressed the doctors, but, on May 22, Forrestal leaped to his death from his window on the 13th floor. Commenting on the suicide, President Truman stated, "This able and devoted public servant was as truly a casualty of the war as if he had died on the firing line."

—JB

Foster, William C(hapman)

(1897–1984) *undersecretary of commerce; deputy administrator, European Cooperation Administration; administrator, European Cooperation Administration; deputy secretary of defense*

William C. Foster was born on April 27, 1897, in Westfield, New Jersey. He graduated from the Massachusetts Institute of Technology in 1918, after serving briefly as a military aviator in World War I. From 1922 to 1946 he worked for the Pressed and Welded Steel Products Company, where he rose from secretary-treasurer to president. During World War II he served on several government agencies, coordinating small business production.

Impressed with Foster's knowledge of the problems of small business, Secretary of Commerce W. AVERELL HARRIMAN convinced President Truman to appoint him undersecretary of commerce in late 1946. The Senate confirmed the nomination in January 1947. Foster handled the day-to-day affairs of the department, while Harriman tried to continue influencing foreign policy. During his tenure Foster proposed changes in the tax laws to aid small businesses and advocated increasing U.S. imports to provide other nations with the currency necessary to buy American exports. He also served on a committee concerned with furthering international cooperation in the aviation industry and developing civil aeronautics.

When Harriman became ambassador at large to Western Europe to oversee the operation of the Economic Cooperation Administration (ECA) in 1948, he chose Foster as his assistant and head of the ECA mission in France. Foster successfully integrated Greece into the Marshall Plan during the summer of 1948 and prepared reports on Europe's economic needs for presentation to Congress. He was appointed deputy administrator of the ECA in June 1949 and administrator in June 1950. As deputy administrator, he encouraged the British not to oppose the formation of a continental economic union (Fritalux) and supranational coordination of the economies of Europe. As administrator he advocated continuing the European Recovery Plan, and he stated, in late 1950, that aid funds were to be directed in the future toward European rearmament. Foster believed in early 1951 that the ECA would continue to be an independent agency even after the scheduled ending of the Marshall Plan in mid-1952. However, the Truman administration proposed that the State Department be put in charge of allocating funds to the ECA. Foster angrily noted that the bill would end the agency's independence and make it hardly more than a "country desk" in the State Department. Congress, however, decided to terminate the ECA altogether, with its functions to be taken over by a new Mutual Security Administration, which would coordinate all aid programs.

Foster praised the Organization for European Economic Cooperation for its "European Manifesto" to expand production in Western Europe by 25 percent, saying it identified "the real answer to many of Europeans difficulties—to expand production and to increase productivity." He advocated the elimination of trade barriers and cartels and the creation of a single market in Western Europe to effect the manifesto's goals.

During the early months of the Korean War, Foster negotiated loans with U.S. allies to increase their contribution to the war effort. He also served as chairman of an 11-member committee to advise CHARLES E. WILSON, director of defense mobilization, on coordinating supplies with U.S. allies.

In 1951 Foster was chosen deputy secretary of defense. Five months after his appointment he testified before a House Armed Services subcommittee investigating procurement policies in the armed forces. He defended the military against charges of waste and loose management. While acknowledging that mistakes had occurred, he emphasized that the Pentagon was improving operations. Foster opposed pending legislation that would have required the reorganization and simplification of procurement policies, maintaining that the secretary of defense already had the power to make necessary changes. Despite his plea Congress passed the Defense Cataloguing and Standardization Act, establishing an agency to simplify procurement procedures.

During his two years with the Defense Department, Foster was primarily concerned with defense policy in Asia. After traveling to Korea in the fall of 1952, he warned that South Korea could not win the war without increases in U.S. military forces in the near future. He also reported that the security of Southeast Asia was endangered because of the absence of cooperative efforts against Communists by governments in the area. In January 1953 Foster ordered the Joint Chiefs of Staff to consider broadening American military assistance to Indochina, especially through training native troops and maintaining equipment supplied by the United States.

Foster was also involved in decisions about U.S. military activities in Europe. As acting secretary of defense, Foster approved, on March 24, 1952, the appointment of a temporary Joint U.S. Military Group (Spain) to start negotiations with Spain to secure its cooperation in defending Europe. He also approved a Joint Chiefs list of American military requirements.

Foster left office in January 1953, and, during the next decade, he served as an executive for a number of large chemical corporations. In 1958 he headed the U.S. delegation to the Geneva Conference on the Prevention of Surprise Attacks. From 1961 to 1968 Foster was director of the U.S. Arms Control and Disarmament Agency. Foster died on October 14, 1984, in Washington, D.C. (See *The Eisenhower Years, The Kennedy Years* Volumes)

—AES

Foster, William Z(eboulon)
(1881–1961) *chairman, Communist Party, U.S.A.*
The son of Irish-Catholic immigrants, William Z. Foster was born on February 25, 1881, in Taunton, Massachusetts. He grew up in the slums of Philadelphia and at age 10 quit school. Over the next decade, he traveled widely "on the hobo" and as a merchant seaman. In 1900 he joined the Socialist Party but was expelled in 1909 for disagreeing with its philosophy. He then joined the Industrial Workers of the World. After a trip to Europe, where he met with syndicalist trade unionists who converted him to the strategy of "boring from within" labor unions, he founded the Syndicalist League of North America and worked as a business agent for a Chicago railroad union. He successfully organized packinghouse workers during 1917–18 and because of his success he was put in charge of the American Federation of Labor's effort to organize the steel industry in 1919. The strike was an attempt to gain union recognition and involved 350,000 people. This effort to form an industrial union was crushed by the industry and authorities. He founded the Trade Union Educational League (TUEL) in 1920. The following year Foster was a TUEL delegate to the Red International of Trade Unions, or Profintern, conference in Moscow. Upon his return to the United States, he joined the Communist Party.

As head of the TUEL, Foster quickly rose to a leadership position within the party. He served as its presidential candidate in the 1924, 1928, and 1932

elections. In 1930 Foster served a six-month prison term for leading a rally of unemployed in New York City. After suffering a heart attack in 1932, he passed the party's leadership to EARL BROWDER at the order of Moscow, which seemed to have seen Foster as compromised from the intraparty fighting of the 1920s. Foster obeyed the Soviets' diktat to follow the Popular Front strategy of the 1930s, then the isolationist party line during the period of the Nazi-Soviet Pact of 1939–41, and then support for interventionism after the German invasion of Russia. He was, however, moderately critical of Browder's decision in 1944 that the party abandon its function as a political unit and turn itself into the Communist Political Association (CPA). The party reprimanded Foster for his criticism, and he retracted it. He then served as CPA chairman.

In April 1945 Browder, who promised that the CPA would not raise the issue of socialism in the postwar period, "in such a form and manner as to weaken national unity," was assailed by a leading French Communist and ousted as head of the American movement for "revisionism." Several months later the party was reconstituted, Foster elected national chairman, and a new, more militant line introduced. By October Foster was attacking the nomination of JAMES F. BYRNES as secretary of state as a "concession to imperialism." He also assailed Truman for "yielding to the monopolistic forces behind American imperialism." As the number of strikes increased during the winter of 1945–46, Foster wondered whether American capitalists were "heading the world toward a fresh debacle of economic chaos, fascism and war?" To impede this crisis Foster called for an alliance of poor farmers, professionals, middle-class Americans, veterans, and blacks, all led by the working class. Foster denounced the Truman Doctrine of 1947 for establishing a policy for containment of the Soviet Union and called the Marshall Plan a "cold blooded scheme of American monopolists to establish their ruthless domination over harassed humanity."

By 1947 the administration had instituted a series of actions designed to destroy the Communist Party. In March Secretary of Labor LEWIS B. SCHWELLENBACH proposed outlawing the party, and Truman issued Executive Order 9385 requiring a loyalty oath from all civil service employees. In addition, Congress passed the Taft-Hartley Act requiring all unions to file noncommunist affidavits.

In the winter of 1947 Foster initiated a two-pronged strategy to counteract these developments. The party threw its support behind HENRY A. WALLACE's presidential candidacy. However, with Wallace's defeat, the party lost much of its base within the trade unions. Following the revelations in November 1947 by former assistant attorney general O. John Rogge that roundups of Communists were expected, Foster began preparing the party's underground organization. Eight months later, on July 20, 1948, Foster and 11 other party leaders were indicated for criminal conspiracy in violation of the Smith Act of 1940. The indictment charged that they had conspired, in the 1945 reconstitution of the party, to form an organization that advocated the violent overthrow of the government. Foster attacked the indictment as a step by Truman to crush electoral opposition. Shortly before the trials opened in January 1949, he and party general secretary Eugene Dennis issued a statement urging Americans in case of war between the United States and Soviet Union to refuse support for their country. Truman denounced Foster and Dennis as traitors, further inflaming the pretrial atmosphere. When the trial opened Foster's case was severed because of his heart condition. During the nine-month trial Foster traveled throughout the country to raise money and lead the party in its defense.

When Congress passed the McCarran Act in 1950, Foster bitterly attacked its provisions for the imprisonment of Communists in case of national emergency and swore that the party would never comply with its registration requirements. After the party's final appeals were denied by the Supreme Court in 1950, four of the party leaders ordered to prison went underground. Foster continued as national chairman, but the party faced continued governmental investigation and prosecution. As a result, membership shrank from its postwar height of nearly 85,000 to only several thousand by the mid-1950s.

With the lessening of cold war tensions following the Korean armistice and with Nikita Khrushchev's 1956 revelations of the excesses of the Stalinist period, Foster came under increasing internal party criticism. He was removed from his leadership position in September 1956 and was elected chairman emeritus. However, Foster's hard-line stance came back into vogue with the Soviet Union's crushing of the Hungarian Revolution in November 1956. Foster increasingly withdrew from party life

after suffering a heart attack in 1957. He went to the Soviet Union in 1961 for medical treatment and died there on September 1.

—DMR

Frankfurter, Felix
(1882–1965) *associate justice, U.S. Supreme Court*

Born to Jewish parents on November 15, 1882, in Vienna, Austria, Felix Frankfurter immigrated to America at the age of 12. He graduated from the City College of New York in 1902 and from Harvard Law School in 1906. A member of the Harvard Law School faculty from 1914 to 1939, Frankfurter became a noted scholar on the Supreme Court and on administrative law. He also established a national reputation as a liberal by aiding organizations such as the NAACP and the American Civil Liberties Union and by protesting what he considered miscarriages of justice in the Tom Mooney and Sacco and Vanzetti cases. Frankfurter was co-writer of a book on the abuses of the labor injunction, which contributed to the passage of the Norris-LaGuardia Act. Throughout the New Deal he served as an adviser to Franklin D. Roosevelt on legislation, appointments, and speeches. Roosevelt named Frankfurter to the Supreme Court in January 1939.

During most of his tenure on the bench Frankfurter was the Court's foremost exponent of a philosophy of judicial restraint. He insisted that judges must avoid reading their own policy preferences into law and must try to decide cases based on reason and impersonal principles. They must accord other branches of government all the power due them and sustain legislation that has a reasonable basis. These views led Frankfurter to uphold most New Deal and state economic and social welfare laws. They also caused him, however, to accept much government action that infringed on civil liberties. Frankfurter rejected the notion that First Amendment freedoms were absolutes or had a "preferred position" that afforded them special protection against any government intrusion. He argued that in civil liberties as well as economic cases, the Court must practice restraint. When he did vote to overturn government action affecting individual freedoms, Frankfurter usually offered narrow procedural or statutory reasons rather than broad constitutional grounds.

In free speech cases Justice Frankfurter weighed the rights of the individual against the state's claims of order or security. Because of such balancing, he voted in February 1947 to uphold the Hatch Act's ban on political activity by federal employees and, in *Saia v. New York* (1948) and *Kovacs v. Cooper* (1949) to sustain local ordinances regulating the use of sound trucks. In *Dennis v. U.S.* (1951) the justice concurred when the Court upheld the convictions of American Communist Party leaders under the Smith Act, although his opinion made clear that he considered the act unwise. His opinion for the Court in *Beauharnais v. Illinois* (1952) case also upheld an Illinois law prohibiting group libel, which had been challenged on First Amendment grounds. However Frankfurter dissented in January 1950, when a majority held that an alien war bride could be denied entry to the United States without a hearing because of accusations that she was a security risk. He also concurred in *Joint Antifascist Committee v. McGrath* (1951), when a majority ordered lower court hearings be held for three organizations that had sued to be taken off the Attorney General's list of subversive organizations. Frankfurter believed the groups' placement on the list without notice or hearing denied them due process.

Frankfurter was more of an activist in federal criminal cases where the Supreme Court had special supervisory responsibilities and where relatively specific constitutional clauses were available to guide the justices. He showed a strong concern for procedural fairness and was particularly insistent that the Fourth Amendment's prohibition of unreasonable searches and seizures be strictly observed. In a series of Fourth Amendment cases decided between 1947 and 1950, Frankfurter voted to limit the scope of the search federal officers could make incident to a valid arrest. For example, in *Harris v. U.S.* (1947) Frankfurter dissented from the majority's upholding a conviction based on evidence collected by the FBI without a search warrant, even though it could have obtained one. He argued if the search was illegal then the seizure committed during the search was illegal, too. He was meticulous in other cases involving the federal government and criminal procedure. For instance, in *Fisher v. U.S.* (1946), Frankfurter dissented from the majority opinion when a first-degree murder conviction of an African American was upheld. The man had struck and killed a woman in the District of Columbia who had called him a racial epithet. Frankfurter argued

the murder had been the result of the epithet, which he quoted in his dissent to some controversy, and was not premeditated. The justice applied less rigid standards to state criminal procedure, however. Unlike Justice HUGO L. BLACK, who argued that all of the Bill of Rights guarantees applied to the states, Frankfurter contended that state proceedings had to meet only certain basic standards of decency and fairness to be constitutional. In *Adamson v. California* (1947), a trial judge in his instructions to the jury made note of the murder suspect's invoking the Fifth Amendment. The suspect objected that this indication violated the due process clause of the Fourteenth Amendment. The Court upheld the conviction. Justice Black dissented, arguing for complete incorporation of the Bill of Rights. In his concurrence with the majority, Frankfurter challenged Black's broad definition of due process by stating it was rather unlikely the states ratified the Fourteenth Amendment believing they were overturning their own criminal procedures. He wrote, "A construction which gives to due process no independent function but turns it into a summary of the Bill of Rights would . . . tear up by the roots much of the fabric of law in the several states." His opinion for the Court in a June 1949 case held the Fourth Amendment applicable to the states under this approach but also declared that state courts did not have to exclude illegally seized evidence the way federal tribunals did. The justice decided state cases involving allegedly coerced confessions or a denial of the right to counsel on the basis of whether events in each instance had resulted in a lack of due process.

In accord with his commitment to judicial restraint, Frankfurter was very attentive to jurisdictional limits on the Court's work. In June 1946, for a four-man majority, he ruled that questions of legislative apportionment were outside the Court's domain. In *Colgrove v. Green* (1946), for a four-man majority, he ruled that questions of legislative apportionment were outside the court's jurisdiction. He said that since the courts' domain are nonpolitical institutions, they "ought not to enter this political thicket." Although in the early 1940s the justice had twice voted to sustain compulsory flag-salute laws against charges that they violated freedom of religion, Frankfurter repeatedly sought during the Truman era to maintain strict separation of church and state. In *Everson v. Board of Education of Ewing Township* (1947) he voted against state payments for the transportation of children to parochial schools, and in *Illinois ex rel. McCollum v. Board of Education* (1948) and *Zorach v. Clauson* (1952), he objected to released-time programs of religious instruction for public school children. Frankfurter joined in a series of Vinson Court rulings that advanced the constitutional rights of racial minorities. In 1948 he chose William T. Coleman as his law clerk—the first African American in the Court's history. When people congratulated him for crossing the color line, Frankfurter dismissed such talk, saying he had hired Coleman because he was the best man for the job.

In succeeding years Frankfurter maintained a center position on the Court on loyalty-security matters, sometimes sustaining and sometimes objecting to government antisubversive efforts. He supported the Court's judgment in May 1954 that racial segregation was unconstitutional and protested bitterly in 1962 when a majority upset his 1946 decision and entered the "political thicket" of legislative apportionment. He resigned from the Court in August 1962 because of ill health and died in Washington on February 22, 1965.

An ebullient, energetic man who delighted in lively conversation and correspondence, Frankfurter was a charismatic figure whose friends included outstanding persons of his day from a variety of fields. Frankfurter could be combative during deliberation with his fellow jurists, pounding the table, reading from a large stack of books, and tossing them around in excitement. He would interrupt colleagues and deride their arguments. His many questions to counsel during oral argument in the Court gave evidence of his professorial background, and his scholarly opinions exhibited his concern for craftsmanship and excellence. In assessing his judicial career, critics asserted that Frankfurter showed more restraint than was necessary or wise, especially in civil liberties cases, in an era when individual freedoms were under considerable attack. His defenders have contended that Frankfurter's judicial philosophy, which reflected his desire to protect the Court's authority and his belief in the efficacy of popular democratic government, helped keep an activist trend among other justices within reasonable bounds. Virtually all observers agreed with a *New York Times* editorialist that as "a philosopher and scholar of the law, a judicial craftsman, a master of prose style and a formative influence on a generation of American lawyers and public officials, Felix Frankfurter was a major shaper of the history of his age." (See *The Eisenhower Years, The Kennedy Years* Volumes)

—CAB

Fulbright, J(ames) William
(1905–1995) *member of the Senate*

J. William Fulbright, the son of a banker and successful businessman, was born on April 9, 1905, in Sumner, Missouri. He graduated from the University of Arkansas in 1925 and then attended Oxford University on a Rhodes Scholarship, receiving a B.S. in history and political science with honors in 1928 and an M.A. in 1931. Three years later Fulbright earned an LL.B. from George Washington University. In 1934 he joined the Antitrust Division of the Justice Department, where he helped prosecute the Schechter chicken case. He left the Justice Department the following year to become an instructor of law at George Washington. In 1936 he returned to Arkansas to teach law at the university and to manage the family business. Three years later Fulbright, then 34, was appointed president of the university.

President Truman signing the Surplus Properties Act of 1946 (*left to right*) President Truman, Senator J. William Fulbright, and Assistant Secretary of State William J. Benton *(Harry S. Truman Library, Harris and Ewing Photos. Gift of John O. Hamilton)*

He was the youngest university president in the United States. Fulbright's efforts to raise the standards of the university gained him national attention. However, his outspoken opposition to isolationism won him some local emnity, including that of Homer Adkins, who, after his election as governor in 1940, forced Fulbright from his post.

In 1943 Fulbright won a seat in the U.S. House, where he was appointed to the Foreign Affairs Committee. As a representative, he supported the war policies and postwar plans of Franklin D. Roosevelt and, several months after beginning his term, defended them in floor debate against the attack of Representative CLARE BOOTH LUCE (R-Conn.). In June 1943 Fulbright introduced a resolution giving House support to U.S. participation after the war in an international organization dedicated to the preservation of peace. The Fulbright-Connally Resolution, which passed both houses by overwhelming margins, was an important step toward the creation of the United Nations. The next year Fulbright served as an American representative to an international conference on education held in London. There he presented a four-point program for reconstructing essential education facilities. The conference accepted his proposal and urged that an organization be established to implement it. These recommendations became the foundations for the UN Economic and Social Council.

In 1944 Fulbright, in a campaign that emphasized his conservative record on domestic issues, defeated his old adversary, Homer Adkins, for a seat in the Senate. Fulbright refused to give a blanket endorsement to Truman's 21-point program of 1945—later known as the Fair Deal—saying he was "neither a New Dealer nor anti–New Dealer" and contended moderation was the best course. He voted against increasing the minimum wage and civil rights legislation and for the Case labor disputes bill and the Taft-Hartley Act. However, he did support the administration on its price control proposals and the Full Employment bill. Despite being assigned initially to the Banking and Currency Committee and not the foreign relations panel, Fulbright's primary interest was in foreign policy. (He won a seat on the Foreign Affairs Committee in 1949.)

During his first year Fulbright sponsored one of the major legislative accomplishments of his Senate career, securing the passage of what came to be known as the Fulbright Scholarship Program. Fulbright introduced the bill to establish the program in the fall of 1945. He had been discussing the need of promoting academic exchange for six months but had hesitated to introduce legislation calling for a program to be financed directly from the Treasury, believing he could not command support sufficient to carry. In September, however, an exchange bill with the problem of disposing of unnecessary American military equipment overseas provided an opportunity. Fulbright proposed to devote funds from the sale of surplus equipment to finance the exchange of scholars, students, and educators. Any country purchasing part of the American surplus would be eligible for up to $20 million for the exchanges. As much as $1 million a year could be spent in each country. Americans going abroad under the program were to receive travel money, tuition, books, and an allowance. Foreign students coming to the United States received travel money and in some cases an allowance; tuition and books were assumed in most cases to be provided under scholarships from American universities. After some hesitation and alterations giving the secretary of state greater control over disbursements, the State Department supported the bill as did various veterans groups and educational organizations. Seeking bipartisan support, Fulbright secured the endorsement of HERBERT HOOVER, who had used the Belgian war debt following World War I to establish a similar program. The measure passed both houses without debate. Truman signed it on August 1, 1946. This program became Fulbright's passion, he fought for higher funding and saw it as a panacea to international conflict.

Fulbright became distressed by the diplomacy of the postwar world. He was particularly unhappy with the United Nations Charter. He had hoped for a tempering of the concept of sovereignty, which the agreement failed to consider. In a November 1945 radio address he proposed that the UN be empowered to limit armaments and the atomic bomb. He recommended abolition of the veto in the Security Council because he saw it as a barrier to the effective working of the United Nations. He wanted to see a stronger World Court empowered to make binding decisions and an ascendance of law and legal forms rather than power in international affairs. "Our government," he said, "does not seem to appreciate the function of law in the makings of peace." Fulbright voted for the charter because of the lack of an alternative course, but the speech marked his break with the administration. Prior to it Fulbright had been mentioned as a possible vice presidential or even presidential candidate for 1948. His speech, because of its harsh criticism of Truman, ended all such talk.

During this period Fulbright became increasingly critical of the Truman administration's policy toward the Soviet Union. He had supported Roosevelt's attempts to mollify the Russians and assure the Soviet Union of the United States's peaceful intentions. He found the Truman administration's policies increasingly belligerent. In his November 1945 radio address, Fulbright charged that the Truman administration's policy was drifting. The United States was demanding strategic concession from the Soviets without offering any of its own. Increasingly an atmosphere of confrontation was developing, he said. In April 1946 Fulbright criticized the administration for antagonizing the Soviet Union with continued atomic tests. The planned test on Bikini Island, he charged, had no military or other value, but was simply a device for displaying American strength.

Fulbright's views changed when the Soviet Union rejected an American plan for the internationalization of atomic weaponry. The USSR became, in Fulbright's eyes, a confirmed adversary. In a May 1946 speech discussing this change of view, Fulbright said, "there are doubts in the minds of many of us that Russia will ever submit to rules of conduct in any field." Fulbright endorsed the Truman Doctrine in March 1947 and voted for aid to Greece and Turkey. He supported full funding of the Marshall Plan in 1948 while lamenting that it would act to restore the separate countries of Europe rather than promote European unity of which he was an advocate. Fulbright voted for the North Atlantic Treaty in 1949. Yet the broad commitment of the administration to containment worried Fulbright, and he thought the United States should encourage a European federation. He thought such a federation would return war-devastated Europe to prosperity and suppress rabid nationalism, control Germany, and contain communism. Keeping Germany down might encourage Moscow to end its expansionism and loosen its control over Eastern Europe. Fulbright biographer Randall Bennett Woods has argued that Fulbright's ardent support for the United Nations and European federation put him in the center of the suprana-

tional movement of the war and postwar eras. Also Woods noted that as Fulbright developed doubts about the UN he shifted his faith to a politically more realistic regional confederation in Europe. He hoped the Marshall Plan would pave the way for a political federation.

Fulbright's relations with Truman deteriorated further after the Republicans took control of Congress in 1947. In a conversation with friends, the senator, influenced by the British system of party rule, suggested offhandly that Truman appoint a Republican secretary of state (who in the absence of a vice president would be first in line to succeed the presidency). He then recommended that the President resign. He based this proposal on the belief that executive and legislature worked best when of a single party. This statement, uttered with a reporter present, found its way into the press. Truman was furious and he called the senator that "overeducated Oxford s.o.b.," saying, "A little more U.S. land grant college education on the U.S. Constitution and what it meant would do Fulbright a lot of good." From then on Truman usually referred to Fulbright as "Senator Halfbright" and the two rarely spoke after the Arkansan's comment.

Fulbright won reelection without opposition in 1950. His support of Truman's foreign policy continued into his second term. Although he had made no public statement about the Korean conflict in 1950, when the administration came under fierce public attack for the recall of General DOUGLAS MACARTHUR in 1951, Fulbright became a vocal administration supporter. He denounced both MacArthur's insubordination and the military strategy the general espoused. Fulbright proved an effective inquisitor of MacArthur when he appeared before a joint meeting of the Senate Armed Services and Foreign Relation committees.

In 1950 Fulbright chaired a subcommittee of the Banking and Currency Committee investigating the Reconstruction Finance Corporation (RFC). His original goal had been to have the agency concern itself more with small businesses that had trouble getting loans. During routine hearings, however, the panel discovered that, after resigning, several RFC officials had taken high-salaried positions from companies to which they had loaned government funds. Over a number of months the subcommittee uncovered evidence that officials had accepted bribes in the form of mink coats and trips to Florida. It uncovered influence-peddling on the RFC board, in the Democratic National Committee, and at the White House. In December he and Senators PAUL H. DOUGLAS (D-Ill.) and CHARLES W. TOBEY (R-N.H.) took the findings to Truman and suggested that he quietly reorganize the RFC. Fulbright offered the president a plan to reorganize the RFC and recommended that, to prevent embarrassment, Truman himself present it to the public. A few days later Truman announced that he would reappoint the sitting RFC directors when their terms expired, signaling his rejection of the senator's plan. This move prompted Fulbright to make public the panel's findings in February 1951. Truman labeled the report "asinine." Fulbright reopened the hearings, and in April Truman backed down. He initiated a reorganization of the RFC similar to that proposed by the senators. It replaced the five-man board with a single administrator. Truman appointed STUART SYMINGTON, to supervise the agency.

During the early 1950s Fulbright had several confrontations with Senator JOSEPH R. MCCARTHY (R-Wisc.). Fulbright found that McCarthy had accepted $10,000 for writing a pamphlet for a company financed by the RFC and consequently under the supervision of the Banking and Currency Committee of which the Wisconsin Republican was a member. McCarthy had not, however, violated the law and the investigation was not pursued.

In October 1950 Fulbright and McCarthy openly quarreled during hearings on the nomination of PHILIP JESSUP to be a delegate to the United Nations. McCarthy charged that Jessup, a high State Department official and a distinguished professor of international law, had an "unusual affinity for Communist causes." The Wisconsin senator appeared before the Foreign Relations Committee to oppose the nomination. Fulbright defended Jessup against the charges and sharply interrogated McCarthy. Their exchange became extremely bitter, ending with an oblique implication by McCarthy that Fulbright was a subversive because his wife had belonged to the Red Cross when GEORGE C. MARSHALL, another McCarthy target, was its chairman.

McCarthy and Fulbright became unforgiving adversaries. During the Eisenhower administration he successfully defended the Fulbright scholarship program against McCarthy's attack. In early 1954 Fulbright was the only senator to vote against further appropriations to McCarthy's Permanent Investigations Subcommittee. That year Fulbright unobtrusively took the lead in the move to censure McCarthy.

In domestic affairs Fulbright remained a consistent, if unenthusiastic, opponent of civil rights throughout the 1950s. He supported the "Southern Manifesto" in 1956 and voted against the Civil Rights Acts of 1957 and 1960.

Fulbright denounced the Eisenhower administration's foreign policy as too ideologically oriented and not sufficiently attentive to big power interests. He questioned the doctrine of massive retaliation and emphasized the need for economic and technical over military aid to American allies. During the 1960s he remained critical of what he saw as an ideologically guided foreign policy. He opposed the Johnson administration's conduct of the Vietnam War and became a preeminent symbol of congressional discontent with the conflict. In 1974 Fulbright lost the Arkansas Democratic primary. His defeat was attributed to his preoccupation with foreign policy at the expense of his constituents' interests. He died in Washington, D.C., on February 9, 1995. (See *The Eisenhower Years, The Kennedy Years, The Johnson Years, The Nixon/Ford Years* Volumes)

—CSJ

Gabrielson, Guy (George)

(1891–1976) *chairman, Republican National Committee*

The son of a shopkeeper, Guy Gabrielson was born on May 22, 1891, in Sioux Rapids, Iowa, and grew up in a small farming community. He received a B.A. from the University of Iowa and an LL.B. from Harvard in 1917. Following military service in World War I, Gabrielson was admitted to the New Jersey bar and opened law offices in Newark and New York City. After serving three terms in the New Jersey Assembly, Gabrielson became Republican majority leader in 1928. The following year he was elected speaker of the New Jersey Assembly.

Leaving elective office in 1930, Gabrielson managed state Republican campaigns and continued to expand his law practice and business interests. In 1944 he was named Republican national committeeman from New Jersey. Two years later Gabrielson was elected president of Carthage Hydrocol, Inc., a gasoline manufacturing company organized with $10 million of Texas oil capital and $18.5 million in loans from the Reconstruction Finance Corporation (RFC).

Gabrielson backed Senator ROBERT A. TAFT (R-Ohio) for the 1948 Republican presidential nomination. When New York governor THOMAS E. DEWEY was nominated, Gabrielson supported him, although personally unsympathetic to Dewey's policies. A conservative Republican from Arizona, C. Budington Kelland, plotted to oust moderate Republican HUGH D. SCOTT from the chairmanship of the Republican National Committee and replace him with Gabrielson, who helped put pressure on Scott. Scott stepped down in August 1949, but supporters of Tom Dewey put forward a challenger,

Axel J. Beck, to Gabrielson, and the latter barely won the chairmanship. Although a Taft conservative, the new party leader sought to unify the liberal and conservative wings of the GOP. In April 1950, he issued a statement of Republican principles which was aggressively anticommunist and defensive of free market capitalism. The following month he accused Truman of promoting "a program of socialism." Shortly After Senator JOSEPH R. MCCARTHY's (R-Wisc.) speech in Wheeling, West Virginia, accusing the administration of harboring Communists, Gabrielson said the search for Communists would be the new focal point of the Republican Party.

In March 1951 Representative Wayne L. Hays (D-Ohio) charged that Gabrielson had received $100,000 in fees from Carthage Hydrocol for obtaining the RFC loans. Gabrielson replied that the loans were granted before he had become company president or national chairman. At the time of Hays's allegations, a Senate banking subcommittee, led by Senator CLYDE R. HOEY (D-N.C.), was investigating political influence in the granting of RFC loans. Subcommittee reports supported Gabrielson's defense, and its staff director stated he had found no evidence of a $100,000 fee or political pressure applied to the RFC by the national chairman.

The following September Senator JOHN J. WILLIAMS (R-Del.) accused Gabrielson of "highly improper" action in representing Carthage Hydrocol before the RFC after he had become GOP chairman. Gabrielson had continued to receive a $15,000 salary as Hydrocol president and additional legal fees. While Williams conceded there was nothing wrong with Gabrielson representing the company before his political post, he denounced Gabrielson for contacting RFC administrator W. STUART SYMINGTON in an attempt to extend repayment of Carthage Hydrocol's loans after he had become chairman.

Gabrielson denied any impropriety. He said the charges were intended to "confuse the public in the hope of protecting crooks . . . within the Truman administration." Testifying before the Hoey panel in October, Gabrielson admitted he tried to get former RFC director Harvey J. Gunderson elected president of the New York Stock Exchange when Gunderson quit his post in 1950. He denied this had anything to do with the loans.

The charges of improper use of influence continued to hamper Gabrielson until January 1952, when the Hoey panel released its report. The legislators found no evidence of improper influence by Gabrielson in representing Carthage Hydrocol before the RFC. However, the subcommittee said he should not have continued as the firm's counsel after becoming national chairman. Meeting the same month, the Republican National Committee rejected a demand for Gabrielson's resignation and gave him a vote of confidence.

Gabrielson was a controversial figure during the struggle for the 1952 Republican presidential nomination. As the contest shaped up into a race between Senator Taft and General DWIGHT D. EISENHOWER, Eisenhower partisans voiced fears that Gabrielson would favor Taft. Their fears were reinforced when the chairman chose Senator EUGENE D. MILLIKIN (R-Colo.), a Taft backer, as platform committee chairman in June. A few days before the convention opened in July, Gabrielson ruled that delegates whose own seats were in dispute could vote on the seating of other contested delegates. This decision favored the Taft forces. He apparently, however, reversed his decision to rule favorably on a point of order by Taftite Clarence Brown to exclude Louisiana's delegation from the Fair Play resolution, which would have prohibited disputed delegates from being allowed to vote until the convention determined their legitimacy. Brown then had to ask for an amendment doing the same thing—something Taft did not want done but was powerless to stop from his hotel room—because it would mean a premature test of strength for both sides. The amendment's defeat foreshadowed Taft's own defeat by Eisenhower. Shortly after his nomination, Eisenhower chose Arthur E. Summerfield to replace Gabrielson as national chairman.

Gabrielson resumed his private law practice and in 1959 he became president of the John Wood Company. Gabrielson died on May 1, 1976, in Point Pleasant, New Jersey.

—MJS

Galbraith, John Kenneth
(1908–) *economist*

John Kenneth Galbraith was born on October 15, 1908, in Iona Station, Ontario, into a political family, leaders of the Scots farmers in their isolated Canadian town. He received a B.S. in agricultural economics from the University of Toronto in 1931 and won a research scholarship to the University of California at Berkeley. Shortly after earning his Ph.D. in 1934, he took a post as an instructor at Harvard University. While at Harvard Galbraith was introduced to the writings of John Maynard Keynes, which, along with those of Marshall, Veblen, and Marx most strongly influenced his thinking. He adopted U.S. citizenship during this period. Galbraith was appointed assistant professor of economics at Princeton in 1939 but left two years later to join the Office of Price Administration. He was named deputy administrator in 1942. The young economist became widely disliked for his support of a comprehensive control system, and, in 1942, Roosevelt asked him to resign. "The most popular single thing he did that entire term," Galbraith called it.

Rejected from the army because of his height (6'8"), he joined the board of editors of *Fortune* magazine. In 1945 he took a leave from *Fortune* to serve as director of the U.S. Strategic Bombing Survey, a post he shared with George W. Ball. Their report concluded that the bombing of Germany had been relatively ineffective in hampering German production of war materials. In one case, an industry produced more in the month after bombing than before. These findings influenced Galbraith's later attitudes toward air power and war. After completing the survey—he had to fight hard to get approval of a reasonably unvarnished report—Galbraith spent several months in the State Department as an adviser on economic policy. He then returned to *Fortune*, where he remained until 1948.

In 1949 Galbraith became professor of economics at Harvard, his more or less permanent home for the rest of his academic career. Two years later he published *The Theory of Price Control*, which he later termed his best book. "The only difficulty," he said, "is that five people read it." The study's limited reception in the academic world prompted Galbraith to aim his later works at a broader, general audience.

During the 1950s he published several widely read analyses of the American economy. His deft style and delight at debunking the "conventional wisdom" won him a large audience for his controversial theories. In 1952 Galbraith published *American Capitalism: The Concept of Countervailing Power*, an analysis of the postwar American economy. He asserted that the success of the U.S. economy after World War II defied the laws of classical economics. The classical competitive model was a free market, one so fragmented that no purchaser or producer could dominate. Competition among these small units kept prices down and generated research. The American economy, he maintained, no longer conformed to this model; it was dominated by large powerful combinations. Yet the evils of concentration had not developed because, according to Galbraith, these powers were "countervailing." Big business gave rise to powerful unions; large manufacturers to large retailers and suppliers. The result was a workable system in which each side got much of what it wanted. Prices and profits tended to be higher in oligopolistic industries but these served a useful function in generating research, which had become increasingly expensive. Galbraith viewed government as the countervailing force to business and labor, the protection of those too weak to organize. "This," he argued, "has become in modern times perhaps the major peacetime function of the federal government." He offered the Wagner Act and farm price supports as illustrations. The economist maintained that government should, rather than vigorously pursue antitrust suits and regulations, direct its attention to more energetically filling this support role.

Response among economists to *American Capitalism* was mixed. Galbraith's writing was widely acknowledged to be stimulating, and he was hailed for calling attention to forces other than competition as shapers of the market. Yet some economists criticized him as sloppy in his use and analysis of historical evidence and inconsistent in his argument, particularly when trying to explain the movement of the postwar economy. Rather than the forces that Galbraith discussed, postwar prosperity and inflation were commonly viewed as flowing from factors such as pentup consumer demand, massive monetary liquidity, consumer doubts about the continu-

ation of prosperity, and federal surpluses and deficits. Nevertheless, his acceptance of bigness per se helped shape U.S. attitudes on this issue during the 1950s.

Galbraith served as a speech writer for ADLAI E. STEVENSON during the 1952 presidential campaign, but he returned to Harvard and his teaching duties before the race was over. Galbraith later claimed the attacks on Stevenson by Senator RICHARD M. NIXON (R-Calif.) and Senator JOSEPH R. MCCARTHY (R-Wisc.) that he was soft on communism, froze Stevenson into a "cold war orthodoxy," which led him to denounce Dwight D. Eisenhower's pledge to go to Korea as a mistake because one had to deal with Moscow to end the Korean War. During the Eisenhower years Galbraith became a vocal critic of administration economic policy and served on the Democratic Advisory Council formed to provide alternatives to the Eisenhower program. In 1955 he published *The Great Crash: 1929* and in 1958 *The Affluent Society*, a major critique of national priorities as he saw them emerging from a society and economy such as that described in *American Capitalism*.

Galbraith became an early supporter of John F. Kennedy and played a major role in winning academic and liberal support for the young senator. He served as Kennedy's agricultural adviser during the 1960 campaign and was ambassador to India during the administration. After Kennedy's death he returned to Harvard and published a number of books over the next several years, of which the most widely acclaimed were the *New Industrial State* (1967) and *Economics and the Public Purpose* (1973). He also produced a television series on economics that was entitled *The Age of Uncertainty* and which was adapted for publication.

Galbraith continued to be active in liberal and Democratic Party politics. He served as president of the Americans for Democratic Action in 1967. He was a vocal critic of the war in Vietnam and was an early supporter of George McGovern for president in 1972. Galbraith retired from his post at Harvard in 1975. (See *The Eisenhower Years, The Kennedy Years, The Johnson Years, The Nixon/Ford Years* Volumes)

—CSJ

Gallup, George H(orace)
(1901–1984) *public opinion analyst*
George Gallup was born on November 18, 1901, in Jefferson, Iowa, the son of a speculator in ranch and

farmlands. After attending the University of Iowa, he became an instructor in journalism. His doctoral dissertation ("An Objective Method for Determining Reader-Interest in the Content of a Newspaper") was on the sample measurement of newspaper readers' reactions, techniques that he soon used in surveys for several midwestern newspapers. In 1932 the New York advertising firm of Young and Rubicon hired him to test their clients' radio and newspaper audiences. Within three years he set up his own marketing research company, the American Institute of Public Opinion, an organization with many public as well as private clients. AIPO polled on a variety of questions, including alcoholism, religion, positions on women's issues, though politics were at the heart of its business. In 1936 Gallup gained prominence by predicting Franklin D. Roosevelt's victory more accurately than any other survey, in particular the infamous *Literary Digest* poll predicting Roosevelt's defeat. Despite his accuracy, he was called before a congressional committee investigating the consistent underestimation of the Democratic vote by pollsters. In 1940 Gallup wrote *The Pulse of Democracy*, a book that attempted to prove that opinion polling was an important aid to representative democracy.

Gallup's surveys manifested overwhelming public approval of Truman's succession to the presidency and his performance during the first months of the administration. However, by early 1946, following the massive labor strikes and the general disenchantment with the postwar world, the president's poll ratings plummeted, hitting 50 percent by April 1946. It did not rise again until after the disastrous Democratic losses suffered in the November congressional elections. By 1947 the Gallup poll revealed that two major concerns were dominating public thinking: the rise in the cost of living and the growing threat of the Soviet Union.

Gallup, as well as his competitors, failed to predict the winner in the 1948 presidential election. They uniformly saw the Republican candidate, THOMAS E. DEWEY, as the victor in a confused four-way race. The Gallup organization stopped interviewing voters 18 days before the election (betraying Gallup's own belief that political campaigns had little effect on election results). It thus did not detect the huge last-minute switches to the incumbent by midwestern farmers, disillusioned supporters of HENRY A. WALLACE, and other uncertain voters. A few days before the election Truman said that people would "throw the Galluping polls right into the ashcan—you watch 'em." Following the election pollsters were ridiculed by Truman and widely criticized for their faulty sampling methods. Gallup responded in an address before the Social Science Research Council. He asserted that polls "constitute the most useful instrument of democracy ever devised . . . [providing] almost our only check today on the increasing strength and influence of pressure groups."

Gallup's polls played an important role in the 1952 presidential primary. By charting the declining popularity of General DOUGLAS MACARTHUR and the relative lack of support for Senator ROBERT A. TAFT (R-Ohio) when pitted against DWIGHT D. EISENHOWER and potential Democratic opponents, the poll assisted the general's chance for the Republican nomination.

The Gallup poll continued to be a major political indicator during the 1960s. John F. Kennedy used it to allay fears about the inelectability of a Catholic during his run for the presidency in 1960. A dramatic last minute Gallup poll before the 1968 Republican National Convention was important in showing Richard M. Nixon's voter appeal. Reflecting on the phenomenal growth, self-assurance, and influence of the polling industry, Gallup told an audience in 1962 that "the only department in which we may have an advantage over the Russians is in our research methods for pre-testing propaganda issues and for measuring their sources in use." Gallup continued to be chairman of the board and CEO of Gallup Organization up to the time of his death on July 26, 1984, while vacationing in Switzerland.

—GB

Gates, John
(1913–1992) *Communist Party official*

The son of Polish Jewish immigrants, Israel Regenstreif was born September 28, 1913. He joined the Communist Political Association at the age of 17. In 1931, while a student at City College in New York, he became a member of the Young Communist League (YCL). He left college in 1932 and obtained a job in a radio parts factory but was soon laid off. Determined to become a full-time Communist organizer, he relocated in Warren, Ohio, in 1933 in order to work with the YCL's midwestern chapter.

Prior to his departure he changed his name to John Gates.

After a brief period in Warren, he moved to Youngstown, Ohio, and was promoted to the leadership of the YCL in 1933. From that year until 1937 he worked for various public works projects. Gates fought on the side of the Loyalists during the Spanish Civil War and rose to lieutenant colonel, the highest rank attained by an American. In his absence the YCL had elected Gates to its National Council. From 1939 until 1941 he held the post of national educational director for the YCL. In 1941 he joined the army but was not stationed overseas because of his Communist background.

Gates supported the reorganization of the CPUSA in 1945. While still in the army, he was elected to the party's National Committee. Upon his return from the war in 1946, he assumed the post of national veterans director of the Communist Party and was responsible for helping Communist veterans readjust to civilian and party life. The following year he became editor-in-chief of the *Daily Worker*.

In 1948 a federal grand jury indicted Gates along with 11 other members of the National Committee on charges of conspiracy to organize a party that advocated the violent overthrow of the U.S. government in violation of the Smith Act. Gates's trial began in 1949. According to the prosecution, the reconstitution of the Communist Party in 1945 meant "the return to a policy of advocating force and violence." As the main evidence of this charge, the government introduced the testimony of FBI informers. As the first defense witness, Gates testified that the party stood for "a peaceful transition to socialism," and that "the party constitution called for expulsion for anyone advocating force and violence." Although Gates was not present at the 1945 convention and there was conflicting evidence that the defendants actually incited violent action, all were convicted. In 1949 Gates was released from prison pending appeal. He returned to the editorship of the *Daily Worker*. In 1951 the Supreme Court upheld the convictions six to two. Gates, together with nine other defendants, was sentenced to the maximum penalty of five years in prison and was sent to the Atlanta Penitentiary.

In 1952 Gates was subpoenaed to testify before the Subversive Activities Control Board, meeting to determine whether the Communist Party should register as a foreign agent. He stated that the Communist Party in the United States was "fully autonomous" but had views identical to the Soviet Communist Party because "there is no difference between the national interests of the people of the U.S. and . . . of Russia." Of course, it was later revealed that the party was subsidized and controlled by the Soviets, who also used the Communist Party USA for infiltration and spying purposes. In April 1953 the board ordered the Communist Party to register its membership and financial facts with the U.S. government.

Gates was released from prison in 1955 and resumed his post as editor in chief of the *Daily Worker*. He remained there until 1958 at which time he resigned from the Communist Party after a failed attempt to democratize the party and wrest control of its affairs away from Moscow. Also in 1958 Gates published his memoirs and admitted that he believed the Stalin-era purge trials were legitimate and the people must have committed the crimes they confessed to and Stalin was doing the most to help the Loyalists in Spain. Gates could not believe Stalin could do that and also coerce false confessions. For a period of two years, Gates had opposed the party's dominant faction, headed by WILLIAM Z. FOSTER. Regarding the Communist Party as a "mummy," he stated in his resignation speech that the party had become "a futile and impotent political sect with no importance in our country." In 1962 Gates assumed a position with the Research Department of the International Ladies' Garment Workers Union. Gates died of heart disease and a stroke on May 23, 1992, in Miami Beach, Florida.

—DGE

George, Walter F(ranklin)
(1878–1951) *member of the Senate*

The son of a tenant farmer, Walter F. George was born on January 29, 1878, in Preston, Georgia. He distinguished himself in intercollegiate contests while attending Mercer University, a Baptist institution, from where he graduated in 1900. He received his law degree a year later and for the next two decades pursued successive careers as a lawyer, solicitor general for the Cordele judiciary circuit, and state judge. He retired as a judge of the Georgia Supreme Court in 1922 and ran for the Senate seat left vacant by the death of the fiery populist Tom Watson. Supported by Atlanta business interests as well as South Georgia Watsonites, George was elected by a landslide vote and reelected in each of five subsequent contests.

In the Senate George gradually rose to power through diligence, seniority, and quiet promotion of conservative policies. Although a supporter of some early New Deal measures, including the Tennessee Valley Authority, the Social Security Act, and the Wagner Labor Relations Act, by Roosevelt's second term he had emerged as a leading foe of reform legislation, mobilizing opposition to housing and wage-hour bills and managing the defeat of Roosevelt's court-packing plan. In the election of 1938 Roosevelt campaigned against George as part of the so-called purge of key congressional conservatives obstructing his program, but the strategy backfired. George won reelection over New Deal supporter Lawrence Camp and rural demagogue Eugene Talmadge.

Assuming the chairmanship of the Foreign Relations Committee in November 1940, George helped win passage of the president's lend-lease program. In August 1941 he resigned the Foreign Relations chairmanship to take over that of the Finance Committee. Except for the 1947–49 session, he held that position until 1953. As head of the tax panel, George generally opposed progressive tax reforms and favored lower tax rates and preferences for corporate income; nevertheless, he was one of the key congressional architects of the system of high taxes enacted to finance World War II.

Throughout the Truman years George worked in his cautious and methodical manner to roll back the wartime rates. In October 1945 he favored elimination of the excess profits tax because he wanted "the young men of this country to have a chance to engage in business enterprises," his stand reflected his belief that the tax injured small business. In the 1947–48 battle over the Republican-sponsored tax cut, George, then ranking Democrat on the Finance Committee, threw his considerable influence behind the sweeping tax slash, which was opposed by the Truman administration. He voted for both 1947 versions, successfully vetoed by the president, and played an important role in revising the 1948 tax reduction so as to win a two-thirds congressional majority sufficient to override Truman's veto in April.

Early in 1949 Truman proposed a tax increase in order to close an anticipated budget deficit. In February George urged delaying action on any tax boost and on March 29 declared that a tax increase was the "one thing which will bring us a sizable depression in 1949." Two days later Truman answered George by saying that a budget deficit would endanger the economy more than his suggested $4 billion tax hike. George strongly favored closing the budget gap by cutting spending instead. The two conducted another public colloquy in August, when George called for an immediate reduction in taxes, especially wartime excise rates, in order to stimulate business expansion. Truman replied a few days later that he would be willing to cut taxes, provided George found other ways of financing the government.

In August 1950 the Senate Finance Committee reported an amended version of a tax bill passed by the House to raise revenue for the Korean War. Unlike most tax measures this one provoked extended and at times acrimonious debate on the Senate floor. As the chairman of the Finance Committee, George defended the measure against attacks by a group of liberal Democrats, led by PAUL H. DOUGLAS (D-Ill.), HUBERT H. HUMPHREY (D-Minn.), and HERBERT H. LEHMAN (D-N.Y.), that the bill was filled with loopholes for special interests.

Humphrey charged that the committee's bill, which George had played a key role in drafting, had converted President Truman's request for higher taxes into "a smoke screen" for private relief amendments. The Minnesotan attacked, and George defended, a provision reducing the capital gains holding period from six months to three; an amendment allowing capital gains treatment for income from oil, gas, and mineral rights; a retroactive "family partnerships" provision that ignored the age of any partner; and the deletion of a House section that extended withholding to dividend income. (Interestingly, George congratulated Humphrey on his hard work, which signaled the Minnesotan's acceptance in the Senate.) George also strove successfully to delay enactment of an excess profits tax on the grounds that the issue needed further study. He argued that a stiff corporate income tax was preferable to an excess profits levy, which he felt was inflationary and injurious to small businesses, but he recognized that an excess profits tax was inevitable.

The tax debate recurred in September 1951, and again George defended his committee's handiwork against the vigorous criticism of the small band of tax reformers. "We have the highest tax rates in the world," he declared in response to charges that the bill failed to provide sufficient revenue to finance the administration's budget. George advocated reduced spending together with wage and price controls, instead of higher taxes, as the remedy for inflation. In one role reversal George defended, in a sharp exchange with Lehman, a section of the bill raising $140 million by taxing the undistributed profits of savings banks and building and loan associations, many of which were New York institutions. As in 1950 the heat generated by floor arguments did not affect the fate of the tax bill; the Senate generally approved the provisions of the committee bill by wide margins.

As a staunch believer in private enterprise, reduced government and fiscal conservatism, George was frequently at odds with the Truman administration in the domestic area. He often led a conservative coalition of Republicans and Southern Democrats in blocking or pruning Fair Deal programs. He fought all attempts to modify the filibuster rule, arguing that majority cloture instead of two-thirds was intended only to clear the way for the administration's civil rights proposals, which he claimed were unconstitutional and not worth discussion. He strenuously opposed the anti–poll tax, antilynching bills, and proposals to establish a Fair Employment Practices Commission.

George voted against public housing and in favor of a bill to renounce federal title to tidewater oil lands. He also voted for the Portal-to-Portal Pay Act and for the Case Labor Disputes bill of 1946. He did support the Senate version of the Full Employment bill. He was a strong backer of the Taft-Hartley bill regulating labor unions, and, along with HARRY F. BYRD (D-Va.) and JOSEPH M. BALL (R-Minn.), proposed amendments that would have made the measure even more restrictive. One, which would have banned industrywide bargaining, was defeated, 44 to 43, and another, which would have forbidden secondary boycotts and jurisdictional strikes and allowed unions to be sued for damages under the antitrust laws, lost 62 to 38, although a revised substitute without the drastic last feature passed, 65 to 26. Like most southerners, George favored low tariffs; in 1949, he worked successfully on behalf of a three-year extension of the reciprocal trade agreements. He also sponsored a number of laws providing federal aid for vocational education.

In 1951 the *U.S. News and World Report* identified George as one of the "quiet bulwarks" of a "stop-Truman" campaign being managed by southern conservatives. (He had backed the Twenty-second Amendment limiting the president to two

terms, but, due to its wording, it did not apply to Truman.) At the Democratic National Convention the following year he made a presidential nominating speech for his junior colleague, Senator RICHARD B. RUSSELL (D-Ga.).

The second-ranking Democrat on the Foreign Relations Committee, George often proved an influential ally of the administration's foreign policy initiatives. He backed the postwar loan to Great Britain and voted to ratify the United Nations Charter. He lent crucial support to such pillars of the postwar containment strategy as the Marshall Plan, Greek-Turkish aid, and the North Atlantic Treaty. At times his fiscal conservatism, prevailed over his internationalism, as in September 1949 when he proposed an amendment to the Mutual Defense Assistance Act to cut cash aid to Europe from $500 million to $300 million. The effort failed by a 46 to 33 vote. He also opposed a $45 million authorization to establish Truman's Point Four program, and threw his support behind the 1951 McClellan Amendment, stating the sense of the Senate that any additional troops sent to NATO beyond the initial four divisions planned should be done only with the approval of Congress.

In January 1953 George responded to the outgoing Truman administration's $78.5 billion budget with the statement, "The principal duty of this Congress is to see to it that the budget is cut." Over the next four years he found the domestic conservatism and foreign policy restraint of the Eisenhower administration more congenial to his own inclinations than the actions of its Democratic predecessor. George devoted himself more to foreign affairs during this period, particularly after assuming the chairmanship of the Foreign Relations Committee in 1955. There he assumed the role of respected elder statesman and spokesman on behalf of the peaceful settlement of international disputes. Following George's retirement from the Senate in January 1957, President Eisenhower named him ambassador to the North Atlantic Treaty Organization. George died of heart disease on August 4, 1957, in Vienna, Georgia. (See *The Eisenhower Years* Volume)

—TO

Gilpatric, Roswell L(eavitt)

(1906–1996) *assistant secretary of the air force, undersecretary of the air force*

Roswell L. Gilpatric was born on November 4, 1906, in New York City. He received his bachelor's degree from Yale University in 1928 and a law degree from the same institution in 1931. The following year he joined the New York law firm of Cravath, deGersdorff, Swaine & Wood, where he specialized in corporation and financial law. During World War II Gilpatric was a legal adviser to corporations engaged in war production. This work brought him into contact with the Defense Plant Corporation and many military officials. On May 28, 1951, President Truman appointed Gilpatric assistant secretary of the air force for materiel. He directed the production and procurement program of the air force, conducting analyses of materiel requirements, and setting targets for future aircraft production. Gilpatric's skill in solving aircraft procurement problems resulted in his promotion to undersecretary of the air force in October 1951.

That fall a House Armed Services subcommittee began an investigation of the Pentagon's procurement practices during the first two years of the Korean War. Critics had charged that the Pentagon's practices resulted in duplication and the waste of tax dollars. Gilpatric testified before the subcommittee on February 8, 1952. He had made a decision to award a multibillion-dollar order for turret lathes to the Fisher Body Company, a subsidiary of General Motors. Fisher was heavily subsidized by the government in obtaining the equipment needed to produce the lathes, yet it produced them at a higher price than that available elsewhere. Six months after the contract was signed, it was suddenly canceled. During the hearings it was revealed that the individual who advised Gilpatric to award the contract to Fisher, Harold R. Boyer, was, in addition to being the chairman of the government's aircraft production board, a former General Motors executive. Gilpatric testified that the $69 million contract was canceled because of cutbacks in jet aircraft procurement and the use of new engineering techniques for producing jet engines, which reduced the need for tools.

Gilpatric became known as a critic of military practices and policies. Intent on modernizing the armed forces, he pushed for American jet fighters, which were as light and maneuverable as the Soviet MiG-15. In March 1952 he outlined, for the first time, a four-year production schedule. He criticized armed forces competition and duplication in aircraft production. He also complained to Defense Secretary ROBERT A. LOVETT in March 1952 that diverting anymore military aid funds from American

aircraft manufacturing to offshore procurement in fiscal years 1952 or 1953 would harm both regular and military aid programs from January 1953 through 1955. Gilpatric later agreed unenthusiastically to offshore procurement if certain conditions were met regarding evaluation, specifications, price, contract administration, and acceptability of the aircraft.

Gilpatric resigned his government post at the beginning of the Eisenhower administration and resumed his law practice, representing many defense contractors in their dealings with the government. He resumed government service when President John F. Kennedy appointed him deputy secretary of defense. He played a critical role in advising Kennedy during the Cuban missile crisis. In January 1964 Gilpatric went back to his law practice. During the Johnson administration he served as a member of panels which advised the government on national security and nuclear disarmament. He retired from his law practice in 1977. He died of prostate cancer on March 15, 1996, in New York City. (See *The Kennedy Years, The Johnson Years* Volumes)

—MLB

Gold, Ben

(1898–1985) *president, International Fur and Leather Workers Union*

The son of a watchmaker, Gold was born on September 8, 1898, in Bessarabia, Russia. He immigrated to the United States in 1910 and eventually found a job in a New York fur shop. After abandoning plans to enter law school, he joined the International Fur Workers Union (IFWU), an affiliate of the American Federation of Labor (AFL), and began a career as a labor agitator and union official. When he was 14 he joined a committee that held the first strike in the New York fur industry. Gold joined the Communist Party at the time of its founding in 1919. In the bitter conflicts between Socialists and Communists that tore through the garment industry during the 1920s, he was one of the party's leading strategists and public spokesmen. In 1926, Gold was in charge of a 17-week strike that led to the institution of a 35-hour workweek in the New York fur industry.

A gifted organizer, Gold won the strong and enduring loyalty of furriers. In 1925 he was elected manager of the IFWU's New York Joint Board, making it the first union in the United States to come under outright Communist control. In 1927, the AFL tried to break Gold's power by dissolving the Joint Board and expelling its leaders. However, in the shop-and-street war that followed, the Communist group managed to retain the support of rank-and-file fur workers. In 1929 the New York furriers joined the Communist-sponsored Needle Trades Workers Industrial Union. Six years later this organization was dissolved and the Gold group instructed to return to the IFWU. In 1937 Gold was elected president of the International, which then left the AFL to join the new Congress of Industrial Organizations (CIO). After a merger in 1939 it became the International Fur and Leather Workers Union (IFLWU). During the 1930s and 1940s Gold was one of the few openly avowed members of the Communist Party among the leaders of American unions. For a time he served on the national and New York State committees of the party, and, in 1931 and 1936, he ran for the New York State Assembly on the Communist ticket.

Relations between Gold and the national CIO remained largely untroubled through the war years—although CIO president Philip Murray was infuriated with Gold's enthusiasm for the No-Strike Pledge. But by 1948, as Murray moved toward a purge of Communist-dominated affiliates, conflict became sharp and open. The IFLWU's outspoken denunciation of the Marshall Plan and the Truman Doctrine and its enthusiastic endorsement of HENRY A. WALLACE's third-party presidential candidacy prompted Murray and his supporters at the CIO national convention in October 1949 to condemn the furriers' leaders. As labor historian Robert H. Zieger has noted, there was disagreement as to what to do about the Communist-dominated union. Murray wanted to drive them out at the 1949 CIO convention. However, CIO general counsel Arthur Goldberg thought a trial of these unions would reveal Gold and others to be dupes of the Communists, and lead to membership revolts. This approach was adopted, and, through this procedure, Gold—who was defiant throughout—was meeting secretly with officials of the Communist Party. Gold and his union were expelled from the CIO in 1950. Along with the officers of nine other pro-Communist unions, they were attacked for their "blind and slavish willingness to act as puppets for the Soviet dictatorship and its foreign policy."

The expulsion of the IFLWU had no effect on its strength in the New York fur trade, which was the center of the industry. It continued to maintain harmonious relations with employers and successfully repulsed all efforts to weaken its position. Threats to locals outside New York, however, made it necessary for the IFLWU to submit to the provisions of the Taft-Hartley Act to protect itself against raiding from other unions. In August 1950 its officers signed the noncommunist affidavits required by the law as a condition for utilizing the services of the National Labor Relations Board in representation elections. To comply with the law Gold announced his resignation from the Communist Party, although at the same time he proclaimed his continuing loyalty to the party's politics. In 1954 Gold was indicted on a charge of perjury in connection with the Taft-Hartley affidavit.

Internal opposition from locals outside New York and efforts by the CIO to set up a rival furriers union during the early 1950s forced the IFLWU to merge with the AFL Amalgamated Meat Cutters in 1954. As one of the conditions for the merger, Gold gave up his post in the union. He returned to work as a furrier. Gold died in Miami Beach, Florida, on July 23, 1985. (See *The Eisenhower Years* Volume)

—TLH

Gore, Albert (Arnold)
(1907–1998) *member of the House of Representatives, member of the Senate*

Albert Gore was born on December 26, 1907, in Granville, Tennessee. He worked as a country schoolteacher from 1926 to 1932. That year he received a B.S. from Middle Tennessee State Teachers College and was elected county schools superintendent. He attended night law classes at the Nashville YMCA and was admitted to the Tennessee bar in 1936. Active in politics since 1932 as an organizer of Young Democratic clubs, Gore was appointed state commissioner of labor after the 1936 election. Casting Secretary of State Cordell Hull as his political ideal, Gore was elected to the House of Representatives from Hull's old district in 1938.

In Congress Gore was a strong supporter of an internationalist foreign policy, voting against the arms embargo amendment to the Neutrality Act in 1939 and in favor of lend-lease in 1941. In domestic issues he combined populist rhetoric with diligent study of economic matters. In 1941, as a substitute for what was called the administration's "weak-kneed" price control bill, Gore introduced a sweeping measure mandating a ceiling on the nation's entire price structure. The House rejected the proposal, 218 to 63. In 1942 Gore denounced the "scandalous" compensations and bonuses paid to executives of corporations with defense contracts, and, in 1943, he led the fight against rescinding President Roosevelt's salary limitation order.

During the Republican-controlled 80th Congress (1947–49) Gore was one of a handful of young Democratic members acting as a "watchdog team" spotlighting mistakes of the opposition. Gore criticized the Republicans' budget-cutting campaign along two lines: the first that budget slashing was crippling essential services and the second that some of the budget reductions were illusory. From his seat on the Appropriations Committee he tried, often in vain, to restore funds to various appropriations. In 1947 Gore fought Representative HAROLD KNUTSON's (R-Minn.) 20 percent across-the-board tax cut, saying that the theory of the cut came "right out of the Andrew Mellon primer of special privilege." The House rejected a substitute favored by Gore and other liberals that would have raised the personal exemption from $500 to $700 or $1,000, a method more advantageous to lower income taxpayers. Gore supported President Truman's vetoes of the Knutson plan, but Congress finally overrode Truman in April 1948.

In 1949 Gore led a House Democratic revolt against the farm plan of Secretary of Agriculture CHARLES F. BRANNAN, which would have altered the system of farm price supports. Calling the Brannan Plan "dangerous," Gore declared that "we cannot afford to run the risk with the farmer's welfare . . . by taking this leap in the dark and throwing overboard a program that has been built out of 16 years of experience and farmer cooperation." In July the Brannan Plan was defeated in the House. The Gore substitute, continuing existing rigid price supports at 90 percent of parity, was passed, 239 to 170.

Gore generally followed a middle-of-the-road course on domestic policy. He voted for the Case labor disputes bill of 1946 and the Taft-Hartley Act of 1947, as well as the Mundt-Nixon anticommunist bill of 1948 and the McCarran Act of 1950. He favored the administration's public housing plan and greater funds for hospital construction. While voting against a Fair Employment Practices Commis-

sion, he was one of the few southern representatives to vote in favor of a bill to outlaw the poll tax. He supported the move to allow committee chairmen to bypass the obstructionist Rules Committee in 1949. He was a strong supporter of the Tennessee Valley Authority and backed larger appropriations for the Atomic Energy Commission. He voted for the Employment Act of 1946. He supported federal claims to the tidelands and Truman's veto of the Price Control Act of 1946, which the president thought did not give him enough power to control prices. He voted against limiting a president to two terms in office.

A reliable supporter of the Truman administration's foreign policy, Gore endorsed the 1946 loan to Great Britain, Greek-Turkish aid, the Marshall Plan, and the 1950 Korea Aid Act. He was a proponent of a liberal trade policy and consistently favored extension of the reciprocal trade agreements originally negotiated by Cordell Hull. During the Korean War Gore attracted attention with his suggestion that the United States use atomic weapons in the Korean conflict to "dehumanize" an area across the width of Korea in order to halt the fighting. He supported the Administration in its efforts to pass Point Four legislation.

In 1952 Gore challenged and defeated the aged chairman of the Senate Appropriations Committee, Senator KENNETH D. MCKELLAR (D-Tenn.), who represented Tennessee's once powerful Crump machine, in the Democratic senatorial primary. Elected in November Gore served three terms in the Senate. In his Senate career Gore stood out as an outspoken southern liberal, a populist maverick outside the Senate "establishment." Along with Senator PAUL H. DOUGLAS (D-Ill.), he was the body's most determined tax reformer and waged a long, usually unsuccessful struggle to close tax loopholes that favored corporations and wealthy individuals. Gore was a supporter of Great Society social legislation and liberal monetary policies and a foe of the Vietnam War. He lost his Senate seat in 1970 to a conservative Republican. In 1972 he became chairman of the Island Creek Coal Company. He also ran a successful cattle-breeding farm. Gore died on December 5, 1998, in Carthage, Tennessee. (See *The Eisenhower Years, The Kennedy Years, The Johnson Years, The Nixon/Ford Years* Volumes)

—TO

Grady, Henry F(rancis)

(1882–1957) *ambassador*

Henry F. Grady was born on February 12, 1882, in San Francisco, California. He received his bachelor's degree from St. Mary's University in Baltimore in 1907 and his doctorate in economics from Columbia in 1927. After a brief teaching career at the City University of New York and Columbia from 1916 to 1918, Grady became a statistical expert for the U.S. Shipping Board. Grady later claimed that World War I had made him attentive to war and its prevention. During 1919 and 1920 he served as a commercial attaché in London and Amsterdam and traveled throughout Europe to report on postwar economic conditions. From 1928 to 1937 Grady was professor of international trade and dean of the college of commerce at the University of California at Berkeley. As chairman of the Foreign Commerce Association of San Francisco and trade adviser to the Chamber of Commerce during the 1920s and 1930s, he opposed the Chinese exclusion laws and favored free trade. Grady joined the State Department as chief of the Trade Agreements Division in 1934 and played an important part in formulating the reciprocal trade program. He was vice chairman of the U.S. Tariff Commission from 1937 to 1939, and he served as assistant secretary of the state for economic and trade affairs from 1939 to 1941.

In January 1941 Grady resigned from the State Department to become president of the American President Lines. As head of an American technical mission in India in March 1942, he tried to increase

Henry F. Grady taking the oath of office as ambassador to India (*left to right*) Stanley F. Woodward, Dean Acheson, and Henry F. Grady (*Harry S. Truman Library, Harris and Ewing Photos, Beth Gore*)

that country's contribution of war materials. Grady was in charge of economic affairs for the Allied Control Commission in Italy from December 1943 to July 1944 and headed the U.S. delegation to the International Business Conference in November 1944.

In October 1945 President Truman appointed Grady head of the U.S. section of the Allied mission observing the Greek elections. He supervised the 600-man U.S. inspection group, which, along with French and British teams, surveyed Greece's nationwide elections in March 1946. The commission's report concluded that the elections had been fair. Later critics claimed the abstention of the left from the election meant the new government was not representative.

As chairman of the board of alternates of the Cabinet Committee on Palestine and Related Problems, Grady met with British officials in London during July and August 1946. He supported the British plan for federation, in which there would be a binational government with autonomy for the Arab and Jewish populations. Grady hoped to prevent the creation of a separate Jewish nation, which would anger Palestinians. Both Jews and Arabs rejected the British plan. It was also criticized by American Zionists who wanted the immediate entry of 100,000 Jews in Palestine, which Grady wanted to put off until both sides in Palestine accepted the plan. According to author Michael J. Cohen, facing pressure from pro-Zionist lobbyists and fears that its acceptance would hurt Democrats at the polls in 1946 and himself in 1948, especially in New York, an exasperated Truman refused to endorse the plan.

Grady became the first U.S. ambassador to India in May 1947. Believing that America's greatest service to world peace would be supplying technological knowledge to underdeveloped nations, he vigorously pushed India to increase industrial production. Replying to the Moslem League's criticism of his alleged pro-Hindu stance and ardent support of American investment in India, he denied that America was seeking control over other countries through the extension of capital assistance to them.

Grady became ambassador to Greece in May 1948. He was responsible for administering the American program of military and economic aid to that nation and giving advice to the Greek army, then fighting Communist insurgents. In January 1949 Grady became a member of that nation's war council, formed to direct the military effort. The

ambassador also put pressure on the government to institute needed economic, social, and political reforms. Grady wrote Greek premier Sophocles Venizelos in March 1950 urging social reforms and the elimination of special privileges, government inefficiency, excessive subsidies, high interest rates, and overcentralized power. In April the U.S. aid mission suspended new power and industrial projects on the grounds that Venizelos had not organized a stable Greek government. In 1949 Grady had to fight off a plan of Greek monarchists, endorsed by some American officials, to make General Alexander Papagos a dictator under King Paul. Grady thought such an act would deal a severe blow to the Truman Doctrine, and with the help of British vice admiral Lord Mountbatten, who dissuaded the king, and Papagos's lack of enthusiasm for the plan, was able to defeat the proposal. Grady also had problems with the Economic Cooperation Administration's director in Greece, John Nuveen, who Grady said wanted to "dictate, in effect, the personnel and method of operation of the government of a sovereign country." Grady failed to persuade Nuveen that this sort of attitude would only validate criticism that the United States was using aid to gain political influence throughout the world. Grady later convinced the administration to recall Nuveen. Grady's administration of the Greek aid program, which totaled about $1.5 billion from 1947 to 1950, was commended by Truman in May 1950.

President Truman appointed Grady ambassador to Iran in June 1950. At that time the English and the Iranians were negotiating over the distribution of revenues of the Anglo-Iranian Oil Company. Grady tried to convince the British to give more of the profits to the Iranian government to assist that nation's development. The British refused. The Truman administration did not follow Grady's advice to increase aid to Iran during the negotiations for fear of offending the British. In March 1951 Iran nationalized the British-owned Anglo-Iranian Oil Company, thus precipitating a crisis with the Western allies. Grady insisted that nationalization would halt the flow of oil to the West and also endanger Iran's economy. He called for "friendly" negotiations between Iran and Great Britain. In response the Iranian government told him not to meddle in the country's internal affairs. Grady's negotiations with Premier Mohammed Mossadegh were unsuccessful, and he believed Iranian Anglophobia rendered compromise impossible for the country's leaders. At the same time, he felt that the United States had put more pressure on Iran to make concessions to the British than was warranted. Thoroughly disillusioned and believing that "old-style colonialism does not work" any longer in the Middle East, Grady resigned in September 1951. At that time he told reporters that negotiations with Mossadegh were useless and prophesied a bleak future for Iran, which he felt was dominated by terrorists.

Grady came out of retirement briefly in 1955 to serve as a member of the Citizens Conference for International Economic Union, an organization advocating the reduction of trade barriers between Communist countries and the West. He died on September 14, 1957, on a cruise to the Far East on board the ship *President Wilson*.

—AES

Gray, Gordon

(1909–1982) *assistant secretary of the army, secretary of the army, special assistant to the president*

Gordon Gray was born on May 30, 1909, in Baltimore, Maryland. His family held a controlling interest in the R. J. Reynolds Tobacco Company of Winston-Salem, North Carolina. First in his class at the University of North Carolina at Chapel Hill, Gray received his B.A. in psychology in 1930. His father wanted him to learn the tobacco business "from the bottom up," and so Gray worked for a time in the Winston-Salem sorting houses. He earned his degree at Yale Law School in 1933 and entered practice in New York City.

With the death of his father in 1935, Gray returned to North Carolina. There he continued to practice law until 1937, when Winston-Salem's two daily newspapers, the *Morning Journal* and the evening *Twin City Sentinel* were for sale. Gray used his inheritance to purchase the controlling Piedmont Publishing Company, which also owned radio station WSJS. With the motto "I consider myself a trustee for the community" as a guiding inspiration, Gray built up the newspapers and radio station into vigorous, influential political organs. In 1938 he first entered politics, serving in the North Carolina state Senate. He resigned in 1942 to join the army. Four years later Gray was again elected to the North Carolina Senate.

In 1947 President Truman appointed Gray assistant secretary of the army. He was brought to

Washington by KENNETH C. ROYALL, the first secretary of the army in the newly created Defense Department and a fellow North Carolinian. Gray's principal duties were to handle relations with other departments of the government.

As assistant secretary, Gray was in charge of army procurement, and he served as the army member on the Armed Forces Munitions Board. In November Secretary of Defense JAMES V. FORRESTAL named Gray to head a six-man interservice committee to study the reorganization and modernization of the nation's National Guard and reserve forces. The committee, known as the Gray Board, examined the role the reserves were to play in future defense preparedness and the question of control of the National Guard. After seven months of hearings, the board's report, submitted early in August, recommended principally that the National Guard be incorporated in the U.S. Army Reserves. The panel also called for strengthening the reserve forces. It also recommended setting up a permanent interservice committee to make recommendations on a continuing basis regarding reserve policy. Truman told Forrestal that the report was "filled with political dynamite" and wanted to put off a decision on it until after the 1948 election. The recommendation for a federalized National Guard met with strong opposition from National Guard officers and from state governors. Legislation subsequently left the states with primary control over the National Guard, while allowing the President to call it into active service.

When Royall resigned in April 1949 due to his hindrance of desegregation in the military, Gray became acting secretary. Gray backed Truman's integration policy, and Truman appointed him secretary of the army in June. During his year at that post, he defended army employees against charges that they were Communist sympathizers. As a step to fulfill Truman's 1948 directive against discrimination in the armed forces, in January 1950 Gray ordered all field commanders to assign qualified blacks to white combat units. Gray criticized NSC-68, which he thought should be more definite on the size of the military force required and the amount of money needed to implement the report's recommendations.

In March 1950 Truman named Gray a special presidential assistant to find ways of narrowing the gap between U.S. imports and exports. Gray also examined how the United States could maintain international trade and alleviate foreign dollar shortages when the European Recovery Program ended in 1952. Gray submitted a report to Truman in November calling for continued U.S. economic aid to Western Europe for another three or four years. He also urged that the United States aid only those countries specifically requesting assistance. At the same time, Gray advocated domestic action to allow other nations to buy essential U.S. supplies at lower prices. He left office to become president of the University of North Carolina in September.

Gray returned to government service in June 1951 to direct the newly formed Psychology Strategy Board. He oversaw the board's handling of psychological warfare activities. This involved the propaganda, political, and economic aspects of the cold war. He left the board in December to return to the University of North Carolina.

President Eisenhower named Gray to the Psychology Strategy Committee in 1953 to participate in war studies. In the same year he served on Eisenhower's nine-member committee on International Information Activities, charged with planning a "unified and dynamic" psychological cold war strategy. In 1954 Gray headed a special panel for the Atomic Energy Commission (AEC) that held secret hearings in April on charges that Dr. J. ROBERT OPPENHEIMER represented a security risk. In May the panel cleared him as "loyal" but decided against his reinstatement as an AEC consultant. Gray also served the Eisenhower administration in several other defense and national security posts in the late 1950s. He resigned in January 1961 to become chairman of the board of the Piedmont Publishing Company. First appointed a member of the consulting Foreign Intelligence Advisory Board by President Kennedy in May of the same year, Gray continued to serve in the same capacity in the Johnson and Nixon administrations. In 1975 Gray became chairman of the board of Summit Communications, Inc. Gray died of cancer on November 26, 1982, in Washington, D.C.

—SF

Green, Dwight H(erbert)
(1897–1958) *governor*

Dwight "Pete" Green was born on January 9, 1897, in Ligonier, Indiana. After serving in the armed forces during World War I, Green attended Stanford University and then the University of Chicago,

where he received his law degree in 1922. He practiced in Chicago until 1926, when he was appointed to the staff of the Bureau of Internal Revenue in Washington. The following year Green became special representative to the bureau's counsel in Chicago and was placed in charge of the income tax prosecutions of underworld figures. His work led to the conviction in 1931 of Al Capone and other Chicago gangsters on charges of income tax evasion. In 1932 Green was appointed to a three-year term as U.S. district attorney for Chicago. He ran unsuccessfully for mayor in 1939. He was elected governor in 1940 on the Republican ticket as a reformer opposed to the corrupt governorship of Democrat Henry Horner.

As governor, Green took a leading role in encouraging economic planning for postwar reconversion. In 1943 he presided over the Midwest planning conference of state governments and established the Illinois Postwar Planning Commission, which brought together representatives of business, labor, higher education, and citizens groups to plan for reconversion. A strong proponent of balanced budgets, Green imposed austerity on Illinois during World War II in order to have a sufficient surplus to guarantee jobs and needed services after the war.

Following the war's end in 1945 Green presented the legislature with a massive capital improvement budget. He won appropriation of funds to expand the state university campuses, to build new hospitals and other public institutions, and to construct new government office buildings. In 1946 Green gained legislative and voter approval for a $385 million bond issue to provide the nation's largest state bonus for veterans. He also sponsored the state enabling legislation that created the Chicago Metropolitan Transit Authority and led, in 1947, to the integration of Chicago's competing bus and trolley lines into a single, publicly owned and operated system.

An outspoken foe of New Deal and Fair Deal liberalism, Green took an active role in the national Republican Party. In December 1945, at a Republican National Committee meeting, he attacked liberal Republicans for their support of New Deal measures and urged the party to remain true to conservative principles. He helped draw up a statement in 1946 signed by Republican governors endorsing the principle of a balanced federal budget. Early in 1947 he sharply criticized Truman's foreign policy as too conciliatory toward the Soviets.

Green's statements on national and international issues led many to speculate that he was seeking his party's presidential, or perhaps vice presidential, nomination. But in August 1947 he declared his support for Senator ROBERT A. TAFT (R-Ohio). When it appeared that Governor THOMAS E. DEWEY's strength might lead to his first ballot nomination, Green pushed for a favorite son strategy among Republican governors in order to prevent the victory. Selected as keynote speaker for the 1948 Republican National Convention, he uncompromisingly attacked the "radicalism" of the New Deal. He charged that Roosevelt and Truman had harbored "crackpots" in public office and that the 16 years of Democratic rule had been a thinly disguised "tryst" with communism. Green also accused Truman of losing the peace to Russia and of being responsible for the Soviet Union's control of Eastern Europe.

Meanwhile in Illinois Green had been busy building a political organization—the "Green Machine"—made up of patronage sinecures. He was known as a puppet of the conservative *Chicago Tribune*. There was corruption in the administration, such as graft in state purchases of supplies and land. For months Green was warned that a mine in Centralia was dangerous; miners begged Green to do something about it. He did not, and the mine blew up in 1947, killing 111. An investigation showed that many of Green's mine inspectors—although not the one at Centralia—had asked mine operators for political contributions. In 1948 a mobster was murdered in Peoria. A reporter, Ted Link of the *St. Louis Post-Dispatch*, which opposed Green, was looking into the murder when politicians associated with Green arrested him on trumped-up charges. As John Barlow Martin has noted, the Green Machine's reputation was as low as that of the Cook County Democrats. Green ran for a third term as governor in 1948, but ADLAI E. STEVENSON soundly defeated him. He returned to private life and the practice of law. Green died on February 20, 1958, in Chicago, Illinois.

—JD

Green, William

(1873–1952) *president, American Federation of Labor*

William Green was born on March 3, 1873, in Coshocton, Ohio. His father was an immigrant coal miner from England. His parent's meager income prevented the young man from realizing his ambition to study for the Baptist ministry. Instead, he left school at age 14 to work as a water boy on a railroad gang. Two years later he went to work in the mines. Green became secretary of the local miners union while still in his teens and within a short time began a steady ascent through the hierarchy of United Mine Workers of America (UMW). He won the presidency of the strategic Ohio district in 1906 and was elected secretary-treasurer of the union in 1913. In the latter year he was also appointed by American Federation of Labor (AFL) president Samuel Gompers to a seat on the federation's Executive Council. Green was active in the Ohio Democratic Party as well, serving two terms in the state senate, where he sponsored a pioneer workmen's compensation law. Green argued for industrial unionism, offering resolutions to that effect in AFL conventions before and during World War I. He also thought the AFL should advocate for labor legislation rather than rely solely on voluntarism.

Green became president of the AFL in 1924, following Gompers's death. Throughout his long tenure he was overshadowed by such powerful figures as WILLIAM ("Big Bill") L. HUTCHESON of the carpenters and DANIEL J. TOBIN of the Teamsters, who dominated the Executive Council. Having no personal machine and wielding no direct influence in any international union, he served mainly as a faithful spokesman for others in the federation hierarchy. He willingly subordinated his own views to those of his more conservative peers. Since the Executive Council rejected industrial unionism, he believed he had to accept its will. He saw himself as a spokesman, and that his job was not to initiate policy, only to execute it. During the late 1930s and 1940s, Green led the opposition to the rival Congress of Industrial Organizations (CIO) and increased organizing drives in industries to meet the challenge it imposed. He seldom lost an opportunity to criticize the influence of Communists in the CIO's top councils. Green's campaign against the CIO was centered on an opposition to worker militancy. He saw the sit-down strike as "sabotage beyond the wildest dreams" of the syndicalist International Workers of the World.

During World War II both organizations cooperated in the war effort. However, Green and spokesmen for the CIO warned against allowing the emergency to be used as a pretense to undermine the legal rights and economic standards of organized labor. As a member of the War Labor Board (WLB), he resisted pressure for a freeze on wages and urged upward revision of the wage formulas to allow rates to catch up with inflation. The federation leadership was less closely linked politically to the Roosevelt and Truman administrations than the heads of the CIO and, as a result, was less willing to subordinate questions of wages and hours to government's demand for continuous production and stable industrial relations.

The AFL faced the problem of postwar reconversion with considerable anxiety. Green complained that, while generous tax treatment was being prepared to smooth the transition for manufacturers whose war contracts were to be cut or canceled, few provisions were made to cushion the impact on workers. He accepted the view that preventing a postwar economic collapse depended upon maintaining high levels of consumer purchasing power and looked to public works and housing programs to provide jobs. Green called for lifting all economic control and abolishing the WLB as soon as hostilities ended. In the fall of 1945, however, with industry profits high and no sign of mass unemployment, Green seized the opportunity to force wage rates up to compensate for the decline in wartime earnings. While arguing that industry could afford to raise hourly rates from 20 percent to 30 percent without substantial price increases, he denounced the Truman administration's policy of disapproving those wage increases employers used as the basis for requesting price relief. Instead, he recommended a relaxation of the price line, even if this lead to an inflationary spiral.

During the massive strike wave of 1945–46 the AFL, while regarding the administration as friendly to labor, spurned the president's persistent efforts to create machinery for minimizing strikes and settling industrial disputes. Green was stunned by Truman's response to the railroad strike of May 1946. The president asked Congress for the power to seize any essential industry threatened by a strike and declare the existence of a national emergency; any striker failing thereupon to return to work would lose his employment rights and become subject to induction into the army. Green bitterly denounced the measure, claiming that it constituted "nationalization of industry, not under socialism, but under fascism." As a result of opposition not only from unions but from employers as well, the bill was allowed to die.

Green worked vigorously against congressional efforts to impose government restrictions on union actions made in response to the strike wave. The federation greatly expanded its legislative activities and engaged for the first time in organized electoral efforts. In testimony before the House Labor Committee in February 1947, Green indicated his willingness to accept some changes in the Wagner Act granting workers the right to organize, but he vigorously condemned the more than 250 labor bills then in both houses of Congress. In the late winter of 1946 and spring months of 1947, the federation and the CIO sought to mobilize all available political pressure to defeat the Taft-Hartley bill. Speaking before mass rallies and on a nationwide radio broadcasts, Green labeled the measure a "slave labor" bill. After Taft-Hartley passed over the president's veto, he promised a campaign to repeal the statute and to defeat members of Congress who had voted for it, saying they were immoral.

Since the Gompers era the AFL had pursued a "nonpartisan" electoral policy, publishing the labor records of leading candidates but making no recommendations for voting. As a direct result of its 1947 defeat, however, the federation established a permanent political auxiliary, Labor's League for Political Education (LLPE). Concentrating on the 1948 elections, the league hired a professional staff and began mobilizing thousands of volunteer canvassers on the model of the CIO's Political Action Committee. Its efforts were weakened by the federation's political inexperience and by the reluctance of Green and other pro-Democratic AFL leaders to offend such powerful Republican members of the Executive Council as William Hutcheson. In the end the AFL and Green did not endorse Truman.

After the return of a Democratic controlled Congress in 1948, Green worked with other leaders for the repeal of Taft-Hartley. However, the AFL legislative campaign was poorly coordinated; Green insisted on personally directing lobbying efforts but could not decide on strategy and left his aides confused. In May 1949 he refused to endorse publicly a House compromise bill that proposed repeal of Taft-Hartley and the restoration of the Wagner Act but with amendments including authority for the presidential use of strike injunctions. However, he privately supported attempts to pass it. As a result, federation lobbyists took different courses; some sought a vote for the measure, some declined to suggest any action, while others simply did not appear on Capitol Hill. In the end Congress ignored the federation completely. The House approved a bill making slight concessions to labor but substantially reenacting the main provisions of Taft-Hartley. In the Senate the Thomas-Lesinski bill, which was backed by the AFL and the administration, never came to a vote, while a substitute measure sponsored by a conservative coalition led by Senator ROBERT A. TAFT (R-Ohio) was passed in its place.

AFL relations with the White House, which had greatly improved with Truman's veto of Taft-Hartley, deteriorated sharply after the outbreak of the Korean conflict. Believing that labor's interests were being ignored by the administration's domestic mobilization programs, the AFL joined the CIO, railway brotherhoods and machinists union in forming the United Labor Policy Committee (ULPC) in December 1950. The committee demanded a voice in the mobilization effort decree and insisted that existing agreements in industry provide for orderly adjustment of wage rates. On February 16, 1951, the three labor members of the Wage Stabilization Board (WSB) resigned after the board adopted a formula fixing a 10 percent ceiling above basic wage levels of January 15, 1950, instead of the 12 percent ceiling demanded by the unions. Twelve days later the ULPC withdrew all its representatives from mobilization agencies, calling for a reconstituted WSB and a more equitable wage policy. The crisis ended in April after the WSB approved the United Auto Workers' escalator clause agreement with the General Motors Corporation. Citing "a significant change of attitude in Washington," the ULPC agreed to resume all posts from which its members had withdrawn. Green and other officials also agreed to serve on a National Advisory Board on Mobilization Policy. Shortly afterward, the AFL dissolved the ULPC on the ground that it had "accomplished its purpose."

The last few years of Green's life were marked by a sense of mounting frustration. Prospects for repeal of Taft-Hartley seemed virtually nil after 1949. He became mostly a figurehead, and claimed he did not have the power to intervene in unions to stop corruption and racketeering. He also said he was powerless when the AFL was criticized for failing to organize women and African-American workers. Often in ill health during this period, Green increasingly abdicated his functions to AFL secretary-treasurer GEORGE MEANY. The federation's vigorous support of governor ADLAI E. STEVENSON's

1952 presidential campaign failed to stem the Eisenhower landslide. Shortly after the election, Green died on November 21, 1952, in Coshocton, Ohio.

According to his biographer Craig Phelan, Green failed as a labor leader because he advocated labor-management cooperation as an organizing strategy, his overwhelming desire for middle-class respectability, and his belief that the differences between owners and workers were in the end moral rather than economic.

—TLH

Greenewalt, Crawford H(allock)
(1902–1993) *president, E. I. du Pont de Nemours & Company*

Crawford H. Greenewalt was born on August 16, 1902, in Cummington, Massachusetts. After graduating from the Massachusetts Institute of Technology in 1922, Greenewalt started as a control chemist at E. I. du Pont de Nemours & Company. In 1926 he married Margaretta du Pont, daughter of president Irenee du Pont. Greenewalt moved up to research group leader in 1927. Six years later he was promoted to research supervisor, in charge of a number of groups. Greenewalt was active in developing the commercial production of nylon, which was first marketed in 1939. In 1941 he was elected to the board of directors and in 1942 was named chemical director of the Grasselli chemical department of the Du Pont firm.

During World War II Greenewalt served as a consultant to several government agencies: the Office of Scientific Research and Development, the Chemical Warfare Service, and the Manhattan District Project. He was present at the University of Chicago in 1942 when ENRICO FERMI engineered the first self-sustaining atomic reaction. Greenewalt was assigned, as head of the development department, to represent the Du Pont leadership in the atom bomb project. He served as a liaison between Du Pont's engineers and the talented group of theoretical physicists that had been assembled. Du Pont's main role in the project was the design, construction, and operation of a huge ($350 million) plutonium plant near Hanford, Washington. Later, in August 1950, Greenewalt was instrumental in obtaining an Atomic Energy Commission contract for Du Pont to develop the hydrogen bomb and operate its plant production. Du Pont also that year took on a $1 billion government contract to design, construct, and operate the Savannah River atomic energy plant.

In 1948, at the age of 45, Greenewalt was appointed president of Du Pont. He was also made chairman of the executive committee and a member of the finance committee. During Greenewalt's presidency from 1948 to 1962, Du Pont's sales volume more than tripled to $2.4 billion. Much of this was due to the company's heavy emphasis on research under his leadership. In his first year as president Du Pont expanded its research program by $30 million. During Greenewalt's tenure Du Pont developed many new products, such as Dacron polyester fibers, Orlon acrylic fibers, titanium, and pure silicon.

As president, Greenewalt faced a number of antitrust suits against the company. A suit begun in 1947, charging monopolistic practices in the manufacture and sale of cellophane, was thrown out in December 1953. Federal judge Paul Leahy ruled that Du Pont should not be "punished for its success" in developing the product. A second suit, filed in 1949, was aimed primarily at Du Pont's $560 million investment in General Motors. The government maintained that this gave Du Pont a controlling share of the stock and was in violation of the Sherman and Clayton antitrust acts. Greenewalt responded in a letter to 275,000 customers, employees, and stockholders calling the suit an "unjustified attack" and asserting "your company will fight." He argued that "bigness" itself should not be attacked because only the biggest corporations could provide the necessary capital to fund the risky research and development that led to new products and industries. Without companies like Du Pont there would have been no atomic energy program and no victory in World War II. The antitrust suit dragged on in the courts until 1961, when the Supreme Court ordered Du Pont to yield its 63 million shares of General Motors (at that time worth over $3.5 billion) within 10 years.

While acknowledging the need for active government involvement in the economy, Greenewalt was a consistent opponent of high taxes. In his book, *The Uncommon Man*, published in 1959, Greenewalt maintained that "the greatest threat to industry, and to the aggressive drive of our people, lies in our steeply progressive system of taxes on personal income." He stressed the need for individual incentives, especially in large organizations like Du Pont, to stimulate the greatest personal effort.

After resigning as president in 1962, Greenewalt maintained close ties with Du Pont. He was chairman of the board until 1967 and chairman of the finance committee until 1974. He retired from the board of directors in 1988 and died on September 27, 1993, in Wilmington, Delaware. (See *The Eisenhower Years* Volume)

—TFS

Grew, Joseph (Clark)
(1880–1965) *undersecretary of state*

A descendant of some of New England's most distinguished families, Joseph Grew was born on May 27, 1880, in Boston, Massachusetts. Reared in affluence in Boston, he graduated from Harvard in 1902, and he joined the Foreign Service as a clerk in the American embassy in Cairo. Before the American entry into World War I, he served in both Vienna and Berlin. In 1918 he returned to Washington as chief of the State Department's Division of Western European Affairs and the following year attended the Versailles Peace Conference. After a series of diplomatic posts in the Near East, he became undersecretary of state in 1924 and oversaw the transition of the Foreign Service from an agency based on patronage to one grounded in professional qualifications. In 1927 he was named ambassador to Turkey and five years later ambassador to Japan.

During his tenure Grew observed Japanese expansion in Asia, and he urged the United States not to become prematurely involved in a war with that nation. Early in 1941 Grew warned of a possible Japanese attack on Pearl Harbor. The Roosevelt administration, however, appeared to ignore his warnings. Grew urged a meeting between Roosevelt and the Japanese premier, Prince Konoye Fumimaro, to resolve the nations' differences peacefully. After the attack Grew was interned until the spring of 1942, when he and his staff were traded for Japanese diplomats. He then returned to Washington to head the Far Eastern Division of the State Department. In January 1945 Grew became undersecretary of state. When Truman assumed the presidency in April, Grew sent a letter of resignation effective upon the armistice with Japan.

During his last months in the Foreign Service, Grew became embroiled in the debate over proposed treaties for the surrender of Japan. He opposed Truman's call for unconditional surrender, the forced abdication of the emperor, and the use of the atomic bomb on Japan. Grew told the president and his top planners that the latter demand would be unacceptable to the Japanese and would prolong the war by making a negotiated surrender impossible. He said it would turn power over to the fanatics in the Japanese army who would raise the cry that the war must continue to save the monarchy. The United States would then have to invade Japan and ask Russia to enter the war in Asia. Grew feared that its needless intervention would enhance Soviet power in the East. Truman rejected the diplomat's criticism. Grew's prediction proved correct. Even after the dropping of the second atomic bomb on Nagasaki, the Japanese refused to accept the dissolution of the monarchy. Reluctant to attempt a costly invasion of Japan, the United States was forced to agree to the dynasty's perpetuation. In his memoirs Grew claimed that if Truman had listened to him in the spring, the United States would not have had to use the atomic bomb, and Soviet expansion in Asia would have been checked.

Along with JAMES V. FORRESTAL and W. AVERELL HARRIMAN, Grew emerged as one of the earliest advocates of a hard-line policy toward the Soviet Union. In May 1945 he wrote a memorandum outlining what he believed would be the course of future Soviet-American relations. He saw the growth of Communist totalitarianism as a threat to the West as great as the fascist menace. Grew accepted as a certainty a future war between the United States and Russia, and he advised the United States to be militarily strong by maintaining strategic air and naval bases developed during the war. "The most fateful thing we can do," he suggested, "is to place any confidence whatsoever in Russia's sincerity, knowing without question that she will take every opportunity to profit by our clinging to our ethical standards. She regards and will continue to regard our ethical behavior as a weakness to us and an asset to her." The administration began adopting some of Grew's recommendations in 1946.

Grew retired in August 1945. He then wrote his memoirs and served as chairman of the board of Radio Free Europe. Ill health curtailed his activities until his death on May 25, 1965, in Manchester, Massachusetts.

—JB

Griswold, Dwight P(almer)

(1893–1954) *director, American mission for aid to Greece*

The son of a Nebraska homesteader, Dwight P. Griswold was born on November 27, 1893, in Harrison, Nebraska. He graduated from the University of Nebraska in 1914. He began a career in banking but left in 1916 to serve in the army. He became editor and publisher of the *Gordon* (Neb.) *Journal* in 1922. Griswold entered politics in 1920, when he won election to the state assembly. He was defeated for reelection two years later but won a seat in the state senate in 1925. In 1940 he was elected governor for the first of three two-year terms. A member of the internationalist wing of the Republican Party, he ran unsuccessfully for the Republican senatorial nomination in 1946 against the conservative incumbent, HUGH BUTLER. Griswold was appointed director of internal affairs and communications for the U.S. Military Government in Germany in November 1946. He supervised communications, public health and welfare, safety, denazification, and education and religious affairs. He remained in Berlin until June 1947.

On June 5, 1947 President Truman appointed Griswold director of the American Mission for Aid to Greece. In addition to administering the $300 million in U.S. military and economic assistance, Griswold was expected to achieve reforms within the Greek government. He was to convince government officials to simplify the tax structure, raise and collect progressive income taxes, which had been previously evaded by big business and by the wealthy, reduce the civil service, eliminate waste from the military budget, and establish a wage-price structure in order to strengthen the government against internal subversion. As head of the American mission, he was also responsible for the spending of United Nations Relief and Rehabilitation Agency and Export-Import Bank funds within Greece. It was this economic and financial power that gave him political power and earned him the title "most powerful man in Greece."

The Truman administration's decision in late 1947 to create a separate agency to give operational advice to the Greek army miffed Griswold. He told Secretary of State GEORGE C. MARSHALL that he had not been foretold of the decision and that economic and military issues were related to one another and of equal significance. But as historian Howard Jones has pointed out Griswold's anger was unjustified. The purpose of the military mission, headed by General Stephen J. Chamberlain, was to provide strategic and tactical advice to the Greek army that a civilian like Griswold was unqualified to offer. He was still in charge of the economic aid—both civilian and military—to the Greek government.

A vigorous anticommunist, Griswold warned that Greece was being undermined by "fellow travelers, the pinko intellectuals," as well as guerrillas. To prevent a Communist takeover, he worked to build up the economy, supply the Greek army, and unify rival political factions. In August he immediately took over British responsibilities for feeding the Greek armed forces and police.

Griswold was anxious to stabilize the Greek government by broadening its base of support. He opposed the rightist regime, led by the Populists, which was committed solely to a military solution to the civil war. Convinced that political measures—amnesty, conciliation, and liberal reforms—must also be used to defeat the Communists, he worked to include the Liberal Party, which shared his views, in a coalition government. When Populist leader Constantine Tsaldaris tried to form a government composed solely of Populists, Griswold convinced Stephanos Stephanopoulos, a former minister of economic coordination and an important member of the Populist Party, not to join. He also attempted to convince younger members of the party not to support Tsaldaris. Griswold's actions paved the way for a Populist-Liberal coalition headed by Liberal Party leader Themistocles Sophoulis, who shared his views. Ambassador LINCOLN MACVEAGH secretly clashed with Griswold because of his methods, which the ambassador considered "rude," and because of Griswold's influence in Washington.

In October 1947 Griswold helped formulate the Greek emergency tax program designed to take greater sums from the rich. Pursuing his goal of government economy, he told Greek officials in January 1948 that 15,000 unnecessary civil officers must be dismissed and anti-inflation measures adopted. Charging the army with ineffectiveness, he approved large increases in the civilian national defense corps in the wake of military defeats. In May Griswold announced that "Communism is stopped in Greece" and praised the Greek army. Griswold left Greece in July 1948.

Griswold was elected to the U.S. Senate in 1952 to fill out the term of KENNETH S. WHERRY (R-Neb.). He died of a heart attack on April 12, 1954, in Washington, D.C., after a dinner party.

—AES

Groves, Leslie R(ichard)
(1896–1970) *chief executive officer, Manhattan Project*

Leslie R. Groves, the son of an army chaplain, was born on August 17, 1896, in Albany, New York, and grew up on various posts throughout the country. After spending two years at the Massachusetts Institute of Technology, he received an appointment to the U.S. Military Academy at West Point. In 1918 Groves graduated fourth in his class and was commissioned a second lieutenant in the U.S. Corps of Engineers. Groves completed the basic and civil engineering courses at army schools and served on various construction teams in the United States and abroad. In November 1940 he was appointed special assistant to the quarter-master general for the army construction program. A short time later, as deputy chief of army construction, Groves helped supervise all military construction in the United States, which at that time totaled $600 million a month. He was directing the construction of the Pentagon when he was appointed executive officer of the Manhattan District Project in 1942.

Groves was responsible for coordinating the thousands of separate projects carried out by universities, corporations, and the military for the production of the atomic bomb. He had complete executive responsibility for all spending, which by the end of the project totaled $2.19 billion.

During 1945 Groves played an important role in the decision to use the atomic bomb against Japan. Anxious that the weapon be used despite doubts by scientists about the need for it, he proposed in early 1945 that detailed plans for the bomb's deployment be drawn up. In the spring of 1945 General GEORGE C. MARSHALL gave him responsibility for choosing the targets in Japan and training special crews to carry out the mission. In conjunction with a group of Manhattan District Project scientists, Grove recommended four targets, including Hiroshima and Kyoto. Secretary of War HENRY L. STIMSON succeeded in having Kyoto later stricken from the list because of its religious significance.

Groves was not a member of the civilian Interim Committee that advised President Truman on the decision to drop the bomb, but he attended all meetings and greatly shaped its deliberations. Instead of focusing on whether or not to use the weapon, the panel concentrated on the conditions under which it would be used. The committee recommended that the bomb be dropped as soon as possible, without warning, on a target of both military and civilian importance. On August 6, 1945, the atomic bomb was dropped on Hiroshima causing an estimated 71,000 missing and dead. After a second device was dropped on Nagasaki, the Japanese surrendered. Groves was awarded a Distinguished

Service Medal and a temporary promotion to lieutenant general for his successful leadership of the Manhattan Project.

During the postwar period Groves was a major advocate of strong military involvement in the control of atomic energy. In October 1945 he testified for the May-Johnson bill, which guaranteed military participation in an Atomic Energy Commission (AEC). This proposal was defeated by a determined lobbying effort led by LEO SZILARD, who had worked under Groves in the Manhattan Project. In July 1946 Szilard succeeded in getting Congress to pass the McMahon bill, which mandated complete civilian control. Groves criticized the measure because it gave each commissioner equal power and did not designate one chief executive.

Groves was involved in a variety of activities after the war as head of the atomic program. Groves was a member of the committee that drafted the Acheson-Lilienthal Plan for international control of atomic weaponry. In 1946 Groves arranged a series of atomic bomb tests off the Bikini Atoll in the Marshall Islands. The bombs' destructive capacity was tested on obsolete American and captured Japanese and German warships. Two of the bombs were tested, but Groves cancelled a third test so as to have more bombs available in case of emergency. Richard Rhodes argued the reason for this was the worsening relations between the United States and the Soviet Union, and this action was indicative of the deterioration of the wartime alliance. Groves predicted that it would take 15 to 20 years for the Soviets to build an atomic bomb; the Russians proved him wrong by exploding one in 1949. He headed the atomic program until it was turned over to the AEC in January 1947.

In 1947 Groves was chosen to organize the Armed Forces Special Weapons Project (AFSWP), an interservice unit for training officers in the problems involved in the military uses of atomic energy. He retired from active duty in February 1948 at the rank of lieutenant general. Soon after he joined the Remington Rand Company as a vice president in charge of its advanced research laboratory. He left in 1961 and became a business consultant. He died on July 13, 1970, in Washington, D.C.

—TFS

Gruening, Ernest H(enry)
(1887–1974) *territorial governor*
Born the son of a prominent physician on February 6, 1887, in New York City, Ernest H. Gruening

received his medical degree from Harvard in 1912 but chose to pursue a career in journalism. He worked as a reporter and editor prior to World War I. When the United States entered the war in 1917, Gruening relocated to Washington and organized the War Trade Board's Bureau of Imports. He returned to journalism after the war. In 1920 he assumed the position of managing editor of the *Nation*, a liberal journal, where he crusaded against U.S. military intervention and financial exploitation in Central and South America. In 1921 Gruening helped initiate a Senate investigation into the U.S. military occupation of Haiti and Santo Domingo. Having traveled extensively throughout Mexico, he published his views on the country's history and conditions in *Mexico and Its Heritage* (1928). He founded the *Portland* (Me.) *Evening News* in 1927 and wrote *The Public Pays*, a muckraking study of American public utilities in 1931.

In 1933 Gruening was adviser to the U.S. delegation at the Seventh Pan American Conference in Montevideo, Uruguay, where the "Good Neighbor Policy" was officially formulated. He was appointed to a commission on Cuban affairs sponsored by the Foreign Policy Association in 1934. Gruening's recommendations for Cuba's economic and social rehabilitation were subsequently published in a report entitled *Problems of the New Cuba*. That year he became director of the Division of Territories and Island Possessions in the U.S. Department of Agriculture. In 1935 he headed the Puerto Rican Reconstruction Administration.

In the course of his duties, Gruening visited Alaska in 1936 and was impressed by what he regarded as "a kind of democracy that had long since vanished from many other parts of our country." Three years later he became Alaska's territorial governor. Gruening initially met opposition from the Alaskan legislature, in part because of his imposition of property and income taxes in a territory that for over a quarter of a century had gone without taxation. Nevertheless, he soon won the general respect of Alaskans because of his executive ability. As governor he sought to improve transportation to connect Alaska's isolated cities. The result was the Alcan Highway, completed in 1942. Gruening called for an end to discrimination against Alaskan natives in housing, education, and economic life. With his encouragement and support, two native representatives were elected to the legislature in 1945 and an antidiscrimination bill passed the same year.

Gruening's postwar program called for the legislature to enact veteran's benefits, establish a department of health with a full-time health commissioner, a department of agriculture, and a department of taxation to ensure that taxes levied would be collected. The legislature appropriated funds for these agencies in 1945. After initial opposition from the territorial senate, the World War II Veterans Act was passed in 1946. It gave thousands of veterans economic stability and, as a result, aided the territory's economy.

Gruening also recommended passage of legislation that would allocate funds for the development of Alaska's natural resources. Although he was concerned with developing the region, Gruening was an outspoken conservationist who abolished bounties on eagles in 1945 in an attempt to prevent their extermination. He introduced legislation in 1941, 1945, and again in 1947 to regulate fish traps in a way that would favor individuals and residents rather than the large absentee corporate interests, but he was unsuccessful because of the canned salmon industry's lobbying efforts.

In the territorial legislative election of 1946, Republicans captured the Alaska House of Representatives and gained control of the Senate due to a split between Democrats. The new GOP territorial legislature, began cutting the budget, much to the liberal Gruening's frustration. The legislature opted to eliminate over time the territorial sales tax, while the Senate voted down Gruening's proposed income tax. In all, the legislature rejected 17 tax measures.

Because of the 1946 Republican victory in the national midterm elections, Gruening looked like a lame duck as the GOP seemed assured of winning the presidency in 1948, and would undoubtedly replace Gruening, originally appointed by Franklin Roosevelt, with one of their own. Meanwhile Gruening struggled to keep good relations with President Truman, since they had no previous personal or political relationship and because the president was friendly with some of his enemies in Seattle, Washington—mostly absentee owners and their political representatives. Soon there were rumors that Truman would replace Gruening with someone closer to Gruening's foes in Seattle. Truman kept Gruening, but only because he feared liberals would attack him for replacing a reformer.

In the 1948 territorial legislative elections, Gruening campaigned vigorously to oust his conservative opponents. Many Alaskans were upset

about the budget cuts made by the Republicans and the Democrats won back both houses. The new legislature passed a host of tax measures, mostly aimed at absentee owners, and raised spending for education and public works.

Gruening was up for reappointment and his Alaskan opponents tried to derail it by getting Republicans on the U.S. Senate Interior Committee to demand public hearings. But the inept testimony of the governor's foes only served to embarrass the Republicans.

Gruening used the heightened national security concerns of the cold war to advance his efforts for more federal funding for the territory. Ironically he would tout cold war policies he would later oppose. Even though he believed in a nonmilitary resolution to the cold war and was afraid the country's fear of the Soviet Union would help conservatives, Gruening used a strident anticommunism and stressed the Soviet military threat to advance federal funding for Alaska. It worked. Spending for Alaskan defenses increased dramatically after 1950 and peaked at $512.9 million in 1953. Yet Gruening would oppose other cold war policies that interfered with his "Alaska agenda." He condemned the armed forces' tendency to take land away from territorial government control for military reserves and opposed foreign aid, saying the money should be spent for Alaskan defenses.

From the beginning of his term Gruening strove for Alaskan statehood. In 1946 Alaskans voted in favor of statehood in a territorial referendum, and Gruening proceeded to gather moderate support for the issue at the Governors' Conferences of 1947 and 1952. However, he began to deemphasize the cold war argument to assist Alaska when he found it was not bringing the territory any closer to statehood. He especially did this after an incident in 1950 when his friend, Democratic Senator Joseph O'Mahoney of Wyoming, said that if World War III came it would "make very little difference whether we have two United States senators from Alaska or not."

Despite his cynical use of the anticommunist hysteria to advance the cause of Alaska, Gruening himself almost became a victim of it. Republican senator Andrew Schoeppel of Kansas accused the "governing authorities" of the Alaska Statehood Committee, which Gruening chaired, of being "Communists or Quislings" because they had hired Randolph Feltus, a public relations specialist who had been a lobbyist for the Polish government for a brief time following World War II. Schoeppel also noted that Gruening had been one of the leaders of the Garland Fund, which the House Un-American Activities Committee had deemed a Communist-front. The Senate rejected Schoeppel's accusations after it investigated them, but then the FBI launched an investigation. Most witnesses noted it was ridiculous to accuse the governor of communism when he had spent the past few years using anticommunist rhetoric to gain defense money for the territory. But his Alaskan opponents were quite willing to testify to their belief that he was a Communist. Although the FBI cleared Gruening, Truman aide JOHN STEELMAN told the president he should disassociate himself from the governor as much as possible. President Dwight D. Eisenhower did not reappoint Gruening in 1953.

In 1956 Gruening began a two-year term as a provisional senator, lobbying for Alaskan statehood in Congress. He was retained after statehood was attained in 1958 and held his seat until 1968, when, at the age of 81, he was defeated in the Democratic primary by Michael Gravel. As senator, Gruening fought U.S. military involvement in Vietnam and called all acts of resistance to the Vietnam war "fully justified in whatever form they take." After leaving the Senate, Gruening rejoined the *Nation*. He campaigned for McGovern in 1972. Gruening died on August 26, 1974, in Washington, D.C. (See *The Eisenhower Years, The Kennedy Years, The Johnson Years* Volumes)

—DGE

Grunewald, Henry W.

(1893–1958) *investigator*

Henry W. Grunewald was born in South Africa in 1893. He arrived in the United States in 1906 and enlisted in the navy. He worked for the Justice Department during World War I. Grunewald was a Prohibition enforcement agent from 1921 to 1922, when he was dismissed after being indicted on charges of conspiring to violate the Prohibition laws. He won acquittal on the charges. Grunewald served the Republican National Committee as an investigator in the early 1920s. In addition, he did work for the Senate Foreign Relations Committee and later for the House Un-American Activities Committee. In 1919 Grunewald reportedly met insurance magnate Harry W. Marsh, who hired him

as an investigator. Through the influential Marsh, Grunewald cultivated the powerful and rich of Washington. Although he called himself a private investigator and public relations man, by the start of the Truman administration, Grunewald was considered one of the most "well-connected" influence peddlers in the city. He owned a principal residence in Washington, a $100,000 winter home in Florida, and a summer retreat in Spring Lake, New Jersey.

Grunewald always remained secretive about his sources of income and avoided publicity. However, the emerging tax scandals in 1951 focused national attention on him. In testimony before a House Ways and Means subcommittee chaired by Representative CECIL R. KING (D-Calif.), Abraham Teitelbaum, a Chicago real estate lawyer and former counsel for gangster Al Capone, linked Grunewald to a Washington clique of tax fixers. Teitelbaum claimed the group had tried to extort $500,000 from him to prevent income tax fraud prosecution. He implicated several top Bureau of Internal Revenue (BIR) officials, including Chief Counsel CHARLES A. OLIPHANT and former commissioner GEORGE J. SCHOENEMAN. Oliphant admitted having accepted loans from Grunewald, but denied any involvement with Teitelbaum's case, as did all other officials named. However, he had given BIR jobs to applicants endorsed by Grunewald.

During a December appearance before the King subcommittee, Grunewald refused to answer questions about the alleged extortion. He read a long statement accusing the subcommittee of "violating the fundamental rights of our country." In January 1952 he again refused to answer questions. The panel recommended his citation for contempt of Congress. Senator OWEN BREWSTER (R-Maine) appeared before the subcommittee in March to explain that he had Grunewald "transmit" $10,000 in campaign contributions in 1950 to Senator RICHARD M. NIXON (R-Calif.) and Senator MILTON R. YOUNG (R-N.Dak.). That month Grunewald pleaded guilty to a single count of contempt of Congress. He appeared before the King subcommittee later in the spring and cooperated fully with the panel.

In April Grunewald detailed the various fees he had collected for "investigative" work for several corporations and legislators. Grunewald named the American Broadcasting Company, Pan American Airways, and the United Mine Workers as a few of his clients. He refused, however, to describe the kinds of investigations he had conducted. Grunewald denied he had received $60,000 for "fixing" a 1948 criminal tax fraud case brought against a New York meat company. He also claimed that his involvement with Senator STYLES BRIDGES (R-N.H.) had been limited to introducing Bridges to Schoeneman. Bridges had been criticized for his interest in the tax-fraud case of a Baltimore liquor dealer. Grunewald did admit accepting money from businessmen under tax fraud probes for "investigative work and introductions."

On June 4, 1953, Grunewald was fined $1,000 and given a suspended 90-day jail sentence for contempt of Congress. Five months later he went to jail for "serious" violations of his parole. In 1955 he and two other defendants were convicted of taking $160,000 to kill federal tax prosecutions against two companies. Grunewald and the two men won a retrial on appeal from the Supreme Court because of a technicality. The retrial ended in a hung jury in July 1958. Grunewald died of a heart ailment in Washington, D.C., on September 25, 1958, two weeks before another scheduled trial.

—JF

H

Hague, Frank

(1876–1956) *mayor*

The son of Irish immigrants, Frank Hague was born on January 17, 1876, and raised in a tenement district of Jersey City. He left school at an early age and worked as a machinist for the Erie Railroad; at the same time he became actively involved in local Democratic politics. In 1911 he was elected to the Street and Water Commission and two years later won election to the Jersey City Commission, from which the mayor was chosen. Six years later the commissioners chose Hague as mayor, a position he held until 1947. He quickly expanded his power beyond Jersey City, becoming Hudson Company party chairman and, in 1919, state party chairman. His control of the state Democratic Party was completed in 1922, when he had himself selected national committeeman for New Jersey. Two years later he led the New Jersey delegation to the Democratic National Convention, where he was elected vice chairman of the national committee.

For three decades Hague was the undisputed boss of New Jersey's Democratic Party. His virtually dictatorial sway over the party organization in heavily Democratic Hudson Company gave him decisive influence in statewide elections. His ability to elect governors provided access to tremendous patronage powers, which he used to cement the loyalty of local ward and precinct leaders. The Hague machine was able to deliver favors and services extensively in Jersey City. Throughout the 1920s and the 1930s there were no serious challenges to his power locally or in the state. He famously declared in 1937, that in Jersey City, "I am the law." His minions harassed CIO organizers and civil liberty advocates, until the Supreme Court forced Hague to stop hindering the exercise of constitutional rights.

Hague's fortunes began to decline after World War II. The years of depression and war had strained the city's ability to provide basic services, and the city desperately needed more schools and hospitals, improved public transportation, and modern housing. Hague's ability to win government jobs for his party loyalists, moreover, declined. In the early 1940s he had broken with Democratic governor Charles Edison over the issue of tax relief for the railroads. The party's lack of unity allowed the Republicans to win the gubernatorial election in 1943. In 1946 another Republican, ALFRED E. DRISCOLL, was elected governor. Driscoll's victory closed many avenues of patronage formerly available to Hague. On June 4, 1947, Hague abruptly and unexpectedly announced his retirement as mayor. In his place he had installed his nephew, Frank Hague Eggers.

Hague's retirement was a mere formality. He continued to make major administrative decisions for Jersey City through his chief lieutenant, Deputy Mayor John Malone, and he retained his leadership of the county and state party, as well as his position on the Democratic National Committee. But challenges to his power quickly emerged. Hague was often absent from the mayor's office, living it up at his summer home on the Jersey Shore and rented Florida villas. Also, Hague had not endeared himself to the Truman White House by opposing his nomination in 1948. In addition Jersey City had the highest tax rate of any U.S. city its size in order to feed the patronage job holders, particularly the police, who were the highest paid in the country. Yet he neglected public education. An important weak point in the machine's armor was Hague's refusal to supply patronage to anyone but Irish Americans. When Hague purged a ward leader, John V. Kenny, from the party organization for his opposition to the selection of Eggers as mayor, Kenny decided to run a full slate of candidates in the 1949 municipal elections. Making Hague's "bossism" the main issue, Kenny put together a coalition of Jewish, Italian, and Polish voters that better mirrored the shifting demographics of the city. He emerged victorious.

Having lost the core of his power base, Hague's influence rapidly eroded. In November 1949 Hague's candidate for governor was defeated, with the Republicans actually carrying Jersey City. The day after the election Hague resigned as county and state party leader, ending his grip on politics at those levels. He attempted a political comeback in 1951, fielding a full slate of candidates for Jersey City's municipal elections, but he was soundly defeated. The following year Hague lost his last remaining position of power, when he was ousted as Democratic national committeeman for New Jersey.

Hague returned to private life in 1952, living comfortably off an estimated two million dollar fortune that he had accumulated during his years in public office. His final years were troubled by legal difficulties. In 1953 the Jersey City government filed a civil suit against Hague to recover $15 million allegedly extorted from city employees from 1917 to 1949. Although Hague won a dismissal in 1954, the New Jersey Supreme Court ruled in 1955 that the city had the right to sue Hague. Before action could be taken, however, Hague died of a hearth attack, on January 1, 1956, in his home in New York City.

—JD

Halleck, Charles A(braham)

(1900–1986) *member of the House of Representatives*

Charles A. Halleck was born on August 22, 1900, in Demotte, Indiana, and grew up in Rensslaer, Indiana, where his parents practiced law and were active in the Republican Party. Halleck served briefly in the infantry during World War I before matriculating at Indiana University. He received his B.A. in economics in 1922 and graduated first in his law school class in 1924. Ambitious and bright, he immediately sought and won election as prosecuting attorney of the Indiana 30th judicial circuit, a post that he held until 1935. In addition to much active trial work, Halleck spoke throughout the state on behalf

of Republican candidates. This exposure helped him win a 1935 special election to fill a House vacancy created by the death of Frederick Landis.

Halleck was known as a conservative who opposed Roosevelt's program. Truman once remarked that Halleck stood "just a little to the right of King George III." However, Halleck first gained national prominence by nominating Wendell L. Willkie, leader of the Republican Party's Eastern internationalist wing for president, at the 1940 Republican National Convention. However, he broke with Willkie's internationalism and voted against lend-lease in 1941. In the presidential election of 1944 he served as chairman of the Republican Congressional Campaign Committee, advising presidential nominee THOMAS E. DEWEY on campaign strategy. During the 1940s Halleck rose steadily on House seniority lists. In 1947 he was elected House majority leader for the Republican-controlled 80th Congress.

Halleck was a foe of organized labor. In an attempt to deal with strikes during 1946, he helped draft the Case labor disputes bill, which provided for a 30-day cooling off period before a strike could begin, permitted injunctions against certain union activities, and made both unions and management liable for breach of contract. In 1947 Senator ROBERT A. TAFT (R-Ohio) asked him to aid in the drafting of other antistrike legislation. Halleck hired Gerry D. Morgan, an expert in legislative drafting, to assist in writing the bill, which became the Taft-Hartley Act. Providing for the first peacetime restraints on union power, the measure was passed by Congress, which later overrode Truman's veto to enact it into law.

Halleck supported most of Truman's foreign policy. He worked to win backing among Republicans for the Truman Doctrine and the proposed $400 million program of economic and military aid to Greece and Turkey. Halleck was highly praised by Democrats for his role in ensuring the bill's passage in May of 1947. However, the following year he voted to slash the European Recovery Program to relieve the U.S. taxpayer.

Halleck's failure to win the Republican vice presidential nomination in 1948 represented one of his greatest political disappointments. The 1948 Indiana Republican convention nominated Halleck a presidential favorite-son candidate to keep the state's delegation to the national convention united and to be able to take advantage of any deadlock at the convention. Halleck saw himself as good as the other candidates running. Because Dewey wanted Indiana's 29 delegates, Halleck told one of Dewey's managers, J. Russell Sprague, that the price for Indiana's support was his nomination as vice presidential running mate. Sprague said he would discuss Halleck's name with Dewey. Halleck withdrew his candidacy to swing his and his delegation's support behind the New Yorker. The votes helped give the governor the nomination. Dewey, however, had not heard of the conversation Sprague had with the Hoosier until the evening he was nominated. At a meeting that night between Dewey and other GOP bigwigs, a majority rejected Halleck as having been too ardent a prewar isolationist, and because of his effort to cut the budget for the European Recovery Program. Halleck was thus passed over in favor of California governor EARL WARREN. During Truman's 1948 whistlestop campaign, the president denounced Halleck and the 80th Congress, accusing him of facing "backwards instead of forward." Dewey's campaign, on the other hand, ignored what Halleck felt to be the considerable achievements of the Republican Congress.

During Truman's second term Halleck served on the House Committee on Small Business and on the Committee on Executive Expenditures, where he denounced Truman's large 1949 budget and called for the reorganization of the executive branch. The representative was instrumental in reviving the Republican–Southern Democrat coalition to block Truman's social welfare program. In 1951 he spearheaded a successful floor drive to repeal the "21-day rule," which had been instituted to circumvent the conservative dominated Rules Committee. Under the rule a committee chairman could bring a bill to the floor if the Rules Committee had not acted on it within 21 days.

Halleck strongly criticized U.S. entry into the Korean War, believing that the president's decision had been politically motivated and had deprived Congress of its constitutional war-making power. Shocked and angered at Truman's dismissal of General DOUGLAS MACARTHUR in 1951, Halleck joined other leading Republicans in inviting the general to vindicate his actions before a joint session of Congress.

In 1952 Halleck, barred from the Republican National Convention by Indiana politicians who had favored Taft, went to the Chicago convention to work behind-the-scenes for DWIGHT D. EISEN-HOWER. He campaigned avidly against Truman over the issues of the Korean War and Communists in government. Halleck won reelection in 1952 by the largest margin of his career.

During the Eisenhower administration the White House often sought Halleck's help with legislative proposals. In a January 1959 secret ballot, Halleck narrowly defeated JOSEPH W. MARTIN, JR., for the House minority leadership. During the Kennedy administration he joined Senate minority leader EVERETT M. DIRKSEN (R-Ill.) in a weekly press conference review of presidential proposals, attracting national news coverage for the Republican Party. Halleck continued to lead his conservative coalition in opposition to most of Kennedy's legislative program until, challenged by his younger and more liberal colleagues, he was finally unseated as Republican minority leader in 1965 by Gerald Ford (R-Mich.). Halleck announced his retirement in 1968. Halleck died on March 3, 1986, in Lafayette, Indiana. (See *The Eisenhower Years, The Kennedy Years, The Johnson Years* Volumes)

—DAE

Hallinan, Vincent
(1896–1992) *attorney; presidential candidate, Progressive Party*

The son of a cable-car brakeman who had belonged to an outlaw Irish nationalist organization before emigration to America, Vincent Hallinan was born in 1896 in San Francisco, California. At St. Ignatius College he edited the college magazine and was the captain of the football team as well as the school boxing champion. He also collected money and weapons for nationalist rebels in Ireland and India. After serving in the navy during World War I, Hallinan returned to finish his law studies, gaining admittance to the bar in 1921 and setting up a practice in San Francisco.

Resourceful and flamboyant in the courtroom, Hallinan prospered in the field of personal injury law, battling insurance companies and taking as his fee a sizeable percentage of the damages awarded to his clients. He gained publicity defending individuals in a number of sensational murder cases; his pugnacity won him several short sentences for contempt of court as well. He developed a new defense strategy of long and emotional opening statements as opposed to the traditional short and restrained ones. He did not want to wait until the summation to be passionate after the prosecutor had made its case.

Early in the 1930s Hallinan assembled considerable real estate holdings by purchasing apartment buildings at depressed prices. Their eventual appreciation combined with his lucrative law practice to make him a millionaire by 1940. Hallinan was vocal on such local issues as jury reform.

From the age of 23 he was a fierce opponent of the Catholic Church. Hallinan fought a long legal battle to invalidate a will bequeathing money to the church on the grounds that the falsehoods of Catholic doctrine amounted to the perpetration of fraud on the testator. He even sued the church for fraud "demanding that it prove the existence of heaven and hell."

In 1949–50 Hallinan won national attention with his vehement defense of West Coast labor leader HARRY A. BRIDGES. Bridges, president of the International Longshoremen's and Warehousemen's Union, was on trial for perjury for denying that he had been a Communist at naturalization hearings. In the course of his defense, Hallinan accused the government of fraud and corruption, castigated the prosecutors, insulted government witnesses, and argued frequently with the judge. In April 1950 Bridges was found guilty of perjury; the Supreme Court overturned the conviction in 1953 on the grounds that the statute of limitations had run out by the time of his 1949 indictment. The trial judge also sentenced Hallinan to six months in jail for contempt of court for his harsh conduct during the trial. Hallinan's appeals as far as the Supreme Court failed, and he began serving his sentence on April 1, 1952.

Hallinan became active in the Progressive Party, energetically supporting that party's presidential candidate, HENRY A. WALLACE, in 1948. After the election he spoke widely, defending San Francisco city employees who had refused to sign loyalty oaths, arguing that the Chinese were not guilty of aggression in Korea, and calling the Japanese peace treaty a U.S. attempt at colonization. Hallinan was nominated as the Progressive Party's candidate for president in March 31, 1952, the day before he started serving his prison term. In his acceptance speech he blamed the two parties for "leading the nation to bankruptcy, for depressed living standards and loss of freedom, and war." He claimed the Democratic Party "was disintegrating and was being deserted by labor, the farmers and the Negro people." His candidacy was later endorsed by the American Labor Party and the Communist Party.

Released from jail on August 17, Hallinan called for an immediate cease-fire in Korea and urged enactment of a civil rights program. In a speech that same month he said the Progressive Party was "the political instrument to be wielded for peace, for civil rights, for the rights of labor." He praised Franklin Roosevelt and said the Democrats had "completely repudiated" the late president's policies. He opened his campaign in September by declaring "the bipartisan program of the Republicans and Democrats is leading America down the road to a bigger, deadlier war." He claimed during the campaign that the "refusal to accept peace in Korea" formed part of a business plan to create "a great American empire out of the ruins of the British and Japanese empires." Hallinan had a plan to end the war: a cease-fire should be reached between the two sides, recognizing the lines as they stood as the new border and a commission of civilian delegates should find a solution to the question of exchanging prisoners of war. "Peace, economic security, equality, and freedom are wrapped up in a single bundle . . . and that is why the Progressive Party, makes peace the No. 1 issue of 1952," he said on September 6. Hallinan claimed that his Republican and Democratic opponents were indistinguishable and both controlled by big business. He declared the programs of both parties "reactionary." Hallinan maintained that the threat posed by the Soviet Union was "mythical" and that the North Atlantic Treaty Organization was "a provocative, sword-rattling alliance." He charged that the Korean War was an imperialist venture from which big business profited. In November Hallinan received a disappointing total of 140,000 votes, compared to Wallace's 1,157,000 in 1948.

In 1953 Hallinan was convicted of evading $36,739 in income taxes. He was in prison from January 1954 to March 1955 for this offense. Over the next two decades Hallinan remained a prominent, controversial figure in San Francisco affairs, a legal maverick and a political radical, and, in the 1960s, a defender of antiwar dissidents and radical activists. Hallinan died in San Francisco, California, on October 2, 1992.

—TO

Hammett, (Samuel) Dashiell
(1894–1961) *novelist*

The creator of the modern detective novel, Dashiell Hammett was born on May 27, 1894, in St. Mary's County, Maryland, and raised on the state's eastern shore. He attended Baltimore Polytechnic Institute for three years before leaving at age 13. Hammett then moved from job to job. He was, at one time, a detective for the Pinkerton Company. While in the army during World War I, he contracted tuberculosis, which eventually forced him to quit his detective work and turn to writing as a living. Hammett achieved great success as an author of detective novels during the late 1920s and early 1930s. It was during this period that his 30-year friendship with playwright LILLIAN HELLMAN began. At the age of 48, Hammett enlisted in the army and served for two years during World War II. Before and after the war he plunged into left-wing political work. He backed the Loyalists during the Spanish civil war. He helped in the attempt to put the Communist Party USA on the ballot in 1940. He was president of the New York Civil Rights Congress from 1946 to the mid-1950s, a group that defended dissidents.

Hammett's involvement with radical causes led finally to jail. In July 1951, along with three others, Hammett was sentenced for refusing to name contributors to a bail fund for four Communist leaders. Hammett was a trustee for the Civil Rights Congress, which had posted the bail money and which was designated a Communist front by the Attorney General. In her book, *An Unfinished Woman*, Lillian Hellman wrote that Hammett had never set foot in the Civil Rights Congress office, nor did he know the names of any of its contributors. Nevertheless he refused to answer any of the questions posed in court. Hammett was sent to jail in a judgment that allowed no bail. Subsequent court appeals failed, and he served six months in a federal prison.

In April 1953 Hammett appeared before the Senate Permanent Investigations Subcommittee, chaired by Senator JOSEPH R. MCCARTHY (R-Wisc.), probing charges that overseas libraries maintained by the State Department circulated pro-communist books. The libraries under consideration stocked 300 copies of Hammett's novels. Hammett would not say whether he was a Communist and held that it was "impossible to write anything without taking some sort of stand on social issues." That year, 73 American overseas libraries removed Hammett's novels from their shelves at the direction of the State Department. Soon after President Eisenhower stated he personally would not have ordered their removal, Hammett's books were returned to the shelves.

Two days after he went to jail in 1951, Hammett's income was attached by the Internal Revenue Service for back taxes. He had no income from that time until his death on January 10, 1961, in New York City.

—EF

Hand, (Billings) Learned
(1872–1961) *judge*

Acclaimed during the last 25 years of his life as America's greatest living jurist, Learned Hand was born in Albany, New York, on January 27, 1872, into a distinguished legal family. He graduated from Harvard College in 1893 and from Harvard Law School in 1896 with highest honors. After practicing in Albany, New York, and New York City, Hand was named a judge on the U.S. district court for the Southern District of New York in 1909. He served there until 1924, when President Calvin Coolidge appointed him a judge on the U.S. Second Circuit Court of Appeals. In 1939 Hand became the senior judge on the Second Circuit.

In his more than 50 years on the federal bench, Judge Hand wrote nearly 3,000 opinions on every conceivable subject of law. Considered models of legal craftsmanship, they invariably presented a clear and concise statement of the facts and of the legal principles involved in a case. They offered an incisive and illuminating analysis of the law in relation to the facts. His opinions were written in an original and brilliant style and were universally ranked as among the best American legal prose of the century. In his rulings Hand made important contributions in a variety of fields, including admiralty, antitrust, conflict of laws, and patent and trademark law. Under his leadership the Second Circuit was regarded as the foremost appellate court in the nation. Hand himself was quoted in Supreme Court opinions and in academic publications more than any other U.S. jurist. He was also influential as a member of the American Legal Institute, an organization that prepared model statutes and restatements of law in many fields. He participated in the drafting of, among others, model codes of criminal procedure, of evidence and restatements of torts, and of conflicts of law. Despite his excellence as a judge, Hand harbored serious doubts about his ability and thought praise that was awarded him was undeserved.

Hand was involved in some of the most famous Red Scare cases. In *U.S. v. Coplon*, a case involving a government employee handing over sensitive information to the Soviets, Hand asserted that her warrantless arrest was wrong because she was not a flight risk. He also found the wiretap used against her illegal under the Communications Act of 1934, and that information from the wiretaps should have been turned over to her counselors so they could determine if it was crucial to her defense. The trial judge had ruled the information could not be released to the defense on national security grounds. Hand believed such a ruling violated the Sixth Amendment and reversed the conviction. He did not, however, dismiss the indictment since at a future trial more evidence might be found suggesting a flight risk, and the prosecution might change its mind and reveal to the defense the information gathered by the wiretaps. Hand voted to overturn the conviction of WILLIAM W. REMINGTON, accused of lying on the stand about his alleged involvement in the Communist Party, because of what he saw as the unconstitutional acts of the grand jury. The court as a whole, however, upheld the conviction. Remington was beaten to death in prison, and the case haunted Hand.

On August 1, 1950, Hand delivered his most famous and most controversial opinions in *Dennis v. U.S.* In October 1949, 11 leaders of the American Communist Party had been convicted under the Smith Act of conspiring willfully to advocate and teach the forceful overthrow of the U.S. government. The defendants charged that the Smith Act violated their First Amendment guarantee of free speech. The prevailing legal doctrine at the time held that government could curtail political speech only when it posed a "clear and present danger" of causing some substantive evil, which the government had a right to prevent. In his opinion Hand restated the "clear and present danger" rule. He declared that in each case the courts "must ask whether the gravity of the 'evil,' discounted by its improbability, justifies such an invasion of free speech as is necessary to avoid the danger." He then examined the nature of the Communist Party and the international situation that existed from 1945 to 1948. Applying his test, Hand concluded that the defendants' conspiracy created "a danger of utmost gravity and of enough probability to justify its suppression." For a unanimous three-judge panel, Hand thus upheld the validity of the Smith Act and of the defendants' conviction under it. Less than a year later, in June 1951, the Supreme Court sustained the convictions by a six to two vote. In the plurality opinion Chief Justice FRED M. VINSON adopted Hand's interpretation of the clear and pre-

sent danger rule. Critics of both the Hand and Vinson rulings in *Dennis* have charged that Hand's formula widened the scope of permissible government infringement on the right of free speech.

Judge Hand was himself a humane and innately liberal man who doubted the wisdom of a law like the Smith Act. His *Dennis* opinion upholding the statute reflected in part his beliefs about judicial review. To Hand the judiciary's power to declare statutes unconstitutional was extremely limited. He almost never held laws invalid under the very general provisions, such as freedom of speech, found in the Bill of Rights. In addition, as Hand biographer Gerald Gunther has noted, the judge believed himself obligated to follow the precedents of the Supreme Court, in the *Dennis* case its doctrine of the "clear and present danger" test.

In other types of cases, however, Hand thought the judge's role a broadly creative one. Within his philosophy a judge always had to be detached and impartial to avoid reading his own political or economic views into law. But in deciding cases of common law or statutory interpretation, Hand believed a judge had much room to exercise his analytic and creative powers in evaluating and weighing the different factors that would lead him to the result.

Hand was devoted off the bench to advocating tolerance even to the intolerant and opposed proposed group libel laws. Despite his decision in the *Dennis* case, Hand also feared the effects the cold war would have on freedom of expression in the United States.

Hand retired from active service on the bench on June 1, 1951, but he kept his office and continued to hear cases on special assignment for the Second Circuit through the rest of the decade. Following his retirement the Judge gave more time to speaking and writing, which again expanded general public awareness of him and his views. Hand spoke out in defense of the right of free discussion and of the right to dissent during the 1950s. He died on August 18, 1961, in New York City.

—CAB

Hannegan, Robert E(mmet)

(1903–1949) *Postmaster General*

The son of a police captain, Robert E. Hannegan was born on June 30, 1903, in St. Louis, Missouri. He earned a law degree from St. Louis University in 1925. Following his graduation he coached football and swimming at St. Louis University and played professional football and minor league baseball. In 1929 he established a law practice in St. Louis and became active in Democratic politics. During the 1930s Hannegan served as a chief aide to Mayor Bernard F. Dickman, head of the Democratic machine in St. Louis. He helped elect Harry S Truman to the U.S. Senate in 1934. Six years later he supported Truman's reelection over Dickman's opposition. Hannegan's political career was marred by charges of corruption and vote stealing. His support of Truman in 1940 lost him Dickman's support and his patronage and power base in St. Louis.

In 1942, at Truman's urging, Hannegan was appointed the collector of internal revenue for the eastern district of Missouri. He revitalized and streamlined the office, making it the best in the nation. In 1943 Secretary of the Treasury HENRY MORGENTHAU, JR., appointed Hannegan commissioner of internal revenue. Hannegan became Democratic National Committee chairman in 1944. At that post he rebuilt the party from the bottom up by reestablishing contacts with precinct workers and state and local politicians by hearing their complaints and taking some of their suggestions.

Hannegan also played a vital role in securing the vice presidential nomination for Truman. Party leaders were troubled by Vice President HENRY A. WALLACE's inchoate liberalism, and he had little backing in the conservative South. The leaders wanted an alternative because they sensed Roosevelt would not survive a fourth term. The president put Hannegan and other solicitors off, but on the evening of July 11, 1944, Hannegan secured a written statement that Roosevelt would accept Associate Justice William O. Douglas or Truman as an alternative to Wallace. Truman was reluctant to make himself available for the nomination until the president rather bluntly issued an ultimatum saying that "if he wants to break up the Democratic party in the middle of a war, that's his responsibility." Truman then thought he had no choice but to accept. Roosevelt himself, however, did not discourage Wallace or "assistant president" JAMES F. BYRNES, director of the Office of War Mobilization, from seeking the nomination too. In a rather chaotic convention Hannegan secured Truman's nomination on the second ballot. Later Hannegan claimed, "I was the man who kept Henry Wallace from becoming president of the United States."

When Truman became president he appointed Hannegan U.S. Postmaster General, a position tra-

ditionally reserved for leaders of the president's party. Hannegan proved to be a liberal cabinet member; he was one of two officers who recommended that Truman veto the Taft-Hartley bill. He was also an excellent administrator. Hannegan decided to install modern equipment at the Post Office, to eliminate the air mail stamp and send all mail by air mail because it was the most efficient method, and to improve rural postal service. He also supported postal workers' requests for wage increases. At the beginning of 1947 he underwent a heart operation and in November resigned from all government and party posts. He played no part in Truman's 1948 reelection campaign.

When Hannegan retired he bought an interest in the St. Louis Cardinals baseball team. In January 1949 he sold his interest in the team for a reputed $1 million. On October 6, 1949, Hannegan died in St. Louis of heart failure.

—GB

Harriman, W(illiam) Averell

(1891–1983) *ambassador; secretary of commerce; special assistant to the president; director, Mutual Security Agency*

The son of railroad industrialist Edward Henry Harriman, W. Averell Harriman was born on November 15, 1891, in New York City. He graduated from Yale in 1913. Two years later he became a vice president in his father's railroad company, the Union Pacific. In 1917 Harriman founded the Merchant Shipping Corporation and, in 1920, W. A. Harriman Company, a private bank. Harriman became chairman of the board of the Union Pacific in 1932 and astonished the nation by modernizing the company during the Great Depression, but the move had only mixed success financially.

In 1932 Harriman, initially a Republican, joined the Democratic Party. He entered government service the following year when, upon the advice of HARRY L. HOPKINS, President Franklin D. Roosevelt appointed him an administrator of the National Recovery Administration. Harriman was chairman of the Business Advisory Council of the Department of Commerce from 1937 to 1940. In 1941 he coordinated lend-lease aid with Great Britain and the Soviet Union. During his numerous trips to Moscow, he won the trust of Joseph Stalin. In 1943 Harriman became ambassador to the Soviet Union, where he worked to continue aid to that

W. Averell Harriman *(Harry S. Truman Library, Mitchell Papers)*

nation. He attended the Tehran and Yalta conferences of allied leaders called to plan the postwar world.

Harriman was an early advocate of a firm policy toward the Soviet Union. Just before Roosevelt's death in 1945, he cabled the president analyzing Soviet policy in the postwar world. Ideology, he maintained, had replaced security as the chief determinant of Soviet policy. The Soviet Union wanted cooperation with the United States at the UN. However, he warned, Stalin would attempt to create a security ring of friendly nations on Russia's western border to prevent a third major invasion during the century. The USSR would control not only foreign policy in these nations but also regulate their internal affairs. Democratic government would not be permitted. The ambassador predicted that the Soviets would attempt to penetrate other nations and, through Communist parties in those countries, try to establish governments friendly to Russia. Harriman advised Roo-

sevelt that Stalin viewed American acquiescence to the Soviet occupation of Eastern Europe as a sign of weakness. He recommended that the United States take a firmer stand, tying economic aid to Soviet political concessions in that area. The Soviets, he predicted, would not react violently because they needed assistance.

Harry Truman, who assumed the presidency a few days after Harriman's cable had been received, was deeply impressed with the analysis. The ambassador briefed Truman before the president's meeting with Soviet foreign minister V. M. Molotov in April. On Harriman's advice Truman took a tough position during the talks. Using "words of one syllable" he berated the foreign minister for Soviet failure to live up to the Yalta Accords. His directness horrified Molotov, who protested being lectured by the president. Harriman had thought Truman had been too rough with the Russian foreign minister and would later claim it was that meeting when the cold war began. To assuage the Soviets Harriman and CHARLES E. BOHLEN suggested Harry Hopkins be sent to see Stalin.

In keeping with his desire to use economic aid as a weapon to gain cooperation with the Soviets, in May 1945 Harriman suggested the United States curtail lend-lease shipments to Russia since the war in Germany had ended. The stoppage, he warned, should be done firmly "while avoiding any implication of a threat or any indication of political bargaining." Truman approved Harriman's recommendation. However, the Foreign Economic Administration dramatically recalled ships already at sea, which neither Truman nor Harriman had wanted. Truman ordered them to proceed once again to the Soviet Union but the damage had been done. Moscow interpreted the abrupt cessation of lend-lease as an unfriendly act.

Truman's conduct with Molotov and the cutback of lend-lease signaled a departure from the policy of conciliation maintained under Roosevelt. Many who did not want a dramatic break with Stalin held Harriman responsible for the anti-Soviet tone of the administration. In his memoirs, *Special Envoy* (1975), Harriman claimed that Roosevelt had already decided a confrontation would be inevitable. He assumed that Roosevelt was more astute politically than Truman and could have postponed the inevitable longer.

Following the end of the war in Japan, Harriman requested permission to resign. Truman persuaded him to remain in Moscow at least until the end of the year. Harriman recommended that the United States recognize the Communist-dominated government of Poland, and one of the last things he did as ambassador was to convince Stalin to agree to convene the Council of Foreign Ministers in Moscow after the disastrous session in London. On January 23 Stalin had his last meeting with Harriman. The ambassador requested help in trying to effect a truce between the Nationalists and Communists in China. Stalin coolly replied that his government recognized the Nationalists and had little contact with the Communists. When he came back to the United States, Harriman gave a copy of GEORGE F. KENNAN's Long Telegram to Secretary of the Navy JAMES V. FORRESTAL, saving it from being pigeonholed in the State Department.

Truman appointed Harriman ambassador to Great Britain in March 1946. He served there seven months before Truman made him secretary of commerce to replace HENRY A. WALLACE, whose advocacy of conciliation with Russia had led him to be ousted by the president. Biographer Ruby Abramson has pointed out that as commerce secretary, Harriman was Truman's liaison with businessmen. He revived the Business Advisory Council and appointed William C. Foster as undersecretary to handle the day-to-day affairs. Much to the irritation of the State Department, Harriman intruded upon foreign affairs, continuing to warn against the designs of the Soviets. Following Secretary of State GEORGE C. MARSHALL's call for a massive economic recovery program in Europe in June 1947, Truman appointed Harriman chairman of the President's Committee on Foreign Aid to translate Marshall's proposal into a program and lobby for its passage in Congress. The committee report, "European Recovery and American Aid," released in November, claimed that if Congress refused to provide aid, all of Europe, the Middle East, and North Africa would fall to the Communists. The panel stressed the importance of Germany in the success of the aid program and recommended special emphasis be put on assistance to that nation to redevelop its purchasing and producing power and prevent it from falling into the hands of the Soviet Union. The committee report also contended that the Marshall Plan was needed to support the continuation of American trade with Europe. It predicted serious problems if Europe's 1948 projected seven billion dollar deficit with the United States was not cor-

rected. The committee recommended a $12 to $17 billion amount to aid Europe. Harriman used his connections with the business community to convince them to accept the Marshall Plan. European Cooperation Administration chief PAUL G. HOFFMAN insisted that Harriman head his agency's Office of the Special Representative in Europe, and Truman agreed, sending Harriman to Europe in 1948. In this post Harriman supervised distribution of Marshall Plan funds. He also pushed for economic unity among European nations, but he found it difficult because Britain wanted to dominate the process even though its empire was fading. In particular, Harriman wanted the Europeans to work out the distribution of aid among themselves rather than deal with the United States on a one-to-one basis, which irked the British who wanted to deal with the Americans directly rather than negotiate with other nations that had been defeated in the war. But Harriman had his way.

In 1950 Harriman became special assistant to the president and acted as troubleshooter for Truman. He served as liaison between Truman and General Douglas MacArthur during the Korean War. Harriman sensed that MacArthur and the Joint Chiefs of Staff did not fully understand each other. Harriman became part of the effort to keep MacArthur from publicly contradicting the presidential policy, which in the end failed with Harriman being the first to recommend firing the general. Harriman was also instrumental in the resignation of the increasingly erratic secretary of defense LOUIS A. JOHNSON. Harriman also was part of the group that reviewed NATO's requirements and recommended it have 50 divisions and eventually 95—a goal Harriman expected would never be met (he was correct)—but the report lent credibility to NATO. He failed in his attempt to mediate the conflict between Iran and Great Britain over the nationalization of the Anglo-American Oil Company. Harriman in 1951 became head of the Mutual Security Administration, which was in charge of foreign aid.

Harriman ran for the Democratic presidential nomination in 1952 and 1956 as holder of the flame of the New and Fair Deals, but he was a poor campaigner and lost the nomination to ADLAI E. STEVENSON both times. From 1954 to 1958 he was governor of New York. He served as assistant secretary of state for Far Eastern affairs from 1961 to 1963 and undersecretary of state for political affairs from 1963 to 1965. He negotiated the agreement neutralizing Laos in 1962 and the nuclear test ban treaty with the Soviet Union in 1963. Harriman served as ambassador-at-large in the Johnson administration and headed the U.S. delegation at the Paris Peace Talks in 1968. He retired in 1969. In 1983 he traveled to the Soviet Union as a private citizen to talk with Soviet leader Yuri V. Andropov. Harriman blamed the Reagan administration for the rocky relations between the Soviet Union and the United States and urged a return to a more congenial relationship. Harriman died on July 26, 1986, in Yorktown Heights, New York. (See *The Eisenhower Years, The Kennedy Years, The Johnson Years, The Nixon/Ford Years* Volumes)

—JB

Hartley, Fred A(llen), Jr.
(1902–1969) *member of the House of Representatives*

Fred A. Hartley, Jr., was born in Harrison, New Jersey. He attended Rutgers University but left after two years and became active in local politics. After serving in municipal offices in Kearny, New Jersey, during the 1920s, he was elected to the U.S. House of Representatives in 1929 as a Republican in a very close race. Hartley was assigned to the Labor Committee, where he voted for amendments to the Wagner Act that strengthened the stand of the American Federation of Labor. However, during the 1940s he voted for strike control bills and a ban on all strikes against the government. Opposed to Franklin D. Roosevelt's price control policy, he rallied a growing group of conservative Democrats behind his interests, a coalition that provided a basis for his power during the Truman era.

Hartley was reported to have said that he stood "a little to the right of Senator Taft." He voted for civil rights bills but continued to support legislation to restrict the activities of unions, such as the Case labor disputes bill and the Portal-to-Portal bill of 1946. He was paired for the dramatically weakened Full Employment bill of the same year. The CIO became a particularly vigorous opponent of Hartley because of his record. Hartley backed the establishment of a House Un-American Affairs Committee on a permanent basis and voted for the Mundt-Nixon bill of 1948. He was a consistent supporter of tax reduction and backed the 1946 bill renouncing federal claims to tidelands.

In 1947 Hartley became chairman of the Education and Labor Committee, and he became the youngest committee chairman at the time at 44. Shortly thereafter he asserted that the Republican victory was a mandate for reform of the labor law in the face of dramatic strikes during the previous year. What Hartley and other conservatives sought was to end what they saw as the overly pro-union interpretations of the Wagner Act by the National Labor Relations Board and restore balance in labor-management relations. In April a coalition of Republicans and Southern Democrats on the Labor Committee reported the Hartley bill. The measure contained provisions barring the closed shop and restricting the conditions for permitting a union shop. It deprived foremen of rights already guaranteed employees under existing legislation, made unions liable for damages for violations of contract, banned secondary boycotts, mass picketing and jurisdictional strikes, and prohibited industrywide bargaining. It created an independent Federal Mediation and Conciliation Service and denied National Labor Relations Board recognition to unions whose officers refused to sign a noncommunist affidavit. In addition it authorized the president to declare a "cooling-off" period and strike votes by employees for walkouts.

The measure touched off a storm from organized labor and liberals, who termed it "a slave labor" bill. Democrats charged the bill had shackled labor in collective bargaining disputes and tipped the balance of strength in bargaining in favor of management. Hartley maintained the bill would prevent labor abuses and help democratize unions. He denied charges that the measure was written by the National Association of Manufacturers. Some Congress watchers saw Hartley's bill as more conservative than what the National Association of Manufacturers had asked for. Hartley's strategy was to come into the conference committee with so many radical proposals to trade that he would still end up with a fairly strong bill. The bill passed the House on April 15 by a vote of 319 to 47.

The measure was softened in the Senate, which passed its own bill formulated by Senator ROBERT A. TAFT (R-Ohio). In conference the House conferees, led by Hartley, surrendered their measures' provisions on industrywide bargaining, welfare funds, the union shop, and subjecting the unions to the antitrust laws. Both houses quickly approved the measure in June. Truman vetoed the bill two weeks later on the grounds that it was unfair to labor and unworkable, but Congress overrode the veto.

In 1949 Hartley resigned his seat to become a business consultant and lobbyist. He also toured the nation defending the Taft-Hartley Act, which in his words "represents the greatest single contribution made by any political party for the past two decades. It corrects in a single piece of legislation the outstanding mistakes of the New Deal." In 1952 Hartley supported Robert A. Taft as the Republican candidate for president, but later in the campaign he switched to DWIGHT D. EISENHOWER. In 1954 Hartley ran an unsuccessful write-in campaign for the Senate seat occupied by Clifford P. Case. Retired from politics, he raised cattle in Frenchtown, New Jersey. On May 11, 1969, he died in Linwood, New Jersey, after a long illness.

—RSG

Hayden, Carl T(rumbull)
(1877–1972) *member of the Senate*

Carl T. Hayden was born in Hayden's Ferry (now Tempe), Arizona, a town named for his father, on October 2, 1877, 35 years before Arizona became a state. After attending Stanford from 1896 to 1900, Hayden returned to Tempe, where he worked in the flour milling business and served as a member of the town council from 1902 to 1904. In 1904 he was a delegate to the Democratic National Convention in St. Louis. He also served as treasurer of Maricopa County, and, in 1907, he was elected sheriff of that county, a post he held until he won a seat in the U.S. House of Representatives in 1912. During his tenure, he played a major role in establishing the Grand Canyon National Park, and he also supported women's suffrage. Hayden was elected to the Senate in 1926. He made few speeches during his career, preferring to play a quiet role, using his seniority and influence in private discussions with senators rather than seeking publicity through dramatic speeches on the Senate floor.

During the Truman administration Hayden served as the ranking member of the Appropriations Committee and as chairman of the Rules and Administration Committee. He supported the president's foreign policy, voting for the $3.75 billion loan to Great Britain in 1946, the Truman Doctrine in 1947, and the Marshall Plan in 1948. The senator established a generally liberal record on domestic legislation, opposing the Case labor disputes bill

and the Taft-Hartley Act and supporting aid to education. He voted against a bill renouncing federal claims to offshore oil and backed most of the president's fiscal program. Hayden established a mixed record on civil rights. In 1947 and 1949 he supported efforts to limit filibusters, often used to defeat civil rights legislation. However, Hayden voted against the elimination of the poll tax in 1948, explaining that he thought a constitutional amendment the proper method of eliminating such disabilities.

Hayden was best known as one of the Senate's strongest proponents of irrigation and water rights legislation. Always conscious of Arizona's need for water, he and his fellow senator from Arizona, ERNEST W. MCFARLAND (D-Ariz.) proposed a bill in 1947 to authorize the construction of the Central Arizona Water and Power project, known as CAP. The project entailed the construction of a dam in the Grand Canyon National Park. With the dam an aqueduct system would be built to divert some of the Colorado River to the dry areas of central and southern Arizona. California legislators opposed the bill to the frustration of Hayden, who noted that he had backed many such water projects for California. He declared, "Each one of these reclamations projects in California is a good investment, and nobody in Arizona begrudges the development over there." Hayden just wanted Arizona to receive its fair share.

Hayden reintroduced the bill two years later. The bill, the largest irrigation proposal of the Truman years, passed the Senate but failed to pass the House. When California representatives proposed a resolution that would have brought the question before the Supreme Court, Hayden was able to head off their effort by shrewd parliamentary maneuvering. By means of a Senate vote, which Hayden instigated, the resolution was placed before the Senate Public Lands Committee where it was never reported. However, the matter finally did go before the high court, and, in 1963, it handed Arizona a victory on its claims on the Colorado River. Hayden finally won passage of the bill in 1968, his last year in Congress, which assured water supplies for the region around Tucson and Phoenix.

In 1951–52 Hayden served on the Privileges and Elections Subcommittee investigating Senator JOSEPH R. MCCARTHY (R-Wisc.). The probe stemmed from criticism leveled against McCarthy for his role in the 1950 Maryland election in which Senator MILLARD E. TYDINGS (D-Md.), a foe of the Wisconsin Republican, went down to defeat. McCarthy challenged the committee's investigation, and Hayden tested the Senate's confidence in the panel by offering a resolution to discharge it of its responsibilities. Hayden led a fight to defeat his own motion, and the Senate voted 60 to 0 to continue the investigation. Hayden then went on to supervise the writing of the subcommittee's final report. Although it made no direct charges of wrongdoing against McCarthy, it did raise questions about McCarthy's personal conduct and his use of funds. Hayden's opposition to McCarthy continued in January 1953, when he tried to challenge the seating of McCarthy in the new Congress. However, he could not muster the support to do so.

Hayden helped write the Federal Highway Act of 1956, which called for the construction of 42,000 miles of highways connecting major cities by 1970. The following year he was named dean of the Senate, an unofficial title given to the member who has served the longest. He served as President Pro Tempore from 1957 to 1969. Hayden retired in 1969, after 42 years in the Senate, and died in Mesa, Arizona, on January 25, 1972. (See *The Eisenhower Years, The Kennedy Years, The Johnson Years* Volumes)

—GMS

Heath, Donald R.

(1894–1981) *ambassador*

Donald R. Heath was born on August 12, 1894, in Topeka, Kansas. He attended Washburn University and then pursued graduate studies at the University of Montpelier in France. Following action in the army during World War I, he worked briefly as United Press White House correspondent and then became a member of the Foreign Service. Heath was vice consul at Bucharest from 1921 to 1923, consul at Warsaw from 1923 to 1925, and at Berne from 1925 to 1929. In December 1929 he was transferred to Haiti, where he served until 1933. During the Roosevelt administration Heath rose to assistant chief of the division of Latin American Affairs in the State Department, where he remained until transferred to Berlin in 1938 as first secretary of the American embassy. Shortly after Pearl Harbor he was transferred to Santiago, Chile, where he served as embassy counselor until 1944. He returned to Washington that year as political director of the Office of Military Government for Germany.

Heath was appointed American minister to Bulgaria in 1947. Two years later the Bulgarian government charged that he was the leader of a Western spy network and had conspired with former prime minister Preicho Kostov, whom the Soviets had deposed because of his support of Marshal Tito. The Communists claimed that before his execution for treason, Kostov had named Heath as his co-conspirator against Bulgaria and the USSR. In January 1950 the Bulgarian government demanded Heath's recall. Denying that he was a spy but merely an ambassador who had endured many "indignities and restrictions" at the hands of the Communists, the State Department in February 1950 broke diplomatic relations with Bulgaria.

President Truman appointed Heath the first American minister to the Associated States of Indochina in July 1950. American policy toward the French colony was ambiguous. On the one hand the administration had announced that it opposed colonialism and wanted independence for Vietnam. To aid the developing area the United States sent economic assistance, expanding it on the village level. On the other hand, the United States did not want to pressure the French. The administration was anxious to convince the French to join the proposed European Defense Community but was well aware that they could not fulfill their role in the alliance and carry on a war against the Vietnamese Communists at the same time. Therefore, the United States gave military support to the French. Following the outbreak of the Korean War, the State Department became more pro-French. Heath reflected this change in policy. He was by nature pro-French and reluctant to disturb the situation in Vietnam. He was totally under the influence of General Jean DeLattre, who attempted to maintain French dominance in the area. He clashed with other members of the mission over increased aid to Vietnam. Robert Blum, head of the American aid program, insisted that further assistance be contingent on the withdrawal of the French or at least the guarantee of French withdrawal by a specific date. Heath disagreed, advocating a policy of continuing aid while pressuring the French. After increased French military disasters during late 1950 the United States gave assistance to the military.

Heath had to deal with the nominal and reluctant ruler of Vietnam, Emperor Bao Dai. On January

20, 1952, he said to Heath that the French should reveal their true intentions. Heath said the French government would offer Vietnam "some economic assurances and preferences" similar to that of the British imperial preference system. The ambassador added the French wanted remnants of their culture and language in Indochina. Bao Dai was dismissive of the latter desire, saying the French had to deal with reality in Indochina and suggested it might be better if the Red Chinese invaded Vietnam. Then he, as emperor, could develop a resistance to "the hated traditional enemy." This idea shocked Heath, who replied that the Chinese Communists would crush any resistance, and only French forces kept Vietnam out of the hands of the Chinese.

In June 1952 Heath became ambassador to Vietnam. He continued at this post during the Eisenhower administration. He had at least an initial skepticism about Ngo Dinh Diem as a leader. In 1954, following the signing of the Geneva Accords dividing Vietnam, Heath carried on negotiations that resulted in direct U.S. military aid to the government of South Vietnam.

Heath was appointed ambassador to Lebanon in January 1955 and was sent as ambassador to Saudi Arabia and Yeman in 1957. The following year the U.S. government rejected overtures for renewal of diplomatic relations with Bulgaria, demanding that its government first retract the old spy charges against Heath. In March 1959 the Bulgarians complied, and diplomatic relations were restored. Heath retired in 1961. He then tried to help Americans trying to be repaid on the defaulted bonds of foreign governments. He was also a professor at the University of California at Los Angeles. He died on October 15, 1981, in Orinda, California.

—AES

Hébert, F(elix) Edward

(1901–1979) *member of the House of Representatives*

The son of a streetcar motorman and a schoolteacher, Hébert was born on October 12, 1901, in New Orleans, Louisiana. He attended Tulane University from 1920 to 1924 but did not complete the required work for his degree. While at Tulane he was an assistant sports editor of the *New Orleans States*. He became a political editor on the *States* in 1929 and was made the city editor eight years later. In 1939 he wrote a series of articles exposing cor-

ruption in Louisiana business and politics that led to the imprisonment of a number of the associates of the late Senator Huey Long. In 1940 Hébert ran successfully for a House seat as a Democrat from the First Congressional District, which included the eight wards of New Orleans and Plaquemines and St. Bernard's parishes. During the war years Hébert was assigned to the Naval Affairs Committee, where he was the chairman of a subcommittee on naval fighter production. Although he supported a strong armed forces, he was most concerned with efficiency and economy in government.

After the committee was merged with the Military Affairs Committee to form the Armed Services Committee in 1947, Hébert was involved with significant investigations. He conducted an investigation of labor and financial problems at Brewster Aeronautical Corporation. Hébert was selected after World War II by Representative LYNDON B. JOHNSON to tour devastated Europe. He kept a diary of his trip, which he later published.

Hébert joined his fellow southern Democrats in opposing most of the Truman administration's legislative program. A strong defender of segregation, he opposed various anti–poll tax and fair employment practices bills. In 1950 he voted for a measure changing House rules to give legislative control to the Republican–southern Democratic coalition. Hébert was a supporter of states' rights, voting for a proposal returning the U.S. Employment Service to the control of the states and a bill renouncing federal ownership of tidelands. He later claimed he supported the Dixiecrat ticket in 1948 because of states' rights, not civil rights. He favored such antilabor legislation as the Case labor disputes bill and the Taft-Hartley Act and voted with Republicans to reduce taxes.

In 1948 Hébert was appointed to the House Un-American Activities Committee (HUAC). Shortly thereafter he attacked the panel for placing higher value on headlines than national security. Although sympathetic to the goals of the group, he opposed its methods. Hébert was particularly distressed with HUAC's treatment of scientist EDWARD CONDON, accused of being a security risk. The Louisiana Democrat was not reappointed to HUAC in 1949 because, he later claimed, he had supported the States' Rights ticket during the 1948 presidential election. (The leadership at the time said from that time on one had to be a lawyer to sit on the committee.)

In 1951 Hébert chaired the Armed Services subcommittee charged with investigating wasteful military expenditures. The purpose of the probe, as Hébert outlined it, was to make all branches of government adopt a uniform purchasing catalog to avoid paying different prices for the same items. During the course of his investigation, Hébert put together an exhibit he called "The Chamber of Horrors," which featured examples of the waste in military procurement. In addition to duplication and mismanagement, he discovered outright fraud. In one case a defense contract involving millions of dollars "was awarded to a concern without plant, personnel or experience." The subcommittee's final report revealed that between 1945 and 1952 the Munitions Board had spent $100 million to develop a single supply catalog while the military departments spent an additional $87 million on separate cataloging systems. Hébert pushed for the passage of the defense supply standardization bill to force the Pentagon to standardize and systematize acquisitions. It became law in June 1952.

Despite his crusades against waste, Hébert was a leading advocate of a strong military establishment. He opposed the Kennedy administration's attempts to assert stronger civilian control of the Pentagon and to modernize the army by switching from manned aircraft to missiles. Hébert consistently argued the Pentagon position for the superiority of manned aircraft and helped stave off the reorganization of the Army Reserve and the National Guard. He was a key supporter of the war in Vietnam and was one of the first members of Congress to advocate the bombing of North Vietnam. Hébert fought the social programs of the Kennedy and Johnson administrations. Hébert became chairman of the Armed Service Committee in 1971, but, in 1975, because of his hawkishness he was stripped of his chairmanship by liberal members in a revolt against seniority. He decided not to seek reelection in 1976. Hébert died in New Orleans on December 29, 1979.

—SJT

Hellman, Lillian
(1905–1984) *dramatist*
Hellman was born on June 20, 1905, in New Orleans, Louisiana. During her youth Lillian Hellman generally spent six months of the year in New Orleans and six in New York. After dropping out of New York University she took a job with the Horace Liveright publishing house. Over the next few years she wrote book reviews for the New York *Herald Tribune*, and traveled around Europe. She married playwright Arthur Kober, with whom she went to Hollywood in 1930 and found a position reading scripts for Metro-Goldwyn-Mayer. Two years later she divorced Kober, returned to New York, and read plays for a Broadway producer.

Hellman won prominence in 1934 with the production of her play, *The Children's Hour.* Other Hellman works, such as *The Little Foxes* (1939), also won critical and popular acclaim and established her as America's most successful woman playwright. Her Broadway successes led to a second lucrative career as a screenwriter in Hollywood.

Beginning in the late 1930s Hellman became involved in various causes on the political left. During a European trip in 1937, she spent a month in Spain to observe the Civil War firsthand from the Loyalist side. Returning to the United States she denounced the right-wing Franco regime and helped raise funds for the Loyalists. In 1941 Hellman's passionate anti-Nazi play, *Watch on the Rhine*, won the New York Drama Critics Circle Award as the best drama of the season; it was made into a popular film in 1943. In 1944 Hellman was invited to visit Russia on a cultural mission; she was one of the few Westerners permitted to accompany the Russian forces in their victorious advance on the Germans.

After the war Hellman was a prominent member of the left-wing intelligentsia dissenting from the cold war anti-Soviet policies of the Truman administration. In 1947 she joined the leftist Progressive Citizens of America. During the 1948 presidential election she campaigned full-time for HENRY A. WALLACE, candidate of the Progressive Party. The following year she sponsored the Cultural and Scientific Conference for World Peace, a conclave organized and attended by Communist and left-wing intellectuals from around the world. Hellman's close companion for 30 years, detective-fiction writer DASHIELL HAMMETT, was sent to prison in 1951 for his refusal to answer questions at a House Un-American Activities Committee (HUAC) hearing concerning contributors to a bail fund of the Civil Rights Congress.

In 1952 HUAC summoned Hellman to testify about her past political activities and associations. Not wanting to cause trouble for former associates or to go to jail for contempt of Congress, Hellman suggested to committee members that she would answer any questions about herself if they did not ask her about anyone else. In a letter to HUAC Hellman said: "I do not like subversion or disloyalty in any form and if I had ever seen any I would have considered it my duty to have reported it to the proper authorities. But to hurt innocent people whom I knew many years ago in order to save myself is, to me, inhuman and indecent and dishonorable. I cannot and will not cut my conscience to fit this year's fashions, even though I long ago came to the conclusion that I was not a political person and could have no comfortable place in any political group."

The committee rejected Hellman's offer. On May 21 she appeared before the panel and was asked whether she had been a member of the Communist Party. She declined to answer on Fifth Amendment grounds. She also took the Fifth Amendment on several other questions concerning former meetings and associations. Hellman's appearance as a witness was brief. She was not called back or prosecuted. HUAC chairman Representative JOHN S. WOOD (D-Ga.) said, "Why cite her for contempt? After all, she's a woman. . . ."

In 1976 Hellman published *Scoundrel Time*, a popular account of the months surrounding her committee appearance. Saying, "I don't want to write about my historical conclusions—it isn't my game," she defended her refusal to testify and painted an unflattering portrait of "friendly" witnesses while criticizing intellectuals for not publicly condemning McCarthyism. She scorned the anticommunist journals *Commentary* and *Partisan Review* for not including articles critical of HUAC and Senator JOSEPH R. MCCARTHY (R-Wisc.). Explaining why "almost all" American intellectuals "either by what they did or did not do, contributed to McCarthyism," she said, "The children of timid immigrants . . . make it so good they are determined to keep it at any cost. . . ." Among her other historical conclusions were that McCarthy "was finished long before the [Army-McCarthy] hearings began" because America was "bored" with him. Anticommunist liberals such as Diana Trilling, Nathan Glazer, and JAMES WECHSLER disputed Hellman's judgments and criticized her for failing to denounce Stalinist Communists with the same vigor as she excoriated anticommunist crusaders.

During the years following her committee appearance, Hellman was blacklisted in Hollywood and found little outlet for creative work as remunerative as her previous efforts. By 1958 she had

begun to receive movie-writing offers again, and, in 1960, her play *Toys in the Attic* was a great success on Broadway. Over the next decade and a half, Hellman taught at several major universities and produced her bestselling memoirs, *An Unfinished Woman* (1969), winner of the National Book Award, and *Pentimento: A Book of Portraits* (1973). In her later years Hellman fell under considerable criticism for alleged fabrications in her memoirs. Mary McCarthy claimed it was all lies, and Hellman sued her, but the apparent dishonesty of her memoirs damaged Hellman's reputation. She died in Martha's Vineyard, Massachusetts, on June 30, 1984.

—TO

Henderson, W(esley) Loy
(1892–1986) *State Department official*

W. Loy Henderson, the son of an itinerant Methodist minister, was born of a farm near Rogers, Arkansas, on June 28, 1892. After graduating from Northwestern University in 1915, Henderson entered Denver University Law School. Upon the entry of the United States into World War I, he volunteered for military service but was rejected for medical reasons. As an alternative he joined the Red Cross. After the war Henderson served as a member of the Inter-Allied Commission to Germany, which was responsible for the repatriation of prisoners of war and the inspection of prisoner of war camps. During 1919–20 he was a member of the American Red Cross (ARC) Commission to Western Russia and the Baltic States. In 1920 and 1921 he was in charge of the ARC in Germany. The following year he began a career in the Foreign Service as vice consul in Dublin. In 1925 he began service in Eastern Europe. Henderson was transferred to Moscow in 1929, where he remained until 1938 when he became assistant chief of the Division of European Affairs of the State Department.

From 1945 to 1948 Henderson was director of the Division of Near Eastern and African Affairs, supervising U.S. policy in Africa, India, Pakistan, Burma, Ceylon, Iraq, Iran, Syria, Lebanon, Palestine, Greece, and Turkey. In this capacity Henderson was involved in the formulation and administration of the Truman Doctrine, developed in response to the Communist insurgency in Greece and Turkey.

In February 1947, following the British announcement of their impending withdrawal from

Greece and Turkey, Henderson—who, as historian Howard Jones has pointed out, made no secret of his anticommunism—headed a special committee to study the problem of U.S. economic and military assistance to the area. As Jones also noted the committee came to the conclusion that the president should present the economic program to the two countries as part of a global strategy in its presentation to Congress. The panel outlined the action to be taken by the president and suggested a detailed plan to implement its decision and justify it to the public and Congress. The panel's recommendation was presented in "Position and Recommendation of the Department of State Regarding Immediate Aid to Greece and Turkey." The report recommended that the administration make every effort to maintain the political and territorial integrity of Greece and Turkey and extend all aid necessary to assure the development of these countries toward democratic states with sound economies. It suggested a number of specific recommendations: passage of legislation authorizing the Export-Import Bank to extend credits free from the bureaucratic procedures normally involved; extension of all available military supplies to the nations and passage of bills permitting further support; and, development of plans for the American administration of economic aid. The report formed the basis for Truman's proposal requesting $400 million in assistance to the two nations. The plan passed Congress in May.

In August 1947 Henderson visited Greece to confer with Ambassador LINCOLN MACVEAGH to discuss methods of implementing the program and effecting a broadening of the Greek cabinet to stabilize the tottering central government. His success in helping formulate a two-party cabinet was regarded as a diplomatic triumph.

Henderson played a major role in the debate over U.S. policy toward Palestine. He was acutely aware of the importance of Near Eastern oil to the United States and Western Europe. "An unfriendly foreign power in possession of these reserves," he warned, "would be in a position to hamper, if not prevent, the rehabilitation of Western Europe and to retard the economic development of Africa and Southern Asia." Therefore, he and other members of the State Department, including Secretary of State GEORGE C. MARSHALL, opposed the immediate partition of Palestine into autonomous Jewish and Arab states, suggesting that the United States support a continuation of the British mandate. Fearing continued violence in the area, he was reluctant to grant requests from prominent Zionists to lift the U.S. arms embargo against Palestine and spearheaded the assault on the idea of partition. In 1948 the administration shifted its position toward one favoring Israel. As part of the change General JOHN H. HILLDRING, a strong advocate of partition, was appointed to the newly created post of special assistant for Palestine affairs, a move apparently designed to remove Henderson from supervision of that area.

In July 1948 President Truman appointed Henderson ambassador to India and minister to Nepal. The Indian government proposed to him (as well as to other people in other venues) a peace initiative to end the Korean War, in which the United States would allow the Chinese Communists to sit on the Security Council, and then the Chinese and the Soviets would back a cease-fire, withdrawal of North Korea troops above the 38th parallel, and creation of an independent and unified Korea. Neither the Soviets nor the Americans would agree to all these terms, and the initiative came to nothing.

In 1951 Truman appointed Henderson ambassador to Iran. He served at this post during part of the crisis over the Iranian seizure of the Anglo-Iranian Oil Company, which had led to tension between Great Britain and Iran. The State Department told Henderson to look into possible alternatives to the nationalist Mosadeq government and what might be needed to replace the latter with one of the former. Henderson's report of July 1952 convinced Secretary of State DEAN G. ACHESON to ask Truman for a direct approach to Mosadeq by Britain and the United States. Nothing came of it at first until Prime Minister Winston Churchill took over supervision of Iranian affairs and a joint attempt was made. Mosadeq shunned it. Henderson on Christmas Day 1952 talked to Mosadeq with the hope of ending the deadlock. Mosadeq seemed amendable to arbitration or compensation to Anglo-Iranian, and Henderson said, if that happened, the United States would advance payment against future oil delivery to help Iran. Henderson's hopes were raised for a few days, but another talk with the prime minister at the end of the year lowered them. The Truman administration could not solve the problem, and the situation was resolved with the CIA-inspired overthrow of Mosadeq during the Eisenhower administration.

Henderson remained in Tehran until 1955, when he was promoted to undersecretary of state for administration. Henderson served the government in various capacities throughout the 1950s. He was a member of the American delegation to the Second Suez Canal Conference in 1956 and chief of the mission to establish diplomatic and counselor offices in the newly emerging African states. After his retirement from the Foreign Service in January 1961, Henderson entered the academic world. He was professor of international relations and director of the Center of Diplomacy and Foreign Policy at the American University from 1961 to 1968 and president of the Washington Institute of Foreign Affairs from 1961 to 1973. Henderson died on March 24, 1986, in Bethesda, Maryland.

—MLB

Herter, Christian A(rchibald)

(1895–1966) *member of the House of Representatives*

Christian A. Herter was born in Paris, France, on March 28, 1895, the son of expatriate American artists. He graduated from Harvard College cum laude in 1915 and entered the Columbia University School of Architecture but left to join the Foreign Service in 1916. He was assigned to the U.S. embassy in Berlin. Upon America's entry into World War I, Herter was reassigned to Washington, D.C., and served on a special commission that negotiated a prisoner of war agreement with Germany. He was also secretary of the U.S. delegation to the Versailles Peace Conference. He then became an assistant to Secretary of Commerce HERBERT HOOVER, serving as secretary to the European Relief Council from 1920 to 1921, and participating in a 1922 relief mission to the USSR. Herter left government service in 1924 to edit *The Independent*. From 1927 to 1936 he was associate editor of *The Sportsman*. He also lectured on international affairs at Harvard from 1929 to 1930.

A Republican, Herter represented Boston's fifth ward in the Massachusetts House of Representatives from 1930 to 1943. He was Speaker of the House from 1939 to 1943 and impressed a young Thomas P. "Tip" O'Neill—later Speaker of the U.S. House of Representatives. A member of the internationalist wing of the Republican Party, Herter called for repeal of the arms and ammunition embargo in the fall of 1939. In 1942 Herter chal-

lenged the renomination of Representative George H. Tinkham, an isolationist Republican representing the Massachusetts 10th Congressional District. Tinkham bowed out before the primary, however, and Herter was subsequently elected.

Herter served on the House Food Committee and toured the major cities of America in 1945 to survey the nation's food problems. Later that year he made an inspection trip to Europe on behalf of the War Food Administration. Herter advocated the formation of the United Nations and urged Congress to support the UN and its agencies. He also approved the Greek-Turkish aid bill and endorsed a $370 million foreign aid appropriation in early 1947. Herter believed, however, that more detailed information was needed to assure the proper spending of these funds. On March 27, 1941, he put forward a resolution for a special committee with a budget of only $125,000, to look into the conditions of the European economy. Congress approved the resolution on July 22, 1947, following the proposal of the Marshall Plan. It established a 19-member Select Committee on Foreign Aid to look into European needs and a possible American aid program. House Foreign Affairs Committee chairman CHARLES A. EATON of New Jersey decided to stay home and allowed Vice Chairman Herter to head the junket.

Herter led a delegation of the committee to Europe in September 1947. They visited 18 countries and recommended immediate interim aid to France, Germany, Austria, and Italy. Herter noted that although British needs were less urgent, Britain's long-term economic problems were the most serious. Although the Truman administration decided against the panel's proposal of a foreign aid agency similar to the domestic Reconstruction Finance Corporation, *Time* magazine observed that without the "... committee's groundwork the program of foreign aid would never have been passed." Herter advised the administration not to promise commodities to Europe that were presently unavailable, arguing that failure to deliver such goods would be a "cruel disappointment" to the intended recipients. He warned the Europeans against "unwanted optimism," however, and added that "no program of American aid can achieve the objectives desired unless each country sets its own house in order to the maximum of its ability." Herter favored limiting the Marshall Plan to 18 months as an incentive to European self-reliance, and he blamed much of Europe's economic disarray on the Soviet blocking of trade between Eastern and

Western Europe. Herter tried to foster greater understanding of foreign countries by helping to found the John Hopkins School of Advanced International Studies.

On domestic legislation Herter voted against a permanent House Un-American Activities Committee in 1945, for the Taft-Hartley Act of 1947, for a two-term limit to the presidency in 1947, for rent control extension in 1948, for natural gas exemptions in 1949, and against a $2 billion farm subsidy in 1950. He favored several cutbacks of federal spending in 1951 and he supported the use of Taft-Hartley in the steel strike of 1952.

In 1951 Herter met with General DWIGHT D. EISENHOWER in Paris and advised him to seek the Republican presidential nomination in 1952. Herter later served as co-chairman of the Eisenhower for President Committee. In the fall of 1952, Herter was elected governor of Massachusetts and was reelected in 1954.

Herter discouraged an effort by liberal Republicans in 1956 to nominate him to replace RICHARD M. NIXON as the vice presidential candidate, and he personally nominated Nixon at the Republican convention that summer. Herter was appointed undersecretary of state in 1957 and succeeded JOHN FOSTER DULLES as secretary of state in 1959. He retired from politics in 1961 and was named chief U.S. trade negotiator by President John F. Kennedy, a position he held until his death on December 30, 1966, in Washington, D.C. (See *The Eisenhower Years* Volume)

—DB

Hickenlooper, Bourke B(lakemore)
(1896–1971) *member of the Senate*

A native of southwest rural Iowa, Bourke B. Hickenlooper was born on July 21, 1896, in Blockton. He served in the army during World War I and received his bachelor's degree in 1920 from Iowa State College. Two years later he earned a law degree from the University of Iowa. Admitted to the state bar in 1925, Hickenlooper worked for private law firms until elected to the Iowa state legislature in 1934. He served as lieutenant governor from 1938 to 1942 and as governor from 1942 to 1944. He won election to the U.S. Senate in 1944.

In the upper house Hickenlooper became the leading spokesman for a program of atomic energy control. He supported legislation in August 1946 that created a five-man civilian commission to supervise atomic energy operations and granted the government a monopoly on atomic patents and inventions. In 1947 he backed President Truman's controversial nomination of former Tennessee Valley Authority (TVA) head DAVID E. LILIENTHAL as chairman of the Atomic Energy Commission (AEC). The senator dismissed allegations that there was widespread Communist activity in the TVA. However, in May 1949 Hickenlooper attacked Lilienthal's "mismanagement" of the AEC. He charged that fellowships were going to Communists, that full security clearance was granted personnel before FBI checks, and that employees were maintained on the payroll despite unfavorable reports from the AEC security office. In September 1949 Hickenlooper disagreed with a joint congressional committee report that cleared Lilienthal of the charges.

Although usually opposed to the administration's domestic measures, Hickenlooper generally supported Truman's foreign policy, which included the British loan in 1946, the Greek-Turkish aid bill in 1947, and the Marshall Plan in 1948. He continually advocated a strengthening of the nation's military preparedness and approved of the North Atlantic Treaty in 1949. On a Far Eastern tour in January 1952, Hickenlooper urged increased technical and material aid to the region and recommended the assignment of an ambassador to Taiwan.

Hickenlooper was a member of the Special Tydings committee that looked into Senator JOSEPH R. MCCARTHY's (R-Wisc.) allegations of Communists in the State Department in 1950. Hickenlooper was known for bewildering and ineffective way of interrogating witnesses, which had let reporters to joke about "pulling a Hickenlooper." McCarthy's one true ally on the Tydings committee was the Iowan. Occasionally, such as during the testimony of Ambassador-at-Large PHILIP JESSUP, McCarthy would provide Hickenlooper with questions to ask. His backing of McCarthy was seen as rewarded by his renomination to run again for his Senate seat by a four-to-one margin. Hickenlooper became angry when Chairman Millard E. Tydings (D-Md.) proclaimed a summary of Owen Lattimore's FBI file had cleared him. Hickenlooper had not read it yet, and, when he did, he dissented. Hickenlooper refused to sign the majority report of the committee, which condemned McCarthy.

Hickenlooper successfully campaigned for reelection in 1950 by attacking Truman's "socialized" domestic programs and the Brannan Plan for farm prices. His election victory over former undersecretary of agriculture Albert J. Loveland, along with other GOP victories in the farm belt, was interpreted by some to mean that Secretary of Agriculture CHARLES F. BRANNAN should be dropped from the cabinet.

Reflecting the strong work ethic of many of his constituents, Hickenlooper continued to vote against welfare measures such as medicare, aid to education, and antipoverty programs of the Eisenhower, Kennedy and Johnson years. He supported defense and military assistance bills and some civil rights legislation. Until his retirement in 1969, Hickenlooper worked to maintain Republican support of American policy in Vietnam. Hickenlooper died on September 4, 1971, in Shelter Island, New York. (See *The Eisenhower Years, The Kennedy Years, The Johnson Years* Volumes)

—TML

Hill, (Joseph) Lister
(1894–1984) *member of the Senate*

The son of a leading American heart surgeon, Lister Hill was born on December 29, 1894, in Montgomery, Alabama. He obtained his bachelor's and law degrees from the University of Alabama in 1914 and 1915, respectively. Hill went to New York City to obtain his second law degree from Columbia University in 1916. He then began practicing in Montgomery. After two years in the army during World War I, he resumed his practice and was active in the city's civic affairs and Democratic politics. Reared a Catholic, Hill publicly converted to Methodism to give himself a chance politically in Protestant Alabama. In August 1923 he was elected to the House of Representatives in a special election. Hill served in the House for several terms, championing the Tennessee Valley Authority (TVA) and other New Deal measures. In 1937 he ran successfully for the Senate seat vacated when HUGO L. BLACK was appointed to the Supreme Court. Three years later he became Democratic whip. In 1940 Lister Hill placed Roosevelt's name in nomination at the Democratic National Convention.

Hill enthusiastically supported Roosevelt's foreign policy. He backed lend-lease, supported the president's defense program, and urged the repeal of the Neutrality Act. In 1943 he helped write the Ball-Burton-Hill-Hatch Resolution, putting the Senate on record in favor of a future United Nations.

During the postwar period Hill became a major proponent of national health care legislation. In 1945 Hill, in conjunction with Representative HAROLD H. BURTON (R-Ohio), introduced a bill authorizing $75 million annually in federal grants to state and local nonprofit organizations for hospital construction. Major health care groups such as the American Medical Association, Council on Medical Education, and American Hospital Association as well as labor and farm organizations supported the measure. The Senate passed the bill by voice vote in December 1945; the House in July 1946. Under the program, one of the most important of the postwar period, the federal government was to spend $75 million annually for a period of five years. The states were to match grants on a two-for-one basis. Hill thought the passage an extraordinarily precedent: "[I]t represents the first time Congress ever has approved various grants to the states, and sets a precedent of distributing federal funds on the basis of need." In 1949 he successfully offered amendments enlarging the funding of the original bill. The program was extended several times in the 1950s and 1960s.

As one of the leading southern liberals during the Fair Deal, Hill supported extension of public power projects as the TVA. He endorsed the campaign of his fellow Alabama senator JOHN J. SPARKMAN (D-Ala.) to expand the public housing programs of the administration. Hill opposed the Taft-Hartley Act and in 1950 cosponsored an unsuccessful attempt to make it more acceptable to unions and the administration.

It was in the civil rights area that Hill broke with the administration. Throughout the Truman presidency he was an ardent segregationist. Rather than support the administration's civil rights program as Democratic whip, Hill resigned from that position and lost his chance to succeed Allen Barkley as majority leader. He opposed an amendment to his hospital bill, barring aid to hospitals discriminating in employing doctors, on the grounds that hiring was a state matter. He participated in the numerous filibusters against the creation of the permanent Fair Employment Practices Commission. Because of the administration's civil rights record, Hill joined Sparkman in April 1948 in calling for Truman's retirement. He joined the pro-Eisenhower forces prior to the 1948 convention. However, Hill refused to join the conservative Dixiecrat defection from the Democratic Party that year.

In 1952 Hill supported Senator RICHARD B. RUSSELL (D-Ga.) in the Democratic presidential primary race. In the aftermath of the 1954 *Brown v. Board of Education* case desegregating public schools, Hill supported the Alabama legislature's attempt at interposition and signed the Southern Manifesto denouncing the Court decision and calling for legal, peaceful resistance. The Alabaman became chairman of the Senate Labor and Welfare Committee and chairman of the Appropriations Committee's Subcommittee for Health and Welfare in 1955. In both capacities he was able to substantially increase federal health expenditures based on the original Hill-Burton Act. He also was one of the authors of the National Defense Education Act of 1958.

Hill grew more conservative after 1962, when he nearly lost his seat to a conservative Republican. He voted against most urban social programs and continued to oppose civil rights legislation. He retired in 1969. Hill died in Montgomery, Alabama, on December 20, 1984. (See *The Eisenhower Years, The Kennedy Years, The Johnson Years* Volumes)

—JB

Hilldring, John H(enry)
(1895–1974) *assistant secretary of state for occupied areas*

The son of Swedish immigrants, John H. Hilldring was born on March 27, 1895, in New Rochelle, New York. He attended Columbia University and the University of Connecticut, where he graduated in 1917. That year he joined the army as a second lieutenant and saw action in France and Germany. During the 1920s he served as an infantry officer in the United States and the Philippines. Hilldring was placed in charge of Civilian Conservation Corps districts in Texas and Arizona during the depression and helped formulate army personnel policy in the late 1930s. In 1942 Hilldring, by then a brigadier general, was assistant chief of staff of the Officers' Branch of the Personnel Division. The following year he became chief of the Civilian Affairs Division of the War Department. At that post he coordinated political and economic planning in areas under military government.

After the Allied victory over Germany in May 1945, Hilldring worked to restore local government in occupied areas of that nation. He was also responsible for de-nazification and de-cartelization in the U.S. zone. Under his direction free press and radio were reinstituted, the educational system was reorganized, and political parties and trade unions were restored. Unwilling to make policy for the occupied areas and yet anxious to prevent civilians from interfering, the army simply evaluated occupation policies in terms of the amorphous idea of "military necessity." Hilldring defended the slow progress toward democratization, asserting, "It is the opinion of our government that the German mind simply cannot be turned inside out overnight." In October 1945 he suggested that German prisoners of war still in the United States should be trained to work for the military government in Germany. The military governor of the American sector, General LUCIUS D. CLAY, was dubious. He feared these people would appear to be collaborators, which would ruin their future usefulness.

When responsibility for occupied areas was turned over to the State Department in February 1946, Hilldring resigned his commission and accepted the post of assistant secretary of state for occupied areas. During his year at that assignment, he urged increased aid to refugees from both private sources as well as national and international organizations. He also received protests from Clay in August 1946 about the War Department's desire to end de-nazification trials. Clay also objected to Hilldring's proposal to send State Department officials to look into how the occupation was going. Hilldring also supported the resettlement of displaced European Jews in Palestine. As chairman of the State, War, and Navy Coordinating Committee, he guided the research for the formulation of the Marshall Plan. He resigned his post in September 1947 due to financial problems.

That month Truman, on the advice of DAVID K. NILES, made Hilldring adviser and alternate delegate to the United Nations, where he helped develop U.S. policy toward Palestine. The appointment was designed to insure that a strong advocate of partition would be present in the U.S. delegation to counter opposition from the State Department, which disapproved of the formation of a Jewish state.

In the spring of 1948 Truman's political advisers, fearful of the president losing the Jewish vote if partition did not happen, pushed the appointment of Hilldring to the State Department, which opposed partition. Hilldring was reluctant to accept the job for that reason, but pleading by ELEANOR ROOSEVELT, HENRY MORGENTHAU, and prominent Zionist Chaim Weizmann convinced him to take the job. Zionists were happy about the appointment because Hilldring would now be in charge of Palestine policy instead of W. LOY HENDERSON, who opposed partition. But Hilldring received a chilly reception at State, and, at the request of friends in the Department, who told him it would help Marshall if he stepped down, resigned from State, claiming ill health made it impossible to carry out such duties. Hilldring subsequently pursued a career in business. He died in 1974.

—MLB

Hillenkoetter, Roscoe H(enry)
(1897–1982) *director, Central Intelligence Agency*

Roscoe H. Hillenkoetter was born on May 8, 1897, in St. Louis, Missouri. He graduated from the U.S. Naval Academy in 1920. After sea duty aboard both submarines and surface ships, he was ordered to Europe in the fall of 1933, where he served as assistant naval attaché at the American embassy in Paris. In 1938 he was given the additional assignment of assistant naval attaché in Madrid and Lisbon. Hillenkoetter was designated naval attaché in Paris in April 1940. After the fall of France in June, he undertook the same duty with the Vichy government. By this time Hillenkoetter could speak five languages and was working with the French underground.

As assistant and then full attaché, Hillenkoetter was in the intelligence branch of his service. He drew on that experience during World War II when he served as officer in charge of intelligence on the staff of Admiral Chester W. Nimitz, commander of the U.S. Pacific Fleet. In 1942 and 1943 he worked to set up a wartime intelligence network in the Pacific. He saw action in the South Pacific later in the war as the captain of the USS *Dixie*. After the war Hillenkoetter returned to his post as naval attaché in Paris. He was made a rear admiral in 1946.

President Truman broke up the Office of Strategic Services and fired its chief, William J. "Wild Bill" Donovan, whom he despised, in 1945. He then set up the Central Intelligence Group, which was to coordinate the government's intelligence agencies. In May 1947 Truman named Hillenkoetter to succeed General HOYT S. VANDENBERG as director of Central Intelligence (DCI) and head of the Central Intelligence Group (CIG). Truman had established the CIG by presidential directive in January 1946. Its purpose was to serve as an intelligence coordinating body. As DCI, Hillenkoetter was responsible for minimizing duplicative efforts between the intelligence services of the different uniformed services and the State Department. The CIG had as its goal to review the raw data gathered by the departmental intelligence services and to provide objective intelligence estimates for the use of senior policymakers. By the time of Hillenkoetter's appointment, the CIG also had emerged as a current intelligence producer, collecting its own information and generating its own summaries of events.

When Congress passed the National Security Act in July 1947, the CIG was reconstituted as the Central Intelligence Agency (CIA). Hillenkoetter became its first director. The CIG had been an extension of several executive departments, with its personnel and budget allocated from the Army, Navy, and State Department. Under the National Security Act the agency Hillenkoetter headed became an independent department responsible to the newly formed National Security Council (NSC).

Under Hillenkoetter the CIA continued to expand, albeit slowly, its independent intelligence production. This included both the overt and the clandestine collection of intelligence. Hillenkoetter, like Truman, did not like paramilitary operations or plots to overthrow governments that had been democratically elected, and the admiral was criticized by some of Donovan's partisans for not being enthusiastic enough in increasing the agency's capability to carry out covert operations. However, he did believe in the idea of psychological warfare, and he ignored the counsel of the agency's lawyers in stopping the political advance of the Communists in elections in Italy and France. The 1949 Central Intelligence Act, designed to assist the agency's clandestine activities, exempted Hillenkoetter and future directors from all federal laws that required the public disclosure of the functions, titles, names, salaries, or numbers of personnel employed by the agency. It gave him the right to allocate at his discretion the extensive sums in the agency's secret annual budget. Preserving the personnel and structure of its CIG predecessor, the CIA likewise attempted to supervise interagency coordination for national intelligence estimates. The efforts were hampered by Hillenkoetter's difficulties in asserting the agency's position relative to the other more established departments.

Hillenkoetter frequently had disagreements over administrative questions with FRANK G. WISNER, director of the Office of Policy Coordination (OPC). The OPC was created in 1948 for the execution of covert operations. Concerned over a global Soviet threat, senior U.S. officials saw covert action as a supplement to the traditional alternatives of diplomacy and war. Although OPC was a CIA component, with its budget and personnel appropriated within CIA allocations, Hillenkoetter had no authority in determining OPC activities. Policy guidance came to Wisner from the State and Defense departments. Hillenkoetter tried to build up the agency's Office of Research and Evaluation (ORE), which had been designed to provide the president the information he needed to decide issues of national security. Unfortunately the ORE had to deal with the obstructionist tactics of the other intelligence agencies of the State Department and the military. Some observers began to criticize Hillenkoetter's seeming inability to manage the intelligence community.

Only six months after the CIA had officially come into existence in September 1947, Hillenkoetter found himself under fire for the agency's alleged failure to predict a major international upheaval. The assassination of Jorge Eliecer Gaitain, a popular liberal Colombian leader, on April 9, 1948, on a street in Bogotá had touched off the "Bogotazo," two days of bloody riots that disrupted the Ninth Inter-American Conference. Embarrassed by the riots, Secretary of State GEORGE C. MARSHALL, who headed the American delegation, blamed them on Communist agitation. Hillenkoetter, called before a subcommittee of the House Committee on Expenditures in the Executive Department on April 15, maintained that although the Communists had seized on Gaitain's assassination, the Colombian leader was slain in "a purely private act of revenge." He testified that the CIA had predicted trouble in Bogotá as early as January of that year. He then told the subcommittee that a March 23 CIA dispatch from Bogotá, warning of Communist agitation, had been withheld from Secretary Marshall by a State Department advance man in Bogotá, acting with the support of the American ambassador there. The agency also corrected the CIG's original assertion that the Soviets would not explode an atomic bomb until 1951.

When North Korea launched its surprise invasion of South Korea in June 1950, Truman summoned Hillenkoetter to the White House as the official assumed to have had the most advance knowledge about what had happened. After meeting with the president, Hillenkoetter told newsmen that his agency had warned about the possibility of such an attack for a year. Asked whether the attack had been anticipated over the weekend, he replied that it was not possible to predict the exact timing of the invasion. He went to Capitol Hill to give the same explanation in secret testimony to the Senate Appropriations Committee. Afterward, committee members said they were satisfied with Hillenkoetter's explanation.

The agency did have some clear-cut successes. They foretold problems in the Philippines, were able to note divisions within the leadership of Russia, and discovered that an air force intelligence report of an imminent Soviet invasion of Scandinavia were unfounded.

In August of the same year the White House announced that General WALTER BEDELL SMITH, former ambassador to Moscow, would succeed Hillenkoetter as CIA director at the end of September. Hillenkoetter, who had previously requested a return to sea duty, took command in November of the navy's Seventh Task Force, assigned to the protection of Taiwan. He was also involved in Korean War operations, such as the Inchon landings. In 1952 he became commander of the Brooklyn Navy Yard and the Third Naval District. He retired from the navy a vice admiral in 1957 and became a director of Electronic and Missile Facilities, Inc. Hillenkoetter died on June 18, 1982, in New York City.
—SF

Hiss, Alger
(1904–1996) *president, Carnegie Endowment for International Peace*

Born on November 11, 1904, in Baltimore, Maryland, Hiss was raised there by his mother, his father having committed suicide when Alger was two. He excelled academically at Johns Hopkins University and was elected president of the student council, among other campus laurels. He earned his law degree from Harvard Law School in 1929, attaining the prestigious position of law secretary to Supreme Court Justice Oliver Wendell Holmes upon the recommendation of Professor FELIX FRANKFURTER. After serving Holmes for a year, Hiss practiced law in Boston and then New York until 1933, when he returned to Washington to join Jerome Frank's staff at the Agricultural Adjustment Administration (AAA), the first of a succession of jobs Hiss held in the New Deal. In the legal division of the AAA, Hiss worked ultimately unsuccessfully to build into the standard contract between farmers and the government protections for poor tenant farmers and sharecroppers to cut back crop production. Hiss was associated with the AAA's left wing, a band of reformers ultimately ousted in the famous "purge" of the AAA in 1935.

By that time Hiss had left the AAA to serve as a legal assistant on the staff of the Nye Committee during its highly publicized investigation of the role of the armaments industry in America's entry into World War I. Disenchanted with the isolationist direction of the Nye Committee, Hiss in mid-1935 joined the Justice Department to aid Solicitor General STANLEY F. REED in defending the constitutionality of the AAA before the Supreme Court. The Court ruled in January 1936 that the AAA was unconstitutional. Hiss also worked on the legal defense for the State Department's tariff-lowering reciprocal trade agreements, an assignment that led to his leaving the Solicitor General's office in mid-1936 to join the State Department as assistant to Francis B. Sayre, assistant secretary of state for economic affairs. After three years working on foreign trade problems with Sayre, Hiss in 1939 became assistant to Stanley Hornbeck, State Department adviser on Far Eastern political relations.

In March 1944 Hiss joined the new Office of Special Political Affairs, rising in a year to the post of director. In this post Hiss played a central role in the creation of the United Nations. As executive secretary to the Dumbarton Oaks conference laying the foundations of the UN, Hiss supervised such matters as transportation, communications, and the recording of minutes. He also served as an adviser to the American delegation. He accompanied President Roosevelt to the Yalta Conference in February 1945, advising the American delegation on matters of UN procedure and the forthcoming organization of the UN at San Francisco. At the San Francisco Conference Hiss was elected temporary secretary general. As at Dumbarton Oaks he handled the administrative and procedural matters and advised the U.S. delegation. It was Hiss who carried the UN charter for its formal presentation to President Truman in June.

After ratification of the charter by the Senate, Hiss went to London as principal adviser to the U.S.

delegation to the first session of the General Assembly early in 1946. At the end of the year, he left the State Department to become president of the Carnegie Endowment for International Peace, a position he held until May 1949. During his tenure at the Carnegie Endowment, a 36-year-old fund for projects that might contribute to the eventual abolition of war, Hiss tried to guide the endowment to support the UN and its objectives.

In 1948 Hiss became a leading actor in a postwar political and legal drama growing out of congressional investigation of Communist infiltration of the U.S. government. On August 3 WHITTAKER CHAMBERS, an ex-Communist currently employed as a senior editor of *Time* magazine, testified before the House Un-American Activities Committee (HUAC) that during the 1930s he and Hiss had belonged to an underground Communist organization in Washington. Chambers named several other former second-echelon New Deal officials as members of this secret network. The list included such individuals as LEE PRESSMAN, HARRY DEXTER WHITE, and Hiss's brother Donald, but the name of Alger Hiss was the most notable.

On August 5 Hiss appeared before the committee and denied Chambers's accusations. He stated that he had never belonged to the Communist Party or any Communist-front organization, or adhered to the tenets of communism. He added that he had never known anyone named Whittaker Chambers. On August 17 he was brought before Chambers at a special committee session held at the Hotel Commodore in New York. Hiss then said that Chambers resembled a "George Crosley" he had known in 1934–35, a freelance journalist who had subleased Hiss's apartment for a time and borrowed money from Hiss without repaying. Chambers admitted that Hiss had not known him by his real name, but said that his pseudonym was "Carl," not "George Crosley." Chambers agreed to take a lie detector test, but Hiss declined.

On August 25 the two appeared before HUAC in a dramatic televised confrontation and gave radically conflicting accounts of their relationship. Chambers characterized Hiss as "a dedicated and rather romantic Communist" in 1934–35; Hiss emphatically denied ever being a Communist. Chambers said they were introduced in 1934 by the head of the Communist underground in Washington; Hiss said he had met Chambers as "George Crosley," a writer preparing a series of articles on subjects being investigated by the Nye Committee, for whom Hiss was working at the time. Chambers testified that Hiss had paid his party dues to him; Hiss stated that the only money he ever gave him was about $30 in personal loans. Chambers said that their meeting had been in 1938, when he unsuccessfully tried to persuade Hiss to join him in repudiating communism; Hiss testified he last saw "Crosley" in 1935. The session lasted 10 hours and produced a welter of contradictory testimony. Chambers accused Hiss of lying, while Hiss castigated Chambers as a "self-confessed liar, spy and traitor." At the hearing Hiss dared Chambers to repeat his charges outside the committee and thus gave Hiss an opportunity to sue for slander. Chambers met the challenge by declaring on an August 27 "Meet the Press" broadcast, "Alger Hiss was a Communist and may still be one." Hiss did not answer until one month later, after harsh criticism from major newspapers for his delay. He then filed a suit for slander against Chambers, claiming damage at $75,000.

The case sharply escalated when, during the pretrial discovery process in November, Chambers accused Hiss of espionage. Until that time Chambers had maintained that Hiss and his cohorts had intended only to promote Communist influence in the New Deal. As evidence to support his charge that Hiss in the early part of 1938 had given him classified State Department documents for delivery to the Soviet Union, Chambers produced a cache of papers connected to Hiss in that period. There were four memorandums in Hiss's handwriting summarizing confidential government material and 65 pages of retyped State Department documents that Chambers said Hiss had given him.

This startling development went unpublicized until early December, when, in response to a HUAC subpoena, Chambers dramatically handed over to committee investigators additional evidence in the form of five roles of microfilm, which he had hidden in a hollowed-out pumpkin the day before. The microfilms, two rolls of which contained classified State Department material initialed by Hiss, were thereafter referred to as the "Pumpkin Papers." Their release was orchestrated with sensational press coverage by HUAC member Representative RICHARD M. NIXON (R-Calif.) and coincided with public disclosure of some of the first group of documents. President Truman, as he had in August, blasted the HUAC probe as a "red herring"; Nixon criticized Truman's statement as

"a flagrant flouting of the national interests of the people."

For a week in December, Hiss and Chambers testified before a New York grand jury. On December 15 the grand jury indicted Hiss on two counts of perjury, alleging that he had lied when he said that he had not seen Chambers after January 1, 1937, and when he denied passing government documents to Chambers. (The charge was perjury because the statute of limitations had run out on espionage.) Hiss pleaded not guilty.

The central issue at the trial, which began on May 31, was the veracity of Chambers and Hiss. The former displayed an intimate knowledge of Hiss's affairs during the 1930s. Another State Department employee of the period, Julian Wadleigh, testified that he, too, had delivered documents to Chambers. The most compelling evidence corroborating Chambers's account was the documents and microfilms unquestionably connected to Hiss, either by handwriting, initials, or typewriter. It was established at the trial that the retyped documents had been typed on a Woodstock typewriter owned by Hiss in the 1930s.

The primary tactic of Hiss's defense was to attack Chambers's credibility. Hiss's counsel, the flamboyant trial veteran Lloyd Paul Stryker, castigated Chambers as "a thief, a liar, a blasphemer and a moral leper." Under cross-examination Chambers admitted lying on numerous occasions in the past; Stryker got Chambers to admit that he had testified falsely before a grand jury in October 1948 when he denied any knowledge of espionage activities. In his summation Stryker called Chambers a "psychopathic . . . sadist" whose spy charges against Hiss were "preposterous."

In court the patrician, distinguished Hiss, an elegant, composed, Harvard-trained lawyer, presented a sharp contrast to the rumpled, portly Chambers with his unstable past, fretful disposition, and melodramatic manner. Hiss's defense began with character witnesses of formidable eminence, Supreme Court Justices Felix Frankfurter and Stanley Reed, praising his character and record. On the witness stand Hiss testified at length about his relationship with Chambers, whom he said he had not seen after mid-1936. He again denied ever being a Communist or a Communist-sympathizer, or having given any secret documents to Chambers in 1937–38. Under cross-examination Hiss acknowledged that there were dozens of discrepancies between his trial testimony and previous statements to the FBI and HUAC. He maintained that his wife had given away the Woodstock typewriter in December 1937, so that it was not in their possession when the 1938 documents produced by Chambers had been typed in it.

The first Hiss trial ended July 8 in a hung jury. The jurors were split, eight to four, for conviction. The second trial lasted from November 17, 1949, to January 21, 1950. In addition to the documentary and oral testimony presented at the first trial, the prosecution introduced as a witness a woman who claimed she knew Hiss to be a Communist in the 1930s. The defense featured new testimony from two psychiatrists who characterized Chambers as a "psychopathic personality." Neither had ever directly examined Chambers, however, and the prosecution made an effective attack on their testimony.

The main strategic difference in the two trials was the effort by Hiss's new attorney, Claude Cross, to discredit the documentary evidence, which Stryker had for the most part ignored. Through lengthy and detailed interrogation of government witnesses, Cross tried to establish that Chambers could have procured the documents from various other "confederates" in the State Department; he also speculated that Chambers could have secretly purloined the Hisses' Woodstock typewriter from the people they had given it to, and retyped the documents in order to frame Hiss. The jury found Cross's arguments confusing and unpersuasive. On January 21 they found Hiss guilty of perjury. On January 25 Judge Henry Goddard sentenced him to five years in prison.

The Hiss case was a cauldron of political controversy, generating headlines and often strident public debate. For both his defenders and detractors Hiss was a symbol; each side saw broad implications in his situation that went far beyond his personal fate. To Republicans and others disaffected by the New Deal, Hiss represented the arrogant elite shaping radical policies in the Democratic administrations of the 1930s and 1940s. To many his conviction was a confirmation of charges of Communist infiltration into the New Deal and the subversion of American foreign policy by Communist agents such as Hiss, who was now given a crucial responsibility for the cold war as the "architect" of the "sellout" at Yalta. For many on the left Hiss was a different symbol: the innocent victim of a postwar antiradical witchhunt designed to repudiate the New Deal, place personal blame for Soviet gains on prominent

Democrats, and whip up public hysteria for the benefit of right-wing politicians.

The most salient beneficiary of Hiss's conviction was Representative Nixon, who had relentlessly pressed HUAC's investigation of Hiss. Having gained the reputation of being a nemesis of Communist subversives, Nixon used the Hiss case as a launching pad for his turbulent career in national politics, winning election to the Senate in 1950, the vice presidency in 1952, and the presidency in 1968. The Hiss affair also fertilized the soil for the anticommunist crusade of Senator JOSEPH R. MCCARTHY (R-Wisc.). Only a month after Hiss's conviction, McCarthy first broadcast his charges about the existence of Communists in the State Department. The Hiss case was one of several postwar spy cases that led some sections of the public to believe McCarthy's sweeping accusations of domestic subversion. Hiss became a stock nefarious example for a generation of Republican orators.

His appeals having failed, Hiss started serving his prison sentence in March 1951 at the Lewisburg federal penitentiary in Pennsylvania. He was released 44 months later in November 1954. Disbarred from law practice, Hiss worked for a time for a manufacturer of women's hair accessories and then spent 15 years as a salesman of office supplies and stationery while living in New York City. He won readmission to the Massachusetts bar in 1975.

Hiss continuously insisted upon his innocence of any espionage or Communist affiliations in the 1930s. In 1957 he published his own brief in his defense, entitled *In the Court of Public Opinion*. After his conviction the debate over his guilt or innocence continued to rage in books and periodicals. The publication in 1978 of historian Allen Weinstein's long-awaited study of the Hiss case dealt a forceful blow to Hiss's contention that he was the victim of a miscarriage of justice. Weinstein examined previously unreleased FBI material and the files of Hiss's attorneys and interviewed members of the Communist underground in the 1930s. He concluded that Chambers was telling the truth, and that Hiss was lying when he denied being a Communist and handing over secret documents to Chambers. Weinstein's conclusions sparked an often-acrimonious exchange with Hiss's defenders in a number of national magazines.

The question of Hiss's guilt or innocence was resolved in the 1990s with the release of the Venona decryptions. Venona was the code name for the military's effort to decipher messages from Soviet embassies and consulates in the United States to Moscow. Venona showed conclusively, despite all his denials, that Hiss was a spy. A Venona intercept of a March 1945 talked of an agent, "Ales," who had been working for Soviet military intelligence since 1935 and had recently been "awarded Soviet decorations." He and his group, mostly relations, worked to obtain military information only, and the documents he purloined regarding the State Department did not interest the GRU much. He had also recently been to the Yalta Conference, after which he went to Moscow and was congratulated on his work by a high Soviet official, whom "Ales" thought was the deputy foreign minister. A process of elimination showed that "Ales" could only have been Hiss. Hiss died on November 15, 1996, in New York City.

—TO

Hoey, Clyde R(oark)
(1877–1954) *member of the Senate*

The son of a Confederate army captain, Clyde R. Hoey was born on December 11, 1877, in Shelby, North Carolina, attended public schools there, and then began his apprenticeship in a printing shop. At the age of 16 he purchased the town newspaper. Hoey won a seat in the North Carolina House of Representatives as a Democrat in 1899, the same year he completed a five-month law course at the University of North Carolina. In 1902 he won election to the North Carolina Senate for one term. President Woodrow Wilson appointed him assistant U.S. attorney for the western district of the state in 1913. Six years later he was elected to fill an unexpired term in the U.S. House of Representatives. Hoey chose to return to North Carolina in 1921 to practice law rather than seek reelection. As governor from 1937 to 1941, he instituted a broad welfare program, increased school spending by 30 percent, and started major highway construction. Yet, he still managed to cut the state debt.

Hoey won election to the U.S. Senate in 1944. He defeated four opponents, carrying 97 out of 100 counties, including the home counties of his rivals. Historian John W. Malsberger has called Hoey a "new conservative." According to Malsberger these senators saw themselves as adapting their conservative philosophy to modern domestic and foreign economic realities. On the issue of federal aid to education, Hoey noted the discrepancies among the

states in education and the large number of draft rejections and believed that the federal government should extend some aid in this area, while local and state government retained control. He did support the Case labor disputes bill and the Taft-Hartley Act, which placed restrictions on union activities. He took a moderate approach to price controls in 1946, wanting some eliminated and others maintained temporarily. As a southerner, he opposed the administration's civil rights program, but he did not join the Dixiecrats, who bolted the Democratic Party in 1948 over that issue. On foreign policy he supported the Greek-Turkish aid bill.

Hoey gained nationwide prominence through his investigations of corruption and graft in the Truman administration. Given to wearing a "frock coat, high shoes, wing collar and red boutonnière," Hoey presided over hearings with stern dignity. As chairman of the Senate Investigations Subcommittee, he led a 1949 probe into the activities of "five percenters" who arranged the awarding of government contracts for a fee. Most of the time Hoey was the only Democrat on the committee in the room, as other Democratic members tended to be absent, giving the Republicans largely a free hand, with only occasional interruptions from the North Carolinian. Thus, Hoey did not effectively control the committee, allowing committee Republicans to embarrass the president as well as uncover corruption. The probe eventually reached high government officials and caused Truman considerable embarrassment when some of his top aides were implicated. In July 1949 the *New York Herald Tribune* reported that James V. Hunt, a former army officer, had obtained government contracts for clients in exchange for a "stiff retainer" and 5 percent of the contract. The Hoey subcommittee then heard testimony in August detailing Hunt's efforts to secure government jobs, contracts, and favors. The hearings indicated that presidential aide General HARRY H. VAUGHAN had become deeply involved with Hunt's influence peddling. One of Hunt's clients had made gifts of deep freezers to Vaughan, Chief Justice FRED M. VINSON, Federal Reserve governor JAMES K. VARDAMAN, and BESS TRUMAN. In addition, Vaughan was linked to JOHN MARAGON, a onetime Kansas City bootblack and reputed "fixer" who was later convicted of perjury.

Truman, angered by the revelations and Republican attacks, criticized the panel's handling of the inquiry. He told an August press conference that "in common fairness" any judgment of Vaughan had to be withheld until after the general testified. He added that testimony favorable to Vaughan had been suppressed. Hoey launched a stinging rebuttal and released all testimony concerning Vaughan. In September 1949 the general denied doing any favors for Hunt and defended his own conduct. The panel's report, issued in January 1950, assailed Vaughan for accepting the freezer and for helping Hunt and Maragon. Mrs. Truman was held blameless in accepting a freezer because of the tradition of gift-giving to the president. Despite the condemnation of Vaughan, Truman allowed him to retain his White House position until the end of his term. Hoey's disclosures helped fuel Republican charges that the Democratic administration was corrupt. Coupled with the emerging scandals in the Bureau of Internal Revenue, the probe damaged the Truman administration's reputation for clean government.

In September 1951 Hoey began a probe of the Reconstruction Finance Corporation (RFC) following a similar investigation by a Senate Banking subcommittee chaired by Senator J. WILLIAM FULBRIGHT (D-Ark.). The Hoey panel focused on reports that the chairmen of the Democratic and Republican National Committees had used political pressure to influence RFC decisions on loans. During hearings in the fall, both Democratic National Committee chairman WILLIAM M. BOYLE, JR., and his Republican counterpart, GUY G. GABRIELSON denied the allegations. Boyle resigned his post in October giving ill health as a reason. Despite pressure from GOP members of Congress, Gabrielson remained in office. The subcommittee's January 1952 report sharply rebuked Boyle and, with greater restraint, criticized Gabrielson. It cleared the two of any illegal activity but cautioned officials of major political parties to avoid "the appearance of wrongdoing."

During his tenure as chairman, Hoey's panel also exposed less publicized instances of official corruption. In April 1951 the unit uncovered evidence that pro-Truman Democrats in Mississippi were selling postal jobs. In a unanimous report in June, the subcommittee blamed the Democratic National Committee for "the vicious job-selling racket." The Post Office dismissed over 50 accused employees. In February and March 1952 the Hoey unit investigated the alleged illegal sale of war surplus tankers. A group of prominent Americans, headed by former representative Joseph E. Casey (D-Mass.), had

leased or sold oil tankers to foreign concerns. NEWBOLD MORRIS, chosen by Truman to direct a cleanup of government corruption, was involved in the high-profit scheme. Because of the subcommittee's work, the government later reclaimed more than 40 surplus ships ruled to have been illegally sold or chartered.

Hoey lost his chairmanship to Senator JOSEPH R. MCCARTHY (R-Wisc.) when the Republicans gained control of the Senate in 1953. He died of a stroke at the age of 76 on May 12, 1954 in Washington, D.C.

—JF

Hoffman, Clare E(ugene)
(1875–1967) *member of the House of Representatives*

Clare E. Hoffman, the descendant of early Pennsylvania Dutch settlers, was born on September 10, 1875, in Vicksburg, Pennsylvania. He grew up on a farm near Constantine, Michigan. Hoffman received his LL.B. from Northwestern University in 1895, but he was not old enough to be admitted to the Michigan bar. So he went to Valparaiso University to take courses in business, and he also practiced law in Indiana. He finally won admittance to the Michigan bar in 1896. His political career began in 1906 when he was elected district attorney for Allegan, Michigan. He served as Republican chairman for Allegan County for several decades. Elected to the U.S. House of Representatives in 1934, Hoffman served 14 consecutive term in Congress.

A man of strong opinions, Hoffman, according to the *New York Times*, "never stood in the middle on any subject. . . . He rarely changed an opinion or a goal." He was known for his vociferous isolationism and opposition to social reform. During the Roosevelt administration he opposed all New Deal programs for city workers, championing the cause of the farmers against the unions and big-city bosses. He voted against the Social Security Act, both Agriculture Adjustment Acts, the Wagner Act, and government subsidized housing. He urged that the best route to economic recovery was to free private initiative and enterprise from a burdensome federal government.

Hoffman also opposed Roosevelt's prewar foreign policy, voting against lend-lease, the 1941 Selective Service Act, and most military spending. He supported defense spending during World War

II, but he was interested in using the war as a rationale to end the New Deal. During the war he was unjustly accused of being pro-fascist because of his and American fascists' prewar opposition to FDR's interventionist diplomacy. After the war he maintained his noninterventionist attitude, voting against aid to Greece and Turkey (as espoused in the Truman Doctrine), the Marshall Plan, and universal military training. During a debate on emergency relief aid to Greece, Italy, Poland, Hungary, and Austria, Hoffman said that "we should be paying more attention to our domestic business." He further stated, "The next thing, United States youths will be sent abroad to settle these troubles in Greece, the Balkans and China."

Hoffman often clashed with JOHN L. LEWIS, president of the United Mine Workers Union, and in 1940 introduced legislation to outlaw strikes in the defense industries and exempt defense workers from the compulsory payment of union dues. Another Hoffman labor bill, his 1947 measure to repeal the Wagner Act, called for outlawing the closed shop, "slowdowns," picketing, union dues deductions from wages, and various types of strikes. He voted for the Taft-Hartley Act that year. Organized labor spent much money during political campaigns attempting to unseat what it termed this "radical anti-labor congressman." The Detroit News claimed that Hoffman was "Enemy No. 1" to unionists from 1937 to 1947.

Hoffman opposed civil rights legislation. He fought Truman's attempts to set up a Fair Employment Practices Commission, eliminate the poll tax, and pass a federal antilynching law, saying these were state matters.

During the 80th Congress Hoffman served as chairman of the House Committee on Expenditures in the Executive Departments, participating in an investigation of surplus war property disposal, a study of the State Department, and a probe of the removal of records by outgoing government officials. Always a prominent opponent of Truman administration measures, Hoffman criticized a 1949 government reorganization plan which President Harry S Truman ordered effective within 60 days if both houses of Congress did not agree to reject it. Believing that the president had usurped the powers of the legislative branch, he introduced a measure, subsequently defeated, that would have required approval of both houses for the projected reorganization.

In an attempt to muzzle criticism of himself and other members of Congress, in 1947 Hoffman initiated an investigation of files on members kept by the Civil Service Commission. Hoffman exacted the commissioners' promise to destroy the files, but President Truman upheld the commission's refusal to permit members of Congress access to them. Hoffman also vehemently opposed the way newspapers editorialized on political candidates. During a 1952 campaign expenditures committee investigation he suggested that Congress limit the "donation" of editorial space to candidates the same way it limited newspapers' donation of money to candidates. However, it failed to win congressional support. Congress also rejected Hoffman's attempt to penalize newspaper reporters for divulging confidential information given to congressional panels. Hoffman also backed the efforts of Senator JOSEPH R. MCCARTHY (R-Wisc.) to root Communists out of government.

Throughout his career Hoffman continued to win reelection by increasing pluralities. He retired in 1962 after having suffered a series of strokes and died in his hometown of Allegan, Michigan, on November 4, 1967. (See The Eisenhower Years Volume)

—DAE

Hoffman, Paul G(ray)
(1891–1967) administrator, European Cooperation Administration

Paul G. Hoffman was born on April 26, 1891, in Chicago, Illinois. He spent two years at the University of Chicago before becoming an automobile salesman for Studebaker Company. He was extremely successful and in 1925 was made vice president in charge of sales and a member of the board of directors. By 1935 he was a millionaire and had risen to the presidency of Studebaker. Hoffman stressed Studebaker's good relations with the labor union to argue that the "Friendliest Factory" produced superior cars than other auto companies where workers were treated as automatons. He remained president until 1948. In the 1940s he coordinated that company's wartime production of military trucks and aircraft engines, which by the end of World War II amounted to 200,000 trucks and 64,000 engines.

In 1948 Congress created the Economic Cooperation Administration (ECA) to oversee the Marshall Plan for the economic revitalization of war-torn Europe. Senator ARTHUR H. VANDENBURG (R-Mich.), the leading Republican internationalist, actively campaigned for Hoffman's appointment as administrator of the ECA. Hoffman was considered a traditional Republican businessman and was thus acceptable to conservative forces in Congress. He was reluctant to accept the post, but Truman forced his hand by publicly announcing the appointment on April 5, 1948. Hoffman's nomination was confirmed April 7 by voice vote.

Hoffman was perfect for the job. As administrator, Hoffman recruited a top-rate staff to run the ECA honestly and efficiently and stressed the importance of returning Europe to prosperity through private business channels. He also believed that investment in European industries was a key step in the rebuilding of the Continent's economy. He backed a U.S. policy of financing only the very basic capital investments that the countries involved could not afford. He did an excellent job of presenting a case for aid. In Senate hearings on the European Recovery Program in 1949, Hoffman outlined his philosophy. He explained that the ECA was trying to distribute Marshall Plan goods through regular commercial means. He assured the Senate that "every person who has gotten one blessed thing, practically speaking, through ECA financing, has paid for it through local currency." He stressed that he was not running a "giveaway" program. As an example of his emphasis on use of the private sector, Hoffman was able to tell the Senate Foreign Relations Committee near the end of the ECA's first year that 84 percent of ECA procurement was through private channels of trade. In 1950 he explained to Congress that the United States had an informal agreement with the Marshall Plan countries that American aid would end if the standard of living in those countries rose above 1938 levels. He pleaded with Congress and taxpayers not to be afraid of a revival of European business competitors and to oppose attempts by special interests to use the European Recovery Plan to obtain advantages in trading.

Hoffman fought a continuing battle against attempts by southern Democrats and conservative Republicans to cut the program. Hoffman explained to Congress in February 1949 that it was "impossible" to cut the second year European Recovery Program budget of $5.58 billion. Later he threatened to resign as ECA head if Congress made any budget cuts. As part of his battle over continuing American aid to Europe, Hoffman found himself reassuring both Congress and the American public

that the program would end on schedule in June 1952. At one point he announced that the program would cost $4 billion less than the original $17 billion estimated.

Hoffman also defended the theory behind the Marshall Plan. He called the ECA, "the first line of defense for Western civilization." In 1950 he explained to a group of college presidents: "Communists have fought us with riots, strikes, terror and sabotage. We've used food, tools, and hope and just beaten the hell out of them." Hoffman tried to avoid becoming involved in political questions in Europe, preferring to consider the Marshall Plan as a strictly economic program. He was willing, however, to offer advice to the European nations involved. In October 1949 he told a group of officials from European nations meeting in Paris that changes in the European economy were needed to assure continued progress. A supporter of the integration of the Western European economy, Hoffman called for the coordination of fiscal and monetary policies, and he attacked quotas and other trade restraints. He also convinced the Europeans to replace their separate national attempts at recovery with one based on cooperative relationships with one another and the ECA. The European Recovery Program never fully achieved economic integration, but it caused European nations to cooperate with one another to revive their economies. He resigned as ECA head in September 1950 to join the Ford Foundation. At the time, after having disbursed some $10 billion, Hoffman said the ECA should spend $8 to $14 billion more before ending on schedule in 1952.

During the early 1950s Hoffman became an outspoken opponent of Senator JOSEPH R. MCCARTHY'S (R-Wisc.) anticommunist crusade. In October 1951, in a speech in New York, he warned that too many Americans were "ready to pillory anyone who holds an unpopular view or supports an unpopular cause." He strongly defended former secretary of state GEORGE C. MARSHALL from McCarthy's attacks in 1952. Hoffman said that McCarthy had made "fantastically false" accusations about Marshall being linked to a mammoth procommunist conspiracy among U.S. foreign policymakers. He later joined in providing important behind-the-scenes help in the McCarthy censure drive in 1954.

An early supporter of DWIGHT D. EISENHOWER for president, Hoffman helped to capture the 1952

Republican nomination for the general. He actively campaigned in New Hampshire for Eisenhower and, after the general's stunning primary victory, Hoffman went to Europe to persuade Eisenhower to return to the United States and campaign.

Hoffman left Studebaker in 1956 to become a member of the U.S. delegation to the United Nations. Despite strong opposition from McCarthy and other conservative Republican senators, Hoffman won confirmation. He continued to be active in UN affairs during the next two decades. Hoffman was awarded the Medal of Freedom by President RICHARD M. NIXON in 1973. He died in New York City on October 8, 1974. (See *The Eisenhower Years* Volume)

—JF

Hoover, Herbert C(lark)

(1874–1964) *chairman, Committee for the Organization of the Executive Branch*

Herbert C. Hoover was born on August 10, 1874, in West Branch, Iowa. Orphaned at the age of nine, he spent the rest of his childhood at the home of various Quaker relatives, first in Iowa and then in Oregon. He was admitted to Stanford University in 1891, the year it opened, and graduated four years later in 1894 with an A.B. in geology. He then joined the London-based mining firm of Bewick, Moering, and Company. For the next 20 years he devoted himself to business, rising to partner before resigning in 1908 to form his own mine consulting firm. By 1914 his work in Australia, China, and Russia, among other places, had made him a millionaire. Hoover directed the American Relief Committee and the Commission for the Relief of Belgium during World War I. In 1917 Woodrow Wilson made him the chairman of the Food Administration Board, where he supervised voluntary food rationing and conservation efforts through the country.

During the immediate postwar period Hoover was the director of the American Relief Administration, which helped avert famine in Europe. His work gained him an unrivaled reputation as a humanitarian. From 1921 to 1928 Hoover served as secretary of commerce. As secretary, he was never an advocate of the unbridled capitalism of laissez-faire doctrine. He pushed regulation of the new aviation and radio industries and assisted in the development of sophisticated theories on the business cycle. He sought to promote a voluntary ratio-

nalization of the American economy that would promote the broadest possible distribution of the benefits of prosperity. In 1928 Hoover was elected president by the largest popular margin to that date.

Hoover had the misfortune of becoming president just prior to the onset of the Great Depression. He took unprecedented action to reverse the economic decline that began after the stock market crash of 1929. He adopted a stimulatory federal budget policy in the 1930–31 fiscal year. He established the Reconstruction Finance Administration to make loans to threatened companies, and he urged the Federal Reserve Board to adopt an easier money policy. But Hoover's concept of the limited role of the national government led him to refuse to permit federal money to be used to finance state and local relief efforts. With little success he attempted to promote voluntary action on the part of business to halt the impact of the decline. Hoover lacked the political acumen and charismatic personality to lead the nation through a great crisis. His cold manner and his frequent assurances of a return to prosperity ultimately destroyed his image as a great humanitarian. For the next generation he was to serve as the personification of heartless, reactionary government ignoring the calls of the desperate. Hoover was turned out of office in 1932.

During the next 12 years he remained out of government, half-heartedly making himself available for the presidential nomination in 1936 and in 1940. Hoover became a severe critic of the New Deal. He doubted the effectiveness of its programs in reversing the depression, insisting later that it was World War II and not the Roosevelt administration that returned the nation to prosperity. Hoover was alarmed by the emerging welfare state and the growth of government, which he maintained threatened personal freedom and restricted the scope of individual initiative. He opposed U.S. involvement in World War II on the grounds that it was out of the American sphere of interest.

Harry S Truman ended Hoover's exclusion from government. In May 1945 Truman met with Hoover to discuss famine relief. Hoover took the opportunity to urge the conclusion of an immediate peace in the Far East without the participation of the Soviet Union in the war against Japan. Hoover wanted to prevent the Soviets from winning a stronger position in the region. In a follow-up memorandum to Secretary of War HENRY L. STIMSON, who had been his secretary of state, he urged that the United States assure the Japanese that it would retain the emperor "who was the spiritual head of the nation." This assurance, he believed, would shorten the war. Truman ignored his advice. Hoover also recommended accepting a Soviet sphere of influence in Eastern Europe so as to have better relations with the Soviets. Truman ignored this suggestion, too.

During early 1946 Truman asked Hoover to draft a program for alleviating world famine. In March he sent Hoover abroad to try to better balance the world's supply and demand for food. The former president traveled 50,000 miles over the next four months and, with his staff of 38 volunteers, worked to improve the distribution of food and arrange loans. As a result, the gap between supply available for consumption and demand was reduced from 11 million tons to 6 million.

In 1947 Truman asked Hoover to become chairman of the Commission on the Organization of the Executive Branch. Hoover worked on the project for the next two years. His report, issued in February 1949, recommended a more efficient, vertical organization of the executive branch. The commission attempted to group all related functions within a single agency. This rationalization, in keeping with Hoover's concepts of government, served to make government more accountable to the Congress and the people for the effectiveness of its performance without increasing the prerogatives of the president. The panel also supported increases in the powers of the various departmental secretaries and, in particular, those of the secretary of defense. It thus endorsed efforts underway at this point to strengthen what had been little more than a ceremonial office since its creation in 1947. In the end the panel, which came to be known as the Hoover Commission, made 273 recommendations, of which 196, by Hoover's count, were adopted.

Despite Truman's cordial relationship with Hoover, the president used Hoover as a whipping boy in the 1948 presidential campaign. Hoover, for his part, was critical of the administration's foreign policy. He urged the economic regeneration of Germany so that it would not be an economic drain on the United States and could take a place among the "major friends of Western civilization." Hoover opposed U.S. attempts to rehabilitate the economy of large segments of the world, a move that he felt was beyond America's capacities and that would make the corporate and democratic institutions of

the United States dependent on foreign expansion. For these reasons he became a critic of the Marshall Plan. He urged limiting its scope and duration and bringing in other economically healthy nations— Canada, Argentina, and Brazil—to share the burden. If combined with a program of conservation at home, he believed, this variant of the Marshall Plan would allow extension of aid to China, Germany, Korea, Japan, Greece, and Turkey as well as the 16 countries not included in the original proposal. While Congress adopted a number of his technical suggestions, it, like the administration, ignored his basic proposal.

Hoover continued to urge a clear definition of the boundaries of American territorial interests, which he asserted to be Britain in the West and Japan, Taiwan, and the Philippines in the East. He opposed the stationing of U.S. troops abroad and the creation of NATO. By the end of 1950 he believed that the American military aid program should be reevaluated. The North Atlantic Treaty Organization, he noted, had been approved on the promise that there would be no American ground troops in Europe. While the administration, in fact, had refrained from a clear commitment against stationing troops in Europe, it had attempted to minimize speculation on the possibility of a permanent garrison abroad.

Although he viewed Asia as more important than Europe, Hoover was critical of America's conduct of the Korean War. He opposed General DOUGLAS MACARTHUR's determination to drive the North Koreans back to China, believing that UN troops should pursue the enemy no further than the 38th parallel. Hoover disliked Sygman Rhee, whom he called a "menace." He criticized the ideological overtones the administration had given the war: he had never approved of making wars into crusades.

Hoover's reservations about the Korean War caused him to reconsider the support he had given to the Truman Doctrine at the time of the crisis in Greece and Turkey. He came to view its open-ended commitment as impractical. Security and internationalism were not, he insisted, of a piece with unlimited foreign expansion and military intervention. "Indeed, they are opposite," he noted in an address in December 1950. Strict limits to intervention, he maintained "would avoid rash involvement of our military forces in hopeless campaigns." He argued that there should be a U.S. program to defend the Western Hemisphere, "this final Gibraltar of Freedom" as he called it. Hoover was generally labeled an isolationist by his contemporary critics, and, for the most part, found himself ignored. But as historian Joan Hoff has noted Hoover was neither a strident anticommunist cold warrior nor an isolationist, as he supported efforts to avoid war and to withdraw from military conflicts. Hoover had great faith that American capitalism could easily beat communism without a resort to arms. Also, Hoover did not join the hunt for Communists after World War II, or think they would seize control of the State Department, but he believed the problem was to be found in the more tolerant attitude in government toward communism that he thought had been brought about by the New Deal.

The election of Dwight D. Eisenhower, the first Republican president since Hoover, increased the former president's national stature. Although Hoover had supported Senator ROBERT A. TAFT (R-Ohio) in the preconvention period and was to disagree with Eisenhower on a variety of policy issues, the new president and the former president became friends. From 1953 to 1955 Hoover conducted a second study into the organization of the executive branch, this time reviewing policy as well as structure. Hoover played the role of elder statesman almost to his death. He was well received at the 1956 and 1960 Republican National Conventions while remaining the rhetorical target of Democratic meetings. In 1959 a Gallup poll found him ninth among most admired Americans. John F. Kennedy, after becoming president, continued the practice of presidential consultations with Hoover. "You will discover," the former president wrote Richard Nixon following the 1960 election, "that elder statesmen are little regarded . . . until they're over 80 years of age—and thus harmless." Hoover died on October 20, 1964, in his apartment at the Waldorf-Astoria Towers in New York City. (See *The Eisenhower Years* Volume)

—CSJ

Hoover, J(ohn) Edgar
(1895–1972) *director, Federal Bureau of Investigation*
The son of a minor official in the Commerce Department, J. Edgar Hoover was born on January 1, 1895, in Washington, D.C. He was raised and educated in the nation's capital. To support himself through National University Law School (later

George Washington University Law School), Hoover worked days as an indexer for the Library of Congress until he earned his degree in 1916. That year he joined the Justice Department as a clerk. In 1919 he became assistant to Attorney General A. Mitchell Palmer. Hoover coordinated the roundup, interrogation, and deportation of thousands of alleged anarchists and Communists during the Red Scare of 1919–20. In 1921 he was appointed assistant director of the department's Bureau of Investigation. (The name was changed in 1935 to the Federal Bureau of Investigation).

Attorney General HARLAN FISKE STONE, based on the recommendations by the law enforcement community and civil libertarians, appointed Hoover the bureau's director in 1924. Impressed by the young man's integrity, Stone hoped he would be the individual to clean up the scandal-ridden, politicized agency. Hoover accepted the position on the condition that he could recruit agents based on the merit system. Stone gladly agreed to his terms. Hoover then revolutionized the bureau by hiring honest, educated, disciplined law enforcement officers. He modernized the agency by establishing a national fingerprint file in 1925, a major crime laboratory in 1932, and a sophisticated training school for his personnel and local police in 1935.

With the increase in crime during the depression and the growing fear of domestic subversion, the bureau's powers were expanded in the 1930s. Originally considered only an investigatory body with a small staff and a meager budget, the FBI was gradually given the authority to solve major interstate crimes such as bank robbery, extortion, and kidnapping. Its agents were permitted to make arrests and carry firearms. Hoover and his "G-men," as the agents were called, became folk heroes. They made spectacular headlines in apprehending such notorious "public enemies" as John Dillinger, "Baby Face" Nelson, "Ma and Pa" Barker, and "Pretty Boy" Floyd.

In 1936 President Franklin D. Roosevelt gave Hoover the authority to investigate espionage and sabotage. He stretched the directive to monitor the activities of the nation's right and left. Hoover also watched Roosevelt's political enemies, including Wendell Willkie, John L. Lewis, and prominent isolationists such as Charles Lindbergh and Senator Burton Wheeler (D-Mont.). Agents even followed the president's wife and Vice President HENRY WALLACE, both of whom had ties to the left. Following

President Truman being greeted by FBI director J. Edgar Hoover (left) and Attorney General J. Howard McGrath Ashe at the Justice Department, 1950 *(CORBIS)*

Pearl Harbor the president permitted the bureau to expand its surveillance of the right, the left, labor unions, civil rights groups, liberal organizations, and the Communist Party, all of which he and Hoover believed could undermine the war effort. Based on authority from the president, the Attorney General, and the Congress, the FBI was permitted to engage in wiretapping that involved national security. The agency also kept a list of American Communists and fascists for possible arrest and detention. Hoover had the additional responsibility of checking the loyalty of federal employees. However, he expanded these operations beyond the president's directives.

In 1940 Hoover promised that the domestic intelligence structure of the bureau would be "discounted or materially curtailed" when the national emergency ended. Hoover failed to keep his pledge as the cold war began in late 1945 and early 1946.

Athan G. Theoharis and John Stuart Cox have noted Hoover employed anticommunism and the backing of allies in the media and congressional conservatives to prevent any rollback of the bureau's domestic intelligence capability. The bureau viewed the American Communists and their sympathizers as tools of the Soviet Union. In Hoover's eyes they were part of a sophisticated espionage ring that had already penetrated the sensitive areas of American government.

During the early cold war the FBI became involved in several prominent investigations of domestic subversion. Through surveillance and the use of double agents and former Communists such as ELIZABETH BENTLEY and WHITTAKER CHAMBERS, it found evidence pointing to subversives in high government office. In 1945 it arrested Foreign Service officer JOHN S. SERVICE for handing secret documents over to a left-wing journal, and investigated HARRY DEXTER WHITE, whom Hoover characterized as the leading Communist in government. Over the next few years the FBI played important roles in investigations of WILLIAM W. REMINGTON and ALGER HISS. Some, such as Service, were cleared because the FBI had failed to prove its case and had infringed on their rights. However, others, such as Hiss and Remington, were eventually convicted of perjury for denying they were Communists. Hoover's FBI dredged up the evidence to put behind bars under the Smith Act the top leaders of the Communist Party USA in the court case *Dennis v. U.S.* Hoover's bureau also exposed the atomic spy ring of Klaus Fuchs (which the director dubbed "the Crime of the Century"), which led to the conviction and execution of Julius and Ethel Rosenberg. Hoover called for clemency for Ethel, having only wanted to use her arrest to obtain the truth from Julius, but the judge sentenced both to death. Hoover did not reveal to the White House the Venona decryptions on Soviet messages back to Moscow regarding Soviet spying in the United States.

The bureau's continued revelations of possible subversion convinced Truman that the government needed an expanded loyalty program for federal employees. Hoover's public campaign to educate the American people about the Communist Party's goal to infiltrate the government also increased the demand for improved anti-espionage measures, as did the Republican's use of the loyalty issue in the 1946 campaign. On November 25, 1946, Truman established the Temporary Commission on Employee Loyalty to review the existing program. Hoover testified before it, calling for a tougher program. Based on his recommendations, the administration instituted a new program that permitted the official in question the right to counsel in front of the loyalty board but protected the confidentiality of his accusers. If found disloyal by his department's board, the individual had the right to appeal to the Civil Service Commission's Loyalty Review Board.

Truman's order left unclear who would do the investigating. Both the Civil Service Commission and Hoover claimed the right. Truman feared that giving the task to the FBI would enhance its power to dangerous levels. Yet the experience of the FBI and the public and the congressional acclaim Hoover enjoyed, convinced Truman that for political reasons he had to permit Hoover to do the investigating. Hoover's agents thus crisscrossed the country to

check on the loyalty of federal officials. Often, to determine whether the subject could be trusted, they asked friends and relatives what he read, what organizations he belonged to, and whether he had voted for Henry Wallace in 1948. The agents then compared the names of the groups to which the individual had belonged with those on the Attorney General's list of subversive organizations (which the FBI had put together). Years later Hoover claimed five million Americans had been checked with 560 removed or denied employment. Throughout the period Hoover always pointed to the small number of Americans forced to leave government as evidence that the agency did not engage in a witch-hunt.

Historian and social critic Bernard DeVoto mocked the manner in which the FBI undertook the loyalty check and surveillance in his October 1949 *Harper's* magazine column. He cited an exaggerated list of questions agents asked and then charged that the Bureau engaged in Gestapo tactics that forced Americans to inform on their families and neighbors. In spite of such liberal attacks, Hoover and the FBI ranked high in American public opinion.

During the Truman era J. Edgar Hoover served as the self-proclaimed government expert on the Communist menace. In numerous speeches and articles (all ghost-written) Hoover outlined the Communist threat to the nation. The party, he maintained, stood determined to infiltrate all expressions of American life. Those who sought to protect the civil liberties of the Communists and their allies, Hoover asserted, were dupes of the party who failed to realize its deceitful practices. He warned Americans to resist Communist propaganda that preached democracy, free speech, and economic reform, believing it a smokescreen for the party's goal of enlisting more Americans. Through a revolution, Hoover predicted, the party would deliver the American people to Stalin, whom he called "The Red Hitler." The FBI encouraged Americans to be on guard for Communists and to expose their operations. Hoover distrusted the attempts of congressional committees and patriotic organizations to undertake this task. Their amateurism, he believed, could undermine the FBI's work. Yet, he established relationships with the House Un-American Activities Committee, which he often fed secret information to aid its work. The committee, in Hoover's view, would expose Communists and their allies in such places as universities and unions while the FBI put together legal charges against them and Russian spies. (Curiously, HUAC member RICHARD M. NIXON (R-Calif.) took the lead in the investigation of Alger Hiss, much to the chagrin of Hoover.)

In 1975 the Church Committee revealed that during the Truman administration the FBI had engaged in covert activities for the political benefit of the administration. The bureau had bugged the telephones of Thomas Corcoran, a prominent New Dealer whose ties to liberals angered Truman. When HAROLD L. ICKES angrily left the administration because he felt it had moved to the right, the White House asked the FBI if it had any damaging information on him in its file. The Church Committee disclosed that Truman and his aides received from Hoover reports labeled "personal and confidential" containing such information as "the negotiating position of a non-Communist labor union; the activities of a former Roosevelt aide who had tried to influence Truman administration appointments; and, reports that a former assistant to the Attorney General had criticized the government's internal security program." In the 1948 presidential election, FBI agents infiltrated Wallace's campaign.

During the Eisenhower era Hoover continued his relentless campaign to ferret out Communists in American life. The administration liberalized his authority to wiretap and investigate government officials. Although Senator JOSEPH R. MCCARTHY (R-Wisc.) praised Hoover as a patriotic American, Hoover remained aloof from the Republican's crusade. As he did with Roosevelt and Truman, Hoover advised DWIGHT D. EISENHOWER, John F. Kennedy, Lyndon B. Johnson, and Richard Nixon on the activities of individuals and organizations he deemed a threat to American security. Hoover considered the civil rights and the antiwar movements to be Communist inspired. His agents and informants kept him and the administration informed of their activities. Through projects such as COINTELPRO, FBI agents, whose conduct Hoover sanctioned, sought to disrupt the activities of the Communist Party and the more extreme expressions of the civil rights and the antiwar organizations. J. Edgar Hoover died on May 2, 1972, in Washington, D.C., four years before the government released evidence of the agency's extralegal activities. (See *The Eisenhower Years, The Kennedy Years, The Johnson Years, The Nixon/Ford Years* Volumes)

—JB

Hopkins, Harry L(loyd)
(1890–1946) *special adviser to the president*

Harry L. Hopkins was born on August 17, 1890. After graduating from Grinnell College in 1922, Hopkins began a career as a social worker. In 1931 New York governor Franklin D. Roosevelt appointed him head of the state's Temporary Emergency Relief Administration. When Roosevelt became president, Hopkins became administrator of the Federal Relief Administration, which, over a five-year period, distributed $8 to $10 billion. He was active in forming the Works Projects Administration and was one of its most vigorous defenders. In 1938 he became secretary of commerce. Hopkins was the closest member of the administration to the president and coordinate his drive for an unprecedented third term in 1940. Hopkins resigned late that year because of ill health. In 1941 he returned to government as lend-lease administrator and became a member of the so-called Little War Cabinet. As a special assistant to the president, he accompanied Roosevelt to all major wartime conferences.

After Truman became president in 1945, he asked Hopkins to undertake a mission to Moscow to help salvage a crumbling wartime alliance, torn by Soviet occupation of Eastern Europe and intransigence on issues regarding the United Nations. Truman, according to Hopkins's biographer, George McJimsey, sent him to Moscow as a sign of a continued desire to cooperate with the Soviets. In his meeting in Moscow in late May, Hopkins demanded that Stalin live up to the Yalta accords promising the inclusion of democratic elements in the Polish government and eventual free elections in that nation. He tried to assure the Soviet leader, who was concerned with having friendly countries on Russia's vulnerable western border, that the United States wanted a government that was both desired by the Polish people and acceptable to the USSR. Stalin did not agree to all of Hopkins's requests, but he did consent to the inclusion of some pro-Western ministers in the provisional Polish government.

The rest of the meeting went smoothly. Stalin promised to honor the Yalta agreements on annexation of Chinese territory when his country entered the war against Japan. Both sides endorsed the agenda for the upcoming Potsdam Conference. The most significant result of the meeting was Stalin's agreement that the future United Nations Security

Council could discuss any issue brought to its attention. Originally the Soviets had sought to enlarge the veto of the council to block even the consideration of an issue.

Following his return from Moscow, Hopkins resigned from the government because of poor health. He then became chairman of the coat and suit industry based in New York City, where he helped mediate disputes between management and labor. Hopkins died there on January 29, 1946.

—JB

Humphrey, Hubert H(oratio)
(1911–1978) *mayor, member of the Senate*
Born on May 27, 1911, in Wallace, South Dakota, Hubert H. Humphrey was the son of a pharmacist who had migrated from Minnesota to the South Dakota prairie town of Wallace. He was born in a room above the family drugstore in Wallace. His father, an active Democrat in a solidly Republican region, taught him to revere William Jennings Bryan and Woodrow Wilson. Humphrey entered the University of Minnesota in 1929 but was forced to withdraw because of financial hardship in his sophomore year and return to South Dakota to help out with his father's business. Six years later Humphrey resumed his studies, graduating in 1939. The following year he obtained an M.A. in political science from Louisiana State University, where he subsequently taught. Humphrey then returned to Minnesota and worked for the Works Progress Administration and other New Deal agencies.

Encouraged by a group of his former classmates and professors from the University of Minnesota, Humphrey became active in Democratic politics in the early 1940s. He and his supporters sought to reinvigorate Minnesota's relatively weak and ineffective Democratic organization. The party, based primarily among Irish Catholics in St. Paul and Duluth, had long been overshadowed by the larger and more left-wing Farmer-Labor Party. Humphrey's own pursuit of political office began in April 1943, when he bumped into George Phillips of the Minneapolis Central Labor Union and George Murk, president of the Musicians Union. The question arose of who ought to run for mayor, and Humphrey was definitely interested. That year he waged a vigorous but unsuccessful campaign for mayor. During the race he garnered important backing from sections of the city's traditionally Republican business

interests and from some labor unions. In the following year he helped effect a merger of the Farmer-Labor and Democratic parties and served as the state campaign manager for the national Roosevelt-Truman ticket.

Humphrey again entered the Minneapolis mayoral race in 1945. Claiming that crime syndicates had taken over the city (gangland-style murders were then a frequent occurrence in Minneapolis, and many municipal officials were thought to be corrupt), Humphrey won election on the basis of an antivice campaign. Humphrey's powers as mayor were quite limited: he could appoint the police chief and use the bully pulpit to try to sway the public and the city council toward his stance on issues. Upon assuming office he appointed an FBI-trained police chief and immediately began cracking down on corruption. Using citizens' committees to make recommendations on housing, veterans' affairs, and law enforcement, the 34-year-old mayor introduced numerous reforms in the city's administration. He also launched a series of innovative, attention-getting projects, including massive construction of prefabricated houses for returning GIs. In 1947 the city council enacted a fair employment practices ordinance, the first legislation of its kind in the United States. The program's antidiscrimination provisions were overseen by a commission and enforced by fines and jail terms for violations. Humphrey's reelection in 1947 (by the largest vote margin in the city's history) was considered a major defeat for former Minnesota governor HAROLD E. STASSEN, who had thrown the full weight of his Republican organization behind Humphrey's opponent.

At the same time Humphrey began to emerge as a prominent spokesman for an aggressively anticommunist liberalism, both in Minnesota and on the national scene. In January 1947, shortly after the Communist-influenced Progressive Citizens of America was organized to promote HENRY A. WALLACE's presidential candidacy, Humphrey joined a group of former New Deal figures and other liberals in founding the Americans for Democratic Action (ADA). With ADA assistance he then launched an intense campaign on the state level to wrest control of the Democratic–Farmer-Labor Party from former governor ELMER A. BENSON and his supporters, who were closely tied to a small, but influential Communist group. As mayor, Humphrey had earlier managed to obtain copies of FBI files identifying most of the Communists in Minnesota; these were used to prepare lists of persons whom his lieutenants endeavored to exclude, often by force, from party meetings in Minneapolis. Beginning in 1947, however, the Benson faction moved openly to put Wallace on the state ballot under the Democratic–Farmer–Labor line and force Truman to run as a third-party candidate. Branding the Wallace campaign a Communist-inspired maneuver, Humphrey mobilized his forces early in 1948 to take statewide control of the party. Wallaceites were barred from precinct caucuses and called upon to resign from county posts. Where these efforts failed, Humphrey partisans simply set up their own rump organizations. By the time of the state convention in June, the Benson faction had been driven from all positions of influence and forced to organize as a separate party. Humphrey was nominated as the Democratic–Farmer–Labor candidate for the U.S. Senate, and several of his aides became party leaders. These included Eugene McCarthy, a future senator and Orville Freeman, later three-term governor of the state and secretary of agriculture.

Humphrey arrived at the Democratic National Convention in July 1948 as leader of the Minnesota delegation and a prominent member of the ADA caucus. At first he backed liberal efforts to swing the presidential nomination to DWIGHT D. EISENHOWER or WILLIAM O. DOUGLAS instead of Truman. However, after the dump-Truman drive collapsed, he joined the ADA's push for a stronger civil rights plank in the party platform. As a member of the platform committee, Humphrey initially agreed to support the administration-sponsored majority report, which urged adoption of a moderate plank similar to the one contained in the 1944 platform. At the urging of the Congress of Industrial Organizations, however, ADA leaders JOSEPH L. RAUH, JR., and Andrew Biemiller drew up a minority report demanding congressional action on fair employment practices, mob violence, and equality in political participation and military service. After a number of powerful northern bosses, including Ed Flynn of the Bronx, JACOB ARVEY of Chicago, and FRANK HAGUE of New Jersey, pledged their support for a strong civil rights statement, the ADA bloc decided to initiate a floor fight. Humphrey thought it was the right thing to do, but it could have split the party disastrously and ruined his career. Many people advised him not to put the minority report up for a vote for fear of dividing the party. But his father,

Hubert Humphrey, Sr., head of the South Dakota delegation, told him to follow his conscience, regardless of the political cost. Speaking for the minority report on July 14, Humphrey delivered a stirring oration that electrified the convention and won him instant national prominence. Arguing that the United States "must be in a morally sound position" to act as "the leader of the free world," he proclaimed, "the time has arrived for the Democratic Party to get out of the shadow of states' rights and walk forthrightly into the bright sunshine of human rights." Following Humphrey's speech the minority report passed by 70 votes and was endorsed by Truman. This prompted a number of southern delegates to bolt the convention and organize the States' Rights Party, which ran South Carolina governor J. STROM THURMOND as the Dixiecrat candidate for the presidency. Many observers have argued that the civil rights plank that Humphrey assisted in getting passed helped the Democrats more than it hurt, because it gave them an issue to rally around and aroused the support of minorities and intellectuals.

Humphrey biographer Charles Lloyd Garrettson III has noted the irony in Humphrey's actions in 1948. His Senate candidacy was made possible through his opposition to the radicals in the Democratic–Farmer–Labor Party. But Humphrey would then make that candidacy successful through the most radical act in his career: his 1948 speech to the Democratic National Convention calling for a stronger civil rights plank. In November 1948 Humphrey routed incumbent Republican senator JOSEPH H. BALL with 60 percent of the vote, becoming the first popularly elected Democratic senator in Minnesota history. He quickly moved into the vanguard of the Senate's liberal minority, promoting a wide variety of social welfare, civil rights, tax reform, aid to education, and pro-labor legislation. The first bill he introduced, in 1949, was a proposal to establish medical care for the aged, financed through the Social Security system—a principle enacted into law 16 years later as medicare.

Regarded by powerful Senate conservatives as a brash, abrasive, and overly voluble crusader, Humphrey's effectiveness was limited at first. Shortly after taking office, Humphrey upset powerful southern senators when he took an African-American staffer, Cyril King, to eat in the Senate dining room. The headwaiter, also black, said he could not let King accompany the senator into the dining room. After Humphrey angrily insisted upon it, King was let in. His exclusion from the Senate's inner circles became complete when, in February 1950, he delivered an attack on the Joint Committee on Nonessential Federal Expenditures, the favorite project of Virginia senator HARRY F. BYRD, one of the most powerful members of the Senate. Even northern liberals walked out of the chamber during his speech, which was considered a shocking breach of Senate etiquette. Senator RICHARD B. RUSSELL (D-Ga.), leader of the Senate southern bloc and a fierce opponent of civil rights, once made derogatory comments about Humphrey within earshot of the Minnesotan. Humphrey believed in personal regard, no matter what ideological differences there might be between him and other senators. This shunning hurt him; he wanted to be needed and to be liked. Stung by this treatment, Humphrey, according to one of his aides, became "obsessed" with a desire to "master the Senate process" in order to increase his effectiveness. During the early 1950s, as a result, he gradually eased his way into the councils of his more conservative colleagues, working closely with Democratic leader Senator LYNDON B. JOHNSON (D-Tex.), who, in turn, used Humphrey as his liaison with labor, intellectuals, and northern liberals. Humphrey broke through the wall of isolation in August 1950. He and PAUL H. DOUGLAS (D-Ill.) took on the Finance Committee barons Chairman WALTER F. GEORGE (D-Ga.) and ranking minority member EUGENE D. MILLIKIN (R-Colo.) on the 1950 tax bill to fund the Korean War that the two had written. Humphrey thought it full of loopholes, studied the issue in-depth, and spoke out on the floor for quite some time in opposition. And although only one of his and Douglas's amendments passed, Humphrey, through his effort, won respect in the Senate, as George and Milliken walked over to him to congratulate him on a job well done. Humphrey came to see that idealism in and of itself would not produce results. Humphrey began to see the value of compromise. But one had to compromise responsibly, being neither too rigid nor too flexible, and combine that with hard work. According to Garrettson, he became an "*institutionalist*" and an "*incrementalist*," working inside the Senate step-by-step toward his goals. To the Minnesota senator, being a good politician and a liberal was not only possible—it was the best possible combination.

At the same time Humphrey began to loosen his ties to grass-roots liberal and civil rights organiza-

tions and draw closer to the political center. In 1949 he rejected pleas from the NAACP to support an amendment to the federal aid to education bill that would have denied funds to those states with segregated schools. The following year he resigned as national chairman of the ADA after its membership refused to allow the organization to become as closely linked to the Democratic Party as Humphrey and other Democratic office holders had wished.

Increasingly, after 1950, Humphrey disappointed his liberal admirers by defending the postponement of Fair Deal legislation, endorsing cuts in domestic spending, and refraining from criticizing the administration's failure to establish the promised Fair Employment Practices Commission. Moreover, as a strong proponent of loyalty-security programs, Humphrey occasionally went further than even the White House was willing to go. In 1950 he was one of the Senate's major backers of a proposal, sponsored by Senator HARLEY M. KILGORE (D-W.Va.), to empower the president to order the internment of suspected subversives during periods of national emergency. The Kilgore bill was first introduced as a substitute and then attached as an amendment to the McCarran Internal Security Act, which passed the Senate over Truman's veto in September of that year. In the atmosphere of McCarthyism, Humphrey reluctantly voted for the McCarran Act, which he thought too restrictive of civil liberties, but after Truman vetoed it decided to help uphold the veto, and assisted with a 32-hour filibuster, which ultimately failed. Humphrey fought to amend the McCarran-Walters Immigration Act. He and HERBERT H. LEHMAN (D-N.Y.) knew they had no chance to eliminate the national origin quotas, which tilted heavily in favor of Northern and Western Europe, even though they found those restrictions abhorrent. Instead, they wanted to pool unfilled quotas from undersubscribed countries to allow in more people from other countries with smaller quotas. Despite a hard fight the two lost on this issue, and McCarran-Walters was passed over Truman's veto.

In the 1952 presidential campaign, Humphrey worried that ADLAI E. STEVENSON was too ethereal and cold, as opposed to the grinning and waving Eisenhower, and he was disappointed by Ike's victory. During the Eisenhower administration Humphrey became a leading advocate of disarmament and economic aid to developing nations. After an unsuccessful try for the Democratic presidential nomination in 1960, he was selected as the party's majority whip in the Senate. Working with his characteristic exuberance to promote the Kennedy administration's legislative program, Humphrey reached the peak of his influence during the early 1960s, winning passage of proposals, such as the Peace corps and the Food for Peace program, which he had been advocating for years. He was chosen to be Lyndon Johnson's running mate in August 1964 and elected vice president in November. Humphrey was an enthusiastic defender of Johnson's domestic and foreign policies throughout the next four years. His unwavering endorsement of the administration's actions in Vietnam cost him much liberal support in his 1968 presidential campaign. Humphrey lost the election to RICHARD M. NIXON by a narrow margin. He returned to the Senate in 1971. Shortly afterward Humphrey developed cancer. He succumbed to the disease on January 13, 1978, in Waverly, Minnesota. (See *The Eisenhower Years, The Kennedy Years, The Johnson Years, The Nixon/Ford Years, The Carter Years* Volumes)

—TLH

Hunt, Lester C(allaway)

(1892–1954) *governor, member of the Senate*

Lester C. Hunt was born in Isabel, Illinois, on July 8, 1892. Raised in that state, he earned a degree in dentistry from St. Louis University in 1917. After service in the Army Dental Corps during World War I, he returned to practice in Lander, Wyoming, where he once had played professional baseball. Besides his dental practice Hunt plunged into civic affairs, becoming active in the American Legion, Masons, and Elks, serving as president of the local Chamber of Commerce and of the state Board of Dental Examiners. Elected to the state legislature in 1932, he thereafter served two terms as Democratic secretary of state from 1935 to 1943 and six years as governor from 1943 to 1949.

As governor, Hunt was a strong defender of states' rights and won national attention by his 1946 fight against a plan by the federal government to take over 221,000 acres of Wyoming land for a national park in Jackson Hole. Hunt was a liberal Democrat, and the conservative Republican legislature shot down most of his proposed legislation. In 1948 he took the unusual step of urging that grants-in-aid from Washington to the states be cut by 20 percent. That year Hunt announced his candidacy for the Senate. Supported by labor and small busi-

ness and campaigning on a platform calling for repeal of the Taft-Hartley Act and more reclamation projects, he crushed his Democratic opponent in the August primary and easily defeated the Republican incumbent, Edward V. Robertson, in November.

Assigned to the Armed Services and Commerce committees, the easy-going Hunt became popular with his fellow senators. However, he refused to serve on the Democratic Senate Steering Committee, saying it would restrict his independence. He was a dependable supporter of the Truman administration's foreign policy and voted against attempts to cut defense appropriations and foreign aid. He voted for the North Atlantic Treaty in 1949 and the Point Four Program and aid to Spain and Yugoslavia in 1950; he voted against cuts in the Marshall Plan authorization and a limitation on a commitment of arms to Western Europe.

Characterizing himself as a "progressive liberal, but certainly not a radical," Hunt backed most of the Fair Deal domestic programs as well. He also supported a federal rent control extension, a constitutional amendment for equal rights for women, federal aid to Wyoming reclamation projects, and the transfer of federal mineral rights to the states. Hunt's major difference with the Truman administration was over national health insurance, which he opposed as "socialized medicine." As an alternative he offered his own plan in 1950, a bill enabling the federal government to sell insurance policies covering medical and dental care to the public. Hunt's bill was bottled up in the Senate Labor Committee. During 1950–51 Hunt was a quiet but diligent member of the Kefauver Committee investigating organized crime.

Early in 1950 Hunt began an unsuccessful campaign to revise the Constitution so that individuals could sue members of Congress for defamatory statements. His anger had been aroused by a prolonged Armed Services Committee investigation into the background of ANNA M. ROSENBERG who had been nominated for the post of assistant secretary of defense. She had been wrongly accused of having Communist connections in her past. Senator JOSEPH R. MCCARTHY (R-Wisc.) argued that Hunt's proposal to abolish congressional immunity would make it impossible to be able to convict Communists.

In December 1952 Hunt announced that he intended to back all legislative proposals of the incoming Eisenhower administration because he considered President-elect Eisenhower's "unheard-of" majority in Wyoming a strong popular mandate for such support. Facing a tough reelection battle in 1954, Hunt announced on June 8, 1954, that he would not be a candidate for office in November. On June 19, despondent over an ailment diagnosed as kidney cancer and that his son had been convicted on a morals charge, Hunt committed suicide in his Senate office in Washington, D.C.

—TO

Hurley, Patrick J(ay)

(1883–1963) *ambassador*

Patrick J. Hurley was born in Choctaw Indian Territory, now Lehigh, Oklahoma, on January 8, 1883. The son of poor Irish immigrants, he worked in the coal mines and as a cowboy before entering Baptist Indian University. He obtained a law degree from National University in 1908 and opened a successful practice in Tulsa. By 1910, at the age of 27, he had become president of the Tulsa Bar Association. Two years later he was appointed attorney for the Choctaw nation. Hurley was an admirer of Theodore Roosevelt and the Rough Riders. During his early years in Oklahoma, he joined the National Guard and in 1917 enlisted in the army. Following service in France he resumed his law practice. Hurley also invested in oil and banking, eventually becoming a millionaire. He ran and financed HERBERT HOOVER's 1928 presidential campaign in Oklahoma. When Hoover unexpectedly carried the normally Democratic state, Hurley emerged as one of the leading Republicans in the nation. In gratitude Hoover appointed him assistant secretary of war. Nine months later he became secretary, when his predecessor in that office, James Good, died. Hurley returned to his businesses when Roosevelt became president in 1933 and also established a lucrative corporate practice in the nation's capital.

During World War II Hurley coordinated the running of the Japanese blockade of Bataan. However, Japanese control of Philippine waters made this impossible, so Roosevelt appointed him minister to New Zealand. Hurley also undertook missions for the president in the USSR and Iran. In August 1944 Roosevelt appointed him his personal representative to China to handle the military and supply problems of fighting the Japanese. That November the president appointed him ambassador. As ambassador Hurley had a disconcerting habit of making a "war whoop," which he said was

a Comanche battle cry, when meeting with Chinese officials, Nationalist and Communist, which made him look faintly ridiculous.

Hurley clashed with Foreign Service personnel working under him over the viability of Chiang Kai-shek's (Jiang Jieshi) government. Unlike such diplomats as JOHN PATTON DAVIES and JOHN S. SERVICE, who believed that Chiang's regime would fall to the Communists because it was corrupt and lacked popular support, Hurley had confidence in the generalissimo's leadership. He opposed a coalition government including Communists and adamantly rejected the suggestion that the United States open contacts with Mao Zedong (Mao Tsetung). The ambassador soon began to believe that the American embassy and the consulates were infiltrated by Communists. Only Communists, he assumed, would take such positions.

In September 1945 Hurley returned to the United States for a vacation. While there he delivered a speech calling on Truman to clarify his views on China and publicly claimed that U.S. Foreign Service personnel in that nation were not carrying out American policy. During his visit Hurley learned that a number of liberal Democrats in Congress had criticized his performance and were pushing to discontinue aid to Chiang. In response he resigned in November in the hope that Truman would refuse to accept his resignation, thus coming out strongly for continued assistance to the Nationalists. In a letter announcing his decision, Hurley charged the professional diplomats with aiding the Communists and interfering with his attempts to save Chiang's regime. Truman accepted Hurley's resignation and in 1946 sent a mission to China in hope of negotiating a compromise between the two sides.

During the last half of the decade, Hurley became one of the leading spokesmen for the "China Lobby," a coalition of American interest groups pressuring the government to support Chiang. In testimony before the Senate Foreign Relations Committee, Hurley reiterated his earlier charges that the U.S. embassy in China had been filled with Communists and specifically mentioned Davies and Service. A State Department investigation failed to substantiate his accusations. Nevertheless, the retired general continued to agitate for a pro-Nationalist policy and for the ouster of those men whom he deemed traitors. In 1950 Senator JOSEPH R. MCCARTHY (R-Wisc.) revived Hurley's charges. As a result of McCarthy's continued prodding, Service and Davies were forced to leave the State Department in 1953.

Following his retirement from government, Hurley returned to his legal practice and business ventures. He ran for the New Mexico Senate seat in 1946, 1948, and 1952. He lost partly because his emphasis on foreign policy did not interest voters. During the 1950s, he remained a prominent Republican conservative, and was a delegate to the Republican National Convention. Hurley died on July 30, 1963, in Santa Fe, New Mexico.

—JB

Hutcheson, William L(evi)
(1874–1953) *president, United Brotherhood of Carpenters*

The son of a ship carpenter, William "Big Bill" L. Hutcheson was born on February 7, 1874, in Saginaw, Michigan. He attended public schools briefly in rural Michigan and then embarked on a career as a carpenter. In 1902 he joined the Brotherhood of Carpenters, and, in 1906, he became the business agent for the union in the Saginaw area. He was elected second vice president of the Brotherhood in 1912 and first vice president the following year. In 1915 he succeeded James Kirby as head of the union. From the time he assumed the presidency, Hutcheson controlled the union with an iron hand. When his autocratic style created internecine conflicts, he employed strong-arm tactics to maintain loyalty and strict adherence to his decisions. Hutcheson's main method of gaining members was through raiding other unions through jurisdictional fights rather than organizing nonunion workers. He was often able to win such struggles by threatening to withdraw his union, the largest in the AFL, from the federation.

In 1918, as a member of the War Labor Board, Hutcheson called off a strike of carpenters at a shipyard on the advice of President Woodrow Wilson. He denied union members an opportunity to vote on the issue of the strike. In 1919 he endorsed government intervention in labor negotiations within the steel industry. Hutcheson was a Republican who supported that party's presidential nominees from 1924 to 1932. Hutcheson also was a foe of communism and other left-wing ideologies.

Hutcheson was elected a vice president of the Executive Council of the American Federation of Labor (AFL) in 1935, but he resigned a year later because of the federation's support of New Deal legislation. He rejoined the AFL as first vice president in 1940. That year Hutcheson was indicted by the Justice Department for criminal conspiracy to restrain interstate commerce as the result of a labor dispute with Anheuser-Busch. The government alleged that the union had prevented further manufacture and distribution of the company's beer—a direct violation of the Sherman Antitrust Act. In 1941 the indictment was dismissed because the government had failed to prove unlawful practices on the part of Hutcheson and the union. The dismissal was upheld by the Supreme Court in *United States v. Hutcheson* (1941). During World War II Hutcheson served on the "peace committee" of the AFL, which dealt with union-management conflicts within the confines of the wartime no-strike pledge. He unsuccessfully sought the Republican vice presidential nomination in 1944.

In 1945 Hutcheson, together with seven other members of the Executive Council of the AFL, headed the federation's delegation to the president's National Management-Labor Conference in Washington. The conference emphasized the importance of resolving differences between management and labor without the stoppage of production. Under Hutcheson's vigorous leadership, the conferees agreed to attempt to settle grievances under existing contracts through arbitration rather than strikes or lockouts. Hutcheson and a number of delegates stressed the need for improved effectiveness in collective bargaining in order to minimize the possibility of government intervention in negotiations. He opposed proposals to appoint fact-finding boards in labor disputes where public health or safety was endangered and turned down a plan that requested strike notices in advance. In 1946 when JOHN L. LEWIS, president of the United Mine Workers (UMW), defied a government injunction designed to prevent a strike and was fined for contempt, Hutcheson bitterly condemned the action.

With the approval of the AFL Executive Council, Hutcheson presented his postwar plan for economic prosperity in 1946. He endorsed the formation of an international organization of nations to provide an enduring peace. He stated that the free enterprise system must be safeguarded and emphasized that international trade controls restricting economic opportunities must be discouraged. A vigorous anticommunist, he warned that, "ideological infiltration into our system by propagandists of foreign nations must not be permitted."

Hutcheson stressed that the nation must maintain a high and ever increasing standard of living measured in "real purchasing power." He regarded the massive construction of urban and rural housing as the country's primary domestic objective. Such a vast plan for housing would provide full employment and sustain high living standards. In 1946 Hutcheson enthusiastically supported the Wagner-Ellender-Taft housing bill, which failed in the House.

Hutcheson was a staunch opponent of all legislation designed to further government intrusion into labor affairs. He opposed the Case labor disputes bill of 1946, which called for establishment of a mediation board, enforced cooling-off periods, outlawing of boycotts and sympathy strikes, and authorization of court injunctions. He criticized the bill's supporters, who he stated, "seemed determined to place legislative shackles on organized labor." Truman subsequently vetoed the bill.

In 1947 Hutcheson appeared before the House of Labor Committee to debate a number of pending bills dealing with labor policy. He stated his opposition to all legislation that would curb labor activities and denounced the committee, headed by Representative FRED A. HARTLEY (R-N.J.), as "useless mandarins attacking an indispensable institution of the community which paid them." Soon after the House Committee hearings, the Taft-Hartley Act became law. Included in the act was a provision allowing the president under certain circumstances to impose a cooling-off period before a union was able to call a strike. The measure also increased the power of the National Labor Relations Board and provided legal redress for the employers or unions over a breach of contract. Hutcheson condemned the bill and said of those who enacted it: "They want a return to the days of 'rugged individualism' which is a fancy name for white slavery." Although he was joined by many prominent labor leaders in his advocacy for repeal, his efforts to undermine Taft-Hartley were unsuccessful.

In 1948 Hutcheson served as a delegate to the GOP National Convention, where he made a serious attempt to get the delegates to adopt a platform plank calling for the repeal of Taft-Hartley. He failed to gain the requisite support. From 1948 to 1949 he wrote numerous editorials in the brotherhood's paper, *The Carpenter*, in which he attacked repressive anti-labor legislation. In 1952 Hutcheson refused to support Senator ROBERT A. TAFT (R-Ohio) for the presidential nomination and endorsed DWIGHT D. EISENHOWER.

Hutcheson retired from the union presidency in 1951 and was succeeded by his son, Maurice. He continued to serve as a vice president of the AFL and his influence within the brotherhood never waned. Hutcheson opposed the proposed merger with the CIO because it included a no-raiding agreement. When he did not get his way he left the Executive Board of the AFL and withdrew his union from the federation. The *New York Times* called him, "a conservative member of a conservative group. He was an old school labor leader devoted to the bread and butter philosophy." During his years as head of the brotherhood he was responsible for the carpenters' increased income, better working conditions, and greater job security. He helped reduce the nationwide work week from 44 to 40 and then to 35 hours. Hutcheson died of a heart ailment on October 20, 1953, in Indianapolis, Indiana.

—DGE

I

Ickes, Harold L(eclair)
(1874–1952) *secretary of the interior*

Born on a farm in Blair County, Pennsylvania, on March 15, 1874, Harold L. Ickes moved to Chicago at the age of 16 to work in his uncle's drug store. He worked his way through the University of Chicago, graduating cum laude in 1897. He then became a newspaper reporter for the *Chicago Record* and later the *Chicago Tribune*. In 1907 he obtained a law degree from the University of Chicago but practiced infrequently. Ickes's primary interest was reform politics, and he soon emerged as one of the leading progressive Republicans in the city. In 1912 he supported Theodore Roosevelt's quest for the presidential nomination and then chaired the Progressive Committee of Cook County. At the 1920 Republican National Convention he opposed the nomination of Warren G. Harding. Four years later Ickes supported Senator Robert La Follette's (P-Wisc.) third run for the presidency. Following his victory in 1932, Franklin D. Roosevelt, anxious to generate support from midwestern progressive Republicans, and liking "the cut of his jib," appointed Ickes secretary of the interior. He held this post for 13 years, the longest term of any cabinet official. Later Roosevelt appointed him director of the Public Works Administration as well. Ickes gained a reputation as an excellent administrator whose parsimony earned him the nickname "Honest Harold." As PWA chief he managed the spending of $6 billion for the construction of hospitals, dams, bridges, highways, and more. Along with HENRY A. WALLACE, he was considered the leading liberal in the administration. His abrasive, quick-tempered, often vengeful personality alienated many. To obtain his way Ickes frequently submitted letters of resignation; Roosevelt humorously refused to accept them.

Along with many others, Ickes questioned President Truman's liberal credentials. The secretary viewed him as a product of the political clubhouse who, as a senator, had allied himself often with conservative interests. Truman's first few months in office seem to confirm Ickes's fears. The president was increasingly influenced by conservative businessmen such as EDWIN W. PAULEY and JOHN W. SNYDER. Liberals accused him of abandoning the New Deal and antagonizing the Russians.

Ickes was the first cabinet member to leave the administration in protest against its conservative direction. In February 1946 Truman nominated Pauley to be undersecretary of the navy. Ickes protested, fearing Pauley's control of the naval oil reserves could lead to another Teapot Dome scandal.

In testimony before the Senate Naval Committee, Ickes recalled Pauley telling him in 1944 that he could collect large campaign contributions if the federal government dropped its suits to claim offshore oil deposits. Pauley had convinced Roosevelt not to allow Ickes and Attorney General FRANCIS B. BIDDLE to sue in federal court to assert federal over state control of the continental shelf. Pauley was an oilman interested in exploiting this area and he believed he could get a better deal from the states than the Interior Department, which would be the case as long as Ickes was secretary, as Ickes's biographer T. H. Watkins noted. In addition Pauley, as treasurer of the Democratic Party, told Roosevelt and Ickes that he could raise money from California oil men if title was left to the states. Roosevelt would not let Ickes proceed. Truman, however, allowed the suit to go forward and, further, asserted federal control of offshore land that would stand until such time as the Supreme Court over-ruled him. Truman backed Pauley, charging to reporters that Ickes had been mistaken. Ickes resigned stating, "I don't care to stay in an adminis-tration where I am expected to commit perjury for the sake of the party. I do not have a reputation for dealing recklessly with the truth." When Truman protested Ickes's questioning of his integrity, the former secretary stated that the president was "nei-ther an absolute monarch nor a descendant of the putative sun goddess." Truman had asked Ickes to be "gentle" with Pauley, but that is hardly the same as suborning perjury, as Watkins noted, and there is the question as to why Ickes just did not tell the president of Pauley's attempted bribery, but, as Watkins notes, Ickes had good reason to be suspi-cious of Pauley. He asked that his nomination be withdrawn, and it was. Ickes retired to a career as a newspaper columnist, writing, "Man to Man" for the *New York Post.* Liberals praised Ickes's resignation. The *Chicago Post* wrote, "Here is the old struggle between the machine politician and the independent; between those who hold office for its own sake and those who see it as a means to public end; between expediency and progressive principles."

Out of office Ickes consented to head the Inde-pendent Citizens Committee of the Arts, Sciences and Professions (ICCASP), one of the leading lib-eral lobbies organized to pressure Truman to move to the left. Unlike the Americans for Democratic Action (ADA), this group permitted Communists to become members. Ickes refused to join the ADA because he considered it a tool of the Democratic Party. However, he soon resigned from the ICCASP because of the growing power of Communists and a personality conflict with the leadership. Its double standard in foreign policy also disturbed Ickes. He deplored its calls for free elections in Spain and Greece while it refused to ask for elections in East-ern Europe. When the ICCASP joined Henry Wal-lace's Progressive Citizens of America, Ickes warned that having Communists in the organization would be alien to the goals of American liberals.

In March 1948 Ickes requested that Truman resign or face the eventuality of being defeated by a "disillusioned and indignant citizenry." However, when confronted with the choice of supporting Wallace or Governor THOMAS E. DEWEY, Ickes backed Truman. Privately he believed Truman could not win. He had little respect for the president, but

his endorsement helped Truman win many liberal votes from Wallace. In 1949 Ickes stopped writing his column to devote attention to writing books. He died on February 3, 1952, in Washington, D.C.

—JB

Impellitteri, Vincent (Richard)
(1900–1987) *mayor*

Vincent Impellitteri, the son of Italian immigrants, was born on February 4, 1900, in Isnello, Italy, and was brought to the United States one year after his birth. The family settled in Ansonia, Connecticut, where his father was a shoemaker. Upon gradua-tion from high school in 1917, Impellitteri joined the navy, serving overseas as a radioman on the destroyer USS *Stockton.* Discharged in 1919, he entered Fordham Law School and worked nights as a bellboy in the Ansonia Hotel. He received his law degree in 1924 and was admitted to the New York bar the following year.

From 1924 to 1929 Impellitteri practiced law, serving for several years as counsel to Local 282 of the Teamsters and Chauffeurs Union. As assistant district attorney of New York Company from 1929 to 1938, he directed a number of prosecutions of rack-eteers. He was appointed secretary to state Supreme Court Justice Peter Schmuck in 1941 and in 1943 became secretary to Justice Joseph A. Gavagan.

A longtime member of the Tammany Hall Democratic machine, Impellitteri was chosen as can-didate for New York City Council president in 1945 ostensibly to balance a ticket headed by WILLIAM O'DWYER, then running for mayor. However, histo-rian Oliver E. Allen claimed the real reason was that mobster Thomas "Three Finger Brown" Luchese told Congressman VITO MARCANTONIO (ALP-N.Y.) to pass word to O'Dwyer to put Impellitteri on the ticket, and O'Dwyer did so. Swept into office along with O'Dwyer, Impellitteri presided over the New York City Council and served as acting mayor in O'Dwyer's absence. He had all mayoral powers except those of appointing new officials and signing laws. In the 1949 city elections Impellitteri polled more votes to win reelection for council president than did O'Dwyer, who was reelected mayor.

In August 1950 O'Dwyer resigned, amid a police scandal and a grand jury investigation of organized crime, to accept an appointment as ambassador to Mexico. Impellitteri became acting mayor pending a special election set for November. At the time Impellitteri was not taken seriously—he would warm the mayor's seat until New Yorkers elected the Tammany-picked candidate, Justice Ferdinand Pecora, in a special election in November. However, Impellitteri upset the machine's plans and tried to win in his own right. The Democratic Party, split between Impellitteri and Pecora, finally nominated Pecora, leaving Impellitteri to run as an independent. With just a few weeks in which to campaign, Impellitteri formed his own "Experience" ticket. His campaign capitalized on his independent status to create an "anti-boss, anti-politician, anti-corruption" image. Dubbed "Impy" by the press and endorsed by the powerful ROBERT MOSES, who had controlled city planning and construction during O'Dwyer's administration, Impellitteri won the race, as Pecora proved a poor candidate. He was the first mayoral candidate ever to win without major party support. Pecora's loss dealt the Tammany Executive Committee a severe blow. Tammany boss Carmine De Sapio attempted to recover by selling judgeships and coming out in favor of social welfare legislation.

Timid in dealing even with his subordinates—Carmine De Sapio had predicted he would be a nonentity—Impellitteri relied heavily on Moses's ideas about city spending and construction. An aide remarked, "Impy never understood that he had any power at all." The mayor appointed Moses's men to key government positions and allowed him to select routes for a dozen new expressways and sites for Title I housing projects. Moses engineered an "understanding" with Governor THOMAS E. DEWEY allowing the city to raise sales taxes and to hike the subway fare from 10 to 15 cents. The increased revenues were directed away from service functions and into the public works construction projects that Moses favored. During Impellitteri's term the city's last large spaces were developed as Moses wished. The implementation of his plans left the city unable to pay for the maintenance of its own physical plant. Schools went onto split shifts, the city college system declined, and hospitals and libraries were neglected. Even the highways planned and newly built by Moses could not be maintained.

Impellitteri also had bequeathed to him scandals of the previous administration, such as gamblers' bribes to police and firefighters' shakedowns of businesses. Inflation also posed problems for him. Impellitteri proposed what later became the independent Transit Authority to take public transportation affairs out of politics. He also appointed Thomas F. Murphy, a former U.S. attorney, as police commissioner with a mandate to stop corruption. But the mayor's staff members were caught in scandals, though Impellitteri himself was never accused of corruption. Still, it hurt his administration, as did his timidity in dealing with the Republican state legislature and Governor Dewey.

With public concern running high over rent hikes, tax and transit fare increases, and overcrowding in the schools, Robert F. Wagner, Jr., defeated Impellitteri by a two-to-one majority in the 1953 Democratic primary for mayor. Wagner, as the next mayor of New York, appointed Impellitteri to a criminal court judgeship, a post he held until retiring in 1965. Thereafter, he returned to law practice taking little active part in politics. In 1972 he was one of President Nixon's New York City campaign cochairmen. Impellitteri died on January 29, 1987, in Bridgeport, Connecticut.

—DAE

Ingersoll, Ralph M(cAllister)
(1900–1985) *publisher*

The son of a socially prominent New York family, Ingersoll was born on December 8, 1900, in New Haven, Connecticut. He graduated from Yale in 1921 with a degree in mining engineering. For two years he worked as a miner in California and Arizona before relocating to Mexico, where he became division engineer for a mining company. Largely on the strength of his first book, *In and under Mexico* (1924), he obtained a job as a reporter for the *New York American*. In 1924 he began reporting for the *New Yorker*, where he rose to become managing editor the following year. He remained in this position until 1930 when he became managing editor of *Fortune*. After a five-year affiliation with *Fortune*, he then served as vice president and general manager of Time, Inc., and in 1937 he was appointed publisher.

A tall and argumentative man with a capacious memory and an abiding interesting in his times, Ingersoll in 1940 resigned from *Time* and founded a New York evening daily, *PM*. As founder and editor, Ingersoll maintained the newspaper's avowed purpose of being "against people who pushed other people around." *PM* was the nation's first major paper to call for U.S. entry into World War II. Ingersoll wrote most of these editorials, which he compiled in the book *America Is Worth Fighting For.* In 1946 *Newsweek* noted, "editorially, Ingersoll tried to keep the paper walking the fence which divides the camp where most of *PM*'s readers are bivouacked: Communists and fellow travelers on the left and Socialists, social democrats and anti-Soviet liberals on the right." When *PM*'s original stockholders, most of whom were not leftists, objected to its editorial policy, Ingersoll suggested that they sell their holdings. Since its inception the paper had subsisted on circulation revenue, charging five cents a copy, while other newspapers cost two or three cents.

In 1942 Ingersoll was drafted into the army, and in a series of *PM* editorials, he charged that his induction was a form of persecution. He rose rapidly from private to lieutenant colonel and wrote a best seller on army training, *The Battle Is the Payoff* (1943). After the war Ingersoll resumed editorial direction of *PM*, which was faced with a sharp political division between the New York and Washington bureaus. The New York office sought to mitigate the fear of those opposed to postwar Russian imperialism while simultaneously addressing itself to that sector of the left that gave all Russian policy a blanket endorsement. In contrast the Washington staff maintained a staunch anticommunist liberal position. In an attempt at editorial control, Ingersoll ordered three members of the Washington staff to relocate in New York. When they refused he fired them. Since their dismissal violated their contract, both the New York and Washington chapters of the Newspaper Guild rallied to their defense. The Washington bureau members criticized Ingersoll for "yielding to Communist pressure." Five members quit, including JAMES WECHSLER; one of the replacements was I. F. Stone.

In 1946, when Secretary of War ROBERT P. PATTERSON and Secretary of the Navy JAMES V. FORRESTAL denied accusations that military members advocated an attack on Russia, Ingersoll immediately jumped into the controversy. In a *PM* editorial he maintained, "responsible senior officers of the U.S. Army have expressed themselves in private, to me personally, as advocating an immediate attack."

As the paper's circulation declined and its deficit increased, management began accepting paid advertising, thus ending the paper's seven-year policy. In opposition to the decision, Ingersoll resigned as editor in 1946. During his final year at *PM* he

wrote *Top Secret,* which was his account of the invasion of Europe.

In 1948 Ingersoll completed *The Great Ones,* a fictionalized love story of a newspaper publisher and his famous wife. The following year he became president of R. J. Company, Inc., a firm specializing in newspaper investments. In 1951 he purchased the *Middletown* (N.Y.) *Times Herald* for investment purposes, and, in 1956, he became the paper's publisher in an attempt to improve the paper's faltering circulation. He resigned as president of R. J. Company, Inc. in 1958 and one year later sold the *Middletown Times Herald.*

Beginning in 1959 Ingersoll purchased and invested in numerous publications, including the *Elizabeth* (N.J.) *Daily Journal,* which was founded in 1779 and once referred to itself as "the organ of the Continental Congress." Ingersoll retired from Ingersoll Publications in 1982. He died from complications from a stroke on March 8, 1985, in Miami Beach, Florida.

—DGE

Ives, Irving M(cNeil)
(1896–1962) *member of the Senate*

Irving M. Ives was born on January 24, 1896, in Bainbridge, New York. He enlisted in the army during World War I, serving in the St. Mihiel and Meuse-Argonne campaigns. After the war he returned to Hamilton College, graduating Phi Beta Kappa in 1920. He then entered the banking business. Ives started his own insurance company in 1930, the same year he won a seat in the New York State Assembly. He was elected minority leader in 1935 and Speaker in 1936, but was ejected from the top post in a party revolt in 1937 and spent the remaining years in the legislature as majority leader. Ives was a conciliator and a craftsman when it came to legislation, and he helped leaven the image of the GOP as standpatters. A liberal Republican, Ives helped write the New York State Fair Employment Act of 1945, making New York State the first to ban discrimination in employment. He also sat on the powerful New York State Joint Legislative Committee on Industrial and Labor Conditions and pushed through a bill creating the State Department of Commerce.

He put through legislation that protected unions and raised the state workmen's compensation and unemployment benefits. He established the

Cornell School of Industrial and Labor Relations and served briefly as its dean in 1946.

Ives had wanted to run for the Senate in 1944; Governor THOMAS E. DEWEY stopped him, believing a Catholic would balance the state ticket. Ives then became dean of the Cornell Industrial and Labor School in 1945 and announced his intention to retire from politics. But the leaders of the New York GOP convinced Dewey that the party should nominated Ives for the other U.S. Senate seat in 1946. Dewey threw his support behind Ives, and the latter's antidiscrimination record earned him the allegiance of African-American and Jewish voters, while his backing of labor legislation won him the support of the American Federation of Labor. He beat former governor HERBERT H. LEHMAN in the general election and became the first New York Republican senator since 1927.

Ives quickly became one of the leading members of the Senate's liberal Republican bloc. Ives, however, was not a rigid liberal, and he preferred being call "realistic" or "progressive." An internationalist, he favored the Truman Doctrine of aid to Greece and Turkey in 1947, the Marshall Plan in 1948, and the North Atlantic Treaty in 1949. Yet he also convinced Republicans to sign on to a resolution in 1950 calling for Secretary of State DEAN G. ACHESON's resignation. Ives was a vigorous supporter of the newly created state of Israel. In domestic affairs he supported a proposed tax reduction for low-income families in 1947, voted for the Educational Finance Act of 1948, and backed the National Housing Act of 1949. In March 1947 Ives introduced a bill banning discrimination in federal employment. Like most Republicans, he opposed Truman's proposals to establish wage and price controls.

During 1947 Ives, as a member of the Labor Committee, became deeply embroiled in the debate over the Taft-Hartley bill. The senator reluctantly supported a moderate bill sponsored by Senator ROBERT A. TAFT (R-Ohio) prohibiting secondary boycotts, jurisdictional walkouts, and the closed shop; increasing the legal responsibility of unions; and authorizing the president to seek injunctions to delay strikes for 80 days. Ives successfully fought attempts to limit industrywide collective bargaining.

Because of Ives's support of the Taft-Hartley Act, American Federation of Labor president WILLIAM GREEN vowed to defeat him in his 1952 reelection bid. Nonetheless, Ives beat his Democratic opponent by 1.3 million votes—the largest plurality obtained by a candidate in New York State to that date.

Ives's liberalism was more evident when he and six other Republican senators signed a "Declaration of Conscience" condemning the tactics Senator JOSEPH R. MCCARTHY (R-Wisc.) in investigating Communists in government.

During the Eisenhower administration Ives played a major role in the development of labor legislation. He ran unsuccessfully for governor of New York in 1954, losing to W. AVERELL HARRIMAN by only 11,000 votes. Ives did not run for reelection in 1958 because of ill health. He died on February 24, 1962, in Norwich, New York. (See *The Eisenhower Years* Volume)

—RSG

Jackson, Henry M(artin)

(1912–1983) *member of the House of Representatives, member of the Senate*

The son of Norwegian immigrants, Henry M. "Scoop" Jackson was born on May 31, 1912, in the mill town of Everett, Washington. He received his LL.B. in 1935 from the University of Washington, and after practicing law for a short time, he entered politics as a Democrat, winning election as prosecuting attorney of Snohomish County at the age of 26. Elected to the U.S. House of Representatives in 1940, Jackson entered Congress determined to aid the British but keep the United States out of the war. He was committed to securing adequate air and shoreline defenses of the Pacific Northwest. In 1943 he enlisted in the army but was ordered back to Congress three months later by President Roosevelt. The war made him see that isolationism was no longer possible and that totalitarianism must be opposed.

During Jackson's six consecutive terms in the House, he established one of the most liberal voting records in Congress. A quiet, methodical man, he seldom made speeches on the floor but was diligent in attendance and committee work. As chairman of the Committee on Indian Affairs in 1945, Jackson pushed through the House a bill creating a commissioner for Indian affairs, thus removing the Indians from the jurisdiction of the bureaucratically tangled Interior Department. In 1946 as chairman of the Indian Affairs Committee he cosponsored and got passed the Indian Claims Commission Act, which gave Native Americans the right to sue for treaty violations, a right denied to them since 1863. In 1946 Jackson was the only one of Washington state's liberal Democratic members of Congress to win reelec-

tion in the Republican landslide of that year. He consistently voted in support of labor, and advocated price controls as a means of combating inflation.

In 1945 Jackson and other congressmen visited Buchenwald. Jackson's tour strengthened his philo-Semitism, and helps explains his later ardent support for Israel and the rights of Soviet Jews. He also went to Norway, and Norwegian fears of the Soviet Union helped develop a belief in Jackson that Soviet totalitarianism had replaced the Nazi variety as the threat to world peace.

Representing a state with more public-power districts than any other, Jackson advocated public ownership in harnessing the energy of the Columbia River. In April 1949, at the request of President Truman, Jackson cosponsored a bill to set up the Columbia Valley Authority as a government corporation to administer power production, flood control, irrigation, navigation, and the systematic development of the region. However, the bill was not passed due to opposition from not only private power companies but also the Interior Department, and the army as they saw the CVA as an encroachment on their prerogatives. Jackson's seat on the Interior Subcommittee of the Appropriations Committee, gained through friendship with House Speaker SAM T. RAYBURN (D-Tex.), gave him control of funds for public works projects and more leverage in his fight for publicly owned power. In 1951 Jackson introduced enabling legislation for the expansion of the Bonneville Power Administration, urging the immediate construction of eight electric plants in the Northwest. Jackson declined an appointment as undersecretary of the interior.

In 1948 Jackson became one of the nine House members of the joint Congressional Committee on

Atomic Energy and soon emerged as an informed congressional spokesman on atomic power and national defense. He favored all-out production of nuclear weapons and in 1949 was a member of the special subcommittee that recommended development of the hydrogen bomb on a crash basis. Jackson later discouraged total reliance on nuclear weapons, stressing the need for continental and civil defense systems in preparing for limited warfare.

As his biographer, Robert G. Kaufman, has noted, Jackson, a man of conservative demeanor, was a typical cold war liberal. He believed in expansive domestic policies: national health insurance, repeal of the Taft-Hartley Act, a higher minimum wage, extension of Social Security benefits, and federal aid to public housing and education. And he was a vigorous advocate of an anticommunist foreign policy: voting for the Truman Doctrine, the Marshall Plan, and an resolution of Senator ARTHUR H. VANDENBERG (R-Mich.) authorizing the United States to join an alliance outside the Western Hemisphere, which was a stepping stone toward NATO. Jackson admired Truman for his tough stand against the Soviets.

Jackson challenged the conservative incumbent Senator Harry P. Cain (R-Wash.) and won election to the Senate in 1952. As a member of the Senate Armed Services Committee, he continued his insistence upon the maintenance of American military superiority over the Soviet Union. Selected to serve on the Permanent Investigations Subcommittee, Jackson opposed Chairman JOSEPH R. MCCARTHY's (R-Wisc.) anticommunist crusade, believing that the true Communist threat was an external rather than an internal one. In July 1953 Jackson and two other Democratic members resigned from the subcommittee in protest against McCarthy's assumption of unlimited power in hiring and firing staff members.

During the Kennedy administration Jackson was critical of its efforts to limit the arms race with the Soviet Union. In 1963 he became chairman of the Interior and Insular Affairs Committee, where he was able to promote his home state's rapidly expanding economy and spearhead passage of major conservation measures. He was an enthusiastic supporter of President Johnson's Vietnam policies. During the 1970s Jackson emerged as a leading supporter of Israel and the rights of Soviet Jews. He ran unsuccessfully for the Democratic presidential nomination in 1972 and 1976. Jackson died on September 1, 1983, in Everett, Washing-

ton. (See *The Eisenhower Years, The Kennedy Years, The Johnson Years, The Nixon/Ford Years, The Carter Years* Volumes)

—DAE

Jackson, Robert H(oughwout)
(1892–1954) *associate justice, U.S. Supreme Court; U.S. chief of counsel, Nuremberg War Crimes Trials*

Robert H. Jackson was born on February 13, 1892, in Spring Park, Pennsylvania. Jackson learned the law mainly as an apprentice to his lawyer cousin, Frank H. Mott. (He would be the last U.S. Supreme Court Justice to become a lawyer through an apprenticeship.) After admission to the bar in 1913 he established a private practice in Jamestown, New York, and became one of the most successful trial lawyers in western New York, although he liked to think of himself as a "country lawyer." A Democrat, Jackson advised Governor Franklin Roosevelt after his election in 1928 and, without enthusiasm, went to Washington to join President Roosevelt's administration, becoming general counsel of the Internal Revenue Bureau in 1934. In 1936 he became assistant attorney general of the Tax Division in the Justice Department, but soon was shifted to head the Antitrust Division. He served as Solicitor General from 1938 to 1939, where he pushed for judicial restraint in his briefs before the Supreme Court. From 1940 to 1941 he was Attorney General, in which post he also acted as a political adviser.

When Chief Justice Charles Evans Hughes retired in 1941, Roosevelt led Jackson to think he would be appointed chief justice. Instead Roosevelt promoted Associate Justice HARLAN FISKE STONE to the top spot and appointed Jackson as an associate justice in June 1941, and the latter took the oath of office the next month.

Jackson early showed himself as a believer in a nationalist interpretation of the Constitution. In *Edwards v. California* (1941) he declared unconstitutional a California law regulating the entry into the state of U.S. citizens without visible means of support, saying it violated the privileges and immunities clause of the Constitution. He upheld an expansive definition of the commerce clause in *Wickard v. Filburn* (1942), upholding the second Agricultural Adjustment Act.

Beginning May 2, 1945, Jackson interrupted his judicial service for 18 months to serve as U.S.

representative and chief prosecutor at the Nuremberg war crimes trials. He had a prominent role in developing the August 1945 London agreement on which the trials were based, and he helped draft the indictments and amass the evidence for the trials. Jackson headed the American prosecution team in the first trial of 22 top Nazis, which began in November 1945. As an exceptionally skilled advocate, he made what was considered a masterful opening statement for the Allied prosecutors. However, his cross-examination of Reich Marshall Herman Goering was less skillful. He also did a poor job in overseeing the administration of the prosecutorial team. His fellow justices on the high court did not appreciate his absence from the Court. Stone thought the war crimes tribunal little more than thinly disguised victors' justice, saying, "Jackson is away conducting his high grade lynching in Nuremberg." After the tribunal found 19 of the Nazis leaders guilty on October 1, 1946, Jackson resigned on October 17. Despite all the controversy that then and later surrounded the Nuremberg trials, Jackson considered them "the most important, enduring and constructive work" of his life. He numbered among their achievements the recognition of aggressive war as a crime under international law and the historical documentation of totalitarian dictatorship in the Nazi era. Several commentators have labeled Jackson the primary architect of the trials. Telford Taylor, who succeeded the justice as chief American counsel at the trials, stated that Jackson contributed more than anyone to the "integrity and dignity of the Nuremberg proceedings."

While at Nuremberg Jackson launched a public attack on Justice HUGO L. BLACK. The two had disagreed in the May 1945 *Jewell Ridge Coal* case where the Court, by a five to four vote, held that coal miners were entitled to portal-to-portal pay. They had also disagreed over the propriety of Black's participation in the case, which had been argued by a former law partner of the Alabaman. When Chief Justice Harlan Fiske Stone died in April 1946, Jackson was considered a possible successor. However reports circulated in the press that Black and one other justice had threatened to resign if Jackson were named Chief Justice; they cited as the reason Jackson's criticism of Black in the *Jewell Ridge* case. On June 10, 1946, after FRED M. VINSON had been appointed Chief Justice, Jackson released a statement from Nuremberg presenting his side of the *Jewell Ridge* story. Jackson's declaration came as

a surprise in the United States, and, though commentators at the time differed on the merits of his charges against Black, many reproached him for turning their difference into a public feud.

The incident reflected deeper doctrinal differences between Jackson and the libertarian and activist Black. Jackson believed that the Court should exercise restraint and leave economic and social policy making to other branches of the government. The justice also thought the Court should normally adhere to precedent. Based on his many years as a practicing attorney, he wanted the Court to strive for clear, consistent interpretations of the Constitution and federal statutes so that lawyers and their clients could know and apply the law with assurance.

On his return to the Court following the Nuremberg trials, Jackson, according to several analysts, showed more conservatism in civil liberties cases. Although he still regarded the First Amendment as a guarantor of the individual's right to believe what he wanted, Jackson did not think it gave anyone the right to express his beliefs in any manner or forum he chose. The Justice thought that government had the authority to deal with threats to the public order. In *Terminiello v. Chicago* (1949) he dissented when the court overturned the conviction of an ex-priest for disturbing the peace with an anti-Semitic and pro-fascist speech, arguing that the Court's majority had set "its eyes on a conception of freedom of speech so rigid as to tolerate no concession to society's need for public order." Jackson contended that "if the Court does not temper its doctrinaire logic with a little practical wisdom, it will convert the constitutional Bill of Rights into a suicide pact." He also voted to uphold government restrictions on the use of sound trucks and street meetings. He viewed the Communist Party as a unique organization posing a special threat. In a separate opinion in *American Communications Association v. Douds* (1950) Jackson supported the Taft-Hartley compulsory pledge of nonmembership in the Communist Party, although he rejected an accompanying oath that required union officials to swear they did not believe in forcible overthrow of the government. Jackson voted in *Dennis v. U.S.* (1951) to sustain the conviction of 11 American Communist Party leaders under the Smith Act. The justice insisted that the government give individuals full and fair hearings in security cases, however, and he refused to uphold the government in several instances where he thought procedural standards had not been met.

In cases involving state aid to religious education, Jackson took a strong stand against any form of government assistance. He voted against state payment for the transportation of children to parochial schools in February 1947 and opposed programs for released-time religious instruction for public school children in March 1948 and April 1952. Jackson tended toward a conservative position in most criminal cases and generally opposed federal court interference in state criminal matters. However, he did favor giving wide scope to the Fourth Amendment. In federal cases he consistently voted to limit the scope of an allowable search conducted without a warrant, and he joined the majority in a June 1949 decision holding the Fourth Amendment applicable to the states.

Jackson was foremost among the justices of his day in insisting that the Constitution had established a national economic market that must be kept free of state and local restrictions. In an April 1949 case, for example, his majority opinion overturned New York State's effort to limit the amount of milk an out-of-state buyer could purchase. He asserted that a state could not burden interstate commerce to protect local economic interests. In April 1952, however, in *Youngstown Sheet & Tube Co. v. Sawyer*, a case involving the question of inherent executive powers over the economy during an emergency, Jackson concurred in the Court's judgment that Truman's seizure of the steel mills was invalid.

A supremely gifted stylist whose opinions reflected his wit and learning, Jackson was considered to be somewhat right of center on the Vinson Court. His votes and opinions exhibited his commitments to judicial restraint and, outside the economic sphere, to the maintenance of federalism. In his final years on the bench, Jackson was occasionally absent because of ill health. However, he made a special effort to be present on May 17, 1954, when the Court unanimously held in *Brown v. Board of Education* racial segregation in public schools unconstitutional. The justice died in Washington, D.C., on October 9, 1954. (See *The Eisenhower Years* Volume)
—CAB

Jenner, William E(zra)

(1908–1986) *member of the Senate*

William Jenner was born on July 21, 1908, in Marengo, Indiana, the son of L.L. "Woody" and Jane MacDonald Jenner. William's father ran a general store and later became the first Ford dealer in the Louisville, Kentucky, district. In 1930, William graduated from Indiana University and two years later earned a law degree from the same institution. In 1934 he won a seat in the Indiana State Senate as a Republican. He became minority leader in 1937 and served as president pro-tempore and majority leader from 1939 to 1941. Jenner then left politics to join the U.S. Army Air Corps during World War II. Upon discharge he became the first veteran to enter the U.S. Senate, when he was appointed to fill the unexpired term of the late senator Frederick Van Nuys (D-Ind.). Jenner served for seven weeks from 1944 to 1945 and then returned to his state to become chairman of the Republican State Committee.

Indiana Republicans nominated Jenner for the U.S. Senate in 1946. In what was called by Speaker SAM RAYBURN a "damned beefsteak election," Jenner ran under the slogan, "Folks, Ain't Ye Had Enough?" He attacked the Democrats for shortages, particularly meat, which he blamed on Franklin Roosevelt's New Deal and Harry Truman's "Mis-Deal," and won the election.

Jenner immediately joined the "Class of 46"—also known as the "meat shortage boys"—Republican legislators who opposed Truman on many issues. In his maiden speech on the floor, Jenner blasted excessive government spending and a burdensome tax system. His constant refrain was that Truman's Fair Deal would bring about a socialist "super-state." He also opposed the Universal Military Training bill, championed by former national guardsman Truman, seeing it as "The camels nose of universal peacetime labor service for all youth, the favorite program of all collectivist societies."

Jenner was a neo-isolationist and fought against most of the elements of Truman's containment policy. He did approve aid to Turkey and Greece because these countries were under direct Communist threat, and he saw aid to them as temporary and bilateral. The senator opposed the Marshall Plan because he perceived it to be permanent and multilateral. From 1948 to 1958 Jenner opposed all foreign aid measures but one. He complained that such programs would bankrupt the United States and bring about another depression, making it easier for the Communists to seize control of the country. He also held European nations in disdain for their social welfare policies and questioned the efficacy of resisting communism by helping socialist governments.

Jenner fiercely resisted passage of the North Atlantic Treaty in 1949, fearing involvement with "the hatreds and the jealousies of the European countries which are masters at making war" would endanger America. Given to apocalyptic oratory, he said joining NATO would be a step "back into the black night of international anarchy." After a worldwide junket in 1949 Jenner claimed that the Soviets were winning the cold war. In an exhibition of fundamentalist provincialism, Jenner at the end of the tour said, "I'm glad I made it but I don't give a hoot if I never see any of those countries again." He said that Europeans used American aid not for international peace, "but to fan the fires of nationalist rivalries." In 1952 Jenner voted against treaties granting Germany increased freedom and linking it with NATO.

Jenner was a member of the "China Lobby," who argued that a small group of conspirators within the Truman administration had betrayed the Nationalists in the Chinese civil war. He indicted the "China Hands," State Department experts on that nation, who had advocated that Nationalist leader Chiang Kai-shek (Jiang Jieshi) form a coalition government with Mao Zedong (Mao Tse-Tung) and the Communists. Curiously, Jenner was skeptical of usefulness of aid to Nationalist China.

The senator was an ardent foe of General GEORGE C. MARSHALL, whom he blamed for Communist expansion and the loss of China. During the fall of 1950, when the Senate was asked to modify the National Security Act of 1947 to permit Marshall to become secretary of defense, Jenner voted against it. Marshall became the target for one of Jenner's most hostile speeches. During the debate over the nomination, Jenner called the general a "living lie" who was an eager "front man for traitors." Marshall, he maintained, had helped set the stage for the Soviet victory that is now "sweeping the earth." Jenner charged that Marshall had contributed to the betrayal of Eastern Europe at the wartime conferences and was the inaugurator of the "sell-China-down-the-river line." The general's advocacy of withholding aid from Nationalist China, he charged, had paralyzed the Chiang government. Jenner angrily proclaimed, "our boys are dying in Korea" as a result of Marshall's policies.

Jenner joined the vocal group of conservative Republican senators who supported General DOUGLAS MACARTHUR in his policy dispute with Truman. When the president fired the popular general

in April 1951, Jenner proclaimed on the Senate floor, "I charge this country today is in the hands of a secret inner coterie which is directed by agents of the Soviet Union. Our only choice is to impeach President Truman and find out who is the secret invisible government." The senator also called for the ouster of Secretary of State DEAN G. ACHESON.

Jenner was a strong supporter of Senator JOSEPH R. MCCARTHY's (R-Wisc.) anticommunist crusade and backed the Wisconsin Republican's allegations that there were Communists in the State Department. In 1950, when the Tydings Committee, formed to investigate the charges, denounced them as a hoax, he called the report "the most scandalous and brazen whitewash of treasonable conspiracy in our history."

In early 1948 Jenner announced his intention to seek the Republican nomination for governor of Indiana. However, the Republican State Convention denied him the spot. Jenner served as chairman of the Republican Speakers Bureau during the election of 1948. He supported Senator ROBERT A. TAFT (R-Ohio) for the 1952 Republican presidential nomination but reluctantly backed DWIGHT D. EISENHOWER after he won the spot. Later when Jenner's reelection looked to be in doubt, he eagerly grasped at Eisenhower's coattails. When the general stopped in Indianapolis during the campaign, Jenner introduced him, and, to Eisenhower's consternation, grabbed his hand in a victory salute. The general later said, "I felt dirty from the touch of that man."

Following Eisenhower's victory Jenner assumed the chairmanship of the Senate Internal Security Subcommittee. Jenner's investigations paralleled McCarthy's probes. He revived the HENRY DEXTER WHITE controversy and probed Communists in the clergy, education, and the army. A loyal defender of McCarthy, Jenner fought his censure in 1954. In foreign policy he continued to support the Nationalist Chinese. During December 1957 Jenner announced he would not seek a third term. He then resumed the practice of law in Indiana, taking the bus every weekday from his home in Bedford to his office in Indianapolis, an hour-and-a-half trip. He died on March 9, 1986, in Bedford.

As Jenner biographer Michael Paul Poder noted Jenner made cogent arguments on the dangers of expanding presidential power, the consequent weakening of Congress, and hyperactive interventionism around the world, but these tended to be lost in his outrageous and shrill demagoguery and conspiracy-theory accusations. (See *The Eisenhower Years* Volume)

—JB

Jessup, Philip (Caryl)
(1897–1986) *ambassador-at-large*

Philip Jessup, the son of a professor of law, was born on January 5, 1897, in New York City. He attended Ridgefield School in Connecticut and Hamilton College and, following service in the army during World War I, obtained his bachelor's degree from that institution in 1919. He received an LL.B. from Yale in 1924, won admission to the District of Columbia bar in 1925, and earned a Ph.D. in international law from Columbia in 1927 for writing a dissertation on maritime law. Jessup worked in the New York law firm of Parker and Duryea from 1927 to 1943. During the late 1920s and 1930s Jessup taught at Columbia, eventually becoming the nation's most prestigious expert on international law. In 1948 Columbia awarded Jessup the Hamilton Fish Professorship of International Law and Diplomacy. Jessup published extensively on his field, and throughout the 1930s and early 1940s, he represented the United States at numerous diplomatic meetings dealing with legal matters. Prior to World War II he was a prominent spokesman for the powerful isolationist lobby, America First.

During the 1940s Jessup held a number of positions dealing with the United Nations and international finance. He was assistant secretary general for the United Nations Relief and Rehabilitation Agency and assistant secretary general of the Bretton Woods Conference of 1944. He served as U.S. representative to the UN Committee on the Progressive Development of International Law and its Codification in 1947. This body was charged with formulating into a set of laws the issues raised by the Nuremberg war crimes trials. The following year Jessup represented the United States at the Little Embassy of the UN. In May 1948 he became deputy to UN ambassador WARREN AUSTIN. He frequently filled in for the ailing ambassador in debates concerning Palestine and particularly distinguished himself when sparring with Soviet ambassador Andrei Vyshinsky over Berlin.

Truman appointed Jessup ambassador-at-large in February 1949. Jessup helped end the Berlin blockade of 1948–49. He was assigned to the job by Secretary of State DEAN G. ACHESON after discovering what importance lay in an omission made by Stalin in a statement to a reporter. The reason Stalin had imposed the blockade was because of the introduction in West Germany and West Berlin of a new German currency, with the aim of building a stable government. The blockade was intended to put pressure on the Allies in West Berlin to withdraw and to prevent the creation of a West German government. The Berlin airlift, however, made the blockade ineffective. Stalin appeared to waver in his commitment to the blockade when he was asked by a reporter what would have to happen for the blockade to end. In his response he did not mention the currency issue that had led to his action in the first place. Acheson, Jessup, and others believed such an omission indicated that Stalin might now be willing to negotiate an end to the crisis. In April 1949 Jessup bellied up the bar at the U.N. with Soviet UN ambassador Yakov Malik and asked if Stalin's omission meant anything. Malik responded that he did not know, but if he found out he would tell him. A few days later Malik told Jessup that the omission was made on purpose, and that, while the currency issue was important, it could be negotiated at a meeting of the Council of Foreign Ministers. Jessup inquired if the blockade could end before or after such a meeting, Malik again inquired and told Jessup that if a date were set for the meeting and if the U.S. would put off plans for the creation of a West German government, the blockade would be ended before the meeting. The date was set, the blockade ended on May 12, 1949, and the meeting was held, but to no end. But Jessup had helped to end the crisis, and only a handful of people knew of his role.

Jessup edited the famous White Paper on China released in the summer of 1949. The report concluded that corruption in Chiang Kai-shek's (Jiang Jieshi) regime was responsible for the fall of that nation to the Communists. From 1950 to 1952 he traveled to UN conferences and meetings of the North Atlantic Treaty Organization. He also held low level discussions with Soviet officials. Jessup participated in the deliberations leading to the U.S. entry into the Korean War and helped formulate strategy.

In 1950 Senator JOSEPH R. MCCARTHY (R-Wisc.), charging that he had a list of known Communists and Communist sympathizers in the State Department, maintained that Jessup had "an affinity for Communist causes." The diplomat had been criticized for some time because of his involvement in the administration's China policy and because he had testified as a character witness for ALGER HISS. Jessup answered McCarthy by producing letters from General GEORGE C. MARSHALL and DWIGHT D. EISENHOWER attesting to his loyalty.

During hearings by the Tydings Committee, formed to investigate McCarthy's charges against the State Department, the Wisconsin Republican elaborated his case against Jessup. He produced the names of six alleged Communist-front organizations to which Jessup had belonged. Of the six, the diplomat had not been affiliated with two and had left two before they were cited as Communist fronts. Two were never designated fronts. McCarthy also repeated charges made by Alfred Kohlberg, head of the "China Lobby," that Jessup was the initiator of a smear campaign against Nationalist China and the originator of the myth that Chinese Communists were merely agrarian reformers. The State Department refuted the charges. In July 1950 the Tydings Committee cleared Jessup.

The following year McCarthy's supporters mobilized to prevent Jessup's appointment as a delegate to the upcoming UN General Assembly meeting in Paris. HAROLD E. STASSEN entered the controversy when he maintained that the late senator ARTHUR H. VANDENBERG (R-Mich.) had told him of a White House meeting where Jessup had pressed for the cessation of aid to the Nationalists and the recognition of Communists. Jessup branded Stassen a liar. State Department records failed to substantiate Stassen's charge. However, the Senate subcommittee charged with approving the UN appointment voted three to two against confirmation. Throughout the hearings Truman and Acheson enthusiastically backed Jessup. The president ignored the Senate vote by giving Jessup a recess appointment, which did not require confirmation.

Jessup left the government in late 1952 to return to teaching. He served from 1961 until 1970 as a judge on the International Court of Justice in Geneva. Jessup continued to lecture and publish books on international law into the 1970s. He died on January 31, 1986, in Newtown, Pennsylvania.

Johnson, Edwin C(arl)
(1884–1970) *member of the Senate*

Edwin C. Johnson, the son of Swedish immigrants, was born on January 1, 1884, in Scandia, Kansas. He graduated from high school in 1903. From 1901 to 1909 he worked as a railroad laborer, a telegrapher,

and a train dispatcher. In 1910 he moved to Colorado to recuperate from tuberculosis. There he homesteaded a cattle ranch. Johnson won election to the Colorado state legislature in 1922, serving there until 1930. He was lieutenant governor from 1930 to 1933 and governor from 1933 to 1937. That year Johnson took a seat in the U.S. House of Representatives as a Democrat.

Describing himself as "a nationalist, an isolationist, an insulationist, and a pacifist," Johnson earned a reputation in Washington as a political maverick. In general he supported the domestic New Deal but fought Roosevelt on foreign policy. Only after Pearl Harbor did he support U.S. involvement in World War II. During the war Johnson worked to increase salaries and benefits for military personnel. He broke with Roosevelt in 1944, when the president decided to run for an unprecedented fourth term. The representative claimed that the decision would lead to tyranny and was "the greatest tragedy of American political history."

Johnson continued to oppose Democratic foreign policy initiatives during the Truman administration. Although he maintained that the United States needed to take "bold action" against communism, he nevertheless labeled the Truman Doctrine an "act of aggression" and charged that, while the Marshall Plan was a "prime deterrent to the causes of war," it would upset the U.S. economy.

Johnson supported America's development of nuclear power and asserted that God had placed the atomic bomb in U.S. hands as a trust to enable America to lead the world to peace. He suggested that the United States employ the bomb to "compel mankind to adopt a policy of lasting peace or be burnt to a crisp." In 1945 Johnson joined Representative Andrew May (D-Ky.) in introducing legislation to regulate atomic power. The measure, drawn up by the War Department, provided for the military dominance of a proposed Atomic Energy Commission. However, as a result of opposition from such scientists as LEO SZILARD and liberal senators, the final bill establishing the Atomic Energy Commission put the agency under civilian control. In 1946 Johnson reversed his stand on the use of the bomb and supported the Baruch Plan for international control and development of atomic power. In 1950 he made a highly controversial radio speech in which he divulged that the United States was working on a hydrogen bomb and that the Soviet Union's atomic bomb was a plutonium device. President

Truman, furious with Johnson's breach of confidence, publicly upbraided him.

Johnson was a major opponent of the universal military training and service bill of 1951, drawn up in light of the Korean conflict. Charging that universal military training was an undemocratic and un-American institution imported from Germany and was "the method of the police state," he argued that young men, who had to learn self-discipline, were "emotionally upset and absolutely ruined" by their military experiences. He claimed that future wars would be fought by scientists and military experts and that there would be no need for the average foot soldier. Johnson's fight was in vain, the bill passed both houses of Congress in June 1951. The law extended the draft to July 1, 1955, lowered the draft age to 18.5, and set up the National Security Training Commission, which was to plan for the implementation of any universal military training that Congress might establish in the future. However, it did not mandate the training itself, and Congress never did establish such a program.

In 1954 Johnson was selected with two other Democrats and three Republicans to serve on the Watkins Committee, formed to recommend action on a resolution to censure Senator JOSEPH R. MCCARTHY (R-Wisc.). McCarthy's lawyer challenged Johnson's credibility as an unbiased committee member because the *Denver Post* had quoted him as saying that all Democrats and all but half a dozen Republicans loathed McCarthy. Johnson stayed on the committee, which recommended McCarthy's censure.

Johnson retired from the Senate in 1955 to become governor of Colorado. He served one term. He died on May 30, 1970, in Denver, Colorado, after a hernia operation.

—SJT

Johnson, Louis A(rthur)

(1891–1966) *secretary of defense*

Louis Johnson was born on January 10, 1891, in Roanoke, Virginia. He graduated from the University of Virginia with an LL.B. degree in 1912 and began practicing law in Clarksburg, West Virginia. In 1917 he was elected to the West Virginia House of Representatives. He enlisted in the U.S. Army during World War I and saw action in France. After the war he returned to the practice of law and became active in Democratic politics. He also

assisted in the organization of the American Legion. President Roosevelt appointed him assistant secretary of war in 1937. Johnson was a vigorous proponent of air power and general military preparedness. Passed over by Roosevelt for secretary of war in 1940, Johnson resigned his post and returned to the practice of law. In 1942 he served as the president's personal representative in India. During 1948 Johnson was chairman of the Democratic Finance Committee in President Truman's uphill election campaign. He immediately underwrote the campaign with $250,000 of his own money and ultimately raised $1.5 million that helped Truman win the election. This assistance positioned Johnson for a federal appointment.

In March 1949 President Truman nominated Johnson secretary of defense (succeeding JAMES V. FORRESTAL), and the Senate confirmed him. Johnson's year-and-a-half time in office was quite controversial. Johnson pledged to continue unification of the armed services as mandated by the National Security Act of 1947. He also promised to maintain the nation's military strength while reducing defense expenditures. Less than a month after assuming office Johnson canceled construction of the navy's 65,000-ton super carrier, the USS *United States*, whose keel had been laid two months earlier. The flush-deck carrier was designed to handle bombers capable of delivering the atomic bomb. Johnson decided, however, that it duplicated the air force's bombing capability, which was based on the new long-range B-36 bomber.

The cancellation of the carrier initiated what came to be known as the "Revolt of the Admirals." Secretary of the Navy JOHN L. SULLIVAN resigned immediately in protest, charging Johnson with "drastically and arbitrarily restricting plans of an armed service without consultation with that service." To replace Sullivan, Johnson appointed FRANCIS P. MATTHEWS, who supported the secretary's plans for unification.

During the spring and summer of 1949 the navy and the air force fought each other to increase their share of a dwindling defense budget. Navy pilots bragged to the press that they could easily shoot down the B-36. In May 1949 Cedric R. Worth, special assistant to the undersecretary of the navy, circulated anonymously to Congress and the press a memorandum listing 55 problems in the air force's B-36 program. The document claimed corruption in the procurement of the B-36. It cited the fact that Johnson had been a director and legal counsel for Consolidated-Vultee, the main contractor, until his appointment as secretary of defense and that FLOYD B. ODLUM, controlling stockholder in the company, was a heavy contributor to the 1948 Democratic campaign.

In a June 1949 speech before the National War College, Johnson said that navy "partisans" were waging "a campaign of terror against further unification of the Armed Forces." A special House investigation in August cleared Johnson of all charges of corruption in B-36 procurement. But Johnson's ill temper had helped bring navy–air force tensions to the breaking point. Johnson's temperament was also afflicted by a strong desire to become president.

Johnson was a strong proponent of centralizing budgetary power to cut defense expenditures. In testimony on the 1949 national security bill, he maintained that the measure, increasing the powers of the secretary of defense, would enable him to save up to $1 billion per year by eliminating waste and duplication. The bill passed in August 1949. It gave the secretary of defense increased powers over the defense budget and over the secretaries of the army, navy, and air force.

The secretary immediately began cutting expenses, focusing on the navy, which he felt played a less important role in postwar defense than the air force. At the end of August Johnson announced that 135,000 civilian workers in the armed services would be cut. The navy was hit hardest, losing 76,000 civilian employees. Congressmen whose districts were affected by the cuts protested vigorously. Truman backed Johnson and said the order would go through but promised that the federal government would give preference in hiring to those let go by the services. In August 1949 Johnson appointed General Joseph T. McNarney chairman of the National Defense Management Committee formed to make recommendations for increased efficiency and savings. Under Johnson's prodding the McNarney Committee announced in the beginning of September 1949 a $929 million cut in the defense budget for 1950. Once again the navy suffered the largest cut—$376 million.

The loud protests by the armed services, especially the navy, over the cuts in the budget finally forced Representative CARL VINSON (D-Ga.) to order a House Armed Services Committee investigation of unification and defense strategy during October. Testifying at these hearings Admiral LOUIS

E. DENFELD, chief of naval operations, accused the Secretary of Defense of "arbitrary" decision-making against "the spirit and concept" of the unification law. On the other hand, former president HERBERT HOOVER praised Johnson's efforts to promote economy in the Defense Department. Vinson concluded that Johnson "deserves the full support of this committee and the country in his difficult task."

A week after the end of the hearings, Secretary of the Navy Matthews, with the support of Truman and Johnson, fired Denfeld. Johnson's efforts to speed unification and cut spending were the center of so much controversy that President Truman in the fall of 1949 was forced repeatedly to deny rumors that Johnson was on the way out. In January 1950 Johnson announced that the $20 billion requested by the services for fiscal 1951 had been trimmed to $13.5 billion, which, he said, was "adequate to defend the nation against any situation that may arise in the next two years." However, in response to congressional criticism, particularly from Vinson, he ordered the Joint Chiefs of Staff to reexamine the 1951 budget to see whether more money was needed for planes. In April 1950 Johnson appeared before the House Appropriations Committee and requested a $553 million increase in the fiscal 1951 arms budget. A $350 million increase was granted. Johnson at first balked, however, at the State Department's attempt to formulate a defense strategy based on anticommunism (later embodied in NSC-68). One particular stormy meeting between State and Defense officials—in which Johnson stormed out of the room and ordered the military officers to follow him—caused Secretary of State DEAN G. ACHESON to doubt his mental balance. Later, however, Johnson signed off on the report. The two men also differed on China policy. Johnson joined with Republicans in decrying Acheson's "loss of China," so as to undercut him in the cabinet. The two did agree, however, that the hydrogen bomb should be built.

In June 1950 war broke out in Korea. Johnson immediately issued a statement saying that South Korean defenses, established with American help, "should assure the security" of that country. As military setbacks mounted in Korea, his economy drive came under increasing attack. Supplemental appropriations passed by Congress increased defense spending from $13 billion in fiscal 1950 to $48 billion in fiscal 1951. Nevertheless Senator LYNDON B. JOHNSON (D-Tex.), chairman of the Armed Services

Preparedness Subcommittee, criticized the slow pace of mobilization in 1950 and the continued wastefulness in the Defense Department. Secretary Johnson replied with statistics attempting to show the combat readiness of the armed services at the time of the Korean outbreak.

Throughout the summer of 1950 Johnson, along with Acheson and Truman, was blamed for U.S. setbacks in Korea. Clyde A. Lewis, national commander of the Veterans of Foreign Wars, charged that the Korean situation had been "bungled" and called for the resignation of Johnson and Acheson. In a lengthy reply to a call for his resignation by Representative Anthony F. Tauriello (D-N.Y.) at the end of August 1950, Johnson said that the attacks on him were aimed "at the administration generally, with an eye to the November elections."

Truman began to question Johnson's competence. His intemperance had worsened interservice relations in the armed forces. He threatened to resign when Truman nominated the independent-minded Thomas K. Finletter—who advocated more money for the air force. Truman ignored Johnson, who withdrew his threat. Then Johnson was heard to have agreed that Acheson should resign. Truman also got wind of a rumor that Johnson had expressed an interest to Republicans in accepting their party's presidential nomination. What finally led to Johnson's ouster was his reluctance to discipline General DOUGLAS MACARTHUR, who was openly critical of the administration's Taiwan policy. Truman finally demanded his resignation on September 11, 1950. In his letter to Truman Johnson admitted that in performing his duties he had made "more enemies than friends." He said in a time of war the country should not be burdened by such controversy. Johnson's economy drive was under heated attack by Republicans and was identified with the inability of the United States to respond forcefully in the early months of the war. Johnson suggested General GEORGE C. MARSHALL be appointed as successor to "promote national and international unity."

Johnson's resignation occurred at the low point of U.S. fortunes in the war. Three days after his resignation the Inchon landing reversed the military fortunes of UN troops in Korea. Johnson later claimed some credit for the Inchon success because he had supported MacArthur's plan over the objections of General J. LAWTON COLLINS, army chief of staff.

After leaving government service Johnson became a senior partner in the Washington law firm of Steptoe and Johnson. He died on April 24, 1966, in Washington, D.C.

—TFS

Johnson, Lyndon B(aines)

(1908–1973) *member of the House of Representatives, member of the Senate*

Lyndon Johnson was born in Stonewall, Texas, on August 27, 1908. He grew up in the rugged hill country of south-central Texas, near Austin. His father, a populist, had been a progressive state legislator as well as a speculator in cattle and real estate. His mother had attended Baylor University and taught debating and elocution in the local high school.

Johnson attended Southwest Texas State Teachers College—to which he barely passed the entrance exam after having failed once—where he procured a job as assistant to the school president, edited the campus newspaper, and played a central role in student politics. Johnson spent his sophomore year teaching in a Mexican-American school and, after graduation in 1930, taught high school in Houston for 15 months. He left Texas for Washington, D.C., to become legislative secretary to Representative Richard Kleberg (D-Tex.). Kleberg was an indifferent legislator, and the energetic Johnson soon took over de facto management of his office. He also won election as speaker of the Little Congress, an organization of congressional assistants.

In 1935 Johnson was appointed state director of the National Youth Administration. As usual he was a whirlwind of activity, aggressively soliciting support for and sponsorship of hundreds of public service projects to employ thousands of young Texans. When a local representative died in 1937, Johnson swiftly announced his candidacy for the seat. He distinguished himself from his seven opponents by strongly endorsing the New Deal, including President Roosevelt's controversial court-packing plan. Elected to the House as a Democrat in April at the age of 29, Johnson won special attention from Roosevelt, who arranged for Johnson to gain a coveted seat on the Committee on Naval Affairs.

Committee chairman representative CARL VINSON (D-Ga.) became one of Johnson's two mentors in the House: the other was Speaker of the House (after 1940) SAM T. RAYBURN (D-Tex.), who had served in the Texas legislature with Johnson's father. Nonetheless, Johnson's primary allegiance was to Roosevelt. He faithfully backed New Deal programs and was a vocal supporter of defense preparedness, a major theme of the administration's foreign policy. With Roosevelt's endorsement Johnson ran for the Senate in a special election in 1941 but lost to Texas governor W. Lee O'Daniel by only 1,311 votes.

Following Pearl Harbor Johnson served for five months in the Naval Reserve. He requested assignment to active duty, which Roosevelt granted and sent the lieutenant commander on an inspection tour of General DOUGLAS MACARTHUR's headquarters. He rode as a passenger in a bomber raid that came under fire. The navy awarded an ill-deserved Silver Star to Johnson, and he exaggerated his combat experience for the rest of his life. He then returned to his duties as a congressman. During the war Johnson was an active chairman of a special investigative subcommittee of the Naval Affairs Committee on the defense program. As the cold war began he was an outspoken advocate of higher defense expenditures, particularly for air power, and he delivered frequent orations on the House floor in support of a firm containment policy. "One thing is clear," Johnson said in 1947, "Whether Communist or fascist or simply a pistol-packing racketeer, the one thing a bully understands is force and the one thing he fears is courage." Likewise, he fervently backed humanitarian measures as weapons in America's mission to combat global communism. In support of the Marshall Plan he said: "By sending food, by sending financial aid, by sending both abroad, we contest with evil in a battle for peace. If despair is replaced by faith, if desolation is replaced by construction, if hunger is answered by food—if those things are done, we shall be victors in the battle."

During the Truman years Johnson slowly shifted toward the right. He voted to pass the Case labor disputes and the Taft-Hartley labor bills over President Truman's vetoes. He opposed civil rights legislation such as the outlawing of state poll taxes and the establishment of a Fair Employment Practices Commission. He voted to sustain Truman's veto of three tax cut bills in 1947–48 and also to restore items in the administrations's budget slashed or removed by the Republican majority in the 80th Congress. He also voted for the Mundt-Nixon bill in 1948.

In 1948 Johnson again ran for the Senate, adopting such novelties as campaigning in a helicopter. He pitched his Stetson out the window as a sign of exuberance, and which aides had to scramble to recover. He was victorious in the Democratic primary over Governor Coke Stevenson by the tiny margin of 87 votes out of total of 988,295. Johnson's victory was sealed by the certification of 201 disputed votes from box 13 in Jim Wells County. Stevenson charged vote fraud had put his opponent over the top, and, as Johnson biographer Robert Caro argued, was outraged by what he considered a flouting of the law when the Democratic State Executive Committee and the State Convention voted to put Johnson on the ballot. On the advice of an attorney, he applied for and received a restraining order from Federal District judge T. Whitfield Davidson preventing Johnson's name from being put on the ballot. Davidson then suggested both Stevenson and Johnson be put on the general election ballot. Johnson's advisers suggested he take the deal, but he refused. Davidson then allowed witnesses to testify to alleged fraud in the Johnson campaign that was damaging to his cause. Davidson announced that a trial might be necessary if Stevenson's civil rights had been violated by vote fraud. However, as Caro noted, through the deft advice and maneuvering of attorney Abe Fortas, Johnson won a stay of the injunction from Supreme Court justice HUGO L. BLACK on September 29, 1948. Johnson then easily overcame his Republican opponent in November.

In July 1977 Luis Salas, the county election judge who, in 1948, confirmed the validity of the 201 disputed votes, disclosed that the ballots were fictitious. "Johnson did not win that election—it was stolen for him and I know how it was done," Salas said. According to Salas, Johnson said on election night, "If I can get 200 votes more, I've got it won." Accordingly, 200-odd Johnson votes were added to box 13; the names were in alphabetical order. Salas said he lied in the original 1948 investigation when he testified the vote had been legitimate, but he chose to break his silence to gain "peace of mind and to reveal to people the corruption of politics."

As a freshman senator, Johnson adopted a more subdued bearing and sedulously courted the leader of the southern delegation, Senator RICHARD B. RUSSELL (D-Ga.). He devoted himself to his committee work, particularly the Armed Services Committee on which Russell was a senior member and who became chairman in 1951. After the Korean War broke out Johnson arranged the formation of an Armed Services Committee preparedness subcommittee to oversee the defense program and the war effort. Shrewd observers compared Johnson's subcommittee to the Truman committee of World War II, that had brought Truman into the vice presidency—which had led, of course, to the presidency—and they had no doubt that Johnson planned to parlay this chairmanship into higher office. Johnson's panel periodically issued reports highlighting waste and inefficiency in such areas as stockpiling of raw materials, manpower, and the sale of surplus equipment. The subcommittee did make useful suggestions, and Johnson was widely praised for his effort.

According to historian Robert Dallek, for Johnson to survive politically as a senator from Texas, he had to appease the oil and gas interests of the state. This meant supporting state ownership of tideland oil, which the Truman administration had ruled in the national domain, which was upheld by the Supreme Court, and the Kerr natural gas bill of 1950, which freed gas producers from regulation by the Federal Power Commission (FPC). The Kerr bill passed Congress but was vetoed by the president. When Truman renominated LELAND OLDS to serve as chairman of the FPC, Johnson campaigned strenuously against Senate confirmation of the liberal, who had earned the enmity of the oil and gas industry by his regulatory policies. On the Senate floor he denounced Olds for his "bias, prejudice and hostility directed toward the oil industry." While maintaining that "I do not charge that Mr. Olds is a Communist," Johnson quoted excerpts from Olds's radical writing from the 1920s to demonstrate his unfitness for the post. The Senate voted to reject his renomination, 53 to 15, in October 1949. Although he defended Texas oil and gas interests and opposed civil rights measures, Johnson did not want to be thought of as a typical southern senator—obsessed with regional affairs—but as a nationalist. So he supported a strong defense policy and Truman's decision to send U.S. troops to Korea in 1950.

The elections of 1950 resulted in the defeats of the Democratic majority leader and majority whip. As Caro reported Johnson hesitated in running for the open whip's post. It had no real power, but Johnson did not have the patience to wait to snare a committee chairmanship—where real power lay at that time—that would take years. So, with Senators Rus-

sell and ROBERT S. KERR's (D-Okla.) backing, he put himself forward for the position and was elected, the youngest party whip in Senate history. Two years later he was chosen minority leader, a remarkably swift ascent for such a junior senator.

With his prodigious energy, exhaustive knowledge of Senate procedures and traditions, and acute and encyclopedic understanding of the strengths, vulnerabilities, and desires of individual senators, Johnson, by force of personality, transformed the formal position of party leader into the fulcrum of Senate business. He deferred to Senate elders while cultivating freshmen with desirable committee assignments and various perquisites. He preferred to work behind the scenes in one-on-one encounters where his powers of persuasion—a shrewd amalgam of cajolery, reasoning, and intimidation that became famous as the "Johnson treatment"—were unmatched. The cumulative result of these sessions was the smooth disposition of the Senate's daily business, which Johnson dominated as no other senator had. A small band of liberal Democrats criticized his leadership as undemocratic and stultifying of social reform, but Johnson's cautious centrist politics and solicitous attention to the wants of the majority smothered any possibilities of revolt in the 1950s.

Johnson was elected vice president in 1960 on a ticket with Senator John F. Kennedy (D-Mass.) as a presidential candidate. He served unhappily in that post until November 22, 1963, when he was sworn in as president immediately after Kennedy's assassination. In office Johnson took the stalemated Kennedy program and with his legislative mastery guided it through Congress in the mid-1960s. His Great Society program, which included civil rights protection, Medicare, federal aid to cities and education, was the most sweeping and bold enactment of social reform measures since the New Deal. Simultaneously, Johnson embarked on a massive military intervention against a Communist insurgency in South Vietnam. The Vietnam War proved to be a disastrous undertaking, eroding Johnson's popularity and eclipsing his domestic goal of ending poverty in America. Isolated and embittered, Johnson withdrew from the presidential race in March 1968 and returned to his vast Texas farm after the inauguration of his successor in January 1969. He died of a heart attack in San Antonio, Texas, on January 22, 1973. (See *The Eisenhower Years, The Kennedy Years, The Johnson Years* Volumes)

—TO

Johnston, Alvanley

(1875–1951) *president, Brotherhood of Locomotive Engineers*

The son of a Scottish emigrant, Alvanley Johnston was born on May 12, 1875, in Seeley's Bay, Ontario. He attended Brookville Business College from 1890 to 1891. The following year he began working for the Great Northern Railway Company as a call boy and then as a clerk and stenographer. From 1897 to 1909 he worked as a locomotive engineer. Johnston became general chairman of the Great Northern Division of the Brotherhood of Locomotive Engineers (BLE) in 1909. He was elected assistant grand chief engineer in 1918 and grand chief engineer in 1925. During his presidency he acquired virtual control of his union. At the 1927 BLE convention Johnston was established as union head while the titles of president, vice president, and secretary were erased from union rolls.

In 1933 Johnston and several other union officials were convicted for misappropriation of BLE funds in the aftermath of a bank failure. Johnston received a sentence of from one to 30 years. However, in 1935 a court of appeals overturned the conviction on the grounds that Johnston had had no direct knowledge of the irregularities. In 1943, when the government temporarily seized the railroads, Johnston and A. F. WHITNEY, head of the Brotherhood of Railroad Trainmen (BRT), served as labor consultants. That same year Johnston was appointed to the Combined War Labor Board as a railroad union representative. Primarily due to his efforts, the BLE emerged solvent in 1945.

During the latter part of 1945, Johnston, Whitney, and leaders of the three operating unions presented wage and rule demands to the railroad companies. The rail unions sought a 31-cent hourly pay increase and a 40-hour workweek, which most industries had already implemented. Negotiations on these demands reached a deadlock in January 1946, and three of the unions agreed to postpone discussions. Johnston and Whitney, however, insisted that both wage and rule demands be resolved.

The two called for a strike for March 16. Truman temporarily averted a walkout by setting up a fact-finding board. The grievances of the two unions were heard publicly before Truman's Emergency Board that same month. The board subsequently recommended that wages be increased and other certain demands of the unions, including the 40-hour workweek. The engineers and trainmen rejected the report and set 4 p.m. May 18 as the strike date. On May 17 Truman seized the railroads under Executive Order 9729. On May 18 Johnston and Whitney postponed the strike again. Truman recommended Johnston and Whitney that they accept a compromise of 16 cents an hour. Johnston and Whitney accused the president of "double crossing" the railroad workers. The membership of the BLE and the BRT voted to start a strike at 4 p.m. on May 23.

On May 24, with the strike already one day old and causing utter chaos in the nation, Truman went on the radio to appeal to the strikers to return to work and threatened to use the army to break the strike. Referring to Johnston and Whitney, Truman said he had warned them that the strike would result in a national disaster: "It is inconceivable that in our democracy any two men should be placed in a position where they can completely stifle our economy and ultimately destroy our country."

On May 25 Truman addressed a joint session of Congress on the matter. He stated that he regarded the railroad crisis as the result of "the obstinate arrogance of two men," Johnston and Whitney, who, he said, "have it within their power to cripple the entire economy of the nation." Truman called for legislation empowering him to draft people striking against the government. Just at that point Secretary of the Senate Leslie Biffle handed Truman a note saying the strike had been settled on his terms. The president announced this but continued to call for the draft legislation. The president's bill did not win approval.

Citing THOMAS E. DEWEY's welfare program and anticommunist stance, Johnston, a Republican, endorsed the New York governor for the presidency in 1944 and in 1948. In 1950, when Senator ROBERT A. TAFT (R-Ohio) was opposed by labor organizations in his reelection campaign, Johnston endorsed the coauthor of the Taft-Hartley Act because of his repeated anticommunist and anti-Truman positions. Taft had also helped stop Truman's 1946 draconian antistrike law from making its way through the Senate. Johnston retired in 1950 after 50 years of membership in the brotherhood. He died on September 17, 1951, in Shakers Heights, Ohio.

—DGE

Johnston, Eric A(llen)

(1896–1963) president, U.S. Chamber of Commerce; president, Motion Picture Association; administrator, Economic Stabilization Agency

The son of a pharmacist, Johnston was born on December 21, 1896, in Washington, D.C. He worked as a longshoreman and law librarian while attending the University of Washington in Seattle. He received his LL.B. in 1917 and served four years in the marine corps. After returning to Spokane, Johnston sold vacuum cleaners door-to-door. In 1923 he bought a small electrical business and built it into one of the largest distributors of household appliances in the Northwest. During the 1930s Johnston organized the Columbia Electrical and Manufacturing Company, turning it into a leading appliance producer; he also revived the bankrupt Washington Brick and Lime Company.

In 1940 Johnston, a liberal Republican, ran unsuccessfully for the U.S. Senate from Washington. Two years later he was elected president of the U.S. Chamber of Commerce, where he quickly reversed its conservative anti–New Deal policies. A strong proponent of profit-sharing and other liberal employment practices, Johnston earned the respect of organized labor. He conferred with President Roosevelt, the American Federation of Labor, the Congress of Industrial Organizations, and farm groups early in his term as chamber president. Through these meetings he developed union support for a "no-strike pledge" and a business "maintenance-of-membership plan," which basically allowed for the establishment of modified union shops. The no-strike pledge caused dissension among workers, who held wildcat strikes while union leaders tried to enforce the pledge according to wartime contracts. While he offered the New Deal qualified support, Johnston objected to what he saw as excessive centralization of government and "efforts to legislate by administrative decree." He also organized the chamber for political advocacy and electoral influence, centralizing control of the organization and creating the departments of Economic Research and Government Affairs.

Johnston advocated what historians would call "corporate liberalism," in which the federal government and unions would play an important role in keeping corporate capitalism stable. Employers would pay high wages and provide job security; the government would only intervene when capitalism failed to meet the country's needs.

During World War II Johnston first entered government service, holding a position on the President's Committee on Deferment of Federal Employees. In February 1943 he toured South America as chairman of the U.S. Commission on Inter-American Development, promoting postwar trade. The following year he traveled through the Soviet Union to inspect the industrial development in Siberia.

In March 1945 Johnston, American Federation of Labor president WILLIAM GREEN, and Congress of Industrial Organization president PHILIP MURRAY put forward the "Charter for Labor and Management," which advocated corporate liberalism. It called for an economy of high employment and high wages in exchange for organized labor's pledge to respect management's control over capitalism's operations. But corporate capitalism proved unpopular with labor and management. Many workers wanted to go on strike for higher pay after the war ended, despite the no-strike pledges of union leaders. Other businessmen, under the aegis of the National Association of Manufacturers wanted to weaken unions. Indeed, within the chamber itself Johnston's ideas were unpopular. Johnston's resignation as head of the chamber in 1946 was met with relief by chamber members.

In 1945 Johnston succeeded Will B. Hays as president of the Motion Picture Association of America (MPAA). The MPAA, a trade organization, acted as a self-regulating policy maker for the film industry. In the late 1940s and early 1950s, Johnston focused his attention on the promotion of international trade and film censorship. He helped to arrange business deals between American film companies and French, Australian, and British distributors. In 1948 he arranged the sale of U.S. films to the Soviet bloc. Johnston also dealt with complaints from groups such as the League of Decency and the American Legion about film content. He helped to establish the Production Code Authority, the industry's self-censoring body.

In March 1947 Johnston appeared before the House Un-American Activities Committee (HUAC) to testify about communism in the U.S. film industry. He discounted fears of Communist influence in Hollywood, noting that foreign Communists hated American movies. But under pressure from Committee member RICHARD M. NIXON

(R-Calif.), Johnston admitted that the film industry had failed to produce a single anticommunist film in the preceding five years. After secret HUAC hearings in May, Johnston and other prominent film leaders were subpoenaed to appear in Washington in October. Before testifying Johnston secretly assured attorneys for writers and actors suspected of Communist or left-wing affiliations that the film industry would not blacklist radicals. When he appeared on October 27, Johnston agreed Communists should be exposed, but he warned of censorship and called for greater protection of civil rights. He also objected to the use of witnesses who could slander without cross-examination and were "immune from subsequent suit or prosecution."

Although he publicly deplored HUAC's tactics and motives, Johnston and others in the film industry worried about public reaction to charges of Communist influence in Hollywood. Many executives feared a boycott of films by conservative groups. Johnston reportedly suggested to the major studios that they agree not to employ "proven Communists." In late November 1947 a conference of film executives met in New York at the Waldorf-Astoria Hotel to discuss possible action on the Communist issue. On November 25 Johnston announced the so-called Waldorf Agreement, which barred Communists from the industry. The Hollywood Ten, a group of writers and directors who had refused to answer questions before HUAC, were to be fired. Johnston also asked Congress to enact laws to "assist American industry to rid itself of subversive, disloyal elements." This ban, an informal blacklist, continued in Hollywood until the early 1960s. In 1951, after pressure from the American Legion, Johnston agreed to investigate more than 200 employees the legion thought might be subversive. Those accused were asked to deny allegations concerning their loyalty.

In January 1951 President Truman appointed Johnston head of the Economic Stabilization Agency (ESA) formed to speed up the imposition of wage and price controls during the Korean War. Wasting little time, Johnston ordered a stop-gap freeze for the U.S. economy on January 26. While he supported temporary wage-price controls, Johnston felt a vigorous fiscal policy, specifically including high taxes, would be "more effective" in combating inflation. In February he put a 10 percent ceiling on pay raises, a limit organized labor considered inadequate. For the most part, Johnston

resisted pressure from labor and blocked wage increases above the ceiling. He allowed special consideration of hardship cases and tried to protect cost-of-living adjustments negotiated by unions before the January ceiling. During February and March first labor and then management groups prevented Johnston from organizing an effective Wage Stabilization Board (WSB). After presidential action, a reconstituted WSB started work in May. In August Johnston approved a new WSB policy of allowing wages to rise with the cost of living. He resigned as ESA head in November 1951 and returned to the MPAA.

In February 1952 Johnston became chairman of the International Development Advisory Board (IADB). The organization was responsible for promoting Truman's Point Four program to bring American technical and financial expertise to underdeveloped nations. When President Dwight D. Eisenhower took office in 1953, he kept Johnston as IADB head. Eisenhower also used him as a special ambassador to the Middle East in an attempt to ease Arab-Israeli tensions. Johnston suffered a stroke in June 1963 and died on August 22, 1963, in Washington, D.C.

—JF

Judd, Walter H(enry)
(1898–1994) *member of the House of Representatives*

Walter H. Judd was born on September 25, 1898, in Rising City, Nebraska. He graduated from the University of Nebraska Medical School in 1923 and two years later became a medical missionary in China. He contracted malaria and was forced to return to the United States in 1931. Judd accepted a teaching position at the University of Minnesota Hospital. In 1934 he returned to China to run a hospital in Shansi Province. When the Japanese conquered the area in 1938, Judd fled to the United States. The doctor then embarked on an extensive speaking tour, informing the nation of the brutality of the Japanese occupation and pleading for more American aid to the Nationalists. Discouraged by the isolationism of the period, he settled down to practice medicine in Minnesota. In August 1942 Judd announced his candidacy for a seat in the U.S. House of Representatives. Endorsed by liberals and labor impressed with his humanitarian concern for the Chinese and his demands for U.S. involvement in the war, Judd defeated his isolationist opponent, Oscar Youngdahl.

Judd quickly emerged as a major spokesman for Chinese interests. His maiden speech deplored the discriminatory exclusion acts and demanded their repeal. He also pleaded for keeping both Russia and China in the war and denounced American diplomacy during the 1920s and the 1930s as based on attempts to impose American ideas on people to whom they were alien. Judd labored to build up the Nationalists as a significant power in Asia so that they would first defeat the Japanese and then the growing Communist movement, led by Mao Zedong (Mao Tse-tung). One of the most vigorous anticommunists in Congress, Judd disagreed with many China experts who assumed that Mao's movement was based more on nationalism than doctrinaire communism. He said in 1945, "I am increasingly convinced that the Chinese Communists are Communist first and Chinese second." He defended Chiang Kai-shek's (Jiang Jieshi) government from charges that it was hopelessly corrupt and reactionary by requesting Americans to understand the difficulties of unifying and governing a large nation.

After the war Judd emerged as a leading spokesman for the "China Lobby," a powerful pressure group composed of officials from the Nationalist embassy in Washington, propagandists, and leading conservative American businessmen, journalists, union leaders, and policy groups. The lobby was formed to pressure the administration to increase aid to Chiang in the face of growing criticism of his regime and Nationalist defeats on the battlefield. Judd considered it hypocritical on the administration's part to provide arms and economic assistance to Europe and not to Asia, where actual battles were being fought. He did win $338 million in Marshall Plan aid to Nationalist China, a further $125 million to be spent at the discretion of the president. He also advocated and gained a quota for Chinese immigrants in 1943. He also pushed for the elimination in immigration laws of all racial discriminatory clauses in the McCarran-Walter Act of 1952.

The former missionary joined the growing number in the lobby who began to believe that only a pro-Communist conspiracy in Washington during and after the war had stymied attempts to aid the Nationalists. These conspirators had portrayed the Chiang government as corrupt while lauding the democratic agrarian roots of Mao's movement. Judd charged

that this conspiracy existed in the Far East desk of the State Department, which he called the "Red Cell." But in his opinion the conspiracy also took place in the high offices of the Roosevelt administration. In 1946 Judd joined 65 other prominent Americans in signing the "Manchurian Manifesto." This document charged that at the Yalta Conference the United States, behind China's back, had promised to turn over Manchuria and Mongolia to the Russians following their entry into the war. Later Judd made JOHN S. SERVICE the focus of his attacks on Chinese experts in the State Department.

Judd continued to criticize Truman's China policy into 1947. He denounced the Marshall Mission, formed to mediate the Chinese civil war, complaining of General GEORGE C. MARSHALL's lack of understanding of the Chinese problem. When the mission failed, Judd pressured the administration into sending General ALFRED C. WEDEMEYER to China to reassess the situation. Truman also lifted the arms embargo to China and replaced the controversial JOHN CARTER VINCENT as director of the Office of Far Eastern Affairs. The president requested a moderate increase in aid to Chiang, but the bill was held up by economy-minded Republicans in the House Appropriations Committee.

Following the fall of China to the Communists in 1949, Judd became one of the most vocal supporters of the new Taiwan regime. He joined many conservatives in denouncing the White Paper on China, which placed the blame for the fall on corruption in the Nationalist regime. Judd praised the Nationalist government for understanding the gravity of the threat of international communism in Asia. He claimed that the White Paper should be read by Americans as "a confession that the leaders of our government possessed no such understanding." Judd further charged that evidence favorable to Chiang was omitted from the document. "We have not tried to win the war in China," Judd proclaimed. "We have tried to end it. But the only way to end the war with Communism—anywhere—is to win the war."

In 1950 Judd backed Senator JOSEPH R. MCCARTHY's (R-Wisc.) charges of conspiracy in the State Department. He repeated his earlier accusation that the responsibility for China's fall lay with "the Communists and their stooges both inside our government and among writers, lecturers, commentators, and so forth." Judd did support Truman's decision to stop the invasion of South Korea by the North, but he agreed with the Wisconsin senator that the war could have been averted if the administration had stood up to the Communists earlier. Judd also opposed Truman's dismissal of General DOUGLAS MACARTHUR. During the war Judd began a campaign, with which he was associated far into the Johnson administration, to pressure Truman not to recognize Communist China and to oppose China's entry into the United Nations.

In 1952 Walter Judd was one of the most admired politicians among conservative Americans. DWIGHT D. EISENHOWER even considered him for the vice presidential nomination. During the Eisenhower period Judd was active in China Lobby affairs and played a prominent role in the founding of the Committee of One Million. Judd delivered the party's keynote address at the 1960 Republican National Convention. In 1962 he lost reelection by a small margin but remained prominent in the Republican Party and continued to speak out on China by authoring articles in *Reader's Digest* and making commentaries on a radio program. President Ronald Reagan awarded him the Presidential Medal of Freedom in 1981. He died of cancer on February 13, 1994, in Mitchellville, Maryland. (See *The Eisenhower Years* Volume)

—JB

K

Kasenkina, Oksana S(tepanova)
(1896–1960) *Russian defector*

Oksana S. Kasenkina, the daughter of a locomotive engineer, was born in 1896 in the Ukrainian village of Glubokaya in the Don region of Russia. She completed her education in the natural sciences in 1914 and launched a teaching career that same year. Her marriage to Demyan Kasenkina was cut short by his abduction in 1937 during Stalin's "Great Purge."

Having secured a teaching position at a school for Soviet children in the United States, Kasenkina arrived in New York City in 1946. When the school was disbanded two years later, all teachers were scheduled to return to the Soviet Union on July 31, 1948. The science teacher, however, avoided the return trip and instead sought refuge at the Tolstoy Foundation's Reed Farm in Valley Cottage, New York. The farm was a community established by Alexandra Tolstoy, daughter of the Russian novelist, for the aid of anticommunist Russians.

Kasenkina's subsequent transport from there to the Soviet consulate on August 7 precipitated a series of incidents that escalated the cold war. Tolstoy accused Soviet consulate personnel of kidnapping the teacher. Russian consul general Jacob Lomakin, on the other hand, charged that the "White Russian Underground" had forcibly detained her at Reed Farm, and Ambassador Alexander Panyushkin exacerbated the situation by accusing U.S. authorities of abetting the abduction. Meanwhile, Kasenkina remained incommunicado inside the consulate. A writ of habeas corpus was requested by Christopher Emmet, chairman of the right-wing organization, Common Cause, Inc., on the grounds that the woman was being held pris-

oner. Although the writ was granted by Samuel Dickstein, justice of the New York Supreme Court, its enforcement was delayed on the advice of the State Department, since there remained an unresolved question of diplomatic immunity. On August 12, the same day as the delay was announced, Kasenkina was critically injured when she jumped from the third-story window of the Russian consulate, an act later labeled by the press as her "leap to freedom." Because of his accusations and his hindrance of a police investigation of this case, Lomakin was asked to leave the United States in a note from Secretary of State GEORGE C. MARSHALL. President Truman signed the expulsion order on August 25. Russia brought the diplomatic dispute to an end by breaking consular relations with the United States.

Over the next 10 years Kasenkina appeared in public as an occasional lecturer for the anti-Soviet cause. She published an autobiography, *Leap to Freedom*, in 1949. A bill was passed and signed in 1951 granting her extended residence in the United States, and in 1956 Kasenkina became a naturalized citizen. In poor health, she retired to Miami, Florida, in 1959; she died there from a heart ailment on July 24, 1960.

An ironic twist occurred when it was revealed in the 1990s that Dickstein had been an agent for the Soviet Union years earlier when he was a congressman. He was supposed to provide information and try to influence policy on behalf of the Russians. He seemed mostly interested in taking money from the Soviets and proved unreliable. The Russians decided to stop using him in the late 1930s.

—LLM

Kaufman, Irving R(obert)

(1910–1992) *district judge*

The son of a small manufacturer, Irving R. Kaufman was born on June 24, 1910, in New York City. He earned his law degree from Fordham University in 1931 and set up practice in New York City. He became a special assistant to the U.S. attorney for the Southern District of New York in 1935 and was appointed Assistant U.S. attorney for the Southern District of New York one year later. Known as the "boy prosecutor," Kaufman gained public attention for uncovering a large ring that had swindled insurance companies out of millions of dollars. He resigned from the post in 1940 and returned to private practice.

In October 1947 Attorney General TOM C. CLARK appointed Kaufman his special assistant to conduct a large-scale investigation into the practice of illegal lobbying procedures. He headed a special unit established to publicize and enforce the Lobbying Act of 1946, which required the registration and reporting of lobbyists. Kaufman's efforts were primarily educative, urging the cooperation of those involved. Only four people and three companies were indicted for willful noncompliance. While in Washington Kaufman became friends with J. EDGAR HOOVER, an association that continued until Hoover's death in 1972. Kaufman left the Justice Department in 1948. The following year President Truman appointed him judge of the United States for the Southern District of New York. The 39-year-old Kaufman was the country's youngest federal judge.

In 1951 Kaufman presided over the trial of ETHEL and JULIUS ROSENBERG, charged with transmitting U.S. atomic secrets to the Soviet Union. After a three-week trial, the Rosenbergs were convicted. On April 5, 1951, Kaufman imposed an unprecedented sentence of death upon the defendants. The judge justified his decision on the grounds that the cold war required such action. "The issue of this case is presented in a unique framework of history," he said, "it is so difficult to make people realize that this country is engaged in a life and death struggle with a completely different system. . . . The punishment to be meted out in this case must therefore serve the maximum interest for the preservation of our society against these traitors in our midst."

The severity of the sentence caused worldwide protest. In the United States a Committee to Secure Justice in the Rosenberg Case was formed and prominent scientists, such as HAROLD C. UREY and ALBERT EINSTEIN asked for mercy. In late 1952 Kaufman received a plea for clemency, requesting that he change the death sentence to one of imprisonment. He refused but granted a stay of execution so that the Rosenbergs could appeal to the Supreme Court. In announcing his decision in January 1953, he maintained: "Their traitorous acts were of the highest degree. They turned over information to Russia concerning the most deadly weapon known to man, thereby exposing millions of their countrymen to danger or death." The Supreme Court rejected a final appeal, and the Rosenbergs were executed on June 19, 1953.

Kaufman was initially praised for his handling of the Rosenberg trial; the Rosenbergs' attorneys even thanked him for his fair treatment. However, during the 1950s several critics maintained that the judge had been anti-Semitic in selecting the jury, that he had favored the prosecution, and that he had delivered sentences that were both illogical and immoral. Kaufman, himself, was acutely conscious of criticism of his handling of the case. Allegedly through his contacts with Hoover, he had writers and playwrights who dealt with the case investigated.

Criticism of Kaufman was not taken seriously until 1976, when the Rosenbergs' sons—Robert and Michael Meeropol—using the Freedom of Information Act, obtained access to previously classified government files on the case. These records appeared to document allegations that during the proceedings Kaufman and the prosecution had held extensive private, out-of-court conversations that may have violated the judicial canon of ethics. Kaufman also apparently asked the prosecution to contact the Justice Department for its recommendations on a sentence. When the Justice Department proved divided on the institution of the death penalty, the judge asked the prosecution to make no recommendation.

The legal community divided sharply in response to the revelations. On the one hand the American Civil Liberties Union, the National Lawyers Guild, and 112 law professors from around the country called for an official inquiry. On the other a New York Bar Association subcommittee worked to "counteract unwarranted criticism" of Kaufman. No official investigation was undertaken.

With the exception of the Rosenberg case, Kaufman had a long and highly respected career as a judge. In 1961, with endorsement of LEARNED

HAND, Kaufman was elevated to the U.S. Court of Appeals, Second Circuit, one of the most important and prestigious posts in the federal judiciary. A liberal on the appeals bench, he supported racial integration, prison reform, minority voting rights, and the constitutional rights of conscientious objectors. In 1971 he sat on the panel that upheld a lower court ruling in favor of the *New York Times* in the *Pentagon Papers* case. Kaufman died in New York City on February 1, 1992.

In their 1983 study of the Rosenberg case Ronald Radosh and Joyce Milton believed Julius Rosenberg had acted as manager of the spy ring that stole information to help the Soviets build the bomb. They believed Ethel was an accessory, at least in convincing her brother David Greenglass to spy. However, they did not think their role as significant as that of Klaus Fuchs. The government's pursuit of the Rosenbergs, according to the two historians, was not only driven by a desire to have the two inform on other spies but also was seen as a way to frighten other potential spies. But Radosh and Milton saw Ethel's arrest as simply a way to pressure Rosenberg to talk, and that the double death sentence was a travesty given that the spying had been on the behalf of an ally during World War II. Some legal experts questioned Kaufman's sentence as a questionable interpretation of the law.

Revelations in the 1990s of the Venona decrypts showed conclusively that the two had spied for the Soviets. But the debate continued as to whether Kaufman's sentence was justified.

—SBB

Kazan, Elia
(1909–2003) *theater and cinema director*

The son of a rug dealer, Kazan was born in Constantinople, Ottoman Empire (now Istanbul, Turkey), on September 7, 1909, and emigrated with his family to the United States. He worked his way through Williams College, graduating Phi Beta Kappa in 1930. In 1932 he received an MFA from the Yale School of Drama. That same year he made his Broadway acting debut in *Chrysalis*. During the ensuing decade Kazan became involved in a number of noncommercial theater groups with left-of-center sympathies, including the Group Theater and the Theater of Action, as an actor, playwright, and director. He appeared in *Men in White* in 1933, *Waiting for Lefty* and *Awake and Sing* in 1935, and

Golden Boy in 1938. During the 1940s Kazan gained prominence as the director of such major Broadway plays as *The Skin of Our Teeth* (1942), *All My Sons* (1947), and *A Streetcar Named Desire* (1947).

Beginning with *A Tree Grows in Brooklyn* in 1945, Kazan embarked on one of the most prestigious film directing careers in postwar American cinema. Like the work of many of his contemporaries, Kazan's films were often influenced by highly controversial contemporary topics. His Academy Award–winning film *Gentlemen's Agreement* (1947) was one of the earliest screen treatments of anti-Semitism. He also directed *Pinky* in 1949, which focused on racial prejudice.

In 1947 the House Un-American Activities Committee (HUAC) began its investigations into alleged Communist activities in Hollywood. Kazan was one of the many leading personalities in the creative branch of the motion picture industry who initially spoke out against the probes and contributed money for the defense of those writers and directors whom the committee cited for contempt. As the investigations continued, however, and an unofficial political blacklist began to appear in Hollywood, Kazan fell silent.

Although Kazan's name was occasionally mentioned in some of the earliest HUAC hearings, it was not until 1952 that he was called to testify. At this point the committee was subpoenaeing Hollywood figures who had begun their careers in the left-wing theater movement during the depression. Kazan appeared before the committee on January 14 and April 11. Along with playwright CLIFFORD ODETS, he was one of the most renowned alumni of New York's progressive theater to break ranks with his former colleagues and cooperate with HUAC.

In his April appearance Kazan stated that he had been a member of the Communist Party from the summer of 1934 to approximately the early spring of 1936. He said that his "unit" was composed of those party members who were associated with the Group Theater and proceeded to supply the committee with the names of several members. Kazan claimed that the party had unsuccessfully attempted to take over the Group Theater and that he had quit the party after concluding that his artistic and political freedoms were being inhibited. Kazan further stated that since he had left the Communist Party in 1936, he had "never been active in any organization since listed as subversive." His only association with "controversial" causes was his support for some of the early witnesses to appear before HUAC. Kazan attributed his subsequent silence to a belief that the protests were organized by Communists.

Kazan's testimony attracted great attention, not merely because of his own stature in the motion picture industry, but also because Kazan himself went to such unusual lengths to justify his cooperation. The day after his appearance the *New York Times* ran a two-column advertisement, written and paid for by Kazan, in which he repeated his statements made in Washington, defended his position and the investigations being conducted by HUAC, and called on liberals to support those probes. Kazan would defend his testimony by saying that while his friend, playwright and fellow traveler Arthur Miller, could continue his writing career behind bars, he, as a film director, could not.

Kazan continued directing films in the 1950s and 1960s. Historian Stephen J. Whitfield has argued that the Kazan-directed film *On the Waterfront*, in which a young dockworker informs on mobsters who run the longshoremen's union and is then ostracized by other dockworkers, indirectly justified Kazan's own informing. While Kazan suffered a certain amount of ostracism for his stance, for the most part his career continued to prosper. In 1955 he directed *East of Eden*, starring James Dean. In 1957 he directed *A Face in The Crowd*. His productivity declined during the 1960s. He turned much of his energies to writing, including his autobiographical novel, *America, America*, which appeared in 1962. Kazan published his autobiography in 1988, and he was awarded an honorary Oscar for lifetime achievement in 1999. He died in New York City on September 28, 2003.

—MQ

Kefauver, C(arey) Estes

(1903–1963) *member of the House of Representatives, member of the Senate*

Born on July 26, 1903, in Madisonville, Tennessee, Kefauver was the scion of a socially prominent Tennessee family. He attended the University of Tennessee, where he excelled in athletics, edited the campus newspaper, and served as president of the student body. After graduating in 1924 he earned a law degree from Yale University. He returned to Tennessee and for the next 12 years conducted a prosperous corporate law practice in Chattanooga. He

served as president of the Chattanooga Jaycees and helped organize the Volunteers, a civic reform group. Defeated in his first run for office in 1938 by the local Democratic machine, Kefauver was appointed state commissioner of finance and taxation the following year. In a special election for a vacant House seat in the summer of 1939, he won the primary with organization backing and defeated his isolationist Republican opponent in the general election.

In the House Kefauver backed the Roosevelt and Truman administrations. Kefauver's relationship with organized labor waxed and waned. He supported the Smith-Connally Act, requiring a 30-day notice before a strike could begin against a war contractor and allowing the government to seize strike-bound plants. He also voted for drafting rail workers during the 1946 shutdown. However, he favored the continuation of wartime price controls, backed federally financed housing and Texas representative WRIGHT PATMAN's full employment bill of 1945, and opposed the Taft-Hartley Act. He was one of only 12 southern Democrats to vote against Taft-Hartley. Other southern congressmen resented Kefauver's liberal tilt. Even though Kefauver supported most of his program, Truman did not like the Tennessee senator, calling him "cow fever." The president was very much an "organization man," as Kefauver biographer Charles C. Fontenay put it, and looked warily upon those who stood apart, independent. Kefauver was a consistent foe of the House Un-American Activities Committee and was one of only 36 members of Congress to oppose consideration of a 1946 bill creating a loyalty review board to investigate, prosecute, and judge anyone whose loyalty was questioned. As head of a TVA bloc in the House, Kefauver ran into trouble with the senior senator from Tennessee, KENNETH D. MCKELLAR. Starting in 1942 and continuing until Kefauver became a senator himself, McKellar kept attaching an amendment to an appropriations bill requiring the TVA to come back to Congress each year for funding, rather than rolling over surplus proceeds into a new fiscal year. The goal was to put the TVA more firmly under the control of McKellar, who was acting chairman of the Appropriations Committee, and with the death of the long ailing Carter Glass of Virginia in 1946 he formally became chairman. Although approved in the Senate, Kefauver and his allies were always able to defeat the amendment in the House.

Kefauver became a champion of internal congressional reform on the floor of the House and in his 1947 book, *A Twentieth Century Congress.* His most distinctive proposal was to establish a formal procedure for the direct questioning of cabinet officers on the floor of the House, an idea that won wide editorial backing but little support in Congress. Kefauver also recommended a four-year term for representatives, House-Senate majority approval for treaties, electronic voting to accelerate roll calls, representation for the District of Columbia, limitation on Senate filibusters, and abolition of the seniority system. Kefauver's proposals were not new, nor did they make much headway during his tenure in the House, but several won enactment in future decades. He unsuccessfully argued against the Twenty-second Amendment limiting presidential tenure to two terms, contending that the third-term decision was best left to the voters.

Kefauver joined in 1945 the Select Committee on Small Business, chaired by Patman. Patman made Kefauver chairman of a subcommittee to look into concentration of economic power in America. The subcommittee's report, "United States versus Economic Concentration and Power," argued that big business in and of itself was not wrong, but that the concentration of economic might could grow to the point where it stifled free enterprise. The report decried the fact that the federal government was abetting this movement by favoring large corporations for defense contracts. The report also pointed out that 1,800 companies had been absorbed through purchase or merger since 1940.

To combat the problem, Kefauver in 1945 and 1947 sponsored bills to close a loophole in the Clayton Antitrust Act that enabled a company to swallow a competitor by buying its assets. The law as it stood only prohibited mergers through buying stocks, but the bill was killed in the Rules Committee dominated by conservative HOWARD W. SMITH of Virginia. This situation prompted Kefauver to make a sharp comparison with Congress's enthusiasm for the Taft-Hartley Act. He asked if Congress was going to make itself ridiculous "by passing a stringent far-reaching bill against the problem of monopoly in labor, while at the same time ignoring the much greater problem of monopoly in industry?" Kefauver did help defeat a bill that would have allowed "voluntary agreements" on prices among sellers. To him the greatest threat posed by monopoly was not in competition or low prices but to those smaller, local businesses that he believed formed the economic and spiritual foundation of most American communities. Growing economic dependence on large economic units, Kefauver warned, would lead to the atrophy of political freedom. Kefauver's antimonopoly fervor harkened back to Woodrow Wilson's New Freedom. In addition to his legislative reforms, he favored increased appropriations for the Federal Trade Commission and the Antitrust Division of the Justice Department.

Kefauver deviated from his outspoken liberalism on civil rights issues. He opposed proposals to establish a Fair Employment Practices Commission to end job discrimination, calling it "a dangerous step toward regimentation." He attacked federal antilynching legislation as "an unjustified encroachment of the rights of the States," since "lynching is murder under every State law." In July 1948 Kefauver contended that "there is no real demand for anti-segregation laws in the South," that southern blacks were more interested in better schools and economic opportunities. He was, however, one of the few southern congressmen to support abolition of the poll tax. Kefauver's desire to eliminate the poll tax had nothing to do with favoring African Americans but because he thought it perpetuated political power of the privileged few, such as Memphis political boss EDWARD H. CRUMP, who would pay the poll tax for those who would "vote right," while it impinged on the ability of organized labor to get out the vote for Kefauver himself. The culmination of his career-long advocacy of this reform was the Twenty-fourth Amendment outlawing the poll tax, finally ratified shortly after his death. Kefauver also opposed the filibuster, which was the southern bloc's principal weapon against civil rights legislation in the Senate.

In 1946 *Collier's* magazine selected Kefauver one of the 10 best members of the House, but by 1948 his independent liberalism had won him the enmity of the powerful Crump machine centered in Memphis. In that year Kefauver entered the race for the Senate against incumbent senator Tom Stewart (D-Tenn.) and Crump-backed Judge John Mitchell. Early in the campaign Crump compared Kefauver to a furtive "pet coon," and said he was too far to the left. In a meeting in June 1948 at the famed Peabody Hotel in Memphis, the heart of Crump country, Kefauver put on a coonskin cap and later said, "I may be a pet coon, but I'm not Mr. Crump's pet coon." He also noted all political opponents of Crump were deemed by the boss to be Communists, fascists, and worse. He outpolled his two conservative opponents in the primary and was elected to the Senate in November over Republican B. CARROLL REECE.

In the Senate Kefauver's outspoken civil libertarian views, populist rhetoric, and liberal voting behavior continued to set him apart as a maverick southerner. In 1950 he was one of only seven senators to vote against the Internal Security Act. "America is never going to find security in suppression," Kefauver said, but only "in free men who have the right to speak and think as they wish." In that year he also opposed the Kerr natural gas bill deregulating prices. As in the House he consistently backed the Truman administration's containment strategy in foreign affairs and spoken often in favor of Atlantic union, a proposal to create a federal system out of the United States, Canada, and Western Europe. His most important legislative achievement of his first term was the 1950 Kefauver-Celler Act, an amendment to the Clayton Antitrust Act closing the loophole allowing companies to purchase the assets of competing firms. In 1950 *Time* magazine chose him as one of the "Senate's most valuable ten."

In 1950–51, as chairman of the special Senate Crime Investigating Committee, Kefauver catapulted to national attention with his sensational probe of organized crime. Amid widespread press coverage the Kefauver Committee conducted hearings in 14 major cities, eventually hearing over 800 witnesses whose testimony ran to thousands of pages. Kefauver angered Truman by taking his committee to Kansas City, once controlled by the corrupt political machine of the late Boss Tom Pendergast, the president's mentor in politics. The committee's investigation of organized crime in Chicago helped bring down the uncorrupted Senate Majority Leader SCOTT W. LUCAS (D-Ill.). The hearings catapulted the senator into the national consciousness, but it also earned him powerful enemies within the Democratic Party. The climax of the probe was the New York City hearings, with committee members interrogating such well-known underworld figures as Frank Costello and politicians such as former New York City mayor WILLIAM O'DWYER. The New York session was carried over nationwide television to record audiences. For the American people, said *Life* magazine, it was "the first big television broadcast of an affair of their government," while the Academy of Television Arts and Sciences awarded the hearings an Emmy for special achievement.

Although the committee's investigation uncovered little evidence that was genuinely new to law enforcement experts, it highlighted the corruption of politicians and police on a local level and dramatized for the nation the networks and syndicates controlling such illegal activities as gambling. Twenty-four aliens or naturalized citizens mentioned by the committee were deported, and Frank Costello served over a year in jail for contempt of the committee. However, most of its contempt citations were dismissed or overturned. Little remedial legislation resulted. The Bureau of Internal Revenue created a Special Rackets Squad, and, by 1957, the Justice Department had obtained hundreds of convictions for criminal fraud originating from the committee's exposures. Kefauver published his own account of the investigation in a book entitled *Crime in America*, ghostwritten by journalist Sidney Shalett; it was a best seller in 1951.

Capitalizing on his new national prominence as a crimefighter and on popular dissatisfaction with the Truman administration, Kefauver declared his candidacy for the 1952 Democratic presidential nomination. His campaign became distinctive for its homespun style. Voters identified the Tennessean by his coonskin cap, his trademark since his 1948 Senate race. Another Kefauver technique was the prodigious handshaking tour, as the candidate tried to establish some personal contact with as many voters as possible. Refraining from direct criticism of the Truman administration, Kefauver emphasized instead his special aptitude to clean up corruption in government.

Given little chance of coming close to Truman in his first test, the March New Hampshire primary, Kefauver won a stunning upset by 3,873 votes. Two weeks later the president announced that he would not be a candidate for reelection. Suddenly cast in the role of frontrunner, Kefauver won a string of primary victories against only nominal opposition. In the Nebraska primary he did overcome a well financed opponent, Senator ROBERT S. KERR (D-Okla.), but he lost the Florida primary to Senator RICHARD B. RUSSELL (D-Ga.) and the District of Columbia contest to W. AVERELL HARRIMAN. Nevertheless, Kefauver went to the July convention in Chicago with an overwhelming majority of the popular primary votes and a plurality of primary selected delegates.

Despite his demonstrated popular appeal, Kefauver was never able to overcome the hostility of party professionals and urban leaders, who were alienated by his independence and bitter over the results of his crime investigation, which many felt had injured city Democratic organizations. All the southern delegations, except Tennessee's, rejected Kefauver for his liberalism. The Truman administration's antagonism was a vital convention factor. Kefauver's convention floor leadership was poorly organized. There was not even a phone connecting the floor leaders to Kefauver, who was across the street watching the convention on television. A golden opportunity for Kefauver was lost over the seating of the Virginia delegation, which had refused to support a resolution pledging to put the nominee on the state's ballot. Kefauver sent a note over to the convention to support Virginia, but it was lost in transit and Kefauver's delegates voted against Virginia. After some confusion, vote switching, and because of the pro-Stevenson tilt of the convention leadership, the Illinois governor's delegates came out in favor of Virginia, and thus Stevenson looked like the moderate and unifier. Kefauver led on the first two ballots but lost the nomination on the third to Illinois governor ADLAI E. STEVENSON.

Kefauver made a second unsuccessful run for the presidency in 1956, a bid that effectively ended with his defeat by Stevenson in the crucial California primary. Voted vice presidential nominee by the convention at large, Kefauver went down to defeat with Stevenson in November under the Eisenhower landslide. Thereafter he devoted himself to his Senate duties and won recognition as a knowledgeable critic of monopoly power. Fontenay has argued that he became the most effective opponent of monopoly in Congress in American history. As chairman of the Antitrust and Monopoly Subcommittee, Kefauver conducted a series of well-publicized investigations into economic concentration, probing the steel, automobile, bread, drug, and electrical equipment industries, among others. In 1962 he clashed with the Kennedy administration over its communications satellite program, maintaining that its plan to turn part of the industry over to AT&T encouraged monopoly. His most noteworthy legislative accomplishment was the Kefauver-Harris Act strengthening regulation of drugs. Kefauver died of a burst aorta on August 10, 1963 in Bethesda, Maryland. (See *The Eisenhower Years, The Kennedy Years* Volumes)

—TO

Kennan, George F(rost)

(1904–2005) *chairman, Policy Planning Staff; counselor, State Department; ambassador*

George Kennan was born on February 16, 1904, in Milwaukee, Wisconsin. He graduated from Prince-

ton in 1925 and entered the Foreign Service the following year. After duty in Central Europe, he was transferred to Eastern Europe. In anticipation of the eventual recognition of the Soviet Union, the State Department sent Kennan to the University of Berlin, where he studied Russian language and culture from 1931 to 1933. He served with the first embassy to Moscow from 1933 to 1936. In this position Kennan soon emerged as a hardened anticommunist who was particularly troubled by Stalin's repression of religion and civil liberties. The young diplomat was stationed in Prague and Berlin during the opening years of World War II. Kennan was interned by the Nazis from December 1941 to May 1942. During the early years of the war he served at the American embassy in Portugal. In 1943 he joined the European Advisory Commission in London, where he worked on plans for a postwar Germany. The following year he became counselor to W. AVERELL HARRIMAN, ambassador to the Soviet Union.

Throughout the war Kennan warned against a close alliance with the Soviet Union. Just after the German invasion of Russia, he wrote, "It seems to me that to welcome Russia as an associate in the defense of democracy would invite misunderstanding." In 1944, after the Soviets had repulsed the Germans, Kennan pleaded for a "full-fledged and realistic political showdown with the Soviet leaders" and advocated ending land-lease aid. He thought that Soviet-American collaboration would be unnecessary after the war. Although he opposed the Communist occupation of Eastern Europe and recommended that economic aid to the Soviet Union be cut off to encourage Soviet withdrawal from that area, he felt that there was little the United States could do about the situation. He believed that the Soviets could not maintain their hegemony in Eastern Europe and recommended that, for the time being, the two nations recognize each other's spheres of influence. The State Department ignored his advice.

In February 1946, in light of the collapse of the wartime alliance and growing domestic anticommunism, the State Department asked Kennan to draft a report analyzing American policy toward the Soviet Union. Suffering from sinus trouble, a toothache, and an ulcer attack, a rather ill Kennan replied from his sickbed. In the "Long Telegram"— which he later likened to "an 18th century Protestant sermon"—he pressed views long ignored.

Kennan's analysis created a sensation. Truman was believed to have read it, and Secretary of the Navy JAMES V. FORRESTAL made it required reading for high military officers. It provided the administration with an intellectual framework upon which to base Soviet-American policy for the remainder of Truman's presidency.

Soviet policy, Kennan asserted, was based on the ideological conviction of the inevitability of socialist-capitalist conflict. The origin of the Soviet's "neurotic" outlook on international relations was the "traditional and instinctive Russian sense of insecurity." To avoid being encircled by capitalist powers, Stalin would strengthen his control at home and surround himself with friendly client states. Kennan assumed that Russia was too weak to attack the West militarily and would attempt to subvert the capitalist nations politically, thereby isolating the United States. As Wilson D. Miscamble noted, the telegram was a catalyst to the department's strategizing, particularly on the subject of whether good relations could be maintained with the Russians, and helped build the argument for a hard-line stance against the Soviets that had already been developing. (Winston Churchill's "Iron Curtain" speech in March was also a factor in this development.) Yet as Miscamble further noted, the administration still floundered about the exact policy to pursue despite the Long Telegram. Unfortunately Kennan did not express his view that nonmilitary action rather military would be sufficient to meet the Soviets. He would repeat this mistake in his *Foreign Affairs* article.

Kennan was called back to Washington in April 1946 to lecture on foreign affairs at the National War College. During the early months of 1947, he took part in discussions over the framing of the Greek-Turkish aid proposal. Kennan opposed recommendations by Senator ARTHUR H. VANDENBERG (R-Mich.) and DEAN G. ACHESON to couch the plan in terms of a moral crusade against communism. He argued that the Soviet Union was not a military threat in Turkey. However, his reservations were ignored.

In April 1947 Secretary of State GEORGE C. MARSHALL invited Kennan to head the department's newly created Policy Planning Staff and charged him with the responsibility for long-range planning of U.S. actions in foreign policy. His first task was to formulate a proposal for the massive reconstruction of Europe. Given only two days in which to draft suggestions, Kennan outlined in general terms a two

George F. Kennan with his two-year-old son Christopher, 1952 *(Harry S. Truman Library, Harris and Ewing Photo, Beth Gore)*

stage proposal of rehabilitation; short-term action to eliminate immediate needs and a long-term program to rebuild the European economy. While the short-term project could be primarily the responsibility of the United States, the long-term program must, according to Kennan, be evolved by Europeans with minimum American influence. He urged studies in Europe and the United States to delineate needs, conditions, and terms of assistance. Kennan emphasized that the rehabilitation of Germany must be a primary consideration while avoiding the specter of a rearmed Germany. He recommended that the program be offered to all nations, including the Soviet Union. However, by making conditions for inclusion stringent, he promised Moscow would never accept the offer. Kennan's memorandum and follow-up reports provided the material for the secretary's Harvard University address in June 1947 during which he proposed the Marshall Plan.

Kennan wrote a justification for the plan in a July issue of *Foreign Affairs* in an article titled, "The Sources of Soviet Conduct." Preferring to remain anonymous, he signed the article "Mr. X," but his identity quickly became known. As he had in the "Long Telegram," Kennan outlined the basis for Soviet foreign policy and discussed probable Russian action. He foresaw the Soviet Union probing for weak links in the Western alliance. To meet this threat Kennan recommended "a long-term patient but firm and vigilant containment of Russian expansive tendencies through . . . the adroit and vigilant application of counterforce at a series of constantly shifting geographical and political points, corresponding to the shifts and maneuvers of Soviet policies." For the near future, he thought containment did not promise victory over the USSR but the preservation of the status quo. Kennan hoped that when Moscow saw the determination of the West to stand up to future aggression, tensions could eventually be reduced. When this occurred the Kremlin leaders would lose their justification for a police state and liberalize their regime.

Kennan's ambiguous use of the term *counterforce* prompted many in Washington to think the diplomat recommended military measures to contain Soviet expansion. In subsequent articles and speeches Kennan argued that he had never viewed containment in this manner. Reiterating that he did not see the USSR as a military threat, he maintained that he had attempted to justify the economic redevelopment of Western Europe and Japan to serve as buffer states against Russia. Despite his protestations, policy makers began viewing the struggle in terms of military force. In 1948 Kennan did call for covert political warfare against the Soviets, but he later came to regret his suggestion.

When Dean Acheson became secretary of state in 1949, Kennan assumed the post of counselor of the department. His brief tenure was marked by constant clashes with the secretary over containment. Kennan questioned the need for the formation of the North Atlantic Treaty Organization, reiterating his belief that the Soviet threat was primarily political. He maintained that a military alliance based on conventional weapons "obsolete in the nuclear age" would be not only useless but also an additional source of aggravation in the cold war. Kennan also clashed with Acheson over the role of Germany. Although he had initially considered the redevelopment and integration of Germany into Europe necessary to contain communism, by 1949 Kennan had concluded that tensions in the area could be reduced by joint U.S.-USSR troop withdrawal and the development of a neutralized, demil-

itarized state. Kennan proposed this at a time when the administration believed that Germany should play a strong role in NATO. When the Soviets exploded their own atomic bomb in 1949, the question arose as to how to respond. Kennan had disdained making the atomic bomb a part of U.S. strategy. In the aftermath of the Soviets' success he thought the administration should attempt once more to negotiate international control of atomic energy with the Russians. He worked with feverish passion on a paper advocating international control at the end of 1949. However, because of his preoccupation with the more general questions of international control and nuclear weapon strategy Kennan was not put in the working group that would work on the more narrow question of whether to build the hydrogen bomb. As Miscamble noted, this probably made the task of super bomb proponents easier. PAUL H. NITZE was a member of the group and he pushed for testing an H-bomb. Kennan disagreed, which led to a debate between the two men that would last for decades to come. Kennan doubted the utility of relying on atomic weaponry and pointed out the danger of both the United States and the USSR possessing such fearsome explosives. He advocated a return to negotiations for international control. He also argued against first use of nuclear weapons in the face of a conventional warfare attack. Acheson, however, sided with the proponents of the Super.

Kennan had shown Acheson in his report the incoherent nature of U.S. nuclear strategy and the overreliance on the bomb. These arguments convinced Acheson that a full review of strategy was necessary. His aim was to show the need for a buildup of conventional arms. Truman approved the H-bomb and the review, which, of course, resulted in NSC-68. Kennan was not directly involved in the formulation of the study, but he did have an indirect influence on it from his noting the overreliance on atomic weaponry. Nitze also used an earlier NSC document (NSC 20/4) that had evolved out of a Kennan draft. Nitze reiterated Kennan's warning of the Russian threat but made the danger more immediate. Miscamble argued that NSC-68 indicated the rejection of Kennan's views on containment. Kennan himself later contended that NSC-68 rested on what the capabilities of the Soviets were, rather than on their intentions, which he thought more crucial. He reasserted his belief in the March 1950 issue of *Reader's Digest* in an article titled "Is War with Russia Inevitable?" But by now no one in officialdom was listening.

Acheson and Kennan also disagreed over policy in Korea. Kennan had originally supported U.S. intervention in the area. However, he opposed Acheson's decision to order the troops to cross the 38th parallel on the grounds that this would invite Communist Chinese entry into the war.

Kennan resigned his post in 1951 to become a member of the Institute of Advanced Studies at Princeton. The following year Kennan became ambassador to the Soviet Union. He found service in Moscow frustrating. Washington failed to ask his advice, and he thought living in the Soviet Union under Stalin's rule to be stifling. When Kennan left Moscow in September 1952 to attend a Conference in London, the Soviets declared him persona non grata. This apparently resulted from Kennan's comment made comparing life in the American embassy to that in a Nazi internment camp during the war. Kennan returned to the United States to await a new assignment from the incoming Eisenhower administration. However, Secretary of State JOHN FOSTER DULLES refused to appoint him to a new post, thus forcing the diplomat into early retirement.

Kennan returned to the institute at Princeton and wrote on foreign policy. He was a forceful critic of the administration's diplomacy, opposing massive retaliation and the expression of foreign policy in terms of a moral crusade.

President John F. Kennedy named Kennan ambassador to Yugoslavia in 1961. Kennan resigned in 1963 to once again return to Princeton. During the mid-1960s he became one of the most prominent critics of the Vietnam War. In addition to teaching, he published numerous books and articles, delivered lectures, and appeared often on radio and television as an analyst of American foreign policy. George Kennan died in Princeton, New Jersey, on March 17, 2005, aged 101. (See *The Eisenhower Years, The Kennedy Years, The Johnson Years* Volumes)

—JB

Kenney, George C(hurchill)

(1889–1977) *commander, Strategic Air Command*

The son of a carpenter, Kenney was born in Yarmouth, Nova Scotia, on August 6, 1889, during his parents' vacation. He studied at the Massachusetts Institute of Technology from 1907 to 1911 and was employed as an engineer by several railroad companies in the United States and Canada for the next three years. Kenney distinguished himself as a flyer during World War I and was commissioned as a captain in the U.S. Army Air Force in 1919. He moved up through the ranks, attaining the permanent rank of general by 1946. During World War II Kenney commanded the air force in the Southwest Pacific area for two years and then the Far Eastern Air Force. In the last three years of the war he was General DOUGLAS MACARTHUR's top air commander. The force under Kenney's command contributed significantly to the success of MacArthur's "leap frogging" counteroffensive designed to take the Philippines and finally Japan. He led the Pacific Air Command from 1945 to 1946 and after the war was the first senior U.S. representative on the military staff commission of the United Nations. He left in November 1946 to lead the Strategic Air Command (SAC).

SAC was officially established on March 21, 1946, when the War Department directed that the continental air forces be divided into three distinct units—Air Defense Command, Tactical Air Command, and Strategic Air Command. SAC's mission was to be prepared to carry out long-range offensive operations anywhere in the world and conduct reconnaissance missions either independently or in conjunction with other branches of the service. As head of SAC, Kenney attempted to upgrade standards and increase U.S. air power. He stated in September 1948 that the U.S. bomber force was twice as effective as in 1947 and four times as effective as in 1946 but that it was "still a one-shot show."

The general supported unification of the armed services. In his opinion "only through an organization which centralizes responsibility for our entire military structure—land, sea, air, guided missiles, atomic power—[could the U.S.] develop the vision to use all these resources to their fullest." However, he sided with those who proposed that the air force be the prime deterrent against Soviet aggression. He backed increased production of the B-36 bomber, designed to carry nuclear weapons.

Kenney urged the United States to be continually vigilant against Soviet attack. In January 1947 he warned that the United States was vulnerable to attack from across the North Pole by pilotless planes bearing atomic bombs. Two years later he urged the manning of U.S. radar and fighter defensive systems 24 hours a day. He noted that although the Soviet Union had no long-range bomber comparable to the B-36 it did have planes that could carry an atomic bomb over the ocean. The explosion of an atomic device in the Soviet Union in 1949 worried Kenney, and, in May 1950, he stated that Russians had probably "set the year for starting World War III."

In 1948 Kenney became commander of the Air University at Alabama. He served at that position until 1951, when he retired. He was president of the National Arthritis and Rheumatism Foundation for 12 years. He died on August 9, 1977, in Bay Harbor, Florida.

—MLB

Kennon, Robert F(loyd)
(1902–1988) *Louisiana politician*

Robert Kennon was born on August 21, 1902, in Minden, Louisiana. He studied at Louisiana State University, receiving his bachelor's degree in 1923 and a law degree in 1925. He practiced law in his home town of Minden and ran successfully in 1925 for a two-year term as mayor. Elected district attorney in 1930 and again in 1936, Kennon became an appeals court judge in 1940. He was known by the sobriquet "Judge" because of his service on the bench. After serving in the army during World War II, he was appointed to the Louisiana Supreme Court in 1945 to fill a term that expired in January 1947.

Although virtually unknown in most of the state, Kennon in 1947 declared his candidacy for governor, heading an all-veterans slate. The campaign marked the return of the Long family to power in state politics, after eight years of reform-oriented state government, with the late Huey Long's brother Earl running for governor. Kennon appealed to good government forces opposed to the machine politics of the Long family and to business interests fearful of the costs of Long's welfare proposals. He promised to lower taxes on industry, abolish the state property tax, and maintain the six-year-old state civil service system. Long mercilessly ridiculed Kennon, in particular, he mocked Kennon's large ears: "Judge Kennon's got the best ears around. He can stand in a court house in Ville Platte and hear a dollar bill drop in Opelousas." He lost to Long, who was elected in the Democratic primary in January 1948 and elected governor in April. A senatorial primary

later that year pitted Kennon against Huey Long's son, RUSSELL B. LONG. The anti-Long forces backed Kennon against the inexperienced Russell, who was in trouble because of the unpopularity of Earl's high tax increases. Russell barely won with a 2 percent margin. (There were allegations that Earl stole the race for his nephew.)

Kennon also supported the attempt of the boss of Plaquemine Parish, Leander Perez, to replace Truman with Dixiecrat J. STROM THURMOND as the official candidate of the Democratic Party in Louisiana. Earl Long managed to keep Truman on the ballot, but Dixiecrats in the legislature would not allow the word Democrat to be associated with Truman. Thurmond won the state.

After his defeats in 1948 Kennon returned to the private practice of law. The campaigns had given him statewide publicity, however, and Kennon took advantage of this to cement his ties to the anti-Long reform wing of the Democratic Party in Louisiana. When New Orleans reform mayor DELESSEPS S. MORRISON opposed Long's efforts to increase the governor's power at the expense of municipalities, Kennon gave the mayor strong support. In return Morrison pledged himself to support Kennon's candidacy for governor in the next election.

Kennon entered the 1952 Democratic gubernatorial primary, campaigning against Long's handpicked candidate, Judge Carlos Spaht. (Louisiana law prevented a governor from succeeding himself.) He ran on a platform calling for tax cuts, efficiency in government, and the restoration of civil service. He also promised to support state constitutional amendments to decrease the power of the governor's office. Kennon defeated Spaht in the second primary in February 1952, capturing more than 60 percent of the votes, and easily defeated his Republican opponent in the April elections. Earl Long had anticipated Spaht's defeat, believing that four years of boring "reform" government would make people hanker for his showmanship. He proved correct as he was elected again in 1956. Kennon immediately fulfilled his campaign pledges by winning legislative approval for reducing taxes, cutting the state highway budget, and restoring civil service.

Kennon was a leader of the Democrats for Eisenhower movement in 1952, breaking with ADLAI E. STEVENSON's candidacy after he spoke in favor of federal claims to tidelands oil reserves. In 1953 Kennon testified before Congress in favor of a bill that turned control of offshore oil to the states. After the 1954 Supreme Court decision declaring school segregation unconstitutional, Kennon pledged to enforce state and local segregation laws. In 1956 he again backed Eisenhower against Stevenson. Following his term of office, Kennon returned to his law practice. In 1964 he was an unsuccessful candidate for the Democratic gubernatorial nomination. Kennon died on January 11, 1988, in Baton Rouge, Louisiana. (See *The Eisenhower Years* Volume)

—JD

Kenny, Robert W(alker)

(1901–1976) *Democratic Party politician, attorney*

The son of a wealthy banker, Kenny was born on August 21, 1901, in Los Angeles, California. He studied law on his own and passed the California bar in 1926. He entered politics during the later 1920s, developing a flashy campaign that helped reelect Governor James Rolph, Jr. in 1930. The following year he was appointed a municipal judge of Los Angeles County. He later won election as Superior Court Judge on an anti-Prohibition platform. He resigned from the post to become a state senator in 1939 and won election as state attorney general four years later. The left-wing National Lawyer's Guild elected him president in 1940.

During the 1940s Kenny emerged as a leading spokesman of the left. He opposed the Dies Committee's investigations of domestic subversion and defended HARRY A. BRIDGES during the government's attempts to deport the left-wing labor leader. Kenny was a leading supporter of civil rights, working for the end of discrimination against Chinese in California and calling for a "relentless drive into every nook and cranny of discriminatory practices" to give blacks equality.

During the postwar period Kenny became a member of the National Citizens Political Action Committee (NCPAC), formed to bring nonlabor reformers into the Congress of Industrial Organizations' (CIO) efforts to mold a progressive lobby. With the backing of the CIO and NCPAC, he made an unsuccessful bid in 1946 for governor of California against Republican incumbent EARL WARREN. Kenny's defeat was attributed to the general voter disapproval of the Truman administration and fears that Kenny was too closely associated with the left and the Communist Party. Following his defeat,

Kenny announced he no longer considered himself a Truman supporter. He resigned his post as attorney general in 1947 and returned to his law practice.

Kenny remained active in state and national liberal politics. He denounced the Truman Doctrine in 1947 and led a faction that split the California Democratic Party over the issue. During 1947 he organized the California Democrats for Wallace. Anxious for HENRY A. WALLACE to win the Democratic presidential nomination, he denounced Truman and maintained that there was little difference between him and the Republicans. "We can't win with Truman," he said, "because he has already chloroformed the independent voters. But we can win with Wallace backed by the Democratic Party." Kenny insisted that if progressive Democrats could choose only between "Tweedledum and Tweedle Dewey," they would not vote. The state Democratic Committee rejected the bid for Wallace in July.

Kenny was elected co-chairman of the Progressive Citizens of America (PCA) in January of 1948. The PCA was a coalition of anti-Democratic liberals formed to fight for civil rights, social welfare, disarmament, and reconciliation with the Soviet Union. Unlike its fellow liberal lobby, the Americans for Democratic Action, PCA permitted Communists to join the organization. Kenny worked for the election of Wallace on the Progressive Party ticket that summer but withdrew from that organization in October because of growing Communist influence in the movement.

Kenny achieved a reputation as a leading civil liberties lawyer during the later half of the decade. In 1947 he served as counsel for members of the Hollywood film community who were called before the House Un-American Activities Committee, then investigating Communist influence in the movie industry. Kenny criticized the probe as an attempt at "censorship of the screen by intimidation." He told clients to tell the committee it had no right to ask whether they were or had been Communists. J. Parnell Thomas told Kenny that if he doubted the committee's constitutionality he should take the question up with the courts. After the establishment of an industry blacklist in December, he denounced the Motion Picture Producers Association for "taking the position that a man is guilty until he is proven innocent." In a later investigation of California lawyers, Kenny advised them to assert their Fifth Amendment rights. Kenny served as a superior court judge from 1966 to 1975. During the late 1960s he became a vocal critic of the Vietnam War and was honorary chairman of the Lawyers' Committee on American Policy toward Vietnam. Kenny died on July 20, 1976, in La Jolla, California.

—SBB

Kenyon, Dorothy
(1888–1972) *attorney*

Dorothy Kenyon was born on February 17, 1888, in New York City. She graduated from Smith College in 1908 and obtained a law degree from New York University in 1917. That year she served as a research specialist for a group of lawyers advising delegates to the Versailles Peace Conference. In 1919 she joined the firm of Pitkin, Rosenson & Henderson. Eleven years later she formed her own law firm.

During the 1930s and 1940s Kenyon gained a reputation as a champion of women's rights and labor. She headed a committee studying New York's Women's Court in 1936 and was named a member of the New York State Committee on Minimum Wage Legislation that same year. In 1939 Kenyon was appointed a judge of the New York City Municipal Court. She was legal adviser to the Cooperative League of the United States and supported the cooperative movement. She argued against expelling Elizabeth Gurley Flynn for being a Communist from the ACLU's national board of directors in 1940. During World War II she was a member of the New York State Advisory Commission on Women's Wartime Problems and was also a proponent of a draft for women. Kenyon served in the League of Nations Committee on the Status of Women from 1938 to 1943. When the United Nations formed a similar committee in 1946, she represented the United States on that body. She served at the post until 1950, where she advocated for a more important role for women in the UN, particularly in its World Health Organization.

During Senate committee hearings held in 1950 on Senator JOSEPH R. MCCARTHY's (R-Wisc.) charges that there were Communists in the State Department, the Wisconsin Republican accused Kenyon of being affiliated with 28 Communist-front organizations. These included the League of Women Shoppers, the National Council of American-Soviet Friendship, and the American Russian Institute. Journalist Jack Anderson pointed out that her relationship with the State Department had been cursory and was at the time of the hearings nonexistent.

Of the 28 organizations Kenyon was supposed to have been involved with, only four were listed by the Attorney General as subversive, and she had left three of them before the designation had been made.

Kenyon's response to McCarthy was swift. Calling him a "low down worm" and "unmitigated liar" she brought distinguished New York lawyers to testify on her behalf. Speaking before the committee headed by Senator MILLARD E. TYDINGS (D-Md.), in March 1950, she produced a *New York Times* article reporting a Russian statement against her. The statement, in response to her disagreement with a Soviet position at a UN committee meeting, called for her to stop "endeavoring to conceal her reactionary stand." The final committee report, released in July 1950, denounced McCarthy as a liar and cleared Kenyon of the charges. But she never received a governmental appointment after her testimony.

Kenyon continued her activities in civil rights causes throughout the 1950s and 1960s. In 1965 she spoke out for a liberal abortion law. Six years later, as a member of the board of directors of the American Civil Liberties Union, she fought sex discrimination on college campuses. Kenyon died on February 12, 1972, in New York City.

—RB

Kerr, Robert S(amuel)
(1896–1963) *member of the Senate*

The son of an ardent Bryan Democrat, Robert S. Kerr was born in a log cabin in Ada, Indian Territory, on September 11, 1896. He attended three Oklahoma colleges, taught school, sold magazine subscriptions, and clerked at a law firm until the United States entered World War I in 1917. After the war Kerr returned to Oklahoma and began a law career. During the 1920s he entered the oil-drilling business with his brother-in-law. In 1932 they struck it rich drilling within Oklahoma City, where other oil firms feared possible property damage. Kerr's business successes made him a millionaire by the end of the depression. Out of a partnership with geologist Dean McGee he formed Kerr-McGee Industries, Inc. Fueled by Kerr's aggressive financial dealings and McGee's technical expertise, the company expanded into most phases of the oil business, and into other natural resources as well.

During the 1930s Kerr was active in religious and fraternal organizations and became prominent as a spokesman for the petroleum industry. He also became a significant force within the Democratic Party in the 1930s. Kerr ran for governor in 1942. The primary was bitter as Oklahoma Democrats had split over Franklin D. Roosevelt's policies. Kerr ran as a supporter of the New Deal and America's involvement in World War II and won by narrow margins in the primary and general election. Kerr traveled widely outside the state, extolled Oklahoma products, and argued for federal aid to promote the state's economic development. In 1944 he gave the keynote address at the Democratic National Convention and helped in selecting Truman as Roosevelt's running mate. In his 1948 Senate race he stressed as his major theme an ambitious plan to bring prosperity to Oklahoma by the multipurpose development of the Arkansas, White, and Red River basins. He denounced his Republican opponent for opposing public power and called him a "tool of the special interests" for sponsoring a bill to remove independent natural gas companies from the jurisdiction of the Federal Power Commission (FPC). Kerr won election with 62 percent of the vote.

Kerr made a powerful impact in the Senate during his first year by his aggressive sponsorship of a bill to remove independent gas producers from FPC regulation, the same measure he had derided his senatorial opponent for advocating the year before. Although not a member of the Interstate and Foreign Commerce Committee considering the bill, Kerr dominated the hearings, testifying as a witness as well as cross-examining other witnesses. He argued that natural gas prices should be allowed to rise unimpeded by governmental restraint. According to the senator, his bill was intended merely to "clarify" the Natural Gas Act of 1938, which, he said, did not provide for FPC regulation of "independent" gas producers. The committee reported the measure favorably, seven to five.

The Senate floor debate over the Kerr bill took place in March 1950 along sectional lines, with southern and western senators generally favoring the measure, which would chiefly benefit the seven southwestern gas-producing states, and northern and eastern senators opposing. The bill's opponents contended that it would allow astronomical price hikes that would injure consumers and bestow windfall profits on a handful of monopolistic petroleum producers. Leading the measure's proponents, Kerr argued that higher prices were necessary to stimulate exploration and increased production. The

debate was often rancorous, with Kerr, mixing his formidable command of the data with ad hominem abuse, fueling the acrimony. At one point he threatened New England with a gas cutback. The Kerr bill passed on March 29 by the unexpectedly close vote of 44 to 38. Declaring that "authority to regulate . . . is necessary in the public interest," President Truman vetoed the measure in April. Kerr commented that the president had been "misled and misinformed," but owing to the closeness of the vote, made no move to overturn the veto. (Deregulation of the natural gas industry would not occur until the 1980s.)

Kerr played a key role in the rejection of LELAND OLDS's reappointment as chairman of the FPC. An outspoken proponent of strict governmental regulation of the petroleum industry, Olds had testified against the Kerr bill in 1949. When President Truman renominated him for another term as FPC chairman, Kerr and pro-oil senators fought against confirmation, pointing to Olds's youthful radicalism and alleged inconsistency. The Senate rejected the nomination, 53 to 15.

As the Senate's leading champion of the oil and gas industry, Kerr gained a strategic wedge in August 1949 with his appointment to the Finance Committee. Throughout his career he waged a vigorous and successful defense of those tax provisions cherished by the industry: the 27.5 percent depletion allowance, the deduction for intangible drilling costs, and the credit for foreign tax payments. Kerr also worked for high oil import quotas in order to keep out cheaper foreign oil.

Unabashedly grasping and provincial, Kerr bluntly stated his purpose in politics, "I represent myself first, the state of Oklahoma second, the people of the United States third—and don't you forget it." He was the wealthiest man in the Senate. His personal fortune, estimated at $10 million when he entered the Senate in 1949, swelled to an estimate $40 million by the time of his death 14 years later.

The most important project Kerr undertook on behalf of his constituents was his promotion of federal projects to develop Oklahoma's natural resources. Having witnessed the dust bowl of the 1930s and the calamitous cycle of flood and drought that afflicted his region, Kerr determined that the key to future prosperity for his state was the development and control of water resources. The core of his regional development plan was the Arkansas River Navigation System, a vast project that included flood control, irrigation works, hydroelectric plants, improved inland waterway systems, pollution control, and recreational facilities.

From his seat on the Rivers and Harbors Subcommittee of the Public Works Committee, Kerr worked assiduously to divert federal funds to Oklahoma. He won approval for the Arkansas River project in piecemeal fashion, constantly bartering his votes on other issues or his support for other senators' water projects for their backing. The Arkansas River project was finally completed in 1971. Federal spending in Oklahoma mushroomed during Kerr's tenure, and his chairmanship of the Rivers and Harbors Subcommittee after 1955 became the cornerstone of his power.

Although he supported the Truman administration's program more often than not, Kerr generally displayed little interest in broader issues like foreign policy, civil rights, or civil liberties. He made an exception in April 1951, when President Truman dismissed General DOUGLAS MACARTHUR as supreme commander of U.S. forces in Korea. Kerr, who had been critical of MacArthur's strategy of risking war with Communist China a month before, vigorously defended Truman's action; for several days he was the only Senate Democrat to speak in favor of the controversial firing. A prime factor influencing Kerr's outspoken anti-MacArthur stance was the fact that Oklahoma's 45th National Guard Division, then en route to Japan, represented one-half of the troops available for fighting on the Chinese mainland, a danger their senator wished to avert.

In 1952 Kerr made an unsuccessful bid for the Democratic presidential nomination. He chose the Nebraska primary as his crucial test, spending large sums on advertisements, campaigning exhaustively around the state, and hurling "soft on communism" accusations at his opponent, Senator ESTES KEFAUVER (D-Tenn.). Kefauver's victory on April 1 by a vote of 65,531 to 42,467 had a crushing impact upon Kerr's presidential hopes. Relying on the possibility that a deadlocked convention might turn to him as a compromise choice, the Oklahoman remained in the race until July. The meager total of 65 votes he received on the first ballot, however, laid to rest Kerr's aspirations for higher office. He seemed too parochial, particularly in the eyes of the press. Columnist Marquis Childs called him "the big boom from Oklahoma: the richest and loudest man in the United States Senate." Kerr biographer Anne

Hodges Morgan has contended that neither major party in 1952 would nominate an unpolished candidate—like Kerr—who was reminiscent of an earlier day in American politics.

After the campaign Kerr returned to the Senate and devoted himself to expanding and consolidating his influence in that body. His close relationship with such senators as LYNDON B. JOHNSON (D-Tex.), whom Kerr promoted for formal leadership positions, placed him at the center of the directorate that dominated the upper house. He was a spirited adversary of the Eisenhower administration on a number of issues involving his state's interests. During the Kennedy years he became the administration's most potent ally, particularly on matters relating to taxes, trade policy, and the space program, although he did oppose Medicare. In his later years, said Senator PAUL H. DOUGLAS (D-Ill.), Kerr was the "uncrowned king of the Senate." He died of a heart attack on January 1, 1963, in Washington, D.C. (See *The Eisenhower Years, The Kennedy Years* Volumes)

—TO

Keyserling, Leon H.
(1908–1987) *member, acting chairman, and chairman, Council of Economic Advisers*

Leon H. Keyserling was born on January 22, 1908, in and raised in Charleston, South Carolina. He entered Columbia University at the age of 16, where he studied under economist and future Roosevelt Brain Trust member REXFORD G. TUGWELL. Upon graduating Phi Beta Kappa, he went to Harvard Law School. He was admitted to the New York bar in 1931 and shortly thereafter became an assistant in the Columbia economics department. An attempt to earn a Ph.D. in economics was scuttled when he moved in May 1933 to Washington to join the new Roosevelt administration as an attorney with the Agricultural Adjustment Administration. Within a few months he became secretary and legislative assistant to Senator ROBERT F. WAGNER (D-N.Y.).

With Wagner he helped draft such important New Deal legislation as the National Industrial Recovery Act of 1933 (he was particularly responsible for Section 7a, which encouraged collective bargaining), the Railway Retirement Act of 1934, and the National Labor Relations Act of 1935. In 1937 Keyserling became general counsel of the U.S. Housing Authority. He remained in central positions in federal housing programs. Keyserling drafted the Democratic Party's platform for the presidential campaigns of 1936, 1940, and 1944. In 1944 Keyserling won second place is an essay contest of the Pabst Beer Company. He wrote on the future of the American economy, and many of the ideas in the essay, particularly the creation of a governmental economic council, found its way into the Full Employment bill of 1945, which would have committed the government to maintain full employment, forcing it to use fiscal policy, including deficit financing, to reach its goal. Its provisions were weakened considerably before passage, and what emerged was declaration of intent. The final bill established the Council of Economic Advisers to keep the president informed of changes in the economy. Truman appointed Keyserling to the newly created three-man council in July 1946. Three years later he became chairman.

According to historian Herbert Stein, Keyserling did not care about fiscal policy or fiscal decisions. For him the major problem of economics was not maintaining aggregate demand but balancing economic sectors, assuring that wages, profits, and farm income did not get out of line with one another and eliminating industrial surpluses and bottlenecks. Keyserling warned against excessive preoccupation with overall conditions like inflation. As a consequence of his orientation, the council's tax proposals tended to emphasize economic restructuring rather than economic stimulation or restraint. The 1948 Truman tax program—reported at the time to be the work of Keyserling and his colleagues—raised corporate taxes almost as much as it lowered personal income taxes. However, Truman put up only a lackadaisical fight for it in Congress.

Although Keyserling was not a Keynesian, he did believe the U.S. economy could sustain a large military necessary for cold war diplomacy and still have the money for more domestic program ("guns and butter"). His input was vital for the drafting of National Security Council Directive 68 (NSC-68), which called for a massive increase in defense spending.

Until the Korean War Truman generally ignored the advice of the council. He and Secretary of the Treasury JOHN W. SNYDER wanted to balance the budget and finance the federal debt cheaply. They did not attach much importance to the broad economic consequences of their fiscal and monetary policies. More than advice, they expected the council members to give support for their decisions. For example,

the council's first report to the president called for a budget surplus to dampen inflation. Truman, upon receiving this recommendation, merely noted his gratification that the panel had endorsed existing administration policy. Keyserling accepted his role as advocate. In 1949, several months into the first postwar recession, with prices falling, Keyserling, in the face of contradictory analysis by the council's staff, continued to support Truman's contention that the major economic problem remained inflation.

Keyserling was a major force behind the development of Fair Deal legislation. Late in 1946, in the aftermath of the disastrous 1946 mid-term elections, a group of liberals in the administration began holding meetings to develop legislative proposals. CLARK CLIFFORD and Keyserling, because of their access to Truman, emerged as leaders. All these men were concerned about the influence of John Snyder and other conservatives on Truman and resolved to coordinate their efforts to move Truman to the left. The group's first major victory was to persuade Truman to adopt a liberal political strategy in the 1948 presidential election campaign and, as part of that strategy, to veto the Taft-Hartley bill. Once the administration had developed a liberal social program, Keyserling became a vigorous advocate of the Fair Deal. With the outbreak of the Korean War, Keyserling took a strong role in developing and advocating such war related proposals as increased taxes and new economic controls. He became a forceful proponent of rapid rearmament, even at the cost of budget deficits and inflation.

Keyserling's role in the formation of monetary policy was small. He endorsed the administration's opposition to the Federal Reserve Board's attempts to raise interest rates to dampen inflation. The council's report to the president in 1952 contended that raising interest rates "might tend to press prices upward." In seeing climbing rates as inflationary, Keyserling and his associates stood in opposition not only to the Federal Reserve but also to the virtually unanimous judgment of the other professional economists. Keyserling's recommendations were unpopular with Republicans in Congress, who eliminated funding for the staff of the council after they gained control of the legislature in the 1952 elections. Keyserling had selected most of the staff, and, with Eisenhower taking office, Republicans wanted to purge it of what they considered his excessive partisan influence. Only after his appointees were gone did they restore funds.

In 1953 Keyserling returned to his law practice and became a consulting economist. During the 1960s he criticized the Kennedy administration for being too timid in pursuing full employment and full capacity production. He also pushed for liberal programs during the Johnson presidency and helped draft the Full Employment and Balanced Growth Act of 1977 (the Humphrey-Hawkins Act). He died in Washington, D.C., on August 9, 1987. (See *The Kennedy Years* Volume)

—CSJ

Kilgore, Harley M(artin)

(1893–1956) *member of the Senate*

Harley M. Kilgore was born on January 11, 1893, in Brown, West Virginia. During World War I he enlisted and rose to become a captain in the army. After his discharge he resumed his law practice, which he continued until 1932. He served as judge of the Criminal Court of Raleigh County from 1932 to 1940 and helped shift the emphasis in state juvenile court system from punishment to rehabilitation and prevention. In 1940 he was elected to the U.S. Senate on a Democratic ticket, beating Republican Thomas Sweeney. Kilgore was an ardent New Dealer and supporter of organized labor. During the early 1940s he was a member of the Senate Committee to Investigate the National Defense Program, headed by Harry S Truman. His proposal in January 1943 to create an Office of War Mobilization to organize production on the homefront was adopted in modified form as the War Production Board. His effort in assisting the mobilization process convinced him of the need for a national policy to encourage technological and scientific research.

Kilgore faced a tough reelection in 1946. Republicans were on the ascendancy with their charge of "Had enough?" referring to the difficulty the Truman administration was having in reconverting the economy back to a peacetime mode. In addition, JOHN L. LEWIS, president of the United Mine Workers, opposed his reelection because of his unclear position on the Smith-Connally Act. He had missed vital votes due to his service on the Truman Committee during the war. He had also supported federal hydroelectric plants in West Virginia, which Lewis thought threatened mine workers. Kilgore beat Sweeney again, but by fewer than 4,000 votes, helped in part by mine workers who ignored Lewis's advice.

Kilgore gained a reputation as President Truman's liberal spokesman in the Senate. He supported most Fair Deal legislation and in July 1945 introduced Truman's extended unemployment insurance compensation bill, which increased benefits to $25 a week for 26 weeks and extended them to federal and maritime workers. Fearful of the onset of the cold war, Kilgore condemned Winston Churchill's 1946 "Iron Curtain" speech and opposed confrontation with the Soviet Union. However, he supported the Truman Doctrine and the Marshall Plan, designed to contain Soviet expansion and rebuild Europe.

Kilgore was a vigorous opponent of the Taft-Hartley Act and led a filibuster against the bill in June 1947 after President Truman vetoed it. He sought to postpone the vote to override the veto until Truman could address the nation and gain support for his position. The filibuster lasted 31 hours but failed. The Senate voted to override by a vote of 68 to 25. Kilgore also supported Truman's Fair Deal, including such things as national health insurance, rural electrification, public housing, extension of Social Security, raises in the minimum wage, and federal aid to education.

Kilgore was a strong opponent of the anticommunist crusade that developed during the late 1940s. In October 1947 he defended motion picture figures under investigation by the House Un-American Activities Committee, questioning "the right of Congress to ask any man what he thinks on political issues." Three years later he pointed out discrepancies in Senator JOSEPH R. MCCARTHY's (R-Wisc.) charges that there were a large number of Communists in the State Department. In September 1950 Kilgore offered an alternative to Senator PATRICK A. MCCARRAN's (D-Nev.) internal security bill, then under consideration. McCarran's measure provided for the registration of Communists and Communist-front organizations. Kilgore suggested a measure that included President Truman's recommendation for strengthening existing sabotage and espionage laws and extending the federal government's powers to deal with deportable aliens. His bill also included a detention plan that would have given the president power to intern all Communists and subversives during national emergencies.

Kilgore had presented this plan, derogatively referred to as the "concentration camp" bill by Truman's advisers, at a meeting with the President, Senator HUBERT H. HUMPHREY (D-Minn.), and other liberal senators, but Truman was noncommital about the measure. As a result of the efforts of Senate Majority Leader SCOTT W. LUCAS (D-Ill.), Kilgore's bill was added to the McCarran measure as an amendment rather than a substitute. The McCarran bill was passed by overwhelming majorities in both houses of Congress in late September. Kilgore voted against the bill and subsequently voted to sustain Truman's veto of the measure.

In 1952 Kilgore faced what again would be a Republican year with Dwight D. Eisenhower running for president, and the public angry over Truman's conduct of the Korean War. But campaigning on his liberal record, he beat Republican Chapman Revercomb, despite the latter's outrageous charges that Kilgore was a Communist sympathizer.

Kilgore remained a prominent liberal Democratic during the Eisenhower administration. He voted against the Bricker amendment, which would have limited the treaty-making power of the president, and opposed the Dixon-Yates contract. From 1955 to 1956 he was chairman of the Judiciary Committee. Kilgore died of a cerebral hemorrhage on February 28, 1956, in Washington, D.C.

—AES

Kimball, Dan A(ble)

(1896–1970) *assistant secretary of the navy for air, undersecretary of the navy, secretary of the navy*

Dan Kimball was born on March 1, 1896, in St. Louis, Missouri. He attended Soldan High School, but it is unclear whether he graduated. He did take correspondence courses in engineering and joined the U.S. Army Air Corps in 1917. The following year he received a commission as a second lieutenant and, before the end of the war, had piloted pursuit planes. In 1919 Kimball moved to California, where he began a long career with General Tire and Rubber Company, eventually becoming manager for the company of a district comprised of 11 Western states. After moving to Washington in 1941, Kimball recommended that the company buy the Aerojet Engineering Company, which made jet assisted takeoff apparatus. General Tire did so and it proved profitable; the company made Kimball director of the subsidiary. During his directorship Aerojet worked jointly with Douglas Aircraft Company and other firms to develop high-altitude research rockets. Kimball became the executive vice

president and general manager of Aeroject and vice president and director of General Tire.

A moderate Democrat, Kimball worked hard for the reelection of President Truman in 1948. In gratitude the president named him assistant secretary of the navy for air in February 1949. Kimball entered the department in the midst of a dispute over the role of the navy in national defense generated by Truman's attempts to lower the Pentagon budget. Air force leaders as well as such prominent members of the administration as Secretary of Defense LOUIS A. JOHNSON contended that emphasis should be placed on strategic bombers as the nation's prime deterrent. Supporters of the navy, on the other hand, maintained that, because of the carrier and the submarine, that service had the flexibility to wage modern warfare. Soon after Kimball arrival in the department, Johnson cancelled the building of the supercarrier USS *United States*, which would have given the navy the ability to deliver nuclear weapons to Russia. Instead, Johnson ordered the building of more B-36 strategic bombers. In protest Secretary of the Navy JOHN L. SULLIVAN and Undersecretary W. John Kenny stepped down. Johnson prevailed upon Kimball to stay and promoted him to undersecretary in May—after only six weeks in the department. Kimball's amiability proved a great asset, particularly in the aftermath of the Admirals' Revolt, when top navy brass openly protested the cancellation of the supercarrier. Also useful was his background in the defense industry and in dealing with the government because of his work.

As Jeffrey G. Barlow has noted, Undersecretary Kimball, in the aftermath of the cancellation of the supercarrier, pushed for the conversion of World War II *Essex*-class carriers to a more updated type, and Johnson agreed to this proposal. Barlow contended that Johnson's decision was part of an implicit quid pro quo, by which the navy would stop complaining about his alleged antinavy bias. Kimball wanted to accept such a compromise, believing interservice difficulties could be resolved amicably.

Kimball supported Truman's defense policy and warned the nation that too high a defense budget would lead to economic collapse and too low a budget to another world war. However, he quickly asserted the importance of the navy. One of his first public statements was affirming the importance of aircraft carriers in future defense. In December 1949 he said that the navy was giving top priority to antisubmarine warfare in order to insure the safety of American ships in any waters at any time.

Kimball was only tangentially involved in the dispute between the navy and air force. As undersecretary, he worked primarily to insure cooperation between civilian and uniformed leaders of the service. During his tenure he approved a new policy permitting the department's civilian employees to join unions and participate in union meetings. The House Civil Service Committee commended him for the way he handled the delicate problems created by the loyalty-security program.

Kimball was nominated as secretary of the navy in June 1951; he was confirmed the following month. As secretary, he continued to defend the role of the navy in modern warfare as a deterrent against Communist nations. In August he recommended that the navy double the number of Forrestal-class supercarriers authorized, which could carry planes that could deliver nuclear weapons. The Kimball administration also saw the beginning of construction of the world's first nuclear powered submarine—a weapon system that Kimball had advocated. "Strong naval forces," he maintained, "are the cheapest form of national security insurance." Kimball oversaw the buildup of the navy during the Korean War. He was a strong supporter of Nationalist China, recommending in 1952 the United States increase military aid to Taiwan. He also implied his support for suggestions that a Nationalist force invade the Chinese mainland.

Kimball retired from government service in January 1953 to return to Aerojet. He died on July 30, 1970, in Washington, D.C.

—MLB

King, Cecil R(hodes)
(1898–1974) *member of the House of Representatives*

King was born on January 13, 1898, in Youngstown, New York, but grew up in Los Angeles. He served in the Canadian army during World War I and then went into business. He also became active in politics. In 1932 King was elected to the state assembly. Ten years later he won a special election to fill a House seat left vacant by the death of Representative Lee Geyer (D-Calif.). A liberal Democrat, King easily won reelection from his industrialized, predominantly working-class district during the Truman years. King supported most New Deal and Fair

Deal legislation, and he backed President Truman's foreign policy.

King won national attention in 1951 when, as chairman of the Subcommittee on Administration of the Internal Revenue Laws, he began probing reports of corruption in the Bureau of Internal Revenue (BIR) and the Justice Department. The King subcommittee was formed in response to statements by members of the Senate Crime Investigating Committee, headed by Senator ESTES KEFAUVER (D-Tenn.), that irregularities were occurring in the BIR. The subcommittee uncovered a pattern of corruption and bribery extending to the highest levels of the bureau. During 1951, 166 officials in the BIR were fired or forced to resign. The BIR's chief counsel, CHARLES A. OLIPHANT, left his post after testimony revealed he had accepted gifts from defendants in tax fraud cases. King was critical of Oliphant's poor discretion. As a result of the King probe, two former bureau commissioners were later convicted for income tax evasion. A number of regional collectors left their jobs under sharp criticism.

The Tax Division of the Justice Department also came under scrutiny, and Assistant Attorney General T. LAMAR CAUDLE resigned at President Truman's request. Testimony in December 1951 showed that Caudle had taken loans, gifts, and free vacations from defendants in tax cases. Caudle later served a prison term for conspiracy. One of the more damaging and sensational allegations surfaced in December, when Abraham Teitelbaum, once gangster Al Capone's lawyer, told the King subcommittee that Caudle, Oliphant, former BIR head GEORGE J. SCHOENEMAN, and other government officials were part of a Washington clique accepting bribes to fix tax cases. All those named denied involvement, but some, such as Caudle, Oliphant, and GSA administrator JESS LARSON, admitted close friendships with alleged Capitol fixers.

As historian Andrew J. Dunar has noted, the president did have better relations with King than he had with Senator J. William Fulbright, who had investigated the Reconstruction Finance Corporation and was disturbed by the committee's revelations, but differences did develop with King nonetheless. Truman would only allow access to Department of Justice files on a case-by-case basis, which led to constant battles over which files were relevant.

King himself came under investigation in November 1951 when rumors started that he had intervened in three tax cases pending in Southern California. While the subcommittee investigated the charges, King disqualified himself from the panel. After two days of hearings the subcommittee cleared him of any wrongdoing. In December columnist DREW PEARSON accused the King unit of "whitewashing" its chairman. Pearson claimed King had intervened in a Justice Department investigation of a Long Beach, California, bank president. Following a second probe, the panel formally cleared King in April 1952.

In January 1952 Truman, stung by Republican charges that his administration was corrupt, announced a reorganization plan for the BIR. The plan abolished the politically appointed offices of collectors of internal revenue and replaced them with 25 district commissioners chosen through civil service and forbidden to have outside jobs. Only the BIR commissioner would be appointed by the president. King endorsed the plan, which became law in March.

King's subcommittee continued its investigation of the tax scandals during 1952. In January HENRY W. GRUNEWALD, a reputed Washington influence peddler, refused to answer questions before the subcommittee. He was later cited for contempt of Congress. In February the hearings shifted to San Francisco, where King concluded that the local BIR office was run by incompetent political appointees. He also attacked the Treasury Department in February for holding special grand jury hearings on activities in the New York BIR office. King claimed he had "clear evidence" that the Treasury Department hoped to "stifle" his unit's probe, scheduled for March. Secretary of the Treasury JOHN W. SNYDER denied the charge. Later in the spring King's group explored the relationship between Senator OWEN BREWSTER (R-Maine) and Grunewald. Brewster admitted he had used Grunewald as a "conduit" to donate large sums to Senate primary campaigns in 1950. Also in the spring, hearings uncovered the intervention of Senator STYLES BRIDGES (R-N.H.) in the tax case of a liquor dealer. Bridges claimed his repeated inquiries into the case were not out of order.

In May 1952 King introduced a bill to plug loopholes in the income tax laws with specific provisions to discourage improper intervention in tax cases. The measure was not reported. The final report of the King subcommittee in December 1952 recommended that the BIR increase salaries and make promotions on merit. It praised the bureau's

efforts at reform and questioned whether the BIR should remain part of the Treasury Department or become an independent agency. King lost his chairmanship when the Republicans took control of Congress in 1953. Although he remained on the Ways and Means Committee, he did not continue his membership on the investigations subcommittee.

King backed the administration's foreign policy. He supported aid to Greece and Turkey, the Marshall Plan, Point Four, the Korean Aid Act, and military assistance to the North Atlantic Treaty Organization. He consistently voted to extend the Trade Agreement Act of 1934. He supported many liberal initiatives, such as the Employment Act of 1946, the National Housing Act of 1949, and the elimination of the poll tax. Although he supported the Case labor disputes bill, he voted against the Taft-Hartley Act of 1947. He also opposed the Mundt-Nixon bill, the McCarran Act, and the McCarran-Walter Act.

King was one of the principal architects of Medicare, instituted in 1965. He retired in 1969 and died on March 17, 1974, in Inglewood, California. (See *The Kennedy Years* Volume)

—JF

Kirchwey, Freda
(1893–1976) *publisher*

Kirchwey was born on September 26, 1893, in Lake Placid, New York. She attended Barnard College where she showed her egalitarian spirit by railing against sororities because of their discriminatory actions, especially against Jews. After graduating from Barnard in 1915, she worked as a reporter for the *New York Morning Telegraph*. In 1918 Kirchwey helped edit the literary magazine *Every Week* and the *New York Tribune*. In August 1918 she joined the *Nation*, where she worked as editorial assistant in the International Relations Section. In 1922 she became managing editor. During the decade, the *Nation* shifted its editorial policy to the left and emphasized social and economic reform. Kirchwey contributed numerous articles on international relations, but as interest in social mores grew, she also wrote articles on the changing status of women. In 1925 she published *Our Changing Morality*, a popular book of articles by prominent American women who described their youth, early sexual experiences, and marriages.

Eight years later the *Nation*'s owner, Maurice Wertheim, infuriated with the magazine's editorial support of Franklin Roosevelt's court-packing scheme, sold it to Kirchwey. Kirchwey recruited some of the most promising young crusading reporters to the staff, including Robert Bendiner, James Wechsler, and I. F. Stone. Under her direction the magazine supported both New Deal social and economic policies and popular leftist politics. She abandoned the journal's pacifism and advocated collective security and then war against fascist nations. The *Nation* opposed American neutrality in the Spanish Civil War and supported the repeal of the Neutrality Act in early 1941.

During the war Kirchwey became an advocate for war refugees and supported the creation of a Jewish state in Palestine. She condemned the dropping of atomic bombs on Hiroshima and Nagasaki. She established a public forum to debate the peaceful use of atomic power and the need to control nuclear activity.

In the postwar period Kirchwey criticized both American and Soviet foreign policy, which she thought contributed to an arms race and the likelihood of global nuclear war. She charged that American foreign policy was failing in Asia because the United States had allowed the Communists to ally with the popular forces. This, she thought, forced America to adopt a counterrevolutionary stance. She criticized the administration's foreign policy for not recognizing the USSR's legitimate security needs, and she favored the division of the European continent into spheres of influence that recognized Soviet fear about its own security. Yet Kirchwey condemned the Soviet Union's incursion into Czechoslovakia and charged that Jan Masaryk's "suicide" was, in fact, murder. Kirchwey thought that the Truman Doctrine was an incursion into national sovereignty and democratic liberties as well as a threat to U.S. security. She saw it as a sham that hid the real U.S. concern about the threat to American capitalist interests in Eastern Europe. Similarly, she believed that the North Atlantic Treaty Organization contributed to an escalation of the arms race, which would also cause "a period of economic dislocation, strikes and demonstrations, severe repression, and growing political reaction" throughout Europe.

Kirchwey charged that Truman's domestic programs pandered to the interests of the ruling class and that his loyalty program, under which 10 State Department employees were dismissed in 1947, represented "thought control" worthy of the most

totalitarian state. She supported HENRY A. WALLACE for the Democratic presidential nomination in 1948 and asserted that the nomination of Truman represented a triumph of the reactionary forces within the Democratic Party.

In 1951 Freda Kirchwey turned over the editorship of *The Nation* to Carey McWilliams, although she continued as publisher until 1955. During the 1960s and 1970s she remained active in liberal causes. She died on January 3, 1976, in St. Petersburg, Florida.

—SJT

Kline, Allan B(lair)

(1895–1968) *president, American Farm Bureau*

Allan B. Kline was born on November 10, 1895, in Dixon County, Nebraska. He grew up in the northeastern part of the state. He received a B.A. from Morningside College in 1917. After service in the army during World War I, he returned to school and obtained a B.S. in 1920 from Iowa State College. He then began farming, eventually becoming a very successful hog raiser.

An active member of the American Farm Bureau Federation, Kline served as its vice president from 1945 to 1947. The Farm Bureau, the largest general farm organization in the United States, had 1.2 million members in 1947. That year the organization split on the question of price supports: Southern cotton and tobacco interests favored high rigid supports, while midwestern corn farmers supported less government intervention in the market. Kline, who backed the latter position, won the presidency at the 1947 convention. In an important break with its past history he led the Farm Bureau to demand phased withdrawal of price supports. Kline urged a "policy of abundance," with farm production running full tilt and foodstuff consumption subsidized by the government. Kline thought price supports should be employed only as a floor during hard times, rather than to maintain high prices artificially.

In speeches across the country Kline advocated a free market system and increased foreign trade as the key to continued farm prosperity. He testified before the Senate Committee on Agriculture and Forestry in 1948 in favor of a sliding scale for price supports between 60 percent and 90 percent of parity. At the 1948 bureau convention, Kline again led the fight against the South—he threatened to resign if he did not get his way—and got the organization to support the Hope-Aiken Act, which provided a sliding scale. He sent a letter to President Truman in December 1948 reminding him that his victories in key midwestern farm states had come from farmers who wanted flexible price supports. But Kline was a Republican, who had been touted as Governor THOMAS E. DEWEY's choice as secretary of agriculture, and thus had virtually no influence on the administration.

Kline was a bitter foe of the policies of Secretary of Agriculture CHARLES F. BRANNAN. The Brannan Plan, proposed in 1949, called for high farm production. It recommended subsidizing low prices to consumers by making up the difference between the market price and parity with direct cash payments to farmers. Kline said Brannan's policy represented the "egalitarian approach" while the existing system was based on the "decision of the individual as to what is best for him." He warned that the costs of the plan would be "staggering." Under his leadership the Farm Bureau played a crucial role in defeating the proposal. Kline opposed all price controls, calling them "the handmaiden of inflation." He supported the Defense Production Act of 1950, which exempted most agricultural products from price control, and the following year he lobbied against an extension of Truman's authority to regulate food prices.

Kline was a vigorous supporter of aid to Europe during the postwar period, believing it was a means of disposing of America's agricultural surplus. He spoke out in favor of the Marshall Plan. In 1948 Truman appointed the Republican to a 12-member board to assist in administering the effort.

Kline retired as president of the Farm Bureau in 1954 and returned to farming. He continued to speak out against government interference in agriculture. During the 1960 presidential campaign he criticized Senator John F. Kennedy's (D-Mass.) farm program as one "that would lead toward socialized agriculture." Kline died on June 14, 1968, in Vinton, Iowa.

—TFS

Knowland, William F(ife)

(1908–1974) *member of the Senate*

Born on June 26, 1908, in Alameda, California, William F. Knowland was the son of a six-term California congressman. Following graduation from the University of California in 1925, he joined the editorial staff of his father's newspaper, the *Oakland* (Calif.) *Tribune*. In 1933 Knowland won a seat in the California Assembly; two years later he moved to the California Senate. In 1938 Knowland was elected to the Republican National Committee and three years later became chairman of its executive committee. California governor EARL WARREN appointed Knowland to finish the term of the deceased senator Hiram Johnson (R-Calif.) in 1945. Warren wanted an internationalist, as Knowland, to replace the fiery isolationist Johnson. According to Knowland biographers Gayle B. Montgomery and James W. Johnson, Warren was also repaying a debt to the elder Knowland for the support he gave him early in the governor's career. Knowland believed in certain principles, held to them stubbornly and, in doing so, earned the sobriquet, "Mr. Integrity" for his honesty.

In the upper house Knowland compiled a mixed record, voting for such antiunion legislation as the Case labor disputes bill and the Taft-Hartley Act, as well as the liberal Full Employment bill of 1945, raising the minimum wage from 40 cents to 65 cents an hour, and increasing unemployment compensation. He supported the creation of a permanent Fair Employment Practices Commission and anti–poll tax legislation. In 1947 he offered a bill to invoke cloture by a majority vote rather than the traditional two-thirds. It failed to pass. A strong states' rights advocate, he voted for a measure renouncing federal claims to lands lying beneath tidewaters. After the Republicans lost control of Congress in the 1948 election, Knowland and a group of other Young Turks challenged the entrenched senatorial leadership. HENRY CABOT LODGE (R-Mass.) ran against ROBERT A. TAFT (R-Ohio) as head of the Republican Policy Committee and Knowland went up against KENNETH S. WHERRY (R-Neb.) for floor leader. The Young Turks lost badly.

Knowland was primarily known as an ardent supporter of Nationalist China. An opponent of the senator, Asian expert and State Department adviser OWEN LATTIMORE, dubbed him "the senator from Formosa," a nickname he detested since he supported containment in Europe, too. As a spokesman for the "China Lobby," he defended Chiang Kaishek's (Jiang Jieshi) government against charges of corruption and demanded increased aid to the regime. According to Montgomery and Johnson, in his foreign policy speeches, Knowland almost always used the line " 'the road to Paris is through Peking,' " which he attributed to Lenin. Although he voted for much of the legislation enacting Truman's policy of containment toward the Soviet Union, Knowland initially opposed such measures as the Marshall Plan unless they were coupled with increased assistance to Chiang.

Knowland opposed the nomination of DEAN G. ACHESON as secretary of state in 1949 because he had assisted in establishing the policy that pressed Chiang to negotiate with the Communists just after World War II. Later that year Acheson's State Department issued its White Paper on China, blaming the fall of that country on the Nationalists. Knowland decried it as a "whitewash" of a "do-nothing" policy. With the possibility of a Communist invasion, Knowland publicly called on Truman to use the navy to protect Taiwan. Truman refused and, under Acheson's prodding, declared Taiwan should be returned to China as laid out in the Cairo Declaration of 1943 and the Potsdam Declaration of 1945. The California senator opposed recognition of the new Beijing government and urged all-out military aid for Chiang to reconquer the mainland. Acheson wanted to recognize Communist China, but the opposition of Knowland and others like him made that impossible.

Knowland maintained that Communists and Communist sympathizers in the State Department were responsible for the fall of China. He pointed particularly to Owen Lattimore. In 1949 he charged Lattimore with advocating a "policy of appeasement" in Asia. The following year he maintained that the scholar was espousing the Communist Party line. Knowland was never able to generate national publicity for his charges until Senator JOSEPH R. MCCARTHY (R-Wisc.) took up the campaign.

Knowland initially applauded Truman's intervention in Korea but soon joined General DOUGLAS MACARTHUR and his supporters in charging that the president's policies prevented a military victory. (Ironically Knowland was the first person to refer to the conflict as a "police action." A reporter in the Senate press gallery heard that, ran to the White House, and, without attributing Knowland, asked if that was what this intervention was. Truman agreed in an assertion that would haunt his presidency.) Of all the Republican critics of the administration, Knowland was the most bellicose on the war. He even welcomed a full-scale war with the Chinese as an alternative to what he

called a "Far Eastern Munich." Knowland opposed any truce that would lead to a permanent partition of the Korean peninsula.

Knowland supported Warren's favorite son candidacy for the presidency in 1952. Taft supporters offered Knowland the vice presidency if he would switch his support to the Ohioan, but Knowland would not break with Warren unless the governor released him. Both Knowland and Warren were angered by what they saw as RICHARD M. NIXON's attempt to win delegates over to DWIGHT D. EISENHOWER, even though Nixon was pledged to Warren. Nixon biographer Irwin Gellman has asserted that this perception was mistaken, and that Nixon only wanted the delegation to be in the position of "kingmaker" if Warren released it. But Knowland distrusted Nixon because of what he thought had happened. When running mate Nixon ran into trouble over his slush fund, Eisenhower asked Knowland to be prepared to take Nixon's place. Nixon, of course, saved himself through his Checkers speech, and Knowland did not become Ike's running mate.

When Senate Majority Leader ROBERT A. TAFT died in 1953, Knowland succeeded him. Following his party's loss of the upper chamber in 1954, he became minority leader. Knowland failed to work closely with the White House. His inflexibility toward possible accommodation with Russia and China often embarrassed the administration, which sought to reduce tensions. In addition, Knowland's defense of McCarthy during the 1954 censure proceedings prolonged the controversy, which the administration wanted to end. In 1958 Knowland ran for governor of California. He was defeated by Democrat Edmund Brown. Knowland then returned to his newspaper business. In 1964 he served on the campaign staff of Senator Barry Goldwater (R-Ariz.), and attended the 1968 Republican National Convention. Knowland died on February 23, 1974, at his summer home near Guerneville, California, the victim of an apparent suicide. (See *The Eisenhower Years* Volume)

—JB

Knutson, Harold
(1880–1953) *member of the House of Representatives*
Born in Skien, Norway, on October 20, 1880, Harold Knutson moved to America with his parents

at age six and grew up on a dairy farm near Clear Lake, Minnesota. He began a career in the newspaper business as a printer's devil, became associate editor of the *St. Cloud* (Minn.) *Daily Journal-Press*, and then publisher of two other papers. He also acquired the two other papers. He also acquired the *Wadena* (Minn.) *Pioneer-Journal*, which he published throughout his political career. During 1910 he served as president of the Minnesota Editorial Association. Active in local Republican affairs, Knutson in 1916 was elected to Congress from Minnesota's agricultural Sixth Congressional District.

One of 50 congressmen to vote against a declaration of war on Germany in 1917, Knutson maintained his staunch isolationist stance for over 30 years. In 1920 he advocated a two-year ban on immigration, arguing that foreign laborers would exacerbate unemployment and spread radical ideas. In the late 1930s Knutson served as vice chairman of the National Committee to Keep America Out of War and denounced all moves to aid opponents of the Axis. Although he voted to declare war on Germany and Japan in 1941, he opposed all lend-lease measures and accused the Roosevelt administration of responsibility for the Pearl Harbor attack.

Few Republicans matched Knutson's unwavering opposition to all manifestations of New Deal and Fair Deal liberalism. An advocate of limited government and a balanced budget, he consistently attacked outgrowths of federal influence, filibustering against the Federal Deposit Insurance Corporation, opposing social security and arguing that the Agriculture Adjustment Act would "sovietize American agriculture." Knutson was a constant critic of governmental economic controls during World War II and once said that "the only difference between a Nazi and a Communist is that a Nazi cannot get a job in the New Deal."

Joining the tax writing Ways and Means Committee in 1933, Knutson was a persistent vocal opponent of tax increases to finance federal spending, whether for social programs or for military appropriations. In 1942 he attacked a measure raising taxes on corporations to finance the war. The next year he led the fight for the Ruml Plan to forgive all 1942 individual income taxes and served as ranking Republican on the conference committee that put together a compromise forgiveness bill. In 1943 he denounced a request by the Treasury for $10.5 billion more in taxes as an increase that would "threaten the future solvency of American business

and bring about the liquidation of the middle class. . . ."

During the first term of the Truman administration Knutson stood out as the most determined congressional advocate of a sweeping tax cut. In August 1946 he promised voters a 20 percent reduction in taxes, along with a balanced budget if the Republicans won control of Congress in the 1946 elections. The Republicans won majorities in both houses, and Knutson in January 1947 was installed as chairman of the Ways and Means Committee.

Knutson's 20 percent across-the-board tax cut was the first bill introduced in the 80th Congress. The Truman administration vigorously opposed the measure as inflationary, while congressional Democrats criticized as inequitable the blanket nature of the reduction, which would give thousands to upper bracket taxpayers but only a few dollars to lower income persons. Knutson refused to modify his plan, however, despite pleas from the Republican leadership. In reply to criticism, he said that the tax cuts of the 1920s had encouraged business investment, fostered prosperity, and ultimately resulted in greater revenue for the Treasury.

In March 1947 the Ways and Means Committee passed a slightly revised version of Knutson's measure, cutting personal income taxes by 30 percent for taxpayers earning less than $1,000, by 20 percent for all others up to $300,000, and 10.5 percent for those over that figure. The new schedule was to have been retroactive to January 1; the revenue loss to the government was estimated at $3.8 billion. The House and Senate passed the Knutson bill, but it was vetoed by President Truman in June. The House sustained the veto by a two-vote margin.

Knutson immediately reintroduced his tax reduction bill, altering it to take effect on January 1, 1948. The House passed the new bill, 302 to 112, in July; Senate passage followed. Truman again vetoed the measure. On this occasion the House overrode the veto, but the Senate sustained it.

In December Knutson put forth a third tax cut measure with more progressive features. Individual exemptions were to be raised by $100, those over 65 were to receive an extra exemption, and married couples would be able to split their income for tax purposes. In February 1948 the House, by a 297 to 120 vote, passed a bill that incorporated these features and cut income taxes by 10 percent for incomes up to $1,000, by 20 percent on those up to $4,000, and 10 percent on those over $4,000, for a total reduction of $6.3 billion. In March the Senate passed a similar measure, but by lowering cuts for higher incomes they decreased the total reduction to $4.7 billion. The House, 289 to 67, concurred with the Senate version. It was sent to Truman, who again vetoed it. Both houses overrode the veto in April, and the Knutson tax cut finally was enacted. Later in the month Knutson decried the House's repeal of the 62-year-old tax on oleomargarine long favored by dairy farmers.

In virtually all areas of foreign and domestic policy Knutson was an outspoken foe of the Truman administration, and according to the *New York Times*, "was said by colleagues not to have voted support for Mr. Roosevelt or Mr. Truman on a single major issue." He was one of only two members of Congress in December 1947 to vote against emergency aid for France, Italy, Austria, and China. He denounced Greek-Turkish aid, the Truman Doctrine, and the Marshall Plan, maintaining that communism could not be halted with money. He was against the draft, extending the Reciprocal Trade Agreements Act by three years, and the 1946 loan to Great Britain. Knutson found the Fair Deal wanting. He opposed the Employment Act of 1946 and federal ownership of coastal tidelands. He supported the Taft-Hartley Act.

A surprise defeat in the election of 1948 ended Knutson's political career. Only a year and a half before, *Business Week* had said that "the Minnesotan has a grip on his district that other legislators regard with awe and envy." Knutson ascribed the defeat to his tax bill and the success of opponents' charges that the measure "gave a horse to the rich man and a rabbit to the poor man." Knutson died on August 21, 1953, in Wadena, Minnesota.

Krock, Arthur
(1886–1974) *journalist*

Krock, the son of a bookkeeper, was born in Glasgow, Kentucky, on November 16, 1886. He was raised in a small town in Kentucky and entered Princeton University in 1904. However, financial circumstances forced him to finish his education at Chicago's respectable Lewis Institute. He graduated with an Associate in Arts degree in 1906 and shortly thereafter became a general assignment reporter for the *Louisville Herald*. In 1908 the *Herald* sent him to cover the national conventions of the Republican and Democratic parties. That same year he became night editor in Louisville for the Associated Press.

In 1910 Krock arrived in Washington as the special correspondent for the *Louisville Times*, thus beginning a focus on national and international affairs that would be his major interest in journalism. Within a year he was also representing the *Louisville Courier-Journal*. Five years later he returned to Louisville as editorial manager for the two papers.

From 1919 to 1923, Krock served as editor-in-chief for the *Louisville Times* and covered the Versailles Conference. In 1923, following an editorial dispute, Krock left for New York City, eventually becoming an assistant to Ralph Pulitzer, editor of the *New York World*. In 1927 Krock joined the editorial staff of the *New York Times*, and, in 1932, he became head of the paper's Washington bureau. Besides his administrative duties he remained a correspondent and wrote his column, "The Nation."

A political conservative, Krock was often critical of the New Deal, which he felt was a menace to states' rights and free economy. Realizing the importance of economics in Roosevelt's domestic program, he became an acknowledged expert on the president's fiscal policies. In 1935 he won his first Pulitzer Prize for general excellence in reporting. Despite Krock's opposition to his domestic program, Roosevelt granted the journalist a personal interview in 1937 in which he revealed his plans for the future, including his decision to enlarge the Supreme Court. The interview resulted in Krock's second Pulitzer. The fact that Krock was given an exclusive interview resulted in a negative reaction on the part of the rest of the Washington press corps, and Roosevelt never again granted that type of interview.

Krock enjoyed a particularly close relationship with President Truman, which began when Truman was a senator and continued after he retired from politics. Krock had been impressed that Truman, as head of the committee to investigate the defense program, was willing to blame the Roosevelt administration for the delay in full mobilization after the bombing of Pearl Harbor, regardless of the partisan disadvantage of such an admission. Nevertheless, their friendship did not dissuade Krock from frequently leveling stern criticism at the administration. Krock admired Truman's personal integrity and the strong self-determination with which the president pursued his various programs. But Krock also believed that Truman too often gave federal posts to political friends and allies rather than to those truly qualified for the job, thus leaving himself open to criticism of "cronyism." Krock admitted Truman could be petty and quite willing to pass the buck.

Truman's action on organized labor pleased Krock. His vigorous stance against the nationwide strikes of coal miners, railway workers, and steel workers in the postwar era drew Krock's praise. But he strongly opposed Truman's Fair Deal legislation. Krock said that the wide range of social programs would inevitably lead to "more federal paternalism and new ways of centralization" while at the same time making a balanced budget virtually impossible. As he had been during the Roosevelt years, Krock was a prominent opponent of deficit spending.

Krock demanded a firm policy toward the Soviet Union and backed Truman's efforts to contain communism. He thought that Truman had been far too conciliatory to the Russians and that such a stance was based on the fallacious assumption that the basic foreign policy of the Soviet Union would be a peaceful one. In April 1948 Truman himself conceded to Krock that he regreted the rapidity with which the armed forces in Europe had been demobilized following the war. Krock was also on good terms with JAMES V. FORRESTAL, America's first secretary of defense, who shared his conservative outlook on foreign policy. The journalist was among the first to notice the signs of the impending mental breakdown, which was to result in Forrestal's suicide in 1949.

In February 1950 Krock received an exclusive interview with President Truman, the result of a personal invitation extended to the correspondent at a Washington social gathering the previous month. Truman gave a general optimistic prognosis of the international and domestic situations and defended his administration in such areas as balanced budgets and the loyalty program for federal employees. At Truman's next weekly news conference reporters reacted even more strongly than they had to Roosevelt's exclusive interview. Truman's strong defense of his actions ultimately weakened further his already poor relationship with the press.

In November 1951 Krock revealed that Truman had approached General DWIGHT D. EISENHOWER with an offer to support him for the Democratic presidential nomination in 1952. Both Eisenhower and Truman strongly denied the claims. So vehement was the president's response that most

commentators accepted his word over Krock's, despite the journalist's characterization of his source as an "eminent Northern Democrat . . . thoroughly reliable and informed." Years later Krock identified the source as Supreme Court Justice WILLIAM O. DOUGLAS. (Truman had offered to support Eisenhower as a Democrat for the 1948 presidential election, something revealed in a Truman diary discovered in 2003.) Krock also implied that Eisenhower was thinking of supporting Senator ROBERT A. TAFT (R-Ohio) in 1952. Eisenhower revealed this to be true in his book *At Ease*, but Taft's refusal to commit to collective security scuttled this idea, and Ike ended up defeating Taft for the Republican presidential nomination.

In 1953 Krock stepped down as head of the *New York Times* Washington bureau. He continued writing his column, however, up until his retirement in 1966. He was a supporter of Richard Nixon, but was greatly disillusioned during the last months of his life by the mounting scandals of Watergate. Krock died on April 12, 1974, in Washington, D.C. (See *The Eisenhower Years* Volume)

—MQ

Kroll, Jack

(1886–1971) *director, Political Action Committee, Congress of Industrial Organizations*

The son of a tailor, Jack Kroll was born on June 10, 1885, in London, England. He immigrated with his family to the United States in 1886. After completing two years of high school in Rochester, New York, he entered the tailor trade as a cutter in 1900. Three years later he joined the Rochester local of the United Garment Workers of America. Because of his role in an unsuccessful strike in 1904–05, Kroll was forced to leave Rochester. He went to Chicago only to discover that he had been blacklisted and could find work only under an assumed name. In 1910 he joined Sidney Hillman in leading a strike of garment workers against Hart, Schaffner and Marx. The strike ultimately led to the formation of the Amalgamated Clothing Workers of America (ACWA) in 1914.

After helping to organize men's garment workers in Chicago for several years, Kroll was named an ACWA national organizer in 1919. He became a vice president and executive board member in 1928. In 1933 his former ally, Sidney Hillman, helped found the Committee for Industrial Organizations

(CIO). The following year the ACWA was suspended from the American Federation of Labor (AFL) and joined the CIO. Kroll became a vice president of the Ohio CIO Industrial Union Council in 1938 and one year later was named its president.

In 1943 Hillman appointed Kroll regional director for the Ohio-Kentucky-West Virginia area of the newly formed Political Action Committee (PAC) of the CIO. The following year he was appointed vice chairman of PAC. After Hillman's death in July 1946, he was named the organization's director.

In an October 27, 1946, article for the *New York Times*, Kroll labeled the advocacy of progressive legislation the primary objective of CIO-PAC. He listed the specific demands contained within the PAC program. These included controlling the high cost of living, providing adequate housing for all, and passing the Wagner-Murray-Dingell health bill. The PAC demands also included improving education without discrimination, enacting the 65-75 cent minimum wage bill, developing effective antilynching legislation, abolishing the poll tax, establishing a permanent fair employment practices code, and promoting a foreign policy that insured peace. Kroll announced that to obtain desired legislation PAC would encourage people to take an active part in primary elections and county committee activities of both parties. Earlier that year Kroll had announced that PAC would "spare no effort in the reelection of a militant group of fighting progressives in the House and Senate and the retirement to private life" of conservative members of Congress.

Following setbacks in the November 1946 elections, Kroll declared PAC would redouble its efforts to carry on the "Roosevelt tradition" and enact social welfare legislation. The following year Kroll denounced the National Association of Manufacturers and Senator ROBERT A. TAFT (R-Ohio) for their role in the passage of the Taft-Hartley Act. He accused them of removing "all the protection the New Deal gave labor and the common people." Kroll strongly supported President Truman's veto of the measure.

The PAC director carried his program of labor and civil rights proposals to the July 1948 Democratic National Convention. The Platform Committee adopted a plank opposing the Taft-Hartley Act. However, its civil rights proposal fell far short of Kroll's expectations. He spent most of July 12 pressing Minneapolis mayor HUBERT H. HUMPHREY

to push for a tougher civil rights plank which would call for congressional action to stop lynching, abolish the poll tax and segregation, and obtain fair employment practices in the states. Following Humphrey's dramatic speech demanding the stronger measure, the CIO helped round up the necessary votes for its passage.

Kroll did not think Truman could win in 1948. He and other CIO officials tried to convince General DWIGHT D. EISENHOWER and then Justice WILLIAM O. DOUGLAS to run for the nomination; both efforts failed. At the Democratic National Convention in Philadelphia, Kroll and other CIO delegates pushed for Senator CLAUDE PEPPER (D-Fla.). Kroll, "the de facto convention spokesman" of the CIO according to historian Robert H. Zieger, was equivocal in his public statements on Truman and advocated for an open convention. Truman won, but the CIO would wait until the end of August before endorsing him.

The CIO-PAC was not always successful in attempts to influence politics. Kroll admitted implicitly that PAC's problems in appealing to union workers to support its political program, which came from the leadership down rather than from the grass roots up. Kroll wanted equal time to proclaim the CIO-PAC message as opposed to others. He allowed that unionists and their families were too often hostile, and he and other CIO-PAC members saw themselves as enlightened leaders and the union members as passive followers, who had to be persuaded to follow the organization's agenda.

In August 1949 Kroll and CIO President PHILIP MURRAY began developing a campaign for unseating Taft in the 1950 Ohio senatorial election. During the race PAC released a speaker's "fact book" denouncing the Ohio Republican. Labor worked hard for Joseph Ferguson, but he lacked sufficient strength throughout the state to defeat the incumbent.

Kroll played a key role in lining up labor support for ADLAI E. STEVENSON at the 1952 Democratic National Convention. During the presidential campaign he urged the CIO to back a massive PAC effort to convince voters that the Republicans were responsible for unemployment and breadlines. Despite Kroll's efforts Republicans scored landslide victories that November. Following the election Kroll blasted the Democrats for barring the CIO from holding an official position on the National Committee. He also criticized them for allowing too many conservative members of Congress to carry the party banner.

After the 1955 AFL-CIO merger Kroll became co-director, with James L. McDivitt, of the Committee on Political Education (COPE). When the AFL-CIO executive board split over whether to endorse the 1956 Democratic presidential ticket, Kroll persuaded the group to back Stevenson. The following year Kroll resigned his position with COPE but remained active in union affairs until 1966. He died on May 26, 1971, in Cincinnati, Ohio.

—EF

Krug, Julius A(lbert)

(1907–1970) *secretary of the interior*

The son of a police officer, Julius Krug was born on November 23, 1907, in Madison, Wisconsin. He graduated from the University of Wisconsin in 1929 and received an M.A. in utilities management from that institution in 1930. Shortly after graduation he worked on the Wisconsin Public Utilities Commission under DAVID E. LILIENTHAL. Lilienthal, who admired Krug's intelligence and reliability, brought him in as chief power engineer of the Tennessee Valley Authority in 1937.

During World War II Krug served as program chief of the War Production Board (WPB) and as head of the office of War Utilities. He became head of the WPB in 1944. To the growing consternation of New Deal liberals, Krug pushed for a release of wage and price controls following the defeat of Germany. He hoped in this way to stave off recession while ensuring adequate production for the defeat of Japan.

In March 1946 Truman chose Krug to replace HAROLD L. ICKES as secretary of the interior. Truman made the appointment to appease liberals who opposed what they saw as a conservative trend in the administration and to answer criticism that a large number of his appointments were political "cronies." Although some support had cooled because of Krug's policy on controls, most liberals felt him ideal for the post. Krug's extensive knowledge of energy qualified him to become one of Truman's chief advisers on the issue.

During his early months in office, Krug played a major role in contract negotiations between mine owners and the United Mine Workers (UMW), headed by JOHN L. LEWIS. Among Lewis's "negotiable suggestions," as he termed them, were wage

increases of an unspecified amount, various improvements in the miners' working and living conditions and, most important, a health and welfare fund financed by royalties on each ton of coal. When negotiations came to a halt on April 1, 1946, the coal workers went on strike. Truman ordered Krug to take possession of the mines on May 21. The secretary then met most of Lewis's demands. The Lewis-Krug Agreement included establishment of retirement and welfare funds, an 18.5-cent-per-hour wage increase, and a promise that the federal government would formulate a mine safety code.

Over the summer Krug attempted to get the mine owners' approval of the pact. Before this could be done, Lewis notified Krug that he would terminate the contract in November. The secretary resentfully reopened negotiations. While doing this Krug, Attorney General TOM C. CLARK and presidential aide CLARK CLIFFORD advised Truman to stand firm. Krug opposed the government reaching

Portrait of Secretary of the Interior Julius A. Krug
(Harry S. Truman Library)

a new agreement with Lewis on the grounds that it would be interpreted as a surrender, would imply the administration's sponsorship of inflationary wage increases, and would postpone the return of the mines to the owners. Instead, he recommended that the president inform the union that the government would not negotiate but would return the mines to the operators shortly after the UMW resumed negotiations. Lewis rejected the proposal and implied the miners would strike. The Justice Department issued an injunction against the proposed termination of the agreement. When the miners struck, Lewis and the union were found guilty of contempt of court. On December 7 Lewis called off the strike.

Krug continually advocated the expansion of government power projects and the establishment of conservation measures in Western states. In 1946 he pushed for experiments to determine the feasibility of extracting oil from lignite and oil shale and the following year estimated that $9 billion would be needed in a five-to-10-year period to build up the synthetic oil industry. That same year Krug reported on the long-term problems of oil reserves, warning that in 10 years they could be dangerously low unless intensive procurement plans were established. In 1949 Krug expressed his enthusiasm about eventually harnessing solar energy.

Krug followed the principles of public power laid out in January 1946 by his predecessor Harold Ickes. Since taxes had built federal dams, the public interests would come first in the distribution of power and water from those dams. The preference of the people would be enunciated in all contracts between federal agencies and consumers. The department would favor local cooperatives' needs over those of private companies that wanted to profit from government facilities. There would be no contracts that would favor sales to specific users or restrict them to specific areas.

Beginning in 1947 Krug became enmeshed in a series of political problems that eventually led to his resignation. In July 1947 a congressional committee determined that the secretary was entertained at a lavish party given by Howard Hughes, then under investigation for wartime activities. Krug's name also appeared on the expense accounts of Johnny Myers, a contact man for Hughes. Krug called any attempts to implicate him by association a "swindle." Krug lost party favor following the 1948 election because of his failure to campaign for the Democrats.

Most important, Krug, enthusiastic about keeping energy production high, became involved in politically questionable methods of offshore oil leasing and dam building. In 1949 he sought to transfer the U.S. Army Corps of Engineers's dam-building authority to the Interior Department's Reclamation Bureau. That same year Krug granted California the right to give offshore leases on public lands. More antagonism was created when he went over the head of the director of budget in appealing to Congress for Interior Department funding. In addition, Krug devoted time to his own private business transactions, borrowing a large sum in order to gain control of a Tennessee cotton mill, a loan that attracted attention when its foreclosure became a danger. Under mounting pressures, including the possible congressional probe, Krug resigned in November 1949 and became president of Volunteer Asphalt Company of Brookside Mills. Krug died in Knoxville, Tennessee, on March 26, 1970.

Landis, James M(cCauley)

(1899–1964) *chairman, Civil Aeronautics Board*

The son of missionary parents, James M. Landis was born in Tokyo, Japan, on September 25, 1899. He graduated from Princeton University in 1921 and earned his law degree from Harvard three years later. From 1925 to 1926 he served as secretary to Supreme Court Justice Louis Brandeis. There he did research for Brandeis's dissent in *Myers v. U.S.* (1926), during which he began to develop an interest in federal regulation, on which he would concentrate for the rest of his career. He then returned to Harvard to accept an assistant professorship of law; he was promoted to full professor in 1928. He joined the Roosevelt administration in 1933 and he, Thomas Corcoran, and Benjamin Cohen put together the Federal Securities Act, which gave the federal government the power to regulate stocks. Roosevelt then appointed him to the Federal Trade Commission in 1933. The three men also drafted the Securities and Exchange Act of 1934. The same year Roosevelt appointed Landis to head the agency this law created, the Securities and Exchange Commission, which was to regulate the stock market. Landis served as chairman of the commission from 1935 to 1937. He resigned from the SEC to accept the position of dean of the Harvard Law School. He contended in his book *The Administrative Process* (1938) that federal regulation was the happy medium between state ownership of business and government inaction. During World War II, he served as director of the Office of Civilian Defense, in which he organized air raid wardens nationwide. After the war he returned to Harvard. Then he left Harvard Law School in 1946 due to the controversy aroused by his effort to leave his wife to marry his secretary.

(He did and then later divorced her, too). He then accepted an appointment by President Truman as chairman of the Civil Aeronautics Board (CAB).

Landis's tenure was surrounded by controversy. The acerbic chairman feuded openly with leading members of the agency and made enemies among CAB employees by lambasting their views. His demand that large airline companies spend more on safety and his encouragement of small operators in developing freight service on unscheduled lines angered the larger airline companies such as Pan American. Its president, Juan Trippe, a leading contributor to the Democratic Party, was rumored to have threatened to leave the party if Landis remained at the CAB. Airlines also objected to what they considered Landis's arbitrary awarding of new routes. In addition, the State Department was angered because of his handling of international agreements. The chairman once boasted of "slipping one over" on Argentina, which promptly shelved the pact.

In late December 1947 Truman invited Landis to the White House to discuss what he believed to be his reappointment. Truman began the meeting by congratulating him on having done a "hell of a job" but informed the chairman that he would not be reappointed. Landis requested an explanation but Truman refused. Landis circulated rumors that the large airline companies had had him fired. The Truman administration had been more amendable to business than Roosevelt's and the major airlines campaigned for his dismissal by pointing to his drinking, marital problems, and contributions to the Democratic Party. Others suggested that Secretary of Commerce W. AVERELL HARRIMAN, who wished to abolish the CAB, had pushed for the action to facilitate the organization of a department of transportation. Landis became a hero among liberals disenchanted with Truman and searching for an alternative to the president.

The former chairman moved to New York City, set up a lucrative law practice, and entered into a number of financial deals with his friend, Joseph P. Kennedy. During 1961 he advised John F. Kennedy on the reorganization of the federal regulatory agencies. In 1963 Landis was convicted of income tax evasion. During his tax trial he suffered a neurological disorder, which required hospitalization. He died from an accidental drowning in Harrison, New York, on July 30, 1964. (See *The Kennedy Years* Volume)

—JB

Lane, Arthur B(liss)

(1894–1956) *ambassador*

Born in the Bay Ridge section of Brooklyn, New York, on June 16, 1894, Arthur B. Lane was a descendant of Pilgrim governor William Bradford. After graduating from Yale in 1916 he studied briefly at the Ecole de Ile de France in Liancourt and then joined the diplomatic service. He became the private secretary to the ambassador to Italy, Thomas N. Page, in 1916, and during the next five years he held various diplomatic posts in Rome, Warsaw, London, and Paris. He was in Poland during the Russo-Polish War of 1920 and came to detest the Bolsheviks, a sentiment that was reinforced by later postings in Riga and Belgrade. During the 1920s and 1930s he served as counselor and minister to posts in Europe and Latin America. (In Nicaragua he found himself increasingly drawn into the internal politics of the country.) Lane was transferred to Eastern Europe in 1936 as minister to Estonia, Latvia, and Lithuania. As minister to Yugoslavia from 1937 to 1941 he helped King Peter in an unsuccessful uprising against pro-Nazi Prince Paul. He served as minister to Costa Rica in 1941 and ambassador to Colombia from 1942 to 1944.

In September 1944 Lane was appointed ambassador to the Polish government in exile in London. The mission was postponed as a result of the uncertain situation in Russian-occupied Poland. In February 1945 he was deputed as ambassador to the Warsaw Provisional Government of National Unity. The government, created by the Yalta Conference, was controlled by the Soviet-dominated Lublin Committee, which had competed during the war with the Polish government in exile supported by the United States and Great Britain. The Yalta agreement on Poland stipulated that the Lublin Committee was to be reorganized with the inclusion of democratic leaders from Poland and abroad. This new Government of National Unity was to hold free elections as soon as possible, in which all anti-Nazi parties were entitled to participate. The voting would be observed by the British and American ambassadors to confirm its legality. However, at the Moscow Conference in April 1945, the Lublin group refused to permit other Polish leaders to join the new coalition government pending free elections.

From the beginning of his tenure as ambassador, Lane opposed U.S. policy toward Poland, viewing it as appeasement of the Soviet Union. Immediately after his arrival in Warsaw in August, he asserted the U.S. commitment to free elections and condemned the Communist-backed government's system of repression and police terrorism, the arrests of liberal political leaders, and censorship of the press. He urged Washington to insist on immediate free elections involving an unlimited number of political parties. He also asked the United States to demand withdrawal of Soviet troops before the voting. However, Secretary of State JAMES E. BYRNES merely suggested that Lane remind the Polish government of the guarantees of free elections as soon as possible. He also refused to object to the six-party limit imposed by the Warsaw government under the assumption that splinter-party groups had often contributed to East European weakness and disorganization.

Lane was particularly interested in withholding economic aid from Poland. In October 1945 he opposed giving Export-Import Bank credits pending elections on the grounds that world opinion would interpret the loan as U.S. approval of the existing regime. Nevertheless, to Lane's dismay, the Ex-Im Bank extended $180 million in credits to the Poles with no concessions from the Communists. The following year he opposed Poland's application for a U.S. loan of $500 million. He contended that the Communist's nationalization of basic industries violated the 1931 commercial treaty between Poland and the United States. Nevertheless, the loan was negotiated in April 1946 in exchange for renewed Polish guarantees of free elections, compensation for American property seized in the nationalization, and a trade agreement favorable to American business.

Lane's outspoken views made him increasingly unpopular in Poland. His protests against Polish takeover of German territory north and west of the Oder-Neisse line before free elections were held led to riots in August 1946 against the American embassy.

In June 1946 the Communists staged a referendum concerning nationalization, the change to a one-house legislature, and the desirability of the retention of the new frontiers. Ballot boxes were stolen in areas where the issues were unpopular, and electioneering was prohibited on the part of the referendum's opponents. This repression led to a violent pogrom against Polish Jews who were regarded as leaders of the Communist movement in the country. Shocked by the fraudulent nature of the referendum and the ugly pogrom, Lane advised the withdrawal of further financial assistance. Elections were finally held in January 1947, but they were marked by terrorism, use of the Soviet army, and intimidation of the voters. The State Department protested ineffectually against the violation of previous agreements. Lane and the British ambassador voiced their opposition by boycotting the opening of Poland's first postwar parliament in February. Believing his continued presence would be construed as a tacit acquiescence in Communist repression, he began to look into another post. None being available, he submitted his resignation on March 25, 1947.

Lane carried on his campaign against U.S.-Polish policy after his retirement. His books, *How Russia Rules Poland* (1947) and *I Saw Poland Betrayed* (1948), angrily depicted what he regarded as the Democratic administration's appeasement of Soviet imperialism. (Lane has been criticized for being unrealistic about the extent to which the Truman administration could affect the situation in Poland with Soviet forces dominant there.) He bitterly lamented the rejection of his proposals by Truman and advocated a policy of armed liberation of Eastern Europe and denounced containment. An active Republican, Lane joined Senator JOSEPH R. MCCARTHY's (R-Wisc.) attack on Secretary of State DEAN G. ACHESON, who had been undersecretary when he was in Poland. Lane helped frame the 1952 Republican Party platform plank advocating a U.S. policy of liberation of Eastern Europe. He also campaigned for McCarthy, praising him as "a patriotic hard-hitting ex-Marine" who exposed "treason and subversive activities in government no matter how

much they may hurt." He joined the board of the National Committee to Free Europe, co-chaired the Committee to Stop World Communism, and chaired the American Committee to Investigate the Katyn Forest Massacre. Lane died of hepatitis on August 12, 1956, in Washington, D.C.

—AES

Langer, William
(1886–1959) *member of the Senate*

William Langer was born on September 30, 1886, in Everest, North Dakota. His father was a member of North Dakota's first state legislature in the 1890s. Langer received a law degree from the University of North Dakota and passed the state bar examination in 1906. Too young to practice law, he went East and earned a B.A. with honors from Columbia University in 1910. Langer then pursued a law career in North Dakota. With the backing of the Non-Partisan League (NPL), a populist farmers' alliance, Langer was elected as state attorney general in November 1916. Defeated in a race for the governorship in 1920, Langer returned to private law practice. He helped to reorganize the NPL, which during the decade gained a measure of control over the state Republican Party.

Aided by his unorthodox endorsement of Franklin Roosevelt, Langer, a Republican, was elected governor of North Dakota in 1932. Two years later the state Supreme Court ousted him after his conviction for illegally soliciting political contributions from federal employees. The verdict was overturned on appeal, and Langer was elected governor again in 1936. However, he was to be plagued throughout his career by allegations of corruption and unethical dealings.

Langer was elected to the U.S. Senate on his second try in 1940, but because of a petition by North Dakota voters he was allowed only a provisional seat. After hearing charges of bribery and obstruction of justice leveled against Langer, the Senate Privileges and Elections Committee voted 13 to 3 for his expulsion. When the issue came to the floor in early 1942, the Senate voted to allow Langer to retain his seat.

A desk-pounding, roaring orator, Langer was a Senate rebel who became known for his dissenting stands on national issues. Nicknamed "Wild Bill," he championed the often unpopular cause of civil liberties during the Truman years and took independent positions on foreign policy and domestic issues. During the late 1940s and early 1950s Langer was responsible for several prolonged filibusters on legislation he opposed. Langer also had a genius for disorienting opponents in debate. Once a fellow senator on the opposite side of an issue from Langer was speaking on the floor of the Senate. Langer came up to him and began pulling cigars out of the pocket of the other solon, who then retreated in confusion. On several occasions during his Senate career he spoke out forcefully against presidential appointments because he felt the smaller states were slighted in the selection process.

Langer generally agreed with the noninterventionist Taft wing of the Republican Party on foreign policy matters, although he sometimes took even more extreme positions. He voted against the UN Charter and opposed both the Marshall Plan and the North Atlantic Treaty. In 1948, he argued for an "American Recovery Plan" that would have taken aid aimed at Europe and sent it back to the United States to pay for pensions, education, farm price supports, and reclamation. He was one of the few senators voting against the Vandenburg Resolution of 1948, which stressed U.S. determination to protect itself through collective security. In June 1949 he joined Senator GLEN H. TAYLOR (D-Idaho) in a futile all-night filibuster to try to block passage of new draft legislation. He also voted against the Universal Military Training Act of 1951. Langer remained critical of Truman policy, joining other Republicans in 1952 to protest defense treaties with West Germany.

Langer lined up with the Democrats on most domestic issues. He supported public housing, most pro-labor legislation, attempts to give the president wage-price control powers, and increased aid to education. Langer pressed for expanded benefits for federal employees and servicemen during the Truman years and helped write a bill providing for pay increases for federal workers in 1951. Langer maintained a warm friendship with Truman, endorsing him in the 1948 presidential election, backing him in the steel seizure crisis, and often supporting his vetoes on legislation he believed imperiled civil liberties.

Langer opposed the Internal Security Act of 1950 and paired against the bill during the final vote. He was also in the forefront of the battle against the McCarran-Walter Act of 1952, legislation designed to regulate and restrict immigration. Langer told Truman that the measure was "one of the most vicious, most dangerous pieces of legislation that has ever been passed by any Senate." He joined Senator HUBERT H. HUMPHREY (D-Minn.) in an unsuccessful filibuster to prevent a vote on Truman's veto. Langer spoke for some five hours before he collapsed. The final vote was 57 to 10, with Langer the lone Republican backing the president.

During Langer's 1952 reelection campaign he received Senator JOSEPH R. MCCARTHY's (R-Wisc.) endorsement. The controversial Wisconsin senator sent a tape-recorded message denouncing charges that "his friend" was a "Communist, socialist, fellow traveler" or "a front man for various subversive organizations." Langer himself failed to endorse Republican presidential candidate DWIGHT D. EISENHOWER, avoiding Eisenhower when he toured North Dakota. He boarded Truman's train when the president arrived in the state to campaign for Democrat Adlai E. Stevenson, whom Langer endorsed.

Langer faced another attempt to bar him from the Senate in 1953. This time he was accused of taking "substantial cash contributions" to introduce legislation legalizing the status of illegal aliens. Since 1947 Langer had proposed 301 such bills, more than any other member of Congress. The Senate Privileges and Elections Subcommittee cleared him of the charges in March.

During the Eisenhower years Langer compiled the poorest overall record of support for White House proposals of Republicans in the Senate. It was often said during this period that the Republicans should trade Langer for the conservative Democratic senator Frank Lausche of Ohio. He continued to be an isolationist, voting against mutual security pacts with China and the Philippines and supporting the 1954 Bricker Amendment to restrict presidential executive agreement–making powers. He also violently disagreed with the Eisenhower administration's emphasis on private development of utilities. Although a foe of McCarthy's anticommunist crusade, Langer opposed the Senate's censure of the Wisconsin Republican in 1954. The senator felt personally obligated to McCarthy because of his help in the 1952 elections. When the Nonpartisan League switched its allegiance to the Democrats in 1956, Langer backed Eisenhower that year for a second term. Langer's health declined in his later years, and he suffered a fatal heart attack on

November 8, 1959, in Washington, D.C. (See *The Eisenhower Years* Volume)

—JF

Lardner, Ring (Wilmer), Jr.
(1915–2000) *screenwriter*

Ring Lardner, Jr., the son of the famous sports writer, newspaper columnist, and short-story writer, was born on August 19, 1915, in Chicago, Illinois. He entered Princeton University in 1932. He left college at the end of his sophomore year and in the summer of 1934 traveled in Nazi Germany and the Soviet Union. Lardner later credited much of his left-wing political development to what he learned on the trip. He felt that Germany was heading "resolutely backward to barbarism" and came to believe that "the best hope for mankind lay with the Soviets."

In 1935 Lardner worked as a reporter for the *New York Daily Mirror*; and, the following year, he was a press agent for motion picture producer David O. Selznick. In 1937 Lardner and Budd Schulberg collaborated in rewriting scenes for *A Star Is Born*. Recruited into the Communist Party that year by Schulberg, he began attending Marxist study groups. Lardner also was made an executive member of the left-wing Screen Writers Guild in 1937. In 1942 he earned an Academy Award for his screenplay *Woman of the Year*.

During the House Un-American Activities Committee (HUAC) investigation of Communist influence in Hollywood in the spring of 1947, he was accused by several witnesses of being a Communist. In September the committee subpoenaed Lardner and 18 others as "unfriendly witnesses." Lardner and nine other writers and directors, led by screenwriter and novelist DALTON TRUMBO, refused to answer questions on the grounds that HUAC had no constitutional right to probe their political affiliations. Supported by many liberals and by the Committee for the First Amendment, a Hollywood group headed by Lauren Bacall and Humphrey Bogart, the Hollywood Ten, as they were known, were confident that their stand would be upheld by the Supreme Court.

On October 21 Lardner appeared before the committee. When Senator J. PARNELL THOMAS (R-N.J.) pressed him about whether he was a Communist, Lardner replied, "I could answer it, but if I did, I would hate myself in the morning." Angered by the response Thomas ordered Lardner removed.

On November 24, the House voted overwhelmingly to cite the Hollywood Ten for contempt of Congress. The next day the leaders of the American film industry announced they would bar Communists from the industry and inaugurated a blacklist of radical actors, screenwriters, directors, and producers. Twentieth Century Fox discharged Lardner three days later.

In January 1948 Lardner and the others pleaded innocent to the contempt charges. He then sued Twentieth Century Fox for $1.3 million for discharging him. (After the sum had been reduced to about $25,000, the suit was settled out of court in 1955.) A year later, in May 1949, the Hollywood Ten filed a $52 million antitrust suit against 10 film producers.

On June 29, 1950, Lardner was convicted of contempt in the U.S. district court in Washington, sentenced to a year prison term, and fined $1,000. He later said that after his conviction he "quietly terminated his membership in the Communist Party." Lardner entered Danbury Federal Prison in Connecticut, his sentence eventually shortened to 10 months for "good time." While in prison he met Thomas, the former chairman of HUAC, who was serving time for padding his congressional payroll. Lardner was released from prison in April 1951. He then spent six months in Mexico among a group of blacklisted writers. In January 1952 MGM, Universal, Columbia, and Warner-Brothers reportedly paid $107,000 to settle the suits brought by the Hollywood Ten. RKO, Twentieth Century Fox, and Paramount refused settlement.

In 1955 Lardner completed a novel he started in prison, *The Ecstasy of Owen Muir*. The book was first published in England. Because of the blacklist both Lardner and his wife, an actress, had difficulty finding employment. During the late 1950s Lardner anonymously wrote television scripts. With Ian Hunter he created the television series *The Adventures of Robin Hood*, *Sir Lancelot*, and *The Pirate*. During this period the government did not allow him to travel abroad. Only after a Supreme Court decision in 1958 liberalizing the issuance of passports was he able to leave the country.

In 1961 Lardner contributed an article to the *Saturday Evening Post* in which he admitted his Communist Party membership in the 1940s and discussed his battle to make a living after his prison sentence. He received his first major post-blacklist screen credit in 1965 when, with Terry Southern, he wrote *The Cincinnati Kid*. In 1970 he won his second Academy Award for *M*A*S*H*. In 1976 he published, *The Lardners*, an account of his family. Lardner died October 31, 2000, in New York City.

Although most reviewers of the Hollywood Ten episode are sympathetic to the Ten, a study by Kenneth Lloyd Billingsley argued that the Communists were trying to infiltrate Marxist propaganda into films, and that the Hollywood Ten were not quite the innocent victims they insisted they were.

—JF

Larson, Jess
(1904–1987) *administrator, General Services Administration; director, Defense Materials Procurement Agency*

Jess Larson was born on June 22, 1904, in Mill Creek, Indian Territory (now Oklahoma). After attending the University of Oklahoma and Emerson College, Larson established a ranching and dairy business. In 1929 he was elected mayor of Chikasha, Oklahoma, and served until 1934. Larson practiced law for a year before beginning a five-year term as the director of the Oklahoma State School Land Committee. Long active in Democratic politics, during the 1930s he also served as president of the Oklahoma Municipal League and of the Oklahoma Young Democrats.

As a member of the National Guard, Larson was called to active duty in 1940 and saw action in Italy during World War II. He was appointed general counsel of the War Assets Administration (WAA) in 1946 and administrator in January 1949. During his year at that post, Larson helped dispose of approximately $8 billion in government property declared surplus at the end of World War II.

In June 1949 Truman appointed Larson to head the newly established General Services Administration (GSA). He was in charge of buying supplies for all civilian federal agencies. Under Larson the GSA reduced major government expenditures for equipment made from scarce materials, decreased the number of purchasing offices, and moved some offices to buildings with lower rents. He also decentralized the agency, establishing 10 regional GSA offices where manufacturers could negotiate contracts with the government. In August 1951 Truman formed the Defense Materials Procurement Agency to increase supplies of critical materials in the

United States during the Korean War. Larson became its first head, a position he held until 1953.

During his tenure at the GSA, Larson's name was mentioned in conjunction with two influence-peddling scandals. In 1949 James V. Hunt, implicated as a member of a group which sold influence in getting government contracts for 5 percent of the contract price, mentioned Larson as one of his contacts. The administrator denied any connection. In testimony before the Senate Permanent Investigations Subcommittee, he said that the GSA required a warranty from all contractors stating that they had not used anyone except bona fide employees or commercial agencies on a contingency fee basis.

Two years later a Chicago lawyer testifying before a House Ways and Means Subcommittee investigating tax scandals stated that he had been told that Larson was a member of a group of federal officials who offered to fix tax cases for a fee. Larson denied that he had discussed tax matters with any alleged members of the group. He pleaded with the subcommittee "to give us some legislation to protect officials from being ruined" by false charges and people who pretend to be able to sell their influence. Ironically Truman wrote a letter to the head of the Justice Department Tax Division, T. LAMAR CAUDLE—also charged with influence peddling—before the scandal broke, saying, "Men like you and Jess Larson make it possible to carry on in this job."

Larson left government at the end of the Truman administration to return to private law practice in Washington. He acted as chairman and president of the Air Force Association from 1964 to 1971. Larson died on February 25, 1987, in Washington, D.C.

—RSG

Lattimore, Owen
(1900–1989) *China scholar*

Lattimore, whose father served as an educational adviser to the Chinese government, was born on July 29, 1900, in Washington, D.C. He spent his early years in Asia. At the age of 20 he took a newspaper job in Shanghai and two years later worked for an export firm in Beijing. During the 1930s Lattimore studied China's culture and history. By 1941 he had written six books on China and had become one of America's leading experts on that nation. He had developed a particular interest in the nomadic Mongol, and his concern for them as a people would help shape his foreign policy views. He would come to believe that the cold war would undermine the interests of his beloved Mongols, as they would become pawns in the struggle among the Chinese, Russians, and Americans. In 1937 John Hopkins University appointed Lattimore director of the Walter Hines Page School of International Relations. Lattimore also belonged to the Institute of Pacific Relations (IPR) in Washington and edited its journal, *Pacific Affairs*. At the institute Lattimore associated with a number of Americans who were targets of the right during the McCarthy era. Many were either Communists or advocates of close relations with Russia and the Chinese Communists. Lattimore agreed with many of their foreign policy views, but he was not a Communist.

In 1941 President Roosevelt appointed Lattimore political adviser to Chiang Kai-shek (Jiang Jieshi). The following year Lattimore returned to Washington to accept a post with the Office of War Information (OWI) as deputy director of the overseas branch in charge of Pacific operations. In 1944 Lattimore accompanied Vice President HENRY A. WALLACE on his trip to China and Siberia. Both reported favorable impressions of Russian and Chinese Communists. The following year Lattimore published *Solution in Asia*, one of his most controversial books. In it he appealed to Chiang to rid his government of corruption and introduce true democracy to his people. Lattimore also asked the American people to be patient with China's desire to free itself from the past yoke of Western imperialism. He resigned from the OWI in 1945 to return to teaching. From 1945 to 1946 he served as an economic adviser to EDWIN W. PAULEY on the Reparations Mission to Japan.

During the last half of the decade Lattimore became one of the principal targets of the "China Lobby," a powerful pressure group demanding continued U.S. support of Chiang. His association with the IPR, under FBI investigation as part of a sabotage ring, and his travels with Wallace, considered by many a Communist puppet, made Lattimore a vulnerable target for their attacks. Also, he had advocated rapprochement with the Soviets and contended that Mao Zedong (Mao Tse-Tung) was not a puppet of the Russians. In 1949 he agreed with the State Department that the United States should delay any policy decision in regard to China until the outcome of the civil war was clearer. He also argued that recognition of Communist China might

not be a bad idea in the future. It did not help Lattimore's cause when Red Chinese attacked U.S. forces in Korea a year later. In a series of speeches and articles, members of the lobby charged that Lattimore was pro-communist and had sabotaged help to Nationalist forces. No inquiry into his conduct was made until 1950, when Senator JOSEPH R. MCCARTHY (R-Wisc.) pointed to Lattimore as one of the principal elements in a Communist conspiracy in the State Department.

In testimony before the Tydings Committee, a Senate panel formed to investigate the charges, McCarthy pointed to Lattimore as the "chief Soviet espionage agent in the United States." McCarthy presented the committee with a summary of charges that had been leveled against Lattimore, primarily by the China Lobby. He announced that he would stake his reputation on the substance of his case against Lattimore. The panel then heard evidence about Lattimore and the IPR from two former Communists, LOUIS F. BUDENZ and Freda Utley. Budenz, former editor of the *Daily Worker*, claimed that the Kremlin had selected Lattimore to organize a campaign in the United States to convince the American people that the Chinese Communists were merely agrarian reformers. When asked for details Budenz could not provide them.

In response Lattimore characterized the testimony as a "plain, unvarnished lie," and maintained that he had always portrayed the Chinese Communist leaders as sincere Marxists. He warned that freedom in America would be destroyed as long as the Wisconsin senator and the China Lobby abused freedom of speech to vilify their enemies. The hysteria they produced in the nation, Lattimore claimed, prevented Americans from presenting diverse views in policy discussion. Only through such debates, he added, did a sound foreign policy emerge. In its final report the panel, led by Senator MILLARD E. TYDINGS (D-Md.) exonerated him. It found that Lattimore did have ties to the left but that there was no evidence he was a Soviet agent. Lattimore himself answered his critics in his book *Ordeal by Slander* (1950) in which he portrayed himself as an innocent martyr in an era of hysteria.

The following year the Senate Internal Security Subcommittee, headed by Senator PATRICK A. MCCARRAN (D-Nev.) revived the Lattimore investigation. McCarran's panel concluded that "Lattimore was for some time, beginning in the middle of the 1930s a conscious, articulate instrument of the

Soviet conspiracy." It recommended that he be indicted for possible perjury. A grand jury issued the five-count indictment, but three years later, after complicated legal maneuvers, a federal court threw out most of the key counts for being vague. The Justice Department dropped the rest of them. Still, Lattimore remained the target of the right.

Lattimore remained at Johns Hopkins until 1953. He then resumed writing books and scholarly articles on China for American and European journalists. In 1963 he accepted a professorship at the University of Leeds. He retired in 1970 and returned to the United States, leading a somewhat unsettled life. He died on May 31, 1989, in Providence, Rhode Island.

—JB

Lausche, Frank J(ohn)
(1895–1990) *governor*

Frank J. Lausche, the son of a Slovene immigrant, was born in Cleveland, Ohio, on November 14, 1895. When Lausche was 12 his father died, and he worked as a lamplighter and court interpreter to support his family. He also played semiprofessional baseball. Lausche served in the army during World War I. In 1920 he earned a law degree from John Marshall University and practiced in Cleveland until 1932, when he was appointed a municipal judge. He was elected to that bench the following year. In 1941 Cleveland voters elected him mayor. An honest, popular official, he worked to improve municipal transit and reduce taxes. He also sponsored health programs and city beautification projects. Lausche, a Democrat, easily won election as governor of Ohio in 1944, despite the fact that the state went to THOMAS E. DEWEY in the presidential race. He was defeated for reelection in 1946 as a result of anti-Democratic sentiment that year but regained the governorship in 1948.

Lausche's popularity was tied to his political independence and pragmatism. During his campaigns he ignored offers of aid from regular Democratic groups and organized labor and campaigned as a nonpartisan in nominally Republican areas. He was skillfully able to accommodate himself to the needs of big business, vitally important in Ohio politics, while appealing to the average voter through his homespun image and reputation for rectitude and incorruptibility. As governor, Lausche was able to undercut criticism from the fiscally conservative

GOP by insisting on a pay-as-you-go philosophy. He initially benefited from a wartime generated surplus in the Treasury but later adamantly refused to raise taxes despite the growing need for capital investments and financing basic state services. He avoided tax hikes by having the state borrow heavily, a course that led to large budget deficits in the 1950s. Lausche positioned himself as an independent on many issues. For example, although a proponent of civil rights and fair employment legislation, he favored right-to-work legislation. In 1950 he voted for Republican senator ROBERT A. TAFT, who was under fire from unions for the Taft-Hartley Act. Ironically, Taft did not appreciate Lausche's conservatism, thinking there should be a clear distinction between the parties. In 1956 President Eisenhower briefly toyed with the idea of a bipartisan ticket with Lausche as his running mate, but such talk came to nothing.

During his unprecedented five terms as governor, Lausche worked for improvements in health and welfare programs, education, and conservation of national resources. He increased state aid to local schools, established a mental health program, reformed the municipal court system and created a state department of natural resources. However, his refusal to increase taxes limited the effectiveness of his programs. Only highway construction, which provided patronage, was adequately funded. By the time Lausche left office in 1957, Ohio, according to journalist Neil Peirce, had lost ground in terms of services provided its citizens and was not meeting the standards of other large wealthy states.

From 1957 to 1969 Lausche served in the U.S. Senate, where he established a conservative record. He opposed much of the Kennedy and Johnson domestic programs, but supported the Vietnam War. In May 1968 Lausche lost the senatorial primary to John J. Gilligan, a young liberal. Estranged from the Democratic Party, he supported Richard Nixon and Gerald Ford for president in 1972 and 1976, respectively. Lausche died on April 21, 1990, in Cleveland, Ohio. (See *The Eisenhower Years, The Kennedy Years, The Johnson Years* Volumes)

—SBB

Lawrence, David L(eo)
(1889–1966) *mayor*

The son of a teamster who was a precinct leader for the Democratic Party, David L. Lawrence was born on June 18, 1889, in Pittsburgh, Pennsylvania, and was raised in the Irish working-class district of the city. After completing a commercial course in high school, Lawrence became a clerk-stenographer to labor attorney William Brennan. Brennan took Lawrence to the 1912 Democratic National Convention, where, as he later said, he "became devoted to politics." His late night political discussions with Brennan, other Democrats, and Republicans, would make him a believer in social welfare legislation, but with an eye toward balancing the budget. Lawrence rose in the ranks of the party organization, becoming Allegheny County chairman in 1920. The 1920s were a difficult time for Democrats in Pennsylvania, as Republicans outnumbered them eight to one. Lawrence reversed this trend with his support for presidential candidate Franklin D. Roosevelt in 1932. Under the burden of the Great Depression and factional squabbling, the city's Republican machine fell apart and Lawrence's hand-picked mayoral candidate for Pittsburgh, William McNair, won the 1933 election, as Lawrence had tied the campaign closely with the new popular president. From then to the present, Democrats have dominated the politics of the city. Lawrence's backing of Roosevelt won him an appointment as collector of internal revenue for western Pennsylvania. In 1934 he became state party chairman. As secretary of the commonwealth of Pennsylvania from 1935 to 1939 under Governor George H. Earle, Lawrence was considered the most powerful politician in the state and helped run Earle's "Little New Deal." He was indicted in 1939 on charges of graft and corruption but was acquitted of all charges in two lengthy trials. Lawrence ran successfully for mayor of Pittsburgh in 1945.

Lawrence's first year in office was plagued by labor strife that created havoc for the heavily industrialized Pittsburgh economy. National strikes in steel and coal, a 115-day walkout at Westinghouse, a major hotel strike, and stoppage by transport and power company workers brought the economic life of the city almost to a halt. His close relationship with organized labor allowed Lawrence to play a mediating role in local strikes. In February 1946 he convinced striking workers at the Duquesne Light Company to return to work while mediators tried to reach a settlement. The intransigence of the employers, however, prevented a settlement, and, in September, the workers struck. Lawrence declared a state of emergency and imposed mandatory power cutbacks in Pittsburgh until the strike was settled the following month.

As mayor from 1946 to 1958 Lawrence played a major role in what became known as the Pittsburgh Renaissance. When the war ended the future of the Pittsburgh economy looked bleak. Property values were declining in the downtown area, the industrial plant was old, major corporations were considering relocating elsewhere, and the city had a reputation as one of the grimiest and dirtiest in the United States. Lawrence formed a close working relationship with Richard King Mellon, head of the Mellon family business interests, and together they worked to transform Pittsburgh. Mellon used his influence in the business community to establish the Allegheny Company Development Conference, and Lawrence pledged the backing of the county Democratic organization for a massive program of redevelopment. The mayor enforced a 1941 smoke-control law that had been suspended during the war to compel industries and residential property owners to use smokeless fuel. With Mellon he successfully lobbied in the state legislature to reverse the exemption won earlier by the powerful Pennsylvania Railroad. Within two years the effects were noticeable as smoke pollution was cut in half.

Lawrence won labor backing for a state law to create an Urban Redevelopment Authority (URA) for Pittsburgh with the power to condemn property and finance new construction. Through URA blighted areas of downtown Pittsburgh were demolished and replaced by the 36-acre Point Park and the 23-acre Gateway Center. Lawrence also used his influence in the national Democratic Party to win federal funds for a number of important projects, including construction of a new airport, a major highway to ease traffic congestion, a flood control program, and low-rent housing units. Mellon, meanwhile, used his power in the corporate world to stimulate construction of new office buildings and industrial plants; by 1949 almost one billion dollars in corporate expansion had been planned. In 1958 *Fortune* magazine judged Pittsburgh one of the eight best administered cities in the country. Lawrence won recognition for his achievements from the nation's mayors when they elected him vice president of the United States Conference of Mayors in 1948 and president two years later.

Lawrence was reelected mayor three times, in 1949, 1953, and again in 1957. He was an ardent supporter of ADLAI E. STEVENSON's presidential campaigns in 1952 and 1956, and, in 1960, he kept the Pennsylvania delegation unpledged until it was clear that Stevenson would not seek the nomination. Lawrence then supported John F. Kennedy. Elected governor of Pennsylvania in 1958, he lobbied for increased federal aid to localities with high rates of unemployment. Lawrence was prevented by state law from succeeding himself. After retiring he remained active in state and national politics, chairing the credentials committee at the Democratic National Convention in 1964. He suffered a heart attack during a campaign speech for gubernatorial candidate Milton Shapp in early November 1966, and he died a few days later on November 21 in Pittsburgh, having never regained consciousness.

—JD

Leahy, William D(aniel)

(1875–1959) *senior military adviser to the president*

The son of a lawyer, William D. Leahy was born on May 6, 1875, in Hampton, Iowa. He wanted to go to West Point, but since no appointment was available, he entered the Naval Academy at Annapolis. Graduating in 1897 at the bottom third of his class, he served on the battleship *Oregon* in the Spanish-American War and became a dedicated "battleship man." During the next two decades he held commands at sea and studied technical ordnance and gunnery. In 1918 he befriended Franklin D. Roosevelt, then assistant secretary of the navy, and the two men became close friends. Nineteen years later Roosevelt appointed Leahy, by then an admiral, chief of naval operations. During his time as CNO, Leahy pushed successfully for money for battleships rather than for aircraft carriers. He served until 1939, when he reached the mandatory retirement age of 64. That year Roosevelt selected him to be governor of Puerto Rico. From 1940 to 1942 Leahy was ambassador to the Vichy government. Roosevelt recalled him in July 1942 to be his chief of staff and promoted him to fleet admiral, the highest rank in the navy. On the recommendation of Army Chief of Staff general GEORGE C. MARSHALL, Roosevelt appointed Leahy also to be the chairmanship of the Joint Chiefs of Staff, which had no formal powers other than to preside at meetings of the Joint Chiefs, but in which position Leahy was able to smooth interservice rivalries and to act as a liai-

son for the chiefs with the commander in chief. Until Roosevelt's death, he was the president's closest military aide. He accompanied the president on his domestic and foreign travels and was Roosevelt's senior military adviser at the important wartime conferences.

President Truman asked Leahy to continue serving in the new administration, where he helped formulate policy toward Japan and the Soviet Union. During the spring of 1945 he joined the faction led by HENRY L. STIMSON and JOSEPH C. GREW; which opposed the demand for unconditional surrender of Japan and the abdication of the emperor. He argued that the army would not have to invade and occupy Japan to win the war. Instead, Leahy suggested a naval blockade of the country and massive bombings of the cities to force Tokyo to capitulate.

The admiral questioned the use of the atomic bomb. As an old ordinance man, he thought the bomb would be a dud, said it was "a lot of hooey," and dubbed it "a professor's dream." Leahy was reported to have charged that the only reason Truman had planned to use the weapon was to justify the vast sums of money spent on it. Later he came to view the bomb in the same light as he did gas and bacteriological warfare. By being the first nation to use the bomb, he maintained, the country had "adopted an ethical standard common to the barbarians of the dark ages." However, there is no evidence from 1945 that he objected to the atomic bomb on moral grounds.

Leahy was an early proponent of a firm policy toward the Soviet Union. (He thought Roosevelt had trusted the Russians too much.) Truman, in referring to another anticommunist, said that at the Potsdam Conference of 1945 he was "the only hard-boiled hitting anti-Russian around except the tough old admiral, Bill Leahy." He was particularly troubled by the Russian occupation in Poland and felt that the Declaration of Liberated Europe, formulated at Yalta, did not adequately guarantee that the Soviets would permit free elections in Poland. While he recognized that the United States could not prevent Soviet domination of the area, he recommended that the administration maintain a strong stand and at least insist that the Polish government give an external appearance of independence. He backed the president's pressure on the Soviets to leave Iran and the Truman Doctrine. He opposed ending aid to the Nationalist Chinese and fought against reductions in the defense budget in the late 1940s. (He would prove prescient in his opposition when the Korean War broke out and American forces found themselves ill-equipped.)

Leahy regarded anyone who considered coming to an agreement with the Soviets an appeaser. He was especially worried about "pinkies" in the State Department and was particularly critical of Secretary of State JAMES F. BYRNES, who, he thought, had compromised too much at the Moscow Conference of December 1945. Privately Leahy wondered whether Byrnes's efforts to effect a coalition between Communists and Nationalists in China was a result of his domination by procommunist elements in the State Department. After Byrnes's resignation in 1947, rumors persisted that the admiral had lobbied for his dismissal.

During the last years of the decade, Leahy's influence diminished as Truman turned increasingly to high State Department officials for advice. He remained a military aide until 1949 and was active in the reorganization of the armed forces. After his retirement, Leahy published his memoirs and led a reclusive life until his death from a cerebral vascular accident on July 20, 1959, in Bethesda, Maryland.

—JB

Lehman, Herbert H(enry)
(1878–1963) *member of the Senate*

The son of wealthy German-Jewish immigrants, Herbert H. Lehman was born on March 28, 1878, in New York City. He joined his family's investment banking firm in 1908. During World War I he headed the relief programs of the Jewish Joint Distribution Committee. He then resumed his work at Lehman Brothers and also acted as a labor mediator in the garment industry. During the 1920s Lehman became involved in New York State Democratic politics. When Franklin D. Roosevelt was elected governor in 1928, Lehman captured the lieutenant governor's office. Roosevelt was often absent, retreating to Warm Springs, Georgia, leaving Lehman as acting governor. He and Roosevelt were reelected in 1930, and Lehman worked well with the governor, who said he was "my good right arm." In 1933 Lehman succeeded him in the state house. Throughout the 1930s Lehman maintained his close association with Roosevelt and developed his own "Little New Deal" of social legislation for New York. In 1943 Roosevelt appointed him head of the United

Nations Relief and Rehabilitation Administration. In this post Lehman built an organization that tried to rise above narrow national interests on behalf of international refugees. The agency delivered relief to the 16 countries and helped revive agriculture and industry. He lobbied the U.S. government hard for money, and snared large appropriations for the agency. After the war, the growing tensions between the Soviets and the Americans made providing relief ever more difficult, although Lehman tried to distribute relief aid on the basis of need rather ideological compatibility. Finding this increasingly hard to do, Lehman resigned on March 12, 1946, to run unsuccessfully for the U.S. Senate. Three years later he defeated JOHN FOSTER DULLES in a special election for the Senate seat vacated by the resignation of ROBERT F. WAGNER (D-N.Y.). Lehman was elected to a full six-year term in 1950.

Lehman backed the president's foreign policy of containment of the Soviets and most of his Fair Deal. He also championed numerous liberal causes. He supported changes in the Taft-Hartley Act to benefit labor, backed the administration's civil rights program, and favored higher taxes to implement Truman's social legislation. Because he felt Congress should impose heavy taxes on companies that had earned enormous profits during the war, Lehman supported Senator Joseph C. O'Mahoney's (D-Wyo.) excess profits tax amendment to the 1950 revenue bill. Lehman also favored a measure that provided that profits garnered from federal ownership of offshore oil operations be used to support public education.

The senator was an outspoken critic of Senator JOSEPH R. MCCARTHY's (R-Wisc.) anticommunist crusade. In 1950 he stood almost alone in promptly denouncing McCarthy's assertions that he had examples of security risks in the State Department. Subsequently, Lehman exposed some of McCarthy's false charges and stood behind many of those wrongly accused by the Wisconsin senator. Lehman viewed McCarthy's crusade as an evil undermining basic freedoms. In October 1952, while campaigning for ADLAI E. STEVENSON, he told a Chicago audience that McCarthy, in the guise of Americanism, was fostering totalitarianism. In addition, he opposed the Internal Security (McCarran) Act of 1950.

Lehman fought vigorously but unsuccessfully for liberalized immigration policies. He opposed the 1950 McCarran-Walter Act, which imposed restrictive measures on immigration and which some liberals claimed was biased in favor of northern Europeans. During the 1951–52 session of Congress, Lehman joined forces with HUBERT H. HUMPHREY (D-Minn.) and others in preparing a bill to counter the McCarran-Walter legislation. The measure proposed that immigrant quotas be based not on national origin but on more objective criteria, including family unification, job skills, asylum from oppression, and consideration for the plight of friendly overcrowded nations. The Lehman-Humphrey bill was defeated in May 1952. Lehman continued, year after year, to introduce liberal immigration bills. All were voted down.

During his final Senate years, Lehman focused much of his energy on civil rights legislation. He also continued to denounce McCarthyism and voted to condemn the Wisconsin senator in 1954. He did not run for reelection in 1956. In the late 1950s, with the aid of ELEANOR ROOSEVELT and New York mayor Robert F. Wagner, Jr., he attempted to reform the New York Democratic Party. Lehman remained a significant force in New York reform politics, helping to oust Tammany boss Carmine De Sapio in 1961, until his death on December 5, 1963, in New York City. (See *The Eisenhower Years, The Kennedy Years* Volumes)

—EF

LeMay, Curtis E(merson)

(1906–1990) *commander, U.S. Air Forces in Europe; commander, Strategic Air Command*

Curtis E. LeMay was born on November 15, 1906, in Columbus, Ohio. He studied engineering at Ohio State University, where he joined the Reserve Officers Training Corps. He left Ohio State prematurely to accept a second lieutenant commission in the artillery reserve in June 1928. Charles Lindbergh's solo flight across the Atlantic inspired LeMay to enroll in the Army Air Corps School, where he earned his wings. In 1937 he joined the 49th Bombardment Squadron and became one of the first qualified pilots of the B-17 bomber. During World War II LeMay played a major role in formulating tactics used in the European theater and planned the devastating B-29 firebombing raids on Tokyo in 1945. As chief of staff to General Carl Spaatz, leader of U.S. Strategic Air Forces, he played a leading role in planning the use of the atomic bomb on Hiroshima and Nagasaki. He supported research on supersonic craft—introducing

the first jet bombers—missiles, space ships, and atomic energy.

LeMay was ordered to Germany in October 1947 to take command of the U.S. Air Force in Europe. In this capacity he was the primary organizer of the Berlin airlift. From the spring of 1948 to the fall of 1949, "Operations Vittles," as it was called, delivered an average of 8,000 tons of supplies per day to the beleaguered city, a two million ton total made in 300,000 flights. (Ironically LeMay thought the United States should have forced its way into Berlin.)

In October 1948 LeMay became head of the Strategic Air Command (SAC), succeeding General George C. Kenny. When he took over the post, LeMay found SAC still unorganized. Morale and training were poor, and SAC was using leftover planes and material from World War II. To improve the service LeMay instituted a rigorous training program. He led mock-bombing raids over American cities, conducted unannounced operational readiness inspections, and started a comparison rating system. LeMay's objective was to put all personnel in SAC into a wartime frame of mind with around-the-clock crews ready to strike the Soviets. He established the Management Control System in which airman would detect potential problems and prevent them from occurring. He was able to secure development of new bombers, such as the B-47 Stratojet, the first all-jet aircraft in the U.S. Air Force. By 1954 he had created a fleet of 1,000 bombers that could devastate Russia within days of the outbreak of war.

LeMay was a strong supporter of the air force's demand that strategic nuclear weapons be the prime deterrent to Soviet aggression. This was based on the service's claim that modern warfare would be characterised by quick strikes won or lost by strategic air power. At a meeting of the National Aeronautics Association in 1946, LeMay claimed that U.S. survival and "the peace of the world" depended on a strong air force. In August 1949, when the role of the air force was discussed during hearings on the proposed B-36 bomber, LeMay defended the SAC as prime deterrent.

LeMay retained his post as head of SAC even after he was appointed air force vice chief of staff in April 1957. In 1961 President John F. Kennedy promoted him to air force chief of staff. After his retirement in 1965 LeMay became an outspoken critic of the Johnson administration's restrictions on bombing raids in both North and South Vietnam. In 1968 LeMay was George Wallace's vice presidential running mate on the American Independent Party ticket. His loose talk of using nuclear weapons in the Vietnam War cost Wallace support. LeMay died in Riverside, California, on October 1, 1990. (See *The Eisenhower Years, The Kennedy Years, The Johnson Years* Volumes)

—MLB

Lerner, Max(well) (Alan)

(1902–1992) *journalist*

The son of an itinerant Hebrew teacher, Max Lerner was born on December 20, 1902 in Minsk, Russia. He and his parents immigrated to the United States in 1907 and settled in New Haven, Connecticut. He received an A.B. from Yale in 1922 and an A.M. from Washington University in 1925. Lerner studied law at Yale from 1923 to 1924; he won his doctorate from the Robert Brookings Graduate School of Economics in 1927. Lerner then became assistant editor of the *Encyclopedia of the Social Sciences.* From 1932 to 1935 he taught social science at Sarah Lawrence College and, in 1935–36, was a lecturer in government at Harvard. He became editor of *The Nation* in 1936 but resigned after two years to join the faculty of Williams College as professor of political science. During these years Lerner also wrote many articles on economics and political and literary problems for periodicals including the *New Republic* and the *Yale Review.*

In 1938 he incorporated a selection of these in *It Is Later Than You Think*, an analysis, according to one reviewer, "by a 'neo-Marxian liberal' of the plight of the liberal." In the work Lerner urged a peaceful but rapid transition from capitalism to "democratic collectivism, in which basis industries would be carefully planned but private property and profits maintained." Lerner believed in what later would be called "the Third Way" in regard to the economy: state intervention to keep the nation prosperous, but not state ownership of the means of production. Subsequently, Lerner published *Ideas Are the Weapon* (1939), a collection of essays and reviews on a variety of topics including law, literature, and social psychology. In addition, in 1941 he wrote *Ideas for the Ice Age*, essays concerned with economic strategy for a democracy in time of war.

Lerner left academia in 1943 to become a radio commentator and editorial director for *PM*, the New York evening daily published by RALPH M. INGERSOLL. As *PM*'s principal editorial voice in New York, he explained Russia's postwar expansion in terms that were soothing to the readership, which feared Soviet imperialism and yet cautionary to those who gave a blank endorsement to all Russian policy. Although he recognized the totalitarianism of the Russian state, he felt that the people had been given "a sense of participation in a process of social and economic construction."

After Harry S Truman assumed the presidency in April 1945, Lerner supported him writing, "No man in the history of the vice presidential succession has grown in stature so fast or so visibly." However, he soon came to question Truman's ability. He saw in the president no grasp of real social cleavages and struggles, and a naivete in attempting to deal with Congress. In 1946 the journalist compared Truman's recommendation that striking railroad workers be drafted to similar action Hitler had taken in Germany.

Lerner opposed Truman's policy of containment of the Soviet Union, maintaining that the president was in the grip of a "war party." He warned that "partnership between a military caste and an industrial caste spelt fascism in Japan and Germany both. Can it in the end spell anything less in America?" The journalist denounced the Truman Doctrine as a demagogic appeal to the anticommunist right. However, he defended the Marshall Plan against Communist criticism. In 1947 he scored Truman's firing of HENRY A. WALLACE in part because the secretary of commerce had advocated reconciliation with the Soviets. By 1948 Lerner had concluded "in order to find itself, the Democratic Party must first shake off the burden of Harry Truman."

Lerner attended the Progressive Party National Convention in July 1948 and initially supported Wallace for President. However, he eventually broke with Wallace because of the secretary's close ties to Communists. Disillusioned with Truman and Wallace, Lerner voted for NORMAN THOMAS.

In 1948 Lerner became a columnist for the *New York Star*, the short-lived successor to the defunct *PM*. The following year he became a syndicated columnist for the *New York Post*. In 1949 he began teaching at Brandeis University, where he served from 1954 to 1956 as dean of the graduate school. In 1959 and 1960 he was a professor of American civilization at the University of Delhi in India.

In 1957 he published his most famous work, *America as a Civilization*, which he had labored on for a decade. In the 1960s Lerner increasingly devoted himself to cultural criticism. In 1980 he initially supported Senator Edward Kennedy (D-Mass.) for the presidency. But in 1984 and 1988 he backed Ronald Reagan and George H. W. Bush. He fought unsuccessfully for the nomination of Robert Bork to the Supreme Court in 1987. He died of cancer on June 5, 1992, in New York City.

—DGE

Lewis, John L(lewellyn)

(1880–1969) *president, United Mine Workers of America*

Of Welsh parentage, John L. Lewis was born in the coal-mining community of Lucas, Iowa, on February 12, 1880. He quit school after completing the seventh grade and entered the mines at the age of 15. A man of commanding presence with a talent for oratory and fondness for Shakespeare, Lewis considered going on stage before deciding to pursue a career in the labor movement instead. In 1909 he moved with his family to the coal fields of central Illinois, where he began to rise rapidly in the local hierarchy of the United Mine Workers of America (UMW). In 1911 Lewis was made a field representative of the American Federation of Labor (AFL), a job that enabled him to travel widely through the mine fields and to build up a strong personal machine within the miners' union. As a result, he became UMW vice president in 1917, acting president in 1919, and president of the largest union in the AFL the next year.

In the years following World War I, Lewis emerged on the national labor scene as a dynamic but ambiguous figure. A champion of industrial unionism, he headed an unsuccessful challenge to the conservative leadership of AFL president Samuel Gompers in 1921. At the same time, however, Lewis exemplified a tough, pragmatic business unionism that was rooted in the AFL tradition. A Republican and a firm believer in free enterprise capitalism, he simply ignored UMW positions in favor of the formation of a labor party and the nationalization of the mines and ruthlessly crushed the strong radical opposition to his personal rule. Lewis's autocratic methods, combined with a fierce antiunion drive by the coal operators during the 1920s, nearly destroyed the UMW by the end of the decade. With the advent of the New Deal, however, Lewis took advantage of the provisions of the 1933

National Industrial Recovery Act to launch a massive organizing drive in the coal fields, recruiting 300,000 miners to the UMW in two months.

After unsuccessfully attempting to persuade the AFL to open its doors to unskilled and semi-skilled workers, Lewis brought together the leaders of 10 other unions in the Committee for Industrial Organization (CIO) in 1935. The CIO proceeded at once to initiate a sweeping organizing campaign in auto, steel, rubber, and other basic industries. When jurisdictional conflicts with AFL craft unions led to the expulsion of the committee from the federation in 1938, it became the independent Congress of Industrial Organizations. As head of both the UMW and the CIO, Lewis lent vital support to President Franklin D. Roosevelt's 1936 reelection campaign, but he was increasingly at odds with the White House during the late 1930s. When World War II began he opposed American intervention and endorsed Wendell Willkie for the presidency in 1940. Promising to step down from the CIO's top post if Roosevelt won a third term, Lewis resigned immediately after the November elections and was replaced by his former UMW protégé PHILIP MURRAY, who was also head of the steelworkers' union.

Following the Japanese attack on Pearl Harbor Lewis announced his support of the American war effort and joined other labor leaders in a no-strike pledge for the duration of the conflict. He soon became a leading critic of the administration's domestic mobilization policies, however, denouncing the domination of regulatory and policy boards by conservative businessmen and administrators and, in 1942, pulling the UMW out of the pro-Roosevelt CIO. When in 1943 he concluded that the government had taken advantage of the no-strike pledge to impose an unfair wage formula on unions, Lewis led a series of epic strikes in defiance of the president's threat to use federal troops to keep the mines in operation. Lewis was vilified by the press as a dictator, racketeer, and near-traitor and specifically targeted in congressional passage of the Smith-Connally Act, which made it a felony to advocate a wartime strike in government-held industries. He nevertheless won a 35-hour workweek, pay for underground travel time, and improved mine safety for UMW members. Moreover, the miners' strikes encouraged workers in other industries to resist wage controls and thus contributed significantly to wartime labor unrest. During the latter part of the war, Lewis also pressed for readmission to the AFL, but he was repulsed by key leaders close to the White House, such as DANIEL J. TOBIN and GEORGE MEANY, who feared the strengthening of anti-administration forces within the federation.

In March 1945 the UMW opened negotiations on its contracts with the bituminous (soft coal) industry. In April the union and the operators agreed on a compromise wage increase. In the anthracite (hard coal) talks that followed, Lewis sought the travel time pay won by bituminous workers in 1943. When the old contract expired at the end of April with no new agreement in sight, 72,000 miners went on strike. On May 4 the administration seized the mines, but the miners defied the government by continuing their walkout. Since Lewis had not officially ordered the strike, the Attorney General could find no violation of the Smith-Connally Act. The stalemate was finally broken when the Supreme Court, in a case pending since 1943, ruled in favor of portal-to-portal pay for bituminous miners and, by implication, for anthracite workers as well. On May 20 agreement was reached on most of the UMW demands. Commenting on both contracts, editorial writers bitterly echoed the opinion of the *Washington Post* that the government had "humiliated itself once more before John L. Lewis and virtually invited other union leaders to apply his rule-or-ruin techniques."

With the end of the war, Lewis called on the administration to lift all restrictions on free collective bargaining. In contrast to CIO leaders, he opposed tying wage increases either to the cost-of-living or to business's "ability to pay." Since the AFL shared Lewis's concern for unfettered wage bargaining and was also increasingly at odds with the Truman White House over reconversion policy, the obstacles to reunification with the UMW were quickly removed. As a result, the miners union was readmitted to the organization in January 1946, and Lewis was elected a federation vice president.

In March 1946 Lewis reopened negotiations with the bituminous operators in an effort to win improved mine safety and a union-run health and welfare fund. The press largely ignored Lewis's specific demands, however, and instead interpreted his action as a bid to destroy federal wage-price policies and outdo Philip Murray, who had just secured substantial wage increases for his steelworkers. Little progress was made in the talks, and, on April 1, the miners struck. Within a month coal shortages forced a national brownout to save fuel and a severe

curtailment of auto and steel production. As pressure against Lewis rose, he announced on May 10 that the miners would return to work in the interests of national safety. On May 21, however, after Truman's proposal for arbitration was rejected by both sides, the president ordered Secretary of the Interior JULIUS A. KRUG to seize the mines and negotiate a settlement with the union. The miners ignored Krug's appeal to continue working after the expiration of the strike moratorium. Eight days after the seizure, the government yielded to the union's demands. Krug and Lewis signed a temporary agreement providing bituminous miners with a welfare and retirement fund jointly supervised by the UMW and the government and financed by a five-cent royalty on every ton of coal mined. A medical and health fund was also established, administered solely by the union and financed by the operators from money previously deducted from miners' wages for company-run health programs. The anthracite miners went on strike two days after the Krug-Lewis agreement was signed, and, on June 8, an accord was reached on a similar package.

In late October, with the mines still under government control, Lewis made a surprise demand for new talks on shorter hours and further wage increases. After some initial hesitation the administration abandoned all attempts at conciliation and instead decided, in the president's words, to "slap that no good so-and-so down hard." The government took the position that the contract could not be reopened, and, on November 17 a White House spokesman informed the press of Truman's orders to "fight John L. Lewis on all fronts." The next day federal Judge T. Alan Goldsborough issued an order restraining UMW officials from calling a strike until there was a judicial review of their new demands. When the bituminous miners nevertheless walked out on November 20, Goldsborough found Lewis and the union guilty of civil and criminal contempt. Denouncing the strike as "an evil and monstrous thing," he fined the UMW $3.5 million and Lewis $10,000 and granted the government's request for a preliminary injunction. Lewis called off the strike on December 7, pending an appeal to the Supreme Court.

Truman's "showdown" with Lewis became a national controversy. The UMW's financial penalty—the heaviest in American history—and the government's willingness to risk violating the 1932 Norris-LaGuardia anti-injunction law, provoked sharp criticism from labor unions. But the administration's aggressive strategy also earned the president broad press and public acclaim and brought him great personal satisfaction. Presidential adviser CLARK CLIFFORD later described the battle as "the moment when Truman finally and irrevocably stepped out from the shadow of FDR to become president in his own right." Moreover the episode brought into public view an intense personal feud between Lewis and Truman, which continued for the next several years. Lewis pronounced Truman "a malignant, scheming sort of an individual" who was "totally unfitted" for the presidency. The president, in turn, labeled Lewis a "headline hunter." When a reporter jokingly suggested that Truman appoint the miners' leader ambassador to Moscow, the president publicly quipped that he would not make that man chief dogcatcher of this country. Lewis replied: "The president could ill afford to have more brains in the Dog Department than in the Department of State, and from this standpoint, his remarks to you are eminently justified." However, Truman's widely publicized exchanges with Lewis, while doubtless stemming from genuine personal animosity, also betrayed political calculation. The move to stand up to Lewis was inspired by the disastrous mid-term elections of 1946, in which the Democrats, due to the ineffectiveness of Truman's reconversion efforts, had lost their majorities in the House of Representatives and the Senate. This, of course, was evidence of Truman's unpopularity, and his aides, such as Clark Clifford, encouraged the president to take on the one American more unpopular than himself, John L. Lewis, to revive his sagging fortunes.

When the Taft-Hartley labor reform bill came up for congressional consideration in 1947, Lewis, to whom government control of union affairs in any form was anathema, mobilized the UMW's flagging political power to attempt to defeat the measure. Warning that it would represent "the first step toward creating a corporate or absolute state," he attempted to make Taft-Hartley unworkable after the act passed over Truman's veto on June 23. The law required union officials to sign noncommunist affidavits in order to utilize the services of the National Labor Relations Board (NLRB) in representation elections. In addition, the NLRB ruled that AFL officers had to file as well. Lewis called for labor leaders, including his fellow AFL vice presidents and executive council members, to collectively refuse to take the oath, in the belief that a show of resistance would elicit popular sympathy and force repeal of the law. His pleas fell on deaf ears among the federation hierarchy, who wished to avoid any confrontation over the issue. In fury and disgust, Lewis subjected the delegates at the AFL's national convention in October to a scathing denunciation for what he regarded as their timid acquiescence to antilabor legislation; after comparing the organization to the biblical parable of "lions led by asses," he concluded: "I don't think the federation has a head. I think its neck has just grown up and haired over." Six weeks later, in a curt, pencil-written memo, he contemptuously informed AFL president WILLIAM GREEN of the UMW's disaffiliation from the federation.

After government management of the mines expired in June 1947, Lewis forced the operators to accept the welfare and retirement fund established by the Lewis-Krug agreement of the previous year. In January 1948, however, the neutral member of the three-man board of trustees, which had been set up to activate the fund, resigned, leaving Lewis and the industry representative, Ezra Van Horn, deadlocked. With Lewis's unofficial encouragement, 200,000 miners struck on March 14. Two weeks later the President instructed Attorney General TOM C. CLARK to obtain an 80-day Taft-Hartley injunction. Seeking to avoid either recognizing the injunction as valid or exposing himself and the union to another contempt conviction by refusing to order the miners back to work Lewis resorted to a complicated political maneuver. After first bringing in as arbiter Speaker of the House JOSEPH W. MARTIN (R-Mass.) he got Van Horn to accept Martin's suggestion of Senator Styles Bridges (R-N.H.) as the fund's new neutral trustee. Bridges then immediately sided with Lewis against Van Horn, and, on April 12, the two men agreed upon a pension plan. However, despite Lewis's insistence that he had purged himself of contempt charges by settling the dispute, he was ordered to stand trial. On April 20 Judge Goldsborough fined the union $1.5 million and its president $20,000.

Meanwhile Van Horn petitioned Goldsborough to suspend Bridges plan, but, before a decision could be reached, Lewis and Bridges voted to activate the fund. Lewis then opened talks on a new contract with the coal industry, demanding that the operators honor the pension provisions of the 1947 contract as a "condition precedent" to a new agreement. After several days of stalemated discussion, the administration again prepared to secure an injunction. On June 22, however, Goldsborough unexpectedly upheld the legality of Bridges's plan and dismissed Van Horn's suit. The ruling undermined the operators' case against the fund, and they promptly conceded most of Lewis's demands.

Although coal began to decline as a major energy source immediately after World War II, exports to Europe in the postwar years offset the deterioration of domestic markets for some time. By the end of the decade, however, the industry considered it imperative to reduce prices by cutting labor costs, particularly the expensive welfare and retirement fund. As a result, separate negotiations in 1949 between the UMW and the operators of the northern, southern, and so-called captive mines, which were owned by the steel corporations, produced a 10-month conflict that was finally resolved only under the threat of a new government seizure.

After the 1948 contract expired on June 30 with no new agreement in sight, Lewis imposed a three-day workweek on the industry. The southern operators responded by halting payments to the welfare and retirement fund, which led to a two-month strike in the bituminous coal fields. Early in December groups of miners in the captive mines began walking out without union authorization, and, by early January 1950, 66,000 had joined the wildcat in defiance of Lewis's instructions to end the strike. Additional operators, in a move apparently aimed at transforming the scattered walkouts into an industrywide strike that would force Truman to invoke Taft-Hartley, also began withholding royalty payments.

On January 31 the president appealed to the miners to return to work for 70 days while a fact-finding board investigated the issue. Since this procedure would have benefited the operators by guaranteeing them full production during the peak winter season and depriving the union of its ability to reduce coal stockpiles in preparation for a possible full-scale strike, the industry representatives accepted Truman's plan and walked out of negotiations with the UMW on February 2. Within three days, as a result, the month-old rash of wildcats became a nationwide strike. The administration quickly obtained an injunction, but was stymied when a federal judge ruled that it had failed to prove the union in contempt of court. Truman then asked Congress for authority to seize the mines, whereupon the disputants reached a compromise settlement in order to avoid a government takeover. In return for increased royalty payments and personal control over the welfare and retirement fund, Lewis agreed to a two-and-a-half year contract, providing the operators with their first opportunity for an extended period of industrial peace since the 1920s.

During the 1950s Lewis increasingly pursued cooperation rather than conflict with the coal industry. In 1952 he was joined by the bituminous operators' association in a successful effort to pressure Truman into approving a contract increase that exceeded the guidelines set by the administration's wartime economic stabilization program. Thereafter the UMW leader spoke increasingly of partnership with the operators for the good of the industry. He allowed the 1952 contract to remain in force until 1955 and requested a new accord only when coal's financial fortunes seemed to improve. Most important, Lewis never again seriously used the threat of a strike. Instead, he encouraged the largest owners to introduce mechanization and close inefficient mines, even at the cost of massive miner unemployment; the financing of welfare benefits by a tax on coal mined gave the UMW a strong incentive to back increased productivity. In 1960 Lewis resigned the union presidency and became president emeritus. Lewis died on June 11, 1969, in Washington, D.C. (See *The Eisenhower Years* Volume)

—TLH

Lilienthal, David E(li)

(1899–1981) chairman, Tennessee Valley Authority; chairman, Atomic Energy Commission

The son of immigrant Jews, David E. Lilienthal was born on July 8, 1899, in Morton, Illinois. He earned his LL.B. degree from Harvard in 1923, where he had studied with Felix Frankfurter. He worked in the law firm of David R. Richberg, a Chicago progressive who specialized in labor law, and, in 1926, started his own practice specializing in public utilities law. There he won some high-profile cases against utility companies in regard to high rates they charged. During this period he also contributed articles to the *Nation* and edited *Public Utilities and Careers Service.* Governor Philip LaFollette appointed him to the Wisconsin Public Service Commission in 1931, where he drafted a model utility regulation program for the state in which he lowered the rates charged by telephone companies and other utilities. This work, hailed by liberals throughout the nation, captured the attention of Franklin D. Roosevelt, who appointed Lilienthal a director of the Tennessee Valley Authority (TVA) in 1933. Eight years later Lilienthal became the agency's sole director. Under his tutelage, the TVA constructed dams, power facilities, and flood control projects along the Tennessee River valley network from Tennessee to northern Alabama. It provided cheap power for the area and aided poor farmers in reclamation projects. It also served as a "yardstick" to evaluate private utility company rates. Lilienthal thought of the authority as a business owned and managed by the people of the region, an idea he termed "grass roots" democracy. However, the TVA was viewed as socialism by many observers and he earned the mistrust of a large number of powerful members of Congress and the anger of private utility company head and future Republican presidential candidate Wendell Willkie.

During the opening months of 1946 Lilienthal, in conjunction with DEAN G. ACHESON, drew up a proposal on International Atomic Energy Control which the United States was to present before the UN Atomic Energy Commission. Their report, issued in March, called for the establishment of an international atomic development agency to survey nuclear raw materials and to assume control of dangerous fissionable material and production plants. The agency would make its resources available for peaceful uses and control, inspect, and license all nuclear activities. It would report any attempt to build atomic weapons to the UN, whose members could take appropriate action. The report stipulated that the United States would end the manufacture of nuclear devices at some point in the future and transfer atomic energy to the UN agency in stages. However, it stressed that there must be no immediate release of atomic knowledge.

BERNARD M. BARUCH, asked by Truman to present the plan to the United Nations, refused to accept the proposal. To insure Soviet compliance in disarmament, he demanded that a provision prohibiting Security Council members from using their veto power when discussing atomic energy be included in the American plan. Despite Lilienthal's and Acheson's objections that this was unnecessary and would lead to the defeat of the proposal, Baruch's recommendations were added. In June the Soviet Union rejected the Baruch Plan.

In February 1947 Truman appointed Lilienthal chairman of the Atomic Energy Commission (AEC). The protests from disgruntled Tennessee senator KENNETH D. MCKELLAR (D-Tenn.) and con-

servative Republicans made the Lilienthal choice a surprisingly controversial one. McKellar had had a feud with Lilienthal since the beginning of the TVA because of the director's refusal to give him patronage power over the project. In addition, McKellar had been representing private interests opposed to the authority. In an effort to deny confirmation, McKellar maintained that, while director, Lilienthal had treated Congress with contempt and charged that he was a friend of Communists. Conservative Republicans joined McKellar's attacks on Lilienthal's links with the left. Republican leader ROBERT A. TAFT (R-Ohio) considered the Lilienthal vote a test on whether the New Deal should continue. Pointing to Lilienthal's support of nuclear disarmament, Taft asked whether he could be trusted to run the AEC at the height of the cold war. There was also talk that he could not be trusted because his parents were from Czechoslovakia, which had fallen to the Communists.

In contrast to McKellar's and Taft's opposition, liberals and business interests, impressed with Lilienthal's managerial abilities, supported the appointment. President Truman added his pressure for confirmation. Twenty-three Republicans and seven Democrats voted against Lilienthal. His margin of victory came from 19 moderate Republicans, led by Senator ARTHUR H. VANDENBERG (R-Mich.), who were skeptical of the charges made by the conservatives.

Lilienthal served as chairman of the AEC until December 1949. Under his directorship the agency prepared for the eventual testing of the hydrogen bomb and studied the peaceful use of nuclear energy. Lilienthal did raise the concern that developing the hydrogen bomb would curtail atomic bomb construction, although he did not oppose the H-bomb in and of itself. Lilienthal still remained a controversial figure. The military resented the fact that he had control of atomic weapons research. Business interests were angered that he had a monopoly on research and development. McKellar continued his vendetta. Most important, the charges that some uranium was missing from one of the plants and that a Communist had been given an AEC fellowship again raised questions of Lilienthal's loyalty. All these factors convinced him not to seek a second term.

Lilienthal retired to New York to practice law. In 1955 he founded the Development and Resource Corporation, which advised non-Western nations on how to construct agencies like the TVA. He was CEO of that company until it was dissolved in 1979. Lilienthal remained active in liberal Democratic politics. He also published his five-volume memoirs, which offered important historical insights into the Roosevelt-Truman years. He died on January 14, 1981, in New York City.

—JB

Lincoln, Murray D(anforth)
(1892–1966) *president, Nationwide Insurance Company*

Murray D. Lincoln was born on April 8, 1892, in Raynham, Massachusetts. He was brought up on a farm near Brockton and graduated from Massachusetts Agricultural College in 1914. He organized one of the first cooperative milk distributing plants in New England. For the remainder of his life, Lincoln devoted himself to the cooperative movement. In 1920 he resigned his position as agricultural agent for a Cleveland bank to become executive secretary of the Ohio Farm Bureau Federation, where he served until 1948. When farmers complained about the high cost of insurance, Lincoln organized the Farm Bureau Mutual Automobile Insurance Company in 1926 with $10,000 in capital borrowed from Farm Bureau members. In the 1930s he formed two other companies for fire and life insurance. Named the Nationwide Insurance Companies in 1955, they had $500 million in assets by 1961. One of Nationwide's slogans was "People working together can do anything." In 1941 Lincoln was elected president of the Cooperative League of the United States, which he had helped organize. The League used his hotel room in Columbus, Ohio, as its first headquarters. He served in that position until 1965.

During World War II Lincoln was a leader of the liberal bloc of the American Farm Bureau Federation. He advocated the "cooperative way" as a solution to the problems on both the national and the international levels. In September 1945, at the International Cooperative Alliance Conference, he called for expanded trade along cooperative lines as a deterrent to the "intrusion of governments into the regulation of foreign commerce." In April 1949 he urged the government to make "sound business-like loans" to provide for cooperatives in American cities. Lincoln believed their formation would increase consumer-buying power and ease the lag in the economy.

Lincoln took his appeal to labor in January 1950 when, in an address to the convention of the Ohio Congress of Industrial Organizations (CIO) Council, he asked labor to back cooperative housing and start buying processing plants to lower the cost of food. He told the audience: "Literally, I think there is not a field of human endeavor that can not be improved as to price, service or quality if we applied the cooperative way." Later that month he went before the U.S. Senate to back President Truman's middle-income cooperative housing plan.

After World War II Lincoln was prominent in the distribution of U.S. agricultural surpluses to needy nations. He was the founder of the Cooperative for American Remittance to Europe, the nonprofit food-distributing agency commonly known as CARE. Lincoln served as its president from 1945 to 1957. He also served on many advisory committees for President Truman, among them committees on higher education, rural electrification, and farm tenancy.

Although a registered Republican during the 1940s, Lincoln joined and became a director of the liberal Americans for Democratic Action. Labor leaders, including CIO president PHILLIP MURRAY, considered him a viable candidate to oppose ROBERT A. TAFT (R-Ohio) in the 1950 U.S. Senate election, but Lincoln refused to run. He joined the Democratic Party in January 1950.

In the 1960s Lincoln headed a task force on the proposed Food for Peace program. He also served on the Peace Corps Advisory Council. Lincoln retired as president of Nationwide in 1964 and died on November 7, 1966, in Columbus, Ohio. (See *The Kennedy Years* Volume)

—EF

Lippmann, Walter
(1889–1974) *journalist*

Walter Lippmann, the son of well-to-do Jewish parents, was born on September 21, 1889, in New York City. He entered Harvard and was influenced by William James, George Santayana, and Graham Wallas. He graduated in 1910 and worked briefly for Lincoln Steffen's *Everybody's* magazine. He then went to work for the socialist mayor of Schenectady, New York, in 1912. In 1914 he joined Herbert Croly in founding the *New Republic*, a liberal journal supporting Woodrow Wilson's progressivism and internationalism. He broke with socialism and came out for the more conservative Progressive dream of an elite-run, scientifically managed society. Three years later he was appointed assistant secretary of war and contributed to the formation of the Fourteen Points and the Treaty of Versailles. The vengeance that was carried out against the Germans in the final version of the Treaty of Versailles caused Lippmann to abandon for a time Wilsonian internationalism. After the war Lippmann joined the *New York World*, soon becoming its Washington correspondent. During the 1920s he also published a number of books expressing his growing pessimism with popular democracy. The public was too easily manipulated, and experts should rule the nation with the role of the people limited to voting.

In 1931 the journalist began his long association with the *New York Herald Tribune*. In his column "Today & Tomorrow," Lippmann analyzed contemporary issues in relation to the problems of American democracy. He initially supported Franklin D. Roosevelt but by 1935 increasingly criticized what he thought was the president's move toward socialism. Nevertheless, he applauded Roosevelt's foreign policy. He deplored the isolationism and pacifism of the nation in the face of Hitler's expansion and supported Roosevelt's attempts to aid U.S. allies.

During the war Lippmann outlined his goals for American diplomacy. In *U.S. Foreign Policy: Shield of the Republic* (1943) and *U.S. War Aims* (1944), he criticized the Wilsonian ideas of internationalism. Lippmann advised Americans to base their diplomacy on realpolitik. National interest, he asserted, was determined by geopolitical and economic factors, not abstract theories of right versus wrong. Lippmann proposed that the United States, USSR, and Great Britain recognize each other's spheres of influence to prevent future conflict. These three nations could then form a coalition to check the rise of Germany and Japan, the only two nations that could threaten the status quo. Lippmann ridiculed the idea of an international organization formed to keep the peace, maintaining that only treaties based on geopolitics could create a stable world.

The journalist warned the Western allies not to challenge the future Soviet hegemony in Eastern Europe. Lippmann acknowledged that Soviet repression in the area could strain his proposed coalition. However, he reasoned that the Soviet Union would not quickly move to suppress freedom because its foreign policy was not determined by ideology but by a desire to protect its western border. He hoped for a neutralized Eastern Europe under Soviet influence but not oppression. His hope of continuing the alliance was finally destroyed after the Communist takeover of Czechoslovakia in 1948.

During the postwar years Lippmann continued to opposed Truman's concentration on Eastern Europe. He also criticized the administration's desire to build a strong Germany as creating an unnecessary source of tension in the cold war—a term he allegedly originated. The only way to allay Soviet fears and introduce stability in Central Europe was, in his opinion, to keep Germany decentralized and neutralized. If the West pushed too hard for unification of Germany, he warned, the Soviets might use their military power to unite the nation under a Communist regime.

Lippmann believed America's major interest was in the Eastern Mediterranean, on the vital oil routes to Western Europe. In 1947 he endorsed the president's request to send aid to Greece and Turkey, then threatened by Communist rebels. However, he attacked the Truman Doctrine, promising American aid to nations fighting communism, because it was couched in terms of a Wilsonian moral crusade.

During the latter half of 1947 Lippmann engaged in a major debate with GEORGE F. KENNAN over foreign policy. The Soviet expert maintained that Russian diplomacy was based on Stalin's paranoia of capitalist encirclement and a desire to extend communism, as well as traditional Russian security concerns. To meet Soviet aggression, Kennan recommended a policy of containment. By placing American power and aid in shifting areas of conflict, the West would soon show the Soviet Union its determination to prevent Communist expansion.

Lippmann dismissed irrationality as a motive for Soviet diplomacy, reiterating his belief that it was based on geopolitical considerations. He supported the Marshall Plan of economic aid to Europe but condemned containment because he thought it would lead to "unending intervention" and would allow the Soviet Union to maintain the initiative in the cold war. Instead of containment, he proposed disengagement by both powers: a U.S. withdrawal from Western Germany to be matched by a Soviet withdrawal from the East. Disengagement, he predicted, would restore some democracy to Eastern Europe because Russia would not have to fear penetration from the West.

In the late 1940s and early 1950s Lippmann devoted less time to foreign affairs. However, when the Eisenhower administration came to power, he once again began to attack American foreign policy. He ridiculed the administration's attempts to couch foreign policy in terms of a moral crusade and denounced JOHN FOSTER DULLES's call for the liberation of Eastern Europe. Lippmann considered involvements in Southeast Asia and Quemoy-Matsu unnecessary overextensions of American power. Disengagement and the American willingness to cooperate with neutral nations, he maintained, were the best ways to ensure a pro-American stable world. Lippmann supported John F. Kennedy for president in 1960 but became increasingly disillusioned with his foreign policy. He was impressed with the early Johnson administration but broke with the president over the war in Vietnam. From 1963 to 1968 Lippmann worked for *Newsweek* magazine. The dean of American journalism died on December 14, 1974, in New York City. (See *The Eisenhower Years, The Kennedy Years* Volumes)

—JB

Lodge, Henry Cabot, Jr.
(1902–1985) *member of the Senate*

Henry Cabot Lodge, Jr., was born in Nahant, Massachusetts, on July 5, 1902, into a distinguished family, which traced its ancestry back to the Massachusetts Bay Colony and later included several cabinet members and congressmen. After his father's death in 1919, Lodge was raised by his grandfather Senator Henry Cabot Lodge, Sr., (R-Mass.). Following graduation from Harvard in 1924, young Lodge pursued a career in journalism, writing for the *New York Herald Tribune*. In 1933 he was elected as a Republican to the Massachusetts House of Representatives and in 1936 to the U.S. Senate. During World War II Lodge served two duty tours: from 1941 to 1942 and 1944 to 1945. In 1946 he once again won a Senate seat from Massachusetts, defeating the Democratic incumbent, David I. Walsh.

Lodge returned from wartime service convinced that the United States could no longer remain isolated from world affairs. He urged American support of the United Nations and assistance for European reconstruction while hoping for an "efficient working relationship" with the Soviet Union. On domestic issues, he was critical of what he saw as the New Deal's interference in the private

sector, its makeshift programs, and the bulging bureaucracy. He also chided the Republican Party for its negativism and what he thought were sometimes reactionary policies. He advocated continued business expansion and federal social programs beneficial to all society.

In 1950 Lodge was a member of the special committee chaired by Senator MILLARD E. TYDINGS (D-Md.), which looked into the allegations made by Senator JOSEPH R. MCCARTHY (R-Wisc.) about Communists in the State Department. In the minority report Lodge was critical of the partisanship showed by Tydings and other Democrats in the hearings.

Lodge developed a close friendship with Senate Foreign Relations Committee chairman ARTHUR H. VANDENBERG (R-Mich.), who had shed his isolationist views and was committed to a bipartisan foreign policy. Lodge supported the Truman administration's policy of containment toward the Soviet Union and, in March 1947, played a significant role in rallying liberal Republican support for the Truman Doctrine. He and Vandenberg were instrumental in steering the Marshall Plan through the Foreign Relations Committee and Senate floor in 1948. He also supported Truman's Point Four program of aid to the developing world.

In the spring of 1948 Lodge often joined Secretary of State GEORGE C. MARSHALL, Undersecretary ROBERT A. LOVETT, and Vandenberg in planning a possible Western military alliance. Negotiations became official following Senate approval of the Vandenberg Resolution in June 1948 and culminated with the signing of the North Atlantic Treaty in April 1949. Along with Vandenberg and Senator TOM CONNALLY (D-Tex.), Lodge was instrumental in obtaining Senate approval of the pact. Lodge was a constant supporter of military preparedness. He urged an increase in the air force in 1951 and charged the United States with failure to deliver promised aid to the North Atlantic Treaty Organization later that year.

The senator was also active on domestic issues. To eliminate government waste he and Representative CLARENCE BROWN (R-Ohio) proposed in 1947 the creation of a nonpartisan Commission on the Organization of the Executive Branch of Government. Subsequently 68 percent of the commission's recommendations were passed by Congress, saving $10 billion in tax expenditures. Much to Senator ROBERT A. TAFT's (R-Ohio) consternation, Lodge also cosponsored a constitutional amendment to abolish the Electoral College and provide for direct election of the president. In 1950 the Senate approved the measure, but the House rejected it. Lodge was frustrated in his efforts to bring about public financing of presidential elections, a move he thought essential to help eliminate corruption. He voted against deregulation of the natural gas industry and for the Fair Employment Act, but against federal aid to education and for the Portal-to-Portal Pay Act, which did not count transit time to the worksite and back as covered by the minimum wage. (Its main application was in the coal-mining industry.)

Lodge's moderate views brought him into direct conflict with the Republican Party's "Old Guard," led by Senators Taft, WILLIAM E. JENNER (R-Ind.), KENNETH S. WHERRY (R-Neb.), James Kem (R-Mo.), and JOHN W. BRICKER (R-Ohio). This conflict sharpened during the 80th Congress as Lodge opposed proposed provisions in the Taft-Hartley Act that permitted injunctive action by private employers against jurisdictional strikes and outlawed union shops, although he did vote for the final version of the bill. He voted for DAVID E. LILIENTHAL as chief administrator of the Atomic Energy Commission in 1946, despite the "Old Guard's" charge that Lilienthal was an example of "creeping socialism" and was "soft on communism."

As chairman of the resolutions committee at the 1948 Republican National Convention, Lodge played an important role in formulating the party platform. The foreign policy section was internationalist in its sentiment, calling for "collective security against aggression," United Nations control of atomic energy, and friendship with Nationalist China. The 1948 GOP platform further reflected Lodge's views promising better labor-management relations, improved farm programs, extension of old age benefits, adequate medical facilities, slum clearance, and an end to racial discrimination.

As a result of the Republican defeats in November, Lodge rationalized the demise of the party unless it modernized, and he personally took the lead to do so. Although he failed to unseat Taft as chairman of Senate Republican Policy Committee in the 81st Congress, he continued to battle. Writing in the *Saturday Evening Post* in 1949 and in the *Atlantic Monthly* in 1950, Lodge charged that the GOP was viewed as a "rich man's club" and a "haven for reactionaries." Pointing to the party's historic progressive roots—slave emancipation, conservation laws,

bank deposit insurance—he urged the party to move forward on the basis of its 1948 platform.

Lodge also believed a new party leader was needed to insure such progress and urged Dwight D. Eisenhower to seek the presidential nomination. Lodge was encouraged by Eisenhower's response at a September 4, 1951, meeting, although the general gave no firm commitment to enter the presidential race. That November Lodge organized an Eisenhower campaign committee, which included THOMAS E. DEWEY, James H. Duff, General LUCIUS D. CLAY, Russell Sprague, and Herbert Brownell. In January 1952, after Lodge had placed his name in the New Hampshire primary as a Republican candidate, Eisenhower admitted Republican Party affiliation. Thereafter, Lodge and his group skillfully managed Eisenhower's primary campaign and presidential nomination over Taft at the Republican National Convention.

Because of his efforts on behalf of Eisenhower, Lodge had left his own political fences unmended. His senatorial defeat to John F. Kennedy in 1952 was attributed largely to loss of the support of Massachusetts conservatives, who were infuriated by his success in securing Eisenhower's nomination over Taft. After serving as chief liaison officer between the Truman and Eisenhower administrations, Lodge was appointed ambassador to the United Nations, serving from 1953 to 1960. Lodge was the Republican Party's vice presidential candidate in 1960 and from 1963 to 1967 was ambassador to South Vietnam. In 1969 and 1970 he headed the U.S. delegation to the Paris peace talks. In his later years he lectured and composed his memoirs. Lodge died on February 27, 1985, in Beverly, Massachusetts. (See *The Eisenhower Years, The Kennedy Years, The Johnson Years, The Nixon/Ford Years* Volumes)

—TML

Loeb, James I(saac), Jr.

(1908–1992) *executive secretary, Americans for Democratic Action*

James I. Loeb, Jr., was born on August 18, 1908, in Chicago, Illinois. He obtained a doctorate in Romance languages from Northwestern University in 1936 and began teaching in the New York City school system. His abhorrence of the Spanish fascists soon drew him into liberal politics. In May 1941 he joined with theologian REINHOLD NIEBUHR in creating the Union For Democratic Action (UDA), a socialist organization formed to fight fascism. As executive director, he successfully led the fight within the UDA to deny membership to American Communists on the grounds that they would disrupt the organization and render it ineffective.

In May 1946 Loeb wrote a historic letter to the *New Republic* that foresaw the split in the liberal community. He denounced many liberals for refusing to hold the Soviet Union as well as the U.S. responsible for the cold war. Liberals, Loeb then warned, had to make a choice whether to collaborate with Communists or not. If they chose to do so, they should expect an ineffective popular front that would strengthen reactionary forces. Loeb appealed for a noncollaborationist liberal coalition for reform.

Six months later Loeb initiated a UDA membership drive to attract such liberals. In January 1947 more than 400 responded to his plea and attended a UDA-inspired conference in Washington to consolidate reform forces. The participants decided to create a new organization, the Americans for Democratic Action (ADA), to replace the UDA. James Loeb was elected its executive secretary and ELEANOR ROOSEVELT its honorary chairman. Founding sponsors included WALTER P. REUTHER, DAVID DUBINSKY, and Marquis Childs. The ADA emphatically rejected any cooperation with Communists. After the formation of the new group, the Progressive Citizens of America (PCA) emerged as the umbrella organization of liberals willing to permit Communists in their ranks. The ADA and the PCA, with its leading spokesman, HENRY A. WALLACE, competed for the support of many progressive Americans disenchanted with President Truman.

Initially the PCA grew faster than the ADA. Wallace's association with it drew many new members and the inclusion of Communists provided it with many more dedicated workers. Yet the decision to create a third party to challenge Truman in 1948 ultimately hurt the PCA. Loeb, who had been a fan of Wallace, had begun to change his attitude in late September 1946 after Wallace's Madison Square Garden speech that called for rapprochement with the Soviets. He began to warn that the PCA's action would guarantee a Republican victory by splitting the liberal vote. He also maintained that Communists dominated the PCA and would control its inevitable presidential candidate, Wallace. As a result of his attacks many liberals did defect to the ADA.

Loeb reasoned that the ADA had the power to influence the selection of the 1948 Democratic candidate because the party needed liberal support to counter Wallace's candidacy. He originally ruled out backing Truman because he felt the president had no way of winning. In addition, Loeb thought his liberal qualifications questionable. The ADA hoped to convince General DWIGHT D. EISENHOWER or Supreme Court Justice WILLIAM O. DOUGLAS to run. He wanted an open convention. Loeb said, "We feel strongly that the nation has a right to call upon men like Dwight D. Eisenhower and William O. Douglas if the people so choose." However, when Eisenhower declined to run and Douglas entertained fruitless hopes of a draft that did not come and Truman started his own successful campaign to raise his standing among liberals, Loeb and his organization decided to support him.

Assuming that the president could win the labor-liberal coalition only if he could neutralize Wallace, Loeb set out on an ambitious campaign to discredit the former vice president. He wrote a friend in regard to his efforts: "Every strategy should be used, both the soft strategy and the tough strategy." In July 1948 he attended, uninvited, the PCA convention to speak before the platform committee. Loeb asked the party to repudiate its alleged ties to the Soviet Union by condemning Stalin's totalitarian and expansionist policies and by backing the Marshall Plan. He further requested the party to pull out of state races in which its candidates jeopardized the election of ADA liberals. If the PCA did not comply with his request, Loeb proclaimed, it would show that its loyalty was with Moscow. Failure to withdraw from the race would do what Russia desired: elect a reactionary government in America. Loeb's appearance received a great deal of publicity and made "red-baiting" a respectable pursuit among liberals. The ADA worked hard for Truman, who won an unexpected victory in November.

Believing Truman owed part of his success to the ADA, Loeb expected progress in liberal reform. Following the election he wrote confidently that the president and Congress would cooperate to pass needed legislation. Loeb soon discovered that a Southern Democratic–Republican coalition prevented action on such measures as public housing, construction, civil rights, repeal of the Taft-Hartley Act, and passage of a national health insurance program. ADA lobbying attempts failed to sway Congress. A number of the organization's endorsed candidates lost in the election of 1950 as a conservative reaction set in. Frustrated, Loeb and the ADA held Truman responsible for not providing inspired leadership.

During Truman's second term Loeb served as a foreign policy adviser specializing in Latin America. He initially supported ADLAI E. STEVENSON for the Democratic presidential nomination in 1952, but when Stevenson refused to commit himself to a race, Loeb backed W. AVERELL HARRIMAN. In the general election campaign he enthusiastically worked for Stevenson.

Following Eisenhower's victory Loeb purchased an upstate New York newspaper. He continued active in ADA affairs, often speaking out for liberal reforms. Loeb originally supported HUBERT H. HUMPHREY's run for the 1960 Democratic presidential nomination but worked for John F. Kennedy in the campaign. During the Kennedy administration he served as ambassador to Peru and to Guinea. In 1965 Loeb left the diplomatic corps to return to his newspaper. Loeb died on January 10, 1992, in Lebanon, New Hampshire. (See *The Kennedy Years* Volume)

—JB

Long, Earl K(emp)
(1895–1960) *governor*

Born on August 25, 1895, in Winnfield, Louisiana, in the poor farmland of northern Louisiana, Earl K. Long grew up in the shadow of his older brother Huey. He left high school early to become a traveling salesman, a charmer who was good at his craft. After briefly attending Louisiana Polytechnic Institute, Earl followed Huey through law school at Tulane and Loyola universities and was admitted to the bar in 1926. Two years later Earl helped Huey win the governorship. He was named inheritance tax collector, his first political post. When Huey, then a senator, refused Earl a place on the 1932 Democratic gubernatorial ticket because he thought his younger brother headstrong, Earl ran against the Long machine's candidate. Badly beaten, Earl testified against Huey at a 1933 Senate investigation of Louisiana voting fraud. The brothers reconciled before Huey's assassination in September 1935. After the senator's death Earl picked up the mantle of Long populism and fitted it to his own career.

Elected lieutenant governor in 1936, Long served as governor in 1939–40 following the resignation of his corrupt predecessor, Richard D. Leche. He was narrowly defeated for reelection in 1940.

Earl Long planned his next campaign carefully. In the fall of 1947 he opened his 1948 gubernatorial race with 29-year-old RUSSELL B. LONG, Huey's son, at his side. This convinced voters that any split in the Long family had healed. He campaigned in Huey Long's "share the wealth" tradition, winning black and labor support with promises of a $50-a-month old age pension, a veterans' bonus, an improved school system, and an increased public works program. He promised to finance this by cutting waste in government and pledged not to raise taxes. In the January 1948 Democratic primary, Long polled 41.5 percent of the votes but was forced into a runoff against conservative runner-up Sam H. Jones. All three major New Orleans newspapers supported Jones. They accused Long of accepting $45,000 in deductions from state employees' salaries and echoed the charge of Jones partisan Representative James Domengeaux (D-La.) that Long had evaded income tax payments. In the February runoff, Long achieved a record-breaking 200,000 vote majority over Jones. The following month Representative Domengeaux's House resolution to investigate Long's income tax returns was defeated.

Long opposed several important Truman administration policies. Although no racist, the governor disapproved of the president's civil rights program. He also opposed Truman's position favoring federal ownership of offshore oil lands. By 1948 Louisiana had earned $34 million from leasing the oil-rich tidelands. However, before the July 1948 Democratic National Convention, Long stated he would support the party's presidential nominee. When Truman was nominated on a strong civil rights plank, a number of southern delegations walked out and nominated South Carolina governor J. STROM THURMOND for president on the States' Rights (Dixiecrat) ticket. Violently opposing Truman on the tidelands oil and civil rights issues, Leander Perez, district attorney of oil-rich Plaquemines Parish, pressured Long into backing Thurmond for president on the regular Democratic Party line. When national Democratic officials protested this, Long compromised. In September he convened a special session of the state legislature and allowed the Truman-Barkley ticket a line on the voting machines. The Dixiecrats carried Louisiana in November, but Truman was elected president.

Between April and November Long started fulfilling his campaign promise of greater benefits. However, he raised taxes to pay for them by more than 50 percent or $70 million in June. He increased sales and gasoline taxes and placed a $100 tax on Louisiana's 10,000 illegal slot machines. Long made no attempt to camouflage his tax package, which fell most heavily on lower and middle-income voters. This was in sharp contrast to Huey Long's tax policy during the 1920s and indicated Earl's closer alliance with the business community. When Russell asked him what to tell outraged constituents, Earl said, "Tell them I lied." The Long faction's popularity suffered a precipitous decline. Russell Long, running as a Dixiecrat for the two remaining years of John H. Overton's Senate term in November, won by only 10,000 votes.

During his first year as governor, Earl Long also had the legislature repeal the Goff Act, which prohibited certain kinds of strikes. In September he repealed the state's six-year-old civil service system so he could increase his number of political appointments, dismissing people for such weighty malfeasances as "political halitosis." Anxious to establish political respectability, Long appointed a number of Huey's foes to posts in the port of New Orleans, the Democratic committee, and the state liquor authority.

By 1952 he had fulfilled most of his campaign promises financed by the enormous tax increase. He had also—under pressure from the NAACP's threat to sue—increased the number of African Americans registered to vote to more 90,000, giving the state the highest percentage of registered blacks in the South. He reached this number by convincing local registrars to stop using discriminatory literary tests. He also equalized pay between white and African-American schoolteachers. However, he also tried to take control of the state universities and tried to crush the independence of New Orleans, which was run by a foe, Mayor DELESSEPS S. MORRISON. The governor also permitted mobsters Carlos Marcello and Frank Costello to spread illegal operations by opening gambling joints throughout the southern half of the state. Prohibited by law from succeeding himself, Long backed Carlos G. Spaht for governor. In February 1952 Spaht lost the Democratic nomination to state appeals court Judge ROBERT F. KENNON, who was running on a "good government" reform ticket backed by big business. Long had anticipated Spaht's defeat, believing that after four years of boring "good government" people would want the entertaining Uncle Earl back. He was proved right when he won another term in 1956.

Earl Long opposed zealous white supremacists following the 1954 Supreme Court decision that outlawed school segregation and reshaped Louisiana politics in racial terms. After his 1956 reelection he reluctantly signed new segregation legislation into law. During a struggle in May 1958 with segregationists who were trying to purge his black supporters from the voter rolls, Long suffered a nervous breakdown. His power further waned the following year when the legislators vetoed a law that would have permitted him to succeed himself. After losing a December 1959 bid for lieutenant governor, Long won the Democratic nomination for a seat in the U.S. House of Representatives. Increasingly given to erratic behavior, Long entered the hospital for treatment as a paranoid schizophrenic in 1959. Long died of a heart attack on September 5, 1960, in Alexandria, Louisiana. (See *The Eisenhower Years* Volume)

—MJS

Long, Russell B(illiu)

(1918–2003) *member of the Senate*

Russell B. Long was born on November 3, 1918, in Shreveport, Louisiana, the oldest son of Huey Long, the Louisiana governor and U.S. senator whose political machine dominated the state in the 1920s and 1930s. Groomed for a political career, he received a B.A. from Louisiana State University in 1941 and a law degree from that institution the following year. After serving in the navy during World War II, Long opened a law practice in Baton Rouge. He made his political debut in 1948, when he assisted his uncle EARL K. LONG's campaign for the governorship. In April 1948 the newly elected governor appointed Russell Long his executive counsel. In this capacity he helped formulate Long's welfare program supported by an $80 million tax increase.

In May 1948 Russell Long announced his candidacy for the Senate seat vacated by the death of Senator John Overton (D-La.). Three months later he narrowly defeated anti-Long candidate ROBERT F. KENNON in the Democratic primary on the basis of a strong rural showing. Russell Long supported the States' Rights (Dixiecrat) Party presidential candidate, J. STROM THURMOND, in the November election. Although Thurmond carried the state by a large majority, Long won election by a scant 10,000 votes. This 95 percent attrition of the Long family's power base within eight months of Earl's victory was attributed to the 50 percent tax increase Russell helped engineer.

Long was assigned to the committees on Rules, Banking and Currency, Post Office, and Civil Service when he took his seat as the Senate's youngest member in January 1949. He established a reputation as a southern moderate. According to biographer Robert Mann, Long gained acceptance in the Senate through hard work on committees and acting mild-mannered, whereas his father had disdained committee work and was ruthless. He consistently supported the administration on federal aid to housing and education and increased social security benefits. He opposed, however, the administration's call for flexible price supports for farm products.

In April 1949 Long voted for a $1.5 billion public housing construction program over a five-year period. One year later he successfully opposed an amendment providing government loans for middle-income housing. In April 1951 the senator cosponsored an amendment to the housing act that prevented builders from obtaining government-insured loans that exceeded building costs. Long opposed Truman on federal ownership of offshore oil properties and price regulation of the oil and natural gas vital to Louisiana's economy. In March 1950 he voted to exempt sales of natural gas by independent producers from federal regulation. The measure was vetoed by Truman as was an April 1952 tidelands oil bill giving states title to land up to the three-mile limit.

While voting to ratify the North Atlantic Treaty in July 1949, Long voted against appropriating $1.3 billion in military aid to the North Atlantic Treaty Organization the following September. In May 1950 he supported Truman's Point Four program for technical aid to underdeveloped countries. He voted to extend the Trade Agreements Act, to ratify the Japanese peace treaty, to confirm GEORGE C. MARSHALL as secretary of defense, and to enact the McCarran-Walter immigration bill. He voted against the McClellan Amendment, which stated the sense of the Senate that no soldiers beyond the initial four divisions planned should be sent to NATO in Europe without Congress's okay. Long favored the anticommunist legislation of the period, including the Internal Security Act of 1950.

In November 1950 Long won election to a full Senate term. He expressed growing independence from his family's political dynasty by supporting anti-Long candidate Hale Boggs in an unsuccessful gubernatorial bid in July 1951. A year later Long was one of a handful of Louisiana delegates to the Democratic National Convention to oppose Governor Robert Kennon and sign a loyalty oath pledging to support the convention's nominees regardless of their stand on civil rights.

Throughout the Eisenhower years Long consistently favored the oil depletion allowance, increased social security payments to the elderly, and tax cuts for the poor. He increasingly opposed foreign aid as "treating foreigners better than Americans." During the 1960s Long generally opposed administration domestic policy while supporting an aggressive stance in foreign affairs. Long died on May 9, 2003, in Washington, D.C. (See *The Eisenhower Years, The Kennedy Years, The Johnson Years, The Nixon/Ford Years, The Carter Years* Volumes)

—MJS

Lovestone, Jay

(1898–1990) *executive secretary, Free Trade Union Committee*

Born in 1898 in Lithuania to poverty-stricken Russian-Jewish parents, Jacob Liebstein came to the United States at the age of nine. A socialist from youth, he was a leader of the Intercollegiate Socialist Society while a student at the College of the City of New York. He became a supporter of Leninist ideology after the success of the October Revolution. In 1919 he was a delegate to the founding convention of the American Communist Party. Changing his name to Jay Lovestone, he worked in the party's underground apparatus during the Red Scare of 1919–20 and later became a leading Communist functionary. He edited the party's underground periodical *The Communist* in 1921. He later became a member of the Executive Committee of the Comintern. Lovestone developed an altered Marxist-Leninist ideology into what was later called "American exceptionalism," which argued there would be a long period of capitalist dominance in the United States, which he believed meant Communists should advocate nonrevolutionary policies in the union movement and elsewhere in the United States. In the bitter intraparty disputes of those years, which reflected the post-Lenin struggle for power in the USSR, Lovestone's faction was aligned with the so-called Right Communists headed by Soviet leader Nikolai Bukharin. As general secretary of the party in 1928, Lovestone carried out the

Moscow-ordered expulsion of the American followers of Leon Trotsky. The following year, however, Bukharin in turn fell from power and Lovestone was ordered to abdicate in favor of a Stalinist minority led by WILLIAM Z. FOSTER, even though Lovestone was known as the "American Stalin." Although he repudiated Bukharin in an effort to mollify Stalin, Lovestone refused to give up his post. He was promptly expelled along with about 200 followers.

Lovestone then organized a dissident Communist group of his own. The "Lovestoneites," as they were popularly known, sought readmission to the parent organization for several years but were branded as "right deviationists" and shunned by the party faithful. Becoming virulently anticommunist, the group remained in existence until 1940, when it dissolved. In the meantime, however, Lovestone pursued a career as an adviser and "troubleshooter" for DAVID DUBINSKY, the head of the International Ladies Garment Workers Union (ILGWU) and a founder of the Committee for Industrial Organization (CIO). In return for Lovestone's assistance in exposing Communists operating within the labor movement and curbing their influence, Dubinsky helped place him and his followers in strategic union jobs. In 1937–38 a group of Lovestoneites emerged in Detroit on the staff of United Auto Workers (UAW) president Homer Martin, who was embroiled in a bitter internal battle with an opposing coalition of Communists, socialists, and nonpolitical UAW militants. Although details have remained obscure, Lovestone apparently encouraged Martin, with secret support from Dubinsky and American Federation of Labor (AFL) president WILLIAM GREEN, to split the UAW and bring part of the union back into the AFL. (The ILGWU left the CIO in 1938 and rejoined the AFL two years later.) The episode earned Lovestone a reputation among many UAW and CIO activists as an unscrupulous operator.

Prior to American entry into World War II, Lovestone also directed the ILGWU's aggressive international relations program. Lovestone and Dubinsky feared that if the Nazis eliminated most of Europe's noncommunist political and labor leadership, the Russians and the Communist underground would control Europe even if Germany were eventually defeated by the Allies. As a result, the ILGWU, with some AFL support, helped rescue hundreds of union officials, politicians, and intellectuals from Axis-occupied Europe. During the war

Lovestonites worked with the Office of Strategic Services and later the Central Intelligence Agency. While working out of ILGWU headquarters in New York, Lovestone also became an unofficial, but highly influential foreign policy adviser to GEORGE MEANY, Matthew Woll, and other internationally oriented AFL leaders. At their behest the AFL in 1944 created a fund to assure assistance for the organization of "democratic" unions in Europe, Asia, and Latin America. Lovestone administered it through a Free Trade Union Committee (FTUC). A quasi-independent body, the FTUC was financed by the ILGWU and the federation, but it was not obliged to report its activities to the AFL Executive Council. Consequently, Lovestone was able to carry on the committee's work without interference from the many powerful federation leaders who were initially skeptical of international involvement and suspicious of his political past. The FTUC's anticommunist initiatives gradually won broad support among the AFL hierarchy in what has been called a "premature" cold war policy. Although others held the top posts, Lovestone became the formulator of AFL foreign policy.

As the war came to an end, Lovestone began establishing a network of overseas representatives, many of them former political associates. IRVING BROWN, the FTUC's leading operative in Western Europe, quickly launched an extensive program of AFL aid to noncommunist union groups in France and Italy. The FTUC encouraged opposition leaders within the Communist-dominated French Confédération Générale du Travail to form an independent union structure and successfully lobbied the American military government to permit the organizing of centralized unions in the American zone of occupied Germany. AFL representatives, many of them attached to American embassies or military missions, others employed directly by the federation or the FTUC, were also active in Japan, Indonesia, India, and the Middle East.

Lovestone also continued the AFL's involvement in Latin America. In 1945 Serafino Romualdi, an antifascist Italian emigré who had worked for the ILGWU and the office of Inter-American Affairs, traveled extensively through Latin America as the FTUC's representative. Romualdi sought support for a new inter-American labor federation to rival the Confederation of Latin American Workers (CTAL), which was dominated by radical Mexican union leader Vicente Lombardo Toledano. With assistance and encouragement from Assistant Secretary of State SPRUILLE BRADEN and with support from union groups in Chile, Venezuela, Peru, and other countries, Romualdi's efforts led to the creation of the Inter-American Confederation of Labor in January 1948.

Lovestone's objectives also included breaking up the World Federation of Trade Unions (WFTU), which was founded in 1945 and joined by both Communist and noncommunist unions (including the CIO). In the spring of 1948 the WFTU split over Soviet-initiated attempts to block implementation of the Marshall Plan in Western Europe. The British Trade Union Congress convened a separate meeting of noncommunist unions in London, to which both the AFL and CIO sent delegates. This conference formed the nucleus of the International Confederation of Free Trade Unions (ICFTU), organized formally in December 1949. Two years later the Inter-American Regional Labor Organization was founded as the ICFTU's affiliate in the Western Hemisphere.

During the early postwar years Lovestone believed that U.S. policy makers, either from naivete or procommunist sympathies, were insufficiently aware of the danger of Communist domination of foreign, particularly European labor movements. With the onset of the cold war, however, AFL and government policy became closely linked. The exact nature of these links was only uncovered in 1967, when Thomas Braden, former head of the Division of International Organization Activity of the Central Intelligence Agency (CIA), revealed that, beginning in 1947, FTUC projects in France and Italy received CIA subsidies averaging $2 million annually. The ICFTU was also subsidized by the CIA.

During the 1950s Lovestone's operations came under increasing criticism from many CIO officials who demanded his removal from any policymaking position as a condition for unity with the AFL. However, Lovestone maintained his control of overseas labor operations after the 1955 AFL-CIO merger. As federation president George Meany's chief foreign policy adviser, he was made AFL-CIO director of international affairs in 1963, a post he held until his retirement in 1974. Lovestone also helped build the Committee on the Present Danger of the mid-1970s, which called for higher defense spending and a more strident anticommunist diplomacy, and later provided personnel for the Reagan administration. Lovestone died on March 8, 1990, in New York City. (See *The Eisenhower Years, The Kennedy Years* Volumes)

—TLH

Lovett, Robert A(bercrombie)

(1895–1986) *undersecretary of state, deputy secretary of defense, secretary of defense*

Robert A. Lovett was born on September 14, 1895, in Huntsville, Texas. His grandfather had been an officer in the Confederate army. His father was a lawyer who eventually became president of the Union Pacific and Southern Pacific railways. Lovett entered Yale in 1914. In his junior year his studies were interrupted with U.S. entry into World War I. Lovett helped organize the Yale unit of pilots and commanded the first U.S. Naval Air Squadron, which initiated a lifelong interest in air power. He returned to Yale after the war, in 1919, receiving his B.A. degree that summer. After college Lovett studied for one year at Harvard Law School and Harvard Graduate School of Business Administration. In 1921 he joined his father-in-law's banking firm, Brown Brothers, as a clerk and rose to become a partner in 1926. That year he was elected a director and member of the executive committee of the Union Pacific Railroad. In 1931 helped arrange the merger between Brown Brothers and the Harriman banking house to form Brown Brothers, Harriman & Company.

During the 1930s Lovett's chief business activity was in the field of international investments. Frequent trips to Europe gave him an insider's view of European industry and convinced him that Hitler was building up Germany in preparation for war. Convinced of the importance of air power in the coming war, during 1939 Lovett made a personal tour of most of the aircraft plants in the United States. He recommended ways of improving production to Undersecretary of the Navy JAMES V. FORRESTAL, who passed these along to Undersecretary of the Army ROBERT P. PATTERSON. Patterson was so impressed that he asked Lovett to come to Washington as his special assistant in 1940. In April 1941 Lovett was made assistant secretary of war for air. He helped obtain for the air arm the preferential semi-autonomous status it enjoyed within the army. He also pushed for priority on bomber production in the war effort. Lovett's chief responsibilities during World War II were in the

(left to right) President Truman, Undersecretary of State Robert Lovett, George Kennan, and Charles E. Bohlen, 1947 *(CORBIS)*

area of procurement and production. He encouraged aircraft manufacturers to construct long-range bombers and was a key figure in approving B-36 development. Patterson was quoted as having said, "The fact that our air forces achieved their huge expansion in time was due more to Bob Lovett than to any other man." In November 1945 Lovett resigned from his government post to resume his banking career.

Two years later Secretary of State GEORGE C. MARSHALL asked Lovett, with whom he had become a close friend during the war, to be his undersecretary. Lovett began to serve in this position in July and became known as Marshall's "trouble-shooter." The two men worked well as a team. A Marshall aide once remarked, "he [Marshall] and Lovett were the perfect combination. Lovett was the best description I've ever seen of an alter-ego." Marshall biographer Forrest Pogue contended the two developed a mental connection similar to that of identical twins. Lovett, like Marshall, was a conservative and an internationalist, but also a pragmatist who did not care for either one-world idealists or fanatical anticommunists and saw the connection

between national security and economic stability throughout the world. With similar motives, intent, and dedication, the two men guided the State Department during some of the most difficult years of the cold war. Lovett helped administer the department and served as acting secretary of state during Marshall's frequent absences from Washington. During the summer of 1947 Lovett oversaw the preparation of the Marshall Plan, pressing for assistance based on self-help and mutual aid, and negotiating with Europeans on the rehabilitation of Germany. He was also responsible for getting the U.S. military government in Germany to accept its expanded role in administering the plan.

Lovett proved quite useful in keeping Marshall from publicly denouncing U.S. recognition of Israel. When White House counsel CLARK CLIFFORD argued in behalf of this policy in May 1948, Marshall privately denounced it as a transparent political ploy and said that, if it were adopted, he would vote against Truman if he violated his oath not to become involved in electoral politics. Lovett, who agreed with Marshall on the politics of the policy, feared, as did Clifford, that his strong disagreement would wreck the administration's foreign policy if it became public. Lovett was able to convince Marshall not to come out publicly against de facto recognition and saved the administration from a crisis.

Also in 1948 Lovett became deeply involved in the efforts leading to the formation of the North Atlantic Treaty Organization. In response to growing cold war tensions and the Berlin blockade, the United States moved to form a mutual defense alliance in Western Europe that would also include Germany. In order to overcome opposition from Republican members of Congress who opposed abolishing America's historic position of no entangling alliances and feared the rearmament of Germany, Lovett worked closely with Senator ARTHUR H. VANDENBERG (R-Mich.) to develop the plan. The result of the Lovett-Vandenberg talks was Resolution 329, the Vandenberg Resolution passed in June 1948. The measure gave senatorial approval to the establishment of a regional defense agreement by the United States with other countries under the UN Charter. During the summer of 1948 Lovett headed the American delegation at secret meetings with diplomats from the Brussels Pact countries and Canada in discussions that led to the signing of the North Atlantic Treaty in 1949.

When Marshall resigned in January 1949, Lovett also left to return to banking. After his appointment as secretary of defense the following year, Marshall asked Lovett to accept the post of deputy secretary. Lovett's duties were myriad. He was, as Marshall said, "in complete charge of operations." While Marshall was present at the daily briefings with the Joint Chiefs of Staff and the president, Lovett handled the internal administration, the budget, and the procurement programming of the Pentagon. He was adept at dealing with suppliers, having built up a close rapport with defense industries during the war. One of Lovett's main tasks was the execution of the details of the scheme, proposed by Marshall, to develop an industrial base, which could convert rapidly to munitions production in case of war. Lovett also backed the president and Marshall's decision to cashier DOUGLAS MACARTHUR. He also thought it better to forcibly repatriate prisoners of war to North Korea so as to end the war, whereas Truman insisted on voluntary repatriations.

When Marshall resigned as secretary of defense in September 1951, Truman nominated Lovett as his successor. The banker accepted the position only because Marshall had asked him to stay. Lovett's accomplishments during his short tenure were limited by the slow nature of change in a large bureaucracy. As Lovett commented, "You don't bend the massive defense organization sharply. It will turn only in gradual shifts." In addition, Congress was reluctant to approve dramatic change because of the general belief that a Republican administration would be inaugurated in 1953.

The principal tool Lovett used for directing the Pentagon was the budget. He insisted on seeing not only the final figures for requests by the services but also the figures that demonstrated how the totals were reached. "We're not questioning your assumptions," he told the military, "we just want to know the basis for your decisions." One of Lovett's contributions to long-range defense strength was to firmly establish the preparation of a coordinated defensewide budget. Lovett expanded research and development programs while in office to include missile development and biological and chemical warfare research. Under his direction production of the *Atlas* intercontinental ballistic missile, abandoned in the late 1940s, was started again.

Before the end of his service as secretary of defense, Lovett wrote a long letter to President Truman in which he made recommendations for improving the administration and operation of the Defense Department. This document was released to the press in January 1953, as Truman and Lovett were leaving office. Lovett called for a clarification of the secretary of defense's "direction, authority and control" in relation to the requirement that the three service branches be "separately administered." He argued that the secretary of defense should be, in effect, the deputy of the commander in chief. In addition, he favored universal military training as the most cost efficient method of keeping military forces in the United States to a minimum, while providing an immediately available, basically trained reserve. He also favored a reorganization of the technical services of the armed forces, which he felt overlapped in several areas, thus adding to the difficulties of administration and control.

With the coming of a Republican administration in January 1953, Lovett left government service and returned to banking. During the 1960s Lovett, termed "a leader of the American establishment" by historian ARTHUR M. SCHLESENGER, JR., served as an adviser to John F. Kennedy. He was also a member of several presidential advisory commissions during the decade. Lovett died on May 7, 1986, in Locust Valley, New York. (See *The Kennedy Years* Volume)

—MLB

Lucas, Scott W(ike)
(1892–1968) *member of the Senate*

The son of a southern Illinois tenant farmer, Scott W. Lucas was born on February 19, 1892, in Chandlerville, Illinois. He earned an LL.B. from Illinois Wesleyan University in 1914. After practicing law in Havana, Illinois, he joined the army in World War I as a private and rose through the ranks to be discharged as a lieutenant in 1918. He subsequently became widely admired as the state commander of the American Legion, an important ingredient in his later political popularity. Lucas was state attorney for Mason Company from 1920 to 1925 and chairman of the Illinois State Tax Commission from 1933 to 1934. He attempted to win the Democratic Party's nomination for U.S. senator in 1932, but he was stopped by Chicago's political machine. In 1935 he won a seat in the U.S. House of Representatives that had been left vacant by the death of Lucas's idol, Speaker of the House Henry T. Rainey. Lucas backed Roosevelt's New Deal and later his interventionist foreign policy. Lucas created a national name for himself in 1938 by defeating the Kelly-Nash Democratic machine in the Illinois Democratic senatorial primary. He went on to win the general election that year and was reelected in 1944 with the help of Chicago mayor Edward Kelly.

In the Senate Lucas established an independent voting record. He supported much Fair Deal legislation, including the Employment Act of 1946, the Barkley Amendment of 1948, and the National Housing Act of 1949. Although known as a friend of labor during the early 1940s, he voted inconsistently on that issue during the Truman administration. In 1946 he supported the Case labor disputes bill and declared during the United Mine Workers strike of that year, "If this government has not the power to outlaw strikes of this character, then this government has no power of self-preservation." He crystalized labor's distrust of him when he voted for the Taft-Hartley Act in the Republican-controlled Senate of 1947. However, he reversed himself and voted against the successful attempt to override Truman's veto of the bill. In 1948 Lucas unsuccessfully sought to delete the injunction provision of the act. Lucas supported Truman's foreign policy, including containment, the Marshall Plan, and the North Atlantic Treaty Organization.

Lucas was a strong Democratic partisan who possessed conservative political instincts in the field of civil rights. He supported the unsuccessful 1946 attempt to make the Fair Employment Practices Commission (FEPC) into a permanent body. Four years later, the Senate, at that time nominally under Lucas's leadership, failed to muster the necessary 64 votes to kill a filibuster on a motion to consider new FEPC enabling legislation. Black labor leader A. PHILIP RANDOLPH asserted that Lucas's public affirmations of support involved "transparent, hypocritical tactics" that masked weak sponsorship of the bill. During the 1948 Democratic National Convention, the Illinois senator was greatly angered by the move on the part of the Americans for Democratic Action and its leading spokesman, HUBERT H. HUMPHREY, to insert a strong civil rights plank into the platform. He called Humphrey a "pipsqueak" for pushing what Lucas saw as unnecessary divisive proposals.

In 1946 his Democratic colleagues elected him majority whip and made him majority leader for the 81st Congress when Senator ALBEN W. BARKLEY (D-Ky.) became vice president. Lucas considered this period, 1949–51, the unhappiest of his life. A well-liked Senate colleague, acceptable to Southern Democrats as an honest broker between party sections, he only controlled 40 of the 54 Democratic votes in the Senate. He proved an ineffective leader who could not muster support for the administration's programs. He possessed neither the prestige of his predecessor, Alben Barkley, nor the manipulative skills of his eventual successor LYNDON B. JOHNSON (D-Tex.). His attempts to maintain party unity opened him to charges that he put political loyalty before issues. His weakness was compounded by Truman's lackluster lobbying efforts for his own legislative proposals and by the fact that effective controls in the Senate had been decentralized since the late 1930s, with major power residing in the southern-controlled Democratic Steering Committee dominated by Senator RICHARD B. RUSSELL (D-Ga.). Finally, Lucas's leadership was hurt by the conservative reaction to the dramatic social welfare programs of the Fair Deal.

The 81st Congress passed a new housing bill, increased the minimum wage from 40 cents to 70 cents per hour, and broadened Social Security coverage to include 10 million additional nonagricultural workers. However, the Democratic leadership, often preoccupied with foreign policy and domestic subversion, was unable to pass many of Truman's original proposals on health care, agriculture, civil rights, and federal aid to education. Lucas himself did not agree with Truman's plan for national health insurance. By the fall of 1949 Lucas was warning the president that an increasingly hostile Senate would not even confirm LELAND OLDS to another term as chairman of the Federal Power Commission because he had been too militant an advocate of tough government regulation of private utility ratemaking. Truman ignored Lucas's advice, sent the nomination to the Senate, and then left Lucas virtually alone to lobby on Olds's behalf. The Senate voted against Olds with the Democrats dividing 21 to 13 against him.

During 1950 Lucas became embroiled in the controversy generated when Senator JOSEPH R. MCCARTHY (R-Wisc.) charged that there were a number of Communists and Communist sympathizers in the State Department. In order to avoid having McCarthy's charges become a powerful partisan issue for the Republicans, Lucas proposed Senate Resolution 231 in February, which authorized a bipartisan committee, led by conservative senator MILLARD E. TYDINGS (D-Md.), to investigate the allegations. On the Senate floor Lucas badgered McCarthy about the conflicting number of Communists he had cited to two different audiences. At one point the majority leader stated that if he had made McCarthy's statements, "I would be ashamed of myself for the rest of my life." Not surprisingly, McCarthy later labeled Lucas as a "dupe of the Kremlin."

That same year Lucas played an important role in the passage of the Internal Security Act of 1950, sponsored by Senator PAT MCCARRAN (D-Nev.). The law required all Communist and Communist-front organizations to register with the Attorney General, barred the employment of Communists in defense plants, prohibited the issuance of passports to Communists, and forbade aliens who had been Communists from entering the United States. Truman had wanted to keep the forerunner of this measure, the Mundt-Nixon bill, off the Senate floor in order to kill it by inaction. But Lucas made the parliamentary mistake of failing to schedule another bill, so the Senate was forced to deal with the issue. As a substitute for the measure's registration provisions, Lucas offered an emergency detention plan, sponsored by Senator HARLEY M. KILGORE

(D-W.Va.), which was rejected. Lucas then offered it as an addition to the registration plan. This, too, failed to pass, but a modification of the detention plan was eventually added to the bill by voice vote. The conference report added the Kilgore modification, and the measure was passed in September.

During 1950 Lucas ran for reelection against his old friend EVERETT M. DIRKSEN, a conservative Republican. He lost by a 294,000 margin. Lucas attributed his defeat to his opposition to McCarthy and to a political scandal in Chicago where the Democratic candidate for sheriff had close associations with gangsters, which was publicized by Senator ESTES KEFAUVER's (D-Tenn.) Crime Committee. (Lucas glowered at Kefauver when seeing him after his defeat.) After leaving the Senate Lucas became a prominent lobbyist. He died of a cerebral hemorrhage on February 22, 1968, in Rocky Mountain, North Carolina.

—GB

Luce, Clare Boothe
(1903–1987) *member of the House of Representatives*

Clare Boothe, the daughter of a dancer and a violinist, was born on April 10, 1903, in New York City. She left home at age 16 to work in the city and enroll in a drama school. Four years later she married George T. Brokaw, the millionaire son of a clothing manufacturer. The marriage ended in divorce in 1929. The following year Boothe joined *Vogue* magazine as an editorial assistant and in 1931 became associate editor of *Vanity Fair*. She was promoted to executive editor in 1933. Boothe left the magazine in 1934 to write for the theater. In November 1935 she married HENRY R. LUCE, president of Time, Inc. Over the next five years she devoted most of her time to writing a number of successful Broadway plays, including *The Women*, which ran for 657 performances, *Kiss the Boys Goodbye*, and *Margin for Error*.

Both Clare and Henry Luce were leading Republican internationalists who were critical of President Franklin Roosevelt for not preparing the nation for war. In 1941 on a trip to China she wrote reports for her husband's magazine *Life* on the Sino-Japanese War. After U.S. entry into World War II she traveled to Burma, India, China, and Africa to report on the war. She interviewed for *Life* such significant people as Jawaharlal Nehru, General Joseph

Stillwell, and Chiang Kai-shek (Jiang Jieshi) and his wife. She developed a close relationship with the generalissimo and Madame Chiang. Luce ran for a seat in the U.S. House of Representatives from Connecticut in 1942. Using the slogan "Let's fight a hard war instead of a soft war," she won the November election by a small margin. As Luce's biographer Sylvia Jukes Morris has noted, if a Socialist had not been running, incumbent Democratic congressman Leroy Downs almost surely would have won. Known for her sharp tongue, she became a prominent conservative critic of Franklin Roosevelt. She opposed the president's conduct of the war and his postwar plans and challenged the expansion of government power. In her maiden speech in the House she blasted Vice President HENRY A. WALLACE's "freedom-of-the-air" proposal as "globaloney."

After Harry S Truman became president, Luce continued to criticize Democratic foreign policy. She charged the Roosevelt administration with selling out the Eastern Europeans at Yalta, and she held the Truman administration responsible for Chiang's setbacks in his civil war with the Communists. The Democratic administrations' confused and ambivalent policies toward Moscow, she maintained, encouraged further aggression. In 1945 Luce introduced a bill to acknowledge the national responsibility of the United States for the Yalta surrender of Poland to the Soviet Union. She was also disturbed by the failure of the administration to send economic aid to war-ravaged Europe shortly after the fighting had ended. In 1946 she joined Representative EVERETT M. DIRKSEN (R-Ill.) in introducing a bill to provide food, clothing, and drugs to Europe. Her measure was a forerunner of the Marshall Plan. On domestic legislation Luce was a conservative in economic matters, but she supported civil rights and women's rights legislation. She was a member of the Joint Committee on Atomic Energy and backed the establishment of a civilian-controlled Atomic Energy Commission.

Luce decided not to run for reelection in 1946 because she had been separated from her husband too much. She resumed her career as a playwright, devoting her attention to writing screenplays. One, *Come to the Stable* (1949), was nominated for an Oscar in 1949. The former representative continued active in Republican politics. In her nominating address for Senator ARTHUR H. VANDENBERG (R-Mich.) at the Republican National Convention in

Clare Boothe Luce, 1932 *(Library of Congress, Prints and Photographs Division, Carl Van Vechten Collection)*

1948, she engaged in a blistering attack on the president, whom she called a "man of phlegm, not fire." The Democratic Party, Luce charged, consisted of three wings: "the extreme right, or Jim Crow group, led by lynch-loving Bourbons, sheet-shirted race supremists of the [THEODORE] BILBO ilk; the left, or Moscow, wing of the party, currently masterminded by Stalin's Mortimer Snerd, Henry Wallace; and the center, or Pendergast gang, run by the Wampum and Boodle boys." In contrast, Luce said, the Republican Party stood unified in its desire to elect a President who would be honest and forthright in his positions. She campaigned for Governor THOMAS E. DEWEY during the 1948 race.

Four years later Luce enthusiastically supported the nomination of DWIGHT D. EISENHOWER and actively campaigned for him. In reward, Eisenhower appointed her ambassador to Italy, where she served until 1956. During her tenure she worked with pro-Western politicians and their supporters in the United States to reduce the power of the large

Communist Party in Italy. She was also involved in the Trieste negotiations between Italy and Yugoslavia. Luce resigned her post for reasons of health in 1956. Three years later Eisenhower appointed her ambassador to Brazil. Senator WAYNE MORSE (D-Ore.) waged a vigorous campaign against her confirmation because of her involvement in Italian politics. Although the Senate confirmed the nomination, Luce decided to decline the post because of the trouble Morse had created. During the 1960s Luce continued writing and remained active in Republican politics. She campaigned for Barry Goldwater in 1964. She died in Washington, D.C., on October 9, 1987. (See *The Eisenhower Years* Volume)

—JB

Luce, Henry R(obinson)
(1898–1967) *editor in chief, Time and Time, Inc.*

Henry R. Luce, the son of a Presbyterian missionary, was born in Tengchow, China, on April 3, 1898. He lived in China until he was 14. At 15 he attended the Hotchkiss School in Connecticut and later entered Yale. Luce edited the Yale *Daily News* with classmate Britton Hadden. He called for American intervention in World War I and served a stint stateside in the army. He went back to Yale in 1919 and graduated Phi Beta Kappa a year later and was voted the "most brilliant" member of his class. In 1923, after a brief career as a reporter for the *Chicago Daily News* and the *Baltimore News*, Luce teamed with Hadden and founded *Time*, "a weekly news-magazine aimed to serve the modern necessity of keeping people informed."

Both men considered themselves editors, but during the magazine's formative years, Luce reluctantly served as *Time*'s business manager as a result of losing a coin toss to Hadden. Hadden died in 1929, and Luce took over both the editorial and the business sides of the magazine. Luce was shaken by the death—and the depression—but Time, Inc. continued to prosper with the publication of *Fortune* in 1930 and *Life* in 1936.

Time had no editorial page, but its presentation of the week's news clearly reflected the strong free enterprise, anticommunist, God-fearing philosophy of Luce. "I am biased in favor of God, the Republican Party and free enterprise," he once said. He mixed religion with politics. During a speech to the United Council of Church Women, Luce said, "I

believe that once the Church has accepted its responsibility, it will . . . make its voice clear and strong so that the war-making power of our nation is put under Christian judgment, Christian restraint—and the courage of Christian conviction."

Luce believed the United States should intervene in World War II. After the fall of France in spring 1940, Luce met with President Roosevelt and urged the destroyer-for-bases deal with Great Britain, which FDR implemented. As part of his campaign for intervention, Luce wrote an essay for *Life* titled "The American Century," in which he contended that the United States could decide who won the war, and then create a free and stable world in the aftermath of an Allied victory. He also moved the Republican Party toward an interventionist foreign policy by strongly supporting, if not creating, the candidacy of Democrat-turned-Republican Wendell Willkie. As James L. Baughman has noted Luce would spend the years after the war trying to clarify his brand of American international leadership.

Luce was a vigorous critic of President Truman. Truman had been featured on a *Time* cover and lauded for his efforts as a senator on the War Productions Board (WPB) during World War II. But when Truman became president in 1945, *Time* reported that "he was a man of distinct limitations . . . In his Administration there are likely to be few innovations and little experimentation." Luce thought Truman was "too soft" on communism. Although Luce applauded the Truman Doctrine and the Marshall Plan, he preferred confrontation with the Soviet and Chinese Communists rather than the president's policy of containment.

Because of his childhood there, Luce was always concerned about China. During and after the war Luce was probably the staunchest and most influential supporter of Chiang Kai-shek (Jiang Jieshi), the Nationalist Chinese leader. Luce had orchestrated Madame Chiang's tour of the United States in 1943. Determined to destroy world communism, Luce overlooked the corruption and unpopularity of the Chiang government and often rewrote dispatches from *Time* correspondents in China that portrayed Chiang in a negative light. Dispatches from Theodore H. White, *Time*'s Chunking correspondent, were so severely altered that he protested to Luce what he described as "making *Time* a Chiang house organ." White hung a sign on his office door reading, "Any similarity between this correspondent's dispatches and what appears in *Time* is purely coincidental." White was eventually recalled from China. When Luce returned to China after the war, he believed the United States could avert a civil war between the Nationalists and Mao Zedong's (Mao Tse-tung) Communists. But after a second trip in 1946 Luce became convinced that war was inevitable and blamed Mao and the Soviets. He argued early on for U.S. resistance to the march of communism in Asia and Europe. Luce featured Chiang on *Time*'s cover on seven occasions and constantly lobbied Washington to send more monetary and military aid to Chiang.

When Chiang's government fell in 1949 and he was forced to flee to Taiwan, Luce blamed the Truman administration. His publications singled out Secretary of State DEAN G. ACHESON. *Life* magazine wrote: "It was Acheson who was Truman's chief adviser on basic policy, and Acheson was also Truman's chief alibiist. It was Acheson who was mixed up with the . . . crowd in the State Department who stupidly or deliberately played into Communist hands in Asia."

Luce often used his publications to influence the election of the candidate of his choice. In 1948, dissatisfied with Truman's policy in China, Luce hoped to elect Republican candidate THOMAS E. DEWEY, and perhaps win a cabinet position for himself, by painting Dewey as the frontrunner and Truman as the bumbling incumbent. A Republican administration, Luce believed, would give Chiang the money and manpower he needed to defeat the Chinese Communists. He backed DWIGHT D. EISENHOWER's 1952 candidacy, infuriating conservative champions of Senator ROBERT A. TAFT (R-Ohio) with his magazine's accusation of his camp's "stealing" of southern delegates. Luce became a supporter of assistance to South Vietnam and American intervention in the war there.

Luce fought hard against world communism but ultimately did not support Senator JOSEPH R. MCCARTHY's (R-Wisc.) anticommunist "witch hunt" in the early 1950s, considering it too internally divisive. A conservative on most issues, Luce found himself in the liberal camp on civil rights. Until his death in 1967 Henry Luce believed it was his and America's mission to "help establish Freedom and Order in the world." He died on February 28, 1967, in Phoenix, Arizona.

—SRB

Luckman, Charles

(1909–1999) *president, Lever Brothers Company; chairman, Citizens Food Committee*

Charles Luckman was born on May 16, 1909, in Kansas City, Missouri. He worked his way through the University of Illinois architectural school and graduated as a licensed architect in 1931. There were few construction opportunities in that depression year, so Luckman took a job selling soap for Colgate-Palmolive-Peet. Assigned to Chicago's poor neighborhoods, Luckman set sales records and before long was placed in charge of the Chicago district, then Wisconsin, and then a six-state midwestern sales territory, the company's largest district, by the age of 25.

In 1935 Luckman joined the Pepsodent toothpaste company as national sales manager. At the time Pepsodent was facing a potential nationwide boycott by independent druggists because discount chains were using the toothpaste as a loss leader to attract customers. Luckman embarked on a personal public relations campaign around the country and by the end of his first year had turned Pepsodent's declining sales around. He continued his swift ascent up the corporate ladder, winning a succession of vice presidencies. In 1943 he was named company president. In 1946, at the age of 37, Luckman became president of Lever Brothers, the giant manufacturer of household products, at a salary of $300,000 a year. *Newsweek* cast him as "a boy wonder whose meteoric career rivaled any [Horatio] Alger ever imagined." *Forbes* featured him as one of "America's Fifty Foremost Business Leaders."

With his latest advance Luckman started actively participating in public affairs, becoming a leading business ally of President Truman. In December 1946 Truman appointed him to the 15-member President's Committee on Civil Rights. Luckman helped write the group's report issued in October 1947. Strongly critical of abuses of civil rights throughout the country, the report recommended legislation outlawing the poll tax, lynching, and racially discriminatory practices, and proposed a permanent Fair Employment Practices Commission.

In September 1947, during a severe food shortage in Europe, Truman appointed Luckman chairman of the Citizens Food Committee to launch a food conservation program in America to aid starving Europeans and slow the rise in food prices. Luckman stirred controversy with his attempts to persuade the public to observe meatless Tuesdays and poultryless Thursdays. He urged cattlemen to conserve grain through efficient feeding of livestock and tried to convince such leading industrial users of grain as distillers and bakers, to cut back. He met with mixed success, but upon his resignation in November, he maintained that the committee had achieved its goal of saving 100 million bushels of grain.

During this period Luckman was the author of a large number of magazine articles on national issues. In a *Harper's* article entitle "Labor Relations on a Hard-Boiled Basis," he called on his fellow businessmen to recognize that "labor unions are here to stay" and to stop complaining about high wages and strikes. "Civil Rights Mean Good Business," he argued in *Collier's*. Speaking before the Super Market Institute in November 1946 Luckman urged greater cooperation between management and labor. Luckman also directed the Freedom Train, which was part of Truman's program to resuscitate Western Europe.

In 1950 Luckman left Lever Bros. Profits had declined during his tenure, while the company had fallen further behind its chief competitor, Procter & Gamble, whose earnings had doubled in the same period. With rumors circulating that he was going to Montgomery Ward or the Atomic Energy Commission, Luckman surprised everyone and returned to architecture, his original vocation. He formed a partnership with an old schoolmate and designed $850 million worth of buildings by the time the firm split in 1958. In the 1960s Luckman's projects included New York's Madison Square Garden (to much controversy the much beloved Penn Station was razed to make way for it), the Manned Spacecraft Center in Houston, and the Sports Forum in Los Angeles. In 1967 *Business Week* characterized him as a "conservative Democrat" in an article titled, "He Sells Architecture the Way He Sold Soap." He died on January 25, 1999, in Los Angeles, California.

—TO

M

MacArthur, Douglas

(1880–1964) *supreme commander of Allied powers in the Pacific; commander, United Nations forces in Korea*

The son of a Union army general, Douglas MacArthur was born in Little Rock, Arkansas, on January 26, 1880. The younger MacArthur followed his father into a military career. MacArthur ranked first in the 1903 West Point graduating class. He served in several stateside army posts until U.S. entry into World War I in 1917. During the war he was decorated on 13 occasions and was cited seven times for bravery. In 1918 MacArthur was promoted to brigadier general. After serving as West Point superintendent from 1919 to 1922, MacArthur was assigned to the Philippines. In 1930 he became a four star general and army chief of staff, the youngest in U.S. history. He was responsible for crushing the Bonus Army in 1933. Roosevelt kept him as chief of staff even though he thought him one of the "three most dangerous men in America." From 1935 to 1941 he served as military adviser to the Philippine government. He became a friend of future Filipino president Manuel Quezon. This and his friendship with other high status Filipinos, MacArthur said, had given him an understanding of what he called "Oriental Psychology." In July 1941 MacArthur was named commander of United States Army forces in the Far East. From the outbreak of the war in December 1941 until March 1942, he directed the defense of the Philippines against the Japanese. Ordered to Australia by President Roosevelt, MacArthur became commander of Allied forces in the Southwest Pacific. Starting in late 1942 he opened a three-year offensive against the Japanese, returning to the Philippines in October 1944. He became a five star general in December 1944 and in April 1945 received command of all army forces in the Pacific. Following Japan's surrender in August 1945, President Truman named MacArthur Supreme Commander of the Allied Powers in the Pacific (SCAP) with responsibility to accept the Japanese surrender on the battleship *Missouri* on September 2, 1945.

President Truman approved the Allied occupation policy for Japan that month. Policy was to be determined by the Far Eastern Commission representing the 11 nations that had been at war with Japan. MacArthur was simply to carry out its decisions. The general, however, almost completely disregarded the Far Eastern Commission and paid little attention to advisers and directives sent from Washington. Instead he administered Japan's occupation with the help of trusted men who had been trained in war and experienced in military operations rather than government.

MacArthur's chief aims included the elimination of Japanese militarism in all its forms and the initiation of political, economic, and social reforms to pave the way for a democracy. Rather than vindictive, as the Japanese expected, MacArthur's firm but fair leadership gained him much respect. The military was quickly disarmed, war industries rapidly destroyed, and war crimes trials conducted for those deemed responsible for the war. Under MacArthur's direction the old Diet passed a new constitution, which went into effect on May 3, 1947. It provided for a number of democratic rights, including free press and free speech. The document also stated that Japan renounced forever the right to make war and banned the maintenance of land, sea, and air forces. MacArthur was quite proud of the constitution.

Portrait of General of the Army Douglas A.
MacArthur *(Harry S. Truman Library)*

Thereafter SCAP functioned through directives
that were incorporated into law by the new Japanese
Diet. The police force and school system were
decentralized, large land holdings were broken up,
and some effort was made to destroy the large
industrial combines (Zaibatsu). However, democratic reform remained incomplete, as Truman
and MacArthur wanted the emperor to retain his
position—albeit now only as a symbol. The conservative political parties from before the war and the
old bureaucracy remained largely intact. Business
contributed heavily to these parties that dominated
postwar politics. In late 1947 MacArthur referred to
Japan as the "Switzerland of the Pacific."

At first the administration thought Japan would
become a secondary economic power, alongside
China and Southeast Asia. But civil war and the
Communist victory in the former and colonial war
in the latter destroyed plans to have a pro-America
China dominate the region. So instead, the Truman
administration started a "reverse course" policy to
build up Japan's industries while postponing any further social reform. As Michael Schaller noted, a
conservative MacArthur ironically resisted this policy in order to court liberal support for his own
campaign for the Republican presidential nomination in 1948. However, MacArthur's bid was
crushed in early 1948 by primary defeats, and he
then accepted the new policy. After Truman won
reelection, MacArthur turned economic control of
Japan over to administration officials.

As early as 1946 MacArthur had urged that the
occupation last no longer than three years, but the
Big Four wartime partners failed to conclude a
Pacific peace accord. Following the fall of China in
1949, Russia militated against Japan's recovery. Following the outbreak of war in Korea in June 1950,
MacArthur successfully encouraged the Japanese
government to restrict Communist groups in the
country. To guard against sabotage a 75,000 man
police reserve was established. Without Russian participation, and as a bulwark against communism in
the Pacific, the United States completed a general
peace treaty in September 1951, after MacArthur's
departure.

An ardent anticommunist, MacArthur was
anguished by the fall of China in 1949. He was critical of the United States failure to provide adequate
assistance to Chiang Kai-shek (Jiang Jieshi). He
maintained that the Chinese Communist victory
encouraged further Communist imperialism on
which would jeopardize U.S. security. His beliefs
that the fall of China marked the beginning of
America's crumbling power in Asia was later reen-
forced by its Korean War policy. Ironically, he had
called for withdrawing troops from South Korea
due to his obsession with Taiwan and argued against
defending South Korea from outside attack.

When the Republic of South Korea (ROK) was
formed in August 1948, MacArthur's official connection with the peninsula ceased until North Korean
forces invaded ROK in June 1950. MacArthur
claimed that Washington officials ignored his intelligence reports that such an invasion was impending. With war at hand President Truman named

him commander in chief of United Nations forces in Korea. Truman himself had nothing but scorn for MacArthur, calling him "Mr. Prima Donna, Brass Hat, Five Star MacArthur." Unprepared and undermanned, the UN army was quickly pinned to the Pusan perimeter. In a daring plan MacArthur directed a successful landing behind enemy lines at Inchon on September 15, 1950. MacArthur was confident of victory by the year's end and also confident that the Chinese Communists would not enter the war. He reported this to President Truman at their Wake Island meeting in October 1950.

In late November 1950 UN forces were deep into North Korea and were caught with their overextended lines by contingents of Chinese Communist troops, which had crossed the Yalu River. By early 1951 the Communists had regained much of North Korea. MacArthur charged "that there is no substitute for victory" and demanded that the Yalu River bridges and Manchurian supply depots be destroyed. He also urged that Chiang's Nationalist Army be permitted to invade the mainland. MacArthur related these views by letter to Representative JOSEPH W. MARTIN, JR., (R-Mass.) on March 20, 1951. The administration denied MacArthur's requests. Committed to European reconstruction, fearing Russian intervention if the Nationalist Chinese entered the war, Truman determined to keep the war localized in Korea. MacArthur's public statements on the matter strained his relations with the president. When Representative Martin read MacArthur's letter on the floor of Congress on April 5, 1951, President Truman decided to dismiss MacArthur, which was done on April 11, 1951. But as D. Clayton James and Anne Sharp Wells observed, MacArthur was hardly an "American Caesar"—as he is sometimes depicted—as he stepped down from power and did not try to take over the government.

The general received a tumultuous welcome upon his return to the United States. Although he told a joint session of Congress on April 19, 1951, "that old soldiers never die, they just fade away," MacArthur remained a public figure for some time. He testified before a congressional committee that his plan to take the war to the Chinese mainland would have resulted in total victory. But the chairman of the Joint Chiefs of Staff General of the Army OMAR BRADLEY famously quipped that a war with China would be the "wrong war, at the wrong place, at the wrong time, and against the wrong

enemy" and feared Europe, which the chiefs and the administration considered more important than Asia, would become endangered. He delivered the keynote address to the Republican National Convention in 1952 and also was a candidate for the party's presidential nomination. But the keynote address fell flat, and he was not nominated. In the same year he became chairman of the board for Remington Rand. He spent his later years quietly living at New York's Waldorf-Astoria. For service to his country, Congress ordered a gold medal struck for MacArthur in 1962 and in the same year he received West Point's Sylvanus Thayer Award. MacArthur died on April 5, 1964, in Washington, D.C.

—TML

McCabe, Thomas B(ayard)
(1893–1982) *chairman, Board of Directors, Federal Reserve System*

McCabe was born on July 11, 1893, in Whaleyville, Maryland. He earned a B.A. in economics from Swarthmore in 1915. He joined the Scott Paper Company as a salesman a few months after graduation. Following service in the army during World War I, he rejoined Scott Paper, becoming assistant sales manager and, within a decade, president of the company. He reinvigorated the company. In 1916 Scott Paper had only one factory with 500 employees; by 1950, it had 60 mills worldwide with 40,000 workers. His success in business convinced President Franklin Roosevelt to bring him into the public sector. In 1937 McCabe accepted the part-time post of director of the Federal Reserve Bank in Philadelphia. He remained an officer of the Philadelphia bank for the next 11 years.

During World War II McCabe took leave from Scott Paper to serve with the government. He was a member of the Business Advisory Council of the Department of Commerce, a deputy director of the Office of Production Management, and deputy lend-lease administrator. Between 1945 and 1946 he was the army-navy liquidation administrator, charged with the disposal of military surplus materials overseas and the settlement of lend-lease accounts. His handling of the sales of supplies to China was later criticized by both the left and the right. The Chinese Communists maintained that delivery of goods exclusively to the central government at Nanking constituted "civil war aid." A

Senate committee charged that the items sold had included airplanes without tails. McCabe denied irregularities.

McCabe was a lifelong Republican with a reputation as a conservative. Nevertheless, in January 1948 Truman asked him to become the chairman of the Federal Reserve Board. The president had offered the job to several others before McCabe, but all, anticipating Truman's defeat in the November elections, declined. McCabe accepted. The appointment raised a furor. McCabe was to replace MARRINER S. ECCLES, who had been chairman for 12 years and had been widely supposed secure for a fourth term. Eccles was attempting to block the growth of the Bank of America at the time, believing the bank's acquisition policies were in violation of the antitrust laws. During confirmation hearings several senators questioned McCabe about his willingness to continue actions related to the Bank of America case. After two-and-a-half months of testimony and deliberation, the Senate confirmed him.

The Federal Reserve System under McCabe did not depart from the policies pursued under Eccles, who remained on the Reserve Board and continued to have a major role in shaping decisions. McCabe carried forward Eccles's struggle to end Treasury domination of the Federal Reserve and free it from supporting interest rates on government securities. These efforts initially had only limited success.

With the onset of the Korean War, Secretary of the Treasury JOHN W. SNYDER attempted to appeal to patriotism to persuade the board to agree to honor its World War II commitment to support the price of treasury bonds. McCabe thought keeping interest rates artificially low just to help the Treasury Department, "feeds the fires of inflation" and preferred open-market operations that were concerned with the whole economy and not those devoted solely to keeping government payments low. During meetings in 1950 and 1951, McCabe attempted to avoid a confrontation with the administration without giving the specific commitments that the president and secretary were seeking.

In January 1951 Snyder attempted to force the board's hand. Without consulting McCabe he announced that the board had conceded to support long term Treasury bonds at 2.5 percent, the existing rate. McCabe privately protested to Truman. However, as a Truman appointee, he felt that he could not make a public protest without resigning.

Therefore Eccles stated the Federal Reserve's position to the public.

Truman, attempting to resolve the dispute, met with the board and its Open Market Committee (which made day-to-day interest rate decisions) on January 31, 1951. Truman supported Snyder's position. He recalled his own experience as an investor with falling bond prices after World War I and said he did not want a similar drop in the value of government obligations to happen again. He wanted to maintain public confidence in government credit. McCabe, in reply, affirmed that he and his associates understood the importance of public confidence. He again avoided confrontation and commitment saying that he would consult Snyder before acting on interest rates and would appeal differences to the president.

Following this meeting the Reserve Board members gathered in executive session. Several denounced McCabe's circumspection. A motion to support interest rates as the president had requested was taken up and defeated by a two-to-one margin. The next day the White House announced to the press that the Federal Reserve had committed itself to stable interest rates. Eccles denied this assertion to reporters. The board assembled a day later and instructed McCabe to meet with the president and to show him the board's own written account of the January 31 meeting. McCabe failed to see Truman and early that evening the White House released to the press a letter from Truman to McCabe asserting once again that the Reserve had agreed to support prices on bonds. The chairman was out of Washington at the time. Eccles, therefore, took it upon himself to release the board's memorandum concerning the meeting with Truman to the newspapers. Publication of the account coalesced public and congressional opinion behind the Federal Reserve. McCabe and others for the board negotiated through February with the Treasury. In early March Truman approved an agreement ending the Reserve's commitment to support government security prices. He proclaimed that the Fed had "maintained its integrity" by not having been made a victim of political maneuvering.

Six days after "The Accord" was announced, McCabe resigned. In reality Snyder and Truman told McCabe that he was ineffective, and he resigned under pressure. He returned to Scott Paper, where he had remained as president throughout his time as Federal Reserve chairman. He also continued to be active in public affairs. Between 1960 and 1963 McCabe served as public governor on the Board of the New York Stock Exchange. In 1962 he became chairman of Scott Paper. He retired in 1968. McCabe died on May 27, 1982, in Swarthmore, Pennsylvania.

—CSJ

McCarran, Patrick A(nthony)
(1876–1954) *member of the Senate*

Pat McCarran was born on August 8, 1876 in Reno, Nevada. After graduating from the University of Nevada in 1901, McCarran began ranching and, in his spare time, studying law. He was elected to the state legislature in 1903 and two years later set up a legal practice in the boom mining towns of Nevada. In 1912 he won a six-year term on the Nevada Supreme Court, spending his final two years as chief justice. McCarran then returned to private practice in Reno. His first attempt to capture the Democratic nomination for the U.S. Senate failed in 1926. He gained the nomination and defeated Tasker Oddie, a popular Republican, in the Roosevelt landslide of 1932.

McCarran quickly emerged as a leader of conservative anti–New Deal forces in the upper house. He led the fight against Roosevelt's 1937 bill altering the composition of the Supreme Court. McCarran fought from 1939 to 1941 what he saw as FDR's move toward war. Because of his opposition to the president, McCarran had to fight for renomination in 1938 and 1944. He won each time. By 1945 McCarran was the top politician in the state of Nevada. McCarran supported Truman in 1948. In 1950, McCarran easily swamped his Democratic opponent in the primary, and he went on to crush the Republican candidate in the autumn. Yet as McCarran biographer Jerome E. Edward reports, although McCarran was top politician in Nevada by the mid-1940s, he was too divisive to excel at being a political boss. A representative of a silver mining region, he continually agitated for higher silver prices, prompting one critic to describe him as "silver-haired, silver-tongued and silver-minded." During World War II, after Senator Key Pittman's (D-Nev.) death, McCarran became the acknowledged head of the silver bloc in Congress. He led many filibusters to make the government unnecessarily stockpile silver. This activity diminished his reputation. He also called for an expansion of Amer-

ican aviation, and, during World War II, he championed a separate air arm in the national defense force. He wrote the 1946 Airport Act, which allocated federal funds for building airports. On other domestic issues he maintained a pro–organized labor record and voted against the Taft-Hartley Act of 1947. The senator won the support of the American Federation of Labor and the railroad brotherhoods, but the Congress of Industrial Organizations strongly opposed McCarran, mostly because of his prewar isolationism and opposition to much of Roosevelt's domestic policy.

In the postwar years McCarran led a coalition of conservative Republicans and Democrats pressing for tougher anticommunist legislation. McCarran was convinced of a "colossal" Communist conspiracy intent on subversion and espionage. While he was often compared to Senator JOSEPH R. MCCARTHY (R-Wisc.), McCarran's approach to anticommunism differed in style and emphasis. McCarthy offended many of his colleagues with his controversial investigations. McCarran, on the other hand, had an unquestioned instinct for the quieter "traditional levers of congressional power." He focused his energy on developing comprehensive antisubversion legislation. As chairman of the Judiciary Committee, his influence grew out of his specialization and expertise in the areas of internal security and immigration. Another factor in his success lay in his freedom from Democratic Party discipline. He willingly challenged President Truman and liberal Democrats and often aligned himself with conservative Republican legislators. At the end of his third term McCarran was one of the most powerful senators in Congress. In 1944–46 and again from 1949 to 1953, he chaired the Judiciary Committee. Herbert Block (Herblock) began depicting him unfairly as an unshaven slob, a precursor of the cartoonist's later depictions of RICHARD M. NIXON and Joseph McCarthy. *Time* listed him as an "expendable" senator: "pompous, vindictive, and power grabbing."

McCarran's interest in national security legislation remained constant throughout the Truman years. In 1947 he introduced a rider to the State Department appropriations bill that allowed the department to fire any employee whose actions it considered harmful to the national interest. McCarran sponsored the most comprehensive and controversial anticommunist bill of the period. The internal security bill of 1950 incorporated provisions from several antisubversion bills, including the unsuccessful Mundt-Nixon bill of 1948. The main weapon of McCarran's measure was the exposure of alleged subversives through registration of legally determined Communist and Communist-front groups. It also tightened safeguards against espionage and sedition, stiffening penalties, and extending the statute of limitations. Provisions in the bill allowed the Justice Department to bar from immigration, detain, or deport subversive aliens. McCarran reported the measure from committee on August 17, just days after Truman had characterized the legislation as "unnecessary, ineffective and dangerous." In response to critics of his Internal Security bill, McCarran said, "This bill does not contain one iota of hysteria, nor is it the cry of alarmists, nor does it contravene any of our basic Constitutional concepts."

Liberal and moderate opponents argued that the registration procedures were cumbersome and would endanger American liberties guaranteed by the First and Fifth Amendments. A group of Senate liberals, led by PAUL H. DOUGLAS (D-Ill.) and HARLEY M. KILGORE (D-W.Va.) proposed a substitute emergency detention plan as a means of undercutting the McCarran proposal. The "concentration camp bill," as it became known, permitted the attorney general to intern suspected subversives when the president declared an internal security emergency. The liberals were embarrassed, however, when, in a series of complicated parliamentary maneuvers, Kilgore's proposal was added to the McCarran legislation. The bill passed both houses on September 17 by lopsided margins. The *New York Times* reported that many legislators who had criticized the bill in debate voted for its final passage because they felt it was "too risky politically to vote against anti-Communist legislation in this election year." Truman vetoed the bill with a strongly worded message on September 22, but Congress overrode his veto.

In 1951, as head of the newly created Internal Security Subcommittee, McCarran began investigations into Communist influence and activities in unions, the entertainment industry, and communications. He also probed the influx of "subversive" aliens and possible espionage by Communist-bloc diplomats. The subcommittee's investigation of Professor OWEN LATTIMORE received the most public attention. McCarran believed Lattimore had acted as a "conscious agent of the Communist conspiracy" in

undermining and betraying the cause of the Nationalist Chinese. Lattimore denied the charges in the spring of 1952. That year the panel investigated possible Communist influence in higher education and subversive activities by U.S. citizens employed by the United Nations. The probe produced controversial firings of several UN employees. McCarran also investigated the International Union of Mine, Mill and Smelter Workers, which had opposed him in Nevada and had been expelled from the CIO for being Communist-dominated. When Truman tried to appoint a commission headed by refined admiral Chester Nimitz to look into the issue of internal security (set up mainly as a counterweight to McCarran and McCarthy) McCarran manuevered to keep in the Judiciary Committee he chaired routine conflict of interest legislation for commission members and staff. The commission resigned without any action.

McCarran backed Truman's resistance to communism in Europe, voting for the Marshall Plan and the North Atlantic Treaty. A conservative Catholic, McCarran sympathized with the Franco dictatorship in Spain. He often advocated the improvement of American relations with the Madrid government. He did attack the administration's Far Eastern Policy. He criticized the handling of American-Chinese relations, charging that Chiang Kai-shek (Jiang Jieshi) had been abandoned to the Communists. He denounced "desk-bound intellectuals" who, he claimed, had produced "statesmanship at the level of the psychopathic ward." He successfully pressed for loans and U.S. military aid to the Nationalists in 1949 and 1950.

McCarran traced much of the alleged domestic subversion to immigrants from Communist-dominated areas of the world. He expressed his concern by spearheading congressional efforts to obtain more restrictive immigration and nationality legislation. In 1948 the senator helped formulate the displaced persons bill, permitting the admission of some 200,000 refugees. Critics claimed that the measure discriminated against Jews and Catholics from Eastern Europe. McCarran successfully blocked liberal revisions of the bill in committee until 1950, when new legislation was passed allowing freer immigration.

In the winter of 1952 McCarran and Representative FRANCIS E. WALTER (D-Pa.) introduced a complete codification and revision of U.S. immigration, naturalization, and nationality laws. The McCarran-Walter Act eliminated race as a bar to immigration and to naturalization but retained the principle of national origins. The census of 1920 was used for allocating immigration quotas. Critics of the bill, such as Representative EMANUEL CELLER (D-N.Y.), pointed out that the census formula discriminated against Asians and Eastern, Central, and Southern Europeans who were not present in great numbers in 1920. In response McCarran warned against "opening the gates to a flood of Asiatics." He claimed the bill was framed with the security of the United States in mind, because "if this oasis of the world should be overrun, perverted, contaminated, or destroyed, then the last flickering light of humanity will be extinguished." The measure also broadened the grounds for the exclusion and deportation of aliens. After passage of the bill in late May 1952, Truman vetoed it, claiming the legislation would "intensify the repressive and inhumane aspects of our immigration procedures." McCarran said Truman's veto measure conformed to the Communist Party line and called it "one of the most un-American acts I have ever witnessed in my public career." Congress overrode the veto.

The new legislation became a major campaign issue in the fall, as both presidential candidates disassociated themselves from the act. In October Democratic candidate ADLAI E. STEVENSON tried to "read" McCarran out of the party. McCarran responded that the liberal Stevenson "wouldn't know a Democrat if he saw one," and refused to support the Illinois governor whom he thought was a Fabian Socialist.

During the Eisenhower administration McCarran continued his attempts to limit immigration. In 1953 and 1954 he backed the unsuccessful Bricker Amendment, a constitutional revision aimed at curbing presidential treaty-making power. One of McCarthy's few Democratic backers, he attacked censure moves against the Wisconsin senator in 1954. Had he lived he would have voted against censuring McCarthy and might have carried other Democrats with him.

As Edwards noted, the senator was at the peak of his power in Nevada in 1950, but it began to wane as more and more people flooded the state. The industry McCarran had been associated with the most, mining, was in decline, and he was caught off guard by the rise of the gambling and tourism industry. By 1954 McCarran's status in the Nevada Democratic Party was increasingly moribund; he

had no protégé running for governor. That year, Vail Pittman, Key Pittman's son, won the gubernatorial primary, and McCarran announced he would support the whole Democratic ticket—probably because of his weakening position in the Nevada Democratic Party. He probably wanted a fifth term in 1956 and may have been put under pressure by the AFL and the party to campaign. He had run for office 12 times and did not want to give up the power he had accumulated in Congress. Also McCarran may have seen himself as indispensable in fighting Communists. But reelection would have been tough. On September 28, 1954, after addressing a political rally in Hawthorne, Nevada, McCarran collapsed and died instantly—a nitroglycerin pill still in his hand. One critic later said McCarran damaged the Democratic Party in Nevada with his divisiveness, and his machine did not survive him. (See *The Eisenhower Years* Volume)

—JF

McCarthy, Joseph R(aymond)
(1909–1957) *member of the Senate*
Born on November 14, 1909, in Grand Chute, Wisconsin, Joseph R. McCarthy, Jr., was the fifth of seven children. He spent his early years on his father's northwestern Wisconsin farm. A shy, awkward, and unattractive child, McCarthy was favored by his mother, who admonished him to succeed. McCarthy quit school after completing the eighth grade. A brief chicken farming venture failed after personal illness, and, at age 19, McCarthy returned to school; he completed four years of high school in one year. McCarthy attended Marquette University, where he excelled as an athlete and student leader while holding numerous odd jobs. He earned a law degree in 1935.

McCarthy never prospered as an attorney and soon turned to politics. As a Democrat, he ran unsuccessfully for Shawano County attorney in 1936. Three years later he became a Republican and won election as 10th circuit court judge. On the bench McCarthy created controversy because of his quick divorce settlements and overall tempestuous conduct.

With U.S. participation in World War II, McCarthy waived deferment and joined the marines. He served as an intelligence officer, briefing and debriefing marine pilots stationed on the Solomon Islands in the South Pacific. He voluntarily flew on combat flights, and in his political campaigns thereafter billed himself as "Tail Gunner Joe."

In 1944, while still in uniform, McCarthy ran for the Republican senatorial nomination against incumbent Alexander H. Wiley. U.S. Marine Corps regulations forbade McCarthy from seeking public office and giving political addresses. McCarthy disregarded both dictums. Although Wiley won, McCarthy ran second in a field of four and ingratiated himself with many Republican voters.

Two years later McCarthy outmaneuvered several prospective foes for the 1946 senatorial nomination and faced incumbent senator Robert F. La Follette, Jr. (R-Wisc.). La Follette, heir to Wisconsin's greatest political family, had been, though originally a Republican, reelected in 1934 and 1940 on the Wisconsin Progressive Party line. His independence alienated the conservative Republican state party leaders, who drew upon their immense organizational and financial advantages to defeat him. His opportunistic switch back to the Republican Party also angered them. McCarthy campaigned tirelessly and criticized La Follette for his close ties to organized labor (then especially unpopular because of postwar strike), his role in winning congressional salary increases, his wartime profits from a 25 percent interest in a Milwaukee radio station, and what McCarthy viewed as his general inattention to constituent needs. Furthermore, McCarthy assailed La Follette's isolationism before 1941 and contrasted it with his own, somewhat exaggerated, war record. In a historic upset, McCarthy narrowly beat La Follette by 5,500 votes after cutting into the senator's normally strong urban, working-class support. In the fall campaign McCarthy faced little difficulty because of Wisconsin's strong GOP following and voter dissatisfaction with the Democratic Party's economic policies. He easily won election in November with 62 percent of the vote and thus became a member of the GOP Senate's freshman "Class of 1946."

From the time of his inaugural press conference in Washington, McCarthy set himself apart as a flamboyant, bombastic figure. On Capitol Hill in December 1946, he called upon President Truman to draft striking mine workers into the army. If the miners through their union leader, JOHN L. LEWIS, then refused to return to work, he advocated their court-martial. During the writing of the Taft-Hartley Act in 1947 McCarthy proposed an amendment compelling union leaders to inform employers of any union members belonging to loosely defined "Communist" associations and approve their dismissal. The bill's Senate sponsor, Senator ROBERT A. TAFT (R-Ohio), quickly dismissed the proposition.

McCarthy's position on labor and other domestic affairs generally resembled that of the conservative Republican wing. He did, however, hold to his more internationalist foreign policy views. He endorsed aid to Greece and Turkey, the Marshall Plan, and the North Atlantic Treaty. But despite his Irish-German-Catholic, working-class background and rough-hewn appeal, McCarthy possessed no "populist" pretensions in his Senate votes. He consistently voted for legislation favored by business interests.

McCarthy associated with some of Washington's most notorious lobbyists from the very outset of his Senate service. Pressed by sugar interests, he forced a lifting of sugar rationing five months ahead of schedule after confusing, through insult and innuendo, the Department of Agriculture and supporters of rationing during a March 1947 debate. In return a Pepsi Cola lobbyist endorsed a $20,000 note for McCarthy, whom wags dubbed "the Pepsi-Cola Kid." In 1959 Richard Rovere wrote that McCarthy "fought like a tiger for full production of soft drinks."

At no time did McCarthy better reveal his skill and allegiance to special interests than in the 1947–48 fight for housing legislation. McCarthy helped to weaken an omnibus housing bill sponsored by Senators Taft, ROBERT F. WAGNER (D-N.Y.), and ALLEN J. ELLENDER (D-La.). Appointed to a special joint committee formed to investigate the problem and recommend legislation, he managed in August 1947 to deny the chairmanship to Senator CHARLES W. TOBEY (R-N.H.), a proponent of public housing. Through a close reading of the rules, he forced the election of Representative Ralph A. Gamble (R-N.Y.), who held no expertise in the field but was much less inclined toward federal aid. McCarthy worked hard on the Gamble panel and used its regional open hearings as a forum against public housing by hand-picking witnesses and foes of the Taft-Wagner-Ellender measure. McCarthy disapproved of the bill's provisions for slum clearance, veterans' cooperatives, public housing generally, and middle-class units specifically. After the House refused to act on the measure, both chambers agreed to McCarthy's substitute, which replaced public housing and slum clearance sections with federal loans to private builders. Truman reluctantly signed the measure into law in August.

McCarthy gained personally from his role in that legislative battle. A Milwaukee construction firm gave him $10,000, ostensibly for writing a brief pamphlet defending private housing. Actually his staff penned the short pamphlet with research assistance from the Federal Housing Authority and the Library of Congress. Still another housing lobbyist presented McCarthy with $5,400 to pay for crap-game losses.

During 1948 McCarthy aided the presidential nomination campaign of HAROLD E. STASSEN. McCarthy had modeled his foreign policy stance after Stassen's internationalism; Stassen in turn may well have been influenced by McCarthy in his attempts to make domestic communism an issue in the GOP primaries. Helping Stassen in the Wisconsin contest, McCarthy sent out numerous letters critical of one of Stassen's rival candidates, General DOUGLAS MACARTHUR. MacArthur was due "for retirement," he wrote, not the burden of the presidency; McCarthy obliquely noted the general's divorce and remarriage. In an upset, Stassen won the primary.

McCarthy increasingly alienated his Senate colleagues—both Republican and Democratic—and found himself groping for power in the 1949 session. One of McCarthy's most controversial actions came during the June–May probe of the army's prosecution of German SS soldiers for the execution of 150 U.S. prisoners of war at Malmédy, Belgium, during World War II. Encouraged by a wealthy Milwaukee German American and mindful of Wisconsin's large German-American population, he first disrupted proceedings, and then quit the panel over its alleged bias in favor of the army. He attacked the special subcommittee chairman, Senator RAYMOND E. BALDWIN (R-Conn.), for "a deliberate and clever attempt to whitewash the American military" for which he held Baldwin to be "criminally responsible." The distraught chairman resigned from the Senate shortly after the incident. Reporters soon voted McCarthy the upper chamber's "worst senator."

In February 1950 McCarthy found an issue that rapidly made him one of the most powerful and controversial men in the Senate.

According to Richard M. Fried, McCarthy had not planned a career of anticommunism when he

went to Wheeling, West Virginia, to make a Lincoln Day address before a group of Republican women on February 9, 1950. McCarthy had been trying to come up with a vehicle for political self-promotion and survival. Having dismissed crime and pensions as issues, he came to Wheeling with two speeches: one on housing, the other on communism. With the host's encouragement, he used the latter. It is not clear what exactly McCarthy said in Wheeling. Critics claimed he said: "I have here in my hand a list of 205" Communists that Secretary of State Dean Acheson knew to be subversives, "who nevertheless are still working and shaping the policy" of the State Department. McCarthy at one point confirmed using the 205 figure, then later denied using it and said it was 57, and a witness at the speech claimed that he said "over fifty persons of known communistic affiliations." However, a radio station employee present claimed he had said 205, and the Associated Press and the United Press reported the number as 205, and that quickly caused a stir. In reality, he had no list of names.

According to historian Thomas C. Reeves, McCarthy apparently did not realize the uniqueness of using exact numbers and claiming to have the names of subversives—Republicans had been contending the presence of Communists in government for some time—although he was quite happy with the attention he received. The State Department denied the charge and demanded that he name the names of the alleged Communists. Truman dismissed the speech's claim as fraudulent. The press reveled in a controversial and newspaper-selling story and puffed McCarthy up. Although admitting McCarthy had raised a legitimate issue, Democrats launched broadsides at him for recklessness.

A short time later McCarthy named four people in Reno, Nevada, who, according to writer Arthur Herman, were security or loyalty risks, despite the denial of the State Department: Gustavo Duran, Mary Jane Keeney, JOHN STEWART SERVICE, and Harlow Shapely. Duran had been a soldier in the Loyalist army during the Spanish Civil War and had been accused of being a part of the Stalinist secret police that worked to eliminate Trotskyites and anarchists. McCarthy's critics dismissed the accusation as Francoist propaganda, despite testimony against him by Spain's former Socialist prime minister. However, he no longer worked at the State Department at the time of McCarthy's accusations. Mary Jane Keeney and her husband

Philip had become agents for Soviet military intelligence just before he entered the Office of Strategic Services, and she entered the Bureau of Economic Warfare during World War II. They were later transferred to KGB control, and Philip by then had transferred to MacArthur's staff in Japan and Mary Jane to the Allied Staff on Reparations in Germany and then the Federal Economic Administration, which became part of the State Department in 1946. FBI agents broke into her apartment and found her diary, which listed her meetings with KGB agents. The Keeneys were dismissed but later Mary Jane found employment with the U.S. delegation to the UN. She was still a State Department employee in 1950. Service had been one of the China Hands, experts on China who served there before the Communist takeover. He had become convinced that Mao Zedong (Mao Tse-tung) and his Communist followers were agrarian reformers and democrats. He was sent back to Washington from China because of his views in 1945. Here he began to hand over sensitive State Department documents to the staff of the journal *Amerasia*, even though he knew one of its staff members had Communist connections. Although he had been cleared of any espionage charge, at the very least Service was guilty of gross indiscretion, and he was still at State in 1950. Shapely was an astronomer and a member of the U.S. delegation to UNESCO. He also was a fellow traveler who had joined various Communist-front organizations, eight of which were on the Attorney General's list of organizations to which government employees could not belong.

McCarthy recounted what he had said in Wheeling later that month on the Senate floor and read excerpts from summaries of State Department loyalty files. By changing their wording, he made the cases sound more ominous than they were. At the urging of both parties, a Senate investigative subcommittee was established with MILLARD E. TYDINGS (D-Md.) as chairman. Tyding's committee tried to discredit McCarthy more than to determine the truth of his charges. The hearings quickly became a partisan free-for-all, which undermined their credibility as being objective, and caused McCarthy supporters to say the Democrats were engineering a whitewash of the State Department. The administration's initial unwillingness to surrender its loyalty files on government employees weakened the panel's case further.

McCarthy named 10 people to the committee as security risks. He seemed to flounder for a time, but conservative Republicans who were still angry from Truman's demagogic attacks on them in the 1948 election egged McCarthy on, and soon he received assistance in his crusade from FBI director J. EDGAR HOOVER and Representative RICHARD M. NIXON (R-Calif.). Senator ROBERT A. TAFT (R-Ohio) was alleged to have said he should keep "talking, and if one case doesn't work out he should proceed with another." (He denied ever making the statement.) Many moderate Republicans disliked McCarthy's tactics, but feared any attack on him would further divide the GOP between its eastern, internationalist, and moderate wing from its midwestern, isolationist, and conservative wing. McCarthy took a risk to regain the initiative by naming an academic and occasional State Department adviser, OWEN LATTIMORE, as the "top Russian spy." He backed off the espionage charge later and simply referred to him as the " 'architect' of our far eastern policy" (i.e., he had helped "lose" China to the Communists.) Lattimore denounced McCarthy and was informed after he testified that an FBI file summary had cleared him and had been available to the committee. McCarthy then produced former Communist LOUIS F. BUDENZ. Budenz claimed that Lattimore had been in charge of formulating the Communist line that Mao and his followers were mere agrarian reformers. Yet Budenz's testimony could not be verified and, even though the FBI had debriefed him countless times, he never mentioned Lattimore until just before he was to testify. Yet Budenz raised doubts about Lattimore and made even State Department spokesman John Peurifoy waver. Lattimore was not proved to be a spy but he did lean to the left in his views on China and Russia (including a defense of the Soviet purges in 1938.) Lattimore had adhered to the Communist anti-intervention line during the Nazi-Soviet Pact and changed to an interventionist tone when Germany invaded Russia in 1941. He backed Chiang Kai-shek (Jiang Jieshi) when the Russians did, and shifted when the Russians reversed course. Lattimore had advised Marshall at a critical 1948 meeting and convinced the secretary to cut aid to Chiang because support for the generalissimo had damaged America's image in the Far East. He also urged pulling out of Korea and Japan, and saying the latter could stay afloat by coming to terms with Communist China. Although the Democrats on the

Tydings Committee proclaimed Lattimore's innocence, many observers held him in suspicion and later the Senate Internal Security Subcommittee of virulent anti-communist Democrat PAT MCCARRAN (D-Nev.) was more critical of Lattimore.

Lattimore was never proven to be a Soviet agent. However, the Institute of Pacific Relations (IPR), where he edited one of its journals, *Pacific Affairs*, hired at least eight people who turned out to be Communist agents. Lattimore also had a close friendly relationship with Franklin Roosevelt adviser Lauchlin Currie, later revealed to be a Soviet agent, who had sent Lattimore to Chinese Nationalist leader Chiang as Roosevelt's representative and who later told Lattimore to hire spy Michael Greenberg as his successor as editor of *Pacific Affairs*. Lattimore also hired Chen Han-shen to help him edit the journal in the 1930s. Chen also turned out to be a Communist spy. Chen said he never told Lattimore his true mission, but Herman has argued that given that he had hired him through Comintern channels, it is difficult to believe he did not know what kind of person he would receive. Ronald Radosh and Harvey Klehr have argued that even if Lattimore was not a Communist, he was certainly an "opportunist."

McCarthy next named PHILIP JESSUP, a former Columbia University professor and ambassador at large. McCarthy had mentioned Jessup on the first day of testimony as some one with an "unusual affinity for Communist causes." Jessup was brought from a mission to Pakistan to refute the case. Jessup claimed that McCarthy's accusations undermined American foreign policy and denied being a member of Communist-front organizations in the 1930s. McCarthy was not allowed to cross-examine the ambassador.

McCarthy went to the Senate floor to make his charges. He pointed to Jessup's membership in some pro-Soviet front organizations in the 1930s, a rather weak case for treason in this instance. Jessup had also been vice chairman of the IPR and research editor for the institute's official journal, *Far Eastern Survey*. McCarthy claimed the ambassador had originated the journal's attacks on Chiang, which had actually been the work of Communists. Jessup undoubtedly had knowledge of such essays, but that connection was too tangential to matter. In the end, McCarthy called Jessup "a well-meaning dupe." According to Herman, Jessup's willingness to listen to the pro-communist ideologues at the IPR could have led him to take positions that aided Communists like Mao. For instance, Jessup had urged the cutting of aid to Chiang in 1948 and recognizing Red China when the Communists took over in 1949.

Meanwhile, support for McCarthy grew with Republicans and the public. Tydings urged the president to allow the committee to see the loyalty files, and he reluctantly agreed. But this did not resolve the issue as McCarthy claimed they had had incriminating information removed to protect the guilty. The committee's Democratic majority—over the sharp dissent of Republican members—finally issued a report that sharply condemned McCarthy for a "hoax." Senators lined up along party lines for and against the majority report.

In late June North Korea invaded South Korea. The Korean War and the earlier fall of China to the Communists made charges of a betrayal of America's Far Eastern policy seem plausible to many people. McCarthy went on the hustings for Republican candidates in the autumn of 1950, charging Democrats with being soft on communism, or worse. Particularly notable was the loss of McCarthy's bête noire, Tydings. McCarthy had spent considerable time and effort on behalf of Tyding's GOP opponent JOHN MARSHALL BUTLER. The results shocked experienced observers, virtually all of whom had expected the incumbent to win easily in the traditionally Democratic state. Several other Democratic critics of McCarthy, including Senate Majority Leader SCOTT W. LUCAS of Illinois, also went down to defeat. Although McCarthy's effect in these elections has been greatly exaggerated, he appeared at the time to have great clout with the electorate, making Senate colleagues even more timid to attack him.

Yet even prior to Tydings's loss, McCarthy had assumed a position in the national Republican leadership. In July 1950 he had reluctantly endorsed American involvement in the Korean conflict, a war he deemed the end product of past policy made by "that group of Communists, fellow travelers and dupes in our State Department." In April 1951 he accused Truman of allowing the British prime minister to make U.S. foreign policy as well. Informed of General Douglas MacArthur's dismissal as U.S. commander in Korea, McCarthy forgot his 1948 belief that the general should retire and told reporters that "the son of a bitch [Truman] ought to be impeached." Through 1950–52, however, he concentrated most of his fire on Secretary of State DEAN G. ACHESON, who had earned the suspicion of many Republicans as early as January 1950 when he defended ALGER HISS, a former assistant accused of espionage.

No person in America was beyond McCarthy's rebuke. In June 1951 McCarthy accused Secretary of Defense GEORGE C. MARSHALL of near treason for his role in formulating America's China policy in the late 1940s. Marshall, head of the Joint Chiefs of Staff during World War II, had enjoyed a tremendous following which viewed him as the personification of the best in America's military tradition. But McCarthy spoke of Marshall's "affinity for Chinese Reds," thus shocking his colleagues into a muted response that denoted, historian Robert Griffin wrote, "the fear and irresolution of honorable men."

In August 1951 freshman Senator WILLIAM B. BENTON (D-Conn.), angered at the attack on Marshall, proposed that the Rules Committee inquire into McCarthy's conduct and determine if he should be expelled from the Senate. McCarthy retorted by describing Benton as "a hero of every Communist and crook in and out of government." The Senate leadership had been prepared to ignore Benton's unusual request until another spirited McCarthy assault on the State Department infuriated Majority Leader ERNEST W. MCFARLAND (D-Ariz.). At McFarland's order, the Rules Committee's Subcommittee on Privileges and Elections, which had just denounced McCarthy's role in the Tydings-Butler election, formally commenced hearings on Benton's motion. Committee members displayed scant enthusiasm for Benton's resolution, however, and not until January 1953 did the panel present its report. Written by Senator Thomas Hennings (D-Mo.), it criticized McCarthy on a number of counts, including his personal financial dealings with lobbyists, but without calling for specific actions against him.

Benton's virtual one-man battle against McCarthy characterized the Wisconsin Republican's strength. Senate colleagues on both aisles, whether unsympathetic to McCarthy's crusade or merely detesting him personally, stood by Senate tradition in refraining from personal attacks on him, even though McCarthy himself freely assailed his colleagues on the Senate floor. Then too, partisanship protected McCarthy from many Republicans like Taft and HENRY CABOT LODGE (R-Mass.), whose despair over the incumbent Democratic administration, life-long aversion to communism, and fear of constituent enthusiasm for McCarthy-

ism, limited their public criticisms of the senator. Truman tried to refute McCarthy without avail. His own popularity had fallen badly by the time McCarthy rose to prominence, and he thus lacked a president's normal command of public opinion. Truman himself had fueled fears over domestic subversion through his own ambitious loyalty campaign of 1947 and his attack against his left-wing political foes in the 1948 campaign. Thus McCarthy inherited a political situation, partisan and legislative traditions that rendered him a well-guarded figure as well as possessed of enormous influence over policy and opinion.

McCarthy had benefited additionally from tensions arising out of the cold war. Several "shocks" immediately preceded his Wheeling speech: the perjury conviction of Alger Hiss, the Soviet Union's development of a nuclear bomb and revelations that American spies had expedited it, and the fall of China to the Communists. These episodes created a climate of opinion ripe for McCarthyism. Although McCarthy had used anticommunism in past campaigns, a careful analysis by historian Jim Watts of his addresses in the *Congressional Record* showed that very few dealt with domestic subversion until the Wheeling speech. Thereafter, McCarthy concentrated his energies on the issue.

McCarthy played no part in the campaign for the 1952 Republican presidential nomination.

One notable incident involved the senator and Eisenhower's campaign in the autumn. Eisenhower expunged from his speech a defense of Marshall at the insistence of Wisconsin politicians when he was to be on the same platform in Madison as McCarthy. (He had defended Marshall earlier in Denver.) Word leaked out about the change, which made it look like Eisenhower cowered before McCarthy. In fact it is more likely that Eisenhower's perfunctory and nameless endorsement of McCarthy helped the senator more than the other way around. Yet Republicans still considered him electorally potent, and his seeming success in campaigning for Republicans in 1952—the GOP recaptured the Senate—maintained an image of political influence with the public, from which his power flowed. With the election of a Republican Congress, his powers momentarily grew. But he ultimately miscalculated his strength when, in 1954, he attacked the U.S. Army and the Eisenhower administration. The Senate voted to censure him in December 1954. Cut off from better committee work, ignored by his colleagues and the news media that had unwittingly aided his rise, McCarthy spent his last years in the Senate in ill health and personal frustration. He died of a liver ailment—undoubtedly brought on by heavy drinking—in Bethesda, Maryland, on May 2, 1957.

Commentaries on McCarthyism—a term originated by *Washington Post* political cartoonist Herbert Block—vary. Seeing the period as a dark time, Ellen Schrecker argued that McCarthy's critics weakened their attempts to squelch the senator by announcing they agreed with his goal to eliminate Communists in the government, just not his methods. Arthur Herman claimed that McCarthy was not as off base as his liberal critics contended—that Truman's loyalty board had not done a thorough job of investigating and eliminating security risks. Herman did admit that McCarthy was irresponsible at times. Reeves said McCarthy frequently lied and disrupted the Truman and Eisenhower administrations, but that he hardly threatened the constitutional edifice of the republic. (See *The Eisenhower Years* Volume)

—JLB

McClellan, John L(ittle)
(1896–1977) *member of the Senate*

The son of a country lawyer, John L. McClellan was born on February 25, 1896, on a farm near Sheridan, in southern Arkansas. He studied law in his father's office and was admitted to the bar in 1913 at the age of 17, becoming the youngest lawyer in Arkansas. After serving in the army stateside during World War I, he practiced law in Malvern, Arkansas, and served as city attorney from 1920 to 1926. From 1927 to 1930 he was prosecuting attorney for the state's seventh judicial district. McClellan was elected to the House of Representatives in 1934 and served two terms, during which he supported most New Deal measures. After losing the Democratic senatorial primary in 1938, he won election in 1942.

With the end of the depression, McClellan adopted a conservative position on domestic issues and opposed most of President Truman's Fair Deal programs. He voted against the Employment Act of 1946, for the Taft-Hartley Act of 1947, and against the administration's multibillion-dollar public housing measure in 1949. A consistent foe of civil rights legislation, McClellan filibustered in 1946 against a bill sponsored by Senator DENNIS CHAVEZ (D-

N.Mex.) to make permanent the Fair Employment Practices Commission. He filibustered again in 1949 against attempts to amend the Senate's cloture rules.

With the Democrats in control of the Senate after the 1948 elections, McClellan became chairman of the Committee on Expenditures in the Executive Departments, a watchdog committee in charge of most Senate investigations. The committee had to implement the recommendations of the Hoover Commission on the Organization of the Executive Branch. Although McClellan had been a member of the panel, he took issue with some of its recommendations. He tended to oppose increasing the power of the federal government at the expense of the states and giving more power to the executive branch at the expense of Congress.

In January 1949 McClellan introduced an administration bill to give the president authority to reorganize executive departments and agencies. At the same time, however, McClellan announced that he would press for certain limits on the powers delegated to the president. In particular, he introduced an amendment to exempt the U.S. Army Corps Engineers from any reorganization attempt and to have the president's reorganization power expire on April 1, 1953. While the latter was accepted unanimously by the Senate, the former was rejected. Instead, a compromise was worked out that provided for no exemptions, but allowed only one house to veto any reorganization plan. With these changes, the Reorganization Act of 1949 finally became law in June. McClellan continued, however, to oppose specific reorganization plans submitted by Truman. In 1950 he led the fight against proposals to increase the independence of the Interstate Commerce Commission and Federal Communications Commission; in May, the Senate rejected the president's proposals.

McClellan supported containment up to the point where he thought it too expensive. He backed aid to Greece and Turkey, the Marshall Plan—at least initially—and NATO, and the Japanese Peace Treaty. But he was against the 1946 British loan and a $45 million authorization to set up Truman's Point Four program.

As a member of the Senate Appropriations Committee, McClellan fought to reduce government spending at home and abroad. In 1949 he sponsored an unsuccessful amendment to the military appropriations bill instructing the president to cut 5 percent to 10 percent from all government expenditures. He also supported the attempt in April 1949 to cut funds for the European Recovery Program (ERP) by 10 percent. When that effort failed, McClellan countered by introducing an amendment to the ERP appropriations bill requiring that $1.5 billion of ERP funds be used to purchase surplus agriculture products from the United States. Despite heavy pressure from the administration to defeat the amendment, the Appropriations Committee retained the proposal. Another attempt in 1950 to cut foreign aid funds was defeated by the Senate in August.

During 1951 McClellan played an important role in the bitter three-month debate over the president's constitutional power to send troops overseas. The debate was provoked by Truman's decision to send four divisions of troops to Western Europe at the request of General DWIGHT D. EISENHOWER. McClellan introduced an amendment to a Senate resolution that would have expressed general support for the president's decision to send troops to Europe. However, McClellan's amendment qualified the expression of support by declaring it the sense of the Senate that no troops beyond the four divisions already committed by President Truman "shall be sent . . . without further senatorial approval." Heavy lobbying by the administration to defeat the McClellan amendment failed, and the Senate accepted the measure.

On domestic affairs McClellan trended conservative. He was a consistent opponent of civil rights legislation. He voted to discontinue the wartime Fair Employment Practices Commission in 1945 and voted against cloture during the 1946 debate over the creation of a permanent FEPC. He voted against the Employment Act of 1946, for the Case labor disputes bill of 1946, the Taft-Hartley Act, and the Portal-to-Portal Pay Act of 1947. Despite later run-ins with Senator JOSEPH R. MCCARTHY (R-Wisc.), McClellan backed the McCarran Internal Security Act of 1950.

During the 1950s and 1960s McClellan achieved prominence by heading several major investigations. In 1957 he began a three-year probe into the activities of organized labor, which exposed widespread corruption and led to the imprisonment of Teamster president James Hoffa. He conducted a highly publicized investigation of organized crime in 1963. McClellan also led several investigations into charges of graft and corruption in the awarding of defense contracts and the procurement of military supplies. In 1973 he relinquished his role on the Government Operations Committee to become chairman of the powerful Senate Appropriations Committee, a post he retained until his death from a heart attack on November 27, 1977, in Little Rock, Arkansas. (See *The Eisenhower Years, The Kennedy Years, The Johnson Years, The Nixon/Ford Years* Volumes)

—JD

McCloy, John J(ay)

(1895–1989) *assistant secretary of war; president, International Bank for Reconstruction and Development; military governor for Germany; high commissioner for Germany*

Born on March 31, 1895, in Philadelphia, Pennsylvania, John J. McCloy graduated from Amherst College in 1916 and entered Harvard Law School. He left in May 1917, after the United States entered World War I, to enlist in the army. McCloy returned to Harvard two years later and, upon graduating in 1921, practiced law in New York City. His work took him to Europe frequently, and between 1930 and 1931, he headed Craveth, DeGersdorff, Swaine & Wood's Paris office. Between 1930 and 1939 he was associated with the famous Black Tom Case, involving a 1916 explosion at a munitions plant in New Jersey. McCloy's investigation helped establish that German secret agents had sabotaged the factory. His work in this case gave him an expert knowledge of German espionage techniques and brought him to the attention of Secretary of War HENRY L. STIMSON. Stimson appointed him a consultant on counterespionage in October 1940. In December he promoted McCloy to special assistant to the secretary and five months later made the lawyer assistant secretary of war. Over the next four years McCloy played an important role in the development of lend-lease, the internment of Japanese Americans, and the establishment of the Nisei units in the army. He was also one of the few members in the administration to know of the existence of the atomic bomb and the plans for its use before it was actually dropped on Hiroshima.

During World War II McCloy was deeply involved in the debate over policy toward Germany after the victory had been achieved. He and his colleagues in the War Department anticipated a brief period of military government followed by a civilian-controlled occupation. They found the prospect of prolonged military government distasteful because of the inability of the army to deal with the economic and social problems of postwar Germany. The war had brought glory to the military. Its leaders did not want to risk this prestige in an operation for which none had a background.

Despite this sense of its own limitations, the War Department did not want any civilian interference during the period of military government. McCloy effectively blocked all attempts by the State Department and other civilian agencies to develop long-range policies for the occupation. He received passive support from the White House. As a consequence, when the German government began to disintegrate in late 1944, the only issue that had been settled was the delineation of Allied zones.

Although he wanted a tough peace for Germany with political decentralization and perhaps even dismemberment, after the war McCloy and the War Department joined the State Department in opposing Secretary of the Treasury HENRY MORGENTHAU's plan for the pastoralization of Germany. Between September 1944 and May 1945 McCloy, representing the War Department, negotiated with various members of the Treasury and State departments on the character of military occupation. McCloy, Morgenthau, and HARRY DEXTER WHITE (a Soviet agent as it turned out) managed to scotch a plan that did not even mention the dismemberment of Germany. The final directive pleased Morgenthau, but McCloy had designed such a flexible one that it could be used to justify just about any kind of policy. It stated the Germans would have to pay reparations but could not rebuild their heavy industries to pay for them. The army was to take no role in bolstering the German economy; that task was to be left to the Germans. It was to do all it could to arrest former Nazis. No Nazi was to remain in any government position, and the German military establishment was to be disbanded. Other than these provisions, the army was directed not to become involved in German political affairs although it was to administer the territory "with a view to political decentralization." However, the plan did allow for centralization in each zone to control critical national services. The agreement limited the army's liability, as McCloy, Stimson, and the military wanted. However, it virtually insured economic and political chaos in Germany. As the cold war developed this policy was gradually abandoned. Working closely with McCloy General

LUCIUS D. CLAY, the military governor, carried out policies designed to revive the German economy and rebuild its industrial base.

McCloy argued in the spring of 1945 that the Japanese were seeking a negotiated peace that would allow the emperor to remain in place. He recommended the Allies drop their insistence on unconditional surrender. He became convinced by mid-June that an invasion of the home islands would be unnecessary. He told Secretary of War Stimson he should urge the president to appeal to Emperor Hirohito to surrender with the assurance he could remain as a constitutional monarch. Such a message would note that the Americans would employ a weapon that could destroy entire cities if the Japanese government did not accept the offer. Stimson agreed, but then made a rather weak argument for the case. Truman asked McCloy his opinion and he forcefully made his case. He thought the United States could obviate entrance of the Soviets into the Pacific war by negotiating a settlement with the Japanese. Truman exclaimed that he wanted just such an option examined. But when McCloy argued the president should warn the Japanese specifically about the atomic bomb, military leaders objected that they were not sure the bomb would work yet. McCloy then argued for a more vague ultimatum that merely warned of the capacity to destroy a city in a single blow. Truman decided against mentioning the bomb at that time. Later McCloy and Stimson agreed with acting Secretary of State JOSEPH C. GREW that a message could be issued to the Japanese that they could eventually choose their own type of government as long as they did not base it on militarism. But Secretary of State JAMES F. BYRNES worked to prevent any mention of McCloy's proposal. He succeeded.

McCloy participated in the formulation of the United Nation Charter and supervised the drafting of Article 51, giving nations the right of collective self-defense even if the Security Council had not acted in a particular conflict. Article 51 would be the basis for the various regional security alliances of both the Soviets and the Americans.

Early in Truman's administration McCloy emphasized the need to work with the Soviets. According to his biographer Kai Bird, McCloy disliked Truman's tendency to see life through Manichean glasses. Although McCloy thought it natural for the two most powerful nations to eye each other warily, he believed "peaceful coexistence"—to use a term from the Eisenhower years—was possible. He realistically noted the dominance of Soviet military power in Eastern Europe but believed the United States should have some access to nations in the region. Stimson had McCloy draft a memo urging the president to share the scientific secrets of the atomic bomb with the Soviets. According to Bird, McCloy felt the same frustrations as the hard-liners toward the Soviets, but there was a difference between their attitude and his, namely, how McCloy viewed the impact of atomic weaponry. McCloy believed another war would be an atomic one that would end civilization. He thought the talk of a preemptive strike against the Soviets immoral and such a blow unnecessary. He never thought the Soviets would invade Western Europe in the early years of the cold war. McCloy thought Soviet-American relations would go well enough if the United States kept sufficient troops in Europe. But the pressure to demobilize was tremendous and made difficult any attempt to implement a "Pax Americana" that McCloy preferred. McCloy supported international control of atomic weaponry, and in January 1946, he was a member of the committee that helped draw up the Acheson-Lilienthal proposal for the international control of atomic energy. He was appalled when Truman appointed BERNARD M. BARUCH to present the plan. Baruch demanded changes that virtually guaranteed Soviet rejection. McCloy blamed Baruch for the failure to set up an international atomic control agency and the beginning of the nuclear arms race. McCloy did not think Truman a great president, and that he was maladroit in atomic diplomacy.

During the same period McCloy participated in the formulation of policies toward Latin America, Europe, and the Far East. In May 1945 in conjunction with Stimson, he pursued sanctions within the UN Charter allowing mutual security groups. These provisions were designed, in part, to protect American "preclusive rights" in the Western Hemisphere. The following month he took part in discussions leading to establishment of the 38th parallel as the line delineating Communist-controlled North Korea from the South.

In November 1945, after a worldwide tour of American military positions, McCloy left the Pentagon to practice with the firm of Milbank, Tweed, Hope, Hadley and McCloy. He remained associated with government affairs. During the latter part of that year, McCloy negotiated terms for the unification of the military under a new Department of Defense.

In February 1947 McCloy accepted appointment as president of the National Bank for Reconstruction and Development (World Bank). McCloy had been offered the post several weeks earlier but had turned it down because of his fears that he would not have the support of the American representatives on the board of executive directors. He had been prevailed upon to reconsider and had spent several weeks negotiating the conditions of his appointment. He accepted the post only after receiving reassurances that he and not the directors would have control over the institution. He also successfully insisted upon the removal of liberal executive director Emilio G. Collado and that the bank base its operations on sound business principles. When McCloy took office the bank had not yet made a single loan or sold a debenture. It had little credit with investors; its accomplishments, in the words of one Swiss newspaper, were "Zero."

The new leader set out to build a reputation for the bank on Wall Street. McCloy's appointment in itself reassured the financial community that the bank was in sound hands. He bolstered this impression by assuring investors that the institution would not become a political agency to dispense foreign aid. In April he announced, "We can't and won't grant loans in order to accomplish political objectives. We can and will refuse loans where political uncertainties are so great as to make a loan economically unsound." In preparation for the first sale of securities, scheduled for July, McCloy, EUGENE R. BLACK, the new executive director, and Robert Garner, the new vice president, gave a series of speeches to persuade the investment community of the soundness of their management. McCloy also directed the assembling of a consortium of 1,700 securities dealers across the country, the largest such network ever organized, to market the July issue. He persuaded the comptroller of the currency to endorse the World Bank's soundness as an investment for national banks. His efforts succeeded. The two note issues, totaling $250 million, came to market on June 15 and within two hours were oversubscribed. With the exception of a small ($4 million) private placement with a bank for international settlements about a year later, this was the only time the World Bank went to the capital market while McCloy was president, but it established the bank with the investment community.

McCloy sought to discourage World Bank participation in relief programs to Europe on the grounds that it would alienate Congress and the investment community, from which much of its capital came. Nevertheless, by April McCloy was persuaded that some bank money would be required to keep Europe from collapse until a massive U.S. relief effort could be devised. In May he approved a $250 million loan to France to help the government in the face of rising popularity of the Communists. The U.S. State Department, however, warned the French that they would have to eliminate the Communists within the government to receive American approval; within hours after the Communists were expelled, McCloy announced the loan would be made. In August he allowed loans to the Netherlands, Denmark, and Luxembourg totaling another $247 million. However, some observers, particularly British and French, thought McCloy too conservative in his loan policy. When Secretary of State GEORGE C. MARSHALL requested that he be more liberal with loans, McCloy responded that he had to run the bank as a business to keep in good graces with the investment community. The bank president recommended the U.S. government take up the slack through an aid program. This suggestion helped lead to the Marshall Plan. McCloy subsequently became a vigorous proponent of the Marshall Plan, testifying for it before Congress and speaking for it at a White House conference of business, industrial, and labor leaders. After the plan was inaugurated in April 1948, the bank ceased further recovery loans to Europe.

McCloy began to channel funds to developing countries. Chile received two loans, amounting to $16 million, in March 1948. Mexico and Brazil received loans the next year. However, the number of loans was limited by the conditions McCloy imposed. He was determined that borrowers demonstrate a capacity to repay and that the specific projects for which the money was requested be soundly conceived, planned, and administered. He also demanded that all national debt and default be settled before an application would be considered. Few developing nations could meet these requirements.

While capacity to repay was the principal criterion for approving a loan, during McCloy's tenure politics was occasionally a factor. McCloy initially supported a $128.5 million loan to Poland to rebuild its coal industry but eventually told the Poles it would be voted down because of U.S. government

pressure. A petition from Czechoslovakia suffered the same fate. In March 1949 Poland complained to the United Nations that the Bank discriminated against Communist Eastern Europe. McCloy, in testimony before the Economic and Social Council, denied the charge. The UN was not capable of dealing with the problem. Although the World Bank was a specialized agency of the UN, the terms of association that had been negotiated in 1947 had accorded the UN little more than observer status at the bank. It was, in the words of one bank official, "more a declaration of independence from than cooperation with the United Nations."

In May 1949 President Truman appointed McCloy military governor and U.S. high commissioner for Germany. McCloy supervised the transition, then underway, from military to civilian rule, and the transformation of West Germany into a free-market economy and parliamentary democracy. He served as civilian high commissioner for three years. McCloy's first major decision was to promulgate a law paying 850 million German marks in compensation to victims of the Nazis. McCloy many times became exasperated by those recalcitrant Germans who seemed unrepentant for the Nazis years, but he believed that Europe required an economically strong Germany to counter the Soviet threat. He, therefore, resisted and often abandoned policies that he believed jeopardized attempts to rebuild the German economy. When denazification and decartelization threatened recovery, McCloy moved to modify these policies. While he worried about neo-Nazi movements and spoke often of this concern, he believed that a prosperous Germany integrated into Europe was sufficient insurance against a Nazi insurgence. He could not completely ignore the cry for imprisonment of all former Nazis, but he gradually eased denazification and began commuting sentences. He told the Senate Foreign Relations Committee in January 1950 that he did not believe that "little Nazis" who changed their views should be denied employment with the West German government. He freed German industrialists (including the famed Alfred Krupp) imprisoned in the American zone on the grounds that they were necessary for the nation's recovery. In October 1949 McCloy proclaimed his intent to proceed with "expedition and energy" to dissolve the large business combinations that had supplied the Nazi military. But by the end of the year, he had signed an agreement with the German government transferring to it responsibility for moving against cartels. At the same time he ended the dismantling of German factories.

McCloy took an active role in the negotiations between Germany and France that led to the adoption of the Schuman Plan and to the formation of the European Coal and Steel Community. The Germans had resisted proposals to prohibit a steel producer from owning coal mines that supplied more than 75 percent of his coal requirements. McCloy broke this impasse by threatening to reclaim supervision of decartelization and impose even stricter measures against German industrial combinations. His implied threat of continued international occupation of the Ruhr gave the Germans another powerful incentive to come to terms. Upon concluding the agreement, both the Germans and the French praised McCloy's role as mediator.

McCloy proved himself an attentive politician during his service in Germany. He paid little attention to the administrative aspects of occupation and spent most of his time with German political leaders. McCloy worked with both the Christian Democrats and the Social Democrats, although he favored the more conservative Christian Democrats because Social Democratic Party leader Kurt Schumacher wanted a reunited, but neutral, Germany, whereas Christian Democratic chief Konrad Adenauer preferred alignment with the West, even if that meant an indefinite division of Germany. McCloy saw the threat to America's interests coming from the left, which wanted reunification, rather than the right. He believed he needed to build up Adenauer among West Germans by showing he was winning back sovereignty for the nation. A way to do that was to make concession to national pride like quickly ending the unpopular de-nazification process.

Russia offered a plebiscite on German reunification, which worried McCloy. A reunified, neutral, and demilitarized Germany was not in the West's interest even though it was popular among some Frenchmen and many West Germans. McCloy made it clear that reunification would have to be on Western terms, and Germany would not be allowed to become a neutral power playing the East off the West and vice versa.

The invasion of South Korea convinced McCloy that some sort of German rearmament had to take place. McCloy and his staff came up with the idea of integrating German units within a European Defense Force (EDF). McCloy believed the EDF would serve as a deterrent, keep Germany divided, and tie the Federal Republic to the West. The EDF, however, was later rejected by the French legislature. In 1955 West Germany was allowed to establish its own army and join NATO.

As high commissioner, McCloy approved the collection of intelligence from a broad array of agents in West and East Germany. Part of McCloy's policy was to use such agents to help root out Communist subversives. One of those agents was Klaus Barbie, who had been Gestapo chief of Lyon (the "Butcher of Lyon") who had tortured and killed prisoners and deported thousands of French Jews to the death camps. However, he had also developed an intelligence network during the war that the Americans thought valuable in the fight against Communists. A French lawyer, defending an alleged collaborator of Barbie's during the war, claimed U.S. intelligence was protecting the former Gestapo member. The question was whether to accede to French requests for his extradition. Barbie by May 1950 knew U.S. counterintelligence operations well, and he had directed American infiltration of French intelligence. The High Commissioner's Office, fearing damage to French-American relations, decided to conveniently lose Barbie. He was smuggled out of Europe in 1950 to South America. Barbie never was the intelligence asset that the Americans thought at the time, and American involvement with Barbie was revealed in the 1980s when he was extradited to France and tried.

McCloy directed contractual negotiations with West Germany to officially end the state of hostility with the West, return most of the Federal Republic's sovereignty, and allow it to rearm. In May 1952 the contractual agreements were signed, and West Germany regained control over much of her own affairs. The Western Allies, however, could still intervene in West Germany if a crisis arose, and they continued their control over West Berlin, reunification, and their troops' security in the Federal Republic.

McCloy returned to private life in August 1952. He became chairman of Chase National Bank of New York in January 1953. McCloy engineered the merger of Chase with the Bank of Manhattan, consummated in March 1955. The combined entity was the second largest bank in the United States. He also served during the 1950s as director of a number of major corporations, including American Telephone and Telegraph, Westinghouse Electric and United Fruit. In addition, he was chairman of the Ford Foundation and of the Council of Foreign Relations. McCloy's quiet prominence in business and national affairs led Richard Rovere to dub him the "chairman of the Establishment."

During the 1950s McCloy served as a foreign affairs adviser to President Dwight D. Eisenhower. Eisenhower had considered him for the office of secretary of state, but Republicans successfully pressed him to accept JOHN FOSTER DULLES. He also was a consultant on disarmament during the late 1950s and early 1960s. In 1966 he was President Lyndon Johnson's special envoy to the U.S., German and British mutual defense talks. Two years later he was a member of the Special Advisory Group on Vietnam, which recommended the de-escalation of the war. McCloy died on March 11, 1989, in Stamford, Connecticut. (See *The Eisenhower Years, The Kennedy Years, The Johnson Years* Volumes)

—CSJ

McCone, John A(lex)
(1902–1991) *undersecretary of the air force*

John A. McCone was born on January 4, 1902, to a prosperous San Francisco, California, family. He received an engineering degree from the University of California at Berkeley in 1922. He then went to work for the Llewellyn Iron Works as a riveter and boilermaker. By 1933 he had become executive vice president and director. McCone left Llewellyn in 1937 to organize his own engineering firm, Betchel-McCone. During World War II Betchel-McCone modified B-24s, B-29s, and other military aircraft. At the same time McCone became president and director of the California Shipbuilding Corporation. The company produced over 450 ships during the war. His wartime contact with government officials would lure him into public service.

In 1947 President Truman appointed McCone to the Air Policy Commission. Truman had formed the panel in response to the widespread debate in the defense community over the role of American air power. The commission examined the tactical and strategic application of military aviation and its relative position in the separate armed services. As a commission member, McCone helped THOMAS K. FINLETTER write its 1948 report, "Survival in the Air Age." He particularly contributed to the military

phases of the report, which advocated expanded U.S. air power and helped to update air defense policies. The first real postwar step toward an independent air service, the report called for a 70-group air force. One of the key witnesses before the commission was General DWIGHT D. EISENHOWER. He and McCone formed a close friendship that continued through McCone's service in the Eisenhower administration.

In 1948 McCone became a special deputy to Secretary of Defense JAMES V. FORRESTAL. He brought his expertise in engineering and military production to bear on his responsibility for the preparation of the department's first two budgets. McCone also worked closely with Forrestal in forming the Central Intelligence Agency (CIA).

McCone left the government in 1948 to return to private business. In June 1950, at the outbreak of the Korean War, he was appointed undersecretary of the air force under Finletter. The following year he sent Truman a memorandum calling for an embryo guided-missile program under an administrator "with full authority and control of funds to exercise absolute power over the entire effort." In 1958 the *New York Herald Tribune*, referring to this memorandum, called McCone a "prophet with honor," and claimed the United States would not have trailed the Soviet Union in guided missiles if his recommendations had been carried out. McCone fought tirelessly for a larger slice of the defense budget for the air force. A hard-nosed executive with a reputation for setting and meeting production goals, he was given responsibility for accelerating the production of war planes. By the time he resigned in October 1951, the production of military planes had doubled.

During the 1950s McCone often returned to government service from private enterprise. In 1954 he sat on the Wriston Committee examining the modernization of the diplomatic service. McCone served the Eisenhower administration as chairman of the Atomic Energy Commission. President Kennedy named him head of the CIA in November 1961. An able administrator, McCone emphasized the coordinating role of the agency in the intelligence community. He opposed the introduction of American combat troops into Vietnam under the administration's imposition of military restraints. McCone resigned in April 1965 and later headed a commission investigating the causes of the Watts riot. He became a director of International Telephone and

Telegraph in 1969. Four years later the Senate Foreign Relations Committee questioned McCone as to whether he had contributed $1 million in ITT funds to defeat Chilean presidential candidate Salvador Allende. McCone claimed the money was meant for agricultural and social reform. President Ronald Reagan awarded him the Presidential Medal of Freedom in 1987. McCone passed away on February 14, 1991, in Pebble Beach, California. (See *The Eisenhower Years, The Kennedy Years, The Johnson Years* Volumes)

—SF

McCormack, John W(illiam)
(1891–1980) *member of the House of Representatives*

The son of a Boston contractor, McCormack was born on December 21, 1891, in Boston, Massachusetts. He left school in 1904 in order to help support his widowed mother. He worked at various unskilled jobs while attending night school and, in 1913, he was admitted to the Massachusetts bar. He then entered private practice. McCormack—a gifted public speaker—began his career in 1920 when he was elected. He served as a Democrat in the Massachusetts Senate from 1923 to 1926, with his last two years spent as state senate floor leader for the Democratic majority. Although his attempt to win the Democratic congressional primary in 1926 failed, McCormack was elected to the U.S. House of Representatives in 1928.

McCormack's loyalty to the party and his rigorous approach to committee assignments, won him the support of Representatives SAM T. RAYBURN (D-Tex.) and John Nance Garner (D-Tex.). In 1931, with the House under Democratic rule, McCormack was appointed to the prestigious Ways and Means Committee. He was influential in gaining support for Rayburn's succession to majority leader in 1936. In 1940 McCormack ascended to that post when his political ally became Speaker of the House, launching the alliance between urban northerners and rural southerners that dominated congressional Democratic leadership for decades to come. McCormack's early tenure was marked by his consistent endorsement of New Deal and Fair Deal domestic legislation and a staunch anticommunist stance in foreign affairs. He had headed up the original Special Committee on Un-American Activities in 1934 and used it as a battering ram against Com-

munists, whom he despised, and would later support the Mundt-Nixon bill. During World War II he stressed that "international machinery" must be "devised and established to assure to the future world permanent peace."

An aggressive and at times vituperative debater, "the fighting Irishman" gained a reputation as an ardent liberal who remained loyal to his political supporters. On domestic issues McCormack supported the Employment Act of 1946 although he considered it an innocuous version of the much-needed Full Employment bill of 1945. He undauntedly defended the Office of Price Administration (OPA) at a time when Republicans regarded the OPA as the "chief promoter of inflation in America." Although he favored legislative restrictions on labor activities during the war, McCormack voted against the Case labor disputes bill of 1946, and he opposed any attempt to override Truman's veto of the Taft-Hartley Act of 1947. Unlike many of his Democratic counterparts in the House, he voted against limitation of the presidency to two terms. In support of Truman's anti-inflation program, he advocated the extension of rent control in 1948. The extension became law the same year.

An ardent foe of Communist expansion, McCormack backed military and economic appropriations for Greece and Turkey in 1947, in order to avoid the threat of Soviet intervention. He backed the extension of the draft in 1948, the Marshall Plan in 1948 and its extension a year later, aid to Korea and Taiwan in 1950, and opposed cutting aid to Europe in the Mutual Security Act of 1951. In 1951, when Communist China refused a UN appeal for a cease-fire in Korea, McCormack introduced a resolution which implored the UN to "immediately act and declare the Chinese Communist authorities an aggressor. . . ." He supported the extension of the Trade Agreements Act in 1945, 1949, and 1951.

In 1952, as chairman of the Democratic platform committee, McCormack stressed the importance of party unity and was able to bridge the gap of dissension between southern and northern Democrats created by the party's civil rights plank. After the death of Rayburn, McCormack was elected Speaker of the House in 1962. During the 1960s he came under criticism for his lack of decisive leadership and his support of the Vietnam War. In 1970, after more than four decades of active service in the legislative branch, he announced his retirement from politics. After his wife's death in

December 1971 he returned to Boston, where he died on November 22, 1980. (See *The Eisenhower Years, The Kennedy Years, The Johnson Years, The Nixon/Ford Years* Volumes)

—DGE

Macdonald, Dwight
(1906–1982) *author*

Dwight Macdonald was born on March 24, 1906, in New York City. His mother was the daughter of a wealthy merchant and his father was a lawyer. Educated at Phillips Exeter Academy and Yale, from which he graduated in 1928, Macdonald devoted his professional life to writing and editing. He served as managing editor of the *Yale Literary Magazine* during his college career. Although his early interest was in literary criticism, he turned to writing about politics in the 1930s. He worked for HENRY R. LUCE as a writer for *Fortune* magazine from 1929 to 1936. He later said his writing on capitalism for Luce drove him to the left. In the 1930s he became a left-wing radical writer and a member of the Trotskyite party but broke with them in 1941. He served as an editor of *Partisan Review* during the late 1930s.

In 1944 he founded *Politics*, a small magazine that lasted for five years. He was, in his own words, its "editor, publisher, owner, proofreader, layout man and chief contributor." Although *Politics* had a small circulation, it contained articles by some of the leading political writers of the times, such as Albert Camus, Simone Weil, Brunn Bettelheim, Lewis Coser, C. Wright Mills, and Paul Goodman and had a devoted following. Always anti-Stalinist, Macdonald often attacked in *Politics* both Stalin's policies and supporters. He made the magazine out to be anarchist and pacifist. Macdonald delivered scathing attacks on liberal and left-wing publications, such as the *Nation*, the *New Republic*, and *PM*. He particularly ridiculed what in his view was a characteristic of some liberals to perceive themselves as morally superior to their opponents. In 1948 Macdonald wrote *Henry Wallace: The Man and the Myth*, in which he portrayed the former vice president and then Progressive Party candidate for president as a mystic, an amateur politician, and an opportunist.

Macdonald was often acclaimed as an individualist, a moralist, and an original critic who avoided doctrinaire politics. His targets were not only Communists and liberals but capitalists, fascists, militarists, and some supporters of religion, as well.

His independence was shown in many articles. A pacifist in World War II, he described himself as a "libertarian socialist." Although a pacifist, he did not regard the United Nations as being an alternative to war, but rather he described it as "a bore." He was a critic of the crusading elements of the Truman Doctrine although he was an anticommunist himself.

Macdonald became disenchanted with political writing during the 1950s and turned to literary criticism and journalistic profiles. He wrote many articles for the *New Yorker*. Macdonald died on December 19, 1982, in New York City. (See *The Johnson Years* Volume)

—HML

McFarland, Ernest W(illiam)
(1894–1984) *member of the Senate*

Ernest McFarland was born on October 9, 1894, in Earlsboro, Oklahoma, to a homesteading family. He graduated from East Central Normal School, and for a brief time taught in the countryside. When the United States declared war on Germany he joined the Navy. Discharged in 1919, he settled in Phoenix, Arizona, due to bronchial illness he had developed in the navy. He then resumed his studies at Stanford University. He earned his law degree in 1921 and a masters degree in political science the following year. For the year 1923–24 McFarland served as assistant attorney general of Arizona. The following six years he was the attorney for Pinal County. At the same time McFarland, who had made an extensive study of the problems of irrigation and water law, acted as attorney for the San Carlos Irrigation and Drainage District. From 1935 to 1940 he sat as judge of the superior court of Pinal County, where he tried many important cases involving most of the water rights of Arizona. McFarland defeated Senator Henry Fountain Ashurst in the 1940 Democratic Senate primary. McFarland went on to win the general election and enter the Senate in 1941. McFarland's main consideration during the war was veteran's affairs. As the putative "Father of the GI Bill," the senator had drafted a section of the law dealing with free education for veterans as well as business and home loans.

As a freshman senator, McFarland was appointed to the Interstate Commerce Committee. He found himself immediately involved with a subcommittee probe into "alleged warmongering" in American films. McFarland opposed government regulation in the movie industry, supporting the administration's view that the constitutional questions of freedom of expression and governmental control of thought and expression were at stake.

McFarland developed an interest in communications during his tenure in the Senate. As chairman of the Interstate Commerce Committee's Subcommittee on Communications Matters, he initiated extensive domestic and international studies in the field. McFarland advocated strong American-owned international communications enterprises. He believed that inexpensive worldwide communications would aid international relations and trade. To further this idea he headed a Senate investigating committee, which recommended the creation of the Special Presidential Communications Policy Board in 1950. His efforts in this area led to the Communications Act of 1952, which changed the 1934 law, setting new guidelines for the Federal Communications Commission.

As the junior senator from a mining state, the Arizona lawmaker was careful to protect extractive industries. In 1949 he sponsored a tariff on copper that put American mines on an equal basis with their Chilean counterparts. The bill drew criticism for endangering trade agreements. In his second term McFarland paid more attention to reclamation projects such as diverting Colorado River water for irrigation and reclamation, and, although he won support in the Senate for the Central Arizona Water and Power Project in 1950 and 1951, it failed to pass both Houses of Congress until the later 1960s. As a senator from Arizona he was concerned with Indian affairs and saw to the passage of the Navajo-Hopi Rehabilitation Act of 1950, which provided money for schools, hospitals, and roads in these tribes' reservations.

A loyal middle-of-the-road Democrat preoccupied first by the issues affecting his state, McFarland tended to back the administration in foreign affairs. During the Truman administration he voted for the United Nations charter, interim aid to Europe, aid to Korea, the Marshall Plan, the North Atlantic Treaty, and military aid to NATO, and he opposed the McClellan Amendment. However, he did not support the administration-backed 1946 loan to Great Britain and in 1952 he voted to override the president's veto of the McCarran-Walter Act.

McFarland tended to support the president on domestic affairs. He opposed the Case labor disputes bill of 1946, the Taft-Hartley Act of 1947, and the GOP tax cuts of the 80th Congress and supported the Employment Act of 1946, federal aid to education, and the National Housing Act of 1949. He also pushed through Congress the only three increases in Social Security to occur from 1946 to 1952. But he abandoned the administration when he voted against cloture in the debate over the establishment of a permanent Fair Employment Practices Commission and backed the McCarran Internal Security Act.

In 1951 McFarland defeated Senator Joseph C. O'Mahoney of Wyoming for the post of majority leader. In the vote the support of southern senators, who believed his views on states' rights closer to their own, proved decisive. As a consequence, McFarland as majority leader found himself tyring to balance the legislative program of the Truman administration and the opposition of the Southern Democrats who had helped bring him to sudden eminence.

By nature genial and friendly, McFarland presided over a Senate preoccupied with the Korean War and the activities of Senator JOSEPH R. MCCARTHY (R-Wisc.). McFarland had little influence or impact; his role was chiefly parliamentary. He oversaw the debate in the Senate in 1951 over the U.S. role in the North Atlantic Treaty Organization (NATO) and the stationing of troops in Europe. The same year McFarland facilitated the passage of a Senate measure strongly condemning the Chinese intervention in Korea, declaring that "action now is needed to put backbone into the UN." While McFarland was majority leader, Truman relieved General DOUGLAS MACARTHUR of his command in Korea. McFarland defended Truman's decision in the Senate, saying he had "no other choice." In 1952 he helped gain the ratification of the peace treaty with Japan and the treaty bringing Greece and Turkey into NATO.

McFarland was defeated in his bid to win reelection in 1952 by Republican Barry Goldwater. He returned to politics in 1954 when he became governor of Arizona. He was elected to a second term in 1956. McFarland again lost to Goldwater in the 1958 Senate race. With his defeat he returned to law practice and then became chief judge of the Arizona Supreme Court. In 1969 McFarland served on the National Commission on the Causes and Prevention of Violence. He finished his autobiography,

Mac, in 1979. McFarland died in Phoenix, Arizona, on June 8, 1984.

—SF

McGranery, J(ames) P(atrick)
(1895–1962)   *U.S. Attorney General*

The son of Irish Catholic immigrants, J. P. McGranery was born on July 8, 1895, in Philadelphia, Pennsylvania. He worked for a time as a union electrotyper, and from which time he received a union card that he carried with him the rest of his life. Earning a law degree from Temple University in 1928, he set up practice in Philadelphia and became active in local Democratic politics. After losing three elections McGranery captured a seat in the U.S. House of Representatives in 1936; he was a party regular and staunch New Dealer who supported virtually all administration measures. In October 1943, while serving his fourth term in the House, McGranery was named an assistant to the Attorney General. During his three years in that post McGranery supervised the major units in the Justice Department and U.S. attorneys and marshals. He also reviewed decisions of the Selective Service Act Board of Appeals. For his wartime service he won a Medal of Merit in 1946.

In 1946 McGranery became a U.S. district court judge for the Eastern District of Pennsylvania. During his five-and-a-half years on the bench, Judge McGranery won publicity for refusing to let Representative Earl Chudoff (D-Pa.) appear as defense attorney in his court in 1949 on the ground that no member of Congress had the right to represent a client in a federal court proceeding. McGranery also handled the case of Harry Gold, who pleaded guilty in July 1950 to charges of having participated in a Soviet spy ring and who later testified against JULIUS and ETHEL ROSENBERG. In December 1950 McGranery sentenced Gold to a maximum term of 30 years in prison.

Truman named McGranery attorney general on April 3, 1952, following the sudden resignation of J. HOWARD MCGRATH. McGranery took over the Justice Department at a time when it was under fire for alleged corruption. McGranery promised to expose and prosecute corruption, but there were charges that, as an old friend of the president's, he would simply whitewash the issue of malfeasance and favoritism in the department. Some anticommunist Republican senators opposed him for his criticism of the FBI's handling of the *Amerasia* investigation of 1945. Sworn in May, McGranery began what historian Alonzo Hamby has called "a quiet and fairly effective effort to weed out corruption." He cooperated with a House Judiciary subcommittee investigating the Justice Department and eventually won the panel's praise for his work in developing and imposing "strict rules of conduct" in the department. McGranery changed the top personnel in several divisions of the department and got Truman to oust a number of U.S. attorneys and marshals involved in questionable activities. He issued an order, effective January 1954, barring U.S. attorneys from engaging in private practice or other work interfering with their duties, and he recommended that both the attorneys and marshals be placed under civil service.

McGranery was active in other fields as well during his 10 months in office. He continued the loyalty-security program set up by his predecessors and expanded the Internal Security Section of the Justice Department. He initiated the prosecution of several second-string Communist Party leaders under the Smith Act. The attorney general ordered a federal grand jury investigation of charges that OWEN LATTIMORE, Far Eastern expert at Johns Hopkins University, had lied to a Senate committee. McGranery secured indictments against former Communist Party leader EARL BROWDER and his wife for perjury and started denaturalization and deportation proceedings against alleged Communists. The attorney general also ordered immigration officials in September 1952 to bar the readmission into the United States of Charlie Chaplin until the filmmaker's fitness of reentry under immigration laws was established.

McGranery started a series of antitrust proceedings, including a grand jury investigation of an alleged international oil cartel and a suit against three leading soap manufacturers for restraint of trade. He established a program to denaturalize and deport some 100 underworld figures and began actions against Frank Costello and Thomas Luchese among others. On December 2, 1952, McGranery submitted an amicus curiae brief to the U.S. Supreme Court in a set of cases challenging racial segregation in public schools. The U.S. brief argued that compulsory racial segregation was inherently discriminatory and urged the justices to hold the separate but equal doctrine unconstitutional. The Court eventually took that position when it decided

Brown v. Board of Education in May 1954. After Dwight D. Eisenhower won the election of 1952, McGranery advised incoming attorney general Herbert Brownell of 25 politically connected department lawyers, whom Brownell should fire, which he did.

After leaving office McGranery practiced law in Washington and Philadelphia. He was active in the Catholic Church and was named a Knight Commander of the order of St. Gregory the Great. He died on December 23, 1962, while vacationing in Palm Beach, Florida.

—CAB

McGrath, J(ames) Howard

(1903–1966) *U.S. Solicitor General, member of the Senate, U.S. Attorney General*

J. Howard McGrath was born on November 28, 1903, in Woonsocket, Rhode Island. He began working his way up through the ranks of the Rhode Island Democratic Party while a student at Providence College. He was president of the Rhode Island Young Democrats from 1924 to 1928. After graduating from Providence College in 1926 he attended Boston University, where he received a law degree in 1929. McGrath then returned to Rhode Island, where he was city solicitor for Central Falls and chairman of the Democratic State Committee from 1930 to 1934. He served as the U.S. attorney for the state from 1935 to 1940. Elected to the first of three terms as governor in 1940, McGrath seconded Harry S Truman's nomination for the vice presidency at the 1944 Democratic National Convention.

McGrath resigned as governor after Truman chose him to be U.S. Solicitor General on September 28, 1945; the Senate confirmed the appointment on October 3. As solicitor general, McGrath successfully defended the constitutionality of the Public Utility Holding Company Act and the war crimes conviction of Japanese general Tomoyuki Yamashita before the Supreme Court. He resigned from the post a year later, in October 1946, after winning the Democratic nomination for U.S. senator from Rhode Island. McGrath won election despite a Republican sweep of New England that year.

In the Senate McGrath was an administration loyalist who voted along party lines on both foreign policy and domestic issues. According to *Congressional Quarterly*, he had a 99 percent record of backing the administration. McGrath built a liberal record by voting against the Taft-Hartley Act, supporting the expansion of social security, and sponsoring bills for national health insurance and federal aid to education.

In October 1947 McGrath was elected chairman of the Democratic National Committee. He took over the job at a time when the Democratic Party was in need of revitalization. A softspoken but hardworking politician who was considered a shrewd strategist, McGrath from the start saw the election of Truman in 1948 as his main task. He was in charge of arrangements for the July 1948 Democratic National Convention in Philadelphia, where Truman secured the presidential nomination. McGrath then helped plan Truman's campaign strategy. He sought to contain defections to the Progressive Party and to the Southern Dixiecrats. Working out of Democratic headquarters in New York City, McGrath mobilized the party machinery throughout the country to raise money, arouse interest in Truman, and get out the vote. His management of the Democratic campaign helped produce Truman's surprising upset victory in November.

In July 1949 Truman asked McGrath to become U.S. Attorney General, replacing TOM C. CLARK, who had been appointed associated justice of the Supreme Court. Clark, a Protestant, had replaced FRANK MURPHY, a Catholic, and it was thought then that a Catholic should at least be attorney general. McGrath reluctantly agreed to serve. He was not considered an effective attorney general. He reportedly did not keep adequate control over the Justice Department and left much of its administration to subordinates.

In loyalty-security matters McGrath generally followed the path laid out by Clark. He supported the use of wiretaps by the FBI and added to the attorney general's list of subversive organizations. McGrath considered the administration's loyalty program for federal employees basically sound. He opposed an independent review of it proposed by liberals who were concerned about the program's infringements on civil liberties. While McGrath was attorney general the Justice Department backed a severe bill allowing the administrative internment of aliens under deportation orders and another measure providing for the summary dismissal of "suspect" civilian employees. The department also supported the use by the federal loyalty board of a standard that made suspicion of disloyalty, without

President Truman and J. Howard McGrath   *(Harry S. Truman Library)*

any tangible evidence, grounds for dismissal of federal employees.

McGrath defended the administration's loyalty program against charges of inadequacy made by Senator JOSEPH R. MCCARTHY (R-Wisc.). He denounced the Wisconsin Republican and his tactics as a danger to American liberties. McGrath also recommended that Truman veto the 1950 Internal Security Act, which the Justice Department believed to have constitutional and administrative defects. When the bill became law over the president's veto, however, McGrath said the department would "vigorously" enforce it. The Justice Department also proposed additional internal security legislation in 1951.

Throughout the Truman years McGrath worked to promote civil rights. He ended racial segregation of the staff at Democratic national headquarters in August 1948 and introduced the administration's civil rights bills in the Senate on April 28, 1949. While he was attorney general the

Justice Department for the first time submitted briefs challenging the constitutionality of racial segregation in three Supreme Court cases. McGrath personally argued for a Court ruling against segregation when the cases were heard in April 1950. He also successfully prosecuted the Great Atlantic and Pacific Company for violation of antitrust laws.

McGrath left the Justice Department abruptly on April 3, 1952, as a result of developments in a government corruption probe. During 1951 a House Ways and Means subcommittee had uncovered evidence of corruption within the Bureau of Internal Revenue and the Justice Department's Tax Division. In January 1952 Truman announced that McGrath and the Justice Department would handle the job of cleaning up corruption in government, but critics pointed out that the department was itself suspect in the tax scandals. On February 1, Truman appointed NEWBOLD MORRIS, an independent New York Republican, as special assistant to the Attorney

General to investigate corruption. Morris made the Justice Department his first target and, in March, demanded that over 500 top Justice officials, including McGrath, answer detailed financial questionnaires. On March 31 McGrath told a House Judiciary subcommittee that he might not answer the questionnaire, which he considered an invasion of privacy and individual rights and would not reappoint Morris if he had to do it over. On April 3 McGrath fired Morris. Shortly afterward Truman announced that the Attorney General had resigned. In reality Truman had forced him out. McGrath told the new Attorney General, J. P. MCGRANERY, "Bring a pair of asbestos trousers with you." In a report on the McGrath-Morris episode released on October 1, 1952, a House Judiciary subcommittee investigating the Justice Department stated that McGrath had shown a "deplorable lack of knowledge" of the department, and it criticized his lack of "enthusiasm" for ridding the department of "wrongdoers and incompetents."

After leaving government McGrath returned to the practice of law and the management of his many business interests. He was campaign manager for Senator ESTES KEFAUVER (D-Tenn.) in 1956 in his unsuccessful try for the Democratic presidential nomination and stayed on to help with the campaign when Kefauver was nominated for the vice presidency. In 1960 McGrath entered and lost a Democratic primary for U.S. senator from Rhode Island. He died of a heart attack on September 2, 1966, in Narragansett, Rhode Island.

—CAB

McKellar, Kenneth D(ouglas)
(1869–1957) *member of the Senate*

The son of a Tennessee country lawyer, Kenneth D. McKellar was born on January 29, 1869, in Richmond, Alabama. McKellar worked his way through the University of Alabama, graduating magna cum laude in 1891 with both a bachelor's and a master's degree. He received his law degree from the same university in 1892. McKellar established a practice in Memphis and in 1911 was elected to the U.S. House with the backing of the local Democratic machine. Six years later he moved up to the Senate with the help of Memphis political boss EDWARD H. CRUMP. The two formed a political alliance that lasted for the rest of McKellar's time in office. McKellar supported the liberal policies of Woodrow Wilson and voted with rural Democrats during the 1920s to aid farmers.

An ardent New Dealer at its outset, McKellar was one of the legislative architects of the Tennessee Valley Authority (TVA), the semi-private corporation that irrigated land, controlled floods, subsidized agricultural projects, and provided inexpensive electric power to the people of seven southern states. McKellar helped guide the legislation through various congressional committees. However, after Senator George Norris (R-Neb.) was acclaimed by the president and the press as the "father of the TVA" McKellar was so incensed that he began to wage a personal vendetta against the project. McKellar's former ideological commitment to the TVA was also questionable. He saw the agency as a source to enhance his patronage power, but the TVA's governing structure, created by Norris and the administration, prevented McKellar from gaining control.

During the Truman administration McKellar was one of the Senate's most powerful members. As chairman of the Appropriations Committee, he passed on the budgets of the military, the regulatory agencies, and the executive departments. The Senate also designated him President Pro-Tempore, a post that gave him procedural power in debate. McKellar's last years in the Senate were undistinguished except for his continued feud with the TVA and its former head, DAVID E. LILIENTHAL. Sitting on the Atomic Energy Committee, in 1947 he waged a one-man campaign to prevent Truman's appointment of Lilienthal as chairman of the Atomic Energy Commission. McKellar accused Lilienthal of being pro-communist, pro-Soviet, and responsible for turning the TVA into a haven for subversives. The Tennessee senator pointed to the fact that Lilienthal's parents were Czech immigrants. Since their nation of origin was at present Communist, he maintained this was sufficient grounds to question the loyalty of their son. Although few in the Senate took McKellar seriously in the debates, his opposition to the appointment created the momentum for a number of conservatives to question the nomination because of Lilienthal's association with the New Deal. Senator ROBERT A. TAFT (R-Ohio), for example, called for the defeat of the Lilienthal appointment as a signal to Washington that the Senate opposed having more liberals in government. The Senate, however, approved the Lilienthal nomination.

McKellar voted against aid to Turkey and Greece in 1947. He initially came out against the

Marshall Plan, but the Communist coup in Czechoslovakia converted him into a supporter, and in 1949 he voted for the North Atlantic Treaty. However, he opposed a $45 million authorization to start Truman's Point Four program.

In the postwar period McKellar, a crusty, often bitter, old man, earned the reputation of being a spoiler whose style was marked by his "dark coat, pin striped trousers, white-edged waistcoat and black bow tie and his use of vicious epithets in debates." McKellar almost came to blows with House Appropriations Committee chairman CLARENCE CANNON (R-Mo.) in 1950. In a conference committee meeting, they argued over an omnibus spending bill. McKellar shouted that Cannon was "blind," "stupid," and "pig-headed." Cannon charged at McKellar, who took up his heavy silver-headed cane, which he also used as a gavel, and moved to strike Cannon. Other committee members had to intervene to prevent an unseemly brawl. Growing older, McKellar frequently fell asleep during the sessions and seemed to curtail his activities. In 1952 Representative ALBERT GORE (D-Tenn.) defeated him in the Democratic primary running on the sole issue of his age. McKellar died on October 26, 1957, in Memphis, Tennessee.

—JB

McMahon, Brien

(1903–1952) *member of the Senate*

The son of a carpenter, James O'Brien McMahon was born on October 6, 1903, in Norwalk, Connecticut. He attended Fordham University and Yale Law School. After receiving his LL.B. in 1927, he practiced law in Norwalk for a private firm. In 1933 he served as a judge of the Norwalk City Court for less than a year, leaving to go to Washington as special assistant to Attorney General Homer Cummings, formerly a powerful Connecticut politician.

From 1935 to 1939 McMahon served as assistant attorney general in charge of the Justice Department's Criminal Division, giving him supervision of the 96 U.S. attorneys throughout the country. McMahon argued 20 cases before the Supreme Court and won every one. Among his most important cases was the prosecution of the Horlan County Coal Operators Association under the Wagner Act for violating employees rights to unionize. Marked by bombings and shootings outside the courthouse, the sensational 1938 trial ended

in a hung jury. However, the mine operators shortly thereafter signed a contract with the United Mine Workers.

McMahon left the Justice Department in 1939, and, for the next five years, practiced law in Washington and Connecticut. In 1944 he received the Democratic nomination to run for the U.S. Senate against the incumbent Republican, Senator John Danaher (R-Conn.). Campaigning as an ardent New Dealer and backer of President Roosevelt's foreign policy, McMahon attacked Danaher as an isolationist. After a spirited campaign McMahon, in his first try for public office, won a surprise victory.

Less than a year into his first Senate term, McMahon took the lead in the congressional battle to establish a policy for dealing with the nascent field of atomic energy. Although only a freshman, he was appointed chairman in October 1945 of a special committee to study the problem of controlling atomic energy, following Senate custom that awarded chairmanship of a special committee to the senator who sponsors the resolution creating it. McMahon's prime objective, and achievement, was to wrest atomic energy from the hands of the military and put it under civilian supervision. His chief obstacle was the May-Johnson bill, which had been prepared by the War Department in 1945. McMahon held hearings in which he argued for civilian control. Truman supported the bill, but backing for civilian control faltered in early 1946, when physicist Alan Nunn May was arrested as a Soviet spy by the British. McMahon then worked with Republican senator ARTHUR H. VANDENBERG of Michigan to strengthen the bill. The bill passed the Senate in June 1946 and was approved by a conference committee in July 1946.

The Atomic Energy Act of 1946, also known as the McMahon Act, set up a five-man civilian Atomic Energy Commission (AEC) as the sole owner of fissionable material with full control over atomic research. The president would appoint its members who would be subject to Senate confirmation. The law also created a military liaison between the committee who could appeal all AEC decisions to the president. The bill provided drastic penalties for the unauthorized disclosure of atomic secrets. Congressional supervision was vested in a Joint Committee on Atomic Energy. Except during the Republican-controlled 80th Congress, McMahon served as chairman of the joint committee until his death.

As joint committee chairman and a self-educated atomic authority, McMahon exerted a powerful influence on the development of atomic policy during the Truman administration. He supported the AEC's first two chairmen, DAVID E. LILIENTHAL and Gordon Dean, a former law partner. His vigorous advocacy was a key element in President Truman's decision to develop the hydrogen bomb. In September 1951 McMahon called for a sixfold expansion of the country's atomic energy program, from an annual expenditure of $1 billion to $6 billion. Nine months later Truman asked Congress for $4.2 billion for atomic expansion.

Parallel to his efforts on behalf of developing atomic weaponry, McMahon waged a less fruitful campaign to bring about a global effort to halt the armaments race and neutralize atomic weapons. In a well-publicized speech before the Senate early in 1950, he warned that "piling 'secret weapon' on top of 'secret weapon' tends increasingly to exclude both public and Congress, and more and more to leave terrible decisions in fewer and fewer 'expert' hands." McMahon urged that the United States set aside $10 billion yearly for the next five years for a global Marshall Plan of atomic development for all nations, including the Soviet Union, under United Nations control and inspection. Nothing came of his proposal.

McMahon fretted over the military monopoly over atomic weaponry as a danger to democracy as late as January 1949 in a speech to the Detroit Economics Club. But the Russian detonation of an atomic bomb in September disturbed McMahon, and he began to push the president to build a hydrogen bomb and told Lilienthal that the only thing that could avert World War III was a preemptive nuclear attack on the Soviet Union. He was disgusted when the AEC's General Advisory Committee recommended against building the hydrogen bomb. He condemned the GAC's position to Truman and called for an "all-out effort" to build the H-bomb. He wrote the president: "If we let Russia get the Super first, catastrophe becomes all but certain." Although he said disarmament was a worthy long-term goal, he blasted physicists Isidor Rabi and ENRICO FERMI's call for negotiations with the Soviets to keep the arms race in check. After winning reelection in 1950, McMahon called for a massive buildup in arms, saying the country needed "thousands and thousands" of nuclear bombs.

McMahon was a partisan Democrat and a stalwart Truman supporter. A member of the Foreign Relations Committee, he was committed to an internationalist foreign policy and free trade and voted in favor of the Marshall Plan, the Greek-Turkish aid program, the British loan, the North Atlantic Treaty Organization, military aid to NATO, the reciprocal trade program, and the Japanese peace treaty. He voted against the McClellan Amendment of 1951. In 1950 McMahon and Senator HUBERT H.. HUMPHREY (D-Minn.) led the fight for adoption of the administration's Point Four program giving American technical aid and economic assistance to underdeveloped nations. He also criticized the restrictive immigration act sponsored by Senator PAT MCCARRAN (D-Nev.) and cosponsored a more liberal measure that failed to win Senate approval. In the domestic arena McMahon worked on behalf of the administration's Fair Deal program, voting for civil rights laws, the Employment Act of 1946, public housing, and federal aid to education. He was against the Portal-to-Portal Pay Act, the Case labor disputes bill, state ownership of tideland oil, and deregulation of the natural gas industry. He was one of 25 senators who voted to sustain Truman's veto of the Taft-Hartley bill.

McMahon's 1950 reelection contest took place amid an anticommunist ferment stoked by Senator JOSEPH R. MCCARTHY's (R-Wisc.) sensational charges about the presence of Communists in the U.S. government. McMahon served on the Tydings Committee investigating McCarthy's contention that the State Department was infiltrated by Communists. In public hearings McMahon repeatedly clashed with McCarthy and became a prime target of the Wisconsin senator's denunciations. McCarthy went to Connecticut to campaign for McMahon's defeat, but McMahon won reelection to a second term with 53 percent of the vote.

McMahon obviously had presidential pretensions but before he could fulfill them he died of cancer on July 28, 1952, in Washington, D.C.

—TO

McNutt, Paul V(ories)
(1891–1955) *ambassador*

The son of an Indiana judge, Paul V. McNutt was born on July 19, 1891, in Franklin, Indiana, and had aspirations of becoming president of the United States while still a child. He received a bachelor's degree from Indiana University in 1913 and a law degree from Harvard three years later. He became a member of the Indiana University Law School faculty in 1917. Following service in World War I McNutt returned to IU to teach law. He was appointed dean of the law school at the age of 34, the youngest man in the history of the school to hold the post. During the 1920s McNutt became active in the American Legion, eventually becoming national commander from 1928 to 1929. These efforts enabled him to develop a political base in Indiana. In 1933 he became the first Democratic governor since 1916. During his four-year term he centralized and streamlined government and helped guide Indiana during the depression.

McNutt's interest in presidential politics was never far beneath the surface. He had led an uninstructed delegation to the 1932 Democratic National Convention. The delegation shifted to support Franklin Roosevelt late in the process, and there is some evidence that McNutt wanted to be the choice of a deadlocked convention. This incident ruined McNutt's relationship with Roosevelt.

From 1937 to 1939 McNutt was the high commissioner to the Philippines. He was federal security administrator from 1939 to 1945, director of defense, health, and welfare services from 1941 to 1943 and chairman of the War Manpower Commission from 1942 to 1945. The strikingly handsome governor, who earned the sobriquet "the Adonis of American Politics," had not given up his childhood dream of running for the presidency. McNutt attempted to win the Democratic presidential nomination in 1940 and 1944 but despite his sizeable backing was thwarted each time by Franklin D. Roosevelt. Roosevelt also denied him the vice presidential spot on the ticket in 1940, insisting instead on HENRY A. WALLACE.

In September 1945 McNutt was reappointed high commissioner to the Philippines because, according to historian Nick Cullather, Secretary of War HENRY L. STIMSON wanted a counterbalance to General DOUGLAS MACARTHUR's civil authority and was able to convince Truman to act. His purpose there, President Truman stated, was "to speed the islands toward independence." Truman's choice of McNutt was controversial. The former governor had long been an advocate of reexamining the U.S. decision to grant independence in July 1946. As early as 1941 he had pointed out that the Philippines was economically dependent on the United States, and he advocated domestic autonomy for the nation while maintaining U.S. control of trade and foreign policy.

The destruction wrought by the war reinforced his views. Shortly before his appointment he had stated: "If the Philippines step off into an uncharted sea, as some of their leaders seem to be advocating, the islands are surely destined for trouble." However, McNutt acknowledged that "we may have to let the Philippines take their freedom now and learn the hard way. It is more than possible that if they get their freedom now they may never again attain their pre-war economic stability and may destine themselves to a permanently lowered standard of living."

While publicly supporting the president's decision to grant independence as scheduled, McNutt continued to warn of the consequences. During testimony before the House Appropriations Committee, he described the damage the war had inflicted on the Philippines and warned "that the Philippines faced problems that would shake any people and especially a people who are about to become an independent nation. . . ." McNutt's perception of the nation's economic status was reflected in his proposals for U.S.-Philippine trade. He and an aide drafted a bill that was introduced in the House of Representatives in September 1945. It called for 20 years of preferential tariffs, absolute quotas on Philippine goods imported into America, limits on the ability of the Philippines to make trade deals with third countries, and unique legal protection of U.S. citizens and companies in the archipelago. Philippine leaders backed McNutt's proposals because they, according to Cullather, "preferred dependency and bilateralism to equality and economic sovereignty." After some changes Congress passed the Philippine Trade Act, which provided for an eight-year period of duty-free trade, then a 20-year period of gradually increasing duties on Philippine imports. To ensure the Philippine legislature would pass the trade act, the Philippine Rehabilitation Act—extending aid to the war-torn islands—was made contingent on its passage of the trade bill. The State Department officials opposed the trade bill because they thought it could cause embarrassment for the United States in negotiations with other nations and would provoke criticism from anti-imperialists and nationalists everywhere. Some members of Congress opposed the trade bill because it smacked of imperialism. Nevertheless both bills were signed into law in April 1946.

Following the Philippines independence on July 4, 1946, McNutt became the first U.S. ambassador to the nation. He continued negotiating diplomatic relations between the Philippines and the United States. By March 1947 he had concluded a 99-year U.S.-Philippine treaty guaranteeing the U.S. military and naval bases in the islands, and a plebiscite granting the U.S. equal trading rights until 1974 in return for rehabilitation funds. In May 1947 he resigned to return to his law practice.

During the final months of the year, he assumed the position of counsel for the Motion Picture Association and the Association of Motion Picture Producers. He represented these groups before the House Un-American Activities Committee, investigating alleged Communist infiltration in Hollywood. McNutt pressed the committee to bring forth a list of specific offenders instead of casting "suspicion on all pictures."

By the 1948 Democratic Convention McNutt had given up his childhood dream of becoming president. He withdrew from political life completely after having served as economic adviser to Korea for two months in 1951. He then became chairman of the Philippine-American Life Insurance Company. McNutt died on March 24, 1955, in New York City.

—SBB

MacVeagh, Lincoln
(1890–1972) *ambassador*

Lincoln MacVeagh was born on October 1, 1890, in Narragansett Pier, Rhode Island. He received his B.A. from Harvard in 1913. The next year he studied languages at the Sorbonne. He worked for the publishing company of Henry Holt and Company from 1915 to 1917, when he enlisted in the army. Here he served as one of General John Pershing's aides. After World War I MacVeagh returned to Holt, where he remained until 1923. He then formed his own publishing company, the Dial Press, Inc. President Franklin D. Roosevelt appointed him envoy extraordinaire and minister plenipotentiary to Greece and Yugoslavia in 1933. In Greece he engineered the extradition of speculator Samuel Insull back to the United States. He served until 1941, when he became minister to Ireland. The following year he was appointed minister to the Union of South Africa.

In 1943 MacVeagh was made ambassador to the Greek and Yugoslavian governments in exile. Before the Greek government returned to Athens, he predicted there would be conflict in both nations,

but the situation there did not interest Roosevelt. By 1947 he became convinced that the United States would have to take dramatic action to prevent a Communist takeover. The economy was in severe difficulty, and the Greek government unstable, lacking support. Great Britain, which had backed and supplied the central government, was itself in serious economic difficulty and was preparing to pull out of Greece, cutting off what little aid it could give. Even before the formal announcement of the British withdrawal, MacVeagh sent a dispatch to Secretary of State GEORGE C. MARSHALL urging that the United States give immediate aid to Greece. Truman, after consultation with high administration and congressional officials, accepted the proposal. During the spring the State Department formulated a legislative proposal for $400 million in assistance. Congress passed the measure in May. MacVeagh then negotiated Greek acceptance of the plan, which gave the United States complete administrative authority over aid expenditure.

The ambassador played little part in administering the program, which was directed by DWIGHT G. GRISWOLD, head of the American mission of aid to Greece. The two men frequently clashed over policy toward the Greek government. As historian Howard Jones has noted, Secretary of State Marshall told Griswold that although his views on the Greek situation were welcome, MacVeagh's opinion would still be "a principal determinant." Yet as Jones further noted Griswold had more power in that he, as head of the mission, could cut off aid if the Greek government did not follow his advice. MacVeagh's authority was hard to pin down, whereas Griswold's was not. MacVeagh supported the narrow-based government of Constantine Tsaldaris, which was composed primarily of members of the Populist Party. The Populists refused to broaden the government to include center and leftist elements and demanded a strong military program to defeat the Communists. Griswold, on the other hand, demanded a coalition of Populists with the Liberals, who shared his desire to use amnesty, political reform, and conciliation to strengthen the central government. Griswold eventually used his economic power and connections with Washington to form a coalition in September 1947.

MacVeagh then formally negotiated formation of the new government headed by liberal Themistocles Sophoulis.

In 1948 MacVeagh was made ambassador to Portugal, where he remained until he was reassigned to Spain in 1952. The following year he retired from the Foreign Service. MacVeagh died on January 15, 1972, in Adelphi, Maryland.

—MLB

Magnuson, Warren G(rant)
(1905–1989) *member of the Senate*

Warren G. Magnuson was born on April 12, 1905, in Moorhead, Minnesota. Orphaned at a young age, he was adopted by a Swedish family and raised in North Dakota. In his late teens he moved to Seattle, where he received his law degree from the University of Washington in 1929. He practiced law in Seattle before being elected to the state legislature in 1932. Magnuson sponsored and won passage of the first state unemployment compensation bill in the nation. He served as county prosecutor in Seattle from 1934 to 1936, when he was elected to the House of Representatives as a Democrat. Magnuson was a staunch supporter of New Deal policies, especially of public works programs to increase employment. He also took an active part in the effort to pass an anti–poll tax law. He won election to the Senate in 1944. He would build an electoral coalition in Washington made up of agricultural and shipping interests, public power advocates, and labor.

In the upper house Magnuson supported the Truman administration's foreign policy, including containment of the Soviet Union and resisting attempts to cut defense spending. He voted for the United Nations Charter, the 1946 British loan, aid to Greece and Turkey, the Marshall Plan, the North Atlantic Treaty, and military aid to NATO, Point Four, and the Japanese Peace Treaty. Magnuson also proved to be a consistent enthusiast for liberal domestic programs. He supported the Full Employment bill and federal claims to tideland oil. He voted for federal aid to state unemployment funds in 1945 and for retention of price controls in 1946. He had opposed the Portal-to-Portal Pay Act, the Case labor disputes bill of 1946, and was among the most vocal foes of the Taft-Hartley Act of 1947. He voted to impose cloture on the debate over the bill to create a permanent Fair Employment Practices Commission. He supported federal funds for housing, extension of Social Security coverage, and rent control legislation.

Magnuson worked hard to channel the increasing government spending of the postwar years to his home state, which was heavily dependent on shipping, aircraft, fisheries, and timber for its prosperity. He advocated government funds for commercial fisheries, reclamation projects, rural electrification, and for a Columbia Valley Authority similar to the Tennessee Valley Authority.

As a member of the Senate Commerce Committee, Magnuson chaired its Merchant Marine and Maritime Affairs Subcommittee. In 1949 he conducted an extensive probe of the conditions of the U.S. merchant marine. The subcommittee's report found that the merchant marine played a "vital role" in national defense but that it was "rapidly disintegrating" due to foreign competition. The report urged extensive government aid to the shipping industry.

In order to help the industry Magnuson successfully amended the Military Appropriations Act of 1949 to require that 50 percent of U.S. arms shipments abroad be carried on American vessels. In 1950 he introduced legislation to expand federal aid to the shipping industry through a program of construction subsidies. Despite extensive hearings on the bill, no action was taken by the Senate in 1950. Magnuson sponsored similar legislation in 1951, however, and won passage of it in July 1952. In its final form the measure liberalized the Merchant Marine Act of 1936 by allowing government subsidies to shipbuilders regardless of whether the ships operated over essential trade routes.

Magnuson also took a lead in the initial attempts to establish a National Science Foundation. In July 1945 Dr. VANNEVER BUSH, head of the wartime Office of Scientific Research and Development, urged creation of a permanent peacetime foundation to support scientific research. President Truman endorsed the recommendation in his message to Congress in September, and Senators Magnuson and HARLEY M. KILGORE (D-W.Va.) introduced legislation embodying the recommendations. The proposed foundation was to promote scientific research by awarding research contracts, providing scholarships and fellowships, and disseminating research findings to the scientific community. Magnuson took the lead in pushing the measure through the Senate. However, the House failed to take any action on it. Legislation establishing the National Science Foundation was finally signed into law in May 1950, but Magnuson played little role in its passage. Magnuson also cosponsored the legislation that established the National Institutes of Health in 1948.

Throughout his career Magnuson continued to channel lucrative government contracts in aerospace and shipping to Washington. This allowed him to retain the support of business interests despite his consistent advocacy of liberal social welfare and labor legislation. During the 1960s he took an increasing interest in environmental and consumer affairs and played a major role in passage of cigarette labeling and auto safety laws. Magnuson also figured prominently in the passage of the controversial public accommodations section of the Civil Rights Act of 1964. In the 1970s he promoted a system of national health insurance. In the 1980 election, Republican Slade Gorton defeated Magnuson, who died nine years later on May 20, 1989, in Seattle, Washington. (See *The Eisenhower Years, The Kennedy Years, The Johnson Years, The Nixon/Ford Years* Volumes)

—JD

Malone, George W(ilson)
(1890–1961) *member of the Senate*

George W. "Molly" Malone was born on August 7, 1890, in Fredonia, Kansas. While an engineering student at the University of Nevada, he formed the King and Malone Construction Company, a firm of construction engineers. He graduated from the university in 1917. Following service in the army during World War I, Malone returned to engineering. From 1927 to 1935 he was chief engineer of Nevada. He also served as a member of the Public Service Commission and the Colorado River Commission. He then resigned his post to return to engineering. During World War II Malone was special consultant to the secretary of war and various Senate committees. In 1946 he won election to the Senate on a conservative platform.

An "Old Guard" Republican, Malone gained attention as a vigorous opponent of foreign aid and reciprocal trade agreements. He opposed the Truman Doctrine and derided the Marshall Plan as a "world-wide WPA." The Senate defeated his amendment to reduce the program of aid to France, Italy, and Austria from $597 million to $400 million in November 1947. The following year, as debate on the European Recovery Program (ERP) continued, Malone joined a group of 20 Republican senators called "revisionists" in an attempt to unite the

party against the Marshall Plan. Later, nine of the senators voted for the ERP. Malone, however, stood against it, regarding it as "the most amazingly brazen and preposterous idea for a world-wide redistribution of wealth which has yet been proposed, even by the socialistic European governments, to lower our living standards down to their own. . . ." In March 1948 he charged that the Marshall Plan would help spread socialism in Europe and predicted that ERP countries would sell their surplus products to Russia. He voted against the North Atlantic Treaty, military aid to NATO and GEORGE C. MARSHALL's appointment as secretary of defense, and he supported the Dirksen Amendment to Mutual Security Act of 1951 to cut $250 million in aid to Europe.

Despite his conservatism, Malone voted against the Taft-Hartley Act of 1947, opposed turning the tidelands over to the states, and supported the Housing Act of 1949. More predictably he voted for the 80th Congress's Republican tax cut, the McCarran Internal Security Act, the McCarran-Walter Immigration Act, and opposed cloture on the debate over the Fair Employment Practices Act.

As a senator from a leading mining state, Malone was eager to promote the interests of the extractive industries. In June 1948 he introduced a mining subsidy bill to create a mine incentive payments division in the Department of Interior to stimulate production and conservation of ores and metals. The Reconstruction Finance Corporation was empowered to purchase metal surpluses arising from the act. Malone stressed that the measures was essential for national defense. However, the bill was attacked as socialistic and no action was taken. In 1951 he voted against the bill to extend the Reciprocal Trade Act, fearing that Nevada's miners would be injured by foreign competition. When the Senate proposed suspending the import duties on zinc, lead, and tungsten in 1951 and 1952, Malone objected.

A vigorous anticommunist, in 1950 Malone introduced a bill to prohibit U.S. financial assistance to any country trading with the USSR or its satellites. He was a foe of the Point Four Program of assistance to underdeveloped countries on the grounds that it would aid Communists. Malone voted against the American peace treaty negotiated with Japan in September 1951, warning that it would result in a Communist takeover of the Far East. The Senator castigated Secretary of State

DEAN ACHESON as a Communist fellow traveler who had lost Asia to communism. He was cosponsor of a bill, passed by the Senate in May 1951, cutting off U.S. economic aid to countries that shipped war materials to the USSR and Communist China.

Reelected in 1952, Malone became a strong defender of Senator JOSEPH R. MCCARTHY (R-Wisc.) and opposed his censure in 1954. In 1958 he led an unsuccessful effort to have the Senate resolution of censure expunged from the record. Malone's political career ended in 1958, when he was defeated in his campaign for a third Senate term by Howard W. Cannon, a Las Vegas city attorney. He returned to his engineering firm in Reno and in 1960 was defeated as Republican candidate for the House of Representatives. Malone died of cancer on May 19, 1961, in Washington, D.C.

—AES

Maragon, John F.

(1894–?) *government official*

John Maragon was born in 1894 on the Greek island of Levkes. At age 13 he emigrated from the island and settled in Kansas City, Missouri, where he worked as a bootblack. During Prohibition he smuggled liquor for several senators, one of whom got him a job with the FBI. In the 1930s he held obscure posts with the National Recovery Administration and the Bituminous Coal Commission. From 1939 to 1945 Maragon was the Washington agent for the Baltimore and Ohio Railroad. He became a close friend of President Truman's military aide, General HARRY L. VAUGHAN, and helped plan trips for members of Congress. Maragon had a pass and a desk in the White House, although he was not on the executive payroll. In 1945 and 1946, despite Truman's removal of his name from the mission list, he was a member of the Allied Mission to Greece, appointed to oversee elections there. He was later fired for being a "nuisance."

During the early postwar period Maragon made several trips to Europe to purchase perfume for the Albert Verley Perfume Company in Chicago. He was aided by Vaughan, who provided army planes for his use at a time when civilian air travel was still prohibited. Radio commentator and newspaper columnist DREW PEARSON accused Vaughan and Maragon of corruption.

In 1949 Maragon's name was linked with the "five percenters," men who sold influence in getting government contracts for 5 percent of the contract price. When the Senate Permanent Investigations Subcommittee, chaired by CLYDE R. HOEY (D-N.C.), investigated these influence peddlers, many of Maragon's questionable dealings came to light. Maragon was accused of attempting to help companies gain government contracts by using his influence with Vaughan. The subcommittee also charged him with collecting income from private corporations while working for the U.S. government in Greece. Maragon denied that he had ever represented private firms before government agencies. In testimony before the panel in August, Vaughan admitted having done favors for Maragon. The general called him a "lovable sort of chap" but predicted that his White House pass would "probably" be revoked for "fumigation." But he did not think Maragon had done anything illegal, saying: "I don't think Maragon ever did anything dishonest. He was always too busy doing something stupid." The subcommittee report, issued in January 1950, denounced Maragon as an "outright fixer."

Maragon was indicted for lying to the subcommittee and convicted of perjury in April 1950. He was given the minimum two-year sentence. In 1956 the Democratic-controlled House of Representatives approved Maragon as a clerk at $1.61 an hour. He was dismissed from the post in 1959.

—AES

Marcantonio, Vito

(1902–1954) *member of the House of Representatives*

Born on December 10, 1902 in East Harlem, New York, Vito Marcantonio began his political career at the age of 18 when he became a leader of the East Harlem Tenant League's successful rent strike. He graduated from New York University Law School in 1925 and managed Fiorello LaGuardia's congressional campaigns in 1926 and 1930. During 1930 Marcantonio was appointed assistant U.S. attorney, specializing in immigration cases. He resigned in 1933 to work in LaGuardia's mayoralty campaign. The following year he took over LaGuardia's seat in the U.S. House, where he represented a district of blacks, Italians, and Puerto Rican immigrants.

Marcantonio joined the left-wing coalition of garment unions in New York, which formed the American Labor Party (ALP) in 1936. Although Marcantonio was not a Communist Party member, the CPUSA gave the ALP considerable help in New York City. Marcantonio generally followed the Communist Party line, and, by the late 1940s, the Communists had become a strong presence in the ALP. The ALP supported Marcantonio through the rest of his political career. He won reelection to the House as a Republican in 1938 and 1940 but was refused the party's nomination in 1942. Nevertheless, by 1942 Marcantonio had become so adept in using LaGuardia's gift of police control, which regularly protected Harlem gamblers and loan sharks, that Tammany Hall leaders gave him the Democratic nomination in exchange for Marcantonio's assurance of protection for whatever rackets Tammany's friends operated. There was another reason why Marcantonio received the support of the Democratic, Republican, and American Labor parties. As Marcantonio's biographer, Gerald Meyer noted, Marcantonio's ALP would endorse this or that Republican or Democrat for local or state legislative offices that had patronage appointments—which is what the local Republicans and Democrats cared about. Meanwhile, Republicans and Democrats would endorse the ALP's Marcantonio, and what the ALP wanted as a left-wing ideological party was having a national spokesman in Congress: Marcantonio. Marcantonio reportedly took money and talent from mobsters, Communists, and Republicans alike but only to maintain his political machine. He lived frugally on his $10,000 a year congressional salary.

During his stormy congressional tenure Marcantonio became known as a Communist sympathizer. Isolated in the House and subjected to overwhelming political pressures from New York politicians, he achieved little legislative success. He was primarily known as a social critic and a vocal opponent of what he received were the forces of "fascism" and "Wall Street imperialism."

In 1940 and early 1941 Marcantonio voted against such defense measures as peacetime conscription and alien registration until the Nazi invasion of the Soviet Union in June 1941. He then became a strong advocate of American intervention and was an early supporter of Stalin's call for a second front. He fought wage freezes and antistrike legislation. He also played a prominent role in creating support for a Fair Employment Practices Commission and anti–poll tax and antilynching legislation and generally supported President Roosevelt's wartime measures.

Marcantonio's foreign policy stand during the Truman years was pro-Soviet, and he analyzed U.S. diplomacy from a Marxist-Leninist perspective. He approved Soviet control of Eastern Europe, applauding the peasants for "throwing off the yoke of their capitalist masters." He opposed the administration's containment policies. He identified the Truman Doctrine as "the cause of world disagreement and possible war" and called the Marshall Plan a military and political program of imperialism and war. Marcantonio warned that "this so-called anti-Communist policy is driving this nation not only into war but also into fascism." In 1949 he proposed that the $1.314 billion authorized for military aid to China and Spain be used instead in research to protect Americans against polio. He disdainfully termed U.S. involvement in Korea "operation desperation" and in June 1950 was the only member of Congress to vote against appropriations strengthening the defense of Western Europe.

Marcantonio was a strong supporter of organized labor. In April and May 1946 he defended striking railroad and sugar workers. Protesting the "lynch labor spirit" of Congress, he called on fellow House members to make business its target. The following year he voted against the Taft-Hartley Act, which, he warned was marching the United States toward fascism. In 1950 Marcantonio likened Truman's threat to take over the coal mines to dropping a "hell bomb on the heads of coal miners and their families." He proclaimed that "all working people know that President Truman can no longer be counted upon as a friend of labor . . . [and] serves the steel oligarchy."

Marcantonio was the leading critic of the antisubversive legislation of the late 1940s. In 1948 he denounced the Mundt-Nixon bill, which would have required the registration of Communists, terming it a "bill of attainder." He also campaigned against the Internal Security Act of 1950 and the loyalty bills that were designed to eliminate Communists from government employment. Marcantonio conducted the successful legal defense of W. E. B. Dubois, who was indicted for failure to register under the Foreign Agents Registration Act.

Opposition to Marcantonio grew during the late 1940s. In 1944 the New York State legislature abolished Marcantonio's old district and created a new one that included, besides his stronghold in

East Harlem, an area called Yorkville, whose residents were largely German-American, had been Coughlinites before the war, and would become McCarthyites after the war. Marcantonio was still able to win the Democratic and Republican primaries, as well as the ALP's, with the usual arrangement with local politicians. Two years later Republican governor THOMAS E. DEWEY threatened New York Republican politicians with investigation and exposure if they endorsed Marcantonio. The GOP ran Frederick Van Pelt Bryan III, a highly decorated veteran. Although East Harlem Republicans hardly helped Bryan, he still won the primary. But Democratic Tammany Hall came to Marcantonio's rescue and gave him its endorsement, in exchange for the ALP's endorsement of its congressional candidates in Manhattan's other districts. Marcantonio still nearly lost the Democratic primary, despite Tammany's endorsement, but he won reelection to his seat, again with Tammany Hall help (including vote stealing and ballot tampering, and reportedly with the assistance of mobster friends).

In 1947 the state legislature passed the Wilson-Pakula Act, prohibiting any candidate who was not a party member from running in a primary without the permission of the party's county committee. Again Tammany came through, nominating a straw candidate whose campaign office was shuttered most of the time and who only made three speeches. Again the ALP endorsed a number of Democratic candidates for other offices. His Republican opponent, John Ellis, ran with the additional endorsement of the Liberal Party and on a staunchly anticommunist platform. Marcantonio still won in a three-way race. Marcantonio ran for mayor on the ALP ticket in 1949, and, although he lost overall, he won a smashing victory within East Harlem. It became apparent that only a fusion candidate could defeat Marcantonio. By 1950 the rising tide of McCarthyism made the old political arrangements between the two major parties and the ALP impossible, and Marcantonio was beaten by James Donovan, who ran under the Democratic, Republican, and Liberal parties' banners. He resigned from the ALP in November 1953 and formed the Good Neighbor Party in February 1954. Marcantonio died on August 9, 1954, in New York City while campaigning for his old seat.

—SP

Marshall, George C(atlett)

(1880–1959) *secretary of state, secretary of defense*

George Catlett Marshall was born the son of a coal merchant on December 31, 1880, in Uniontown, Pennsylvania. He attended the Virginia Military Institute, where he graduated in 1901. The following year he joined the army. From 1902 to 1906 he was stationed in the Philippines and the American Southwest. Marshall attended the Infantry-Cavalry School from 1906 to 1907 and graduated from the School of the Line (the forerunner of the Command and General Staff School) in 1908. For the next two years, he served as instructor at the school. During World War I he held high administrative and planning posts with the American Expeditionary Force. In 1918, as chief of operations of the First Army, he helped prepare the Meuse-Argonne offensive.

Impressed with Marshall's ability, General John Pershing appointed him aide de camp; Marshall served at that post from 1919 until the general's retirement in 1924. He saw duty in China from 1924 to 1927 and was stationed at the Infantry School at

Portrait of Secretary of Defense George C. Marshall, 1950 *(Harry S. Truman Library, Ralph N. Stohl Papers)*

Fort Benning, Georgia, from 1927 to 1932. As assistant commandant in charge of instruction, he strengthened the curriculum and revamped instruction techniques. His work influenced several generals, including J. LAWTON COLLINS and W. BEDELL SMITH, who became prominent in World War II. During the 1930s Marshall organized Civilian Conservation Corps camps in South Carolina, Georgia, Washington, and Oregon. Marshall became chief of the War Department's War Plans Division in 1938. The Brigadier General was appointed army chief of staff a few months later. In September 1939 he was jumped in rank to full general.

At that post Marshall directed the American military buildup for World War II. Under his command the army grew from 200,000 to 8.3 million men. He helped train an excellent fighting force, chose outstanding officers, and coordinated the procurement of material necessary for the war effort. An aloof, confident, self-disciplined man, Marshall impressed Allied military leaders with his air of command. He led the opposition to Churchill's Mediterranean strategy, pressing instead for a cross-channel invasion route for the conquest of the Axis powers. His diplomatic ability broke many deadlocks between the Allied leaders. Because President Roosevelt felt him too valuable to leave his post, Marshall did not lead the Normandy invasion. The campaign was headed by his protégé, General DWIGHT D. EISENHOWER. During late 1944 Marshall was named general of the army with rank over all other five-star military men except Admiral WILLIAM D. LEAHY. When Soviet-American relations began to disintegrate in the spring of 1945, Marshall warned Truman against a belligerent policy toward the Soviet Union, because the general believed the Russians were needed to fight the Japanese. Having dealt with Marshall while chairman of the wartime Senate committee that investigated the defense program, the president had come to respect the chief of staff greatly. Since Truman's assertiveness had not brought any better behavior on the part of the Soviets, the president began to strike a more conciliatory pose with the Soviets in June. Marshall emerged from the war a hero, representing to many the best in the nation's military tradition. Winston Churchill called him "the true organizer of victory." When Marshall retired as chief in November 1945 at the mandatory age of 65, Truman awarded him his only medal for service in the war: a second Oak Leaf Cluster to his World War I Distinguished Service Medal. (He had refused to accept any during the war while men were dying in the field.)

On November 27, a week after Marshall retired, Truman requested that he go to China on a mission to negotiate a coalition government between Nationalist Chiang Kai-shek (Jiang Jieshi) and Communist Mao Zedong (Mao Tse-tung) so as to avoid civil war. Although anxious to leave government service, Marshall reluctantly agreed out of a sense of duty, and was named Truman's special emissary with the personal rank of ambassador. Truman had chosen the general because of his own respect for Marshall, whom he publicly called "the greatest living American." The president thought that Marshall's wartime experience in dealing with military leaders would aid him in negotiations between Mao and Chiang. More important, the president believed that Marshall's stature and reputation for objectivity would blunt already growing criticism by the China Lobby that the administration was willing to "sell out" China to the Communists. Marshall's friends thought Truman had given him an impossible task, given the deep-seated animosity the two sides held for each other, which virtually precluded the formation of a coalition government.

Marshall had two contradictory goals: he was to be a disinterested mediator building a coalition government composed of all political parties while at the same time he was to build up Chiang so as to minimize the power of the Communists. The only leverage he had was the threat to assist or not to assist the Nationalists in moving back into Manchuria. He could motivate the Nationalists by threatening not to aid them in any move, or the Communists by threatening to help Chiang's forces. Another problem was that even if Chiang refused to make concessions, the United States would aid him in any case. This took pressure off Chiang, as he suspected this to be the case, and it made Mao, who also believed this was America's policy, wary of Marshall's claims of impartiality. He was also to develop a comprehensive and impartial economic assistance program to aid all of China. During 1946 Marshall, against difficult odds, worked to assemble the coalition. Each side deeply distrusted the other. The Nationalists refused to accept Communists into the government until Mao disbanded his army. The Communists, in turn, refused to disarm without guarantees of their status in the government. Nevertheless, by late February Marshall had negotiated a truce, set up a date for convening a National Assembly and a council to draft a constitution, and secured agreement from both sides to a plan for integration of their armies.

In March 1946 Marshall returned to Washington to consult with Truman and work out a Chinese aid program with various government agencies. In his absence the shaky accord disintegrated. Conservative Kuomintang elements rejected coalition with the Communists. In addition, when Mao's forces moved into areas of Manchuria abandoned by the Soviet Union, the Nationalists attempted to prevent the takeover. Warning that Chiang was overextending his supply lines, Marshall attempted to stop the offensive and negotiate a truce. His efforts failed. Both Communists and Nationalists stiffened their attitudes, forcing him to conclude that his peace efforts had reached an impasse and that he should be recalled. Truman ended the mission in January 1947. In his reports Marshall warned that if the United States would try to save Chiang it would "virtually [have] to take over the Chinese government. . . . It would involve [the United States] in a continuing commitment from which it would practically be impossible to withdraw." Anxious not to become pulled into such a war, the president gradually withdrew American aid, granting only token assistance in response to domestic criticism.

During an inspection tour of U.S. Army posts in the Far East, Chief of Staff General DWIGHT D. EISENHOWER passed word to Marshall in Nanking that Truman wanted him to replace JAMES F. BYRNES as secretary of state. Marshall, who again wanted to retire, felt duty-bound to accept, but he wanted to put off the appointment until later because he still dimly hoped he could bring about a settlement. When all hope of restoring peace vanished, Marshall left for home to become secretary of state. Marshall enjoyed high standing on both sides of the congressional aisle, which would be important because the Republicans had regained control of Congress in the 1946 elections. The Senate, disregarding precedent, unanimously approved the nomination without a hearing on January 8. Marshall became the first military leader to head the State Department.

Most Americans praised Truman's choice, but a few criticized the appointment of a career officer to the senior cabinet post and warned of a trend toward militarism in the conduct of foreign affairs. To these doubters Marshall retorted, "It is not with brass hats but with brass heads that the danger to our country lies." He quickly stopped speculation that he might use his position to run for high elective office, arguing that his cabinet post was not political and assuring the nation that he would not become involved in partisan matters.

Marshall's appointment gave the administration prestige at a point when its popularity was low and aided Truman's drive for a bipartisan foreign policy. He had immense authority with Congress and received the support of many conservative Republicans who had opposed the administration's conduct of foreign affairs. The public admired him as a man of integrity and wisdom who stood above politics. Foreign leaders, many of whom he had dealt with during the war, respected him. Marshall quickly developed a close working relationship with Truman, who, in the words of historian Alexander DeConde, "virtually adored him." Truman was so in awe of the man that he never seemed relaxed with Marshall. The president placed such trust in Marshall's judgment that the secretary later admitted he found it frightening. In the general, Truman found a man of ability and prestige who was deeply loyal even when others deserted him. During 1948, when Truman's popularity was low, Marshall resisted suggestions by his subordinates that he divorce foreign policy from the president. Even though the two men occasionally differed on details of foreign policy, they hardly ever quarreled over fundamental issues.

One of Marshall's first tasks as secretary was the reorganization of the department to clarify the lines of authority. He developed a structure similar to that of the military with the undersecretary of state acting in effect as a chief of staff. He did not concern himself with the day-to-day workings of the bureaucracy or the details of foreign policy planning. Only major policy questions came to his desk. Most recommendations were made by his undersecretaries, DEAN G. ACHESON and later ROBERT A. LOVETT. Marshall thought his function was to determine broad policy objectives. To advise him, he created a Policy Planning Staff outside the department hierarchy. Its task was to analyze trends in foreign affairs and make long-term policy suggestions. Marshall helped rebuild State Department influence, which had become a policy backwater under Roosevelt and then Byrnes.

The selection of Marshall as secretary of state signaled a firmer Administration policy toward the

Soviet Union. Marshall shared Truman's growing belief that Soviet communism was a threat to the Western world and that the United States had a responsibility to resist Soviet expansion. Marshall was oriented toward Europe and recommended that the United States stop Soviet expansion there before directing attention toward Asia. Endorsing the concept of a bipartisan foreign policy, he criticized the lack of American intensity and unity of purpose to meet the Soviet challenge. Yet Marshall initially did not think cooperation with the Soviets on all issues entirely out of the question. As Marshall biographer Forrest C. Pogue pointed out he was the last important American leader to give up on the Soviets as utter obstructionists. But he soon came to the opposite conclusion when he had to deal with them as secretary.

Marshall was away at conferences during much of the time and could not give close attention to molding the administration's containment policy toward the Soviet Union. Dean Acheson, therefore, played a major role in policy formulation. Nevertheless, Marshall determined broad policy objectives and offered suggestions on specific proposals when he thought necessary. When the British notified the administration in early 1947 that it no longer could support the Greek government against a Communist insurgency and the Turks against pressure from the Soviets over control of the Dardanelles, Marshall agreed that Communist success in these places might lead to Soviet domination of Europe, the Middle East, and Asia. He told congressional leaders that America must stop the Communists and recommended a program of American aid to the beleaguered nations. Because he was preparing for the Moscow Foreign Ministers Conference, he entrusted the formulation of the plan to Acheson. The undersecretary proposed a $400 million program of assistance to the nations. Marshall presented the plan to Congressional leaders, but Acheson did not think him forceful enough in arguing the case with the congressmen, and he put the crisis in more apocalyptic terms, affirming that Western civilization itself was at stake. At Senate Foreign Relations Committee chairman ARTHUR H. VANDENBERG's (R-Mich.) urging, Truman chose the more dramatic approach to call for aid to Greece and Turkey. Marshall thought the tone of the speech overblown and that the country's rapid demobilization—which he had opposed—made such a rhetorical commitment not

credible. Despite his opposition to the manner in which the plan was presented, Marshall lobbied for the proposal, which was passed in May.

Marshall worried that the crusading tone of the Truman Doctrine speech was also bad timing, as he was going to Moscow for negotiations and still had hope for an agreement. The Moscow Foreign Ministers Conference of April 1947 finally convinced him such could not be attained. At the meeting, called to discuss the future of Germany, the Russians proposed the political centralization of that defeated nation. They asked for Russian participation in the control of the Ruhr and settlement of reparation issues favorable to Moscow. Soviet foreign minister Vyacheslav Molotov refused to yield ground, and Stalin, unlike during the war, seemed unconcerned that the conference accomplished little over a five-week period. Marshall now agreed with his subordinates that the Soviets had no interest in reaching a settlement over Germany. Further, he became convinced the Russians were stalling in the negotiations and thus impeding the important task of rebuilding Germany, hoping rather for the economic collapse of Western Europe, thus making it ripe for Communist subversion.

On April 28, two days after his return, Marshall delivered a national broadcast address on the conference. Europe, he said, was not recovering from the war as quickly as expected and would need immediate U.S. aid. "The patient is sinking," he said, "while the doctors deliberate." The following day, working on ideas advanced by planners in the State, War and Navy departments, he asked GEORGE F. KENNAN, head of the Policy Planning Staff, to begin formulation of an aid proposal. Kennan, Acheson, and Undersecretary of State for Economic Affairs WILLIAM L. CLAYTON worked through the spring to develop the plan. Kennan recommended a long-term aid program directed primarily by Europeans. Clayton, on the other hand, urged immediate aid under the control of the United States. Both men insisted that the participation of Germany was vital even though it might make permanent the division of that nation and increase tensions with the USSR. Marshall agreed with Kennan's insistence on European initiative. He also accepted Kennan's recommendation that the Soviet bloc be invited to join the plan despite the risk that the Russians might try to block German economic resurgence with demands for a joint administration of the Ruhr. Extending an invitation to all of Europe to participate was done to avoid the suggestion of an American division of Europe, but it was done with the expectation in the State Department that the Soviets would reject it for fear of losing control of Eastern Europe and in opposition to the verification process the Americans would require to see if funds were used properly. These controls eventually prevented Russian acceptance of the proposal.

Marshall carefully timed the public announcement of the plan. It must, he insisted, break with "explosive force" to overcome isolationist opposition. "It is easy to propose a great plan," he maintained, "but exceedingly difficult to manage the form and procedure so that it would have a fair chance of political survival." Although many details remained undeveloped, Marshall announced the European Recovery Program (ERP) after he received an honorary degree at Harvard in June of that year. "It is logical that the U.S. should do whatever it is able to do to assist in the return of normal economic health in the world, without which there can be no political stability and no assured peace," he said. "Our policy is directed not against any country or any doctrine but against hunger, poverty, depression and chaos." Marshall then invited the Europeans to draft a joint proposal for economic aid that would "provide a cure rather than a mere palliative." Europeans responded enthusiastically to the plan, eventually requesting a four-year program of $17 billion in aid.

Marshall's belief that the Soviets intended to wreck European recovery was reinforced during the fall of 1947. Not liking the requirements to list their nation's resources and needs, the Russians denounced the plan and forced the rest of Eastern Europe to reject it. Moscow launched a propaganda campaign against the ERP, created Cominform, and approved Communist-inspired violence in Western Europe. The final breakdown in East-West cooperation came at the London Conference in December 1947. Marshall was weary of continued Russian demands for German reparations, abolition of the joint British-American sectors called Bizonia in western Germany, and participation in the occupation of the Ruhr. He, therefore, abruptly asked for adjournment of the meeting. No plans were made to call another one.

During the first half of 1948 Marshall worked for the passage of the ERP. He encountered intense opposition from a hostile Congress dominated by Republicans unwilling to give the administration a

major diplomatic triumph during the election year and reluctant to grant large amounts of foreign aid. With the help of Senator Vandenberg, Marshall gradually gained acceptance of the proposal. An effective witness before committees and an excellent impromptu speaker, he convinced Congress of the need for the plan. His reputation as a nonpartisan also helped the proposal on Capitol Hill. Marshall explained that an economically stable Western Europe would correct adverse socioeconomic conditions that had served to breed communism. To congressmen fearful that German participation might lead to a return of militarism, he pointed out that the plan contained controls to insure use of German natural resources and industrial capabilities solely for Europe's economic rehabilitation. Marshall disagreed with those who warned that the program would be a drain on the U.S. economy. Rather, he maintained that a revitalized Western Europe would stimulate U.S. production and trade. He expressed concern over continued Russian expansion westward, fearing the collapse of Western civilization if Soviet aggrandizement were not checked. Marshall rejected Senator J. WILLIAM FULBRIGHT's (D-Ark.) suggestions that the European nations be required to create a continental federation before becoming eligible for aid. Although he hoped that economic integration might eventually lead to political unity, Marshall counseled caution. He noted that European nationalism might prove an insurmountable obstacle. Forcing the issue might bring accusations of American imperialism. By the spring of 1948 Marshall had convinced a majority in Congress to back his plan. Events in Europe coalesced support. The Communist coup in Czechoslovakia during February convinced many of the need to take action on the proposal. Congress passed the Marshall Plan in March.

According to historian Michael Hogan, the Marshall Plan, although not the sole reason for Western European economic recovery, did help make the difference.

Because of his respect for the man, Truman rarely acted against Marshall's advice. However, he did do so on the issue of the division of Palestine and the recognition of Israel. Because of the Holocaust there was widespread sympathy for the creation of a Jewish state. Palestine had been a British mandate since the end of World War I, but, with increasing conflict between Jewish immigrants and native Arabs, London decided to leave the problem to the

UN in 1947. The UN partitioned the province into Jewish and Arab sections, with both the United States and the USSR agreeing to the plan. When Britain announced it would withdraw completely in May 1948, intercommunal violence rose and war was imminent. Marshall and the State Department's Near East Division opposed partition because of the unavailability of American troops for reinforcement and because it would alienate Arabs, giving the Soviets an opening to the oil-rich region. The Defense Department and U.S. intelligence agreed. These groups tried to reverse administration support of partition in the spring of 1948.

By March Marshall had convinced Truman to acquiesce to the continuation of trusteeship status in the area if negotiations over partition failed. However, in early May, days before the British mandate terminated and the Jews declared independence, Truman reversed himself. White House officials David Niles and Clark Clifford argued that denying support for partition would be wrong given the Holocaust. Niles and Clifford not only advocated support for partition but also for the immediate recognition of Israel when it was formed. Marshall denounced the presidential adviser recommendations as election year politicking, and if the president followed Niles and Clifford's advice, he would break his lifetime pledge not to vote, and he would do so against Truman. (Clifford in his memoirs denied politics as the motivation for his position.) The president resumed his support of the secretary's position and told Clifford that he wanted recognition but not immediately. Clifford persuaded Truman to reconsider, and he managed to get Undersecretary of State ROBERT A. LOVETT to secure Marshall's acquiescence but not support. Just minutes after Israel declared independence on May 14, Truman granted de facto recognition. What caused Truman to make this decision and how it affected the election is still a matter of dispute.

Marshall successfully clashed with Truman's political advisers over the handling of the Soviet blockade of Berlin in June 1948. He rejected the suggestion of such military leaders as General LUCIUS D. CLAY that the United States force entrance into Berlin with armed convoys. Marshall convinced Truman to support an airlift to supply the beleaguered city. As fear of war increased and criticism of the president's handling of foreign policy mounted during the election year, Truman's policy advisers urged him to take dramatic action on Berlin to gain

support. They were concerned that the public considered Marshall the dominant force in foreign affairs. Marshall, one of Truman's advisers said, was always associated with diplomatic victories, Truman with defeats. They suggested that Truman send Chief Justice FRED M. VINSON to Moscow to conduct direct talks with Stalin on Berlin. Truman agreed. Marshall, however, opposed the mission, arguing that it would undercut negotiations on the issue at the UN. Truman cancelled the mission. His advisers tried to convince him that the secretary did not understand the political importance of the move but the president refused to ignore Marshall's advice.

Although Marshall focused much of his attention on Europe, he played a major role in developing policies toward other areas. His actions were shaped, in part, by the growing cold war. Marshall pushed for the unification of the armed services and the establishment of an agency to coordinate military and foreign policy. Some of his suggestions were incorporated into the National Security Act of 1947, which created the National Security Council. The body was composed of the president and the secretaries of state, defense, army, navy, and air force. It was to advise and coordinate defense and foreign policy. Marshall advocated universal military training to expand the army, thus increasing its effectiveness as a diplomatic weapon. He also championed rearming Western Europe to bolster the region against potential Soviet aggression. Just one month after becoming secretary of state, Marshall had spoken in favor of international control of atomic energy and supported the Baruch Plan, which called for UN control and inspection of atomic sites. When it became apparent in 1948 that the Russians had no interest in atomic controls, Marshall expressed no reservations about increasing U.S. experimentation with atomic weapons and cautioned against unilateral atomic disarmament.

Marshall had little interest in Latin America, and, according to one critic, during his tenure Latin American affairs temporarily fell in eclipse. He did, however, initiate a series of alliances designed to prevent Communist expansion in the area. In 1948 he persuaded the Latin American nations to join together in the Rio Pact. The treaty stipulated that an attack against any hemispheric nation would be considered an attack against all but that members would not be required to use their armed forces without their consent. It also defined the pact's security zone to include all the Americas. The following year Marshall helped formulate the Pact of Bogotá, establishing the Organization of American States. The meeting reaffirmed the principle that an attack against one member was aggression against all.

While the political and military needs of the hemisphere were central to Marshall's thinking, the economic problems resulting in part from the end of the war received only verbal attention. American wartime investment contributed to the Latin American economic boom, which abruptly ended after the armistice. By 1947 Latin American political leaders were seeking U.S. economic assistance. Speaking for the administration in 1947 at the Rio Conference, Marshall explained that Europe, being "threatened with starvation and economic chaos" must receive attention first, and he predicted that European rehabilitation would contribute to "the economy of this hemisphere." At the 1948 Bogotá meeting, Marshall asked for Latin Americans to understand that the United States alone was carrying almost the entire burden of world recovery and reiterated a promise for future economic aid.

During his tenure Marshall began discussions on the formation of a North Atlantic alliance, which he thought necessary in light of Soviet intransigence at the UN and Russian conduct in Europe. The result was the Brussels Pact, a 50-year mutual defense agreement signed in March 1948 by Britain, France, and the Benelux countries. Although Marshall advocated supplying American arms and reviving lend-lease to assist in meeting the alliance's military needs, Congress refused funding. In the spring of 1948 he held secret meetings with Senators HENRY CABOT LODGE (R-Mass.) and Arthur Vandenberg on possible U.S. involvement in a European defense pact. The result of these conversations was Senate Resolution 239, which supported the principle of U.S. participation in regional collective arrangements. Throughout the summer and fall of 1948, at Marshall's direction, Robert Lovett held secret talks with Brussels Pact representatives over U.S. involvement in the organization. The result was the North Atlantic Treaty signed in 1949, after Marshall had left office.

As secretary of state, Marshall was careful to avoid increasing U.S. involvement in the Chinese civil war. He made no policy statements on China and resisted demands from the powerful China Lobby to increase aid to Chiang, fearing that such a commitment would jeopardize the U.S. position in Europe. Neither Truman nor Marshall believed that

increased aid would save Chiang. Marshall had told the Chinese leader that "the fundamental and lasting solution to China's problems must come from the Chinese themselves."

Nevertheless, Marshall was forced to make some concessions to right-wing pressure on the issue. In July 1947 he sent General ALBERT C. WEDEMEYER to China to investigate the situation and to make policy recommendations. Wedemeyer's report suggested increasing aid to the Nationalist regime. Believing the general's assessment inadequate and impractical, Marshall urged the report's suppression. Truman agreed. Nevertheless, during the debate on the European Recovery Program, the administration, seeking to placate critics, asked for a slight increase in aid to China. At the same time Marshall abandoned advocacy of a coalition government although he would not acquiesce to Republican calls for intervention in the war. Marshall and his advisers did not believe the fall of China would mean Soviet domination there and the defeat of the Nationalists would not be equivalent to the loss of Western Europe to the Soviets. Aid to Chiang would be useless without reform. Chiang would cost the United States so much in military and economic strength that it would amount to an impossible task. Any such aid to the Nationalists would have to come out of the European Recovery Plan budget, and the United States did not have the military forces to save Chiang. Marshall agreed with Kennan's assessment that the United States had to choose wisely the places where it would resist communism, and both did not see China as a region as vital as Western Europe. But Marshall conceded that Chiang's allies in Congress could block the ERP if no support was extended to the Nationalists. Congress passed and Truman signed in 1948 the China Aid Act, which extended $400 million in aid in order to satisfy the American public and hopefully ward off temporarily a Communist victory.

Despite Republican opposition to the administration's China policy, Marshall escaped personal criticism while at the State Department. Conservatives vigorously attacked Truman and other high officials in the department. Vandenberg, while denouncing administration policy, refused to say anything that reflected on Marshall's personal role. He merely stated that he thought Marshall was "somewhat misled by the boys on the Far East desk." However, after China fell to the Communists in 1949, Republican conservatives pointed to

Marshall as one of those responsible for Mao's victory. Senator WILLIAM E. JENNER (R-Ind.) described him as "either an unsuspecting stooge or an actual co-conspirator with the most treasonable array of political cut-throats ever turned loose in the executive branch of government."

The stress of his position and the continual round of conferences eventually undermined Marshall's health. His doctors told him in mid-1948 that a kidney had to be removed, and by his own reckoning he had had only 19 days off since 1939. He stayed on the job until December, when he had the operation. Acheson succeeded him in January 1949. Truman arranged Marshall's appointment as head of the American Red Cross. Marshall crisscrossed the country promoting the agency and investigating its extensive bureaucracy.

In July 1950, while vacationing in Michigan, Marshall received a call from Truman asking him to become secretary of defense, replacing the bumptious LOUIS A. JOHNSON. Once again out of a sense of duty Marshall agreed. Truman again turned to Marshall during a period of crisis. The administration was under extreme criticism for its handling of the Korean conflict. Morale in the army was low. Military strength had not reached the numbers needed, many units were staffed by poorly trained draftees, and soldiers were fighting with antiquated weapons, which were in short supply. Officers decried the limited defense budgets of the late 1940s and the lack of coordination between military plans and foreign policy. Many, most notably General Douglas MacArthur, bridled against carrying on a limited war.

Marshall's appointment lifted morale in the department. He was a symbol of past military victory, of stability, and of achievement. As he had done in the State Department, the new secretary reorganized the Pentagon, forming the same kind of hierarchical structure he had utilized before. He gradually eased out many political appointees and brought in such experienced men as Robert Lovett with whom he had established a good working relationship. Marshall also reopened communications between the State and Defense departments at the lower levels to coordinate policy. (Relations between the two departments had deteriorated badly because of Johnson.)

Marshall's immediate task was to rebuild America's military posture. He thought it useless to rely exclusively on atomic weapons. Ground troops, he believed, were the deciding element in any conflict. In 1950 he asked Congress to place 2.7 million men

under arms by June 1951 and requested a $6.5 billion military program to meet the needs of his department. He continued to advocate universal military training, which Congress approved in June 1951.

Marshall supported the administration's limited war policy in Korea, although shortly after MacArthur's successful invasion at Inchon in September 1950, he wavered. On October 1, in one of his first acts as secretary, he cabled MacArthur to "let action determine the matter." Nevertheless, he ultimately backed Truman's decision to repel the Communist invasion of South Korea and not extend the war into China. His stand was consistent with the "Europe first" policy he had advocated while secretary of state.

Following Communist Chinese intervention in Korea in late 1950, MacArthur called for the bombing of Communist sanctuaries in Manchuria and the "unleashing" of Chiang's Nationalist troops against mainland China. MacArthur reasoned that the defeat of Asian communism would persuade the Soviets to abandon their European ambitions. Marshall and the administration disagreed. They maintained that Chiang's small force offered little promise of success, while expansion of the war increased possibilities of Russian intervention and left Western Europe vulnerable to attack.

By the spring of 1951 MacArthur's policy disagreements with the administration had become public. The general openly criticized Truman's decision to fight a limited war and, in essence, challenged the president's position as spokesman on foreign policy. With Marshall's approval Truman relieved MacArthur of his command in April 1951. The nation was shocked by the action. Although the Joint Chiefs of Staff had also supported the action, critics contended that the firing was a result of a feud between Marshall and MacArthur that could be traced back 40 years. In May 1951 Marshall testified at congressional hearings on the dismissal. Through almost a week of questioning, he reiterated the theme that MacArthur had been called home for publicly disagreeing with the foreign and military policy of the United States. Marshall's explanation quieted most congressional criticism. However, the Republican right vigorously attacked him and the administration for the failure of policy in Asia. Senator JOSEPH R. MCCARTHY (R-Wisc.) was the most vociferous of these critics. He alleged that Truman, Marshall, and Acheson had permitted the fall of

China to the Communists and had tolerated known Communists in the State Department. He also implied that Marshall and Truman should be impeached. Congress ignored his advice.

In September 1951 Marshall retired to Leesburg, Virginia. He spurned a lucrative offer to write his memoirs. In 1953 President Eisenhower gave Marshall the honor of representing the United States at the coronation of England's Queen Elizabeth II. That same year he won the Nobel Peace Prize for having developed the European Recovery Plan. Marshall took no part in foreign or defense affairs during the 1950s. He received, however, the brunt of criticism from the China Lobby and right-wing Republicans who accused him of harboring Communists in government. He died in Washington, D.C., on October 16, 1959.

Marshall, Thurgood

(1908–1993) *director-counsel, NAACP Legal Defense and Educational Fund*

Thurgood Marshall was born on July 2, 1908, in Baltimore, Maryland. His father was a steward at the Chesapeake Bay Club, and his mother taught school in Baltimore. Marshall graduated in 1930 from Lincoln University and in 1933 from Howard University Law School, where his mentor Charles Hamilton Houston convinced Marshall that the law was a type of social engineering that could be used to assist African Americans. After practicing law in Baltimore he joined the NAACP as assistant special counsel in 1936. He was named special counsel two years later. When the NAACP Legal Defense and Educational Fund was established in 1940, Marshall was appointed director and counsel. As head of the fund, he led the legal battle against racial discrimination for three decades. He gained attention as one of the nation's foremost civil rights attorney. Marshall personally argued cases before the Supreme Court on 16 occasions, losing only three times. He participated in almost every major civil rights case in the second half of the century.

After World War II Marshall at first thought desegregation efforts should concentrate on transportation, as it involved less the issue of social equality, which would confuse the justices' deliberations. NAACP lawyer Robert Carter wanted an all-out strategy while another association lawyer, William Hastie, thought the early attacks should concentrate

on postsecondary education. There was also a debate on what to pursue as far as desegregating education: Carter thought a broad attack at all levels should be attempted, whereas Hastie said universities should be tackled first because he feared the Supreme Court would uphold school segregation. In this area Marshall wanted to go after segregation in postsecondary education first and thought the association should challenge "separate but equal," and not try to make separate but equal work, which would concede the validity of such laws.

In the end Marshall directed a broad attack on segregation during the Truman years, winning victories in suits challenging segregated housing and transportation as well as discrimination in voting and jury selection. He was known for his conversational approach, avoiding legal jargon and presenting his case with "great courtesy and deference." His arguments were tightly reasoned, backed by intense research. In 1944, in *Smith v. Allwright*, he successfully argued that the "white primary" of the Democratic Party in Texas, which excluded blacks, was unconstitutional. Two years later, in *Morgan v. Virginia*, he persuaded the Supreme Court to invalidate segregated interstate bus travel under the commerce clause of the Constitution. The decision in *Shelley v. Kraemer* (1948) struck down state court enforcement of racially restrictive real estate covenants. In 1950 he attacked the doctrine of "separate but equal" in graduate education in *Sweatt v. Painter* and *McLaurin v. Oklahoma State Regents*. Marshall argued that white education was superior to black, even with physical equality, because of "intangible" qualities. The Supreme Court agreed, unanimously ruling that blacks had not had "substantial equality in educational opportunities."

Shortly after the Court's decision the NAACP Fund launched a drive to end all segregated public education. Marshall supervised the preparation of five cases challenging racial segregation in public schools. The Truman administration joined the NAACP action by filing an *amicus* brief in the case. Marshall personally represented the black plaintiffs from Clarendon Company, South Carolina, in one of the suits during oral arguments before the Supreme Court. "Slavery is perpetuated in these statutes," he said in discussing mandatory segregation laws. In December 1952 Marshall argued that state-enforced segregation violated the Fourteenth Amendment to the Constitution. He also repeatedly maintained that if the Court declared segregation unconstitutional "the rank and file people in the South" would obey the decision. During December 1953 he reiterated his attack on the doctrine of "separate but equal." In a unanimous decision on May 17, 1954, the Supreme Court ruled that segregation in public education was unconstitutional. The case, *Brown v. Board of Education* (1954), was a landmark decision in American judicial history and was, perhaps, Marshall's most important victory. Marshall and the NAACP then moved to secure the *Brown* decision.

Marshall did not confine his advocacy of civil rights to the courtroom. While he opposed a "disobedience movement" by southern blacks, claiming in 1946 that such a campaign would result "in wholesale slaughter with no good achieved," he forcefully spoke out against racial discrimination. Concerned with other areas of civil liberties law, he was critical of the decision to intern Japanese Americans during World War II and attacked the House Un-American Activities Committee. In 1947 he sent a telegram to New York members of Congress calling on them to vote against contempt citations for the Hollywood Ten. He denounced Truman's federal loyalty program in 1949 as "blatantly unconstitutional."

In 1951 Marshall went to Japan and Korea to investigate charges that black soldiers convicted by Army courts had received unfair trials. He discovered that few of those convicted had been treated impartially, and he was disturbed by the harsh sentences blacks received. Marshall, in arguing appeals for black servicemen, had sentences reduced for 22. In his final report to the army's Far East Command, he criticized General DOUGLAS MACARTHUR for permitting segregated facilities.

Marshall continued to argue civil rights cases during the Eisenhower years. He handled suits extending the *Brown* decision to public recreation and transit and aided in the defense of students arrested during the first nonviolent protests against segregation. In September 1961 he was named a judge on the U.S. Second Circuit Court of Appeals. President Johnson appointed him Solicitor General in July 1965 and nominated him to the Supreme Court in June 1967. The first African-American Supreme Court justice, Marshall charted a liberal course on the nation's highest judicial body, tending to vote against the more conservative Burger and Rehnquist majorities. He died on January 24, 1993, in Bethesda, Maryland. (See *The Eisenhower Years*,

The Kennedy Years, The Johnson Years, The Nixon/Ford Years Volumes)

—JF

Martin, Joseph W(illiam), Jr.
(1884–1968) *member of the House of Representatives*

Joseph W. Martin, Jr., was born on November 3, 1884, in North Attleboro, Massachusetts. Following the death of his father, he went to work at the age of six delivering newspapers to support his family. He graduated from high school in 1902 and declined a scholarship to Dartmouth College to become a full-time reporter for the *North Attleboro* (Mass.) *Sun*. In 1908 Martin and several other individuals purchased the local Republican paper, the *Evening Chronicle*. As editor and publisher he more than quadrupled circulation until it included virtually every home in the city. Eventually he bought out his partners and acquired a weekly, the *Franklin* (Mass.) *Sentinel*. He remained owner of these papers until his death.

Through newspaper work Martin became interested in local politics. He ran successfully for the Massachusetts House of Representatives in 1911 and served three terms before election to the Massachusetts Senate in 1914. He was a delegate to the Republican National Convention in 1916 and served as chairman of the state legislative campaign the following year. In 1922 he was made executive secretary of the Massachusetts Republican Party.

Martin ran for the U.S. House of Representatives in 1924. He lost the Republican primary, but the man who won died before the election. A district convention selected Martin to take his place on the ballot, and Martin won the race. As a result of his friendship with Calvin Coolidge, Martin rose quickly in the House. In 1929 he was assigned to the powerful Rules Committee and became an assistant to the Speaker of the House. The election of Franklin Roosevelt did little to hurt the Republican's career. He soon became a friend of the new president, who provided his district with ample federal services. Never an ideologue and always following the advice he gave new members to "vote your district," Martin supported those New Deal measures that aided New England while opposing such measures as the Agricultural Adjustment Administration in which his constituents had little interest.

Martin was elected minority leader in 1939. He quickly set out to construct a strong organization among the House Republicans and to build an anti–New Deal alliance with the increasingly disaffected Southern Democrats. Martin's leadership became an important factor in the setbacks the Roosevelt administration suffered during the late 1930s and early 1940s. Martin tended to be conservative on economic issues, maintaining the outlook of a small businessman of a small town. On foreign policy he took largely isolationist positions, opposing lend-lease, repeal of the Neutrality Act, and extension of the draft. Yet he carefully maintained contacts with the internationalist faction of the GOP, which supported these measures.

The death of Roosevelt and the ascension of Harry Truman to the presidency brought Martin new power. "We could not stop the New Deal," he wrote in his memoirs. "When we tried it ran over us." However, because of the growing conservative reaction, he was able to block much of Truman's Fair Deal legislation, including national health insurance, extension of public housing, and federal aid to education. Other Fair Deal legislative proposals he opposed included the Full Employment bill, the permanent school lunch program, the 1949 Housing Act, and federal government ownership of the tidelands.

With the election of a Republican Congress in 1946, Martin became Speaker of the House. Although he ruled House Republicans with a gentle hand, he did say in his memoirs that "no Republican went on an important committee without my approval." His pragmatic bent made him acutely aware of constituent pressures on his colleagues. He generally did not pressure Republican representatives to vote for bills unpopular in their districts. Martin was a legislative technician, not an initiator or shaper of proposals. He acted as a catalyst and was known more for his facilitation of the work of other members and of his party than for legislation he developed. Under his leadership the House passed the Taft-Hartley Act and overrode Truman's veto, cut income taxes despite administration opposition, and passed the Twenty-second Amendment to the Constitution limiting presidents to two terms in office. Although he was at odds with Truman on almost every major item of domestic policy during the 80th Congress, Martin generally supported a bipartisan foreign policy and oversaw the passage of the Truman Doctrine and the Marshall Plan. He did, however, vote to eliminate a $25 million authorization to establish the president's Point Four program.

In July 1948 Truman called the 80th Congress back into special session as part of his strategy to make the Republican Congress the central issue of the presidential campaign that fall. Martin charged that Truman's action was "a last desperate gasp of power by an administration which already had lost the confidence of the people in domestic policies." He helped shape the Republican leadership's response to Truman's challenge. Instead of passing the measures that Truman demanded or simply adjourning immediately and going home, the leaders decided to stay in session for two weeks and act on a few minor bills. This strategy backfired. Truman successfully branded the 80th Congress the "Do-nothing Congress." Partially on this issue, he defeated the Republican candidate, THOMAS E. DEWEY, that November, bringing a Democratic Senate and House to office with him. Martin became minority leader once more.

In 1951 Martin played a central role in the events that led to Truman's recall of General DOUGLAS MACARTHUR from Korea. In April 1951 he released a letter he had solicited from the general in which MacArthur disagreed with the administration policy toward Korea and Taiwan. MacArthur implied an endorsement of a speech by Martin urging the use of Nationalist Chinese troops against mainland China. The publication of this statement and that of others the general had made, contributed to Truman's decision to recall him from his command in the Far East.

Martin later viewed these developments with mixed feelings. While regretting that MacArthur had lost his post in the field, Martin viewed him as a potential Republican presidential nominee in 1952 and considered his recall by the unpopular Truman an advancement of this candidacy. MacArthur was, wrote Martin, "The most distinctively Republican of all the commanders in our armed forces." Martin was partially responsible for the invitation that brought the general before a joint session of Congress in which he delivered a speech saying, "Old soldiers never die, they just fade away." Martin helped arrange the congressional hearings into the dismissal. He intended to use the probe as a further promotion of MacArthur as a presidential prospect. The investigation served instead to discourage MacArthur's supporters, airing as it did instances of insubordination in the field.

From 1940 to 1956 Martin served as permanent chairman of the Republican National Convention. At every meeting from 1940 to 1952, he was mentioned as a darkhorse candidate for the presidency. He relished this role, and, while never promoting his own candidacy, said, "I regarded the presidency about the same way that a man who joins the fire department regards the red car in front of the fire house; it would be nice to be chief."

In 1953, following the Eisenhower landslide, Martin became Speaker once more. Despite his disappointment with much of Eisenhower's legislative program, which he believed too liberal, Martin supported the president on a wide range of issues.

During the Eisenhower years Martin's leadership became a cause for discontent among congressional Republicans. As a result, he failed to win reelection as minority leader in 1959. Following this defeat Martin lost all significant influence in Congress and in the party. In 1966 he was defeated in his district's Republican congressional primary. On March 6, 1968, he died in Hollywood, Florida, of peritonitis. (See *The Eisenhower Years* Volume)

—CSJ

Martin, William McChesney, Jr.

(1906–1998) *president, Export-Import Bank; assistant secretary of the Treasury; chairman, Board of Governors, Federal Reserve System*

William McChesney Martin, Jr., was born into a banking family on December 17, 1906, in St. Louis, Missouri. His father had been among those who had drafted the Federal Reserve Act of 1913 and had subsequently become president of the Federal Reserve Bank of St. Louis. Martin attended Yale University. For a time he considered entering the ministry, but, after graduating with a degree in English and Latin in 1928, he returned to St. Louis to join the bank examiners' office of the Federal Reserve Bank. A year later he entered the brokerage firm of A. G. Edwards & Son and in 1931 purchased the firm's seat on the New York Stock Exchange. In New York he took evening courses at Columbia, completing all the work necessary for a Ph.D. but never taking the degree. He also helped establish and edit the *Economic Forum*. In 1935 Martin was elected to the board of governors of the exchange and two years later was appointed to a commission to rewrite the rules of the exchange. In 1938 he became the first salaried president of the New York Stock Exchange, a position established by the constitution he had helped write. He was 31, the youngest man ever to hold the post. Although he

called himself merely "a bond man," he would become known as "the boy wonder of Wall Street."

Martin was drafted into the army in 1941 as a private. He was promoted rapidly; he served as an aide to the Joint Chiefs of Staff and eventually supervised much of the lend-lease program to Russia. Lend-lease gave Martin contact with a number of New Deal officials, and, in 1945, Leo Crowley and HARRY L. HOPKINS recommended him to be a director of the newly created Export-Import Bank. Shortly after this appointment the presidency of the bank fell vacant, and Martin was named to fill it. Martin proved to be a conservative banker, granting loans on the basis of financial soundness. He resisted pressures to give aid on purely political grounds. Martin opposed a loan to prop up the Nationalist Chinese regime but granted one to Communist-dominated Poland, which was eventually blocked by the State Department. His performance impressed Secretary of the Treasury JOHN W. SNYDER, who convinced Truman to appoint Martin assistant secretary of the Treasury for international finance in January 1949.

In June 1950 Martin was drawn into the long smoldering controversy between the Treasury and the Federal Reserve System over the reserve's World War II commitment to support the price of government securities. After the war the Federal Reserve had become increasingly uneasy with this arrangement, because it destroyed the reserve's control of the money supply. Both MARRINER S. ECCLES, chairman of the board until 1948, and THOMAS B. MCCABE, his successor, pushed for the reserve's independence from the Treasury. Snyder, who was trying to keep down the government's cost of borrowing in light of the Korean War, opposed the move. Martin, the secretary's close adviser, sided with the Federal Reserve. He considered a free capital market a necessary underpinning for the economy and urged a return to an unrestricted market as soon as the military situation permitted, even if it meant higher interest rates for government borrowing.

The conflict became heated in August 1950, when the Federal Reserve raised the short-term interest rates and blocked a Treasury attempt to engineer a $13.5 billion refunding. A series of public and private confrontations between the Federal Reserve on the one hand and Snyder and Truman on the other followed during January 1951. By early February congressional and public support for the Federal Reserve was so strong that the administration was forced to compromise.

When the Federal Reserve Board informed the Treasury that it would no longer back government security prices, Martin asked Synder's permission to conduct sessions to make the change to an unsupported market as smooth as possible. As Donald F. Kettl has noted, Martin worked with Federal Reserve chief career economist Winfield Rieller and, by early March 1951, the two had reached an agreement known as "The Accord." On the surface it had something for each side. Martin won the Reserve's agreement to spend up to $600 million in open market purchases, to assure a "satisfactory" volume of exchange in the refunding of matured Treasury issues and to raise its rediscount rate no higher then $1\frac{1}{2}$ percent before 1952 to hold the discount rate at $1\frac{3}{4}$ percent and not adjust it without consulting Treasury. The Treasury agreed to the neutralization of long-term bonds through the issuance of a nonmarketable $2\frac{3}{4}$ percent 29-year bond redeemable before maturity only through conversion into a five-year marketable note. After the transition, the Fed would no longer support the short- or long-term market for government bonds.

Despite the appearance of balance in the agreement, the Federal Reserve got all that it wanted. Three days after the agreement went into effect in March, the $600 million support fund had been exhausted, and the securities exchange had been executed. There was no pressure to raise the new discount rate until well beyond the end of 1951. Thus the Fed ended its support for low-interest federal government borrowing.

On March 3 McCabe resigned. He recommended that Martin take his place as chairman of the board. Snyder also recommended Martin. Truman initially wanted the chairman of the Securities and Exchange Commission to fill the job, but he was ineligible because somebody on the board was from his Federal Reserve district, and so Truman went with Martin. Despite considerable apprehension in the Senate that Martin might act as the Treasury's agent in the Federal Reserve board room, the upper house confirmed Martin's nomination.

By the time his first term as chairman had expired in 1955, Martin had become an internationally recognized symbol of sound money and an independent Federal Reserve. He had presided over a moderate rise in the rediscount rate. He was also beginning to consolidate the open market activities of the system in the Open Market Committee and the Federal Reserve Board, thus weakening the tra-ditionally strong hand of the New York branch in these operations.

Martin's credit policies became more severe during the last half of the decade. In 1960 the rediscount rate stood at 3 percent, and John F. Kennedy chose Martin as a target for criticism in his presidential campaign. Nevertheless, Martin got along well with Presidents Kennedy and Johnson and eased monetary policy for a time in an accommodation to their stimulative fiscal policies. During the Vietnam War interest rates rose to their highest level since the 1920s, and Martin was again at the center of a storm of controversy. He retired from the Federal Reserve in 1970. After retirement from the Fed, Martin served on the boards of corporations and nonprofit organizations, such as IBM, American Express, and the National Geographic Society. He died on July 27, 1998, in Washington, D.C. (See *The Eisenhower Years, The Kennedy Years, The Johnson Years, The Nixon/Ford Years* Volumes.)

—CSJ

Matles, James (J)
(1909–1975) *union leader*

James Matles was born on February 24, 1909, in Soroca, Romania. He left Romania for the United States in 1929 and settled in New York City, where he found work as a machinist. He soon became involved with the International Association of Machinists and, in 1933, began organizing workers in major electrical-equipment companies for the newly formed Committee for Industrial Organization (CIO). Four years later Matles joined the United Electrical Workers Union (UE) and was elected its director of organization.

Following World War II the government and big business accused many of the CIO's affiliates of being Communist-dominated. Matles recommended that the organization not attempt to clear itself of what he termed "the damnable slander of Communism." (Matles was in fact a Communist.) The union leader also refused to comply with the provision of the Taft-Hartley Act requiring leaders to sign noncommunist affidavits. He stated, "We will not rush to that Taft-Hartley line-up for the simple reason it is not a chow line. It is a line where they are dishing out poison." If CIO leaders surrendered on this point, workers would wonder about their courage and would be reluctant to join them in the effort to repeal Taft-Hartley. By not signing the affidavits these unions were in danger of decertification, but Matles argued that strong unions could use their power to force management to negotiate with them.

Matles in 1948 personally endorsed HENRY A. WALLACE but indicated that the UE did not formally back any candidate. He also opposed the CIO's endorsement of the Marshall Plan.

In 1948 Matles charged that other CIO unions were raiding the UE because of its unpopular political stands. The UE was particularly concerned over raids conducted by WALTER P. REUTHER's United Automobile Workers Union. Despite assurances from CIO president PHILLIP MURRAY that this was not the case, the raiding increased and eventually led to the UE's withdrawal from the November 1949 CIO convention. At that conference Murray and Reuther denounced the UE as "Communist-dominated" and declared the union expelled from the CIO. A new union with jurisdiction in the electrical, radio, and machine industries was quickly established with JAMES B. CAREY, CIO secretary, at its head. Following this action a long era of jurisdictional disputes ensued between the rival unions.

Matles continued to defend his union's political stand. In testimony before the Senate Labor Committee in 1952, he reiterated the UE's position of giving equal rights to all members regardless of political belief. The following year Matles, at his own request, testified at hearings held by Senator JOSEPH R. MCCARTHY (R-Wisc.). The UE leader accused McCarthy of cooperating with the management of General Electric in its efforts to defeat the UE in the National Labor Relations Board election in Lynn, Massachusetts. Matles charged that McCarthy had used terror tactics to "browbeat decent working people."

In December 1952 the government began attempts to denaturalize and deport Matles. The Justice Department claimed that he had become a citizen by fraud, because when he was naturalized in 1934, he had sworn that he was not a member of an organization teaching or advocating violent overthrow of the U.S. government. Matles vehemently denied the charges. The U.S. Supreme Court dismissed the case in 1958.

In 1962 Matles was named UE general secretary-treasurer. He remained a union leader until his death from a heart attack on September 15, 1975, in Santa Barbara, California.

—EF

Matthews, Francis P(atrick)
(1887–1952) *secretary of the navy*

Francis P. Matthews was born on March 15, 1887, in Albion, Nebraska. His father was a country merchant who died before his son finished elementary school. At the age of 19 Matthews enrolled at Creighton University in Omaha. He worked his way through school, receiving a B.A. in 1910, an M.A. in 1911 and an LL.B. in 1913. That year he was admitted to the Nebraska bar and began a law practice in Omaha. In addition Matthews held executive positions in several business firms. In 1932 he was elected chairman of the Democratic Committee for Douglas Company, Nebraska. The next year he was appointed a counsel for the Reconstruction Finance Corporation, a post that he held until 1949, when he was appointed secretary of the navy.

Matthews was surprised by the appointment—he had wanted to be ambassador to Ireland—and had no experience in the military. He quipped that the only experience he had with the navy was that he owned a rowboat. Naval personnel derisively dubbed him "Rowboat Matthews." As historian Jeffrey G. Barlow has noted defense secretary LOUIS A. JOHNSON picked Matthews because his predecessor, JOHN L. SULLIVAN, had been a high-profile Catholic in the administration, and Matthews was a Catholic. Barlow saw Matthews's appointment as a disaster for the navy because of his inexperience and subservience to the defense secretary.

As director of the Chamber of Commerce of the United States, Matthews was appointed chairman of a committee on socialism and communism, which, in 1947, published a pamphlet entitled "Communism within Government." The document charged that "a real service to the community could be rendered if the secret stories of Yalta and Teheran could be made public" and that forces within the State Department were "pushing the cause of the Communist Chinese." Matthews served as a member of President Truman's Committee on Civil Rights, headed by CHARLES E. WILSON. The panel's report, issued in 1947, found that educational, political, economic, and social discrimination existed against minorities and asked for the passage of laws to protect individuals against violation of their rights.

Matthews was credited with having swung Nebraska's 12 votes to President Truman at the 1948 Democratic National Convention. During the ensuing campaign he became well acquainted with

Johnson, who became secretary of defense the following year. When Sullivan resigned in a dispute with the secretary over the place of the navy in postwar defense, Johnson convinced Truman to appoint Matthews to the post.

Matthews immediately became embroiled in the debate over the navy's role in warfare and in the unified defense establishment. A large number of naval officers, led by Chief of Naval Operations LOUIS E. DENFELD, felt that the administration was placing too much reliance on the air force as America's prime deterrent and that cuts in the navy budget were destroying the effectiveness of that service. Matthews, who had no knowledge or personal affection for the service, was loyal to the president. Shortly after his appointment he announced that he believed that unification of the armed forces could be accomplished "without impairing Navy prestige."

The secretary tried, often unsuccessfully, to stop uniformed personnel from protesting policy. During the fall of 1949 he ordered marine guards and investigators from the Inspector General's Office to seize Captain Arleigh Burke's office, where the uniformed service had set up an informal public relations department to push its stand. The marines held Burke and his men under virtual house arrest for three days. The official reason for the crackdown was to find the source of a leak to a *Washington Post* reporter; according to Barlow, what Matthews really wanted to do was silence navy personnel over a controversy on the procurement of the B-36, the air force's strategic bomber. Part of the problem was that Matthews remained distant from naval officers and that he did not know the extent of discontent over the cancellation of the supercarrier.

As a result of Denfeld's public opposition to the administration's defense policy before congressional committees, Matthews asked Truman to dismiss the admiral. "Either Denfeld goes or I do," he said. Truman removed the chief of naval operations in October. Matthews's action precipitated a storm of protest from the right. In January 1950 Senator JOSEPH R. McCARTHY (R-Wisc.) contended that Matthews had no power to dismiss Denfeld and suggested that he should be impeached by the Senate. However, in February 1950 the Senate Armed Services Committee heard Matthews's explanation for Denfeld's ouster and closed the case after apparently agreeing that Matthews's action was justified. Denfeld himself retired in March 1950 and wrote three articles for *Collier's* accusing Matthews and

Johnson of favoring the air force over the navy and vindictiveness.

Matthews appointed Admiral Forrest Sherman as chief of naval operations; Sherman approved a supercarrier in early 1951. By this time Matthews appreciated the worth of public relations officers to counteract those of the other services; morale and Matthews's reputation improved.

Matthews believed fervently that the threat of Soviet aggression was acute, a "graver threat [than] . . . when Hitler's legions overran France." In August 1950 he declared that the United States should be willing "to pay any price" for world peace, "even the price of instituting a war to compel cooperation for peace." He touched off a controversy when he suggested a program that would "cast us in a character new to a true democracy—an initiator of a war of aggression." Matthews was of the conviction that this "would win for us a proud and popular title. We would become the first aggressors for peace." The speech irritated Truman.

In June 1951 Matthews retired. The following month he was appointed ambassador to Ireland. Matthews died of a heart attack on October 18, 1952, while vacationing in Omaha, Nebraska.

—MLB

May, Andrew J(ackson)
(1875–1959) *member of the House of Representatives*

Andrew J. May was born on June 24, 1875, in Langley, Kentucky. He taught in Kentucky country schools for five years before graduating from Southern University Law School in 1898. He opened a private law practice in Prestonburg, Kentucky, in 1900. Pursuing a business and a political career at the same time, May obtained appointment as Floyd County attorney and special circuit court judge while serving as president of the Beaver Valley Coal and Greenbrier Mining Company. Firmly allied with the coal and oil interests of Kentucky's Seventh Congressional District, May was elected to the House of Representatives in 1931.

Like other Southern Democrats, May voted consistently against civil rights legislation, criticized what he viewed as the government and executive encroachment on congressional power, and voted only reluctantly for Roosevelt's New Deal policies until the mid-1930s. Anxious to defend the coal interests of the state, in 1938 he used his position as chairman of the Military Affairs Committee to cut appropriations to the Tennessee Valley Authority, one of the area's leading electricity producers. He supported Roosevelt's war policies, sponsoring and backing legislation for civilian and industrial mobilization, expansion of the military, subsidization of the munitions industry, relaxation of cash-and-carry policies, and centralization of federal wartime authority.

In regard to domestic policy May did not stand firmly on either side of the ideological divide. He voted for the Case labor disputes bill and the permanent school lunch program. He tended to support the administration's foreign policy. He voted for the British loan of 1946 and the three-year extension of the Trade Agreement Act in 1945. In early 1945, he saw passed in the House his manpower draft bill, which assessed penalties on essential workers, who were also liable to the draft, if they refused to work in the essential position.

May was a major advocate of military control of atomic energy. Following President Truman's request in October 1945 for legislation creating an atomic energy commission, he immediately introduced a bill drafted by the War Department that secured control of atomic energy for the military. He engineered the bill's referral through his committee and, in an attempt to quickly push the bill through Congress, arranged for immediate hearings with only a few supportive witnesses. Dr. LEO SZILARD, physicist on the Manhattan District Project, learned of May's maneuvering and demanded to be a witness at the hearings in opposition to military control. Although May managed to report the bill out of his committee intact, Szilard, along with other alarmed atomic scientists, mobilized a campaign in the Senate to defeat the measure. In February 1946 Truman came out publicly against military control. The Senate opposition succeeded in slowing the progress of May's bill by creating a special committee, chaired by BRIEN MCMAHON (D-Conn.), to hold hearings on atomic energy. McMahon introduced his own bill in December. Structured around civilian control, it became the basis for the Atomic Energy Act of 1946.

In July 1946 the Senate Special Committee to Investigate the National Defense Program, chaired by Senator James W. Mead of New York, heard charges that May had used his influence to obtain army contracts totaling $78 million for a combine of 19 Illinois manufacturers. Further charges of impropriety followed. May admitted to acting as an agent for and endorsing the checks of the Cumberland Lumber Company, which was connected with the combine. However, he protested that he had made no profits on the contracts and was the victim of political opportunism. He was finally subpoenaed by the committee but suffered a heart attack one day before he was to appear.

May was defeated for reelection the following November and, in January 1947, was indicted by a federal grand jury. Six months later he was convicted of accepting $54,000 in bribes to use his influence in obtaining war contracts. He served nine months of his eight-to-24 month sentence before being paroled in September 1950. In June 1952 the Kentucky Court of Appeals restored May to the bar. President Truman pardoned him in December and May retired to his law practice in Prestonburg. He died there of a kidney ailment on September 6, 1959.

Meany, George
(1894–1980) *secretary-treasurer, American Federation of Labor*

George Meany was born on August 16, 1894, in New York City. He grew up in the Bronx, the son of an Irish Catholic plumber and union official. At age 16 he became a plumber's helper and later joined the union when he became eligible as a journeyman. At first he was not interested in unionism, but, in 1919, he ran for the local's executive board. His father's years as an official in the union helped George win a seat. Meany was elected as an opponent of corrupt unionism. He was elected to his first full-time union office in 1922 as business agent of the plumber's union Local 463, which encompassed the Bronx and Manhattan. After this point he no longer worked as a plumber. Business agents in the building trade unions stuck to plain-and-simple unionism: guarding against jurisdictional raiding against the local, maintaining union standards at worksites, and helped settle conflicts. Meany became secretary in 1923 of a new city building trades council, chartered to battle rampant corruption in the construction union. In 1932 Meany was elected to the executive board of the New York State Federation of Labor. Here Meany helped put together an unemployment insurance bill and convinced the 1934 state convention to adopt it. This aided him in winning the presidency of the state federation. Meany proved a skilled lobbyist and able executive. As head of the state federation, Meany studied first AFL president Samuel Gompers's ideas on unionism, and he was an anticommunist and against the formation of a labor party. His new position made him the chief labor spokesman in Albany and put him in close contact with the Roosevelt administration and the national leadership of the American Federation of Labor. In 1935 Meany thought the AFL leadership had handled the question of industrial unionism poorly but opposed the establishment of the Committee on Industrial Organization for fear it would split the labor movement. In 1940 AFL president William Green named him secretary-treasurer of the federation.

After serving on the National Defense Mediation Board and the War Labor Board during World War II, Meany emerged as the most prominent AFL spokesman on reconversion problems. Within the federation he advocated an immediate postwar return to aggressive collective bargaining without government controls. At an executive council meeting in August 1945, he succeeded in quashing a proposal by Green that the wartime no-strike pledge be extended for six months after the Japanese surrender. Meany argued that higher wages were justified in order to maintain the purchasing power needed for a full-production economy. He thought they were particularly necessary because, with the elimination of premium overtime-paid night shifts and downgrading from high-wage war jobs, union members experienced substantial reductions in take-home pay. Meany also called for a 30-hour week to help absorb returning veterans into the job market.

In 1947 the Taft-Hartley bill, barring a number of what its proponents termed unfair labor practices by unions, came to the forefront in Congress. Meany denounced the legislation as the work of "profit-greedy industrialists . . . attempting to destroy workers' organizations as the first step in their plan to control the economic life of America," He helped organize the most vigorous lobbying campaign in AFL history in an unsuccessful effort to prevent its passage. Nevertheless, at the AFL convention in November, shortly after the bill became law over President Truman's veto, he led a fight to win compliance with the noncommunist affadavits that the act required of union officials. The National Labor Relations Board (NLRB) had earlier ruled that if any official refused to sign the affa-

davit his union could not use its assistance in representation elections. Meany and other AFL leaders supported the oath, partly because they believed it would cripple the Communist-dominated unions affiliated with the rival Congress of Industrial Organizations (CIO). They also viewed the NLRB's ruling, which applied to federation officials as well as union officers, as an issue with which to discredit JOHN L. LEWIS, controversial leader of the United Mine Workers. Meany received wide publicity when, in a dramatic confrontation on the convention floor, he implied that Lewis's opposition to the oath stemmed from his willingness in the past to cooperate with Communists, in contrast to the undeviating anticommunism of those who had never been "comrade to the comrades." Lewis's defeat on the issue led to his withdrawal from the AFL several weeks later. AFL unionists were grateful for the tongue-lashing Meany gave Lewis and his aggressiveness helped make him the most likely successor to Green.

At the 1947 convention Meany spearheaded the founding of Labor's League for Political Education (LLPE), the AFL's first formal venture into electoral politics. Hitherto the federation had been officially nonpartisan, although most of its leaders were Democrats. The election of the Republican 80th Congress and the consequent passage of the Taft-Hartley bill, however, convinced AFL leaders of the need to create a political arm with campaign goals and a congressional district structure similar to that of the CIO's aggressive Political Action Committee (PAC). As head of LLPE Meany hired a permanent staff with authority to raise money from affiliated unions to inform AFL members of candidates voting records and get them to the polls at election time.

In the 1948 elections the league endorsed anti–Taft-Hartley congressional candidates and assisted state legislative candidates who opposed state "right-to-work laws." However, because of the AFL's conservative traditions, the LLPE did not match PAC's vigorous efforts on behalf of the Democratic Party nationally. A proposal to endorse Harry S Truman's presidential candidacy was deleted from its official report to the 1948 convention in order not to offend such powerful Republican executive council members as WILLIAM L. HUTCHESON of the carpenters' union. Unofficially LLPE worked closely with the Truman campaign. Meany, however, claimed the AFL was not abandoning its nonpartisanship, but strengthening it.

Meany, like other union leaders, interpreted the election of Truman as a popular mandate for the repeal of Taft-Hartley, and he urged Congress to proceed immediately on the issue. However, although liberal representation was heavily increased in both houses of the 81st Congress, labor greatly overestimated its support from the outset. By early 1949 the Republican–Southern Democratic coalition had regained the initiative, eliminating any possibility of repeal. During the second Truman administration the AFL and CIO barely managed, through their combined lobbying efforts, to prevent the strengthening of the act. Bitterly disappointed, Meany occasionally suggested that a third party might be needed to achieve labor's goals. More often, he argued for intensified LLPE activity on behalf of pro-labor Democrats, pressing the federation to divert funds used for organizing drives to subsidize more campaign literature and radio programs. In the 1950 elections the LLPE participated for the first time in united labor committees with PAC in a number of states.

During the Korean conflict Meany emerged as a central figure in organized labor's conflicts with the Truman administration. In August 1950 he offered a no-strike pledge on behalf of the AFL but demanded in return price controls to forestall inflation. The administration, instead, announced a price freeze several months in advance of its implementation, thereby allowing business to raise prices before the effective date. This is turn set off an inflationary spiral. In addition, AFL and CIO recommendations were persistently ignored or rejected by the Office of Defense Mobilization (ODM), which labor charged was composed of a large number of antiunion businessmen. Discontent came to a head early in 1951 during attempts by the ODM's Wage Stabilization Board (WSB) to fix a limit on pay increases. At Meany's urging the board's labor members resigned, charging that the administration had denied them any real voice in the economic controls program. In April, after a White House conference with Meany, Green and PHILIP MURRAY of the CIO, Truman appointed Meany to a 17-man Advisory Board on Mobilization Policy, which included representatives from labor, business, and the public. The board approved wage increases in the auto, packing house, and shipyard industries that surpassed the guidelines imposed by the ODM.

Another area in which Meany assumed increasing responsibility during the Truman years was foreign policy. Critical to his future success was his institution of an anticommunist foreign policy for the AFL. Along with DAVID DUBINSKY, president of the International Ladies Garment Workers Union, Matthew Woll, a federation vice president, and JAY LOVESTONE, Dubinsky's foreign affairs adviser, Meany set up the Free Trade Union Committee (FTUC) in 1944 under AFL sponsorship. In the aftermath of the war, the FTUC sent its agents into European and Asian countries with offers of leadership and funds to help rebuild shattered trade unions and sabotage Communist efforts to control labor in France, Italy, and Japan. In 1946 an international labor relations department of the federation was created to widen the scope of AFL union contacts abroad. Although the AFL had accepted the wartime alliance with the USSR as a military necessity—Meany had been critical of it even then—Meany bluntly rejected any suggestion of postwar cooperation with Communist governments. In contrast to the CIO, the AFL boycotted the World Federation of Trade Unions (WFTU) because it included Communist labor groups. Warning that the Soviet Union was trying to use the WFTU as a fifth column to undermine democratic nations, Meany called instead for a confederation of noncommunist unions. In January 1949 the AFL joined the CIO and British and Dutch unions in organizing the International Confederation of Free Trade Unions (ICFTU). Meany was chosen a member of its executive board in 1951.

Meany strongly backed Truman's anticommunist initiatives abroad. In return, the White House placed AFL representatives on advisory committees throughout the foreign policy apparatus and gave the federation veto power over the selection of labor attachés to U.S. embassies. Although Meany insisted that the AFL's far-flung foreign activities were financed strictly by American union funds, many contemporary observers privately suspected, and later publicly claimed, that the FTUC and the federation's international department received lavish subsidies from the Central Intelligence Agency.

During his tenure as secretary-treasurer, Meany gradually assumed de facto leadership of the AFL as the often-ailing William Green progressively withdrew from the day-to-day affairs of the federation. Innovative, yet careful not to break too sharply with AFL tradition, Meany earned the trust of the powerful building trades leaders who dominated the Executive Council. In 1952 he succeeded in persuading the federation to give formal endorsement to a presidential candidate, Illinois governor ADLAI E. STEVENSON, for the first time in its 67-year history. On November 20, 1952, William Green died. Meany automatically became acting president and was elected president by the Executive Council five days later.

Meany's first important act as head of the AFL was to negotiate a merger with the CIO. This took place in 1955, with Meany assuming the presidency of the united AFL-CIO. With the support of the former CIO unions, he took the lead in 1957 in the expulsion on corruption charges of the federation's largest affiliate, the International Brotherhood of Teamsters. During the 1950s Meany also continued to deepen organized labor's involvement in anticommunist activities abroad.

Meany enthusiastically endorsed the social welfare legislation of the Kennedy and Johnson administrations. He was also a strong supporter of the war in Vietnam. Despite mounting criticism of his leadership during the 1960s, Meany's control of the AFL-CIO remained virtually unchallenged. Meany died on January 10, 1980, in Washington, D.C. (See *The Eisenhower Years, The Kennedy Years, The Johnson Years, The Nixon/Ford Years, The Carter Years* Volumes)

—TLH

Medina, Harold R(aymond)
(1888–1990) *federal judge*

Of Mexican and Dutch heritage, Harold R. Medina was born on February 16, 1888, in New York City. He attended Princeton University, graduating summa cum laude in 1909. At Columbia University Law School he received the Ordronneaux Prize for the highest standing in his class. Medina graduated with a LL.B. in 1912 and joined a New York law firm. He supplemented his income by giving series of six-week "cram" courses for law school graduates planning to take the state bar examination. Medina also taught law at Columbia during this period. He was something of a showboat; many quipped he was meant for Hollywood.

Medina founded his own law firm in 1918. Until 1931 he specialized in appeals work, arguing over 1,400 cases covering, *Time* magazine reported, "every imaginable kind of law from bas-

tardy to bankruptcy." Starting in 1931 Medina began trial work and, over a span of 14 years, did not lose a case. During World War II he defended Anthony Cramer, charged with treason for aiding Nazi agents. Medina fought the case all the way to the Supreme Court, winning a reversal of Cramer's conviction.

After a campaign by the bar association to have him nominated, President Harry S Truman announced in May 1947 Medina's appointment as a judge on the U.S. District Court, Southern District of New York. He was appointed even though he was opposed by local party bosses, and his appointment was seen as a victory of professionalism over politics. Although he was despised by the left, the public adored him. The news media deemed him Judge Patience, and he became the most well-known trial judge of his time. Medina, who reportedly was mystified by the unexpected nomination, gave up a $100,000 a year law practice to accept the $15,000 a year post. He quickly emerged as a national figure when he was assigned to preside over the trial of 11 members of the national committee of the American Communist Party (CP). The 11 were charged with violating the Smith Act, a 1940 law making it a crime to teach or advocate the violent overthrow of the U.S. government, or to conspire to commit such acts. The defendants held key positions in the party. Eugene Dennis, the Communists' leader, Irving Potash, vice president of the furriers' union, and JOHN GATES, editor of the *Daily Worker*, were members of the Politburo. A 12th defendant, the party chairman, 67-year-old WILLIAM Z. FOSTER, avoided trial because of a heart ailment.

Medina prepared for the trial legally, mentally, and physically, for he was aware that the Washington sedition case of 1944 had ended in a mistrial when, after constant defense harassment, the exhausted judge, Edward C. Eicher, had died. The lawyers for the Communists opened the trial in January 1949 with a challenge to the jury system. They charged that federal juries, especially "blue ribbon" juries, were composed of the upper classes and were discriminatory. Two of the defendants, Henry Winston and Benjamin Davis, were black. Medina, who once argued against "blue ribbon" juries before the Supreme Court and narrowly lost, allowed the defense to argue its point for six weeks. Then after constant prodding failed to present proof of discrimination, Medina insisted the pretrial challenge end. By March 21 a jury of three blacks and nine whites had been selected, and the government commenced the presentation of its case.

The prosecution focused on the reorganization of the Communist Party in 1945. It claimed that the party had trained a corps of professional revolutionaries ready to destroy the "bourgeois state." The government's star witness was Herbert Philbrick, an FBI agent who had infiltrated the party. Along with six other FBI informants, Philbrick testified that the party believed in violent revolution. He said it was a conspiracy that had planned sabotage of the nation's economy in the event of war with the Soviet Union. The defense challenged the government, claiming the CP believed in a peaceful transition to socialism. The party, the defense claimed, was a "working-class movement" fighting for the rights of labor. Furthermore, it said, the Smith Act was a "thought-control" law and, as such, unconstitutional. During the trial Medina and the five defense lawyers repeatedly clashed in often acrimonious exchanges. Medina jailed defendants John Gates, Henry Winston, Carl Winter, and Gus Hall for refusing to answer questions or for disturbing the peace of the court.

In his charge to the jury, Medina made it clear that the constitutionality of the Smith Act had no bearing on the guilt or innocence of the defendants. He stressed that the 11 individual leaders, not the Communist Party, were charged with criminal conspiracy. He carefully drew a distinction between the secret actions of a conspiracy and freedom of speech. He also said he thought there was "sufficient danger of a substantive evil" in their activities to justify the nation using the Smith Act in self-defense.

On October 14, 1949, the jury found all 11 Smith Act defendants guilty. Immediately after the verdict, Medina said he would turn to "some unfinished business." He found the six defense lawyers in contempt of court. (Dennis had acted as his own attorney.) He told them, "I find you guilty of willful, deliberated, and concerted effort to obstruct the trial for the purpose of causing such confusion as would prevent a verdict." Medina sentenced three of the lawyers to six months in jail; two to four months; and one to 30 days. His sentences for the Smith Act defendants were more severe. He fined them $10,000 each and sentenced 10 of the 11 to five years in prison. Robert G. Thompson, New York state chairman, was given three years because of military service in World War II.

In June 1951 the Supreme Court, in a six-to-two decision, upheld the convictions. Chief Justice FRED M. VINSON's basic opinion rejected the plea that the Smith Act violated freedom of speech guarantees. The Court refused to review the contempt of court sentences Medina had imposed on the Communists' lawyers. Shortly thereafter Medina succeeded Judge LEARNED HAND as a judge of the U.S. Circuit Court of Appeals, Second Circuit. In March 1952, in a five-to-three vote, the Supreme Court upheld the contempt sentences. But Justice HUGO L. BLACK, in a dissenting opinion, criticized Medina for "repeatedly" calling one of the lawyers a "liar." Another dissent, written by FELIX FRANKFURTER, said Medina "should not have combined in himself the functions of accuser and judge."

In September 1953 Medina dismissed antitrust charges against 17 leading investment banking firms after a 34-month trial. He said he was convinced the defendants had not conspired to monopolize their field. A year later Senator KARL E. MUNDT (R-S.Dak.) revealed that the Senate Permanent Investigations Subcommittee had sought Medina as a special counsel for the Army-McCarthy hearings. Mundt said the Supreme Court had unanimously opposed the idea. Medina retained his seat on the appeals court during the 1960s and 1970s. In 1967 he joined with the court in ruling that local draft boards could not punish Vietnam War protestors by reclassifying them into 1-A status. He was also involved in a 1973 decision limiting class action suits. He died on March 14, 1990, in Westwood, New Jersey.

—JF

Miller, Arthur
(1915–2005) *playwright*

The son of middle-class Jewish parents, Arthur Miller was born on October 17, 1915, in New York City. In his youth Miller preferred athletics over academics; his scholastic record was poor and he displayed little interest in drama or literature. During the depression Miller went to work in his father's garment business, where he came to loathe the inhumane treatment of workers. After he left this position he wandered from job to job. During this time Miller became deeply involved in literature, plunging into the Russian classics. In 1934 the University of Michigan granted him probationary acceptance. While attending college Miller held several jobs, but he still found time to write plays and won the university's playwriting award in 1936 and 1937.

In January 1947 Miller won critical and commercial success with the production of *All My Sons,* which captured the New York Drama Critics' Circle Award. The main character in the drama was Joe Keller, a small factory owner who, in order to hold on to a wartime government contract, permitted a shipment of cracked cylinder heads for airplane motors to go out to the air force. Twenty-one fliers plunged to their deaths in the faulty planes. The play's theme, the individual responsibility and the effect of a corrupt society on the individual, was one Miller returned to continually in later plays.

With the production of *Death of a Salesman* in February 1949, Miller was acclaimed a major force in American theater. The play won both the Circle Award and the Pulitzer Prize. Willy Loman, the work's protagonist, was a traveling salesman whose dreams went unrealized. Despite the almost universal praise from critics, the play was attacked from both the left and the right. One critic claimed that "it is, of course, the capitalist system that has done Willy in" and then went on to berate Miller for clouding this truth "behind an air of pseudo-universality." Another resented the use of Willy's capitalistic friend Charley as a eulogist and Miller's apparent empathy for the success that Charley's son wins within the capitalist system. Miller maintained that *Death of a Salesman* was neither a radical critique of American capitalism nor an implicit approval of it.

In the early 1950s Miller became interested in the story of Peter Panto, a dockworker who tried to fight racketeering in the port of New York. He was murdered and his body dumped in the East River. Miller thought that this story would make for a good movie. Elia Kazan joined with Miller in offering the latter's screenplay, titled "the Hook," to Hollywood. Columbia president Harry Cohn did not like the film but okayed it with the hope that Kazan would direct a more profitable movie in the future. But Cohn wanted the blessing of Hollywood's most powerful labor boss, the chairman of the Federation Film Council, Roy Brewer. Cohn told Miller if Brewer turned it down union projectionists would not show it or any other Columbia movie. Brewer said the International Longshoremen's Association would not be involved in such crimes, especially with his friend JOSEPH P. RYAN as its president. (Ryan later went to prison for his involvement in organized crime.) Brewer suggested that the film

would be acceptable if Communists, rather than racketeering unionists, were the villains. Miller would not hear of it and withdrew the script. Kazan, however, persisted and eventually the story became the movie *On the Waterfront.*

The production of *The Crucible* in 1953 propelled Miller into the center of political controversy. Many people saw the play, which dealt with the Salem witch hunts of the 17th century, as an attack on McCarthyism. Analogies were drawn between McCarthyites and the Puritans whose paranoia led to the deaths of innocent people charged with being witches.

In 1956 Miller was called before the House Un-American Activities Committee. He was accused of having signed statements circulated by procommunist organizations and of having applied for membership to the Communist Party. Miller admitted that he had attended five or six meetings of Communist Party writers in 1947 but maintained he had done so to clarify his position on Marxism. He claimed he could not recall the exact nature of the application he had signed. While disavowing support for communism, he refused to provide the committee with the names of those present at the meetings he had attended in 1947.

Miller continued to write plays in a style known as "social realism." One of these, *A Memory of Two Mondays,* which appeared in 1955, was based on his work experience in an auto parts warehouse. In 1964 Miller was elected president of PEN, the International Association of Writers. During the late 1960s Miller was an opponent of the Vietnam War. Miller published his autobiography *Timebends* in 1988. Miller died on February 10, 2005, in Roxbury, Connecticut. (See *The Eisenhower Years* Volume)

—EF

Millikin, Eugene D(onald)
(1891–1958) *member of the Senate*

Eugene D. Millikin was born on February 12, 1891, in Hamilton, Ohio. He left Ohio at age 19 to enroll in the University of Colorado Law School. Upon graduation in 1913 he became executive secretary to George Carlson, who was soon elected governor of Colorado. After army service in France and Germany during World War I, he formed a law partnership with a politically ambitious oil man, Karl Schuyler. Both men left their prosperous practice for Washington, D.C., in 1932, Schuyler as the newly elected senator from Colorado and Millikin as his secretary. Schuyler was killed in an automobile crash in 1933. Millikin returned to Colorado, resumed his corporate law practice, and served as president of the Kinney-Coastal Oil Company.

In 1941 Millikin was appointed to fill a Senate vacancy created by the death of Alva Adams (D-Colo.). He was elected to serve the remainder of Adams term in 1942 and won reelection in 1944 and 1950. A strong conservative, Millikin took a special interest in taxation and trade questions and joined the Finance Committee. The Republican successes in the congressional elections of 1946 thrust him into a leadership position in the 80th Congress. Millikin's close associate and ideological ally, Senator ROBERT A. TAFT (R-Ohio), was senior to Millikin on the Finance Committee, but Taft chose the chairmanship of the Labor Committee instead. This paved the way for Millikin, a senator only five years, to become chairman of the powerful Finance Committee. As chairman of the Republican Conference and a member of the Joint Committee on Atomic Energy, he was a key figure in the formulation of Republican policy and exerted influence over a broad span of legislative matters. Millikin preferred working behind the scenes and avoided being quoted in the press by the constant use of profanity.

Millikin found almost all of the Truman administration's domestic program objectionable. He voted against the Employment Act of 1946, the Fair Employment Practices Commission, the anti–poll tax bill, and public housing measures. He also opposed federal aid to education. Millikin voted in favor of the various bills to control labor union activities and was an outspoken supporter of Senator Robert S. Kerr's (D-Okla.) bill to free natural gas producers from federal regulation.

On other aspects of domestic policy, Millikin was a typical conservative Republican. He voted for the Case labor disputes bill, Taft-Hartley, the Portal-to-Portal Pay Act, flexible agriculture price supports, giving the tidelands to the states, and the McCarran Internal Security Act. He voted against the Housing Act of 1949. However, Millikin, the fiscal conservative, cooperated with his fellow senator from Colorado, Democrat Edwin C. Johnson, to bring home pork to the state. The two set up a "joint projects" office when the Korean War broke out. They split the costs of the office and used it to receive requests from constituents. The administrator was told to credit whichever senator needed it the most at

that moment. With this operation they secured the Air Force Academy for Colorado Springs.

On fiscal issues Millikin moved to the forefront of congressional action. He consistently joined in efforts to cut Democratic budgets, but, during the 80th Congress, he exerted a moderating influence on his Republican colleagues, some of whom favored larger budget slashes than he or Taft deemed prudent. Millikin fought to cut a $6 billion budget reduction passed by the House of $1.5 billion. He also worked strenuously to pass the Republicans sweeping tax cut in 1947–48. During 1947 the measure twice passed Congress and was twice vetoed by President Truman. In 1948 Millikin helped to alter the bill by adding provisions, such as income-splitting for married couples, to broaden its appeal among Democrats. The strategy succeeded; Congress overrode Truman's veto to the Revenue Act of 1948 which cut taxes by $4 billion.

Millikin often devoted his technical expertise and formidable debating skills to the creation and preservation of tax preferences for corporations and wealthy individuals. During 1950–51, when a small band of liberal Democratic senators attacked "loopholes" in the tax code, Millikin plunged into the debate with characteristic acerbity. He vigorously defended such provisions as the special treatment of capital gains income and the depletion allowance for oil and other minerals. In response to Sen. HUBERT H. HUMPHREY's (D-Minn.) spirited attacks on the "legalized stealing" of the well-to-do, Millikin expressed his sympathy for the man earning $500,000 a year.

Millikin adhered to a protectionist trade policy and voted against renewal of the reciprocal trade program in 1945. In 1947–48, however, faced with a House Republican movement to gut the program entirely, Millikin worked with administration officials to moderate protectionist changes in trade policy. In 1948 he managed a compromise bill that extended the Trade Agreements Act for one year, instead of three as the administration requested. But it did not subject trade agreements to congressional veto, as did the House-passed version. The House accepted and Truman signed the Senate version of the measure in June.

Millikin was more likely to line up behind the foreign policy moves of the Truman administration than its domestic actions. He voted for ratification of the United Nations Charter, the Marshall Plan, and the North Atlantic Treaty. He also supported the McMahon bill giving the government control of atomic energy development, despite his usual hostility to federal regulation, on the grounds that there was no sound alternative to government direction of the revolutionary possibilities of atomic power.

Like many Republicans Millikin often found the implementation of an internationalist, anticommunist foreign policy to be at odds with his desire for economy in government. Hence, he often took part in congressional efforts to slash appropriations for foreign aid and military assistance. For instance, he opposed the $3.75 billion loan to the British in 1946. In November 1947 he supported an unsuccessful move to cut the stop-gap relief program for France, Italy, and Austria from $597 million to $400 million. In 1948 he promised that Republicans would support the Marshall Plan but would work to strip it "clean of hysteria, waste, extravagance, overswollen aims, and scatteration." He criticized Truman's Point Four program as a "concoction of patronage, intrusion and imperialism." In 1951 he supported the McClellan Amendment and opposed the nomination of GEORGE C. MARSHALL as secretary of defense in 1951. He voted for the Japanese Peace Treaty.

Millikin backed Taft in 1952 for president. When Eisenhower beat Taft for the GOP nomination, Millikin mediated between the disgruntled Taftites and the supporters of the nominee. During the Eisenhower years Millikin served as an influential Senate ally of the Republican administration, a proponent of fiscal conservatism, and a champion of the billion-dollar Colorado River Storage Project, approved in 1956.

Despite his power and ability Millikin never betrayed any presidential ambitions and spurned opportunities to be Senate Republican leader. "He was valuable to the interests he represented," said his frequent adversary Senator PAUL H. DOUGLAS (D-Ill.), "but he failed to become a national figure because of his natural indolence and the narrowness of his concerns."

Millikin retired from the Senate in 1957 and died of pneumonia on July 26, 1958, in Denver, Colorado. (See *The Eisenhower Years* Volume)

—TO

Mills, Wilbur D(aigh)

(1909–1992) *member of the House of Representatives*

The son of a country banker, Wilbur D. Mills was born on May 24, 1909, in Kensett, Arkansas. He attended Arkansas public schools and Methodist-affiliated Hendrix College before entering Harvard Law School in 1930. He returned to Arkansas without receiving a degree in 1933 and took a job as a cashier in his father's bank. In 1934 he was elected county and probate judge for White Company on a pledge to balance the budget. He fulfilled the campaign promise and was reelected. In 1938 the 29-year-old Mills ran successfully for a seat in the U.S. House of Representatives as a Democrat. He was returned to office in every subsequent election with little or no opposition. A protégé of Speaker of the House SAM T. RAYBURN (D-Tex.), Mills gained appointment under Rayburn's sponsorship to the Ways and Means Committee in 1943, an uncommonly swift ascension to the prestigious tax-writing panel. Through exhaustive study and attention to the details of government finance and trade legislation, Mills by the 1950s became the House's foremost tax expert. According to Mills biographer Julian E. Zelizer, Mills and others of his generation believed in the primacy of specialized knowledge. Mills himself asserted that the federal tax code relied on the expertise of accountants and economists.

While by no means a tax reformer, Mills's fiscal conservatism and Democratic loyalties generally placed him in opposition to Republican plans to ease taxes on upper- and upper-middle-income groups. In March 1947 he assailed a Republican proposal to replace the income tax with a "manufacturer's excise tax." "Why don't they call it a sales tax and be done with it," Mills asked. "Any excise tax inevitably would fall on the consumers."

In the same month Mills voted against a bill sponsored by Ways and Means Committee chairman HAROLD KNUTSON (R-Minn.) that would cut income tax by 20 percent. Many Democrats charged that the bill gave unnecessary relief to the affluent. The measure passed both houses of Congress but was vetoed by President Truman. Mills voted against overriding the veto in June but supported a new tax cut plan a few weeks later. The new measure was likewise a sweeping cut, although it moderated relief for the upper brackets. Truman vetoed the latter version as well; Mills voted with a two-thirds House majority overriding the veto in July, but the Senate sustained the president's action. In April 1948 Mills was in the majority of a 311 to 88 vote overriding Truman's third veto to a major tax cut, which became the Revenue Act of 1948 when the Senate followed the House's vote. In the same month Mills voted to repeal the margarine tax.

In 1949–50 Mills sponsored a plan to increase federal revenue quickly by accelerating tax payments by corporations (compelling companies to pay their 1949 income taxes early in 1950). The so-called Mills Plan was not adopted in 1949 but won acceptance the following year, despite criticism that it was merely "figure-juggling." In August 1950 Mills's proposal for immediate consideration of an excess profits tax to help pay for the Korean War was defeated, 15 to 8, in the committee. The excess profits tax, however, won House passage in December.

Mills followed a generally moderate course on other domestic questions. He voted for the Employment Act of 1946 and endorsed many of the social welfare programs, such as the Housing Act of 1949. However, he voted to overturn President Truman's veto of the Taft-Hartley Act and, in 1952, voted to request the president to invoke the act to halt the steel strike. He voted for turning over the tidelands to the states in 1951 and for deregulation of the natural gas industry. Along with his southern colleagues Mills opposed all civil rights proposals of the Truman administration.

He was a reliable supporter of administration foreign policy, voting in favor of the British loan, Greek-Turkish aid, the Marshall Plan, military aid to the North Atlantic Treaty Organization, and the Korean Aid Act. However, he did support a measure in 1951 reducing aid to Europe. He was a strong proponent of free trade and worked in the Ways and Means Committee to extend the low-tariff reciprocal trade agreements and block protectionist amendments.

Mills believed in the fight against communism at home as well as abroad, supporting making the House Un-American Activities Committee a permanent body, the Mundt-Nixon bill, and the McCarran Internal Security Act.

Assuming the chairmanship of the Ways and Means Committee at the end of 1957, Mills, with his unmatched mastery of the tax code, dominated tax policy over the next decade and a half. In this position he achieved greatest prominence when he stood as a roadblock to various fiscal and social measures desired by Democratic administrations, ultimately exerting great influence over the shape of tax, Medicare, social security, and trade policy when he decided it was appropriate to move forward. One of the most powerful figures in Congress throughout the 1960s, Mills retired from Congress in 1977 after a scandal involving his relationship with an Argentine stripper and public displays of drunkenness. Following his retirement Mills made speaking tours on behalf of Alcoholics Anonymous and practiced law in Washington for the firm of Shea, Gould, Climenko, and Casey. He retired in the early 1980s and returned to Kensett. Mills died there on May 2, 1992. (See *The Eisenhower Years, The Kennedy Years, The Johnson Years, The Nixon/Ford Years* Volumes)

—TO

Minton, Sherman
(1890–1965) *associate justice, U.S. Supreme Court*

Sherman Minton was born on October 20, 1890, in Georgetown, Indiana. An outstanding student and athlete at Indiana University, Minton received a law degree from that institution and another from Yale Law School the next year. He practiced law mainly in New Albany, Indiana, until 1933, when he was named counselor of the state Public Service Commission. Elected to the U.S. Senate as a Democrat in 1934, Minton was a consistent and outspoken supporter of the New Deal. Defeated for reelection in 1940, Minton was appointed a presidential assistant in January 1941 and, four months later, a judge on the U.S. Seventh Circuit Court of Appeals. As circuit judge, Minton wrote several significant antitrust and pro-labor opinions. In a 1948 case he upheld the anticommunist oath requirement in the Taft-Hartley Act.

Minton had become good friends with Harry Truman during their Senate years. He sponsored the bill establishing the Truman Committee to investigate the defense program, which had garnered the attention that led to Chairman Truman's nomination as vice presidential candidate. In March 1948 President Truman named the judge to a three-man board set up to investigate a 10-day strike by JOHN L. LEWIS's United Mine Workers. On September 15, 1949, Truman nominated Minton to the Supreme Court. Because of his liberal tendencies, some conservative senators wanted Minton to be questioned by the Judiciary Committee-Minton refused to appear, citing the precedent of FELIX FRANKFURTER's refusal when he was nominated. The following month the Senate confirmed the appointment. Minton was sworn in as an associate justice on October 12, 1949.

Minton's Senate record led many observers to believe he would be a liberal justice, but he soon emerged as one of the most conservative members of the Court. The Court fight of the 1930s had convinced him that judges must allow other branches of government to use the powers given them in the Constitution and refrain from ruling on the wisdom of executive or legislative action. As a result, the justice supported a policy of judicial restraint. He applied it not only to economic and social welfare measures but also to the civil liberties questions that increasingly came before the Court during the cold war era. Minton believed many government restrictions on individual freedoms were permissible under the Constitution. His appointment to the bench helped create a five-man conservative bloc, which dominated the Court for the next four years.

On loyalty-security matters Minton almost always supported the government against individual rights claims. In one of his first major opinions, Minton, in *U.S. ex rel. Knauff v. Shaughnessy* in January 1950, upheld the exclusion of an alien war bride from the United States without a hearing because the Attorney General considered her a security risk. His opinion for the Court in a March 1952 case—*Adler v. Board of Education of the City of New York*—sustained New York's Feinberg Law (barring members of subversive organizations from teaching in public schools) against a First Amendment challenge. Minton also voted in *Dennis et al. v. U.S.* in June 1951 to uphold the conviction of 11 Communist Party leaders under the Smith Act and, in March 1952, to allow alien Communists facing deportation to be held without bail if the Attorney General thought them a danger to national security. He voted to uphold Truman's loyalty program in the 1951 case *Bailey v. Richardson.* The justice also dissented in the June 1952 case, *Youngstown Sheet & Tube Co. v. Sawyer,* when the majority invalidated Truman's seizure of the steel industry and rejected the president's claim of an inherent executive power to seize private property in a national emergency.

In free speech cases that did not involve security questions, Justice Minton was somewhat more likely to support the individual against the government. In January 1951, for example, he voted to overturn a New York City ordinance requiring preachers to get a police permit for religious services held in city streets and parks. On the same day Minton dissented when the Court, in *Feiner v. New York,* upheld the arrest of a public speaker who was being threatened by hostile members of his audience. However, the justice also voted in the April 1952 case, *Beauharnais v. Illinois,* to approve an Illi-

Portrait of Senator Sherman Minton *(Harry S. Truman Library, Messall Papers)*

nois law prohibiting group libel against a challenge that it denied free speech.

Minton generally favored the government in criminal cases and was very reluctant to interfere with state criminal proceedings. He also hesitated to upset convictions when the defendant did not make any claim of innocence but only charged the government with procedural errors. In an important February 1950 case, *U.S. v. Rabinowitz,* Minton wrote for a five-man majority to approve the warrantless search of a defendant's office following his arrest there. The Court overturned a 1948 decision that required law enforcement officials to obtain search warrants wherever "reasonably practicable."

Justice Minton believed the states had no power to practice racial discrimination, and he joined in a series of important rulings that outlawed discriminatory government practices. For example he joined the majority in striking down restrictive covenants in *Shelley v. Kraemer* (1948) and voted that the University of Texas Law School could not exclude a person on the basis of race in *Sweatt v. Painter* (1950). However, he did not think the Constitution prohibited discrimination by private parties and, on that ground, dissented in June 1952 when the Court ruled against the discriminatory practices of a railway labor union.

Under Chief Justice EARL WARREN, a more liberal trend gradually developed in loyalty-security decisions, and Minton found himself dissenting far more than he had on the Vinson Court in such cases. He remained a conservative on criminal rights issues and a liberal on most racial questions. He joined the May 1954 *Brown v. Board of Education* decision holding public school segregation unconstitutional. Because of ill health, Minton retired from the Court in October 1956. He died on April 9, 1965, in New Albany, Indiana. Although a friendly, down-to-earth man who was well-liked by all of his judicial colleagues, Minton was not a leading figure on the bench. He did not contribute significantly to the development of the law, in part because his conception of the Court's role discouraged any legal creativity. His judicial career has not been highly rated by scholars. (See *The Eisenhower Years* Volume)

—CAB

Monroney, A(lmer) Mike

(1902–1980) *member of the House of Representatives, member of the Senate*

The son of a pioneer Oklahoma family, A. Mike Monroney was born on March 2, 1902, in Oklahoma City, Oklahoma. He showed an early interest in journalism and worked for a local newspaper while still in high school. After graduating from the University of Oklahoma in 1924, he became a political reporter for the *Oklahoma News*. His father's ill health forced him to abandon his career as a journalist, and he took over the family's furniture business in 1928. He quickly assumed a position of leadership among the younger businessmen of Oklahoma City. In 1938 Monroney was elected to the House of Representatives as a Democrat, where he was an early supporter of military preparedness. During World War II he took a firm stand in favor of a strong Office of Price Administration to fight inflation.

Monroney earned a reputation in Congress as an independent, supporting some liberal Fair Deal measures while opposing others. He was a strong proponent of extending price controls in 1946 and

also played a leading role in the fight for Truman's housing subsidy plan in 1946. In 1949 he led the successful fight on the House floor for the extension of rent control. He also supported the Employment Act of 1946 and the law to make the school lunch program permanent. In 1949 he led the successful fight on the House floor for the extension of rent control. He voted for the Case labor disputes bill of 1946 and the Taft-Hartley Act of 1947 and opposed the establishment of a Fair Employment Practices Commission and proposals for a national health insurance plan. Monroney largely supported the efforts to fight Communists on the home front. Although he voted against making the House Un-American Activities Committee permanent, he did support the Mundt-Nixon bill and as a senator voted for the McCarran Internal Security Act.

He supported Truman's foreign policy, voting for the British loan in 1946 and to extend the Trade Agreements Act in 1945. He backed aid to Greece and Turkey, the Marshall Plan, and military aid for NATO. As a senator he voted against the McClellan Amendment, and voted for the Japanese Peace Treaty.

Monroney received a great deal of public attention and praise for his role in congressional reorganization. In November 1943 he and Senator Francis Maloney (D-Conn.) introduced resolutions to set up a Joint Committee on the Organization of Congress. When the panel was finally established in December 1944, Monroney was chosen vice chairman. After extensive hearings during 1945, the committee submitted its report in March 1946, recommending major changes in the rules, procedures, and organization of Congress. Monroney introduced legislation embodying the group's major recommendations. These included a large reduction in the number of congressional committees, the appointment of staff experts to aid members of committees, and the establishment of procedures for drawing up a legislative budget early in each fiscal year. The bill also required that congressional lobbyists register and disclose their sources of funds. Monroney had hoped to modify seniority rules, limit the power of the House Rules Committee, and eliminate the filibuster, but he lacked sufficient support to include these measures in his legislative proposals. Most of his recommendations were incorporated in the Congressional Reorganization Act, passed in August 1946. For his role in securing passage, Monroney was awarded *Collier's* Congressman of the Year Award.

In 1950 Monroney ran against incumbent senator ELMER THOMAS stressing Thomas's old age as a reason to oust him. He noted that Thomas had voted to cut air force spending just before the Korean War. Elected to the Senate, Monroney was one of the earliest critics of Senator JOSEPH R. MCCARTHY (R-Wisc.). In February 1951 the Senate Rules Committee authorized its Subcommittee on Privileges and Elections to investigate the Tydings-Butler campaign of 1950 in Maryland. Monroney headed the investigation. Monroney invited McCarthy to testify in response to the allegations that he had improperly intervened in the election, but McCarthy refused. After a long delay, the subcommittee finally issued its report in August 1951. It exonerated Senator JOHN MARSHALL BUTLER (D-Md.) of any improprieties but was extremely critical of McCarthy's involvement in the campaign. Because of partisan differences, however, the report failed to make any recommendations.

Three days later, Senator William B. Benton (D-Conn.) introduced a resolution calling on the Rules Committee to investigate whether to initiate action to expel McCarthy from the Senate. The resolution was sent to the Subcommittee of Privileges and Elections, and Monroney pushed hard for its favorable consideration. In April 1952, after McCarthy attacked the panel, Monroney demanded a vote of confidence from the Senate. On April 10 the Senate unanimously voted to keep the Benton Resolution before the Rules Committee. When the 82nd Congress expired on January 3, 1953, the subcommittee still had not completed its investigation, and the resolution died in committee. Monroney continued to criticize publicly McCarthy's smear tactics against other senators and Senate institutions. He remained a vocal critic of McCarthy during the early years of the Eisenhower administration.

During the rest of his Senate career, Monroney continued to support foreign aid and defense spending, and he backed American policy in Southeast Asia. He also voted for most of the liberal domestic programs of the Kennedy and Johnson administrations. In 1965 he co-chaired the Joint Committee on the Organizations of Congress, which conducted the first major review of congressional operations since the passage of Monroney's reorganization bill in 1946. Campaigning for reelection in 1968, he lost to his Republican opponent by 33,000 votes. Monroney died on February 13, 1980, in Rockville, Maryland. (See *The Eisenhower Years, The Kennedy Years, The Johnson Years* Volumes)

—JD

Moody, (Arthur Edson) Blair
(1902–1954) *member of the Senate*

Blair Moody was born on February 13, 1902, in New Haven, Connecticut. He graduated from Brown University in 1922 with a degree in economics. After a year of teaching and coaching baseball and football, he became a sports-writer with the *Detroit News*. Within a year he left the sports desk to cover city hall. In 1933 he became the Washington correspondent for the *News* and wrote the column, "The Lowdown on Washington." Moody served as war correspondent in Italy, Iran, and North Africa. From 1944 to 1945 he was an economic consultant for the Committee for Economic Development, which attempted to develop policies to maintain a high level of production and employment.

Moody was a strong supporter of a bipartisan foreign policy. He assisted Senator ARTHUR H. VANDENBERG, (R-Mich.) in the preparation of his famous 1945 speech that laid the foundations for interparty cooperation between Republicans and Democrats. Along with his assignment with the Washington bureau of the *News* in 1946, Moody became moderator of the broadcast program, "Meet Your Congress." After the war he traveled through countries that were benefiting from the Marshall Plan to report on their economic progress.

In 1951 Moody, a Democrat, was appointed to the Senate seat vacated by the death of Vandenberg. He became the first working reporter to sit in the Senate. Although he had no prior political affiliation, when he took the oath of office he allied himself with liberal Democrats. Because of his background in economics, Moody was named to the Banking and Currency Committee and the Committee on Expenditures in the Executive Branch. A few months later he became chairman of the Senate Small Business Committee, known as the "Watchdog Group." As head of this panel, Moody investigated black market activities in scarce steel, nickel, and aluminum. Moody was a firm supporter of price controls as a means to curb inflation. He also backed supplementary unemployment benefits to areas affected by the business shift to defense work. He voted against the Byrd Amendment to the Defense

Production Act Amendments of 1952, which requested Truman to invoke the Taft-Hartley Act after the Supreme Court struck down his seizure of the steel industry during a labor dispute during the Korean War. He voted against the McCarran-Walters Act and giving the tidelands to the states.

Truman could rely on Moody to support his foreign policy. He supported the Japanese Peace Treaty and voted against the Dirksen amendment to the Mutual Security Act of 1951, which would have cut aid to Europe by $250 million.

He opposed Senator JOSEPH R. MCCARTHY's (R-Wisc.) anticommunist crusade, regarding it as an attempt to "undermine for political reasons our foreign policy—which is fighting Communism." In 1952 Moody served as the head of the anticensorship committee of the Senate Permanent Investigations Subcommittee, which sought to reconcile security requirements with the free access to government information by journalists. He left office before the investigation was completed.

At the Democratic National Convention in 1952, Moody led the fight for a civil rights plank in the party's platform that included the demand for equal protection under the law for all racial minorities and desegregation of the armed forces. He also sponsored a loyalty pledge requiring all delegates to support the convention's candidates. The move was an attempt to compel Southern Democrats to support the party's nominee despite their opposition to its civil rights program. Although the convention voted in favor of the pledge, southern moderates bound by state party regulations requested that they be exempt from it. As a result Moody's resolution was virtually suspended.

Moody lost his bid for reelection to Representative CHARLES E. POTTER (R-Mich.) in the landslide Republican victory of 1952. He then returned to his position as moderator of "Meet Your Congress." In 1954 he began a race for a full term as senator but died of viral pneumonia in Ann Arbor, Michigan, on July 20, 1954, one month before the Democratic primary.

—DGE

Morgenthau, Henry, Jr.
(1891–1967) *secretary of the Treasury*

Henry Morgenthau was born on Manhattan's Upper West Side on May 11, 1891. His father, who had become wealthy in real estate ventures, was promi-nent in the Democratic Party and served as ambassador to Turkey during the Wilson administration. Morgenthau studied architecture at Cornell University but withdrew after three semesters. Deciding to become a farmer, he purchased some acreage in the Hudson River valley. In 1922 he bought up a weekly magazine, the *American Agriculturalist*, which he used to promote conservation, reclamation, and modern farming methods. He became a close friend and confidant of Franklin D. Roosevelt, a Dutchess County neighbor. After Roosevelt was stricken with polio in 1921, Morgenthau aided him in his political comeback. When Roosevelt became governor of New York in 1928, he appointed Morgenthau chairman of his agricultural advisory commission, with the task of winning support for his administration among upstate Republican farmers.

During the early months of the New Deal, Morgenthau headed the Federal Farm Board and its successor, the Farm Credit Administration. In this post he worked to expand credit as a means of easing the burden of mortgages and other debts contracted by farmers during the pre-depression years. Although he was not a banker, a broker, or a lawyer, and thus lacked the usual qualifications for this cabinet position, Morgenthau was appointed secretary of the Treasury in December 1933. He quickly proved to be the most activist secretary in the history of the Treasury. Under his direction the department intervened in world financial markets to an unprecedented extent, buying and selling gold and foreign currencies in order to stabilize the devalued U.S. dollar. Morgenthau favored a balanced budget rather than a deliberate Keynesian countercyclical fiscal policy. He was part of a circle of presidential advisers who revised New Deal measures in a conservative direction. However, although his colleagues regarded him as too economically orthodox, they were usually able to enlist his support for their spending programs.

During World War II the need to finance the vast economic and military efforts of the Allied coalition brought Morgenthau and the Treasury Department to the center of foreign as well as domestic economic planning. When Germany invaded Poland in 1939, Morgenthau set up a procurement service that facilitated the purchase of American munitions by Britain and France. After the United States opened hostilities against the Axis powers, he concentrated on the sale of war bonds. At the Bretton Woods Conference in 1944, he took a leading role in establishing postwar economic and currency policies, and in providing for U.S. participation in the International Monetary Fund and the Bank for Reconstruction and Development (World Bank).

At the same time Morgenthau became involved in a controversy over the dispositon of Germany after the war. Early in 1944 he put forward a plan to "pastoralize" Germany by destroying its heavy industry and forcing most of its population into agricultural pursuits. The Morgenthau Plan, as it was known, proposed separating German children from their parents in order to reeducate them in special schools. It also recommended partitioning the country into northern and southern states with the annexation of western industrial regions by France and eastern regions by Poland. The plan never became official U.S. policy; it was strongly opposed by elements in the War and State departments, which believed that German industrial prosperity would play an essential role in the postwar economic reconstruction of Europe. Just what President Roosevelt's plans for Germany were was never clear, but by early 1945 the center of economic decision making in the administration began to shift to the State Department.

Morgenthau's entire public career had hinged on his friendship with Roosevelt. After the president's death he planned to remain in office under the Truman administration only for as long as it would take to advance his program for Germany. However, Truman favored a postwar restoration of German industry, and he replied evasively to Morgenthau's pleas for support. In addition, Morgenthau was shunted out of control over lend-lease shipments to Great Britain and replaced by Truman's close friend FRED M. VINSON, head of the Office of War Mobilization and Reconversion. Vinson reduced the aid previously promised to Britain and shelved Morgenthau's plans for converting lend-lease into a massive program of U.S. economic assistance to postwar Europe, proposing instead a series of individual loans. Consequently, Morgenthau found his position increasingly untenable. On July 5, 1945, he resigned, and, on the following day, Truman announced his intention to appoint Vinson his successor. Accounts of Morgenthau's resignation differed: the former secretary claimed afterward that he had hoped to serve until the victory over Japan but was asked by Truman to retire. The president, in his memoirs, recalled that Morgenthau had threatened to resign unless allowed to accompany him to the Potsdam Conference. Truman had little regard

for Morgenthau. In an unsent letter he described the secretary as a "blockhead, nut!" Council of Economic Advisers member LEON H. KEYSERLING thought Truman's later Treasury secretary, JOHN W. SNYDER, was better at the job than Morgenthau.

During his last year in the cabinet, Morgenthau had been a leading supporter of the Soviet Union's request for a multibillion dollar U.S. loan, which he hoped might ease Russian demands for German reparations. Consequently, his departure from the administration was considered a sign of the new anti-Soviet mood in Washington. Over the following years Morgenthau occasionally criticized what he regarded as Truman's reversal of Roosevelt's policy of compromise with the USSR, complaining, in particular, that the rebuilding of Germany impaired peaceful Soviet-American relations. He joined the anti-Truman Conference of Progressives in 1946. However, he refused to support either the Communist-influenced Progressive Citizens of America or the anticommunist Americans for Democratic Action when the liberal movement split at the end of the year. Increasingly disillusioned by the cold war and liberal disunity, Morgenthau withdrew from politics and devoted himself to philanthropies. From 1947 to 1950 he was general chairman of the United Jewish Appeal and from 1951 to 1954 chairman of the board of governors of the American Financial and Development Corporation for Israel. Morgenthau died on February 6, 1967, in Poughkeepsie, New York.

—TLH

Morris, Newbold (Augustus)
(1902–1966) *special assistant to the U.S. Attorney General*

The son of a patrician New York family, Newbold Morris was born on February 3, 1902, in New York City. He attended Groton School, received a B.A. from Yale University, and an LL.B. from that institution in 1928. The following year Morris joined his father's law firm and the New York County Republican Committee. A liberal Republican, he was appointed assistant corporation counsel by New York mayor Fiorello LaGuardia in 1934. Morris was elected New York City Council president as a Republican, Liberal and Fusion Party candidate in 1937, and reelected in 1941. During World War II he served as chairman of the New York City War Council. He ran unsuccessfully for mayor in 1945 and 1949.

On February 1, 1952, President Harry S Truman appointed Morris special assistant to Attorney General J. HOWARD MCGRATH. Morris's father-in-law, Judge LEARNED HAND, had recommended him. Morris was to direct a cleanup of corruption in government, much of which was alleged to center in the Justice Department. The scope of Morris's job, the powers he would be given, and his place in the government were not spelled out. McGrath saw Morris as a good choice because he had a reputation as a reformer. Also, as historian Andrew J. Dunar has argued, McGrath appreciated that Morris had had no experience in investigation and therefore as someone whom the Attorney General could easily direct so as to avoid an in-depth inquiry. Morris's liaison with the White House, Harold Seidman of the Bureau of the Budget, told Morris he was being played for a sucker. Morris himself proved to be inept and indecisive. Morris considered himself answerable only to Truman, although the president, seeking to avoid Senate confirmation proceedings, had made him McGrath's assistant. McGrath himself said at the outset that Morris "owes no allegiance whatsoever . . . to myself or to the present administration."

Following the appointment, Senator CLYDE R. HOEY (D-N.C.), chairman of the Senate Permanent Investigations Subcommittee, pointed out that Morris's law firm was the subject of a current investigation for alleged involvement in surplus oil tanker deals. Morris stated that he never received "a single dollar" from the tanker leases. He antagonized the Attorney General immediately by stating on the television show "Meet the Press" that an investigation of the Justice Department was at the top of his agenda. He then refused McGrath's offer of desk space and established an independent headquarters with his own staff.

On February 14 Truman asked Congress to give Morris power to subpoena witnesses and grant immunity from prosecution to those whose testimony was crucial. Morris had not asked for authority to grant immunity and publicly said so later. By presenting both requests to a Congress resentful at being circumvented by his roundabout appointment of a special investigator, the president made it likely the legislature would grant neither. The following week a House judiciary subcommittee denied Morris immunity power. Morris believed someone had betrayed him by putting in the immunity request, which was sure to sink the bill. At the same time the special investigator found himself implicated in the "Casey tanker case" by the Senate's Hoey panel.

In 1947 a distinguished group headed by former representative Joseph E. Casey (D-Mass.) bought eight oil tankers worth $3 million each from the government for half price. Such sales to speculators were illegal. Through a complicated arrangement Chinese Nationalists hired Morris's law firm to obtain use of three tankers for fees approximating $40,000 a year. Morris's law partner, Houston H. Wasson, testified that Morris shared in the fees. This contradicted Morris's earlier statement, and he volunteered to testify. Complicating his position, in public broadcasts on February 28 and March 2, Morris denied working for McGrath despite his title. Without presenting evidence he asserted McGrath, Secretary of the Treasury JOHN W. SNYDER and Truman's military aide, General HARRY H. VAUGHAN, were priority targets for investigation. Without clear legal authority Morris also announced that all officials involved in granting government contracts would be required to fill out lengthy questionnaires revealing their financial resources.

On March 12 Morris testified before the Hoey panel on his connection with the Casey oil tanker controversy. United Tanker Corporation, the company counseled by Morris's law firm, had carried oil to Communist China under Soviet charter before the Korean War. When Senator JOSEPH R. MCCARTHY (R-Wisc.) accused Morris of profiting from the blood of American soldiers, Morris denounced "diseased minds" in the Senate chamber. He said he had cleared the oil shipments with the State Department. He denied making money from the tankers themselves but did not deny that his legal fees could amount to $30,000. Morris claimed he was being probed because he was the corruption investigator. Following Morris's testimony, Senator RICHARD M. NIXON (R-Calif.) accused him of "one of the most disgraceful performances I have ever seen before a congressional committee." McCarthy said he didn't think Morris "was responsible for what he was saying."

On March 18 the Senate Judiciary Committee voted unanimously not to give Morris subpoena power. The same day Morris delivered his financial questionnaire to McGrath and other top Justice Department officials. A week later the House Judiciary Committee's special panel to investigate the Justice Department, chaired by Representative Frank Chelf (D-Ky.), called McGrath to testify. He said he had not decided whether to answer Morris's questionnaire but stated he would not appoint Morris as investigator if he had to do it over again.

Following heated discussions with Truman, McGrath fired Morris without notice on April 3. He, himself, was dismissed as Attorney General by Truman the same day. Testifying before the Chelf Subcommittee in April, Morris stated he had uncovered no evidence of corruption during his brief tenure. The following month former deputy Attorney General Peyton Ford and others told Chelf that both Morris and McGrath had known the Justice Department was investigating Morris's involvement in surplus tanker deals before his appointment. This contradicted testimony by the two former Justice Department officials. In its report released in September 1952, the Chelf Subcommittee expressed the conviction that McGrath had appointed Morris to investigate corruption in the belief that he "might be susceptible to pressure" because of the tanker deal.

Following his dismissal Morris returned to private life. In 1960 he was appointed New York City parks commissioner by Mayor Robert Wagner, Jr. and held that post for nearly six years. Morris died of stomach cancer on March 31, 1966, in New York City.

—MJS

Morrison, DeLesseps S(tory)
(1912–1964) *mayor*

The son of a Louisiana district attorney and a descendant of Ferdinand deLesseps, the builder of the Suez Canal, Morrison S. DeLesseps was born on January 18, 1912, in New Roads, Louisiana. He worked as a bookkeeper and cotton sorter to pay his way through Louisiana State University. After graduating from Louisiana State Law School in 1934, he joined the National Recovery Administration (NRA), where he was responsible for enforcing wage and hour statutes. One year later he left his post at NRA to join his brother Jacob and future U.S. representative Hale Boggs in organizing a New Orleans law firm.

In 1936 Morrison became active in city reform politics. Four years later he was elected to the state legislature as a reform candidate opposed to the late Huey Long's Democratic machine. Morrison pushed various progressive measures, including the installation of voting machines in New Orleans. He was reelected to his seat in 1944 while serving in the army.

With the support of veterans organizations, women's clubs, and blacks, Morrison ran as the reform candidate for mayor of New Orleans in 1946 and defeated Robert S. Maestri, who enjoyed the backing of the Long machine. Morrison assumed office that May, beginning the first of four terms as mayor of the Crescent City.

Having won the election by a small majority, Morrison recognized the importance of the growing number of registered black voters in the city. In September 1947 he announced that slum clearance and the construction of public housing projects would be part of his program for New Orleans. Facilities were built to upgrade black areas. Yet the mayor supported segregation. He made few attempts at integration, and the efforts he did make were often termed token. After years of evading the issue, he agreed, in June 1949, to permit very limited integration of the police department. The following year two black men were appointed to the force but were quickly tucked out of sight in plain clothes in a predominantly black district. Despite their addition to the force, there were continued instances of police brutality against blacks.

In 1948 Morrison backed Sam Jones for governor on a good government platform. The mayor, however, hurt Jones's campaign by making the sort of behind-the-scene deals that EARL K. LONG made. He promised three prominent Democrats state jobs for their support of Jones. He also convinced Jones to raise New Orleans's sales tax and increase the number of patronage jobs for the city if he was elected governor. He convinced his friend HENRY R. LUCE to contact Louisiana newspaper editors and publishers and press them to endorse Jones. He had a private detective investigate Long. The investigator accused Long of receiving $46,000 that was deducted from the paychecks of state employees. Morrison claimed Long was the puppet of gangsters. Despite Morrison's efforts, Long defeated Jones.

Morrison was also active in expanding the movement for increased foreign trade through the port of New Orleans begun by business leaders before World War II. By the time the International Trade Mart opened in June 1948, he had assumed the leadership role in attracting international trade, and he had created the nation's first municipal department of international relations. Because of the city's location, Morrison emphasized trade with Latin America. During his tenure he made many visits there and was instrumental in establishing new air routes from New Orleans to Caracas, San Juan, and Havana.

The mayor's program to attract commerce gave the New Orleans economy a tremendous boost. New port facilities were built, and, by 1947, the Crescent City ranked second in dollar value of trade among the nation's ports. In 1948 officials estimated an increase of $1 billion in annual trade volume since 1940. Paralleling its commercial expansion, New Orleans enjoyed fantastic industrial growth. In 1951 industry worth over $200 million entered the Crescent City area.

Despite the expansion of the economy and his popular construction and recreation programs, Morrison's administration was tarnished by charges that his reform program was more image than substance, by scandals in the police department, and by increased agitation over school integration.

Morrison made two unsuccessful attempts to capture the Louisiana governorship, in 1956 and again in 1960. In June 1961 President Kennedy appointed him ambassador to the Organization of American States (OAS). Two years later, Morrison resigned this post to make another fruitless run for the governorship. He died in a plane crash in the Mexican mountains on May 22, 1964, near Ciudad Victoria, Mexico. (See *The Eisenhower Years* Volume)

—EF

Morse, David A(bner)

(1907–1990) assistant secretary of labor, undersecretary of labor, director-general, International Labor Organization

David A. Morse was born in New York City, on May 31, 1907. An All-American end on the 1926 Rutgers College football team, he graduated from that institution in 1929 and received his law degree from Harvard in 1932. Following practice in Newark, New Jersey, during 1932 and 1933, Morse moved to Washington to join the solicitor's staff of the Department of the Interior. From 1934 to 1938 he held a number of other legal positions in the Interior and Justice departments. In 1938 Morse became the regional mediator for the National Labor Relations Board for an area covering New York, New Jersey, and Connecticut. Morse left government in 1940 to resume his law practice and served as a labor mediator in the New York City area. During service in the army in World War II, he had the responsibility for formulating labor policy for the Allied occupational forces in Italy and Germany. Upon his discharge in September 1945,

Morse became general counsel to the National Labor Relations Board. As a result of Morse's reputation as an expert on labor, President Truman appointed him an assistant secretary of labor in June 1946. He was responsible for formulating policy on labor for U.S. delegations to various United Nations commissions and was one of the federal mediators in the numerous strikes that plagued the early Truman years. Morse also sat on an ad-hoc committee of administration liberals, headed by CLARK CLIFFORD, that planned the Fair Deal policies of the administration. Morse was one of a coterie of liberals in the administration who tried to move Truman to the left on domestic policy after the disastrous mid-term elections of 1946. They met Monday evenings in the Wardman Hotel apartment of the acting chairman of the Democratic National Committee, OSCAR R. EWING.

Morse along with White House counsel Clark Clifford advised the president on labor legislation after the 1946 election and the egregious strikes of that year. They told him that if he sent draft legislation to Congress the administration would like it to be backed "whatever monstrosity might result." Yet just to veto such legislation would risk being accused of negativism. In the end, Truman decided to let Congress take the lead, which resulted in the Taft-Hartley Act. Truman's veto of the bill—it was overridden by Congress—helped patch relations with organized labor, which had been strained because of Truman's harsh reaction to the railroad strike of 1946.

Morse represented the United States at the 13th Conference of the International Labor Organization (ILO), which met in Switzerland during the summer of 1947. There he chaired the committee that drew up a report on the possibility of international machinery guaranteeing the right of freedom of association. Morse returned to Washington to receive a promotion to undersecretary. During 1947 he aided in attempts to defeat the Taft-Hartley bill. After its passage Morse helped administer the Labor Department's functions under the measure.

In June 1948 the ILO elected Morse its director general. He resigned his administration post to head the Geneva-based organization beginning in September. Under Morse's direction the ILO passed a series of conventions designed to improve the conditions of workers. These treaties, which were eventually ratified by most of the member states, pledged to protect the right of organization and to establish international minimum wage standards. They also promised to provide equal pay for men and women for work of equal value, to offer social security and maternity protection and holidays with paid benefits, and to establish strict on-the-job safety procedures. Morse supervised the ILO's technical assistance program for the developing nations. In 1969 he accepted the Nobel Peace Prize on behalf of the ILO. He remained with ILO until 1970, when he returned to New York to practice law and serve as a mediator for the ladies garment industry. He also was a member of a number of United Nations committees dealing with economic assistance. Morse died on December 1, 1990, in New York City.

—JB

Morse, Wayne (Lyman)
(1900–1974) *member of the Senate*

Wayne Morse's populist beliefs had their origins in Wisconsin, where he was born on October 20, 1900, in Madison. He graduated from the University of Wisconsin in 1923 and then taught argumentation at the University of Minnesota from 1924 to 1928. He earned a law degree from the institution and, in 1929, became an assistant professor of law at the University of Oregon. Two years later he was named dean of the university's law school.

In this position he often was called on to mediate West Coast labor disputes. He soon became one of the nation's leading authorities on labor relations and, in January 1942, was appointed to the National War Labor Board. Although he sympathized with labor interests, Morse resigned his post two years later to protest what he considered unwarranted concessions to JOHN L. LEWIS's United Mine Workers.

In 1944 Morse, running on the Republican ticket, was elected to the Senate from Oregon. He soon established his reputation as an independent liberal who refused to compromise his convictions. While respecting his character and expertise, many senators were antagonized by what they considered his abrasive personality.

Taking his Senate seat in January 1945, Morse quickly allied himself with ARTHUR H. VANDENBERG (R-Mich.) and his internationalist stance on world affairs. Following the ratification of the UN charter, Morse introduced a measure in July 1945 that called for American adherence to the authority of the World Court. The bill was severely weakened when it was amended to demand U.S. compliance only when in the nation's interest. Morse also supported the Marshall Plan and when the Czechoslovak Communist Party seized power in 1948, he called for an increase in defense spending.

Morse was initially worried by the attitude of many government officials that the United States should not share the secrets of the atomic bomb. The senator believed that spread of science and technology of the bomb was inevitable, and that what was needed was international control of atomic energy. However, by 1948 Morse had shifted to the predominant cold war position that the United States should not share the secrets of the bomb, even with the British.

Morse soon antagonized the conservative wing of the Republican Party, which advocated an aggressive Asian policy. He supported the removal of General DOUGLAS MACARTHUR from his command, and he called for a congressional inquiry into the operations of the pro-Nationalist China lobby in Washington. Yet during the Truman years Morse opposed American recognition of Communist China and its admittance to the United Nations.

On the domestic front, Morse's view consistently paralleled those of organized labor. On the Labor Committee Morse formed an alliance with Republicans GEORGE D. AIKEN of Vermont and IRVING M. IVES of New York and the four liberal Democratic members to tone down ROBERT A. TAFT's (R-Ohio) attempt at restricting union activity, although he had to agree to some measures to appease the public. But much of this victory was lost on the floor of the Senate, where Taft offered four committee-rejected amendments. Morse rounded up enough votes to defeat the one that would have outlawed industrywide collective bargaining, but Taft won his other amendments, which put tight restrictions on labor unions. Morse voted against the final Taft-Hartley Act.

Morse was more successful in efforts to stop raids on the Treasury through the disposal of land purchased by the military during the war, but which it no longer needed. Morse found members of Congress taking the land for constituents in private bills without paying the government. The Oregonian established the "Morse Formula," which stipulated that if state or local governments bought the land for a public purpose, it would have to pay half the fair market value. If private interests bought it they would have to pay the full price. Soon the formula was being applied to the disposal of any type of federal government surplus. Another sign of his probity came when, during the scandals of the Truman administration, the president secretly offered Morse the post of Attorney General, but he rejected the offer.

It was something of a surprise when Morse, who supported the Tennessee Valley Authority, declined to back a similar project for the Columbia River valley in 1949. To the disappointment of liberals, Morse argued that the Southeast was different from the Northwest and, in the latter region, a combined effort of states and private interests would do a better job than the federal government.

Morse backed President Truman's seizure of the steel mills in 1952. He introduced two bills related to the crisis: the first outlined procedures for the president to seize industrial property; the second proposed a settlement of the steel strike by granting wage and price increases. The Senate acted on neither proposal, and Morse was embarassed when the Supreme Court ruled Truman's action unconstitutional.

Morse took inconsistent stands on the issue of civil liberties. In 1949 he said it was perfectly acceptable to keep Communists and Communist sympathizers out of university faculties, and he voted for Pat McCarran's Internal Security Act a year later and the Communist Control Act of 1954. However, in June 1950 he joined with five other Republicans to sign MARGARET CHASE SMITH's (R-Maine) "Declaration of Conscience," which condemned JOSEPH R. MCCARTHY's reckless tactics. Later Morse chastised McCarthy for making accusations without proof, and he recommended that all witnesses have the right to counsel when called to testify before Senate investigators. He also opposed the Defense Department's use of lie detectors in screening job applicants and the FBI's use of wiretaps. His criticism of McCarthy fluctuated during 1953 and 1954.

Morse initially supported DWIGHT D. EISENHOWER for the 1952 Republican presidential nomination but reversed himself and backed ADLAI E. STEVENSON when Eisenhower met with Taft in September and agreed to support a conservative program drawn up by the Ohioan. A month later Morse resigned from the party and became an independent. Early in 1955 he crossed over to join the Democratic Party. Morse maintained a liberal stance throughout the 1950s, voting for civil rights

bills, measures to restrict wiretapping, and proposals to develop natural resources.

Morse ran unsuccessfully for the Democratic presidential nomination in 1960. He supported most of the Kennedy and Johnson administration's domestic legislation, but he was an early and vociferous opponent of the Vietnam War. Republican Robert Packwood unseated Morse in the 1968 Senate race. Four years later he tried an unsuccessful comeback. In 1974 Morse won the Democratic primary, but kidney failure cut short a possible return to the Senate. Morse, the Senate's "lone tiger," died in Portland, Oregon, on July 22, 1974. (See *The Eisenhower Years, The Kennedy Years, The Johnson Years* Volumes)

—EF

Moses, Robert
(1888–1981) *chairman, Triboro Bridge and Tunnel Authority; chairman, New York State Council of Parks*

Robert Moses was born on December 18, 1888, in New Haven, Connecticut. He was a graduate of Yale and Oxford and received a doctorate in political science from Columbia University in 1924. From 1913 to 1918 he worked for the New York City Bureau of Municipal Research; and in 1919 Governor Alfred E. Smith appointed him adviser on the revision of the state constitution. In 1924 Moses became president of the New York State Council of Parks and chairman of the Long Island State Commission. He soon built a series of widely praised beaches and parks on Long Island and two major parkways connecting the island to New York City.

Moses ran unsuccessfully for governor in 1934. That year he became New York City's first citywide commissioner of parks while retaining his various state posts. Mayor Fiorello LaGuardia also appointed him a member of the Triboro Bridge Authority. In 1936 he became chairman of the authority. With the help of federal money, Moses undertook a massive program of park and bridge construction. He considered New York City a "magnetic core" around which the rest of the state revolved and built a series of highways connecting it with upstate and Long Island. A hard-nosed pragmatist, Moses accepted the urbanization of American life and denounced "long-haired green belt boys" who sought to decentralize the city. He had little nostalgia for historical landmarks, many of which he did not hesitate to demolish to build his projects.

Moses's power increased during the postwar period. In 1946 he was appointed city construction coordinator with authority over postwar housing construction. His supporters were appointed members of the city housing authority, consolidating his control. Moses used his many posts to build an independent power base largely outside of the control of elected officials. During the late 1940s, when the city and borough governments lacked funds to create jobs and placate their constituents, Moses, who controlled revenues from the state and federal government, held the reins of power. The *New York Times* dubbed him "the strongman" of the O'Dwyer administration. When WILLIAM O'DWYER left the mayoralty in August 1950, Moses became the guiding hand of the new mayor, VINCENT IMPELLITTERI, who won election in November 1950 with Moses's endorsement.

During the late 1940s and early 1950s, Moses began an urban renewal project for New York City and persuaded O'Dwyer to appoint a Mayor's Slum Clearance Committee, with him as the head. Since the city was on the verge of bankruptcy, Moses suggested that money for new housing be obtained from the state legislature. To win the support of the conservative-dominated legislature, he recommended yielding to their demands for less extravagant facilities for the poor. Moses opposed the community-oriented ideas of Jerry Finkelstein, chairman of the City Planning Commission, whose rezoning efforts sought to give neighborhoods a role in planning their future development. Following Moses's recommendation, Finkelstein was removed from the commission. Although the building program began slowly, during Impellitteri's 40-month tenure, 24 housing projects were constructed.

Moses also continued his highway construction program and developed a plan for the expansion of Idlewild Airport. To finance many of his projects Moses used independent public authorities. Seeking to win support from the wealthy sections of the city, he sold authority bonds through private placement to the large city banks. He recommended supporting mass transit by doubling fares and urged increased sales taxes to generate funds for construction projects.

Moses's projects and methods offended a large number of individuals. His highway program resulted

in the eviction of thousands of families. His recommendations for tax increases elicited complaints that they fell chiefly on the poor. Liberals also denounced his emphasis on highway building while postponing school, library, and hospital construction.

Moses continued to control New York development through the 1950s. He resigned his city posts in 1960 in the wake of scandals involving his slum clearance program. By 1967 he had resigned from his state park posts as well, retaining only the chairmanship of the Triboro Bridge and Tunnel Authority. After the formation of the Metropolitan Transit Authority (MTA) and the abolition of the Triboro Authority in 1968, Moses became a consultant to the MTA. Moses died on July 29, 1981, in New York City. (See *The Kennedy Years, The Johnson Years* Volumes)

—AES

Muccio, John J(oseph)
(1900–1989) *ambassador*

John J. Muccio was born on March 19, 1900, in Valle Agricola, Italy. His parents immigrated to the United States from Italy when he was a child. They settled in Providence, Rhode Island, where Muccio attended high school. He then entered Brown University, interrupting his education in 1918 to serve in the army. He returned to Brown and graduated in 1921 with a bachelor of philosophy degree.

That same year Muccio became a naturalized citizen and entered the Foreign Service as a consular assistant. He received a master's degree from George Washington University two years later and was appointed a Foreign Service officer in November 1923. Muccio became vice consul at Hamburg, Germany, in 1924 and held the same post in Hong Kong starting in 1926. From 1928 to 1935 he served as consul in a series of Far Eastern ports, including Hong Kong, Foochow, and Shanghai. In February 1935 he was shifted to Latin America. Over the next 10 years he held various diplomatic posts in Bolivia, Nicaragua, Panama, and Cuba.

In 1945 Muccio became assistant to ROBERT D. MURPHY, U.S. political adviser to Germany. Muccio returned to Washington a year later and, in July 1947, was named Foreign Service inspector. In August 1948, when the Truman administration gave conditional diplomatic recognition to the Republic of Korea, Muccio went there as personal representative of the President. Considered by Secretary of

State DEAN G. ACHESON to be an experienced and "level-headed" officer, Muccio was known as a modest, unassuming career diplomat with an extensive background in Far Eastern affairs.

Muccio announced in December 1948 that the United States would provide economic aid to South Korea through the Economic Cooperation Administration (ECA). John C. Caldwell, deputy director of the U.S. Information Service, later criticized Muccio's role in administering American assistance. Caldwell claimed that the American Mission's efforts were uncoordinated and that Muccio and his aides were hostile to Dr. Arthur Bunce, head of the ECA in Korea. He reported in *The Korean Story* (1952) that Muccio provided little supervision of the aid and that, despite widespread corruption, "the Department of State and the Ambassador frowned upon any intervention in Korean affairs."

Early in 1949 Muccio disclosed that the United States was considering the withdrawal of American military forces from Korea. He announced that the "best information available from military experts indicate that Korean forces are already competent to maintain internal stability." The South Korean government opposed the withdrawal. In April 1949 Muccio became the first American ambassador to the Republic of Korea. According to *Newsweek* he "initially used the velvet glove to restrain President Syngman Rhee." In mid-1949 Muccio reportedly advised members of the South Korean national assembly, angered by Rhee's near-dictatorial rule, to abandon a constitutional amendment freeing cabinet members from the power of the president. Muccio reportedly argued a change in the new constitution would be interpreted as lack of unity within the Korean government.

In January 1950 the ambassador and Korean representatives signed a $10 million agreement providing the republic with military aid, and Muccio was able to assuage some of Rhee's fears about the American withdrawal. He convinced the South Korean president to take steps to control inflation. Four months later Muccio and the State Department took a harder line with Rhee, threatening to withhold economic and military aid if South Korea did not hold elections scheduled for May and if corruption and mismanagement were not attacked. Muccio was recalled to Washington in April for consultations on the aid programs. He argued for more military aid to South Korea with some success. While in Washington, according to columnist

DREW PEARSON, he warned of a possible invasion by Communist North Korea. In June he called on Congress to continue military aid, noting guerrilla warfare had been started by the Communists.

On June 25, 1950, Muccio cabled the State Department that North Korean forces had crossed the 38th parallel in "an all-out offensive against the Republic of Korea." As Communist troops moved south, the embassy staff debated evacuating Americans from Seoul with the ambassador reportedly against withdrawal from the capital. He contemplated staying himself but Acheson convinced him that his capture would serve no useful purpose. By June 27 Muccio had directed the evacuation of all Americans. John C. Caldwell later claimed the evacuation was confused and poorly managed. He also charged that the personnel records of South Korean embassy employees were mistakenly left for the Communists, providing "a ready-made list for persecution and execution."

Muccio accompanied the Korean government to Taegu. He later said that if the North Koreans had not halted in Seoul for a week they could have pushed to Pusan without encountering effective military opposition. In August Muccio was forced to retreat to Pusan. During the headlong retreat there, the ambassador contended the war could yet be won, which boosted the morale of the Rhee government. He convinced the U.S. Army to place Korean troops in its understrength battalions. In September, with the advance of UN troops, he was able to return to Seoul. In October he joined General DOUGLAS MACARTHUR and Truman in their Wake Island meeting and called for allowing Rhee to participate in the occupation of the North. Later in October he returned to the United States to confer with several UN committees. When Chinese forces mauled the UN army in late 1950, sending it flying southward, Muccio took the embassy once again to Pusan, where it stayed for the rest of his time as ambassador. Muccio could not convince Rhee that the United States would not allow the South to be conquered and that a negotiated end to the war was in his country's interest. He also could not persuade Rhee to adopt democracy, as he tightened his iron grip on power in June 1952. During the first American attempts at negotiations with the Communists, Muccio provided a channel to Rhee, indicating to the Korean leader that American peace initiatives came before hopes for reunification.

Ellis O. Briggs, former U.S. ambassador to Czechoslovakia, replaced Muccio in November 1952. After serving on the UN Trusteeship Council in 1953, Muccio went to Iceland as an envoy extraordinary in 1954. From 1956 to 1959 he was ambassador to Iceland and then assumed the same post in Guatemala. In 1961 he left public service. Muccio died on May 19, 1989, in Washington, D.C.

—JF

Mundt, Karl E(rnest)

(1900–1974) *member of the House of Representatives, member of the Senate*

The son of pioneers, Karl E. Mundt was born in Humboldt, South Dakota, on June 3, 1900. He went on to be educated at Carleton College in Minnesota and earned a master's degree at Columbia University. From 1928 to 1936 he served as chairman of the speech department at Beadle State Teachers College in his home state. During this period he also worked in his father's insurance, real estate, and investment business. Elected to the U.S. House in 1938, Mundt, a proponent of conservation, introduced legislation aimed at curtailing water pollution. He was an isolationist until Pearl Harbor, when he became a vigorous backer of the war effort.

During the mid-1940s Mundt toured Europe and returned to the United States highly critical of Soviet activity in Poland and Czechoslovakia. He urged President Truman to take a hard line with the Soviet Union and cosponsored legislation to establish the Voice of America to counter Soviet influence. Mundt also supported the Marshall Plan. Mundt also supported some other parts of Truman's foreign policy. He voted for Greek-Turkish aid, to extend the draft, and for the North Atlantic Treaty and the Japanese Peace Treaty. However, he voted against the British loan, a $45-million authorization to set up the Point Four program, and supported the McClellan Amendment of 1951.

On domestic policy Mundt tended to be conservative. He voted for the Case labor disputes bill of 1946, the Taft-Hartley Act of 1947, the Republican tax reduction of 1948, the McCarran-Walters Immigration Act of 1952, and the 1952 measure requesting the president to halt the steel strike. However, since he was from a northern farming state, he supported high fixed price supports for agriculture as opposed to flexible ones, and opposed deregulation of the natural gas industry.

Mundt gained national prominence for his involvement in the ALGER HISS hearings and for his sponsorship of anticommunist legislation. He presided over the 1948 House Un-American Activities Committee (HUAC) investigation into alleged Communist infiltration of government agencies. There he helped obtain information leading to the grand jury indictment of Hiss, a State Department official accused of collaborating with the Soviets. Mundt claimed that HUAC had definite evidence of one of the most elaborate spy rings in U.S. history.

The HUAC inquiry was attacked by Truman as a "red herring" designed to distract attention from the Republican-controlled Congress's failure to combat inflation. Mundt responded to the president's accusation by challenging him to authorize publication of all the documents the committee had obtained.

As early as April 1947 Mundt called for a program to protect America from "Godless Communism and red fascism." His proposal, outlined in a radio speech, called for such measures as compulsory registration of American Communists and denial of federal labor law rights to Communist-led unions. Mundt said he opposed legislation outlawing the Communist Party at that time, because the FBI and HUAC were gaining valuable information by infiltrating the party. The following year, however, he cosponsored with RICHARD M. NIXON (R-Calif.) legislation requiring the registration of organizations named by the Attorney General as Communist or Communist-fronts. The measure also barred members of such political organizations from federal employment and called for stiff punishment of convicted subversives. The bill passed the House but was killed in the Senate Judiciary Committee. Responding to criticism from the left, Mundt, who had been elected to the Senate in 1948, introduced a slightly modified version of the original bill. He compromised again in 1950, agreeing that labor unions would be excluded from registration. Congress eventually overrode a presidential veto and passed the omnibus McCarran Act, which incorporated many of the provisions Mundt had introduced.

Mundt served as chairman of the Permanent Investigation Subcommittee during the 1954 Army-McCarthy hearings. He continued to back Senator JOSEPH R. MCCARTHY (R-Wisc.), even as support for the senator eroded, and he voted against Senate censure of McCarthy.

During the Kennedy administration Mundt was involved in the 1962 investigation into the activities of Texas financier Billie Sol Estes and the 1963 hearings on the Defense Department's role in the awarding of TFX fighter/bomber contracts. While supporting the war in Indochina, Mundt condemned the 1968 mission of the spy ship *Pueblo*.

In 1969 Mundt suffered a crippling stroke that cut short his Senate activities. It ultimately led to the Senate's relieving him of his post as ranking Republican on the Government Operations Committee and as second-ranking minority-member of the Foreign Relations and Appropriations Committees. Mundt died on August 16, 1974, in Washington, D.C. (See *The Eisenhower Years*, *The Kennedy Years*, *The Johnson Years* Volumes)

—EF

Murphy, Charles S(prings)
(1909–1983) *administrative assistant to the president, special counsel to the president*

Charles Murphy was born on August 20, 1909, in Wallace, North Carolina. He received his B.A. degree from Duke University in 1931 and his LL.B. from that institution three years later. During the last five years of his education, he worked a full night shift at the Durham post office. Upon graduation Murphy worked as assistant counsel in the Office of the Legislative Counsel of the Senate, where he helped draft bills in the legal language suitable for introduction. As a newly elected senator, Harry S Truman often called upon Murphy, a Democrat, for assistance. Murphy helped draft the resolution formulating the Senate War Investigating Committee, which Truman later chaired.

In 1947 Truman brought Murphy to the White House to help draft legislative proposals and occasionally to shepherd them through Congress. Murphy thus served informally as liaison between the White House and Congress, a position not formalized until the 1950s.

A self-effacing and inconspicuous member of the group of administrative assistants dubbed the "Little Cabinet," Murphy became known for his meticulous treatment of detail and his understanding of Congress and current legislation. As an excellent speech writer and deft politician, he became one of Truman's chief political lieutenants in the White House and played a leading part in planning

Undersecretary of Agriculture Charles Murphy, 1961 *(Harry S. Truman Library, USDA Office of Information)*

the strategy and famous "whistle-stop" speeches of Truman's 1948 campaign. He was one of the staff members who encouraged the president to speak extemporaneously. Upon the resignation of CLARK CLIFFORD as special counsel to the president, Truman appointed Murphy to that post. He was sworn in on February 1, 1950. He recommended to Truman to form a commission to examine the internal security problem. Murphy told the president that such a body would likely condemn Senator JOSEPH R. MCCARTHY (R-Wisc.), recommend the repeal of the McCarran Internal Security Act, and arrest the developing anticommunist hysteria. Truman tried to establish such a commission in 1951, but Senator PAT MCCARRAN (D-Nev.) refused to report the necessary legislation out of the Judiciary Committee for the committee to function. Murphy was influential in formulating presidential policy on major issues. In addition, he continued to write the straight-forward speeches that were Truman's trademark. Although he initiated no major policy changes, he was widely viewed as the most able member of Truman's staff and was responsible for monitoring the progress of the president's programs in Congress.

Murphy was one of a group that advised Truman not to run for the presidency again in 1952. Dithering over whether to run for the Democratic presidential nomination, Governor ADLAI E. STEVENSON in March 1952 wrote Murphy a letter saying he would not run but would accept a draft.

Murphy spent the Eisenhower years practicing law in Washington, but he returned to government in 1961 as undersecretary of agriculture for the Kennedy administration. He served as chairman of the Civil Aeronautics Board from 1965 to 1968 and as counselor to the president during the later year. In 1969 he returned to his law practice but remained a respected and influential behind-the-scenes figure in the Democratic Party. Murphy died on August 28, 1983, in Anne Arundel County, Maryland.

—DAE

Murphy, Frank

(1890–1949) *associate justice, U.S. Supreme Court*

Frank Murphy was born into an Irish Catholic family in Harbor Beach, Michigan, on April 13, 1890. Murphy received a law degree from the University of Michigan in 1914, served in the American Expeditionary Force in World War I, and returned to the United States to begin his public career in 1919 as an assistant U.S. attorney in Detroit. He served as a judge on the Detroit Recorder's Court from 1923 to 1930 and became mayor of the city in 1930. A supporter of Franklin Roosevelt for the presidency in 1932, Murphy was named governor-general of the Philippine Islands in June 1933. Elected governor of Michigan in 1936, Murphy took office just as the sit-down strikes in Michigan auto plants began. He persistently refused to use force against the strikers and helped negotiate a settlement to the disputes. After losing a reelection bid in 1938, Murphy was appointed U.S. Attorney General in January 1939. A year later Roosevelt named him to the Supreme Court. He took the oath of office in February 1940.

Initially Murphy was often indecisive and diffident, looking to senior justices for guidance. By 1943, however, he had come into his own on the Court and had developed self-confidence as a justice. He started to carve out a role for himself as an ardent defender of civil liberties. Over the next six years he espoused the view that the Supreme Court

had a duty to act as spokesman of the national conscience and protector of the weak. Murphy frankly asserted that reaching just, equitable, and compassionate results in a case mattered more than adherence to legal rules and precedents. In perhaps the most famous instance of his use of these standards, he objected in December 1944 when the majority upheld the wartime relocation and internment of Japanese Americans. The justice wrote a passionate dissent in *Korematsu v. U.S.* (1944) condemning the racial prejudice underlying the program.

In the postwar years Murphy emerged as the foremost civil libertarian on the bench. Although often part of a four-man liberal "bloc" on the Court, the Michigan justice surpassed all others in the consistency of his support for claims of individual liberty and civil rights. In February 1946, only he and Wiley Rutledge, the justice with whom Murphy was closest personally and judicially, voted in *In re Yamashita* to overturn the war crimes conviction of Japanese general Yamashita on the ground his trial lacked basic constitutional guarantees of due process. A strong foe of racial discrimination, Murphy joined in several decisions advancing the rights of blacks and upsetting California anti-Japanese laws. From 1942 to 1949 he repeatedly voted to sustain the rights of Jehovah Witnesses to practice their religion freely (e.g., *Jones v. Opelika*, 1943, *West Virginia State Board of Education v. Barnette*, 1943). He wrote the opinions for the 1945 cases *Marsh v. Alabama* and *Tucker v. Texas* giving the Witnesses relief. One of the justices allegedly said, "If Frank Murphy is ever sainted, it will by the Jehovah Witnesses." The Catholic Murphy's decisions favoring the Witnesses' rights was ironic, given the latter's virulent anti-Catholicism. Despite criticism from some fellow Catholics, Murphy joined the majority in two decisions in 1947 and 1948 (*Everson v. Board of Education* and *Illinois ex rel. McCollum v. Board of Education*, respectively) involving state aid to parochial schools in which the Court held that the First Amendment placed a high wall of separation between church and state.

Murphy went beyond the position advanced by Justice HUGO L. BLACK that the Fourteenth Amendment made all of the Bill of Rights applicable to the states and insisted that the amendment also protected individuals against government intrusion on rights not specifically listed in the Bill of Rights. Murphy favored strict observance of the constitutional rights of the criminally accused and almost always voted in favor of a defendant's claim in criminal cases. Favoring strong protection of the Fourth Amendment's guarantee against unreasonable searches and seizures, Murphy agreed when the Court in *Wolf v. Colorado* (1949) applied the principle of the amendment (although not the amendment itself through incorporation) because such searches were against "the concept of ordered liberty" as laid out in *Palko v. Connecticut* (1937). However, he objected when it also held that illegally seized evidence did not have to be excluded from state courts as it was in federal courts.

Murphy voted to sustain New Deal legislation and argued that these statutes should be interpreted in accord with the humanitarian and reform goals of the New Deal. In 1944 and 1945 he wrote the opinion of the Court in two cases (*Tennessee Coal, Iron and Railroad Company v. Muscoda* and *Jewell Ridge v. Local No. 6167 UMWA*) that ruled that iron and coal miners were entitled to portal-to-portal pay under the Fair Labor Standards Act.

Murphy, who had been in declining health for several years, died of a heart attack in Detroit, Michigan, on July 19, 1949. Both before and after his death, the justice was deeply respected by libertarians for his devotion to civil liberties, but his reputation was low in professional legal circles. To his critics Murphy was a misfit on the Court, a doctrinaire libertarian without intellectual depth or a regard for legal traditions who decided cases on the basis of his own sympathies rather than the law. He became a symbol of the partisan and activist judge who voted his personal policy preferences into law. For example, according to historian Sydney Fine his concurrence in *West Virginia State Board of Education v. Barnette* added little to the debate—he simply wanted to vent his emotions on the subject. Murphy was quite willing to invoke the Constitution in his opinions, whereas his colleagues on the Court were reluctant to do so when a case could be decided on other grounds. Later scholars have argued that Murphy was technically competent as a jurist and that his votes were independent of his personal politics and religious affiliations. (It has to be noted, though, that he left the drafting of opinions largely to his law clerks.) Moreover, many of the views he expressed in dissent concerning civil liberties and criminal rights were ultimately adopted by the Court. Fine has noted that to Murphy "the freedom of the individual" and what he saw as "a just result" were more important than stare decisis. Fine

is also dismissive of criticism that Murphy often decided cases with his heart rather than his head, arguing that there are not "a fixed body of legal principles that has only to be understood to yield a correct result." Yet Murphy still is rated as only an average justice, in part because he frequently was indifferent to legal technicalities when they stood in the way of achieving larger goals. This frankly instrumental view of the law remains rather unorthodox. He also often wrote, especially in dissent, in a crusading, evangelistic style that was consistent with his view of the Court as public conscience but seemed to some sanctimonious cant devoid of legal analysis. According to his biographer J. Woodford Howard, Jr., and others, Frank Murphy most resembled the ideal of the just judge who puts humane results and public policy ahead of book law and legal formalities. He was the "most underestimated member of the Supreme Court in our time," according to John P. Frank. Murphy, wrote another commentator, stands in the forefront of Supreme Court justices who have "applied their great talents, courage and devotion to the increase of individual liberty under law and to the amelioration of social and economic hardship."

—CAB

Murphy, Robert D(aniel)

(1894–1978) *political adviser for Germany; director, Office for German and Austrian Affairs; ambassador*

The son of an Irish laborer, Robert D. Murphy was born on October 28, 1894, in Milwaukee, Wisconsin. He worked his way through Marquette University and entered George Washington University Law School in 1916. Prevented by injuries suffered in an industrial accident from enlisting in the army when the United States entered World War I, he joined the State Department instead as a consular clerk at Bern. Upon returning to the United States in 1919, he reentered law school and received his degree in 1920.

Wanting to live abroad once again, Murphy joined the Foreign Service that same year and was assigned to Zurich as a vice consul. Six months later he was transferred to Munich, where he observed the early political career of a neighbor, Adolf Hitler. After a brief term as consul in Seville, in 1925 Murphy was reassigned to the United States. He was sent to Paris in 1930 and remained there until the Germans overran France in 1940. That year Murphy became chargé d'affaires at Vichy, where, in the absence of WILLIAM C. BULLITT, he was ambassador. He returned to Washington in September. During World II Murphy became, in effect, the president's secret agent, helping to lay the ground work for the North African invasion and performing a variety of other missions, such as serving as General DWIGHT D. EISENHOWER's political adviser.

In September 1944 Murphy was appointed U.S. political adviser for occupied Germany. Murphy opposed various proposals that called for the partitioning of Germany because he believed that partition would make the occupation more expensive for the United States. Murphy was reassured when Admiral WILLIAM D. LEAHY told him the subject concerned Truman, who did not want to repeat the interwar pattern whereby the United States would loan money to Germany with which it paid reparations. He established himself in Berlin along with the Deputy Military Governor, General LUCIUS B. CLAY, who directed the occupation until 1949. For most of that time Murphy was the ranking American civilian in Germany, heading the State Department office there. Murphy served as a consultant to Clay, who supervised all political and military aspects of the occupation. In close cooperation the men molded policy toward Germany. During the early months of the occupation, they carried out administration policies outlined by Secretary of the Treasury HENRY MORGENTHAU, JR., who wanted the "pastoralization" of the defeated nation. However, both Murphy and Clay became early proponents of the economic rehabilitation of the Western sectors of Germany and agitated for a change in U.S. action.

Murphy attended part of the Potsdam Conference, which foreshadowed some of the difficulties the United States would face in Germany. It occurred to him at the conference that no peace treaty might be made with Germany as he listened to Stalin lay out his intentions for Eastern Europe. Murphy was also frustrated that the U.S. military government in Germany never received any record of what exactly happened at the Potsdam Conference—the confidential protocol of which dictated how the United States would administrate Germany. Murphy noted later the irony of postwar governance of Germany. Eisenhower's directive JCS 1067 prohibited him and the deputy governor, General Lucius Clay, from doing the things that had to

be done. The Potsdam Protocol ordered them to do the impossible. For example, JCS 1067 forbade the employment of executive or skilled workmen who had been Nazis. But most of these people had been Nazis and their services were essential to reconstruction. Clay eventually loosened the restrictions. The Potsdam Protocol called for treating Germany as an economic unit. However, the French were not bound by the protocol, as they had not been allowed to participate in the conference. Yet they were members of the Control Council and could thwart such goals as economic unity—as when they vetoed a proposal to centralize railroad control in Germany. Despite these obstacles, Murphy and Clay were able to achieve their goals of changing U.S. policy and rehabilitating the economy of West Germany. As American-Soviet relations deteriorated during the last half of 1945 and the first months of 1946, the administration and military emphasized the need for a strong Germany as a buffer to the Soviets in Central Europe. By the latter half of 1947 Clay and Murphy won approval for the assignment of Marshall Plan aid to Germany. The two men also pressed for currency reform as a prelude to uniting the divided sectors. Although progress on the issue was stalled during 1946, reform proceeded quickly after the London Conference of 1947 in which the Soviet Union had refused to negotiate the issues of Germany and Eastern Europe.

When currency reform was introduced in the spring of 1948, the Soviets, protesting the dramatic step toward unification, blockaded Berlin. Murphy, on the advice of Ernest Reuter, the first mayor of West Berlin, became an advocate of "calling the bluff" of the Russians. He believed that the Soviets were neither willing nor capable of conducting a major military operation. He joined Clay in advocating a show of force and sending armed convoys if necessary across the roads leading from the West to Berlin to guarantee land access to the city. They were consistently overruled by a president unwilling, Murphy believed, to take a stand on Berlin during an election year without the backing of the Joint Chiefs of Staff. The Joint Chiefs, in turn, did not share Murphy's confidence in the reluctance of the Soviets to fight and believed the United States was not capable of staging a war in that area. Murphy's frustration on this issue was so intense that he later wrote he should have resigned at that time. The breaking of the blockade with an airlift was not, he believed, a victory for the West, for the principle of right of access by the ground was never raised and never established by the Western powers. Murphy became convinced that the refusal to force full access to West Berlin caused the Soviets to lower their respect for the Americans' determination and eventually led to the Korean War. In February 1949, with the blockade still in effect, Murphy was recalled to Washington. At the end of that year he was appointed ambassador to Belgium. While he was in Brussels a national controversy was raging over the return of King Leopold III. Many Belgians thought he should have led the government in exile after Germany crushed the Belgian army in 1940 rather than having remained in the country. Eventually Leopold abdicated in favor of his son, Crown Prince Baudouin, who became king on his 21st birthday.

After an uneventful year and a half at this post, he was named the first postwar ambassador to Japan in 1952. Because of the growing controversy over U.S. policy in Asia, Truman wished to appoint someone who had not been involved in the area and so might win rapid Senate confirmation. Murphy, with no experience in the Far East and considerable stature as a diplomat, received quick approval. Admiral Arthur Radford, commander in chief, Pacific, persuaded Murphy not to return the Bonin Islands to Japan, as they were useful for naval and military bases. Turmoil occasionally engulfed the ambassador, as when left-wing demonstrators on May Day 1952 stoned his car as he traveled the streets of Tokyo. He was recalled when President Eisenhower took office, but before he could leave Japan he was reassigned to General Mark Clark as political adviser. Clark and Murphy directed completion of the Korean armistice negotiations, settling the sensitive issue of exchange of prisoners. The armistice was signed in July 1953, and Murphy left Korea soon afterward.

During the Eisenhower administration Murphy served as a State Department troubleshooter. He became involved in such matters as the Italian-Yugoslavian negotiations over the division of Trieste, the Suez Crisis, and the aftermath of the landing of American troops in Lebanon. Murphy retired from the Foreign Service in 1959 and was named a director of the Corning Glassworks. During the 1960s he was a member of several presidential commissions on foreign intelligence activities. In 1964 he published his autobiography, *Diplomat among Warriors.* Murphy died on January

9, 1978, in New York City. (See *The Eisenhower Years* Volume)

—CSJ

Murray, James E(dward)
(1876–1961) *member of the U.S. Senate*

James E. Murray was born on a farm near St. Thomas, Ontario, Canada, on May 3, 1876. At age 18, he moved to the American West, eventually settling in Butte, Montana. He earned an LL.B. degree from New York University in 1900 and a master's in law in 1901. He won election as Silver Bow county attorney in 1906 but did not run for reelection in 1908. In 1933 Franklin Roosevelt appointed him to the Montana's advisory board for the Public Works Administration. In 1934 Murray was elected to the U.S. Senate as a Democrat. He proved an avid New Dealer. Before World War II Murray was an isolationist; however, as war drew near, he changed his attitude and supported revision of the neutrality laws. He supported the alliance with the Soviet Union during the war and hoped after the conflict that good relations could be maintained. He voted against aid to Greece and Turkey in 1947, but he did support the Marshall Plan as a humanitarian measure.

Murray's major piece of legislation was the Employment Act of 1946. The idea for the federal government maintaining full employment germinated within the National Farmers Union; its leader JAMES G. PATTON showed a copy of the plan to Murray. The senator's staff crafted it into legislation, and Murray introduced the full employment bill in January 1945 with Senator ROBERT F. WAGNER (D-N.Y.) as a cosponsor. The Murray bill said the federal government was responsible "to provide such volume of federal investment and expenditure as may be needed to assure continuing full employment." It detailed how the government would use spending to cure unemployment. Under the proposed law, the president would submit to Congress a National Production and Employment Budget at the start of each year. The president would estimate the volume of government and private expenditures and investment for the coming year, and the amount of which would be needed to attain full employment. If spending and investment by both the private and public sectors could not meet the goal, the president would work to promote private expenditures. If that did not work, then he would send to

Congress a spending plan to attain the goal. The legislation would also have established the Joint Committee on the Congressional National Budget, which would study the president's proposals and submit a resolution to assist congressional committees crafting tax and spending bills. Under the bill, the president would also review every three months the level of federal expenditures and, if necessary, adjust their rate to provide employment for those who wanted to work.

Business generally opposed the bill, while union heads gave it their support. Murray was able to pick up a handful of Republican cosponsors. The National Farmers Union tried to counteract the opposition from the American Farm Bureau Federation and the National Grange. Murray's bill also picked up the support of the liberal Union for Democratic Action. Hostile editorial writers called the Wagner-Murray bill "state socialism."

When in August 1945 the Office of War Mobilization and Reconversion advised President Truman that 8 million people could be put out of work by the coming spring, Truman said the Murray bill needed to be passed. Opponents attempted to weaken the bill, particularly its provision for federal expenditures to raise employment. One amendment, the Hatch Amendment, was attached to the bill. It said any federal spending under the law had to be "consistent with the needs and obligations of the federal government and other essential considerations of national policy." This amendment softened the focus on full employment, but it did assure Senate passage. However, the House of Representatives was bent on weakening the measure even more. The rationale for the bill also diminished when the predicted postwar depression did not occur. The House committee on expenditures in executive departments rejected the Senate version. The committee added a provision to its version creating a three-member Council of Economic Advisers (CEA) to counsel the president, but it stripped from the bill the declaration of a right to work, federal responsibility to full or even maximum employment, and the national employment and production budget. The law was "to promote a high level of employment," not full or even maximum employment, and stated that the government should not compete with the private sector.

The president supported the Wagner-Murray bill but did little to advance its prospects in the House. The compromise that came out of the conference committee proclaimed the federal government would act to maintain "maximum" rather than full or high employment. The CEA and the Joint Congressional Committee on the Economic Report were retained but all mention of presidential control of federal expenditures to maintain full employment were eliminated. The name of the bill was changed to the Employment Act of 1946 from the Full Employment Act. Murray, a Keynesian, believed the law could fulfill its original purpose of full employment if administered properly, and he secured the appointment of University of Chicago economist EDWIN G. NOURSE as the CEA's first chairman.

Another area of concern for the Montana senator was national health insurance. In June 1943, Murray, Senator Wagner, and Representative JOHN D. DINGELL (D-Mich.) introduced a bill, the heart of which was compulsory national health insurance. The people covered by the proposed program would be all those enrolled in Social Security and their dependents. Up to 30 days a year of hospital care and doctor services would be provided by the insurance. Taxes on employees and employers would pay for the plan.

An American Medical Association (AMA) offshoot, the National Physicians Committee, led the charge against the Wagner-Murray-Dingell bill. Murray did have support from organized labor and liberal magazines such as the *New Republic* and *PM*, and a Gallup poll showed 60 percent of Americans wanted Social Security expanded to pay for hospital and doctor bills. Murray and other sponsors realized there was little chance of passing such a bill in the immediate future. The bill did force doctors—who could not afford to oppose all health-care legislation—to come out eventually in favor of federal funding of hospital construction and maternal and child care.

In 1945, dental and nursing care benefits were added to Wagner-Murray-Dingell, as well as an extension of hospital time from 30 to 60 days. It was unlikely, however, that Congress would pass this new version of the bill. But the AMA did begin to advocate private insurance, disease prevention, and more doctors in rural areas. Because the new bill contained funding provisions, it went to the Senate finance committee, where chairman WALTER F. GEORGE (D-Ga.) pigeonholed it.

Then Murray and Wagner in September 1945 separated the funding provision from the health insurance plan, and the bill went to the Senate education and labor committee chaired by Murray. In November, Truman requested Congress to pass national health insurance, after which Wagner and Dingell introduced the revised bill. Although the AMA denounced Truman's proposals just as much as Murray's, it came out even more strongly for voluntary private insurance and also endorsed hospital construction funding, federal aid for maternal and child care, and sickness compensation for workers. Part of the Murray bill was enacted when the Hill-Burton Construction bill became law; it provided $375 million to the states for the building of non-profit hospitals.

In the Republican-majority 80th Congress, Murray introduced a different bill, with the hope of satisfying conservative critics. States and localities would distribute federal insurance monies, and the Surgeon General was no longer accorded the role of sole administrator. Doctors' and dentists' rights and the role of private insurance would be expressly recognized. Senator ROBERT A. TAFT (R-Ohio) countered with a means-tested health programs for the poor, which Murray argued would make the United States "a nation of public charity patients." In hearings before the Senate health subcommittee, it was clear the Republicans were less interested in advocating Taft's plan then in heaping calumnies on Murray's plan.

Murray reintroduced his insurance plan in the Democratic-controlled 81st Congress, but the conservative coalition would not let it out of committee. Murray then backed a bill introduced by ELBERT D. THOMAS (D-Utah). This bill was a potpourri of different public health proposals including insurance, hospital construction funding, physician and dentist training grants, and an enlarged role for the federal government in medical research and disease prevention. But the bill had no chance of passage either, and Murray decided to put off a battle on national health insurance until 1950. Murray pursued a strategy of pushing other health proposals, but only funding of hospital construction was enacted.

In 1950 Murray again conceded there was no possibility of passing an insurance bill and decided to make the 1950 elections a referendum on the issue. However, the elections disappointed the Montana senator. Truman and Murray did not seriously try to pass national health insurance in the 82nd Congress. Instead Murray concentrated on passing a five-year emergency plan to fund the edu-

cation of doctors, dentists, and nurses. The Senate never held a vote on the bill. Murray introduced another bill in April 1952 to extend insurance coverage for up to 60 days of hospitalization per year to all those eligible for Social Security benefits. This proposal eventuated in Medicare in 1965.

During the Eisenhower administration Murray realized comprehensive national health insurance stood no chance of passage but continued to push a variety of public-health proposals.

Another concern for Murray was the Missouri River valley. It was subject to disastrous periodic flooding, and there was a need for hydroelectric power in the upper reaches of the region. Irrigation of the valley's farms was another concern for Murray. In 1937 Murray introduced a bill establishing a Missouri Valley Authority (MVA), modeled after the Tennessee Valley Authority. It would have established a three-person board to have control over dams and other federal projects in the valley. However, Murray did not succeed in passing the bill.

The senator was still pushing the project when Truman became president. The new president was lukewarm—to say the least—toward such a project. Flooding in the valley in 1947 did cause Truman to call on Congress to provide $4 billion for flood control. Murray complained this would be deleterious to the cause of the MVA, but Truman continued his course. (He did, however, make a general endorsement of valley authorities.) Truman never fully got behind the MVA, and after the start of the Korean War, opposed beginning any large reclamation projects. This attitude disappointed Murray, but major flooding of the Missouri River basin caused Truman to request more money for reclamation. There were signs late in his administration that Truman was changing his attitude toward the MVA, as he created the Missouri Basin Survey Commission to study the problems of the valleys. The commission, while arguing better coordination between federal agencies regarding the region, did not recommend an MVA, and President DWIGHT D. EISENHOWER largely ignored the commission's findings.

Murray continued to be a firm liberal during the Eisenhower years. He focused his attention on irrigation, federal power projects, conservation, land use, and American Indians. In his last years in Congress Murray was in failing health, but he announced in 1959 his desire to run for reelection the next year. However, his son convinced him to stand aside. Murray died on March 23, 1961, in Butte, Montana.

Murray, Philip
(1886–1952) *president, Congress of Industrial Organizations; president, United Steel Workers of America*

The son of an Irish-Catholic coal miner, Philip Murray was born in Blantyre, Scotland, on May 25, 1886. After a few years of schooling, he entered the mines at the age of 10. In 1902 the family immigrated to the United States, settling in the coal fields of western Pennsylvania. The 18-year-old Murray became involved in his first labor dispute when he punched a weigh-master whom he accused of cheating him and was fired, prompting a protest strike by his fellow miners. The Murrays were evicted from their company house and run out of the county; Philip became a hero and was elected president of his local union. In 1912 Murray advanced to the executive board of the United Mine Workers of America (UMW). Four years later he became president of the union's Pittsburgh district.

A skilled negotiator with detailed knowledge of the economics of the coal industry, Murray was elected vice president of the UMW in 1919. In this post he served as right-hand man to the UMW's president, JOHN L. LEWIS, during the 1920s and 1930s. Lewis appointed him to head the Steelworkers Organizing Committee (SWOC) in 1936. Although Murray succeeded in bringing the giant U.S. Steel Corporation to the bargaining table in 1937, SWOC was defeated in its efforts to organize the "Little Steel" companies—Bethlehem, Republic, Inland, and Youngstown Sheet and Tube—in the same year and entered a period of stagnation that lasted until the outbreak of World War II. He succeeded to the presidency of the Congress of Industrial Organizations (CIO) when Lewis broke with President Roosevelt in 1940. Murray, unwilling to end the CIO's close alliance with the administration, repudiated Lewis's isolationist stance and endorsed the government's war-production effort.

Beginning in 1941 the CIO experienced a second wave of growth, doubling in size by the end of the war and putting its bargaining relations in basic industry on a routine basis. Crucial assistance was provided by the Roosevelt administration, which sought to guarantee the stability of CIO unions in return for their leaders' help in promoting uninterrupted production and labor discipline. In 1942 the War Labor Board (WLB) awarded CIO organizations dues checkoff and "maintenance of membership"—a modified union shop. These actions resolved the unions' chronic financial problems and assured their steady wartime growth by providing for the automatic enrollment of new workers in the defense industries. The centerpiece of CIO cooperation was the no-strike pledge, ratified shortly after Pearl Harbor.

Beginning in 1943 the tasks of upholding the no-strike pledge and defending the authority of the WLB became increasingly onerous to Murray and other CIO leaders, especially because they had to enforce government wage standards, which they regarded as unfair and inadequate. In 1943 the Political Action Committee (PAC) was created as the CIO's permanent political arm. Although aimed at assuring Roosevelt's reelection, it was also formed to deflect a growing demand for some form of independent political action by organized labor. Under the direction of Sidney Hillman, the national PAC attacked the labor party idea and encouraged its state units not to challenge local Democratic machines.

The CIO's moderate wartime policies were partly a result of Murray's belief that, during the immediate postwar period, the nation would experience a major recession and an aggressive business-initiated open shop drive of the kind that had followed World War I. Hoping to minimize a potentially disruptive strike wave, he proposed a new government board to replace the WLB. This panel would impose an accommodation with industry under a continuing no-strike pledge and a more liberal wage formula. Murray had to abandon these plans, however, when a surge of unauthorized strikes, involving especially the United Automobile Workers (UAW), followed the Japanese surrender in August 1945. The return of the 40-hour week brought workers' incomes almost back to prewar levels while prices continued to escalate. Speaking as president of the steelworkers union, which had reorganized three years earlier as the United Steelworkers of America (USWA), Murray argued in October that corporations could afford to pay a 31 percent wage boost without increasing prices and still earn twice as much profits as in the 1936–39 period. Management in steel and other industries contented that it could not absorb sizable pay increases without price relief. The Truman administration's Office of Price Administration (OPA), however, refused to permit firms to include the cost of wage raises until a six-month accounting period established the need for higher prices. By late fall negotiations had broken down in the oil, auto, electrical goods, meat, and steel industries.

The administration responded to the strike threats by temporarily seizing oil refineries and meat packing plants but tried to settle the dispute in steel without factory takeovers. At the president's request the USWA resumed bargaining with U.S. Steel on January 10, 1946. Murray later reported that he offered a deal to U.S. Steel president BEN-JAMIN F. FAIRLESS for a raise of 19.5 cents an hour in which U.S. Steel would raise their offer from 15 cents an hour to 17.5 cents and the USWA would reduce its claim for correction of wage inequities from 5 cents an hour to 3 cents, with the 2-cent difference being applied to the regular hourly wage hike. Murray claimed that Fairless had personally been willing to go along with the deal, but he had to present it to the executive committee of U.S. Steel. Fairless denied this and claimed that he had never offered anything more that a 15-cent-an-hour raise and had dealt with Murray only as a representative of U.S. Steel, not the entire industry, and that the steel industry as a whole only came up in regard to negotiations regarding the settlement of wage inequities, which had to do with a directive of the National War Labor Board against the entire industry. Fairless's claim that he only negotiated for U.S. Steel was, however, disingenuous, as the U.S. Steel settlement would set the pattern for Little Steel. Fairless said he needed time to discover the sentiments of his company's executive committee and other steel corporations, and he asked for the strike deadline of January 14 to be postponed for a week. Murray refused. Truman then called the two together for a White House conference on January 12. The president convinced Murray to give Fairless the extra time to present the proposal to his executive committee and the other steel companies. However, the U.S. Steel executive committee and Little Steel would not accept a settlement of 19.5 cents an hour, and Fairless reported this impasse to Truman and Murray when they met again on January 16. On January 17 Truman proposed an 18.5 cent an hour raise retroactive to January 1, 1946. The union agreed, but the steel companies would not. The strike began January 21, 1946, as 750,000 steelworkers walked off the job. Negotiations did not

recur until early February, and serious talks did not occur until later that month, after Truman decided to allow wage increases and a price hikes to companies afflicted with an undue burden because of such wage increases. Murray offered to extend the termination date of the new contract from October 1946 to February 1947. In exchange he obtained the continuation of maintenance-of-membership and check-off provisions of the old contract. After a White House conference, agreement was quickly reached on a 18.5 cent hourly increase, with a 9.25-cent-an-hour increase applied to all work performed from January 1, 1946, to February 17, 1946, when the strike ended, as Fairless would not agree to a retroactive 18.5 cent increase. Three days later the government authorized a steel price increase of $5 a ton—more than double the price relief OPA chief CHESTER BOWLES had recommended.

The steel strike coincided with a wave of walkouts by other CIO unions in basic industry. At its peak in early 1946 two million workers were involved, more than in any year since 1919. In vivid contrast to the violence, organized strikebreaking and militant tactics that had often accompanied prewar labor conflicts, however, picket lines were orderly. The government intervened through fact-finding boards rather than injunctions and troops, and almost no struck industry attempted to operate. In the auto dispute, WALTER P. REUTHER, head of the UAW's General Motors division, demanded a wage increase without an increase in the price of cars and called for the company to open its books to prove inability to pay. Murray had promoted a similar anti-inflation wage policy during the immediate post-war months. However, he had offered it to the government for tripartite negotiation and had not demanded it directly of particular corporations. Moreover, by the winter of 1946 most CIO leaders were less concerned with industry prices and inflation and were content to let the companies fight with the OPA on these issues. Murray and the more conservative CIO officials strongly opposed the idea of making profits and prices subject to collective bargaining. Consequently, most CIO strike leaders, including Reuther, were finally forced to settle for the 18.5 cent pattern increase set by the USWA—far less than the raises they had originally sought.

The demand for a second round of wage increases rose steadily in the fall of 1946 in response to the mounting cost of living. Though hinting that it would ask for a 20 to 30 percent per hour increase,

Murray's USWA accepted in April 1947 a 15-cent-an-hour wage increase and fringe benefits package without a strike. In the following year a third round settled on an 11 to 13 cent increase pattern. In 1949 a month-long strike ended, after intervention by a presidential fact-finding board, with agreement by the steel companies to contribute to a pension plan and a health and welfare fund, but without a fourth round of wage increases.

Under Murray's presidency the CIO suffered a series of painful political defeats. No sooner had PAC demonstrated its ability to mobilize and coordinate CIO support behind Democratic candidates in the 1944 election than Congress and the state governments launched an offensive against many of the rights that organized labor had won during the New Deal era. In June 1945 the Ball-Burton-Hatch bill, calling for compulsory arbitration of "national emergency" strikes, was introduced in the Senate. At the same time several state legislatures began consideration of "right-to-work" laws, which aimed at outlawing both closed and union shop contracts. Vigorous CIO opposition to the Senate measure, which was dubbed the "Ball and Chain bill," prevented it from reaching the floor, but state bans on union security agreements proliferated during the next three years. In December 1945 President Truman, responding to the mounting strike wave, added his voice to the call for new labor legislation. He asked Congress for the power to certify national strikes as contrary to the public interest and to force strikers back to work for a 30-day period while fact-finding panels investigated disputes. Murray charged that the proposal represented "appeasement" of industry and that it was designed to "weaken and ultimately destroy labor union organizations." Congress, however, went further than the White House wished. In May 1946 it passed the Case labor disputes bill, which extended the cooling-off period from 30 to 60 days and added a provision forbidding union interference with the movement of interstate commerce. Truman vetoed the measure in June.

Following the wholesale defeat of PAC-supported candidates in the fall 1946 elections, efforts to revise labor laws in the 80th Congress were spearheaded by a group of outspokenly anti-CIO legislators led by Representative FRED A. HARTLEY, JR. (R-N.J.) and Senator ROBERT A. TAFT (R-Ohio). As the two houses debated the Taft and Hartley bills in April 1947, the CIO mustered its forces to defeat the legislation. Murray declared

a "Defend Your Union Month" and instructed state and local councils to initiate a massive letter writing campaign and public protest rallies. However the Taft-Hartley bill was sent to the president in June. Its provisions included bans on the closed shop and certain kinds of secondary boycotts; 80-day injunctions were authorized for use against public interest strikes; unions were forbidden to make political campaign contributions or endorse candidate; unions were to be held liable for contract violations in federal court for their agents' action, and bargaining agent certification was denied to any union that had any officer who was a Communist. On June 20 Truman vetoed the measure, citing the ban on union political expenditures as a "dangerous intrusion of free speech." The House overrode the president within hours, the Senate three days later.

Denouncing Taft-Hartley as an "unprincipled piece of dirty legislation," Murray, together with 13 other CIO officials, refused to sign the noncommunist affidavits required by the law. In addition, he ordered the *CIO News* to endorse a Maryland congressional candidate in an attempt to test the constitutionality of the statute's political expenditures provision. Murray was indicted by a federal grand jury in February 1948. In March a federal court upheld the CIO's challenge, but the Supreme Court, to which the government appealed the case, refused to rule on the question of constitutionality. The tribunal dismissed the indictment against Murray, however, since it held that the ban on political activities had not been violated.

During the postwar period the issue of communism in the CIO was continually raised in Congress and the press. John L. Lewis had relied on skilled Communist organizers during the founding years of the CIO, and, by the end of the war, and estimated one-fourth of the total CIO membership was enrolled in unions whose leaders were either members of, or strongly influenced by, the Communist Party. Foremost among them were the United Electrical Workers (UE), National Maritime Union (NMU), International Longshoremen's and Warehousemen's Union (ILWU) and the Mine, Mill and Smelter Workers. Since the Communists and their followers had been the most passionate defenders of the no-strike pledge and official CIO policy, they were closely allied with Murray during the war. By the end of 1945, however, as the cold war began to develop, anti-Communists within the CIO began to mobilize. Murray's role in the emerging dispute was highly equivocal. A devout Catholic and firm opponent of communist ideology, he was nevertheless chiefly concerned with avoiding a split in the CIO. His own entourage included such prominent spokesmen for the Communist wing as CIO general counsel LEE PRESSMAN and *CIO News* editor Len DeCaux. In 1946 Murray endorsed the Communist-supported leadership group in the UE and threw his prestige behind incumbent UAW president R. J. Thomas, who was backed by the union's small, but well-organized Communist caucus, against Reuther. Reuther won the UAW presidency and soon emerged as the leader of the anticommunist forces within the CIO. Meanwhile, in the national office JAMES B. CAREY, former president of the UE and now secretary-treasurer of the CIO, worked with the Association of Catholic Trade Unionists in encouraging Murray to take a stand against the Communists.

In late 1947 Murray began to show signs of ending his policy of cautious neutrality. In large part, he was forced to act by the Communists themselves, who chose to wage an open fight in the CIO on the issues of compliance with the Taft-Hartley Act and support of a national third party. Although the CIO protested the provision of Taft-Hartley requiring union officers to sign noncommunist affidavits to be eligible for the services of the National Labor Relations Board (NLRB) in representation elections, most of its affiliates were obliged to take the oath as a means of self-protection. By taking a stand against compliance, the Communists exposed the unions under their control to raids by the AFL and by other CIO units. It seriously ruptured the relations between the party and those of its members who were heads of unions and therefore had a stake in their survival. As a result, in 1947 JOSEPH E. CURRAN of the NMU and MICHAEL J. QUILL of the Transport Workers, both of whom had been supported by the Communists, turned on their associates and ousted them from their unions.

With their union base eroding, the Communists further weakened their position by defying CIO policy during the 1948 elections. Murray viewed the third party candidacy of HENRY A. WALLACE as a serious threat to the CIO's political program. While only lukewarm toward Truman (PAC successively promoted DWIGHT D. EISENHOWER, WILLIAM O. DOUGLAS, and Florida senator CLAUDE PEPPER for the Democratic nomination) Murray believed that

Wallace might drain off enough liberal votes to allow the Republicans to win the presidency. Making support of the Democratic ticket a test of loyalty within the CIO national office, Murray dismissed Pressman, who favored the Progressives, and replaced him with Arthur Goldberg. In November 1949 the UE, which had endorsed Wallace, was expelled and the CIO constitution amended to permit the executive board to remove any union that worked in behalf of "a totalitarian movement." Charges were brought against 10 other unions, and, by March 1950, every Communist-led affiliate had been thrown out. In addition, the CIO withdrew in 1949 from the World Federation of Trade Unions, which had been dominated by representatives of Soviet labor organizations and European Communist unions since its formation in 1945. The same year it joined the new International Confederation of Free Trade Unions.

In 1949 Murray demanded that U.S. Steel set up a noncontributory insurance and pension plan. U.S. Steel refused, and the union set a strike deadline of July 16. The company believed that the Taft-Hartley Act gave them an edge in the negotiations. But Truman, instead of imposing the 80-day cooling off period, set up a fact-finding committee and convinced the two sides to extend the existing contract 60 days in order to give the board time to work out a resolution. In September it recommended that the union drop its demand for higher wages, but also said that U.S. Steel should pay for health insurance and pensions. The union agreed, but the company would not. Murray switched tactics and negotiated a settlement with Bethlehem Steel in October. The contract established health insurance benefits and improved an existing pension plan. The Bethlehem agreement set the pattern for the industry.

Murray, along with the most other labor leaders, came into conflict with the economic controls program set up by the administration during the Korean conflict. In January 1951 the president issued a general freeze order to hold the line on wages and prices, and the Wage Stabilization Board (WSB) ruled that wage increases of more than 10 percent over the previous year's levels required its approval. Murray and AFL president WILLIAM GREEN then objected that prices had risen far more than wages during the base period. Shortly afterward the two federations withdrew all their representatives from defense agencies. They returned two months later after the WSB approved a cost-of-living escalator clause in the auto contract of that year, and Truman promised a larger voice for labor in policy making.

The problem of the USWA's contract, which expired at the end of 1951, proved more intractable. At the president's request, the union postponed a strike until the WSB could rule on its wage demands. In March 1952 the board proposed that the steelworkers be granted 12.5 cents an hour immediately, with additional raises in installments by the following January. However, the steel companies refused to agree to the increases unless awarded sizable price relief. CHARLES E. WILSON publicly supported the industry's position and resigned as director of the Office of Defense Mobilization. On April 8, in a controversial effort to avoid a strike without having to invoke an 80-day Taft-Hartley injunction, Truman took over the steel mills under his wartime authority as commander in chief. The president's action provoked a storm of protest. CLARENCE B. RANDALL, head of Inland Steel, accused Truman of seizing the mills to pay a political debt to the CIO, while Senator Taft declared that the move was grounds for impeachment. The Supreme Court ruled the seizure unconstitutional on June 2. Truman returned the mills to the corporations, and 600,000 steelworkers immediately struck. A settlement was reached in July embodying roughly the terms approved by the wage board four months earlier. It also granted the industry a price increase of $5.65 per ton of steel.

Murray and the CIO vigorously supported Illinois governor ADLAI E. STEVENSON for president in 1952. Shortly after the election on November 9, 1952, Murray died suddenly in San Francisco, California. His demise left the CIO almost evenly divided between two candidates for the presidency: Walter Reuther, spokesman for the more liberal leaders of most of the large industrial unions; and Allan S. Haywood, an aging Murray protégé who represented the national office staff and the conservative heads of the USWA. In a close contest, Reuther won the office.

—TLH

Muste, A(braham) J(ohannes)
(1885–1967) *clergyman, peace activist*

A. J. Muste was born on January 8, 1885, in Zierikzee, Netherlands. He grew up in Michigan in an atmosphere of religious conservatism. He was ordained a minister in the Dutch Reformed Church in 1909. From 1909 to 1913 he studied at the Union Theological Seminary, receiving a bachelor of divinity degree. Muste left his New York ministry because he no longer believed in Calvinism or literalism. He then served a Congregational Church in Newtonville, Massachusetts. Increasingly influenced by Christian pacifist thought, Muste proclaimed his own pacifism, which conflicted with the beliefs of his congregation. He resigned as pastor in December 1917 and embraced Marxist ideas. He moved to Providence, Rhode Island, where he became a Quaker minister. In 1918 he went to Boston to work for the Fellowship of Reconciliation (FOR), which sought to mediate in labor disputes and other social conflicts. In this role he led the Lawrence textile strike of 1919, becoming interested in the techniques of nonviolent direct action as part of his pacifist program. He was elected general secretary of the Amalgamated Textile Workers, but his organizing drives in the East and Midwest were largely unsuccessful. In the 1920s he directed the Brookwood Labor School, where he educated workers in nonviolent techniques. Muste helped organize the successful Toledo Auto-Lite strike of 1934. FOR workers established the Congress of Racial Equality in 1942 and Muste influenced Martin Luther King, Jr., in his advocacy of nonviolence.

Muste opposed U.S. entry into World War II, but he cooperated with the Civilian Public Service (CPS) which set up work camps for conscientious objectors as an alternative to military service. By 1944 he came to think that FOR and other peace organizations cooperating with the CPS were "simply administering conscription for the government," and he convinced FOR to stop its work with the National Service Board for Religious Objectors. Muste then adopted an absolutist position on conscription, counseling pacifists to refuse to register for the draft. In 1947 he joined a group of pacifists in a draft card burning ceremony in front of the White House. The following year he began his practice of refusing to pay federal income tax because he felt that payment supported atomic and biological warfare.

Following the war Muste traveled throughout Europe to keep pacifists there aware of American peace activities. In December 1949 he attended the World Pacifist Meeting in India, where he espoused his conviction that mass nonviolent action could become the most effective means to prevent war. He joined an international liaison committee whose purpose was to organize an international nonviolent movement. Back in the United States Muste worked for peace by participating in the April 1950 "Fast for Peace" in Washington, D.C. The fast spread to over 20 American cities and eventually to Japan. During that same year Muste toured the United States, urging unilateral disarmament. He was one of the first prominent anti-Communists to take that stand. He believed if the United States were attacked, nonviolent resistance would lead to "creative" victory.

Muste's attempts to organize the nonviolence movement through political means met with little success. The "Third Way International Movement," which he promoted in 1954, eventually dissolved. This group tried to gather under one umbrella all organizations opposing the policies of the United States and Soviet Union. In the late 1950s Muste shifted his energy into staging civil disobedience demonstrations at nuclear testing sites.

During the mid-1960s Muste traveled widely for pacifist causes. He actively opposed U.S. involvement in Southeast Asia and helped organize rallies, vigils, and marches to protest the war. Before his death in 1967 he met with Ho Chi Minh to discuss the possibility of negotiations between North Vietnam and the United States. He died on February 11, 1967, in New York City while trying to organize an anti-war rally. For his efforts for peace he has been called "America's No. 1 Pacifist" and the "American Gandhi." (See *The Eisenhower Years* Volume)

—EF

N

Nathan, Robert R(oy)

(1908–2001) *economist*

Robert R. Nathan was born on December 25, 1908, in Dayton, Ohio. After receiving an M.A. in economics from the Wharton School in 1933, he joined the Department of Commerce to work on the original National Income Study. He resigned in June 1934 to work with the Pennsylvania Emergency Relief Board and with the president's Commission on Economic Security, which developed the statistical data used to guide the drafting of the Social Security Act. He returned to the national income section in December. Nathan became its chief in June 1935 and remained there until 1940. Among his most important works was *National Income in the United States, 1929–1935*, published in 1939. He also wrote articles for encyclopedias and labor magazines. In 1940 Nathan became chairman of planning on the War Mobilization Board. Two years later he was appointed deputy director of the Office of War Mobilization and Recovery (OWMR).

Nathan resigned his post in December 1945 in protest over the Truman administration's conservative fiscal policies. The director of the OWMR, Truman's friend and longtime political associate JOHN W. SNYDER, was moving quickly to remove all wartime controls on the economy. Nathan, with many other liberals, believed this course wrong. It was, in his opinion, certain to lead to inflation and the destruction of small business by large corporations, which had the power to demand priority on delivery of scarce materials. Nathan's departure was part of an exodus from the administration of liberals angry over what they saw as its conservatism. Many liberals lobbied for Nathan to be appointed to the first Council of Economic Advisers, formed in

1946. When Truman did not follow their request, they argued that government had lost one of its brightest young economists. Nathan did become a member of a liberal brain trust established by Postmaster General ROBERT E. HANNEGAN. The group advised administration on reconversion policy. Liberals hoped it might influence the president.

Out of office Nathan founded his own company, the consulting firm of Robert Nathan Associates, Inc. During 1946 Nathan conducted a study of wages and prices for the Congress of Industrial Organizations (CIO). The report, released in December, found that "total corporate business [could] support a 25 percent increase in wages" without raising prices. The CIO announced that its members would use the report as a guide during the wage negotiations of the coming year.

The findings created a brisk controversy. On the one hand, the National Association of Manufacturers denounced it as "economic absurdity." On the other, Secretary of Commerce HENRY A. WALLACE said he thought the conclusions accurate. In March 1947 Nathan, appearing before a presidential fact-finding board as a CIO witness, said that the steel companies could grant a 21-cent-an-hour wage increase without raising prices. The president of U.S. Steel countered that it was impossible for the industry to lower prices because of the size of the wage demand.

Nathan helped found the Americans for Democratic Action (ADA) in 1947 and sat on the organization's Economic Stabilization Committee. In May of that year the panel called for a vigorous national program against inflation. It urged a 10 percent cutback in retail prices, a general 15-cent-an-hour wage increase, a national 65 cent minimum wage, and a tax cut for lower income groups. In December 1947 Nathan told the Senate Banking Committee, in hearings on Truman's anti-inflation program, that there would be "dubious" justification for new pay increases if the cost of living could be lowered by 15 percent.

For the next year and a half, Nathan remained busy with his business and with the ADA. However, in 1949, he again entered the controversy over wages and prices. During July, in another report that he wrote for the CIO, Nathan asserted that business profits were sufficiently high to permit wage increases and, possibly, price decreases. He applied this view directly to the steel industry later in the month. In testimony before a presidential fact-finding board established to recommend the terms of an industry settlement, Nathan said that the companies could grant a 30-cent-an-hour package without raising prices because of large profits and lower costs. Later in the year he joined other liberal economists in advocating massive federal spending to pull the United States out of a recession that had begun in early 1949.

Nathan was a vocal liberal critic of the Eisenhower administration, calling for greater attention to economic stimulation during recessions and greater tax relief for lower income groups. He became an advocate opposed to military aid. He argued that "hundreds of millions for economic development could save billions for defense and the war." In 1960 Nathan served as an economic adviser to Senator HUBERT H. HUMPHREY (D-Minn.) during his campaign for the Democratic presidential nomination. Later he served on John F. Kennedy's economic transition team. Kennedy often consulted Nathan on economic matters. He advised Humphrey's 1968 presidential campaign. Nathan died on September 4, 2001, in Bethesda, Maryland. (See *The Eisenhower Years* Volume)

—CSJ

Niebuhr, Reinhold
(1892–1971) *theologian*

Born on June 21, 1892, in Wright, Missouri, Niebuhr followed his father, a German-born pastor, into the ministry. After graduating from Yale Divinity School in 1915. Niebuhr was ordained by the Evangelical Synod Church of North America. His first pastorate was in Detroit, where he became active in left-wing and pacifist causes.

Although his early training had led Niebuhr to embrace the optimistic liberalism of the Social Gospel, his 13 years in Detroit made him more radical in his demands for social change. In 1928 he joined the faculty of the Union Theological Seminary in New York. There he continued his criticism of Establishment Protestantism first expressed in his 1927 book, *Does Civilization Need Religion?* During the early 1930s Niebuhr joined the Socialist Party. He coupled his advocacy of political reform with forceful attacks upon American liberalism. In *Moral Man and Immoral Society* (1932) he insisted that large social groups, such as nations, operated according to the demands of their particular interests and without regard for morality. This "realistic" view of politics led Niebuhr to qualify his earlier pacifism. He refused to rule out "a season of violence" if necessary to create "a just social system."

Disturbed by Hitler's rise in Germany, he had begun to question the wisdom of the Socialists' isolationism by the end of the 1930s. In June 1940 he resigned as a party leader over the issue of American aid to the Allies. Niebuhr felt the United States should risk war because the Nazis were a threat to Western civilization. In 1941 he founded *Christianity and Crisis*, a bi-weekly publication that held that "the halting of totalitarian aggression is a prerequisite to world peace and order." That same year he helped organize the Union for Democratic Action, a group of ex-pacifists active in mobilizing public support for the war effort.

Niebuhr's neo-orthodox theology, developed from the conservative perspective of St. Augustine, complemented his pragmatic view of international politics. He combined a distrust of "the sentimental optimism" he saw embodied in liberalism and socialism with a theological emphasis on original sin. Niebuhr attacked the 20th century belief in human perfectability and moral progress in human events. Communism was especially dangerous, he felt, because it theorized that a better society could be created by altering economic relationships. Convinced of "the inevitable tragedy of human existence, the irreducible irrationality of human behavior," Niebuhr called for a "tough," practical approach to international affairs. He argued that the United States could best preserve its freedoms by seeking a balance of power with the Soviet Union. He rejected recognition of the United Nations as a legitimate international authority because he felt the organization masked the reality of nations in conflict.

Niebuhr did not immediately become a cold war warrior at the end of World War II, and for the first year after it, he condemned both the United States and the USSR for the rise in tensions, but he placed the burden of responsibility on the United States, which could afford to be patient with the Soviets since it had the atomic bomb. But a trip to Germany in 1946 convinced him that the Soviets were the greater threat, as German Socialists and Christian Democrats told him the Russians were imposing communism in their country (and Niebuhr's ancestral land), and that it needed U.S. assistance to avoid a totalitarian seizure of power. Niebuhr thought that, because communism did not have the overt heinousness of Nazism, it was a less obvious threat, and therefore more dangerous. "Russia hopes to conquer the whole of Europe strategically or ideologically," he wrote in 1946. That year he entered the dispute between the Truman administration and Secretary of Commerce HENRY A. WALLACE. Wallace charged that the State Department was betraying American chances for peace by antagonizing the Soviets. In response Niebuhr warned of "sentimental liberalism," which "refused to contemplate the tragic effects of human existence honestly." He claimed that "in resistance to Soviet expansion . . . all non-Communist Europeans, whether left or right, see the only real hope of peace." In the late 1940s he argued for the revitalization of Europe and the rebuilding of Germany. GEORGE F. KENNAN invited Niebuhr to participate in the discussion of the State Department's Policy Planning Staff in 1949. However, Kennan later claimed that Niebuhr did not make any substantive policy contributions and could not recall uttering the famous quotation that Niebuhr was the "father of us all" in regard to those fighting the cold war. What Kennan appreciated about Niebuhr was his philosophical viewpoint. For his part, Niebuhr preferred Kennan's foreign policy "realism" to a Wilsonian moralistic one, although he did worry about the United States becoming too infatuated with "national interest" goals. Publicly Niebuhr provided strong support for President Truman's overseas initiatives. He backed the Marshall Plan, arguing that it offered not only economic aid to Europe but also a peaceful method of containing communism. Later, he called for the passage of the North Atlantic Treaty, observing that "the frontiers of our interests and responsibilities lie far beyond our geographic boundaries." "For peace we must risk war," he wrote. "We cannot afford any more compromises. We will have to stand at every point in our far-flung lines."

Niebuhr was an influential member of the Liberal Party and a founder of the Americans for Democratic Action (ADA) in 1947. The ADA, which banned Communists from its membership, was meant to occupy the "vital center" of American politics. In the 1948 presidential campaign, the organization provided vocal opposition to Henry Wallace's Progressive Party candidacy. Niebuhr criticized the Progressives as "a party in which Communists and their sympathizers hold all the levers of power." In October he drafted an "Appeal to Liberals," attacking Wallace's foreign policy ideas as a "betrayal of free people throughout the world." Niebuhr scored the Progressive movement as "a corruption of liberalism."

In the early 1950s Niebuhr began to temper his advocacy of American interventionism. In *The Irony of American History* (1952), he argued that Americans could be blinded by their own idealism. He advised against U.S. involvement in mainland conflicts in the Far East. Niebuhr believed that Asians wanted Western technology while rebuffing Western civilization. Confronted by new "social forces," a military adventure would fail like "the spears of the knights when gun-powder challenged their reign." He thought Asian communism could be contained by fortifying Japan and the Philippines. Niebuhr concluded that if the United States remained patient, communism would be destroyed in underdeveloped nations by its own "inner corruption." In 1952 he backed ADLAI E. STEVENSON for president. Niebuhr was disturbed by the forces, "partly drawn from the Army and partly from business," he felt DWIGHT D. EISENHOWER represented.

Although, starting in 1952, he suffered a series of minor strokes, Niebuhr continued his social, political, and religious commentary. During the Eisenhower years he consistently advocated a strong American presence abroad. On domestic issues, he advanced the cause of civil rights. Niebuhr became an early critic of U.S. policy in Vietnam, calling the war "a fantastic adventure of U.S. imperialism." He did not, however, rule out the need for a continued American influence in Southeast Asia. Niebuhr took a less active role on *Christianity and Crisis* after 1966 because of advancing age. He died on June 1, 1971, in Stockbridge, Massachusetts. (See *The Eisenhower Years, The Kennedy Years* Volumes)

—JF

Niles, David K.

(1890–1952) *administrative assistant to the president*

David K. Niles, born David Neyhus in 1890 in Boston, Massachusetts, was the son of poor Russian immigrants who had settled in the slums of North Boston. Niles finished high school and then found work in a department store. In his spare time he attended lectures at Boston's Ford Hall Forum. There he came into contact with the director of the lecture series, George Coleman, who made Niles his assistant. In 1921 Niles became associate director of the Forum Hall. During this period he also worked with the information office of the Labor Department.

Niles directed the speaker's bureau of the Progressive Party during the 1924 presidential campaign. Three years later he began an unsuccessful crusade to prevent the execution of Nicola Sacco and Bartolomeo Vanzetti. In 1928 Niles directed the National Committee of Independent Voters for Al Smith. He began work as general assistant in charge of labor liaison under HARRY L. HOPKINS in 1935. Later he became administrative assistant to the president, specializing in the problems of minorities.

Truman retained Niles in this capacity when he became president. Virtually unknown to the general public, Niles cultivated an air of mystery about himself, masking his position in the Washington power structure. He wrote little and culled his office files every year. During the early years of the Truman administration, he was involved in federal investigations of violent racial incidents in the South, and he convinced the president to seek the establishment of a permanent Fair Employment Practices Committee and to create the President's Committee on Civil Rights, which issued the report "To Secure These Rights."

Niles was extremely influential in furthering the Zionist cause in the administration. Truman, half-jokingly, once said that Niles was so emotional about the subject of a Jewish homeland in Palestine that he would often break into tears when discussing the subject. He was in close contact with the members of the Executive of the Jewish Agency and served as liaison between Jewish leaders and the president.

It was Niles who, in the summer of 1947, recommended JOHN M. HILLDRING as an adviser and alternate delegate to the United Nations. The appointment of a man known to support the establishment of the Jewish state was meant to offset pro-Arab sentiment in the U.S. delegation. In November 1947 Niles helped arrange a secret meeting between Truman and Chaim Weizmann in order to give the Jewish leader a chance to persuade the president to support a Jewish homeland in Palestine.

Niles resigned his post in May 1951. He died of abdominal cancer on September 28, 1952, in Boston, Massachusetts. After he passed away, Truman paid him this tribute: "Presidents have been served by many able men, but seldom one so truly selfless. His passion for anonymity was matched only by his sense of public responsibility. David Niles' quick mind and warm heart were always in the service of humanity."

—MLB

Nitze, Paul H(enry)

(1907–2004) *chairman, Policy Planning Staff, State Department*

The son of a professor of romance languages, Paul H. Nitze was born on January 16, 1907, in Amherst, Massachusetts. Nitze graduated from Harvard in 1928 and the following year entered the banking firm of Dillon, Read, and Company. With the exception of the years 1938 to 1939, when he headed his own company, he remained there until 1941 when he entered government service as a financial director of the office of the coordinator of inter-American affairs. From 1942 to 1944 he held top administrative posts in the Board of Economic Warfare and the Foreign Economic Administration. Nitze served as vice chairman of the U.S. Strategic Bombing Survey from 1944 to 1946. After the war he accepted the post as deputy director of the office of international trade policy in the State Department. His negotiations with Sweden and Canada over renewal of the Reciprocal Trade Agreements made him realize that America's massive trade surplus was gobbling up other nation's dollar reserves, making it increasingly difficult for them to fund their debts. He called for a global aid plan to bail these nations out. Others were coming to the same conclusion—though usually on political grounds of anticommunism and they focused on Europe. All of this concern led to the formulation of the Marshall Plan in 1947. In helping to put together the Marshall Plan, Nitze was concerned with the economics—such as reviving production, restoring trade, strengthening financial markets, and controlling inflation. Marshall stressed to Nitze that the program be self-liquidating, as Americans would not support such a program for years on end. When it came time to get approval from the Republican Congress, Nitze and his staff composed "brown books," which described the economic situation in the different recipient nations and the amount of aid the administration thought Congress should give. The chairman of the House Appropriations Committee, JOHN TABER (R-N.Y.) dispensed with using them. Taber went through each country talking about minute details to stall action. A call from Undersecretary of State ROBERT A. LOVETT convinced Taber to allow Nitze to bring experts into the committee room to answer such questions. Nitze became deputy to the assistant secretary of state for economic affairs in 1948.

During 1949 Nitze became the assistant to GEORGE F. KENNAN, director of the State Department's Policy Planning Staff. The two men worked on the proposals for the 1949 Paris meeting of the Council of Foreign Ministers. They offered two plans. Plan A called for the withdrawal of virtually all foreign forces from Germany and reunification. Plan B advocated no military withdrawal and to move toward reunification as much as possible under that condition. Secretary of State DEAN G. ACHESON went with Plan B, because he believed the Soviets would not agree to any withdrawal of their troops. In fact he had CHARLES E. BOHLEN sound out the Soviets about Plan A, and the Soviets replied they would not pull out. It became evident early on at the conference that no agreement on the fundamental issues would be reached. Before the end of the year, Kennan had resigned in a dispute with Acheson. The Soviet expert opposed the formation of a military alliance with Western Europe, believing that it would antagonize the USSR and provide little protection in a nuclear age. Nitze, a long time advocate of a hard-line position toward the Soviet Union and a supporter of the alliance, took his place. He helped formulate the basic structure for the North Atlantic Treaty Organization (NATO) and pushed for the passage of the North Atlantic Treaty in Congress.

Nitze was also involved in Asian policy. He and the State Department's Far Eastern Affairs chief William Walton Butterworth, Jr., argued that because the wartime agreement made the United States the sole financial support of Japan and its economy was restricted under the occupation, it would be impossible for Japan to recover on its own. The two argued that industrial constraints should be ended. This was done; as Nitze had foreseen, the Soviets protested for a few days then ceased complaining. Nitze postulated that the Soviets were surprised that it had taken so long for the Americans to do the obvious.

In response to the Soviet Union's successful detonation of an atomic bomb and the fall of China to the Communists in 1949, Acheson asked Nitze in January 1950 to head an interdepartmental study group to review American foreign and defense policy. Given to the president in April, the report, NSC-68, was the first comprehensive review of U.S. national security policy. Nitze's analysis was based on the assumption that the Soviets were dedicated to world conquest and would, by 1954, have the nuclear capability of destroying the United States. To meet the challenge, the United States would have to accept primary responsibility for the security of the noncommunist world. NSC-68 recommended a massive development of free world military capabilities "with the intention of righting the power balance and in the hope that through means other than all-out war [the U.S.] could induce a change in the nature of the Soviet system." The report recommendation a two to fourfold expansion of American arms spending to strengthen NATO's conventional forces and develop nuclear weapons. This increase would enable the alliance to meet a full-scale invasion and permit the United States to engage in peripheral limited conflicts. NSC-68 argued that because of its wealth, the United States could afford the increased expenditures, estimating that 20 percent of its gross national product could be used for arms without suffering severe economic dislocation. Nitze also asserted that the United States had to rebuild the West until it surpassed the Soviet bloc. Only then could it stand at the "political and material center with other free nations in variable orbits around it." In his memoirs Nitze indicated that the report—as widely misperceived—did not anticipate a war in 1954. It really said 1954 would be the year of "maximum danger"; when the Soviets would have the capacity in nuclear weapons and long-range aircraft to devastate the United States. He also noted that NSC-68 merely echoed NSC 20/4, which had been formulated by Kennan.

Truman was initially reluctant to accept the program and refused to allow publication of the report. However, after the Korean War began, he started implementing its recommendations. NSC-68 fell from favor during the Eisenhower years, when the administration attempted to cut the defense budget and rely on strategic nuclear weapons as America's first deterrent.

Truman also wanted advice on whether to build a hydrogen bomb. A special committee of the National Security Council was established to advise the president. Members included the secretaries of state and defense and DAVID E. LILIENTHAL, chairman of the AEC. These people appointed a group of deputies to come up with recommendations. Nitze was part of the State Department group. Defense wanted a crash program; Lilienthal wanted none. Nitze and the State Department delegation decided that a deliberate program was needed. The group recommended to its superiors that work on a fusion bomb should proceed in conjunction with a review of U.S. policy toward Russia—which would eventuate in NSC-68. Acheson, Secretary of Defense LOUIS A. JOHNSON, and Lilienthal presented these recommendations to the president. Truman agreed.

Nitze was originally slated for a top defense post in the Eisenhower administration, but his name was dropped because of protests by the Republican right. During the 1950s he lectured and wrote on foreign policy. In 1957 he advised the Gaither Committee, formed to study U.S. defense needs. Two years later Nitze served as an adviser to the Senate Foreign Relations Committee. He was assistant secretary of defense and secretary of the navy in the Kennedy administration. Nitze served as deputy secretary of defense from 1967 to 1969. President Nixon appointed him a member of the U.S. delegation to the Strategic Arms Limitation Talks in 1969. Nitze served until 1974. Nitze helped form the Committee on the Present Danger, a hawkish group of conservative Democrats against SALT II, and served as an arms negotiator in the Reagan administration. Nitze died on October 19, 2004, in Washington, D.C. (See *The Kennedy Years, The Johnson Years* Volumes)

—JB

Nixon, Richard M(ilhous)

(1913–1994) *member of the House of Representatives, member of the Senate, Republican Party vice presidential nominee*

Richard M. Nixon was born on January 9, 1913, in Yorba Linda, California. His mother was a Quaker from Indiana and his father a Methodist from Ohio.

They met and married in California. The Nixon family, despite a good income from the gas station and grocery store, encountered persistent financial problems due to the 10-year illness of Richard's older brother. Nixon himself worked part time in the family store beginning at about age 10. He excelled in his academic work at Yorba Linda and Whittier public schools and received his B.A. from Whittier College in 1934. Nixon attended Duke University Law School on a scholarship and graduated third in his class in 1937. He returned to Whittier to establish his own practice, having rejected a chance to work for a New York law firm and having been denied appointment as an FBI agent because of the bureau's then limited budget. During World War II Nixon worked in the Office of Price Administration for eight months, an experience that left him forever distrustful of government bureaucracy. He then served as a noncombat naval officer stationed in the South Pacific.

An accomplished speaker, Nixon had campaigned for the 1940 Republican presidential nominee, Wendell L. Willkie. Nixon's family had been Republican from the days of William McKinley. Nixon offered himself as a candidate for the House of Representatives in response to the suggestion of a family friend, Herman L. Perry, bank manager of the Bank of America and a member of a committee soliciting Republican candidates for the 12th district of California. As Irwin Gellman has noted, contrary to myth, Murray Chotiner did not manage Nixon's 1946 campaign for Congress. He produced 10 news releases for the primary and did not even work in the general election. Nixon successfully associated the five-term incumbent, Representative JERRY VOORHIS (D-Calif.), with widespread voter dissatisfaction with the Truman administration over meat and housing shortages and economic controls. Nixon's campaign literature and five public debates with Voorhis also noted his opponent's endorsement by the local Congress of Industrial Organizations's Political Action Committee (CIO), which had been charged with Communist affiliation. Nixon upset Voorhis with 57 percent of the votes. In June 1948 he netted both the Republican and the Democratic nominations through California's cross-filing primary rule. He hence won reelection in November without formal opposition.

In the House Nixon voted in favor of Republican Party positions. *Congressional Quarterly* measured Nixon's support for the GOP leadership on selected legislation at 91 percent in 1947–48 and 74 percent in 1949–50. At his request Nixon gained appointment to the Labor Committee and to the subcommittee that drafted the House version of the Taft-Hartley Act of 1947. Although he claimed he wanted balance in labor-management relations, as Gellman had indicated, he ran on a platform that opposed the CIO-PAC's influence and the rampant strikes of 1946. He wanted the balance of power to shift more toward management. In other domestic legislation he supported the Republican tax cut of 1948 and voted for raising the minimum wage to 75 cents an hour in 1949. That year he served on a special panel, headed by Representative CHRISTIAN A. HERTER (R-Mass.), which toured Europe in September and returned endorsing the Marshall Plan. The experience contributed much to Nixon's support of an international foreign policy. He backed aid to Greece and Turkey, the Marshall Plan, and the North Atlantic Treaty Organization.

Nixon gained a national reputation as a strong anticommunist. He belonged to the House Un-American Activities Committee (HUAC) but did not participate in its controversial 1947 inquiry into communism in the motion picture industry. However, the following year he emerged as a leading proponent of strong action against possible domestic subversion. He and Representative KARL E. MUNDT (R-S.Dak.) sponsored a bill to require the federal registration of Communists and Communist-front groups. Congress eventually incorporated parts of this measure into the Internal Security Act of 1950.

Washington colleagues such as Representative Charles Kersten (R-Wisc.), a fellow member of HUAC, reinforced Nixon's concern over domestic subversion. In 1947–48 Kersten introduced Nixon to several Roman Catholic clergymen, including Monsignor Fulton J. Sheen, who were engaged in church-sponsored investigations of domestic communism. One of these men, Father John Cronin, reported to Nixon that Communist Party members and sympathizers had been working in the State Department. Cronin maintained that one of these secret party followers was ALGER HISS, who had left the State Department to become president of the prestigious Carnegie Foundation for Peace. HUAC counsel Robert Stripling similarly advised Nixon of Hiss's past affiliations.

Hiss's possible connection with the left became national news on August 3, 1948, when WHITTAKER CHAMBERS, subpoenaed by HUAC, declared that in the 1930s Hiss had been a close friend and like him,

a Communist. Hiss, testifying two days later, denied ever knowing Chambers or having been a Communist. The handsome Hiss possessed an excellent academic and professional background and close ties to the leaders of government, academia, and business. Chambers, rotund and a poor speaker, paled by comparison. So effective had Hiss's presentation been that HUAC, already under fire for its movie inquiry, appeared all the more foolish and in danger of abolition at the start of the next session for having permitted Chambers to testify.

Nixon refused to accept Hiss's innocence. On the one hand, he was impressed with the fact that Chambers could detail so much of Hiss's personal life. On the other hand, as Robert Stripling later remembered, Nixon, who lacked Hiss's background and polished demeanor, found Hiss insolent toward him. But despite Stripling's claim that the congressman "had his hat set for Hiss," Nixon tried to be fair in weighing the evidence. At Nixon's insistence, Mundt, then HUAC's acting chairman, named him head of a subcommittee to pursue Chambers's allegations.

Methodically, Nixon forced Hiss into acknowledging a past association with Chambers. At a subcommittee hearing held in New York City on August 17, Nixon arranged a personal confrontation between Hiss and Chambers. There, and publicly later in August, Hiss confessed to having befriended Chambers briefly in the mid-1930s; he reiterated his non-involvement in Communist activities. This change in Hiss's testimony revived national interest in HUAC and in Chambers. After being called before a grand jury, Chambers provided more information and some material evidence. In December Nixon forced Chambers's hand further. At Nixon's direction, HUAC investigators subpoenaed materials hidden on Chambers's Maryland farm. Stored inside a pumpkin was microfilm of classified State Department documents from early 1938 that, Chambers maintained, Hiss had stolen for transmission to spies. A grand jury in 1949 indicted Hiss for perjury on the grounds that he had lied in his testimony about his relations with Chambers. (The statute of limitations prevented an espionage indictment.) After a second trial Hiss was found guilty.

Hiss's fate greatly embarrassed the Truman administration. Nixon, in turn, strove to capitalize on the case. Initially Truman dismissed the Hiss inquiry as a "red herring." Secretary of State DEAN G. ACHESON stood by Hiss even after he was found guilty. In the fall of 1948, well before Hiss's case had been fully developed, Nixon decried the administration's stance and attempted to use the issue to aid the Republican Party. He urged GOP presidential candidate THOMAS E. DEWEY to make the Hiss scandal a campaign issue. Nixon wrote a high Dewey aide in September 1948, "The record of the [Truman] Administration [on domestic subversion] is completely vulnerable and should be attacked." Dewey, however, declined Nixon's suggestion and rarely mentioned the matter.

Nixon's role in the Hiss case received severe assessments in the years after the probe. Hiss continued to profess his innocence and assail Chambers through the 1970s. A large body of liberals and intellectuals sympathetic to Hiss contended that Nixon dishonestly plotted his fall for the most base of political motives. Hiss and his defenders argued further that Nixon worked in close collaboration with the FBI or right-wing cliques, groups that sought to associate some Roosevelt-Truman administration members with communism.

Most of these theories, as well as Nixon's own claims, were undermined by the research of historian Allen Weinstein. In *Perjury* (1978), Weinstein disassociated Nixon from the FBI, which, the historian maintained, held him in contempt. Although Catholic clergy apparently influenced Nixon into pursuing the investigation, many in Washington, Weinstein discovered, had suspected Hiss of Communist inclinations long before Chambers testified. Weinstein assembled much proof of Hiss's culpability. He also revealed Nixon to have been both clever and lucky. In 1962 Nixon described himself as the cold, tough-guy detective in the case. Actually, Nixon, according to the historian, had banked heavily on Chambers long before he had very definite proof of Hiss's guilt and was concerned about the reliability of his witness. "The combination of accident, good luck, inside information, fear and panic," Weinstein wrote, characterized Nixon's work on Chambers and Hiss. In the 1990s with the release of the Venona decrypts, it was conclusively shown that Hiss was a spy for Soviet military intelligence.

For Nixon the Hiss case proved worth the risk. In 1950 he felt sufficiently well-known to run for the U.S. Senate. The bitter Democratic senatorial primary provided him with ample ammunition for his own race. Democratic opponents of liberal representative HELEN GAHAGAN DOUGLAS (D-Calif.), who eventually won the party's nomination, freely accused her of Communist sympathies. Nixon closely patterned his own fall campaign after those waged by the Democrats against Douglas, his own 1946 effort against Voorhis, and GEORGE A. SMATHERS's successful, red-baiting campaign against liberal senator CLAUDE PEPPER (D-Fla.) in the May 1950 Florida Democratic primary. As in 1946 Murray Chotiner helped manage Nixon's race and distributed literature grouping Nixon's foe with American communism. Some 580,000 pink-colored sheets noted similarities in the voting records of Douglas and Representative VITO MARCANTONIO (ALP-N.Y.), commonly considered to be procommunist. (Ironically, Marcantonio detested Douglas and encouraged this anti-Douglas tactic.) Douglas herself conducted an inept campaign. Voter disillusionment with the Truman administration and the outbreak of the Korean conflict also aided Nixon, who triumphed with a 680,000 vote margin.

Nixon emerged from his 1950 victory a national party leader and a favorite for the Republican vice presidential nomination in 1952. A sought-after speaker, he harshly rebuked Truman's wars against communism at home and abroad. During a Senate debate on Korea in April 1951, he accused Truman of "bare-faced appeasement" in his attempts to resolve the conflict. As before, he stressed the issue of Communists in government. "The most vulnerable point" of the Democratic record, he said in June 1951, was the Truman administration's "failure" to deal with the American Communist "fifth column."

In May 1951 Nixon met with General DWIGHT D. EISENHOWER, a likely candidate for the GOP presidential nomination. Eisenhower commended Nixon on the firmness of the Hiss hearings while impressing upon the senator his own familiarity with foreign policy. Convinced that Eisenhower alone could win in 1952, Nixon quietly aided the general's candidacy; he did so despite his formal commitment to California governor EARL WARREN. But Gellman has argued against the contention that Nixon undermined Governor Earl Warren's favorite-son candidacy. Nixon campaigned for the governor in the primary, and the delegation was legally bound to support the favorite son on the first ballot. Nixon and others were quite open that they would support Eisenhower when or if Warren dropped out and believed the general would win. Nixon did not have the votes in the delegation to revolt against Warren, and the senator had pledged he would support the delegation. He did say the governor was the strongest dark horse candidate. Warren's maladroitness was what destroyed his chance, according to Gellman, not Nixon. In May 1952 Dewey, a key Eisenhower supporter, suggested to Nixon that he consider second place on an Eisenhower ticket.

After Eisenhower's nomination in June Dewey successfully recommended Nixon to Eisenhower for the vice presidential nomination. Despite his wife's opposition, Nixon accepted Eisenhower's offer. Dewey felt that Nixon's youth—he was 39—would aid the party among younger voters. Furthermore, Nixon's place on the ticket, Eisenhower strategists correctly anticipated, would reconcile the "Old Guard" wing of the party to the nomination of internationalist Eisenhower since its members much admired Nixon's active anticommunism. In his acceptance speech Eisenhower described Nixon glowingly as "a man who has a special talent and ability to ferret out any kind of subversive influence wherever it may be found."

During the fall 1952 campaign, a political fund scandal jeopardized Nixon's rising political fortunes. Nevertheless, Nixon survived the crisis after an emotional television appeal, made famous by his maudlin reference to a gift from a Texas supporter to the senator's daughters of a dog, Checkers, that the family would keep no matter what. In November the Eisenhower-Nixon ticket won by a landslide. Nixon served as vice president for two terms and enjoyed unprecedented powers. His campaign tactics and utterances, and certain shifts in his policy positions, kept him a controversial figure. In 1960 Nixon ran as the Republican nominee for president and narrowly lost to Senator John F. Kennedy (D-Mass.). Two years later Nixon nearly wrecked his career by losing the California gubernatorial election. He survived and won election as president in 1968.

Despite some successes, Nixon eventually left office in disgrace. Nixon initiated several major changes in American foreign policy, while slowly ending U.S. involvement in the Vietnam War. The Democratic Party's consistent control of Congress, however, frustrated the president's domestic proposals. Scandals involving his 1972 reelection campaign, and Nixon's clumsy attempts to obstruct criminal investigations of them, resulted in his resignation from office under threat of impeachment in August 1974. Despite this setback, Nixon went

on to become an elder statesman consulted by presidents. Nixon died in New York City, on April 22, 1994. (See *The Eisenhower Years, The Kennedy Years, The Johnson Years,* and *The Nixon/Ford Years* Volumes)

—JLB

Nourse, Edwin G(riswold)
(1883–1974) *chairman, Council of Economic Advisers*

A descendant of Salem witch trial victim Rebecca Nurse, Edwin Nourse was born on May 20, 1883, in Lockport, New York. He received a bachelor's degree in agricultural economics from Cornell in 1906. He taught finance at the Wharton School and was a professor and chairman of the department of economics at the University of South Dakota before entering the graduate program of the University of Chicago. He received his Ph.D. in 1915 and joined the faculty of the University of Arkansas shortly after graduation. Nourse moved to Iowa State College in 1918 and to the Institute of Economics in Washington, D.C., in 1923 as head of the agricultural division. He became director of the institute in 1929, two years after it was merged with other research organizations to form the Brookings Institution. In 1942 he became vice president of Brookings, where he remained until July 1946. That month Truman asked him to become chairman of the Council of Economic Advisers.

Nourse's appointment was not viewed with enthusiasm by liberals who saw him as a conservative, or at best a moderate. Nourse was opposed to government intervention in the economy but had said that federal control was growing inevitably. He tended to be concerned with the interrelationship of wages, profits, and farm incomes and believed that, through cooperation with one another, the private sectors—agriculture, labor, and business—might achieve a proper balance. In his widely praised book, *Price Making in a Democracy,* published in 1944, he called for business, through raising productivity, to increase profits and lower prices. This emphasis on balance of sectors ran against the dominant themes of current economic thought. Most economists had turned their attention to economic measures related to the aggregate demand for goods and services. They were interested in how to influence demand through the manipulation of the federal budget and, to a lesser extent, the money supply.

Called "the first and last faceless economic adviser," Nourse believed that the Council of Economic Advisers should point out and explain issues to the president. He was not inclined to formulate policy or to defend administration programs before congressional committees. He believed that the council should not take a political role. These attitudes particularly irked the president who valued members more as advocates for his programs than consultants. Nourse's refusal to commit himself to programs became increasingly frustrating to Truman, who had no clear understanding of economic theory and was impatient with economists and their ideas. He liked to be presented with concrete proposals, which he could reject or accept. Walter Heller, chairman of the council under President John F. Kennedy, termed Nourse the classic "on the one hand on the other hand economist." Nourse frustrated Truman by failing to present clear policies for adoption. Truman, as Heller recalled, once lamented, "Why can't somebody bring me a one-handed economist?"

During his first two years in office Nourse remained on good terms with Truman. The council's reports, emphasizing the dangers of inflation rather than recession, implied policies that the administration was inclined to adopt anyway. However, in 1949 Nourse dissented from the administration's position that no recession was in sight.

That year, as a result of a tax cut imposed by the 80th Congress and a downturn in the economy, the federal budget slipped into a deficit for the first time since the end of World War II. Truman was loathe to cut expenditures as revenues fell below projections, but Nourse opposed federal deficit spending. On October 18 he finally spoke out publicly in an address to the National Retail Farm Equipment Association. He asserted that, despite the recession, employment and production were high. A federal deficit was inappropriate, he said, under such circumstances. "The slippery road to misery," he called it. Truman accepted Nourse's resignation the next day. In an off-the-record press conference that day, the president said, "I am certain that Dr. Nourse didn't know what he was talking about. Although he is an economist, he knows absolutely nothing about government financing." Truman allegedly said to new CEA chairman LEON H. KEYSERLING about Nourse: "Well the Doctor was a very nice old gentleman but he wasn't very practical."

Early the next year Nourse again spoke against Truman's fiscal policies, calling deficit spending "artificial and dangerous." He never again entered public life and, except for some contribution to economic journals and reviews, lived in retirement until his death on April 7, 1974, in Bethesda, Maryland.

—CSJ

Odets, Clifford

(1906–1963) *playwright*

The son of a painter, Clifford Odets was born on July 18, 1906, in Philadelphia, Pennsylvania, and grew up in the Bronx. He left high school after two years, considering it a waste of time. After a brief spell as a fledgling poet, Odets became interested in theater and radio, advancing from amateur groups to small professional companies as an actor. In 1928 he began playing small roles in Broadway productions of the Theater Guild. Three years later he and other guild members formed the Group Theater, which became a major force in American theater during the depression. The Group Theater tried to have seven or eight actors portray equal characters, rather than use the star system that was typical of the time. In 1935 Odets joined the Communist Party.

It was during his years with the Group that Odets became a playwright. In 1935 his first major work, *Waiting for Lefty*, about different characters trying to survive as cabbies, was presented on Broadway after scoring major successes in New York's Labor Theater circuit. The play, about unions banding together to fight the depression, associated Odets with radical political theater. That year he also premiered *Awake and Sing*. Critics generally acclaimed him the most promising young American playwright.

Following the failure in 1936 of his next major work, *Paradise Lost*, about an upper-middle-class family struggling during the depression, Odets began the first of many periods in Hollywood as a screenwriter. He returned to Broadway in 1937 with his greatest stage hit, *Golden Boy*, the story of a violinist who wanted to become a prizefighter. Succeeding years saw Odets alternating between several unpopular plays such as *Rocket to the Moon* in 1938 and *Night Music* in 1940, and trivial screenwriting jobs in Hollywood. He finally settled in California, following the failure of *Clash by Night* in 1941.

Kept out of military service by an arthritic condition, Odets contributed to the war effort by translating a Russian play for the American stage. He was increasingly disenchanted with the commercial aspects of his life as a Hollywood screenwriter after the war. In 1949 he revealed his anger and frustration in the Broadway production of *The Big Knife*, a blistering anti-Hollywood work. The play also made glancing references to the blacklisting of those accused of Communist sympathies.

Odets was among those writers who initially opposed the House Un-American Activities Committee (HUAC) hearings into alleged Communist influence in the movie industry. In 1947 he publicly supported the "Hollywood Ten," who refused, on First Amendment grounds, to cooperate with the investigations. By 1952 Odets's position had changed dramatically. When he appeared before HUAC in executive session during the spring, he testified freely and at length. He conceded that he had been a member of the Communist Party for a brief period in the mid-1930s, after being approached by another member of the Group Theater, and he proceeded to name numerous other Group Theater actors as members of the party. Odets frequently quoted poor reviews of his plays from left-wing newspapers as proof of his basic disagreements with Communist policy, and he told the committee that he had left the party after deciding that there had been too many attempts to influence the content of his plays. He disavowed responsibility for subsequent productions of his plays under Communist Party auspices.

Odets's last theater piece was produced on Broadway in 1954. He spent the next years writing screenplays and television scripts. When he died of cancer on August 14, 1963, in Los Angeles, California, he was working on the drafts of three new plays. At the time of his death, critics believed that his work had never lived up to its potential and had been detrimentally influenced by Hollywood.

—MQ

Odlum, Floyd B(ostwick)
(1892–1976) *financier*

The son of a Methodist preacher, Floyd B. Odlum was born on March 30, 1892, in Union City, Michigan. He earned a law degree from the University of California in 1914. He then worked as a legal clerk for the Utah Power and Light Company. In 1923 he and some friends started the Atlas Corporation, a private investment pool, with a net capital of $39,600. The company prospered and, before pulling out of the stock market just before the 1929 crash, was worth $6 million. Odlum then proceeded boldly to buy up troubled companies at bargain prices as the depression deepened. Within a few years he was one of the richest men in the United States with major interests in banking, real estate, manufacturing, motion pictures, and aviation. He became known as "Fifty Percent Odlum," as his friends jokingly remarked that "he buys everything for fifty cents on the dollar."

Odlum was a supporter of the New Deal and gave $10,000 to Franklin Roosevelt's reelection campaign in 1936. In 1941 Roosevelt selected him to head the defense contracts distribution division of the Office of Production Management. Odlum remained as a dollar-a-year man until the end of World War II.

Odlum became increasingly interested in aviation after his second marriage in 1936 to Jacqueline Cochran, who at one time held more speed, distance, and altitude records than any other pilot. In 1947 he bought control of Consolidated-Vultee Aircraft Corporation (later Convair Division of General Dynamics), which had lost $35.7 million that year. Consolidated became profitable in 1949 when the air force doubled its contract for the B-36, the largest airplane in the world. The B-36 became the backbone of U.S. defense strategy based on its ability to deliver the atomic bomb to distant targets.

In May 1949 Representative James E. Van Zandt (R-Pa.) charged that political influence was involved in the nearly 1 billion contract. Van Zandt's charges were based on the so-called Anonymous Document—a scissors-and-paste report written by Cedric Worth, special assistant to the undersecretary of the navy, and Tom Davies, special assistant to the assistant secretary of the navy for air, on the alleged scandal behind the procurement of the B-36 bomber. He maintained that Secretary of Defence LOUIS A. JOHNSON had been legal counsel for Consolidated prior to his appointment and had solicited two contributions from Odlum of $3,000 each for President Truman's 1948 election campaign. The House Armed Services Committee conducted an investigation and, in August 1949, concluded that there was "not one scintilla of evidence" of corruption in procurement of the B-36.

Odlum played an important role in the development of U.S. missile and space programs. After the military stopped funding research and development of missiles in July 1947, he pumped Consolidated's own funds into the program. At the end of 1952, with the development of lighter weight hydrogen bombs, the missile program again received top priority. Odlum's company then received the main contract to develop the Atlas missile, the first intercontinental ballistic missile in the U.S. arsenal.

In April 1950 Odlum said in a speech that the cold war had become "a plain, undiluted war [leading to] destruction." He charged Stalin with stirring group prejudices in the United States to bring about a political revolution. Odlum was one of the first Americans to aid the economic recovery of Franco's Spain, selling planes to the nation and agreeing to leave the profits in the country for investment.

In 1953 Odlum sold Consolidated-Vultee, doubling the $10 million investment that his Atlas Corporation had originally made. In 1954 he used this money to invest heavily in uranium mines, relying on projections that the country would turn increasingly to nuclear power plants for electricity. After he resigned from the Atlas Corporation in 1963, he worked for two years as a deputy to Howard Hughes. He spent the last six years of his life in retirement at his ranch in California. Odlum died on June 17, 1976, in Indio, California.

—TFS

O'Dwyer, William
(1890–1964) *mayor, ambassador*

The son of two schoolteachers, William "Bill-O" O'Dwyer was born on July 11, 1890, in Bohola, Ireland, one of 11 children. He received his early education in his father's class in Bohola, Ireland, and attended St. Nathys College in Boscommon before going to Spain to study for the priesthood at the Jesuit University of Salamanca. Abandoning his ambition to become a priest, young O'Dwyer booked passage for America, arriving in New York in 1910 with $25.35 in his pocket. In the years that followed he held a variety of jobs, among them grocery clerk, stoker on a South American freighter, fireman on a Hudson River steamer, plasterer, and bartender at the Vanderbilt Hotel. While working as a longshoreman in 1916, O'Dwyer began attending evening classes at the Fordham University Law School. In 1917 he joined the New York police force, becoming a patrolman on Brooklyn's toughest waterfront beat. By the time he received his LL.B. degree in 1923, O'Dwyer had already become head of the police legal bureau. In 1925 he resigned from the force to establish his own law practice, often representing policemen in departmental trials.

O'Dwyer's political career began in 1932 with his appointment as a New York City magistrate by acting mayor Joseph V. McKee. From 1935 to 1937 he presided over the Brooklyn Adolescent Court, and, in 1938, he was elected to a 14-year term as a Kings Company Court judge. He gave up his seat on the bench, however, to run for district attorney of Brooklyn on the Democratic ticket in 1939.

As district attorney, O'Dwyer immediately began to "clean house," bringing new men into his department. One of the men O'Dwyer hired was his long-time friend James F. Moran, whose associations with the underworld were well known at the time. Within a few months, using police techniques to solve 56 underworld murders, O'Dwyer made national headlines by announcing that he had smashed "Murder, Inc.," the infamous underworld execution squad. However, the key criminal figure in Murder, Inc., Albert Anastasia, was never called for questioning. Moran and the policemen assigned to the district attorney's office ordered certain "wanted" cards and arrests sheets taken out of the police files. Two witnesses who had agreed to testify against Anastasia were mysteriously killed, one while in protective custody. One observer asserted that top mob leaders sacrificed hitmen to take the pressure off themselves. At the time these irregularities were overshadowed by O'Dwyer's spectacular success in breaking the murder ring. O'Dwyer lost

his first mayoral bid against incumbent Fiorello H. LaGuardia in 1941 but was reelected district attorney two years later with the endorsement of all major parties.

During World War II O'Dwyer was commissioned a major in the Army Inspector General's office and assigned to investigate graft on army contracts. He was later promoted to colonel and then brigadier general and was chosen to represent the Foreign Economic Administration in Rome as President Roosevelt's personal envoy. Roosevelt also appointed O'Dwyer to the War Refugee Board. Returning to civilian life in 1945, O'Dwyer was nominated for mayor of New York, by both the Democratic and the American Labor parties. When his opponents brought up the rumors of his past underworld dealings, some of which had already been confirmed by a Brooklyn grand jury, O'Dwyer dismissed the charges as political. He was elected mayor in 1945 by the largest majority ever given a mayoral candidate to that date. As mayor, O'Dwyer quarreled with the leaders of Tammany Hall to show his independence, but his attempts to reform the Democratic Party in the city had little lasting impact.

As New York's first postwar mayor, O'Dwyer faced major labor problems, including a strike of tugboat workers, which cut off the city's oil supplies in the winter of 1946, a severe truck strike, and a threatened subway strike. O'Dwyer settled these by the use of tripartite panels composed of representatives of the public, industry, and labor to aid in bargaining. He worked 10- and 12-hour days. At one point during his time as mayor he confessed to the *New York Times* what a burden running the city was. During the war construction had ceased, and, by 1946, the need for new schools, hospitals, libraries, and subways was urgent. Funds for new construction, however, were unavailable. The shortage was due to a heavy city debt accumulated through the graft of Tammany Hall politicians and the projects of ROBERT MOSES, whose enormous behind-the-scenes influence in the areas of city planning and construction had already begun to change the shape of New York.

Through Moses, O'Dwyer was able to work out a deal with the state government that allowed him to generate revenue by imposing new city taxes and by raising subway fares from five to 10 cents. Much of this revenue was poured into the mammoth expressways and other construction projects favored by Moses, such as slum clearance.

O'Dwyer did not want to run for reelection in 1949, but Bronx political boss Ed Flynn convinced him to run by getting President Truman—despite his dislike of Bill-O—to agree to appoint him ambassador to Mexico in 1950. Flynn's belief was that since 1950 was a gubernatorial election year, more people would come out to vote in a special election for mayor, helping the Democratic candidate.

O'Dwyer won his 1949 reelection bid easily, despite opponents' accusations of corruption and inefficiency. However, by that date evidence began to surface of past improprieties. Harry Gross, a Brooklyn bookmaker, testified before a grand jury investigating racketeering in Brooklyn that he had been a big contributor to O'Dwyer's mayoral campaigns. As the grand jury began to question O'Dwyer's connections with underworld figures, a Senate committee prepared to investigate links between organized crime and New York politicians. On August 1, 1950, citing poor health, O'Dwyer filed his application for retirement. Within two weeks President Truman announced his appointment as ambassador to Mexico. O'Dwyer left the country on August 31, 1950. The special election proved a disaster for Democrats as their candidate lost.

In March 1951 O'Dwyer voluntarily testified before the Senate Crime Investigating Committee, headed by ESTES KEFAUVER (D-Tenn.) The ambassador was charged with appointing friends of racketeers to high office, with accepting underworld money for his mayoral campaigns, and with taking a bribe of $10,000 from John Crane, president of the Uniformed Firemen's Association, in return for promising to support measures favorable to firemen. He was also accused of failure to prosecute key criminal figures during his tenure as district attorney. In defending his career O'Dwyer testified that he fought against Tammany Hall and corruption. While he admitted meeting with mobster Frank Costello and appointing to office men with underworld connections, O'Dwyer denied accepting any money from John Crane.

In May 1951 the Senate Crime Committee issued a report charging O'Dwyer with aiding crime while a New York official. It stated that during his terms as district attorney and mayor, "neither he nor his appointees took any effective action against the top echelons of the gambling, narcotics, waterfront, murder or bookmaking rackets." The report also claimed that O'Dwyer's failure to follow up evidence of organized crime actually led to its growth in New York. From his post in Mexico City O'Dwyer denied the charges, saying that he was a victim of "inference and innuendo."

Despite increased pressure on Truman to recall O'Dwyer, the president supported him. The ambassador remained in his post until the advent of the Eisenhower administration. A highly successful diplomat, O'Dwyer became an expert in Mexican affairs. He stayed on in Mexico City after giving up the ambassadorship, serving as a consultant to a law firm there. He returned to New York City in 1960 and died of a heart attack there on November 24, 1964.

—DAE

Olds, Leland

(1890–1960) *member, Federal Power Commission*

The son of the president of Amherst College, Leland Olds was born on December 31, 1890, in Rochester, New York. He graduated from Amherst in 1912 and did postgraduate work in economics and sociology at Harvard and Columbia. Before World War I he served as a statistician on the Shipbuilding and Labor Adjustment Board and was also researcher for the Council of National Defense. Olds became a member of the National War Labor Board in 1918 and was head of the research bureau of the railroad employees department of the American Federation of Labor from 1920 to 1922. During the remaider of the decade, Olds wrote for the Marxist labor news service, the Federated Press. He contributed essays that denounced capitalism and capitalists as "a privileged class of parasites whose idleness and dissipation become an increasing stench in the nostrils of the people." A specialist in public utilities, Olds also represented the Community Councils of the City of New York before the Public Service Commission, where he advocated the consumers' view on utility regulation. During the 1930s Olds worked with a New York State Power Commission, eventually becoming executive secretary in 1939.

President Roosevelt appointed him to the Federal Power Commission (FPC) in June 1939 despite his membership in the leftist American Labor Party. Olds was chairman of the FPC from January 1940 to December 1946. As head of the agency he worked for strict regulation of utilities and government competition with private power producers to protect the consumer and got utilities to use uniform accounting practices, which allowed them to collect information across the nation and discover methods to lower rates. He contended that government regulation by itself was "futile because the utilities companies always find ways to circumvent it." Nevertheless, he explained to the Senate during the debate over his confirmation for a second term in 1944 that his main interest was in preserving a modified free enterprise system.

During the war Olds and the FPC stressed the building and expansion of power plants to aid the war effort. Olds did not think such facilities would be underutilized after the war ended, but, rather, would facilitate and encourage the sale of appliances to keep the economy humming.

In 1949 President Truman renominated him for a third five-year term. Senators from oil producing states, led by ROBERT S. KERR (D-Okla.), vigorously fought the reappointment on the grounds that Olds was a former Communist. Democratic representative John Lyle of Texas pointed to articles from the 1920s to portray Olds as a Communist sympathizer. Senator LYNDON B. JOHNSON (D-Tex.) also pointed to Olds's earlier writing as cause to disqualify him for confirmation. The true reason for their opposition was the regulatory power of the FPC over natural gas wellhead prices. Just before his confirmation hearings, Olds had fought a bill introduced by Kerr, a millionaire oil producer, to exempt independent producers from the commission's oversight. When the nomination's defeat seemed likely, Truman put great pressure on Democratic leaders to push through the appointment. He asked ELEANOR ROOSEVELT for assistance and sent a public letter to the Senate in October praising Olds as the people's friend, a "nationally recognized champion of effective utility regulation" who was opposed only by "powerful corporations" for his service to the consumer. Truman told the chairman of the Democratic National Committee, WILLIAM M. BOYLE, JR., to put pressure on state and local party leaders to persuade Senate Democrats to vote for Olds. Despite Truman's effort, which was applauded by the liberal press and the Americans for Democratic Action, Olds was defeated. The Senate Interstate and Foreign Commerce Committee voted 10 to 2 against his reappointment, explaining that it had been "shocked beyond description" by the "radical views" he had expressed in the 1920s. The full Senate voted down the appointment in a vote of 53 to

13. Olds bitterly remarked that the vote showed his earlier criticisms of capitalism had some validity. Truman in turn vetoed the Kerr bill.

Undaunted, Truman continued to utilize Olds's talents. In 1950 the president used emergency funds to appoint Olds the only full-time member of the Water Resources Policy Commission formed to conduct a year-long study of the nation's water supply. During 1951–52 he was the Interior Department's representative on a committee to study development of natural resources in New England. Olds left office when the Republicans came to power in 1953, but he served as a power and natural resources consultant to the Public Affairs Institution from 1953 until his death. Speaking before Democratic groups he condemned the Eisenhower administration's energy and public utilities policies as favoring big business. He launched an attack on the Dixon-Yates agreement of 1954 as a precursor to the ultimate abolition of the Tennessee Valley Authority. Olds died of a heart attack on August 4, 1960, in Bethesda, Maryland.

—AES

Oliphant, Charles A.
(1909–1960) *chief counsel, Bureau of Internal Revenue*

The son of a government lawyer and law professor, Oliphant was born on July 26, 1909, in Kirklin, Indiana. He attended Wabash College, Johns Hopkins University, and Columbia University. In 1934 he received a law degree from the University of Maryland. During the 1930s Oliphant worked for the Federal Land Bank and the Regional Agricultural Credit Corporation as well as the Farm Credit Administration. In 1939 he joined the Bureau of Internal Revenue (BIR) as special attorney in the office of chief counsel. He remained there until 1942, when he became an assistant general counsel of the Treasury Department. In 1947 Oliphant was made BIR chief counsel. During his three years tenure the BIR brought income tax evasion charges against several organized crime figures, including Ralph Capone, brother of Al Capone.

In the fall of 1951 a House Ways and Means subcommittee, chaired by Representative CECIL R. KING (D-Calif.), began investigating reports of irregularities in tax collection and in prosecution of tax fraud. On November 29, T. LAMAR CAUDLE, former head of the Justice Department Tax Division, testified that he and Oliphant had accepted a free plane ride in 1947 from North Carolina textile executive Troy Whitehead, who was under investigation for tax fraud. Caudle said they had flown to Florida for a fishing trip. He added that in 1949 he had successfully pressured Oliphant to have tax liens removed from the executive's property. On December 4 Abraham Teitelbaum, once gangster Al Capone's laywer, told the King subcommittee that Caudle, Oliphant, and other BIR officials were part of a Washington clique accepting "shakedowns." Teitelbaum claimed that Frank Nathan and Bert K. Naster had tried to extort half a million dollars from him in 1950. According to Teitelbaum, the two men said he would have "trouble" if he did not pay and claimed influence with Oliphant, Caudle, and two former BIR commissioners.

All those named denied involvement. On December 5 Oliphant resigned his post. He insisted he was not part of any clique seeking bribes or payoffs and wrote an angry letter to President Truman denouncing the panel for providing a "forum" for "sensational and irresponsible statements." Oliphant claimed the "attacks, vilification, rumor and innuendo [were] beyond the point of human endurance." He further contended: "Without inquiry of me, without a shred of credence to link my name to the alleged plot, the forum of a responsible Congressional Committee was made available for hurtling sensational and irresponsible charges throughout the country." At the same time he released a financial statement that revealed he had accepted a $1,300 loan from a Washington investigator, HENRY "The Dutchman" GRUNEWALD, who had been mentioned several times in the Teitelbaum case. Oliphant demanded a public hearing, but when King quickly scheduled one, his attorney announced he was sick, "suffering from shock."

When Oliphant finally testified on December 13–14, he claimed his friendship with Grunewald was "essentially social" but admitted that he had given BIR jobs to applicants suggested by Grunewald. He testified that upon Grunewald's urging he had speeded up prosecution of the Teitelbaum case. Oliphant admitted accepting a trip to the Kentucky Derby, tickets to the World Series, and other gifts and loans from defendants in tax cases. He traveled to the World Series in the private plane of a friend, Poncet Davis, who was being investigated for tax fraud. He denied any improper actions on behalf of his friends, claiming he had always disqualified himself. *Time* magazine later characterized him as "Washington's most diligent freeloader." King remonstrated him for his poor discretion. After the conclusion of Oliphant's testimony, King criticized him from protecting his friends and granting them considerations not afforded the average citizen. Oliphant responded, "I know of my own integrity, and I know of my pride in my name." Further testimony in 1952 showed that Oliphant had interceded in several tax cases upon the request of members of Congress.

Oliphant returned to private practice after his resignation. In 1952 he received temporary permission to represent clients before the Treasury Department. He died of a heart attack on March 29, 1960, in Washington, D.C.

—JF

Olson, James B. E.
(1895–1957) *Bureau of Internal Revenue official*
James B. E. Olson was born on March 1895 in Brooklyn, New York. After attending Holy Cross, he began a career as an insurance solicitor. In 1934 he was named a deputy chief of the Income Tax Division of the Bureau of Internal Revenue's (BIR) New York office. He rose though the ranks of the New York BIR, becoming deputy chief collector of the first district, which included Long Island and Staten Island. Olson left the bureau in 1944 when he was passed over for the open collector's position because Brooklyn Democratic chief Frank V. Kelley insisted to Commissioner of Internal Revenue ROBERT E. HANNEGAN that his man, James P. Marcelle, be given the position. He then went to work for a wine producer named Joseph Applebaum, who paid Olson $100,000 for public relations work from early 1945 to the middle of 1946.

In 1946 Olson founded the J. B. E. Olson Company to sell aluminum automobile and truck bodies. The following year BIR commissioner Joseph Nunan appointed Olson district supervisor of the Alcohol Tax Unit (ATU) in the BIR's third district, which included all of Manhattan north of 34th Street. As supervisor, Olson was responsible for collecting millions of dollars in liquor taxes each year. In 1948 Olson and Nunan became vice presidents of the American Lithofold Corporation, a St. Louis printing firm that later obtained a loan from the Reconstruction Finance Corporation (RFC). The RFC loan was allegedly obtained through political pressure exerted by high Democratic officials.

In 1951 Olson was implicated in a series of emerging tax scandals. On August 24, 1951, following newspaper stories questioning the legality of his association with Lithofold and his own company, Olson resigned as New York ATU head. A House Ways and Means subcommittee, chaired by Representative CECIL R. KING (D-Calif.), investigating charges of corruption in the BIR and the Justice Department, then focused on his activities. On August 28 King charged that Lithofold had paid Olson for landing printing contracts from liquor companies under his jurisdiction. He also said Olson's truck and automobile body company had made sales to breweries in the Third District. The next day Lithofold confirmed it had paid Olson commissions in 1949 and 1950. In September Olson testified before the King subcommittee and admitted having earned sales commissions but said all he had done was "make two phone calls." Lithofold officials disputed his testimony, claiming that Olson was deeply involved with their liquor accounts. Olson also testified that he split the commissions with Nunan and James P. Finnegan, a former BIR collector in St. Louis. On September 25 he admitted that he earned his Lithofold commissions by "influencing" liquor dealers but denied his actions were improper or illegal.

In April 1952 the King subcommittee uncovered evidence that suggested Olson had interceeded with Nunan on behalf of his friends. King charged that in the mid-1940s Nunan had twice reversed unfavorable findings of ATU field agents to grant Joseph Applebaum, Olson's employer, federal permits to sell wine. On April 29 Olson refused to testify on the grounds of possible self-incrimination. The next day tax agents revealed that he had spent more than $213,000 during 1947–50 although his total known income was $178,000.

Olson returned to his truck company after his resignation. In September 1956 he pleaded guilty in Brooklyn Federal Court to cheating the government of $22,000 in income taxes in a five-year period. He was given a suspended sentence in November. Olson died on October 4, 1957, in New York City.

—JF

O'Neal, Edward A(sbury), III

(1875–1958) *president, American Farm Bureau*
Edward O'Neal was born on his grandfather's Alabama cotton plantation in Florence, Alabama,

on October 26, 1875. He received an A.B. from Washington and Lee University in 1898 and then began farming his own 1900-acre plantation. Elected vice president of the Alabama Farm Bureau Federation in 1922, he became its president the next year. From 1924 to 1931 he was vice president of the American Farm Bureau Federation, which represented large farmers. In 1931 O'Neal was elected president of the bureau; he held the post until 1947. Under his direction the bureau's membership grew from 276,000 in 1931 to 1.12 million in 1946. He developed the organization into a powerful lobby molding farm policy in the New and Fair Deals. *Time* called him "the most powerful spokesman U.S. farmers ever had." During the 1930s he supported attempts to increase farm income by limiting production. O'Neal was also an originator of the idea of parity, by which prices farmers received for crops were tied to prices paid for manufacturered goods during a specific period of farm prosperity. This formed the basis of Roosevelt's agricultural policy.

During the immediate postwar period O'Neal opposed continuation of price controls. Appearing before the Price Decontrol Board in April 1946, he advocated free markets for the farmer as in the "long-term interests of the nation." However, shocked by the postwar fall in cotton prices, O'Neal quickly reversed his stand and urged a return to the government restrictions on growth. At the annual convention of the Farm Bureau in December 1946, he demanded that "the ever-normal granary, commodity loans and all price stabilizing features of the old farm program be continued, because they proved their worth in peace as well as war." He dismissed the idea of postwar liberals that farm prosperity depended upon industrial full employment. He argued that since there were only slightly more industrial laborers than farm workers, prosperity depended upon farmers receiving parity. O'Neal opposed the theory, propounded by many midwestern farmers, that low farm income could be met by expanding demand and subsidizing food for the poor. Instead, he predicted a postwar farm depression unless there was a return to rigid parity. In 1947 the issue came to a climax at the annual Farm Bureau Convention. O'Neal was stepping down after 15 years at the helm of the Farm Bureau, and southerners, who championed O'Neal's gospel of high, fixed price supports, could not find an ideological heir willing to run. The midwestern farmers succeeding in electing ALLAN B. KLINE and in getting the convention to endorse a policy of flexible price supports.

O'Neal continued active in agricultural affairs during the 1950s. Although a life-long Democrat, he urged farmers to vote for DWIGHT D. EISENHOWER in 1952 because of Truman's emphasis on flexible parity. O'Neal died on February 26, 1958, in Florence, Alabama.

—AES

Oppenheimer, J. Robert
(1904–1967) *physicist; chairman, General Advisory Committee, Atomic Energy Commission*

The son of German-born textile importer, J. Robert Oppenheimer was born on April 22, 1904, in New York City. He graduated from Harvard summa cum laude in 1925 and went on to pursue graduate studies at Cambridge. He received his doctorate in physics from the University of Göttingen in 1927. In 1929, after additional studies in Leyden, Zurich, and a Harvard, Oppenheimer began teaching concurrently at the University of California at Berkeley and the California Institute of Technology at Pasadena. He was highly respected for his comprehensive mastery of atomic physics and his theoreti-

(*left to right*) Leslie Groves and J. Robert Oppenheimer, Alamogordo, New Mexico, 1945 (*Harry S. Truman Library, Lansing Lamont*)

cal work during the 1930s on the positron and the theory of "gravitational collapse." Oppenheimer was nevertheless most noted for his inspirational and lucid teaching.

Oppenheimer first became interested in the possibility of an atomic bomb in 1939 after hearing Niels Bohr's explanation of the vast amount of energy that could be liberated during uranium fission. He spent much of his spare time making rough calculations of the critical mass that could cause an explosion, and, in 1941, he began on his own initiative to work on the problems of fission at the Lawrence Radiation Laboratory in Berkeley. Because of his impressive work there, Oppenheimer was asked by scientist Arthur Compton to devote himself full time to the Manhattan District Project, the atomic bomb research project Compton had helped organize. Oppenheimer's suggestion that all Canadian and U.S. atomic research efforts be concentrated in one spot led to the creation of a "super" laboratory at Los Alamos, New Mexico, in March 1943. Appointed director of the laboratory, Oppenheimer used his personal magnetism to persuade top nuclear physicists to join the project, despite the stringent security regulations to which they had to submit.

Because of his former left-wing political associations, Oppenheimer had trouble receiving security clearance for his post as director of Los Alamos in 1943. However, General LESLIE S. GROVES, convinced of Oppenheimer's indispensibility to the Manhattan Project, demanded immediate security clearance for him. Later that year Oppenheimer volunteered to army counterintelligence officers his knowledge of a Soviet attempt to gain U.S. atomic secrets and eventually named his friend Haakon Chevalier, a language lecturer at Berkeley, as the intermediary. In 1942 Chevalier had been approached by George Eltenton, a British engineer, who suggested an interchange of scientific information with the Russians. Chevalier had mentioned this to Oppenheimer, and both men had dismissed the idea as out of the question.

During 1944 and 1945 the development of the atomic bomb progressed at Los Alamos under Oppenheimer's supervision. In April 1945, before the first bomb had been tested, Oppenheimer was appointed to a panel of scientists to advise President Harry S Truman's Interim Committee on Atomic Policy. Despite the hope of many of the Manhattan Project scientists that the bomb would be given a purely technical demonstration, Oppenheimer and the other panel scientists advised "direct military use" of the weapon against Japan to end the war quickly and save American lives. They recommended that a dual military and civilian target be chosen to demonstrate the bomb's destructive power and suggested it be dropped without prior warning. On July 16, 1945, the first atomic bomb was successfully tested in the desert near Los Alamos, shocking Oppenheimer and other scientists present with the magnitude of the explosion. The United States dropped the A-bomb on Hiroshima on August 6. Criticized for the failure of the advisory panel to protest the use of the weapon without warning on a civilian target, Oppenheimer later wrote, "What was expected of this committee of experts was primarily a technical opinion. . . ."

After the war Oppenheimer was heralded by the public as the "father of the atomic bomb" and awarded a Medal of Merit by Truman for his direction of the Los Alamos laboratory. While enjoying the prestige and influence generated by his wartime work, Oppenheimer became increasingly ambivalent about atomic weapons research. At first he stressed the importance of secrecy and of continuing the work of weapons development in the face of an almost certain Soviet atomic rivalry. But while he claimed he felt no guilt for the creation of the bomb, he later wrote ". . . the physicists have known sin, and this is a knowledge they cannot lose." In the autumn of 1945 he resigned his post at Los Alamos and helped draw up the Acheson-Lilienthal proposal, which called for international controls for atomic energy and a free interchange of scientific information among countries. Oppenheimer served as consultant to BERNARD M. BARUCH, who presented the plan to the United Nations in 1946. The proposal was rejected by the Russians.

In 1947 Oppenheimer returned to the academic world as director of the Institute for Advanced Study at Princeton. He also continued to advise officials of the State Department and the Pentagon. That year he was appointed chairman of the General Advisory Committee (GAC) to the Atomic Energy Commission (AEC). After the successful test of the first Russian atomic bomb in 1949, the GAC was asked for recommendations on the advisability of producing a hydrogen or fusion bomb, a project abandoned during the war due to technical difficulties. EDWARD TELLER, who had worked under Oppenheimer on the Manhattan Project, urged a crash program to develop the weapon. However, the GAC scientists felt that such a move was both morally and economically unjustifiable and advised against production. Nevertheless, Truman approved the project. When, in 1951, Teller presented new ideas that made the bomb technically feasible, the GAC became enthusiastic. Attempting to explain this reversal, Oppenheimer later wrote that when a project becomes "technically sweet," you go ahead with it and worry about what to do with it "only after you have had your technical success."

During the early 1950s the GAC, under Oppenheimer, remained dominated by scientists who believed that the United States must strengthen itself militarily to resist Soviet aggression but must not pour all its resources into ever larger and more powerful nuclear arms. Hoping to limit the arms race and keep the door open for negotiation of atomic controls, these men stressed the need to develop strategic alternatives to nuclear weapons.

During the Korean War Oppenheimer worked in Project Vista, which proposed the development of small tactical nuclear weapons for conventional ground warfare as an alternative to massive strategic bombing. In 1952 Truman named Oppenheimer chairman of a special State Department Advisory Committee on Disarmament. The committee's report, published in 1953, urged the Eisenhower administration to educate the public about the realities of nuclear warfare and to share atomic weapons information with America's Western European allies. Committed to a decrease in overall arms spending, the Eisenhower administration chose instead to center U.S. defense policy on massive nuclear weapons.

After 1952 Oppenheimer's influence in the government waned. He served only occasionally as a special consultant, though he maintained top level security clearance, allowing him access to atomic secrets. In 1953, however, in the midst of Senator JOSEPH R. MCCARTHY's (R-Wisc.) anticommunist crusade, William L. Borden, former executive director of the Joint Committee on Atomic Energy, sent FBI director J. EDGAR HOOVER a letter indicating that Oppenheimer was probably a security risk. As a result, President Dwight D. Eisenhower suspended Oppenheimer's security clearance pending a review of his past Communist associations. In April 1954 Oppenheimer received a hearing before a special board appointed by the AEC. Almost all of his former colleagues at Los Alamos attested to his loyalty. However, his leftist ties during the 1930s, his equivocation about the Chevalier matter in 1943, and his ambivalence toward the production of the hydrogen bomb led the board to uphold the suspension of his security clearance. When Oppenheimer filed an appeal with the AEC, the commission upheld the decision.

After the 1954 hearing Oppenheimer devoted himself to directing the work at the Institute for Advanced Study and to investigating the spiritual and intellectual problems raised by modern nuclear physics. In December 1963 President Lyndon B. Johnson, acting on the wishes of President John F. Kennedy, presented Oppenheimer with the Enrico Fermi Award. Oppenheimer died of cancer on February 18, 1967, in Princeton, New Jersey.

There is a disagreement as to whether Oppenheimer gave information to the Soviets. Authors Allen Weinstein and Alexander Vassiliev have noted Soviet cables decoded by the military intelligence's Venona Project, indicate Oppenheimer was a member of the American Communist Party, but said there is no corroborating evidence. The two contend the Soviets had hopes that Oppenheimer would spy for them, but further argue that NKGB station chief Grigory Heifetz's inability to have any of the Manhattan Project's scientists spy for him would seem to indicate Oppenheimer did not spy for the Soviets.

Another pair of Venona scholars, John Earl Haynes and Harvey Klehr, point out that while Oppenheimer was talked about in the Soviet cables back to Moscow, there has not appeared any Venona transcripts showing him talking to the Russians. Haynes and Klehr also cast doubt on the spy story, but they do note Oppenheimer had strong ties to the Communists in the late 1930s and early 1940s, and that while nothing so far has been proved about him personally spying, he may have been indifferent early in the Manhattan Project to spying that was occurring until he reported in mid-1943 his conversation with Chevalier.

Venona researchers Herbert Romerstein and Eric Breindel point to a list a top Soviet agent sent to Moscow of the site where atomic research was taking place. All the names but one were in the clear, and that one was Oppenheimer, whose code name was "Veskel." The NKVD in March 1945 ordered its New York office to send agent "Guran" (unidentified) to go "re-establish contact with 'Veskel'... as soon as possible"—evidently indicating there had been previous contact. But this was only circumstantial evidence. Romerstein and Breindel point to

the 1994 revelations of Soviet chief of atomic bomb espionage Pavel Sudoplatov that Oppenheimer had handed over classified information. This caused an uproar in the United States and the American Physical Society denounced Sudoplatov's accusations as false. Sudoplatov's coauthors of the book found that Sudoplatov was trying to get back in favor with the Soviet leadership after he fell from grace with Lavrenti Beria in 1953. In 1982 he appealed to Soviet leader Yuri Andropov and the Politburo, reminding them of his achievements—including obtaining classified information from Oppenheimer, Klaus Fuchs, ENRICO FERMI, and others in Enormous (the Soviet code name for the Manhattan Project). Romerstein and Breindel insist that it would have been foolhardy to lie to the former KGB head and then dictator Andropov, who could have easily checked on the veracity of Sudoplatov's boasting. But Sudoplatov's accusations are still shrouded in controversy, and it may not be until all relevant Soviet intelligence files are opened that this case will be resolved, if even then as any such records might have already been destroyed. (See *The Eisenhower Years* Volume)

—DAE

Oxnam, G(arfield) Bromley
(1891–1953) *Methodist bishop; president, World Council of Churches for North and South America*

The son of a mining executive, G. Bromley Oxnam was born on August 14, 1891, in Sonora, California, and traveled all over the world with his father. He graduated from the University of Southern California in 1913 and received a bachelor of theology degree from Boston University two years later. Oxnam was ordained in 1916 and first served as pastor in rural Poplar, California. From 1917 to 1927 he was the pastor of the Church of All Nations in Los Angeles. He supported labor unions and longshoremen in their 1923 strike, and the Bureau of Investigation (later the FBI) began a file on him. In 1927 Oxnam became professor of practical theology at Boston University. In 1928 he was appointed president of DePauw University, a post he held until 1936. While president, Oxnam abolished the Reserve Officers Training Corps, and permitted the students to dance.

Elected a Methodist bishop in 1936, Oxnam was assigned to the Omaha, Nebraska, area. He came under attack from conservatives for his policies at DePauw and his liberal positions in politics and theology. Some conservative religious groups felt Oxnam's beliefs unorthodox and thought he did not espouse the divinity of Christ. In 1939 Oxnam became bishop of the Boston area; five years later he became bishop of New York. In 1952 he was chosen to head the prestigious Washington area.

The Truman administration in late 1945 convinced Oxnam to chair a commission to look into relief and refugee conditions in war torn Germany. This body gave Truman a report that influenced America's occupation policy.

By the late 1940s Oxnam had become recognized as a champion of minority groups and organized labor as well as a left-wing proponent of a "new postwar world order." Oxnam denounced the influence of the military in the formation of American foreign policy. Although he had defended the use of the atomic bomb in ending World War II, Oxnam opposed the use of force against communism, claiming only the "dynamic faith of Christ" could conquer it. He urged the use of economic aid to stop Communist expansion, saying in 1946 "Communism makes no headway where plenty exists." He created and led the Methodist Crusade for a New World Order, which advocated that Methodists favor U.S. leadership in founding the United Nations. For this work he received praise from Presidents Franklin Roosevelt and Harry Truman. As a member of the World Council of Churches, Oxnam urged negotiations between the United States and the Soviet Union and called for an end to the arms race.

Because of his politics Oxnam came under a great deal of criticism, much of it focused on his affiliation with so-called Communist-front groups, such as the Council of American-Soviet friendship. Oxnam repeatedly denied that he was a Communist or involved with Communist-front organizations. In 1949 he attacked "Red-baiting," calling the "labeling of patriotic citizens as Communists" a new form of lynching. And yet he had helped found the anticommunist Americans for Democratic Action.

After World War II Oxnam became the spokesman for Protestants concerned with the political aims of the Roman Catholic Church. He bluntly attacked what he considered Catholic attempts to break down separation of church and state. As president of the Federal Council of Churches, in 1946 Oxnam warned of a Catholic threat to religious freedom. He claimed that behind a public willing-

ness to accept religious tolerance, the Catholic Church actually wanted to impose its faith through the government. In response the *Pilot*, a Catholic publication, scored Oxnam for creating "confusion and pain" among Christians with his views. In 1948 Oxnam helped found an organization called Protestants and Other Americans United for Separation of Church and State. Catholic Archbishop Richard J. Cushing termed the group "a refined form of the Klu Klux Klan." The following year Oxnam warned of a "worldwide crisis" facing Methodists, and he compared the Catholic Church and the Communist Party. He claimed Catholics did not believe in "religious liberty as we understand it," and Communists "in civil liberty as we understand it."

In 1950 and 1951 Oxnam was in the forefront of a Protestant effort to end U.S. representation at the Vatican. Oxnam and other Protestant leaders urged Truman not to replace the wartime envoy to the Vatican on the grounds that such recognition would show favoritism toward the Catholic Church and would jeopardize church-state separation. Truman eventually abandoned the idea of reappointing a personal representative to the Holy See. An envoy was not sent until 1970.

Oxnam was also a vocal critic of Catholic attempts to gain federal funds for parochial education. He frequently clashed with FRANCIS CARDINAL SPELLMAN and other Catholic leaders over the issue. In 1952 he joined other Protestants in defending the government's decision to withhold tax money from church schools. He warned against drawing the conclusion "that because religion is essential to the free society, therefore the hierarchy should be permitted to get its prehensile hands in the public treasury."

In 1953 Oxnam angrily attacked the House Un-American Activities Committee (HUAC) after Chairman HAROLD H. VELDE (R-Ill.) suggested a probe of possible Communists in the American clergy, and Representative Donald Jackson said Oxnam was "to the Communist front what Man O'War was to thoroughbred racing." Oxman scored anticommunist crusaders who he said "created as much national distrust" as the Communists. HUAC reluctantly cleared Oxnam of any Communist Party affiliation.

Oxnam retired from active leadership in the Methodist Church in 1960. While recuperating from a successful operation to correct Parkinson's disease in 1962, Oxnam caught bronchial pneumonia. He died on March 12, 1963, in White Plains, New York.

—JF

P

Pace, Frank, Jr.

(1912–1988) *director, Bureau of the Budget; secretary of the army*

Pace, the son of a prominent Little Rock, Arkansas, attorney, was born in that city on July 5, 1912. He graduated from Princeton University in 1933 and received his LL.B. degree from Harvard three years later. In 1936 he became assistant district attorney in Arkansas's 12th judicial district. From 1938 to 1940 Pace was general counsel to the state department of

Portrait of Frank Pace, Jr. *(Harry S. Truman Library)*

revenue. During World War II he served in the U.S. Army Air Corps's Air Transport Command. Pace left the army in early 1946 and worked for a brief period as a special assistant on tax matters to Attorney General TOM C. CLARK. In May of that year he became executive assistant to the Postmaster General. President Truman appointed him assistant director of the Bureau of the Budget in January 1948. The following year he became director.

At 36 Pace was the youngest man ever to occupy the post. As director, he helped Truman formulate the record peacetime budget needed to support the administration's Fair Deal and military preparedness programs. Although a believer in the principle of a balanced budget, Pace rejected the annually balanced budget and the cyclical budget. He warned that as long as the cold war existed, the United States would have to accept deficit spending. Pace also instituted the "performance budget" recommended by the Hoover Commission, published a readable summary of the 1,500-page budget, and established the President's Management Appraisal Program and the President's Advisory Committee on Management Improvement. He also prepared for Truman 29 plans for simplifying the organization of federal agencies.

In April 1950 Truman named Pace as GORDON GRAY's successor as secretary of the army. Pace helped formulate U.S. policy toward the war in Korea. He supported Truman's decision to limit military operations above the 38th parallel in order to make it clearly understood that U.S. operations in Korea "were designed to restore peace there and to restore the border." In May 1953 Pace was called before the Senate Armed Services Committee's Preparedness Subcommittee during an investigation of ammunition shortages in Korea. He testified that, until January 1953, fighting in Korea was done solely with World War II surplus, leaving the reserves severely depleted. The subcommittee's final report determined that the shortages had resulted in the "needless loss of American lives" but that "revised procedures had replenished stocks."

As secretary of the army, Pace intensified military research and development in nuclear weapon technology. He established a long-range estimates program and instituted a performance budget for the army.

Pace did not like the fact that, while the army chief of staff reported to the secretary of the army, in that capacity, he, as a Joint Chief of Staff executive agent, bypassed the secretary to report to the JCS and thence to the defense secretary and the president. Pace thought he was not being fully informed, and he was embarrassed when he could not answer questions about the problems at a prisoner of war camp in South Korea. He also disagreed with Defense Secretary ROBERT A. LOVETT when the latter wanted the army to become the executive agent for construction in the U.S. European Command. Pace told Lovett that joint commanders reported to the chief of staff, not to him and that he, as secretary, did not have authority in the matter. But observers thought he did, which put the army secretary in an untenable situation. Lovett rejected Pace's argument, and made him executive agent. Pace reluctantly agreed, but only if his authority was established in the matter. Pace also advocated that the service secretaries should have cabinet status and should sometimes be allowed to attend National Security Council meetings.

Pace resigned his post with the coming of the Eisenhower administration. He was then elected executive vice president and director of General Dynamics Corporation, one of the main defense contractors in the United States. In 1955 he became chief executive officer of the company. Pace resigned his post in 1962 to join the International Executives Services Corps. He served as the first chairman of the Corporation of Public Broadcasting. Pace died of a heart attack on January 8, 1988, in Greenwich, Connecticut. (See *The Eisenhower Years* Volume)

—MLB

Patman, (John) (William) Wright

(1893–1976) *member of the House of Representatives*

The son of a Texas tenant farmer, Wright Patman was born on August 6, 1893, in Patman's Switch, Texas. He studied law while working as a sharecropper and obtained his degree from Cumberland University in Tennessee in 1916. Between 1920 and 1924 he served two terms in the Texas House of Representatives as a Democrat. After an additional two years as district attorney in Texarkana, Patman was elected to the U.S. House in 1928 as an anti–Ku Klux Klan candidate from the poor northeastern corner of Texas.

Patman quickly emerged as a populist opponent of big business and banking interests. In 1932 he called for the impeachment of financier Andrew Mellon, then secretary of the Treasury, for conflict of interest. He repeatedly introduced a veterans' bonus bill as an economic stimulant against the depression. The bill was finally passed over President Roosevelt's veto in 1936. In the same year Patman sponsored the Robinson-Patman Anti–Chain Store Act, which prevented chain stores from unfairly undercutting smaller rivals by discriminatory price reductions.

During World War II Patman fought to win a fair share of defense contracts for small business. After the war he was a prominent figure on the Committee on Small Business, established to solve the problems of peacetime reconversion. In February 1945 he introduced to the House a companion measure to the Full Employment bill of 1945, sponsored in the Senate by Senators ROBERT WAGNER (D-N.Y.) and JAMES E. MURRAY (D- Mont.), and, in September, the representative publicly attacked attempts to prevent or dilute full employment legislation. Patman's original bill was seen as too liberal to pass, but Patman realized the importance of getting a compromise bill to the floor with the hope of making improvements with floor amendments and in the conference committee with senators. The law finally passed as the Employment Act of 1946, which Patman voted for. The federal government, in pursuit of the law, tended to rely on countercyclical spending measures and the Federal Reserve's manipulations of monetary policy and interest rates.

Patman had a demagogic tendency to label conservative opponents as fascists. When a group called the Committee for Constitutional Government planned to defeat Patman in 1944, the congressman denounced its officials as fascist. He argued that when Republicans labeled people or groups as communists, they were using the tactics of Adolf Hitler and Joseph Goebbels and were working to destroy American democracy.

Patman's concern with the problems of small business was intensified in the postwar period. Much of the legislation he personally sponsored during the Truman years involved antitrust laws and the protection of small businessmen from unfair competition. Patman introduced several new bills dealing with the business practices of chain stores. He drafted legislation for measures against price discrimination, for the strengthening of the Sherman Antitrust Act, for the liberalization of federal credit unions loans, and for a fair share of government contracts to small firms. In the immediate postwar period he fought for the extension of the Smaller War Plants Corporation and, with the outbreak of the Korean War, for the establishment of a Small Defense Plants Corporation. He opposed government divestiture of rubber plants and attacked big business for marking up its prices in sales to the federal government. According to Patman's biographer Nancy Beck Young, this Texas representative of the mid-20th century still held to antitrust tenets that were more common in the 19th century.

In other areas as well, Patman's legislative activities represented a furthering of New Deal policies in the postwar period. Between 1945 and 1947 he introduced or supported legislation for appropriations to the federal mortgage insurance fund, price ceilings on new and old construction, and preservation of the tax-exemption status of cooperatives. His interest in housing culminated in the Patman Emergency Housing Act of 1947, making cheap housing available to middle- and lower-income groups. He had also wanted to place a limit on the price of new and used homes, but this provision was eliminated in the House. According to Young, community was central to Patman's idealism and home ownership was a critical part of his goals. He opposed all postwar extensions of rent control passed by Congress. In 1948 Patman clashed with Republican senators during hearings on transportation prices, stating that "selfish, greedy big interests" wanted to maintain the wartime "basing point" system of calculating freight prices. The representative favored uniform national "free-on-board" charges, which he thought

would prevent discriminatory pricing. He voted against the Republican tax cut of 1948 and supported raising the minimum wage to 75 cents an hour in 1949. In 1950 and 1951 Patman voiced reservations about the emancipation of the Federal Reserve Bank from the U.S. Treasury, believing that institutional freedom for the Federal Reserve would mean higher interest rates. Yet he was pleased to see the Federal Reserve emancipated from the Treasury in one sense: it opened the way for more congressional oversight of the central bank.

When SAM T. RAYBURN said he would not run for minority leader after the Democrats lost the House of Representatives in the 1946 mid-term elections, Patman was one of a group of congressmen who prevailed upon him to serve in that post.

Patman followed the pattern of Southern Democrats of the time and opposed civil rights legislation, such as the anti–poll tax bill, the antilynching bill, and the Fair Employment Practices Commission bills. Young says that Patman viewed northern meddling in southern race relations in the same resentful way he viewed northern economic dominance of the South.

Patman generally supported the Truman administration's global containment policies. He voted for the loan to Great Britain in 1946, aid to Greece and Turkey in 1947, and the Marshall Plan in 1948. The following year he voted for the Mutual Defense Assistance Act, which authorized $820 million in military aid to the newly founded North Atlantic Treaty Organization.

A vigorous opponent of organized labor, Patman supported the Case labor disputes bill of 1946, which provided for the creation of a permanent labor-management mediation board to seek injunctions against strikes or lock-outs affecting the public interest. Although he did not cast a vote on the Taft-Hartley bill in 1947, he did support the Defense Production Act Amendment of 1952, which requested President Truman to invoke Taft-Hartley against the steel strike of that year.

During subsequent administrations Patman continued to advocate the populist policies that had brought him prominence during the Roosevelt and Truman eras. He maintained his fight for government support of small business and attacked the Federal Reserve Bank. In the 1950s Patman conducted an important investigation into tax-exempt foundations and the interlocking ownerships of the large commercial banks. He held the chairmanship of the House Committee on Banking and Currency from 1963 to 1975. In January 1976 Patman announced that he would not seek reelection; he died on March 7 of that year in Bethesda, Maryland. (See *The Eisenhower Years, The Kennedy Years, The Johnson Years, The Nixon/Ford Years* Volumes)

—JD

Patterson, Robert P(orter)
(1891–1952) *secretary of war*

Robert P. Patterson was born on February 12, 1891, in Glen Falls, New York. After graduating from Union College, Patterson went to Harvard Law School, where he received his degree in 1915. He left his New York law practice the following year to join the army. Patterson fought in World War I and was cited numerous times for bravery. He left the army in 1919 and returned to his practice. Patterson was appointed judge of the U.S. District Court for Southern New York in 1930 and judge of the Second Circuit Court of Appeals nine years later. President Roosevelt appointed the Republican assistant secretary of war in July 1940 and undersecretary of war that December.

A dynamic, effective administrator, Patterson supervised the army's $100 billion procurement program during World War II. To speed things along Patterson awarded most contracts to large corporations. Some observers see this as the beginning of the military-industrial complex. He worked closely with Undersecretary of the Navy JAMES V. FORRESTAL, and the two men became known as an effective team. Upon Forrestal's recommendation, President Truman in September 1945 offered Patterson his choice of a seat on the U.S. Supreme Court or appointment as secretary of war. When Patterson replied that he would serve where he was most needed, Truman appointed him to succeed HENRY L. STIMSON in the War Department.

Patterson was immediately faced with the problem of demobilization. In September General GEORGE C. MARSHALL promised that all men with two or more years service would be discharged by late winter. Patterson, however, favored a large army to meet U.S. commitments abroad and to check Soviet expansion. The Pentagon declared that the rate of demobilization was too rapid and, in January 1946, announced the discharge date for two-year men would be pushed back. During an inspection tour of Pacific bases, Patterson faced angry demonstrations of up to 10,000 soldiers and sailors. On Guam angry soldiers burned him in effigy.

During the same period Patterson was forced to defend the Army against charges by the Senate War Investigating Committee that the occupation of Germany was ineffective. A committee report, issued in December 1946, charged that there was widespread corruption by army personnel and declared that denazification was a glaring failure. Patterson called the report "distorted" and "erroneous." He sent the editor of the *Saturday Evening Post*, Forest Davis, to Germany to report on conditions. In a 10-page letter to Senator ROBERT A. TAFT (R-Ohio), Davis praised the U.S. commander, General LUCIUS D. CLAY for avoiding "vindictiveness in his attitude or policies" and called the overall record "magnificent."

The secretary was an important advocate of the military control of atomic energy. His stand put him at odds with Truman, who had come out strongly for civilian control provided by the McMahon bill in February 1946. However, after an amendment was added to the bill to establish a military liaison committee, Patterson reversed his position and, in April 1946, deemed it "wholly acceptable." The measure was passed in July 1946. Patterson then took part in the transfer of atomic energy from the War Department to the Atomic Energy Commission in January 1947.

Patterson supported desegregation in the armed forces, and WALTER F. WHITE, the leader of the National Association for the Advancement of Colored People, saluted him as "one of our generation's noblest and most unselfish men."

Patterson was a strong advocate of the use of military aid to prevent Communist expansion. In February 1947 he, Forrestal, and Marshall sent a memorandum to President Truman advocating immediate aid to Greece and Turkey in order to stop Communist aggression. Patterson testified before the Senate Foreign Relations Committee in March 1947 in support of the $400 million assistance plan. He maintained that sending combat troops to either Greece or Turkey was "not contemplated." However, he advocated that $100 million be made immediately available to strengthen the Greek army against guerrillas. In June 1947 Patterson testified before the House Foreign Affairs Committee in favor of military aid to Latin American countries to prevent them from seeking weapons and training "elsewhere."

Throughout his 10 years in the War Department, Patterson was a vigorous spokesman for unification of the armed forces. As undersecretary, he had urged the creation of a single Department of Defense, and, as secretary, he emerged as a major proponent of a strong, centralized defense establishment. Patterson supported a proposal to provide a single secretary of the armed forces and a single military chief of staff with subordinate chiefs for each branch of the services. Under the plan a secretary of defense would determine policy and have primary responsibility for administration and budgeting aspects of the department.

Legislation embodying his views was reported out of committee in April 1946. However, Patterson's old friend, Forrestal, criticized the measure as administratively illogical and a hindrance to research and development. Instead, he recommended that the secretary of defense be primarily a coordinator and that most power reside in the service secretaries. Truman asked Forrestal and Patterson to resolve their differences. The result was the National Security Act of 1947, a compromise. The secretary of defense was authorized to set "common policies" and supervise and coordinate the budget. However, the individual service secretaries had the right to appeal his decisions. The act also established the Joint Chiefs of Staff. Truman asked Patterson to accept the post of secretary of defense, but he declined for financial reasons. He returned to his law practice.

Patterson remained active in politics. He helped found a national committee in November 1947 to support passage of the Marshall Plan. He also spoke frequently in favor of universal military training. At congressional hearings in 1949 he called the North Atlantic Treaty Organization "a pact to preserve peace." After leaving government Patterson was elected president of the New York City Bar Association and the Council on Foreign Relations.

Patterson died in an airplane crash in Elizabeth, New Jersey, on January 22, 1952.

—TFS

Patton, James G(eorge)

(1902–1985) *president, National Farmers Union*
The son of an unsuccessful small farmer and mining engineer, James G. Patton was born on November 8, 1902, in Bazar, Kansas. He attended Western State College at Gunnison, Colorado. After a brief career as a physical education instructor in Colorado and Nevada schools, he returned to Western State as assistant business manager from 1927 to 1929. He

was cooperative insurance organizer for the Colorado Farmers Union from 1932 to 1934. Patton became the union's executive secretary in 1934 and its president in 1938.

In 1940 Patton rose to the presidency of the National Farmers Union (NFU), which had been founded in 1902 to represent the small farmers ignored by the American Farm Bureau Federation and the Grange. A supporter of the New Deal and cooperation between the "family farmer" and organized labor, Patton served on the Economic Stabilization Board and other wartime agencies. He was a steadfast supporter of the Farm Security Administration against the efforts of congressional and Farm Bureau conservatives to abolish it. Patton opposed inflated farm prices during World War II and demanded a "full employment" economy as a solution to the farm problem. His proposal in 1944 that government intervene in the economy to guarantee a minimum $40 billion investment to maintain full employment provided the theoretical base for the Employment Act of 1946. As representative of the small farmers of the Great Plains and Mountain States, he insisted that the family farm was the backbone of the nation's virtue and charged that its demise would result in "rural fascism." He advocated the creation of a Farmer-Labor Party to unite the "producing classes."

Patton was a major figure in American liberalism, with interests that extended far beyond the area of farm policy. After World War II he advocated federal aid to education and a national health plan. A member of the National Citizens Political Action Committee (NCPAC), Patton worked closely with liberals and labor groups to establish a reform coalition built around the producing classes. Although officially neutral, Patton leaned toward those segments of the liberal movement that advocated opening the liberal coalition to Communists. However, when Communists gained power in the NCPAC, he left the organization. Patton supported Secretary of Commerce HENRY A. WALLACE's demands for a reconciliation with the Soviet Union and the destruction of nuclear weapons. When the president announced the Truman Doctrine, the farm leader joined ELEANOR ROOSEVELT and other liberals in deploring his failure to first consult the United Nations. He went on radio to attack the administration in broadcasts sponsored by Wallace's Progressive Citizens of America, but he refused to support Wallace's third-party presidential bid, backing Truman in the election of 1948.

Patton clashed frequently with the Truman administration over farm policy. Patton maintained a friendship with Secretary of Agriculture CLINTON P. ANDERSON as long as their mutual goal was increased production—especially in the last months of the war. But after the war's abrupt end Anderson obsessed over falling farm goods' prices caused by high production. He began to argue for production restrictions, which led to complaints from Patton over Anderson's apparent leaning toward the American Farm Bureau's restrictionist philosophy. He opposed Anderson's decision to cut back production in order to maintain farm prices. Patton advocated a program of increased food production and consumption to keep farm income at wartime levels. He warned that "this country no longer will stand for the destruction of food or the restriction of its production while people are hungry and undernourished." As Allen Matusow noted, although the postwar food shortage shelved temporarily any talk of production quotas, the incident showed Anderson and Patton differed substantially over farm policy. Patton was further antagonized when Anderson appointed a conservative—rather than Patton's nominee—to head the Farm Security Administration, an agency that focused on poor farmers and agricultural laborers and which had long been the target of conservatives in Congress and the America Farm Bureau. Congress would disband the FSA in 1946 without complaint from Anderson, replacing it with the nonthreatening Farmer Home Administration. Anderson and Congress then gutted another preserve of liberals, the Bureau of Agricultural Economics. The gap between the secretary and Patton was widened further by Anderson's apparent refusal to testify to Congress on behalf of farmer and farm workers to be covered by Social Security. By May 1946 Patton was calling on Truman to oust Anderson. Truman refused. Soon the Farmers Union came out against the president himself. Patton wrote President Truman in May 1946 demanding Anderson's resignation. When the president refused, he announced, in July 1946, that Truman had permitted inflation, abandoned the New Deal, and was no longer in the NFU's confidence.

As leader of the small farmers, Patton criticized what he considered Anderson's favoritism toward wealthy corporate farm interests. In December 1945, when Anderson appointed a conservative to head the Farm Security Administration, Patton denounced

the action as a "bitter betrayal of millions of small farmers." He also attacked Anderson for weakening the Bureau of Agricultural Economics.

Patton became reconciled to the administration during 1948, when his friend CHARLES F. BRANNAN became secretary of agriculture. Brannan had long supported Patton's ideas on full employment, increased farm production, and the expansion of foreign markets. Truman easily secured Patton's backing for the Marshall Plan despite his qualms about failure to work through the United Nations, and the president appointed him to a special 12-man advisory board to administer the program.

Patton's views on agricultural policy were inconsistent in the late 1940s. He had spoken in congressional hearings during October 1947, simultaneously supporting rigid price supports at 90 percent of parity and increased production without government controls. In the spring of 1948 he appeared favorable to flexible price supports, backing the Hope-Aiken bill, which provided sliding controls on price/production ratios. This stand brought an outcry from the NFU, and he soon returned to backing rigid price supports. He was said to be the author of the Brannan Plan of 1949, which would have directly subsidized farmers but not curtailed production and would thus have aided the consumer by reducing food prices. He called it "a milestone in the history of agriculture."

Regarding the nuclear contest between the United States and Soviet Union as potentially disastrous, Patton responded with a plan for general disarmament to be followed by an annual U.S. contribution of $10 billion to a world development fund over a 15-year period. With ALBERT EINSTEIN and others, he signed a protest in February 1950 as a member of the National Council against Conscription, which attacked "the military establishment's infiltration" of the nation's colleges. Following the introduction of the Tydings Resolution which urged a new UN disarmament conference, Patton, in March 1950, proposed a U.S.-Soviet peace conference.

The invasion of South Korea put an end to Patton's pacifism, and, by 1951, he was suggesting an armed crusade against Communist "tyranny." As a member of the National Advisory Board on Mobilization Policy, he opposed CHARLES E. WILSON, head of the Office of Defense Mobilization, for what he saw as favoritism toward big business interests and neglect of farmers' needs. In a public letter to Wilson and ERIC A. JOHNSTON, head of the Economic Stabilization Agency, he demanded anti-inflation credit restrictions and profit limits on business.

Patton was a government consultant during the Eisenhower administration but was at odds with Secretary of Agriculture Ezra Taft Benson's program of flexible price supports. During the Kennedy administration he helped form Secretary of Agriculture Orville Freeman's program, designed to preserve the small family farm. As he had in the past, he supported a plan to sell wheat to the USSR and favored increased American food exports aboard and lower trade barriers. He retired from the NFU presidency in 1966. Between 1967 and 1969 he was president of the United World Federalists and from 1971 to 1973 served as a special consultant to the Pennsylvania Department of Agriculture. Patton died on February 17, 1985, in San Francisco, California. (See *The Eisenhower Years, The Kennedy Years* Volumes)

—AES

Pauley, Edwin W(endell)

(1903–1981) *U.S. reparations commissioner, adviser to the secretary of state on reparations*

Pauley was born on January 7, 1903, in Indianapolis, Indiana. To support himself through college and graduate school, Pauley worked as a laborer in California's oil fields. In 1923 he earned an M.S. from the University of California's College of Commerce and Business. During the next 15 years he amassed a fortune in the oil business. Pauley was active in Democratic politics and in 1932 and 1936 was a top fund-raiser for Franklin D. Roosevelt. Four years later he coordinated Democratic fund-raising in the West. As a result of Pauley's success, Roosevelt requested him to be the party's treasurer in 1942. Within two years the California oil magnate wrote off the party's $750,000 debt. A power in the inner ranks of the party, Pauley worked for the nomination of Harry S Truman as vice president in 1944. He and the president's appointments secretary, Major General Edwin M. "Pa" Watson, brought people into the White House who would criticize Vice President HENRY A. WALLACE, who wanted a second term, and kept out those who would have spoken well of him. When it looked like Wallace supporters were going to stampede the 1944 Democratic National Convention on behalf of the Vice President, Pauley told an aide to stop the organist

who was playing the Iowa state song—Iowa being Wallace's home state—even if it meant using an ax, presumably to cut the organ's cable. Pauley and other party leaders stopped the stampede, and the next day Truman was nominated on the second ballot. In addition to his political work, Pauley was a special representative on petroleum supplies with Great Britain and the Soviet Union during World War II.

In April 1945 President Truman appointed Pauley, whom he considered a trusted friend and adviser, to represent the United States on the Allied Reparations Commission. The new president chose Pauley because of his reputation as a tough bargainer with the Soviets and because of his help in the 1944 campaign. At Potsdam Pauley successfully renegotiated the reparations agreements promised by Roosevelt at Yalta. Roosevelt had agreed that Germany would be required to pay $20 billion in reparations, $10 billion to the Soviets, $10 billion to the West. However, following the Yalta Conference, the administration had come to realize that the agreement would cripple the German economy and create a dangerously weak state in the strategically vital center of Europe. Pauley, therefore, renegotiated a percentage settlement rather than an absolute sum. The Russians were guaranteed 40 percent of the reparations, the Western nations divided the remainder. Pauley then represented the United States for the next two years at reparations meetings over German and Japanese responsibilities.

In January 1946 Truman announced his intention to appoint Pauley assistant secretary of the navy with the hope that he would eventually succeed to the top position in the department. Liberals deplored this appointment because the oil magnate would have control of the vast naval oil reserves. In a series of articles, the *St. Louis Dispatch* implied a connection between Pauley's efforts to convince the federal government to stop its suit to assert ownership over the tidelands oil off California with his successful fund-raising activities among oil companies in 1944. During his confirmation hearings, Pauley testified that he had openly made known his belief that the states owned the tidelands, but that he never lobbied anyone on the matter. He said he never discussed the issue with Roosevelt or Secretary of the Interior HAROLD L. ICKES. Ickes had promised Truman he would not speak out against Pauley, but if he were called to testify he would have to tell the truth. It turned out that Ickes had let one of the senators on the committee know how he could tease damning information out of him on Pauley. Consequently, the secretary contradicted Pauley—not only was he interested in tidelands oil but had also tried to stop the federal case. According to Ickes, Pauley told him he could raise several thousand dollars from California oilmen for the Democrats if the suit were dropped. Pauley denied ever saying such a thing, asserting his regret that Ickes might have misinterpreted what he had said. Then Ickes produced memos purporting to show Pauley's attempts to pressure the secretary. Despite such devastating revelations, Truman would not withdraw his name. In a February 1946 press conference, Truman said Ickes could be mistaken. At that Ickes resigned, and he said the president had encouraged him to commit perjury to save Pauley's nomination. Initially the administration responded calmly to Ickes's resignation. Privately, Truman fumed that the attacks on Pauley were really meant for him. He was certain that Pauley had never lobbied him.

The Pauley affair soon proved to be a political liability for the president. Republicans raised the issue of corruption and cronyism. Editorial opinion, led by the *New York Times*, opposed the nomination. Although the Naval Affairs Committee affirmed Pauley's personal integrity, confirmation of the nomination appeared doubtful. Pauley asked Truman to withdraw his name from consideration in March. The incident, with the charges of cronyism, reminded many observers of Truman's past as part of Thomas J. Pendergast's political machine in Missouri. Yet others admired Truman's loyalty to a friend.

In December 1947 HAROLD E. STASSEN, a contender for the Republican presidential nomination, charged Pauley with being one of several "insiders in the national administration profiteering in food." This charge was prompted by a recent speech by Truman that inflation in food prices resulted from commodity speculators. Senate Appropriations Committee chairman STYLES BRIDGES launched an investigation into Stassen's allegations. Pauley conceded that while serving on the Reparations Commission he had speculated in food and clothing. He also acknowledged that in September 1947, when he had been temporary special assistant to Secretary of the Army KENNETH C. ROYALL, he had holdings in grains, hides, and other agricultural products. He called them "little transactions." They "were peanuts in the whole scheme of things . . . something less than one million dollars." He maintained

the investments were a wise and legitimate way "to protect my family" against the dollar's declining value. Pauley denied the charge that he had inside information to help his speculation endeavors and flatly refuted the accusation that the commodity traders pushed prices up. His clash with Stassen ended Pauley's hopes of acquiring any major posts in government. Following the termination of his service on the Reparations Commission, Pauley returned to business. Pauley died on July 28, 1981, in Beverly Hills, California.

—JB

Pearson, Drew (Andrew) (Russell)
(1896–1969) *syndicated columnist*

The son of an English professor, Drew Pearson was born on December 13, 1896, in Evanston, Illinois. He graduated from Swarthmore College in 1919. He served as a foreign correspondent until 1926, when the *United States Daily* (later *U.S. News and World Report*) hired him as its foreign editor. In 1929 he joined the staff of the *Baltimore Sun*. Two years later Pearson gained renown for his book *The Washington Merry-Go-Round*, an exposé written with journalist Robert Allen. In 1932 the two men began writing a column of the same name, which by 1942 was syndicated in 350 papers. In addition the two men had a popular radio program. In the mid-1930s they collaborated on two books, *Nine Old Men* and *Nine Old Men at the Crossroads*, both muckraking accounts of the U.S. Supreme Court. Pearson, a self-proclaimed liberal, supported civil rights, domestic welfare programs, foreign aid, and closer relations with the Soviet Union. However, his column usually focused on exposing corrupt political figures, often with ruthless zeal. President Franklin D. Roosevelt once labeled Pearson "a chronic liar." He was often sued for libel, but he frequently slipped the noose, and when he did not, damages were minimal.

Following World War II Pearson launched an attack on the Ku Klux Klan, then experiencing a revival. Challenged by the grand kleagle to air his opinions publicly, Pearson broadcast on July 26, 1946, from the steps of the Georgia State Capitol building. Frequently heckled by onlookers, he charged that the Klan was advancing the same policies of hate that Hitler had used in Germany. He went on to accuse gubernatorial candidate Eugene Talmadge of promising to place a Klan official at the head of the state bureau of investigation.

In the fall of 1947 Pearson organized a transcontinental Friendship Train to collect donations for the hungry in France and Italy. He contributed $10,000 to start the train rolling. The operation mushroomed, and Pearson supervised the distribution of 700 carloads of food. The idea for the Friendship Train coincided with the development of the Marshall Plan.

Pearson continued to be known primarily for his exposure of corruption and incompetence in government during the postwar period. He kept a close watch on the president's staff, criticized by liberals as court-house politicians, and ran a series of columns exposing some of their more questionable dealings. In 1949 Pearson attacked General HARRY H. VAUGHAN, Truman's military aide, for accepting a medal from Argentine dictator Juan Perón and suggested Vaughan should be removed. In response, Truman replied, "any S.O.B. who thinks he can cause any of these people to be discharged by me by some smart-aleck statement over the air or in the paper, he has another think coming." Pearson revealed the existence of an influence-peddling ring with connections to the White House, which sold government contracts for 5 percent of the contract price. Henry Vaughan was again involved in this scandal as was JOHN F. MARAGON.

Pearson did not confine his probes to the executive branch. During the campaign against commodities speculation in the late 1940s, he revealed that Senators John Bankhead (D-Ala.) and ELMER THOMAS (D-Okla.) were involved in cotton speculation. Pearson's taunts were often merciless. Senator KENNETH D. MCKELLAR (D-Tenn.) was so incensed by Pearson's references to his age that he punched the reporter.

Pearson was an early opponent of Senator JOSEPH R. MCCARTHY (R-Wisc.). In 1950, when the senator charged that members of the Communist Party were shaping State Department policy, Pearson systematically showed that only three of the 205 persons on McCarthy's presumed list were suspect. Pearson then opened his column to McCarthy's enemies, and one personal exposé after another appeared.

McCarthy counterattacked by dubbing Pearson "an instrument of international Communism." Pearson was vulnerable to such charges, because he used Communists and fellow-travelers as informants and, at times, as staff workers. The senator collected his most harmful accusations in a booklet which he distributed to the public. He also pressured Pearson's radio sponsor into terminating his contract. The antagonism between the two men climaxed in December 1950, when McCarthy slapped and kneed Pearson in the groin at the Sulgrave Club.

The exploits of General DOUGLAS MACARTHUR were also of special concern to Pearson. The columnist reported that MacArthur had ignored orders from the Pentagon and even from the White House while he commanded U.S. and UN military forces in Korea. In January 1951 Pearson reported on a secret conference between MacArthur and Truman, which had taken place the previous October. At the meeting MacArthur predicted victory in Korea by Christmas.

During the Eisenhower administration, Pearson shifted his attention to conflict of interest within the executive branch, such as that of presidential assistant Sherman Adams. In the 1960s he investigated such public figures as Adam Clayton Powell and Senator Thomas Dodd (D-Conn.). Pearson died on September 1, 1969, in Washington, D.C. (See *The Eisenhower Years, The Kennedy Years, The Johnson Years* Volumes)

—EF

Pepper, Claude (Denson)
(1900–1989) *member of the Senate*

Born September 8, 1900, in Dudley, Alabama, Claude Pepper taught elementary and high school in that state. He also worked in a steel mill. After graduating from Alabama State University he went to Harvard Law School. He earned his LL.B. in 1924 and then taught law at the University of Arkansas for a year. In 1925 he moved to Perry, Florida, to open his own law practice. Pepper soon became active in Democratic politics and, in 1929, was elected to the Florida House of Representatives. He became a member of the State Board of Public Welfare in 1931 and of the State Board of Law Examiners two years later.

Pepper ran for the U.S. Senate in 1934 as a Democrat and was defeated by a narrow margin. Two years later he ran without opposition for the seat vacated by the death of Duncan Fletcher (D-Fla.). In 1938, running as a champion of the working class and poor, he was elected to a full six-year term. In the Senate Pepper consistently backed Roosevelt's New Deal programs. An interventionist,

Pepper called for "aid short of war" to the Allies and he urged the United States to enter World War II months before Pearl Harbor.

In 1944, following Pepper's support of Roosevelt's veto of a tax bill favoring special interests, big business, industry, and oil companies, there began a campaign to oust him. The effort was led by Edward Ball, a representative of the DuPont interests. That year Pepper defeated an unknown opponent to retain his Senate seat. However, his victory margin was surprisingly slim.

Pepper maintained a consistently liberal voting record during the Truman administration. He backed legislation calling for an increase in the minimum wage. As a senator Pepper in 1937 supported a southern filibuster of a national antilynching bill, but he became more progressive on the issue of civil rights by backing the Fair Employment Practices Committee and, after 1937, he refused to participate in southern filibusters to block civil rights measures. As early as 1935 he spoke for a national health insurance plan tied to social security. This earned him the enmity of the medical associations. In foreign policy Pepper favored cuts in the military budget and accommodation with the Soviet Union. He criticized aid to Greece and Turkey to prevent a Communist takeover, reminding the Senate that Greek insurgency had developed from deep, legitimate grievances.

Angered at what he considered the conservative trend of the administration, and thinking very little of Truman in comparison to Roosevelt, Pepper proposed that Truman be replaced as the 1948 presidential candidate with HENRY A. WALLACE or DWIGHT D. EISENHOWER. On July 11, 1948, just before the Democratic National Convention, he announced his own candidacy. Pepper picked up several liberal backers, including JOSEPH L. RAUH, JR., but he was unable to unite the diverse factions of the party, and his candidacy in the words of historian Alonzo Hamby, "simply added a comic touch to the dump-Truman effort."

Business intensified its campaign against Pepper in preparation for the 1950 election. An effort was made to characterize him as a reckless proponent of civil rights and a backer of Russia. The anti-Pepper forces initially approached Governor MILLARD F. CALDWELL to run against the senator, but when he and several others refused, they settled on GEORGE A. SMATHERS, Pepper's former political ally.

Florida's 1950 Democratic senatorial primary was one of the dirtiest in U.S. history. Through insinuation and distortion Pepper was pictured as a pervert and a procommunist. Smathers dubbed him "Red Pepper" for his leftward political views. (He was also called that because of his red hair.) In one memorable speech Smathers insinuated: "Are you aware that Claude Pepper is known all over Washington as a shameless extrovert? Not only that, but this man is reliably reported to practice nepotism with his sister-in-law, and he has a sister, who was once a thespian in wicked New York. Worst of all, it is an established fact that Mr. Pepper, before his marriage, practiced celibacy." (Smathers claimed he never said that.) Ads came out calling Pepper all but a traitor. A week before the campaign Smathers's supporters blanketed the state with a little book entitled "The Red Book of Senator Claude Pepper." Pictures appeared of Pepper standing near left-wing entertainer PAUL B. ROBESON, and newspaper, clippings from 1946 were circulated in which Pepper had asked Americans to pray for Stalin. Although there has been much speculation on the subject, Pepper did not believe the president tried to oust him in 1950 for the senator's efforts to eliminate him from the 1948 Democratic presidential ticket.

Pepper attempted to defend his record, but with the conservative backlash of the late 1940s, won little support. Smathers went on to defeat him in the primary, which attracted the largest voter turnout ever recorded in Florida to that date. Pepper's loss was a major blow to Fair Deal forces and was cause for celebration among right-wing elements across the nation. But Pepper biographer Tracy Denese has argued that Smathers, despite his outrageous rhetoric, raised a legitimate issue in questioning Pepper's rather tolerant view of Soviet postwar actions.

In 1958 Pepper made an unsuccessful attempt to unseat Senator Spessard Holland (D-Fla.). Four years later he easily won in the newly created 11th congressional district. During the 1960s and 1970s Pepper consistently supported measures benefiting the elderly, who comprised a large portion of his constituency. He favored increasing Social Security benefits and worked for the establishment of a nutrition program for older Americans. Pepper backed Medicare and supported every measure aimed at increasing the scope of the program. For this activity he became known as "Mr. Social Security." One of the last major laws he shepherded through Congress was a 1986 act eliminating mandatory retirement because of age. During the early years of the Vietnam war, he supported most of President Johnson's wartime policies. However, in 1968, when he heard that the number of American troops in Vietnam might be increased to 700,000, he began calling for withdrawal of American forces. Because much of his House district constituency became Cuban American over time, Pepper opposed normalizing relations with the government of dictator Fidel Castro and supported aid to the Nicaraguan contras. Pepper died on May 30, 1989, in Washington, D.C.

—EF

Perlman, Philip B(enjamin)
(1890–1960) *U.S. Solicitor General, acting U.S. Attorney General*

Philip B. Perlman was born on March 5, 1890, in Baltimore, Maryland. He began his career as a journalist. While working as a newspaper reporter, he received his law degree from the University of Maryland in 1912. He became city editor of the *Baltimore Sun* in 1913 but left journalism in 1917 to become an assistant to the state attorney general. He was secretary of state of Maryland from 1920 to 1923 and city solicitor of Baltimore from 1923 to 1926. Perlman then entered private law practice and became active in Democratic politics. He was a delegate to several Democratic national conventions during the decade and was an adviser to Maryland governors on legal matters.

In January 1947 Truman appointed Perlman solicitor general, a position usually regarded as the most important in the Justice Department next to the attorney general. Perlman's confirmation was delayed for six months by Senator HOMER FERGUSON (R-Minn.), chairman of a judiciary subcommittee that was studying the appointment. Ferguson believed that Perlman had wielded undue political influence in Maryland and was in fact the Democratic boss of the state. Despite his objections, the Senate ratified the appointment in July by a vote of 58 to 21.

As solicitor general, Perlman argued 61 cases before the Supreme Court, losing only 12. He was particularly involved in the cases extending civil rights. In 1947 he filed an *amicus curiae* brief against socially restrictive real estate covenants. He argued that the covenants hindered the work of government agencies, injured national prestige, and threatened the general welfare because of hardships

placed on blacks. This sociological approach would be repeated in future cases. The Court ruled, two years later, that restrictive covenants were unenforceable in the courts. The brief in the case, which Perlman wrote with Attorney General TOM C. CLARK, was published in 1948 under the title, *Prejudice and Property.*

During 1949 Perlman filed a brief supporting the plaintiff in a case (*Henderson v. United States*) challenging railroad segregation in which the Interstate Commerce Commission was a codefendant. The solicitor general argued that segregated facilities could never, in fact, be equal and that segregation itself was "a negation of citizenship." Again he employed a sociological brief as well as legal arguments, saying such practices stunted the personal and social growth of blacks and attenuated the morality of whites. He later challenged the constitutionality of the "separate but equal doctrine" in educational facilities in *Sweatt v. Painter* and *McLaurin v. Oklahoma State Regents.* The Supreme Court eventually upheld his views in each of these cases.

Perlman successfully argued the government's case on several loyalty-security issues. He defended the Taft-Hartley Act's requirement for noncommunist oaths by labor leaders and the establishment of the attorney general's list of subversive organizations. He opposed the appeals of ALGER HISS on conviction of perjury and of 11 Communist Party leaders on conviction of conspiracy to overthrow or advocate the overthrow of the government. In other areas Perlman represented the United States in cases of ownership of tidelands oil, rent control, and antitrust cases against motion picture companies.

In 1952 Perlman spoke for the government in arguments on the constitutionality of President Truman's seizure of the steel mills. He defended the move against assertions by JOHN W. DAVIS, who represented the industry, that Truman had acted under no statutory authority and had therefore constitutionally usurped the power of the legislative branch. Perlman asserted that because of the crisis of the Korean War, Truman had no choice but to resort to seizure to prevent a strike in a vital industry. In fact, he took a swipe at Davis for barely mentioning the current national emergency, and instead relying on constitutional interpretations. When the Court ruled against the administration, Perlman recommended against implementing the Taft-Hartley 80-day cooling off period because it would anger the unions.

Perlman was appointed acting attorney general in April 1952 upon the resignation of J. Howard McGrath. He served until June of that year. In September 1952 Truman appointed him chairman of a special commission on immigration and naturalization. The commission sharply criticized the McCarran-Walter Act as being discriminatory. Perlman practiced law in Washington until his death there on July 31, 1960.

—HML

Petrillo, James C(aesar)

(1892–1984) *president, American Federation of Musicians*

The son of an Italian immigrant who was a city sewer digger, James C. Petrillo was born on March 16, 1892, in Chicago, Illinois. He attended Dante Elementary School in Chicago for nine years but never progressed beyond the fourth grade. In 1900 he began playing the trumpet and took free lessons at Chicago's Hull House. At the age of 14 Petrillo organized a four-piece band and in 1906 joined the American Musicians Union (AMU) in Chicago. He was elected to a three-year term as president of the AMU in 1914 but was defeated for reelection three years later. Disappointed over his defeat, he resigned from the AMU and joined the Chicago Federation of Musicians Local 10 of the American Federation of Musicians (AFM).

Petrillo became vice president of Local 10 in 1919 and president in 1922. One of the first important actions he took after assuming the presidency was to require that radio stations pay musicians. Previously they had played merely for the advantage of publicity. In 1932 Petrillo was elected to the National Executive Board of the AFM and eight years later became national president. From 1942 to 1944 Petrillo led a 27-month strike against the recording industry in an attempt to secure royalties for union members. President Roosevelt thought Petrillo's wartime strike set a bad precedent and believed music kept morale high. Despite presidential appeals, however, Petrillo continued the strike. Roosevelt then had the War Production Board order a halt to the walkout. But the board had no enforcement powers, so Petrillo just ignored its order. The strike succeeded and, as a result, a welfare fund was established for the receipt of royalties. Because of accusations of improper conduct during the strike, a Senate subcommittee investigated

Petrillo and the AFM. Concerned with effective demonstrations of his patriotism during World War II, Petrillo required all orchestras to play the "Star Spangled Banner" before and after every program.

During the mid-1940s Petrillo increased demands on the radio industry at a time of acute manpower shortages. As a result, Congress investigated charges that the union was pressuring companies to employ standby musicians in the event a hired musician was unable to perform. In 1946 Representative Clarence F. Lea (D-Calif.) sponsored legislation to curb Petrillo's power and activities. The measure, known as the Lea Act or Anti-Petrillo Act, abolished the standby practice and made it unlawful to threaten or compel a broadcaster to employ more persons than was needed or to pay more than once for services. The union could not force a station to refrain from broadcasting noncommercial educational programs or radio communications which originated outside the United States. The law prohibited payment for the production or use of recordings and payment for the rebroadcast of programs.

Petrillo declared the act unconstitutional and proceeded to challenge it by demanding that a Chicago radio station hire three additional musicians it did not need. The station refused, and Petrillo called the musicians out on strike. The Justice Department decided to prosecute. In response Petrillo stated, "I'm ready to face the music, gentlemen." Labor rallied to the union's support, and the American Federation of Labor's (AFL) convention in 1946 voted to fight the Lea measure. Although the government argued that AFM was a "racketeering organization that had extorted millions of dollars from the radio industry" a U.S. district court declared in December 1946 that the Petrillo Practices Act was unconstitutional. The ruling cited violation of the First Amendment "because the law prohibited a form of speech" and the Thirteenth Amendment "because it regarded as coercion the refusal of some employees to work unless additional employees were engaged." The government appealed the case directly to the U.S. Supreme Court, and, in June 1947, the district court was overruled. The following year Petrillo was acquitted of violating the act on the grounds that the government had not proved he had coerced a Chicago broadcaster into hiring the three musicians.

In 1947 a subcommittee of the House Education and Labor Committee conducted hearings into charges that an AFM local in Los Angeles had coerced a restaurateur to maintain an orchestra larger than he needed. At the conclusion the subcommittee recommended that "the continued exercise of such tyrannical power by any individual or group should not be countenanced nor tolerated in a free republic." The Labor Committee proposed legislation to forbid monopolistic practices of labor unions, but Congress took no action.

In 1951 Petrillo was elected a vice president and member of the executive council of the AFL. In 1958 he resigned all union positions except the presidency of AFM Local 10 in Chicago. Four years later he was defeated for reelection of Local 10. Although he maintained considerable influence within the AFM, after his defeat he retired from active union participation. Petrillo died on October 23, 1984, in Chicago, Illinois.

—DGE

Peurifoy, John E(mil)

(1907–1955) *assistant secretary of state for administration, deputy secretary of state for administration, ambassador*

A member of an old southern family, John Peurifoy was born on August 9, 1907, in Waterboro, South Carolina. He attended West Point from 1926 to 1928, but, following his father's death and his own near-fatal bout with pneumonia, he withdrew and worked for a Kansas City, Missouri, land bank. From 1929 to 1934 he was an insurance underwriter and cashier in New York. In 1934 he obtained a minor post in the Treasury Department. During the late 1930s and early 1940s, Peurifoy held various positions in the Labor and State departments. As assistant to Undersecretary of State DEAN G. ACHESON, he made the physical arrangements for the San Francisco Conference in April 1945. In 1946 he became deputy director of the Office of Public Affairs and briefly served as UN deputy secretary-general. He rose to assistant secretary of state for administration in 1947.

In that post Peurifoy was responsible for 6,000 State Department personnel and 18,000 Foreign Service officers. He was in charge of hiring and firing, loyalty investigations and security, as well as preparation of the budget. Peurifoy reorganized the department, putting the Foreign Service under closer department scrutiny and giving the four assistant secretaries of state policy-making powers.

During his tenure Peurifoy became deeply involved in the issue of domestic subversion. He served on President Truman's Temporary Commission on Employee Loyalty in 1947, which dismissed 10 State Department workers suspected of disloyalty or questionable associations. The following year he appeared before a subcommittee of the House Committee on Executive Expenditures to ask for funds to employ more loyalty investigators in the Foreign Service. However, he insisted that dismissals must be based on reliable evidence not "spiteful, unsupported, or irresponsible allegations." In May 1949 the Senate Judiciary Committee subpoenaed Peurifoy to produce files on 168 Foreign Service officers suspected of subversive activity. He withheld them at Truman's direction, contending that disclosure was not in the public interest.

Peurifoy clashed with Senator JOSEPH R. MCCARTHY (R-Wisc.) in 1950 over the loyalty issue. Following McCarthy's speech in Wheeling, West Virginia, in which the senator charged that there were a large number of Communists in the State Department, Peurifoy telegrammed McCarthy in Reno, challenging him to reveal the names of the disloyal individuals. The assistant secretary also stated that if he found any Communists in the department they would be "fired before sundown." In response, McCarthy named four people in Reno he accused of being Communist: one worked at the United Nations (and who did turn out to be a Soviet spy); another had, on behalf of Stalin, eliminated Trotskyites and anarchists during the Spanish Civil War; one was a communist sympathizer; and the fourth, John Stewart Service, a State Department China expert, had given classified documents to a journal published by a man in contact with Soviet intelligence, although Service's motive appears to have been one of simply leaking information to the press rather than spying. Peurifoy defended many of the Asian specialists in the department accused of being Communists. He derided the senator's tactics, saying that McCarthy "roared like a lion when he wore the cloak of congressional immunity but bleated like a lamb" in public speeches in which he could be sued for slander. In June 1950 McCarthy charged that Peurifoy had given a suspected Communist legal advice in return for the man's promise not to implicate him in an anticommunist probe. Peurifoy denied any deal had occurred.

President Truman appointed Peurifoy ambassador to Greece and head of the Economic Aid Mission (EAM) in July 1950.

His assignment was to strengthen the Greek government against a second possible left-wing invasion, facilitate operation of the EAM, and keep Greece cemented to the West, Greek anticommunist forces unified, and Communists out of the government. Peurifoy became known as a "man of action," who, despite protests from the Greek government, always and many times brusquely advanced American interests. During 1950 the Greek parliament passed most of the enabling legislation the EAM needed to do its work.

Relations between Peurifoy and the Greek government deteriorated during 1952. Charging that parliamentary leaders were corrupt and their administration weak, in August he called for new elections and received State Department backing for this request. The coalition cabinet, headed by Premier Nicholas Plastiras, won a vote of confidence in Parliament on August 22. Peurifoy left Greece the following year.

President Eisenhower appointed him ambassador to Guatemala in 1953. There he was instrumental in the overthrow of the left-wing Arbenz regime. Peurifoy served as ambassador to Thailand from December 1954 until his death in an automobile accident on August 12, 1955, in Bangkok.

—AES

Pine, David A(ndrew)

(1891–1970) *U.S. District Court judge*

David A. Pine was born on September 22, 1891, in Washington, D.C. He graduated from Georgetown University Law School in 1913. He became an employee of the Justice Department, working first as a confidential clerk and later as special assistant to Attorney General Thomas W. Gregory. From 1921 to 1934 Pine engaged in private practice in Washington, D.C., handling cases for labor unions and management groups. In 1934 he accepted an appointment as chief assistant to the U.S. attorney for the District of Columbia. Four years later he became U.S. attorney for District of Columbia. Pine was an aggressive prosecuting officer fighting racketeers and corruption in the U.S. marshal's office.

In April 1940 President Roosevelt appointed him to the U.S. District Court for the District of Columbia. In the late 1940s and early 1950s Pine handled many cases involving the Communist Party, and he supported the House Un-American Activities Committee (HUAC) in many of its investiga-

tions. In 1945 he was one of three judges who found eight Hollywood writers and producers guilty of contempt of court for refusing to tell the HUAC whether they were members of the Communist Party. In 1950 he imposed the maximum sentence of a year in prison and $1,000 fine on Eugene Dennis, secretary of the Communist Party, for contempt of Congress in refusing to testify before HUAC.

On April 8, 1952, President Truman, using what he believed were presidential emergency powers, ordered Secretary of Commerce CHARLES SAWYER to seize steel plants as a means of preventing a strike by 650,000 members of the United Steelworkers of America. The refusal of the steel company owners to accept the wage recommendations of the Wage Stabilization Board unless they were coupled with increases in steel prices; the threatened walkout of the steelworkers as a result of this breakdown in negotiations; and the strategic importance of steel in national defense programs were the three factors that led to President Truman's order.

The lead attorney for the steel industry, Theodore Kiendl (representing U.S. Steel), in his argument before Pine for a preliminary injunction against the government, wanted the judge to enjoin Sawyer not to change the terms and conditions of employment until the final disposition of the case. Pine reminded Kiendl that the moving papers in the U.S. Steel brief had asked for the seizure to be enjoined. The judge asked the other steel companies' attorneys if they wanted a similar injunction that Kiendl was now asking for, or one that enjoined the seizure itself. Only one, Bruce Bromley for Bethlehem Steel asked to enjoin the seizure itself. Pine showed a willingness to hear arguments covering the constitutional issue of the seizure itself, which surprised the steel industry's attorneys. After much confusion and much prodding from Pine, one of the attorneys, Charles Tuttle, representing Armco Steel Corporation, began to tackle the constitutional issues head on, saying Truman's seizure of the steel plants constituted usurpation of congressional powers. Assistant Attorney General Holmes Baldridge floundered badly in his response coming across as if the president had unlimited power on that day and the next. Truman, in a public letter, implicitly repudiated Baldridge, but the damage was done.

On April 29, 1952, ruling on the steel owners' request for a temporary injunction, Pine declared

President Truman's action unconstitutional and issued an order restoring the steel industry to its private owners. Although nearly 70 similar seizures of private property had been made by the president since 1941 (most under wartime conditions) this was the first such seizure to be questioned on the grounds that the constitutional powers of the president were limited in this respect.

The *New York Times* described Pine's decision as "the most precise and firmest restraints on executive power that have been stated by a federal court in our history." Pine found that there was a complete lack of authoritative support in the law and the Constitution for the government's position. There was no grant of power in the Constitution authorizing the president to direct the seizure, no grant of power from which it could be implied, nor any "inherent" powers permitting the order to seize private property. Pine ruled that the president had no more authority to assume powers not granted by the Constitution than had Congress and the courts, no matter how grave the emergency. Furthermore, the power of eminent domain and the power "to provide for the common defense and general welfare" was lodged in Congress. The Supreme Court would on June 2, 1952, affirm Pine's decision in *Youngstown Sheet and Tube Co. v. Sawyer.*

Judge Pine continued his career on the bench until 1965. Later that same year he became a member of the President's Commission on Crime in the District of Columbia. In January 1967 he submitted one of two dissenting opinions to the commission's report. In the dissent Pine reproached the panel for having avoided the question of whether court decisions favoring defendants contributed to the rise in crime. Pine died on June 12, 1970, in Washington, D.C.

—BF

Pollock, James K(err)

(1898–1968) *diplomat*

James K. Pollock was born on May 25, 1898, in New Castle, Pennsylvania. He received a bachelor's degree from the University of Michigan in 1920 and a master's degree in political science from the same institution a year later. He was granted a Ph.D. from Harvard in 1925. During the 1920s and 1930s Pollock pursued an academic career, becoming an expert in international, particularly German, politics. In 1925 Pollock became an instructor of polit-

ical science at the University of Michigan; nine years later he was promoted to professor. Deeply involved in Michigan politics, he served as chairman of the Michigan Civil Service Study Commission from 1935 to 1937.

After the Allied victory over Germany in May 1945, Pollock was chosen special adviser to General LUCIUS D. CLAY, deputy military governor of the U.S. zone in occupied Germany. During his year at the post, Pollock played a significant role in the political reorganization of that nation. His goal was the quick restoration of German self-government under a democratic political system. Under his guidance the American military government created three German states in the U.S. zone—Würtemberg-Baden, Hesse, and Bavaria—and appointed cabinet ministers and presidents for each. To coordinate their activities Pollock helped establish a Council of States (Länderrat), composed of the presidents of these areas. Their decisions on such internal matters as food distribution, transportation, and communication were subject to the approval of the military government. Pollock also helped in the formulation of constitutions for these states.

Pollock became coordinator of regional government, providing direct communication between Clay and the Länderrat. At Clay's insistence elections were held at the village level in January 1946 and at the county and city levels during the spring. Pollock was entrusted with the inspection of the voting. Pollock also assured Clay that a new university could be established in West Berlin. This became the Free University.

Pollock resigned his post in August 1946 to resume his academic career. Shortly thereafter he reported that, in his opinion, de-nazification was proceeding well and that the United States was "far ahead" of the USSR in giving Germans political freedom. During 1947 Pollock served as a member of the Commission on the Reorganization of the Executive Branch. Pollock dissented from several commission recommendations. Pollock supported a single chief of staff for the military rather than joint chiefs suggested by the commission. He also favored a new cabinet-level department of natural resources and opposed the liquidation of the Reconstruction Finance Corporation.

Pollock continued to advise the government on Germany. In February 1948 he chided the USSR and France for blocking increased German production in their zones and urged the French to merge their zone with the American and British under American supervision. He contended that this would aid the Marshall Plan. In May he returned to Germany as adviser to Clay during the Berlin blockade. During 1950 Pollock served as special adviser to the U.S. high commissioner for Germany, JOHN J. MCCLOY. Pollock died on October 4, 1968, in Ann Arbor, Michigan.

—AES

Porter, Paul A(ldermandt)

(1904–1975) *administrator, Office of Price Administration; chief, American Economic Mission to Greece*

The son of a Baptist minister, Paul A. Porter was born on October 6, 1904, in Joplin, Missouri, and grew up in Winchester, Kentucky. At age 14, upon his father's death, he took a part-time job as a reporter for the *Winchester Sun*, a position he held during high school and his years at Kentucky Wesleyan College. He worked as city editor of the *Lexington Herald* while studying at the University of Kentucky for his law degree, which he received in 1929. Porter then became general counsel for Oklahoma Newspapers, Inc., leaving in 1931 to take a similar position with General Newspapers, Inc.; both chains served primarily rural areas. Porter also wrote editorials for some of the chain's newspapers.

Impressed by Porter's editorials on farm policy, Secretary of Agriculture HENRY A. WALLACE invited him to Washington in 1933 to serve as special legal assistant. Porter organized a publicity staff within the Agricultural Adjustment Administration (AAA) to sell the new agency to the public. Besides his legal duties Porter was a prolific producer of radio speeches for delivery by AAA spokesmen. He left the government in 1937 to become Washington counsel for the Columbia Broadcasting System, a position he held until 1942.

During World War II Porter served the Roosevelt administration in a variety of capacities. In 1940 he took a leave from CBS to join the National Defense Advisory Commission as a legal assistant to CHESTER C. DAVIS, who was studying U.S. food requirements should the country be drawn into the war. After a year teaching administrative law at the Catholic University College of Law, Porter returned to the government in 1942 as deputy administrator for rent control in the Office of Price Administration (OPA). A year later he left the OPA to become

associate war food administrator, a post he soon left for the associate directorship of the Office of Economic Stabilization. President Roosevelt made Porter publicity director of the Democratic National Committee for the 1944 presidential campaign. Following his election to a fourth term, the president appointed Porter chairman of the Federal Communications Commission (FCC). In addition to his legal ability and his wide-ranging experience in administration and public relations, Porter approached his official tasks with an affable charm and story-telling skill that enabled him to carry out potentially controversial duties while engendering a minimum of hostility.

In his one year as FCC chairman, Porter endeavored to get radio stations to broadcast fewer commercials and more public service programs. In February 1946 President Truman named him head of the Office of Price Administration. Porter took over the unpopular office at a most difficult time. Businessmen and farmers vehemently attacked the idea of a price control agency continuing in peacetime, while labor and consumers lobbied to maintain price ceilings. Porter labored to persuade Congress to extend the OPA for another year. When Congress in June passed a measure continuing the OPA but drastically weakening its power, Porter helped to persuade Truman to veto the bill. While issuing public exhortation to hold the line in prices, Porter found it necessary in his 11-month tenure to preside over the dissolution of his agency and the removal of price controls.

In the winter of 1946–47 Porter went to Greece at Truman's behest as head of a special mission to assess the deteriorating political and economic situation there. Porter found intense poverty, a corrupt and ineffective government, and a chaotic relief program. Profiteering, black marketing, and speculation beset the nation. Long-term reconstruction programs found it difficult to find investors because people did not have confidence in the Greek government. Greeks had become helpless and believed the Allies were obligated to aid them because of the hard times of World War II. But U.S. ambassador LINCOLN MACVEAGH argued that the main threat came from external and internal Communist forces in the North rather than any internal malaise. MacVeagh convinced Porter that the insurgency and any possible invasion from the North had to be stymied first. Porter finally agreed, but he insisted that any aid be made contingent on economic reform.

Returning to Washington in March, Porter warned Congress that, because of the incapacity of the Greek government and the menace of the Soviet Union, Greece would fall to communism unless America intervened with massive economic and military aid. However, he insisted that such aid had to be made on the condition of economic reforms on the part of Greece. Returning to Washington in March, he warned Congress that, because of the incapacity of the Greek government and the menace of the Soviet Union, Greece would fall to communism unless America intervened with massive economic and military aid. In his final report released in April, Porter put forth a five-year program of reconstruction and development that became the foundation of the Greek-Turkish aid package submitted by Truman and approved by Congress.

In 1947 Porter joined a Washington law firm recently established by New Deal veterans Thurman Arnold and Abe Fortas. Arnold, Fortas & Porter soon established itself as one of the most talented and successful firms in the city. While Arnold and Fortas shared a scholarly bent, Porter excelled at charming clients and swaying judges. "Though Porter is unquestionably astute," said journalist Louis Cassels, "no one would describe him as an intellectual. His greatest asset is a gift of gab that makes him a persuasive conversationalist in private and an eloquent advocate in court."

In its early years Arnold, Fortas & Porter distinguished itself by its defense, without fee, of government employees discharged for disloyalty during anticommunist probes of the federal government. Over and over again the firm went to court challenging firings based merely on charges made by anonymous accusers. A critical case was that of Dorothy Bailey, a government employee dismissed on the basis of anonymous accusations that she had attended Communist meetings. Bailey denied the charges, but Porter was unable to persuade the Loyalty Review Board or the Court of Appeals that the nameless informant should be confronted or that his client's constitutional rights had been violated. He argued the appeal before the Supreme Court, but the Court's four-to-four division in *Bailey v. Richardson* had the effect of upholding the lower court's decision. In a similar case, Porter appeared before the Supreme Court on behalf of Dr. John Peters, a government scientist whose dismissal the Court overturned on technical grounds.

Parallel to its *pro bono publico* civil libertarian advocacy, Arnold, Fortas & Porter built up a prosperous corporate practice. Its clients included such established companies as Coca-Cola, Lever Brothers, Western Union, and the American Broadcasting Company. By the time of Porter's death the firm was one of the largest and most thriving in Washington. He died on November 26, 1975, after choking on a piece of lobster in a restaurant in Washington, D.C.

—TO

Potofsky, Jacob S(amuel)

(1894–1979) *president, Amalgamated Clothing Workers of America*

Jacob S. Potofsky was born on November 16, 1894, in Radominsol, Russia. He immigrated to New York City in 1905 and went to work at Hart, Schaffner, and Marx, a men's clothing manufacturer, in 1910. He joined the pantsmaker union and took part in a strike against Hart, Schaffner led by Sidney Hillman. Potofsky continued his association with the union during the next decade. After Hillman founded the Amalgamated Clothing Workers of America (ACWA) in 1916, Potofsky served as assistant general secretary-treasurer of that organization. During the 1930s, under Potofsky's direction, the union organized 5,000 cotton garment workers in the South and Middle Atlantic. In 1934, after Hillman became a government adviser, Potofsky was appointed assistant president of the Amalgamated Clothing Workers. He again took control of the union in 1940–41. In 1941 when United Mine Workers president JOHN L. LEWIS attacked Hillman in his association with President Roosevelt, Potofsky sharply rebuked him as causing division within the ranks of the CIO.

Potofsky was unanimously elected general president of the union in 1946 following the death of Hillman and pledged to continue the progressive policies of his predecessor. In late 1946 Potofsky announced with the president of the Clothing Manufacturers Association the establishment of a pension program allowing workers in the men's and boys' clothing industry with service of 20 years of service to retire at the age of 70. In 1947 the two groups announced a wage hike of 12.5 cents an hour—raising the average wage to $1.50 an hour—and a second week of vacation for 150,000 workers in the industry. Potofsky deplored the fact that the union had to negotiate a wage hike every year to try to keep up with the rising cost of living. He called for price controls to end such a situation. During the Truman administration he joined other labor leaders in opposing passage of antiunion legislation, particularly the Taft-Hartley Act. When Truman vetoed the bill Potofsky telegrammed him saying the president's action was "in the highest American tradition." He also pressed for an increase in the minimum wage and unsuccessfully tried to gain government contracts for his union. Potofsky was a strong supporter of the state of Israel and urged increased aid to that nation.

In 1947 he rejected calls for a third party for the 1948 elections, saying his union would try to influence the Democratic Party to take a more pro-labor stand, and would not back HENRY A. WALLACE in his bid for the White House. However, he evaded comment on a Truman candidacy for some time, only finally endorsing him at a CIO Executive Board meeting in September 1948. In 1951 in the midst of the Korean War, Potofsky warned that a third party might be formed in 1952 if "wrongs in the mobilization program are not righted." In the end, though, he campaigned for Democratic nominee ADLAI E. STEVENSON.

In 1950 Truman appointed Potofsky to the Point Four Advisory Board, formed to make recommendations on the allocation of funds to the receiving countries. Potofsky argued that the growth of voluntary labor unions should be encouraged wherever private investments were made.

With the formation of the AFL-CIO in 1955, Potofsky was chosen vice president and became a member of the Executive Council. He was the first major union leader to endorse John F. Kennedy in 1960 and HUBERT H. HUMPHREY in 1968, and he attacked RICHARD M. NIXON's Southeast Asia policy in 1970. In 1972 Potofsky retired as head of the Amalgamated Clothing Workers. He still remained active in union affairs. Potofsky died on August 5, 1979, in New York City.

—MN

Potter, Charles E(dward)
(1916–1979) *member of the House of Representatives*

Charles E. Potter was born on October 30, 1916, in Lapeer, Michigan. Following his graduation from Michigan State Normal College in 1938, Potter became a social worker in Cheboygan County. He served with distinction in the army during World War II and lost both legs during the invasion of France. Following his discharge in 1946 Potter worked as a vocational rehabilitation representative for the Department of Labor. In 1947 he won a special election as a Republican for a House seat from northern Michigan's 11th Congressional District.

Potter compiled a conservative record in the lower house, voting to override Truman's veto of the McCarran-Walter Act in 1952 and supporting the use of the Taft-Hartley Act against striking steel workers the same year. He also favored the Mundt-Nixon bill, the McCarran Act, state ownership of the tidelands, the 1948 tax cut, raising the minimum wage to 75 cents an hour in 1949, and opposed the Housing Act of 1949. He opposed many aspects of Truman's foreign policy, such as military aid to NATO in 1949, a $25 million authorization to establish Point Four, and the Korean Aid Act. However, he did support the Marshall Plan, although he backed an effort to reduce aid to Europe in 1951. During the Korean War he advocated "unleashing" Nationalist Chinese troops to attack the Chinese mainland.

In 1950 Potter was given a seat on the House Un-American Activities Committee (HUAC). There he led an investigation Communist activities in the film industry and in Detroit's labor unions. He became known, in the words of one senator, as "something of a junior McCarthy." During 1952 Potter objected to the appointment of NEWBOLD MORRIS as a special investigator of corruption in government. He asked that Morris refuse the appointment because he was a supporter of Communist-front organizations. Speaking before the House in February 1952, he pointed out that HUAC had labeled as subversive six organizations with which Morris was associated. Attorney General J. HOWARD MCGRATH fired Morris in an unrelated dispute over the investigation in April.

Potter sought election to the Senate in 1952. His campaign was supported by such conservative Republicans as Senator JOSEPH R. MCCARTHY (R-Wisc.) and Colonel Robert R. McCormick, publisher of the *Chicago Tribune*. Running as a strong anticommunist and opponent of organized labor, he charged the Democratic incumbent, BLAIR MOODY, with being "a captive of the little band of overlords who rule the CIO" and a tool of "Moscow-trained"

WALTER P. REUTHER. Moody, in turn, questioned Potter's anticommunism, claiming he was frequently absent from HUAC meetings and denouncing him as a puppet of the National Association of Manufacturers and the monopolistic automakers. Riding on DWIGHT D. EISENHOWER's coattails, Potter narrowly won the election.

During the Eisenhower administration Potter served on the Senate Permanent Investigations Subcommittee, headed by McCarthy. There he tried to prevent an open break between the senator and the administration. Potter finally voted for McCarthy's censure in 1954. The senator was a marginal supporter of the administration during Eisenhower's first term. In seeking reelection in 1958 he strove to separate himself from the increasingly unpopular president. He lost his reelection bid to Philip Hart by a 170,000 vote margin. Potter died in Washington, D.C., on November 23, 1979. (See *The Eisenhower Years* Volume)

—AES

Pressman, Lee

(1906–1969) *general counsel, Congress of Industrial Organizations*

The son of Russian immigrants, Pressman was born on July 1, 1906, in New York City. He graduated from Cornell University in 1926. He received a law degree from Harvard in 1929, and he joined a prestigious New York law firm, handling cases involving corporations, receiverships, and labor. In 1933 Pressman went to Washington as an assistant general counsel of the Agricultural Adjustment Administration under Secretary of Agriculture HENRY A. WALLACE. He also served as counsel of the Works Progress Administration and the Resettlement Administration.

In 1936 Pressman became general counsel of the Committee (later Congress) of Industrial Organizations (CIO). That same year he also assumed the position of general counsel for the Steelworkers Organizing Committee, which became the United Steelworkers of America in 1942. Pressman directed the CIO's legal affairs and was active in contract negotiations for several unions. He was an articulate, controlled negotiator and lawyer who was known for his forcefulness. Once described by Joseph and Stewart Alsop as "the hero of the CIO's Communists and pro-Communists," Pressman was an eloquent representative of the left wing within the labor movement.

Pressman often served as a labor spokesman. In 1940 he warned that workers in national defense industries would not refrain from striking and would base their demands on industry's increased profits. He moderated this view during World War II, supporting President Roosevelt's wage and price freeze in 1943. After the war Pressman attacked Congress for seeking "to stifle labor organization" and resisting tax reform. He was a vocal opponent of the Taft-Hartley Act of 1947, which banned the closed shop and imposed other restrictions on organized labor. Pressman argued that the law reduced labor-management relations to legalistic proceedings because of its denoting unfair labor practices, giving employers more access to employees in the representation election process, and making the National Labor Relations Board approach fact finding in a more legally formal fashion. Pressman explained to the leadership of the CIO that the Wagner Act "has not been weakened or emasculated." Instead it maintained only a nominal existence. Pressman led the CIO's legal fight against the bill, challenging the constitutionality of provisions in the law in both federal and state courts. In April 1947 he assisted CIO president PHILIP MURRAY in negotiations with U.S. Steel. The United Steelworkers of America received a new contract, with a 15 cent hourly wage increase for some 140,000 production employees of the corporation's five principal operating subsidiaries.

Murray reluctantly fired Pressman in February 1948 as CIO and USWA general counsel after Pressman announced he would back HENRY A. WALLACE's bid for the presidency and that he would run for Congress in a Brooklyn district. Murray and other CIO officials opposed Wallace's third party as divisive, and they feared he would act as a spoiler, aiding the Republican candidate. At the Progressive Party Convention in July 1948 Pressman served as secretary of the platform committee. He was said to have written much of the platform that called for the abolition of both the Marshall Plan and the Truman Doctrine and blamed the United States for the cold war. The platform came under criticism from some Progressive Party members and from liberals for being too pro-Soviet. Historian Zachary Karabell, however, has argued that Pressman believed in Wallace's ideas, not Stalin's. In the fall election Pressman ran unsuccessfully for the U.S. House from Brooklyn's 14th Congressional District as a candidate of the American Labor Party (ALP).

In August 1948, during testimony before the House Un-American Activities Committee (HUAC), WHITTAKER CHAMBERS named a group of former government officials as members of a prewar Communist underground cell. Chambers said Pressman was one of the three leaders of the cell, whose membership included ALGER HISS. Pressman denied the charges in early August and called Chambers's testimony a "smear." When called before HUAC, however, he refused to answer questions on constitutional grounds. Pressman attacked the hearings as an effort to discredit Wallace's campaign and smear the memory of Franklin Roosevelt. He elicited from the committee the admission that he had never been accused of espionage. On August 26, only a few days after Pressman's appearance, HUAC released the secret testimony of LOUIS F. BUDENZ, the former editor of the *Daily Worker*. Budenz said that during World War II he had regarded Pressman as "under Communist Party discipline." Pressman's name was mentioned by Alger Hiss in December 1949, during Hiss's perjury trial. He said he had known Pressman and four other men Chambers had cited as members of a Communist underground in Washington. But he denied he knew the men, including Pressman, to be Communists.

Pressman quit the ALP in August 1950, attacking its pro–North Korean stance. He said organized labor refused to support the ALP because its "policies, activities and political direction" were Communist influenced. Representative VITO MARCANTONIO (ALP-N.Y.), claimed Pressman left the ALP because he was not getting big legal fees from the movement. That month Pressman admitted before HUAC that he had been a Communist Party member in 1934–35. He named three other New Deal attorneys, all previously identified by Chambers, as members of his Communist cell in the Agriculture Department. Pressman refused to name any others and said he had never known Hiss to be a Communist. (He had.) He admitted privately that the group had been part of Communist Party operation. The three Pressman named, John J. Abt, Charles Kramer, and Nathan Witt, all refused to answer questions posed by HUAC on Communist activities.

Pressman left public life after his HUAC testimony in 1950. After leaving the CIO in 1948, he became a partner in the law firm of Pressman & Scribner. His firm represented several unions, including the Marine Engineers Beneficial Association. He died on November 19, 1969, in Mount Vernon, New York.

—JF

Quill, Michael J(oseph)

(1905–1966) *president, Transport Workers Union*
Michael J. Quill was born on September 18, 1905, in Gourtloughera, Ireland, and grew up amid the Irish rebellions. As a child he saw members of his family carried off to British jails, and in his teens he carried a rifle in the Irish Republican Army (IRA). He came to New York in 1926 and four years later got a job as a station agent on the city's subway system. Quill was one of a small group of Irish workers and Communist Party organizers who founded the Transport Workers Union (TWU) in 1934. In 1935 he was elected union president. Two years later the TWU affiliated with the Congress of Industrial Organizations (CIO). Between 1937 and 1949 Quill also served three terms on the New York City Council, twice as a representative of the American Labor Party and once as an independent.

As TWU president, Quill was a close ally, if not ever an actual member, of the Communist Party. (He was even called "Red Mike.") However, Communist influence in the union depended almost solely upon a core of secondary officials—chief among them John Santo, a Communist from Hungary who had served as TWU secretary-treasurer since 1934. The party was never able to muster a strong rank-and-file grouping among the union's overwhelmingly Irish Catholic membership, which considered Quill's claim to service in the IRA more significant than his Communist proclivities.

Always a flamboyant personality with a flair for publicity as well as a tough negotiator, he repeatedly issued strike threats in the form of dramatic ultimatums, but he rarely authorized an actual work stoppage. When New York mayor WILLIAM O'DWYER suggested in 1946 selling the city's power plants to Con Edison, Quill vowed to strike because his control over TWU workers at the plants assured him of the power to shut down the subways, and he did not want to lose that bargaining chip. Quill forced the mayor to hold a referendum on the proposal. Quill threatened another strike if his demand for a $2-a-day wage hike and exclusive bargaining rights for his union over transit workers were not met. O'Dwyer asked Congress of Industrial Organization president PHILIP MURRAY to mediate. Quill won the pay raise but not exclusive bargaining power. When the state legislature outlawed strikes by public servants and the city became indifferent to workers demands, Quill told his members to strictly adhere to the safety regulations of city ordinances. This dramatically slowed the city's transit system, yet legally could not be deemed a strike.

During the postwar years Quill's willingness to cooperate with the Communists increasingly came into conflict with his desire to maintain control of the TWU. At the CIO national convention in October 1947, he vigorously attacked the Truman administration and called on labor to consider supporting a possible third-party ticket headed by HENRY A. WALLACE. When Wallace announced in December that he would accept the Progressive Party's presidential nomination, Quill was elected, with strong Communist support, to head the New York CIO Council as Wallace's foremost union backer. Quill later claimed his support for Wallace was a ploy to force the Democrats to nominate a different candidate than Truman. At the time Quill noted his endorsement of Wallace was personal and not institutional and privately feared that the Progressive campaign would divide the CIO and alienate his own membership. In addition the Communist Party believed it could elect American Labor Party congressman and fellow traveler VITO MARCANTONIO (ALP-N.Y.) mayor on a promise not to raise the nickel subway fare, and party officials told Quill, a city council member, to oppose any fare hike, even though that was the only way the city could afford raising the wages of transit workers. According to Quill, Communist Party chairman WILLIAM Z. FOSTER at one point ordered him to campaign for Wallace even "if it splits the last union down the middle." As a result, after some hesitation, he decided to make a clean break with the Communists. He also informed CIO head Murray that the Communist Party was forcing its labor cadres to back Wallace.

In March 1948 Quill resigned the New York Council presidency and publicly announced that he was breaking with the Communists. At a TWU meeting he climaxed a speech by seizing a copy of the *Daily Worker*, holding it aloft, and tearing it to shreds, crying "that's what I think of them." Quill then mobilized a frantic purge of the TWU's Communist officials, employing physical violence, stacked meetings, and trickery. He also used his personal friend, Mayor O'Dwyer, who was popular with the union's Irish members, to intercede on his behalf. Within a year all his former Communist associates had been ousted from the TWU. In 1949 Quill also

served as a key witness in CIO hearings concerning charges brought against other Communist-influenced affiliates. His testimony against HARRY A. BRIDGES, president of the International Longshoremen's and Warehousemen's Union, led to that union's expulsion from the CIO. He also noted the Communists, in their promotion of government employee unions, had worked against the interests of the TWU. Quill said a party leader in 1941 had told him to stop the organization of Detroit street railway men and instead assist in the establishment of a government employee union headed by a party member.

After 1948 Quill avoided political involvements, deciding in the following year not to seek reelection to the New York City Council. He concentrated instead on a long, bitter, and ultimately successful campaign to win a 40-hour, five-day workweek for New York bus and subway workers as opposed to the normal 48 hour, six-day workweek. Despite all the strike threats, until 1965 there was no major disruption of New York's transit system. In that year Quill led a 12-day shutdown of the city's buses and subways, during which he was jailed. Quill died shortly afterward of a heart attack on January 28, 1966, in New York City. (See *The Kennedy Years, The Johnson Years* Volumes)

—TLH

R

Randall, Clarence B(elden)

(1891–1967) *president, Inland Steel Company*

Born on March 5, 1891, in Newark Valley, New York, Clarence Randall was reared in a small town society that emphasized self-reliance, ambition, and hard work. Before attending Harvard, Randall studied at Wyoming Seminary, a Methodist preparatory school. He graduated from Harvard College in 1912 and Harvard Law School three years later. Turning down an offer from a prestigious New York law firm, Randall chose instead to enter practice with a cousin in Ishpeming, Michigan. After serving in the army during World War I. Randall returned to his practice and in 1925 joined Inland Steel Company. He was promoted to vice president in 1930 and president in 1949. Although a supporter of big business and industrial freedom, he insisted that industry be responsive to human needs. He upgraded company mining towns in West Virginia and helped draft Michigan's workmen's compensation law.

Randall went to Europe in 1947 as steel and coal consultant to the Economic Cooperation Administration under the Marshall Plan. During the postwar period he served as a spokesman for the steel industry in its dealings with the government. Following an impasse in negotiations between the steel industry and the steelworkers during the summer of 1949, President Truman proposed a three-man board to investigate the dispute and prevent a strike.

Randall assailed the action as a forerunner of a socialist state, and he opposed the panel's subsequent recommendation that the steel companies pay the full cost of pension and welfare benefits for their workers. "In a free America," Randall stated, "no man should be fully relieved by others of the duty of providing for his future and of his family." On October 1 the steelworkers struck over the pension dispute. The strike was settled in November with the industry agreeing to pay for the pension program and share the cost of the welfare program.

The 1952 steel industry dispute propelled Randall to national attention. In March, when the Wage Stabilization Board recommended an 18-month contract with an increase of 12.5 cents an hour retroactive to January 1, 1952, and an additional increase of 2.5 cents an hour effective June 30, 1952, and another increase of 2.5 cents an hour on January 1, 1953, Randall denounced the suggestion, saying it would raise employment costs by 30 cents an employee hour and total costs by 60 cents an employee hour. Although a government economist disagreed with this assessment, the steel industry demanded the government allow it to raise prices by $12 a ton to meet such a wage hike, which the government would not grant. Wage negotiations broke down and, on April 8, President Truman ordered the seizure of the steel industry to prevent a strike. Randall told journalists that if the courts upheld the seizure it would be "the end of the road for free enterprise." The next day Randall, chosen as the industry's spokesman, appeared on national television to condemn the president's move. He charged that Truman had "transgressed his oath of office" and taken over the industry without the support of any specific law. The president, he maintained, had been part of a "corrupt political deal." He suggested that Truman was paying back a "political debt to the Congress of Industrial Organizations." Randall asserted that Truman had been pro-labor in his explanation of the seizure. The steel executive then went on to name PHILIP MURRAY, president of the United Steelworkers of America, as the man who called the strike by obstructing a last-ditch effort at a settlement. On April 29 U.S. District judge DAVID A. PINE ruled that Truman's action was illegal and ordered the industry returned to its owners. Randall hailed the decision and said, "This is a great day for America. The country will take new hope for the future." However, execution of the order was indefinitely stayed by a court of appeals ruling giving the government time to appeal to the Supreme Court.

In May Truman summoned Randall to the White House to attend a meeting between the leaders of the industry and the union. The conference, which was aimed at negotiating an end to the walk-out, failed. After a battle in the federal courts, the Supreme Court, in June 1952, declared the seizure of the mills unconstitutional and ordered them returned to private ownership. The union then launched a strike. The strike was settled the following month.

In August 1953 President Dwight D. Eisenhower appointed Randall chairman of the Commission on Foreign Economic Policy, which urged tariff reductions to stimulate trade. After retiring from Inland Steel in April 1956, Randall served as a government consultant in foreign economic policy for the Eisenhower and Kennedy administrations. He died of a heart attack on August 4, 1967, in Ishpeming, Michigan. (See *The Eisenhower Years* Volume)

—EF

Randolph, A(sa) Philip
(1889–1979) *president, Brotherhood of Sleeping Car Porters*

The son of a Protestant minister, Randolph was born on April 15, 1889, in Crescent City, Florida. He left his Florida home in 1911 to join the burgeoning prewar migration of southern blacks to Harlem, where he hoped to become a stage actor. Soon after his arrival he abandoned his show business dreams and turned to socialist politics. In 1917 he helped found the antiwar journal, *The Messenger*, which became a mainstay of Harlem's Negro Renaissance in the early 1920s.

Long a supporter of black trade unionism, Randolph began organizing Pullman Company porters in 1925. The effort culminated in August 1937, when the Brotherhood of Sleeping Car Porters signed a contract with Pullman, the first such agreement between a black union and a major American company. With this success Randolph became the most widely respected black leader of his time. In June 1941 his threat of a march on Washington by 100,000 blacks prompted President Roosevelt to issue an executive order banning racial discrimination in federal employment and in the defense industries and establish the Fair Employment Practices Committee to monitor compliance.

Randolph delayed launching a campaign against segregation in the armed forces until two years after the war, when President Truman called for a peacetime draft. With Grant Reynolds he founded the Committee against Jim Crow in Military Service and Training in November 1947. In early 1948 the committee became the League for Nonviolent Civil Disobedience against Military Segregation.

Appearing before the Senate Armed Services Committee in 1948, Randolph stated he would counsel youth to choose imprisonment rather than cooperate with a segregated conscription system. In response to questioning from Senator WAYNE MORSE (R-Ore.), he said he would recommend a program of civil disobedience "to make the soul of America democratic." He followed his appearance with a series of streetcorner meetings in which he urged young men to refuse induction in a segregated army. Randolph continued his campaign by picketing the Democratic National Convention held in Philadelphia during July 1948. His action, combined with the liberal battle for a strong civil rights plank in the party's platform and Truman's need to win the black vote, prompted the president to sign an executive order calling for an end to discrimination in the military. In response to the order, issued July 26, Randolph called off the civil disobedience campaign, a decision opposed by the more radical branch of the movement.

During the late 1940s Randolph was also active in leading an unsuccessful struggle for a permanent Fair Employment Practices Commission to insure equal rights in the labor market. He had already established, in 1943, the National Council for a Permanent FEPC. But a permanent FEPC would need congressional authorization since the wartime agency operated only on emergency funds that would expire when the conflict ended.

A 1945 bill to extend the agency's life was filibustered in the Senate until a compromise was reached that slashed the FEPC appropriation to $250,000, and mandated that the agency close when its funds ran out or at the end of the fiscal year (July 1946), unless Congress approved the establishment of a permanent FEPC. However, the House Rules Committee blocked consideration of establishing a permanent commission and the agency would expire in the autumn of 1945. As industries began to reconvert they reverted back to discrimination—a pattern Randolph confirmed during a tour of the nation in the autumn of 1945. He denounced the move of industries back "to their old habits of discriminating against Jews and Catholics, Negroes and Mexicans. Their policy once more is to divide the worker and build cheap labor markets." Randolph tried to see Truman in late 1945 and early 1946 to appeal personally for a permanent FEPC, but he failed. However, the president did announce his support for such a body. In February 1946 at a rally for a permanent FEPC, Randolph said Truman had not expended enough energy on passage. The labor leader further said that supporters of the FEPC "shall rightly apply the rule of rewarding our friends and punishing our enemies." In 1948 Truman issued an executive order for an FEPC for the federal government, but attempts to pass legislation for an FEPC to cover private business failed.

In January 1949 Randolph called upon blacks to press their senators for a change in the rules to end filibusters against civil rights legislation. An attempt by Senate liberals to change the rules to make it easier to invoke cloture failed. Randolph wrote the president that should blacks be disappointed in the defeat of civil rights legislation they might disappoint the Democrats in the 1950 midterm elections. But any attempt to bring legislation to the floor of the Senate in 1950 was met with a filibuster, upheld by Republicans and Southern Democrats and Truman gave up on civil rights legislation. When the Korean War broke out, Randolph asked the president to issue an executive order to create a wartime FEPC, as Roosevelt had done. But previous legislation did not give the president the funds to create a wartime FEPC. By 1951, Randolph, seeing that no FEPC legislation was going to be passed, pressed Truman to establish the Committee on Government Contract Compliance through an executive order, but it had no enforcement powers, relying on persuasion. An attempt in 1952 to change the Senate filibuster rule, supported by Randolph, also failed.

In the 1940s Randolph became interested in the establishment of a socialist-democratic party,

and he accepted the chairmanship of the National Education Committee for a New Party. It supported an anti-Soviet policy and called for the backing of liberalism throughout the world. He denounced the Progressive Party as being dominated by Communists, and he supported Socialist NORMAN THOMAS in 1948. Most blacks, however, voted for Truman.

The early 1950s marked Randolph's decline within the black movement. He no longer enjoyed preeminence in the broad battle for African-American rights, but he remained the leading black spokesman for political and trade union democracy. In the latter part of the decade. Randolph pressed the newly formed AFL-CIO to end discrimination within its affiliated unions. His criticism often brought him into conflict with federation president GEORGE MEANY. In 1959 Randolph helped organize the Negro American Labor Council (NALC) to fight for change within the federation. He served as NALC president for four years.

In the 1960s Randolph worked to eliminate the economic barriers that blacks faced. He helped BAYARD RUSTIN organize a march for "jobs and freedom" in 1963. Randolph backed Lyndon Johnson's War on Poverty, but he opposed the president's Vietnam policy because it diverted funds from poverty programs. In September 1968, aged and ailing, Randolph retired as president of the Brotherhood of Sleeping Car Porters. Randolph died May 16, 1979, in New York City.

Randolph's biographer Paula F. Pfeffer has argued that while he and other African-American leaders did not bring about equality in the 1940s and early 1950s, they had laid the basis for the civil rights movement of the late 1950s and 1960s. (See *The Eisenhower Years, The Kennedy Years, The Johnson Years* Volumes)

—EF

Rankin, John E(lliot)
(1882–1960) *member of the House of Representatives*

John E. Rankin was born on March 29, 1882, in Itawamba County, Mississippi. He worked on a local newspaper before enrolling in the University of Mississippi Law School. After graduating in 1910 he set put practice in Tupelo, Mississippi. Ten years later he successfully ran for a seat in the House of Representatives on a white supremacist program. Rankin, a Democrat, represented a strongly segregationist district in northeastern Mississippi where blacks were excluded from voting by the highest poll tax in the United States.

One of the most colorful legislators in the nation, Rankin became known as a leader of the forces of "Southern racist reaction." He was vehemently anti–African American, anti-Semitic, and anticommunist, professing, in the words of the *New York Times*, "to see a Communist plot behind everyone and everything he disagreed with." He frequently resorted to tirades against "New York Jews" and "damn Yankee interference." During World War II Rankin charged that the Communist Party conspired with the Red Cross to "mongrelize" the white race by refusing to segregate blood used for transfusions.

A vigorous opponent of monopolies and private utilities, Rankin sponsored the bill creating the Tennessee Valley Authority. As a member and from 1949 to 1953 as chairman of the Veterans' Affairs Committee, he sponsored several bills to extend benefits. However, some groups considered his support of questionable value because of the extreme nature of the measures he advocated. One would have given pensions to all survivors of deceased veterans.

During the Truman administration Rankin continued his conservative voting pattern. He opposed all civil rights legislation and supported the Case labor disputes bill of 1946 and the Taft-Hartley Act of 1947, both measures opposed by organized labor. He also supported requesting the president to invoke Taft-Hartley during the steel strike of 1952 and state ownership of tidelands. He opposed the Employment Act of 1946, the Housing Act of 1949, raising the minimum wage to 75 cents an hour in 1949, and making the school lunch program permanent. Being from a cotton-farming region, however, he backed high rigid price supports for agricultural products. He also voted for the Republican tax cut of 1948. He mostly opposed Truman's foreign policy. He voted against the 1946 British loan, Greek-Turkish aid, the Marshall Plan, the Korean Aid Act, a $25-million authorization to set up Point Four, and for sharply reducing aid to Europe in 1951.

In January 1945 Rankin pushed through the House a bill making the House Un-American Activities Committee (HUAC) a permanent body. Rankin did not choose to head the panel, a position to which he was traditionally entitled as sponsor of the resolution. However, for years he remained a dominant force on the committee. His first target was Hollywood, which he claimed was dominated by Jews and therefore by Communists. He also led the investigation of the Communist Party's role in many liberal organizations during the 1930s. Throughout these hearings Rankin persisted in interrupting witnesses with racist slurs, often to the annoyance of his fellow committee members. After J. PARNELL THOMAS (R-N.J.) became chairman of the Committee in 1947, he effectively restrained Rankin's outbursts.

In 1947 Rankin introduced a bill that would have made it a criminal offense to advocate communism in schools or send Communist material through the mail. During hearings before HUAC many conservatives, including J. EDGAR HOOVER, testified against the measure because of the constitutional questions it would have raised and the difficulty in enforcing it. The panel voted down the bill. Ironically, for all his redbaiting, he at first doubted the guilt of ALGER HISS when he first testified before HUAC, and in fact rushed to congratulate him when he finished answering questions on his first day of testimony. Following the 1948 election the Democratic leadership of the House removed Rankin from the panel. He blamed liberals and Communists for the effort to silence him. Party leaders said a chairman of another committee could not sit on HUAC, although it might have been because Rankin supported the Dixiecrat ticket in 1948. As might be expected, he supported the Mundt-Nixon bill and the McCarran Internal Security Act.

As a result of a loss in population, Rankin's district was combined with a more moderate one in the early 1950s. The representative was defeated in the 1952 Democratic primary by a close friend. He died on November 26, 1960, in Tupelo, Mississippi, of a heart attack after a long illness.

—JB

Rauh, Joseph L(ouis), Jr.
(1911–1992) *chairman, Executive Board, Americans for Democratic Action*

The son of a German immigrant businessman, Joseph L. Rauh, Jr., was born on January 3, 1911, in Cincinnati, Ohio. Rauh graduated from Harvard Law School in 1935 and served as secretary to Supreme Court justices Benjamin Cardozo and Felix Frankfurter until 1942, when he went into the army. While clerking he also worked as a counsel to various New Deal agencies. From 1946 to 1947 he was deputy to WILSON WYATT, head of the Veterans Emergency Housing Program. In 1947 Rauh joined Wyatt and other disenchanted liberals in leaving the Truman administration in protest against the growing conservative influence in Washington.

According to his friend ARTHUR M. SCHLESINGER, JR., Rauh's liberalism was traditional: "liberalism without mawkishness, without self-pity, without guilt, without illusion, but with zest in the struggle and unquenchable hope for all humanity."

Rauh was one of the founders of Americans for Democratic Action (ADA), formed in January 1947 as a liberal anticommunist lobby. The new organization elected him chairman of the executive board. Rauh and the ADA played an important role in getting liberal support for Truman during the 1948 presidential election. During Truman's second term he spoke forcibly for the passage of civil rights, housing, national health insurance, and public works legislation.

Rauh also provided legal assistance to a number of liberals, but he would not defend avowed Communists. In 1948 he represented William Remington, a Commerce Department economist charged with being a Communist. After the economist was convicted of perjury for denying the accusation, Rauh represented him in a series of unsuccessful appeals. Throughout the legal maneuvers Rauh claimed that the prosecution had failed to prove that Remington was actually a member of the Communist Party and that it had withheld and suppressed evidence. Remington was eventually murdered while serving a prison term. In 1952 the lawyer represented LILLIAN HELLMAN during her testimony before the House Un-American Activities Committee.

When United Auto Worker leader WALTER P. REUTHER was shot, Rauh, Washington counsel for the union, contacted Attorney General TOM C. CLARK to have the FBI investigate, but J. EDGAR HOOVER would not look into it, saying it was a state matter.

Rauh served as vice chairman of the ADA from 1952 to 1955 and as chairman from 1955 to 1957. He was so closely identified with the organization that he was given the informal title "Mr. A.D.A." As spokesman for the organization he criticized much of the Eisenhower administration's foreign and domestic program. He was a strong supporter of civil rights and, during the 1950s and 1960s and was

an early supporter of the Vietnam War. Rauh died on September 3, 1992, in Washington, D.C. (See *The Eisenhower Years, The Kennedy Years, The Johnson Years, The Nixon/Ford Years* Volumes)

—JB

Rayburn, Sam(uel) T(aliaferro)
(1882–1961) *member of the House of Representatives*

One of 11 children, Sam T. Rayburn was born on January 6, 1882, in Roane County in the Clinch Valley of Tennessee. When he was five the Rayburn family moved to a cotton farm near Bonham, Texas. Rayburn worked his way through East Texas State Normal College, earning a B.S. degree in 1903. At the age of 24 Rayburn won election to the Texas House of Representatives. He served from 1906 to 1912 and was chosen speaker in 1910, the youngest person in Texas history to hold that position. He ran a populist campaign for the U.S. House of Representatives in 1912, winning both a close Democratic primary and the general election. Rayburn gave both Woodrow Wilson and Franklin Roosevelt strong support in the House. He played a major role in the passage of such controversial legislation as the Securities and Exchange Act of 1934, the Public Utility Holding Company Act of 1935, and the bill establishing the Rural Electrification Administration. After serving as a lieutenant of Speaker of the House John Nance Garner, in 1937 he became majority leader. Three years later Rayburn was unanimously chosen Speaker.

Rayburn provided firm support for Roosevelt's wartime measures, except for gas rationing, an unpopular proposal in oil-rich Texas. During the war Rayburn's friendship with Senator Harry S Truman blossomed and Rayburn backed the Missouri Democrat as a moderate replacement for Vice President HENRY A. WALLACE in 1944. (Rayburn's own hopes for the vice presidency were crushed by conservative Texas Democrats.) When Truman assumed the presidency Rayburn became his chief protector in Congress. As Speaker of the House during most of the Truman administration, he championed the often-controversial White House legislative programs. A fiercely partisan Democrat, he expected firm loyalty from members of his own party. "To get along, go along," his famous advice to incoming representatives, also represented Rayburn's attitude toward veteran members of the House. Rayburn did claim, however, that he never asked a member of Congress to vote against his principles. He became one of the strongest Speakers in American history through a combination of tact, informal influence, shrewd political sense, and a reputation for integrity. During the Truman years he forged a close working relationship with Republican leader JOSEPH W. MARTIN, JR. (R-Mass.), who supplanted Rayburn as Speaker in 1947 when the GOP gained a majority in the House.

It was at Rayburn's Capitol building hideaway that Truman returned an urgent call from Franklin D. Roosevelt's press secretary Steve Early, who then told Truman to come to the White House immediately, where he learned the president was dead. Rayburn was stunned by the news of the president's death, although hardly surprised. The Speaker early on showed confidence in Truman as president while most others, including Truman himself, had doubts. Truman invited Rayburn to attend cabinet meetings, but Rayburn declined saying, "Even if the changing balances of power in the government raise the Speakership to a prestige it hasn't enjoyed in years, it won't change Sam Rayburn."

Rayburn faced an immediate test of his powers of persuasion when Truman proposed a 21-point social program with provisions for extended unemployment benefits, full employment, and continued price and rent controls. Rayburn doubted the wisdom of introducing the comprehensive package to a war-weary Congress. His misgivings proved accurate; a coalition of Southern Democrats and Republicans combined to defeat or delay much of the legislation. In June 1946 he counseled Truman not to reject a weak price-and-rent control bill. Truman vetoed the bill, and food prices and rents skyrocketed until a measure imposing controls was passed two months later.

According to his biographers D. B. Hardeman and Donald C. Bacon, Rayburn by 1946 had restored much of the power that had been stripped from the Speaker's post in the rebellion against Uncle Joe Cannon in 1910. Rayburn had transformed a job that had for three decades been a comparatively powerless and internally focused office into a powerful and prestigious position whose reach went beyond the House of Representatives. He stood watch jealously over the position's regained preeminence and when a 1946 reorganization bill threatened it, he refused to move on it until all provisions tempering its power were eliminated.

Rayburn went into the 1946 mid-term elections with anxiety, as a meat shortage threatened to turn the event into "damned 'beefsteak election.'" His fears proved correct as the Democrats lost control of Congress for the first time since 1930. At first Rayburn did not want to be minority leader, preferring instead to be a mediator between the Democratic president and the Republican Congress; however, he yielded to enormous cajoling by his fellow Democrats to serve in the position. Rayburn was of a mind not to oppose every Republican bill that came to the floor but to save fights for important issues. As minority leader he made many more speeches than he did as Speaker, and people in the House were galvanized when he approached the podium.

He battled a conservative Republican-dominated House for two years, trying to block or delay the revision or destruction of New Deal legislation. He also resisted Republican efforts to cut taxes. He focused much of his criticism on JOHN TABER (R-N.Y.), the chairman of the Appropriations Committee. Taber's desire for cuts in social services, public housing, and education prompted Rayburn to say that Taber behaved like "a man with a meat axe in a dark room." Rayburn also engineered a behind-the-scenes fight against the Taft-Hartley Act of 1947, legislation considered antilabor by unions and liberals. In a brief speech Rayburn gave before the final vote he said: "I do not know what is in this bill. Few do, or can. But from what I know of it, I know what you are doing here is not fair . . . I'm not going to vote for it." Despite Rayburn's opposition, Taft-Hartley passed. He also voted against the 1948 Republican tax cut.

Rayburn generally supported Truman's foreign policy, although he initially was reluctant to accept containment. He felt that Truman's hard-line policy toward the Kremlin was "hasty" but later changed his views and championed White House proposals for Greek-Turkish aid, the Marshall Plan, and the North Atlantic Treaty Organization. Later he argued for an additional $17 billion of foreign aid over four years. "These are dangerous days," he said. "Let us not do too little."

Rayburn disapproved of Democratic attempts to draft General DWIGHT D. EISENHOWER for the presidential nomination in 1948. While he liked the general, Rayburn felt the Eisenhower boom was ill-advised with an incumbent president available to run. "No, won't do," he said. "Good man but wrong business." As permanent chairman of the Democratic National Convention, Rayburn roused the delegates in July with a passionate speech extolling the Roosevelt and Truman administrations. After HUBERT H. HUMPHREY successfully introduced a progressive civil rights plank to the platform, Rayburn refused to allow the Southern Democrats to disrupt the convention with their protests. He believed the Democrats who walked out of the convention and formed the States Rights' Democrats were disloyal. Rayburn was one of the few people who believed Truman would win the election of 1948.

Rayburn found Truman a more assertive president after his surprising 1948 reelection victory. Truman wanted a purge of the Dixiecrats in Congress but Rayburn, fearing a realignment of the two major parties that would favor the Republicans, suggested instead a reduction in the power of the Rules Committee. Southern Democrats and Republicans dominated the Rules Committee and were able to determine which bills reached the floor. Rayburn masterfully engineered a rules change in 1949, allowing committee chairmen to bring bills directly to the floor if the Rules Committee failed to clear them for House action within 21 days. Rayburn attached a condition to the 21-day rule. Committee chairmen would have to receive his approval of the bills before bringing them to the floor. Rayburn found that the 21-day rule led to foolish legislation and backed an effort by Southern Democrats to repeal it in 1951. The Fair Deal legislative program Truman proposed for the 81st Congress again ran into resistance from more conservative Democrats and the Republicans. Rayburn stumped the South for Truman's Fair Deal, but the response there, and in Washington, was disappointing.

Rayburn avoided one stalemate by substituting a voluntary federal employment Practices Commission for the compulsory one Truman had proposed. It was only on the issue of civil rights that Truman and Rayburn disagreed; the Texas congressman remaining constantly aware of the pressure brought to bear on southern and Southwestern representatives when this type of legislation reached the floor of the House. Rayburn opposed Truman's civil rights legislation, and with president's understanding, would not introduce the president's program in the House. It would have to be introduced in the Senate first. He was also skeptical of federal aid to education fearing its effect on school segregation. But he began to show discomfort at the continued denial of political equality to African Americans and asked Texas state officials to repeal the state's poll tax.

Truman's desire to eliminate the 27.5 percent oil depletion allowance and his support of federal ownership of offshore tideland oil brought political headaches to Rayburn, who saw the oil industry as critical to Texas prosperity. The oil interests strongly favored state ownership and reacted violently to attacks on the oil depletion allowance. In 1951 Rayburn offered a compromise bill, which sought a federal-state sharing of offshore oil resources. But Texas leaders rejected compromise, and the Supreme Court ruled the tidelands belonged to the federal government. Rayburn then threw his support behind a bill to grant all of the tidelands to the states, which passed Congress, but was vetoed by Truman. Rayburn also supported the natural gas industry's call for federal price deregulation.

He supported Truman's program for priority and allocation of war materials for the Korean War. Rayburn defended the administration's dismissal of General DOUGLAS MACARTHUR in 1951 when the president and MacArthur clashed over strategy in Korea. When MacArthur returned to the United States, Rayburn and Senator TOM CONNALLY (D-Tex.), agreed to give the flamboyant general a chance to defend himself before Congress. They hoped the publicity would quickly turn a possible conservative hero into an overexposed, and even boring, figure. A critic of the excesses of the anti-communist crusades of the late 1940s and early 1950s, Rayburn was disturbed by the conduct of the House Un-American Activities Committee (HUAC). Early in 1952 he angrily instructed HUAC chairman FRANCIS E. WALTER (D-Pa.) to halt the television and radio broadcasting of committee hearings. Rayburn objected to the circuslike atmosphere he felt the open hearings produced.

Rayburn's national stature grew in the later years of the Truman administration. In January 1951 he passed Henry Clay's record for length of service as Speaker of the House. Rayburn was proposed as a possible presidential candidate in 1952, but the opposition of Allan Shivers, the Dixiecrat governor of Texas and Rayburn's political enemy, doomed his chances. Without any measurable support from Texas, he lacked credibility as a candidate. As chairman of the convention, he used his power to gain the nomination for Truman's candidate, ADLAI E. STEVENSON. Rayburn called a recess at a key moment during the convention to allow Truman to reach Chicago and meet with party leaders. The recess stalled Senator ESTES KEFAUVER'S

(D-Tenn.) drive and propelled Stevenson to the nomination. Rayburn grew to greatly respect Stevenson as a leader.

At the convention Rayburn also, as permanent chairman, kept the party from splitting up. The issue was whether to exclude from participation the South Carolina, Virginia, and Louisiana delegations because of their refusal to take a loyalty oath to back whoever was nominated. Rayburn stalled as pro-Stevenson delegates, wanting support from the South, rounded up votes for a motion that the three states had complied in spirit with the oath. The maneuver worked and the three delegations were allowed to vote.

Rayburn returned to the position of minority leader in the 83rd Congress. During the 1950s he supported the Eisenhower administration against moves by the conservative wing of the GOP that Rayburn felt represented a misguided isolationism. He did oppose Eisenhower proposals he considered socially regressive, such as a 1954 tax cut Rayburn thought favored corporations. When the Democrats regained power in the House in 1955, he continued his policy of cooperation with the administration on foreign policy issues, and he pushed through some civil rights and domestic legislation.

In the late 1950s Rayburn came under attack by liberals as an "Eisenhowercrat." His inability to promote liberal legislation was caused not by preference but by friction with Representative CHARLES A. HALLECK (R-Ind.), the new minority leader. Beginning in 1959 Rayburn was a strong backer of Senator LYNDON B. JOHNSON (D-Tex.) for the Democratic presidential nomination. He eventually urged Johnson to accept the vice presidential nomination after initially counseling him to reject Senator John F. Kennedy's (D-Mass.) offer. Rayburn campaigned for the ticket, insuring that Texas voted Democratic. He died on November 16, 1961, in Bonham, Texas. (See *The Eisenhower Years*, *The Kennedy Years* Volumes)

—JF

Reece, B(razilla) Carroll

(1889–1961) *member of the House of Representatives*

B. Carroll Reece was born on December 20, 1889, and raised on a farm in Butler, Tennessee, in the Great Smokey Mountains. He obtained his B.A. degree from Carson and Newman College in 1914 and then studied economics at New York University

(NYU). During 1916 and 1917 Reece taught economics at NYU and then enlisted in the army. Reece saw action in Europe, where he distinguished himself as a war hero. After the war he resumed his teaching career in New York. In 1920 he returned to Kentucky and won a seat in the House of Representatives from his home district.

A quiet man, Reece was one of the chamber's most inconspicuous members, seldom speaking and sponsoring little legislation. Throughout the 1920s and 1930s he consistently voted as a conservative on domestic legislation. In foreign affairs he was an isolationist who opposed Franklin Roosevelt's efforts to prepare the nation for war. Reece continued his conservative voting record during the first years of the Truman administration. He opposed the continuation of price controls and supported attempts to weaken the Full Employment bill of 1945, although in the end he voted even against the completed weakened bill, the Employment Act of 1946. He also voted to restrict the power of unions through the Case labor disputes bill, to make the Special House Committee on Un-American Activities permanent, and to turn tidelands over to the states.

In April 1946 Reece, a supporter of Senator ROBERT A. TAFT (R-Ohio), assumed the chairmanship of the Republican National Committee. His victory was considered the first step by Taft forces toward winning the 1948 presidential nomination. Republican liberals opposed the appointment because Reece's conservatism would not attract crucial labor support needed to win future elections. Former governor HAROLD E. STASSEN, a leader of the party's liberal wing, criticized Reece's voting record and challenged his leadership qualifications.

Reece resigned his seat to accept the party post. Attempting to heal the rift between the liberals and conservatives, he announced his job was to "elect" not "select" candidates and promised that all Republicans up for election would receive the support of the national organization. Looking at the party's chances in the 1946 election, he believed they could win the House but not the Senate. Throughout the spring and summer he traveled extensively to coordinate the campaigns of the candidates. In Washington he put together an efficient research, publicity, and fund-raising staff to assist the candidates in the localities. During the fall Reece targeted for national aid those districts and states that Republican candidates had lost by less than 5 percent in the 1944 election. Reece campaigned hard for party members. He promised that with Republicans in control of Congress, the party would enact legislation to end "the present rules of controls, confusion, corruption and Communism." If Truman vetoed the measures, Reece warned, an "outraged Congress" would override him. Reece's strategy paid off. The Republicans won control of both Houses of Congress in November, and Reece was hailed as the architect of the victory.

After THOMAS E. DEWEY won the presidential nomination in 1948, he replaced Reece as chairman with HUGH D. SCOTT. Reece ran unsuccessfully for a Senate seat from Tennessee in 1948 against the popular ESTES KEFAUVER. He returned to the House in 1951, and that same year put through a cut of $350 million in aid to Europe from the Mutual Security Act. He also voted for the relatively restrictive McCarran-Walters Immigration Act of 1952. However, he devoted most of his attention to helping Robert Taft secure the 1952 Republican presidential nomination. Reece was Taft's campaign coordinator in the South. He fought a surge of Republican support for General Dwight D. Eisenhower in the area, particularly in Texas, Louisiana, and Mississippi. Through his control of the state parties, Reece, after bitter struggles, sent regular party delegations loyal to Taft to the Republican National Convention. However, several dissident factions sent rival groups supporting Eisenhower. After Eisenhower won the presidential nomination, Reece returned to his duties in the House. During the 1950s he continued to be one of the leading conservative representatives in Congress. Reece died of cancer on March 20, 1961, in Washington, D.C.

—JB

Reed, Daniel A(lden)

(1875–1959) *member of the House of Representatives*

Daniel A. Reed was born on September 15, 1875, in Sheridan, New York. He received his law degree from Cornell University in 1898 and practiced law for a few years in Dunkirk. From 1903 to 1909 he was employed as an attorney for the New York State Excise Department. He then served as coach of Cornell's football team for the next nine years. In 1918 Reed was elected to the first of his 21 terms as representative of a solidly Republican upstate district.

Reed's most notable accomplishment in his first decade in office was his sponsorship in 1928 of a bill creating a federal Department of Education. Over the next 30 years, nevertheless, he stood out as a constant critic of the growth of the federal government, particularly the social welfare programs of the New Deal and Fair Deal. From his seat on the influential Ways and Means Committee, Reed consistently fought tax increases. He was also an advocate of high protective tariffs and a staunch opponent of foreign aid.

During the Truman years Reed was a vocal Republican foe of much of the administration's foreign and domestic policies. Having been one of the few members of Congress to vote against the renewal of the Lend-Lease Act in 1944, he maintained his anti–foreign aid stance into the cold war. Reed voted against the 1946 British loan, Greek-Turkish aid, the Marshall Plan, Point Four, Korea-Formosa economic aid, extension of the military draft, universal military training, the admission in 1948 of 200,000 displaced persons, and an emergency loan to India in 1951 for the purchase of U.S. grain. He supported drastically cutting aid to Europe in 1951.

A lifelong proponent of high tariffs, Reed persistently argued that low tariffs allowed a flood of foreign imports to damage the American economy. He repeatedly and unsuccessfully sought to overturn the reciprocal trade agreements originally negotiated by Secretary of State Cordell Hull and reaffirmed by the Truman administration. In 1949 he charged that the trade agreements had been written by Communists, who formed "a nest of vipers" in the State Department.

Reed's adherence to traditional orthodox Republicanism placed him in opposition to most modern social programs and regulatory policies of Democratic administrations. In June 1945 he was one of a handful of members of Congress voting against an extension of wartime price controls to June 30, 1946. He backed the Case labor disputes bill and voted in favor of the Taft-Hartley Act opposed by labor unions. He supported making the House Un-American Activities Committee permanent, the Mundt-Nixon bill, and the McCarran Internal Security Act. He opposed the creation of a permanent Fair Employment Practices Committee and ending the poll tax. He voted against even the water-downed House version of the Full Employment bill of 1945. He was for state ownership of tidelands and, in 1949, backed a bill exempting natural gas producers from regulation by the Federal Power Commission. He opposed the National Housing Act of 1949 and a bill proposed in 1950 to create a federal Department of Health. In that year he favored a $600 million across the board cut in the federal budget. Yet in 1949 he had supported raising the minimum wage to 75 cents an hour.

As ranking Republican on the tax-writing Ways and Means Committee, Reed was in the forefront of efforts to lower taxes or to block increases requested by the Truman administration. In 1947 he sponsored a bill to freeze the social security tax at its 1 percent rate for the next two years; the House passed the measure unanimously. Reed was a strong supporter of an income tax reduction bill passed by Congress in 1947 but vetoed by the president. Congress passed the bill over a third Truman veto in 1948. In 1950 he was the author of a tax proposal, which he called "a Republican answer to . . . President Truman," which would have cut excise taxes by 10 percent to 20 percent, raised the personal exemption to $700 and put a 50 percent ceiling on the highest tax rates. The measure did not pass. In 1951 he denounced the tax increase Revenue Act of 1951 as "a bill to authorize the bureaucrats to turn the taxpayers' pockets inside out." He demanded that the administration cut spending instead of raising taxes.

Generally favorable toward business interests, Reed in 1950 presented the Republican alternative to the excess profits tax put forth by the Democrats to help pay for the Korean War. The Republican version, which would have allowed corporations to elect to pay either the excess profits tax or a higher corporation tax, was defeated in the Ways and Means Committee by a 15 to 10 vote along party lines. On the House floor Reed criticized the excess profits tax as inflationary and branded it "the CIO [Congress of Industrial Organizations] tax program." His motion to recommit the bill to committee lost. Early in 1953, as the new chairman of the Ways and Means Committee, Reed fought an isolated campaign to defeat a six-month extension of the excess profits tax. The Eisenhower administration and the House Republican leadership circumvented Reed by the unconventional step of bypassing the Ways and Means Committee and routing the excess profits bill to passage on the House floor via the Rules Committee.

From 1950 to 1959 Reed was the House's most senior Republican. He continued to support his party's legislative program, although his stance on tariffs and foreign aid, for example, frequently placed him in conflict with the administration. He died of a heart attack on February 19, 1959, in Washington, D.C. (See *The Eisenhower Years* Volume)

—TO

Reed, Stanley F(orman)
(1884–1980) *associate justice, U.S. Supreme Court*

The son of a doctor, Stanley F. Reed was born on December 31, 1884, in Minerva, Kentucky. He graduated from Yale University in 1906 and went on to earn a law degree from Columbia. In 1910 he was admitted to the bar in Kentucky, where he set up a private practice and became involved in local Democratic politics. He served as counsel to the Federal Farm Board from 1929 to 1932 and as general counsel for the Reconstruction Finance Corporation from 1932 to 1935. Chosen U.S. Solicitor General in March 1935, Reed defended such major New Deal legislation as the National Industrial Recovery Act before the Supreme Court. President Franklin Roosevelt's second Supreme Court appointee, Reed had a reputation as a liberal Democrat with sound legal training and a judicious character when he was named a justice in January 1938.

As solicitor general, Reed had seen a conservative Court majority overturn important New Deal measures. Probably as a result of that experience, the Kentuckian generally adhered to a policy of judicial restraint while on the bench. He regularly voted to uphold federal economic and social welfare laws and thus helped to legitimize the expansion of government regulatory powers that occurred during the 1930s. Although his belief in judicial deference to the executive and legislative branches produced a liberal record on economic matters, the same attitude led Reed to conservative positions on the civil liberties issues that became increasingly important during his years on the Court. Indeed, Associate Justice William O. Douglas later described Reed as "one of the most reactionary judges to occupy the Bench in my time." The Justice voted to uphold most government security efforts against charges that they violated individual rights. He established one of the lowest records of support for civil liberties among the members of the Vinson Court. Reed voted with the majority in May 1950 in *American Communications Association v. Douds* to sustain the noncommunist oath provision in the Taft-Hartley Act and in June 1951 in *Dennis v. United States* to uphold the convictions of American Communist Party leaders under the Smith Act. He wrote the majority opinion in *Carlson v. Landon* (March 1952) in which a closely divided court ruled that the Attorney General could hold without bail alien Communists who were facing deportation charges. In June 1952 in *Youngstown Sheet & Tube Co. v. Sawyer* Reed dissented when the majority decided that President Truman's seizure of the steel industry was unconstitutional.

Outside the field of national security, Reed proved more responsive to individual rights claims involving the First Amendment. His majority opinion in a June 1946 case (*Pennekamp v. Florida*) reversed the contempt of court conviction against a Miami newspaper for its criticism of local judicial proceedings. In March 1948 in *Winters v. New York*, Reed's opinion for the Court overturned a state law barring publications that featured stories of violent crime. In April 1952 in *Beauharnais v. Illinois* the justice voted to invalidate an Illinois law against group libel. However, Reed also wrote the majority opinion in a February 1947 case (*United Public Workers v. Mitchell*) sustaining the Hatch Act's ban on political activity by federal employees against a First Amendment challenge. He upheld a city ordinance prohibiting door-to-door sales in *Breard v. Alexandria* (June 1951) and in *Saia v. New York* (1948) and *Kovacs v. Cooper* voted to sustain local laws regulating the use of sound trucks.

Reed favored a narrow interpretation of the First Amendment's clause barring the establishment of religion. He was the sole dissenter in *McCollum v. Board of Education* (March 1948) in which the majority upset a program of released time religious education in public schools. He took a conservative position on most criminal rights issues. In an important June 1947 case (*Adamson v. California*) he defended the traditional view that the Fourteenth Amendment did not extended all Bill of Rights guarantees to the states. Although a southerner, Justice Reed joined in a series of decisions expanding the constitutional rights of blacks. He wrote for the Court in a June 1945 case (*Railway Mail Association v. Corsi*) sustaining the application of New York State's civil rights law to a labor union and in *Morgan v. Virginia* (June 1946) holding state segregation laws inapplicable to interstate buses.

Justice Reed was not easy to categorize because his liberalism in most economic labor and civil rights cases was offset by his general conservatism on civil liberties and criminal rights issues, and academics have tended to rate Reed an average justice based on his opinions in these types of cases. He was seen as a swing vote, even a waverer. The unifying thread in his decisions, however, was a belief that the Court must give broad powers to the other branches of the federal government and to the states. During the tumultuous Stone Court years Reed generally maintained cordial relations with his brother justices. Throughout the Vinson Court years Reed occupied a position at the center of the bench, usually voting with Truman's judicial appointees. On the Warren Court Reed continued to support government loyalty-security programs, and he joined in the celebrated *Brown* decision invalidating racial segregation in public schools. Reed retired from the Court in February 1957. Reed died on April 2, 1980, in Huntington, New York. (See *The Eisenhower Years* Volume)

—CAB

Remington, William W.
(1918–1954) *government economist*

The son of an insurance supervisor and an art teacher, William W. Remington was born in 1918 in Ridgewood, New Jersey. He graduated from Dartmouth College and earned an M.A. in economics from Columbia University. Remington joined the War Production Board in 1942 and entered the navy in 1944. The navy placed him in the Office of War Mobilization and later with the Office of Naval Intelligence, where he specialized in Soviet affairs. In 1946 Remington joined the staff of the President's Council of Economic Advisers. From there he was transferred to the Department of Commerce, where he served as director of the exports program for Eastern Europe in the Office of International Trade.

In 1948 ELIZABETH BENTLEY, an ex-Communist turned FBI informer, named him as one of several former Communists holding federal positions. Remington denied Bentley's allegations, including her claim that while at the War Production Board, he regularly supplied her with classified material concerning aircraft production figures and also paid her his Communist Party dues. In fact he had been a Communist and had wanted to link up again with the party but realized open membership would damage his career. So instead he had passed on information to Bentley. (Bentley later said Remington thought he was spying for the American Communist Party—she later claimed he knew it was going to the Soviets.) Following his testimony Remington was suspended without pay. Although his superiors testified he was anti-Russian, the Fourth Regional Loyalty Board found reasonable doubt as to his loyalty. During the summer and fall Remington continued to defend himself against Bentley's charges. He admitted that he had been introduced to Bentley by Communist reporter Joseph North—although he claimed he did not know he was a Communist at the time—and that she went by the name Helen Johnson and said she was a reporter from the newspaper *PM*. He maintained he had supplied her only with unclassified material. The money he had given her, Remington testified, was for the Joint Anti-Fascist Refugee Committee. He denied ever being a member of the Communist Party. In September Bentley repeated her charges on the NBC radio program "Meet the Press." Bentley did not appear before the Loyalty Board. During that same month a regional loyalty board sustained Remington's suspension without summoning Bentley for cross examination.

With the aid of JOSEPH L. RAUH, JR., a prominent civil liberties lawyer, Remington sued NBC and Bentley for $100,000. He also appealed the decision of the regional loyalty review board. Rauh pointed out that there was never any corroborating evidence offered for Bentley's charges, nor did any other witnesses come forth to support her version of the events. Bentley never appeared at the hearings. The federal board cleared Remington in February 1950. The board said, "Our government's attitude toward Russia in 1942 was such that giving the Russians information with respect to the progress of our war effort wouldn't necessarily spell disloyalty." His civil suit was settled out of court shortly thereafter for a reported $10,000.

In May 1950 Howard Allen Bridgeman and Kenneth McConnell both appeared before the House Un-American Activities Committee and testified that they had attended Communist Party cell meetings with Remington. Remington conceded that he had met Bridgeman but again denied that he had ever been a Communist. Before a grand jury, the defendant's divorced wife, Ann Remington, at first denied William was a Communist agent. The foreman of the grand jury threatened her unless she changed her testimony to implicate her ex-husband.

In June Remington was indicted for perjury by a New York grand jury and forced to resign by the secretary of commerce.

Remington's trial took place in January 1951. The chief witness for the prosecution was Ann Remington, who had turned state's evidence. She claimed that both she and Remington had been Communists and that her ex-husband had given Bentley a formula for manufacturing explosives out of garbage. The defense countered by saying that Remington was a fighter for the underprivileged, with a taste for radical affectations, but he was not a Communist. (According to historian Ellen Schrecker, he had been involved in the Tennessee Communist movement.)

In February Remington was found guilty and sentenced to the maximum penalty of five years imprisonment and a two thousand dollar fine. In August the U.S. Court of Appeals overturned the conviction on the grounds that the presiding judge had given inadequate instructions to the jury. The court also noted that Elizabeth Bentley was planning to write a book with the foreman of the grand jury that had originally handed down the indictment. It criticized U.S. Attorney Irving Saypol for possibly arousing anti-Semitism in the jury against a defense witness.

In August, while appealing to the Supreme Court to have the original indictment dismissed, Remington was again indicted for perjury on the basis of statements made during the first trial. Judge LEARNED HAND dissented, noting the intimidation employed by the grand jury foreman. He was found guilty and, in April of 1952, began serving a three-year sentence in the federal penitentiary at Lewisburg, Pennsylvania. In his 1954 application for parole Remington admitted giving information to someone he knew was a Communist. On November 24, 1954, just months before his scheduled release, three prisoners beat Remington to death.

—MQ

Reuther, Walter P(hilip)
(1907–1970) *president, United Automobile Workers*

The son of an immigrant German brewery worker and Ohio Valley union leader, Walther P. Reuther was born on September 1, 1907, in Wheeling, West Virginia, and raised in a closely-knit family. After completing high school in Wheeling, West Virginia,

United Auto Workers president Walter P. Reuther
(Harry S. Truman Library)

Congress of Industrial Organizations (CIO) allied themselves more closely with the Roosevelt administration and the Democratic Party. He continued to champion social democratic goals, however, partly to win support for his own career ambitions from the UAW's activists and secondary leaders.

At the beginning of World War II, Reuther attracted considerable attention with a plan to convert the auto industry to airplane production under joint employer-union management. With its collectivist implications, the proposal won acclaim from many socialists but was shunned by the administration. Reuther firmly supported the CIO's wartime no-strike pledge. At the same time, however, he sought to ameliorate growing UAW rank-and-file discontent with government-imposed wage restraints. In early 1945 he urged the CIO to boycott the War Labor Board until the agency adopted a more liberal pay policy.

In September of that year, Reuther wrote an article for *New York Times Magazine.* In it he claimed the trouble with American capitalism was that, though it had perfected the production process, it had failed in the sale of goods to consumers. According to Reuther's biographer Nelson Lichtenstein, after the war larger production capacity of industry had shifted the battle between management and labor from the work site to the size of the paycheck. Reuther was to lead the labor movement away from a prewar focus on industrial democracy to one of Keynesian ideas of maintaining purchasing power.

Shortly after the fall of Germany, Reuther insisted on an immediate industrywide strike vote to back CIO demands for an end to the administration's wage ceilings. Reuther's militancy greatly increased his popularity among UAW members but placed him in conflict with most of the union's leaders, including President R. J. Thomas and Secretary-Treasurer George Addes, who were closely allied with a small, but influential Communist group. Thomas and Addes opposed any initiatives by the auto workers until CIO president PHILIP MURRAY had time to work out a new postwar wage-price formula at a labor-management conference called by the Truman administration for November. However, with a rash of unauthorized work stoppages spreading to one UAW local after another, Reuther recognized the futility of maintaining the no-strike pledge and came forward with a proposal for an early strike against the General Motors Corporation (GM). Reuther wanted

he moved to Detroit in 1926 and got a job as a skilled tool and die worker at the Ford Motor Company. Discharged for his union activity in 1931, Reuther joined the Socialist Party, attended Wayne State University for two years, and campaigned enthusiastically for NORMAN THOMAS's 1932 presidential candidacy. With his brother Victor he then set out on a world tour, which included a 16-month sojourn as skilled workers in a Soviet auto factory. Returning to Detroit in 1935 the two Reuthers joined another brother, Roy, in the movement to organize the new United Automobile Workers (UAW). Within a year Walter and Victor helped bring 30,000 workers on Detroit's West Side into UAW Local 174, thus establishing themselves as important leaders of the union.

Politically pragmatic, Reuther quit the Socialist Party in the late 1930s as the UAW and the a postwar wage pattern produced under the guidance of the government, but he saw that only by wielding the strike weapon could he force industry to give in and prompt the Truman administration to be firm in standing by price guidelines of the Office of Price Administration. The plan was reluctantly endorsed by the union's executive board. (After it became clear that the strike was popular among the rank and file the executive board became more enthusiastic.)

The UAW's dispute with GM dramatized the sharp postwar decline in workers' purchasing power as industry reverted to the 40-hour week, ending the overtime and premium pay of war work. Reuther demanded a 30 percent wage boost with no increase in the price of cars, unless GM was willing to open its books and publicly demonstrate that it could not afford to meet the union's demand. Although other labor leaders, including most UAW and CIO officials, were wary of Reuther's "open the books" slogan, his program was viewed by many in union ranks and liberal circles as an answer to the problem of inflationary wage-price spirals. GM firmly rejected Reuther's suggestion of direct union intervention in corporate decision making as an intolerable invasion of its management prerogatives. George Romney of the Automobile Manufacturers' Association expressed the fear of American capitalists when he claimed that "Walter Reuther is the most dangerous man in Detroit because no one is more skillful in bringing about the revolution without seeming to disturb the existing forms of society." A bitter stalemate ensued, and, on November 21,200,000 GM workers walked out of 96 plants in the first major strike of the postwar period.

The strike lasted for 113 days and became something of a touchstone for social opinion. Conservative newspapers attacked Reuther's program as a threat to free enterprise, while prominent liberals, including ELEANOR ROOSEVELT and HENRY MORGENTHAU, JR., viewed the company's intransigence as an attempt to force the auto workers into submission and wipe out price controls. Rallying to the union's defense, they formed a committee to raise money for the strikers. President Truman first condemned the walkout as an obstacle to his reconversion program, but then appointed a fact-finding board to investigate the dispute. After the president included "ability to pay" within the board's jurisdiction, GM, which refused to allow its profit structure and price policy to become collective bargaining issues, withdrew from the panel's hearings. The

board's report, released in January 1946, proposed a lower wage figure than the UAW demand, but supported the union's contention that the company could pay the increase without raising prices. The dispute helped precipitate a massive strike wave of steel, electrical, packing house, and other workers, creating strong industry pressure on the White House to relax its policy on prices. Early in February the administration indicated that a rise in steel prices would be approved if the companies settled with the union in that industry. This led other CIO unions to abandon the Reuther formula. On February 12 the United Electrical Workers (UE) signed a contract with GM for 30,000 workers under its jurisdiction, accepting the president's proposal of an 18.5-cents-an-hour wage increase. UAW members regarded the UE action as a "double-cross," and many felt that JAMES MATLES, a leader of the union who was close to the Communist Party, had settled, at least partly in order to discredit Reuther with a lost strike. Another issue had been the effect of seniority on employee transfers. Reuther won the right for arbitration of such disputes, but umpires generally sided with GM. On March 13 the auto workers returned to their jobs with the "pattern" increase set by the electrical and steel unions. Lichtenstein argued Reuther's failure to obtain his goals in the 1945–46 strike signaled "an end to the New Deal's capacity for a direct and progressive reconstitution of the nation's political economy." With the demise of wage and price controls later in 1946 the UAW wage gains disappeared in real terms.

Despite the failure of his anti-inflation program, Reuther's aggressive conduct of the GM strike won him the support of most noncommunist UAW militants in his subsequent bid for control of the union, which had been one his objectives in calling the strike. But the main objective had been to push a Keynesian economic structure on GM and by extension the rest of industry.

While the ensuing battle between the Reuther caucus and the Thomas-Addes faction, which included most UAW top officers, was waged principally around the issue of Communist influence in the union, the Reutherites, on the whole, attacked their opponents from the left. They condemned the Communists not as a "radical" group (during the war they had supported piecework and incentive pay schemes, which Reuther opposed as destructive of trade unionism), but as agents of a totalitarian power. At the 1946 UAW convention Reuther narrowly defeated Thomas for the presidency but failed to gain a majority for his caucus on the union's executive board. After another year of intense factional struggle, however, his supporters completed their victory with a clean sweep of the UAW governing council.

Reuther's campaign for the UAW presidency helped initiate the postwar split in the CIO over the Communist issue. Supported by such CIO officials as JAMES B. CAREY and Emil Rieve, Reuther put pressure on Philip Murray to abandon his role as a neutral conciliator within the federation and openly repudiate those on his staff and in the leadership of affiliated international unions who adhered to Communist policies. In 1948 he helped lead the fight in the CIO for support of the Marshall Plan and on behalf of withdrawal from the Communist-dominated World Federation of Trade Unions. At the federation's 1948 convention Reuther advocated expelling "those who put loyalty to the Communist Party ahead of their loyalty to the CIO and loyalty to the Soviet Union ahead of loyalty to their own country," although within the UAW he had previously opposed political purges. In the following year Murray finally moved against the electrical workers, longshoremen, and other unions in which Communists exercised a predominant influence.

As UAW president, Reuther emerged in the postwar years as one of organized labor's most aggressive and imaginative leaders. In each of the major wage disputes after 1946, the auto contracts set the dominant pattern for the CIO and usually featured important collective bargaining innovations. However, negotiations for a "third round" of wage increases in 1948 were conducted in Reuther's absence; in April he had been seriously wounded in an assassination attempt. (A short time later his brother Victor was also gunned down and nearly killed.) Lichtenstein traced these assassination attempts to gangster Santos "the Shark" Perrone, who worked with industry and with some union leaders to line his own pockets through a variety of rackets backed up by violence. At first the Big Three auto makers—Ford, Chrysler, and GM—offered only six cents an hour, but in May, after the UAW began a strike against Chrysler, GM suddenly broke industry ranks with a proposal for annual wage increases and a cost of living escalator provision in exchange for a two-year contract. The concepts of an "annual improvement factor," to be added to workers' pay each year as their share of rising out-

put per man hour, and an escalator formula, under which wages would be adjusted up or down according to the Bureau of Labor Statistics's cost of living index, were devised by GM president CHARLES E. WILSON. Wilson had long sought to move the industry away from annual bargaining, which encouraged unstable labor relations, toward a system of longer range settlements; he regarded the 1948 contract concessions as necessary to winning UAW support for a two-year agreement.

In 1949 the UAW launched a campaign for company-paid pensions, during which Reuther coined the popular phrase, "too old to work and too young to die," to describe workers forced into a bleak retirement on Social Security payments. While GM insisted that pensions were a management prerogative not subject to bargaining, Ford indicated a willingness to negotiate the issue. In October the company agreed to pay the entire cost of pensions by putting $20 million a year into a special fund that guaranteed retirement benefits to auto workers.

In May 1950 the UAW signed an unprecedented five-year contract with GM, which included a modified union shop. Hailed by *Fortune* magazine as the "treaty of Detroit," the agreement survived only two years. By 1952 the Korean War had sent prices soaring, shrinking the buying power of auto workers despite the contracts' cost of living provisions. Responding to growing rank-and-file unrest reflected in a wave of wildcat strikes, Reuther moved to reopen talks with the industry in the fall, arguing that the agreements were "living documents" that should be revised to meet changed conditions. Key plants were struck over local grievances, virtually halting production at GM and Ford and finally forcing the Big Three to agree to raise pensions and wage rates.

During the Truman years Reuther was also actively involved in politics as the leading union spokesman for the liberal-labor coalition. Along with such left-wing New Deal figures as Leon Henderson, ARTHUR M. SCHLESINGER, JR., and HUBERT H. HUMPHREY, with whom he maintained close political connections, Reuther proposed extending the social reforms of the Roosevelt era toward the creation of a "mixed economy" along the lines of the British Labor Party's program. Instead of a trade union–based third party, however, he generally favored a "political realignment" of the Democratic Party by drawing into it liberal Republicans and excluding southern conservatives. In 1947 the UAW joined Michigan reform clubs in a successful takeover of the state's weak and relatively conservative Democratic organization. The union's large Detroit auto worker constituency and control of the Michigan CIO Political Action Committee, which functioned as a powerful partisan campaign organization, enabled it to revitalize and liberalize the party and to win a series of dramatic electoral victories for Democratic gubernatorial and congressional candidates.

The passage of the Taft-Hartley Act in 1947 caused a shift in Reuther's attitude toward the state's involvement in labor's struggle against capital, according to Lichtenstein. He became ever more entangled in collective bargaining and upholding contracts, which constrained the social ideals and political movement that the laborite left had once called for. For instance, Reuther in the spring of 1947 called for a political rally against Taft-Hartley to occur during the workday—which would violate the GM contract. Reuther began to have second thoughts and, although he did not cancel the event, he now saw it as a mistake. When many GM workers left early for the rally, they were fired or laid off. To get their jobs back, Reuther had to admit the political strike was a violation of the contract. The Taft-Hartley Act also required labor leaders to sign noncommunist affidavits or their union would lose the right to participate in certification elections of the National Labor Relations Board. Although Reuther did not like the law, he felt obliged to obey it so as to continue organizing—particularly when the American Federation of Labor readily agreed to take the oath.

During Truman's first two years in office, Reuther frequently criticized the administration and occasionally indicated a willingness to entertain the idea of a national third party. Declaring in the spring of 1946 that the New Deal was a "spent force in the Democratic Party," he joined the National Committee for a New Party, which included civil rights leader A. PHILIP RANDOLPH, farm leader James Patton, and Socialist spokesman NORMAN THOMAS. With the emergence of HENRY A. WALLACE's independent candidacy early in the following year, however, Reuther, who regarded the Wallace movement as a Communist maneuver, helped form the Americans for Democratic Action (ADA), a coalition of anticommunist liberals organized to work as a pressure group within the national Democratic organization. An outspoken proponent of the "dump Truman" drive prior to the 1948 Democratic National Convention, he joined Humphrey, CHESTER BOWLES, and several other ADA figures in an unsuccessful last-minute effort to draft Supreme Court justice WILLIAM O. DOUGLAS for the party's presidential nomination. Afterward Reuther endorsed Truman and even campaigned for him. At the same time he considered Republican candidate THOMAS E. DEWEY's victory a virtual certainty and the disintegration of the Democratic Party its probable outcome. As a result, he scheduled a conference on political problems for January 1949, following Dewey's expected inauguration, at which the first steps were to be taken to form a new party. Reuther abandoned these plans after the president's upset victory in November.

Reuther's relations with the administration remained somewhat cool through Truman's second term. At the 1952 Democratic National Convention, he played a key role in discouraging Vice President ALBEN W. BARKLEY from seeking the party's nomination and delivering important labor support to Illinois governor ADLAI E. STEVENSON. Shortly after Stevenson's defeat in the November elections, Reuther further enhanced his national standing by winning election to the presidency of the CIO, made vacant by the death of Philip Murray.

Reuther headed the CIO until its merger with the American Federation of Labor in 1955. He became a vice president of the new AFL-CIO and was put in charge of its Industrial Union Department. Reuther also continued to negotiate pacesetting bargaining agreements for the UAW until 1958, when the recession of that year cut the union's membership from 1.5 to 1.1 million. As working conditions in the auto industry deteriorated during the late 1950s and early 1960s, Reuther began to face growing internal opposition as well as recurrent wildcat strikes following negotiation of each companywide contract. At the same time he clashed repeatedly with AFL-CIO president GEORGE MEANY over foreign policy and domestic issues. In 1968 Reuther formally withdrew the UAW from the federation. On May 10, 1970, he and his wife were killed near Pellston, Michigan, when their chartered jet crashed on landing. (See *The Eisenhower Years, The Kennedy Years, The Johnson Years, The Nixon/Ford Years* volumes)

—TLH

Richardson, Seth W(hitley)

(1880–1953) *chairman, Loyalty Review Board; chairman, Subversive Activities Control Board*

The son of a Methodist minister and a descendent of early New England settlers, Seth Richardson was born on February 4, 1880, in Otterville, Iowa. After obtaining a law degree from the University of Wisconsin in 1903, Richardson began practice in Kenmare, North Dakota. He served as assistant state attorney for Cass County, North Dakota, from 1904 to 1908 and was special assistant to the attorney general of North Dakota in 1919 and 1920. A Republican, he was appointed U.S. district attorney for North Dakota in 1923 and assistant attorney general in 1929. Richardson returned to private practice after the Democratic victory of 1932 and represented a number of large corporations in antitrust suits. He also served as counsel for airlines before the Civil Aeronautics Board.

Richardson became chief committee counsel for the Joint Congressional Committee Investigating the Pearl Harbor Attack in January 1946. The panel's final report, prepared by Richardson and signed by eight of 10 committee members, exonerated the Roosevelt administration from culpability for the surprise attack. It stated that Roosevelt had not deliberately provoked war with Japan. He had expected a surprise attack on the British and Dutch colonies in Southeast Asia. Admiral Husband E. Kimmel and General Walter C. Short, respectively the army and navy commanders at Pearl Harbor, were faulted for "errors of judgment," but not "dereliction of duty," Richardson later claimed that after about August 1941 responsible officials began to think less and less of any imminent danger to Pearl Harbor from such an attack. Historians Gordon W. Prange, Donald M. Goldstein, and Katherine V. Dillon, however, disagree, saying Washington continued to warn military and naval officials at Pearl of possible Japanese military action.

In November 1947 President Truman appointed Richardson chairman of the Loyalty Review Board, a 20-member group that was responsible for investigating disloyal activity or membership in subversive organizations by government employees. It was the highest panel of appeal for employees dismissed from government jobs as security risks. Truman pledged the board would not be guilty of "witch-hunting." He instructed the panel to hear appeals in individual cases of dismissals for disloyalty as well as to develop the standards for determining loyalty and investigative procedures.

By September 1948 Richardson's panel was responsible for the discharge or resignation of 883 government employees out of a total of two million. According to a report Richardson submitted in

January 1950, out of 2.8 million employees screened during his tenure, 10,359 were sent to the FBI for investigation but only 139 were formally dismissed. Richardson recommended that the Loyalty Review Board be granted permanent status to enable the government to handle the growing number of new federal employees hired annually. Along with members of the Justice Department, he urged Truman to tighten and clarify dismissal standards for employees. He believed that any doubts about any individual's loyalty should be sufficient to result in his dismissal since he viewed federal employment as a valuable privilege rather than as a right. Following advice from Richardson and others, Truman issued Executive Order 10241, which denied employment to those "who are potentially disloyal or are bad security risks."

Several of the Loyalty Board's decisions came under attack from right-wing elements. In 1949, for example, the board reversed the decision of a subordinate panel that Commerce Department employee WILLIAM W. REMINGTON be dismissed from the federal government because of former Communist association. Richardson's clearance of the Commerce official made him something of a hero among liberals. By May 1950 Richardson's board had overturned the findings of subordinate panels of suspected disloyalty in 143 out of 451 cases. During the Tydings Committee hearing of 1950 regarding Senator JOSEPH R. MCCARTHY's (R-Wisc.) accusations of subversion in the State Department, Richardson said, "We have not received any evidence of any card-carrying Communists in the State Department, up to the present time." After Richardson's death, Senator Joseph R. McCarthy contented that he had conducted the Loyalty Review Board by the principle "not to discharge any employees merely because they were Communists."

Richardson was involved in the court case *Bailey v. Richardson*. The case concerned Dorothy Bailey, a former government employee trying to be reemployed. She had to undergo a Loyalty Review Board hearing, and found she had been accused of being a Communist and a member of two groups on the Attorney General's subversive list. She denied she was a Communist but the board did not reinstate her. Bailey went to court to reverse the decision, claiming she had been denied due process, as she had not been able to confront her accusers, see the evidence against her, nor did the board explain its decision. The U.S. Court of Appeals upheld the board's action, saying government employment was a privilege, not property, and thus not subject to due process rights. The Supreme Court, in 4-4 decision, upheld the appeals court's decision.

The question arose of how adverse an Loyalty Board decision affected future employment in the private sector. In 1947 Richardson said, "this loyalty program applies only to government employees and of course not to citizens in general." He later admitted, however, that after a disloyalty dismissal "a man is ruined everywhere and forever. No reputable employer would be likely to take a chance in giving him a job."

Richardson opposed the idea of creating a Subversive Activities Control Board in response to growing criticism that the administration was not handling the problem of domestic subversion properly. He felt the proposal was a personal affront to him and the Loyalty Board. "Any step taken now in the hope of allaying hostile criticism [of the Truman administration as procommunist], would, in my opinion, only make a bad matter worse," he wrote in June 1950.

When the board was formed to administer the Internal Security Act of 1950, Truman chose Richardson chairman. The panel was a bipartisan commission responsible for deciding which organizations should register with the Justice Department as subversive groups under the act. After his appointment Richardson, who agreed with Truman that the board was an impracticable idea, said, "If I wasn't 70 and curious to see whether the president or congress is right about the workability of the law, I wouldn't have touched this job with a 10-foot pole."

Richardson's first assignment was the review of Justice Department charges that several Communist organizations considered subversive had not registered under the McCarran Act. On April 23, 1951, the Subversive Activities Control Board began hearings to decide whether the Communist Party should register as a foreign agency controlled by the Soviet Union. Representative VITO MARCANTONIO (ALP-N.Y.) and John Abt, attorneys for the party, challenged the board's authority to act, but Richardson overruled them. The board's investigation was not completed when Richardson resigned in 1951 because of ill-health. In April 1953 the panel ruled that the party was a Communist action group and hence had to register with the Attorney General.

In retirement Richardson opposed President Dwight D. Eisenhower's plan to terminate the Loy-

alty Review Board and decentralize administration of employee loyalty investigations within the executive departments with dismissed employees having recourse to appeal to federal courts. Richardson protested that the plan would give federal courts, rather than the president "real power" over dismissals. He died on March 17, 1953, in Washington, D.C.

—AES

Ridgway, Matthew B(unker)

(1895–1993) *commander in chief of the United Nations Command and supreme commander for the Allied powers, supreme commander for the Allied powers in Europe*

Ridgway, the son of an army colonel, was born in Fort Monroe, Virginia, on March 3, 1895, and raised on various military posts. In 1917 he received a B.S. degree from the U.S. Military Academy at West Point and, during the next two decades, served on numerous assignments in Central America, the Far East, and the United States. By 1936 he was deputy chief of staff. In September 1939 Ridgway was assigned to the War Department general staff in Washington, D.C., to work with the War Plans Division. He remained there until January 1942, when he became assistant division commander and, shortly thereafter, commander of the 82nd Infantry Division. Ridgway headed one of the army's first airborne units and participated in the invasion of Sicily, the Italian campaign, and the assault on Normandy. In late 1945 he was appointed a representative of General DWIGHT D. EISENHOWER on the Military Staff Commission of the United Nations. This body was created by the UN Charter to advise the Security Council on military matters. Ridgway assisted in the preparation of a report that formulated the general principles for the organization of an armed force controlled by the Security Council. The document was described by the *New York Herald Tribune* as marking "the first, and albeit faltering step toward the establishment of an international police force." Critics pointed out it had serious limitations: the international force would not be used against any of the permanent nations of the council or the allies because they had the right to veto military sanctions. Ridgway felt that the guarantees of world peace were the hope and objective of the future, but he warned Americans not to think "that they can confide their military security today to the UN."

While serving on the Military Staff Commission, Ridgway also was an adviser to the U.S. civilian delegation to the UN General Assembly and senior delegate to the Inter-American Defense Board. This latter body was formed to plan the standardization of organization, training procedure, and equipment among Western allies. In August 1948 Ridgway was made commander of the Caribbean Defense Command and the Panama Canal Department.

At the outset of the Korean War Ridgway was deputy chief of staff, and he became frustrated at the Joint Chief of Staff's unwillingness to control UN commander general of the army DOUGLAS MACARTHUR.

At MacArthur's request Ridgway took over the Eighth Army after the death of its commander, Lieutenant General Walton Walker, who died in an auto accident. Ridgway took command after the Chinese had driven the UN forces into a pell-mell retreat southward. There was even talk in Washington and Tokyo of evacuating the peninsula. Ridgway, however, never considered such an option. He quickly set about to restore the confidence and morale of the troops. A man of great persuasive ability, Ridgway traveled among the soldiers to encourage them and relieved officers he thought were not aggressive enough. Known for carrying a grenade and first-aid kit worn on a paratrooper shoulder strap, Ridgway was given a free hand in Korea by MacArthur. He quickly stopped the retreat to the south of Seoul, and in offensives in January, February, March, and April 1951, Ridgway began to drive the communists back, retaking Seoul on March 21.

On April 11 Ridgway was ordered to take the place of the cashiered MacArthur as Commander of UN forces in Korea, as well as the U.S. Far East Command, the U.S. Army in the Far East, and the Allied occupation of Japan. Seeing what had happened to MacArthur, Ridgway was determined to communicate better with Washington and follow its orders to the letter. Ironically, he began making demands similar to MacArthur in the way of asking for more troops. Ridgway kept a close eye on his successor as Eighth Army commander lieutenant general James A. Van Fleet, whom he thought too aggressive, whereas Ridgway wanted to abide by the limited war doctrine of Washington. In late April and early May Eighth Army stopped the Chinese spring offensive and again drove north; however, Ridgway cancelled a proposed offensive of Van Fleet

to drive up to the narrower waist of the peninsula. He saw this as keeping in line with Washington directives, but historians D. Clayton James and Anne Sharp Wells noted the decision might have lengthened the war by reducing pressure on the Chinese and North Koreans. Ridgway ordered an end to major U.S. offensives in November 1951, as peace talks got under way at Panmunjon, after having failed in Kaesong. Ridgway left the Far East in April 1952, after the Japanese Peace Treaty with the United States became effective.

Ridgway succeeded Eisenhower as Supreme Commander of Allied Forces in Europe on June 1, 1952. He warned the "lords of communism" not to mistake Western "tolerance and magnanimity" in the face of cold war provocations for weakness and said that another world war "could bring dreadful suffering to us but it would bring destruction to them and their power." In July 1952 Truman widened Ridgway's command to include the European, Eastern Atlantic, and Mediterranean naval and air forces. The following year Ridgway said that the "threat" posed by the military strength of "potential aggressors had not diminished one iota in the last two years."

Ridgway was relieved as supreme Allied commander in Europe in May 1953. Two years later he retired from the army to become director of Colt Industries. During the Johnson administration Ridgway was one of a number of military men who attempted to persuade the president to limit U.S. involvement in Vietnam. Ridgway died on July 26, 1993, in Fox Chapel, Pennsylvania. (See *The Eisenhower Years, The Johnson Years* Volumes)

—MLB

Robertson, A(bsalom) Willis
(1887–1971) *member of the House of Representatives, member of the Senate*

A. Willis Robertson was born on May 27, 1887, in Martinsburg, West Virginia. A member of a distinguished Virginia family, he received his B.A. degree in history from the University of Richmond in 1907 and his LL.B. there the following year. Robertson first entered politics when he served in the Virginia Senate from 1916 to 1922. For the next six years he was the attorney for Rockbridge County. In 1932 Robertson won election to the U.S. House of Representatives, where he was returned until his election to the Senate in 1946.

During his tenure in the House, the Virginia Democrat developed the reputation as a champion of conservationist causes. He sponsored an influential and policy-setting House resolution in 1934 providing for the establishment of a Select Committee on Conservation of Wild Life Resources, and he helped lead the fight for the resultant Wild Life Conservation Act of 1937. In the same year Robertson became the first Virginian in 37 years assigned to the powerful Ways and Means Committee. For his remaining 10 years in the House he focused on the problems of taxation. He voted against the Roosevelt administration on the central elements of the New Deal and with it on questions of defense and foreign affairs. In the postwar era he continued this conservative and internationalist voting trend. As a representative he voted for the Case labor disputes bill and the British loan of 1946. There were exceptions, however, such as when he voted for the Employment Act of 1946.

Robertson saw himself as a man working for the preservation of states' rights and individual constitutional freedoms. A conservative in the manner of his fellow Virginian, Senator HARRY F. BYRD (D-Va.), Robertson opposed the general extension of federal power, social welfare programs, and racial integration. But Robertson was not on close terms with Byrd or the other organization leaders. It was the strength of his own extensive, informal network of supporters and friends that forced the Democratic machine in Virginia to back him in 1946 when he won an election to fill the unexpired term of the late senator Carter Glass.

As a senator, Robertson maintained his conservative voting pattern, opposing social and labor legislation. He supported the Taft-Hartley Act of 1947 and the Republican tax cut of 1948. In 1949 he voted against the public housing features of the Truman housing bill. During the coal strike of 1950, Robertson introduced a bill to subject unions to civil and criminal action under the antitrust laws if they threatened the nation's economy, health, or safety. With the settlement of the strike, no action was taken on the measure. He was among three Democrats voting against Truman's plan to reorganize the Reconstruction Finance Corporation, preferring its abolition. Typical for a southern Senator of the time, he opposed civil rights for blacks, and he voted against cloture in the debate over establishing a Fair Employment Practices Commission in 1950.

Robertson supported the Truman administration's foreign policy, voting for the 1946 British loan, Greek-Turkish aid in 1947, and the Marshall Plan in 1948. He was a strong supporter of the North Atlantic Treaty Organization, and supported sending military aid to it in 1949. He also supported extensions of the Trade Agreement Act of 1934. In the 1951 debate over the U.S. role in NATO, Robertson favored the stationing of U.S. troops in Europe. He endorsed Truman's call for universal military training and supported the draft bill. Robertson backed the extension of foreign aid programs. He opposed making Marshall Plan aid contingent on the foreign trade policies of prospective recipient nations, calling it "dollar diplomacy." He helped lead the successful opposition against the proposal to include fascist Spain in the plan. He occasionally differed from the administration, such as when he backed a cut in aid to Europe in 1951.

In 1948 Robertson was an early, behind-the-scenes proponent of General DWIGHT D. EISENHOWER for president. He believed Eisenhower was the only candidate who could unite the nation and deal with the Soviet Union. Robertson visited Eisenhower privately early in the year, and he came away from the meeting with the belief that the general would succumb to a draft. He urged southern colleagues to join him in persuading Truman to step aside in favor of Eisenhower. They declined to act on his advice.

With Eisenhower unavailable Robertson, in July, became the first of the major Virginia Democrats to announce support of Truman for a second term. He felt the Dixiecrats, who had broken with Truman over civil rights, would hurt the cause of states' rights. At the same time Robertson stated that he had "no idea of accepting the interpretation of our Democratic platform with respect to a civil rights program which Mr. Truman has placed upon it." Again, in 1951, Robertson worked to promote an Eisenhower candidacy. When it became clear that Eisenhower was a Republican, Robertson confidentially asked the financier BERNARD M. BARUCH to help support the general as the 1952 Republican candidate.

During the Eisenhower years Robertson continued to build a reputation in the Senate as an expert on foreign trade, banking and currency, and tariffs and taxation. He obtained the chairmanship of the Banking and Currency Committee in 1959. In this post Robertson was among the leading critics and opponents of the programs of the Kennedy New Frontier and the Johnson Great Society. In

1966 Robertson lost the Democratic primary to William B. Spong, Jr., a moderate state senator. After the defeat he resigned from the Senate in order to give Spong seniority and became a consultant to the International Bank for Reconstruction and Development. Robertson died on November 1, 1971, in Lexington, Virginia. (See *The Eisenhower Years, The Kennedy Years, The Johnson Years* Volumes)

—SF

Robeson, Paul B(ustill)

(1898–1976) *entertainer, political activist*

Paul B. Robeson was born on April 9, 1898, in Princeton, New Jersey. His father was an ex-slave who later became a minister, and his mother was a Philadelphia schoolteacher. Robeson won a four-year academic scholarship to Rutgers College in his senior year at Somerville (N.J.) High School. A brilliant scholar-athlete, he was only the third black stu-

Actor and activist Paul Robeson, 1942 *(Library of Congress, Prints and Photographs Division, FSA/OWI Collection, Photographed by Gordon Parks)*

dent in the school's history. After graduating in 1919 he supported himself through Columbia Law School by playing professional football on the weekends. He graduated in 1923 and began a law career but soon decided to enter the theater, a field in which he had displayed great talent while in law school. In the ensuing decades he earned fame as a stage and motion picture actor and as a singer. He made recordings of folk songs and spirituals in over 20 languages, and his rich baritone became familiar to millions of people.

As his career progressed, Robeson became increasingly identified with left-wing causes. He was outspoken in his condemnation of the treatment of blacks in the United States. He left the United States in 1928 to tour Europe and was impressed by the social climate there. During the 1930s Robeson spent a great deal of time in England, where he joined several left-wing anti-fascist groups. He visited the Soviet Union, returning convinced that the communist experiment of a classless society was succeeding. Robeson learned Russian and became a folk-hero to the Soviets, but his espousal of the Soviet cause damaged his reputation in the United States. In the mid-1930s he entertained Loyalist troops fighting in the Spanish Civil War. When Robeson and his family returned to the United States in 1939, he said he found the racial climate had improved with the New Deal. During World War II he was active in the Popular Front against fascism.

He was disappointed after the war when only the defeated powers' colonies where put under UN trusteeships, rather than all colonies. As chairman of the Council of African Affairs, he called on the administration to act in this matter, but Secretary of State EDWARD R. STETTINIUS, JR., evaded his questions. When he received the National Association for the Advancement of Colored People Spingarn Medal in 1945, he proclaimed the hostility toward the Soviets by the U.S. and Great Britain presaged the rising once again of fascism. According to biographer Martin Bauml Duberman, his reception of the Spingarn Medal marked the zenith of his public acclaim and the beginning of the decline of reputation in the United States.

Robeson lost much of his popularity as the cold war intensified. At the height of his success, in 1947, he was earning $100,000 a year; by 1952 his income had dropped to an annual $6,000. Rather than mute his criticism of American foreign policy and racial practices, Robeson actively entered the political forum. For example, he led a delegation that urged baseball commissioner Kenesaw Mountain Landis to drop racial bars in professional baseball. In 1946 he visited the White House to pressure President Truman to protect the civil rights of African Americans in the South. Robeson was particularly interested in an antilynching bill. After heated discussion, in which Truman said the timing had to be right before an antilynching law could be passed, Robeson declared that if the federal government would not protect blacks against lynch mobs, they would defend themselves. Truman abruptly ended the interview. That year he denied membership in the Communist Party before a committee of the California State Legislature.

In April 1947 Robeson went to Peoria, Illinois, during a concert tour. Two days before his performance, the House Un-American Activities Committee (HUAC) declared him—along with nearly 1,000 others—as one "invariably found supporting the Communist Party and its front organizations." The Peoria City Council resolved against the appearance of a performer who they said was "an avowed propagandist for Un-American ideology." The authorities did not give him a place to sing. Other cities imposed restrictions on what Robeson could say. He traveled in the Deep South, speaking at no inconsiderable risk, about the need for civil rights for blacks.

In 1948 Robeson became a founder and cochairman of the Progressive Party and delivered an emotional speech at the party's convention in July. There was even talk of Robeson being Wallace's running mate, but Robeson withdrew his name at the convention. He added that everyone was employed in the USSR and discrimination did not exist. He actively participated in the Progressive campaign for presidential candidate HENRY A. WALLACE by raising funds and performing. In 1949 he provoked controversy when he was misquoted by the Associated Press as saying to the World Peace Congress in Paris that American blacks would not go to war "on behalf of those who have oppressed us for generations against a country [the USSR] which in one generation has raised our people to full dignity of mankind." In fact he had said that America's wealth had been made "on the backs of white workers from Europe . . . and on the backs of millions of blacks. . . . And we are resolved to share it equally among our children. And we shall not put up with

any hysterical raving that urges us to make war on anyone. Our will to fight for peace is strong. We shall not make war on anyone." The mistakenly attributed comments brought on a storm of criticism in the United States. HUAC heard the testimony of several black leaders, including baseball star JACKIE ROBINSON, who denied blacks were less patriotic than other Americans. Former Communist Manning Johnson claimed Robeson dreamed of becoming "a black Stalin." WALTER F. WHITE said many blacks would be happy if Robeson's words led to equality, but further noted that blacks were Americans who would fight for their country. In fact the black civil rights establishment blasted Robeson. In August 1949 he attempted to appear for a performance at a music festival in Peekskill, New York, sponsored by the radical Civil Rights Congress. It was postponed when protesters put 20 concertgoers in the hospital. The concert went forward in September with unionists providing security for Robeson, but there was another riot, and many attendees were injured.

Robeson's unpopular political views caused him other problems. In March 1950 the National Broadcasting Company barred him from appearing on a television show with ELEANOR ROOSEVELT. In August Madison Square Garden refused a rally for the Council on African Affairs backed by Robeson. That month the State Department demanded he surrender his passport. It would not issue him a new one unless he signed a noncommunist oath and promised not to give political speeches overseas. Robeson refused, claiming that the government had no right to base his freedom of travel on his political beliefs. He was unable to leave the country until 1958, when the Supreme Court, ruling in a similar case, found the government's demands unconstitutional.

Robeson continued his strident denunciations of American policy in the early 1950s, protesting U.S. involvement in Korea and attacking what he called the "genocide" of blacks in America. In 1952 the Soviet Union awarded him the Stalin Peace Prize. In 1956 Robeson appeared before HUAC during hearings on the revocation of U.S. passports. He refused to answer most questions on constitutional grounds. HUAC threatened him with a contempt citation, but no action was taken.

Before leaving the United States in 1958, Robeson gave a farewell concert at Carnegie Hall in New York City. He remained abroad until 1963 when, back in New York, he announced his retirement from the stage and all public affairs. At a 75th birthday celebration for the singer, Mayor Richard Hatcher of Gary, Indiana, called Robeson "our own black prince and prophet." Robeson died on January 23, 1976, in Philadelphia, Pennsylvania. (See *The Eisenhower Years* Volume)

—JF

Robinson, Jackie (John) (Roosevelt)
(1919–1972) *baseball player*

The son of sharecroppers, Jackie Robinson was born on January 31, 1919, in Cairo, Georgia. His father abandoned him at the age of 18 months. His family moved to Pasadena, California, where his mother worked as a domestic. Robinson attended the University of California at Los Angeles on an athletic scholarship and became a star player on its football team. In 1941 he was invited to play professional football with the Los Angeles Bulldogs. Robinson served in the army during World War II.

After an excellent year in the Negro National League, in August 1945 Robinson was signed by coach Branch Rickey to the Brooklyn Dodgers top farm team, the Montreal Royals. On the way to training camp in Daytona Beach, Robinson and his wife had to face the petty humiliations of Jim Crow. As his biographer Arnold Rampersad noted, Robinson's success with the Royals caused people to try to employ him to fight for racial equality in other areas. For instance, in 1946 the organizing committee of the United Negro and Allied Veterans of America asked Robinson to be its chairman. Robinson said he would accept the post and come speak to the group at Harlem, saying, "The burning problems of discrimination in housing, employment, education and on-the-job training facing Negro veterans demand an immediate solution." However, Robinson did not go because Rickey usually did not allow players to make public speeches during the playing season and, as a Republican and anticommunist, would not have approved an organization started by leftists.

In the runup to the 1947 season, Rickey urged New York City black leaders not to overplay Robinson's ascension to the majors, as it would antagonize whites. The officials agreed and word was passed through African-American newspapers and pulpits counseling moderation. Some Dodger players, particularly those from the South, resisted playing with a black man at first. Manager Leo Durocher balled them out, and Rickey made it clear he would decide

who was on the team and Durocher would decide who played, Rickey signed Robinson in April 1947. Rickey was determined to make Robinson the first African American in the major league. Assuming that success would be based not only on Robinson's baseball skill but also on his ability to cope with prejudice, the two staged a series of potential confrontations so that Robinson could practice tolerance when confronted by militant whites.

A man of fiery temperament, Robinson displayed an incredible amount of self-control during his career. Hotels refused him accommodations and airlines cancelled his reservations. Players threw balls at his head and deliberately spiked him. Verbal abuse was common. With few exceptions teammates refused to accept him during his first year.

In 1949 the House Un-American Activities Committee called Robinson to testify on black loyalty to the United States. In contrast to Paul Robeson, who allegedly claimed that blacks would not go to war against the USSR because of the dignity with which he said they were treated in Russia, Robinson supported America's stand in the cold war. "You can put me down as an expert on being a colored American," he said. "We can win our fight without Communists, and we don't want their help."

In 1947 Robinson was named rookie of the year and two years later the National League's most valuable player. While Robinson was with the Dodgers, the team won six National League pennants. He retired in 1956 and was elected to the National Baseball Hall of Fame six years later. Robinson was the first black so honored.

Upon his retirement he became vice president of Chock Full O' Nuts Corporation and was active in the civil rights movement. He died of a heart attack on October 24, 1972, in Stamford, Connecticut.

As Rampersad noted, Robinson did more than end segregation in the major leagues. Robinson "had revolutionized the image of black Americans in the eyes of many whites," and, as writer Jules Tygiel indicated, the ballplayer had become "a symbol of pride and dignity" to African Americans.

—SB

Rockefeller, Nelson A(ldrich)
(1908–1979) *assistant secretary of state for Latin American Affairs*

The grandson of oil magnate John D. Rockefeller, Nelson A. Rockefeller was born on July 8, 1908, in

Bar Harbor, Maine, and graduated from Dartmouth College in 1930. He began his apprenticeship in the family's financial empire as a clerk in the International Division of Chase Manhattan Bank and worked in the rental department of New York City's Rockefeller Center. From 1935 to 1940 Rockefeller was a director of the family's Creole Petroleum Company, an affiliate of Standard Oil. Creole had large holdings in Latin America, especially Venezuela. During his visits to Latin America in the late 1930s, Rockefeller was shocked to see the poverty often caused by Creole's callous treatment of the people. Convinced that future U.S. capital investments in Latin America must be tied to an increase in the standard of living there, Rockefeller set out to change American economic policy toward that area. After a business trip to Latin America in 1937, Rockefeller and a group of associates wrote a memorandum calling for business to humanize its practices and asking the government to encourage an improvement in cultural and political relations between the United States and its neighbors. Such an improved environment, Rockefeller believed, would make Latin America even more conducive to American investment. Franklin D. Roosevelt, impressed with the report, made Rockefeller coordinator of the Office of Inter-American Affairs in 1940.

Known for his ebullience and unbridled energy, Rockefeller turned his agency into an efficient and effective operation. Before the American entry into World War II, he coordinated the successful American blacklist of Latin American businesses favoring the fascist powers. Rockefeller also improved cultural contacts between the American and Hispanic peoples and further increased American humanitarian aid. In December 1944, in reward for his performance, he was appointed assistant secretary of state for Latin American affairs.

During World War II Rockefeller clashed with Secretary of State Cordell Hull over the department's policy of publicly ostracizing Argentina for its sympathy to the fascists. He preferred to quietly woo Argentina away from fascism. Rockefeller's biographer Cary Reich argued that Rockefeller had followed an incremental strategy to move the United States and Argentina closer together. Hull deeply resented Rockefeller's intrusion in State Department affairs. When EDWARD R. STETTINIUS, JR., succeeded Hull in 1944, he accepted Rockefeller's recommendations. These recommendations were that the Argentines would have to declare war on Ger-

many and Japan, adhere to the "principles and declarations" of the Chapultepec Conference of early 1945, and sign the Act of Chapultepec, which called for a regional peace-keeping alliance in order to reestablish relations with the United States and to gain its support to join the UN. Rockefeller's plan succeeded. Argentina belatedly declared war against the Axis powers and nominally agreed to the other requirements. In return the United States agreed to support the admission of Argentina into the United Nations. This pledge repudiated Roosevelt's promise to Stalin to oppose the entry of any nation that collaborated with the Nazis. Franklin Roosevelt had okayed Rockefeller's plan, but Reich believed FDR did not realize the full import of what he had agreed to—going back on a promise to the Soviet dictator and he would not have gone along with the agreement if he had.

A number of high officials in the Truman administration urged the new president not to support Argentina's admission. W. AVERELL HARRIMAN, for example, argued that for the United States to break its promise to Stalin would morally justify Soviet policies in Poland that were equally reprehensible. Nelson Rockefeller emerged in the early days of the Truman administration as a one-man lobby for the Argentines. Harriman recalled asking him, "Nelson, are you the ambassador to the Argentine or the ambassador of the Argentine? HENRY A. WALLACE wrote in his diary that U.S. delegation aide ADLAI E. STEVENSON told him that "Nelson Rockefeller places the unity of the hemisphere above the unity of the world." He worked to construct a unified Pan-American alliance in an uncertain world in which he anticipated trouble with the Soviet Union. He argued that Argentina had to be in the alliance to make it effective. In addition, to win support of other conservative Latin American states, Rockefeller insisted that the United States must show them it was willing to forgive Argentina for its past mistakes. Rockefeller lobbied successfully for admission of Argentina during the San Francisco Conference. Soviet foreign minister Vyacheslav Molotov demanded that the Ukraine and Byelorussia, both Soviet republics, be given their own membership in the United Nations, saying he would leave if this promise of the Yalta Agreement was not met, meaning the collapse of the meeting. Secretary of State Edward Stettinius agreed, but he had to round up the votes. The best place for those was Latin America, and the person to unlock the key was Rockefeller. But the Latin Americans demanded Argentina be invited to the UN conference and admitted to the UN itself. Truman reluctantly agreed. (Some observers suspected Rockefeller had orchestrated Latin America's demand for a quid pro quo.)

Rockefeller had been looking for a way to exempt regional alliance of the Americas called for by the Act of Chapultepec from the veto of the Big Five in the Security Council. His main concern was a Communist threat to Latin America. Much to Stettinius's ire, Rockefeller had secretly worked with delegate senator ARTHUR H. VANDENBERG (R-Mich.) to draw up the exemption. Such an exemption was sure to provoke a hostile response from the Soviets. HAROLD E. STASSEN worked a way out the imbroglio—a country's right to defend itself could be extrapolated to include mutual security pacts. At first there was to be a specific exemption for Chapultepec and the Monroe Doctrine. But this was dropped upon objections from other nations, and, in the end, the Americans privately assured the Latin Americans there would a treaty conference after the UN meeting was finished to form a regional pact. (This became the Rio Pact of 1947.) The Soviets agreed to the new clause, Article 51, which allowed for regional defensive alliance. This led to a plethora of pacts that made the UN somewhat superfluous to international collective security.

Rockefeller's critics claimed that his interest in Article 51 was based on his financial holdings in Latin America. Having a future defense alliance with the conservative states there would protect the continent from social change. The alliance could justify future American military intervention there to protect its investments. Rockefeller's apologists defended his dream for a unified Latin America as a needed weapon to contain communism. They pointed out that because of Rockefeller's humanitarian interests in Latin America, it was wrong to link his name with more reactionary forces.

In May 1945, while the San Francisco Conference was in session, Rockefeller testified before a congressional committee requesting a $2 million appropriation for Latin American affairs to make the region a bulwark against Soviet expansion. Rockefeller's stand made him the enemy of the American left and those internationalists who thought the admission of Argentina and the passage of Article 51 undermined the United Nations. Believing he had been misrepresented, Rockefeller

attempted to repair the damage. He had an aide try to arrange a meeting between him and Cordell Hull. Hull, resentful of the way "Little Rockefeller" handled the Argentine matter, responded to the overture with, "You can tell the young whippersnapper to go to Hell!" Because of his aggressiveness, Rockefeller also antagonized the career professionals of the State Department. When JAMES F. BYRNES became secretary of state in the summer of 1945, he offered the post of undersecretary to DEAN G. ACHESON. Acheson accepted it on one condition, Rockefeller must go. The president and Byrnes gladly complied.

Rockefeller returned to his financial interests but continued to be involved in Latin American affairs. Backed by his family's money, he founded the American International Association for Economic and Social Development (AIA) in July 1946 and the International Basic Economy Corporation (IBCE) in January 1947. He served as president and director of both groups. Rockefeller hoped they would raise the standard of living in Latin America through help from the American private sector. AIA sought to distribute money directly to the people in the form of agrarian aid. IBEC funded capital investments in Latin American industry. Critics of the programs charged that money never reached the poverty-stricken areas Rockefeller intended it to; instead, the Latin American rich and middle class benefited from the assistance. However, Rockefeller's AIA and his interest in getting the United States to extend aid to the developing world helped initiate Truman's Point Four program.

In November 1950 President Truman appointed Rockefeller chairman of the Advisory Board on International Development of the Point Four program. Rockefeller argued that a centralized agency was needed to run the program and that it should be a private-public cooperative effort. The aim of the program would be to raise living standards in the developing world so as to diminish the allure of communism. However, the administration would not establish a centralized foreign aid agency, nor would it give incentives to the private sector to invest in developing nations. Congress, however, pushed through a bill that created the Mutual Security Administration, which was to handle all foreign aid, economic and military, except for Point Four technical assistance, which would be handled by the State Department. Rockefeller had argued against combining economic and military aid under one roof.

Rockefeller quietly resigned from the advisory board, telling the press he preferred to focus his attention on the private sector's role in foreign assistance.

Rockefeller supported DWIGHT D. EISENHOWER for the presidency in 1952. He expected a cabinet position in return for his aid, but Eisenhower appointed him undersecretary of health, education, and welfare. Rockefeller left the post in 1954, frustrated with the administration's slow progress in social welfare programs. Eisenhower then named him a special assistant on foreign policy.

Rockefeller resigned from the federal government in 1955 to pursue the governorship of New York. He won election in 1958 and served until 1973. A leading Republican liberal, Rockefeller made great strides in improving the health, education, and social services of New York. But his administration was characterized by huge budget deficits and high taxes, which made him the enemy of his party's conservatives. Rockefeller sought the Republican nomination for the presidency in 1960, 1964, and 1968 but lost all three times to more conservative members of his party. He resigned the governorship in 1973 to devote his attention to a study group, which he formed, called the Commission for Critical Choices for Americans.

From 1974 to 1977 Rockefeller served as vice president in the Ford administration. He retired from politics in 1977 but continued to speak out on public issues. During the Carter administration he advised the president on efforts to ratify the Panama Canal treaty. Rockefeller died in New York City on January 26, 1979. (See *The Eisenhower Years, The Kennedy Years, The Johnson Years, The Nixon/Ford Years* Volumes)

—JB

Roosevelt, (Anna) Eleanor
(1884–1962) *delegate to the United Nations*

Eleanor Roosevelt was born on October 11, 1884, in New York City. Her parents died when she was young, and she was raised by her maternal grandmother. She was privately tutored and then sent to finishing school in London. In 1905 she married her distant cousin Franklin D. Roosevelt. Mrs. Roosevelt encouraged her husband's political career and, during the 1920s, when polio forced him to temporarily retire, she stood in for him in Democratic Party functions. It was during this period that she developed her own interests such as world disarma-

Eleanor Roosevelt *(National Archives)*

ment, the creation of an international organization to keep the peace, protection for female and child labor, and advancement for American blacks. By the time Roosevelt became governor of New York in 1929, his wife had already developed her own political power base among women and reformers. She campaigned hard for Roosevelt in 1932, stressing the issues that had become her special interest.

Mrs. Roosevelt was the nation's first politically oriented first lady. In her "My Day" column, her nationwide radio show, and her magazine articles, she discussed the major issues of the day. She served as Roosevelt's "eyes and ears" and became the unofficial advocate in the White House of help for the nation's youth, blacks, and agrarian poor. When Roosevelt died in April 1945, liberals encouraged the former first lady to remain politically active, even suggesting she run as Truman's vice presidential candidate in 1948. She ruled out pursuing any elective office and decided to continue to speak out though her column. She also was a presence in the Democratic Party. Truman requested that she evaluate for him individuals who had served her husband. She pressed the president for more liberal actions: civil rights, more women in government, and greater efforts toward world peace.

Roosevelt accepted President Truman's invitation to join the American delegation to the UN conference held in London in December 1945. Although she as well as other members of the delegation were uneasy about the appointment because she lacked diplomatic experience, Roosevelt proved a major asset to the mission. She was assigned to Committee Three, charged with humanitarian, social, and cultural matters. During 1946 and 1947 Roosevelt forcefully countered Soviet demands that Eastern European refugees be returned to their country of origin. In the debate she bested Soviet Andrey Vyshinsky—who had directed the Great Purge Trials—by deftly playing to the South American delegates in discussing Simón Bolívar's fight for freedom. She defended UN aid to displaced persons camps and asserted that refugees should have free choice in deciding where to reside.

Roosevelt served as chairman of the Commission on Human Rights formed to draft a universal statement on human rights. The panel decided to write two separate statements: one, a declaration of human rights, which would express in general terms the goals mankind should strive to reach. The General Assembly would vote on the proposal but it would not be binding. Following this a binding covenant would be drafted pledging the signatories to uphold human rights. According to biographer J. William Youngs, Roosevelt's diplomacy combined idealism and realism. She skillfully guided the commission through two years of stormy debate over the nonbinding declaration. The American delegation insisted that the document include those rights guaranteed citizens in the British, American, and French constitutions. The Russians resisted the Western demand, which they considered dangerous to the supremacy of the state, and, instead, wanted a declaration that stressed the primacy of economic rights: to a job, shelter, food, unionization, medical care, and education. Since the Western nations out-voted the Soviet bloc in the commission, the final document focused on civil rights, but at Roosevelt's urging, it did include most of the economic rights the Soviets wanted. On

December 10, 1948, the General Assembly approved the Declaration of Human Rights with the Soviet Union and its bloc abstaining. Roosevelt's commission then undertook the more difficult task of writing the covenant. She sat in on the lengthy proceedings until President Dwight D. Eisenhower replaced her in January 1953 with a Republican appointee. The General Assembly did not approve a covenant until 1966.

During the early postwar years Roosevelt supported HENRY A. WALLACE's attacks on Truman administration foreign policy and his demands for closer relations with the USSR. She joined many other liberals in deploring the administration's willingness to shore up right-wing anticommunist dictatorships in Spain, Greece, Turkey, and Latin America. However, as a result of her experiences with the Soviets in the UN and Russia's repression in Eastern Europe, she gradually came to support Truman's containment policies. Although Roosevelt questioned the ability of military means to prevent Communist expansion and deplored the growing arms race, she supported the Marshall Plan, designed to prevent the spread of communism through economic aid.

Roosevelt broke with Wallace because of his close association with Communists and his refusal to speak out against Soviet repression. In January 1948 she helped form the liberal Americans for Democratic Action (ADA) as anticommunist alternative to Wallace's Progressive Citizens of America. Roosevelt served as its first honorary chairman. The organization campaigned for Truman in the 1948 presidential election.

Roosevelt also traveled as a good-will ambassador throughout the non-Western world. The former first lady continued to condemn Soviet repression and aggression, especially in Korea. At home she advocated the continuation of New Deal programs started by her husband. She was particularly interested in establishing a national health insurance program and in ending segregation. Roosevelt also joined the small chorus of liberals condemning McCarthyism.

Roosevelt supported ADLAI E. STEVENSON's unsuccessful campaign for the presidency in 1952. Following Eisenhower's election she returned to private life but continued to travel, write, and deliver speeches for the UN and the ADA. The former first lady was also active in New York City's reform Democratic Party. President Kennedy appointed Mrs. Roosevelt to a number of advisory committees and asked her once again to serve on the American delegation to the UN. Roosevelt died on November 7, 1962, in New York City. (See *The Eisenhower Years, The Kennedy Years* Volumes)

—JB

Roosevelt, James
(1907–1991) *Democratic Party politician*

James Roosevelt was born on December 23, 1907, in New York City. He was the eldest son of Franklin Roosevelt. Following in his father's footsteps, he attended Groton and graduated from Harvard in 1930. Roosevelt attended Boston University Law School for a short time but decided to enter the business world instead. In 1930 he worked for a Boston insurance company, moving up to be its vice president by 1938. He then left to be president and partner of his own firm, Roosevelt and Sargent, Inc.

Roosevelt also worked on behalf of his father and the Democratic Party in numerous campaigns. In 1937 the president requested him to leave his company to serve as his administrative assistant and press secretary. Many opposed this appointment as an example of nepotism. However even the anti-Roosevelt DREW PEARSON praised the young man's performance at the White House. Roosevelt resigned in 1938 to become vice president of Samuel Goldwyn Productions. He remained in the movie business until his reserve unit was called up in 1940. Roosevelt was released from the army in August 1945 and moved to Beverly Hills to resume his career as a motion picture executive.

Determined to continue his father's fight for liberal reforms, Roosevelt tried to enter politics in California. In January 1946 he accepted the $25,000-a-year position as head of the Independent Citizens Committee of the Arts, Sciences and Professions (ICCASP). That year Roosevelt also began a syndicated weekly broadcast of news commentary. Roosevelt soon became disenchanted with the ICCASP because the liberal lobby organization favored admitting Communists into its rank. In late July he resigned to accept the chairmanship of the California State Democratic Central Committee.

Roosevelt inherited a state organization torn between two factions, one allied to HENRY A. WALLACE, the other led by EDWIN W. PAULEY, allied to Truman. Roosevelt tried to persuade the liberals and conservatives to unify in order to capture the governorship in 1948 and win the state for the Democratic presidential candidate. However his efforts at compromise only deepened the divisions. For example, he tried to fashion a foreign policy plank agreeable to both sides. It stated that the organization endorsed the goals of the Truman Doctrine but opposed the means used to achieve the goals. This reflected liberal opposition to providing military aid to the conservative governments of Turkey and Greece. The position so angered Pauley that he persuaded Secretary of the Treasury JOHN W. SNYDER and director of the Democratic National Committee Gael Sullivan to refuse to speak at the party's annual dinner. Rather than the unity dinner he had hoped for, Roosevelt faced a faction-ridden meeting which featured his mother as guest speaker.

Roosevelt enthusiastically worked for the draft-Eisenhower movement in 1948. This enraged Truman so much that reportedly he told Roosevelt at a private meeting, "If your father knew what you were doing to me, he would turn over in his grave. But get this straight, whether you like it or not, I am going to be the next President of the United States. That will be all. Good day."

Following the Democratic National Convention James Roosevelt resigned his post to prepare for the California gubernatorial primary in 1950. Truman endorsed Roosevelt's opponent in the primary. Eleanor Roosevelt considered resigning from the United Nations in anger over Truman's behavior. Nevertheless, Roosevelt won the primary and then waged a spirited campaign, defending the Fair Deal against his Republican rival, the incumbent EARL WARREN. Roosevelt's mother and the rest of his family helped him in the race, but his campaign failed to generate enthusiasm. He drew large crowds but observers noted that people came out of curiosity. Warren easily defeated Roosevelt in the election.

In 1954 Roosevelt was elected to the House of Representatives, where he established a liberal voting record. He supported ESTES KEFAUVER in 1956 for the Democratic presidential nomination, while Eleanor backed ADLAI E. STEVENSON. James backed John F. Kennedy in 1960. He retired from Congress in 1965 and became a delegate to the UN Economic and Social Council. A year later he left that position for the private sector to resume his career as a financial consultant. In his later years, Roosevelt zigzagged in his party preferences for presidents. In 1972 he went for Richard Nixon; in 1976, Jimmy Carter; and, in 1984, Ronald Reagan.

Roosevelt died on August 13, 1991, in Newport, California. (See *The Johnson Years* Volume)

—JB

Roper, Elmo B(urns), Jr.

(1900–1971) *public opinion analyst*

Elmo B. Roper, Jr., was born in the small midwestern town of Hebron, Nebraska, on July 31, 1900. He began a career in the jewelry business in Creston, Iowa. In 1931 he left to become a salesman for the Seth Thomas Clock Company and constantly quizzed his customers as to their preferences in clocks. Two years later Roper moved into marketing research in New York, where he later formed his own firm. By 1935 publisher HENRY R. LUCE had engaged Roper's firm to conduct public opinion surveys to be published in *Fortune* magazine. The 1936 presidential election brought Roper to national attention with his scientific use of sampling methods. These, in contrast to the subscriber mail-in technique of the famous *Literary Digest* poll, made a correct forecast of Roosevelt's victory. In 1940 his prediction in the presidential election was only .2 percent off the actual vote. During World War II Roper held various governmental posts and his polls were used for their propaganda value at home and abroad. By the end of the war, he was deputy director of the Office of Strategic Services, and his firm had grown to serve such companies as Standard Oil, Spiegel Mail Order, and the American Meat Institute.

Roper's influence in the early Truman years grew with his column "What People Are Thinking," syndicated by the *New York Herald Tribune.* His poll results showed, for instance, that in 1945 80 percent of the American people were in favor of a Jewish state in Palestine, in 1946 voters were narrowly in favor of leaving legislative initiatives on civil rights issues to the states, and in 1950 73 percent supported President Truman's commitment of U.S. troops to Korea.

As did other pollsters, Roper predicted that THOMAS E. DEWEY would defeat Harry Truman in the 1948 election. The dramatic failure of his poll was due to the perception gained in the previous three national campaigns that there had been a "constant" Roosevelt, whose popularity had not shown week-to-week fluctuation from the nomination to election day. Proceeding on that assumption, the Roper organization published its final

results in early September based on interviews conducted between August 2 and 7. He related to his readers that to conduct further polls would be fruitless. The election results left Roper's firm the most embarrassed of all the pollsters. He had predicted that Truman would receive 37.1 percent of the popular vote; Truman's actual tally was 49.4 percent. Roper said another error was assuming that those who wanted HENRY A. WALLACE and J. STROM THURMOND to win would vote for them. Many realized their preferred candidate would not win and saw Truman as the lesser of two evils. Another mistake was assuming the undecided voters would divide proportionately between Dewey and Truman. In reality three-quarters of those undecided voted for Truman. A final reason was erring on the size of the turnout and its composition. More blue-collar workers voted than had been anticipated and an indeterminate number of Republicans may have stayed home, perhaps because of complacency created by the polls. Roper speculated this was probably a major factor in Dewey's downfall.

In his book *You and Your Leaders* (1957), Roper wrote that "I have always felt that the polls helped defeat Dewey. If so, this raises grave questions because if a measuring rod alters the size of what it purports to measure, its effectiveness is reduced. And if it helps defeat a candidate for office, it is stepping out of its character in what to me is a harmful manner." Another explanation Roper offered for Dewey's defeat was that he simply did not stimulate enough sentiment among people to elect him. Roper said there were two reasons for this: people did not find Dewey likable; the other was his equivocation. Another factor was Truman's hard-hitting campaign in which he distinguished himself form the GOP 80th Congress.

Although editorially condemned by numerous newspaper for its poor performance in the election, Roper's firm lost no clients. In the long run, as Roper related, the results of the debacle were beneficial because "practitioners learned more about the limitations of the technique and, from past errors, how to avoid future errors."

In the years following the Truman administration, Roper continued to work as a pollster and market consultant until his semiretirement in 1966. He was the chairman of the liberal Fund for the Republic in the late 1950s and active in business. For the rest of his life, Roper spoke out against the improper use of polls by politicians. He died on April 30, 1971, in Norwalk, Connecticut.

—GB

Rosenberg, Anna M(arie)
(1902–1983) *assistant secretary of defense*

Anna Lederer, the daughter of a prosperous furniture manufacturer in Budapest, Hungary, was born in that city on June 19, 1902. In 1912, after the family lost its fortune, it emigrated to the United States. Seven years later she married a young serviceman, Julius Rosenberg. While her husband was overseas Rosenberg did volunteer work in a state hospital. In 1919 she became a naturalized American citizen. During the early 1920s Rosenberg entered politics and became involved in settlement work. By 1924 she had the political contacts that enabled her to become a public relations, personnel, and labor consultant. She was so successful in dealing with labor matters that Governor Franklin D. Roosevelt often consulted her.

In 1934 Rosenberg was appointed assistant to the regional director of the National Recovery Administration and the next year was made regional director. She was appointed a member of the New York City Industrial Relations Board in 1937. Mayor Fiorello H. LaGuardia said of her, "She knows more about labor relations and human relations than any man in the country."

During World War II Rosenberg held several posts, among them director of the Office of Defense, Health, and Welfare Services and regional director of the War Manpower Commission. In July 1944 President Roosevelt sent her to the European theater as a personal observer. The following summer President Truman sent her on a similar mission to report on the problems involved in repatriation and demobilization of American troops.

During the mid- and late 1940s Rosenberg served on several federal committees. In September 1946 she was a member of the advisory commission of the War Mobilization and Reconversion Board's subcommittee examining wage stabilization policy. That December she was named to the Presidential Advisory Commission on Universal Military Training. From 1946 to 1950 Rosenberg was a member of the American Commission for UNESCO and served as an alternate delegate in 1947 at Mexico City. In August 1950 the chairman of the National Security Resources Board, STUART SYMINGTON,

appointed Rosenberg to a 12-member committee to advise him on mobilization policy for the Korean War. In November 1950 Secretary of Defense GEORGE C. MARSHALL offered Rosenberg the post of assistant secretary of defense in charge of coordinating the department's manpower activities. Marshall particularly liked her backing of universal military training.

The Senate Arms Services Committee approved the nomination but recalled its approval because of accusations by Benjamin Freedman and ex-Communist Ralph de Sola that Rosenberg had once been associated with Communist-front groups. Freedman later said he had confused her with another woman of the same name. Witnesses could not corroborate de Sola's accusations. Therefore, the committee unanimously reapproved the nomination. As a result of her case, Senator LESTER C. HUNT (D-Wyo.) announced that he would sponsor legislation to abolish congressional immunity for slanderous statements or at least to allow those damaged to sue the government. Senator JOSEPH R. MCCARTHY (R-Wisc.) responded that this would make it impossible to convict Communists.

Rosenberg had a vivacious personality and was the only Pentagon official Marshall called by first name. The defense secretary gave her the power to coordinate policies on civilian personnel and military manpower. She inspected military installations throughout the nation and the world, taking prompt action to solve any problems she discovered.

As assistant secretary of defense, Rosenberg was responsible for preparing a universal military service and training bill for submission to Congress. Its main provision called for the drafting of 18 year olds in order to increase the armed forces for the Korean conflict. Rosenberg felt that this was the best method for supplying a pool of trained soldiers for the next decade because it would cause the least dislocation of national economic life and the expense to the government would be reduced since payments to dependents would be virtually eliminated. The Universal Military Training and Service Act was passed by a 79 to 5 vote in the Senate in 1951. The final version raised the draft age to $18\frac{1}{2}$ but barred drafting anyone under 19 until the 19–26-year-old manpower pool was filled. However, in regard to universal military training, Congress agreed only to establish the National Security Training Commission to draw up a UMT program that it might okay in the future. It never did.

In 1952 Rosenberg launched a drive to increase the number of women in the military. She said that "when men are being drafted and women are not, women should insist upon and assume some equality of rights." However, she also called for improved use of women, saying that the military should offer women recruits a sufficient variety of activities, making full use of their skills.

Rosenberg's office also proposed legislation to enhance the quality of life for servicemen. The Veterans Readjustment Act provided Korean War veterans the same benefits as those given to veterans of World War II. The Combat Duty Pay Act of 1952 compensated men not receiving any other incentive pay an additional $45 a month to those who worked in combat situations for six or more days a month. She tried to have pay for soldiers raised by 10 percent in 1952. Congress increased it by 4 percent.

In 1953 Rosenberg was replaced by Eisenhower appointee, John Hannah. After leaving office she returned to her personnel management practice. In 1955 and 1956 she was co-chairman of the Stevenson for President Committee in New York City and was throughout the Eisenhower period a leading liberal Democrat in New York State. During the 1960s and 1970s Rosenberg continued to serve on the boards of a number of organizations dealing with civil rights, the United Nations, and municipal problems. Anna Rosenberg divorced Julius in 1962 and married PAUL G. HOFFMAN later that same year. She died on May 9, 1983, in New York City.

—MN

Rosenberg, Ethel (Greenglass)
(1915–1953) *convicted espionage agent*

The daughter of a sewing machine repairman, Ethel Greenglass was born on September 28, 1915, in New York City and grew up on the Lower East Side. After graduating from high school in 1931, she took a six-month stenographic course and then got a low-paying clerical job. In her spare time she studied singing and performed in local theatrical productions. She became active in union affairs and was fired from a job for organizing a strike. In 1939 she married a fellow radical activist, Julius Rosenberg, who soon took a position as a junior engineer with the Army Signal Corps while Ethel settled into the life of housewife and mother.

In mid-1950 the Rosenbergs were arrested for conspiracy to commit espionage. The government charged them with being at the center of a Soviet spy ring that included British physicist Klaus Fuchs, Harry Gold, MORTON SOBELL, and Ethel's brother, David Greenglass. The spy ring's chief accomplishment was the theft in 1944–45 of information relating to the construction of an atomic bomb from Los Alamos, New Mexico, where the most advanced experimentation was taking place. Fuchs, Gold, and Greenglass had confessed their involvement after being arrested. The Rosenbergs and Sobell emphatically denied any connection with an espionage ring.

The 1950 trial of the Rosenbergs took place in an atmosphere of intensive public preoccupation with domestic subversion and the threat posed by the Soviet Union and international communism. In September 1949 the Soviet Union had exploded its first atomic device, thereby ending America's monopoly on atomic weapons. In January 1950 former State Department official ALGER HISS had been convicted of perjury for denying his role in delivering classified documents to agents of the Soviet Union, and a month later Senator JOSEPH R. MCCARTHY (R-Wisc.) launched his anticommunist crusade before a public made receptive by similar investigations conducted by the House Un-American Activities Committee. Since June 1950 U.S. troops had been fighting Communist forces in Korea.

The prime witness against the Rosenbergs was David Greenglass. He claimed that Julius had recruited him for espionage work while Greenglass was in the army serving as a machinist at Los Alamos. He testified that he had delivered to Rosenberg several times and to Harry Gold once diagrams and sketches of the lens, the detonating mechanism, of the bomb. Greenglass also said that he had informed Rosenberg in June 1945 of the impending explosion of the atomic bomb at Alamogordo, New Mexico. Greenglass also maintained that he had ceased spying after 1945, rejecting Rosenberg's offer to continue espionage while studying nuclear physics at the Russians' expense. He likewise rejected the Rosenbergs' urging to flee to Mexico when Fuchs and Gold were arrested. Greenglass's wife, Ruth, an indicted co-conspirator, also testified in confirmation of her husband's account.

The Rosenbergs' attorneys, Emanuel and Alexander Block, subjected the Greenglasses to a blistering cross-examination. They accused David Greenglass of being a liar and a traitor and an "animal" for betraying his sister. He had implicated the

Rosenbergs, they said, to win a reduced sentence for himself. The defense charged that Ruth Greenglass had conceived the scheme to escape prosecution. The Greenglasses' testimony, nevertheless, remained unshaken by the defense's assault.

The defense was also unable to dislodge Max Elitcher, a college classmate of Julius Rosenberg, from his testimony that Rosenberg had tried to recruit him into espionage during World War II. Harry Gold corroborated Greenglass's statement that Greenglass had passed documents to him, but he testified that he had never met the Rosenbergs. The prosecution also produced other witnesses who corroborated elements of the Greenglasses' story. Former Communist ELIZABETH BENTLEY testified for the prosecution about Russian control of the American Communist Party.

Testifying on their own behalf, the Rosenbergs denied all the government's allegations and contradicted all the incriminating testimony given by the Greenglasses and Elitcher. When questioned about Communist affiliations, they refused to answer on the grounds of the Fifth Amendment's privilege against self-incrimination. The strategy was pursued against the advice of their lawyers and soon backfired. Pleading the Fifth Amendment damaged their protestations of complete innocence and did not succeed in keeping evidence of their Communist background away from the jury. The prosecution managed to introduce it anyway. Sobell elected not to testify at all.

On March 29, 1951, the federal jury found all of the defendants guilty. Judge IRVING R. KAUFMAN sentenced Sobell to 30 years and Greenglass to 15. He sentenced Julius and Ethel Rosenberg to die in the electric chair. Calling their crime "worse than murder," Kaufman said to the Rosenbergs, "I believe your conduct in putting into the hands of the Russians the A-bomb years before our best scientists predicted Russia would perfect the bomb has already caused, in my opinion, the Communist aggression in Korea, with the resultant casualties exceeding 50,000 and who knows but that millions more of innocent people may pay the price of your treason."

The Rosenbergs' execution was put off for two years while their attorneys argued a series of appeals to higher courts. Their appeal brief to the U.S. Circuit Court of Appeals cited numerous grounds on which they believed their verdict should be reversed. They charged that the espionage statute was too vague, and that giving information to a for-

eign government was speech protected by the First Amendment. The brunt of the appeal, however, alleged that Kaufman had been biased in favor of the prosecution. They maintained that, among other errors, he had questioned witnesses to the disadvantage of the defense, that he had inadequately instructed the jury and that he had admitted inadmissible evidence, most importantly regarding the Rosenbergs' Communist beliefs, which would tend to inflame the jurors against them.

The Court of Appeals decision, written by the distinguished jurist Jerome Frank and announced on February 25, 1952, rejected these contentions and upheld the conviction of the Rosenbergs and Sobell. Judge Frank, in his opinion, ruled that Kaufman's questioning of the witnesses had been appropriate, since a judge in a federal court had far greater latitude in such matters than a judge in a state court. Regarding Kaufman's charge to the jury, Frank found the claim that it was inadequate to be without merit and cited the defense counsel's praise of Kaufman immediately after the trial. The appellate opinion also held that the matter of the defendants' communism was relevant, because it pertained to the motive for the crime, and pointed to Kaufman's repeated stricture to the jurors not to determine guilt or innocence merely on the basis of the Rosenbergs' Communist beliefs.

The affirmance of the conviction by a respected liberal judge writing for a prestigious appellate court was a powerful blow to the Rosenbergs' case. On September 7, 1952, the Supreme Court unanimously denied the Rosenbergs a writ of certiorari, stating that the case raised no legal question that had not been previously decided. Judge Kaufman set a new execution date of January 12, 1953.

In the two years between the Rosenbergs' conviction and execution, their case became an international cause celebre. Protest against their death sentence swelled and intensified as each successive legal appeal failed and the date of execution drew near. The movement to save the Rosenbergs included Communists and non-Communists, some of whom believed that the Rosenbergs were the innocent victims of an anticommunist witch-hunt and others of whom accepted their guilt but felt that the death penalty was too harsh. Pope Pius XII, French president Vincent Auriol, and scientists ALBERT EINSTEIN and HAROLD C. UREY were among the prominent individuals who made public pleas for clemency for the Rosenbergs.

President Truman left office without responding to the appeals. In the first six months of President Dwight D. Eisenhower's tenure, pleas, rallies, and petitions on behalf of the Rosenbergs reached a crescendo as the final execution date approached. The last judicial hope of the Rosenbergs was extinquished on June 18, 1953, when the Supreme Court overturned a stay of execution granted by Justice WILLIAM O. DOUGLAS a few days before. President Eisenhower then refused a plea for clemency from Ethel Rosenberg. On June 19 the Rosenbergs were executed at Sing Sing prison in Ossining, New York.

Controversy over the guilt or innocence of the Rosenbergs and to the appropriateness of the death sentence continued to rage in the decades following their deaths. The release of FBI files on the case in the mid-1970s renewed the campaign to reopen the case. Although the new documents added little to the case for the Rosenbergs' innocence, some raised questions as to the fairness of the trial and the propriety of Judge Kaufman's conduct. The Rosenbergs' sons, Robert and Michael Meeropol, spearheaded the movement to win vindication for their parents.

The guilt of the Rosenbergs was settled in the 1990s with the release of the Venona decrypts. The military had been intercepting and decoding messages from the Soviet embassies and consulates to Moscow under the code name Venona. The intercepts showed the Soviets asking Julius for people working on "Enormous" (i.e., the atomic bomb project) who could be induced to be spies. Julius and Ethel recommended that Ethel's sister-in-law Ruth Greenglass be recruited to establish a "safe house" for the spy ring. One of the messages also showed Julius requesting the Soviets send an agent to speak with David Greenglass about what information he had on the atomic bomb, and Greenglass later did meet with Gold. Venona also revealed that Julius was engaged in photographing confidential U.S. government documents for the Soviets.

One of the Venona decrypts has a Soviet agent telling his boss that Ethel was dedicated, but because of her poor health did not work; yet, she did play an ancillary role. For instance, once she signaled a Soviet agent to come to their apartment by buying something at a drugstore, and another time she acted as a courier, taking a Leica camera and $7,000 in cash to a Soviet agent to get them out of the apartment for safe-keeping. Allen Weinstein and Alexander Vassiliev argue that execution of the Rosenbergs was excessive given that their roles in the atomic spy ring, particularly that of Ethel, were somewhat limited. The authors believe it was the supercharged anticommunist atmosphere of the time that led to their death sentence. (See *The Eisenhower Years* Volume)

—TO

Rosenberg, Julius
(1918–1953) *convicted espionage agent*

Born on May 12, 1918, in New York City, Julius Rosenberg was the son of a garment worker, and grew up on city's Lower East Side. In his teens he was attracted to radical politics and became a Communist while attending City College, from which he graduated with a degree in electrical engineering in 1939. That year he married a fellow Communist, Ethel Greenglass, and soon obtained a job as civilian junior engineer in the Army Signal Corps. He held this position until 1945, when he was fired on charges that he was a Communist. He worked as an engineer at the Emerson Radio Corporation until he formed his own hardware company with his brother-in-law Bernard Greenglass. When this venture failed he operated a small machine shop with his wife's other brother, David Greenglass. On June 16, 1950, Rosenberg was arrested and charged with being a central figure in a wartime espionage ring that had stolen secret information on American atomic research for delivery to the Soviet Union. (See ROSENBERG, ETHEL)

Royall, Kenneth C(laiborne)
(1984–1971) *undersecretary of war, secretary of war, secretary of the army*

A descendent of colonial settlers, Kenneth Royall was born in July 1894, in Goldsboro, North Carolina. He received his bachelor's degree from the University of North Carolina in 1914 and his law degree from Harvard three years later. In May 1917 he joined the army and served in France. He returned to North Carolina in 1919 to begin a law practice. Over the next 20 years Royall became a successful trial lawyer and involved himself in Democratic politics. He served as state senator in 1927 and as a Democratic presidential elector in 1940. In 1942 Royall was appointed chief of the Army Service Forces legal section; the following year, he became deputy fiscal director of the Army Service Forces. From April to November 1945 Royall served as a special assistant to Secretary of War HENRY L. STIMSON.

In October 1945 President Truman named Royall undersecretary of war. The new undersecretary was a vigorous defender of department policy. One newspaper commentator called him, ". . . the War Department's Number 1 bulldog—its main attacker of those who criticize the system." In response to mass meetings and protest demonstrations by U.S. soldiers abroad, Royall defended the pace of demobilization. He also defended the War Department against charges that it was handling poorly the disposition of war surplus material and that the court-martial system was unjust. In April 1946 Royall conceded that the courts-martial made under the pressure of war were often harsh, and he announced his agreement that the system be revised. In the fall of that year, during clemency reviews held under Royall's direction, hundreds of incarcerated American soldiers were released.

In July 1947 Truman appointed Royall secretary of war to replace ROBERT P. PATTERSON, who was resigning. The following month, after the formal restructure of the military was completed and the post of secretary of defense established, Royall's title was changed to secretary of the army. In this capacity he supervised the drafting of a series of formal agreements that divided personnel and operations of the army and the newly created air force. He cautioned that too much reliance should not be put on air power in providing for a strong defense establishment and that capable ground forces were vital. Under his direction the army requested an additional $500 million to support U.S. occupation troops in Europe. In November 1947 Royall enlarged the U.S. military mission in Greece, which he felt was essential to provide stability and protect U.S. interests in that country.

In May 1948 Truman asked the Joint Chiefs of Staff to develop a non-nuclear war plan, given that any international agreement to control atomic energy would preclude the use of nuclear weapons. He added that Americans might not allow the government to use atomic bombs for "aggressive purposes." Secretary Royall objected to the possibility that the United States would abandon the use of nuclear weapons, and he called for a review of atomic strategy by the National Security Council. Secretary of Defense JAMES V. FORRESTAL showed reluctance to do so but eventually discussed the

issue of weapons use with the president, who agreed that the policy should be flexible.

During the fall of 1947 Royall told Truman that if DWIGHT D. EISENHOWER became a candidate for the presidency on either party ticket he would feel compelled to support the general. Royall thought that it might be best if he resigned quietly before this actually happened. Truman reportedly asked him to stay. The president also instructed Royall to tell Eisenhower that if the general were receptive to the Democratic nomination, he would run on the same ticket as vice presidential candidate.

In 1948 Royall clashed with civil rights leaders over the issue of desegregation of the military. During the spring, Truman, prompted by threats of massive civil disobedience campaigns, announced steps to begin desegregation through conferences and discussion. Royall declared that he would not consider any change in the army's segregation policy. In June the NAACP adopted a resolution calling for his resignation. The following month Truman issued an executive order barring racial discrimination in federal employment and inaugurating a policy of equal opportunity in the armed forces.

Royall resigned in April 1949 to resume his law practice. Although a Democrat, he came out openly in 1952 in support of Eisenhower's candidacy for the presidency. In 1960 he supported John F. Kennedy's bid for the presidency and eight years later backed the unsuccessful candidacy of HUBERT H. HUMPHREY. Royall died on May 25, 1971, in Durham, North Carolina.

—MLB

Rusk, Dean

(1909–1994) *assistant secretary of state for UN affairs, deputy undersecretary of state, assistant secretary of state for Far Eastern affairs*
The son of an ordained minister and schoolteacher, Dean Rusk was born on February 9, 1909, in Cherokee County, Georgia. He attended Davidson College, where he graduated Phi Beta Kappa in 1931. He went to Oxford on a Rhodes scholarship, receiving his B.S. in 1933 and M.A. in 1934. Rusk returned to the United States later that year and accepted a position as assistant professor of government at Mills College in California. During World War II he served in the army, eventually becoming deputy chief of staff to General Joseph Stillwell.

Rusk was assistant chief of the State Department's Division of International Security. Here he was involved in the failed attempt to establish a UN Security Force, including Russians and Americans, which Rusk later admitted would have been unworkable anyway. Rusk played a role in the establishment of the Korean border. At the end of World War II, the State Department wanted U.S. troops to go as far north on the mainland as possible in occupying Japanese-held territory. The army, however, did not want responsibility for places where it had few or no troops. Rusk and Colonel Charles Bonesteel came up with a compromise by which the army would occupy Korea up to the 38th parallel. This would put Seoul, the capital, in the American sector. The Soviets would occupy the rest of Korea. In 1946 he became assistant to the secretary of war. In this post he was involved with securing postwar desegregation of the army, creating a centralized intelligence agency, and procuring food for occupied Japan and Germany.

At the request of Secretary of State GEORGE C. MARSHALL, Rusk returned in 1947 to become director of the Office of Special Political Affairs, also known as the UN desk. Rusk thought initially that the Marshall Plan should have been administered by the UN. This was rejected as countries in the General Assembly other than European ones might demand aid, too. He also advocated the Baruch Plan to control atomic weapons, although he later admitted it was understandable why the Soviets rejected it. Rusk urged UN involvement during the Greek-Turkish crisis of 1947, and, at the insistence of Senator ARTHUR H. VANDENBERG (R-Mich.), it was Rusk who worked with the senator on the aid legislation. Rusk and others at State convinced the UN General Assembly to urge nations north of Greece to stop aiding the insurgency. During 1948 Rusk was active in formulating policy toward Palestine. Rusk opposed partition of the area into Arab and Jewish states, fearing that such action would precipitate a war in which the United States would have to become involved. Instead, he proposed that the United Nations temporarily assume an administrative trusteeship in the area. Truman eventually accepted the plan, and, on May 3, Rusk submitted a formal proposal to extend the British mandate and negotiate a settlement between Jews and Arabs. Less than two weeks later Truman, on the advice of CLARK CLIFFORD, reversed his stand. Minutes before Israel announced its independence on May

14, the president recognized the nation. The following year Rusk was appointed assistant secretary of state of UN affairs. In February he was appointed deputy undersecretary of state, coordinating all policy work in the department. He also dealt with Far Eastern affairs.

Rusk took the post of assistant secretary of state for Far Eastern affairs in March 1950, later saying that since Senator JOSEPH R. MCCARTHY (R-Wisc.) had not attacked him and since he had experience with the Far East, he volunteered for the job. He did so despite the fact that technically it was a demotion and that the administration was under intense criticism for its Asian policy in light of the fall of China to the Communists.

Rusk played a leading role in formulating policy in Korea. Following the outbreak of war in June 1950, he recommended the United States take all action through the UN. He suggested that America submit a resolution to the UN to try to force the North Koreans from the South and urged strong action to prevent further Communist aggression in Asia. He described the situation in Korea as analogous to that in Europe during the late 1930s. Rusk demanded that the United States prevent another "Munich" and contain the spread of communism before it engulfed other areas of the East. He warned "If we run away from it [the Korean War], the aggressor will learn that there is great profit in crime, that he will not be resisted, and that his victims are weak and can be destroyed at will." Rusk recommended going into North Korea after its soldiers had been driven across the 38th parallel and helped convince DEAN G. ACHESON that it was a good idea. Rusk feared that any halt would give the North Koreans time to regroup and renew the offensive. Also, the UN had called for reunification before the war, but the North Koreans had stymied all efforts. Here was an opportunity to complete the task. After the Chinese attacked, Rusk said the United States should stay the course and not abandon the peninsula. He also argued against taking the war to China and advised Truman that General DOUGLAS MACARTHUR should be relieved.

The assistant secretary was a strong supporter of Chiang Kai-shek (Jiang Jieshi), whom he believed represented the Chinese people. Communist China, he insisted, was a satellite of the Soviet Union. Rusk supported a policy of nonrecognition of the Communist regime and opposed admission of that nation to the UN. In a speech in 1951 he emphasized his support of Chiang and insisted that the Nationalist regime was the legitimate representative of China. "We can tell our friends in China that the United States will not acquiesce in the degradation which is being forced on them" he said. "We do not recognize the authorities in Peiping for what they pretend to be. The Peiping regime may be a colonial Russian government—a Slavic Manchukuo on a larger scale. It is not the government of China. It does not pass the first test. It is not Chinese." He admitted later he spoke less factually than polemically.

As assistant secretary of Far Eastern affairs, Rusk was involved in the signing of the Japanese Security Treaty of 1952. However, he had little role in formulating the document. The agreement permitted the establishment of U.S. Army bases in Japan with the Japanese paying $155 million per year in yen for their up-keep and providing the real estate. In return the Americans paid for the cost of maintaining troops.

As president of the Rockefeller Foundation during the Eisenhower administration, Rusk directed the distribution of $250 million to Asian, African, and Latin American nations to improve their agriculture and promote social welfare. He also fought to preserve academic freedom during the McCarthy era. During the Kennedy and Johnson administrations he served as secretary of state and played a leading role in formulating and defending U.S. policy on Vietnam. After leaving government in 1969, Rusk became professor of law at the University of Georgia. Rusk died on December 20, 1994, in Athens, Georgia. (See *The Eisenhower Years, The Kennedy Years, The Johnson Years* Volumes)

—RG

Russell, Richard B(revard)
(1897–1971) *member of the Senate*

Richard B. Russell was born on November 2, 1897, in Winder, Georgia. He served as a naval reserve officer in World War I and, in 1918, obtained his LL.B. from the University of Georgia. His political career began in 1921 with his election to the Georgia State Assembly as a Democrat. By 1927 he had become Georgia State Assembly speaker and, in 1930, was elected governor of Georgia on an austerity program. After two years in office, during which he reduced his own salary, drastically cut the state budget, and eliminated many state commissions, Russell was elected to a vacant seat in the U.S. Senate.

Like many southern Democrats under the New Deal, Russell began his career in Congress as a supporter of liberal social legislation. He was instrumental in the creation of the Rural Electrification Administration and the Farmers' Home Administration, and he also drafted legislation for the first nationwide school lunch program. In addition to the New Deal domestic program, Russell supported President Roosevelt's foreign policy prior to U.S. entry into World War II, advocating the end of the mandatory arms embargo, the establishment of the Selective Service, and the implementation of lend-lease.

Russell's liberalism on many social questions did not extend to racial issues. He remained throughout his career an archopponent of racial integration. In 1935 and 1937 he helped filibuster against antilynching laws and in 1942 filibustered against the abolition of the poll tax. During World War II he was a critic of the Fair Employment Practices Commission (FEPC), established by executive decree in 1941 to "eliminate discriminatory employment practices."

The courteous, dignified Russell became one of the most influential members of Congress in the 1940s and was generally perceived as a leader of the Senate. He served as mentor to several generations of senators, including such men as LYNDON B. JOHNSON (D-Tex.).

Russell wielded his tremendous power through his long tenure, ability, and his control of the southern caucus. As Russell biographer Gilbert C. Fite has noted, the senator by 1945 had replaced Texas senator Tom Connally as leader of the group. With his formidable intellect and expert knowledge of parliamentary procedure, he was often capable of controlling the flow of legislation. Despite Russell's identification with the South, he was highly respected by most senators and was widely regarded as the embodiment of the best traditions of the upper house.

At the end of World War II, Russell was one of many southern New Deal Democrats who turned against liberal social policies. As Russell himself put it, "I'm a reactionary when times are good . . . in a depression I'm a liberal." The senator was a particular enemy of unions. He voted for the Case labor disputes bill and the Taft-Hartley Act, both denounced by organized labor. The rise of union influence within the Democratic Party concerned Russell and other Democrats. Despite his comment above, the

Georgian believed in a certain type of liberalism. To Russell liberalism was not always voting at the unions' behest. According to Fite, Russell held to Jeffersonian liberalism in which a liberal was one who backed, in Russell's words, "the greatest measure of individual freedom for each man . . . so long as he does not impinge on the rights of another individual or threaten the welfare of the whole."

Since he was from a farming state, Russell concerned himself with agricultural policy. In March 1946 he successfully pushed for an amendment to the administration's minimum wage legislation that required the government to compute farm labor costs into parity prices for agricultural products. President Truman, citing the inflationary potential of the Russell amendment, threatened a veto. Many southerners from farm states supported the proposal, hoping its inclusion would scuttle a bill that they otherwise did not have the power to stop. Nevertheless, Russell's amendment ultimately became part of the bill, which would have raised the minimum waged to 65 cents per hour. The House of Representatives, however, did not pass this measure, and it was not until 1949 that Russell succeeded on this issue. Russell fought hard in the Republican 80th Congress to reduce cuts in spending for soil conservation, the school lunch program, and the Farmers Home Administration. Russell also preferred fixed price supports of agricultural products—such as cotton—at 90 percent of parity and opposed flexible price supports.

The senator remained an ardent foe of civil rights legislation. In the 1945 debate over the status of the FEPC, Russell introduced an unsuccessful amendment to kill the agency. He opposed the gradual desegregation of the armed forces as proposed by Truman. Russell argued that southerners would refuse to enlist if they were compelled to serve in an integrated unit. In 1949 he introduced a bill that would have provided federal funds to subsidize black migration to northern cities in order to eliminate racial tensions in the South. In that same year Russell successfully resisted an effort by Senator WAYNE MORSE (R-Ore.) to change the rule on cloture so as to require only a simple majority vote to invoke it. In fact, with southern Democratic and Republican support, the rule was changed from needing two-thirds of those present to invoke cloture to two-thirds of all senators.

According to Fite, although Russell supported much of Truman's foreign policy, the senator dis-

agreed with the president on certain issues. He thought the United States was taking on too many burdens for the economic and military security of other nations at a high cost to U.S. taxpayers. He did not believe the United States should become involved in areas where it held no national interests. He thought Great Britain should give the United States bases on British territories as a quid pro quo for a $3.75 billion loan. Because this condition was not met Russell voted against the loan. He advocated a political union between the United States and Britain to open more trade and reduce economic competition. This suggestion was not taken seriously. Although Russell had not stopped seeing the Russians as untrustworthy, he did hope that postwar relations would be peaceful. However, as time drew on and the Soviets oppressed Eastern Europe, he came out in favor of Greek-Turkish aid. But he supported it because he believed keeping Soviet communism out of Greece and Turkey served U.S. interests, and people should not confuse this goal with supporting democracy. He also became critical of those he viewed as Soviet sympathizers. He unenthusiastically voted for the Marshall Plan. He thought the initial appropriation of nearly $600 million was too high and wanted to lower the amount. He also would have preferred temporary humanitarian aid rather than a commitment lasting years. Russell by 1949 had become increasingly critical of foreign aid, believing the money would be better spent on the U.S. military. He voted for NATO, but against the bill to send it $1.3 billion in aid. He believed such huge sums for foreign assistance would bankrupt the U.S. economy. He tried to cut foreign aid by $400 million in September 1949, but Congress rejected his amendment. He also opposed a $45-million authorization to set up the Point Four program of aid to the developing world. Yet he voted against the Dirksen Amendment cutting aid to Europe in 1951.

Russell's attention turned increasingly to national security during the Truman era, and, by 1950, most of his own legislative initiatives were in that domain. He had been an early advocate of national preparedness under Roosevelt, and, in collaboration with the Georgia representative CARL VINSON (D-Ga.), he assured his state its share of defense contracts and military installations. Russell was in essential agreement with Truman on the need to reorganize the armed forces, replacing the cabinet-level posts of secretary of war, army, and navy with a single secretary of defense. He also supported the most controversial implication of this organization, which was to make the air force, and not the navy's air arm, the basis of future U.S. air strike capacity. Russell's main reservations about reorganization concerned the excessive increase in the power of the president in military affairs. In the "Great Debate" of 1950–51 over the numerical limit to the troops the president could commit overseas without consulting Congress, Russell cosponsored an amendment to a Senate resolution that affirmed the president's right to unlimited commitments. His measure would have required the president to consult with Congress on any serious escalation. No action was taken on it.

After Senate Majority leader SCOTT W. LUCAS (D-Ill.) lost his seat in 1950, some of Russell's Democratic colleagues in the Senate urged him to run for the position. But Russell said he disagreed with the administration too much to be floor leader. Besides, he preferred being independent. Russell did support Lyndon Johnson for majority whip, which the Texan used as a springboard to greater power and eventually to party floor leader in 1953.

Russell supported Truman's decision to defend South Korea in 1950, but when the Chinese intervened, he thought U.S. ground troops should be withdrawn from the peninsula. He believed instead that the United States should bomb Chinese cities until China left Korea, but he did not want the bombing to begin until U.S. troops were evacuated. He feared the bombing might lead to Soviet intervention and threaten the American withdrawal.

Russell gained national prominence in 1951 as chairman of the Armed Forces Committee, then investigating the firing of General DOUGLAS MACARTHUR. Like many members of Congress, Russell wanted to avert a showdown injurious either to Truman or to the popular MacArthur. His skillful, even-handed conduct during the probe was widely credited with helping to defuse an explosive political issue. After his role in the MacArthur affair, Russell's national stature, in the view of many commentators, reached its apogee.

Russell made two unsuccessful bids for the Democratic presidential nomination during the Truman administration. His southern origins proved to be an insuperable barrier to nationwide support. In 1948 he was overwhelmingly defeated in every primary outside the South, ultimately receiving only the South's 263 votes at the Democratic

National Convention. Russell did oppose the Dixiecrat bolt from the convention and gave a pro forma endorsement to Truman. Russell wanted to work within the party to halt civil rights legislation. Southern Democrats had the advantage of seniority in Congress and, as Fite noted, Russell was too attached to the Democratic Party to break with it. Russell's 1952 bid for the nomination was no more successful than his previous one. Once again his association with Deep South segregation and general hostility to liberal domestic programs made it impossible for him to win primaries in the North, Midwest, or West, and he received only 294 delegate votes. Russell said he would vote for the nominee, ADLAI E. STEVENSON, but he did not actively campaign for him because he would want the cooperation of Republicans in any attempt to loosen the rules on cloture in the Senate in 1953. Truman later noted in his memoirs that Russell might very well have been president if he had not been from the South. Fite said Russell could, and, to a certain extent, would not become a national leader because he could not separate himself from his southern concerns, which always came first. Russell's biographer also asserted that the senator knew deep down he would not win the nomination. The party was too dominated by liberals to allow someone they saw as too conservative and the fact that he was also a southerner precluded the chance for him to win the top spot on the presidential ticket.

Following the second race Russell became somewhat embittered and declined an opportunity to become Senate Minority Leader in 1953. For the remainder of his career he was the senior southern senator, prominent for his ongoing role in military affairs and hostility to the civil rights legislation of the early 1960s. In the filibuster against the 1963 civil rights bill, Russell declared that "if they overcome us you'll find me in a last ditch." After initial doubts about the U.S. presence in Vietnam, Russell supported the war on the grounds that the United States was obligated to keep its commitments. In 1969 he gave up his chairmanship of the Armed Services Committee to become head of the Appropriations Committee. He became President Pro Tempore of the Senate the same year. Russell died of a respiratory ailment on January 21, 1971, in Washington, D.C. (See *The Eisenhower Years, The Kennedy Years, The Johnson Years, The Nixon/Ford Years* Volumes)

—LG

Rustin, Bayard
(1910–1987) *civil rights leader*

One of 12 children, Rustin was born on March 17, 1910, in West Chester, Pennsylvania. Raised in poverty there by his grandparents, he was early influenced toward pacifism by his grandmother, who belonged to the Society of Friends. Rustin's decision to combat segregation originated when he was physically ejected from a restaurant because of his race.

In 1936 Rustin joined the Young Communist League (YCL), believing it to be an organization committed to pacifist ideals and equal rights for blacks. He moved to New York City two years later and began organizing for the league. At the same time he attended City College at night and sang in nightclubs with Josh White and Leadbelly to earn money. Rustin left the league in 1941 when, after

Civil Rights leader Bayard Rustin, 1963 *(Library of Congress, Prints and Photographs Division, photographed by Warren K. Leffler)*

the Nazi invasion of the Soviet Union, the YCL subordinated its commitment to social protest to the cause of defeating Germany.

Soon after departing the YCL, Rustin joined the Fellowship of Reconciliation (FOR), a pacifist nondenominational religious organization opposed to racial injustice. He subsequently organized the New York chapter of the Congress of Racial Equality (CORE), a secular offshoot of FOR. In 1941 he joined with A. PHILIP RANDOLPH, president of the Brotherhood of Sleeping Car Porters, in organizing a March on Washington for improved job opportunities for blacks. When President Roosevelt issued an executive order banning racial discrimination in defense industries, the march was cancelled. In 1942 Rustin traveled to California to aid Japanese Americans whose property was jeopardized after they were placed in work camps. Imprisoned as a conscientious objector during World War II, Rustin served more than two years in jail.

After his release from prison, Rustin traveled America to, in his words, "make pacifists of people." Audiences at colleges run by pacifist churches and youth camps of the American Friends Service Committee especially welcomed him, according to Rustin's biographer John D'Emilio. However, most Americans believed military preparedness was the best way to preserve peace. But Rustin was uncompromising in his pacifism. When a member of FOR relied on practical arguments to oppose conscription—that no nation threaten the United States to justify the draft—Rustin argued induction should be opposed on pacifist principles alone. In New York Rustin urged men to burn their draft cards while others prepared to lobby Congress.

Rustin also wanted FOR to focus on civil rights for blacks. Rustin believed in Gandhian nonviolent civil disobedience as a way to accomplish the goal of racial equality. Thus to test a Supreme Court decision banning segregation on interstate bus travel, Rustin helped plan and then participated in the 1947 Journey of Reconciliation. The protest served as a model for the Freedom Rides of 1961, the Montgomery bus boycott of 1955–56, and the student sit-ins of the 1960s. Rustin was arrested in North Carolina when he refused to move to the back of a Trailways bus. He subsequently served 22 days on a chain gang. (His account of this experience led to the abolition of chain gangs in the state.)

In 1947 Randolph and Rustin formed the Committee to End Jim Crow in the Military. When the group's effort to end segregation in the armed forces seemed stymied, Rustin and fellow activist George Houser, with Randolph's blessing, established in 1948 the independent League for Nonviolent Civil Disobedience against Military Segregation. As executive secretary of the league, Rustin led a successful campaign that persuaded President Truman to issue his July 1948 executive order calling for an end to discrimination in the military. After this victory Randolph wanted to disband the league. Rustin opposed the action, contending that it would be unfair to blacks still serving prison sentences for refusal to cooperate with the conscription system. In spite of Rustin's position, Randolph withdrew. Without his influence the league collapsed in November of that year.

Rustin found life difficult in the late 1940s and early 1950s. He struggled with his homosexuality, which threatened exposure to the detriment of his work. His left-wing views and even his pacifism became equated with communism and subversion. He met open hostility in many cities where he had come to advocate peace. He believed militarism was gaining the upper hand in America, with liberal FOR pacifists supporting the Korean War and apathy toward the building of the hydrogen bomb, and his pacifism did nothing to stop the cold war. Yet he held true to his Gandhian principles of nonviolence.

In the early 1950s Rustin joined with George Houser to found the Committee to Support South Africa Resistance. In 1953 he resigned his post with the FOR to become executive secretary of the War Resister's League. He traveled to England in 1958 to help mobilize the first of the annual marches for nuclear disarmament. Along with his work for peace, Rustin remained active in the struggle for civil rights, helping to organize the 1955 Montgomery bus boycotts and later drafting the initial plans for the Southern Christian Leadership Conference headed by Martin Luther King.

In 1960 Rustin, at the invitation of King and Randolph, organized civil rights demonstrations at the Democratic and Republican national conventions. As Randolph's assistant, he planned the 1963 March on Washington for Jobs and Freedom, which attracted 200,000 protestors to the nation's capital.

Rustin became director of the newly created A. Philip Randolph Institute in 1964. In that capacity he attempted to improve job opportunities for black youth and to push civil rights groups toward the noncommunist left. In his later years Rustin spoke out for gay rights. He died on August 24, 1987, in New York City. (See *The Eisenhower Years, The Kennedy Years, The Johnson Years, The Nixon/Ford Years* Volumes)

—EF

Rutledge, Wiley B(lount)
(1894–1949) *associate justice, U.S. Supreme Court*

The son of a Baptist minister, Wiley B. Rutledge was born on July 20, 1894, in Cloverport, Kentucky. He graduated from the University of Wisconsin in 1914 and then taught high school for eight years, interrupted once by a bout with tuberculosis. He received a law degree from the University of Colorado in 1922 and began his teaching career there in 1924. Rutledge went on to become professor of law and dean of the law school at Washington University in St. Louis between 1926 and 1935. He served as dean of Iowa College of Law from 1935 to 1939. He was active on the St. Louis Commission for Social Justice and was an ardent supporter of Franklin Roosevelt and the New Deal. A respected and influential figure in legal circles in the Midwest, Rutledge publicly criticized the anti–New Deal decisions of the Supreme Court and backed Roosevelt's Court-packing plan in 1937. His statements brought him to the attention of the president, and, in March 1939, Rutledge was named to a judgeship on the U.S. Court of Appeals for the District of Columbia. In his four years there Rutledge wrote liberal opinions that reflected New Deal views on the economy and social welfare. He was nominated to the Supreme Court in January 1943 and easily won confirmation the next month.

On the bench Rutledge fulfilled expectations that he would be a liberal jurist. He supported the expansion of federal power over the economy and upheld broad interpretations of Congress's commerce and taxing powers. He generally voted in favor of workers in labor law cases and sustained the regulatory authority of federal administrative agencies.

At the same time Rutledge was careful to safeguard individual freedoms against government intrusion. He emerged as one of the foremost defenders of civil liberties in the Court's history. During his tenure Rutledge was part of a four-man liberal bloc—also known as the Axis—along with HUGO L. BLACK, WILLIAM O. DOUGLAS, and FRANK

MURPHY, which sought to expand the scope of individual rights guarantees. He was most closely aligned with Murphy in voting, and, like those of his colleague, Rutledge's decisions were influenced by his humanitarian philosophy and by his concern that the social and individual results of a decision serve justice as well as the law. He believed that the Constitution mandated rigorous protection of personal rights and that the Court was to be the primary guardian of individual liberties. Rutledge's only major lapse from a strong civil libertarian position came during World War II, when he voted to uphold the government program evacuating Japanese Americans from the West Coast in *Korematsu v. United States* (1944).

Justice Rutledge took an expansive view of the guarantees in the Bill of Rights. He insisted that full constitutional protection be given those accused of crime in both federal and state courts. He voted to uphold the right to counsel every time this issue came before the Court, and he took strong stands against coerced confession and denials of the privilege against self-incrimination. Rutledge concurred when the Court held the Fourth Amendment applicable to the states in *Wolf v. Colorado* (June 1949), but he objected when a majority also ruled that state courts could admit illegally seized evidence. The justice thought basic rights of due process should be guaranteed even to an enemy belligerent. In what some consider his most important civil liberties opinion, he dissented in February 1946 in the case *In re Yamashita*, when the majority upheld the conviction of Japanese general Tomoyuki Yamashita who had been tried by a U.S. military commission for violation of the laws of war. Rutledge attacked the legal basis of the commission, argued that its procedures had denied Yamashita a fair trial, and insisted that the military tribunal had to meet the basic standards of fairness of the Anglo-American legal tradition.

Rutledge adhered to the view that First Amendment freedoms have a preferred position and require special protection against government infringement. In *Saia v. New York* (1948) and *Kovacs v. Cooper* (1949) Rutledge twice voted to overturn local ordinances restricting the use of sound trucks and, in *Terminiello v. Chicago* (May 1949), he voted to guarantee the free speech rights even of a man whose statements had stirred up a crown and created a disturbance. Rutledge almost always agreed to sustain the rights of Jehovah's Witnesses to distribute their literature free from government interference, such as in second *Jones v. Opelika* (1943). At the same time he took a strict view of the First Amendment's ban on the establishment of religion and contended that this provision barred the government from making any contributions from public funds to religious organizations. He thus dissented in a February 1947 case, *Everson v. Board of Education*, when the Court approved public payments for the transportation of children to parochial schools and joined the majority in *McCollum v. Board of Education* in March 1948 to overturn a released time program for religious education in the public schools.

Justice Rutledge joined in decisions that advanced the rights of blacks in public education and transit. In February 1948 he wrote for a seven-man majority in *Bob-Lo Excursion Company v. Michigan* to uphold that state's civil rights law to an excursion boat that had excluded African Americans, even though the boat entered Canadian waters during its trips. In one of the more famed cases of the Truman era, Rutledge dissented in March 1947 when the Court in *United Mine Workers v. United States* upheld the conviction of JOHN L. LEWIS and the miners' union for civil and criminal contempt for having violated an antistrike injunction issued by lower federal court at a time when the U.S. government had taken over the coal mines. The justice argued that the 1932 Norris-LaGuardia Act had withdrawn from federal courts the jurisdiction to issue injunctions in labor disputes, even when the federal government was involved, and he objected to the district court's mixing of civil and criminal proceedings in the same case.

Justice Rutledge died on September 10, 1949, while vacationing in York, Maine. By all accounts he was a man of great personal warmth and friendliness who showed a sincere interest and concern for all those around him. Although on the Court for only six-and-a-half years, Rutledge earned high ratings from legal analysts. He combined a strong humanitarian and democratic faith with scholarship, an able command of the law, and prodigious workmanship. One of his brother justices on the Court noted he approached an opinion the way a law professor approached a law journal article—trying to figure out "the total mosaic in which the case appeared in legal literature." All agree that his most enduring contribution came in the field of civil liberties. "Rigid, uniform protection of civil liberties," one commentator has observed, was for Rutledge

"very nearly an absolute general principle." He had profound respect for the dignity of the individual and believed that this must be carefully safeguarded. Rutledge became, next to Frank Murphy, "the most consistent champion of substantive civil liberties on the Court." After both men died in the summer of 1949, the Supreme Court took a conservative turn. Not until the 1960s, when the activist Warren Court adopted many of his views, was the Court again as libertarian as it had been in Rutledge's day.
—CAB

Ryan, Joseph P(atrick)
(1884–1963) *president, International Longshoremen's Association*

Born in the Long Island town of Babylon, New York, on May 11, 1884, Ryan was raised in the rough Chelsea district of New York City's West Side. He attended parochial schools through the sixth grade, and then found work as a clerk and a streetcar conductor. In 1912 he got a job on the Hudson River docks and joined the International Longshoremen's Association (ILA). Within two years Ryan became a full-time union official. He worked his way through the ILA hierarchy, winning election to the vice presidency in 1918 and the presidency in 1927.

A close ally of New York's Tammany Hall, Ryan ran the ILA in the style of an old-time political boss—passing out five-dollar bills as he strolled along the docks, soliciting under-the-table "contributions" from employers, cooperating with the gangsters who began to penetrate the New York waterfront in the 1930s, and getting himself elected president for life in 1943. The "shape-up" hiring system, under which longshoremen were arbitrarily selected for each day's work by the pier bosses, gave Ryan and other ILA officials control over jobs, which they used to enrich themselves through "kickbacks" extorted from the men and to favor supporters of the machine. The systematic shaking down of dockworkers in need of employment and stevedoring companies seeking to avoid delays in the loading and unloading of ships attracted such underworld figures as Albert Anastasia, whose brother dominated the Brooklyn ILA locals.

Although the ILA's Pacific Coast locals broke away in 1937 under the leadership of HARRY A. BRIDGES to form the International Longshoremen's and Warehousemen's Union (ILWU), Ryan's con-

trol of the New York docks was not seriously challenged until the postwar years. In October 1945 a wildcat strike broke out in Manhattan when it became known that Ryan had failed to include a 2,240-pound limitation on the size of sling loads in that year's contract. Led by a rank-and-file committee whose members had to conceal their identities in order to avoid the ILA strong-arm squads, the walkout was supported by the ILWU and the National Maritime Union. In response Ryan charged that the opposition was inspired by Communists, who were influential in these unions. Aided by the American Federation of Labor (AFL) and its affiliated waterfront organizations, Ryan quashed the revolt within two weeks; its leaders were beaten up and expelled from the union.

According to author Vernon H. Jensen, Ryan thought he was acting in the traditional way union bosses operated in gaining what members wanted, but he had ignored or did not know of developments in the labor movement. Ryan undoubtedly believed that a 10-cents-an-hour wage hike he had obtained was a good deal. He did not realize the importance of keeping in contact with the workers about the negotiations.

Although Ryan had triumphed in his internal confrontation in 1945, the insurgency raised rank-and-file expectations and, when the contract expired, the ILA made greater wage and pension demands than it had on previous bargaining occasions. Although a one-year agreement raising pay 10 cents an hour was reached in 1947, 1948 would see confrontation on the docks, as a complex dispute developed over overtime pay. Ryan recommended acceptance of the New York Shipping Association's (NYSA) final offer, but, in early November, the membership of the New York locals voted it down and walked off their jobs. After the strike had spread to other East Coast ports, the union's leadership endorsed the work stoppage, making it the first official ILA strike in 28 years. Pressure from federal mediators and administration appeals to allow grain and coal to move to Europe forced the union to come to terms with the steamship companies at the end of the month. In the settlement, workers gained increased vacation time, a welfare plan, and a wage hike of 13 cents an hour, retroactive to August 21, 1948.

Opposition to Ryan emerged on a larger scale following negotiation of the 1951 contract. A walkout of New York longshoremen on October 15 in protest against the union's wage settlement led to violent clashes between pickets and Ryan loyalists. Federal mediators again entered the dispute, but Ryan refused to reopen talks with the NYSA and, instead, sent a telegram to President Truman complaining of subversive conspiracies. Finally, after a New York State–appointed board of inquiry gave assurances to the insurgents that a full investigation would be made and that no strikers would be penalized, the longshoremen returned to work on November 9. During two weeks of public and private hearings, the board examined a broad range of subjects in addition to the issue of the contract's validity. Although longshoremen opposed to Ryan charged that there had been voting fraud in the ratification of the agreement, the panel ruled that the contract should be recognized as binding. At the same time, however, it found that the union lacked democratic standards.

Shortly after the hearings had gotten under way, New York governor THOMAS E. DEWEY announced that the State Crime Commission would undertake a full-scale investigation of criminal activities on the waterfront. The commission's probe, which received extensive national press coverage, concluded that the high cost of delay in port operations was "an open invitation to blackmail" and that the erratic and unsteady nature of the labor market encouraged exploitation and abuse of longshoremen. Ryan and other ILA officials were shown to have accepted hundreds of thousands of dollars in kickback money paid by employers. Ryan claimed that the funds were donations to "anticommunist" activities, but his bank records revealed the payments to have gone for country club dues, Caribbean cruises, and expensive clothes. Ryan was also charged with using his position on the New York State Pardons Board to place ex-convicts on the ILA staff. Criminal records were uncovered for at least 30 percent of the union's officials, many of whom, it was shown, operated theft, loansharking, and gambling operations on the docks. The commission report, issued in May 1953, strongly condemned the shapeup and proposed replacing it with a hiring and licensing system administered by the New York–New Jersey Port Authority.

The AFL initially attacked the investigation as "biased and dangerous," arguing that corruption was a matter for the police and the ILA itself to resolve. However, the commission's disclosures and the resulting public scandal put pressure on the federation to clear itself of any implication in Ryan's affairs. In addition, AFL president George Meany, who was seeking to merge the federation with the Congress of Industrial Organizations (CIO), felt obliged to respond to CIO demands for a purge of racketeering elements as a precondition for uniting the two organizations. As a result, in 1953 the ILA was ordered by the AFL Executive Council to reform itself and then expelled after refusing to do so.

In November, shortly after the ILA's expulsion, Ryan resigned the union presidency and was named president emeritus with a substantial pension. In the meantime he had been indicted on charges stemming from the Crime Commission's investigations. Two years later he was convicted of violating the Taft-Hartley Act by accepting $2,500 from a stevedoring company and given a six-month suspended sentence. The conviction was later overturned on appeal. Ryan died on June 26, 1963, in New York City.

—TLH

Sabath, Adolph J(oachim)
(1866–1952) *member of the House of Representatives*

The son of a poor Jewish butcher, Adolph J. Sabath was born in Zabori, Austria-Hungary, on April 4, 1866. He emigrated to Chicago at age 15 and worked in a planing mill and a shoe store before graduating from Bryant and Stratton Business College in 1885 and Lake Forest University Law School in 1891. Active in Democratic politics, Sabath was elected in 1907 to his first of 24 terms in the House. He represented Chicago's Fifth Congressional District, an area composed primarily of Southern and Eastern European immigrants.

Sabath accumulated a liberal record in the House, introducing bills for workman's compensation, old-age pensions, and wages and hours regulation. He also fought immigration restriction and Prohibition. Sabath was a major supporter of Franklin D. Roosevelt's New Deal, cosponsoring the legislation establishing the Federal Deposit Insurance Company and working for passage of the Wagner Act, the Social Security Act, and the Securities and Exchange Commission Act. He was also a champion of civil rights and liberties during the Truman administration. He supported Representative VITO MARCANTONIO's (ALP-N.Y.) bill to abolish the poll tax and voted against the extension of the House Un-American Activities Committee, the Mundt-Nixon bill of 1948, and the Internal Security Act of 1950.

Sabath opposed much of the Truman administration's foreign policy. He participated in the Win the Peace Conference in Washington, D.C., in 1946, which sought to promote U.S.-Soviet amity. Sabath voted against much of the legislation implementing Truman's containment policies, including aid to Greece and Turkey, the Mutual Defense Assistance Act of 1949, and the Mutual Security Act of 1951. However, he did support the British loan of 1946 and the Marshall Plan. Sabath also broke with Truman over China policy, maintaining that the Communist uprising there appeared to be legitimate and democratic, not the product of Soviet expansion.

As far as postwar domestic policy, Sabath opposed turning the tidelands over to the states, the Taft-Hartley Act, the 1948 Republican tax cut, and the amendment to limit the president to two terms. He backed the Full Employment bill of 1945, making the school lunch program permanent, raising the minimum wage to 75 cents an hour in 1949, and the Housing Act of 1949.

As chairman of the Rules Committee, Sabath faced a majority coalition of Republicans and Southern Democrats, which repeatedly blocked his attempts to report such bills as a strong fair employment practices measure and an increase in the minimum wage. It also forced him to report the Case Labor Disputes bill in 1946, which he denounced. Sabath vented his frustration on the floor of the House on June 22, 1949, when he opened debate on the housing bill of that year. He decried the "unholy alliance and coalition" of Republicans and Southern Democrats, which had successfully fought the bill for three years. Thereupon Representative E. E. COX (D-Ga.) called Sabath a liar and struck the Illinois Congressman in the mouth. Sabath, then 83, delivered several blows before his colleagues restrained him.

In 1949 Sabath successfully pushed through the House a measure designed to circumvent the Southern Democratic–Republican coalition in the Rules

Committee. The so-called 21-day rule permitted legislative committees under certain conditions to bypass the Rules Committee and bring their bills directly to the House floor. The rule was repealed in 1951.

Sabath died of pancreatic cancer on November 6, 1952, in Chicago, Illinois.

Saltonstall, Leverett
(1892–1979) *member of the Senate*

A descendant of English and Irish colonial settlers, Leverett Saltonstall was born on September 1, 1892, in Chestnut Hill, Massachusetts. A member of one of the wealthiest and most powerful families in Massachusetts, he graduated from Harvard College and received a law degree from that university in 1917. After serving in the army during World War I, he practiced law in the family firm. Saltonstall entered elective politics in 1920 as a Newton, Massachusetts, alderman. At the end of his two year term, he successfully ran as a Republican for the state legislature. Beginning in 1923 he served 13 years in the Massachusetts House, including four terms as the speaker from 1929 to 1936. In 1938 he was elected governor, a post he held until 1944. While governor, the liberal Saltonstall was able to expand services and yet reduce the state debt by cutting back on what he considered wasteful programs. When Senator HENRY CABOT LODGE, JR., (R-Mass.) resigned to enter military service in 1944, Saltonstall ran for the vacant Senate seat. A popular and respected politician, the man "with a South Boston face and a Back Bay name," won election by more than 400,000 votes. He carried Democratic Boston by over 60,000 votes.

In the Senate Saltonstall maintained a low profile, speaking rarely and avoiding controversy. Nicknamed "Salty," he came to represent Yankee integrity to many of his colleagues. LYNDON B. JOHNSON once remarked that Saltonstall would be incapable of "double-crossing" anyone. Although he never exerted great political influence in the Senate, Saltonstall was an effective promoter of the Commonwealth's fishing, electronics, and commercial interests.

During the Truman years he fashioned a moderately liberal record on civil rights and foreign policy. A member of the internationalist wing of the GOP, he was an enthusiastic proponent of the Marshall Plan and supported the $2.7 billion increase for the program in 1949. He voted for the UN Charter in 1945, the British loan in 1946, Greek-Turkish aid in 1947, the North Atlantic Treaty in 1949, and military aid to NATO in the same year. He voted against the 1951 McClellan Amendment. As a member of the Armed Services Committee, Saltonstall supported generous appropriations for the military. He voted for the National Security Act of 1947, which unified the army, navy, and air force under the Department of Defense. In the late spring of 1951, he participated in the joint Foreign Relations–Armed Services Committee hearings on President Truman's decision to relieve General DOUGLAS MACARTHUR of his Korean command. Saltonstall voted with the majority not to issue a report. He later said he thought MacArthur was "difficult and almost insubordinate" and wrong to be dabbling in politics." Saltonstall refused to join the majority of Republicans on the committees who released a statement in August critical of Truman and Secretary of State DEAN G. ACHESON.

While Saltonstall was known as an internationalist who endorsed administration foreign policy, he opposed a large portion of Fair Deal legislation. Some liberal groups felt he aligned himself with the more conservative Republican Senate bloc on domestic matters. An American Federation of Labor (AFL) study in 1954 claimed that between 1947 and 1952 Saltonstall had voted against labor interests on 23 of 30 critical votes. He supported the Case labor disputes bill, the Taft-Hartley Act, the GOP tax cut of the 80th Congress, the Portal-to-Portal Pay Act, the 1952 Byrd Amendment calling on the president to invoke Taft-Hartley in the steel strike, deregulation of the natural gas industry, and turning the tidelands over to the states so they could control access to the oil there. He opposed the Housing Act of 1948 and the Barkley Amendment of 1948 giving the President stand-by rationing and wage-price control powers. In 1950 he voted for the Internal Security Act. That same year, however, Saltonstall defended General GEORGE C. MARSHALL when Senator JOSEPH R. MCCARTHY (R-Wisc.) called him "a pitiful thing" not fit to hold office and attacked him for his support of "appeasement" toward the Soviet Union. When McCarthy scored Acheson along similar lines in 1950, Saltonstall warned against questioning the secretary of state's integrity or loyalty and called for an end to "witch-hunting." He did support some liberal legislation, such as the Senate version of the Full Employment bill of 1945, the Housing Act of 1949, and federal aid to education.

In 1952 Saltonstall joined two other Massachusetts Republicans, Lodge and Representative CHRISTIAN A. HERTER (R-Mass.), in urging DWIGHT D. EISENHOWER to run for the GOP presidential nomination. They were instrumental in promoting the general's candidacy in the early primaries and provided delegate strength at the Republican National Convention in June.

Saltonstall was receptive to the Eisenhower administration's legislative program during the 1950s. As Republican whip and assistant GOP Senate leader, he helped gather congressional support for White House proposals. The ranking Republican on the Armed Services Committee and its chairman in 1953 and 1954, he defended the administration's often controversial military and foreign aid requests. Saltonstall cautiously opposed McCarthy's anticommunist probes and voted to censure the Wisconsin senator in December 1954.

During the Kennedy and Johnson administrations Saltonstall retained his image as a moderate. He generally backed Democratic foreign policy, supporting the nuclear test ban treaty and the Vietnam War. He was also active in pushing for the adoption of civil rights legislation. In 1967 Saltonstall announced he would not seek reelection. His retirement allowed Attorney General Edward Brooke to successfully run for the seat and become the first black senator since Reconstruction. Saltonstall died on June 17, 1979, in Dover, Massachusetts. (See *The Eisenhower Years, The Kennedy Years, The Johnson Years* Volumes)

—JF

Sawyer, Charles
(1887–1979) *secretary of commerce*

The son of teachers, Charles Sawyer was born on February 10, 1887, in Cincinnati, Ohio. He graduated from Oberlin College in 1908 and the University of Cincinnati Law School in 1911. He practiced law in Cincinnati and became the youngest member of its city council in 1911. Following service in the army from 1917 to 1919, he returned to private practice. He served as lieutenant governor from 1933 to 1934 and ran unsuccessfully for the Democratic gubernatorial nomination in 1938. Sawyer campaigned for Franklin D. Roosevelt who appointed him ambassador to Belgium and Luxembourg in 1944.

In May 1948 Truman, impressed with Sawyer's performance, appointed him secretary of commerce

Secretary of Commerce Charles Sawyer *(Harry S. Truman Library)*

following the resignation of W. AVERELL HARRIMAN. The choice of the conservative lawyer was designed not to alienate business leaders. Sawyer held serious reservations about New Deal regulatory expansion and high taxes. In 1949 he stated, "No government official ever will, or can, run a business as well as a businessman can do it." He saw the business world as essentially cooperative but often confused by complex laws. Consequently he attempted to minimize government involvement and sought "voluntary compliance" with regulations. Yet he opposed the Kerr bill, which would have deregulated prices natural gas companies might charge to pipelines. Throughout his tenure Sawyer acted as a liaison between government and big business. His view of the department's role led many in the press to consider him the "weakest" member of the cabinet, who would probably not last in the administration.

Despite his conservatism, or perhaps because of it, Sawyer became caught up in the postwar Red Scare. ELIZABETH BENTLEY accused Commerce Department employee WILLIAM W. REMINGTON of being a Communist agent. Even though cleared by the Loyalty Review Board, Sawyer, under pressure by right-wing congressmen, dismissed him in June 1950.

Despite his emphasis on free enterprise, Sawyer accepted regulation of business during national emergencies and played a major role in regulation during the Korean conflict. In 1950 Truman placed him in charge of all materials and facilities. Sawyer set up a National Production Authority to handle priorities, allocations, and inventory controls. Aware of the necessity of rapid productivity, he announced that government had to use mandatory orders in controlling defense production because voluntary agreements "just won't work."

Following his seizure of the steel mills in April 1952, Truman put Sawyer in charge of the industry. The president had taken the extreme action to prevent a strike after the steel industry refused to accept a wage increase proposed by the Wage Stabilization Board (WSB) without appropriate price rises. The secretary, who had not been consulted on the action, which he resented, reluctantly agreed to the appointment. He disliked the seizure but believed that it was necessary for national defense, saying that he had "neither requested not wanted this job, but when our men at the front are taking orders in the face of great danger those of us further back could do no less." He further noted that the country was "facing a situation of great peril where continued production of steel is essential to our national welfare." Sawyer demanded he be given "a free hand" in running the mills, which Truman agreed to. Sawyer's appointment had been designed to avert industry criticism and to show Americans that the administration only wanted to continue vital steel manufacturing. Sawyer initially hoped that a wage settlement could be concluded through collective bargaining. However, when postseizure negotiations did not succeed, Sawyer said he would look into the wage situation in order to satisfy the steelworkers' union and threaten the steel manufacturers to settle. When this failed, he told the reluctant companies that he would raise wages. At the end of the month, he authorized a wage increase and a rise in the steel price ceiling.

When a federal district court ordered the mills returned to their owners, Sawyer recommended the Taft-Hartley Act's 80-day cooling off period be invoked. But other administration officials pointed out that the public would think the president had been mistaken in not employing the law in the first place. Truman decided against utilizing the act.

The secretary returned the mills to the industry following the Supreme Court's decision, on June 2, that the seizure had been unconstitutional. Still without a contract, the unions then went out on strike. Sawyer again advised Truman to invoke Taft-Hartley to avoid any disruption of steel manufacturing on the grounds that its production was essential to the war effort. He asserted that an injunction would give the two parties time to negotiate. If the measure failed to produce a settlement, Congress, not the president, would then be forced to act. Truman, however, once more refused Sawyer's advice. The strike lasted until July 24, when an agreement was reached similar to that proposed by the WSB and including a steel price increase.

Sawyer retired from public service upon the entry of the Eisenhower administration and returned to private law practice in Glendale, Ohio. Sawyer died on April 7, 1979, in Palm Beach, Florida.

Schlesinger, Arthur M(eier), Jr.
(1917–) *historian*

The son of a distinguished American historian, Arthur M. Schlesinger, Jr., was born on October 15, 1917, in Columbus, Ohio. He graduated summa cum laude from Harvard in 1938. His senior honor thesis, on 19th-century Jacksonian Orestes Brownson, was praised by historians when it was published the following year. After a year of study at Cambridge University, Schlesinger returned to Harvard to join the prestigious Society of Fellows, where he began his book, *The Age of Jackson*. He completed this work, which won the 1946 Pulitzer Prize for history, while serving in Washington with the Office of War Information. In the *Age of Jackson* Schlesinger portrayed the president as the paradigm of a successful leader, an aggressive liberal who used his power in a pragmatic fashion. Schlesinger joined his father on the Harvard faculty in 1947.

The historian was a leading spokesman for the anticommunist left during the postwar era. He was a founding member of the Americans for Democratic Action, a coalition of liberals who opposed the inclusion of Communists in a progressive alliance. In a series of articles he condemned the Communist Party for being authoritarian and helping conservatives by "dividing and neutralizing the left." Schlesinger opposed HENRY A. WALLACE's third party candidacy in 1948. However, believing Truman a sure loser for election, Schlesinger along with many other liberals, wanted to draft, DWIGHT D. EISENHOWER for the Democratic nomination. He later ruefully admitted that he learned from this experience never to support a presidential candidate whose views were unknown. In 1948 Schlesinger also worked temporarily for the Economic Cooperation Administration to formulate information policy.

Schlesinger's most important contribution to the political debates of the period was *The Vital Center* (1949), a book highly influenced by the neo-orthodox Christian theology of REINHOLD NIEBUHR. Schlesinger warned American liberals to forsake utopian solutions propounded either by the extreme left or right and asked them to adopt an "unsentimental" approach to politics. He lamented that many liberals, in their search for a utopia, had idealized communism and the Soviet Union and had joined popular fronts in cooperation with Communists. Schlesinger predicted that such collaboration could only lead to disaster because communism as practiced by the Soviet Union preached the destruction of freedom by the state.

Schlesinger indicated that during the postwar period he had found the "restoration of radical nerve" among the noncommunist left whose perceptions of the Soviet Union derived from Stalin's purges rather than an idealization of the Bolshevik Revolution. He perceived this "revival of American radicalism" in the election of WALTER P. REUTHER as president of the United Automobile Workers, the creation of the Americans for Democratic Action, and the ouster of leftist LEE PRESSMAN from the Congress of Industrial Organizations. Advocating "a new radicalism," these liberals, according to Schesinger, reaffirmed their commitment to the basic civil liberties of the Western world and supported a mixed economy, which featured a blending of capitalism and New Deal regulatory and social reform programs. In foreign affairs they preached an anti-Stalin diplomacy that supported the containment policies of the Truman administration. Schlesinger's title, *The Vital Center,* became the accepted term denoting the liberal creed of the late Truman era.

Believing ADLAI E. STEVENSON to be the potential leader of the center, Schlesinger served as his speech writer during the former governor's 1952 presidential campaign. Although several Republican conservatives denounced Schlesinger as a Communist during the race, Stevenson retained the young historian. Schlesinger also headed the research and speech writing division of Stevenson's campaign during his second try for the presidency in 1956.

During the 1950s Schlesinger was a prominent critic of Senator JOSEPH R. MCCARTHY (R-Wisc.). A friend of John F. Kennedy, Schlesinger worked on his campaign staff in 1960 and was his special adviser on Latin America during the administration. Schlesinger left the White House following Kennedy's assassination. In 1965 he published *A Thousand Days: John F. Kennedy in the White House,* which won him his second Pulitzer Prize.

Schlesinger left Harvard in 1966 to become a Schweitzer professor of humanities at the City University of New York. Still active in liberal Democrat politics, he was a close political advisers to Robert Kennedy and a constant critic of the Vietnam War. In 1973 he published *The Imperial Presidency,* tracing the enormous growth of the executive during the postwar period. (See *The Kennedy Years, The Johnson Years* Volumes)

—JB

Schoeneman, George J(eremiah)
(1889–1966) *commissioner of internal revenue*

Born on March 4, 1889, in a Newport, Rhode Island, lighthouse of which his father was keeper, George J. Schoeneman was reared in that state where he attended public schools. In 1911 he entered government service as a stenographer in the Post Office Department in Washington. He held the position of executive clerk to the Postmaster General from 1913 to 1916 and was assistant superintendent of the Division of Supplies and Equipment from 1916 to 1919. He then became secretary to one of the members of the Federal Reserve Board.

Schoeneman's career with the Bureau of Internal Revenue (BIR) began in 1920, when he was appointed chief of the Bureau's Personnel and Field Procedure Division. There he oversaw tax filing practices of the bureau's branch offices and employee hiring and promotion. He rose through the ranks of the bureau, becoming assistant commissioner of internal revenue in 1944.

Because of his exceptional performance as an administrator, Schoeneman was appointed administrative assistant to President Truman in 1945. From his White House office he supervised personnel and civil service problems. He was soon promoted to the position of executive assistant to the president with the responsibility for supervising and coordinating the work of the White House staff. In 1947 Truman appointed Schoeneman the new commissioner of internal revenue. The appointment was wholeheartedly approved by private industry since, as *Business Week* noted, "as a career man, Schoeneman is welcomed by tax lawyers who respect his knowledge of BIR's functionings." However, historian Andrew J. Dunar has argued that the bureau needed reform and Schoeneman did not have the capacity to launch such a program.

Besides the enforcement of internal revenue laws, Schoeneman supervised the determination, assessment, and collection of all internal taxes. This included levies on alcoholic beverages, income, and profits. He also made decisions on the application of the tax laws. For the duration of his tenure, Schoeneman and his staff brought into the Treasury approximately $110 billion in taxes and handled more than 300 million tax returns. In November 1950 Truman commended the BIR, "From what I hear from George Schoeneman, he says he has the most effective organization that has ever been in existence in the history of the Bureau of Internal Revenue. I am proud of that and I hope you will keep that reputation."

Prior to Schoeneman's appointment the BIR had come under scrutiny because of branch office irregularities. As a result, when he assumed the position of commissioner, Schoeneman provided strong assurances that any irregularities would be fully investigated and that the proper authorities would be notified of employee impropriety. In 1950 Secretary of the Treasury JOHN W. SNYDER began a quiet investigation of the BIR as a result of persistent rumors of bribery and links to the underworld in certain of the bureau's branch offices. His investigation revealed that 55 employees had taken bribes, 24 embezzled government funds, and 21 did not pay their taxes. Snyder subsequently sought to prosecute BIR regional officers for failure to report irregularities and attempted to lodge criminal charges against the employees involved. In March 1951 Schoeneman responded to the Snyder investigation and accusations that BIR branch offices maintained ties to underworld figures by establishing a special fraud section to investigate the tax returns of racketeers. He also stated that only 50 or 60 bureau employees out of 55,000 had been dismissed each year for bribes and other irregularities. But according to Dunar, Schoeneman could not handle the scandals and, in June, he resigned for "reasons of health."

During the fall a House Ways and Means subcommittee headed by Representative CECIL R. KING (D-Calif.) held hearings on alleged corruption within the BIR. It heard testimony by Chicago lawyer Abraham Teitelbaum revealing that a "clique" in Washington fixed important tax cases for a free and that one of those involved was Schoeneman. The commissioner's name also came up in an investigation of Truman's former appointments secretary, MATTHEW J. CONNELLY. For bribes Connelly had allegedly lobbied Schoeneman on a tax evasion case. Schoeneman was later accused of failure to pay taxes on $176,000. He was never indicted for tax evasion or any other irregularity. Schoeneman died in February 1966.

—DGE

Schwellenbach, Lewis B(axter)
(1894–1948) *secretary of labor*

Lewis B. Schwellenbach was born on September 20, 1894, in Superior, Washington, of German-American parents and raised in Spokane, Washington. His father died while Lewis was young, and the family lived on the edge of poverty. He worked his way through the University of Washington Law School, graduating in 1917. When America entered World War I, Schwellenbach joined the army. Following his discharge in 1919 he returned to Spokane and joined the law firm of Roberts and Skeel, specializing in labor law. He left the firm in 1925 to form a law partnership. During the 1920s he became active in state politics, advocating such programs as public pensions for the elderly and public ownership of utilities. In 1932 he ran unsuccessfully for governor, calling for government operation of unused farms and factories for the benefit of the unemployed. With strong support from liberals, labor unions, and the American Legion, Schwellenbach won a seat in the U.S. Senate in 1934. His campaign was based on a liberal reform program he termed "End Poverty in Washington."

In the upper house Schwellenbach rose to the leadership of a group of freshmen Democrats known as the "young Turks," which included Carl Hatch, SHERMAN MINTON, and Harry S Truman, all of whom were strong supporters of Roosevelt's New Deal legislation. In 1938, when economic recovery seemed uncertain, he attacked the inflexible policies of "monopolistic and quasi-monopolistic industries" that kept prices too high to allow for economic stimulation. "If private industry does not take up the slack promptly," he warned, "the government must." In 1940 Roosevelt appointed him district judge for the eastern district of Washington. He assumed the post after finishing out his Senate term in December 1940 and served until 1945.

In 1945 Truman appointed Schwellenbach to succeed Francis Perkins as secretary of labor. His appointment pleased Congress of Industrial Organizations president PHILIP MURRAY and American Federation of Labor chief WILLIAM GREEN. He immediately began reorganizing and revitalizing the department, which had played a relatively passive role during the Roosevelt administration. He consolidated the various agencies dealing with labor matters—such as the National War Labor Board and the War Manpower Commission—in his department.

After the war ended in August 1945, Schwellenbach was faced with a tremendous wave of strikes that swept the nation. He believed in settling disputes through federal mediation, fact-finding boards, and reconciliation within the framework of free collective bargaining, and he opposed government seizures of industry. In a radio speech on Labor Day 1945 he cautioned unions and management that they both had a responsibility to avoid strikes and create jobs.

The first major test for the secretary came when oil workers went on strike in the autumn of 1945. Schwellenbach intervened in what was regarded as an unprecedented manner. Negotiations had broken down, with the union demanding a 30 percent pay increase and the oil companies offering no more than 15 percent. Schwellenbach ordered the parties to submit to arbitration and find a compromise between the 15 percent and 30 percent increases. The companies reacted sharply, charging that they were being forced to exceed their maximum offer. When no peaceful solution could be found and the nation was faced with a potentially crippling oil shortage, Truman seized the refineries, and the workers were ordered back to work.

In early November 1945 a National Labor-Management Conference was convened in Washington, prompted by a letter from Republican senator ARTHUR H. VANDENBERG of Michigan to the labor secretary, and discussions between Truman, Schwellenbach, and other administration officials. It was to provide a forum for business, labor, and government in which problems could be discussed and peaceful solutions found to the critical labor difficulties facing the nation. Schwellenbach played an important role in the meeting, but his attempt to promote constructive dialogue was unsuccessful.

On November 21, 1945, one of the largest strikes in American history began as more than 200,000 auto workers went on strike against General Motors. The next month Truman proposed that fact-finding boards be established to investigate and bring public pressure on labor and management. Schwellenbach strongly supported the proposed boards, which had the power to subpoena witnesses, hold quasi-judicial proceedings, and make recommendations for settlement. In mid-December Truman appointed a fact-finding board to investigate the auto strike, but its efforts and those of Schwellenbach to find a solution were unsuccessful.

The striking auto workers were joined in January 1946 by workers in the steel, meatpacking, electrical equipment, and other industries. That month nearly two million workers were on strike. By late spring labor problems peaked with the strike or threatened strike of the coal miners and the railroad workers. In both these cases the collective bargaining an arbitration processes favored by Schwellenbach broke down, and Truman intervened with government seizures of the industries to force an agreement. Although many of the major strikes were not settled by peaceful arbitration by the Labor Department, some 12,500 strikes were settled in 1946 without compulsory methods. The U.S. Conciliation Service was Schwellenbach's main tool for mediating these disputes.

Congressional opposition to the power of labor grew rapidly during 1946, and many measures were proposed to limit labor's power. The Case labor disputes bill was the first such measure to pass Congress. The bill provided for a 30-day cooling-off period before unions could strike, forbade organized boycotts to force employers to come to terms, and permitted injunctions against certain union activities. Schwellenbach voiced strong opposition to the proposal, objecting that it would take power away from the secretary of labor until a strike was inevitable and then would "dump the controversy in his lap when all the real trouble arises." He admitted that emergency legislation was needed, but he said permanent legislation required more study before adoption. Upon Schwellenbach's recommendation Truman vetoed the bill in June 1946. The secretary also opposed the Taft-Hartley Act, which Congress passed over the president's veto in 1947.

By 1947 the postwar strike wave had subsided, the Schwellenbach was less active in the direct mediation of disputes. He continued to argue publicly for changes in labor laws, especially for a liberalization of Taft-Hartley restrictions on closed shops and for an increase in the extension of minimum wage law coverage.

In March 1947 Schwellenbach called for a ban against Communists in public office and union activity. His suggestion received wide attention and touched off a storm of controversy among labor leaders. In the months that followed many unions began to exclude Communists from holding union office, and several bills were introduced in Congress calling for restrictions on Communists.

Schwellenbach suffered from poor health beginning in late 1947, and his activity in the Labor Department was limited. He died in Washington, D.C., on June 10, 1948.

—DMR

Scott, Hugh D(oggett)

(1900–1994) *member of the House of Representatives*

Hugh D. Scott was born on November 11, 1900, in Fredericksburg, Virginia. He graduated from Randolph-Macon College in 1919 and received a law degree from the University of Virginia three years later. He practiced in Philadelphia and from 1926 to 1941 served as assistant district attorney in that city. In 1940 and 1942 Scott was elected to the U.S. House of Representatives. Following naval service during World War II, he was again elected to the House in 1946.

A member of the eastern, internationalist wing of the Republican Party, Scott supported the administration's Greek-Turkish aid program and the Marshall Plan. However, he voted against military aid to the North Atlantic Treaty Organization and the Korean Aid Act. He backed the resettlement of displaced European Jews in Palestine and opposed the relatively restrictive McCarran-Walter Immigration Act. On domestic issues the representative voted to override President Truman's veto of the Taft-Hartley Act of 1947 and supported efforts to institute voluntary price control. He favored the Republican tax cuts of the 80th Congress and backed anticommunist legislation, including the 1948 Mundt-Nixon bill, which would have required the registration of Communist-front organizations and their officers, and the 1950 McCarran Internal Security Act. He voted for raising the minimum wage to 75 cents an hour in 1949.

Scott strongly supported New York governor THOMAS E. DEWEY, over Senator ROBERT A. TAFT (R-Ohio) for the 1948 Republican presidential nomination. Following his nomination at the June convention, Dewey chose Scott to be national chairman. Scott took little part in managing Dewey's campaign, which was led by the former national Republican chairman, Herbert Brownell. His major role was in attempting to unite the Dewey and Taft factions of the party. Scott asked Taft to liberalize his position on several issues in order to undercut support for Truman, but the Ohio senator refused. Some critics felt Taft's intransigence weakened Dewey's position but the candidate's own lackluster campaign contributed to the GOP defeat in November.

Following Dewey's defeat the Republican National Committee met in January 1949. Scott was assailed as "a symbol of Dewey misrule" by an unusual coalition of Taft conservatives and liberals allied to HAROLD E. STASSEN. Scott defended himself against charges of losing the 1948 election by asserting that Brownell had run Dewey's campaign. He denied any tie to the New York governor and said that Dewey should not run again in 1952. After a bitter intraparty struggle, Scott retained his post by a narrow four-vote margin. As a concession to anti-Dewey factions, he replaced former pro-Dewey members of the GOP Executive Committee with individuals opposed to his leadership. During the spring of 1949 Republican vice chairman Thomas E. Coleman resigned in protest over Scott's leadership. Scott replaced him, but a few days later announced his own resignation. The following month Taft backer GUY GABRIELSON was elected national chairman.

In May 1950 Scott accused conservative Republicans and Taft of forming alliances with Southern Democrats for purposes of patronage and personal advantage. He continued to oppose Taft as the party's 1952 presidential nominee and was an early participant in the "draft Eisenhower" movement. At a Young Republican Convention during the fall of 1951, Scott asserted that Eisenhower was the "one candidate who would be certain to become president on the Republican ticket." In February 1952 Scott was among 19 representatives who wrote DWIGHT D. EISENHOWER urging him to seek the GOP nomination. Scott served as chairman of Eisenhower's headquarters committee during the presidential campaign.

During the Eisenhower administration Scott was instrumental in persuading the president to modify his opposition to civil rights legislation. Over the opposition of the party's Pennsylvania machine, Scott received the 1958 Republican Senate nomination. He won the election despite the Democratic tide of that year. As a senator, Scott continued to stand toward the left of his party. In 1964 he attempted to block the nomination of conservative senator Barry M. Goldwater (R-Ariz.) for president. Scott became Senate minority leader in 1969. Compromised by his persistent defense of President Richard M. Nixon during the Watergate crisis of the 1970s and by the revelation that he had been receiving an annual fee from an oil corporation, Scott did not seek reelection in 1976. Scott died of cardiac arrest on July 21, 1994, in Falls Church, Virginia. (See *The Eisenhower Years, The Kennedy Years, The Johnson Years, The Nixon/Ford Years* Volumes)

—MJS

Seaborg, Glenn T(heodore)

(1912–1999) *nuclear chemist; member, General Advisory Committee, Atomic Energy Commission*
The son of a machinist, Glenn Seaborg was born on April 19, 1912, in Ishpeming, Michigan. He received a doctorate in nuclear chemistry from the University of California at Berkeley and subsequently joined the faculty there. Between 1937 and 1940 his studies of atomic structure led to the discovery of numerous new isotopes of common elements. Seaborg's major achievement, however, was the discovery of plutonium, a transuranium element with fissionable properties, which he was able to produce through uranium bombardment experiments in the cyclotron at Berkeley. Scientists working in Chicago in the summer of 1939 had already proven the possibility of reducing the materials necessary for a nuclear chain reaction to the small format of a bomb. Seaborg's discovery of plutonium provided a new source of potential nuclear fuel.

With the United States's entry into World War II, Seaborg took a leave of absence from Berkeley to continue his plutonium research at the Manhattan District Project, organized in 1941 to develop an atomic bomb. As section chief of the University of Chicago metallurgical laboratory, Seaborg succeeded in developing a separation process for plutonium that contributed to the creation of the bomb.

Even before the first atomic bomb had been tested, scientists working on the project saw the need of some system of control for the awesome new weapon. Seaborg was chosen to serve on a committee to discuss the social and political consequences of atomic energy. He was among seven scientists who, in June 1945, submitted to the secretary of war a memorandum known as the Franck Report. The report contended that America's nuclear monopoly could not last more than a few years. Calling for the prevention of a postwar arms race through a system of international controls based on mutual trust, it also warned that such trust would be violated from the start if the United States were to use an atomic bomb in a surprise attack on Japan. Such an attack would "prejudice the possibility of reaching an international agreement on the future control of weapons." The framers of the Franck Report advocated a demonstration of the bomb in an uninhabited place. However, President Truman followed the advice of his Interim Committee, which recommended that atomic bombs be dropped on Japan without warning. In his memoirs Seaborg admitted that it would have been difficult to prevent a postwar arms race given U.S. relations with the Soviets at the time. He said he understood why the bomb was dropped on Hiroshima and did not argue with the decision. He did doubt the necessity of bombing Nagasaki. However, he had no regrets about his involvement in the project, believing it had saved lives that would have been lost in an invasion.

Seaborg returned to Berkeley in 1946 to teach and to direct nuclear chemical research at the university's Lawrence Radiation Laboratory. Over the next several years he and his staff proved the existence of six additional transuranium elements. A pioneer in the areas of nuclear methodology and instrumentation, Seaborg was awarded the Nobel Prize for Chemistry in 1951.

From 1946 to 1950 Seaborg served on the Atomic Energy Commission's (AEC) General Advisory Committee (GAC), a body established by Truman to advise on atomic energy policy and to determine the direction of future research. The explosion of the first Soviet atomic device in 1949 led the GAC to consider the advisability of instituting a crash program to develop a hydrogen or fusion bomb. Absent from this meeting, Seaborg expressed his support of the project in a letter to GAC chairman J. ROBERT OPPENHEIMER. All the other GAC members, including Oppenheimer, opposed the weapon's development, fearing that it would increase America's dependence on atomic weapons and prejudice attempts to achieve a system of international controls. Truman decided to go ahead with the bomb. When, in 1954, Oppenheimer's alleged leftist leanings led President Eisenhower to suspend his security clearance, Seaborg was the only one of Oppenheimer's former GAC colleagues not to testify in his behalf. Seaborg had no doubt about Oppenheimer's loyalty, but he did tell him that if asked he would say not releasing his letter on the hydrogen bomb to the GAC had been a mistake. Neither the government's nor Oppenheimer's lawyers thought his testimony would help their case. Oppenheimer's alleged failure to publish Seaborg's letter supporting the hydrogen project was influential in the final ruling against the GAC chief.

From 1954 to 1958 Seaborg served as associate director of the Lawrence Radiation Laboratory. He gave up nuclear research in 1958 to become chancellor of the Berkeley campus. In 1959 he was appointed to the President's Science Advisory Committee and, in the same year, was given the AEC's Enrico Fermi Award. In 1961 President Kennedy appointed Seaborg chairman of the AEC; he was the first scientist to hold that post. Seaborg sought to maintain the rapid pace of technological advance begun during World War II through government funded nuclear research programs. He hoped through the development of atomic energy to "advance peaceful national goals." He was instrumental in formulating the 1963 nuclear test ban treaty. In 1971 Seaborg resigned as chairman of the AEC and returned to the University of California. He returned to his work in the classroom and the laboratory and worked in a group that created a new isotope, element 106 on the periodic table, which later was named seaborgium. He died on February 25, 1999, in Lafayette, California. (See *The Eisenhower Years, The Kennedy Years, The Johnson Years*, Volumes)

—DAE

Service, John S(tewart)

(1909–1999) *diplomat*

The son of American missionaries, John S. Service was born on August 3, 1909, in Chengtu, China, and spent his early years in that country. Following his graduation from Oberlin College in 1931, he joined the Foreign Service as a clerk at the Ameri-

can consulate in Kunming. By World War II Service was one of America's leading experts on China.

In July 1944 Service accompanied the Dixie Mission to Yenan, the seat of rebel Communist forces. From there he forwarded policy recommendations on the civil war. He predicted that the Communists would eventually win the war because the corrupt Nationalist government under Chiang Kai-shek (Jiang Jieshi) did not have the people's support. Service advised Washington to change its policy of sending aid only to Chiang in the war against Japan so that if, as he predicted, Mao Zedong (Mao Tsetung) did win the civil war, the Communists would be friendly to the United States. Many read Service's dispatches as a realistic assessment of power in China. However others, most notably PATRICK J. HURLEY, the ambassador to China, and the pro-Chiang "China Lobby," thought that his recommendations were evidence that he was procommunist. Service had been ousted as General Albert Wedemeyer's aide by Hurley and been sent back to Washington to await further assignment. When he later became political adviser to General DOUGLAS MACARTHUR, the China Lobby started to agitate for his ouster from government.

Service's role in the *Amerasia* affair further complicated his difficulties with the right. While he was waiting for reassignment, Service had contemplated quitting and going public with his concerns over the China situation. But the head of the Far Eastern Affairs Office at the State Department, John Carter Vincent, and White House aide Lauchlin Currie—later revealed as a Soviet agent—encouraged him to leak information to the press instead. In Washington Service met Philip Jaffe, editor of a leftist magazine on Asian affairs, *Amerasia*. Jaffe was quite open about his Communist sympathies, which Service knew about, but, unbeknownst to Service, he wanted to serve Soviet intelligence. Service also did not know that the FBI had Jaffe under surveillance for possessing secret government documents. Service offered to lend Jaffe a translation of a document that was in circulation among high officials in China, but which Jaffe could not quote because of its sensitivity. Service then began turning more documents over to Jaffe. The FBI had no proof that Jaffe was passing on Service's documents to a foreign power. But in late April and early May a man describing himself as a Soviet agent, Joe Bernstein, contacted Jaffe about turning government documents over to him. Authors Ronald Radosh and

Harvey Klehr believe Bernstein was an intelligence operative for the Russians. Jaffe met with the unwitting Service, who provided documents to Jaffe, but Jaffe does not appear to have handed them over to Bernstein because he was having trouble determining whether he was in fact a Soviet agent.

When the FBI raided the *Amerasia* office and arrested Jaffe in June 1946, the agents found classified information in the office safe. Following the raid the FBI arrested Service, charging him with passing secrets to Jaffe. Service defended himself by claiming it was normal for government officials to pass certain documents to journalists as background material for articles. Feeling responsible and undoubtedly afraid of exposure, Currie convinced Washington lobbyist Thomas Corcoran to help Service out. Corcoran promised Attorney General–designate TOM C. CLARK that he would help with his confirmation in the Senate, and Clark, seemingly as a quid pro quo, as Radosh and Klehr have argued, went easy on Service. In addition much of the FBI's evidence had been based on illegal wiretaps and was inadmissible. From 1946 to 1948 the State Department conducted four additional loyalty checks on Service in which he was cleared. A House Judiciary subcommittee also examined the *Amerasia* affair and pronounced him innocent.

Senator JOSEPH R. MCCARTHY (R-Wisc.) revived the loyalty question in the spring of 1950. Based on material supplied by the China Lobby, he announced that Service was "a known associate and collaborator with Communists" who had been "consorting with admitted espionage agents." The Wisconsin Republican also revealed that J. EDGAR HOOVER had stated that he thought he had a 100 percent case against Service. Either coincidentally or coordinated with McCarthy's charges, the State Department decided to put Service through another security hearing. The department recalled him while en route to New Dehli to assume the post as counselor of the embassy. Back in Washington he was assigned to a routine desk job until a decision was rendered.

The Loyalty Board once again examined the *Amerasia* incident. It also heard testimony from both GEORGE F. KENNAN and JOHN K. FAIRBANK attesting to Service's anticommunism. In response the FBI provided material designed to convince the panel that Service was a suspected homosexual and that he had fathered an illegitimate child while in China. The board once again cleared Service. Con-

current with that review, a Senate panel led by MILLARD E. TYDINGS (D-Md.), examined McCarthy's charges. Service testified that he had been indiscreet in giving Jaffe material but then repeated that it was routine to do so, and he downplayed his role. He also was dismissive of his meeting with Currie and Corcoran, and, of course, did not reveal the coverup on his behalf. The Tydings Committee cleared the diplomat of any wrong doing.

In the fall of 1951 the Loyalty Review Board, which had the power to examine departmental decisions, took up the case. That December it ruled that there was a "reasonable doubt" about Service's loyalty. It cited the *Amerasia* case as justification for this decision. Secretary of State DEAN G. ACHESON then discharged Service. Radosh and Klehr argued that if Service had been dismissed in 1945 for trying to undermine his superiors thought leaking information, his firing would have been justified. But in 1952 he was dismissed on the false charge of disloyalty.

Service decided to test the constitutionality of his ouster. In January 1957 the Supreme Court found that Acheson had no right to remove him from office. Service returned to work in a bureaucratic position in Washington. Two years later he was transferred to Liverpool as consul. Service retired in 1962 to accept a position as resident China scholar at the University of California at Berkeley. In 1971 he visited Communist China. Service died on February 3, 1999, in Oakland, California. (See *The Eisenhower Years* Volume)

—JB

Small, John D(avid)

(1893–1963) *civilian production administrator; chairman, Munitions Board*

John D. Small was born on October 11, 1893, in Palestine, Texas. He graduated from the U.S. Naval Academy in 1915 and served in the navy for the next nine years. From 1926 to 1941 he was employed in chemical firms. He returned to naval service during World War II as an officer assigned to control of munitions. Small played a role in organizing the Normandy invasion, not only supervising the construction of landing craft but also joining the invasion in its first stages. During 1944–45 he served as executive officer of the War Production Board (WPB) and in April 1945 became chief of staff to WPB chairman JULIUS A. KRUG. At that post he headed a committee formed to handle industrial conversion for the war in the Pacific. He was also concerned with providing increased civilian goods as the war wound down.

When President Truman created the Civilian Production Administration at the end of 1945 to replace the WPB, he appointed Small its administrator. Small's goals were to expand production of scarce materials, conserve raw materials, prevent hoarding, and break production bottlenecks. Anxious to alleviate the serious housing shortage caused by the wartime moratorium on construction, he promised to give priority to veterans housing. A supporter of business interests, Small joined JOHN W. SNYDER, director of the Office of War Mobilization and Reconversion, in backing "incentive price increases" to encourage full peacetime production. For instance, Small supported Snyder when the latter called for an increase in the price of steel to offset wage hikes needed to settle the 1946 steelworkers' strike.

During 1946 Small denounced strikes for reducing output and contributing to continued scarcity. The coal strike, begun in April 1946, particularly aroused his anger. As a result of the fuel emergency he ordered a "dimout" in 22 states. Disturbed by the economic dislocation and worker layoffs resulting from the work stoppage, on May 16 Small asked Congress to outlaw strikes for at least six months. He charged that postwar strikes had already cost $2 billion in lost output of goods. Small's proposal was greeted by labor's demands for his dismissal.

Despite his continued labor problems, by the end of 1946 Small was extremely optimistic about the reconversion process. In November he lifted production controls. The following month he reported that most reconversion problems had "already been licked" and that output and employment were at the highest levels in U.S. history. On December 5, 1946, Small submitted his resignation in reaction to a new coal miners strike. He became president of the Maxon Food System, Inc., where he remained until 1950.

In November 1950, following the outbreak of the Korean War, Truman appointed Small chairman of the Munitions Board. There he created a procurement office to unify the buying of equipment for the armed forces. In early 1951 Small called for a quick increase in the country's stockpile

goals of critical raw materials and speeding up procurement to reach the new goals. Small resigned in 1953 to return to private business. He died in Washington, D.C., on January 23, 1963.

—AES

Smathers, George A(rmistead)

(1913–   ) *member of the House of Representatives, member of the Senate*

George Smathers was born on November 14, 1913, in Atlantic City, New Jersey. He graduated in 1936 from the University of Florida, where he was named "best all-round man." Two years later he received a law degree from the university and entered private practice. With assistance from Senator CLAUDE PEPPER (D-Fla.) Smathers was named assistant U.S. district attorney for Dade County in 1940. Two years later he enlisted in the marine corps. Again with help from Pepper, Smathers was discharged in 1945 and appointed a special assistant to the U.S. Attorney General.

In 1946 Smathers, running with Pepper's backing, won as a Democrat a seat in the House of Representatives where he quickly earned a reputation as a liberal, supporting the National Housing Act of 1949 and raising the minimum wage to 75 cents an hour in the same year. In an aberration to his liberalism he also supported the Taft-Hartley Act, the Mundt-Nixon bill, and the McCarran Internal Security Act. He also offered a motion to recommit a bill for Alaskan statehood to the Interior Committee, instructing it to study making the territory a commonwealth and giving it some form of self-governance. He initially supported HENRY A. WALLACE's policy positions opposing militarism and favoring cooperation with Russia. However, he soon turned toward supporting the administration's foreign policy of containment, voting for Greek-Turkish aid, the Marshall Plan, and military aid to the North Atlantic Treaty Organization. When he sensed the conservative tide mounting against Pepper, Smathers challenged his former political ally for his Senate seat.

Enjoying the support of conservative business interests who abhorred Pepper's liberal position on taxes and labor legislation, Smathers launched a vicious campaign against the incumbent. His tactics included insinuations about Pepper's sexual practices. In one speech Smathers allegedly said: "Are you aware that Claude Pepper is known all over

Washington as a shameless extrovert? Not only that, but this man is reliably reported to practice nepotism with his sister-in-law, and he has a sister, who was once a thespian in wicked New York. Worst of all, it is an established fact that Mr. Pepper before his marriage, practiced celibacy." (Smathers denied he ever said that.) Smathers circulated a newspaper clipping in which Pepper asked Americans to pray for Stalin. At campaign rallies Smathers would read the article and then ask his audience, "Did you pray for Stalin this morning?" Smathers also maintained that the Fair Employment Practices Commission, which Pepper backed, was a Communist-inspired plot to undermine southern segregation. Smathers called the senator "Red Pepper" for his leftist political stance. (He was also called that because of his red hair.) But Pepper biographer Tracy Denese has argued that Smathers, despite his shameful rhetoric, raised a compelling issue in questioning Pepper's rather forgiving attitude toward Soviet actions in the postwar era.

With the support of Republicans, some liberals who feared close association with the left, and conservative Democrats, Smathers defeated Pepper by 60,000 votes in the largest vote ever cast in Florida to that date. In November Smathers won the general election. Pepper's defeat represented a serious blow to the Fair Deal tradition and encouraged the growth of McCarthyism. Right-wing forces across the nation were encouraged by Smathers's victory.

Once in office Smathers continued the anticommunist crusade he had used against Pepper. During the 1952 Democratic presidential primary, he attacked ESTES KEFAUVER (D-Tenn.), for being soft on communism. Smathers subsequently backed the Democratic nominee for president, ADLAI E. STEVENSON, despite his support for civil rights and the repeal of the Taft-Hartley Act. During the 1953 congressional inquiry into the alleged upsurge of Communist influence in Hawaii, Smathers spearheaded a move to deny statehood to the territory. As a senator, Smathers continued his support of Truman's foreign policy, voting against the 1951 McClellan Amendment stating the sense of the Senate that no troops other than the four originally planned by Truman should be sent to Europe without the consent of Congress and the 1951 Dirksen Amendment cutting aid to Europe. He supported the Japanese Peace Treaty.

From the time of his election to the Senate, Smathers vigorously opposed civil rights measures.

During his first year in office, he declared he would defend, for no fee, any police officer indicted for violation of civil rights. In February 1953, in front of television cameras, he stated a Supreme Court decision banning segregation would "set the situation in the South back 50 years."

Through his association with Senate Majority Leader LYNDON B. JOHNSON (D-Tex.), Smathers's political fortunes rose; he was admitted into the inner circle of senators who made important committee assignments and often decided the outcome of legislation. According to journalist Robert Sherrill, Smathers wielded his influence to push bills that favored the interests of oil companies and railroads, some of which were clients of his Miami law firm.

Smathers maintained his conservative voting pattern during the Kennedy administration. He retained his power through the 1960s. However, toward the end of the decade many of his questionable business dealings were brought to light, and he was frequently charged with influence peddling. Claiming ill health, Smathers announced he would not seek reelection in 1968. (See *The Eisenhower Years, The Kennedy Years, The Johnson Years* Volumes)

—EF

Smith, H(oward) Alexander
(1880–1966) *member of the Senate*

The son of a physician-professor, H. Alexander Smith was born on January 30, 1880, in New York City. He graduated from Princeton in 1901 and Columbia University Law School in 1904. After practicing law for 12 years in Colorado Springs, Colorado, he joined HERBERT HOOVER's wartime Food Administration. Smith traveled in England, France, and Italy to study food rationing and participated in postwar relief activities for Belgium, Yugoslavia, and Finland. During the 1920s he was lecturer in international relations and executive secretary at Princeton University. Smith served as treasurer of the New Jersey Republican Committee from 1934 to 1940 and chairman in 1941. In February 1944 Republican leaders endorsed him to run for a Senate seat vacated by the death of Senator Warren Barbour (R-N.J.). Smith won the November election and ran again for a full term in 1946. He won on a platform that stressed his bipartisan, internationalist stance in foreign affairs and his interest in labor-management relations.

Smith built up a moderate record in the Senate. A member of the Labor Committee from 1944 to 1959, he endorsed the Case labor disputes bill of 1946 and the Taft-Hartley Act of 1947 to curb the power of labor unions. He supported the Portal-to-Portal Pay Act and the 1952 Byrd Amendment requesting Truman to invoke the Taft-Hartley Act in regard to the steelworker strike of that year. He voted for the 1948 Republican tax cut. Attacking the growth of federal bureaucracy and its interference in business and the economy, he opposed the Truman administration's request for the extension of price controls and wrote his own national health bill designed to decentralize health care responsibility to the states. Smith supported several civil rights measures during the period, endorsing and sponsoring a fair employment practices bill in 1948 and an equal rights amendment in 1950. He voted for the confirmation of DAVID E. LILIENTHAL as chairman of the Atomic Energy Commission despite accusations that Lilienthal had Communist connections. The senator backed federal aid to education and introduced the bill creating the National Science Foundation.

Senator ARTHUR H. VANDENBERG (R–Mich.), Smith's mentor in the Senate, brought the New Jersey senator into the Foreign Relations Committee, where he became instrumental in gaining support for a bipartisan foreign policy and collective security. He played a major role in the passage of aid to Greece and Turkey, the Marshall Plan, the North Atlantic Treaty, and the Point Four program. Smith voted against the McClellan Amendment of 1951 stating the sense of the Senate that no more troops than four initially planned by the president should be sent to NATO without congressional approval. He opposed the Dirksen Amendment to cut military aid to Europe in 1951 and the Bricker Amendment limiting the treaty-making powers of the president.

During the late 1940s Smith emerged as a major opponent of Truman's China policy and a vigorous supporter of Chiang Kai-shek (Jiang Jieshi). After a trip to the Far East in 1949, in which he conferred with Chiang and General DOUGLAS MACARTHUR, he became convinced that the continent would fall to the Communists because of the failure of U.S. policy. As chairman of the Far Eastern Subcommittee of the Foreign Relations Committee, he joined Senator WILLIAM F. KNOWLAND (R–Calif.), in advocating all-out aid to Chiang. After Chiang's flight to Taiwan, Smith worked to prevent

U.S. disengagement from the Nationalist regime. In an effort to block what he considered the "callous betrayal" of Chiang, he attempted to develop the idea of Taiwan's immense strategic importance. He suggested that the island's international status was undetermined because of the lack of a peace treaty with Japan and therefore Taiwan should be occupied by the United States with the agreement of Nationalist China. This action, he maintained, would forestall a Communist Chinese invasion of the island. The administration, however, took no action on his recommendation.

During the 1950s Smith remained a strong supporter of Chiang and a member of Committee of One Million founded to prevent the admission of Communist China to the U.N. Smith retired from the Senate in 1959 and served as a consultant to the State Department until 1960. He died of a stroke in Princeton, New Jersey, on October 27, 1966. (See *The Eisenhower Years* Volume)

—JMP

Smith, Howard W(orth)
(1883–1976) *member of the House of Representatives*

Howard W. Smith was born on February 2, 1883, in Broad Run, Virginia. Smith graduated from the University of Virginia Law School with a bachelor of laws in 1903. He moved to Alexandria, Virginia, in 1904 to practice law and quickly became involved in local politics. By 1922, he was corporation court judge, and in 1930, he was elected to Congress as a Democrat. He became a member of the powerful Rules Committee in 1933. Smith backed such New Deal measures as the Agricultural Adjustment Act and Social Security, but opposed the National Industrial Recovery Act, the Works Progress Administration, and the National Labor Relations Act. By the late 1930s, he was an affirmed member of the conservative coalition of Southern Democrats and Republicans.

Smith lent his name to two major pieces of legislation: the Smith Act of 1940 and the Smith-Connally Act of 1943. The heart of the Smith Act was the provision to jail or deport undesirable aliens and a prohibition on attempts to overthrow the federal government. The Smith-Connally Act was a World War II measure to deal with violations of the no-strike pledge of labor leaders. The law required for the duration of the war that unions give a 30-day strike notice, made clear the president's power to seize any defense plant affected by a strike, and prohibited union contributions to candidates to federal office. (Ironically, the law only encouraged unions to use the 30-day strike pledge as a club against employers, who feared a government takeover if a strike occurred.)

Smith was much concerned after the war with the power of labor unions. He and fellow rules committee member E. EUGENE COX (D-Ga.) encouraged Representative FRANCIS H. CASE (R-S.Dak.) to submit a bill that would control unions and their ability to strike. Smith and Cox convinced enough of the other rules committee members to attach this bill to another labor bill. Rules committee chairman ADOLPH J. SABATH (D-Ill.) objected to this rather unorthodox maneuver, but it passed the committee anyway. The Case bill passed both houses of Congress, but Truman vetoed it.

When Senator Carter Glass (D-Va.) died in 1946, Smith very much wanted to win his seat. But his virulent anti-labor stand caused the political machine of Senator HARRY F. BYRD (D-Va.) to hesitate. Byrd remained silent—and Virginia Democrats went for Representative A. WILLIS ROBERTSON instead. Smith was deeply disappointed, but as his biographer Bruce J. Dierenfield has noted, the congressman was probably better served by staying in the House. Within nine years he would chair the Rules Committee and have more power than Byrd himself.

When Smith came back to the now Republican-controlled Congress in 1947, he was ready to resume his assault on unions. He introduced legislation to dramatically revise the Wagner Act. Smith wanted to outlaw intimidation or violence in strikes, the closed shop, unionization within the government, and sympathy strikes.

Smith worked in tandem—albeit informally—with Republican leaders Speaker JOSEPH W. MARTIN, JR., of Massachusetts, majority leader CHARLES A. HALLECK of Indiana, and House labor committee chairman FRED A. HARTLEY, JR., of New Jersey. Hartley included many of Smith's proposals in his bill, and the Virginian and Cox helped manage the conservative coalition of northern Republicans and southern Democrats. Smith met with one representative of each southern state to work out strategy on the labor bill. In April 1947, the House approved the Hartley bill by nearly a three to one margin. The Senate passed a slightly weaker bill of ROBERT A. TAFT (R-Ohio), and a conference committee hammered together a compromise bill (Taft-Hartley),

which the president would veto, but which the Congress would override.

Smith did back Truman's anticommunist foreign policy. He supported the Greek-Turkish aid bill, the Marshall Plan, and universal military training. By 1951, however, Smith believed Europe sufficiently recovered that aid funding could be limited.

The Virginia congressman strongly supported the hunt for subversives in America, and the Smith Act played a key role in the process. It was used in the prosecution of Communist Party leaders, whose convictions were upheld by the Supreme Court in *Dennis v. United States* (1951). In the end, 96 people were convicted under the Smith Act for conspiracy. During his 1948 reelection campaign, Smith distanced himself from Truman—although he formally endorsed him—who had introduced civil rights proposals to Congress. Smith included in his campaign references to J. STROM THURMOND, the South Carolina governor running for president on the pro-segregation States' Rights Democratic Party. Smith won with 54.8 percent of the vote, his lowest percentage up to that time.

When Smith came back to Washington, he found Speaker SAM T. RAYBURN (D-Tex.), determined to stop the obstructionism in the Rules Committee. Rayburn got Congress to pass the 21-day rule that allowed a committee chairman to discharge a bill from the Rules Committee. Two years later, the 21-day rule was repealed.

Despite Senator Byrd's refusal to endorse Governor ADLAI E. STEVENSON for the 1952 presidential election, Smith backed the Illinois governor as he had all previous Democratic presidential candidates. But he declared his opposition to such planks of the party platform as the repeal of Taft-Hartley, public housing, and the establishment of a Fair Employment Practices Commission. One reason for supporting Stevenson was to keep his seat on the Rules Committee as a Democrat. Smith again won reelection, and when the new Congress convened in 1953, both Sabath and Cox had died, making Smith the senior Democrat on Rules, which paved the way for his becoming chairman when Democrats regained control of Congress in 1955. Under Smith, the Rules Committee became a graveyard for liberal legislation. However, in 1961, the Rules Committee was enlarged, diluting Smith's power. Smith failed to win the Democratic primary for his congressional seat in 1966. He died on October 3, 1976, at his farm near Broad Run.

Margaret Chase Smith, 1943 *(Library of Congress, Prints and Photographs Division)*

Smith, Margaret Chase

(1897–1995) *member of the House of Representatives, member of the Senate*

The daughter of a barber and a part-time waitress, Margaret Chase was born on December 14, 1897, in Skowhegan, Maine. She taught school upon her graduation from high school and later worked as a clerk for the Maine Telephone and Telegraph Company. In 1919 she became the circulation manager for Skowhegan's *Independent Reporter,* building it in nine years to seventh place in national circulation among rural papers. In 1930 Margaret Chase married Clyde Harold Smith, a founder and publisher of the *Independent Reporter.* When Clyde was elected to the House, Margaret worked as her husband's secretary. In 1940 Representative Smith died of a heart attack, and his wife ran successfully for his seat.

During the war years Smith sponsored legislation for the creation of the Waves (Women

Accepted for Voluntary Emergency Service) and served on the Naval Affairs Committee, where she was involved in investigating destroyer production. Smith helped push through the Army-Navy Act, which made nurses' status permanent and gave them regular rank as commissioned officer with equal pay and benefits. Her concern for women in the armed forces continued into the Truman administration. In 1946 Smith offered an amendment allowing WAVES and women marines to be part of the regular service rather than the reserve. It passed the House Naval Affairs Committee, but Chairman Carl Vinson refused to allow it to the floor for a vote. Smith made another attempt at fuller integration of women into the services in the Republican-controlled 80th Congress before the now-integrated Armed Services Committee. The Women's Armed Services Integration Act was reported out of the Senate Armed Services Committee in July 1947. But House Armed Services chairman W. G. Andrew (R-N.Y.) and Vinson, now ranking minority member, would not hold hearings. Smith angrily confronted Andrews on the issue, and high-ranking officers and Secretary of Defense JAMES W. FORRESTAL appealed for women to have regular status, but the House Armed Services Committee would only allow reserve status. Smith's objections did force the issue to be debated on the floor, and she tried to amend the bill, but only succeeded in having the name of law changed from the Women's Armed Services Integration Act to the Women's Armed Services Reserve Act. Smith made a spirited call upon Forrestal to help in the conference between House and Senate versions, and he emphatically recommended regular status for women. The name of the law was changed back to the Women's Armed Services Integration Act, which mandated regular status for women. Truman signed the law in July 1948. She also voted to defeat a proposal cutting plans for day-care facilities for wartime factory workers.

Although she termed herself a "moderate Republican," she developed an independent record on domestic legislation. She voted against such proposals as the Smith-Connally antistrike bill and attempts to cut the administration budget. She supported a raise in federal salaries and an increase in social security coverage.

During the Truman administration Smith's voting record continued to defy political categorization. She voted for the Taft-Hartley Act and, although she was against the tactics of the House Un-American

Activities Committee (HUAC), she voted for the 1948 Mundt-Nixon bill, which was a product of that committee. Additionally, she opposed her fellow Republicans to vote for universal military training and federal aid to education. In 1948 Margaret Chase Smith won a Senate seat by the largest vote in the history of Maine politics to that date.

Smith decided that in order to obtain respect in the Senate as its only women member, she should not disturb gender stereotypes. She remained feminine, but she did not demand special privileges and she kept a balance between being too friendly and not friendly enough. She dressed like a businesswoman, with dark suits, and groomed herself well. She did wear a rose in her lapel, which became her trademark. On a congressional junket to desolate postwar Europe, Smith acted in a somewhat grandmotherly fashion by distributing lollipops to children.

After Wisconsin Republican senator JOSEPH R. MCCARTHY's speech in Wheeling, West Virginia, in which he accused the State Department of harboring subversives, Smith took him seriously enough to listen to his speeches on this subject and did not immediately discount his veracity. But soon she began to doubt it. She did not like his accusation that Judge DOROTHY KENYON was a security risk. Kenyon supported the Multi-Party Committee on Women, Inc., which had hailed Smith's election to the Senate. There was no truth to the accusation, but McCarthy simply moved on to other targets. Smith especially did not like McCarthy's ruining of people's reputation for political gain while he hid behind congressional immunity. In a speech on the Senate floor in June 1950, she and six other Republicans made their "Declaration of Conscience." They accused their colleagues of allowing individual senators to abuse the power and privileges of the Senate by engaging in "smear tactics" and "character assassination," which had ruined the lives of many innocent people. They also criticized their fellow Republicans for cynically using the anticommunist issue to "ride to political victory on the four horsemen of calumny—fear, ignorance, bigotry and smear," and urged them to desist by opposing McCarthy. Finally, they charged the Truman administration with adding to the anticommunist hysteria by giving credence to McCarthy's charges and ignoring the Communist threat at home and abroad and by issuing "contradictory grave warnings and optimistic assurance" to the American people confusing them and eroding their confidence in government. Republicans received Smith's remarks in silence. The Declaration of Conscience did not stop McCarthy because his fellow senators would not do anything about him, and soon all the signers of it backed off except Smith and WAYNE MORSE (R-Ore.). Smith herself was dropped from the Republican Senate Policy Committee, moved from the District of Columbia Committee to the Rules and Administration Committee, dismissed from the Permanent Investigations Subcommittee of the Expenditures in the Executive Branch Committee by McCarthy, and replaced there by RICHARD M. NIXON (R-Calif.). On the Rules Committee she was appointed to the Subcommittee on Privileges and Elections, which investigated the 1950 Maryland Senate race, in which McCarthy had plotted to bring about the defeat of his nemesis, MILLARD E. TYDINGS (D-Md.). The subcommittee filed a report exposing the foul deeds of McCarthy in assisting JOHN MARSHALL BUTLER's Senate campaign without recommendations in regard to Butler or McCarthy. It did recommend the full Rules Committee establish guidelines for elections and the disciplining of any senators who violated them. McCarthy said the Privileges and Elections Subcommittee was biased because two members had signed the Declaration of Conscience. Smith denounced McCarthy for calling into question her integrity. She later made a dramatic speech defending herself and the subcommittee. When she ran for reelection in 1954, McCarthy encouraged the candidacy of Robert L. Jones, one of his former aides. Smith won an easy victory over Jones. Although she opposed McCarthy, she did support the McCarran Act, which called for the registration of all Communist and Communist-front organizations.

Although Smith was a fervent opponent of McCarthyism, she was a staunch anticommunist herself. She backed the postwar anticommunist bipartisan foreign policy. She supported the Truman Doctrine, the Marshall Plan, and advocated a defense buildup. During the Korean War, after the Chinese attacked UN troops in force in late 1950, Smith advocated using any means necessary to stop them—including atomic bombs. She saw Truman's limited war as appeasement. In August 1953, after a trip to Asia, she declared that the United States should consider dropping "the atomic bomb on those barbarians [the Communist Chinese] who obviously in their past atrocities have proved that they have no concept or desire for decency."

As the 1952 presidential campaign approached, there was talk of a possible Smith vice presidential candidacy, and supporters rounded up votes for her among the delegates to the Republican National Convention. However, DWIGHT D. EISENHOWER, after a bitter nomination fight with Senator ROBERT A. TAFT (R-Ohio), wanted no division with the conservatives on the vice presidential candidate and chose Nixon. Smith, through CLARE BOOTH LUCE, withdrew her name from consideration. After his choosing Nixon and not repudiating McCarthy, Smith was reluctant to help Ike, but she finally wrote an article in support of him for *Woman's Home Companion.* Twelve years later she became the first woman to be nominated at a national convention.

During the 1950s and 1960s Smith continued her strong support of the Pentagon by voting funds for the Vietnam War and by opposing the voluntary army and the reduction of U.S. forces in Europe. She was one of the few Republicans to vote for president LYNDON B. JOHNSON's domestic policies. In 1972 she was defeated in her reelection bid by Democrat Paul Hathaway. Smith died on May 29, 1995 in Skowhegan, Maine. (See *The Eisenhower Years, The Kennedy Years, The Johnson Years, The Nixon/Ford Years* Volumes)

—SJT

Smith, Walter B(edell)

(1895–1961) *ambassador, director of central intelligence*

Walter Bedell "Beetle" Smith was born on October 5, 1895, in Indianapolis, Indiana. He began his military career when he joined the Indiana National Guard. He later enrolled in Butler University but was forced to drop out to support his family. During World War I he saw action in France. He rose in rank in the army in the 1920s and 1930s, serving in the United States and the Philippines. In 1942 Smith, a brigadier general, was assigned to be General DWIGHT D. EISENHOWER's chief of staff. Eisenhower gave him the responsibility for planning and coordinating the invasions of North Africa, Italy, and Normandy. Smith then negotiated the surrender of Italy and received the surrender of Germany. After VE day he served as chief of staff of the American occupation forces in Germany.

In February 1946 President Truman appointed Smith to replace W. AVERELL HARRIMAN as ambassador to the Soviet Union. For almost three years

Smith lived in isolation in the American embassy as relations between the two superpowers deteriorated. He contributed little to policy making because the State Department centralized this function in Washington. Smith was called upon to defend and then report the official Soviet reaction to administration policy. For instance, when Truman and Secretary of State JAMES F. BYRNES reacted to Soviet aggression in Iran, demanding the withdrawal of all Russian troops from that country, Stalin complained to Smith that the president and Byrnes had not objected to his demands in regard to Iran before. Smith also defended the Truman Doctrine, the Marshall Plan, and NATO to the Soviets. He had no illusions about the Soviets. In 1946 Smith contended that the Russians' objective was "to create in Eastern Germany an antifascist republic as a preliminary to a Soviet socialistic state, or at least a state oriented directly towards Moscow."

Smith was intimately involved with negotiations with the Russians when the Berlin blockade began and as senior to the French and British ambassadors to Moscow, he acted as spokesman for the group. Stalin told Smith that the blockade would end when the West replaced the American-introduced deutsche mark in Berlin with the Soviet mark—currency reform was part of the West's plans to create a West German state—and agree to four-power talks over the German question. He also sought to announce that he only wanted to express a desire, rather than a demand, that the London program for the establishment of a West German state not take place. Smith and his colleagues agreed to pass on these terms with recommendations for approval. Washington rejected them because they believed Stalin still had a belligerent intent. Smith presented the counteroffer from the Western powers calling for ending the transportation restrictions, establishing the conditions for use of the Soviet mark in Berlin, and guaranteeing four-power talks over Germany. The Soviets believed the West had gone back on the deal worked out with the ambassadors and thus escalated their demands. The two sides could not reach an unambiguous settlement. Smith thought the United States should not have put itself in such an isolated place as Berlin. The city had become an important political symbol because the West had made it so. But what was done was done and Smith recommended using the offices of the United Nations to find a way to extricate from Berlin. He doubted, however, that the Soviets wanted war. In January 1949 Smith told journalist Kingsbury Smith that the Soviets wanted to end the blockade but that they did not know how to do it. Kingsbury wired Stalin for a reply. The Soviet dictator's answer was that if the West ended their counterblockade—the West had cut off the flow of supplies from West Germany to East Germany—then he would end his of Berlin. This comment led the way to resolution of the crisis.

Following his return from Moscow in March 1949, Smith wrote *My Three Years in Moscow*. The book included his personal observations of the Soviet Union, focusing on its leadership, its culture, its industrial development, and its many problems with nationalities and religion. Smith also assessed the course of future Soviet-American relations. He suggested that the Soviet Union would never seek peaceful coexistence with the West because of a Marxian determination to destroy capitalism. Russia, he maintained, was being readied for the future struggle. He claimed those preparations required the Soviet Union to make up for the years of backwardness under czarist rule. According to Smith, students and factory workers had to be driven relentlessly to compensate for the Soviet Union's backwardness. Smith concluded that there was little likelihood of a Soviet attack on the West unless it could be assured of easy victory. He emphasized that Western resolve to meet this threat had impressed Stalin, and he urged an emphasis on maintaining Western unity and military strength. Smith resumed his military career in 1949 as commander of the First Army.

In October 1950 President Truman asked Smith to head the Central Intelligence Agency (CIA). The agency and Smith's predecessor, ROSCOE H. HILLENKOETTER, had recently come under criticism for failure to predict the North Korean invasion of the South. In addition, Hillenkoetter seemed incapable of asserting the organization's position in disputes with the Defense and State departments. He also failed to administer the agency's growing bureaucracy.

Smith was chosen precisely because he had the qualities Hillenkoetter lacked. A tough-minded, hard-driving man, nicknamed "the American bulldog" by Winston Churchill, he was known as an excellent administrator. In addition, his assertive personality, senior military position, and diplomatic experience assured that he would dominate dealings with other departments.

Smith immediately embarked on a plan of reorganization. He created the Office of National Estimates (ONE) to produce and evaluate intelligence data. He also announced that he would assume control of the Office of Policy Coordination (OPC), which was responsible for covert operations, thus divorcing it from State Department control. The OPC had been a semiautonomous agency whose budget was included in CIA appropriations although the director of central intelligence had no control over its actions. Between 1950 and 1952 Smith took steps to encourage cooperation between the OPC and the Office of Special Operations (OSO), responsible for overt collection of intelligence data. In 1952 Smith began a general reorganization of the agency. He created a directorate for administration to oversee personnel, budget, and security and provide logistic support for overseas operations. That year he also grouped the agency's intelligence functions—those components including ONE that produced intelligence, provided current political research and carried out basic scientific studies—into the directorate for intelligence. Finally, Smith merged the OPC and the OSO into the directorate for plans. Thus, by the end of his tenure, Smith had created the basic structure the CIA would have for the next 20 years.

According to historian Ludwell Lee Montague, Smith, as DCI believed a preoccupation with covert actions would divert the agency from its main mission of collecting and analyzing intelligence. He tried to limit the number of covert operations run by the agency, but only with minimal success. He wanted the Department of Defense to take responsibility for guerrilla warfare; when he lost this battle he insisted that the CIA, in conducting guerrilla warfare, would be acting on behalf of the Defense and State departments, and that they would take full responsibility for such operations.

During Smith's tenure the CIA increased dramatically as the result of the Korean War and continued tensions with the Soviet Union. OPC, for example, grew from 322 people in 1949 to 2,812 persons with 3,142 overseas contract personnel in 1952. The agency also expanded its activities. From a limited number of ad hoc covert operations, Smith began conducting ongoing activities on a massive scale. In 1952 clandestine collection and covert action accounted for 74 percent of the agency's budget and 60 percent of its personnel strength.

CIA personnel tended to regard Smith as one of the best, perhaps the best DCI the agency ever had. He set about to bring the disparate offices of the agency into a coordinated whole. He stressed intelligence operations and asked professor William Langer to help in making the CIA's intelligence operation more effective, and their accomplishment in this area, according to author John Ranelagh, was one of the most significant in the history of the agency. Smith also coordinated the CIA with military and State Department intelligence. Despite agency officials' high regard for Smith, however, most of the activities that would give the agency a bad image in the 1970s began under him.

Smith served as undersecretary of state during the early years of the Eisenhower administration. He had little influence on policy making because JOHN FOSTER DULLES centralized power in the hands of the secretary of state. Smith served primarily as the top administrator in the State Department's bureaucracy. He retired from government in October 1954 but continued to advise Eisenhower and Dulles on disarmament. Smith died on August 9, 1961, in Washington, D.C. (See *The Eisenhower Years* Volume)

—JB

Snyder, John W(esley)

(1895–1985) *director, Office of War Mobilization and Reconversion; secretary of the Treasury*

John W. Snyder was born on June 21, 1895, in Jonesboro, Arkansas. After a year at Vanderbilt University, he entered the army in 1915, serving in Europe during World War I. Following the war he returned to his native Arkansas and became a bank clerk. He remained in the U.S. Army Reserve, where he developed a friendship with another reserve officer, Harry S Truman. Snyder later moved to St. Louis to take up banking. In 1931 he joined the staff of the Controller of the Currency. Six years later Snyder became St. Louis regional director of the Reconstruction Finance Corporation (RFC) and, in 1940, while remaining at the RFC, became executive vice president and director of the Defense Planning Corporation (DPC). He left the DPC in 1943 to join the First National Bank of St. Louis, but he kept his post at the RFC.

During these years Snyder and Truman became professionally close. Snyder was one of Truman's earliest supporters in the senator's 1940 reelection bid, helping to plan the campaign and raise contributions. That same year Snyder also worked with

Truman to develop a proposal for the formation of a Senate committee to examine corruption and irregularities in the awarding and execution of defense contracts. The committee brought Truman, who served as its chairman, national prominence. Snyder was one of several friends who persuaded Truman to accept the vice presidency in 1944.

When Truman assumed the presidency in April 1945, Snyder was one of the first men he consulted. Anxious to keep his friend in Washington, the new president appointed Snyder the federal loan administrator in May. Two months later Snyder became director of the Office of War Mobilization and Reconversion. It was his duty to supervise the dismantling of World War II price controls, the selling of government-owned defense plants, and the granting of government loans to private industry to finance conversion to peacetime production. In June 1946 Truman, without consulting Snyder, named him secretary of the Treasury. Margaret Truman later wrote that the announcement left Snyder "agreeably and very much surprised." Snyder served at that post until the end of the Truman administration.

Snyder was one of Truman's closest advisers on foreign and domestic policy. The two men developed the habit of meeting every morning before the president's first appointment. It was said in Washington at the time that the last person with whom Truman talked before making any decision was Snyder. In a memorandum written in May 1948 Truman ranked Snyder with GEORGE C. MARSHALL as a "tower of strength and common sense" in foreign policy.

Snyder was involved in foreign economic policy in a variety of ways. He chaired the National Advisory Council on International Monetary and Financial Problems, established under the Bretton Woods Agreement Act of 1945. Other NAC members included the secretaries of state and commerce, the chairman of the Board of Governors of the Federal Reserve, and the president of the Export-Import Bank. The council became the main coordinator of international financial and economic concerns during the Truman years. It dealt with many policies, including operations of the World Bank and the International Monetary Fund.

Another concern of Snyder was the international monetary system. The secretary told Congress in early 1949 that because of U.S. foreign aid, America had an interest in European exchange rates. The secretary of the Treasury and secretary of defense in 1948 instituted a stabilization plan for Japan and, in 1949, on the recommendation of NAC, an exchange rate of 360 yen to the dollar was set up.

He assisted in negotiations with the British over the international financial situation in 1949. Faced with economic difficulties the British wanted the U.S. government to stimulate investment overseas, maintain a demand for imports, and conclude international commodity pacts to steady the cost of natural resources exported from the British sterling area—in addition to lowering U.S. tariffs and continued aid. Otherwise, Britain would have to quarantine its economy from U.S. recessions and unfair competition. Snyder did not like the suggested concessions and reported to Truman that the British wanted the dollar area to change to suit their domestic economic planning. According to historian Michael Hogan, Snyder wanted to maintain free enterprise instead of adopting state economic planning on an international scale. All that was agreed to was to continue the talks at a later date.

Snyder's impact on the Truman administration lay in domestic affairs. He emerged as the leader of the conservative faction in the White House. This group advocated the restriction of government involvement in business and the economy and the consolidation rather than the expansion of social programs. Liberals viewed the appointment of Snyder as an indication that Truman was abandoning the social activism of his predecessor. They saw Snyder's rise and the resignation of individuals connected with the Roosevelt administration as an indication that the dynamic men and women who had served FDR were being replaced by what they termed "mediocre party men." As OWMR director Snyder hired a conservative general as one of his aides and later won the merger of the liberal-leaning Office of Economic Stabilization into his agency.

Liberals' fears proved excessive. Truman accepted Snyder's policy recommendations on economic affairs. Both men shared a view of the role of the federal government in the economy and had similar conceptions of how the government should be financed. The president, however, eventually adopted a more liberal view of domestic social policy than Synder would have liked. The president often followed the recommendations of CLARK CLIFFORD, spokesman for the White House liberals, in domestic affairs.

During the summer and autumn of 1945 Snyder and Truman worked to remove many wartime price controls. Snyder's actions brought him into frequent conflict with CHESTER BOWLES, director of the Office of Price Administration, who believed that to discontinue controls so rapidly would precipitate inflation, which might bring in its wake a serious depression. Twice in particular the two clashed. In September Snyder moved to deregulate construction materials. He was backed by several administration liberals who hoped that decontrol would spur housing construction and employment. Bowles, however, warned that materials were scarce and would be diverted from housing to more lucrative commercial construction. Snyder was forced to reinstate regulations in December when Bowles's predictions proved accurate.

In January 1946 the United Steel Workers struck for higher wages. When the industry rejected a presidential fact finding board's recommendations for a wage increase, Truman considered seizing the mills. Snyder, who opposed government coercion of private industry, dissuaded him and suggested that the president investigate raising steel prices to compensate for the wage increase. Bowles opposed the move on the grounds that inflated corporate profits could absorb higher wages with only a moderate price rise. The result was a compromise. On the recommendation of a panel of what Snyder termed "top cost accountants," Truman granted an increase of five dollars a ton—twice what Bowles had recommended. The companies accepted the offer and the strike ended. Bowles, however, resigned in protest to the move. Although he returned to the administration a few days later, his influence with

(*left to right*) Secretary of the Treasury John W. Snyder and President Truman (*Harry S. Truman Library*)

the White House declined after Truman made it clear there was no well-defined position as to who was more powerful—Snyder or Bowles—and that fact angered the latter.

Snyder failed to dissuade the president from presenting a program of social legislation to deal with the effects of reconversion. He opposed Truman's 21-point program of September 1945, which called for such measures as a raise in the minimum wage and increases in unemployment insurance. Snyder thought the president should not commit himself to a program of social legislation.

Although Truman respected Snyder's opinions he frequently ignored his advice on politics. Both men believed that the secretary of the Treasury should be largely nonpartisan. Although Snyder privately gave political advice to the president, he did not make political speeches. Snyder, with many others, interpreted the Republican triumphs in the 1946 elections as a sign of popular rejection of New Deal liberalism. He believed that labor and liberals would always remain loyal to the Democratic Party and recommended that the president court the conservative vote. He tried to persuade Truman to forego a liberal social program and, in particular, recommended that he sign the Taft-Hartley bill of 1947, termed a "slave labor" measure by unions. Truman, however, accepted Clark Clifford's recommendation that he attempt to maintain the New Deal coalition of labor and liberals by vetoing the measure.

In economic affairs Snyder had no rival in the administration. He and Truman worked with complete intimacy in determining the administration's budgetary and monetary policies. In these matters neither paid attention to economists. Both looked at the federal budget and interest rates not as tools for manipulating the economy but as elements of what Truman later termed "good financing," by which he meant producing surplus revenue and, when necessary, acquiring cheap debt. Neither Truman nor Snyder saw much difference between financing a Missouri county and the federal government. As a consequence, when viewed from the perspective of most economic theorists, their positions on budgetary and monetary matters appeared inconsistent and at odds with those suggested by prevailing economic conditions. When viewed, however, from the perspective of "good financing" their policies—if not their pronouncements—always made sense.

In October 1945, for example, Snyder—as director of the OWMR—predicted an employ-ment figure of eight million by spring of 1946. Nine months later, as secretary of the Treasury, he made no recommendation to stimulate the economy through deficit spending. Rather, with the financing of World War II completed, he moved to balance the budget and retire the national debt. By June 1949 he had reduced federal obligations by $18.2 billion or 7 percent.

In keeping with the administration's budgetary policy, Snyder opposed any move that would reduce federal revenues and thereby jeopardize the government's capacity to pay down federal debt. He attempted to bloc the 20 percent across-the-board tax cut proposed by the Republican-controlled Congress in 1947. Snyder argued before congressional committees that the economy was operating at full capacity and required high taxes as a restraint to inflation. Such an argument implied increased tax collections, reflecting that natural expansion of business activity under such circumstances. Nevertheless, Snyder presented these committees with projections of tax collections that presumed no growth. As historian and economist Herbert Stein noted of the period: "Low revenue estimates did not make the administration oppose tax cuts. . . . The truth is more nearly that the administration made low revenue estimates because it was against any tax cut." Congress passed the bill but was unable to override Truman's veto of the measure. The following year the president proposed a $40 across-the-board decrease designed primarily to redistribute the tax burden. Snyder privately opposed the measure and supported it publicly only out of loyalty to Truman. Even congressional Democrats were lukewarm on the plan. Congress, instead, revised and passed the Republican tax proposal and then overrode Truman's veto.

The country entered a recession in June 1949, about the time that the stimulating effects of the tax cut began to be felt. The deficit that the government ran over the next year as a consequence of the cut helped make the recession short. By June 1950 the nation had returned to nearly full employment.

Almost until the recession was over Truman and Snyder continued to insist that inflation, not joblessness, was the nation's primary economic ill. Indeed, in November 1949, in the middle of the recession, Snyder told the American Bankers Association that, "American business is having another tremendous year."

The outbreak of the Korean conflict led Snyder and Truman to ask for tax increases in 1951 and

1952. The Congress, of which the Democrats had regained control in 1948, approved raises, although ones smaller that the administration had requested. The requests were prompted by the desire to prosecute the war without resorting to deficit spending but were justified to the public as restraints upon rising prices.

While raising the spector of inflation whenever discussing tax or budget policy, Snyder pressured the Federal Reserve Board to maintain its World War II agreement with the Treasury to "peg" interest rates at artificially low levels. Although the policy was highly inflationary, Snyder—in conformity with the principles of "good financing"—wanted to acquire such debt as the government needed on the most favorable terms possible. The Federal Reserve, under the direction of MARRINER S. ECCLES and later THOMAS B. MCCABE, pushed for independence from the Treasury, fearing that the arrangement was destroying its control of the money supply. From 1946 until 1949 Snyder unsuccessfully tried to stop the Federal Reserve from abandoning support of short-term Treasury debt instruments.

Following the outbreak of the Korean War in July 1950, Snyder redoubled his efforts to keep down the government's cost of borrowing. He attempted to associate continued Treasury supervision of the Federal Reserve with meeting the Communist threat. "Economic preparedness" he called it. Nevertheless, support for the Treasury's position had dwindled. In an era when inflation was a problem, low interest rates became difficult to defend. During 1950 the Federal Reserve began to renounce its obligation to support long-term rates. These rates, in contrast to those on short-term notes, had a very important impact on the cost of financing the government. Snyder resisted angrily. Over the next six months, in private and sometimes in the press, he struggled with the Federal Reserve, but by early 1951 he was forced to acquiece to its demands. In February the two sides had reached an agreement, negotiated by Eccles for the Federal Reserve and WILLIAM MCCHESNEY MARTIN for the Treasury, that freed the Federal Reserve from pegging. Truman, apparently on the basis of Snyder's recommendation, reluctantly approved the accord.

Snyder and Undersecretary of the Treasury Lee Wiggins worked to reform the Bureau of Internal Revenue—where there had been corruption—to end the appointment of poorly qualified and venal political hacks. With Truman's support the reform bill eventually made its way through Congress.

Snyder left government with the coming of the Eisenhower administration. He never played a prominent role in politics again. From 1953 to 1966 he served as president of the Overland Corporation. Between 1955 and 1973 Snyder was an adviser to the U.S. Treasury and sat on the boards of a number of philanthropic organizations. Snyder died on October 8, 1985, on Seabrook Island, South Carolina.

—CSJ

Sobell, Morton
(1917–   ) *espionage agent*

Born April 11, 1917, in New York City, Sobell graduated from City College of New York as an engineer in 1938. While in college he was a classmate and friend of JULIUS ROSENBERG, who was later convicted and executed for passing atomic secrets to the Soviet Union. Along with another friend, Max Elitcher, also an engineer, Sobell got a job in 1939 with the Navy Bureau of Ordinance. He took a master's degree in electrical engineering from the University of Michigan in 1942. A year later he joined the aircraft and marine engineering division of General Electric (GE) in upstate New York. During the 1940s Sobell left GE and moved to New York City, where he worked with a company that had classified government contracts. Naval intelligence had noted that Sobell had been a supporter of the Communist-front American Peace Mobilization Committee; he had also counseled children at a Communist youth camp and openly admired Soviet dictator Joseph Stalin. Yet as late as 1949 he obtained a security clearance to work on U.S. defense contracts. And Elitcher later told the FBI that he had helped Sobell deliver film to Rosenberg in 1948.

In August 1950 Sobell was arrested on charges of espionage for the Soviet Union. The government claimed that he had recruited for a Russian spy ring and had passed secrets to the Rosenbergs. In a move that was later criticized, Sobell was tried with them. The key witness against him was Max Elitcher. He testified that both Sobell and Julius Rosenberg had asked him to participate in espionage activities from 1944 to 1948. Elitcher also maintained that Rosenberg had told him that Sobell had turned over a number of important classified documents.

The government made much of Sobell's visit to Mexico shortly before his arrest. While there he had used different aliases and had tried to obtain passage out of Mexico without necessary papers. In his rush to leave the United States he had not had time to obtain a passport, which he had not needed to go to Mexico. Sobell contended that the visit was a long overdue vacation. The government, however, claimed he had hoped to flee with his family behind the Iron Curtain. Sobell later maintained that he had been kidnapped in Mexico and delivered illegally to FBI agents at the border. From Ronald Rudosh and Joyce Milton's study of the Rosenbergs, it is unclear who apprehended Sobell and turned him over to the FBI.

Sobell claimed his total innocence of espionage. His lawyers attempted to portray Elitcher as a psychopathic liar, bent on protecting himself. (Elitcher had lied about his own Communist Party membership when working for the government.) On the advice of his lawyers, Sobell did not take the stand in his own defense. He was judged guilty of espionage. However, he was not linked to the Rosenbergs' supposed passage of atomic secrets to the USSR. At the end of the trial, in April 1951, Judge IRVING R. KAUFMAN announced that he did not doubt Sobell's guilt, but he noted that there had been no evidence of Sobell's involvement in the atomic ring. Kaufman imposed a 30-year sentence on Sobell and stated that he felt Sobell should be denied parole.

During the mid-1950s there were several unsuccessful attempts to overturn Sobell's conviction. The Supreme Court refused eight times to review his case. In 1962 Sobell became eligible for parole, but it was refused. After serving 17 years and nine months in prison, he was released in 1969 with time off for good behavior. In 1974 Sobell wrote *On Doing Time*, a book detailing his experiences in prison. During the 1970s he and his wife were active politically and continued efforts to win his and the Rosenbergs' vindication. KGB Agent Alexsandr Feklisov later revealed that Sobell was definitely a member of the spy ring and his role was to gather information regarding the development of sonar. (See *The Eisenhower Years* Volume)

—JF

Souers, Sidney W(illiam)

(1892–1973) *director of Central Intelligence; executive secretary, National Security Council*
The son of a cotton planter, Sidney W. Souers was born on March 30, 1892, in Dayton, Ohio. He completed his B.A. degree in 1914 at Miami University

in Ohio. After a year of newspaper work for the *New Orleans Item*, he turned to a career in finance in the same city. In 1925 he assumed the duties of executive vice president of the Canal Bank and Trust Company. He was appointed commissioner of the Port of New Orleans in 1928. While serving at that post Souers joined the Naval Reserve. He was commissioned a lieutenant commander in 1929. The following year Souers moved to St. Louis to become financial vice president of the Missouri State Life Insurance Company. Souers made the city his permanent home and expanded his activities to include executive positions with several companies (such as the Piggly Wiggly food-store chain), corporate directorships, and memberships in a number of financial associations. In 1932 he was named senior intelligence officer for the Naval Reserve in the St. Louis district.

Souers was called to active service in July 1940. During World War II he was dispatched to the 10th Naval District, headquartered at Puerto Rico. An intelligence officer for the Caribbean Sea Frontier, Souers was responsible for developing countermeasures against enemy submarines. He was promoted to rear admiral in 1943. His achievements attracted the attention of Secretary of the Navy JAMES V. FORRESTAL, who brought Souers to Washington in July 1944 as assistant director of the Office of Naval Intelligence. In November Souers was appointed deputy chief of naval intelligence.

Souers continued in this post after World War II. During the immediate postwar period there was debate in the U.S. intelligence community over the nature and scope of the role intelligence should play in peacetime. President Truman had disbanded the Office of Strategic Services (OSS), the nation's wartime intelligence service, in 1945. He quickly found, however, that the conflicting reports of the various departmental intelligence estimates did not meet the postwar need for coordinated intelligence estimates. Admiral WILLIAM D. LEAHY, Truman's personal chief of staff, informed the president that, in 1944, General William J. Donovan had developed a plan creating an independent centralized intelligence agency patterned after the OSS. The navy in turn had worked out a counterproposal. Much of the original work on the project had been done by Souers. Under the navy proposal there would be a central agency to serve as an overall intelligence organization, but with each of the departments responsible for national security having a stake in its operation. During the debate Truman asked Secretary of State JAMES F. BYRNES for his recommendations on a way to coordinate intelligence among the departments involved. Byrnes maintained that the State Department should be in charge of all intelligence.

Truman turned to Souers to resolve the conflicts of interest. Souers worked closely on the question with Leahy and James S. Lay, Jr., who had been secretary of the Joint Intelligence Committee, on which all current military and foreign intelligence agencies were represented. On January 20, 1946, Truman issued an executive order setting up the Central Intelligence Group (CIG) and placing it under the control of a National Intelligence Authority (NIA), made up of the secretaries of state, war, and navy, and the president's personal representative. Leahy become the first presidential designee. Truman appointed Souers the first director of central intelligence (DCI) and head of the CIG.

Souers did not show enthusiasm for the job. When a reporter queried him on his plans as director, Souers said, "I want to go home." Souers took the job of the DCI with the understanding he would resign and return to private life as soon as a candidate could be found to replace him. As author John Ranelagh has pointed out, Souers had no clear mandate as to what role he was to play and Truman did not give him the power or resources to organize the CIG. His posting and the CIG were stepping stones toward the formation of the Central Intelligence Agency. Ranelagh argued that by being the chief of the CIG Souers "gave force to the idea of peacetime intelligence." However, the military and State Department intelligence agencies were able to outmaneuver him, and Souers merely administrated an interdepartmental group that answered to the National Intelligence Authority, headed by Leahy. Souers did launch an investigation into the legal basis and requisites for a peacetime all-inclusive intelligence organization, and the inquiry proved important. Finished after Souers left office, the investigation's report showed the CIG had no statutory basis and was merely a coordinating body with no authority except in "an advisory and directing capacity." The report also doubted whether the CIG, a presidential-created agency, could continue without a statutory foundation after January 1947.

Six months after Souers's appointment General HOYT S. VANDENBERG was unanimously recommended by both the military and State Department,

and Truman named him the first permanent DCI. Souers continued as a consultant to his successor. The intelligence organization over which Souers briefly presided was an extension of executive departments, with its personnel and budget allocated from the military and State Department. The CIG had as its goal to review the information collected by the various intelligence services and to furnish objective intelligence estimates for the use of senior policymakers.

In May 1947 Souers was recalled to Washington to set up an intelligence service for the Atomic Energy Commission. In September Truman named him the first executive secretary of the new National Security Council (NSC). The NSC replaced the NIA. Comprised of the president and vice president, the secretaries of state and defense and their representatives, the council had as its officially defined function to advise the president on matters of national security and to direct the operation of the newly formed Central Intelligence Agency (CIA). Under the 1947 National Security Act the CIA had superseded the CIG as an independent central intelligence organization. As executive secretary Souers was responsible for assembling the NSC's staff and for seeing that it carried out whatever duties it might be assigned. (Souers himself became a poker-playing friend of the president.)

When Leahy retired as Truman's personal chief of staff in January 1949 Souers assumed the duty of briefing the president daily on "military-politico" developments. Souers had the additional responsibility, as executive secretary, of issuing the president's orders in writing to all members of the NSC. He helped originate and participated in the NSC's major review of America foreign and defense policy in 1949–50. The report, NSC-68, was submitted to Truman in 1950. It concluded that the Soviet Union was an aggressive expansionist power that found its opponent in the antithetic ideas and power of the United States. The report recommended an immediate buildup in U.S. military forces and weapons. Souers also submitted a report as to the duties of the NSC executive secretary. He should be an apolitical adviser of the president and coordinator of the views of other officials with authority and should serve the president and the other members of the NSC while maintaining a low profile himself.

Souers resigned from the NSC in January 1950 to devote himself to personal business affairs. At the time it was announced that he would continue as special consultant to the president on security matters. He spent most of his time in Washington and was de facto supervisor of the NSC even though he was no longer executive secretary. Souers died on January 14, 1973, in St. Louis, Missouri.

—SF

Sparkman, John J(ackson)

(1899–1985) *member of the Senate*

Born on a poor farm in Morgan County, Alabama, on December 20, 1889, John Sparkman supported himself through college and law school. Following graduation from the University of Alabama Law School in 1923, he began private practice in Huntsville, Alabama. Sparkman became active in local Democratic politics, and, in 1936, he was elected to the House of Representatives. Like many Southern Democrats he supported most early New Deal programs. He worked hard for passage of the Tennessee Valley Authority Act, which tied his poor district for the first time to electric lines. Sparkman won a special election in 1946 to fill a Senate vacancy created by the death of Senator John H. Bankhead (D-Ala.). Because of his liberal record he received the endorsement of the Congress of Industrial Organizations' Political Action Committee.

Throughout the Truman years Sparkman was one of the most liberal members of the South's congressional delegation. Although he originally supported the Taft-Hartley Act of 1947, he was convinced by Truman's veto message to sustain the veto. He backed federal rent control, aid to schools, and expansion of rural electrification projects. He did, however, vote for the 1948 Republican tax cut and deregulation of the natural gas industry.

Sparkman supported Truman's foreign policy, voting for Greek-Turkish aid, the Marshall Plan, the North Atlantic Treaty, military aid for NATO, Point Four, and the Japanese Peace Treaty. Although he supported the McCarran Internal Security Act, he defended the administration against charges of it harboring subversives.

During the late 1940s Sparkman developed an interest in housing legislation that became his special focus of attention during his Senate career. As the chairman of the Housing Subcommittee of the Banking and Currency Committee, Sparkman in 1949 lobbied for the passage of a comprehensive housing bill designed to aid low-income groups. The Housing Act of 1949, signed into law in July, made "a decent home and a suitable living environment for every American

family" a national policy goal. It provided for programs to assist slum clearance efforts, extend Federal Housing Authority mortgages, construct 810,000 housing units for low-income families, and grant loans for farm housing. The following year he sponsored the Housing Act of 1950, aimed primarily at aiding middle-income groups by liberalizing Federal Housing Authority and Veterans' Administration programs.

Although a liberal on many domestic issues, Sparkman remained a strong foe of civil rights. Throughout the Truman years he opposed any congressional attempts to outlaw the poll tax, pass anti-lynching legislation, or change cloture rules to facilitate passage of civil rights bills. Sparkman argued that constitutional amendments were needed before Congress could act in these areas. When Truman presented his comprehensive civil rights program in February 1948, Sparkman joined the southern defection from the Democratic Party. Initially he supported General DWIGHT D. EISENHOWER for the Democratic presidential nomination. When the general declined to run, Sparkman supported Governor J. STROM THURMOND, the Dixiecrat candidate. However, he did not actively campaign for the insurgents.

ADLAI E. STEVENSON chose Sparkman as the Democratic Party's vice presidential candidate in 1952. Sparkman's internationalism and liberalism on matters outside civil rights impressed Stevenson, who tried to unify the party. Sparkman toured the nation defending the party's vague civil rights position, condemning Senator JOSEPH R. MCCARTHY (R-Wisc.) and supporting the liberal record of the Truman administration.

During the 1950s Sparkman was a major critic of the Eisenhower administration's foreign policy. He worked for additional housing legislation and aid to small businesses and continued to oppose civil rights measures. He joined other southerners in condemning the Supreme Court's decision in *Brown v. Board of Education*, which struck down segregation in public schools. Sparkman became one of the most powerful senators during the Kennedy, Johnson, and Nixon presidencies. He assumed chairmanship of the Banking Committee in 1957 and succeeded Senator J. WILLIAM FULBRIGHT (D-Ark.) as head of the Senate Foreign Relations Committee in 1975. Sparkman chose not to seek reelection in 1978. Sparkman died of a heart attack on November 16, 1985, in Huntsville, Alabama. (See *The Eisenhower Years, The Kennedy Years, The Johnson Years, The Nixon/Ford Years* Volumes)

—JB

Spellman, Francis J(oseph)

(1889–1967) *Roman Catholic archbishop of New York*

Born on May 4, 1889, in Whitman, Massachusetts, Francis J. Spellman was ordained a Roman Catholic priest in 1916, and named archbishop of New York in 1939 and a cardinal in 1946. He became one of America's most influential and conservative clergymen. His power grew in the postwar years as Catholics moved increasingly into the middle class and took a more active role in national politics. As military vicar general of the U.S. Armed Forces, he visited American troops around the world and was frequently identified with American military interests. The cardinal was an outspoken defender of American politics during the cold war. He consistently spoke for the interests of the church, especially when he felt they were threatened by communism. A successful fund-raiser, he built churches and schools in New York and helped finance Catholic missionary work abroad.

Spellman denounced the spread of Communist influence after World War II. In a speech given in March 1948 he accused the Soviet Union of devouring the "little God-loving free peoples" of Europe and Asia. Spellman was particularly vehement in his condemnation of communism in Eastern Europe. He defended Yugoslavian archbishop Aloysius Stepinac, who was on trial for antigovernment activity, and took an active role in the case of Archbishop Josef Beran of Czechoslovakia, who had expressed his concern over the limitation of church power by the Communist government in his country.

Spellman became most involved in the controversy surrounding Josef Cardinal Mindszenty of Hungary. Mindszenty, a personal friend of Spellman, was a leader of the resistance to the Communist plan to nationalize the Hungarian schools, many of which were run by the church. He was arrested the day after Christmas in 1948. In his confession, which Spellman believed was induced by torture and drugging, Mindszenty named the New York archbishop as a participant in a royalist plot to restore Archduke Otto to the Hungarian throne. He also stated that Spellman was involved in an attempt to keep the Holy Crown of Hungary from the Communists. Spellman denied the first charge, stating that all the money Americans had contributed to Hungary went for food, clothing, and medicine. However he admitted that in July 1946 he had interceded on behalf of Mindszenty to guaran-

tee the Crown would remain in American hands. In February 1949 Spellman delivered a sermon in St. Patrick's Cathedral in which he asked for prayers for the Hungarian cardinal as a protest against the "crucifixion of humanity." Mindszenty was eventually sentenced to life imprisonment.

Spellman sent aid to the Vatican in its struggle to stop communism in Italy after the war. The cardinal tried to calm a pessimistic Pope Pius XII, who worried that the Communists would win the elections of 1947. With Spellman's and the CIA's help the Christian Democrats won in a landslide. The archbishop arranged for the U.S. government to reimburse the Vatican for funds it had expended to defeat the Communists.

Spellman favored the establishment of an independent Jewish homeland in Palestine but only if guarantees could be obtained for equal rights of Palestinian Arabs and Christians. In May 1948, after war broke out between Arabs and Israelis, the cardinal called for the protection of Jerusalem and all Christian holy places. The following year he urged free access to Jerusalem's holy places. Spellman supported the Korean War and, in 1951, began his practice of flying to Korea each Christmas to encourage American troops stationed there. In February 1952 the cardinal said he opposed any further concessions to the Communists in the truce talks then underway.

Spellman was eager to cooperate with the crusade against communism at home. FBI director J. EDGAR HOOVER in 1946 dispatched agents to ask if the prelate would cooperate in cracking down on Communist-infiltrated unions. The soon-to-be cardinal was happy to help. Spellman's biographer John Cooney claimed the archbishop despised unions; actually his hatred seemed to be directed more toward Communist-infiltrated CIO unions. Spellman did not want his part in the program known, and it is not known what he did, but Spellman was involved deeply in alerting Americans to Communist subversion. In an article in *America* in June 1946 he warned that Communists "try to seduce us into believing that Americans can be Communists, but a true American can be neither a Communist nor a Communist condoner, and we realize that the first Loyalty of every America is vigilantly to weed out and counteract Communism and convert American Communism to Americanism. . . ."

Spellman was also involved in New York City politics. He appeared at many city dedications and Mayor WILLIAM O'DWYER began to allow Spellman to assist in the appointment of judges and city officials. In the uncertain days after the war, when employment looked dicey, Spellman began a large construction program that helped workers, made construction companies grateful, and impressed politicians.

Spellman reacted vigorously to a June 1949 column of ELEANOR ROOSEVELT arguing against the use of state revenue to support private or religious schools. Spellman, who very much wanted public aid for parochial shools, became involved in a fierce contretemps with the former first lady, whom Spellman disliked because of her liberalism. He accused Roosevelt of being an anti-Catholic, which she denied. Other Catholic bishops supported the cardinal. The issue became rather troubling for Democrats, so much so that Truman asked Brooklyn Democratic boss Ed Flynn to go to the Vatican to pressure Spellman to reconcile with Roosevelt. Spellman eventually visited Roosevelt, but did not apologize. She, however, extracted a promise from the cardinal not to oppose Democratic Senate candidate HERMAN H. LEHMAN, whom Spellman was angry at for his opposition to the prelate's campaign to ban the leftist magazine the *Nation* from public schools.

During 1949 Spellman became embroiled in a much publicized dispute with the unionized cemetery workers in his archdiocese. The cardinal believed that labor and management had mutual rights and responsibilities and favored cooperation between the two parties as a deterrent to work stoppages, which he thought threatened America's economic stability and security. All construction in the archdiocese was performed by union labor after Spellman became archbishop. In a speech given in August 1948 the cardinal warned that Americans must guard against minority groups within unions who were opposed to democracy and used strikes as "smokescreens to wage political war against America." He advised labor not to break the controversial Taft-Hartley Act.

The cardinal was soon forced to deal with a union strike within his archdiocese. In January 1949 employees of Calvary Cemetery, members of Local 293, of the United Cemetery Workers, CIO, staged a walkout after negotiations with the trustees of St. Patrick's Cathedral had broken down. After six weeks coffins containing hundreds of unburied dead were lying in open trenches. The cardinal met with members of the local and invited them to return to

work as individuals and to form a new union not affiliated with the CIO, which Spellman believed was Communist-dominated. When this offer was rejected, the cardinal led seminarians through a picket line at Calvary Cemetery in order to bury the dead. Spellman and the trustees were attacked for union-busting by Communists as well as the Association of Catholic Trade Unionists. Spellman responded by asking for an injunction against the strike and the pickets. On March 9, 800 members of the local voted to form their own union and join the Building Service Employees Union, AFL. Two days later the strike was settled, and the workers returned to their jobs. Soon after the cardinal sent a check to each of the strikers for 65 dollars.

For the remainder of his life the cardinal was involved in the political arena, taking stands on McCarthyism, peaceful coexistence, the federal school-aid program, and the Vietnam War. His strong support of the war brought him into conflict with Pope Paul VI; but Spellman's offer to resign as archbishop because of his age was refused by the pope. The cardinal died of a stroke on December 2, 1967, in New York City. (See *The Eisenhower Years, The Kennedy Years, The Johnson Years* Volumes)

—EF

Stassen, Harold E(dward)
(1907–2001) *Republican Party leader*

A farmer's son, Harold E. Stassen was born on April 13, 1907, in South St. Paul, Minnesota. He worked his way through the University of Minnesota, where he earned a B.A. in 1923 and an LL.B. in 1929. That year he began a law practice and in 1930 won election as Dakota County attorney. Through the 1930s Stassen and a group of young friends plotted to take control of the Minnesota Republican Party. Although more liberal than the state GOP leadership, Stassen nevertheless won the 1938 Republican gubernatorial primary and the general election. He was 31 years old. Voters reelected him in 1940 and 1942. As governor, Stassen rid the state of corrupt officials left from the previous administration, reorganized state government along rational lines, and, while emphasizing greater efficiency, retained most state-level social welfare programs. Additionally, he secured passage of a bill to regulate organized labor, which anticipated the Taft-Hartley Act of 1947.

Stassen quickly gained national prominence; journalists acclaimed him as "the Boy Wonder of the Republican Party." At the 1940 Republican National Convention, he delivered the keynote address and was convention floor manager for Wendell L. Willkie. In 1943 he resigned as governor to become naval attaché to Admiral William F. Halsey. A year later supporters briefly promoted him for the 1944 Republican presidential nomination.

In February 1945 President Franklin D. Roosevelt named Stassen one of the two Republican members of the American delegation to the first organizational meeting of the United Nations in San Francisco. At the UN Stassen fought unsuccessfully to eliminate the major powers' right to veto. Fellow Republican delegate Senator ARTHUR H. VANDENBERG (R-Mich.) described Stassen as "one of the ablest young men I have ever known."

In December 1945 Stassen commenced an 18-month campaign for the 1948 Republican presidential nomination. Out of office, living off lecture fees, he visited 40 states and traveled over 160,000 miles. Stassen reasoned that only broad electoral support, demonstrated in the state primaries, would offset the antipathies of party leaders, most of whom distrusted him because of his youth, reputation for opportunism, and internationalist positions. In his 1947 activities, Stassen sought to gain the support of both the Eastern, internationalist and the isolationist, "Old Guard" wings of the party. In the process he alienated members of both. In February 1947 he urged Republicans to abandon their long-held preference for high tariffs. Still optimistic about U.S.-Soviet relations, he visited Europe in April and met with Joseph Stalin. He left the encounter declaring that "Russia wants to cooperate" with America in foreign affairs. The following month, however, Stassen was among the first Republicans to endorse the Truman Doctrine, designed to contain Communist expansion (through he dubbed Truman's approach to Communist expansion "negative"). Over the summer of 1947 Stassen argued for the Marshall Plan to save the "entire, deteriorating economic system in Europe." These and other foreign policy positions separated Stassen from many conservative Republicans, particularly in the Mid-West. But Stassen also favored a version of the Taft-Hartley Act to which unions were even more opposed than the final law, and supported measures designed to outlaw the American Communist Party.

Stassen's intensive speechmaking strategy initially worked. Although he did poorly in New Hampshire, winning only two out of eight delegates, people there voted for delegates rather than candidates, and Dewey's delegates were more prominent than Stassen's. Further, he had put New York governor THOMAS E. DEWEY on the defensive. Entering the Wisconsin primary Stassen faced General DOUGLAS MACARTHUR and Dewey. Experienced observers, who had never taken Stassen seriously as a contender, predicted that MacArthur, despite his absence in Japan, would win. Indeed, the party's 1944 nominee, Dewey, was rated ahead of Stassen even though the governor alloted only two days for campaigning in the state. Nevertheless, Stassen secured the help of the GOP state organization—especially its younger members—and with the help of Senator JOSEPH R. MCCARTHY (R-Wisc.), built up a grassroots organization, and traveled for days throughout Wisconsin. On April 4 he won—despite Wisconsin's past affinity for isolationism—19 of its 27 delegates. The Wisconsin victory, coupled with another win in Nebraska a week later, suddenly placed Stassen, the *New York Herald Tribune* noted, "in the first division of contenders." The Gallup poll survey of Republicans nationwide found Stassen's support to have risen from 15 percent in February to 26 percent in June. "To many younger Republicans," historian James Patterson wrote later, Stassen "seemed a dynamic alternative" to the other candidates.

Stassen also ran in the Ohio primary, later claiming that it would have been hypocritical not to run there because of his belief in allowing the people to elect the Republican nominee. Stassen's biographer, Alexander B. Kirby, noted that members of the Minnesotan's staff believed he could win in the home state of Senator ROBERT A. TAFT, who also was running for the nomination. A victory for Stassen here would knock Taft out of the race. This plan went against the usual strategy of not running in primaries where another candidate was the state's favorite son and thus fraught with risk. Although Taft won 44 delegates to Stassen's nine (he had only competed for 23), Kirby saw Ohio as a victory for the former governor, as he had won industrial urban areas. Also Stassen's biographer noted that the Ohio primary's outcome showed that the party leaders had made a mistake in rejecting Stassen at the convention. Stassen had demonstrated he could win city voters, and, since he had previously shown strength with farmers, Republican chieftains should have noted Stassen's ability to compete against President Truman throughout the nation. Also, Stassen had campaigned against Taft on the basis of the Taft-Hartley Act. This strategy helped him with the urban areas, showing a political talent that would have been useful in the fall campaign.

The May Oregon primary all but ended Stassen's chances. For the first time Dewey matched Stassen's labors at campaigning. He also took up Stassen's challenge for a debate, which proved to be the critical factor. On the radio the two men divided over whether the Communist Party should be outlawed. Stassen took the affirmative stance and, with McCarthy at his side, weakly accused Dewey of being "soft on communism." Dewey, an experienced trial lawyer with the better radio voice, systematically destroyed Stassen's arguments. He went on to win the Oregon contest and enter the convention as the favorite.

Stassen went to the convention still optimistic about his chances of gaining the nomination. He refused Senator Taft's request that he withdraw from the race and throw his support behind the Ohio conservative in order to prevent Dewey's nomination. Stassen would only withdraw in favor of fellow internationalist Vandenberg, although Taft's representative offered him the vice presidential nomination. Dewey led after the second ballot, and Stassen's delegate support deteriorated. Taft, his own delegate total increasing, implored Stassen to abandon his candidacy and endorse him to arrest the Dewey momentum. Stassen refused, saying that he would await the third ballot results. Realizing Dewey could not be stopped without Stassen's endorsement of his candidacy, Taft ordered his managers to announce his concession.

Within weeks of the Republican National Convention in July 1948, Stassen accepted the presidency of the University of Pennsylvania, a post he held until 1953. Stassen raised funds and oversaw the expansion of the university's physical plant. He fostered symposia of academicians and leaders from outside the university community. Stassen did not neglect his political future. In Detroit on September 7, 1948, he officially opened the Republican presidential campaign for Dewey. Attacking the Truman labor and diplomatic policies, Stassen accused the president of an extreme demogogic appeal to "set class against class" and faulted him for "colossal failure" at the May 1945 Potsdam Conference.

Dewey's unexpected defeat revived Stassen's status as a party leader. As cold war tensions mounted with the outbreak of hostilities in Korea, Stassen, like most GOP figures, adopted a militant view on foreign policy. In August 1950 he told a national radio audience that the next Communist attack, after Korea, would result in an American retaliation on Russia itself, "War will come to Moscow, to the Urals, and to the Ukraine." On the eve of the 1950 congressional elections he argued that the war had erupted in Asia because of "five years of coddling Chinese Communists" by the Truman administration. In December Stassen asserted that he would use atomic weapons against mainland China if the Chinese army failed to agree to a cease-fire in Korea within 24 hours. He reiterated this position in January 1951 while demanding the resignation of Secretary of State DEAN G. ACHESON. Testifying before the Senate International Security Subcommittee in October 1951, Stassen charged the State Department generally, and advisers PHILIP JESSUP and OWEN LATTIMORE in particular, with the responsibility for the Communist takeover of China in 1949.

Having kept his name in the public eye, Stassen conducted another campaign for the Republican presidential nomination in 1952. But his effort died aborning; his potential voter base of younger Republicans was badly undercut by the rival candidacy of General DWIGHT D. EISENHOWER. Neither the Eisenhower campaign nor that of the other main aspirant, Taft, paid attention to Stassen's entry. Both groups quickly concluded that Stassen ran only as an unofficial "stalking horse" for Eisenhower, with whom he shared common foreign policy views. Stassen's slim 1952 chances suffered an irreparable blow in the March Minnesota primary when a spontaneous Eisenhower write-in campaign almost bested his "favorite-son" slate. Stassen subsequently ran a poor third in the Nebraska primary; in the May Gallup poll, only 3 percent of the Republican voters still favored his candidacy. At the Republican National Convention in July, Stassen, hoping for his selection in the event of a deadlock, resisted demands of Minnesota delegates that they be allowed to switch to Eisenhower. After Minnesota split its vote 19 for Stassen and 9 for Eisenhower, one of the former governor's floor managers calculated that if Minnesota switched all its votes to Ike at the end of the first ballot that it could put him over the top. A call was made to Stassen at his hotel room asking his permission to shift the delegation's vote. Stassen asked that the tally not be changed, with the obvious hope that a deadlock would ensue and he might end up the compromise candidate.

However, he did not order it not to be shifted, and Stassen's floor managers, having power of attorney from him, ignored his wishes and allowed the delegates to switch, nominating Ike.

In 1953 Eisenhower named Stassen director of foreign aid programs and, later, special assistant for disarmament. He resigned from government service in 1958 and practiced law in Philadelphia. Stassen attempted to resurrect his political fortunes in unsuccessful campaigns for the Pennsylvania Republican gubernatorial nomination in 1958, the Philadelphia mayoralty in 1959, presidential nomination efforts in 1964, 1968, and 1976, and the Minnesota Republican senatorial nomination in 1978. He attempted one last run for the White House—his ninth—in 1988. Stassen died on March 4, 2001, in Bloomington, Minnesota. (See *The Eisenhower Years* Volume)

—JLB

Steelman, John

(1900–1999) *assistant to the president*

John Steelman was born on June 23, 1900, in Thornton, Arkansas, and brought up on a small cotton farm. He served in World War I before attending Henderson-Brown College, where he received his bachelor's degree in 1922. Two years later he received a master's degree in sociology from Vanderbilt University and in 1925 a Ph.B. In 1928 the University of North Carolina granted him a Ph.D. in sociology. While a professor of sociology and economics at the Alabama College for Women in Montevallo, Steelman successfully mediated a labor dispute in Mobile. Impressed by the results, Secretary of Labor Frances Perkins in 1937 appointed Steelman a commissioner in the U.S. Conciliation Service. Under Steelman's leadership the service increased its caseload from 1,287 to 25,000 annually, resolving 95 percent of these disputes without a strike.

In the fall of 1945 Truman appointed Steelman a special consultant on labor-management problems. He was brought to the White House to aid Secretary of Labor LEWIS B. SCHWELLENBACH, who had had no previous experience in labor relations. Until Schwellenbach was replaced in 1948, Steelman served, according to historian Patrick Anderson, as de facto secretary of labor. Steelman was appointed director of the Office of War Mobilization and Reconversion (OWMR) in June 1946. Six months later, when OWMR was abolished, he became assistant to the president.

Steelman's power in the White House transcended his assigned tasks of dealing with federal bureaucracies; he gradually became one of Truman's important domestic advisers. A hard-working, aggressively jovial man, he had the trust of Truman, who liked his country-boy manners. Critics, however, were offended by his "jovial evasiveness" to questions and "crude attempts to manage news." Columnists Robert A. Allen and William V. Shannon found him " . . . red-faced, pushy, opportunistic . . . a congenital glad-hander . . . a bombastic hack." His main duties tended to be administrative—paper work and resolving small interdepartmental and interagency problems to keep them from landing on the president's desk, so Truman could deal with the major issues. Steelman was not prominent in foreign policy debates. Although he argued against reindustrializing Germany, Truman proceeded to do so.

Steelman prided himself on being non-political, but he soon emerged as a leading spokesman of the administration's conservative faction, led by JOHN W. SNYDER. He often clashed with CLARK CLIFFORD, who spoke for the liberals. When, in 1947, Clifford urged Truman to institute a program of social legislation and civil rights, Steelman opposed the recommendation, suggesting that the president avoid offending powerful interests and plot a middle course on social issues. But as Truman biographer Alonzo Hamby has noted the conflicts between Steelman and Clifford were less ideological and more about "public recognition and White House turf." Steelman was not ideologically driven and did not appear interested in dueling with Clifford over many policy issues.

The two men's first major clash came over how to handle JOHN L. LEWIS, president of the United Mine Workers (UMW). In the spring of 1946, when the UMW struck for a 10 cent royalty per ton of coal to be used for medical and retirement benefits, Truman seized the mines. Then, following Steelman's advice, he agreed to conciliate Lewis by granting a contract with a five-cent royalty on each ton of coal. This, however, did not satisfy the union leader. Two weeks before the 1946 congressional elections, Lewis hinted a new strike was in the offing. Steelman again advised Truman to compromise, but the president followed the recommendations of Clark Clifford and took a hard stand. When Lewis allowed miners to walk off the job after the election, Truman ordered the Justice Department to ask for an injunction against the walkout and eventually won a $3.5 million contempt-of-court fine against the UMW.

In the spring of 1952 Steelman played a major role in negotiations between the steel industry and the United Steelworkers of America. In March, during the dispute between the government and the steel companies over the wages for steel workers, Steelman replaced CHARLES E. WILSON as director of the Office of Defense Mobilization. Wilson had resigned in protest against the Office of Wage Stabilization's recommendation for an 18-cent-an-hour pay increase without compensating the steel companies. When the government could not get the industry to accept the proposal, Truman seized the steel mills to prevent a strike. However, after the action was ruled unconstitutional by a district court, the workers walked out. Steelman then negotiated a settlement. After 52 days he got the parties to agree to a 16-cent-an-hour pay increase in return for an increase of $5.20 a ton for steel.

After leaving the White in March 1953, Steelman acted as a consultant to industry. He later served as director of the Audio-Dynamics Corporation and as a trustee of the Nationwide Investing Foundation. He died on July 14, 1999, in Naples, Florida.

—RSG

Stennis, John C(ornelius)
(1901–1995) *member of the Senate*

John C. Stennis was born on August 3, 1901, in Kemper County, Mississippi. He began his education in a one-room schoolhouse in Kipling Crossroads, Mississippi. He graduated from Mississippi Agricultural and Mechanical College in 1923 and received a law degree from the University of Virginia in 1928. That year he was elected to the Mississippi House of Representatives, where he served until 1932. From 1931 to 1935 Stennis was a district prosecuting attorney. In 1937 he was appointed a circuit court judge.

During 1947 Stennis ran as a Democrat for the U.S. Senate in a special election to fill the vacancy created by the death of the white supremacist THEODORE G. BILBO (D-Miss.). Claiming to follow the advice of his father not to mention the race issue, Stennis at least downplayed it, campaigning on a platform of agricultural reform, which called for the encouragement of increased mechanization and diversification of farming. He did, however,

make clear his support of "reasonable and proper segregation." Stennis was more a paternalistic segregationist than a rabid racist, as one of his election opponents, Representative JOHN E. RANKIN, was. Rankin hated not only blacks but also Catholics and Jews. In a hotly contested six-man race, Stennis won the seat with the support of liberals and blacks.

In the Senate Stennis compiled a conservative record, voting for the Internal Security Act of 1950, which provided for the registration of Communists. He also backed the McCarran-Walter Act of 1952 restricting the immigration of Asians and Eastern Europeans. The senator opposed housing legislation and the administration's wage-price control policies.

Stennis did introduce some progressive legislation. In 1949 he and MILTON R. YOUNG (R-N.Dak.) offered a bill that would have provided $100 million yearly for making "farm-to-market" roads. Hearings were held, but nothing further was done. Stennis sponsored in 1951 an amendment that would have increased funding for vocational education by $445,000. It was passed and became law.

In 1951 Senators Stennis and JAMES O. EASTLAND (D-Miss.) charged on the Senate floor that pro-Truman Democrats in Mississippi were selling federal jobs. The Committee on Expenditures in the Executive had its investigations subcommittee, headed by CLYDE R. HOEY (D-N.C.), look into the matter, and it found the charges to be true. Several people were later indicted.

Stennis joined other Southern Democrats in opposing the Truman administration's civil rights proposals. During July 1948 he began a filibuster of an anti–poll tax bill. He argued that the measure would not only be unconstitutional but also might bring about federal interference in local elections. The following year he helped defeat the Barkley anti-filibuster amendment, which had been seen as a possible way of facilitating passage of civil rights legislation. He also joined with a majority in voting against a bill forbidding segregation in public housing. Stennis termed civil rights programs as "the selling of our people down the river by bartering away our Constitution."

Stennis opposed Alaska statehood. In 1952 he listed several reasons why the territory should not be allowed to become a state: many Alaskans had opposed statehood in an election; Alaska had few people but would have two senators; allowing statehood for "disconnected" territory was a dubious policy and such areas should not have a significant say in foreign policy as they would have if they had U.S. senators and representatives as a state; admission of Alaska would not end Soviet charges of U.S. imperialism; the federal government would still have to finance much of the Alaskan economy as it did not have the wherewithal to support itself; and statehood would make no difference as to the defense arrangements in Alaska. Another strike against statehood according to Stennis was there were only 75,000 to 80,000 non-native civilians in Alaska. This was an argument that southerners used against admission of not just Alaska but also Hawaii, for fear of non-whites gaining more political power.

A strong anticommunist, Stennis generally backed Truman's foreign policy. He supported the Marshall Plan in 1948, viewing it as a method of combating communism and also rebuilding world markets for U.S. exports. However, he shifted his stand after an inspection trip to Europe the following year and called for a "substantial reduction" in American funding. In 1949 he voted for the North Atlantic Treaty. Two years later he opposed attempts to limit the number of U.S. ground troops committed to Europe without congressional approval.

During the 1950s and 1960s Stennis continued his opposition to civil rights and social welfare legislation. He voted to limit foreign aid and American military involvement overseas. In 1954 he was one of the first Democrats to call for the censure of Senator JOSEPH R. MCCARTHY (R-Wisc.). As a leading member of the Armed Services Committee, he often supported Pentagon budget requests. His views on the Vietnam conflict fluctuated.

During his years in the Senate, Stennis, a courtly, dignified man, acquired a reputation for integrity that transcended his political stands. In 1973, in the midst of President Richard Nixon's battle to withhold the Watergate tapes, the White House suggested that Stennis independently verify their content as an alternative to public release of the documents. The plan was never adopted because the scandal escalated. In his later years Stennis became a mentor to younger senators. He did not run for reelection in 1988 and died on April 23, 1995, in Jackson, Mississippi. (See *The Eisenhower Years, The Kennedy Years, The Johnson Years, The Nixon/Ford Years* Volumes)

—JF

Stettinius, Edward R(iley), Jr.

(1900–1949) *secretary of state, ambassador*

Born on October 22, 1900, in Chicago, Illinois, Edward R. Stettinius, Jr., was the son of a partner of the giant J. P. Morgan banking firm. He attended the University of Virginia but failed to graduate. Rather than devoting his attention to studies, he was active in Christian social service projects, including the Young Men's Christian Association. Stettinius considered becoming a clergyman and often toured the mountains preaching. After working as a clerk, Stettinius, whose father was the director of General Motors (GM), became assistant to John L. Pratt, a GM vice president. He was named one of the corporation's vice presidents in 1931. Three years later U.S. Steel invited him to be vice chairman of its finance committee. By 1938 he was chairman of the giant corporation.

In 1939 Franklin D. Roosevelt, searching for executives to join the administration's future war effort, appointed Stettinius chairman of the War Resources Board. The following year Stettinius left U.S. Steel to devote all his time to his membership in the National Defense Advisory Commission. In 1941 he became director of priorities for the Office of Production Management. That year Roosevelt appointed him lend-lease administrator. Impressed with Stettinius's administrative abilities, Roosevelt asked him to become undersecretary of state in 1943.

As undersecretary, Stettinius set out to reorganize the State Department, which, over the years, had become a confusing array of departments and sub-departments with no central coordinating office. Under his plan, presented in January 1944, the bureaucracy was organized in a pyramid structure with administration centered around the undersecretary of state. Stettinius established well-defined responsibilities for the undersecretary and the four assistant secretaries of state. For coordination of the top officers at State he created a Policy Committee and a Committee on Post-War Programs. Also, he created an Office of Public Information and the Division of Science, Education, and Art, which later became the Division of Cultural Cooperation in July 1944. Stettinius improved the department's liaison with the White House, press, Congress, and the public. Experts considered Stettinius's reorganization his greatest contribution during his stay in the State Department. As undersecretary and secretary of state Stettinius was able to win large appropriations from Congress.

Roosevelt appointed Stettinius secretary of state upon the resignation of Cordell Hull in December 1944. The reasons behind the choice were unclear. However, CHARLES E. BOHLEN surmised that the president wanted a secretary who would continue reform of the department's bureaucracy while FDR and HARRY L. HOPKINS molded foreign policy. The pleasant, easygoing Stettinius, who had little foreign policy background, was willing to follow these men's leads.

Stettinius served only six months at his post. After being appointed secretary of state, Stettinius accepted the resignation of all but one of the four assistant secretaries, this one being DEAN G. ACHESON. He appointed JOSEPH C. GREW as undersecretary. Some of Stettinius's appointments stirred controversy as they included individuals from big business, such as WILLIAM C. CLAYTON and NELSON A. ROCKEFELLER, and they were held up for a few days until Roosevelt insisted on their confirmation. Late in 1944 Stettinius announced another reorganization plan that added two more top officers to the existing assistant secretaries of state: a legal adviser and a special assistant in charge of international organizational and security affairs. In addition to carrying out more bureaucratic reforms, he improved relations with the White House that had been strained under Hull and appointed Bohlen as liaison officer to it.

Stettinius had five objectives as secretary: diplomacy conducted so as to support the armed forces; prevention of Germany and Japan from being able to go to war; creation of an effective United Nations to guard the peace; promotion of free trade so as to maintain full employment at home and raise the standard of living throughout the world; and the encouragement of the development of democracies. During this period he opposed HENRY MORGENTHAU's plan for the pastoralization of Germany and worked for a coordinated effort on the part of the wartime allies during the occupation of that nation. Stettinius demanded the election of representative governments in Eastern Europe. Before the Yalta Conference Stettinius and British foreign minister Anthony Eden agreed on not recognizing the Soviet-imposed Polish puppet Communist government, on the creation of the American and British zones of occupation in Germany, and on giving the French a portion of the U.S. and British sectors. Thanks to Stettinius Roosevelt at Yalta relied more on the State Department than in previous conferences, and he

accompanied the president to the conference. The Big Three—Roosevelt, Joseph Stalin, and Winston Churchill—turned over some problems to their foreign ministers to make recommendations. The Big Three accepted Stettinius's recommendation that a commission be established to determine reparations for Germany. Stettinius demanded the election of representative governments in Eastern Europe and accompanied Roosevelt to the Yalta Conference called to discuss postwar policy. He also participated in the discussions leading to the creation of the United Nations.

When Harry Truman became president Stettinius handed in his resignation. Truman did not personally know him and therefore did not have the confidence in him that Roosevelt did. More important, Truman realized that to have Stettinius in a post, which was next in line for the presidency, would not be politically sound because the secretary had never held elective office. Stettinius was also considered an intellectual lightweight. The president therefore decided to offer the job to JAMES F. BYRNES, who had been a leading contender for the 1944 vice presidential nomination. However, the president postponed the acceptance of Stettinius's resignation until after the United Nations Conference in San Francisco.

The secretary's last official responsibility was the planning of the San Francisco Conference. On the eve of the San Francisco Conference Stettinius was still optimistic about the prospects of the United Nations. He compared the drafting of the United Nations charter to the Philadelphia constitutional convention of 1787 and said he believed the conference was the best way to prevent another world war. The delegation chosen by Roosevelt included Senators TOM CONNALLY (D-Tex.) and ARTHUR H. VANDENBERG (R-Mich.), Representatives SOL BLOOM (D-N.Y.) and CHARLES A. EATON (R-N.J.), former governor HAROLD E. STASSEN and Virginia G. Gildersleeve, dean of Barnard College. Roosevelt selected Stettinius to be the delegation chairman. The secretary found it difficult to work with such prominent personalities. None were willing to accept his leadership or to permit him to speak to the press for the delegation. The group even failed to agree on a daily statement for the media. Stettinius did, however, play a role in the negotiations. He met with the heads of the British, French, Chinese, and Soviet delegations in his penthouse suite at the Fairmont Hotel to iron out differences among the Big Five on the Dumbarton Oaks proposals.

Stettinius remained dominated by his delegates even in policy debates. On April 27 the Czechoslovakian government moved to admit the Soviet puppet Lublin government of Poland as a member. Upon the demand of Vandenberg Stettinius took to the floor to oppose the motion. Stettinius's major clash with the Russians came on the role of the Security Council. The Soviet Union insisted that the permanent members of the council should be able to veto even the discussion of a dispute. Stettinius answered that the United States would not join the world body if this occurred. With the issue deadlocked at the San Francisco Conference, Truman sent Harry Hopkins on a special mission to Moscow, where he obtained a reversal of this position from Stalin.

On June 27, the day after the conference closed, Truman accepted Stettinius's resignation. The president appointed him the first ambassador to the United Nations. Stettinius attended the preparatory conference in London in early 1946, where he again had problems controlling his delegation, which included such major Republicans as JOHN FOSTER DULLES and Senator Vandenberg. In June of the same year Stettinius resigned following reports that he had disagreed with James Brynes over policy. In August 1946 Stettinius was appointed rector of the University of Virginia. In 1947 he helped found the Liberia Company to funnel money to that country for development. Stettinius suffered a heart attack in February 1949 but was able to finish his book on the Yalta Conference, *Roosevelt and the Russians*. He died on October 31, 1949, in Greenwich, Connecticut.

—JB

Stevenson, Adlai E(wing)
(1900–1965) *governor, Democratic Party presidential candidate*

Named after his grandfather, who was vice president in Grover Cleveland's second administration, Adlai E. Stevenson was born on February 5, 1900, in Los Angeles, California. He attended the Choate School and graduated from Princeton in 1922. After working for a short time for his father's newspaper in Bloomington, Illinois, he studied law at Northwestern University, where he received his degree in 1926. The following year Stevenson entered a Chicago law firm.

In 1933 Stevenson moved to Washington to become special counsel to the Agricultural Adjustment Administration. The following year he transferred to the Federal Alcohol Control Administration as assistant general counsel. In 1937 he returned to private law practice in Chicago. Stevenson, a leader of the Chicago Council of Foreign Relations, became one of the most prominent internationalists in the isolationist-dominated Midwest. He was also an important reform Democrat in his city. Stevenson returned to Washington in 1941 as special assistant to Secretary of the Navy Frank Knox. Four years later he became special assistant to Secretary of State EDWARD R. STETTINIUS, JR.

In February 1945 Stevenson became assistant secretary of state and was a press officer to the April 1945 UN Conference at San Francisco. In September 1945 he became deputy delegate in the American mission to the UN's Preparatory Commission in London. Truman appointed Stevenson as an alternate delegate to the 1946 UN session, where he represented the United States before the committee that dealt with social and economic issues, and budgetary and financial matters. When America's UN ambassador Edward Stettinius became ill, Stevenson took charge, and the Americans generally had their way on organizational issues. Stevenson orchestrated a campaign to have himself named U.S. ambassador to the UN after Stettinius resigned in 1946, but Republican senator WARREN AUSTEN of Vermont received the position. During 1947–48 he again represented the United States as an alternate delegate. Throughout this period Stevenson was one of the Truman administration's leading supporters of the UN, justifying it to a nation growing distrustful of internationalism and frustrated with the world body's inability to stem the tide of the cold war.

In 1945 Stevenson worried that the Soviets were becoming alienated because they lost so many votes in the UN. But by mid-1946 Stevenson warned of a return to tension between democracy and communism that had begun with the October Revolution. He backed both the Truman Doctrine and the Marshall Plan.

In 1948 Stevenson ran for governor of Illinois with the backing of the reformist Independent Voters of Illinois and the Chicago Democratic machine, led by JACOB ARVEY. Stevenson waged a liberal campaign, attacking the Republican Party for corruption and called for a new constitution. He promised a state fair employment practices act, the creation of a civil rights division in the Illinois Attorney General's office, and more money for schools and hospitals. Stevenson beat Republican governor Dwight Green by an unprecedented 572,000 votes: 57 percent of the vote and the largest plurality in Illinois history.

As governor, Stevenson brought into his administration an excellent staff of experts independent of political bosses. Outfitted with a surplus from the Green administration and rising tax revenue from a robust economy, Stevenson successfully battled the conservative Republicans, who dominated the legislature, increased spending for public schools, housing, prisons, and highways, and raised the salaries of state employees. However, Stevenson failed in securing a state constitutional convention and a state Fair Employment Practices Commission. The failure of the latter to pass inspired rumors that Stevenson was soft on civil rights; he was hardly in the vanguard on this issue, and his stand was typical of the day. Yet he did desegregate the Illinois National Guard and, when race riots broke out in Cicero, Stevenson sent troops to protect the African-American families that had just moved into the area. Stevenson's positions on civil rights earned him the praise of the nation's liberals. One of the governor's most controversial acts was his order to break up illegal gambling operations, despite the opposition from a large number of prominent citizens who wanted gambling retained. However, he cracked down without enthusiasm.

With his second legislature (1951–53) Stevenson won passage of bills increasing state workers' and teachers' salaries, expanding aid to education, and boosting workers' compensation and unemployment benefits. He also secured funding for a new highway program, paid for with an increase in the low gasoline tax and truck license fees. To avoid GOP criticism he proposed no other tax increase, and he ended his years as governor with a small budget surplus. Stevenson did not strive to build a bureaucratic edifice but rather to secure an efficient government, with moderately expanded responsibilities, and he was actually something of a fiscal conservative. Stevenson became a liberal icon because of his veto of the Broyles bill, which required loyalty oaths for political candidates, schoolteachers, and public employees, and made it a felony to belong to a subversive group. Stevenson remarked, "Does anyone seriously think that a real traitor will hesitate to sign a loyalty oath?" Liberals also admired his attacks

on Senator JOSEPH R. MCCARTHY (R-Wisc.) and his opposition to the Red Scare.

Stevenson's victory as governor made him a serious contender for the 1952 Democratic presidential nomination. He was an expert on foreign affairs and had a progressive record highlighted by his stands on civil rights and loyalty, which made him a favorite candidate among liberals.

Truman originally had wanted Chief Justice FRED M. VINSON to be his successor, but he turned the president down. For a brief time in early 1952, he considered running for another term, but his staff recommended against such a course. Truman began to look to Stevenson as a suitable successor because of his Democratic pedigree, his 1948 victory, and his service in the federal government. Stevenson met with Truman on January 23, 1952, and the president later said the governor rejected his offer. Stevenson announced in early 1952 he would run for a second term as governor and did not authorize the draft movement that began to develop around his name. Although Stevenson never explained his reluctance to fight for the presidential nomination it is believed he saw himself as the one potential candidate upon whom all factions of the party could agree. He, consequently, wanted to avoid becoming associated with any major faction and, in particular, wanted to prevent identification with the unpopular Truman administration. Nevertheless, Stevenson declined to repudiate the burgeoning grassroots campaign for him. In July, when it appeared that the national convention might actually fail to nominate him, Stevenson finally indicated his willingness to accept a draft.

Vice President ALBEN W. BARKLEY dropped out of the race—organized labor thought him too old—and this was a windfall for the governor, as Barkley and he were seen as the only candidates who could unite both southern conservatives and northern liberals. Stevenson won on the third ballot. In his acceptance speech, evidently in as messianic mood, he quoted Jesus in the Olive Grove: "If this cup may not pass from me, except I drink it, Thy will be done."

Stevenson toured the nation defending the administration's foreign policy, especially the unpopular Korean War. He ridiculed the Republican's rhetorical promises to liberate Eastern Europe as irresponsible campaign gestures designed only to garner votes. Stevenson demonstrated the courage to raise unpopular issues in front of unsympathetic audiences. To the American Legion he condemned blind patriotism and McCarthyism. At the United Automobile Workers rally in Detroit, Stevenson refused to commit himself to the total repeal of the Taft-Hartley Act. In Texas Stevenson praised Truman's veto of the bill that would have turned over offshore oil reserves to the states. Stevenson's moderation of his former civil rights position dismayed a number of liberals. Rather than endorse a Fair Employment Practices Commission, he came out with a vague pronouncement that he would prefer the states to establish commissions before the federal government did. His choice of Senator JOHN J. SPARKMAN (D-Ala.), a segregationist, also upset many of his party's liberals. Nevertheless, the governor hoped his choice would hold the South for the party.

GEORGE W. BALL said Stevenson was "never a real liberal." Stevenson biographer Jeff Broadwater said he was more a turn-of-the-century Progressive than a New Dealer. He was committed to the public interest, rather than particular interest groups. He believed that societal problems could be solved through public exposure and education and that the moral uplift was vital for the advancement of society.

Although many observers praised him for being a sophisticated campaigner, Stevenson suffered from the problem of being labeled an "egghead" because of his eloquent discourses on issues. His style made it difficult for him to compete with the simple, down-to-earth, father-figure image of Eisenhower. Stevenson's campaign was further weakened by the relentless attacks of the Republican right, which charged him with being soft on communism and with having former Communists on his campaign staff.

He blundered badly when in responding to Republican charges of corruption in the administration he proclaimed he had experience as governor in cleaning up such messes, which infuriated Truman. Eisenhower won the election by a landslide, capturing 55.1 percent of the vote to the governor's 44.4 percent. Many later observers thought Eisenhower's victory was inevitable, but Truman became convinced that Stevenson's failings as a candidate had cost the Democrats three to four million votes and the election.

Stevenson lost the presidency to Eisenhower again in 1956. Four years later a draft Stevenson movement failed to deliver him the nomination. President John F. Kennedy appointed him ambassador to the United Nations, where he distinguished himself in debates over the Cuban missile crisis.

During the Johnson presidency Stevenson privately questioned the administration's policy in Vietnam. He was planning to resign his UN post when he suffered a fatal heart attack in London on July 14, 1965. (See *The Eisenhower Years, The Kennedy Years, The Johnson Years* Volumes)

—JB

Stimson, Henry L(ewis)
(1867–1950) *secretary of war*

Henry L. Stimson was born on September 21, 1867, in New York City. His family was, as he wrote in his memoirs, "sturdy, middle class people, religious, thrifty, energetic and long-lived." The son of a banker and doctor, Stimson graduated from Yale in 1888 and, after two years at Harvard Law School, was admitted to the New York bar in 1891. He then embarked upon a prosperous law practice with Elihu Root's firm. In 1906 Stimson was appointed attorney for the Southern District of New York, where he prosecuted a number of famous antitrust cases. Four years later he ran unsuccessfully for the governorship of New York. President William Howard Taft appointed Stimson secretary of war in 1911. When Woodrow Wilson became president in 1913, Stimson left government to return to his law practice. He served in the army during World War I.

During the last half of the 1920s Stimson was special envoy to Nicaragua and governor-general of the Philippines. He served as secretary of state during the Hoover administration. During his tenure the administration announced what came to be known as the Stimson Doctrine, in which the United States refused to recognize the Japanese invasion of Manchuria. With the election of Franklin D. Roosevelt, Stimson retired from government but stayed long enough to direct the transition to office for the new president, who was his good friend.

The president called Stimson, a leading Republican internationist, to assume the post as secretary of war in July 1940. The highest ranking Republican in the administration, Stimson, at the age of 73, supervised the mobilization for the American intervention into the war. After Pearl Harbor he was the top American civilian, next to the president, to administer the military's war effort. Stimson participated in the major military and foreign policy decisions of the administration. In addition, after May 1, 1943, he was Roosevelt's adviser on the military employment of atomic energy. Stimson retained his posts when Truman became president.

Stimson mentioned to Truman after he was sworn in as president that the government was building a weapon of "almost unbelievable destructive power." Roosevelt had told Truman about the atomic bomb in August 1944 after he had been nominated as the vice presidential candidate. Stimson, unaware of this, briefed the new president on the details of the bomb on April 25, 1945. The secretary told Truman that in four months the armed forces would have the weapon ready. The device could obliterate a city, and although no other country would be able to produce one for some years, eventually one almost certainly would. He believed the problem of revealing its secrets to other nations was "a primary question of our foreign relations." If this conundrum could be solved "the peace of the world and our civilization can be saved." According to Stimson's biographer, Godfrey Hodgson, these ideas were the result of the secretary's talks with members of the Roosevelt administration, his staff, and the Manhattan Project, and his own contemplation.

During his last months in office Stimson played a major role in the political, military, and diplomatic debates over the use of atomic power. He was ambivalent about Secretary of State JAMES F. BYRNES's recommendation that the United States use its possession of the atomic bomb to pressure the Soviet Union into making concessions in Eastern Europe. Stimson hoped the Soviet Union would be more accommodating to U.S. demands once the bomb had been used. However, he sympathized with the Russian desire to surround itself with friendly states. Although Soviet repression in the area shocked him, he reminded Truman that these countries never had democratic governments. Stimson asserted that it was more important for the United States to maintain the wartime alliance than to break it over the issue of freedom for Eastern Europe.

In June Truman asked Stimson to head the Interim Committee, charged with advising the president on the use of the atomic bomb against Japan. Stimson made the final decision to recommend dropping the bomb on Hiroshima and Nagasaki in early August if Japan did not surrender. He insisted that no bomb be dropped on Kyoto, the ancient capital of Japan, which was of religious and cultural significance to the Japanese. Just before Truman left for the Potsdam Conference in late July, the secretary and his aides drafted a peace proclamation he hoped would be acceptable to the Japanese. In return for surrender the proposal offered the Japanese a quick restoration of civilian government

and the maintenance of a constitutional monarchy. Byrnes rejected the plan, demanding instead that the emperor abdicate. Although uninvited, Stimson attended the Potsdam Conference, where he tried to convince Truman that the military thought the use of the bomb unnecessary. Stimson urged Byrnes to give the Japanese a strong warning about the bomb and to permit them to retain the emperor so that the weapon might not have to be used. Byrnes rejected both requests. After the two bombs were dropped, the Japanese still remained adamant about the emperor's future. Truman then agreed to the monarchy's continuation. However, the emperor would answer to the Allied supreme commander, General DOUGLAS MACARTHUR.

In a *Harper's* magazine article in February 1947 Stimson defended the use of the bomb despite his original reservations: "In the light of the alternatives which, on a fair estimate, were open to us, I believe that no man in our position and subject to our responsibilities, holding in his hand a weapon of such possibilities for accomplishing this purpose and saving those lives, could have failed to use it and afterward looked his countrymen in the face."

In September 1945, just before his retirement, Stimson questioned the American nuclear monopoly in a historic letter to Truman. He maintained that future relations with the Soviet Union would be dominated by the American possession of the weapon. "These relations may be perhaps irretrievably embittered by the way in which we approach the solution of the bomb with Russia. For if we fail to approach them now and merely continue to negotiate with them, having this weapon ostentatiously on our hip, their suspicions and their distrust of our purposes and motives will increase. . . . The chief lesson I have learned in a long life is that the only way you can make a man trustworthy is to trust him; and the surest way to make him untrustworthy is to distrust him and show your distrust." If the United States and USSR failed to develop some means for controlling the spread of atomic weapons, Stimson predicted, a major arms race would begin. The elder statesman recommended the United States propose halting bomb construction, impounding existing weapons, and formulating an international agreement to outlaw nuclear weapons. Stimson argued that the United States should propose this idea to the USSR directly with the support of Great Britain, but not as part of an international coalition of nations, which he did not think the Russians would take seriously. The administration rejected Stimson's proposal.

Stimson retired on September 21, 1945. One year later he reversed himself on disarmament. Disturbed by Soviet intransigence over Eastern Europe, he wrote BERNARD M. BARUCH, "the time has passed for handling the bomb the way I suggested to the President last summer." Stimson told JAMES V. FORRESTAL, secretary of the navy, that the United States should immediately make as many atomic missiles as possible.

Stimson died of a heart attack on October 20, 1950, in Huntington, New York.

—JB

Stone, Harlan Fiske

(1872–1946) *chief justice of the United States*
Son of a New England farmer, Harlan Fiske Stone was born on October 11, 1872, in Chesterfield, New Hampshire. He graduated from Amherst College in 1894 and from Columbia Law School in 1898. He then divided his time between teaching at Columbia, where he was dean of the law school from 1910 to 1923, and private practice as a corporate attorney in Wall Street firms. A Republican, Stone was named U.S. Attorney General in April 1924. In January 1925 he was appointed an associate on the U.S. Supreme Court. Some liberals were hesitant to confirm a lawyer with connections to Wall Street, so, to convince them of his worthiness, he offered to answer questions before the Senate Judiciary Committee—a practice carried on today. The Senate overwhelmingly voted to confirm Stone. On June 12, 1941, President Franklin D. Roosevelt selected Stone as chief justice; the Senate confirmed the nomination later that month.

Throughout his years on the bench, Stone preached a philosophy of judicial restraint. Judges, he believed, must accord the legislature broad powers in social and economic affairs and must not allow their personal views on the desirability or wisdom of such legislation to determine its constitutionality. Stone also opposed the use of rigid legal formulae to settle cases and doubted the validity of solely determining constitutionality on the basis of social justice or conservative skepticism thereof. Therefore he urged, instead, that each decision be based on a careful weighing of all relevant evidence, including such elements as precedents, facts, and legislative intent.

Through the mid-1930s, these views led Stone to dissent repeatedly when a conservative majority overturned various economic and social welfare laws, including many important New Deal measures. In a

particularly sharp dissent written in 1936 in the case *United States v. Butler,* in which the Court invalidated the first Agricultural Adjustment Act, Stone chastised the majority for discarding any economic legislation it considered "undesirable" and thus usurping the function and powers of the legislature. In 1937 the Court began to shift direction, and personnel changes helped create a new majority that sustained New Deal regulatory measures. With this, Justice Stone was more often in the majority, and he helped establish the legitimacy of wide-ranging federal power over the economy. His opinions made important contributions to the law in areas such as intergovernmental tax immunities, commerce clause restrictions on the states, equity, and patents.

In the April 1938 case *Carolene Products Co. v. United States,* Justice Stone said the Court would mostly exercise judicial restraint in regard to economic legislation, but, in the famous Footnote Four, he suggested the Court might practice less restraint and subject to close scrutiny laws that infringed on Bill of Rights guarantees or the rights of racial, religious, or political minorities. This statement was the foundation for the "preferred freedoms" doctrine, the notion that certain rights, particularly those listed in the First Amendment, are fundamental to all other liberties and must be given special protection by the judiciary. Stone's best-known application of the doctrine came in June 1940 in the case *Minersville School District v. Gobitis,* in which the Court upheld a state law requiring public school children to salute the flag against a challenge from Jehovah's Witnesses that this violated their religious scruples. Stone was the sole dissenter in this judgment. Three years later he was vindicated in *West Virginia State Board of Education v. Barnette,* in which several justices reconsidered their previous opinions and overturned a similar flag salute law.

Stone's position in most economic and civil liberties cases won him a reputation as a liberal, but in his final years on the bench, he was often at odds with justices on the Court's left wing. Still a believer in judicial restraint, Stone objected when he thought these jurists were trying to write their own liberal economic and social views into law, especially in cases involving statutory interpretation and the rulings of federal administrative agencies. He also protested when he believed the "preferred freedoms" approach was used simplistically to invalidate any legislation affecting First Amendment rights. Although he generally voted to support civil liberties, Stone did dissent in January 1946 in *Marsh v. Alabama*, in which the majority upheld the right of Jehovah's Witnesses to distribute their literature in a company town. The next month he also joined in a ruling sustaining the legality of the military tribunal that sentenced Japanese general Tomoyuki Yamashita to death in the case *In re Yamashita*.

"As an individual justice," John P. Frank wrote, "Stone was one of the great, dynamic contributors to American law, but as a chief justice, he was strikingly unsuccessful." Although his appointment to head the Court had been universally praised, Stone proved ineffective in the post. He disliked administrative work and lacked the skills needed to direct the Court and keep differences under control. Stone's Court was "the most frequently divided, the most openly quarrelsome in history," according to the Justice's biographer. The conflict included personal sniping and bickering as well as substantive differences on issues. By the end of Stone's tenure, critics asserted that the divisiveness had caused a decline in the Court's dignity and authority.

On April 22, 1946, Stone became ill while on the bench to announce decisions. He died later the same day at his Washington home. Despite his poor record as chief justice, Stone has been ranked as one of the greatest Supreme Court jurists because of his "intellectual acumen" and "perception of constitutional fundamentals." His biographer Alpheus T. Mason contended that Stone was not interested in maintaining an image of unity on the Court, but rather believed it was more important that the justices debate cases, even sharply, to arrive at decisions that did not denigrate the past, did meet the present situation, and did not trip up future attempts to resolve constitutional issues. He was a judge's judge, a superb legal craftsman who could sift through a mass of conflicting precedents to come up with a clear and solidly based rule of law. He was calm, deliberate, and balanced in his approach to issues and independent in his judgments. Stone combined, one scholar noted, "a basic faith in the dignity and worth of the individual with a firm belief in the right and capacity of the people to govern themselves."

—CAB

Strauss, Lewis L(ichtenstein)

(1896–1974) *commissioner, Atomic Energy Commission*

The son of a wholesale shoe manufacturer, Lewis Strauss was born on January 31, 1896, in Charleston, West Virginia. He was an avid student of physics who was forced to forego a college education because of economic problems. Instead, he entered his father's business. During World War I Strauss worked with the U.S. Food Administration, serving as HERBERT HOOVER's secretary. He played a role in arranging the final terms of the armistice agreement. In 1919 Strauss joined the prominent Wall Street banking house of Kuhn, Loeb, and Company. Nine years later he was made a partner. Active in the cultural and philanthropic affairs of the American Jewish community, Strauss was also a promoter of scientific research. In 1926 he entered the U.S. Naval Reserve and was ordered to active duty early in 1941. Strauss became coordinator of ordinance production and procurement during World War II. President Truman made him a rear admiral in 1945, an honor rarely extended to reservists.

In 1946 Truman named Strauss one of the five members of the newly created Atomic Energy Commission (AEC). On the panel he was a strong advocate of maintaining the U.S. monopoly of atomic technology and materials. He feared that security measures outside the United States were not stringent enough to assure that such materials would not end up in the hands of the Soviet Union. In September 1947 Strauss attempted unsuccessfully to have the AEC's ruling permitting isotope exports overturned. Two years later he testified before the Senate Appropriations Committee against the shipment of isotopes to Norway, deeming them "security risks."

In the years following V-J day, Strauss emerged as a major spokesman for a crash program to develop a hydrogen bomb. He was supported by a number of scientists associated with the AEC's General Advisory Committee: EDWARD TELLER, Ernest Lawrence, and Luis Alvarez. Following the first Russian atomic explosion in August 1949, Strauss wrote a memorandum to other members of the AEC saying that producing more atomic bombs would not be a sufficient reaction to the Soviet test. He recommended "a quantum jump in our planning" and to proceed to build the superbomb. He also sent a letter to President Truman arguing that an H-bomb was needed to maintain U.S. strategic superiority. He downgraded the dangers of "fallout" from nuclear explosions and added that, while he believed the AEC could pass judgment on certain technical questions involved in the H-bomb, the actual question of whether or not the weapon should be built was the province of the State and Defense departments.

The majority of the AEC and its General Advisory Committee, chaired by J. ROBERT OPPENHEIMER, opposed the crash program on moral, technical, and strategic grounds. However, Strauss was able to rally support from outside the AEC, and, in January 1950, Truman announced that America was to begin the crash development of a hydrogen bomb. Strauss resigned from the AEC shortly thereafter to take various positions in the business community.

In 1953 President Dwight D. Eisenhower appointed Strauss AEC chairman. He supported the suspension of Oppenheimer's security clearance in 1954 and backed the controversial Dixon-Yates contract the following year. Strauss remained opposed to a nuclear test ban throughout his tenure, despite growing public concern over radioactive fallout. He became the focus of an increasing controversy as proponents of the test ban charged he was attempting to conceal the dangers of such tests. In the wake of growing support in the administration for a test-ban treaty, in 1958 Strauss declined to accept another five-year term as AEC chairman. Eisenhower appointed him secretary of commerce in October, but the Senate rejected the nomination in June 1959. Strauss retired from government and remained active in charitable activities during the 1960s. Strauss died on January 21, 1974, in Brandy Station, Virginia. (See *The Eisenhower Years* Volume)

—MQ

Stuart, John L(eighton)

(1876–1962) *ambassador*

The son of Presbyterian missionaries, John L. Stuart was born on June 24, 1876, in Hangchow, China, but went to the United States for his education. He obtained his degree from Hampden-Sydney College in Virginia in 1896 and returned to China as a missionary. In 1919 he founded and became president of Yenching University—a forerunner of Beijing University—an institution that became noted for its political liberalism. During the 1920s and 1930s he witnessed the growth of civil war in China and the expansion of Japanese power in the East. Imprisoned by the Japanese after the attack on Pearl Harbor, he was released in September 1945. He began rebuilding the war-damaged Yenching University and at the end of the year returned to the United States to regain his health.

On the recommendation of GEORGE C. MARSHALL, Truman appointed Stuart ambassador to China in July 1946. He served as Marshall's adviser during the general's unsuccessful mission to form a coalition government between the Communists and Kuomintang. Even after the State Department abandoned the effort, Stuart continued to support a coalition, believing that, through education and local democracy, China would find a "middle way between capitalism and communism."

Stuart at first tended to minimize ideological conflict between Mao Zedong (Mao Tse-tung) and Chiang Kai-shek (Jiang Jieshi), believing instead that a personality clash was the main issue. However, he soon became convinced that he was witnessing "a gigantic struggle between two political ideologies with the overtones of democratic idealism perverted by bureaucratic incompetence on the one side, succumbing to a dynamic socialized reform vitiated by Communist dogma, intolerance and ruthlessness on the other. And the great mass of suffering inarticulate victims cared for neither but were powerless to do anything about it."

Stuart was an unsympathetic critic of the Kuomintang's corrupt regime, although he absolved Chiang from blame, calling him "the only moral force capable of action." He attacked corruption in the army and government, warning that U.S. aid could not save the Nationalists until the bureaucracy was reformed. In an article in the *China Press* in 1946, he voiced his hope for "another internal revolution" in China against the "narrowly partisan or selfishlessly unscrupulous or ignorantly reactionary forces among her own people."

By 1947 Stuart had insisted that the United States should either actively intervene in the situation with technical or military assistance to Chiang or withdraw entirely from the area. Any such assistance should be conditioned on Chiang instituting needed reforms. In September of that year he reported that the political, military, and economic position of the central government had continued to deteriorate within recent months as a result of U.S. failure to send anticipated military aid and a renewed Communist offensive, which intensified the Nationalist "tendency to panic in times of crisis." He warned in February 1948 that without U.S. aid, appeasers might take over the government and seek Soviet mediation in the conflict.

Stuart became increasingly dissatisfied with American policy in 1948 and 1949. He deplored the failure of the United States to give the Nationalists more effective aid and criticized "its aberrant and contradictory policies," which enervated the Nationalist government when it needed understanding.

Stuart was still in the U.S. embassy when the Communist Chinese took over Nanking in April 1949, but he stayed there for an additional three months. His hopes for good relations between the new People's Democratic Republic of China and America turned futile due to mutual antagonism. A former student of his at Yenching University, Huang Hua, who was head of the Alien Affairs Office in Nanking, told the ambassador that he had received a message from Mao inviting Stuart to visit Beijing. Truman and Secretary of State DEAN G. ACHESON refused to let him go. Stuart sent a letter to Mao saying the United States believed countries governed by different ideologies could coexist peacefully, and that good relations with America would help China. Although repeating his invitation to Stuart, Mao also insisted that China could survive without American trade, and that Russia had helped China more than the United States. Stuart left the country and returned to the United States telling the State Department of the rout of the Kuomintang army. Stuart objected to the discontinuance of American assistance to the Chinese Nationalists on Taiwan after October 1949 and regarded the State Department's White Paper on China as excessively critical of the Nationalists, believing it manifested a desire to place the blame for the fall of China on Chiang. In Stuart's opinion, the United States was partly to blame because it had been deceived by Communist claims to "progressivism" and had failed to recognize "the achievements to date and the potentialities of Chinese democracy." Stuart suffered a stroke in Washington, D.C., in December 1949 and was hospitalized there and in New York City intermittently until September 1950. He officially resigned as ambassador to China in November 1952.

In his autobiography, *Fifty Years in China* (1954), Stuart presented an optimistic view of Chiang and of the potential of the Nationalist government to effect meaningful social reform. He also implied that the Truman administration leaned toward recognition of the new Communist regime and was vaguely leftist, but was deterred by the power of public opinion. Stuart died on September 19, 1962, in Washington, D.C., following years of poor health.

—AES

Sullivan, John L(awrence)
(1899–1982) *undersecretary of the navy, secretary of the navy*

John L. Sullivan was born on June 16, 1899, in Manchester, New Hampshire. His father, a cigar manufacturer and lawyer, once acted as personal counsel to Secretary of the Navy Frank Knox. The younger Sullivan interrupted his studies at Dartmouth College in 1918 to enter the U.S. Naval Reserve as an apprentice seaman. He served for three months until he was released from active duty and was able to return to college. He received a B.A. from Dartmouth in 1921 and an LL.B. from Harvard Law School in 1924. That year he began practice as a member of his father's law firm in Manchester, New Hampshire. During the 1930s he made two unsuccessful attempts to win the governorship of his state.

In January 1940 President Roosevelt appointed Sullivan assistant secretary of the Treasury. He remained at that post until late 1944, when he resigned to return to his law practice. In June 1945 Sullivan was appointed secretary of the navy for air. The following year President Truman appointed him undersecretary of the navy. Sullivan remained in the background during the battle over the unification bill, but he did work with Secretary of the Navy JAMES V. FORRESTAL to prevent too much lobbying by naval officers against the measure.

In August 1947 Sullivan was named secretary of the navy under the new unification plan. Under his leadership the navy began a program of expansion and modernization. He denied charges that the service would play only a secondary role in modern defense and maintained that it should be "a tangible, visible, immediately usable force for stability in an unsettled world." The navy was, in his view, "the only adequate instrument . . . for insuring uninterrupted use of the communications which are vital to the existence of the United States." Under his direction the service focused on the production of guided missiles and submarines. In February 1949 he disclosed that the navy was planning a five-year building program, which included the construction of a 60,000- to 80,000-ton aircraft carrier and of four submarines with double the speed capability of those previously used. The cost of these projects was estimated at $538 million.

As the air force pushed for dominance in the defense establishment during the latter half of the decade, Sullivan continued to defend his service and, particularly, naval air power.

In July 1948 Sullivan asked Air Force Secretary STUART SYMINGTON about his service's attitude toward the Navy's air force having access to nuclear weapons. Symington said atomic bombing should be confined to the air force. Later in the month at a dinner with Secretary of Defense James Forrestal and the other service secretaries, Sullivan admitted that strategic air warfare was the purview of the air force, but that the navy should have the ability to use nuclear weapons on specific targets. Army Secretary KENNETH C. ROYALL said any use by the Navy of atomic weapons should be subordinated to the air force's role.

After the meeting Symington, at Sullivan's request, clarified his views in writing. Symington merely conceded that the navy could use atomic weapons to fulfill its normal roles, which could not be done by the air force, but only if there were a surfeit of resources to do additional operations and if it would result in equal or more efficient use of fissionable material. Navy planes, however, could carry only the less efficient guntype uranium weapons, whereas air force bombers could carry the more efficient implosion plutonium devices. Sullivan responded that no one service should have a monopoly on atomic weaponry.

In rebuttal to critics who believed warfare would be decided by strategic air power and therefore within the purview of the air force, Sullivan insisted in January 1949 that "push-button" warfare "might not fully materialize in our time" and that "a future conflict might involve as many battles under the sea as on the surface."

Sullivan abruptly resigned in April 1949 in protest to Secretary of Defense LOUIS A. JOHNSON's cancellation of plans to complete the proposed supercarrier *United States*. Sullivan accused Johnson of overruling a project approved by the president, the Congress, and top naval strategists. He described Johnson's action as a blow that "will result in a renewed effort to abolish the Marine Corps and to transfer all naval and marine aviation elsewhere." Even of greater significance, Sullivan said, "is the unprecedented action . . . in so dramatically and arbitrarily restricting the plans of an armed service without consultation of that service."

In October 1949, at the end of House Armed Services Committee hearings on disputes between navy and air force officials over defense policies, Johnson defended his cancellation of the carrier and indicated that he had asked Sullivan to resign because the latter had opposed unification. Sullivan, denying Johnson's statement, said that he had

Secretary of the Navy John L. Sullivan *(Harry S. Truman Library)*

supported the unification but was opposed to the abolition of marine and navy aviation and the "slow death" of the marine corps.

After his resignation Sullivan retired from government service and resumed his law practice. He supported Senator HENRY M. JACKSON's run for the presidency in 1976. Sullivan died on August 8, 1982, in Exeter, New Hampshire.

—MLB

Symington, (William) Stuart

(1901–1988) *secretary of the air force; chairman, National Securities Resources Board*
Symington was born on June 26, 1901, in Amherst, Massachusetts, where his father taught romance languages at Amherst College. Still a teenager, he joined the army in the last year of World War I. Symington attended Yale University from 1919 to 1923. Because of a deficiency in a math requirement, he did not receive his degree until 1946, after he had

become a member of the Truman administration. Following college Symington entered his uncle's coupler business. He soon found fault with the company's product and was discharged. In 1925 he bought an almost bankrupt clay products firm, which, by the time he sold it in 1927, had become a success. Symington repeated this process for several other firms during the 1920s and 1930s. He eventually established a reputation as a clever businessman who was able to turn a dying firm into a profitable enterprise.

From 1938 to 1945 Symington was president of the Emerson Electric Manufacturing Company in St. Louis, where he became known as a businessman who was able to deal successfully and amicably with organized labor. He initiated a profit-sharing plan at Emerson with the result that the plant maintained a high production record during a time of labor-management disputes. Symington's work at Emerson brought him into contact with government officials and, as a result, he was appointed an observer for the Office of Production Management.

Upon the recommendation of JOHN W. SNYDER, Symington was appointed chairman of the Surplus Properties Board in July 1945. He was given the responsibility for the liquidation of huge piles of war surplus. Much to his displeasure, Symington acquired the title "$100 million junk man." During his six months at his post, Symington attempted to alleviate housing shortages by turning over to the states surplus material, equipment, and land for emergency housing. Conscious that the agency was a great temptation for influence peddlers trying to use their positions to gain from postwar shortages, Symington had an FBI agent appointed to ferret out corruption.

Despite his precautions Symington and his agency became a target of a full-scale congressional investigation. In December 1946 a House select committee vigorously criticized the program and spoke of "slipshod operations, chaotic administrative conditions and unconscionable delays" in the sale of sites and instances of favoritism if not downright corruption. Symington defended his action, maintaining that he merely set policy and that other agents were assigned to dispose of property. He also said that the six months that he held the post was too short a time to gain complete control of his agency.

By the time of this testimony Symington had been appointed assistant secretary of war for air. He quickly became known as a leading supporter of the reorganization of the military under a single secretary of defense and a vigorous backer of an independent air force. Symington emerged as the master strategist and manager of the campaign to push unification of the armed services through Congress. He was opposed by Secretary of the Navy JAMES V. FORRESTAL and uniformed naval officers who felt that centralization would result in secondary status for the navy. As a result of the clash between the two branches, the final measure creating the post of secretary of defense was a compromise. The secretary was given power over policymaking functions. However, the service secretaries still maintained a large portion of their powers and had the right to appeal the decisions of the secretary of defense. The National Security Act of 1947, which created the office of secretary, also established the air force as a separate branch of the armed services.

Linked to the reorganization controversy was the issue of U.S. defense strategy in the age of nuclear weapons. Symington was a leading voice in the debate, calling for substantial defense budgets and a strong air force as a cornerstone of U.S. defense forces. He felt that the atomic bomb was the most powerful weapon in the world and that the only vehicle capable of delivering it, at least until missile technology was improved, was the airplane. This view was typical of those pro–air force officials in government, military and industry who proposed that the key to the future security of the U.S. rested on American capability to carry out a massive atomic assault on the Soviet Union. This strategy, in turn, depended on a strong air force. Symington, who believed his role was to advocate military strategy, not to make it, therefore, vigorously urged increased spending for air force development and expansion. As part of this campaign, he worked behind the scenes to establish an independent presidential commission to investigate air power in the postwar period. In January 1948 the President's Commission on Air Policy released its report. The document written by THOMAS K. FINLETTER, entitled "Survival in the Air Age," called for an immediate increase in air force funding and warned the nation to be ready by 1953 to defend itself against possible atomic attack. The report added weight to Symington's insistence on a larger air force.

When asked in July 1948 by U.S. Navy Secretary JOHN L. SULLIVAN what role the navy should play in atomic warfare, Symington replied it was the sole business of the air force. When asked to put his beliefs in writing, Symington at first was evasive. When later in the month Sullivan asked Symington to put his thoughts in writing again, Symington was more forthright. The navy should be limited to using atomic weapons in fulfillment of its traditional roles when such missions could not be done by the air force, but only when there were resources available for additional military missions, which would use fissionable material in equal or greater efficiency. Since navy planes could be armed only with less efficient uranium bombs, rather than the more efficient plutonium bombs, this amounted to no concession at all.

President Truman's announcement in September 1949 of an atomic explosion in the Soviet Union reinforced Symington's claims that the United States should rely on atomic power delivered by strategic bombers. When Truman asked for a non-nuclear war plan, Symington opposed, saying an air force would be superfluous without atomic bombs. He declared that within four years the United States needed an air force that was instantly ready for war and that the existing 48-wing force should be expanded to a 70-wing group. The navy, and to a lesser extent the army, disputed the air force doctrine that future wars between the United States and the Soviet Union would be quick battles won or lost by strategic air power. As part of a campaign against an increased role for the air force, the navy attacked Symington's plan to increase procurement of the B-36 bombers, which he had previously thought to be outdated. In 1949 Congress initiated an investigation of "ugly, disturbing rumors" of corruption. It was alleged that Secretary of Defense LOUIS A. JOHNSON—a one-time member of the board of directors of Consolidated Vultee, the company that made B-36s, had asked Consolidated Vultee to give money to Truman's 1948 campaign, presumably in exchange for going ahead with the B-36. There was also allegations that "there [was] a plan underway" for Symington to quit as soon as funds for the bomber were voted in order to head an aircraft combine controlled by Consolidated Vultee.

Symington welcomed the probe, calling the rumors "obviously and demonstrably false." The congressional investigating committee found no corruption or political influence in procurement of B-36s. Chairman of the Joint Chiefs of Staff OMAR BRADLEY blasted the navy officials who led the attack on the air force. Symington charged navy officials with imperiling U.S. security by peddling "falsehoods" about defense plans.

In March 1950 Symington resigned his position as air force secretary in protest against Johnson's slashing of the air force budget. Symington said that the combat effectiveness of the air force had declined because of reductions in numbers and that prospects for defending the United States were bleak because the Soviet Union and its allies had "the world's largest ground army, air force and undersea fleet." In rebuttal to those who demanded a balanced budget, Symington warned that Soviet military power "grows relatively greater as against the strength of the U.S." In his semi-annual report submitted in April, Symington stated that the USSR's possession of the atomic bomb made it imperative for the United States to have a "truly long-range offensive air arm."

In April 1950 Truman nominated Symington to head the National Security Resources Board (NSRB). He was responsible for mobilization for the Korean War. He urged higher taxes, stiffer credit terms, and longer working hours to avert inflation and boost production in the "fight for survival." Nevertheless he was not a strong advocate of price and wage controls. He thought that they should be applied only when other measures of controlling inflation and increasing production had failed. He also directed the effort to help expand the production capacity of critical industries and the amount of vital materials. With the creation of another mobilization agency, Symington's powers began to dissipate.

In April 1951 Truman appointed Symington the administrator of the reorganized Reconstruction Finance Corporation (RFC). One of his major tasks was that of building up public confidence in the RFC after disclosure of alleged influence peddling in RFC loans. He quickly dismissed those employees implicated in the scandal and promoted those uninvolved to improve morale. When Symington resigned this post in January 1952, Truman expressed great satisfaction with his assurance that the agency was in good shape and functioning properly.

After winning the Democratic primary in Missouri in August 1952, Symington waged a successful campaign for senator in November, beating the Republican wave brought on by Eisenhower's campaign for the presidency. In the Senate Symington continued to support high defense spending. By May 1953 he was already charging that the Eisenhower administration's defense budget cuts were endangering the nation and that the Soviet Union's strength in air power and submarines exceeded that of the United States.

Symington served briefly as a Democratic member of Senator JOSEPH R. MCCARTHY's (R-Wisc.) Permanent Investigations Subcommittee. He eventually denounced McCarthy as one who "needed a psychiatrist" and later stated that he was "not afraid of anything about [McCarthy] or anything [McCarthy] had to say, at any time, any place, anywhere."

In 1959 Symington entered the campaign for the Democratic presidential nomination, running on a platform that attacked Eisenhower's defense policies. Although he obtained the backing of former president Truman, Symington lost the nomination. During the 1960s Symington continued to advocate increased military spending, but by the end of the decade, he was an opponent of the Vietnam War. In 1973 Symington reversed his long held position on high defense spending and called on President Nixon to bring home U.S. servicemen throughout the world because of the detrimental effect large scale defense commitments had on the U.S. economy. Symington did not run for reelection in 1976. After his retirement he worked on his memoirs. Symington died on January 14, 1988, in New Canaan, Connecticut. (See *The Eisenhower Years, The Kennedy Years, The Johnson Years, The Nixon/Ford Years* Volumes)

Szilard, Leo
(1898–1964) *physicist*

The son of a construction engineer, Leo Szilard was born on February 11, 1898, in Budapest, Hungary. He studied at the Budapest Institute of Technology from 1916 to 1919 with a year's interruption to serve in the Austro-Hungarian army. His experience left him with a lifelong antipathy toward the military. He became interested in theoretical physics after being exposed to the works of Max Planck and ALBERT EINSTEIN at the Berlin Technical Hochschule. Szilard received a Ph.D. from the University of Berlin in 1922 and then taught there for 10 years. He also worked at the Kaiser Wilhelm Institute, where he was closely associated with Einstein. Following Hitler's takeover in Germany during 1933, he fled to Vienna and then to London, where he obtained a job in the physics department of St. Bartholomew's Hospital in 1934. There he

succeeded in separating isotopes of artificially radioactive elements. From 1935 to 1937 he worked in nuclear physics at Oxford's Clarendon Laboratory. Disturbed by Britain's pact with Hitler at Munich, Szilard settled in the United States, where he became a guest lecturer at Columbia University.

In 1939 Szilard and Dr. Walter Zinn confirmed the theory that atoms could be split under certain conditions. Concerned about the military consequences of his discovery, during 1939 Szilard persuaded Einstein to sign a letter to President Roosevelt urging him to take action so that the United States could develop the atomic bomb before the Germans did. From 1940 to 1942 Szilard and ENRICO FERMI headed the Manhattan District Project to develop the weapon. Excessive publicity resulted in its removal from Columbia University to the University of Chicago Metallurgical Laboratory, where the two men achieved the first atomic chain reaction from a plutonium pile in 1942. After Fermi was transferred to Los Alamos, New Mexico, to work on the project, Szilard remained at Chicago, concentrating on devising a commercially feasible method of extracting plutonium from uranium. Later the two scientists shared the first patent for a nuclear reactor.

Szilard's main aim was to utilize atomic energy, through scientific control, for the good of mankind. Ironically, he thought for a time that the atomic bomb should be used so that its devastating power would convince people of the necessity of international control. However, after Germany's defeat he opposed the use of the atomic bomb against Japan. He wrote a memorandum to President Roosevelt warning that use of the atomic bombs could set off an arms race between the United States and the U.S.S.R. FDR died before Szilard could send the letter. Then Szilard made an appointment to see the new president, Harry Truman, to discuss the same subject. Truman shuffled him off to JAMES F. BYRNES, whom Truman was planning to name secretary of state. Szilard did not know that, but he suspected Byrnes would be given some position in the new administration, perhaps to be chief of the postwar atomic energy program.

In late May 1945 Szilard met with Byrnes. When Szilard argued against employing the weapon, Byrnes indicated that the United States had already spent $2 billion on it, and that funds would not be made available for postwar research of atomic energy unless the bomb was used. Byrnes also emphasized that use of the bomb would frighten the Russians and probably allow the United States to manage them more easily in Eastern Europe. Byrnes asked Szilard if he would want the Soviets to remain in Hungary indefinitely. Szilard said no, but he was more concerned with a potential arms race than with Hungary at that moment. Byrnes noted the contention of Manhattan Project director General LESLIE R. GROVES that the Soviets would not have access to uranium, but Szilard said this was not true. Byrnes in the end did not take Szilard's arguments to heart.

Szilard did not give up. He and other scientists submitted a report to Secretary of War HENRY L. STIMSON about the perils of an arms race and called for a demonstration of the bomb for the Japanese to observe rather that militarily use the bomb. This effort failed. Szilard than circulated among the Manhattan Project scientists a petition against the weapon's use, which affirmed that to do so would be immoral. This, too, changed nothing, and the United States dropped two atomic bombs on Japan.

Szilard was the major scientific opponent of the 1945 May-Johnson bill that would have secured control of atomic energy for the military and limited the dissemination of atomic knowledge. In September Szilard prepared a memorandum suggesting that only atomic scientists be appointed to the projected Atomic Energy Commission (AEC). He insisted on freedom of scientific communication and opposed the rigid espionage provision concerned with restricting the diffusion of knowledge. In testimony against the proposed bill in October, he maintained that only international control could prevent a ruinous arms race.

Concerned that Representative ANDREW J. MAY (D-Ky.) was trying to ram the bill through Congress, Szilard began a major lobbying effort against it. He initiated a write-in campaign by scientists demanding extensive hearings on the bill and called press conferences at which he objected to the brevity of the House Military Affairs Committee's one-day hear-

ing. He succeeded in persuading Edward Levi, a noted legal scholar, to write an article pointing out the legal defects of the bill. As a result of Szilard's pressure, May agreed to continue hearings. Although May managed to report the bill out of committee, Szilard mobilized a campaign in the Senate to defeat the measure. In February 1946 President Truman came out publicly against military control. In December 1945 Senator BRIEN MCMAHON (D-Conn.) introduced an alternative bill structured around civilian control. Szilard and Einstein organized a committee of scientists to raise money to lobby for the proposal. However, Szilard, by that time engaged in teaching biology at the University of Chicago, did not play a major role in securing the bill's passage. Instead, he proposed direct negotiation with Soviet scientists on international control of atomic power. But Szilard's biographers William Lanouette and Bela Silard note that his schemes regarding arms control were "too visionary" and "too quixotic" for the times. He even wrote Soviet dictator Joseph Stalin and urged him to address Americans often over the radio to ease tensions. The U.S. government would not give its permission to send the letter, so Szilard published it, but to no effect. When the Soviets exploded their own atomic bomb in 1949, he called upon the United States to dissolve NATO and negotiate a treaty to eliminate A-bombs. After Truman announced the United States would build a hydrogen bomb, Szilard warned that adding cobalt to H-bombs could lead to a nuclear fallout that would obliterate mankind. This tactic to scare the administration into abandoning the superbomb failed miserably. He continued to pursue his idea of bringing American and Soviet scientists together to discuss arms control, but to no avail.

Szilard continued his campaign for international control of atomic energy during the 1950s. He won the Atoms for Peace award in 1960. Appointed resident fellow at the Salk Institute for Biological Studies at La Jolla, California, in 1964, he died there on May 30 of that year.

—AES

T

Taber, John
(1880–1965) *member of the House of Representatives*

A descendant of New York State politicians, John Taber was, born on May 5, 1880, in Auburn, New York. He received his B.A. from Yale in 1902, and, after a year's study at New York Law School, he was admitted to the state bar and began practice with his father's firm of Taber and Brainerd. He also became active in Republican politics. In 1922 Taber was elected to the U.S. House, where he represented a conservative Republican district in upstate New York.

During his 30 years in the House, Taber established a conservative record, voting against most New and Fair Deal social legislation. He initially opposed Roosevelt's foreign policy but early in 1941 spoke out forcefully for aid to U.S. allies. Taber maintained his conservative domestic stance during the Truman administration. He voted for most antiunion legislation, including the Case labor disputes bill and the Taft-Hartley Act, and opposed the modified full employment bill of 1945. He supported the 1952 Smith Amendment requesting the president to invoke the Taft-Hartley Act against the steelworkers' strike of that year. Taber also backed the anticommunist legislation of the period, including making the House Un-American Activities Committee a permanent body, the Mundt-Nixon bill, and the McCarran Internal Security Act.

The congressman, who was ranking member of the Appropriations Committee during the Roosevelt administration and chairman of the panel from 1947 to 1949 and 1953 to 1955, gained a reputation as a foe of federal expansion and of government spending. In 1946 he opposed continuation of the Office of Price Administration, calling it "the chief promoter of inflation in America." He maintained that its "ridiculous regulation and penalties imposed upon those who would produce" had promoted shortages. The following year he voted for the Republican tax cut vetoed by Truman, who had claimed it would have fanned inflation and given disproportionate relief to persons with high incomes. Taber also opposed raising the minimum wage to 75 cents an hour in 1949.

In his years on Capitol Hill Taber's name became synonymous with vigorous budget cutting. To "taberize" meant to make large cuts in budgets or force large staff reductions. He was variously known as "the watchdog of the Treasury," "John (Cash and Carry) Taber," and "the Fiscal Vigilante." As chairman of the Appropriations Committee, he was one of the most powerful men in Washington. "His influence," wrote Cabell Phillips, "does not extend far beyond the field of appropriations, but in this it is paramount."

During the Truman administration Taber unsuccessfully moved to cut the president's $37.5 billion budget for 1947 by $6 billion. When he failed Taber said, "We will be back and at it again next year. We will hear screams from new directions. If they don't scream we will not know we are doing a job." Three years later he unsuccessfully attempted to reduce the $31.4 billion omnibus funds bill by $600 million. One of Taber's favorite targets was the federal bureaucracy. In 1947 he announced his goal of reducing the number of federal employees by one million, a cut of almost 50 percent. He failed, but a large number of federal workers were discharged because of his budget cuts.

Taber was a vigorous foe of foreign aid. He voted for aid to Greece and Turkey in 1947 and the Marshall Plan in 1948 but consistently demanded reductions in appropriations for the programs. After a visit to Europe in 1947, he announced that he thought an ambitious foreign aid plan was unnecessary. The following year he unsuccessfully attempted to cut funds for the Marshall Plan. The House acquiesced to reductions of $1.5 billion in the program during the spring of 1948, but most of this sum was eventually restored. Taber later voted against funds for the North Atlantic Treaty Organization and for the Point Four program. He also opposed the Korean Aid Act.

Taber remained an important force in the House throughout the 1950s. He continued his opposition to foreign aid and social legislation. During the latter half of the decade, he was particularly vehement in his opposition to public works. Taber opposed most New Frontier legislation. In 1962 he announced he would not seek reelection. Taber died on November 22, 1965, in his hometown of Auburn, New York. (See *The Eisenhower Years* Volume)

—RSG

Taft, Robert A(lphonso)
(1889–1953) *member of the Senate*

Robert A. Taft was born on September 9, 1889, in Cincinnati, Ohio, the son of William Howard Taft, 27th president and 10th chief justice of the United States. Robert Taft attended the Taft School, a prestigious boys preparatory school in Watertown, Connecticut, founded and run by his uncle. Taft graduated first in his class at Yale in 1910 and at Harvard Law School in 1913. He turned down a clerkship with Supreme Court justice Oliver Wendell Holmes and joined the Cincinnati law firm of Maxwell and Ramsey, where he served for three and a half years at token pay. In 1917, having been refused twice for the army because of his poor eyesight, Taft joined the staff of the Food Administration headed by HERBERT HOOVER. He traveled to Europe to organize relief efforts and was at Hoover's side in Paris during the Versailles Conference in 1919.

Taft won a seat in the Ohio State Assembly in 1920. He served for six years, becoming majority leader and finally speaker. He retired in 1926 to devote his attention to his law firm, Taft, Stettinius, and Hollister, with which he was associated for the rest of his career. In 1930 he won election to the Ohio State Senate. He was defeated for reelection two years later, a victim of the Roosevelt landslide and an unpopular tax program he had pushed

through the state legislature. In 1936 he was Ohio's favorite-son candidate for president. His candidacy was designed, in part, to give him statewide exposure in anticipation of a later bid for the Senate.

Taft was elected to the U.S. Senate in 1938. A master of detail and an expert in parliamentary procedure, he immediately emerged as the leader of the Republican minority in the upper house. Taft represented the midwestern, conservative-isolationist wing of the GOP. He repeatedly denounced what he viewed as Roosevelt's wasteful social programs and sloppy administration. Taft warned that the growth of the federal government was hazardous to individual liberties. He resisted Roosevelt's attempts to aid Western allies prior to Pearl Harbor, believing such assistance would drag the United States into the war. His stand earned him the opposition of the Eastern, internationalist, wing of the Republican Party. Combined with his awkwardness as a campaigner, his foreign policy positions helped defeat his 1940 bid for the Republican presidential nomination.

With the death of Senate Minority Leader Charles L. McNary (R-Ore.) in 1944, Taft became de facto Republican leader. He declined to formally accept the post, which carried with it many time-consuming bureaucratic duties. He preferred, instead, to direct the Republicans from his position as chairman of the Republican Policy Committee. The post allowed him to concentrate on the substance rather than the forms of leadership.

In the aftermath of World War II Taft and other conservatives rallied to try to slash Leviathan government. With his help, the Senate did away with the excess profits tax in early 1946. Although he did believe the government played a counter-cyclical role in the economy, he kept faith otherwise with balanced budget dogma to the point where he thought Congress had cut corporate and income taxes too much just after the war ended.

Taft led the battle against Truman's price controls in the postwar era. He succeeded in eliminating them by August 1946. He argued that price controls should be lifted on goods that would permit profit margins that would reflect increases in the cost of living since October 1941. This would increase incentives to produce to meet demand and would stabilize prices. Many senators agreed and Congress passed a bill renewing price controls with that provision. Truman, however, vetoed the bill even though congressional Democratic leaders said that was the best they could get. Prices skyrocketed and a short time later Truman signed a bill similar in effect to the one he vetoed.

To those who did not know him, Taft seemed reserved and cold. He was intolerant of ignorance or obtuseness. Yet he won the respect of many senators from both parties because of his vast capacity for work, his command of issues, his lack of pretense, his trustworthiness, and his willingness to consult all factions. WALTER LIPPMANN said of him, "The inner man was the solidest part of Taft, and at the core he was so genuine and just, so rational and compassionate that he commanded the confidence of men when he could never convince them."

Taft's conservativism was shaped by his reverence for the Constitution and his belief in the freedom of the individual. One of his most controversial stands was his denunciation of the Nuremberg trials of 1946. They "violated that fundamental principle of American law," he said, "that a man cannot be tried under an ex post facto statute. . . . About this judgement there is a spirit of vengeance and vengeance is seldom justice." Taft doubted the worth of many social welfare programs. Yet he believed that the government should ensure an economic "floor" for all citizens because it was a necessity for the enjoyment of freedom. He therefore supported aid to education and became a leader in the fight for federal housing. His views on civil rights reflected the importance he placed on the freedom of the individual. He supported bills against lynching and the poll tax. Yet he opposed the establishment of a Fair Employment Practices Commission with powers of enforcement as an infringement on the employer's rights.

The problems of labor occupied much of Taft's attention during the early postwar years. Taft was distressed by the wave of strikes that engulfed the nation in 1945 and 1946 and supported legislation to curb what he viewed as the excesses of labor unions. During April 1946 he helped guide through the Senate the Case labor disputes bill. The measure, presented by conservative FRANCIS H. CASE (R-S.Dak.), provided for a 30-day cooling off period and fact-finding procedures before strikes could be called. It also permitted injunctions against certain union activities and made both unions and management liable to suits for breach of contract. In addition, the bill prohibited organized boycotts to force employers to come to terms with unions. Truman vetoed the measure in June.

Despite his support of the stringent bill, Taft refused to back Truman's call on May 25, 1946, for power to draft strikers in response to a nationwide railroad strike. The House, influenced by the crisis, approved the legislation within hours. Taft, however, denounced the proposal. It "violates every principle of American jurisprudence," he said. Taft joined New Deal liberal senator CLAUDE PEPPER (D-Fla.) in delaying Senate consideration of the bill. When the Senate took up the measure three days later, the crisis had passed and the bill was defeated.

As leader of the majority party in the 80th Congress, Taft had his choice of committee chairmanships. He relinquished his place on the Finance Committee and accepted the less prestigious post of chairman of the Labor Committee so that he could personally supervise revision of the labor law. Taft wanted to preserve collective bargaining and the right to strike, but he also wanted to define and prohibit unfair labor practices in much the same way that the Wagner Act had defined unfair management practices.

Both the House and the Senate worked on labor revision during the spring of 1947. The Senate bill was molded by Taft. In order to maintain the support of both the conservative and liberal wings of the Republican Party to override an anticipated presidential veto, he produced a moderate measure. It called for an end to the closed shop, prohibited coercion of workers by union leaders, defined unfair labor practices, set up restrictions on welfare and pension plans, and established penalties for mass picketing. Although Taft had little interest in the provision, he accepted an amendment by Senator JOHN L. MCCLELLAN (D-Ark.) requiring an anticommunist oath from union leaders. He acquiesced to demands for an 80-day cooling off period, though he believed that the effects of walkouts had been exaggerated. Taft adamantly opposed conservative demands that the president be given power to seize struck industries. That provision was not adopted.

In order to maintain the support of the more liberal segments of the Republican Party, Taft compromised on the issue of how to control secondary boycotts and jurisdictional strikes. Taft originally wanted to seek injunctions in court. However, liberals such as IRVING M. IVES (R-N.Y.) charged that it might lead to a return to the days of collusion between management and antilabor judges. Taft accepted a compromise merely permitting employers to sue unions for damages incurred from the boycotts. He also acquiesced to a liberal demand by Ives that there be no limits on industrywide bargaining, although he would have liked to restrict the practice. The House, on the other hand, passed a much more stringent measure. It included many of the provisions of the Senate bill but added others banning industrywide bargaining and prohibiting employer contributions to welfare funds in which the union played an administrative role. In the conference committee, Taft was unwavering on those elements he believed central to the Senate position. The result was a bill that reflected his more moderate position. The House provisions on industrywide bargaining and employer contributions were rejected. The Taft-Hartley Act outlawed the closed shop and use of closed shop hiring halls, permitted suits for damages in breach of contract or as a result of economic losses from secondary boycotts, and gave the president the authority to request an 80-day cooling off period in strikes imperiling the national health and safety. It required a noncommunist affidavit from union officials and forbade various types of employer payments to unions. The act also reorganized the National Labor Relations Board. Congress sent the bill to Truman in early June. The president, persuaded that he would need labor's support in the coming election, vetoed it. Both the House and Senate overrode the veto.

Taft was never able to dominate foreign policy as he did domestic. He had reservations about the Truman administration's postwar foreign program. Nevertheless because of a continuation of wartime bipartisanship policy, he never commanded sufficient support to do more than raise questions and voice objections. Taft opposed the establishment of the International Monetary Fund, doubting its effectiveness in establishing stable exchange rates on a multinational basis. He opposed the World Bank even more strenuously, objecting to the concept of official investment abroad. Such investments, Taft suggested, would lead foreigners to think of Americans as "absentee landlords."

Taft voted for the UN Charter in 1945, but only after noting that the Security Council vetoes would make the United Nations effective solely in those matters about which the big powers agreed. He would have preferred establishing a strong international legal order, with a strong international court, rather than an organization based upon a balance of power. Taft also took exception to the appar-

ent absence of a congressional role in determining how to cast American votes at the UN.

During the spring of 1945 Taft voiced his fears that U.S. military and official economic presence abroad would lead to imperialism. He returned to this theme regularly in the next several years. It became among the most consistent objections he raised to the expanding American presence overseas. Taft opposed the 1947 Greek-Turkish aid bill, designed to prevent a Communist takeover in the area. He questioned the strategic importance of the area and pointed out that intervention so near the Russian border might force Soviet retaliation. Nevertheless, when Truman presented his plea for aid in terms of a fight against communism, Taft voted for the measure. He believed that to deny the funds under such circumstances would be a sign of American weakness. Taft raised the same questions about the Marshall Plan in late 1947 and 1948. Again he ultimately voted for the proposal because he thought the circumstances demanded it. But he attempted unsuccessfully to cut funding for the year from $597 million to $400 million. The House tried to cut it further. However Taft, who was seeking the presidential nomination, announced, after consulting with the GOP Policy Committee, that the Senate's appropriation represented a "moral commitment." He warned that the Senate would remain in session until that commitment was met. The House backed down.

Taft refused to support the ratification of the North Atlantic Treaty in 1949. He questioned whether America's willingness to supply arms to Europe would act as more of a deterrent to the Soviets than would the atomic bomb. It would, he insisted, give the Russians the impression that the United States was preparing for eventual aggressive action. Taft foresaw even graver dangers. "We have quietly adopted a tendency," he said, "to interfere in the affairs of other nations, to assume that we are a kind of demigod and Santa Claus to solve the problems of the world . . . It is easy to slip into an attitude of imperialism where war becomes an instrument of public policy rather than its last resort." Taft voted against the treaty and futilely fought subsequent requests for arms for the alliance.

Taft opposed Truman's containment policy not only because it suggested imperialism but also because it expanded the president's power to commit the United States to a position in the world without congressional authorization. During the debate on the North Atlantic Treaty, he warned that the pact would give the president the power to enter into a European war without consulting Congress for the 20-year term of the agreement. Taft also worried about the economic consequences of so active a policy. He suggested that it would distort the federal budget, leading to excessive deficits and drawing money away from domestic needs as the government strained to finance the bloated defense establishment.

Although Taft opposed U.S. intervention in Europe, he was ambivalent about American involvement in the Far East. He never really developed a coherent policy on the U.S. role in Asia. In 1948 he said, "I believe very strongly that the Far East is ultimately even more important to our future peace than is Europe." He supported sending military equipment to Chiang Kai-shek (Jiang Jieshi) and criticized the Truman administration for not doing more to prevent the "fall" of China to the Communists in 1949. After the North Koreans invaded South Korea in June 1950, he charged that the administration's omission of Korea in its statements defining the American defense perimeter had encouraged the attack. He supported Truman's commitment of ground troops to the conflict and joined General DOUGLAS MACARTHUR in recommending that the Nationalist Chinese be permitted to invade mainland China.

Yet while backing the president he also made statements critical of the administration. A month after endorsing Truman's action in Korea, he told reporters, "I would have stayed out," and that if he were the president, "he would get out and fall back to a defensible position in Japan and Formosa." While supporting MacArthur, Taft opposed using either American troops or the atomic bomb in China.

Taft's confusion was a result of his concentration on domestic affairs. More important, he was torn between his desire to stop communism where it appeared most threatening and his opposition to overseas involvement. In part, his ambivalence was due to partisan considerations. Far Eastern policy appeared to be a good election issue.

Partisanship warred with conflicting principles in Senator Taft's response to McCarthyism as well. When Senator JOSEPH R. MCCARTHY (R-Wisc.) first charged in February 1950 that there were Communists in the State Department, Taft ignored him. But in March, while still expressing private reservations about McCarthy's handling of evidence and his harassment of witnesses, Taft endorsed his

allegations of Communist influence in the State Department. Taft's ambivalence about McCarthy continued throughout his career. On the one hand he was genuinely alarmed at American policy in Asia and was an ardent anticommunist. He also felt it a good partisan issue. On the other, his sense of order and belief in the freedom of the individual made McCarthy's measures distasteful. Torn between conflicting emotions, Taft was unable to act.

Known as "Mr. Republican," Taft enjoyed the respect of politicians throughout the nation. Nevertheless, he never achieved his greatest goal: the presidency. Internationalists within the party opposed him, and he lacked the overwhelming popular support to overcome their opposition. His 1944 presidential campaign was a model of bad management. Taft concerned himself with discussing the issues and allowed reactionary party hacks to run his organization. They resisted innovative media techniques and attempts at emphasizing the more liberal portions of Taft's record.

Even more important than the poorly conducted campaign was Taft's own ineptness as a candidate. His speeches were intelligent but uninspiring. A shy man, he had a peculiar air of preoccupation in small groups of strangers. People he met for the first time found him cold and unresponsive. There was a widely held feeling within the party that Taft, whatever his distinction as a senator, was not a magnetic candidate and so a risky nominee.

Taft and Dewey were the strongest candidates at the Philadelphia Convention in 1948. But after two ballots it was clear that unless Dewey opponents could be gathered around a single alternative candidate, the New York governor would win. Taft asked Stassen, who was running a poor third, to quit in his favor. Stassen refused, and Taft withdrew, endorsing Dewey.

In 1952 many of the same factors that had worked against Taft in 1948 hurt him again. His foreign policy stands continued to lose him support and push Republicans closer to the popular general DWIGHT D. EISENHOWER. While improving as a campaigner, Taft continued to be awkward and occasionally insensitive in ways that caught the media's attention. His organization was more efficient in 1952 than it had been in 1948. Still there were blunders that emphasized his weakness. Having decided to remain out of the New Hampshire primary, Taft, at the urging of several advisers, entered at the last moment, too late to defeat the well-organized Eisenhower drive. Taft lost again a week later in Minnesota, where both he and the general were write-in candidates, and then in mid-April in New Jersey. He had entered the New Jersey primary despite the opposition of the Republican governor and the party's organization. He did manage to win the Wisconsin primary, but then became embroiled in a dispute over delegate selection in Texas. There pro-Taft and pro-Eisenhower forces battled it out in the election of delegates. The Taft supporters dominated the small Texas Republican Party, but the Eisenhower backers called upon Independents and Democrats to attend precinct caucuses to overwhelm the pro-Taft regular Republicans. The two sides hurled accusations at each other and sent rival delegations to the Chicago convention. Taft came up with what he thought and later historians have argued was a fair division of the delegates, but Eisenhower supporters claimed the Taftites were trying to steal delegates and made the issue a moral one. At the convention Eisenhower partisan Arthur B. Langlie, governor of Washington, offered a resolution (the "Fair Play" Amendment) stating that disputed delegates could not vote until their fate was decided by undisputed delegates. A loss on this vote would probably presage a Taft defeat. The convention approved the Fair Play Amendment, showing that Eisenhower had the upper hand. Taft then lost a vote on some disputed Georgia delegates, an issue on which he could plausibly argue that his delegates should be seated. This vote effectively dashed Taft's hopes. When the nominating vote came Eisenhower was just short of a majority. Minnesota switched some of its votes to Ike to carry him over the top. As Taft biographer James Patterson pointed out, after 20 years out of the White House, most Republicans were not going to take a chance on a man who, many observers said, could not win, and instead they went with a war hero.

Taft sat out the early stages of the general campaign. By September Eisenhower was anxious for his active support. Taft's coolness had become an embarrassment. After a series of preliminary maneuvers between aides. Taft and Eisenhower met at the general's home on Morningside Heights in New York City. Taft emerged from the meeting with a commitment from Eisenhower that as president he would attempt major cuts in the federal budget, defend the Taft-Hartley Act, and not discriminate against Taft supporters in filling federal positions. The two had also decided that their disagreements

on foreign policy were only "differences of degree." The press labeled the accord "the surrender at Morningside Heights," but it brought Taft aggressively into the campaign and helped Eisenhower.

Taft became majority leader when the Eisenhower landslide brought in a Republican Congress. He did an effective job of uniting his party behind the new administration. He and Eisenhower became extremely close, and Taft, in the first few months of the Eisenhower administration, enjoyed more influence than ever before. By late spring 1953 Taft was seriously ill with inoperable cancer. He retired as majority leader in June, selecting as his successor Senator WILLIAM F. KNOWLAND (R-Calif.). He died on July 31, 1953, in New York City. (See *The Eisenhower Years* Volume)

—CSJ

Talmadge, Herman E(ugene)
(1913–2002) *governor*

Born on August 9, 1913, in McRae, Georgia, Herman E. Talmadge was the son of Eugene Talmadge, a fiery white supremacist and anti–New Deal orator who was governor of Georgia during the 1930s and 1940s. After earning his law degree from the University of Georgia in 1936, Herman managed his father's unsuccessful bid for a U.S. Senate seat in 1938 and his gubernatorial reelection campaign in 1940.

When his father entered the Democratic gubernatorial primary in May 1946, young Talmadge was again campaign manager. As in previous races the Talmadges rallied the poor farmers of Georgia's southern lowlands by promising to restore the white primary, which had been declared unconstitutional by the U.S. Supreme Court. The former governor was renominated, but he became seriously ill shortly before the state Democratic convention. Herman spoke for him, but not too long before the general election—in which Eugene was unopposed—a political ally of the Talmadges asked Herman what would happen if Eugene died before he could take office. The Georgia constitution was not clear on the matter but Talmadge's people thought if one of their own could get second place in a write-in vote he might be chosen by the state legislature if his father died before he could take the oath. So the Talmadge forces arranged a write-in campaign for Herman to counter any such move from anti-Talmadge politicians. Shortly before he was to be inaugurated Eugene Talmadge died.

A fierce controversy then ensued between the Talmadge and anti-Talmadge factions of the Democratic Party.

In January 1947 the state legislature chose Herman Talmadge to succeed his father. The outgoing governor, Ellis G. Arnall, however, refused to surrender his office. Talmadge then seized control of the state capitol building and the governor's mansion with the aid of units of the state police and the National Guard. Shortly afterward Arnall abdicated his claim to the governorship in favor of incoming lieutenant governor Melvin E. Thompson, who took the oaths for both lieutenant governor and governor. Talmadge continued to occupy the executive departments but, after 67 days of dual power in Atlanta, the state supreme court awarded the office to Thompson. In his memoirs Talmadge complained that the Georgia Supreme Court had not been disturbed "by the philosophical difficulties of considering a corpse to be a legal person or declaring a dead man governor." He also noted that Arnall later admitted that he knew how Georgia's high court would rule.

The issue was finally resolved in a special primary election between Talmadge and Thompson in 1948. Adopting his father's campaign trademarks—red suspenders and chewing tobacco—Talmadge managed to project a suitably rustic image and to skillfully exploit the racial fears of rural whites. The voters awarded him a majority of both the popular and the county unit votes (the Georgia Democratic Party considered each county a unit allotted a specific number of votes).

While in office, Talmadge greatly increased expenditures for health, education, and welfare, particularly for vocational schools, roads, and mental hospitals.

However, the tax system did not raise enough revenue to carry out his ambitious program. He wanted to turn state property taxes over to the localities and eliminate "nuisance" taxes. Increasing the highway use taxes would not have raised much money, and hiking the income tax would drive away business. Talmadge opposed a sales tax at first because it was regressive and thought to be political suicide. However, after his reelection in 1950, the governor asked for a 3 percent sales tax. It was approved along with a lower state property tax and

the elimination of 130 nuisance taxes. State tax revenue more than doubled in three years.

At the same time he strove to prevent Georgia blacks from participating in politics. During his election campaign Talmadge had promised to establish a new voter registration system, based on educational requirements, that would have barred 80 percent of the state's blacks from voting. The law was enacted but never enforced after Talmadge's followers discovered that it would disqualify an equally large number of poor white voters. Talmadge also made an unsuccessful attempt to revive the poll tax, which had been repealed in 1945, as an additional means of restricting the black vote.

In 1950 Talmadge's administration faced serious financial problems, and the opposition, again led by Thompson, put up a strong challenge to his renomination in the gubernatorial primary that year. In his campaign Talmadge repeatedly stressed the threat posed to white supremacy by the Truman administration's proposed Fair Employment Practices Commission. Pointing out his own unambiguous commitment to segregation, he portrayed Thompson, who had ties to the administration, as an ally of integrationists. As a result, Thompson spent most of his time denying Talmadge's accusations rather than criticizing the governor's financial policies. Talmadge won renomination, with a majority of county votes and a narrow plurality of popular ballots.

Recognizing that urbanization in Georgia was rapidly eroding his rural base, Talmadge sponsored an amendment to the state constitution in 1952 that would have extended and formalized the county unit system, thus increasing the already disproportionate electoral weight of the least populous counties. The measure was defeated in a referendum by 29,000 votes. At the same time, however, Talmadge made overtures to city voters by encouraging new industries and expanding state services. Ultimately, he won a substantial urban following while retaining the allegiance of rural dwellers.

Talmadge's prestige in Georgia was further enhanced by his reaction to the Supreme Court's 1954 school desegregation decision. Shortly after the Court's ruling the governor put forward a constitutional amendment that permitted private schools to be substituted for the state's public school system. This anti-integration device was overwhelmingly endorsed by Georgia voters. As a result of his fight against desegregation, Talmadge achieved virtually complete domination of the state Democratic organization by the mid-1950s, driving his factional rivals out of politics altogether. In 1956 he won election to the Senate with 80 percent of the popular vote.

Despite his reputation for political demagoguery, Talmadge quickly earned the respect of fellow senators. During the Kennedy and Johnson administrations he compiled a conservative voting record, opposing both civil rights and social welfare legislation while supporting measures favorable to business interests. Although initially a strong supporter of the Vietnam War, Talmadge called on President Nixon to withdraw American troops from Indochina in 1971. During 1973 Talmadge served on the Watergate committee.

In 1978 Talmadge became involved in a scandal concerning an assistant, Daniel Minchew, who had diverted campaign funds and office expense money into a secret account for real estate speculation. Minchew claimed Talmadge had ordered him to do so for the senator's benefit. Talmadge proclaimed his innocence, but the Senate Ethics Committee recommended that he be denounced for his conduct. The full Senate approved the resolution by a lopsided margin. Talmadge ran for reelection in 1980 but was defeated by Republican Mack Mattingly. Talmadge died on March 21, 2002, in Hampton, Georgia. (See *The Kennedy Years, The Johnson Years, The Nixon/Ford Years* Volumes)

—TLH

Taylor, Glen H(earst)
(1904–1984) *member of the Senate*

Glen Taylor was born on April 12, 1904, in Portland, Oregon. He quit school at the age of 13 to work as an Idaho sheepherder. He later went into show business, billed as "the Crooning Cowboy." During the 1930s Taylor developed an interest in radical politics and tried to organize in Nevada and Montana a farmer-labor party. He ran unsuccessfully as a Democrat for a seat in the U.S. House in 1938 and a seat in the Senate in 1940 and in 1942. In all his campaigns he relied on his singing talent and cowboy attire to attract crowds to hear speeches in support of the expansion of the New Deal and the establishment of a United Nations. In 1944 Taylor finally won election to the Senate by less than 4,000 votes.

From 1945 to 1947 the "Cowboy Senator" impressed liberals with his consistent support of progressive legislation. Because of his colorful background and his excellent speaking ability, Taylor gained publicity for his pro–civil rights record and his antipathy toward corporations. He earned labor's respect for his opposition to the Case labor disputes bill, the Taft-Hartley Act, the Portal-to-Portal Pay Act, and his support for the Full Employment bill of 1945. He also backed federal aid to education and public housing.

Taylor broke very early with the Truman administration over foreign policy. Along with HENRY A. WALLACE, he questioned the administration's opposition to pro-Soviet governments in Eastern Europe while the United States wanted pro-American ones in Latin America. Taylor advocated world disarmament and giving the United Nations a monopoly over nuclear weapons. In late October 1945 he introduced a resolution to strengthen the UN "towards the ultimate goal of establishing a world republic based on democratic principles."

As relations with the Soviet Union became strained in 1946, Taylor cited a number of conspiracies he believed responsible for this threat to world peace. Although he voted for the 1946 loan to Great Britain, Taylor blamed part of the deterioration of relations on the British and especially Winston Chuchill, who warned against Soviet expansion. He found Wall Street and the military to have a strong negative role in shaping policy toward the USSR. Both, he maintained, had influenced the formation of the Truman Doctrine, which Taylor deplored. Taylor voted against the Greek-Turkish aid bill that implemented the doctrine. He rejected Truman's premise that the United States was fighting for freedom by aiding these two countries and charged that the governments of both were fascist. The last Greek election, Taylor maintained, was as rigged as the one in Communist Poland. How then, he asked, could the United States condemn the one in Poland and praise the one in Greece. Taylor suggested that the real reason the United States had entered the Greek-Turkish dispute was because of the need to protect sea lanes used by ships transporting Middle Eastern oil. Together with Senator CLAUDE PEPPER (D-Fla.), he introduced a substitute bill calling for the UN to administer the aid program and requiring the Greek government to distribute relief to all political factions in the nation.

Taylor supported Henry Wallace's defection from the Democratic Party in 1947. Two months after Wallace decided to run as the Progressive Party's candidate for the presidency, Taylor accepted the party's second spot. "I am not leaving the Democratic Party," he said. "It left me. Wall Street and the military have taken over. Now I will be free to fight this bipartisan coalition and all its works: Taft-Hartley, universal military training, the drive toward war, high prices and racial discrimination and suppressed civil liberties."

Taylor opened the campaign, as Wallace did, with an attack on the Marshall Plan. He ridiculed the humanitarian justifications for the program and maintained that the real reason for massive assistance was to open up Western Europe as a cheap market for surplus American goods. He introduced a resolution in the Senate to turn over the Marshall Plan to the United Nations. The proposal was defeated.

Liberals portrayed both Taylor and Wallace as unwitting dupes of the Communists. Taylor, however, refused to repudiate the Communist role in the campaign. This, he argued, would be "red baiting." He welcomed any Communist who supported his and Wallace's brand of "progressive" capitalism and the call for peace with Russia. If they were for these ideas, he said, they were good Americans.

Following the 1948 defeat, Taylor returned to the Senate, where he continued to oppose administration foreign policy. He voted against appropriation bills for the Marshall Plan and the North Atlantic Treaty, all of which he considered unnecessary American provocations of the cold war. In early 1950 the Idaho Democratic Party organization mobilized to defeat Taylor in the primary. Taylor belatedly tried to mend fences with the administration by supporting the Marshall Plan, the North Atlantic Treaty Organization, the Point Four program and by endorsing Truman's response to the Korean War. However, he lost the primary by 949 votes to a candidate who ran on an anticommunist platform. Taylor then disappeared from politics and became a successful businessman, establishing a wig-manufacturing company in Millbrae, California. He died of Alzheimer's disease on April 28, 1984, in Burlingame, California.

—JB

Teller, Edward
(1908–2003) *nuclear scientist*

Edward Teller was born on January 15, 1908, in Budapest, Hungary, the son of well-to-do Jewish parents. He acquired an undergraduate degree in chemical engineering in 1928 and went on to earn a doctorate in physical chemistry from the University of Leipzig. Aided by a Rockefeller fellowship, he continued his studies with renowned physicist Niels Bohr. When the Nazis came to power in 1933, Teller fled to England. He accepted an invitation to teach at Washington University in 1935 and became an American citizen six years later.

During World War II Teller worked on the Manhattan District Project, which developed the atomic bomb. Teller also investigated the possibility of producing a bomb through thermonuclear fusion—the merging of hydrogen atoms rather than the splitting of them. However, the work on the H-bomb, as it became known, was delayed because of priority given to the atomic bomb and because of technical difficulties. In 1944 the project encountered major obstacles when scientists found that an explosion would require extremely high temperatures then considered unattainable. Given his later work on the Strategic Defense Initiative (SDI), it is interesting to note that in a 1945 report Teller talked about the possibility of defensive weapons being used against nuclear missiles.

At the end of World War II Teller was invited to remain at Los Alamos, New Mexico, site of the Manhattan District Project, as director of the Theoretical Division. He said he would only accept the post conditional upon approval of a plan for 12 nuclear weapons tests per year. His request was refused, and Teller went to work at the University of Chicago in 1946.

During the postwar period Teller played a prominent role in the debate among nuclear scientists over the role of atomic energy and atomic weapons in defense. Teller was a major supporter of the Acheson-Lilienthal Proposal and the Baruch Plan for control of atomic energy. These plans called for the creation of an atomic development authority, under the auspices of the United Nations, that would control fissionable materials and production plants. The agency would report attempts to build atomic weapons to the UN whose members could take appropriate action. Under the plan the

United States would eventually transfer control of atomic energy to the UN agency in stages.

Teller urged further extension of the measures. Assuming that disarmament could take place only in an open society, he urged that the authority of the UN agency be increased. He proposed that nations be permitted to send an unlimited number of agents to other countries as representatives of the agency with the right of access to all nuclear facilities. He also thought that citizens of all nations should have the right and obligation to inform the agency of illicit atomic activity. Teller summed up his philosophy saying that "one will not gain real confidence in the stability of the world structure until tyranny has disappeared from the earth and freedom of speech is insured everywhere. To reach this goal may not be feasible in the immediate future. If the present proposal is put into effect, at least this much would have been achieved: we shall have a way to protect a man who has raised his voice for the purpose of safeguarding peace."

Soviet refusal to accept the Baruch Plan deeply troubled him. He gradually began to believe that no hope of accommodation with the Soviets was possible and that a nuclear arms race would develop. If this was the case, he asserted, in the United States should work to maintain its lead in part by continuing development of the hydrogen bomb.

Soviet explosion of an atomic device gave him a greater sense of urgency and prompted him to demand a crash program for the H-bomb. Physicist Ernest Lawrence encouraged Teller to promote such a program and Teller began recruiting scientists. He initially won over physicist Hans Bethe, but he backed out, and ENRICO FERMI would not join the project. JAMES B. CONANT wrote to J. ROBERT OPPENHEIMER that an H-bomb would be built "over my dead body"—a letter Oppenheimer shared with Teller. Oppenheimer also came out against the hydrogen bomb. The Atomic Energy Commission's General Advisory Committee (GAC) opposed the plan on moral and technical grounds. These scientists opposed an escalation of the arms race and an increase in U.S. reliance on atomic weapons, which might force the United States into a nuclear war with the Soviet Union. The device was viewed by several on the committee as a danger to humanity. The panel also questioned its cost effectiveness and its theoretical underpinnings. The GAC proposed gradual development. Teller met with Senator BRIEN

MCMAHON (D-Conn.), the author of the law that put atomic energy under civilian control. In his memoirs Teller believed that the meeting "injected enough facts into the political pipeline" to induce President Harry Truman to support Teller's position and order a crash program in early 1950, despite the objection of the GAC. Teller responded to the GAC's recommendation in the February edition of the *Bureau of Atomic Scientists Magazine.* "It is not the scientist's job to determine whether a hydrogen bomb should be constructed, whether it should be used, or how it should be used," he said. "This responsibility rests with the American people and with their chosen representatives."

During 1949, while the debate was raging, Teller had returned to Los Alamos and full-time work on the development of the weapon. His primary concern was overcoming difficulties with the extreme temperatures and the materials needed. These problems were successfully eliminated and a thermonuclear device was tested in the Pacific in November 1952. A completed hydrogen bomb was exploded in May 1954, preceding the first Soviet hydrogen bomb test by seven months.

Teller was not untouched by the Red Scare of the 1950s. He had been hired by the University of California at Los Angeles starting in the autumn of 1950. The university regents had put into effect a loyalty oath that some professors refused to take and who were fired. Teller had no objection to taking the oath himself but did object to dismissing faculty who refused. When he found out that one of the regents was using his acceptance of employment there as proof that the oath would not scare away prospective employees of high quality, Teller rejected the appointment. Fortunately, the University of Chicago was willing to keep him as a professor. In 1952 Teller went to work as director of the laboratory at Livermore, California, in association with the Berkeley Radiation Laboratory.

During the 1950s Teller remained a leading opponent of nuclear disarmament as demands for test ban treaties grew. In 1954 Teller was called upon to testify during hearings on Oppenheimer's security clearance. Although he initially stated his belief that the scientist "would not knowingly and willingly" endanger his country, he advised against reinstating clearance. He pointed to Oppenheimer's opposition to the production of the H-bomb as one of the reasons for his recommendation. In 1966

Teller was presented with the Fermi Award by the U.S. government for notable service in the field of atomic energy. Teller advocated and worked on SDI in the 1980s and 1990s. Teller died on September 9, 2003, in Palo Alto, California. (See *The Eisenhower Years*, *The Kennedy Years* Volumes)

—RB

Thomas, Elbert D(uncan)

(1883–1953) *member of the Senate*

Born on June 17, 1883, in Salt Lake City, Utah, Elbert D. Thomas graduated from the University of Utah in 1906. He then spent five years in Japan as a Mormon missionary. He then traveled and studied in Europe and Asia. Thomas returned to the University of Utah in 1914 and taught Latin and Greek. He obtained a doctorate in political science from the University of California in 1924. During the 1920s and 1930s Thomas was active in Democratic politics. He was elected to the U.S. Senate in 1932 in a campaign against conservative Republican Reed Smoot.

In the upper house Thomas was a vigorous supporter of the New Deal and of Franklin D. Roosevelt's foreign policy. He was a firm advocate of American aid to Great Britain before U.S. entry into World War II and a major planner of the War Labor Board. Thomas urged the bombing and invasion of Japan as the only way of ensuring its defeat. Nevertheless he recommended that Emperor Hirohito's palace be spared because of the reverence in which the emperor was held by the Japanese. He felt that maintaining the emperor in power would preserve some kind of order and stability in Japan at the end of the war. In domestic affairs, Thomas was known as a strong advocate of the rights of labor unions. He cosponsored measures in 1942 to guarantee union advances made during the New Deal in wartime. He was the U.S. delegate to International Labor Organization conferences held from 1944 to 1948. He opposed the Case labor disputes bill, the Taft-Hartley Act, and the Portal-to-Portal Pay Act.

Thomas continued his support of labor and progressive social legislation during the Truman period. As chairman of the Labor and Public Welfare Committee during the 81st Congress, he introduced a bill to raise the minimum wage to 75 cents an hour, which passed, and a measure to repeal the Taft-Hartley Act, which failed. The latter proposal, drafted by Secretary of Labor MAURICE J. TOBIN,

would have replaced the Taft-Hartley Act with a revised Wagner Act. It would have included a ban on certain types of jurisdictional strikes and secondary boycotts, and a means for settling strikes in vital industries and preventing strikes over interpretation of existing contract provisions. Despite Thomas's impassioned defense, the measure failed. He also supported federal aid to education and the National Housing Act of 1949.

Thomas supported Truman's foreign policy of containing the Soviet Union. He voted for the 1946 British loan, Greek-Turkish aid, the Marshall Plan, the North Atlantic Treaty, military aid to the North Atlantic Treaty Organization, and Point Four.

Thomas was a vigorous foe of the anticommunist crusade of the late 1940s. He spoke out against what he termed the House Un-American Activities Committee's violation of personal liberties during its hearings on Communist influence in the Hollywood film-making community. Thomas participated in the nationwide broadcast, "Hollywood Fights Back," in October 1947, in which he denounced the congressional proceedings. An enemy of Senator JOSEPH R. MCCARTHY (R-Wisc.), he joined New York senator IRVING M. IVES (R-N.Y.) in introducing a resolution in June 1950 to remove investigations of subversion from the Senate. They proposed that Congress delegate its authority to congressional investigating commissions composed of outsiders who would look into charges made by McCarthy and others. No action was taken on the bill.

As a result of Thomas's opposition to McCarthy, the right made him a target for defeat in 1950. In one of the dirtiest campaigns of the period, his Republican opponent, Wallace Bennett, castigated Thomas as the "darling of several un-American organizations." Opponents accused him of doing nothing to discourage liquor sales to minors or to end gambling and prostitution in his state. In addition, rumors were circulated that Thomas, a devout Mormon, had deserted his church. Thomas attempted to ignore his attackers and was unwilling to publicly discuss his religious beliefs. Without an issue, he spent most of his time defending his record. Despite the support of organized labor and professional educators, Thomas lost the race in November.

In 1951 Thomas was appointed high commissioner of the Trust Territory of the Pacific Islands. The territory was composed of 96 island groups comprising the Caroline, Marshall, and Marianas Islands. These islands were formerly held by Japan and were under American trusteeship and UN juris-diction preparatory to independence. During his brief tenure Thomas attempted to administer the islands for the benefit of the inhabitants rather than for American interests. Thomas died in Honolulu, Hawaii, on February 11, 1953.

—AES

Thomas, Elmer
(1876–1965) *member of the Senate*

Elmer Thomas was born on September 8, 1876, in Greencastle, Indiana. He graduated from Central Normal College in Danville, Indiana, in 1897 and was admitted to the state bar that same year. Three years later he moved to Oklahoma, where he became a real estate speculator and practiced law. In 1907 he was elected to the Oklahoma Senate and served until 1920. That year he ran unsuccessfully for a seat in the U.S. House. He was elected two years later. In 1926 Thomas won a seat in the Senate as a Democrat.

On Capitol Hill Thomas was a supporter of most New Deal programs. He regarded himself as a representative of the farmer, the "silver bloc," and veterans. He sponsored the "Thomas Amendment" to the Agricultural Administration Act of 1933, authorizing the president to abandon the gold standard. Thomas was a moderate on civil rights. He opposed antilynching and antisegregation bills as an unwarranted interference with states' rights, but he voted for the continuation of the Fair Employment Practices Commission after World War II. He also supported the Full Employment bill of 1945 and opposed the Case labor disputes bill, the Taft-Hartley Act, and the Portal-to-Portal Pay Act. From a state rich in natural gas, Thomas supported fellow Oklahoma senator ROBERT S. KERR's unsuccessful attempt to deregulate federal price controls over part of the industry.

As chairman of the Agriculture Committee, Thomas steadfastly supported the farmers' interests and worked for the removal of price controls on agricultural products. In June 1945 Thomas proposed to amend the Emergency Price Control and Stabilization Act to require a ceiling price for major processed farm products that reflected the cost of production plus a "reasonable profit." It was considered an inflationary scheme because it would apply to individual products rather than aggregate processors' profits. In June 1946 he asked for removal of

price controls on cotton, milk, poultry, livestock, fish, and grains. He supported the Russell amendment to the Minimum Wage Act that included costs of farm labor in computing parity price formulas.

Thomas was a supporter of high, rigid parity payments. During 1949 his committee held hearings on the administration's long-term agricultural policy, formulated by Secretary of Agriculture CHARLES F. BRANNAN. The program was a major departure from previous ones. Brannan called for direct payments to farmers when prices fell below support levels. Thomas's committee unanimously rejected the bill. Instead, it recommended a compromise, proposed by CLINTON P. ANDERSON (D-N.Mex.), that called for a sliding scale of 75 percent to 90 percent parity. The Agricultural Act of 1949 was a compromise between this and the House bill, offered by ALBERT GORE (D-Tenn.), that called for 90 percent parity for basic commodities. The final measure, backed by Thomas, provided ultimately for flexible price supports but for rigid ones during a transitional period.

Although he voted against the 1946 British loan, Thomas generally supported Truman's cold war foreign policy. He backed Greek-Turkish aid, the Marshall Plan, the North Atlantic Treaty, military aid to NATO, and Point Four.

During Truman's first administration, Thomas became involved in a growing scandal over cotton speculation. Denouncing such activity on the exchanges, where prices plummeted in October 1946, Thomas charged that a "bear raid" had depressed cotton prices by $255 million. Two years later a list released by Secretary of Agriculture Clinton P. Anderson revealed that Thomas's wife was a speculator in cotton futures. Thomas, in self-defense, explained that she had her own money "and I don't know what she does with it." In January 1948, a Senate Appropriations subcommittee investigating government officials involved in commodity futures speculation discovered that Thomas himself had been active in the commodity markets. He contented that his investments were "strictly income-producing" rather than speculative. He promised to disclose all his operations to the Senate. However, when Thomas's name was revealed on a subsequent list of speculators, he reversed his earlier statement. Nevertheless the panel tentatively cleared him of charges that he had used inside information to make a profit.

Thomas was defeated in the 1950 Democratic senatorial primary by Representative A. S. Mike Monroney (D-Okla.). He retired from public life at the end of the year and died in Lawton, Oklahoma, on September 19, 1965.

—AES

Thomas, J(ohn) Parnell
(1895–1970) *member of the House of Representatives*

The son of a former state legislator and Jersey City police commissioner, J. Parnell Thomas was born on January 16, 1895, in Jersey City, New Jersey. He was originally named John Parnell Feeney, Jr. His father died when he was young and Thomas later adopted his mother's maiden name. After attending the Wharton School and New York University Law School, he enlisted in the army in 1917.

Thomas became a bond salesman in New York City after the war. He left Wall Street to enter politics, first serving as mayor of Allendale, New Jersey, from 1926 to 1930. He was elected to the New Jersey Assembly in 1935 and 1936. The next year Thomas entered Congress as representative of the Seventh Congressional District. That solidly Republican area was composed mainly of affluent suburbs with a few scattered urban enclaves. Thomas, considered conservative and reliable, usually voted along with the Republican leadership. He quickly established himself as an unyielding foe of the New Deal.

Thomas also voted conservative in the Truman period. He supported the Case labor disputes bill, the Taft-Hartley Act, and the Republican tax cut of the 80th Congress and opposed making the school lunch program permanent and the National Housing Act of 1949. Yet he did vote for a bill of Representative VITO MARCANTONIO of the American Labor Party (ALP-N.Y.) to eliminate the federal poll tax.

A member of the Military Affairs Committee, Thomas supported several moves aimed at preparing the United States for war; he voted for the Selective Service Act and the arming of merchant ships in 1940, and for lend-lease in 1941. After World War II Thomas fought to end wartime wage and price controls. He also was vociferous opponent of private control of the development of atomic energy, maintaining that military control would prevent domination by "subversive" scientists.

Thomas emerged as a strong anticommunist shortly after being named to the original House Un-American Activities Committee (HUAC) in 1938. He backed Representative JOHN E. RANKIN (D-Miss.) in making the committee a permanent body. In 1947, when the Republican Party gained a majority in Congress, Thomas assumed the chairmanship of HUAC. He rose to national prominence in the two years that followed as a vigilant anticommunist crusader, concerned with the menace of internal subversion. A colorful leader and often abrasive interrogator, Thomas at times would become involved in heated arguments with "unfriendly" witnesses appearing before the panel. During one such outburst, Thomas told a lawyer, "The rights you have are the rights given you by this Committee. We will determine what rights you have and what rights you have not got before this Committee." Thomas felt communism had penetrated into all areas of American society, including the government. He remained suspicious of the New Deal, and was interested in links between Communists and liberals. Thomas saw his task as one of ferreting out Communists and "fellow travelers" from their "entrenched bridgeheads" in American life.

The committee made several attempts during Thomas's tenure at evolving legislation to control Communists within the United States. One proposed bill, to outlaw the Communist Party, met opposition from Thomas because he felt it would drive Communists underground. The measure was never reported out of HUAC. Another attempt, the Mundt-Nixon bill of 1948, sought to register the Communist Party and its "front organizations," but it died in the Senate. For the most part, Thomas was more interested in investigating and exposing communism than in creating legislation. HUAC became known for its highly publicized probes of Communist influence: the Hollywood hearings and the Hiss Case were the two most famous investigations launched by Thomas and his committee.

In October of 1947 Thomas turned HUAC to a scrutiny of Communist activity in the film industry. The Hollywood hearings focused national attention on the issue of internal subversion and featured the leaders of the movie industry and its stars. Thomas took the lead in closely questioning a small group of suspected Communists, mainly writers, about their activities. When asked about possible membership in the Communist Party, 10 witnesses, the so-called Hollywood Ten, refused to answer. They disputed

HUAC's right to pose questions about political or religious views. Among the 10 were RING LARDNER JR., son of the famous sportswriter, DALTON TRUMBO, and John Howard Lawson, once described as the "Grand Old Man of Hollywood communism." Many of the Hollywood Ten had been active in left-wing causes and some were, in fact, members of the Communist Party. They believed a constitutional question was involved in the HUAC investigation. Thomas was instrumental in pushing for contempt of Congress citations for the 10. All were found guilty and given light sentences.

The Hiss Case, HUAC's most famous investigation, was seen as proof by some that Communist subversion threatened the security of the nation. A former Communist, *Time* magazine editor WHITTAKER CHAMBERS, claimed involvement with an underground Communist cell in Washington during the early years of the New Deal. One of those Chambers implicated during his 1948 testimony was ALGER HISS, president of the Carnegie Endowment for International Peace. Hiss asked the Thomas Committee for a chance to deny the charges under oath. A respected New Deal lawyer and official, he claimed he had never met Chambers. That same day, August 5, President Truman called the investigation a "red herring." Thomas and several other members of HUAC then wanted to drop the investigation or turn it over to the Justice Department. But Representative RICHARD M. NIXON (R-Calif.) and chief counsel Robert E. Stripling pressed for a continuation. On August 17 Hiss and Chambers were brought together in New York for a face-to-face confrontation. Hiss admitted he had known Chambers in the 1930s as "George Crosley." On August 25 the confrontation was restaged in Washington with Hiss continuing to plead his innocence. Thomas observed that one of the two men would be tried for perjury. After two trials Hiss was eventually convicted on that charge in 1950.

Thomas captured headlines with his handling of other investigations. In 1947 he called attention to Gerhart Eisler, a man Thomas termed the "No. 1 agent of the Communist International." Eisler refused to cooperate with HUAC and fled to East Germany after being found guilty of contempt of Congress. HUAC also investigated the presence of Communists in the labor movement, focusing on the membership of the United Auto Workers and the United Electrical Workers. In March 1948 Thomas released a report characterizing EDWARD

Representative J. Parnell Thomas after being sentenced to 18 months in jail, 1949 *(Harry S. Truman Library, Harris and Ewing Photo, Beth Gore)*

U. CONDON, director of the National Bureau of Standards, as a weak link in America's atomic security. Condon denied any disloyalty and was cleared by both the Commerce Department and the Atomic Energy Commission.

Thomas and the committee came under fire during the Truman years for their tactics and goals. Some liberals and civil libertarians felt HUAC violated the rights of the accused by raising unsubstantiated charges. Thomas was attacked during the Hollywood hearings by the Committee for the First Amendment, a group led by Humphrey Bogart and Lauren Bacall, for jeopardizing personal freedoms. In 1947 four Democratic senators questioned the right of HUAC "to ask any man what he thinks on political issues." After the Condon investigation, in

1948 Truman singled out the Thomas Committee and charged it with creating a "totalitarian climate" and using "smear tactics."

In October 1948 a federal grand jury began investigating accusations of corruption made against Thomas by columnist DREW PEARSON. Thomas called it "cheap Pendergast politics," but took the Fifth Amendment before the grand jury. In November he was indicted on charges of padding his congressional payroll. When his health finally allowed prosecution of the case in 1949, Thomas pleaded no contest to the charges. He was fined $10,000 and sentenced to 6 to 18 months in jail. He resigned from the House on January 2, 1950, and served close to nine months in the federal prison at Danbury, Connecticut, before being paroled. (Ironically he had served in the same prison at the same time as Hiss.) Truman pardoned him in December 1950. Thomas returned to his home in Allendale, where he publicly proclaimed his innocence.

Thomas ran for his old congressional seat in 1954, calling himself "a fighter of the McCarthy type." His attempt at a political comeback was crushed by a large margin. In 1956 he moved to St. Petersburg, Florida, where he was active on the lecture circuit before his death in that city on November 19, 1970.

—JF

Thomas, Norman (Mattoon)
(1884–1968) *Socialist Party leader*

Norman Thomas was born on November 20, 1884, in Marion, Ohio. While he was a student at the Union Theological Seminary, he was influenced by the writings of Dr. Walter Rauschenbusch, whose theology stressed the social responsibility of the Protestant churches. Thomas received a bachelor of divinity degree in 1911 and became a pastor of the East Harlem Presbyterian Church in New York City. In 1916 he joined the Fellowship of Reconciliation, a religious pacifist group. That same year he undertook his first major political action, leading a group of pacifist clergymen in a protest against the draft law. Thomas opposed American involvement in World War I, and with ROGER N. BALDWIN, he helped found the National Civil Liberties Bureau (later known as the American Civil Liberties Union) to aid conscientious objectors.

Thomas joined the Socialist Party in 1918. That same year he ceased his religious activity. During the 1920s he emerged as the party's leader, replacing Eugene V. Debs. From 1928 through 1948 Thomas headed its national ticket in each presidential election. He received his greatest support in 1932, polling 844,000 votes. Afraid of the antidemocratic consequences for American domestic life, Thomas opposed U.S. entry into World War II. However, following Pearl Harbor he gave qualified support to the war effort. With the dropping of the atomic bombs in 1945, he made it his mission to prevent war with the Soviet Union even though he despised the Stalinist system. He worried the United Nations would become a league of empires rather than a democracy of nations. He pleaded with Americans to continue rationing food so devastated Europe could be fed with the surplus and spoke against imposing drastic punishment on Germany and Japan. He urged an end to the draft and a move toward disarmament.

He was delighted when Britain's Labour government granted India its independence, which made Prime Minister Clement Attlee a Socialist hero to Thomas. He tried to dissuade American liberals who were infatuated with Communist Russia. He complained to Secretary of Commerce HENRY A. WALLACE that in his concern to support friendly relations with the Soviets he seemed to ignore "the ruthlessness of Soviet imperialism, both in its treatment of the common man at home and in the occupied territories." According to Thomas's biographer W. A. Swanberg, it appeared the Socialist leader backed an alignment of the party with American conservatives in his aversion to Russia and opposing liberals in this area. Thomas responded he wanted "the liquidation of all forms of imperialism," whether American, Soviet, or European, and one of the reasons he opposed induction was that it was aimed at the Russians. He wanted peace with the USSR, but he wanted Americans to know the truth about it.

In 1946 Thomas appealed to labor and progressive leaders to help form a new political party. A large group of Socialist, labor, and farm organization leaders met to consider Thomas's proposal, but by the middle of that year DAVID DUBINSKY, head of the powerful International Ladies Garment Workers Union, declared his opposition to the proposal, and the movement collapsed.

Although Thomas questioned whether the Socialist Party should run a presidential candidate in 1948, he reluctantly accepted the presidential nomination to divert Socialist and peace votes from

Henry Wallace. Thomas was dubious of Wallace's candidacy because of the latter's naïveté about the Communists. After a poor showing in the election, Thomas called on the party to drop out of electoral politics. However, it was not until 1957, after two disastrous showings in presidential elections, that it voted to do so.

Thomas severely criticized Soviet expansionism and believed that the United States and the Soviets should renounce military force in favor of "competitive coexistence" in which Communists and capitalists would agree to vie ideologically and economically. He disagreed with GEORGE F. KENNAN's containment policy, but he also rejected WALTER LIPPMANN's desire to return to a balance-of-power international system. He wanted the United States to lead the way toward the diminution of national sovereignty and toward disarmament under international controls.

In August 1950 he visited President Harry S Truman and urged him to press the UN General Assembly for world disarmament under strict international inspection carried out by an international police force. Thomas asked Truman to promise that the United States would use the billions of dollars saved through disarmament to promote a greatly enlarged program to attack world hunger and poverty. In October Truman went before the UN Assembly to press Thomas's suggestions.

While Thomas denounced Soviet totalitarianism, he opposed the hysterical brand of domestic anticommunism, which he feared would be exploited by the extreme right wing to suppress civil liberties. He condemned the Mundt-Nixon bill and the House Un-American Activities Committee. He denounced Senator JOSEPH R. MCCARTHY's (R-Wisc.) anticommunist tactics and defended the rights of Communists to engage in legal political activities. However, he agreed with McCarthy that Communists should be expelled from places of responsibility.

In 1951 Thomas published *A Socialist's Faith*, which exposed his loss of fervor for unqualified socialism. Socialism should allow more private ownership than he had earlier propounded while nationalization should be circumscribed to the "commanding heights" of the economy. He did not want complete collectivization, as the Soviet Union had shown what a disaster that would be. He believed that capitalism's life was ebbing, but its death was still distant.

In 1957 Thomas and Norman Cousins helped found the Committee for a Sane Nuclear Policy

(SANE), which favored an end to nuclear testing. Thomas backed ADLAI E. STEVENSON for the 1960 Democratic presidential nomination and reluctantly supported John F. Kennedy in the general elections. In July 1963 he testified before a Senate committee in support of the administration's civil rights bill. He was an outspoken critic of the Johnson administration's Vietnam policy. In the fall of 1967 Thomas suffered a stroke. He died on December 19, 1968, in Huntington, New York. (See *The Eisenhower Years*, *The Kennedy Years*, *The Johnson Years* Volumes)

—EF

Thorp, Willard L(ong)

(1899–1992) *assistant secretary of state for economic affairs*

The son of a New England clergyman, Willard L. Thorp was born on May 24, 1899, in Oswego, New York. He graduated from Amherst College in 1920 with a degree in economics. He obtained an A.M. from the University of Michigan in 1921 and a Ph.D. from Columbia University three years later. He taught economics at Amherst in 1921 and 1922 and, after serving on the research staff of the National Bureau of Economic Research, became professor of economics in 1926. He also served as chief statistician for the New York State Board of Housing in 1925 and 1926. In 1933 Thorp was appointed director of the Commerce Department's Bureau of Foreign and Domestic Commerce. He served with various New Deal agencies from 1933 to 1935 and then became director of economic research for the investment firm Dun & Bradstreet, Inc.

Thorp returned to government service as deputy assistant secretary of state for economic affairs in 1945. That year he served as assistant to Secretary of State JAMES F. BYRNES and Assistant Secretary of State WILLIAM L. CLAYTON at the Paris Peace Conference. As U.S. representative on the Italian Economic Commission during 1946, he advocated leniency in Allied reparation demands on Italy.

Thorp was confirmed as assistant secretary of state for economic affairs in January 1947. At that post, the second highest in the department, he helped promote European reconstruction and defend administration policy before the United Nations. In August 1947 he headed a U.S. delegation to an Anglo-American conference on Ruhr coal production. He helped negotiate an agreement between the United States and Britain in September arranging for the joint operation of the mines (at that point run by Great Britain) in light of the British economic crisis. The pact also provided for improvements in housing, transportation, and labor relations.

Thorp headed up the Committee on the European Recovery Program, which had been established in late June 1947 to consider Secretary of State GEORGE C. MARSHALL's proposal to give assistance to Europe. Representatives of all departmental offices concerned with European recovery met as a group every Tuesday and Thursday evening in the Old State Department Building to discuss this issue. The members generally agreed that Western European economies must be integrated and made self-supporting in a three- to four-year period. Two years later Thorp noted that the United States should chip "away at sovereignty [in European nations] in limited areas" by creating "central institutions" to coordinate and control their economies. He also reviewed NSC-68 and contended that the document overestimated Russian economic capabilities.

During 1947 and 1948 Thorp served as U.S. spokesman before the United Nation's Economic and Social Council (UNECOSOC). He reasserted the Truman Doctrine granting aid to countries resisting communism and in 1948 defended the American system against Communist charges that the plight of workers in the United States was deplorable. Against Soviet opposition he won UN agreement for the International Bank for Reconstruction and Development and the International Monetary Fund to affiliate with UNESCO.

Thorp played a large part in the formulation of Truman's Point Four program of economic and technical assistance to underdeveloped nations. He presented it to UNECOSOC in February 1949 and asked that the UN Secretariat have a program to help underdeveloped countries ready by June to work in conjunction with the American plan. He recommended that the work be financed out of the UN budget and said that the United States would share its technical knowledge and encourage private capital investments in the backward areas. Thorp admitted the timetable for the program should "be measured in decades, not in years." In September 1949 he explained and defended the program before a skeptical House Foreign Affairs Committee. Thorp resigned from the UN Economic and Social Council in June 1950 to administer the plan. During his two years in office he advocated greater U.S. aid to developing nations.

After the Republican victory in November 1952, Thorp resumed his career as professor at Amherst. During the next three decades he served as State Department representative at important international conferences and wrote several books on economics and foreign trade. In *The Reality of Foreign Aid* (1971) he stressed the simultaneous need for the export of knowledge as well as capital to underdeveloped nations in order for foreign aid to be effective. He was critical of both the quantity and quality of U.S. assistance abroad, comparing the American record unfavorably with that of other countries. Thorp became professor emeritus at Amherst College in 1965. Thorp chaired the Pelham (Massachusetts) Finance Committee from 1977 to 1987 and was town treasurer from 1987 to 1990. He died on May 10, 1992, in Pelham, Massachusetts.

—AES

Thurmond, J(ames) Strom
(1902–2003) *governor, presidential candidate*

Born the son of a politician on December 5, 1902, in Edgefield, South Carolina, J. Strom Thurmond received a B.S. degree from Clemson College in 1923 and worked as a high school teacher for the next six years. He was admitted to the South Carolina bar and joined his father's law firm in 1930. Three years later Thurmond won election to the South Carolina Senate. Thurmond staunchly supported President Franklin Roosevelt's New Deal, and while in the legislature he supported a number of social welfare programs, including the state's first bill providing aid to the aged, the blind, and needy children. In 1938 Thurmond became a circuit judge. He enlisted in the army shortly after American entry into World War II, and was part of the airborne assault on D day.

Thurmond resumed his judgeship after being discharged from the service in 1946, but in May he resigned his post to run for governor. His conservative opponents in the Democratic primary charged him with being a New Dealer and hinted that he was receiving money from the Congress of Industrial Organizations. In fact Thurmond did claim the mantle of progressiveness and said he wanted to expand and modernize the state schools and universities and to pay the teachers higher salaries. He also called for higher wages for working people and more public health and social welfare programs. In the race Thurmond hardly mentioned race, although he paid the expected obeisance to segregation. He won his party's nomination, which was equivalent to election in one-party South Carolina. As governor, Thurmond increased appropriations for education and health care facilities, led a successful drive to repeal the poll tax, and backed a minimum wage and maximum hour bill. He made a strong but unsuccessful effort to convict a white mob charged with lynching a black and appointed the state's first African American to the state board of medical examiners.

Although Thurmond was regarded as a moderate by his state's black leaders, he was a segregationist. In October 1947 he criticized the recommendation of President Truman's Committee on Civil Rights, which had called for federal legislation to protect black and other minority rights in voting, housing, and employment. Thurmond believed that such measures would be unconstitutional, an encroachment on states' rights. He also opposed federal control of oil-rich tidelands claimed by certain states. In 1948 he backed Mississippi governor FIELDING L. WRIGHT's call for Southern Democrats to break with Truman and the national party if they continued pressing for civil rights. In February 1948, following the presentation of Truman's civil rights program to Congress, the Southern Governors' Conference appointed Thurmond to head a delegation to call on Democratic National Chairman J. HOWARD MCGRATH. The delegation asked him to have Truman withdraw the offending legislation in return for southern support in the 1948 presidential election. The chairman refused. The southern governors then recommended that the states choose delegates to the Democratic National Convention opposed to Truman and pick presidential electors who would refuse to vote for any candidate favoring civil rights. The governors hoped to deny either of the two major party candidates an electoral majority and throw the election into the House of Representatives, where either a southern president would be chosen or a compromise candidate found.

In May Democrats from Mississippi and Alabama held a conference in Jackson, Mississippi, to solidify plans for the Democratic National Convention. Thurmond delivered a keynote address laden with anti–civil rights emotionalism. He exaggerated Truman's civil rights stance and declared that "all the laws of Washington, and all the bayonets of the Army cannot force the Negroes into Southerners' homes, schools, churches . . . and places of amusement." Thurmond suggested that

the Democratic National Committee be notified that southern delegates would not support civil rights nominees so that they could not be accused of "bolting or breaking faith with the party." The Jackson conference planned to reconvene at Birmingham, Alabama, following the national convention if a strong civil rights stand was not repudiated. Thurmond had the South Carolina state convention instruct delegates to the national convention to vote for him as a favorite son candidate, and not to support the president or anyone else who supported a strong civil rights program.

At the convention members of several southern delegations refused to accept the platform committee's moderate civil rights plank. They moved that the convention adopt the southern view, reject civil rights, and replace Truman at the head of the ticket. When the deadlocked meeting offered to restate the tepid civil rights endorsement of 1944, they refused the compromise. The southern delegations were divided between those who would take their fight outside the party and those who would not. Perhaps moved by southern intransigence, the convention then adopted the strong civil right plank pushed by HUBERT H. HUMPHREY and the liberal Democrats. It even added a commendation for the president's personal role.

At that point Mississippi and half the Alabama delegation walked out. (The Thurmond-controlled South Carolina delegation did not bolt because a largely African-American dissident delegation was ready to take their place.) At the subsequent Dixie caucus Thurmond shouted, "We have been betrayed and the guilty shall not go unpunished!" The remaining southern delegates united behind the candidacy of Senator RICHARD B. RUSSELL (D-Ga.), leader of the southern bloc in the Senate and who had refused any third-party role. Thurmond seconded Russell's nomination, transferring his state's votes to the Georgian. Russell delivered a ringing speech in defense of the South. He received 263 votes to Truman's 947, and the president was nominated.

The dissidents reconvened in Birmingham on July 17. With the exception of Mississippi's congressional delegation accompanied by Wright, almost all southerners in Congress refused to actively support a third-party move. Most southern politicians on the national level who knew Truman thought he had only a limited devotion to civil rights, and believed the fight should remain within the Democratic Party. (In addition they wanted to remain in the party so as not to lose their chairmanships of congressional committees that they were entitled to due to their seniority as Democrats.) Present were state officials, extreme segregationists, anti–New Deal Democrats, and representatives of corporate interests and the petroleum industry in the South. Some people in the oil industry favored Thurmond because of his support for state ownership of tidelands oil. Coastal states with offshore oil taxed companies less for drilling than the federal government did. They adopted a "declaration of principle" that supported segregation and called on "any other loyal Americans" to join in defeating "Harry Truman and THOMAS E. DEWEY and every candidate for public office who would establish a police state" in America. The conference nominated Thurmond for president and Wright for vice president and formally adopted the name of States' Rights Democrats. They were quickly dubbed "Dixiecrats" by the press. In accepting the nomination Thurmond denounced the federal antilynching bill and endorsed racial segregation. He rejected the "white supremacy" mantle, however, saying he would campaign as an "open progressive" on the states' rights platform. Thurmond also refused the support of Gerald L. K. Smith, whom he denounced as a "rabble rouser."

The roots of the Dixiecrat rebellion lay in those one-party states of the Deep South that faced no Republican challenge and so could afford division. The rebels were not primarily motivated by racism but by fear that the southern economic system would be overturned by racial equality. Segregationists with New Deal inclinations, such as Senator Olin D. Johnston (D-S.C.), and followers of the late Mississippi senator THEODORE G. BILBO did not support the movement. Dixiecrat leaders such as Thurmond and Wright were state officials who feared their powers and prerogatives would slowly slip away to Washington. In North Carolina, Virginia, and Tennessee— southern states with a rudimentary Republican threat—local Democrats did not back Thurmond. Florida, Texas, and Arkansas had few Republicans but fewer blacks than Mississippi and South Carolina and a weaker tradition of white supremacy. Here, too, the Dixiecrats did not take hold. Louisiana was a unique case. The Long and anti-Long factions practically formed two parties under the Democratic umbrella. Only by first manipulating the state ballot to exclude Truman's name entirely and then permitting Thurmond to run under the traditional Democratic emblem did the Dixiecrats succeed there.

Thurmond opened his campaign in North Carolina in late July. Refused support by Governor Cameron Morrison, he denounced the three other presidential nominees for supporting civil rights. Thurmond continued his campaign through Texas and Maryland, where the States' Rights ticket had a chance. He did speak in New York, but his campaign was primarily a struggle for control of party machinery between conservatives and progressives in the South. Although they were on the ballot in 13 states and polled 1.2 million votes, the Thurmond-Wright ticket ultimately carried only Mississippi, South Carolina, Alabama, and Louisiana, where they were the official Democratic Party nominees. They won 38 electoral votes from these states, plus one from Tennessee, while Truman won 88 electoral votes in the mid and upper South. Thurmond's biographer, Jack S. Bass, argued that with Thurmond's Dixiecratic candidacy, southern progressives lost a man who could have helped lead the South into a new era of racial reconciliation because he had led in the prosecution of the white lynch mob and had a desire for better education for the state's African-American community. In fact, he had rarely mentioned race in previous campaigns and hardly talked about states' rights before the runup to the 1948 election. So why did he decide to run as a segregationist candidate for the presidency? Ross speculated that in part it had to do with Thurmond's political ambition to win a Senate seat in 1950. He could appeal to whites in the state by being clearly identified as the utmost advocate of segregation.

Following Truman's victory, the States' Rights protest lost much of its popular support and financial backing. In July 1950 Thurmond lost a bitter Senate primary battle to Olin Johnston. Both campaigned against Truman's civil rights program, but African Americans, newly enfranchised to vote in the Democratic primary by a federal court decision, went with Johnston, despite his racist rhetoric, because of his generally progressive record. African Americans in South Carolina were also determined to defeat the man who had been the segregationist candidate for president two years before. Supreme Court decisions in the *Sweatt, Henderson,* and *McLaurin* cases handed down in June 1950 struck at the heart of institutionalized white supremacy. They, together with the final banning of school segregation by the Court in 1954, made white southern voters feel abandoned by the Democratic Party. When South Carolina's Democratic machine kept

Thurmond's name off the Senate primary ballot in 1954, he won election as a write-in candidate, the first person in the state to do so.

During the 1950s Thurmond established a reputation as a conservative southerner who was outside the "club" of conservative southern lawmakers. This was underscored in 1957 when he filibustered against a watered-down civil rights bill the others agreed not to filibuster. In 1964 Thurmond left the Democratic Party for the Republican and supported the presidential candidacy of Senator Barry M. Goldwater (R-Ariz.) He subsequently won reelection to the Senate as a Republican in 1966, 1972, 1978, 1984, 1990, and 1996. After his handpicked gubernatorial candidate, who ran as a segregationist, lost in 1970, Thurmond began to reach out to African Americans to soften their opposition. He voted for the Martin Luther King national holiday and for an extension of the 1965 Voting Rights Act in 1982. He went on to become the oldest person to serve in Congress at 100 years old and the longest-serving senator in U.S. history. Thurmond finally decided to step aside and did not run for reelection in 2002. He died on June 26, 2003, in Edgefield, South Carolina. (See *The Eisenhower Years, The Kennedy Years, The Johnson Years, The Nixon/Ford Years* Volumes)

—MJS

Tobey, Charles W(illiam)
(1880–1953) *member of the Senate*

A descendant of old New England colonists, Charles W. Tobey was born on July 22, 1880, in Roxbury, Massachusetts, and was raised in the suburbs of Boston. After graduating from high school he went to work as a bank clerk. Later, he got a job as a bookkeeper with a shoe company and eventually rose to the presidency of the firm. In 1903 he took up residence in the small village of Temple, New Hampshire, where he farmed and raised flowers while commuting to his job in Boston. Inspired by Theodore Roosevelt and Charles Evans Hughes, Tobey entered politics in 1913 as a "Bull Moose" Republican, serving on the Temple Board of Selectmen. The following year he won election to the New Hampshire House of Representatives on the Progressive ticket. In 1919 he was chosen speaker of the house. Six years later he was elected to the New Hampshire Senate and in 1929 to the governorship. In 1933 Tobey won a seat in the U.S. House of Representatives. Five years later he was elected as a Republican to the Senate on an anti–New Deal platform.

During his first two years in the upper house, Tobey was a strong isolationist, opposing passage of the lend-lease bill and voting against the repeal of the Neutrality Act. After Pearl Harbor he became so unpopular in his state that there were calls for his resignation. These demands subsided, however, when the senator demonstrated his support of the war effort. In 1943 he was named to the Naval Affairs Committee, and, the following year, he was selected a delegate to the Bretton Woods Conference.

During the postwar years Tobey's voting pattern was erratic and seldom conformed to the recommendations of the Senate GOP Policy Committee. In 1946 he provoked the ire of his conservative colleagues by voting for the Employment Act, the loan to Great Britain, and the increase in the minimum wage. That year he antagonized President Truman by leading the opposition to the confirmation of EDWIN W. PAULEY as undersecretary of the navy. Tobey insisted that Pauley, a Democratic fund-raiser with close connections to West Coast oilmen, should not be placed in a position of authority over the navy's large offshore oil reserves. In hearings conducted by the Naval Affairs Committee on February 1, Secretary of the Interior HAROLD L. ICKES revealed, under Tobey's questioning, that Pauley had privately opposed government claims to the tideland oil fields as politically unwise. Four days later Ickes reappeared before the panel with records of a conversation in which Pauley had informed the secretary that he had assured his friends in the oil industry that no federal tidelands suit would be filed if they contributed to the Democratic National Committee. Despite the growing scandal Truman continued to defend his appointment. On February 13 Ickes, who claimed that the president had urged him to "go soft" on Pauley in his testimony, resigned from the cabinet, saying he did not care to "commit perjury for the sake of the party." As a result the committee asked Truman to withdraw the nomination. The president assented but at the same time publicly deplored the aspersions cast on Pauley's integrity by Tobey and Ickes.

In the Republican-controlled 80th Congress Tobey took over the chairmanship of the Banking and Currency Committee. At this post he carried on a one-man crusade against the Reconstruction Finance Corporation, investigating and criticizing an $8-million loan it had made to the Baltimore and Ohio Railroad. He backed the Republican tax cut of 1948, the Taft-Hartley Act, federal aid to education, the National Housing Act of 1949, and the establishment of a permanent Fair Employment Practices Commission. On foreign policy matters Tobey was aligned with the liberal Republican bloc led by Senators GEORGE D. AIKEN (R-Vt.) and WAYNE MORSE (R-Ore.). He supported the UN Charter of 1945, the Truman Doctrine and Greek-Turkish aid in 1947, the Marshall Plan of 1948, the Point Four program of 1950, and the Japanese Peace Treaty of 1951. A member of the American Christian Palestine Committee, Tobey also worked to secure U.S. recognition of Israel.

In 1950 the Republican organization in New Hampshire, led by Senator STYLES BRIDGES (R-N.H.), made an effort to block Tobey's renomination for a third term. After a bitter campaign Tobey narrowly defeated his opponent, a Bridges protégé, in the primary and went on to win the general election in November. In the following year the senator emerged in the national spotlight as a member of the Special Committee to Investigate Organized Crime in Interstate Commerce, chaired by Senator ESTES KEFAUVER (D-Tenn.). Tobey delighted television audiences by quoting the Bible to underworld figures and urging them to "come clean." Revelations linking criminals and high political officials so distressed him that tears flowed down his cheeks as he pleaded to heaven for honesty in public life. Several witnesses were themselves reduced to tears during the senator's emotional outbursts. During hearings in April a confrontation took place between Tobey and former New York mayor WILLIAM O'DWYER. Stung by the senator's charges that he had associated with gangster Frank Costello, O'Dwyer accused Tobey of having received campaign contributions from unknown sources. Tobey passionately denied the allegations, which were never proved.

On July 24, 1953, shortly after his 73rd birthday, Tobey died of a heart attack in Washington, D.C.

—TLH

Tobin, Daniel J(oseph)

(1875–1955) *general president, International Brotherhood of Teamsters*

Born in April 1875 in County Clare, Ireland, Daniel Tobin emigrated to the United States in 1889. He lived in Boston, working at odd jobs in factories and stables, driving streetcars and horsedrawn trucks. He joined the Boston local of the Team Drivers International Union and in 1903 participated in the creation of the International Brotherhood of Team-

sters. He began president of the Teamsters in 1907. By 1910 he was recognized as the undisputed leader of the union. He served as treasurer of the American Federation of Labor (AFL) from 1917 to 1928 and became a vice president of the AFL in 1933.

Over the years Tobin gradually built his union into one of the wealthiest and most powerful in the nation. His success was based, in part, on his adherence to two principles: avoidance of sympathy strikes that would deplete the union treasury and frugal administration of union funds. He opposed the use of strikes except as a last resort. Before he dispersed support payments to striking locals, he would carefully investigate whether the strike was in conformity with union constitutional rules and regulations. A vociferous opponent of Communist infiltration in unions, Tobin was responsible for the provision in the Teamsters constitution that barred them from membership. He minimized the amount of violent crime and corruption in his union—although he did have the Teamsters buy two houses for him. During his tenure the Teamsters grew from about 39,000 in 1907 to 1.2 million with a treasury of $26 million in 1952.

Under Tobin the union remained largely decentralized. He rarely interfered in local affairs, and, in fact, relied on powerful leaders of local Teamster unions to keep him in power. According to Teamster chronicler Steven Brill, Tobin, initially opposed the organization of long-haul drivers for fear this would require centralized decision making and thus alienate local bosses. He preferred to dedicate much of his time to AFL affairs. However, Tobin did have potentially great authority because of his ability to appoint trustees to oversee locals in cases of suspected corruption. Tobin's power rested primarily on his national reputation. He dominated policy making that affected relations with other elements in the labor movement and served as a spokesman for important segments of the labor force.

An ardent Democrat, Tobin was an early supporter of Franklin D. Roosevelt and served as chairman of the labor division of the Democratic National Committee during each of Roosevelt's presidential campaigns. In 1940 he was Roosevelt's administrative assistant and two years later his emissary to London, where he studied labor conditions in Great Britain. Tobin supported Roosevelt's labor policies during World War II. He proudly proclaimed in 1945 that the Teamsters had obeyed the wartime no-strike pledge almost 100 percent. Tobin was a nativist and zealous advocate of alien exclusion laws. Fearing that foreign competition would reduce wages, he opposed the admission of Chinese during World War II and of European Jews after the war.

Tobin advocated the consolidation of the AFL and the Congress of Industrial Organizations (CIO) throughout the 1940s. From 1942 to 1950 he participated in AFL-CIO joint conference committees that unsuccessfully attempted to bring the two organizations together. In 1950 he was chairman of the AFL bargaining group at the meeting. He helped lay the foundation for joint legislative and political action and established machinery for the handling of jurisdictional disputes. He also formulated an agenda for later meetings that led to the union of the two organizations in 1955.

Often critical of the nonpartisan stand of the AFL leadership, Tobin urged organized labor to become politically active. During the early postwar period he charged that Truman had lost the confidence of organized labor and predicted a Democratic defeat in the upcoming congressional elections if the party did not adopt a more pro-labor stand. Like many AFL and CIO leaders, Tobin opposed Truman's nomination in 1948 and would have preferred DWIGHT D. EISENHOWER as a candidate. The Teamster newspaper, *The International Teamster*, later reported that Truman had offered Tobin the post of secretary of labor in June 1948, apparently in an effort to obtain his backing, but he had refused. After the Korean War had begun, Tobin was a vigorous supporter of the administration. In a speech before the AFL in December 1950, he urged the organization to abandon its 65-year opposition to universal military training. In the presidential election of 1952. Tobin supported liberal Democrat Adlai E. Stevenson.

In October 1952 Tobin retired from the presidency of the union after an unsuccessful, and little publicized, attempt to attain the presidency of the AFL. According to GEORGE MEANY, on the death of AFL president WILLIAM GREEN, Tobin wanted to be president for a year or two, but he lost an informal vote to Meany on the morning of Green's funeral. The Teamsters convention selected Executive Vice President Dave Beck, reportedly Tobin's personal choice, as his successor. The convention then elected Tobin president emeritus with a $50,000 salary, the same as Beck's. Tobin continued as a vice president of the AFL and a powerful member of the Executive Council until his death in Indianapolis, Indiana, on November 14, 1955.

—AES

Tobin, Maurice J(oseph)
(1901–1953) *secretary of labor*

Tobin was born on May 22, 1901, in the poor Mission Hill district of Boston, Massachusetts. His father, an Irish immigrant, worked as a carpenter. Tobin left high school in 1919 after two years to go to work in a leather factory. He later took night courses in Boston College. In the early 1920s he joined the New England Telephone Company as a relay adjuster. He eventually became a district traffic manager in 1928.

The politically ambitious Tobin rose swiftly in state politics. In 1926, at the age of 25, he was elected to the Massachusetts General Court, where he served for two years. In 1931 Tobin won election to the Boston School Committee and in 1937

Maurice J. Tobin *(Harry S. Truman Library)*

defeated boss Jim Curley for the Boston mayoralty. As mayor, Tobin concentrated on improving the fiscal status of the near-bankrupt city. He won reelection but resigned to run for governor in 1944.

During his two-year term Tobin challenged the Republican legislature by introducing a liberal social program. Among his reforms were the Fair Employment Practices Act, designed to end discrimination in hiring, and measures instituting rent control, additional unemployment aid, and veterans benefits. The governor was known as a champion of organized labor. Tobin lost his post to Lieutenant Governor Robert F. Bradford, a Republican, in the November 1946 elections. Two years later he was battling for the Democratic gubernatorial nomination when President Truman appointed him secretary of labor. Tobin assumed office in August 1948.

Tobin did not have an immediate impact on the government's dealings with organized labor. He discovered that the Department of Labor had lost much of its power and influence. For example, the National Labor Relations Board and the Mediation Service, two large and active labor agencies, were not under Tobin's jurisdiction. Tobin set out to rebuild and reorganize the department. In 1949 he persuaded Truman to transfer the United States Employment Service and the Unemployment Insurance Service from the Federal Security Agency to his department. A year later the Bureau of Employees' Compensation and the Employees' Compensation Appeals Board were added. In 1950 Tobin also created a Federal Safety Council in the Bureau of Labor Standards.

Tobin was an articulate spokesman for both the Truman administration and the cause of labor. He strongly opposed Republican-sponsored labor legislation, primarily focusing on the Taft-Hartley Act of 1947, and made some 150 speeches in over 20 states on the subject during the 1948 election campaign. A fiery orator, he attacked the legislation as a "blow to unionism" and warned that Taft-Hartley left "the future welfare of workers on dangerous quicksand." He objected to the act's ban on union political activity and its restrictions on a closed shop. In a speech before the New York Liberal Party in New York City, Tobin contended that the Republican 80th Congress "urged on by the NAM [National Association of Manufacturers], took advantage of the emotional and hysterical atmosphere" caused by the postwar strike wave to put

through "discriminatory legislation." He later said the only "protection" the act gave was to the "rugged individualists of the National Association of Manufacturers." As part of his campaign oratory, he pointed out in November 1948 that the earnings of 16 million American workers lagged 9 percent behind the cost of living. He urged the American Federation of Labor (AFL) and the Congress of Industrial Organizations (CIO) to merge as a method of gaining greater bargaining power.

After the election Tobin continued to advance his pro-labor views. In 1949 he was active in the unsuccessful fight to repeal the Taft-Hartley Act. Tobin drafted the bill that would have repealed Taft-Hartley and reinstated the original Wagner Act with certain amendments, such as ones outlawing unjustifiable secondary boycotts and all jurisdictional strikes. Testifying before the Senate Labor and Public Welfare Committee in February, he noted that strikes had gone up 8 percent since enactment of the legislation. He argued that the closed shop ban had made illegal collective bargaining agreements that had prevented strikes for over 100 years, and that the act was inequitable in allowing injunctions to resolve disputes between management and labor. He also called for giving the president power to seize factories, mine, and docks during national emergencies. Later in the year he advocated increased unemployment benefits and a government pension plan for all retired workers. He backed the Fair Labor Standards Amendments of 1949, which increased the minimum wage to 75 cents an hour, strengthened the existing child labor laws, and clarified provisions relating to overtime pay. Throughout his tenure Tobin was active in pressing for congressional action to improve the wages and benefits of railway workers, government employees, and others. In July 1949 he raised the hourly wages of steel and iron workers on government contracts by 19 cents.

After the start of the Korean War, Truman made Tobin responsible for federal civilian manpower. Tobin created national, regional, and area labor-management defense manpower committees and within the Department of Labor instituted the Defense Manpower Administration.

The secretary joined a handful of cabinet members in criticizing the excesses of Senator JOSEPH R. MCCARTHY's (R-Wisc.) anticommunist crusade. Addressing a Veterans of Foreign Wars convention in August 1951, Tobin castigated "slanderers" who used the Senate "to hide in from libel suits."

Although he did not mention McCarthy by name, it was clear Tobin was attacking the senator for charging that Secretary of State DEAN G. ACHESON was in league with Communists. In a less publicized speech that fall, Tobin called on "all Catholics" to repudiate "a campaign of terror against free thought in the United States."

In May 1952 Tobin backed the unions in the steel strike. He felt "the time for impartiality" had passed and that the government should favor the unions. Tobin said that since the workers had accepted the Wage Stabilization Board contract offer, which the steel companies had rejected, the unions were justified in striking. However, after the Supreme Court ruled against Truman's seizure of the steel mills, Tobin ironically thought the administration should invoke the 80-day cooling-off period of the Taft-Hartley Act.

After leaving office in January 1953, Tobin faded from public view. He died of a heart attack on July 19, 1953, at his summer home in Scituate, Massachusetts.

—JF

Truman, Elizabeth Virginia Wallace
(1885–1982) *first lady*

The daughter of a politician and the granddaughter of a flourmill owner, Elizabeth Wallace "Bess" Truman was born on February 13, 1885, in Independence, Missouri. Harry Truman first saw her in Independence's Presbyterian Church Sunday school. The six-year-old boy saw the five-year-old girl, and he fell in love with her instantly, he later recalled. But it was several years before he could summon up the courage to speak to her. Once when Bess saw Harry working at a drugstore when they were children, she commented that she wished he did not have to work so hard. Although they were in the same class in high school and a friendship developed, their paths diverged after graduation. Bess had several boyfriends but nothing came of these relationships. Then in 1903 Bess's father, David Wallace, committed suicide, for reasons unknown. Her mother, Madge Wallace, took Bess and her other children away to Colorado Springs for a time and then moved in with her father in Independence. Bess remained with her mother for several years, during two of which she commuted to Kansas City to attend a finishing school.

In 1906 Harry, who had been working in a bank in Kansas City, was told by his father to come help him on a farm he had taken over from an uncle. This

made it difficult for Harry to visit Independence, but one time he was visiting an aunt—who lived across the street from Bess—when he learned a cake plate had to be returned to Mrs. Wallace. He declared he would return the plate and quickly grabbed it and proceeded across the street to the Wallace home, where Bess answered the door. Thus their courtship began. From the farm Harry would write Bess often, with him relating life there. (Her letters to him from this time have not survived.) In 1911 he proposed to her through a letter, but she turned him down. He persisted, however, and, in November 1913, she promised to marry him if she married anyone.

In 1914 Harry's mother loaned him money to buy a car. Now he had much easier access to Independence and Bess, which he took advantage of. He took Bess with friends and relatives on excursions. After his service in World War I, Harry married Bess at the Trinity Episcopal Church in Independence on June 28, 1919. After his haberdashery failed, Harry ran for judge in Jackson County in 1922 and won. Bess's sentiments about Harry's running for office in 1922 are unknown, but, in 1934,

Wedding portrait of Harry and Bess Truman, 1919
(Harry S. Truman Library)

she opposed his running for Congress, preferring to stay in Independence. Boss Tom Pendergast chose someone else to run for Congress in any event, but he then offered Harry a chance to run for the Senate, which Truman agreed to.

When he was a senator, Truman put Bess on his office payroll in 1941 and in three years she was drawing the highest salary of the staff, even though she did little work. When Truman was being considered for the vice presidential nomination in 1944 this payroll padding worried the senator, which he feared would be reported in the newspapers if he were nominated. Margaret Truman also believed that he feared word of David Wallace's suicide would become known, which was still considered something of a disgrace at that time, and that would cause Bess and her mother anguish. Bess opposed his nomination because she feared his ascending to the presidency, a possibility she loathed. She went through the motions of supporting her husband—even saying she was "reconciled" to his nomination. Her real sentiments were revealed when they had to push through a frenzied crowd to a limousine after his nomination in Chicago; she glared at Truman and exclaimed, "Are we going to have to go through this for the rest of our lives?" She said little on the way back to Independence and Margaret remembered the atmosphere in the car as being quite chilly.

After Truman ascended to the presidency, Bess responded to a reporter's questionnaire in 1947 by bluntly saying she would not have entered the White House if she had any choice in the matter. She spent as much time as she could in Independence. However, Bess gave advice to the president, as she had throughout his political career. Truman discussed with Bess his decision not to run for reelection in 1952. He did consider running for the Senate, but Bess was against the idea, wanting to return to Independence for good. When he made his announcement at the Jefferson-Jackson dinner in 1952 that he would not run again, "Mrs. Truman," reported presidential friend Harry Vaughan to the president, "looked like you do when you draw four aces."

Bess spent the rest of her days quite happily away from the Washington scene. She even changed the plans for Truman's state funeral so that it did not occur in Washington—everything would happen in Independence. She died on October 18, 1982, in Independence.

Truman, Harry S
(1884–1972) *president of the United States*

Harry S Truman was born on May 8, 1884, in Lamar, Missouri, into a family of ardent Democrats. His father worked at various times as a farmer, a livestock trader, and a grain speculator, and, despite several economic reverses, he provided a comfortable life for his family. His mother, a devout Baptist who had a powerful influence on Harry, placed great emphasis on morality and education. When Harry was seven the family moved to Independence, Missouri, where he attended public schools. Anxious to pursue a military career, he applied to West Point but was rejected because of poor eyesight. He then joined the National Guard. Truman lacked the money to pay for a college education and, over the next few years, held a number of jobs, including mailroom clerk and bookkeeper before becoming a farmer at the age of 22. When World War II broke out, he saw action as an artillery officer in France. Following the war he opened a haberdashery with a friend in Kansas City, Missouri; the business failed in the economic downturn of 1921–22.

Truman had been long interested in entering politics. In 1922 he ran for the administrative post of judge of the Jackson County Court. He was backed by the powerful Pendergast machine, which controlled Democratic politics in much of Missouri. He won the contest but lost his reelection bid two years later. In 1926 he was elected presiding judge of the court and occupied that position for eight years. In these posts he supervised public building and carried on an extensive road construction program. Although supporting the Pendergast organization, he was never associated with the scandals that eventually led to its downfall.

With the backing of Tom Pendergast, Truman won a seat in the U.S. Senate in 1934. He was a consistent supporter of Franklin D. Roosevelt's domestic and foreign policies. He played a major role in drafting the Civil Aeronautics Act of 1938 and the Railroad Transportation Act of 1940. His allegiance, however, was primarily to the party rather than to the president's program. He gained a reputation as a pragmatic, middle-of-the-road politician.

After the Pendergast machine crumbled in the late 1930s under the weight of scandal and Boss Tom went to jail, Truman found himself in a difficult reelection campaign in 1940. Governor Lloyd C. Stark, with the covert backing of President Roosevelt, entered the Democratic primary. But so did

Maurice Milligan, the man who had prosecuted Pendergast. This split in the reform vote allowed a hard-campaigning Truman to win the primary. He went on to win the general election in the autumn.

Truman first came to national prominence during World War II when, as chairman of a special watchdog committee, he uncovered inefficiency and corruption in the nation's defense program. As a result of the investigation, he became a power in the Senate and was mentioned as a possible vice presidential candidate in 1944.

The Democratic Party at the time was divided on the question of a running mate for FDR. Party leaders assumed that the next vice president would soon become president and so would determine the direction of the Democratic administration into the next decade. The left wing favored the renomination of HENRY A. WALLACE, who was opposed by big city bosses and southern conservatives who saw him as too liberal. Southern conservatives supported South Carolinian JAMES F. BYRNES, the director of the Office of War Mobilization, who had gained the informal title of "assistant president" during the war. However, organized labor refused to support him.

With powerful sections of the party torn between the two candidates, Roosevelt selected Truman as a compromise. Truman's border-state ties appealed to the South and conservatives while his support of the New Deal won him the backing of labor and northern liberals. His ties to the Pendergast machine made him acceptable to big city bosses. More important, Roosevelt thought that Truman's popularity on Capitol Hill could help him gain ratification of peace treaties and the UN Charter, thus avoiding the problems Woodrow Wilson had faced after World War I. Roosevelt did not think the vice presidential candidate would aid his ticket. Instead, he was anxious to have a running mate who would not lose him votes. Truman, with few enemies, had the necessary qualifications.

Elected in November, Truman served only 83 days. During his short tenure he remained on the edge of decision making. Preoccupied with the war, Roosevelt relied primarily on those advisers, such as HARRY L. HOPKINS, who had been with him throughout his presidency. Truman was not included in discussions, particularly in foreign policy, and spent most of his time presiding over the Senate. He described himself during that period as a "political eunuch."

On April 12, 1945, Roosevelt died of a cerebral hemorrhage and Harry Truman assumed the presidency. Shocked by FDR's death and staggered by the thought of replacing him, Truman asked reporters, "Boys if you ever pray, pray for me now. . . . When they told me yesterday what had happened, I felt like the moon, the stars and all the planets had fallen on me."

Men who had worked closely with Roosevelt worried about Truman's lack of experience and questioned his ability to lead. DAVID E. LILIENTHAL, chairman of the Tennessee Valley Authority, wrote in his diary: "Consternation at the thought of that Throttlebottom Truman. The country and the world doesn't deserve to be left this way, with Truman at the head of the country at such a time." Those who had worked with him in the Senate had a different opinion. "Truman will not make a great, flashy President like Roosevelt," Speaker of the House SAM T. RAYBURN predicted. "But, by God, he'll make a good President, a sound President. He's got the stuff in him."

Truman's first days in the White House won praise both from the public and government officials. They were impressed with his ability and willingness to accept the demands of his office. An early public opinion poll showed that seven out of 10 voters approved of Truman's actions. Even conservative Republican HENRY R. LUCE wrote that he had confidence in Truman. In part this reaction was a result of the traditional "honeymoon" the public gives a new president. Domestic issues were sidelined and the war was proceeding well. Just as important was Truman's style of operating. His informality and his acknowledgment of his limitations made him approachable to the public. His sense of order and direct decision making contrasted sharply with Roosevelt's use of confusion and conflict among advisers to develop policies, and tensions within the presidential staff declined.

As the war in Europe drew quickly to a close, Truman moved to end the conflict in Asia. He was determined to push for the unconditional surrender of Japan and the abolition of the Japanese monarchy. Anxious to end the war quickly, he rejected suggestions that the U.S. blockade the islands to starve out Japan. Roosevelt had informed Truman of the atomic bomb shortly after the convention. When Truman ascended to the presidency, however, the weapon had not been tested, and the planning for an invasion of Japan continued. When a test in July proved the weapon viable, he decided to use it to forestall a bloody invasion. He accepted an advisory committee's recommendation that the bomb be dropped on a military-civilian target without warning. Truman rejected pleas by atomic scientists that the Japanese be shown the force of the bomb before it was used. Anxious to avoid continued U.S. casualties, he maintained there was no time to prepare a demonstration.

The president also refused the recommendations of JOSEPH C. GREW and Cordell Hull that the United States accept the continuation of the monarchy to speed up surrender. During July the Western Allies issued a proclamation calling for the Japanese surrender. They warned that Japan would have to give up its army, its war-making capacity, and its occupied territory but promised the continuation of civil liberties and peacetime industries. The communication made no mention of the future of the emperor. The Japanese refused the ultimatum, and, in early August, Truman approved the use of the weapon. After the destruction of Hiroshima and Nagasaki, and the Russian invasion of Japanese-occupied Manchuria, the Japanese sued for peace but refused to surrender until the United States had given assurances that the monarchy would be returned. Truman allowed that the Japanese could adopt what form of government they wanted, except a militarist, authoritarian one, but that their government would be under the control of the Supreme Allied Commander, General DOUGLAS MACARTHUR. The Japanese surrendered on August 14.

Truman assumed the presidency during a difficult time in international affairs. The war in Europe was drawing to a close but the victorious alliance threatened to disintegrate over the issue of the Soviet military occupation of Eastern Europe. The new president was completely inexperienced in international relations and anxious to assert himself on questions dividing the Allies. His desire to lead pushed him during his first year in office to make hasty decisions. With no background in foreign affairs, he relied primarily on his advisers for counsel. These men were deeply split on their approach to Soviet policy. One group, led by W. AVERELL HARRIMAN and WILLIAM D. LEAHY urged a firm policy to force Russian concessions in Eastern Europe while the other, led by HENRY A. WALLACE, continued to push for cooperation to ensure a peaceful postwar world. Without a basis for determining Soviet motives and uncertain of his own understanding of foreign affairs, Truman followed the advice of first one faction and then the other. His policies, therefore, vacillated.

Truman initially hoped to continue Roosevelt's policy of cooperation with the Soviet Union. He felt himself committed to FDR's efforts and was reluctant to involve the United States in a war over Eastern Europe. Just as important, he viewed Soviet leaders as pragmatic politicians, similar to urban bosses, with whom arrangements could be made through personal diplomacy. Yet his determination to assert himself and his abrasive personality signalled to the Soviets a harsher stand and speeded the development of the cold war.

During the spring and summer of 1945 Truman attempted to take a firm stand toward the Soviet Union while looking for a way to maintain cooperation. He lectured the Soviet foreign minister in undiplomatic language on the need to live up to the Yalta Accords guaranteeing free elections in Eastern Europe. He also slowed down aid to Russia to pressure Stalin on the issue. Yet in an effort to prevent a break, Truman sent Roosevelt's trusted adviser, HARRY L. HOPKINS, to Moscow to try to settle outstanding differences. Hopkins was able to get Stalin's agreement to a compromise government in Poland and his assurances of entry into the war against Japan but could not forestall a worsening of relations. At the Potsdam Conference of July and August, Truman demanded and received a compromise on reparations that limited Soviet claims on Western German goods. More significantly the agreement permitted the redevelopment of the German economy, which Truman considered vital for the economic health of Europe. Still the Soviets refused vigorously to reaffirm support for the Yalta Declaration on Eastern Europe.

Despite Soviet intransigence Truman declined to use American military might to pressure Stalin. He rejected Winston Churchill's suggestion that the U.S. Army push farther into Central Europe during the closing days of the war to give the West a better bargaining position with the Russians after the armistice. He also ignored requests from his advisers that he reverse Roosevelt's decision to ask for Soviet entry into the war against Japan in return for political concessions in Asia. Truman believed that the best way to handle the Soviet Union was "to stick carefully to our agreements and to try our best to make the Russians carry out their agreements."

Congressional pressure and public opinion gradually moved Truman to a more strident position on the Soviet Union by 1946. Revelations of a Communist spy network in Canada and continued Soviet intransigence at international conferences led many to doubt Russian friendship. Powerful senators such as ARTHUR H. VANDENBURG (R-Mich.) demanded an end to compromise. Vandenberg was particularly angered at the conduct of Secretary of State JAMES F. BYRNES, whom he thought too willing to make concessions to Stalin. The secretary's conduct at the Moscow Conference of December 1945 proved a turning point. At that meeting he agreed to diplomatic recognition of the Soviet dominated regimes in Bulgaria and Romania in return for a broadening of the governments. Vandenberg termed it "one more typical American 'give away.' " Truman, also angered at the accord, said that Byrnes had "lost his nerve at Moscow."

By the beginning of 1946 the president had come to believe that a less pliant policy toward the Soviet Union was necessary. Frustrated in efforts to work out settlements to outstanding issues, and under extreme pressure from Congress and the public not to give in further to the Soviets, he developed a stance of "patience with firmness." Negotiations with the Soviet Union could continue, but henceforth any concessions would come from the Russians. Truman accepted GEORGE F. KENNAN's view that the Soviet Union was an expansionist power, which because of a desire for security and because of a paranoiac mind-set was bent on world conquest. To stop its advance, the United States would have to "contain" the USSR. This was to be done primarily through the use of American economic power rather than military might.

During 1946 Truman resisted further concessions to the Soviet Union. He insisted that the USSR remove its troops from Iran, which it had agreed to occupy only until the end of the war. Fearful of Russian penetration into the eastern Mediterranean, he dispatched U.S. warships to Greece and Turkey to discourage Soviet infiltration. He minimized attempts to come to terms with Stalin on Germany and backed unification of the American and British occupation zones to provide for the economic rehabilitation of that nation. Truman continued his commitment to international control of atomic energy, but he did so on terms that made it difficult for the Soviets to accept. He supported the Baruch Plan, submitted to the United Nations in the spring of 1946, which called for inspection of all nuclear sites and disclosure of atomic research

before the United States would give up its nuclear monopoly. In September 1946, when Secretary of Commerce Henry Wallace denounced the administration's "get tough policy with the Soviets," Truman asked him to resign, although he had offhandedly approved Wallace's speech beforehand. Wallace, once out of office, became the leader of liberals' discontent with the administration and began activities that led to his presidential candidacy in 1948.

Truman and his advisers, primarily Secretary of State GEORGE C. MARSHALL and Undersecretary of State DEAN G. ACHESON, established the cornerstones of the containment policy during 1947 and 1948. In the early months of 1947 the president moved to replace the British presence in Greece and Turkey with American aid to prevent a Communist takeover. To win the support of a Congress hostile to U.S. involvement in Europe, Truman couched his aid message in terms of an ideological struggle against Communist expansion. In enunciating what came to be known as the Truman Doctrine, he called for a clear division between democracy and a way of life that "relies upon terror and oppression . . . and the suppression of personal freedoms." Truman stated, "I believe that it must be the policy of the United States to support free peoples who are resisting attempted subjugation by armed minorities or by outside pressures." Three months later Marshall unveiled the European Recovery Program, called the Marshall Plan at Truman's insistence. This proposal called for massive economic aid to war-torn Europe. Although there was a strong humanitarian element in the program, the administration also thought the ERP would reestablish economic prosperity and thus eliminate a breeding ground for Communists.

Truman did not intend to use American military power to challenge the Soviets. He refused to intervene in the Communist takeover of Czechoslovakia in February 1948. When the Soviet Union blockaded Berlin in June 1948, the president ignored both cries of some observers to abandon the city and demands from the military, particularly General LUCIUS D. CLAY, that U.S. troops open supply routes. Instead, he used an airlift to supply the beleaguered city.

Truman pushed hard for the reorganization and modernization of the defense establishment to respond to modern warfare. In order to eliminate waste and inefficiency, he called for the unification of the services in a Department of National Defense with power centralized in a civilian secretary of defense. Because of opposition from the navy, he was forced to compromise. The National Security Act of 1947 gave the secretary of defense only a coordinating role. Yet it established the base upon which Truman could build. He eventually won approval for a stronger secretary in 1949. In keeping with America's greater role in world affairs, the act established the National Security Council to coordinate defense and foreign policy. It also reorganized the American intelligence community into the Central Intelligence Agency.

The victory over Japan brought Truman his first major domestic problem—reconversion. Assuming that the conflict would continue for at least a year, government planners had not prepared for the major transition. Roosevelt and Truman, busy with the war, had also put off dealing with the problem. The confusion and turnover in personnel following Roosevelt's death hampered planning still further.

Truman approached reconversion with the primary goal of preventing a recession. Like many who could remember the economic problems after World War I, he feared that a short period of inflation would be followed by a long recession as men were thrown out of defense-related jobs and soldiers were demobilized. In addition, the president and the nation as a whole were haunted by memories of the Great Depression. Truman could remember that, as recently as 1939, 10 million persons were unemployed. In developing his reconversion policies Truman tried to steer a middle course, which he hoped would win the support of all important segments of the nation—labor, business, agriculture, and the consumer. His policies reflected his own background as a small businessman and as a midwestern progressive.

On the advice of JOHN W. SNYDER, who became his primary economic counselor, Truman announced on August 16 that most economic controls would end promptly except where needed. Reacting to demands by labor for increased wages to offset reductions in the work week, he asked union leaders to continue their wartime no-strike pledge and promised to call a labor-management conference to discuss outstanding differences. He announced that the government would legalize wage increases as long as they did not result in price rises.

On September 6 Truman presented a 21-point domestic program to deal with reconversion. While acknowledging that inflation might become a problem, he focused his attention on dealing with the expected recession. He asked for a full employment bill, an increase in unemployment compensation, a substantial though unspecified rise in the minimum wage, a comprehensive housing measure, legislation establishing permanent farm price supports, a law protecting and encouraging small business so that it could compete for scarce goods, an increase in public works projects, and a limited tax reduction. In addition, Truman requested the establishment of a permanent Fair Employment Practices Commission (FEPC) to end discrimination in hiring.

During the fall and winter of 1945–46 Truman's reconversion program floundered, bringing an end to the honeymoon period and alienating many segments of the nation that he had tried to court. Truman, himself, was in part responsible for the defeat. When he assumed the presidency, he was still a regional politician and he had difficulty developing the national constituency needed to push his plans through Congress. Although many Americans admired his courage in tackling the problems of office, they quickly found his administration lackluster and his decisions inconsistent. His continued protestations of unworthiness focused attention on his faults rather than on his competence. Truman could not shake the shadow of Franklin Roosevelt, whose accomplishments during the depression became magnified and whose domestic failures during the war years minimized. Truman also lacked Roosevelt's ability to inspire. New Deal liberals, who might have been expected to back Truman, were reluctant to aid a man who had been closely associated with an urban machine and had surrounded himself with advisers whom liberals found unacceptably conservative.

Truman was unwilling to use the powers of the presidency to push his program. Hoping to avoid the impasse between Congress and the White House that had characterized the late New Deal, he left priorities up to Congress. Without guidance, the legislature destroyed his program, severely weakening the full employment bill, defeating the FEPC, and increasing the tax cut beyond that which Truman had requested.

Truman's advisers also contributed to his problems. Many seemed to have been chosen not because of experience or ability but because they were old friends of the president. One critic complained that the major criterion for receiving a high administration position was membership in Tru-

President Truman and his Cabinet, 1949 *(Harry S. Truman Library, Abbie Rowe)*

man's old reserve unit. John Snyder, a small Midwest banker who became secretary of the Treasury had been Truman's friend since they had met in the U.S. Army Reserve. Secretary of Agriculture CLINTON P. ANDERSON had been a friend in the Senate, as had Attorney General TOM C. CLARK. At a time when labor problems were acute, LEWIS B. SCHWELLENBACH, a one-time senator and judge, became secretary of labor, although he had had no experience in labor negotiations. JAMES K. VARDAMAN, JR., another Missouri businessman who had been a Truman friend and assistant, was appointed to the largely ceremonial post of naval aide. When Vardaman proved an embarrassment there, Truman, who did not have the heart to fire him, appointed him to the Board of Governors of the Federal Reserve System.

Cabinet members bickered among themselves and often acted contrary to Truman's reconversion policy. Snyder, for example, a proponent of removing controls, feuded openly with CHESTER BOWLES,

director of the Office of Price Administration, who wished controls maintained. Clinton Anderson vigorously supported farmers' demands for price rises and backed moves to hold produce from market in the face of Truman's desire to keep down food costs and send food to famine-stricken Europe. Schwellenbach feuded with Wallace over wage and price increases.

Labor became one of Truman's constant worries during 1945 and 1946. The president was never able to win assurances from union leaders for a continuation of the wartime no-strike pledge. During the summer and fall of 1945, the number of strikes rose as labor, trying to recover income levels lost with the end of wartime overtime, demanded higher wages. At the end of October Truman retreated from his earlier stand that he would back only those wage increases that did not raise prices. He proposed a plan that would enable business to include the cost of wage increases in price rises after a six-month accounting period had demonstrated need. Neither labor nor management liked the suggestion. Truman's proposed Labor-Management Conference, convened in November, failed to settle differences. The president offered no guidance during the meeting, and labor, divided within itself, could not agree on a wage policy to present to management. Attempting to stop the rash of strikes, in late 1945 Truman requested legislation providing for fact-finding boards to investigate disputes and giving the president the power to impose cooling off periods before strikes could be called. The proposal further alienated labor because it limited the right to strike.

The number of strikes continued to grow during early 1946. In April coal miners, led by JOHN L. LEWIS, refused Truman's compromise on a wage increase and walked out at the same time that railroad workers threatened to strike. The public saw Lewis's action in particular as a challenge to the president and a test of Truman's ability to govern. The coal miners' strike crippled the nation. Many states and cities imposed dimouts and in some industries production halted. When both sides refused arbitration, Truman, in desperation, ordered the mines seized. Shortly thereafter the government gave in to most of Lewis's demands.

While negotiating the coal strike, Truman attempted to forestall a railroad strike by the Brotherhood of Railroad Trainmen and the Brotherhood of Railroad Engineers. In May he seized the railroads and began bargaining with the two unions. When negotiations became deadlocked hours before the strike, Truman issued a blistering attack against the unions. In an address before Congress he asked for the power to draft workers "who are on strike against their government." An agreement was reached as Truman spoke. The president's handling of the labor situation was severely criticized. The dislocation caused by the strikes and Truman's apparent impotence before labor leaders hurt his standing with the public. His demand for draconian labor legislation lost him support not only among labor and liberals but also among conservatives such as Senator ROBERT A. TAFT (R-Ohio), who declared that Truman's demands offended "every basic principle for which the American republic was established."

Truman's handling of the economy also proved inept. During the autumn and winter of 1945–46 he had become convinced that inflation and not recession would be the major postwar economic problem. In an effort to keep a ceiling on prices, during the spring of 1946 he asked for continuation of price controls and the extension of the life of Office of Price Administration. He refused to fight for the legislation, however. Congress passed a weak version of his proposal, which Truman signed only reluctantly. He did so hoping that the public would become discontented and pressure Congress into passing a stronger measure. His strategy backfired. As prices rose and a black market developed, the public blamed the president.

Truman did not understand the uses of fiscal or monetary policy as devices for controlling the economy. He looked at the federal budget and Federal Reserve Board policy from the narrowest financial perspective, as if he were still administering a Missouri county. He wanted surplus revenues and cheap debt. He insisted that the Federal Reserve continue its wartime policies and maintain interest rates at artificially low levels, a practice that fanned inflation.

By the 1946 elections Truman and the Democratic Party were in serious trouble. Many liberals had left the administration and were attacking Truman's foreign policy and lack of a strong domestic program. Labor was alienated by his reaction to wage demands and business by his handling of the economy. Shortages of foods angered consumers while low prices for agricultural products irritated farmers. Southerners attacked Truman's racial policies. Soldiers were angered by the slow pace of demobilization. Running on the slogan "Had Enough?" the Republicans won decisive control of the House and a narrow margin in the Senate.

The fall of 1946 was the nadir of the Truman presidency. After the elections the domestic situation began to improve, and Truman, seemingly jolted into fighting by the results, took the initiative in domestic affairs. By the winter of 1946 the reconversion period was over: the number of strikes had declined; shortages had disappeared and wage and price controls had all but ended. On November 9, just four days after the election, Truman ordered the termination of all wage controls. He retained price controls only on rent, sugar, and rice.

Truman had also grown in office and became accustomed to the problems and duties of the presidency. He ended his defensiveness and protestations of inadequacy. In addition, a number of Truman's less competent advisers had left, and CLARK CLIFFORD, whose political insights were to prove an important influence on the Truman presidency, was gaining power. Just as important, Truman no longer felt himself restricted by a

Democratic Congress that opposed his programs. Instead he used the adversarial relationship between the executive and legislature to present himself as a bold leader, hampered by a reactionary Congress. He offered the Republican-dominated 80th Congress a program of domestic legislation, challenging the legislature to destroy it.

Truman's newfound confidence was expressed in his confrontation with John L. Lewis during the winter of 1946. In October Lewis had accused the administration of breaking the contract with the miners it had made during the previous spring. He asked for a reopening of negotiations and hinted at the possibility of a strike. Truman, on Clifford's advice, refused to negotiate a new agreement. He asserted that it would be interpreted as another surrender. Instead, he notified Lewis that the government would return the mines to the owners shortly after negotiations resumed. Truman then ordered the Justice Department to obtain an injunction against the proposed termination of the agreement. When the miners struck in November, Lewis and the union were found guilty of contempt of court and fined $3.5 million. In December Lewis called off the strike.

Truman, on the advice of Clifford, proposed a program of social legislation during 1947 and 1948 that was designed to solidify the New Deal, establish the president's standing with liberals, and lay the basis for the 1948 presidential campaign. He suggested changes in agricultural laws to increase aid to farmers, proposed raising the minimum wage from 40 to 75 cents, asked for increases in Social Security coverage, called for the reenactment of price controls to cut inflation, and requested a tax cut to benefit primarily the lower and middle classes. He also called for a comprehensive housing program to increase the stock of new housing and aid slum clearance. In December 1946, in reaction to a series of vicious racial murders in the South, Truman appointed a President's Committee on Civil Rights. The panel's report, "To Secure These Rights," issued in October 1947, became the basis for his civil rights proposals presented in February 1948. Truman called for an antilynching bill, the elimination of the poll tax, and the establishment of a Fair Employment Practices Commission.

With the exception of the housing program, most of Truman's proposals were ignored. The 80th Congress voted for a tax cut, including relief to the rich, cut funds for crop storage, and enacted dis-placed person legislation that discriminated against Catholic and Jews. Truman countered Congress's attempts to trim back the New Deal by using his veto 62 times during 1947 and 1948. His most important veto was of the Taft-Hartley bill, which limited the rights of organized labor. Explaining his action on national radio, Truman termed the measure "bad for labor, bad for management, and bad for the country." Congress, however, passed Taft-Hartley over the president's veto.

Critics acknowledged that Truman had pulled his administration together and had grown in office. Still the feeling prevailed that he was not competent to do the job. The *St. Louis Post-Dispatch*, a normally Democratic paper, wrote that Truman had shown he lacked "the stature, the vision, the social and economic grasp, or the sense of history required to lead the nation in a world crisis." Prominent Democrats such as CLAUDE PEPPER led efforts to prevent Truman from securing the nomination. They hoped to replace him with General DWIGHT D. EISENHOWER or Supreme Court Justice WILLIAM O. DOUGLAS. When these men declined to run, the anti-Truman drive collapsed, and the president received the nomination on the first ballot. Conservative southerners opposed to the civil rights plank of the party's platform bolted and formed the States Rights' Democrats with J. STROM THURMOND as their presidential candidate. Many liberals, discontented with Truman's foreign and domestic policies, rallied around Henry Wallace, the candidate of the newly formed Progressive Party.

The press, the public, and the professional pollsters predicted that Truman would go down to defeat to the Republican candidate, THOMAS E. DEWEY. Nevertheless, the feisty Truman remained optimistic. He was determined to use his status as the underdog and his quarrels with the 80th Congress to overcome Dewey's lead. Acting on the advice of Clark Clifford, he molded a campaign designed to maintain the New Deal alignment of poor, urban, and agricultural voters that had brought Roosevelt to power. Although Truman felt a moral obligation to recognize Israel upon its independence over the objections of Secretary of State Marshall, he hardly could have overlooked the gratitude that Jewish voters would extend to him at the polls. The president also initiated the desegregation of the armed forces, which won the hearts of the African-American electorate. On his whistle stop tours across the country, Truman stressed his adherence to the New Deal tradition and denounced the "do-nothing" 80th Congress for failure to pass his social programs. He called Congress into special session in order to pass social legislation. Its failure to do so reinforced Truman's contention that it was "the worst Congress" in history. While Dewey ran a restrained campaign, Truman blasted the Republicans. "If you send another Republican Congress to Washington," he told his audiences, "you're a bigger bunch of suckers than I think you are." Crowds, enjoying the combative Truman, would yell back "Give 'em hell Harry."

In November Truman scored what appeared to be one of the biggest upsets in U.S. history. However, author Harold I. Gullman has argued that given the political configuration of the time, the real upset would have been if Dewey had won. The president received 24.1 million votes to Dewey's 22 million and 303 electoral votes to the Republican's 189. Thurmond received only 39 electoral votes while Wallace received none. Truman's victory was based, as Clifford had expected, on the continuation of the New Deal coalition. He received the support of African Americans, labor, and the new "blue-collar" middle class. The President regained many midwestern farmers, who that had been drifting toward the GOP in recent elections, because of anger at the agricultural legislation of the 80th Congress. To a large extent the victory was influenced by the memory of the depression and the fear that a Republican administration would be unconcerned with the problems of the working man.

President in his own right, Truman announced that "every segment of our population and every individual has a right to expect from his government a fair deal." He urged enactment of an extensive domestic program based in part on the one he had proposed to the 80th Congress. At his request Congress passed a comprehensive housing bill designed to aid lower income groups and veterans. It became the basis for most of the government's housing programs in the 1950s. Congress extended Social Security benefits, increased the minimum wage, kept farm price supports high, and expanded conservation programs. Many of these measures seemed little more than a continuation of the New Deal. Critics categorized the years of the 81st Congress as "Roosevelt's Fifth Term." Truman, however, was not content with extending Roosevelt's programs. He also introduced extensive proposals on civil rights, called for aid to education,

asked for the repeal of the Taft-Hartley Act, and continued his appeal, first made in 1945, for national health insurance. Secretary of Agriculture CHARLES F. BRANNAN, in a dramatic policy departure designed to preserve the small farm, proposed a plan based on direct payments to farmers rather than a restriction of production. Congress, however, was reluctant to enact innovative legislation, and the president met defeat on these proposals.

Frustrated by the Congress's refusal to enact civil rights, Truman used executive power to increase the rights of African Americans. He appointed an African American to the federal judiciary and strengthened the Justice Department's Civil Rights Division. Under his direction, the department filed *amici curiae* briefs in support of efforts to end segregation in public schools and stop enforcement of restrictive covenants. Truman also increased the pace of desegregation in the armed forces.

In foreign affairs Truman continued extending the containment policies of his first administration. Hoping to put his own imprint on foreign policy, long dominated by his secretaries of state, he proposed "making the benefits of our scientific advances and industrial progress available for the improvement and growth of underdeveloped areas." The plan, known as the Point Four program, was enacted into law in May 1950. It was designed, as the European Recovery Program had been, to contain communism by eliminating the poverty that led to discontent. Unlike the earlier program, Point Four focused on the transmission of technical skill rather than the use of massive loans to aid developing nations.

Truman worked for the ratification of the North Atlantic Treaty of 1949, which committed the United States for the first time in its history to a mutual defense pact in Europe. To enable the United States to cope with its larger military role, he asked Congress to increase the power of the secretary of defense and support development of a modern air force, capable of delivering nuclear weapons anywhere in the world. Shortly after the Soviets revealed that they had exploded an atomic device, Truman ordered a crash program to develop the hydrogen bomb to maintain U.S. nuclear superiority.

A large portion of Truman's attention in foreign affairs was devoted to China, where Communists and Nationalists were engaged in a bitter civil war. Early in his first administration Truman had sent George Marshall on a mission to try to negotiate a truce and form a coalition government. Marshall had failed and returned predicting that if Chiang Kai-shek (Jiang Jieshi) did not reform his corrupt government no amount of American aid could save him. Truman, on his advice, had attempted to phase out aid to that nation to prevent U.S. involvement in a full-scale war. He was, however, forced to acquiesce to demands from right-wing Republicans for a new mission to China and continuation of some form of assistance. By the summer of 1949 it had become clear that Chiang was losing the war. In an attempt to explain American policy and extricate the United States from the situation, Truman ordered Secretary of State Dean Acheson to issue a White Paper on China. He blamed the imminent Communist takeover on corruption in the Nationalist regime.

The fall of China precipitated a storm of protest from the right, which accused Truman of having "sold-out" Chiang by concentrating U.S. aid in Europe. Influenced by the anticommunist hysteria of the time, the China Lobby insisted that the loss was the result of Communist influence in the State Department. After the formal proclamation of the Communist government, Truman was forced to assure China Lobby leaders that he would not recognize the new regime or permit its admission to the United Nations. Truman rejected demands from Senator WILLIAM F. KNOWLAND (R-Calif.) that the U.S. fleet protect Taiwan from the Communists and announced that he would not provide military aid or advice to the Nationalist Chinese. He would continue only economic aid. However, after the outbreak of the Korean War, he dispatched the Seventh Fleet to the straits between the two nations.

In light of the fall of China and the Soviet detonation of an atomic bomb, Truman in January 1950 ordered a complete reassessment of American defense and nuclear policy. The report, NSC-68, recommended that the United States unilaterally accept responsibility for the defense of the world and begin an immediate large-scale buildup of America's defense forces. Truman initially rejected its recommendations and refused to have the report made public. He reasoned that without a major crisis he could not get Congress or the public to support large defense appropriations. When the Korean conflict began in June 1950, Truman began implementing the report's recommendations.

Truman's handling of the Korean situation undermined his domestic support. In response to the North Korean invasion of the South, he sent U.S. troops under UN auspices to conduct what was termed a police action. Because the United Nations and not the United States alone was officially fighting the war, Truman decided not to ask Congress for a declaration of war. The public initially supported Truman's action, believing that a strong show of force was necessary to contain communism in Asia. Yet, despite his seeming willingness to fight in Korea, Truman was unable to quiet charges that he was "soft on communism." Republicans pointed to a speech by Dean Acheson, in which he had failed to include Korea in the U.S. defense perimeter, as a major factor in the outbreak of the war. Within a few months of the outbreak praise gave way to grumbling as the Chinese Communists intervened and drove the Americans back down the peninsula and the Korean conflict became "Truman's War."

Truman became even more unpopular after he fired General DOUGLAS MACARTHUR as supreme commander of UN forces in Korea in April 1951. Following the general's open opposition to a limited war and his politicking with Republican leaders in Congress, Truman announced that he could "no longer tolerate his insubordination" and dismissed him. Liberals supported his action as a necessary defense of presidential power, but members of the China Lobby and those who wanted an increased emphasis on Asia in foreign policy, denounced him. Senator JOSEPH R. MCCARTHY (R-Wisc.) called the president a "sonofabitch" who made his decision while drunk on "bourbon and Benedictine."

Truman's problems increased as the war dragged on. The conflict fanned an inflationary boom that he failed to restrain. Reluctant to impose wage and price controls, he announced a partial mobilization in July 1950. In his message he called for tax increase, restrictions on credit and the allocation of scarce materials. He did not, however, ask for wage and price controls. The regulations proved ineffective and prices continued to rise.

Truman's inability to control the domestic anticommunist crusade undermined his administration still further. Throughout the 1940s Americans had become increasingly concerned about domestic communism. Revelations in 1945 of the disclosure of State Department documents to a left-wing journal and discovery of a Communist spy ring in Canada heightened tension. Truman was disturbed by secret FBI reports suggesting that there were

Communists in high government offices. During the 1946 campaign Republicans ran on the pledge to "clean the Communists and fellow travelers out of the government." Truman, himself, contributed to the growing hysteria by couching his foreign policy pronouncements in terms of a crusade against communism.

In response to the growing pressure, Truman ordered a broad investigation of Communist activities in 1947 and established a stringent loyalty program for all federal employees. Under Executive Order 9835 every person accepting a civilian federal job was to undergo a loyalty check. If accused of disloyalty, an individual was entitled to a hearing with counsel present. However, he was not able to confront his accusers. During the Truman presidency the attorney general's list of subversive organizations was enlarged and used more formally in loyalty investigations.

Despite his own willingness to institute a loyalty program and to use the issue of domestic communism in his presidential campaign, Truman opposed much of the anticommunist crusade of the 1940s. In 1948 he termed the House Un-American Activities Committee's investigation of ALGER HISS "a red herring" and in 1951 attempted to block a congressional probe of OWEN LATTIMORE by refusing to produce loyalty files on the ground of executive privilege.

Truman opposed most of the anticommunist legislation of the period. He denounced the Mundt-Nixon bill of 1948, which would have required the registration of Communists. He asserted that it "adopted police-state tactics and unduly encroached on individual rights." Truman promised to veto any internal security bill. He sent to Congress a message on the issue and campaigned, unsuccessfully, for moderate legislation. Two years later Congress passed the Internal Security Act of 1950, which incorporated the Mundt-Nixon bill as well as provisions for the internment of suspected subversives in a national emergency. Truman, true to his word, vetoed the measure. In an effort to defeat attempts to override, he sent personal messages to each member of the House explaining his action. The House ignored him and voted to override.

Truman proved an ineffectual opponent of Senator McCarthy. He was angered at the senator's attacks on his administration and particularly the State Department. In addition, he was concerned by what he thought was McCarthy's growing power.

During the spring of 1950 he set up a special task force in the White House to rebut every charge McCarthy made. Truman used his own press conferences and speeches to attack McCarthy. However, he never confronted McCarthy directly, asking him to substantiate his charges. Despite his efforts, Truman seemed unable to restrict McCarthy's power. In the 1950 elections several prominent opponents of the Senator lost their seats in Congress to candidates McCarthy had backed. Historians later pointed out that the defeats were primarily a result of local political conditions and opposition to Truman administration policies, but contemporary observers attributed it to support for the anticommunist crusade. Although the Democrats retained control of Congress, the margin was held by southern conservatives, ending hopes for the continuation of the Fair Deal. McCarthyism continued to grow, and the president failed to quiet charges that he harbored Communists in government.

Domestic scandals contributed to Truman's loss of prestige. As early as 1949 rumors had been spread of conflict of interest at the White House. That year a congressional investigation uncovered proof that men close to the White House were selling government contracts for 5 percent of the contract price. One of Truman's closest friends, HARRY H. VAUGHAN, was implicated. During 1951 further probes revealed widespread corruption in the Reconstruction Finance Corporation and the Bureau of Internal Revenue. Truman's reluctance to reorganize these agencies and his fiery defense of his friends hurt his standing still further.

In March 1952, Truman, his legislative program stalled, and his administration under attack, publicly announced he would not run for reelection that year. He privately offered ADLAI E. STEVENSON, the liberal governor of Illinois, his support for the nomination. Stevenson, however, was reluctant to associate himself with the administration and refused to acknowledge his candidacy until the convention. After he received the nomination Stevenson took care to maintain a distance from the administration. His strategy offended the president who, as a vigorous political fighter, disliked Stevenson's low-keyed campaign. Relations between the two remained strained, and in subsequent years Truman maintained that Stevenson's loss was his own fault.

In his final State of the Union Message in January 1953, Truman warned Stalin against war with the United States and urged continued Western resistance to Communist expansion without plunging the world into nuclear conflict. He also cautioned against legislation aimed at domestic communism that would promote an "enforced conformity."

During the 1950s Truman frequently spoke out in opposition to the Eisenhower administration's foreign and domestic programs. He remained active in Democratic politics, backing Averell Harriman for the presidential nomination in 1956 and STUART SYMINGTON in 1960. When John F. Kennedy received the nomination that year, Truman campaigned vigorously for him despite his personal dislike of the Kennedy family. He was a strong supporter of the Johnson-Humphrey ticket in 1964 and generally backed the Great Society legislative program. In 1965 President Johnson flew to Independence to sign the law creating Medicare at a ceremony honoring Truman, who had proposed national health insurance in 1945. Truman was a consistent supporter of the administration's Vietnam policy. He died in Kansas City, Missouri, on December 26, 1972, at the age of 88.

Historians' assessments of Harry Truman changed dramatically in the 25 years after his administration. During the late 1950s and early 1960s, he was lauded as the man who, thrown into the presidency, was able to lead the nation through the difficult period of reconversion with no severe social or economic dislocations. He was, in the words of Clinton Rossiter, a "highly successful Andrew Johnson." They particularly applauded his demands for aid to education, national health insurance, and strong civil rights legislation. "Truman encountered many reverses," historian William Leuchtenberg wrote, "but he at least raised new public issues that two decades later would still form part of the agenda of Lyndon Johnson's Great Society."

America's involvement in Vietnam and the growth of presidential powers engendered by the conflict strongly influenced assessments of Truman's foreign policy. New Left historians charged that Truman had overreacted to Stalin's legitimate desire for security on his western border and was to a large extent responsible for the development of the cold war. Some questioned his humanitarian motives in instituting the Marshall Plan and maintained that Truman was primarily interested in reestablishing important American markets. More conservative historians such as ARTHUR M. SCHLESINGER, JR., pointed out that Truman's actions in Korea

increased presidential power, contributing to the development of "the imperial presidency."

During the 1970s historians' views of Truman again began to change. While still praising his domestic programs, writers pointed out that Truman's own weaknesses as chief executive contributed to their defeat. Historians have also charged that Truman, while opposing the anticommunist hysteria in the late 1940s, contributed to its development through his loyalty program and his decision to describe the struggle with the Soviet Union in terms of a moral and ideological conflict. He also failed to stop the development of McCarthyism because of inept leadership. Some historians, notably John Lewis Gaddis, became more sympathetic to Truman's cold war policies. They asserted that Truman, as the leader of a democratic society, was constrained by public opinion and congressional demands to pursue a firm policy toward the USSR. Stalin, he pointed out, had a greater opportunity to accommodate himself to the U.S. position because he lacked these restrictions. Therefore, blame for the cold war must be distributed more evenly.

In recent years a wide variety of interpretations of Truman's presidency have arisen, as archives opened more manuscripts for review. Three major biographies of Truman were produced as well as a myriad of monographs. David McCullough, in a sympathetic look at the 33rd president, painted Truman as a hero who had not lost his common touch. Alonzo L. Hamby contended that, despite Truman's snappishness, partisanship, and lack of charisma, he excelled in the usages of power. Despite his fiery campaign rhetoric, he could fashion bipartisan coalitions to meet goals. Truman evolved from an ideology of "insurgent progressivism" to "New Deal–Fair Deal liberalism." Yet his attempt to maintain the Roosevelt coalition led to "a politics of liberal promise and conservative gridlock" that hurt his credibility. His foreign policy suffered in the end because of the expanding commitments he incurred and diminishing military capabilities that his budget cuts imposed. Despite these problems, Hamby concluded that Truman was correct in his advocacy of civil rights and meeting the Soviet threat. Robert H. Ferrell saw Truman as a courageous man, devoted to public service, who stood up to the Soviets, but who could be hot-tempered toward those who disagreed with him. (See *The Eisenhower Years, The Kennedy Years, The Johnson Years* Volumes)

Trumbo, Dalton

(1905–1976) *screenwriter*

The son of working-class parents, Dalton Trumbo was born on December 9, 1905, in Montrose, California. He left the University of Colorado at Boulder after one year for economic reasons. In 1925 the Trumbo family moved to Los Angeles, where Dalton took a job at the Davis Perfection Bakery. He remained there for eight years. Trumbo did not romanticize the poverty of his early years. "I never considered the working class anything other than something to get out of," he later said. His radical political views and his hatred of "bosses" were in part shaped by his experience during the depression.

In 1932 Trumbo became an associate editor of the *Hollywood Spectator* and in 1934 took a job with Warner Brothers as a reader of possible movie properties. The following year he published his first novel, *Eclipse*, which received favorable reviews. In October 1935 Warner Brothers hired him as a junior screen writer. Trumbo worked mainly on B-pictures until he was fired after a year for his membership in the left-wing Screen Writers Guild. In 1938, after signing a contract with RKO, Trumbo wrote *A Man to Remember*, a highly acclaimed low budget film that helped establish him in his profession. The following year he published *Johnny Got His Gun*, an antiwar novel told from the point of view of a crippled and isolated veteran. In 1940 he earned an Academy Award nomination for his screenplay *Kitty Foyle*. Trumbo joined the Communist Party in 1943. He later claimed that the move "represented no significant change in [his] thought or life," since he had been fighting for radical causes with Communists for years. During World War II Trumbo visited the Pacific as a war correspondent. He also contributed to the screenplay for *30 Seconds Over Tokyo* in 1944.

In 1947 the House Un-American Activities Committee (HUAC) began a probe of possible Communist influence in Hollywood. Several movie executives accused Trumbo of "un-Americanism" while others said that he might be a Communist. In October he and nine other screenwriters, including John Lawson, Lester Cole, and RING LARDNER, JR., appeared before the committee. Led by Trumbo, the Hollywood Ten as they became known, refused to answer the panel's questions on the grounds that it was unconstitutional to investigate their political beliefs. Trumbo would not directly respond to questions about his membership in either the Screen Writers Guild or the Communist Party. He sur-prised Committee chairman J. PARNELL THOMAS (R-N.J.) by asking to see any evidence the committee held. The request was denied. As a result of his refusal to answer questions, Trumbo, along with the other nine, was cited for contempt by the House on November 24. The following day, after a meeting of leaders of the American film industry, ERIC A. JOHNSTON, president of the Motion Pictures Association, announced the Hollywod Ten would be discharged and Communists barred from the industry. MGM fired Trumbo on December 2.

Confident that their stand would be upheld in the courts, the Hollywood Ten pleaded innocent to the contempt charges in January 1948. In May Trumbo and Lawson were convicted and sentenced to a year in prison. The remaining eight waived trial and agreed to abide by the outcome of the Lawson-Trumbo appeal. By then Trumbo was in the process of leaving the Communist Party. He later said that in 1948, ". . . I just drifted away. I changed no beliefs. I just quit going to meetings and never went back—with no more feelings of separation than I had before I started with the Communist Party."

In May 1949 the Ten brought a $52 million antitrust suit against 10 major studios. The Circuit Court of Appeals in Washington upheld the convictions the following month. In 1950 the U.S. Supreme Court, in a 6 to 2 decision, supported HUAC's right to force witnesses to divulge Communist Party membership. Trumbo entered a federal prison in Ashland, Kentucky, in June 1953. He served a reduced sentence of 10 months. After his release he found employment scarce and took his family to Mexico. In 1952 several of the studios named in the Hollywood Ten damage suit agreed to an out-of-court settlement. Trumbo later estimated his share of the total was $28,000. In 1954 Trumbo moved back to Hollywood. Because of the blacklist he was forced to find writers to front for his work or to write under an assumed name. That year he rejoined the Communist Party in a gesture of support for 14 party officials in California convicted under the Smith Act. He quit after the convictions were reversed and the defendants freed.

Trumbo was responsible for what has been described as a "personal campaign" against the blacklist. He constantly spoke out against the restrictions placed on writers with radical or left-wing pasts. In 1957 his screenplay for *The Brave One*, written under the pseudonym Robert Rich, won an Academy Award. Since blacklisted writers could not receive Oscars, Trumbo's success, quickly discovered by the press, served to embarrass the Hollywood establishment. Trumbo finally received the award for that screenplay in 1975. In 1961 he "broke" the blacklist when he publicly received credit for *Exodus*. During the 1960s and early 1970s, Trumbo wrote the scripts for such popular movies as *Hawaii*, *The Fixer*, and *Papillon*. In 1971 he wrote and directed the film version of *Johnny Got his Gun*. The film won the Cannes Film Festival International Critics Award. Trumbo underwent surgery of lung cancer in 1973. He died of a heart attack on September 10, 1976, in Los Angeles, California.

Although the Hollywood Ten tend to garner sympathy from most observers, author Kenneth Lloyd Billingsley has contended that Communists were subtly attempting to introduce Marxist propaganda into movies, and that the Hollywood Ten were not as guiltless as they pretended to be. Trumbo himself once said, "Every screen writer worth his salt wages the battle in his own way—a kind of literary guerrilla war" and bragged about preventing the production of anti-Soviet and anti-communist films.

—JF

Tugwell, Rexford G(uy)
(1891–1979) *governor; chairman, Progressive Party platform*

Rexford G. Tugwell was born on July 10, 1891, in Sinclairville, New York. His father, Charles Henry Tugwell, was a successful upstate New York farmer. The younger Tugwell graduated from the prestigious Wharton School, receiving a bachelor's degree in 1915 and a master's degree in 1917. He was assistant professor of economics at the University of Washington until 1918 and then spent two years abroad at the American University in Paris. Returning to the United States he received his doctorate at Wharton in 1922. His dissertation, entitled "The Economic Basis of Public Interest," reflected the primary theme of his entire subsequent career—the need for regulation of the economy, and industry in particular, in order to serve the needs of the nation. He joined the faculty of Columbia University in 1922 and remained there until 1937.

Tugwell served as campaign adviser to Franklin D. Roosevelt in 1932 and, during Roosevelt's first administration, served as undersecretary of agriculture. He was considered by many to be the most radical of the New Deal officials and played a prominent role in the formation of the Agricultural Adjustment Act and the Civilian Conservation Corps, as well as the development of currency regulation. In 1938 New York mayor Fiorello H. LaGuardia asked Tugwell to head the city planning commission. Three years later Secretary of the Interior HAROLD L. ICKES selected Tugwell to lead an inquiry into land disputes in Puerto Rico. Tugwell became acquainted with Luis Muñoz Marín, head of Puerto Rico's Popular Party, a relationship that became important when, in August of the following year, Tugwell became governor of Puerto Rico.

In close cooperation with Muñoz Marín, then president of the Puerto Rico Senate, Tugwell instituted a broad-range program of industrial and agricultural development, eventually dubbed "the little New Deal" by the press. Under President Truman he inaugurated "Operation Bootstrap," an economic development program offering a 12-year tax exemption and general assistance with labor problems and plant construction to new industry. However, his anticolonialist policies came under increasing attacks from the sugar industry and conservative politicians. He resigned in 1946, defended his record as governor in a book *The Stricken Land*, published that same year.

Tugwell then became a professor of political science at the University of Chicago. In March 1948 the university held a conference at which he helped design and present a "Preliminary Draft of a World Constitution," which stated in part that the atomic bombing of Hiroshima had been "the logical and inevitable concomitant of modern technological achievements. Unless we bring them under control of one government, they will destroy us." It also advocated the development of a confederated world government made up of the Federal Convention, the Council, the president, three special units (a Syndical Senate; an Institute of Science, Education and Culture; and a House of Nationalities), the Grand Tribunal, the Supreme Court, the Tribune of the People, and the Chamber of Guardians. Tugwell believed the chief body would be the Planning Agency, which would guide the world's economy.

Tugwell was one of the many progressive Democrats who felt that the Truman administration was betraying the social reforms of the New Deal and pursuing a dangerously militant foreign policy. He supported HENRY A. WALLACE's campaign for the presidency on the Progressive Party ticket during 1948. He believed the Progressives "were starting a true Progressive movement, worthy to succeed that of LaFollette and his co-workers." According to his biographer, Michael V. Namorato, Tugwell thought Wallace's candidacy was intended to bring back into existence the best parts of the New Deal. In the months preceding the party's convention, he appeared at Wallace campaign rallies and attempted to bring other prominent New Deal liberals into the Progressive Party. However, he had little success. Tugwell served as chairman of the party's Platform Committee charged with drawing up the statement of party principles. At the convention in July, he found himself involved in several disputes with other members of the committee. While opposing what he considered to be the aggressive policies of the Truman administration, he felt that the Progressive Party platform was too "pro-Russian" and failed to take into account "power politics considerations" when dealing with defense matters. He was in sharp disagreement with New York Representative VITO MARCANTONIO (ALP-N.Y.), who wished the platform to definitively endorse total independence for Puerto Rico. Tugwell preferred a simple call for "self-determination." Compromise language was eventually worked out.

The final platform called for negotiations with the Soviet Union, repeal of the peacetime draft, repudiation of the Truman Doctrine and the Marshall Plan, and formulation of a disarmament agreement to outlaw the atomic bomb. On domestic issues it demanded full equality for minorities, controls to reduce inflation, nationalization of certain industries, repeal of the Taft-Hartley Act, and establishment of old-age pensions and medical care for all.

While presenting the platform to the full convention, Tugwell delivered a rousing pro-Wallace speech. But in August he conceded to a reporter from the *Baltimore Sun*, in what he thought was an off-the-record conversation, that he felt that extremists had too much influence at the convention. Since the Communist Party had already openly endorsed the Wallace campaign, the press presented Tugwell's statements as a virtual admission that Wallace was "controlled by the Communists." Wallace issued a statement denying any ties to the Communist Party—but not wishing to be a part of what he considered a "red scare," he rejected Tugwell's advice to openly repudiate Communist support.

Tugwell continued to appear on behalf of Wallace and turned down a covert suggestion from Truman supporters in October that he leave the

Progressive Party. By election day, Wallace's support had greatly diminished and his showing was poor.

The Wallace campaign marked the end of Tugwell's active participation in politics. He returned to the University of Chicago, eventually retiring in 1957. In 1964 he became a member of the Center for the Study of Democratic Institutions in Santa Barbara, California. He came to believe strongly that another Franklin Roosevelt was needed to lead the nation and also thought the Constitution should be restructured and updated so that it would allow economic planning. Tugwell died of cancer in Santa Barbara, California, on July 21, 1979.

—MQ

Tydings, Millard E(velyn)
(1890–1961) *member of the Senate*

Tydings was born on April 6, 1890, in Havre de Grace, Maryland, the son of Millard Fillmore, an engineer, and Mary O'Neill Tydings. The future senator earned a B.S. degree from Maryland Agricultural College in 1910 and a law degree from the University of Maryland in 1913. Three years later he won a seat in the Maryland House of Delegates as a Democrat. Tydings served in the army during World War I and then returned to the Maryland legislature. He won a seat in the U.S. House in 1923 and in the Senate three years later. A conservative, Tydings opposed most New Deal legislation. For this reason, Franklin D. Roosevelt personally campaigned against him in the state's 1938 senatorial primary. The Maryland voters ignored Roosevelt and reelected Tydings in the primary and the general election. Tydings's opposition to Roosevelt's wartime domestic social legislation and his identification with the southern white supremacist bloc in the Senate earned him the enmity of labor and of his state's growing black population. Yet support from the state's rural and suburban areas guaranteed him reelection in 1944.

Tydings's political priorities took a dramatic turn in 1945 and 1946. In May 1945 he visited the Philippines, which had been devastated by the recent conflict. He returned home to report to Truman and made a stirring speech in the Senate advocating millions of dollars in aid to the archipelago, which became law. A little over a year later he was present at an atomic bomb test at Bikini Atoll, in which mighty battleships served as targets and were either sunk or badly damaged. The sight made a deep impression on the senator, and spurred on his interest in arms control. He advocated for the complete disarmament of both nuclear and conventional weapons by all nations by 1950.

Tydings became chairman of the Armed Services Committee in 1949 and crafted a law strengthening the power of the secretary of defense, making the secretaries of the three branches of the armed services completely subordinate to the defense secretary. The act also created the chairman of the Joint Chiefs of Staff, who would give integrated military advice to the secretary. The senator also was an advocate of universal military training.

By 1947, Tydings had tired of constantly fighting the party's leadership as he had during Roosevelt's time, and he developed a much closer relationship with President Truman, a friend from when the Missourian was a senator, than he had with his predecessor. He especially supported the president's foreign policy. He backed the various foreign aid measures of the administration, including aid to Greece and Turkey and the Marshall Plan, and even voted against a Republican tax cut proposal in 1947 because he believed the money was needed to help noncommunist Europe. He also supported the creation of NATO.

A fiscal conservative, Tydings did oppose the president's Fair Deal. He backed Republican demands for budget cuts in 1949 and introduced a bill requiring the president to cut spending by at least 5 percent but no more than 20 percent. His proposal was defeated. Tydings remained an adamant segregationist. Tydings had been considered a possible vice presidential running mate for Truman in 1948 but took himself out of the race because of the party platform's liberal civil rights plank. However, he did not join the Dixiecrat revolt of 1948.

On February 9, 1950 Senator JOSEPH R. MCCARTHY (R-Wisc.) delivered a controversial speech in which he announced that he had evidence of subversives in the State Department. A few days later the Senate formed a bipartisan committee, headed by Tydings, to investigate the charges. The Maryland senator approached his assignment confident that McCarthy would be repudiated. A master of invective and a shrewd political operator, according to historian Robert Griffith, Tydings sought to discredit McCarthy by pointing out inconsistencies in his statements and challenging him to give specifics. The senator's tactics elicited criticism from

Republican members of the panel who demanded that Tydings stop harassing McCarthy and let him present his findings uninterrupted. Tydings reluctantly agreed. McCarthy then presented a list of nine names of individuals he considered disloyal, including OWEN LATTIMORE and JOHN S. SERVICE.

During the spring of 1950 the Tydings Committee delved into McCarthy's charges against these individuals. The investigation engendered a struggle with the administration and divided the panel along partisan lines. Truman bitterly opposed the probe and refused to release Lattimore's loyalty files on the grounds of executive privilege. Tydings, however, was able to reach a compromise. He and three other senators were permitted to view summaries of the documents. The four senators, Tydings, fellow Democrats Theodore Green and BRIEN MCMAHON (D-Conn.), and Republican HENRY CABOT LODGE (R-Mass.), said the summaries did not indicate that Lattimore was a communist. Tydings proclaimed Lattimore cleared. However, the committee member who had not reviewed the summaries with the others, Republican BOURKE B. HICKENLOOPER (R-Iowa), after reading them, said they did not say Lattimore was not a communist. Then Lodge, miffed at Tyding's premature clearing of Lattimore, said he had not yet made a decision on the case, and when he did so he would announce it himself. Tydings then convinced a reluctant Truman to allow the committee to see the files themselves, but that hardly satisfied McCarthy, who claimed the files had been "raped and rifled." The committee also reviewed the government's handling of the *Amerasia* case, in which Service was accused of passing classified government documents, and found no wrongdoing.

The Tydings Committee divided on the results of the probe. On June 28 the Democrats issued a final report accusing McCarthy of perpetrating "a fraud and a hoax" and "perhaps the most nefarious campaign of half-truths and untruths in the history of the Republic." McCarthy, they maintained, had "deceived and misled" the Senate by using the "Big Lie." The report cleared Lattimore of any wrongdoing. The Republicans, on the other hand, charged the Democratic members with planning a coverup. Tydings's report precipitated a fierce debate in the Foreign Relations Committee and on the floor of the Senate. Senator WILLIAM E. JENNER (R-Ind.) accused him of conducting "the most scandalous and brazen whitewash of treasonable conspiracy in our history."

Tydings, in turn, angrily defended the report and denounced McCarthy as a "rank demagogue." The report was adopted on a straight party line vote.

Tydings's probe failed to stem the tide of McCarthyism or quell American fears of domestic subversion. The senator became an enemy of the right, and McCarthy set out to defeat him in his 1950 reelection bid. McCarthy personally campaigned for JOHN MARSHALL BUTLER, Tydings's Republican opponent, and helped plan strategy. The race proved to be one of the bitterest and dirtiest of the Truman era. Butler exploited doubts that Tydings had conducted a fair investigation and attempted to discredit his entire record in light of this uncertainty. He accused Tydings of shielding traitors and, at one point, his staff published a photograph of Tydings presumably talking with EARL BROWDER, leader of the Communist Party. The Republicans labeled the photo a composite, but few people noticed.

At first Tydings disregarded his opponent. Winning four terms in the Senate and, in particular, surviving Roosevelt's attacks had made him feel unassailable. He failed to see how vulnerable he was. Maryland's Democratic administration had just passed the state's first sales tax and, in addition, Tydings had already alienated the black vote, which Butler actively courted. Labor and liberals, which had always opposed him, refused to aid his campaign, even though the Americans for Democratic Action endorsed him. Maryland Catholics, an important part of Tydings's previous coalition, were impressed with McCarthy, a fellow Catholic, and resentful of Tydings's elitist image. As a result, Tydings lost the election by 40,000 votes.

Griffith asserted McCarthy's role in Tydings's defeated has been overestimated, but Tydings biographer Caroline H. Keith noted that the Marylander had been the favorite to win before he agreed to chair the committee investigating McCarthy's accusations and claimed that the Wisconsinite was pivotal in the upset. The defeat of Tydings, one of the most powerful members of the Senate, put a chilling effect on opposition to McCarthy in that body for the next four years.

In December 1950 Tydings filed an oral and written complaint with the Senate Subcommittee on Privileges and Elections in which he denounced his opponent's literature as "scandalous, scurrilous, libelous, and unlawful." The Senate permitted Butler to take his seat "without prejudice" pending the conclusion of the hearings on Tydings's charges. Following three months of testimony, the panel exonerated Butler of any wrongdoing but condemned the role of outsiders in the campaign.

Tydings retired to his Maryland farm. He died on February 9, 1961 at Havre de Grace.

—JB

U

Urey, Harold C(layton)
(1893–1981) *chemist*

Harold Urey was born in Walkerton, Indiana, on April 29, 1893, and raised in the Hoosier State by his mother and clergyman stepfather. He taught for several years in country schools before matriculating at Montana State University, where he received a B.S. in zoology in 1917. During World War I he worked as a research chemist, helping to manufacture war materiel. After the war he returned to Montana State to teach chemistry. Pursuing studies in both chemistry and physics at the University of California at Berkeley, Urey received his Ph.D. in 1923. He then received a fellowship to study at the Institute for Theoretical Physics at the University of Copenhagen under renowned atomic physicist Niels Bohr.

Urey returned to the United States in 1924 and taught chemistry at Johns Hopkins University for five years. In 1929 he accepted an associate professorship at Columbia University. Two years later he announced his discovery of heavy water, consisting of one atom of oxygen and two atoms of the heavy hydrogen isotope, deuterium. This discovery, for which Urey received a Nobel Prize in 1934, had a major effect on future research in medicine and biology as well as in physics and chemistry.

When Urey's former teacher, Niels Bohr, arrived from Europe in 1939 bringing news of successful nuclear fission experiments in Germany, Urey was one of the first American scientists to recognize the possibility of developing an atomic bomb. He worked at Columbia, along with ENRICO FERMI, on a diffusion process for the separation of uranium isotopes, and during the war visited Britain in connection with this study. From 1940 to 1945 Urey served as the director of war research on the atomic bomb at Columbia University.

Urey was one of the first scientists to express his fears about the development of atomic weapons. In 1945, when President Harry S Truman created the Interim Committee with its four-man scientific panel to advise him on using the atomic bomb, many younger scientists who favored a public test of the bomb in an uninhabited area agitated for Urey's appointment. Urey was not named to the panel, which later recommended the use of the atomic bomb on a dual civilian-military Japanese target. Earlier in Urey had joined physicist LEO SZILARD in his journey to Spartanburg, South Carolina, in May to see Truman confidant and future secretary of state JAMES F. BYRNES. They argued to Byrnes the case against dropping the atomic bomb on Japan. The mission, of course, failed in its objective.

After the war Urey insisted upon the scientists' responsibility in educating the public on the dangers and values of atomic energy. In 1946 he published a pamphlet entitled "I'm a Frightened Man," in which he called for an international political structure to deal with the new challenge of atomic energy. Urey felt that "here political leaders must pioneer as scientists have pioneered." He stressed that the "secret" of atomic energy would soon be known by all competent scientists and warned that the United States, with its concentrations of population and industry, would be most vulnerable to surprise atomic attack. After the Russians' rejection of the Baruch Plan for atomic control in 1946, Urey came to favor the maintenance of strong American and European defenses, including an arsenal of atomic weapons, to deter Soviet aggression.

Urey returned to teaching and research after World War II, accepting a key position at the newly created Institute for Nuclear Studies at the University of Chicago in 1945. In October 1949, when the General Advisory Committee (GAC) of scientists to the Atomic Energy Commission advised against a crash program to produce a hydrogen bomb, Urey deplored the GAC's decision as being politically and not scientifically motivated. After Truman's decision in 1950 to develop an H-bomb, he began to work on the project but left after a few months to devote himself full time to teaching and other research. He remarked that his study of sea shells to discover past and future climatic changes interested him more than anything he "was able to do in connection with the development of the bomb." In 1952 he published a controversial work, *The Planets, Their Origin and Development*, which set forth a new theory of the origins of the solar system.

When J. ROBERT OPPENHEIMER lost his security clearance in 1954, Urey came to his defense. In 1958 Urey accepted a professorship at the University of California in La Jolla. He continued to teach and do research into the 1960s, receiving in 1965 a National Medal of Science for his work on the origins of the solar system. Urey died on January 5, 1981, in La Jolla, California.

—DAE

V

Valentine, Alan
(1901–1980) *administrator, Economic Stabilization Agency*

Born on February 23, 1901, in Glen Cove, New York, Alan Valentine graduated from Swarthmore College in 1921 and received an M.A. from the University of Pennsylvania the following year. After further study at Oxford as a Rhodes scholar, he became a professor of literature and an administrator at various American universities and colleges. In 1935 he was appointed president of the University of Rochester, a post which he held until 1949. Active in Democratic politics, Valentine served as executive director of the National Committee of Democrats for Willkie in 1940. During the postwar period he was a member of several government committees, and in 1948–49, he served as chief European Cooperation Administration's mission to the Netherlands.

In October 1950 President Truman appointed him administrator of the newly created Economic Stabilization Agency (ESA), established to deal with the inflation stemming from the Korean War effort. The appointment of the conservative Valentine aroused derision among liberals. ARTHUR M. SCHLESINGER, JR., noted his opposition to the New and Fair Deals. The *New York Post* sardonically quipped that the new ESA head might be "exactly the man for the job of non-administering non-existent controls." Valentine's service on the ESA was as short as it was controversial. While fully committed to wage and price controls, Valentine favored a slower pace of implementation than either Truman or the other members of the ESA would support.

On October 31, 1950, two weeks after assuming his duties, Valentine warned in a speech that a long-range defense program required controls as strict as those in force during World War II and that such controls would have to remain in effect "much longer." When on December 5 both General Motors (GM) and Ford announced price increases on new cars, Valentine supported these words with strong actions. On December 7 he requested the major auto companies to withhold such price increases until an ESA investigation could be made. This constituted the first government request for voluntary price restraint since World War II. On the following day GM and Ford announced that they had "regretfully" rejected Valentine's request.

The conflict between government and industry escalated on December 16, 1950, when ESA Ceiling Price Regulation No. 1 rolled auto prices back to December 1 levels. Although the ESA also promised on December 19 to stabilize auto industry pay as quickly as possible, the auto industry called the order "discriminatory" and asked the agency to reconsider. Despite Valentine's offer of possible price relief to auto makers, GM on December 18 halted sale of all 1951 models pending "examination" of the ESA order. On December 21, however, the industry capitulated and resumed sales at December 1 prices. On December 22 Valentine froze auto industry wages through March 1, 1951, the first wage curb since World War II.

Despite this success Valentine had by this time fallen out of favor with the administration. Price Stabilization director MICHAEL V. DISALLE had drafted a plan for a 30-day order to freeze all wages and prices, but, because Valentine insisted that the agency had insufficient staff to enforce such an order, the plan was scuttled. This conflict between Valentine and DiSalle over the implementation of controls quickly became a national political issue.

Valentine had repeatedly attacked DiSalle's proposed 30-day order, characterizing absolute controls as "impossible" but promising overall controls by March 1. He also criticized the public for its lack of support for the ESA. Valentine was in turn criticized by Defense Mobilization director CHARLES E. WILSON for being "too slow" in setting up control machinery.

On January 19, 1951, Truman asked Valentine to resign as ESA administrator. The president replaced him with ERIC A. JOHNSTON of the Motion Picture Association of America and gave Johnston broader powers. In his resignation statement, Valentine asserted that he disagreed with Truman, DiSalle, and Wilson only "as to the precise timing and methods" of controls.

After his ouster as head of the Economic Stabilization Administration, Valentine became president of the Committee for Free Asia. He resigned that post in late 1952. Valentine then turned to more scholarly pursuits and published numerous books, including *The Age of Conformity* (1954), *Vigilante Justice* (1956), and *The Education of an American* (1958). Valentine died on July 14, 1980, in Rockland, Maine.

—LG

Vandenberg, Arthur H(endrick)
(1884–1951) *member of the Senate*

The son of a harness manufacturer, Arthur H. Vandenberg was born on March 22, 1884, in Grand Rapids, Michigan. He took odd jobs as a teenager to help support his family when his father's business failed in 1893. After dropping out of law school in 1902, Vandenberg joined the staff of the *Grand Rapids* (Mich.) *Herald* as a political reporter. In 1907 he became the paper's publisher and editor. He soon emerged to be one of the most prominent citizens of Grand Rapids as well as a leading Michigan Republican. In 1928 Vandenberg was appointed to fill a Senate seat vacated by the death of Woodbridge N. Ferris (D-Mich.).

With the defeat of many incumbent Republicans during the depression, Vandenberg moved up quickly in seniority. By 1940 he was a leader of the party in the Senate. He established a conservative record, opposing most New Deal legislation. In the late 1930s he was the key member of the GOP's isolationist wing. After World War II broke out in 1939 Vandenberg opposed measures giving aid to American allies and led the fight against the modification of the Neutrality Act.

Like many isolationists he supported the president's war measures after Pearl Harbor, beginning what DEAN G. ACHESON later described as "his long day's journey into our times." Vandenberg chaired a committee of leading Republicans that pledged the party's support of the war effort. He also served on a bipartisan committee formed to help the administration plan postwar policy. Vandenberg formally renounced isolationism in a speech to the Senate in April 1944. During the last half of the 1940s, he played a major role in the formation of the United Nations and in gaining congressional support for the organization. President Roosevelt appointed him ranking Republican delegate to the San Francisco Conference of 1945, which drafted the UN charter. When he assumed the presidency, Harry Truman renewed the appointment. At Vandenberg's insistence the U.S. delegation at San Francisco pushed for the adoption of Article 51 of the UN Charter, which permitted member states to enter into regional security pacts for the maintenance of international peace and security. His resolution later served as the justification for U.S. entrance into such alliances as the North Atlantic Treaty Organization and the Rio Pact. Vandenberg then helped secure Senate ratification of the charter.

Along with Secretary of State JAMES F. BYRNES, Vandenberg was the architect of the Truman administration's policy of "talking tough" to the Soviets. As the representative of a state with a large Polish-American constituency, he vigorously denounced Soviet domination of Eastern Europe and backed calls for a firm U.S. stand on Soviet disengagement. His experience in dealing with the Soviets at international conferences reinforced his fears that the Soviet Union would not comply with the Yalta Accords. By the early months of 1946, he had become convinced that cooperation between the two powers was impossible. Returning from a foreign ministers' conference in Paris, Vandenberg somberly reported that a "cold war" now existed and warned that the United States must adopt new policies to meet the crisis. During the spring of 1946 the administration, in the face of growing anti-Soviet feeling, adopted an increasingly firm policy toward Russia. It escalated the rhetoric of the cold war, cut off American economic aid to the USSR, and increased the American nuclear arsenal.

Following the Republican victory in the 1946 congressional elections, Vandenberg assumed the chairmanship of the Foreign Relations Committee. He became, as Acheson wrote, "The key to indispensable Republican cooperation in obtaining legislative approval and the support for policies of the greatest magnitude and novelty." Vandenberg was deeply involved in securing congressional approval of the Truman Doctrine. In February Truman invited Vandenberg and several other influential senators to the White House to discuss aid to Greece and Turkey. During the meeting Vandenberg allegedly told president that if he wanted Congress to appropriate money for the programs he would have to "scare the hell out of the country." Truman accepted this advice and, in his landmark Truman Doctrine address of March 14, 1947, placed his request for aid in terms of a moral crusade against communism. Vandenberg then led the battle for Senate ratification of the aid package. Largely as a result of his efforts the measure passed in April.

Following Secretary of State GEORGE C. MARSHALL's unveiling of the Marshall Plan in June 1947, Truman invited Vandenberg to work closely with the administration to frame the legislation for the program. The senator also advised the administration on the formation of a number of committees to investigate Europe's needs. Vandenberg worked hard to overcome opposition to the Marshall Plan by conservatives anxious to maintain a balanced budget and pro-China senators, who wanted funds given to Chiang Kai-shek (Jiang Jieshi) rather than to European governments. Vandenberg described the plan as a program that would "help stop World War III before it starts." In an impassioned speech to the Senate, he said that if the plan failed, "We have done our final best, if it succeeds our children and our children's children will call us blessed." He obtained enough Republican support to guarantee passage of the program in June 1948.

Vandenberg was a vigorous advocate of U.S. participation in a Western defense alliance. In May 1948 he presented to his committee a working paper calling on the United States to grant military aid to international alliances among its allies. The committee unanimously recommended the proposal, and the Senate passed the resolution in June 1948. The Vandenberg resolution, as it was known, proved the basis for American entrance into the North Atlantic Treaty Organization (NATO). Although suffering from cancer, Vandenberg lobbied for passage of the North Atlantic Treaty in

1949, urging its ratification as the best means for discouraging armed aggression. In a speech to his colleagues in July 1949, he delivered so moving an appeal for support for "the terrifying authority for peace" that members of his party and even some Democrats stood up and cheered him. The Senate passed the treaty that month.

During the last years of his life Vandenberg continued to support what he termed a "un-partisan foreign policy." He advocated cuts in the 1950 foreign aid bill but continued to advocate economic assistance to prevent war. The senator supported nonrecognition of Communist China but broke with other Republican leaders who demanded armed intervention if necessary to protect Taiwan. During the spring of 1950 he urged a complete reconsideration of foreign policy.

Despite his postwar internationalism Vandenberg remained somewhat of a protectionist regarding foreign trade. For instance, he voted to eliminate the ability of the president to cut tariffs by as much 50 percent as they stood on January 1, 1945, in the 1945 extension of the Trade Agreements Act of 1945. He also supported the use of "peril points," by which the Federal Tariff Commission was to recommend the minimum tariff rates needed to protect native industries of various products. If the president cut rates lower than these points, he would have to explain why he did so.

Vandenberg tended to vote conservatively on domestic issues. He backed the Case labor disputes bill, the Taft-Hartley Act, the Portal-to-Portal Pay Act, the 1948 Republican tax cut, turning the tidelands over to the states, and the McCarran Internal Security Act. Yet he did vote for the Full Employment bill of 1945, federal aid to education, the National Housing Act of 1949, and to invoke cloture in the 1950 debate over the creation of a Fair Employment Practices Commission.

Because of his illness Vandenberg was often absent from the Senate in 1950–51. Yet he appeared to vote for funds for the Marshall Plan and for NATO. Vandenberg died on April 18, 1951, in Grand Rapids, Michigan.

—JB

Vandenberg, Hoyt S(anford)
(1899–1954) *director, Central Intelligence Group; air force chief of staff*
Hoyt S. Vandenberg was born on January 24, 1899, in Milwaukee, Wisconsin. After graduating from

West Point in 1923, he immediately joined the U.S. Army Air Corps. Between 1934 and 1938 he completed studies at the Air Corps Technical School, the Command and General Staff School, and the Army War College. During World War II Vandenberg was sent to England as a temporary colonel. In 1942 he worked on the air plans for the invasion of North Africa and flew combat missions in Europe and Africa. In 1943, already a temporary brigadier general, Vandenberg returned to Washington and led an air mission to the Soviet Union. The next year he was promoted to commanding general of the U.S. Ninth Air Force. He attended the conferences of Western leaders at Quebec, Cairo, and Teheran, where he was part of the top-level planning group.

Vandenberg became head of the army's intelligence unit, G-2, in 1945 and later represented G-2 on the Intelligence Advisory Board. In June 1946 President Truman appointed him director of the Central Intelligence Group (CIG), the predecessor to the Central Intelligence Agency. The CIG was created by presidential directive in January 1946 and was made responsible for coordination, planning, evaluation, and dissemination of intelligence. Vandenberg quickly established himself as an

General Hoyt S. Vandenburg being sworn in as Chief of Staff of the U.S. Air Force by Justice Vinson, 1948 *(Harry S. Truman Library, Ralph N. Stohl Papers)*

assertive and aggressive director. The nephew of Senator ARTHUR H. VANDENBERG (R-Wisc.), an influential member of the Senate Foreign Relations Committee, Vandenberg was able to gain access to members of both the House and the Senate. Since the CIG depended upon financial support from the State, War, and Navy departments, he fought for an independent budget. Under Vandenberg, the scope of CIG was also broadened. He gained an espionage capability as well as the authority to conduct independent research and analysis. Vandenberg also wanted the director of central intelligence to become the "executive agent" of the National Intelligence Authority (later the National Security Council) to make sure that policies were put into effect. This plan was met by such fierce resistance from the State Department and the military that Vandenberg's successor as DCI, Rear Admiral ROSCOE H. HILLENKOETTER, dropped the idea. Vandenberg held the post of DCI until May 1947.

In 1947 Vandenberg supported Truman's demand for the passage of the National Security bill. The measure paved the way for a unified armed services, creating a Department of Defense and an independent air force and establishing the Joint Chiefs of Staff. In 1948 Truman appointed him air force chief of staff, and Vandenberg became the nation's youngest full general at the age of 49.

In June 1948 the Soviet Union began a land blockade of Berlin, cutting off supplies to 2.5 million citizens. Vandenberg was reluctant at first to commit the air force to an airlift. He warned Truman that the United States would be spreading its air strength thin. However, Truman believed an airlift had less chance of provoking a Soviet military response than attempts to supply Berlin by ground convoy. Under the president's orders, Vandenberg instituted "Operation Vittles," a massive airlift of supplies. Over 1.7 million tons were transported into Berlin by the time the Soviets lifted the blockade in May 1949.

During the late 1940s Vandenberg became involved in debates on air strategy, international cooperation, and American military preparedness. Throughout his career he remained a firm advocate of a larger and stronger air force. He opposed the navy's proposed supercarrier, saying it duplicated a strategic bombing capability better left to the air force, and such a carrier would not only be vulnerable to air attack but to surface ship and submarine attack as well. The supercarrier was not built. During congressional testimony during the so-called Revolt of the Admirals, Vandenberg insisted upon the strategic bombers deterrent capacity, the effectiveness of strategic bombing as shown in World War II, and the ability of the B-36 bomber to carry out its mission. Toward the end of the decade, he unsuccessfully resisted cuts in the air force budget, arguing that Soviet advances in jet and bomber production were a threat to U.S. security. However, as a result of the Korean conflict, Congress later provided much of the funds Vandenberg had requested. In his annual report issued in February 1950, Vandenberg said America's greatest deterrent to military aggression was "the existence of a strategic force capable of inflicting damage sufficient to make aggression extremely unprofitable."

As head of the air force Vandenberg was responsible for directing the air war against North Korea. When the Korean conflict started in June 1950, he thought the United States could confine its military operations to sea and air support for the South Koreans. As the war progressed he changed his mind and supported the involvement of American troops. Vandenberg publicly stressed American air power in the face of what he called a "massive effort" by the Communists to challenge U.S. air superiority. He advocated "hot pursuit," which would have allowed UN Command aircraft to follow Communist planes across the Chinese border for a limited distance. At one point, in 1951, he claimed that in jet combat, "our boys are knocking their socks off," and later pointed out that UN fliers had an "8-1 kill ratio" over the North Koreans. In October 1951 Vandenberg revealed that the United States believed that Russian pilots were flying North Korean fighters. That November he warned that if truce negotiations stalled, the United States might stop fighting a "war of halfway measures" and begin air raids on Manchuria, the location of Communist airfields.

Vandenberg supported Truman's efforts to discipline General DOUGLAS MACARTHUR. In January 1951 he went to Japan to deliver a letter from Truman to MacArthur instructing the general to restrict his statements about U.S. foreign policy. Vandenberg joined other members of the Joint Chiefs of Staff in backing Truman when he dismissed MacArthur from his Korean command in the spring of 1951.

Vandenberg's scheduled retirement as air force chief of staff in 1952 was delayed when Truman extended his term of office 14 months. During the

Eisenhower administration Vandenberg became a vocal critic of proposed cuts in the defense budget. He attacked a five billion dollar reduction in the air force appropriation advanced by Secretary of Defense CHARLES E. WILSON. Vandenberg warned the Senate Appropriations Committee in 1953 that the cut would "increase the risk to national security beyond the dictates of rational prudence." The reduction went into effect in July 1953. Vandenberg retired on a medical disability and died on April 2, 1954 in Washington, D.C. (See *The Eisenhower Years* Volume)

—JF

Vardaman, James K(imble), Jr.
(1894–1972) *presidential naval aide; member, Board of Governors, Federal Reserve System*

The son of Mississippi senator James K. Vardaman, James "Jake" Vardaman, Jr., was born on August 28, 1894, in Greenwood, Mississippi. He attended the U.S. Naval Preparatory School in Annapolis, Maryland, and the University of Mississippi before receiving his law degree from Millsaps College in 1914. Vardaman practiced law in Jackson, Mississippi, until he entered the army during World War I. During the 1920s he purchased municipal, corporate, and public utility bonds for various banking syndicates in St. Louis and then became a loan officer for the Liberty-Central Trading Company and First National Bank of St. Louis. In 1933 Vardaman became regional manager of the St. Louis branch of the Reconstruction Finance Corporation. Four years later the Tower Grove National Bank appointed Vardaman its president after the Federal Reserve System had called for a change in management. Because of the disagreement with the board of governors of the bank, Vardaman later resigned. He became a troubleshooter for the Hamilton Brown Shoe Company, then in financial difficulties. Despite his efforts the company went bankrupt in 1942.

During the 1920s and 1930s Vardaman also pursued a military career. An active member of the U.S. Army Reserve, he became a friend of Harry S Truman, who was also an officer. He transferred to the U.S. Naval Reserve in 1939 and served in the Naval Intelligence Office during 1941. In 1942 he became security officer on the staff of Admiral Harold Stark, chief of U.S. naval operations in Europe.

Shortly after he assumed the presidency, Truman named Vardaman to the largely ceremonial post of naval aide to the president. According to Margaret Truman the naval aide quickly "acquired an acute case of Potomac fever." Officious, Vardaman assumed himself an expert on administrative practices large and small and proceeded to instruct White House staff on how to run their offices. He eventually tried this management technique with BESS TRUMAN's staff and was promoted out of the way to the Board of Governors of the Federal Reserve System—only five months after his appointment as naval aide. After lengthy debate over alleged dubious practices on the part of Vardaman's St. Louis banking interests, and the suggestion that the appointment was the result of cronyism, the Senate approved the nomination in April 1946. He was replaced at the White House by his young protégé, CLARK CLIFFORD.

Vardaman supported a "pay-as-you-go" fiscal policy and, during the Korean War, advocated "across the board control" of wages and prices "at the earliest possible moment." In 1951 he sided with President Truman and Secretary of the Treasury JOHN W. SNYDER in their dispute with the Federal Reserve Board over interest rates. Vardaman supported the Treasury's opposition to any increase in the interest rate on short-term government obligations and on funding and refunding bonds. Snyder had objected to the increase because it would have raised the government's cost of borrowing. In contrast, most members of the Board of Governors of the Federal Reserve System believed that not increasing the interest rate would be inflationary.

Vardaman played virtually no part in the ultimate resolution of this conflict. Other board members appear to have considered him an outsider in their midst, little more than an administration lackey. The ultimate Treasury-Reserve Accord was negotiated by MARRINER S. ECCLES for the Federal Reserve and WILLIAM MCCHESNEY MARTIN for the Treasury. It represented an almost total victory for the board with a few insubstantial, face-saving provisions for Snyder and Truman.

After the end of his term on the Federal Reserve Board in 1960, Vardaman became a banker in Albany, Georgia. He died on July 28, 1972.

—RSG

Vaughan, Harry H(awkins)
(1893–1981) *military aide to the president*
Born on November 26, 1893, in Glasgow, Missouri, Harry H. Vaughan was the son of a dentist and

graduated from Westminster College in 1916. He then served with the Missouri National Guard stationed at the Mexican border and later worked as a chemist in a wood preservation and treating plant. In July 1917, shortly before U.S. entry into World War I, Vaughan enlisted in the First Missouri Field Artillery of the National Guard. After attending an officers' training camp, he was commissioned a second lieutenant. During military training at Fort Sill, Oklahoma, Vaughan became a friend of Harry Truman, who was also an artillery officer. Vaughan fought in France as a commander of an artillery battery. He was discharged with the rank of captain in 1919.

During the 1920s and 1930s Vaughan served with Truman in the National Guard at Fort Riley, Kansas. When not on summer maneuvers as a reserve officer, he held a variety of jobs: engineer, plant manager for a tie company, railroad inspector, and salesman. In 1939 he became treasurer of Truman's successful 1940 campaign for a second Senate term. He went to Washington as Truman's secretary but, following the Japanese attack on Pearl Harbor, volunteered for active duty. Vaughan served in Australia. After being injured in a plane crash, he returned to Washington. There, he was made the War Department's liaison to the Senate Special Committee Investigating the National Defense Program, headed by Truman.

When Truman became vice president in 1944, Vaughan, by that time a colonel, became his military aide. He remained with Truman after Roosevelt's death in 1945. In June Vaughan was promoted to brigadier general. As military aide, he was liaison with the War Department and coordinator of veterans' affairs with power to cut red tape to help members of the armed services. Truman also made him his liaison with J. EDGAR HOOVER on FBI affairs. Vaughan was utterly loyal to Truman and he helped the president relax with a joke or a good story—no small feat given the tensions surrounding the presidency at that time. The closeness of Vaughan to the president made him the object of press scrutiny and criticism, and he was depicted as a court jester. One journalist described Vaughan's role: "General Vaughan is not interested in government policy. He is interested in Harry Truman and stands by to joke, berate or damn the world according to the president's mood." But he did much more than that, because by being close to the president, he could also be bluntly honest with him about situations.

Vaughan frequently embarrassed the president. On one memorable occasion in 1945 the aide, known to be frank and uninhibited, offered a comparison of the Roosevelt and Truman administrations. "After a diet of caviar," he said, "you like to get back to ham and eggs." He also spoke about the terrible black market prices in occupied Germany and illustrated this by telling how he sold his $55 U.S. watch to a Russian officer for $500. On another occasion, during some hard questioning by reporters, Vaughan told them to ease up because, "after all, I am the president's military aide and you guys will want favors at the White House some day." Truman took Vaughan's remarks in stride and on more than one occasion defended his friend. It was in support of Vaughan that Truman uttered to the press his famous, "No s.o.b. is going to dictate to me whom I am going to have [on my staff]."

Vaughan was generous, perhaps too generous, and people took advantage of him. Vaughan's association with Greek-native John F. Maragon caused the administration many headaches. Maragon had ingratiated himself with Vaughan when the latter was secretary to Senator Truman by doing him various favors. When Truman became president, Maragon soon exploited his friendly relations with the president's military aide, and even received phone calls in Vaughan's office at the White House. Vaughan helped get Maragon a position on a mission to supervise Greek elections in 1946—a job he was hardly qualified for and despite the president having already removed him from the list of mission members. Columnist DREW PEARSON soon targeted Vaughan over his relationship with Maragon.

Vaughan's troubles were not over. A Massachusetts furniture manufacturer and former *New York Herald Tribune* reporter, Paul Grindle, revealed that a Washington influence peddler, James V. Hunt, had told him in 1949 he could assist him in getting government contracts since he knew people in high places who could help, including Vaughan. Hunt said for $1,000 up front, $500 for expenses, and 5 percent of any contract he would use his contacts to secure a deal. The story stunned the nation and put a new word in its lexicon: "five percenter." The Investigations Subcommittee of the Senate Committee on Expenditures in the Executive Department, chaired by CLYDE R. HOEY of North Carolina, launched an inquiry. Republicans attacked Vaughan for his alleged role. Truman's instincts were to circle the wagons and that is what he did,

refusing Vaughan's proffered resignation. Truman had a blind faith in someone as loyal as Vaughan.

The issue that received the most attention in the hearings was the gift of deep freezers to Vaughan and others in the administration, including Mrs. Truman, from an agent of David Bennett, president of a perfume company. Evidence revealed that Vaughan had written letters on behalf of Bennett and one of his employees, none other than Maragon, to expedite the procuring of passports for them or set up visits to military authorities. Maragon was caught at one point smuggling oils necessary for the manufacture of perfume from Greece. No direct link between the deep freezers and the favors was ever uncovered, but Vaughan's discretion was called into question.

Vaughan also worked to expedite the diversion of scarce building materials to restore a racetrack that had been seized during the war to become a Japanese-American relocation camp. One of the track's owners, William Helis, Jr., an acquaintance of Vaughan, had given him money in 1946, which he turned over to the Missouri Democratic Party. Although the federal housing expediter, Tighe Woods, testified that he had decided to send the material before he saw Vaughan in early 1948, and both said Vaughan's request was routine, it again attested to military aide's lack of judgment.

Vaughan was also accused of interceding on behalf of the Allied Molasses Company to have the Department of Agriculture turn over to it a tank car of molasses being held in demurrage. Vaughan could not remember making such a request. His defense was that he simply told people who they had to go to obtain relief for problems they had with the government.

While the "five percenters" greatly profited from Vaughan's good will, there was no evidence that Vaughan received any more than deep freezers, a box of cigars, and hospitality. What Vaughan did, he did for friendship and flattery. According to historian Patrick Anderson, "Vaughan was a dumb but not dishonest man who had been made a fool of in the classic pattern of the country bumpkin and the city slickers." What Vaughan did not seem to realize is that activity on behalf of constituents that would be expected of a secretary to a senator was not appropriate for an aide to a president.

After leaving the White House in 1952 Vaughan went into retirement on his military pension. Vaughan died on May 20, 1981, at Fort Belvoir, Virginia.

—SRB

Velde, Harold H(immel)
(1910–1985) *member of the House of Representatives*

Born on April 1, 1910, in Parkland, Illinois, Harold Velde graduated from Northwestern University in 1931. After teaching high school for four years, he entered the University of Illinois Law School. He received his law degree in 1937 and began practice in his home state. Velde served a year with the U.S. Army Signal Corps and, in 1943, joined the FBI's sabotage and counterespionage division, where he specialized in wiretapping. He left the bureau in 1946 after being elected an Illinois county judge. Campaigning with the slogan "Get the Reds out of Washington and Washington out of the Red," Velde was elected to the House of Representatives in 1948. A member of the conservative wing of the Republican Party, Velde favored the reduction of foreign aid and an end to rent control and public housing. He rarely wavered in his isolationist stance, voting against aid to Korea and Taiwan in the late 1940s and early 1950s.

As might be expected Velde voted conservatively on domestic issues. He quite naturally supported the McCarran Internal Security Act. He voted for the Reece Amendment cutting aid to Europe and against military aid to NATO, Point Four, and the Korean Aid Act. He opposed the National Housing Act of 1949 and backed the Smith Amendment of 1952, calling upon Truman to invoke the Taft-Hartley Act in regard to the steelworkers' strike that year. Yet he did vote to raise the minimum wage to 75 cents an hour and to maintain 90 percent parity for certain agricultural products and against deregulation of the natural gas industry.

Velde saw himself as an investigator, and his assignment to the House Un-American Activities Committee (HUAC) in 1949 provided him the opportunity he sought. A vigorous anticommunist, he actively involved himself in the committee's attempt to root out domestic subversion. Velde, along with Representative RICHARD M. NIXON (R-Calif.), found himself pressing the Democratic majority on HUAC to intensify its investigations. He also sponsored antisubversion legislation, including unsuccessful bills to create a list of sub-

versive books in the Library of Congress and to mandate a loyalty oath for anyone voting in a national election.

In 1949 Velde enthusiastically joined the HUAC probe of wartime espionage, drawing on his experience with the FBI in investigating alleged subversives in the Manhattan District Project. When President Truman announced in September that the Soviets had detonated an atomic device, Velde claimed Russia had gained "three to five years" in producing the atomic bomb, because of a "soft" official attitude toward communism. He called on Americans to "throw out of office those incompetents who regard their political lives as more important than our national security."

In July 1949 Velde joined Nixon in criticizing Judge Samuel F. Kaufman's handling of the ALGER HISS trial and unsuccessfully proposing that HUAC hear testimony from key witnesses. The Hiss conviction in 1950 prompted Velde to charge that Russian espionage agents were "running loose" all over the country. He also ridiculed President Truman's famous remark that the Hiss case was a "red herring" meant to disguise the "do-nothing" nature of the Republican 80th Congress. "This cooks President Truman's 'red herring,' " Velde said. "I hope he enjoys eating it." Velde favored the investigation of the Hollywood film industry by the committee in 1951. He said he was "certain that Communist propaganda had been put into films—perhaps not in an open manner, but in the way the writers think if they are Communists." The HUAC report on the investigation, however, discounted the assertion.

In 1953, when the Republicans gained control of Congress, Velde became chairman of HUAC. He led probes into education, labor, and the clergy. Velde captured national attention in November 1953 when he issued congressional subpoenas to Truman, former secretary of state JAMES F. BYRNES, and former Attorney General TOM C. CLARK. Velde wanted the Democrats to testify about their knowledge of the background of HARRY DEXTER WHITE, a government official accused of having Communist ties. All three men refused to appear. After President Eisenhower expressed displeasure with the subpoenas, Velde let the issue quietly drop. He retired from Congress in 1957. Velde died on September 1, 1985, in Sun City, Arizona. (See *The Eisenhower Years* Volume)

—JF

Vincent, John C(arter)

(1900–1972) *diplomat*

John Carter Vincent was born on August 19, 1900, in Seneca, Kansas. He graduated from Mercer University in 1923 and joined the Foreign Service two years later. During his first decade in the State Department he served extensively in China. In 1935 Vincent was assigned to the State Department's Division of Far Eastern Affairs. He then returned to China and became counselor of embassy in Chungking from 1942 to 1943. During World War II he developed close personal friendships with Chou Enlai, one of the Communist leaders and Chiang Kai-shek (Jiang Jieshi), the Nationalist leader.

In 1944 Vincent was recalled to Washington as Chief of the Division of Chinese Affairs. That year he accompanied Vice President HENRY A. WALLACE on his trip to China. The two men tried to convince Chiang to focus his attention on fighting Japan rather than the Communists. Although Vincent believed that the generalissimo offered the best hope to reunite the nation, he urged Chiang to make needed reforms to consolidate support for the regime. He fought against a postwar military advisory group, saying it would only encourage Chiang to use military means rather than peaceful means to end the conflict with the Communists.

Following his trip Vincent became head of the Office of Far Eastern Affairs. Here he recommended to the administration that it not give Chiang unqualified support and take a hard-and-set attitude. He worried when U.S. troops were sent into northern China to accept the surrender of the Japanese and to keep order, arguing American soldiers putting down civil disorder was a bad idea. He believed Chinese troops flown there in U.S. planes should do that task.

According to Vincent's biographer, Gary May, Vincent was not as agitated by the cold war in later 1945, and he had a low regard for President Truman. He did not think, as others in the administration did, that the Soviets wanted to dominate China. According to him, they were, however, concerned about Chiang's threat to the Chinese Communists and Russia, and Stalin might intervene in the civil war to establish a satellite state in Manchuria and northern China. Vincent believed a liberal Chinese government that could be accepted by both the Americans and the Soviets would solve the problem of Sino-Soviet relations. He was one of the archi-

tects of the Marshall mission to China in 1945. The delegation, headed by General GEORGE C. MARSHALL, was formed to urge Chiang to cooperate with the Communists in establishing a stable government and beginning necessary reforms. Vincent briefed Marshall for the trip and candidly portrayed the Nationalists as hopelessly corrupt. The failure of the mission convinced him of the futility of further American aid, and he recommended the U.S. reduce its commitment. According to May, Vincent had helped the United States avoid greater involvement in the Chinese civil war. But he would pay a price for his "calm realpolitik" in cold war America.

In early 1947 Truman nominated Vincent to become minister to Switzerland, a post that required Senate confirmation. Conservative senator STYLES BRIDGES (R-N.H.), a member of the pro-Chiang "China Lobby" led opposition to the nomination. He issued a list of 12 charges against Vincent that included the accusation that the diplomat had leaked State Department documents to the Chinese Communists. Bridges requested the Senate examine Wallace's report of his China trip "for further indications of Mr. Vincent's approval of the Communist program in China, opposition to the support of the Nationalist government, and furtherance of extension of the influence of Russia in China." Secretary of State DEAN G. ACHESON refuted all 12 of Bridges's charges. Albert Kohlberg, a leader of the China Lobby, then revealed that PATRICK J. HURLEY, former ambassador to China, had heard that Vincent was "a secret Russian espionage agent." Despite the charges, the Senate confirmed Vincent's appointment. He served in Switzerland from 1947 to 1951, after which he was transferred to Morocco.

The China Lobby did not give up its campaign to force Vincent out of government. Following the fall of China in 1949, Senator JOSEPH R. MCCARTHY (R-Wisc.) presented its charges to a very receptive public groping for someone to blame for America's failure in China. On February 9, 1950, the Wisconsin senator claimed in a historic speech in Wheeling, West Virginia, that he had a list of individuals in the State Department who were members of the Communist Party. Vincent was the number two man on the list. McCarthy accused the Foreign Service officer of being a Moscow-controlled Communist who ran an espionage ring in the State Department. McCarthy asserted that Vincent sabotaged the Marshall mission to China by drawing up directives to the general that placed impossible demands on Chiang. Two weeks later McCarthy related to the Senate a bizarre tale of Vincent's alleged Communist link. On one rainy day someone had left a raincoat in Vincent's outer office. It lay there for quite some time. One day it was raining, and, having forgot his own raincoat, he borrowed the lost one to go to lunch. He absent-mindedly left it in a restroom. He then returned to retrieve the coat and found it missing. Vincent called the building superintendent to inquire if it had been found. The office told him that the security people had it because they had found a note with Russian words on it in one of the pockets. The Tydings Committee, formed to review McCarthy's charges concerning the State Department, cleared Vincent.

In 1951 the McCarran Internal Security Subcommittee heard testimony once again accusing Vincent of Communist ties. The hearings led to a State Department Loyalty Board probe, which again cleared him. However, soon afterward, the Civil Service Loyalty Board voted three to two that there was a reasonable doubt as to Vincent's loyalty. Vincent's lawyer appealed to Acheson. Neither Acheson nor Truman wanted to see Vincent leave the State Department. They, therefore, formed a new panel, headed by a respected jurist Learned Hand, to review the case. The Eisenhower administration came to power in the middle of the panel's deliberations. Secretary of State John Foster Dulles dismissed the group preferring to review the case himself. As a result of pressure from the right, he decided that Vincent had to leave government. He convinced the diplomat to resign rather than be fired. Vincent retired to Cambridge, Massachusetts, at the age of 52 to lecture on China at Radcliffe College. Vincent died on December 3, 1972, in Cambridge, Massachusetts.

In 1996 Harvey Klehr and Ronald Radosh revealed in their book, *The Amerasia Spy Case: Prelude to McCarthyism*, that the FBI considered Vincent a suspect in an investigation in which classified documents were being passed on to Andrew Roth, a lieutenant in the Office of Naval Intelligence, who passed them on to Philip Jaffe, editor of the left-wing magazine *Amerasia*. OSS chief William Donovan heard about the investigation and passed word of it to U.S. ambassador to China Patrick Hurley, who, already feeling negatively toward Vincent, believed Donovan. Hurley concluded that Vincent and others in the Foreign Service were conspiring against him and were Soviet agents under orders to wreck U.S. China policy. Vincent was never proven

to be a spy, but he had encouraged JOHN S. SERVICE to leak information to undermine opponents in the State Department, such as Hurley. (See *The Eisenhower Years* Volume)

—JB

Vinson, Carl
(1883–1981) *member of the House of Representatives*

The son of a planter, Carl Vinson was born on November 18, 1883, in Baldwin County, Georgia. After receiving his LL.B. in 1902, Vinson became Baldwin County's prosecuting attorney. A Democrat, he served as a member of the Georgia House of Representatives from 1910 to 1912, when he was elected judge of the Baldwin County Court. In 1914 Vinson won a seat in the House of Representatives.

During his first years in the House Vinson focused his attention on national defense. In 1917 he became a member of Naval Affairs Committee and, in 1931, chairman of the panel. Prior to World War II he pressed for a major enlargement of the navy as America's major deterrent against aggression. In 1934 he wrote the Vinson-Trammell Act, which laid the foundation for the two-ocean navy. He pushed through further naval expansion in 1938, 1939, and 1940. After the outbreak of World War II, he called for legislation requiring industry to curtail commercial production and to speed armament output. The controversial Vinson bill, proposed in 1941 to curb strikes in defense industries, was opposed by labor and the administration. It was never reported out of committee.

On domestic policy, Vinson is hard to pigeonhole as conservative or liberal. Typical of a southerner of that time he opposed civil rights legislation. He also supported laws to restrict the activities of labor, such as the Case labor disputes bill and the Taft-Hartley Act. From a farming region and a farmer himself, he supported 90 percent parity price supports for certain agricultural goods. He voted for anticommunist measures such as the Mundt-Nixon bill and the McCarran Internal Security Act, yet voted against making the House Un-American Activities Committee a permanent body. He backed the Truman foreign policy by supporting the British loan of 1946, Greek-Turkish Aid, the Marshall Plan, military aid to NATO, and the Point Four program.

Following the war Vinson continued to support large military appropriations and the maintenance of modern, well-equipped armed services. President Truman, however, preferred a smaller and less expensive navy, which led to conflict between the commander in chief and the chairman. In late 1945 Truman proposed the unification of the separate military services into a single Defense Department with power centralized in the hands of a secretary of defense. Vinson opposed the measure, supporting instead a proposal submitted by Secretary of the Navy JAMES V. FORRESTAL, which called for the establishment of a National Security Council linking the State Department with the services. According to Vinson's biographer, James F. Cook, the congressman saw the army and the navy as having distinct missions, and wanted coordination, not unification of the services. Under his plan the secretary of defense was a coordinator rather than a policymaker. To support his view, Vinson pushed through the House a resolution endorsing the navy's plans. Vinson demanded that decisions on service rolls and force levels be reached before unification was attempted and promised Forrestal that no unification measure would be passed by the 79th Congress. He kept his promise. However, the measure was subsequently enacted in the Republican 80th Congress. With the creation of the National Military Establishment in 1947, the House's military panels were combined to form the Armed Services Committee, of which Vinson became ranking minority member. In 1949, when the Democrats regained control of Congress, Vinson became chairman.

Known for his cunning and political acumen, Vinson, called "the Swamp Fox," often operated in anonymity. However, he quickly gained dominance of his committee. He abolished all regular subcommittees, divided the full panel into three equal parts, and reserved to himself the right to assign bills. This gave him great power over policy and patronage.

As chairman of the Armed Services Committee, Vinson opposed the further centralization of power in the hands of the secretary of defense as requested by Truman and Forrestal. In 1949 he asked for tighter control by Congress over the secretary of defense's actions to prevent the creation of a "military dictator." Under his proposal the secretary of defense would have to consult the armed services committees before exercising any authority to transfer or consolidate the function of the three services. He attempted to block further legislation until discussion of the roles of the various services had been completed, and conversations between Defense Secretary LOUIS A.

JOHNSON and the chairman became quite heated during the former's testimony. Vinson also objected to a single chief of staff over all the armed forces and the formation of an armed forces general staff. He also wanted to allow service secretaries and chiefs to testify before Congress after informing the defense secretary. However, Truman threatened to put through reorganization by executive order, and Vinson was unable to prevent Congress from acting. The bill creating the Department of Defense and consolidating the power in the hands of the secretary of defense was signed into law in August.

Vinson also pushed for higher defense spending than Truman and the Bureau of the Budget, both of whom had wanted a ceiling of $15 billion, which was less than what the military chiefs had called for. Vinson said, "As between the Bureau of the Budget and the Joint Chiefs of Staff, I will place my confidence in the latter, in regard to what our national defense needs are." The chairman contended that, "If we do too much in the way of arming, we will just lose dollars. But if we do too little, we may lose American lives, we may lose vital engagements with the enemy, we may bring on global war through our indecision and weakness" and called the Truman defense budget "unhealthful and shortsighted." Vinson convinced the Congress to appropriate $851 million more than Truman's request.

During 1949 Vinson's committee held hearings on the role of various services, particularly the navy's air and land branches, in postwar defense. The representative objected to the failure of Congress to boost naval aviation funds saying that, "they are stagnating the navy air arm and they are letting the navy operating air force die on the line." Yet, in the same year he supported the creation of a 70-group air force and the development of the controversial B-36 air force bomber, which the navy maintained would relegate it to secondary status in the defense establishment. Vinson also shocked the admirals by opposing the development of a super aircraft carrier, commenting that in the future the United States must rely on land-based planes and land fighting. He and Secretary Johnson were overruled in 1950, when the House voted to go ahead with the project.

In April 1950, shortly before the outbreak of the Korean conflict, Vinson attacked Johnson's proposed defense reductions, charging that they would cut into the sinew and muscle of the fighting force. Johnson responded by having the Joint Chiefs reexamine Truman's military budget to see if more money should be requested for aircraft procurement. Subsequently Johnson recommended a $350 million dollar increase in the budget. When, with the eruption of the Korean War, Truman asked Congress for money to disperse government agencies to areas outside of Washington to minimize the danger of aerial attack, Vinson won cheers by declaring that the government should spend less on moving the capital and more on defending it. However, Vinson helped the administration by steering through the House a $10.5 billion defense appropriation in response to the war. In 1951 he supported Truman's dismissal of General DOUGLAS MACARTHUR and spoke in favor of the establishment of universal military training, which never came into being.

Throughout the 1950s and into the 1960s Vinson continued to play a crucial role in the formulation and passage of military-related bills. He dominated his committee through patronage, determining who would introduce bills on the House floor and who would be sent on tours of inspection. The lower chamber, in turn, approved almost all legislation reported favorably by his committee. During the Eisenhower administration Vinson supported the army officers who opposed the doctrine of massive retaliation with its reliance on nuclear weapons. In the 1960s he opposed efforts by Presidents Kennedy and Johnson to phase out manned bombers in favor of missiles, and he attacked Secretary of Defense Robert S. McNamara's effort to transfer power from the services to the Defense Department. By the time Vinson decided to retire in 1964, he had exceeded the late Speaker SAM T. RAYBURN's (D-Tex.) record for length of service in the House. Vinson died on June 1, 1981, in Milledgeville, Georgia. (See *The Eisenhower Years, The Kennedy Years, The Johnson Years* Volumes)

—DAE

Vinson, Fred(erick) M(oore)
(1890–1953) *secretary of the Treasury, chief justice of the United States*

Fred M. Vinson was born on January 22, 1890, in Louisa, Kentucky. He received a law degree from Centre College in Kentucky in 1911 and then established a private practice, first in Louisa and later in Ashland, Kentucky. He soon became involved in state Democratic politics and won election to the House of Representatives in 1924. By 1933 Vinson

had become a member of the Ways and Means Committee. Generally loyal to President Franklin D. Roosevelt, he played a key role in the development of New Deal tax and coal programs. Vinson became a judge on the U.S. Court of Appeals in Washington in 1938 but gave up that post in May 1943 to serve as director of economic stabilization. He acted briefly as federal loan administrator in March 1945 and then was named director of war mobilization and reconversion.

When Truman assumed the presidency Vinson quickly became a close friend and adviser. On July 16, 1945, Truman nominated the Kentuckian to be secretary of the Treasury. Vinson soon emerged as the strongest figure in Truman's first cabinet. He counseled the president not only on economic matters but on a broad range of domestic issues. As Treasury secretary Vinson headed a team of American negotiators who worked out the terms of a major postwar loan to Britain in 1945. He was also a chief U.S. representative during the formation of the International Monetary Fund and the International Bank for Reconstruction and Development, and at home, successfully recommended a reduction in tax rates.

He proposed that Congress cut taxes by $5 billion in 1946, which would include the repeal of the excess profits tax for corporations. An assistant that opposed the repeal admitted that it probably helped reconversion, but thought it also may have contributed to high postwar inflation. Vinson also sent to Congress a proposal for a full employment bill, in which the government would expend whatever funds were needed to obtain the bill's goal. However, the final law was watered down. One observer did credit Vinson as probably the one person who could get even this act passed.

On June 6, 1946, Truman named Vinson chief justice of the United States Supreme Court. Aside from his compatible political philosophy and record in government service, the calm, patient, and sociable Vinson was a skilled negotiator and conciliator. Truman evidently hoped he would be able to unify a faction-ridden Supreme Court. Vinson's abilities in conciliation played a critical role in Truman's decision to appoint him chief justice. The High Court was badly divided between "conservatives" and "liberals." James St. Clair and Linda C. Gugin postulate that Truman also wanted to free up the secretary of the Treasury post for his friend and fellow Missourian JOHN W. SNYDER. Although sworn

Chief Justice Fred Vinson and President Truman
(CORBIS)

in as chief justice on June 24, 1946, Vinson remained part of Truman's inner circle and often advised him on political and diplomatic matters.

In 1948 Truman requested that Vinson go to Moscow to talk peace with Stalin, but it was a rather transparent attempt to boost the president's popularity in a tough election. Vinson—who was willing to go if necessary—told Truman that he would have to resign as chief justice if he accepted the mission because he opposed extrajudicial tasks for Court justices. Secretary of State GEORGE C. MARSHALL, however, vehemently opposed this scheme, and it was shelved. Truman, however, appreciated Vinson's loyalty and, in 1952, urged the chief justice to enter that year's presidential race.

A very pragmatic man, Vinson believed that the government needed broad powers to deal with postwar domestic and foreign problems, and he followed a policy of judicial restraint, which gave the government wide scope. In civil liberties cases Vinson's approach led him to sustain government power over claims of individual rights in almost all instances. He voted to uphold state and federal loyalty programs, investigations of Communist activities, and harsher treatment of aliens. He also wrote the opinion of

the Court in two of the most important civil liberties cases of the period. In May 1950 in *America Communications Association v. Douds* Vinson upheld the noncommunist oath requirement in the Taft-Hartley Act against a First Amendment challenge. In June of the following year in *Dennis v. United States* he also sustained the convictions of 11 Communist Party leaders who were charged under the Smith Act with conspiracy to organize a party to teach and advocate the overthrow of the government. Using a formula devised by Judge LEARNED HAND, Vinson held that the government could outlaw a conspiracy to advocate revolution when the individuals intended to overthrow the government as soon as circumstances would permit even though the possibility of a successful revolution was not at all immediate. He said the government did not want to "wait until the putsch is about to be executed, the plans have been laid and the signal is awaited." The two decisions effectively curtailed the scope of the First Amendment's guarantees of free speech and association.

Some observers have argued that in deciding some cases Chief Justice Vinson appeared to be acting specifically to the benefit of the president, a close friend who he still socialized with, and that Vinson had a marked tendency to support government power. Richard Kirkendall pointed to Vinson's long experience in government caused him to believe strong government, rather than weak government, protected freedom better. Government that could not meet the problems of the day and could not shield the people from harmful forces led to the loss of liberty. His trust of government power was displayed in *United States v. United Mine Workers* (March 1947) and *Youngstown Sheet & Tube Co. v. Sawyer* (June 1952), the steel seizure case. In the mineworkers' case Vinson's opinion for the Court sustained a contempt judgment and heavy fines against JOHN L. LEWIS and the United Mine Workers for their defiance of a district court order court order against striking. The order had been issued at a time when the government had assumed control of the coal mines. In the steel seizure case, when a majority of the Court held Truman's takeover of the steel mills unconstitutional, Vinson dissented, arguing that in a time of genuine emergency the president had inherent power to move in defense of the nation's substantial interests.

In criminal cases Vinson gave greater weight to society's interest than to the defendant's. He usually voted to reject claims that a confession was coerced or that counsel was improperly denied. He was particularly conservative in Fourth Amendment cases. In *Harris v. United States* (May 1947), a case that surprised many observers, he wrote for a five-man majority to uphold a conviction based on evidence obtained in long, detailed search of a defendant's apartment that was conducted without a warrant but had been incidental to a valid arrest. Vinson wrote his first dissenting opinion in June of the next year in *Trupiano v. United States* when another narrow Court majority reversed direction and held that search warrants must be obtained wherever reasonably practicable. In February 1950, when the latter decision was overturned in *United States v. Rabinowitz*, he was in the majority.

Vinson wrote several of his most significant opinions in cases involving racial discrimination. In May 1948 in *Shelley v. Kraemer* he held racially restrictive real estate covenants unenforceable in federal and state courts. Speaking for a unanimous Court in *Sweatt v. Painter*, Vinson in June 1950 ordered a black student admitted to the University of Texas Law School because the separate state law school for blacks was unequal. In *McLaurin v. Oklahoma State Regents*, decided the same day, he held that black students could not be segregated within facilities such as classrooms and libraries at a state university. Although these rulings extended the constitutional rights of blacks, Vinson stayed within the traditional legal framework on racial issues and went only as far as necessary to reach the immediate result in these cases. He heard argument in December 1952 in five suits that directly challenged the validity of public school segregation. However, in June 1953 the Court, having reached no decision, ordered the cases reargued in the next term. Vinson died in Washington, D.C., on September 8, 1953, before the second round of arguments was held.

With only seven years as chief justice, Vinson did not have sufficient time to establish a record of prominence. After 1949 he was part of a five-man bloc that largely controlled the Court, especially in civil liberties cases. However, Vinson never succeeded in unifying or personally dominating the Court on which justices of strong intellect and convictions were often divided on basic issues. In fact, according to St. Clair and Gugin, the Court became more riven than under Chief Justice Stone. In addition some of the justices had little respect for Vinson's intellectual capabilities. Vinson had strained relations especially with Felix Frankfurter for this reason. He did endeavor to be in the majority often,

giving him, as chief justice, the right to assign the majority opinion (opinion of the Court), which he valued as a way to establish precedent and win public approval. Vinson earned a reputation in being equitable in assigning opinions. Observers did criticize Vinson in delays in producing opinions, which often resulted from trying to fairly distribute opinions between slow and fast justices. Critics thought Vinson himself produced too few opinions. He also tended to rely on his clerks for drafts, although he expressed his views throughout the process and the final opinion represented his ideas. Frankfurter's keen appetite for concurring opinions bedeviled the chief justice, who wanted to send clear signals to judges and lawyers through unanimous decisions. Vinson and the other justices, who preferred judicial restraint, reduced the number of cases heard by approving fewer writs of certiorari much to the annoyance of liberal activists.

Vinson was recognized as a man of integrity and devotion to the nation, who as chief justice helped advance the rights of racial minorities. However, he was also one of the most conservative members of the Court on other civil liberties issues. Critics charged Vinson and the Court he led with overemphasizing the needs of the state to the detriment of individual rights. C. Herman Pritchett, for example, accused Vinson and those who voted with him of lacking a belief in the importance of libertarian values and an insistence on procedural safeguards. Pritchett also maintained that they failed to scrutinize closely the official rationalizations given for infringements on liberty. Under Vinson the Court followed the policy of restraint he favored, but later analysts questioned whether such a passive Court role was necessary or wise at the time, particularly in civil liberties matters. (See *The Eisenhower Years* Volume)

—CAB

Voorhis, Horace Jeremiah (Jerry)
(1901–1984) *member of the House of Representatives*
Born on April 6, 1901, in Ottawa, Kansas, Jerry Voorhis attended public schools in Kansas, Colorado, Oklahoma, Missouri, and Michigan. He graduated Phi Beta Kappa from Yale University in 1923 and later toured Germany as a representative of the Young Men's Christian Association. After returning to the United States, Voorhis worked as a

cowboy and on an automobile assembly line. He taught school in Illinois from 1925 to 1926 and two years later opened the Voorhis School for Boys in San Dimas, California. He remained headmaster for 10 years, earning a master's degree in education from the Claremont College in the meantime. Voorhis also taught American history at Pomona College during this period.

A LaFollette Progressive during the mid-1920s, Voorhis became an active Socialist during the early years of the depression, advocating the nationalization of both industry and land. He backed Upton Sinclair in his race for the California gubernatorial seat in 1934. By 1936 Voorhis had left the Socialist Party, and he successfully ran for Congress as a Democrat, winning election by some 8,500 votes. He explained his change in politics by saying "I was never a fullfledged Socialist and Mr. Roosevelt has made it possible for me to be a Democrat with a clear conscience." Voorhis represented the predominantly Republican 12th congressional district, which encompassed Whittier, California, and its environs. Voorhis won reelection five times despite gerrymandering attempts by the Republican-dominated state legislature in the early 1940s.

A staunch New Dealer, Voorhis championed the development of economic cooperatives and proposed an alteration of the monetary system that included the nationalization of the Federal Reserve System. He became increasingly conservative on other matters, sponsoring the Voorhis Act of 1940, which required the registration of foreign-controlled political organizations. Near the end of his tenure, Voorhis was chosen by the Washington press corps as the member of Congress with the greatest integrity and was voted the hardest-working legislator by his peers.

For the most part, however, Voorhis remained a committed liberal, voting to end the federal poll tax, to pass the Employment Act of 1946, and to make the school lunch program permanent. He quite naturally voted against making the House Un-American Activities Committee a permanent body and the Case labor disputes bill. On foreign policy he backed extending the Trade Agreement Act for three years in 1945 and the British loan of 1946.

In the election of 1946 Voorhis faced Republican challenger RICHARD M. NIXON, a political novice given little chance of unseating the five-term incumbent. Nixon focused his criticism on Voorhis's liberal voting record and his association with left-wing

organizations. While Voorhis enjoyed a national reputation, he was vulnerable to charges that he had done nothing for his district. The national Republican slogan was "Had enough?" Nixon's followers portrayed Voorhis as an advocate of "Big Government." His literature also claimed that Voorhis had the backing of the Congress of Industrial Organizations' (CIO) Political Action Committee (PAC), which was considered Communist-directed. Voorhis denied CIO-PAC support, but Nixon noted that the National Citizens' PAC, a different group sharing some of CIO-PAC's officers, had endorsed Voorhis. And although national and state CIO-PACs had not endorsed Voorhis, local ones had. Voorhis had accepted only CIO-PAC endorsements from those who were not Communist controlled, but his blunt denial of CIO-PAC was misleading. Nixon capitalized on this issue and on Voorhis's voting record in a series of debates. Nixon carried the district by some 15,000 votes with Voorhis losing to his challenger even in his own home town.

As Nixon's political career advanced, there were repeated charges that he had "red-baited" Voorhis during the campaign. Some Democrats pointed to Nixon's tactics in his senatorial contest in 1950 against HELEN GAHAGAN DOUGLAS as a reflection of the Voorhis campaign. In *Confessions of a Congressman* (1947) Voorhis did not emphasize the questionable aspects of the election, but he did complain that his voting record had been misrepresented and his affiliation with the PAC groups distorted. Voorhis stated that the crucial issue had been the Democratic record during the war years. Nixon later said that communism was not an issue during the campaign. Voorhis provided a different view in *The Strange Career of Richard Milhous Nixon* (1972), charging that Nixon had "smeared" him as "disloyal" and had used the PAC issue to discredit him as following a "Communistic line." Voorhis called Nixon's tactics "an arrant deception of the voters" and "unworthy of a responsible politician." But as Nixon biographer Irwin Gellman has shown some of the accusation hurled at Nixon do not hold up under close examination.

Some observers accused the Nixon campaign of calling up voters and claiming Voorhis of being a Communist. But as Gellman had pointed out these accusations have never been substantiated. Critics like Roger Morris charged that Nixon was a tool of the very rich to oust the liberal Voorhis. But Gellman demolished those charges, too, showing it was unsophisticated grassroots Republicans who had helped elect Nixon.

Gellman explained that Voorhis had been a victim of his own complacency. He had never established a district political organization. He did not come home to campaign during the primary, while Nixon made himself known by barnstorming the district. Finally when Voorhis reappeared in California for the general election, he made egregious mistakes such as trying to hide that fact that several local CIO-PACs had endorsed him.

After his defeat in 1946 Voorhis became involved with the Cooperation League of the USA. He served as executive director from 1947 to 1965 and as president until 1967. He was also active in the Group Health Association, the National Association of Housing Cooperatives, and various consumer action groups. In 1967 he became president of the Co-op Foundation. Voorhis died, on September 11, 1984, in Claremont, California.

—JF

Wagner, Robert F(erdinand)
(1877–1953) *member of the Senate*

Born on June 8, 1877, in Nastatten, Germany, Robert F. Wagner came to the United States when he was eight years old. He worked selling newspapers and in a grocery store after school to help support his family. After graduating Phi Beta Kappa from City College in 1898, Wagner attended New York Law School. He received his degree and was admitted to the bar in 1900. Active in the Algonquin Democratic Club in Yorkville while in law school, Wagner won election to the state legislature in 1904. From 1904 to 1919 he served in the New York State Senate, where he was a floor leader after 1913. Wagner sponsored and fought for some of the most far-reaching legislation in the nation, measures that made New York a model state for reform. These included workmen's compensation, low transit fares, child and woman labor laws, and one of the most advanced factory inspection acts in America. In 1918 Wagner left the New York Senate to sit on the New York State Supreme Court. Eight years later he won a seat in the U.S. Senate.

Over the next 23 years Wagner became a major force in the upper house. He sponsored some of the most significant legislation of the Roosevelt administration. The senator personally fought for the National Industrial Recovery Act of 1933, the Social Security and the National Labor Relations, or Wagner, acts of 1935, and the Wagner-Steagel Act of 1937. He failed to win passage of an antilynching bill and the Wagner-Murray-Dingall bill, which included a national health insurance program, and a federal system of unemployment insurance.

Wagner continued to support important labor, civil rights, and social welfare legislation during the Truman administration, but he was not as active because of failing health. His son, Robert F. Wagner, Jr., represented him at almost all public functions from 1944 on. Wagner joined other liberals in sponsoring the Full Employment bill of 1945. The legislation would have committed the government "to assure the existence at all times of sufficient employment opportunities" to provide jobs for all those willing to work. In order to achieve this goal, the government was to "stimulate and encourage the highest feasible levels of private investment" and complement this with federal investment when necessary. He unsuccessfully battled conservatives in Congress who objected to the sweeping goal of the bill and opposed the deficit spending it would have required. The final measure, adopted in February 1946, committed the nation in very general terms to reach the highest possible level of employment but without intervention to stimulate investment and spending.

Wagner's other proposals received a mixed reception. Congress refused to pass his national health care proposal and his plan for a truly national unemployment insurance program. Although Congress defeated the Wagner-Ellender-Taft housing bill in 1946 and 1947, it passed a similar measure in 1949. This bill expanded the federal government's role in providing housing for the poor and middle class. Quite naturally he opposed the union-restricting modifications to the Wagner Act that eventually became the Taft-Hartley Act.

Wagner enthusiastically supported the Truman administration's containment policies toward the Soviet Union. Like many other postwar liberals, he considered communism an evil that should be fought with the same determination the United

States had fought fascism. He supported Greek-Turkish aid and the Marshall Plan. Wagner was a strong supporter of Zionism. In October 1945 Congress overwhelmingly voted for the Wagner-Taft resolution on Palestine. This guaranteed U.S. support for Jewish immigration to Palestine with the ultimate objective of creating a Jewish state.

In March 1949 Republican leaders called for Wagner's retirement because he had not attended any sessions of the 80th and 81st Congresses. As a result, Wagner resigned, and his seat was filled for the next year by JOHN FOSTER DULLES. Wagner died of a heart attack on May 4, 1953, in New York, City.

—JB

Wallace, Henry A(gard)

(1888–1965) *Secretary of Commerce, March 1945–September 1946; presidential candidate, Progressive Citizens of America, 1948*

Henry A. Wallace was born on October 7, 1888, in Adair County, Iowa. His father, Henry C. Wallace, was a noted agriculturalist and professor at the University of Iowa, where he developed new techniques for breeding livestock and growing grain. The elder Wallace was the editor of the *Wallace Farmer*, an influential newspaper in rural America, and secretary of agriculture under Warren G. Harding. Young Henry grew up in a household that stressed hard work, a love for the land, a thirst for science and a devotion to Christianity. As a young boy, he became a friend of George Washington Carver, the black botanist, who introduced him to plant genetics. While at Iowa State Agricultural College, Henry Wallace pioneered a number of new techniques in the hybridization of corn and in soil conservation. Following graduation in 1910 Wallace educated himself in agricultural economics and mathematics and contributed articles to his father's newspaper on the industrialization of agriculture. Wallace's two books, *Agriculture Prices* (1920) and *Correlation and Machine Calculation* (1925), both called for the modernization of farms.

When Wallace's father assumed the position of secretary of agriculture in 1921, Henry succeeded him as editor of the *Wallace Farmer*. The young man also continued his work in genetics, developing techniques for the hybridization of corn on a commercial scale. He founded the HiBred Corn Company, which became one of the major corn distributing concerns in the nation.

Initially a Republican, Wallace grew increasingly disillusioned with the Republican administrations of the 1920s because of their refusal to subsidize agricultural prices to insure the farmer a stable income. Wallace, therefore, supported Al Smith for president in 1928 and Franklin D. Roosevelt in 1932. The following year Roosevelt, impressed with Wallace's ability and well aware of his prestige among farmers, appointed him secretary of agriculture.

As secretary, Wallace reorganized the Department of Agriculture and helped draft the Agricultural Adjustment Act of 1933, which established the subsidy plan he had championed. Increasingly, Wallace's interests expanded out of the realm of strictly agricultural policy. He became one of the administration's leading supporters of pro-union, civil rights, and welfare legislation. Wallace's liberal position and distance from party politics alienated the leaders of urban machines and the powerful southern wing of the Democratic Party. When Roosevelt chose Wallace for the vice presidency in 1940, these groups threatened to defeat the nomination. Roosevelt was forced to use all his political acumen to win acceptance of his choice.

While vice president, the scope of Wallace's interests continued to grow. He became an outspoken internationalist and a visionary who looked to a postwar world in which the standard of living would be high, government would be democratic, colonialism and economic nationalism would end, and an international body would be formed to promote peace. The world, Wallace proclaimed, could enter "the century of the common man." At home Wallace became the leading spokesman for continuing the New Deal. He advocated ambitious social reforms, including government guarantees of full employment, national health insurance, advancement for women and blacks, increased public housing, and continued subsidies for farmers.

Wallace failed to established the political base he needed to obtain support for his programs. He made few friends outside a small cadre who shared his dream. His aloof manner and his unconcealed contempt for machine politicians made him a Democratic pariah in Washington. In 1944 urban bosses and Southern Democrats successfully pressured Roosevelt into discarding him as vice president. At the Democratic National Convention Roosevelt chose Harry S Truman to take the second spot on the ticket.

As a reward for past service, Roosevelt made Wallace secretary of commerce in 1945. During his early months in that post, Wallace was primarily interested in developing free trade agreements to promote disposal of surplus industrial and agricultural goods. By ending trade barriers, Wallace maintained, the threat of a postwar depression would vanish. The Soviet Union played a major role in Wallace's thought. He believed that good relations with the USSR were necessary to insure free trade as well as the creation of his dream for a peaceful postwar world. Wallace saw the Soviet Union as a devastated nation that needed American help and would eventually become an important market for U.S. goods. Wallace doubted Stalin's commitment to world revolution and downplayed his repressive domestic policies.

On domestic policy Wallace believed attainment of a higher standard of living for Americans necessitated some national economic planning, but not a "planned economy" of socialism. He called for a "national budget" or the "full-employment budget" to regulate spending so as to reduce unemployment or inflation, whichever one pressed the country at the moment. This took shape in the Full-Employment bill, devised by Wallace, industrialists, and economists. Although conservative Republicans and Democrats stripped the bill of its mandatory clauses, it passed, and the nation stepped closer to Keynesian economics.

During the Truman administration Wallace's primary aim became the preservation of Soviet-American cooperation begun by Roosevelt. According to Wallace biographers John C. Culver and John Hyde, both Truman and Wallace wanted to carry out Roosevelt's program, but they approached it differently: Truman from the perspective of a politician and Wallace from that of a philosopher. Thus, a parting of the ways was inevitable. In 1945 and 1946, as the administration adopted an increasingly firm policy toward the Soviet Union, Wallace neglected his Commerce Department duties to concentrate on what he deemed to be deteriorating American-Russian relations. He opposed the administration's decision to suspend aid to the Soviet Union in order to attempt to force the USSR to become more conciliatory in negotiations on Eastern Europe. He felt that the move would sabotage any hope of peaceful relations between the two powers. The aid cutoff also threatened Wallace's plan for the establishment of a free market by jeop-

ardizing Soviet economic revival and forcing Russia toward self-sufficiency.

The Truman administration's decision in September 1945 not to share atomic information estranged Wallace still further. (Wallace was talking about the scientific principles behind the bomb, not the technological secrets in actually building one.) The Soviets would discover the secrets anyway, but a reluctance to share the science, Wallace contended in cabinet meetings, would only deepen Stalin's suspicions of America. He opposed as counter-productive any effort to use the bomb to pressure the Soviet Union to withdraw from Eastern Europe.

Increasingly, Wallace considered himself the only voice for peace and cooperation in an administration dominated by anti-Soviet militarists. He was dissatisfied with Truman's handling of foreign affairs but believed that the president's policies reflected the influence of his advisers more than Truman's own thought. When Wallace urged the president to continue good relations with the Soviets, Truman would nod in agreement, but his actions belied any meeting of the minds had taken place. In spite of Truman's refusal to adopt the policies he recommended, Wallace remained a loyal Democrat. He rejected the advice of many prominent liberals that he leave the cabinet to head a movement against Truman. Wallace opposed the early stirrings in 1945 and 1946 to create a third party. He continued to believe the Democratic Party could be reformed from within. Although he thought Truman inadequate, he felt that with proper advice the president could become a successful chief executive.

Wallace muted his criticisms until the spring of 1946. In March, at a dinner for Russian relief, he publicly debated W. AVERELL HARRIMAN on Soviet policy. Harriman, an early cold war warrior, condemned Soviet domination of Eastern Europe. Wallace defended Stalin's desire to make his boundaries secure from capitalist encirclement. The West, he reminded his audience, had tried to destroy the Bolshevik regime after World War I. He asserted that the United States had nothing to gain in protesting Soviet hegemony in the area "but on the contrary everything to lose by beating the tom toms against Russia."

Wallace held the British in part responsible for the administration's anti-Soviet policies. He blamed Winston Churchill for intriguing with Washington to create an Anglo-American alliance that would commit the United States to protect what Wallace saw as a morally bankrupt British Empire and to oppose the Soviet Union. Churchill's 1946 speech at Fulton, Missouri, provided Wallace with additional evidence of what he viewed as an Anglo-American conspiracy against Russia. During that address the former prime minister had called for "a fraternal association of the English speaking peoples" against communism. Wallace later denounced the speech. He told the president that the United States should not tie itself to the defense of the British Empire, which he predicted was destined to crumble.

On July 23, 1946, Wallace sent Truman a long memo outlining his opposition to administration foreign policy. The secretary noted that Stalin had reasonable grounds to fear and distrust the United States. America's refusal to share atomic knowledge, its development of a large air force with bases all over the world, and its arming of Latin American states, all had anti-Soviet overtones. Wallace maintained that it was only natural for Stalin to view these developments with fear. The American refusal to recognize the Soviet leader's desire for security on Russia's Western border and need for access to warm water ports, intensified Stalin's distrust of the West. Wallace singled out the American proposal for the international control of nuclear weapons as being particularly anti-Soviet. He pointed out that the Baruch Plan, as it was known, called on Russia to reveal its nuclear research and submit to inspection before the United States had turned over its secrets. Wallace again emphasized the Soviet need for extensive economic aid. Summing up, the secretary suggested that if the United States made a number of limited concessions on atomic weapons, granted the loan, and recognized Soviet interests in Eastern Europe, "an atmosphere of mutual trust and confidence" would develop. Truman ignored the letter. Frustrated, Wallace made plans to resign following the November elections.

On September 12, 1946, Wallace delivered a speech in New York's Madison Square Garden to a meeting sponsored by the Independent Citizens Committee of the Arts, Sciences and Professions (ICCASP) and the National Citizens Political Action Committee (NCPAC). The slant of American foreign policy, Wallace told his audience, should neither be for nor against Britain or Russia. The United States should promise the world economic assistance for recovery and work for peace based on a strong United Nations and on mutual trust between the "Big Three." Unfortunately, Wallace asserted, American foreign policy had been influ-

enced by "numerous reactionary elements." The "get tough policy" with the Soviet Union that this group advocated, he maintained, would fail: "The tougher we get, the tougher the Russians get." Wallace called on the United States to recognize the Russian sphere of influence in Eastern Europe. In return, he suggested that the Russians acknowledge American interest in Latin America. Wallace also called on the major powers to recognize the "open door" to trade in China and asked the Soviet Union to keep Eastern Europe open to American trade. He believed that acquiescence to this plan could usher in a period of peaceful competition between the capitalist and the Communist world. As time passed, he hoped, the distinctions between the two systems would blur; capitalism would be socialized and communism would be democratized.

Wallace's speech won a mixed reception. The Communists in the audience booed him for his anti-Soviet remarks and his call for an open door for American capitalism. His demand for acceptance of spheres of influence confused many liberals. On the one hand they supported his desire for good relations with the Soviet Union, but on the other they were unwilling to recognize repressive Communist regimes. They also thought that his recommendations would undermine the United Nations.

Wallace's speech created confusion in the Truman administration. Secretary of State JAMES F. BYRNES, negotiating in Paris with the Russians, threatened to resign if Wallace kept on advocating policies that undercut his bargaining position. Senator ARTHUR H. VANDENBERG (R–Mich.), the leader of Republican internationalists in the Senate, charged that Wallace threatened bipartisan foreign policy. Wallace also embarrassed President Truman. He told his audience that the president had read his speech and endorsed it. When questioned by the press, Truman claimed that he had just endorsed Wallace's right to deliver the address, not the contents of the speech. Wallace responded that Truman had gone over his talk, carefully approving all the sections.

Following protests by Byrnes and Vandenberg, Wallace pledged to refrain from making foreign policy speeches until the Paris conference had ended. This did not satisfy the two men, who demanded Wallace's ouster. On September 19 Truman asked Wallace to resign.

Out of office Wallace proved a focus for liberal discontent with the administration. He continued to give speeches denouncing Truman's domestic and foreign policy. He also used his new post as editor of the *New Republic* to attack the administration and propose policy alternatives. During the spring of 1947 Wallace concentrated on two issues: the administration's loyalty program and its proposal for aid to Greece and Turkey. Following revelations of security leaks, Truman had issued a directive tightening procedures for insuring loyalty within government. Wallace denounced the order as a gross violation of constitutional rights. He feared the program would not drive Communists out of the government. Instead he said, it would bar from public service "the man who has ever read a book, had an idea, supported the ideals of Roosevelt, or fought fascism."

Wallace vigorously opposed U.S. economic and military aid to Greece and Turkey to prevent a Communist takeover in the area. He characterized the Greek government as fascist and reminded the American people that Turkey, neutral during World War II, had been close to the Axis powers. Rather than checking Communist advances, Wallace charged, the United States would aid Moscow by siding with the forces of reaction. He proposed a rebuilding program for Greece that would be administered by a coalition of Western and Communist governments.

During the summer of 1947, it looked like Wallace and Truman might reconcile some of their differences. Wallace praised the president's veto of the Taft-Hartley Act, and he initially endorsed the Marshall Plan as a peaceful, nonpolitical program for rebuilding Europe. Russia, however, rejected the proposal, which Wallace regretted. He then said he would oppose the plan if it became a program to restore Germany as a threat to the Soviet Union. By the autumn Wallace broke with Truman on the program. He termed it an unwarranted attempt by the United States to interfere in the domestic affairs of European nations. The assistance program, he charged, would enhance the power of the rich in those nations. In addition, Wallace maintained, the requirements for receiving aid made it impossible for Communist nations to join. He asserted that the goal of the plan was not to unify Europe but to increase the distance between East and West.

Wallace's attack on the Marshall Plan ended any possibility of reconciliation with the Truman administration. It also lost him the support of the more moderate elements of the liberal movement.

Such prominent members of the Americans for Democratic Action (ADA) as ELEANOR ROOSEVELT, WILSON WYATT, and JOSEPH L. RAUH, JR., attacked Wallace for his criticism of the aid program. However, the Progressive Citizens of America (PCA), a coalition of liberals and Communists, supported Wallace's stand.

In December 1947, the PCA decided to mount a third party drive for the presidency and chose Wallace as its candidate. Wallace announced his acceptance with a stinging attack on the Marshall Plan and a promise for peace with Russia. Recognizing that the party lacked the organization necessary to wage an effective campaign, Wallace, in an evangelical fervor, pledged to assemble "a Gideon's Army, small in number, powerful in conviction" to carry on the fight. Wallace accepted the PCA nomination in order to introduce an ideological element into American politics. He believed that the Democrats under Truman did not offer a clear alternative to the Republican Party. Both, he maintained, backed the politics of reaction. He sought to create a new party that would give the voter a clear choice. Even if he lost in 1948, Wallace hoped, the party would eventually replace the Democratic one. Liberal critics charged that Wallace would draw enough votes from the Democrats to hand the government over to the Republicans. Wallace answered that he preferred seeing a conservative Republican as president than a "Wall Street Democrat." Wallace began his campaign in early 1948. The spring of that year proved to be the high point of his drive. He drew large crowds wherever he appeared; small donations poured in. In speeches he repeated his criticisms of the Truman Doctrine, the Marshall Plan, and the administration's loyalty program. Despite opposition and physical harassment—the former vice president was egged during his campaign swing through the South—he toured the former Confederacy calling for racial equality before integrated audiences.

The growing Communist influence in the PCA gradually undermined Wallace's effort. American Communist Party leader WILLIAM Z. FOSTER endorsement did not help Wallace, and the Communist presence attracted FBI scrutiny of Wallace and his followers. (The bureau composed a hefty file on the candidate.) Although the Communist Party distrusted Wallace because of his espousal of capitalism, it was impressed by his condemnation of the Truman administration and his pro-Russian policies. Many party members flocked to join the

PCA. A number rose to key positions in the campaign, especially in Wallace's research and speech writing staff. Liberals urged Wallace to remove them but he dismissed their advice. He defended Communist involvement in the campaign and announced that as long as they understood he "believed in God and progressive capitalism" Communists would be welcome in his movement. He warned, however, that they must support him on his terms not theirs. He stated, "If the Communists are working for peace with Russia, God bless 'em. If they are working for the overthrow of the government by force, they know I'm against them."

During early 1948 Wallace made a number of tactical errors that undermined his drive. In the tense period following the Communist takeover of Czechoslovakia in February 1948, he blamed the action on the president's issuance of the Truman Doctrine. He charged that the Soviets were merely reacting to American aggression by tightening their control of Eastern Europe. In a press conference on March 14, Wallace blamed the whole Czech affair on the American ambassador, charging that he had tried to engineer a rightist coup. All the Communists did, Wallace claimed, was beat him to the draw. In addition, he dissented from the prevailing view that the Russians had assassinated Czech president Jan Masaryk. Wallace suggested the possibility of suicide. Wallace's views on the Czech coup hurt his position among liberals, particularly those associated with the ADA. Many quickly pointed out the similarity between his position and that of Stalin. Stalin, himself, also helped discredit Wallace. In May Wallace wrote an open letter to the Soviet dictator proposing a six-point plan for peace. Stalin replied that the plan would be a good basis for dialogue. Wallace's enemies used this as an indication that Stalin actually endorsed Wallace for the presidency.

Wallace lost ground in the fall of 1948. Liberal defections hurt him. The ADA mounted an intense campaign to discredit him as a dupe of the Communists. By citing names of those Communists in his campaign and drawing parallels between Wallace's positions and those of the Kremlin, the liberal organization successfully discredited Wallace. A Wallace victory, the ADA predicted, would fit Stalin's plan for an eventual takeover of the United States. Even if he did not win, the organization warned, Wallace would draw enough votes to give the presidency to THOMAS E. DEWEY. This, in turn, would put what it termed the reactionary Republi-

cans in power, making the United States ripe for a revolution. A vote for Wallace, the ADA asserted, was a vote for communism, not at the present but in the future. Both the American Federation of Labor and the Congress of Industrial Organization added their voices to those opposing Wallace. Although many of the member unions had supported him in 1946 and 1947, labor leaders such as DAVID DUBINSKY and WALTER P. REUTHER deserted him because of his failure to repudiate Communists. The defection of the liberals enhanced the power of the Communists in the PCA still further, adding to the plausibility of charges that they dominated Wallace. Truman's electoral strategy also hurt Wallace. The president swung to the left in 1948, endorsing a program for civil rights and bashing the Republican 80th Congress for not passing various social welfare programs. This gave many liberals a reason to stick with Truman.

Wallace failed to carry any state in the November election. He received 1.2 million votes compared to 24 million for Truman, 22 million for Dewey, and one million for Strom Thurmond, the Dixiecrat candidate. Most of Wallace's votes came from urban areas with strong leftist traditions. In the spring of 1948 Wallaces's forecasters had projected a vote of close to four million for him. The slippage revealed what many thought was the success of the ADA's efforts to discredit him and Truman's ability to draw the liberal vote.

After the defeat Wallace sent Truman an eloquent letter congratulating him and imploring him not to forget the liberal mandate he had received in the election. The former vice president retired to his experimental farm, Farvue, in South Salem, New York, but he remained active in the PCA until it disbanded in the early 1950s. He continued to criticize the administration for its reliance on military alliances. However, he joined Truman in denouncing Communist repression in Eastern Europe and aggression in Korea. In fact, the opposition of most of the Progressive Party's leadership to UN intervention in the Korean War led to Wallace leaving the party in 1950.

Wallace became entangled in the Red Scare of the 1950s. In 1951 LOUIS F. BUDENZ accused Wallace of writing a secret report to Roosevelt in 1944 recommending that Chiang Kai-shek (Jiang Jieshi) be forced into a coalition with Mao Zedong (Mao Tse-Tung). Budenz claimed that JOHN CARTER VINCENT and OWEN LATTIMORE urged him to make that recommendation, and that Vincent and Lattimore were Communist agents. Wallace denied the charges before the Senate Internal Security Subcommittee, and released the actual report to prove his case. The committee ignored Wallace's disclaimer in its final report. WHITTAKER CHAMBERS then claimed that a Communist cell led by Harold Ware existed in the Agriculture Department when Wallace was secretary. Wallace pointed out that Ware had been hired during the Coolidge administration and was no longer in the department when he became secretary in 1933. The former secretary further noted that after the cell was formed he fired some of the members and most of the others left because of a department purge in 1935. Wallace said he did not learn they were Communists until Lee Pressman testified to that fact in the mid-1940s. Wallace had to fend off such accusations for years to come

In 1952 Wallace privately voted for Democrat ADLAI E. STEVENSON for president, but in 1956 he backed DWIGHT D. EISENHOWER, thinking the former general could better control the military. In 1960 he lent tacit support to RICHARD M. NIXON's candidacy, by denouncing John F. Kennedy's agricultural policy proposals. Four years later he endorsed LYNDON B. JOHNSON for the presidency. Wallace continued to support liberal domestic politics in the last years of his life. He died on November 18, 1965, in Danbury, Connecticut.

—JB

Walter, Francis E(ugene)

(1894–1963) *member of the House of Representatives*

Francis E. Walter was born on May 26, 1894, in Easton, Pennsylvania. A George Washington University graduate, he served in the U.S. Naval Air Force during World War I. He received a law degree from Georgetown University in 1919, and returned to Easton, Pennsylvania, to open a law office. Walter attended the 1928 Democratic National Convention as a delegate and was appointed county solicitor the same year. In 1933 he entered Congress as representative of a district including the counties of Carbon, Monroe, and Northhampton. Early in his career, Walter supported the New Deal, proposing legislation for flood control, water conservation, and the development of hydroelectric power. All of these proposals directly benefited his district.

By Roosevelt's second term, however, Walter had become increasingly disenchanted with what he saw as an encroaching federal bureaucracy. He found himself challenging presidential policy, a familiar role for Walter in later years. As an attempt to curtail governmental power, he helped write the Logan-Walter bill in 1939. The measure provided for judicial review of regulations issued by federal agencies. Roosevelt, unhappy with the bill, vetoed it in 1940. In 1946 Walter and Senator PAT MCCARRAN (D-Nev.) successfully sponsored the Administrative Procedure Act, which required the publication of agency regulations in the Federal Register. Walter also backed efforts to limit the power of organized labor. In 1941 he pushed for federal jurisdiction over labor walkouts and strikes that might threaten national security. He also supported the Hobbs anti-labor racketeering bill of 1943. Yet he would vote against both the Case labor disputes bill and the Taft-Hartley Act.

After World War II Walter emerged as a strong anticommunist, concerned about domestic subversion and Communist influence in the United States. In 1949 he became the second-ranking Democrat on the House Un-American Activities Committee (HUAC). While he accepted the post reluctantly— he had voted against making HUAC a permanent body in 1945—and later termed it a "stinking job," Walter nevertheless came to view HUAC as essential to national security. He believed communism to be an international conspiracy bent on overthrowing democracy and argued the committee was vital in combating international subversion. In March 1949 he introduced an unsuccessful bill to deprive Communist Party members of their American citizenship. The following year his proposal to force Communists to register with the Justice Department as agents of a foreign government was considered by HUAC and rejected. As chairman of a HUAC subcommittee, Walter led a 1950 investigation into Communist activities in Hawaii. The next year he served as acting committee chairman in the second round of Hollywood hearings into possible Communist influence in the film industry. Both investigations resulted in a series of contempt of Congress citations as witnesses refused to answer questions about their political affiliations. In 1955 Walter became chairman of the committee.

Walter also focused his energies on immigration legislation during the Truman years. As chairman of the House Judiciary Subcommittee on

Immigration Affairs, he was in a position to shape American immigration policy. Known as a politician who "blew hot and cold" on issues, Walter wavered between backing legislation favoring immigration and more restrictive measures. Critics like Representative EMANUEL CELLER (D-N.Y.) charged his efforts tended to discriminate against Asians, and Central, Southern, and Eastern Europeans. In July 1948 Walter introduced a bill doubling the number of displaced persons allowed entry into the United States over the following four years. In the summer of 1949, he traveled to Europe to study the refugee problem. The following year he sponsored legislation increasing the flow of displaced persons into the United States and removing racial barriers to naturalization.

As a delegate to a 26-nation meeting in Brussels on European migration held in 1951, Walter tried to place immigrants in countries other than the United States. The committee established by the conference aided in relocating 165,000 people, including 47,000 refugees, to new homes. Walter also spent time in 1951 investigating the illegal entry of Mexicans into the United States. He proposed amendments to the existing immigration law that would have made it a crime to harbor and employ illegal aliens.

Walter's most controversial piece of legislation was the McCarran-Walter Act of 1952. Despite opposition from both President Truman and liberal members of Congress, the bill was passed on June 11, 1952. The law admitted immigrants under quotas based on the 1920 ratio of foreign born in the nation's population. It also extended the grounds for excluding or deporting aliens. Provisions in the bill allowed the Attorney General to deport those involved in activities "subversive to the national interest." Opponents pointed out the law would effectively discriminate against Asians and others not present in large numbers in 1920. Truman vetoed the measure on June 25, claiming it would "intensify the repressive and inhumane aspects of our immigration procedures." He called upon Congress to allow 300,000 more immigrants over a three-year period. Walter called Truman's veto message "fictional and amateurish." Both the House and Senate voted to override the veto.

The McCarran-Walter Act became an issue in the presidential campaign that fall as Truman attacked DWIGHT D. EISENHOWER for "moral blindness" in "embracing" Republicans who had voted to override. Eisenhower, fearful of being labeled anti-Jewish or anti-Catholic, quickly announced his opposition to the law and called for new legislation.

In other areas of legislation Walter tended to support the Democratic line. He voted to make the school lunch program permanent, and for the 1946 Employment Act, the National Housing Act of 1949, and raising the minimum wage to 75 cents per hour in 1949. As might be expected, he supported the Mundt-Nixon bill and the McCarran Internal Security Act. He backed Truman's foreign policy, voting for the 1946 British loan, Greek-Turkish aid, the Marshall Plan, the Korean Aid Act and against eliminating a $25 million authorization for establishing Point Four.

Throughout the Eisenhower and Kennedy administrations, Walter fought to preserve the quota system of the McCarran-Walter Act. He often defended the law on the grounds that it helped to winnow out foreign subversives attempting to immigrate. Walter did support lifting the immigration quotas for Eastern Europeans and Chinese fleeing Communist rule. As HUAC chairman after 1955, Walter found he was leading a committee rapidly losing prestige and public support. In the early 1960s he successfully rejected pressure from congressional liberals to abolish the panel. Walter died in Washington, D.C., from leukemia on May 31, 1963. (See *The Eisenhower Years*, *The Kennedy Years* Volumes)

—JF

Warren, Earl

(1891–1974) *governor*

Of Scandinavian heritage, Earl Warren was born on March 19, 1891, in Los Angeles, California, and grew up in Bakersfield. As a youth he spent summers working for the Southern Pacific Railroad, which employed his father as a car repairer. He attended college and law school at the University of California at Berkeley, receiving his law degree in 1914. After working a few years for private firms, Warren enlisted in the army in 1917 and spent most of the war training recruits. In 1919 he joined the staff of the Oakland city attorney but left a year later to be a prosecutor for Alameda County.

Here he obtained a reputation for prosecuting gambling, bootlegging, and prostitution. None of his convictions were ever overturned.

In 1938, pledging a nonpartisan regime, he was elected California attorney general as the nominee of the Republican, Democratic, and Progressive parties. For four years Warren carried out his law enforcement duties with the same vigor and sternness he had shown as district attorney. He waged an energetic campaign against racketeering and offshore gambling enterprises. At the outset of World War II, he zealously advocated the internment of Japanese Americans. Warren argued at the time that Americans of German and Italian descent need not receive the same treatment. He later regretted his actions.

In 1942 Warren was elected governor over the Democratic incumbent, Culbert Olson. With his hearty public persona, plain manner of expression, and pragmatic style, Warren created a personal following in the state that transcended party labels. His liberal Republicanism angered conservatives but won over enough Democrats to achieve handsome majorities in his reelection contests. Warren characterized his middle of the road politics as "progressive conservatism." He won reelection in 1946 and 1950.

During Warren's tenure California raised old-age pensions, widened unemployment coverage, and reorganized its penal system. His sponsorship of a plan to enact "prepaid medical care through a system of compulsory health insurance" aroused the vociferous opposition of the California Medical Association, which denounced it as "socialized medicine" and waged a successful campaign to defeat the measure in the legislature. However, he later secured expansion of workers' disability to workers and later won legislation to extend hospital benefits of unemployment compensation.

Presiding over the state government during a period of economic prosperity and tremendous growth, Warren was constantly engaged in expanding public services to accommodate the swelling population. He supported public development of hydroelectric power and pushed through the legislature an increase in the gasoline tax to finance highway construction. He testified before congressional committees in favor of state ownership of offshore oil. In the battle over loyalty oaths at the University of California, Warren opposed the dismissal of professors who refused to sign a special pledge required of faculty members. He did not oppose a loyalty oath per se but argued that the professors had already subscribed to the loyalty oath taken by all state employees. Warren also criticized the clause of the Taft-Hartley Act requiring loyalty oaths from

union officials on the grounds that such oaths "ought to apply mutually to both sides."

Warren's only hope for the nomination was a deadlocked convention, but that did not occur. The California governor swung his state's delegates to New York governor THOMAS E. DEWEY on the final ballot. Dewey chose an unenthusiastic Warren as his running mate, and the convention unanimously endorsed the selection. According to Warren's biographer, Ed Cray, Dewey's rigid and cautious campaign plan dismayed the Californian, who wanted a more flexible approach. At one point in the campaign, President Truman answered Warren's criticism by saying of the California governor: "He is really a Democrat and doesn't know it." The Dewey-Warren ticket went down to defeat in November.

Warren usually remained neutral in other people's political races in California. When he ran for senator in 1950, Representative RICHARD M. NIXON demanded an endorsement, but Warren refused, not wanting to be associated with someone who had helped draft the Taft-Hartley Act. Murray Chotiner, Nixon's campaign manager, however, goaded Nixon's opponent HELEN GAHAGAN DOUGLAS to endorse Warren's Democratic gubernatorial challenger, James Roosevelt. In response, the governor asked her publicly whom she expected he would vote for in the race for the Senate seat. Nixon and Warren both beat their Democratic opponents.

In 1952 Warren ran again for president as California's favorite son for the Republican presidential nomination. But according to Cray, he wanted to do more than to unite a usually fractious California delegation; he wanted to win the nomination. However, he did not have a national political organization. Warren's strategy then was to wait for a deadlock in the convention and offer himself as a compromise candidate. He easily trounced conservative Representative Thomas H. Werdel in the California primary. Because of his limited resources he ran only in the Wisconsin and Oregon primaries and lost in both. The governor's hope was to hold his delegation together for the first three roll calls while the other candidates did not reach a majority. In a fourth roll call, he believed his chance would come. The chairman of the California state American Federation of Labor, Cornelius Haggerty, promised 100 labor-influenced delegates would switch to Warren if no one had won by the third ballot. This might create a bandwagon effect and carry the governor to victory. But it was not to be.

Warren and the California delegation voted for the Fair Play Amendment, in which contested delegates would not vote on their own behalf, which cinched the nomination for DWIGHT D. EISENHOWER, who later won on the first ballot. Warren blamed Nixon for undermining his candidacy, but Nixon biographer Irwin Gellman has made a compelling case that the senator did not. Warren actively campaigned for Eisenhower in the autumn.

In September 1953 President Eisenhower appointed Warren chief justice of the United States. During his almost 16 years on the Supreme Court, Warren presided over a judicial revolution that ended legal segregation in schools, equalized political representation for urban and rural districts, and expanded constitutional protections for criminal defendants in state courts and for political dissidents from government restraint. Warren's tenure has been ranked beside that of John Marshall for its sweeping impact on American society. Warren retired in 1969 and died on July 9, 1974, in Washington, D.C. (See *The Eisenhower Years*, *The Kennedy Years*, *The Johnson Years* Volumes)

—TO

Warren, Fuller

(1905–1973) *governor*

The son of a lawyer, Fuller Warren was born on October 3, 1905, in Blountstown, Florida. He entered the University of Florida in 1922, intending to follow his father's footsteps. His studies were interrupted, however, when he won election to the Florida State Assembly in 1926, becoming the youngest legislator in Florida history. After one term in office, Warren returned to the study of law; he received his degree from Cumberland University in 1928. Warren practiced law in Jacksonville and was elected to the Jacksonville City Council in 1931, where he served three terms. In 1940 he ran unsuccessfully in the Democratic primary race for governor.

After serving in the navy during World War II he returned to the practice of law and entered the race for governor in 1948. His campaign stressed improvement in state education and pension programs, opposition to a state sales tax, reduction of government spending through central purchasing, and development of Florida's tourist attractions. Warren won the Democratic nomination in the May 1948 primary and easily defeated his Republican opponent in the November election.

Warren's legislative program aroused the opposition of business interests in the state. In April 1949 he submitted a 15-point tax proposal to the legislature that called for increased levies on banks, insurance companies, utilities, and capital gains. The affected groups lobbied against the proposals, and the legislature passed instead a sales tax on nonessential items. Warren fared better with his proposals to regulate the citrus industry. Concerned about the quality of Florida products, he won legislative approval of a citrus code requiring state inspection and labeling of citrus products.

Warren's governorship witnessed changes in the area of race. During his term of office black voter registration more than doubled, from 53,000 in 1948 to 112,000 in 1952. Some progress came in the area of education as well. Although the public schools remained segregated, Warren had the pay scales of white and black teachers equalized and doubled the per capita spending on the education of black children. During his administration construction of schools for black children exceeded the cost of new schools for whites for the first time.

Even these small signs of progress aroused antagonism. When mobs of whites set fire to black homes in Groveland, Florida, in July 1949, Warren called out the National Guard. Two years later, in the fall of 1951, a series of bombings occurred in Miami. Directed first at blacks, they soon spread to Jewish synagogues and Catholic churches and were accompanied by Ku Klux Klan cross burnings. Warren pushed through the legislature a bill outlawing cross burning and the public wearing of masks. When one of the bombings resulted in the death of Florida NAACP coordinator Harry T. Moore and his wife, Harriet, Warren offered a $5,000 reward for information on the slaying.

Warren's administration was troubled by serious allegations of corruption. In the summer of 1950 the Senate Crime Investigating Committee under Senator ESTES KEFAUVER (D-Tenn.) heard testimony from witnesses about illegal gambling in Florida. One racetrack operator, William Johnston, said that he had contributed $100,000 to Warren's campaign in violation of state law. The committee's report, issued in February 1951, accepted Johnston's allegations and also charged Warren with "official tolerance" of illegal gambling activities in Florida. Warren denied the charges. When the Committee subpoenaed him in June, he returned the subpoena and refused to testify. As a result the panel dropped its Florida investigations. Although the Florida legislature conducted its own probe, it failed to uncover evidence of corruption sufficient to warrant criminal charges and dropped the matter.

Prevented by Florida law from succeeding himself as governor, Warren returned to the practice of law in 1953. He attempted a political comeback in 1956 but finished a poor fourth in the gubernatorial primary. Warren never again sought elective office. Warren died on September 23, 1973, in Miami, Florida.

—JD

Wason, Robert R(oss)
(1888–1950) *president, National Association of Manufacturers*

Wason was born on May 1, 1888, to poor Irish parents in Ashtabula, Ohio. After graduating from high school he worked as a longshoreman, structural steel helper, and blacksmith's helper. In 1910 he became a reporter for the *Ashtabula* (Ohio) *Independent*, switching after a few months to the advertising side of the business. Three years later he moved to Cleveland and worked in advertising. In 1920 he became vice president and director of merchandising for the Proctor and Collier advertising agency in Cincinnati. Eleven years later Wason accepted the presidency of Manning, Maxwell and Moore, Inc., an engineering firm. Wason's innovative merchandising techniques were credited with increasing the business 17-fold by 1942.

A member of the National Association of Manufacturers (NAM), Wason served as chairman of its Economic Principles Commission from 1942 to 1945. This group prepared a textbook "to present the modern free enterprise system in this country." In August 1945 he became chairman of the NAM Reconversion Council. Several months later he appeared before the special House Committee on Postwar Economic Policy and Planning and recommended removal of all Office of Price Administration (OPA) controls by February 15, 1946.

In December 1945 Wason was elected president of NAM. During his year in office he criticized Truman's reconversion policies. He accused the president of allowing wages to go up while keeping a ceiling on prices. In July 1946 he labeled the OPA "made in Germany" and identified it with the authoritarian methods of Hitler. "OPA has created black markets," he charged, which "undermine the moral standards of your children." He singled out Stabilization Director CHESTER BOWLES for attack, calling him a spokesman for the authoritarian state. Wason also blasted the administration for deficit spending, claiming it helped cause inflation. In September 1946 he attacked Secretary of Commerce HENRY A. WALLACE for "appeasing Russia." "That is the party line of all Communists and fellow-travelers in America," he said.

Once a union member, Wason repeatedly stressed his belief in unions as a means of protecting workers. However, in 1946 he singled out organized labor as a prime cause of the nation's economic problems. In a speech before the Chamber of Commerce in his hometown of Ashtabula, Wason accused the government of making a deal with the Congress of Industrial Organizations "at the expense of the other three-quarters of the laboring economy." The Truman administration has become the "stooge" of unions, he said. He called for changes in the labor laws to end the "economic anarchy" caused by strikes and to bring back equality between management and labor.

In December 1946 Wason was succeeded by EARL BUNTING as the NAM switched to a more liberal policy toward labor. As was customary, Wason was elected chairman of the board for the next year. In June 1947 he accused the president of wanting to spend $24 billion fighting communism in Europe, while encouraging Communist tendencies in the United States. He denounced the administration for promoting collectivism and for following Marxist philosophy by forcing wages up while letting production lag.

Wason remained president of Manning, Maxwell, and Moore until 1950, when he died of a heart attack that year on July 7 in New York City.

—TFS

Wechsler, James
(1915–1983) *editor*

Born on October 31, 1915, in New York City, James Wechsler in 1931 entered Columbia University, where he edited the newspaper and became involved in left-wing politics. He joined the Young Communist League (YCL) in 1934 and, after leaving Columbia the following year, served briefly on the league's Executive Committee. A growing disenchantment with the organization culminated in Wechsler's departure from the league in 1937.

Wechsler soon began writing articles for *The Nation*, a liberal magazine that he helped edit for two and half years. In 1940 he joined the staff of a new left-wing daily, *PM*. Wechsler worked in the labor section of the paper and later headed its Washington bureau. During World War II he served in the Special Services and did public relations work in Germany.

Following the war Wechsler returned to *PM* and in early 1946 interviewed for the magazine an anonymous top progressive figure in the government disenchanted with the president. The disgruntled employee complained, "Truman keeps lamenting that good liberal men won't take top posts in his administration. . . . Who wants to work in a set-up where you have to go through this forward wall of politicians," who were "a lot of second-rate guys trying to function in an atom bomb world." Wechsler too had a jaundiced view of Truman, writing in *PM* in February 1946 in regard to big business arrogance that the president "was still seeking to avoid a showdown, still fearful that direct language would upset the boat, still unwilling to carry his case to the country." Wechsler resigned from *PM* in June 1946 because he believed the paper was Communist-dominated. Wechsler also was a contributor to *Progressive*, in whose pages he condemned Truman's loyalty program, cheered his veto of the Taft-Hartley Act, and bemoaned his lackluster leadership. Later in 1947 Wechsler joined the Washington bureau of the *New York Post*. Wechsler helped found the liberal, anticommunist Americans for Democratic Action (ADA) in 1947. He served on its press committee and helped draft the ADA's first general statement, which included a provision for screening out Communists. He berated the ADA's rival the Progressive Citizens of America for allowing Communists to join and refusing to respond to criticism of its policy: "This, of course, is the way in which Communists traditionally invite themselves into the house and make it illegal for their critics to do anything about it while they take over the furniture."

Wechsler became editor of the *Post* in April 1949. The first editorial printed after his appointment outlined the paper's commitment to liberal journalism and maintained that this orientation was superior to an "absolutist party line." The *Post*'s editorial policy over the next four years conformed to Wechsler's liberal posture. The paper backed the European Recovery Program, supported the attempt to establish a defense community in Western Europe,

and applauded the United Nations's decision to intervene in Korea. In September 1951 the *Post* began a 17-part series, "Smear Inc., Joe McCarthy's One-Man Mob," an exposé of the senator's investigatory tactics and questionable financial dealings.

In the spring of 1953 Wechsler was twice called to testify before McCarthy's Permanent Investigations Subcommittee and was accused of sympathizing with the Communist movement. McCarthy charged Wechsler with using the *Post* as a vehicle for denouncing opponents of communism. Wechsler replied that he had severed his ties with Communists 15 years earlier. He charged that McCarthy was using the hearings as a means of discrediting the *Post* and as a "primitive fishing expedition designed to silence independent newspaper comment." After considerable provocation from McCarthy, Wechsler provided the subcommittee with the names of former members of the YCL.

Wechsler continued as editor of the *Post* until 1961, when he began editing the editorial page and writing a regular column. Wechsler died of cancer on September 11, 1983, in New York City.

—EF

Wedemeyer, Albert C(oady)
(1897–1989) *army officer*

Albert C. Wedemeyer was born on July 9, 1897, in Omaha, Nebraska. He graduated from the U.S. Military Academy at West Point in 1918 and was commissioned a second lieutenant in the infantry in November of that year. After completing the Command and General Staff School in July 1936, he studied abroad at the German General Staff School, the first American to do so. In 1941 he was appointed a member of the Plans Group of the War Department General Staff, serving under General DWIGHT D. EISENHOWER. Three years later Wedemeyer, with the rank of major general, was assigned the command of U.S. Army forces in China. Concurrently, he was named chief of staff to Generalissimo Chiang Kai-shek (Jiang Jieshi), Wedemeyer replaced General Joseph W. Stillwell who had clashed with Chiang about the conduct of the war, the need for government to reform to win the support of the people, and the incorporation of Chinese Communists into the effort against Japan.

Although publicly condemning criticism of China as a hindrance of the war, Wedemeyer privately reported to Washington that reform was necessary if Chiang was to be maintained in power. He reported that the generalissimo could hold power in southern China only if he accepted foreign administrators and technicians, rooted out corruption in his regime, and began a series of social reforms. He concluded that Chiang could not establish himself in the North without a settlement with the Chinese Communists.

During 1945 and 1946 Washington sent several missions to China to arrange a coalition between the two Chinese factions and begin a reform program. All ended in failure, and Truman began substantial cuts in U.S. aid. In July 1947 the president sent Wedemeyer to China and Korea to review the situations there. Wedemeyer held deep suspicions not only about the communists but also toward State Department foreign officers in China whom he thought had an antipathy toward the Nationalists. He wanted to change policy toward China even before he left the United States. He believed he had two objectives: to convince Chiang that American assistance would be ill-spent without his instituting reforms and to persuade the American government that aid must be continued. Pessimistic about the situation in China, the general reported finding apathy and lethargy in many quarters. Chiang's government, he said, was more interested in blaming outside influences for problems than in solving them. He warned that "performance is absolutely necessary. It should be accepted that military force in itself will not eliminate Communism." Wedemeyer also reported that the weakening Nationalist position in Manchuria warranted immediate attention and feared the failure of Chiang's forces would lead to a Soviet satellite government being set up in that province and to the rise of a Communist-ruled China. Wedemeyer thought the United States should have the United Nations make Manchuria one of its trusteeships. Wedemeyer believed Chiang when he said reforms were in the offing, and recommended the resumption of large-scale U.S. assistance, suggesting grants of $1.5 billion over a five-year period, as well as the stationing of military advisers. Although he admitted the Nationalist Chinese were not winning at that moment, he believed it was not too late for them to prevail. Some aid was extended but not as much as Wedemeyer had called for. Otherwise, the administration was confused over how to respond to the report and officials suppressed it. The administration later explained the report was suppressed because it feared the trustee-

ship idea would have hurt relations with the Chinese. Wedemeyer, however, thought Marshall wanted to cover up what he saw as the secretary's intention not to take action. Its findings were later incorporated into a State Department white paper on U.S. policy toward the Chinese civil war. The paper, released in August 1949, marked off Nationalist China as a lost cause.

In May 1951, during the Senate Armed Services and Foreign Relations Committees' hearings into General DOUGLAS MACARTHUR's conduct of the Korean War and removal from command, Truman allowed the release of Wedemeyer's secret report on Korea. The paper predicted the invasion of South Korea and stated that when the Soviet army withdrew from the North, it would leave a North Korean Army "sufficiently well established to carry out Communist objectives without the presence of Soviet troops." Wedemeyer warned against ending U.S. military occupation of South Korea until it was given "an American controlled and officered South Korean Scout force sufficient in strength to cope with the threat from the North." Wedemeyer also argued that it was impossible to make South Korea a self-sustaining state and that the United States should subsidize its economy. Secretary of State DEAN G. ACHESON, commenting on the paper, said that virtually all of Wedemeyer's recommendations had been carried out.

In July 1951 Wedemeyer retired from the army. During the 1952 presidential campaign Eisenhower charged that Truman had "disregarded and suppressed" Wedemeyer's report on Korea. Wedemeyer supported the contention. However, Wedemeyer in early 1949 had recommended withdrawing U.S. forces from South Korea. After his retirement in 1951 Wedemeyer became an official with the Avco Manufacturing Company and later the Rheem Manufacturing Company. Wedemeyer died on December 17, 1989, in Fort Belvoir, Virginia.

—MLB

Welker, Herman
(1906–1957) *member of the Senate*

Born in Cambridge, Idaho, on December 9, 1906, Herman Welker worked his way through the University of Idaho Law School, where he received his degree in 1929. While enrolled at the university, he held the position of prosecuting attorney of Washington County. In 1936 Welker moved to Los

Angeles to open a general law practice. After serving in the U.S. Army Air Force in 1943–44, he returned to Idaho to practice law. In 1948 he ran successfully for the Idaho State Senate.

Two years later Welker entered the race for the U.S. Senate. Running with the backing of Senator JOSEPH R. MCCARTHY (R-Wisc.), he focused on incumbent GLEN H. TAYLOR's (D-Idaho) alleged Communist leanings. Welker was opposed by labor because he refused to take a clear stand on the Taft-Hartley Act. According to the chairman of the Idaho-Farmer-Labor Joint Legislative Council, Welker "sounded too much as if he favored a police state." Welker went on to win the election and later credited his triumph to McCarthy's support. However, historians have suggested that the victory was a result, in part, of the vicious Democratic primary that shattered party unity.

Welker voted with the most conservative faction of the Republican Party in the Senate. He opposed foreign aid and in 1951 backed Senator EVERETT M. DIRKSEN's (R-Ill.) move to slash a half-billion dollars in economic aid to Europe from the administration's Mutual Security Act. That year he also voted in favor of a complete ban on allied trade with the Soviet Union. He also supported the McClellan Amendment of 1951, which stated that it was the sense of Senate that any troops above the four divisions already being sent to NATO in Europe should not be deployed there without congressional approval. He opposed the Japanese Peace Treaty. Welker backed stringent immigration requirements and opposed amendments to the Immigration and Naturalization Act of 1952 that would have liberalized U.S. immigration policy. In November 1952 he supported the selection of JOHN FOSTER DULLES as secretary of state. Welker believed that Dulles, who urged the abandonment of containment and the liberation of Eastern Europe, would "clear up the mess" McCarthy claimed existed in the State Department.

On domestic affairs, Welker backed the bill giving seaboard states title to tidelands oil. He opposed President Truman's request for a $4.3 billion tax hike in 1952; Welker labeled the proposed increase "the same old Truman theme—socialism in government." He also voted against authorizing the president's seizure of the nation's steel mills to avert a strike.

In the Senate Welker became known as a staunch supporter of McCarthy's anticommunist crusade. He believed with the Wisconsin senator

that many of the nation's ills stemmed from Democratic appeasement and fumbling. In July 1951, while most of his Republican colleagues steered clear of public contact with McCarthy, Welker openly backed his position. Welker served on the Subcommittee on Privileges and Elections, which during 1952 held hearings on the Benton Resolution, calling for an investigation of McCarthy with a view toward his expulsion. Welker tried to stall the panel's probe, and, in September 1952, he quit the subcommittee, complaining that it was biased against McCarthy. He acted as McCarthy's self-appointed manager during the 1954 Senate censure debate. Welker was defeated in the 1956 Senate race by Frank Church. He died in Washington, D.C., on October 30, 1957. (See *The Eisenhower Years* Volume)

—EF

Wherry, Kenneth S(picer)
(1892–1951) *member of the Senate*

Kenneth S. Wherry was born on February 28, 1892, in Liberty, Nebraska. The son of a small storeowner, the future senator graduated from the University of Nebraska in 1914 and then studied law and business administration at Harvard. In 1916 he returned to Pawnee City, Nebraska, to become a partner in his father's furniture business, in addition to selling cars, farm implements, and livestock, practicing law, and running several funeral homes. He was nicknamed "Lightning Ken" for his excellent salesmanship. He entered Republican politics as Pawnee County chairman in 1918 and was elected to the Pawnee City Council in 1927. He served as mayor of that city from 1929 to 1931 and 1938 to 1940. During the 1930s he also was a member of the Nebraska State Senate. He soon became known as the most radical Republican in the state capital, backing Nebraska's progressive Senator George Norris (R-Neb.). (Observers dubbed him Norris's "errand boy.") Wherry became a more conservative Republican after Norris left the GOP to become an independent. Wherry became state party chairman and revitalized the Nebraska party. He gained national recognition in 1939 by organizing campaign caravans that helped his party sweep state elections. During 1940 and 1941 he served as Western director for the Republican National Committee, supervising party activities in 22 states. In 1942 he defeated his former mentor Norris in a three-man race, campaigning against the New Deal. Senator KARL E. MUNDT argued Wherry's defeat of Norris foretold the replacement of progressives in the Midwest with conservative Republicans.

Wherry entered the Senate at a time when Republican representation was at a low ebb. Gaining a reputation as one who fought his battles purely on the political and not the personal level, he rose quickly to a position of prominence. Wherry's rise continued in 1944 when, while still a freshman senator, Republicans elected him to the post of minority whip. He was responsible for getting out the party vote in the Senate and holding members to the party line. During the 80th Congress, while Republicans held a majority in the Senate, Wherry became majority whip and many times acted as floor leader because Wallace White (R-Maine), the elected majority leader, was often ill. After the 1948 election fiasco for the Republicans, a group of "Young Turks" waged a campaign to unseat the GOP leadership in the Senate. The Young Turks thought the party needed a more constructive approach as the opposition party. WILLIAM F. KNOWLAND (R-Calif.) challenged Wherry for floor leader and HENRY CABOT LODGE (R-Mass.) ran against ROBERT A. TAFT (R-Ohio) for Senate Republican Policy Committee chairman. The Young Turks failed in their efforts by margins of two to one, and Wherry served as Republican floor leader, from 1949 until his death in 1951. Senator EVERETT M. DIRKSEN (R-Ill.) explained why Wherry rose so far, so fast: "he had a shamrock in his pocket and was forthright as hell." Wherry had great powers of mental absorption and could find weak spots in others' arguments quite well. In debate Wherry was quite dynamic; Senator ARTHUR H. VANDENBERG (R-Mich.) chided him: "The senator from Nebraska can even say 'Good Morning' so vehemently as to make me quail." Wherry did have a tendency toward malapropisms. He called WAYNE MORSE, junior senator from Oregon, "the distinguished senator from Junior." Indochina became "Indigo China" in the speech of Wherry. He once accused Harry Truman of "sugar coating his red ink" and called the Joint Chiefs of Staff "the Chief Joints of Staff."

As a Senate leader, Wherry did not make policy alone but rather executed tactics developed with the help of Taft, chairman of the GOP Policy Committee, and EUGENE MILLIKEN (R-Colo.), chairman of the Conference of Republican Senators. Extremely popular among both Republicans and Democrats

he was known as the "Merry Mortician." Wherry relied on "friendly persuasion" to unify his party and was expert at obtaining "unanimous consents," those agreements that allow Senate business to proceed without hours of debate. Instrumental in the reorganization of the Republican Party in 1944, Wherry published a list of proposals, including the suggestion that the office of national chairman should be a full-time job with a four-year term. He recommended that the chairman be supported by an ongoing Republican organization operating at the state level to achieve fuller voter registration. Wherry stressed the need for grass roots Republican organization to maintain the strong opposition vital to the two-party system. He also asserted that the Republican National Committee should have a top-rate research division, which should assist congressmen with policy questions, and should reach out to urban voters.

Wherry opposed most of the domestic and foreign policies of the Truman administration. Although personally on friendly terms with the president, he labeled Truman's program "the farewell deal," attacking it as a "blueprint for socialism." With the notable exception of government price supports for farmers, Wherry consistently fought Fair Deal legislation, helping to ensure the demise of the Office of Price Controls and supporting the Taft-Hartley Act. He voted against public housing and federal aid to education. He also denounced the Fair Deal's centralization of power in the federal government, which, Wherry felt, would limit individual freedom and undermine free enterprise. For Wherry, who saw his Senate years as a constant battle by Republicans to curb inflation and government spending, the whole system of checks and balances had been eroded by executive encroachment. As Wherry's biographer Marvin E. Stromer noted the senator became the capital's "leading symbol and rallying point of die-hard conservatism." In light of his championing of the legislative branch, it is not surprising that Wherry successfully pushed for a law changing the succession to the presidency from the vice president to the cabinet officers to the vice president to the Speaker of the House of Representatives to the Senate President Pro Tempore, and only then to the cabinet officers.

Similarly, in the area of foreign policy, Wherry sought to uphold congressional prerogatives in the decision-making process. In 1949 Wherry attacked the administration's bipartisan foreign policy. He thought the GOP should oppose Democrat Truman's foreign policy and make a political issue out of it. He voted against the NATO treaty when the Senate rejected an amendment prohibiting the supplying of atomic bombs or information thereof to other member nations. He feared that without this proviso, other laws restricting the imparting of secrets of the atomic bomb would be nullified. He accused Truman in 1950 of having signed a secret accord with the Russians at Potsdam that compromised the freedom of Eastern Europe. He also charged the administration with ignoring Central Intelligence Agency warnings of the impending Communist invasion of South Korea. Although Wherry did vote to ratify the UN Charter, he opposed sending arms to foreign countries and in 1946 toured Europe at his own expense to confirm his suspicions that United Nations Relief and Rehabilitation Agency food that was distributed by the United States in Russian-occupied countries was being diverted to Soviet use.

From 1945 on, Wherry engaged in a running feud with DEAN G. ACHESON. It began with his unsuccessful attempt to block Acheson's nomination as undersecretary of state in September 1945, after Acheson's "rebuke" of General DOUGLAS MACARTHUR. Long a MacArthur supporter, Wherry had been angered when Acheson responded to MacArthur's views on the occupation of Japan with the statement that policy would be made in Washington and not in the field. In 1949 he was one of the few senators to oppose Acheson's appointment as secretary of state. In one Senate committee hearing, Acheson and Wherry engaged in such a heated discussion that the secretary of state readied a punch for the senator, but an aide restrained him. Acheson's relations with Wherry actually improved after the incident, the secretary later wrote.

Although Wherry supported Truman's action in sending troops to Korea in 1950, he continued to challenge the Truman-Acheson views on the conduct of the war, believing that Truman had failed to use MacArthur's keen judgment to maintain U.S. superiority in the Far East. Shocked and dismayed by the president's recall of MacArthur in April 1951, Wherry introduced a resolution to invite MacArthur to present his views and recommendations on Asian policy to a joint session of Congress. Wherry did not question the president's right to remove MacArthur, but rather the wisdom of the decision. While MacArthur's address before Congress, advocating

action against China to contain the Communists, laid bare the issues of the Far Eastern policy debate, Truman held firm to his decision to limit the war to Korea. Wherry continued his criticism of the president's policies, believing Truman ignored the real problem: Communist China's defiance of the United Nations by intervening in Korea and that any action short of ending that defiance was appeasement. The senator pushed for a resolution to hold open hearings on the MacArthur dismissal and on Far Eastern policy. Senator RICHARD B. RUSSELL (D-Ga.), chairman of the Armed Services Committee, wanted a closed hearing, releasing to the public transcripts with information that would endanger national security edited out. Russell prevailed over Wherry.

Long an advocate of strategic air power as America's first line of defense, Wherry, in January 1951, introduced Senate Resolution 8 to restrict the president's power to assign troops to Europe for the North Atlantic Treaty Organization pending the formulation of policy by Congress. Senator Tom Connally (D-Tex.), chairman of the Foreign Relations Committee, supported Wherry's resolution. The measure represented another step in Congress's attempt to maintain its power to declare war and contribute to the formation of foreign policy. The Democratic majorities on the Armed Services and Foreign Relations committees quashed Wherry's proposal, but within 10 years his view of the primary importance of American air mastery had come to prevail in the form of the Ballistic Missile Early Warning System and the North American Air Defense Command. STUART SYMINGTON, then secretary of the air force, later credited Wherry with being the leader in "awakening Congress to the potential of air defense."

Wherry's health began to fail in 1951. His last day in the Senate was August 31, and from then until the end of the session on October 20, his post as minority floor leader was filled by LEVERETT SALTONSTALL (R-Mass.). Wherry died on November 29, 1951, in Washington, D.C., from a sudden attack of pneumonia during his convalescence from a stomach operation.

—DAE

White, Harry Dexter

(1892–1948) *assistant secretary of the Treasury; executive director, International Monetary Fund*
The son of Lithuanian immigrants, Harry Dexter White was born on October 9, 1892, in Boston,

Massachusetts, where he grew up. Following graduation from high school in 1909, he spent the next eight years working in his family's hardware business. He served in the army during World War I and then became director of, successively, an orphan asylum, a settlement house, and a boy's summer camp. White received his B.A. and M.A. in economics from Stanford University. He undertook doctoral studies at Harvard, where he was an instructor in economics. His thesis, entitled "The International Payments of France, 1880–1913," won the David A. Wells Prize for 1931–32. In 1932 White left Harvard to become professor of economics at Lawrence College in Wisconsin.

During the mid-1930s White was special economic analyst for the Treasury Department. In October 1936 he was made an assistant director of the Division of Research and Statistics. Two years later White was appointed director of the newly created Division of Monetary Research.

Hard-working, abrasive, and aggressive, with a thorough knowledge of complicated monetary problems and an ability to translate technical matters into administrative policies, White won the attention of Secretary of the Treasury HENRY MORGENTHAU, JR. Morgenthau came increasingly to rely upon White for special assignments and policy recommendations, particularly in the area of foreign economic policy. White played a major role in the implementation of the silver-purchase program by which the United States tried to support China's currency in the late 1930s. He strongly urged the extension of $25 million in credit to China in 1938 to aid the flagging Chinese resistance to the Japanese invasion. Both White and Morgenthau strove to involve the Roosevelt administration in more active opposition to the expansion of Germany and Italy. In 1939 White pressed for a $100 million additional loan to China ($45 million was extended in 1940) as well as a $250 million loan to Russia to shore up resistance to the Axis. He also proposed that extensive U.S. lending in Latin America would bring about "the establishment of the Americas as a tight economic unit."

In the months before Pearl Harbor, White played an important part in administration efforts to head off the approaching collision with Japan. In two secret memorandums for Morgenthau he advanced bold, sweeping proposals for an accommodation with that nation. Among his recommendations were a 20-year non-aggression pact between the two countries, the withdrawal of the U.S. Navy

from the Pacific, a $3 billion loan to Japan, and the repeal of the 1917 immigration law limiting Japanese entry into the United States. In return, Japan would withdraw her troops from China, grant the United States and China most favored nation status in the Japanese Empire and sell to the United States a large portion of her military output. However, White's proposal for a diplomatic settlement with Japan was ignored.

Immediately after Pearl Harbor Morgenthau raised White's status to the level of assistant secretary and placed him in charge of the Treasury's international operations. In that capacity, White dealt with such matters as continuing gold shipments to China and the creation of currency to use in occupied countries. His major activity was the planning of international financial policy for the postwar period. White and Morgenthau were primarily concerned with the establishment of some stabilizing monetary mechanism that would obviate the currency fluctuations and competitive devaluations that had upset the world economy in the 1930s and injured international trade. White spent many hours in strenuous negotiations over the form of this monetary mechanism with his British counterpart, John Maynard Keynes.

The result of their labors was the International Monetary Fund (IMF) approved at the Bretton Woods Conference of 1944. The aggregate capital of the IMF's currency stabilization fund was set at $8.8 million, with the United States subscribing $2.75 million, Great Britain $1.3 million, and Russia $1.2 million. The fund would fix the rates of exchange of each member's currency in relation to the dollar or gold. In times of liquidity shortages or balance-of-payments difficulties, members could borrow from the fund to acquire foreign exchange. Allied with the general purpose of the IMF was the creation at Bretton Woods of the International Bank for Reconstruction and Development, later known as the World Bank, an institution White had first ambitiously outlined in 1942. The final product, much narrower in lending capacity than White had originally envisaged, was given $10 billion in capital to finance long-term construction and development, as opposed to the short-term needs to be met by the IMF. According to his biographer, David Rees, "the signing of the Bretton Woods Articles of Agreement marked the apex of White's career."

After the Bretton Woods Conference White played a central role in the debate within the administration over Allied policy toward postwar Germany. An advocate of a harsh treatment of the defeated enemy, White promoted the Morgenthau Plan. The plan envisioned the destruction of German war-making capacity, the elimination of other major industries such as steel and chemicals, and the partition of Germany. In this view, the postwar German economy would be essentially agricultural.

President Roosevelt and British prime minister Winston Churchill approved the essentials of the Morgenthau Plan at their Quebec Conference in September 1944. However, when details of the plan became public, it was generally denounced, and the leaders retreated from it. White continued to fight for the plan, but President Truman decisively rejected it soon after he became president. White's January 1945 proposal for a $10 billion postwar loan to Russia was also ignored.

White was officially appointed assistant secretary of the Treasury in January 1945, although he had functioned at that level throughout the war. One year later President Truman appointed him the first American executive director of the International Monetary Fund. White served in this post, for which he left the Treasury in May 1946, until his resignation from government in May 1947. Over the next year White did some financial consulting work, but his activity was limited due to a heart attack suffered in September 1947.

On July 31, 1948, ELIZABETH BENTLEY, a confessed former Communist spy for the Soviet Union, appeared before the House Un-American Activities Committee (HUAC) and gave sensational testimony about an espionage network among government employees during the war. She named White as one of 30 officials involved; he was the most senior and powerful official named. Bentley claimed that White regularly gave secret information during the war to Nathan Silvermaster, a leader of one of the underground espionage groups. She said that she had not known White personally but was repeating what was told to her by Silvermaster and others.

On August 3 another former member of the Communist underground, WHITTAKER CHAMBERS, testified that White during the 1930s had been one of a clandestine Communist "elite group" whose design was to infiltrate the New Deal. Chambers, who maintained that he had been personally acquainted with White, could not say for sure whether White had belonged to the Communist

Party, but "he certainly was a fellow traveler so far within the fold that his not being a Communist would be a mistake on both sides."

White appeared before the committee on August 13 and emphatically denied the charges of Bentley and Chambers. "I am not now and never have been a Communist, nor even close to becoming one," he declared. "I cannot recollect ever knowing a Miss Bentley or a Mr. Whittaker Chambers, nor judging from the pictures I have seen in the press, have I ever met them." He characterized the claim that he had helped obtain Treasury positions for members of the Communist underground as "unqualifiedly false." "My creed is the American creed," White said, before making a patriotic affirmation of the principles he believed in.

Under questioning White acknowledged that Silvermaster was a good friend of his, and that many of the others named by Bentley were acquaintances and had worked for him, but he disclaimed any knowledge of Communist affiliations on their part. Sparring with committee members, White made a strong impression with his vigorous rebuttal. Three days later, on August 16, he died from a heart attack.

After White's death the controversy over his alleged involvement with the Communist underground subsided, eclipsed by the fiery debate surrounding other accused spies such as ALGER HISS and JULIUS and ETHEL ROSENBERG. Over the next few years, Chambers and Bentley added details to their accusations against White. In November 1948, as part of the discovery process in Hiss's slander suit against him, Chambers produced a cache of government documents from the 1930s, one of which was a long memorandum written by White concerning foreign operations of the Treasury. At Hiss's perjury trial the next year, and in his 1952 autobiography, *Witness*, Chambers maintained that until 1938 White regularly transmitted to him for delivery to Soviet agents government documents and weekly summaries of information.

In 1951 Bentley, testifying before a congressional committee, elaborated on the role White had played within the Silvermaster group during the war. Not only did White give confidential information and place Communist contacts within the Treasury, she charged, but he also had tried to influence U.S. policy in a pro-Soviet direction. Bentley claimed the Morgenthau Plan was an example of such influence.

The White case became a headline affair for a few weeks in November 1953, when Attorney General Herbert Brownell, a Republican, resurrected the controversy. "Harry Dexter White was a Russian spy," Brownell declared in a speech in Chicago. "He smuggled secret documents to Russian agents for transmission to Moscow. Harry Dexter White was known to be a Communist agent by the very people who appointed him to the most sensitive position he ever held in government service."

Brownell's charges sparked a vehement denial from former president Truman. Over the next few weeks Truman engaged in a bitter public debate with Brownell, who was supported by FBI director J. EDGAR HOOVER, over the appointment of White to the IMF in 1946. Truman acknowledged receipt of an FBI report about White's underground activities, but he said the charges were "impossible to prove." He maintained that he then allowed White's appointment to the IMF to proceed so as not to disrupt any of the FBI's parallel investigations into security risks or to alert White to the fact that he was under suspicion. Brownell's charges, Truman said, were lies.

Brownell and Hoover appeared before the Senate Internal Security Subcommittee to rebut Truman's version. Brownell quoted from FBI reports to buttress his claim that Truman had been told that White was a subversive before he was named to the IMF. Hoover maintained that he had told Truman's Attorney General, TOM C. CLARK, that the White appointment was "unwise." He also claimed that he was not a party to any agreement to allow the White nomination to proceed for investigatory purposes. The FBI investigation was "hampered" by White's appointment, Hoover said, because the IMF's premises were extraterritorial and FBI agents could not enter them.

The Senate subcommittee took no action and little more was said in public on the affair of Harry Dexter White.

In the 1990s the release of the Venona decrypts settled the question of the charges against White. He did give classified information over to Soviet agents. White's other biographer, R. Bruce Craig, however, argued that the assistant secretary did not subvert U.S. policy on behalf of the Soviets or Chinese Communists. Craig believed White was motivated by a desire to promote cooperation between the Soviet Union and the United States.

—TO

White, Walter F(rancis)
(1893–1955) *executive secretary, NAACP*

Walter White was born on July 1, 1893, in Atlanta, Georgia. He decided to devote his life to civil rights, after his father, an Atlanta mailman, was killed during a race riot. He graduated form Atlanta University in 1916 and briefly sold insurance. In 1918 White joined the NAACP as James Wilbur Johnson's assistant secretary. From 1918 to 1929 he personally investigated 41 lynchings and eight race riots. During the 1920s he gained fame for his novels, one of which, *Rope and Faggot* (1929), was a powerful indictment of lynching. White became executive secretary of the NAACP in March 1931. He served at that post until his death.

As leader of the most prominent civil rights group of that period, White acted as a lobbyist in Washington for antilynching, antisegregation, and anti–poll tax laws. During World War II White condemned discrimination against blacks in the armed forces and defense industries. He drafted President Roosevelt's executive order of June 1941 prohibiting racial discrimination in defense industries. From 1943 to 1945 White toured the war theaters as a special *New York Post* correspondent. An outgrowth of his travels was *A Rising Wind* (1945), a book on the treatment of black soldiers. At the 1945 UN San Francisco Conference, White lobbied for decolonization to the neglect of other NAACP business, such as a planned membership drive. However, the Truman administration had other priorities. W. E. B. DuBois thought the executive secretary's performance at the conference ineffective because of his ignorance of foreign affairs and its implications. It took some time for White to realize that the U.S. government was more interested in keeping the support of the Western imperial powers in the emerging cold war than in decolonization.

Yet, according to his biographer Kenneth Robert Janken, White proved willing to unlink decolonization from the civil rights movement at home in order to keep open channels to the government and continue lobbying. Before imperialism and domestic racial discrimination had been seen as inseparable—both would have to be destroyed in order to end the threat to blacks. Now White was saying civil rights concessions at home would bolster the U.S. image in developing nations as opposed to the Soviets. White also tried to effect this new balance through the suppression of black leftists who still coupled civil rights with decolonization.

A moderate, White advocated the use of legislation and particularly the power of the executive to end segregation. He believed that such action would end discrimination more quickly than violence and direct mass action. During the postwar period he urged Truman to establish a permanent fair employment commission, eliminate segregation in Washington, D.C., end discrimination in the civil service, and abolish "once and for all" segregation in the armed forces. White appeared before the platform committee at the 1948 Democratic National Convention to demand a strong civil rights plank. "The day of reckoning has come," he said, "when the Democratic Party must decide whether it is going to permit bigots to dictate its philosophy and policy or whether the party can rise to the heights of America which alone can justify its continued existence." He praised the strong civil rights plank pushed through by liberal leaders.

During the great strike wave of 1946, the CIO launched Operation Dixie—the Southern organizing drive that would include blacks—the NAACP reversed its traditional distrust of unions. White called upon local chapters of the NAACP to raise money for strike funds, and he represented the association in meetings to force General Motors to negotiate in good faith with the United Autoworkers. White even backed the racist railroad brotherhoods when they went on strike against the government-seized railways and whose workers were threatened with induction by President Truman. White did request the brotherhoods to drop their discrimination.

In the aftermath of a bloody year of racial violence in 1946—including the assault of white national guardsmen on the African-American section of Columbia, Tennessee—White urged Truman to do something about the situation. Truman established the Presidential Committee on Civil Rights, which wrote the 1947 report "To Secure These Rights," which recommended ways to end segregation.

Although he objected to Truman's inclusion of several men whom he considered racist in the cabinet, White generally applauded the president's efforts to end discrimination. He praised Truman's 1947 speech before the NAACP promising to attack racial discrimination, and he supported the executive order of July 1948 barring discrimination in the armed forces and civil service. Despite official NAACP neutrality he vigorously supported Truman during the 1948 presidential campaign. In his syndicated newspaper column White belittled the efforts of HENRY A. WALLACE and THOMAS E. DEWEY on behalf of blacks while praising Truman's frontal attacks on racial and religious discrimination. He condemned southerners as "morons" and the GOP as "transparently dishonest." White was so pro-Truman that he ousted W. E. B. Dubois from his position as research director of the NAACP because of his support for Wallace.

In 1947 White announced that the NAACP would go to court against segregated school systems in 17 states. Although a federal court in Charleston, Supreme Court, upheld public school segregation in June 1951, White was undeterred, predicting that racial segregation would be abolished within 10 years. Following bloody race riots in Cook County, Illinois, in July 1951, he wrote in the *New York Herald Tribune* that the conflict had resulted from black confinement in Chicago's ghettos and whites' opposition to admitting them to suburbia. He attacked the refusal of real estate associations, mortgage companies, and banks to lend money to blacks.

During the 1952 presidential campaign White charged that DWIGHT D. EISENHOWER had advocated racial segregation in the armed forces and opposed admission of black officers since they had received "vastly inferior education" to whites. He also attacked Democratic vice presidential candidate JOHN J. SPARKMAN as a racist. In June 1953 White announced that NAACP policy was no longer "separate but equal facilities" but "total integration." White died on March 21, 1955, in New York City.

—AES

Whitney, A(lexander) F(ell)

(1873–1949) *president, Brotherhood of Railroad Trainmen*

Born on April 12, 1873, in Cedar Falls, Iowa, and brought up on a prairie farm in Nebraska, A. F. Whitney became a train brakeman at the age of 17. In 1896 he joined the Brotherhood of Railroad Trainmen (BRT), where he became in turn master of his local lodge, chairman of the general grievance committee for the Chicago and Northwestern Railroad, and, in 1907, vice president of the brotherhood. Originally little more than a mutual insurance society, the BRT, like the brotherhoods of locomotive firemen, engineers, conductors, and other railway tradesmen, gradually set more ambitious collective bargaining and legislative goals. During World War I all the brotherhoods were strengthened by the government's seizure of the railroads and its attempts to foster a system of national adjustment boards to settle disputes. Provisions for continuing this system were embodied in the 1926 Railway Labor Act. The measure compelled employers to negotiate on matters of pay and working conditions exclusively with representatives of employees who had been freely chosen, and it set up the National Mediation Board to arbitrate disputes.

In 1928 Whitney was elected president of the BRT. Four years later he became chairman of the Railway Labor Executives Association, which included the leaders of all the brotherhoods. By this time railroad workers had become disenchanted with the Railway Labor Act, which provided for no enforcement machinery and, as a result, permitted the proliferation of company unions and antibrotherhood blacklists. With the support of the Roosevelt administration, Whitney fought for and won congressional passage of the Emergency Railroad Transportation Act in 1933. The act strengthened the right of rail workers to organize into unions and contained many provisions later embodied in the 1935 Wagner Act.

After World War II the brotherhoods joined the rest of the labor movement in a simultaneous push for higher wages to compensate for inflation and the end of overtime pay. Handicapped by government regulations, which provided for a time-consuming process of arbitration and fact-finding, railroad workers could not assert their demands with the speed of other unions. After months of negotiations, in April 1946 the National Mediation Board finally awarded a cost-of-living increase of 16 cents an hour, 2.5 cents below the national pattern set in the steel and auto strikes earlier that year. All 20 unions involved condemned the offer, and Whitney and ALVANLEY JOHNSTON of the engineers called a nationwide strike for May 18. On May 17 President Truman seized the railroads, secured postponement of the strike date for a week and offered an additional 2.5 cents. Only the BRT and the engineers refused to accept. Truman conferred with the two men but they would not relent on their demands and, on May 23, they ordered their members to strike.

Faced with open defiance of his authority Truman lashed out at Whitney and Johnston. The day after the strike began, he drafted a violent speech for national radio broadcast, condemning "effete union leaders" who had been "living in luxury" and calling on veterans to form vigilante groups to "put transportation and production back to work, hang a few traitors and make our own country safe for democracy." The president's advisers convinced him to tone down the speech and on the radio he said this was "no contest between labor and management but one between a small group of men and the government." He indicated those men were "not going to tie up the country. . . . If this is the way you want it, we'll stop you." In an address before a joint session of Congress on May 25 he asked for the power to draft strikers into the army. Liberals and union officials denounced the Truman proposal as a form of fascism, and conservative ROBERT A. TAFT (R-Ohio) helped lead the charge against the bill.

Although a settlement was reached in the strike, Whitney vowed to spend the BRT's entire treasury of $47 million to defeat Truman in the next election. (Ironically Whitney had backed Truman in his crucial reelection campaign to the Senate in 1940.) The following year he became a vice chairman of the Progressive Citizens of America (PCA), which he viewed as the nucleus of a possible third party. Although the PCA was strongly influenced by the Communist Party, Whitney remained in it for some time after other liberals and labor leaders switched allegiance to the rival Americans for Democratic Action. The day after the Senate overrode Truman's veto of the Taft-Hartley Act, Whitney wrote other union leaders saying that unions had long relied on the Senate to protect their interests from the "more or less reactionary" House of Representatives. But with the Senate's action the major unions had to work to rectify this misdeed and make a plan that would be to "the mutual advantage of every group of labor." In late 1947, following the president's veto of Taft-Hartley, Whitney left the PCA and reconciled himself to Truman. During the following year, in fact, he emerged as the president's strongest supporter in the labor movement. He was one of the few important union leaders to back Truman's renomination in the early stages of the 1948 Democratic National Convention.

On July 16, 1949, in Cleveland, Ohio, Whitney died suddenly of a heart attack.

—TLH

Williams, G(erhard) Mennen

(1911–1988) *governor*

A product of one of Detroit's wealthy old families, G. Mennen "Soapy" Williams, was born on February 25, 1911, in Detroit, Michigan. His grandfather was a soap manufacturer and his father a pickle magnate. He attended the exclusive Salisbury School in Connecticut and then earned his bachelor's degree from Princeton in 1933. Three years later he received his law degree from the University of Michigan. Williams astonished his Republican family by becoming a Democrat and joining the Roosevelt administration in 1936 as an attorney for the Social Security Board. Governor FRANK MURPHY appointed him assistant attorney general in 1937. When Murphy became U.S. Attorney General in 1939, Williams joined his staff as administrative assistant. He left the Justice Department in 1942 to enlist in the navy.

Following his discharge in 1946 Williams returned to Michigan to become deputy director of the state's Office of Price Administration. Murphy, by then a Supreme Court justice, had recommended him for the position hoping, the young man could use the office as a springboard for advancing in state politics. Williams traveled throughout the state building up political contacts. In 1947 he joined a Detroit law firm and sat on the State Liquor Control Board. There he gained publicity by campaigning in favor of tougher penalties for selling liquor to minors.

After the state's Democratic ticket was defeated in the 1946 election, Williams joined other liberals in forming the Michigan Democratic Club, a reform organization that hoped to revive the party by taking it out of the control of Teamster leader James Hoffa. They initiated a grassroots operation, organizing reform clubs throughout the state. Williams helped establish the clubs and worked with them to plan the 1948 election. The liberals selected Williams in 1948 to run in the Democratic gubernatorial primary against Victor Bucknell, Hoffa's handpicked candidate, and Burnett J. Abbott. Backed by liberals and organized labor, particularly WALTHER P. REUTHER, and with Bucknell and Abbott splitting the old regular Democratic vote, Williams won the primary by a small margin. Following the victory Williams's forces proceeded for the next two years to purge the party organization of Hoffa's backers. During the general election campaign Williams ran on a reform platform, demanding improved and affordable housing, better education facilities and higher teachers' pay, civil rights legislation, farm programs, veterans benefits, road construction, and an increase in the amount and length of time of state unemployment compensation. Williams defeated the incumbent, Kim Siegler—who had become unpopular even within his own party—in November.

Upon being sworn in as governor, Williams—who liked to wear a trademark green and white polka dot bowtie—requested a state corporate and personal income tax to help finance his "Build Michigan" reform program.

The legislature continued to turn down his request for such tax increases to fund expanded education, hospital, health, prison, and unemployment assistance programs. However, because of general revenue increases, Williams was able to make modest improvements in these areas. During the 1948 campaign the governor had promised to establish a Fair Employment Practices Commission to fight racism in job hiring. Once in office he kept his promise. This agency quietly, and with little publicity, hastened the integration of many businesses, especially the automobile industry. The state's Fair Employment Practices Commission became a model for the nation. Williams also took the lead in appointing blacks and ethnic minorities to state positions.

Williams endorsed Senator ESTES KEFAUVER (D-Tenn.) for the Democratic presidential nomination in 1952 in the hope that the senator would select him to be the vice presidential candidate. On the first ballot the Michigan delegation advanced Williams as a favorite son, but on the second roll call the delegation went for Kefauver. On the last tally they voted for ADLAI E. STEVENSON. During the 1950s Williams became one of the most forceful advocates of civil rights within the Democratic Party. Although many liberals mentioned him as a contender for the Democratic presidential nomination in 1956 and 1960, vehement southern opposition removed him from serious consideration. Williams endorsed John Kennedy for the 1960 presidential nomination and aided him in obtaining support from liberals previously committed to Adlai Stevenson. From 1961 to 1966 Williams served as assistant secretary of state for African affairs. He ran unsuccessfully for a Senate seat from Michigan in 1966. President Johnson then appointed him ambassador to the Philippines, where he served from May 1968 to March 1969. In November 1970 Williams won election to the state supreme court. In 1983 Williams was elected chief justice of the Michigan Supreme Court by the other justices on the court. Williams died on February 2, 1988, in Detroit, Michigan. (See *The Eisenhower Years, The Kennedy Years* Volumes)

—JB

Williams, John J(ames)
(1904–1988) *member of the Senate*

John J. Williams was born on May 17, 1904, in Frankford, Delaware. A graduate of Frankford's high school, Williams relocated to nearby Millsboro in 1922 to become involved in chicken farming and a feed and grain business. In 1940 he was elected to the Millsboro town council. "Fed up with what was going on in Washington," as he later recalled, Williams ran for the Senate in 1946. He mounted a zealous, unrelenting campaign against federal regulation of the economy and wasteful government spending and, although initially obscure, was elected in the Republican landslide of that year. Williams took his Senate seat in 1947 and joined the ranks of the conservative wing of the Republican Party.

Williams was determined to reverse the policies of the New Deal. He regarded the ever-growing powers of the unions and the executive branch as severely detrimental to the continued expansion and progress of private business. As a member of the Public Works Committee, he helped draft the final report, which opposed Gordon R. Clapp's succession to the chairmanship of the Tennessee Valley Authority (TVA) on the grounds that Clapp was "soft on communism." Williams also vehemently opposed the appointment of DAVID E. LILIENTHAL to head the Atomic Energy Commission.

Consistent with his campaign pledge to reduce government spending, Williams voted against economic aid to Greece and Turkey in 1947 and implementation of the Marshall Plan in 1948. Although he was in favor of the North Atlantic Treaty in 1949, he endorsed a proposal to cut foreign arms aid to Europe by 50 percent. The following year he opposed a bill providing funds for the Point Four program and a loan for Spain.

On the domestic front he continued his concern for limitation of the federal budget by opposing subsidies for education and funds for the

construction of a TVA steam plant and the St. Lawrence project. Both the private power and railroad industries argued successfully against the two latter proposals. In 1949 Williams voted for a 5 percent to 10 percent decrease in federal spending and a reduction of river-harbor appropriations. Williams opposed a bill to extend federal rent control and supported a cut in nondefense spending in 1950. He also voted for the Taft-Hartley Act, the Portal-to-Portal Pay Act, and the 1952 Byrd Amendment, which called upon the president to invoke the Taft-Hartley Act in regard to the steel strike that year. He also supported the Republican tax cut of 1948 and the McCarran Internal Security Act of 1950.

Because of his fear of the encroaching power of the executive branch, Williams endorsed a measure to restrict the presidency to a two-year term in 1947. The following year he voted against a proposal to give the president stand-by power over wage-price controls. One of the Senate's most vocal critics of government inefficiency, Williams denounced the Commodity Credit Corporation in 1949 for its inept handling of agricultural purchases slated for distribution abroad. He also directed his criticism at the Maritime Commission, maintaining that because of incompetence, surplus war vessels had been sold at an exorbitant loss to the government.

As early as 1946, prior to his senatorial victory, Williams had suspected willful wrongdoing within the Bureau of Internal Revenue (BIR). Several tax payments, including his own, were never properly deposited and credited to taxpayers' accounts, even though bureau officials became aware of the impropriety of this action. In December 1947 Williams disclosed in a Senate speech that a cashier in the Wilmington collector's office had embezzled over $30,000. The cashier, Maurice Flynn, pleaded guilty in January 1948 and the court sentenced him to four years in prison. What had disturbed Williams more than the crime was the fact that he had to prod BIR officials with a public speech. Williams believed Flynn's political ties might have led to forbearance of his misdeeds. The case gave Williams national exposure and soon honest BIR officials were reporting corruption to him. In 1951 Williams joined the Committee on Interstate and Foreign Commerce, where he became a member of an investigative subcommittee that examined tax collection procedures. Williams had at his disposal a compilation of dubious as well as corrupt bureau practices in local offices based on his own investigations in late 1949 and 1950. He maintained that one local collection official had settled a tax matter by accepting a bribe. In another instance, there was sufficient evidence to prove that the Treasury and Justice departments had intentionally withheld information that was vital to build a case against another collector.

Together with the other subcommittee members, HARRY F. BYRD (D-Va.) and CLYDE R. HOEY (D-N.C.), Williams uncovered what was soon labeled as the "Truman tax scandals." After exhaustive, systematic examination, he discovered that the BIR had favored 48 companies with tax settlements at a fraction of their obligation. One claimant's outstanding balance of $800,000 in taxes was settled for a mere $1,000. Bureau offices in all major cities and the business records of all personnel except file clerks were carefully examined in what became the first national shakeup of the BIR in history.

Based on the subcommittee revelations, Secretary of Treasury JOHN W. SNYDER began his own investigation. As a result of his findings, 66 officials were dismissed. Charges ranged from bribe taking and embezzlement to failure to pay taxes. Williams's quiet, thorough investigating technique unearthed widespread corruption, which eventually lead to the resignation of the commissioner of the bureau, GEORGE J. SCHOENEMAN.

In 1951 Williams also began an examination of the Reconstruction Finance Corporation (RFC), a government agency responsible for approving and dispensing loans as well as contracts to private industry. He alleged that the RFC had established a practice of favoring companies with ties to Capitol Hill regardless of whether or not the companies qualified for loans, Williams charged that Lithofold Corporation had received over three million dollars in RFC loans soon after securing WILLIAM M. BOYD, JR., the Democratic national chairman, as its attorney. He also maintained that a former BIR employee had worked for Lithofold for the sole purpose of exerting pressure on the RFC. His allegations lead to the formation of an ad hoc subcommittee that sought the ouster of Boyd and a thorough cleanup of the RFC.

For the remainder of his political career, Williams became an outspoken critic of excessive fringe benefits enjoyed by government employees. After several attempts at passage of a bill designed to curtail employee benefits, Williams finally succeeded in 1960. He also continued his fight against federal corruption and mismanagement. In 1963 he uncovered valuable information on the Bobby Baker

scandal. With the completion of his fourth term in the Senate in 1971, Williams retired at the age of 68. Williams died on January 11, 1988, in Lewes, Delaware. (See *The Eisenhower Years*, *The Kennedy Years*, *The Johnson Years* Volumes)

—DGE

Wilson, Charles E(dward)
(1886–1972) *president, General Electric Company*

Charles E. "Electric" Wilson was born on November 18, 1886, and raised on the edge of "Hell's Kitchen" in New York City. His father, a bookbinder, died when Wilson was only three years old. In 1899, at the age of 12, he left school to go to work as an office boy in the Sprague Electrical Works. Four years later Sprague became a subsidiary of General Electric Company (GE), and in 1918 it was absorbed by GE. Wilson moved his way up steadily through the corporation, mastering many aspects of production and sales. He played an important role in GE's switchover from almost total reliance on heavy machinery to the production of household appliances. In November 1939 he was elected president of the corporation.

In September 1942, at the invitation of President Franklin Roosevelt, Wilson left GE to join the War Production Board. As vice chairman in charge of production scheduling, he cleared the way for the manufacture of a record 93,369 military aircraft in 1944. In August 1944 he resigned over differences with Donald Nelson, head of the War Production Board, concerning what Wilson regarded as an overhasty plan for reconversion. He immediately resumed the presidency of GE.

Even though a registered Republican, Wilson served on many presidential advisory panels under Truman. These included the industrial panel of the National Security Resources Board, the National Labor-Management Panel, and the Taft-Hartley Advisory Board. Wilson was appointed to the Universal Military Training Commission to make sure it did not advocate segregation in training. In 1946 he was appointed chairman of President Truman's Commission on Civil Rights. Truman saw Wilson as the perfect figure to chair the group because of his passion for civil rights and his leading position in the U.S. economy.

The panel's report, entitled "To Secure These Rights," issued in October 1947, found that there was educational, political, economic, and social discrimination against blacks, Jews, Mexicans, Indians, Catholics, Orientals, and other minorities. It stated that lynching was one of the most serious threats to civil rights and maintained that in some sections of the nation a mob could murder "with almost certain assurance" of immunity. The panel recommended the reorganization of the Justice Department's Civil Rights Division, the establishment of federal and state agencies to investigate rights violations, and the appointment of a permanent presidential commission on civil rights. The commission demanded the "elimination of segregation based on race, color, creed or national origin from American life." It asked for the passage of laws to protect individuals against violation of these rights and police brutality. It also recommended the abolition of the poll tax and an end to bias in employment, education, housing, health, public services, and the armed forces. Wilson later said the report looked at "the bad side of our record—on what might be called the civil rights frontier."

Wilson was a strong opponent of labor unions. At the end of 1945 organized labor was pressing for substantial wage increases, which had been severely limited during the war. In December 1945 Wilson offered the United Electrical, Radio and Machine Workers Union a "take it or leave it" 10-cent-per-hour increase. One hundred thousand GE workers went on strike. During the strike Wilson told the Senate Committee on Education and Labor: "These bitter conditions . . . have never been obvious in our own relationship with our people before they were unionized, or after they were unionized. I mean we haven't had bitter and bad controversy between management and the union." Wilson argued that higher wages would have to be accompanied by higher productivity. He also said, "There is entirely too much of the spirit of union representatives holding back workers, even those on an incentive basis, who desire to produce more goods, and therefore get more money, but holding those workers down to predetermined level. . . ." Wilson particularly disliked the union's argument about the company's ability to pay higher wages. After almost two months the strike was settled with a compromise $18\frac{1}{2}$ cent increase. In October 1946 Wilson summed up his reaction to labor agitation: "The problem of the United States can be captiously summed up in two words: Russia abroad, labor at home." Three months later he stated. "The Amer-

ican people have not yet had the benefit of technical progress because of strikes, rumors of strikes and shutdowns." He denounced ROBERT R. NATHAN's report for the Congress of Industrial Organizations, which maintained that further wage increases could be given without increasing prices. Wilson urged a moratorium on wage hikes to give industry a period of adjustment from the wartime economy. During such a period technological advances achieved in wartime could be passed on to consumers in terms of lower prices.

In 1947 Wilson brought in his former wartime assistant, Lemuel Boulware, to devise what GE's opponents called one of the best financed, most highly organized and longest antiunion campaigns in corporate history. It was antiunion in the sense of wanting to reduce the influence of unions rather than eliminate them. Under Boulware GE developed a bargaining formula in which its first offer was generally its last. This technique was combined with the extensive use of marketing and advertising to publicize GE's side in labor negotiations, not just to the public at large but especially to its employees over the heads of their union leaders.

In response to the entry of Communist China into the Korean conflict in December 1950, Truman appointed Wilson to direct the newly created Office of Defense Mobilization. Wilson was ordered to "direct, control and coordinate all mobilization activities of the executive branch . . . including production procurement, manpower, stabilization and transport activities." He accepted the post only after Truman guaranteed that he would have full authority, second only to the president. There were advantages and disadvantages in appointing Wilson. He had shown competency in executive positions and had experience as vice chairman of the World War II War Production Board. It was hoped he could more readily obtain the cooperation of businessmen. He would also bring about bipartisan approval in Congress. Congress saw Wilson as capable, and it became evident early on that it wanted him to use all of his position's powers. However, unions distrusted him, and he came off as rather arrogant. However, he did support the establishment of a wartime Fair Employment Practices Commission.

Wilson favored the use of wage and price controls to prevent inflation and increase the mobilization effort. In February 1951 the rearmament program was threatened by a railroad strike, which slowed down steel mills and limited supplies of materials and food to U.S. forces in Korea and to the domestic population. In a nationwide broadcast Wilson appealed to the patriotism of the workers to end the strike. The walkout, he charged, "can very soon hurt the United States more than all the Communist armies in Korea put together." Wilson left the government in March 1952 in a dispute with Truman over a wage increase granted to steelworkers. He opposed the Wage Stabilization Board's raise package recommendation of $17\frac{1}{2}$ cents per hour, a union shop, and increased fringe benefits as a destabilizing precedent. "Inevitably other unions would demand and probably have to be given like consideration, and . . . the resultant inflationary pressures could [not] be resisted." Wilson thought he had Truman's approval to settle the strike with a wage-fringe benefits package smaller than what the Wage Stabilization Board had recommended and a $4- to $5-per-ton price hike. Truman claimed that he had told Wilson to talk to the steel industry about price increases, but not to surrender totally to their demands. Wilson resigned, saying he believed the president had called him a liar. He said that Truman's willingness to give the steelworkers a raise but deny a corresponding price rise for the companies "violates my sense of justice."

From 1952 to 1956 Wilson served with W. R. Grace and Company, rising to board chairman before resigning. He then served as president for two years of the People-to-People Foundation, a program initiated at the suggestion of President Dwight D. Eisenhower to promote international friendship and understanding. Wilson later acted as a business consultant and was chairman of the industries advisory committee of the Advertising Council. He died on January 3, 1972, in Bronxville, New York.

—TFS

Wilson, Charles E(rwin)
(1890–1961) *president, General Motors Corporation*

Charles E. "Engine" Wilson was born on July 18, 1890, in Minerva, Ohio. After completing an electrical engineering course at the Carnegie Institute of Technology in Pittsburgh, he joined the Westinghouse Electric Company in 1909. At the age of 21 he designed the first automobile starters made by Westinghouse. In April 1919 he became chief engineer and sales manager of the automobile division of the Remy Electric Company, a subsidiary of General Motors (GM). Wilson moved up to vice president of GM in 1928. In 1937 GM's president, William Knutsen, called upon Wilson to settle the sitdown strikes that were paralyzing the automotive industry. In June 1940, when Knutsen was drafted to direct the government's national defense program, Wilson was made acting president. He was elected permanently to that position in January 1941.

Wilson directed the conversion of General Motors to wartime production. The company produced $12 billion worth of war materials representing 8 percent of the total government spending on military hardware during World War II. After the war Wilson became embroiled in controversies over the best way to reconvert the economy to peacetime production. He was heavily criticized in the press in 1945 for urging that the 48-hour week, instituted during the war, be reduced to 45 hours, instead of to 40 hours as most advocated. In October 1945 Wilson endorsed temporary national wage and price controls during the transition to a peacetime economy. He criticized Truman for vacillating in his policy and for attempting to deal with the economic problems of reconversion by "juggling with the value of money." General Motors increased its domestic sales of cars and trucks from 230,000 in 1945 to 1,123,000 in 1946, but this still fell short of planned rates of production. Wilson blamed the Truman administration and labor unions.

During 1945 and 1946 General Motors was hit by a 119-day strike of the United Automobile Workers (UAW). Wilson settled that strike by compromising on an 18.5 cent per hour wage hike. But he sharply criticized unions for demanding wage increases that went beyond increases in productivity. He blamed strikes on the unions and called them the cause of "organized unemployment." Wilson maintained that the labor situation in 1947 was leading to "state socialism." In testimony before the Senate Labor Committee in February 1947, he compared compulsory union membership to a "requirement for membership in the Nazi party." He advocated a 10-point program to curb unions. It included banning compulsory union membership; prohibiting industrywide bargaining; declaring boycotts and sympathy strikes illegal; and, limiting negotiations to wages, hours, and conditions of employment. Wilson was an important force behind the Taft-Hartley Act, passed in 1947 to limit the power of labor unions.

The 1948 contract between General Motors and the UAW set the trend for labor negotiations in the postwar period. Wilson in 1948 believed a long-term accommodation with the UAW could now be had, to keep unionism within what he saw as its "proper sphere." Wilson believed that otherwise the "border area of collective bargaining will be a constant battleground between unions and management." To make negotiations smoother, he shook up his negotiation team. Wilson's primary concern was to maintain stability and control of production, and he was willing to pay a higher price for such predictability. Years earlier, while recovering from a broken hip, he devised a plan for tying wage increases to the Consumer Price Index of the Bureau of Labor Statistics. The "escalator clause" was first introduced into negotiations in 1948. The GM president offered quarterly cost-of-living adjustments linked to changes in the Consumer Price Index. Wilson believed that this would protect employees against inflation, and he maintained it would not cause inflation as some critics claimed Also, GM committed itself to a 2 percent annual improvement factor wage hike each year, made to at least partly reflect the rise in the corporation's annual productivity. These new features allowed for longer-term contracts and greatly reduced strikes. In 1950 GM agreed to a pension of $125 a month and paid half the cost of a new health insurance policy. The 1950 contract, which was to run five years, was called the "Treaty of Detroit" by *Fortune* magazine.

In March 1949 General Motors, along with Standard Oil of California and Firestone Tire Company, was convicted in federal court of having criminally conspired to replace city electric trolley systems with gasoline- or diesel-powered buses. GM was involved in 45 cities, including New York and Los Angeles. The company was fined $5,000.

A Republican, Wilson was appointed secretary of defense by President DWIGHT D. EISENHOWER in 1953. After four-and-a-half controversial years in office, Wilson resigned in 1957. He remained active in business until his death due to coronary thrombosis on September 26, 1961, in Norwood, Louisiana. (See *The Eisenhower Years* Volume)

—TFS

Wilson, Edmund, Jr.
(1895–1972) *author, critic*

Edmund Wilson, Jr., was born on May 8, 1895, into affluent Red Bank, New, Jersey—his father was a successful lawyer and a former attorney general of the state. From an early age Wilson was exposed to the arts and literature. While still 13 he went on the first of many cultural tours to Europe. He was a contributor to Princeton University's *Nassau Literary Magazine* during his years there from 1912 to 1916, when he also met and befriended F. Scott Fitzgerald. He enlisted in the army in August of 1917, serving until 1919.

Wilson's career blossomed during the 1920s. In 1920 he was named managing editor of *Vanity Fair*. The following year he became drama critic for the *New Republic*. During this decade he published major essays on such writers as Ernest Hemingway, Eugene O'Neill, and Willa Cather. In 1926 he became an associate editor at the *New Republic*. Wilson published a novel, *I Thought of Daisy*, in 1929.

The 1930s marked a period of political radicalism and protest for Wilson, beginning with the publication of "An Appeal to Progressives" in the *New Republic* in 1931. He attacked the liberal ideal of gradual reform and openly embraced the basic principles of communism—although not necessarily the Communist Party itself, which he found too dogmatic. *Axel's Castle*, published in the same year, firmly established Wilson as a major literary critic. *The American Jitters* in 1932, examined poverty, racism, and their relationship to capitalism. *Travels in Two Democracies*, based on his 1935 travels through Russia, appeared in 1936 and resulted in his being barred from the Soviet Union. In 1940, Wilson's *To the Finland Station* concluded that marxism could not, in and of itself, prevent human exploitation. That same year he ended his long association with the *New Republic*, claiming that it was printing British, pro-war propaganda. In 1943 he became literary editor for the *New Yorker* and toured Europe as a reporter for the magazine in 1945. During the tour he confessed, "I have become so anti-British over here that I have begun to feel sympathy with Stalin because he is making things so difficult for England." According to his biographer Jeffrey Meyers, Wilson talked of the senseless devastation of the war, and lumped Britain in with the extinct empires of Rome and Greece. He condemned the English for stymieing political development in

Southern Europe and for imposing military governments in Greece and Italy.

One of the great literary controversies of the postwar years began in 1946 with the publication of Wilson's *Memoirs of Hecate County*. The book was a scathing satire on the spiritual and ethical emptiness of affluent America's private and public life. It appeared in March to mixed critical response, with much attention centering on one story, "The Princess With the Golden Hair"—a contrasting study of two love affairs, one working class and one upper middle class. The story included a number of sexual encounters considered quite explicit by the standards of the time.

In July of that year the New York Society for the Suppression of Vice obtained a court order against the publishers, Doubleday & Company, resulting in police raids on New York bookstores. Similar actions occurred in Boston and Philadelphia. The Hearst newspaper chain began a nationwide campaign against the book. It was removed from the New York Public Library in September, and Senator JOSEPH R. MCCARTHY (R-Wisc.) said it was "pro-Communist." Meanwhile, the notoriety of the work resulted in its becoming a bestseller.

In November the Special Sessions Court in New York City fined Doubleday one thousand dollars and enjoined the company from publishing or selling the work, following a two-to-one decision that *Memoirs of Hecate County* was obscene and tended to deprave and corrupt the young. Doubleday appealed to a series of higher courts. The Appellate Division and the U.S. Court of Appeals in Albany upheld the decision of the lower court. The case ultimately reached the Supreme Court, which also upheld the lower court ruling in a tie vote. *Memoirs of Hecate County*, despite the fact that lower courts in other parts of the country had not found it immoral or obscene, was not printed again in an uncut edition until 1959.

Wilson also created a controversy, albeit a smaller one, with his work *Europe without Baedeker*, published in 1947. Based on the essays he had written for the *New Yorker* during his travels through postwar Europe, the book led critics to charge Wilson with Anglophobia for his stinging attacks on England. He criticized the English for their condescension and class snobbery. More seriously, he claimed that England had, as always, manipulated Europe into a balance of power most favorable to her own interests and that this manipulation was largely responsible for the breakdown of relations between the Soviet Union and the other Allied powers after the war.

In 1950 Wilson's *Classics and Commercial* analyzed the state of literature during the 1940s. Other important works of subsequent years included *The Scrolls from the Dead Sea* (1955), which won a gold medal from the American Academy of Arts and Letters; *Apologies to the Iroquois* (1959), a strong attack on America's continuing injustice to the American Indians; *Patriotic Gore* (1962), a classic study of Civil War literature; and *The Cold War and the Income Tax* (1963), which outlined Wilson's tax problems in the late 1940s and early 1950s and criticized the uses to which tax dollars were put. That same year he won the Presidential Medal of Freedom, the highest civilian honor in the nation.

An important cultural figure up to his death at age 77, Wilson was considered the foremost social and literary critic of his time. He died on June 12, 1972, in Talcottville, New York.

—MDQ

Winchell, Walter
(1894–1972) *syndicated columnist*

The creator of the modern gossip column, Walter Winchell was born on April 7, 1894, in New York City and reared in poverty. His first job was selling newspapers on a street corner. At age 12 he made his entertainment debut singing with George Jessel. His formal education stopped in the sixth grade, and Winchell soon began a national tour as part of a revue featuring child performers. Winchell wrote gossip columns for several newspapers before joining the staff of *The Mirror* in 1929.

Winchell had many friends in high places. He often dined at the Stork Club with FBI director J. EDGAR HOOVER. Many of New York's most notorious gangsters were Winchell's companions. He supported the president and his New Deal and was a frequent visitor to the White House in FDR's second term. Winchell also counted President Roosevelt among his friends. Winchell urged the United States to aid the Allies as war threatened in Europe. In December 1941 he entered active duty with the navy's press section.

Following World War II, Winchell was slow to realize the Russian threat, even writing a favorable column on Joseph Stalin in early 1946. Soon, however, he began to see Soviets as he had seen the

Nazis before World War II and began to warn against a Communist conspiracy to take over the world. He urged America to rearm and opposed peace talks with the Russians cautioning, "When Communists say it with flowers, it's because they expect a funeral."

In sharp contrast to his warm relationship with Roosevelt, Winchell's encounters with President Truman were unfriendly, sometimes bitter. Winchell's biographer, Neal Gabler, thought the personality differences between the two men caused the friction. Truman represented the rural Midwest of the 19th century, Winchell, the eastern city of the 20th. The president apparently offended Winchell during one meeting, and the columnist thought Truman incomparable to the great FDR. In 1948, when Winchell visited the White House and suggested that Truman meet with Stalin, he was sharply rebuffed. Anti-Truman items then began to appear in Winchell's column. Winchell began to urge that DWIGHT D. EISENHOWER should run for president in 1948.

Winchell supported the creation of a Jewish homeland in Palestine. Since Secretary of Defense JAMES V. FORRESTAL opposed this, he became a target of Winchell's incessant and vicious attacks, which may have driven him to commit suicide.

By the end of the 1940s, Winchell had reached the pinnacle of his career. He had the nations's most popular radio broadcast and newspaper column. Beginning in 1950 Winchell gave his support to Senator JOSEPH R. MCCARTHY (R-Wisc.) and published anticommunist diatribes leaked to him by the Wisconsin senator. Winchell agreed with McCarthy that the government was Communist infiltrated, and he backed the senator's efforts to remove Communists from high posts. When Truman dismissed DOUGLAS MACARTHUR during the Korean War, Winchell rose to the general's defense and labeled the president "the greatest appeaser in history" for having not stood up to the Soviets in Eastern Europe. According to Gabler, Winchell's condemnation of MacArthur's removal marked his break with the left.

The newscaster's decline began in 1951, when Josephine Baker, a black American expatriate entertainer, charged that the Stork Club had discriminated against her party. Winchell ignored the pleas of friends to intervene on behalf of Baker, and his office was soon flooded with a number of critical letters.

In January 1952 the first in a series of articles condemning Winchell as an egoist and liar appeared in the *New York Post*. Following the 18th article Winchell lapsed into a serious depression and stopped his column and newscasts. After he recuperated, he began attacking the *Post*, and specifically editor JAMES WECHSLER, as procommunist. Winchell turned increasingly to McCarthy and the right for support. He soon came under criticism for dealing in horse and stock tips over the air. Communication executives became wary of him because he was involved in so many feuds. By 1960 his column, which once had run in 800 papers, slipped to under 150. It virtually disappeared when *The Mirror* closed its doors in 1963.

Winchell's demise coincided with the decline of Broadway and the increased influence of television. He died of cancer on February 20, 1972, in Los Angeles, California.

—EF

Wisner, Frank G(ardiner)

(1909–1965) *Central Intelligence Agency official*
Frank G. Wisner was born on June 23, 1909, in Mississippi. He received his B.S. degree in 1931 and his LL.B. degree in 1934 from the University of Virginia. He practiced law in New York, where he made the acquaintance of many who in World War II were to play central roles in the Office of Strategic Services (OSS), the nation's wartime intelligence service. Wisner served during the war as the self-confident and capable head of the OSS station in Bucharest. He was credited with masterminding a number of operations in the Balkans, including the pinpointing of the Ploesti oil fields in Romania for the massive raid the U.S. Air Force launched from Egypt.

In September 1944 while in Romania, Wisner was informed by Romanian intelligence—which had penetrated the Romanian Communist Party undetected—that the Russians planned to impose Soviet-friendly regimes in Eastern Europe. Wisner wanted to act against the Soviet plans, but no one would allow him.

Wisner's experiences with Russian forces in the Balkans laid the groundwork for a growing anticommunism that was reinforced during his tour of duty in postwar Germany. There he was second in command to ALLEN W. DULLES at the OSS station in Berlin. American intelligence agents often encountered hostility in their Soviet counterparts and were impeded in their missions in Russian-controlled areas. By the time the two men were recalled to the United States, Dulles had begun to sympathize with Wisner, who wanted to move on from searching for Nazis to finding out what the Communists were doing.

President Truman disbanded the OSS in September 1945. Wisner returned to New York and law practice with Carter, Ledyard, & Milburn. In 1947 he took a job with the State Department as deputy to the assistant secretary of state for occupied areas. Like his former chief, Dulles, Wisner had continued to work informally as an intelligence agent, and the position gave him an excuse for frequent trips to Germany and Eastern Europe. That same year Congress passed the National Security Act, establishing the Central Intelligence Agency (CIA) under the authority of the National Security Council (NSC).

Wisner reentered the intelligence service in June 1948, when he was appointed director of the Office of Policy Coordination (OPC), a CIA component formed for the execution of covert operations. Author John Radelagh described Wisner as perfect for the job. He had pushed for the establishment of a covert-action organization and, according to Radelagh, Wisner "possessed the experience, operational instincts, active temperament, and sheer physical energy" to set up and build the office. In the wake of the Communist takeover in Czechoslovakia and events in France and Italy, senior U.S. policy makers had sought ways to respond to what they saw as a global Soviet challenge other than the traditional alternatives of diplomacy and war. In 1948 the NSC had issued a paper authorizing special operations, and Truman had created the OPC. Wisner's budget and personnel were appropriated within CIA allocations, but policy guidance came from the State and Defense departments. (Wisner derided the CIA officials, who were concerned with administration and intelligence gathering and analysis rather than covert operations, as "a bunch of old washerwoman exchanging gossip while they rinse through the dirty linen.") The OPC's work included psychological, political, and economic warfare, and paramilitary activities.

Under Wisner the manpower, budget, and scope of activities of OPC skyrocketed. In 1949 the organization had five stations, employed 302 agents,

and had a budget of five million dollars. By 1952 this had increased to 47 stations, a staff of 2,812 plus 3,142 overseas contract personnel, and a budget of $84 million. From an organization designed to provide the capability for ad hoc operations, OPC developed into an independent organization with ongoing activities on a large scale.

Wisner quickly turned OPC into an effective operation with its own unvouchered funds. He formed an intelligence unit under the direction of a former Nazi to provide information on the Soviet Union and raised small private armies of refugees for possible invasions of Russia and Eastern European nations. OPC was involved in the elections in Italy and in breaking the great union strikes in France. In 1950 OPC failed in an attempt to overthrow the Communist government in Albania. Another OPC plan in 1950 was to use troops of Chiang Kai-shek's (Jiang Jieshi) army in Burma for guerrilla raids into China. There was a problem here in that Truman had refused Chiang's offer of troops to send to Korea because he feared it would widen the war; now an OPC operation was sending Nationalist soldiers against the Communists in China itself. Fortunately nothing developed of this scheme because the Nationalist Chinese commander—perchance also a warlord—was more interested in making drugs than fighting, which he never did. However, Wisner did establish a successful program to encourage professionals, like doctors, to abandon the Eastern bloc for the West.

In late 1950 General WALTER B. SMITH, the new director of central intelligence and head of the CIA, announced that the OPC would be brought administratively into the agency and that Wisner would report to him. In 1952 OPC was merged with the Office of Special Operations (OSO), the CIA's clandestine collection component, into the Directorate for Plans. Wisner became deputy director for plans (DDP).

Wisner and Dulles were reunited in 1951 when Dulles came into the CIA as its deputy director. Dulles shared with Wisner an orientation toward the covert operations side of intelligence work. In 1953 Dulles was named to head the agency. That same year the CIA directed the overthrow of Premier Mohammed Mossadegh in Iran, and in 1954 it was involved in the coup against President Jacobo Arbenz Guzmán of Guatemala. The two operations replaced the leaders with pro-Western officials. At this time both Dulles and Wisner believed in a policy of "liberation" for Eastern Europe. As DDP, Wisner recruited and trained agents for espionage, sabotage, and propaganda behind the Iron Curtain from among displaced Russians and Eastern Europeans. He saw the Polish and Hungarian uprisings of 1956 as the fulfillment of the liberation policy. He argued incessantly but to no avail that the United States should intervene in the revolt.

Disillusioned by the Soviet's crushing of the Hungarian uprising and the failure of the United States to take any action, Wisner turned to drink. He was placed on sick leave by Dulles. He returned to active duty to initiate a series of covert activities in Asia. His operation to overturn the government of President Sukarno of Indonesia failed. Wisner suffered a breakdown and resigned as DDP in 1958. In 1959 he was sent to London as station chief. He committed suicide in Galena, Maryland, on October 29, 1965.

—SF

Wolcott, Jesse P(aine)

(1893–1969) *member of the House of Representatives*

Jesse P. Wolcott was born on March 3, 1893, in Gardner, Massachusetts. After attending high school in New England, Wolcott moved to the Midwest in 1912. He entered the Detroit Technical Institute and graduated from the Detroit College of Law in 1915. While in law school Wolcott worked as a drummer in a professional dance orchestra. He practiced law in Detroit until 1917, when he joined the army.

When he returned to the United States in 1919, he began practicing in Port Huron, Michigan. A staunch Republican, he was elected the assistant prosecuting attorney in 1922 and five years later became the county prosecutor. Wolcott ran for the U.S. House in 1930, easily winning election in the traditionally Republican Seventh Congressional District. Wolcott represented the six-county district for 27 years, often running for reelection without opposition. Generally voting with "Old Guard" Republicans, he fought New Deal agricultural policies. However, he backed some social and economic legislation, such as the National Recovery Act, the Social Security Act, and the Wagner Housing bill. An isolationist, Wolcott voted for the munitions embargo in 1937 and against the Selective Service Act in 1940 and lend-lease in 1941. Throughout

World War II he firmly backed economic stabilization. In 1944 he served as a delegate to the Bretton Woods Conference and later successfully fought for Republican acceptance of American participation in the World Bank.

After the war he supported certain aspects of Truman's internationalist and containment foreign policies. He voted for the British loan of 1946, Greek-Turkish aid in 1947, the Marshall Plan in 1948, and military aid to NATO in 1949. On domestic policy he was conservative, supporting the Case labor disputes bill, the Taft-Hartley Act, the 1948 Republican tax cut, the Mundt-Nixon bill, and the McCarran Internal Security Act. Yet he occasionally would take a somewhat more liberal position, such as when he voted for the Employment Act of 1946 and raising the minimum wage to 75 cents per hour in 1949.

The senior Republican on the House Banking and Currency Committee, and chairman during the 80th Congress, Wolcott helped shape Republican economic policy during the Truman years. After 1945 he led congressional resistance to government control of the economy, attacking wage and price controls and public housing proposals offered by the Truman administration. "Price controls, allocations and priorities beget a vast brood of contradictions and uncertainties," he said in 1947. Wolcott felt such measures promoted black markets and deterred production. He favored voluntary measures and fought for greater freedom for business. To attack inflation he supported cuts in federal spending, tax revision, and international currency stabilization. He felt the only "panacea" for American economic problems was "production and more production."

In 1946 Wolcott proposed an amendment to the Office of Price Administration (OPA) extension bill limiting the life of the agency to an additional nine months. He also wanted the OPA to "fix ceilings which would permit a reasonable profit" for business. Wolcott's amendments, opposed by administration Democrats, passed in the House and were modified by the Senate before final passage of the bill in June. Truman vetoed the measure, claiming it provided a choice only between "inflation with a statute and inflation without one." A compromise bill was passed in July. The Michigan congressman also favored continued rent control, with raised ceilings, and proposed the reduction of agricultural subsidies. He strongly opposed the Taft-Ellender-

Wagner housing measure. Objecting to what he called the "socialized" housing provisions it contained, Wolcott prevented the bill from leaving committee.

With the Republican congressional victory in 1947, he became chairman of the Banking and Currency Committee. Wolcott introduced a housing bill in 1947, which substituted assistance to private construction of homes for federal housing. Cosponsored by Senator JOSEPH R. MCCARTHY (R-Wisc.), the measure passed in August. Truman attacked the McCarthy-Wolcott bill as "inadequate" but signed it into law as the Housing Act of 1948.

Wolcott and Representative CLARENCE BROWN (R-Ohio) sharply criticized the Truman administration's proposed rent control extension bill in 1949. Southern Democrats helped to defeat Wolcott's effort to limit the extension to 90 days. That year Wolcott also led opposition to a renewed attempt at passing the Taft-Ellender-Wagner bill. Along with Representatives JOSEPH W. MARTIN, JR., (R-Mass.) and CHARLES A. HALLECK (R-Ind.), he engaged in an unsuccessful floor fight to eliminate the public housing section of the measure, which became the Public Housing Act of 1949. In 1950 Wolcott added two amendments to the Defense Production Act. One curtailed control of credit on real estate construction and the other restricted the government's authority to build and operate defense plants.

Wolcott returned to his chairman's post on the Banking and Currency Committee for two years starting in 1953. He continued his opposition to public housing and government controls during the Eisenhower administration. Wolcott left the House in 1957 and a year later became board chairman of the Federal Deposit Insurance Corporation. He remained there until 1964, when he retired. Wolcott died on January 28, 1969, in Chevy Chase, Maryland.

—JF

Wood, John S(tephens)

(1885–1968) *member of the House of Representatives*

Born on a farm in Cherokee County, Georgia, on February 8, 1885, John S. Wood was one of 14 children. He worked his way through North Georgia Agricultural College and Mercer University from which he received a law degree in 1910. Following brief service in the air force in World War I, he

became a member of the Georgia House of Representatives. He later served as solicitor general of the Blue Ridge judicial circuit court and then circuit judge of the same court. A Democrat, he won election to the U.S. House in 1931, where he represented a backwoods district in which two of the counties had no telephones. Defeated in his 1935 reelection bid, he resumed his law career.

Wood returned to the U.S. House in 1944, where he established a conservative record. A supporter of states' rights, he favored the return of the U.S. Employment Service to state governments, and he opposed anti–poll tax laws and voted against federal aid to state school lunch programs. Wood voted for the Case labor disputes bill, the Taft-Hartley Act, and the 1948 Republican tax cut. In 1949 he offered a bill to repeal the Taft-Hartley Act but to reenact what he called "its best features." The Wood bill would have retained Taft-Hartley's provisions for injunctions for strikes that threatened the national interest and would have extended its anticommunist oath provisions to employers as well as union members. Unlike Taft-Hartley it would have permitted closed shops in states that passed legislation permitting them. The House passed the bill in May, but because of administration pressure, it was recommitted to the Labor Committee for further study. No action was taken on the measure. Wood voted against the rather innocuous 1946 Employment Act, raising the minimum wage to 75 cents per hour in 1949 and the National Housing Act of the same year. He voted for both the Mundt-Nixon bill and the McCarran Internal Security Act. He generally did not back Truman's foreign policy, opposing the Marshall Plan, military aid to NATO, and the Korean Aid Act and supported eliminating a $25-million authorization to start the Point Four program. However, he did vote for Greek-Turkish aid in 1947.

Wood was one of 70 Democrats who voted in January 1945 to make the House Un-American Activities Committee (HUAC) a permanent committee. He accepted the chairmanship of that panel in July, when he pledged to make "no attempt at either whitewashing or witchhunting." During the 79th Congress Wood conducted probes of possible Communist infiltration of left-wing organizations and an investigation of an espionage ring trading in atomic secrets. After a year of study Wood admitted that he had no conclusive proof that such a spy ring existed. He also proposed legislation to deal with subversion. Among his recommendations was a bill to set up rules governing editorial broadcasts, which would be clearly distinguished from "news items."

Wood lost his committee chairmanship during the Republican-controlled 80th Congress but resumed the post in 1949. He frequently clashed with some of his witnesses. In 1949 he investigated possible Communist slants in college textbooks. This resulted in a storm of criticism, and Wood was forced to deny accusations that he had any intention to censor textbooks or interfere with academic freedom.

The highlight of Wood's chairmanship was HUAC's investigation during 1951–52 of alleged Communist infiltration in the motion picture industry. Many of the sessions were televised. Celebrated movie stars, producers, and writers testified concerning their former connections with the Communist Party. Following the hearing 24 people connected with the motion picture business, among them actresses Anne Revere and Gail Sondergaard, charged that they had been blacklisted by movie studios and were denied jobs because of the stigma attached to their appearances before the committee. Twenty-three actors, writers, and film studio employees unsuccessfully sued Wood, HUAC, and the Hollywood studios for over $51 million.

In February and March 1952 the panel investigated communism in the labor movement. In Chicago it investigated the electrical workers union, which had been on strike against International Harvester Corporation. In Detroit the committee investigated the United Automobile Workers' largest local, which represented more than 50,000 Ford employees.

Following the revelation that the USSR possessed the atomic bomb, Wood's fear of Soviet espionage increased, and, in 1952, he published a HUAC report on Soviet spying since 1919 called *The Shameful Years*. As chairman of the committee, he was responsible in February 1952 for a report that recommended the death penalty for spying as a measure to "stem Soviet espionage." The report condemned the Hollywood movie industry's alleged failure to deal with Communist infiltration and financial support of the industry. It cautioned the burgeoning television networks to beware of Communist penetration and berated Harvard University and the Massachusetts Institute of Technology for failure to suspend alleged Communists on their faculties.

Wood did not seek reelection in 1952 and returned to the small town of Canton, Georgia, to practice law. President DWIGHT D. EISENHOWER nominated him for a three-year term on the Subversive Activities Control Board in 1955, but the Senate rejected the nomination after Wood admitted he had been a member of the Ku Klux Klan for a brief period during his youth. Wood died on September 12, 1968, in Atlanta, Georgia.

—AES

Woods, Tighe E(dward)

(1910–1974) *federal housing expediter; director, Office of Price Stabilization*

Tighe Woods was born on August 2, 1910, in Chicago, Illinois. After graduating from Notre Dame University in 1933, he worked for a Chicago real estate firm. He owned a property management office in Chicago from 1936 to 1942 and then joined the government as a rent control examiner for the Office of Price Administration in Chicago. An officer in the U.S. Naval Reserve, Woods saw action in the Pacific from 1944 to 1946. He then joined the Office of the Housing Expediter as director of the Chicago rent control office in May 1946. A year later he was appointed regional rent director and deputy expediter.

In December 1946 Woods was appointed federal housing expediter; he was confirmed in April 1948. At his post, Woods followed the policies of his predecessor, Frank R. Creedon, lifting rent controls only in cases in which the reason for such action could be "appropriately substantiated." Among Woods's criteria for rent hikes was evidence of an increased number of housing facilities in the effected rent control areas. Woods supported demands for the extension, clarification, and strengthening of the Rent Control Act of 1947. During early 1948 he told a Senate Banking and Currency subcommittee that increased rental housing would be necessary before rent control laws could be abandoned. He demanded that the powers of the expeditor and the local rent advisory board be made clear and asked that the boards be composed of representatives of tenants, landlords, and the community. Woods also demanded that the law be strengthened to give the expediter and his tenants the power to sue for damages when the landlords illegally raised rents. In March Congress extended the rent control law and granted Woods the power he requested.

During the remainder of his tenure Woods worked to strengthen laws protecting tenants. In November 1948 he reiterated the need to extend the rent control law, scheduled to expire in March 1949. He called for a law similar to that imposed during World War II. Woods requested restoration of federal control over evictions, authority to collect treble damages for overcharges, and criminal sanctions for violations of the law. A bill that included many of the provisions he requested was passed in March 1949.

While attempting to protect the tenants, Woods increased rents and deregulated housing where circumstances permitted. In July 1948 he announced adoption of modifications in the rent control regulations. These new rules stipulated that no landlord need operate units at a loss and provided hardship adjustments for those owning more than four dwelling units. In May 1949 Woods announced new regulations that guaranteed landlords profits of 25 percent of their gross operating expenses. More than 500,000 landlords immediately applied for rent increases. The following month Woods announced that he was putting into effect four new rules permitting rent increases if "major capital improvements" or other service benefits took place in the accommodations. He ended controls on luxury housing in cases where landlords had converted them into additional housing units. Gradually Woods decontrolled a large number of units in small cities and turned over management of rent control to the states. After prices and wages were frozen in January 1951 in response to the Korean War, Woods announced support for a tough rent control bill similar to the wage and price restrictions in effect. He reimposed full federal rent controls in 54 areas in December 1951.

Woods served as director of Price Stabilization from August 1952 to November 1952. In September he ended price controls on most types of shoes and ordered in October the recontrol of prices of radio, television, and phonograph records—the first such edict of the war. He announced in November controls on apparel would end in December. In late November Woods announced his resignation, dissatisfied over what he said was a "weak control law." He huffed, "It seems all I have done is sign orders increasing prices, and I haven't particularly enjoyed the job." Woods claimed the law establishing the controls did not "impose a fair burden on everybody" and called for reform of the statute to make

it more equitable. After leaving government service he became a land developer and private realtor. He also championed fair housing. Woods died in Washington, D.C., on July 9, 1974.

—AES

Wright, Fielding L(ewis)

(1895–1956) *governor; presidential candidate, States' Rights Democrats*

Fielding L. Wright was born on May 16, 1895, in Rolling Fork, Mississippi, in the Mississippi delta and received a law degree from the University of Alabama. He then joined his uncle's law firm, where he specialized in corporate law. In 1928 Wright was elected to the Mississippi State Senate as a Democrat. Four years later he won election to the lower chamber and in 1936 was unanimously chosen speaker of the house. Wright was considered a supporter of business interests and favored industrial development to supplement Mississippi's overwhelmingly agricultural economy. After briefly retiring from politics, he was elected lieutenant governor in 1943 and succeeded to the governorship three years later upon the death of incumbent Tom Bailey.

Governor Wright first attracted national attention in March 1947, when he convened a special session of the state legislature after the Supreme Court had ruled that blacks be permitted to vote in primary elections. A few months later Wright and the legislature decreed that such eligibility hinged on voters affirming belief in the segregationist principles of the state Democratic Party. In November Wright won election to a full term as governor. Several days before, the President's Civil Rights Commission had recommended legislation to protect rights in voting, employment, and housing.

In his January 1948 inaugural message, Wright attacked Truman's civil rights panel and called for a break with the national Democratic Party. When Truman recommended civil rights legislation to Congress the following month, Wright carried his crusade to the Southern Governors' Conference and called for a March meeting of Southern Democrats in Jackson, Mississippi. The governors initially demurred. They called upon Democratic Party national chairman J. HOWARD MCGRATH and requested he have Truman withdraw the offending legislation. McGrath refused. It was becoming clear that he and the president intended waging the 1948 campaign on a strong civil rights plank to win big-city black and ethnic voters. Wright, meanwhile, continued crusading for solidarity among Southern Democrats by broadening the states' rights issue. In February he condemned Truman not for favoring civil rights but for favoring federal ownership of off-shore oil lands claimed by Mississippi and other states. The following month the Mississippi Democratic Committee recommended that delegates quit the national convention if not given "proper" assurances on civil rights.

In May party leaders in Mississippi and Arkansas convened the states' rights conference Wright sought. In a radio address aimed at blacks on the eve of the meeting, Wright defended segregation and in measured tones advised blacks opposed to it to leave Mississippi. The meeting was dominated by men from those states with the largest black populations. Wright was elected temporary chairman of the conference, and South Carolina Governor J. STROM THURMOND delivered the keynote address. The dissidents sought the restoration of the Democratic Party rule requiring that a presidential candidate be nominated by a two-thirds majority, support of state claims to offshore oil, and abandonment of all commitments to civil rights. Anticipating defeat at the national level, the conference planned to reconvene in Birmingham, Alabama, following the Democratic National Convention.

At the July Convention the Mississippi delegation, which was pledged to support neither Truman nor any civil rights plank, had difficulty getting seated. Later Wright's forces lost the key vote to restore the two-thirds rule by a wide margin. Despite this show of weakness, they were unwilling to compromise and continued their campaign against a strong civil rights platform. When a deadlocked platform committee offered to restate the tepid civil rights endorsement of 1944, they refused the offer. They also rejected a final compromise to eliminate endorsement of federal control of tidelands oils in return for acceptance of a civil rights plank. When the convention adopted a strong civil rights plank, Wright's delegation walked out along with half of that from Alabama.

The dissident Democrats reconvened at Birmingham. Having refused political compromise, the rebels now sought to deny the Democratic and Republican candidates an electoral majority and so throw the election into the House of Representatives. Wright alone was accompanied and supported by his state's congressional delegation. Some Florid-

ians, Alabamians, and the Mississippi delegation had wanted Wright to head the ticket, but Wright demurred, saying "I do not feel that I am a man of sufficient political stature to accept such a nomination." He was nominated for vice president by the newly formed States' Rights Democrats while Thurmond was nominated for president. The two ran on a platform stressing states' rights and listing a "long trail of abuses and usurpations of power by unfaithful" Democratic leaders. The platform called the Democratic civil rights plank "this infamous and iniquitous program" and said it would mean a "police state in a totalitarian, centralized, bureaucratic government" if adopted. It declared that if a foreign power attempted to force the program on the people "it would mean war and the entire nation would resist such effort."

Called "Dixiecrat" by the press, the new movement was the expression of a continuing intraparty Democratic feud. "The race problem," according to Wright was only "a side issue" as anti–New Deal Democrats joined with new southern corporations and oil interests in a campaign for states' rights and laissez-faire economics. However, a large number of southern conservatives feared a Republican victory more than one by Truman and either remained aloof from the Dixiecrats or opposed them outright.

According to historian Kari Frederickson, Wright was a poor choice to help lead the Dixiecrat movement. One Mississippi politician said the governor "wasn't what you'd call a popular man. He wasn't a backslapper." He obviously hated campaigning and one time during the campaign sneaked off a train to dodge a crowd awaiting him.

When, in September, Truman announced his pro-labor Fair Deal and the integration of the armed forces, it fanned Dixiecrat fears that the government would overturn the southern economic order through racial equality. Nevertheless, although the States' Rights Democrats appeared on the ballot in 13 states, the party carried only those where its candidates were the officially designated Democratic nominees. Mississippi, South Carolina, Louisiana, and Alabama combined with one vote from Tennessee to give Thurmond and Wright 39 electoral votes. At the same time Truman won 88 electoral votes throughout the South. The Dixiecrat ticket won 1,169,000 popular votes.

The states' rights protest lost popular support and financial backing following Truman's election. Despite this decline Wright and other Dixiecrat

leaders established a national states' rights committee to propagandize "the Southern way of life" in
May 1949. A year later the Supreme Court began
striking at the heart of institutionalized white
supremacy and the South began the move to massive resistance to school desegregation. In May 1951
Wright declared, "We shall insist upon segregation
regardless of consequences" and made Mississippi
one of the key states in the massive resistance movement. Wright recommended another third-party
effort in 1952, but he said that he was withdrawing
from politics when his term as governor ended.
After he left office that year, he returned to his private law practice. Three years later he was defeated
in the gubernatorial primary. He died of a heart
attack on May 4, 1956, in Jackson, Mississippi.

—MJS

Wyatt, Wilson W(atkins)

(1905–1996) *administrator, National Housing
Agency; national chairman, Americans for
Democratic Action*

Wilson W. Wyatt was born on November 21, 1905,
in Louisville, Kentucky. After dropping out of the
University of Louisville Law School in 1923 for
financial reasons, he worked as a shipping clerk during the day and attended evening classes at the Jefferson School of Law. He received his degree from
that institution in 1927. He then set up practice in
Louisville. Active in Democratic politics, he campaigned for Al Smith in 1928 and Franklin D. Roosevelt in 1932. In addition, he managed a number of
local campaigns. From 1930 to 1934 Wyatt was
president of the Kentucky Bar Association. By 1940
he was considered to be the most powerful Democrat in his part of the state.

In 1941 Wyatt won the mayoralty of Louisville.
In this position he provided progressive leadership
to a city overcrowded with defense personnel from
local army bases. Wyatt modernized the city's
bureaucracy, introduced city planning and zoning
laws, and reorganized municipal finances. He also
increased the number of blacks working in the city's
segregated agencies. His reforms drew national
praise, especially from liberals.

Impressed with Wyatt's record as a mayor,
President Truman appointed him administrator of
the National Housing Agency in December 1945.
He took office in January 1946 and was immediately
asked to formulate a plan for national housing leg-

islation that would meet the increased demand of
discharged veterans. Wyatt's program called for
$400 million for the construction of 2.7 million
housing units by the end of 1947. He suggested
using prefabricated homes to quickly alleviate the
shortage. Under the plan the federal government
would subsidize a large portion of the construction
to keep future mortgage payments or rents down.
Wyatt recommended that ceilings be established on
payments and rents so that they would not be subject to inflationary pressures.

Conservatives attacked the program as socialistic and argued that Wyatt's plan of constructing
great numbers of prefabricated houses would be too
expensive. Despite opposition the bill became law in
May. By late 1946, however, the end of many
wartime economic controls made Wyatt's program
untenable. He told Truman a new program was
needed and that a new housing administrator would
have a better chance of pushing it through. Wyatt
resigned in December 1946.

Wilson Wyatt was one of the original founders
of the Americans for Democratic Action (ADA),
formed in January 1947. He became its national
chairman. The organization was one of two major
liberal coalitions formed to push the administration
to the left. The ADA rejected collaboration with
Communists, while the Progressive Citizens of
America (PCA), led by HENRY A. WALLACE,
accepted them as members. Wyatt spoke for the
ADA in clashes with the PCA over foreign policy.
He supported Truman's policy of containment
toward the Soviet Union and vigorously defended
the Truman Doctrine against charges that it was
designed to support fascist dictatorships. At the
ADA's 1947 convention he said, "If we continue to
allow the ragged and hungry people of Greece to be
exploited, we shall only fan the fires of Communism. But if we assume the burdens of guarding
national independence and supervising economic
reconstruction, we will give the democratic alternative to fascism and Communism new strength and
vitality throughout the world."

Wyatt was one of the earliest ADA backers of
Truman's quest for the 1948 Democratic presidential
nomination. As chairman of the party's Jefferson-
Jackson dinner in early 1948, he endorsed the pres-
ident while other members supported DWIGHT D.
EISENHOWER or Supreme Court justice WILLIAM
O. DOUGLAS. Wyatt was mentioned as a possible
Truman running mate, but he declared that he was

not interested. Instead, he helped organize a movement to make Senator ALBEN W. BARKLEY (D-Ky.) the vice presidential candidate. Truman allowed party bosses to push for Wyatt for the slot, but Wyatt stampeded the convention for Barkley after the senator's keynote address at the convention. As did other ADA members, Wyatt savagely attacked Henry Wallace in the 1948 election. He charged that the former vice president's candidacy would only benefit the Communist Party and the National Association of Manufacturers. Wallace's campaign, he maintained, would split liberals and return the nation to conservatism and isolationism. Wyatt claimed this is exactly what Moscow wanted.

Wyatt joined a growing number of liberals who encouraged ADLAI E. STEVENSON to run for the presidency in 1952, and he later served as Stevenson's campaign manager. Wyatt's role in the campaign became a center of controversy. Republican national chairman Arthur Summerfield offered Wyatt's advocacy of "socialized housing" as proof that the "ultra-left wingers" were controlling Stevenson. This accusation was one of many made by Republicans in attempts to associate Stevenson with possible Communist supporters and subversives. Wyatt defended himself, claiming he was a member of the "right wing" of the ADA and had not been active in the organization for the past three years. He advised Stevenson not to answer the charges.

Following Stevenson's defeat, Wyatt informally advised him on future activities. He was one of many who encouraged the defeated candidate to continue to speak out on the issues and to run again in 1956. Wyatt sat on the 1955 "Steering Committee to Secure AES the Nomination in 1956." This group put together contingency plans for a campaign if the former governor chose to run again. During the 1956 race Wyatt served as coordinator of the campaign. In 1959 he won election as lieutenant governor of Kentucky, but three years later, he lost a bid for his state's Senate seat. During the Johnson administration he served as special emissary to Indonesia to negotiate an oil controversy. Wyatt also remained active in liberal Democratic circles. Wyatt died on June 11, 1996, in Louisville, Kentucky.

—JB

Y

Young, Milton R(uben)

(1897–1983) *member of the Senate*

The son of a grain farmer and real estate dealer, Milton R. Young was born on December 6, 1897, in Berlin, North Dakota. He attended North Dakota Agricultural College and Graceland College in Iowa before operating his own farm. After serving on township and county Agricultural Adjustment Administration boards, Young was elected to the North Dakota Assembly as a Republican in 1932. Two years later he won election to the North Dakota State Senate. He served there until 1945, becoming president pro tempore in 1941 and majority leader in 1943. In March 1945 Young was appointed to the U.S. Senate to fill the vacancy caused by the death of Senator John Moses (D-N.Dak.)

A conservative on domestic issues and generally an isolationist in foreign affairs, Young opposed most Truman administration legislation. He voted against the retention of price controls in 1946 and against giving the president standby wage and price control powers in 1948. He supported the Case labor disputes bill of 1946, the Taft-Hartley Act of 1947, the Republican tax cut of 1948, the McCarran Internal Security Act of 1950, and the McCarran-Walter Immigration Act of 1952. He did, however, vote for the National Housing Act of 1949. Although Young voted for aid to Greece and Turkey in 1947 and the Marshall Plan in 1948, thereafter he consistently voted to cut economic aid to Western Europe. He was one of only 13 senators who opposed the North Atlantic Treaty in 1949. He voted for the McClellan Amendment of 1951 in which the Senate called upon the president to ask for its permission if he sent more than the planned four divisions to Europe. He also opposed a $45-million authorization to set up the Point Four program and voted against the Japanese Peace Treaty.

As a farmer and a senator from a largely agricultural state, Young supported government subsidies for agriculture and other proposals to increase farmers' income. He took a leading role in the congressional debate over farm policy in 1949. In July Senator CLINTON P. ANDERSON (D-N.Mex.) introduced legislation providing for flexible price supports for basic commodities ranging from 75 percent to 90 percent of parity. On October 7, when the bill was on the Senate floor, Young and Senator RICHARD B. RUSSELL (D-Ga.) cosponsored an amendment providing for rigid price supports at 90 percent of parity. Young's amendment carried through the tie-breaking vote of Vice President ALBEN W. BARKLEY, but Anderson won a vote to have the amended bill sent back to committee. The final measure was a compromise. The rigid price supports advocated by Young were accepted through 1950; after that, a system of flexible supports prevailed. Young continued to press for mandatory price supports at 90 percent or parity. In 1952 he successfully sponsored legislation that suspended the sliding scale and restored the 90 percent level of price supports for basic commodities.

Young was reelected to the Senate in 1956, 1962, and 1968. He continued to vote with the conservative wing of the Republican Party and opposed most social welfare legislation and foreign aid programs. His support of legislation to aid farmers remained strong, and, during the 1960s he won important military projects for North Dakota to offset the declining prosperity of the state. In 1974 Young was elected to his fifth full term, defeating his opponent, former governor William L. Guy, by the narrow margin of 177 votes. Young did not run for reelection in 1980. He died on May 31, 1983, in Sun City, Arizona. (See *The Eisenhower Years, The Kennedy Years, The Johnson Years, The Nixon/Ford Years* Volumes)

—JD

APPENDICES

CHRONOLOGY

1945

March 1—John L. Lewis, president of the United Mine Workers (UMW), asks a 10 percent royalty on all coal mined to cover worker benefits.

April 12—President Franklin D. Roosevelt dies in Warm Springs, Ga. Harry S Truman is sworn in as President of the United States.

April 16—Truman addresses a joint session of Congress, promising a continuation of Roosevelt's policies and a quick end to the war.

April 16—Truman signs a bill extending lend-lease for one year.

April 25—U.S. and Soviet forces meet for the first time at the Elba River. The U.N. Charter Conference opens in San Francisco.

May 7—Germany surrenders unconditionally to the Allies in Reims, France.

May 8—V-E Day marks the formal end of the war in Europe.

June 5—The Allies establish occupation zones in Germany. Berlin is divided among the Big Four Powers (Great Britain, France, the United States, and the USSR).

June 12—Truman orders the withdrawal of U.S. troops into the American zone in Germany.

June 21—The Japanese surrender Okinawa after a struggle that took the lives of 100,000 Japanese and 13,000 Americans.

July 5—General Douglas MacArthur reports the liberation of the Philippine Islands after 10 months of fighting and 12,000 American dead.

July 16—The United States explodes the first atomic bomb near Alamogordo, New Mexico.

July 17–August 2—Churchill, Stalin, and Truman meet at Potsdam, Germany, to discuss postwar policy toward the conquered nations.

July 19—The Senate approves U.S. membership in the International Bank for Reconstruction and Development.

July 26—Anglo-American conferees at Potsdam issue an ultimatum of unconditional surrender or complete destruction to Japan.

July 28—The Senate ratifies the UN Charter by a vote of 89 to 2.

August 6—The United States drops an atomic bomb on Hiroshima.

August 9—The United States drops an atomic bomb on Nagasaki. The Soviet Union declares war on Japan.

August 14—Japan surrenders to the Allies.

August 15—Truman proclaims V-J Day.

August 17—Truman orders General Douglas MacArthur to temporarily divide Korea at the 38th parallel. The Soviets occupy the North while U.S. forces move into the South.

August 29—The occupation of Japan begins. Truman names MacArthur supreme commander for the Allied powers in Japan.

August 31—Truman writes to British prime minister Clement Attlee requesting that Britain allow an additional 100,000 Jewish refugees to enter Palestine.

September 2—Japan formally surrenders on board the U.S.S. *Missouri* in Tokyo Bay.

September 28—Truman issues two proclamations and two executive orders asserting federal jurisdiction over natural resources off the continental shelf.

October 22—Truman recommends a universal military training program to Congress.

November 19—Truman sends a message to Congress calling for establishment of a national compulsory health insurance program financed through payroll deductions.

November 20—The Nuremberg War Crimes Trials begin. Twenty-three former Nazi officials go on trial for crimes against humanity.

November 21—In the first strike of the postwar period, the United Auto Workers strike General Motors.

December 15—Truman dispatches General George C. Marshall as special ambassador to China.

December 19—Truman recommends to Congress that the armed forces be reorganized into a single department.

December 31—Truman abolishes the War Labor Board and creates in its place the Wage Stabilization Board.

1946

January 9—Demanding a 5–7 cent hourly wage increase, 7,704 telephone mechanics at Western Electric go on strike in 44 states.

January 15—200,000 United Electrical, Radio and Machine Workers strike in 16 states for a $2 daily wage increase.

January 20—Truman issues an executive order establishing the Central Intelligence Group, the forerunner of the Central Intelligence Agency. He appoints Admiral Sidney W. Souers to head the agency.

January 21—The United Steelworkers Union shuts down the nation's steel mills in a wage dispute with management.

January 25—The American Federation of Labor's (AFL's) Executive Council votes to readmit the

United Mine Workers and elects John L. Lewis a vice president.

January 29—Representative Francis Case introduces a labor bill to set up mediation boards, enforce "cooling-off" periods, outlaw boycotts and sympathy strikes, and authorize court inspections.

February 21—Truman creates the Office of Economic Stabilization to handle the problems of postwar reconversion.

March 5—In a speech at Westminster College in Fulton, Missouri, Winston Churchill warns of an "Iron Curtain" being drawn across eastern Europe.

March 13—The 113-day strike of 175,000 United Automobile Workers against General Motors ends with the union winning a wage increase of $18^1/_2$ cents per hour, pay adjustments, and vacation benefits.

April 1—400,000 United Mine Workers go on strike demanding indefinite wage increases, changes in living and working conditions, and a union-administered health and welfare plan financed through a royalty on each ton of coal mined.

April 29—The Agriculture Department reports that prices received by farmers as of April 15 are at the highest level since July 1920.

May 17—Truman seizes the nation's railroads and directs the Office of Defense Transportation to operate them 24 hours before a scheduled strike by the Locomotive Engineer and Railroad Trainmen Brotherhoods. The strike is called off the following day.

May 21—Truman orders Secretary of the Interior Julius Krug to take over operation of soft coal mines at midnight as the UMW-management deadlock continues.

May 23—Transportation across the nation is paralyzed as 250,000 members of the Railroad Trainmen and Locomotive Engineers Brotherhoods strike.

May 25—Before a joint congressional session, Truman asks for the right to use court injunctions against labor leaders who urge workers to stay away from their jobs after the government has taken over an industry. During his address, he is given a note stating that leaders of the striking rail unions have settled with railroad operators for an $18^1/_2$ cent hourly wage increase.

May 30—The UMW strike ends after 59 days. The settlement includes a wage increase and a welfare and retirement fund financed by the companies.

June 3—In *Morgan v. Commonwealth*, the Supreme Court rules that uniform seating without regard to race must apply on buses engaged in interstate commerce.

June 11—Truman vetoes the Case labor disputes bill. The House immediately upholds the veto.

June 14—At the U.N., Bernard Baruch submits an American plan for international control of atomic energy.

July 4—Truman proclaims the Philippines an independent nation.

July 15—Truman signs the $3.75 billion British loan bill.

July 25—Truman signs a bill extending wartime price controls for a year.

August 1—Truman signs the Atomic Energy Act of 1946, placing control of all phases of atomic energy, including weapons development, in civilian hands.

September 5—More than 60,000 members of the seafarers and sailors union strike, closing U.S. ports. The strike is settled on September 20.

October 1—The Nuremberg War Crimes Tribunal sentences 12 Nazi war criminals to death and seven others to prison terms.

November 5—In the general elections. Republicans win control of the House by 59 seats and the Senate by six. In addition, the GOP wins two governorships, bringing the total number of Republican governors to 25.

December 7—After UMW President John L. Lewis is convicted of contempt of court and fined, he ends a 17-day nationwide coal strike. It is the second walkout of 1946 for the UMW.

December 31—The total number of workers idled by strikes during the year is 4.75 million, the highest number on record.

1947

January 29—Truman announces he is abandoning mediation in China between the Nationalists and the Communists and orders 12,000 Marines home.

March 6—In *United States v. United Mine Workers*, the Supreme Court rules that disobedience to a court injunction is contempt of court, even if there was no authority to issue the injunction.

March 12—In a major address before Congress, the president outlines the Truman doctrine of containment of the Soviet Union. He asks Congress for $400 million in aid to Greece and Turkey to prevent Communist takeovers in those countries.

April 7—The National Federation of Telephone Workers strikes AT&T for a $12 a week wage increase and better fringe benefits. The strike is settled May 10 with little disruption of service. The contract calls for a $4.79 weekly increase.

April 12—United Mine Workers end a 40-day strike protesting a fine of the union for a 1946 strike.

May 19—Truman recommends to Congress the establishment of a comprehensive health-care program for the nation.

May 22—Truman signs the $400 million Greek-Turkish aid bill.

June 5—Secretary of State George C. Marshall proposes "the Marshall Plan" of massive economic aid to Europe.

June 5—The Senate ratifies peace treaties with Italy and with the lesser Axis powers.

June 20—Truman vetoes the Taft-Hartley Act, which calls for notice by labor and management before the termination of a contract and gives the government the right to delay strikes for 80 days if public health or safety are endangered. Secondary boycotts, jurisdictional strikes, excessive dues, and featherbedding are also prohibited. The bill requires union leaders to take a noncommunist oath.

June 23—Congress passes the Taft-Hartley Act over Truman's veto.

June 23—In *Adamson v. California*, the Supreme Court rules that states do not have to effect all guarantees of the Bill of Rights in criminal cases. The Court leaves the door open to modify this decision on a case-by-case basis.

July 17—Truman appoints a 12-person Commission on the Organization of the Executive Branch, to be chaired by Herbert Hoover.

July 18—Truman signs the Presidential Succession Act putting the Speaker of the House next in line when there is no vice president.

July 25—Truman signs the National Security Act establishing a unified Department of Defense and creating the National Security Council.

July 27—Truman appoints James V. Forrestal first secretary of defense.

September 2—The Inter-American Defense Pact, which provides for united defense against aggression, is signed in Rio de Janeiro.

September 19—General Albert Wedemeyer submits a report on his China trip to Truman, recommending a five-year U.S. military aid program and encouragement of internal reforms in the Nationalist government.

October 9—Truman instructs the State Department to support the U.N. plan to partition Palestine into Jewish and Arab states.

October 14—The U.S. becomes the first nation to break the sound barrier.

October 18—The House Un-American Activities Committee opens an investigation of alleged communist infiltration in the movie industry.

October 24—Senator Robert A. Taft formally announces his candidacy for the 1948 Republican presidential nomination.

October 29—The President's Commission on Civil Rights reports its findings in a paper entitled, "To Secure These Rights." Among the report's recommendations are creation of special federal and state investigative units for civil rights cases, elimination of poll taxes and specific laws against bias in housing, education, health, and public services.

November 29—The state of Israel is established by a joint U.S.-Soviet-backed decision in the UN.

December 3—*A Streetcar Named Desire*, by Tennessee Williams, opens in New Orleans.

December 19—Congress votes a $540 million appropriation for interim aid to France, Italy, Austria, and China and receives Truman's request for $17 billion for a four-year European Economic Recovery Program.

December 29—Henry A. Wallace announces his candidacy for the presidency on a third party ticket promising peace and abundance.

1948

January 12—In *Sipeul v. Board of Regents of the University of Oklahoma*, the Supreme Court rules that a state may not deny blacks admission to its law school on the basis of color.

February 2—Truman sends a 10-point civil rights program to Congress calling for an end to segregation in public schools and accommodations and reducing discrimination in employment.

March 6—The U.S. and its Western European allies reach an agreement on the formation of a federal government for West Germany and its participation in the Marshall Plan.

April 20—Federal Judge T. A. Goldsborough fines John L. Lewis $20,000 and the United Mine Workers $1.4 million for criminal contempt of court for their March 1947 coal strike.

May 3—In *Shelley v. Kraemer*, the Supreme Court rules that state courts cannot be used to enforce racially restrictive covenants.

May 10—Faced with a railroad strike, Truman seizes the nation's railroads and orders the Army to operate them.

May 14—Truman gives de facto recognition to the new state of Israel.

May 19—The House passes the Mundt-Nixon bill requiring the registration of all Communist Party members and providing penalties for attempts to establish a dictatorship in the U.S. No Senate action is taken.

May 25—General Motors introduces an escalator clause into its contract with the UAW. It ties wages to cost-of-living indicators.

June 11—The Senate overwhelmingly passes the Vandenberg Resolution stating that the U.S. can associate itself in peacetime with nations outside the Western Hemisphere in collective security agreements.

June 24—The Republican National Convention nominates Governor Thomas E. Dewey of New York for President and Governor Earl Warren of California for vice president.

June 24—Soviet occupation forces begin a blockade of Berlin.

June 26—Truman orders all planes in the American European Command to supply Berlin's needs until the Soviets lift their blockade.

July 15—The Democratic National Convention nominates Truman for president. Alben Barkley is chosen vice presidential candidate. When the convention adopts a strong civil rights plank, some conservative southern delegates walk out.

July 17—Southern Democrats opposed to the Democratic Party's stand on civil rights form the States' Rights Party, which nominates Strom Thurmond for president on a platform calling for racial segregation.

July 22—The Progressive Party nominates Henry A. Wallace for president on a platform urging a conciliatory policy toward the Soviet Union.

July 26—Truman issues an executive order barring segregation in the armed forces and prohibiting discrimination in federal employment.

July 26—Truman calls Congress into special session to pass inflation control and civil rights legislation and repeal the Taft-Hartley Act. None of this is accomplished.

August 3—Admitted former Communist Whittaker Chambers names Alger Hiss as a former member of a Communist cell in Washington.

November 2—Truman unexpectedly defeats Dewey by approximately 2.2 million popular votes and 114 electoral votes. Thurmond receives 39 electoral votes and Wallace receives none. Democrats also win control of both houses of Congress.

1949

March 2—An Air Force B-50 bomber completes its first nonstop flight around the world while refueling aloft. It proves the United States can drop an atomic bomb anywhere.

April 4—Twelve nations, including the United States, sign the North Atlantic Treaty.

April 8—Truman orders the U.S. occupation zone in Germany to be merged with those of Great Britain and France.

May 2—*Death of a Salesman*, a play by Arthur Miller on decline of contemporary values, wins the Pulitzer Prize.

May 12—The Russian blockade of Berlin ends; Truman terminates the U.S. airlift.

June 13—In *Standard Oil v. United States*, the Supreme Court broadens the definition of "monopoly in restraint of trade" under the Clayton Antitrust Act, making it easier for the government to move against exclusive dealerships.

June 20—The UMW ends a seven-day nationwide strike against coal operators for shorter work hours and higher welfare payments.

June 27—In *Wolf v. Colorado*, the Supreme Court holds that evidence seized through illegal search and seizure can still be used to prosecute in state courts.

August 5—With Truman's approval, the State Department issues a White Paper blaming the fall of China to the Communists on Chiang Kai-shek's (Jiang Jieshi) corrupt, inefficient government. It states that no further aid will be given the Chiang government.

August 10—Truman signs a bill organizing the military into the Department of Defense and separate departments of the army, navy, and air force.

September 21—The United States and Western powers end military control of Germany.

September 22—Truman signs the Mutual Defense Assistance Act, which provides for military aid to NATO allies in case of aggression.

September 23—Truman announces that the Soviet Union has exploded a nuclear bomb.

October 1—Steelworkers strike for larger pensions and retirement benefits. The strike ends on December 20 with most companies capitulating.

October 1—A Communist regime under Mao Zedong (Mao Tse-tung) is established in China. It is immediately recognized by France and Great Britain and refused recognition by the United States.

October 14—A federal court in New York convicts 11 leaders of the American Communist Party of violating the Smith Act in advocating the overthrow of the U.S. government.

October 31—Walter Reuther, president of the United Auto Workers, begins a purge of Communist-dominated unions from the CIO.

December 9—Representative J. Parnell Thomas, chairman of the House Un-American Activities Committee, is fined and sentenced to eight to 24 months in prison for payroll padding.

1950

January 21—Hiss is convicted of perjury in denying that he gave U.S. secrets to Communists.

January 31—Truman orders a crash program for the construction of the hydrogen bomb.

February 7—In a speech at Wheeling, W. Va., Senator Joseph R. McCarthy charges that there are numerous Communists in the State Department.

February 20—In *United States v. Rabinowitz*, the Supreme Court broadens the authority of police officers to make seizures of property without a search warrant.

May 8—The Supreme Court, in *American Communications Association v. Douds*, upholds the constitutionality of the noncommunist affidavit requirement of the Taft-Hartley Act.

June 5—In *McLaurin v. Oklahoma State Regents*, the Supreme Court rules that, having admitted a black to its law school, a state cannot deny him equal use of all facilities. In *Sweatt v. Painter*, the Supreme Court holds that a state cannot bar the admission of a black to a state law school on the grounds that there is a black law school available.

June 5—Truman signs the International Development Act (Point Four Program) into law.

June 25—North Korea invades South Korea. The UN Security Council, with the Soviet Union absent, declares North Korea the aggressor.

June 30—Truman orders U.S. ground forces into Korea and extends the draft to July 1951.

August 18—The Special Committee to Investigate Crime in Interstate Commerce, chaired by Senator Estes Kefauver, issues an interim report alleging that organized crime is expanding into legitimate businesses.

August 25—Truman orders the army to seize all railroads to prevent a threatened national strike. They are returned May 25.

September 8—Congress passes the Defense Production Act granting the government wide-ranging powers to impose wage and price controls because of the Korean War.

September 23—Congress passes the Internal Security Act over Truman's veto. The act provides for registration of members of Communist-action and Communist-front groups, detention of Communists in national emergencies, and establishment of the Subversive Activities Control Board.

October 26—Chinese Communist troops intervene in the Korean conflict.

November 1—Puerto Rican nationalists attempt to assassinate Truman.

November 7—Republicans increase their representation in the House and Senate, picking up five and 31 seats respectively. Nevertheless, Democrats retain control of the Senate 49 to 47 and of the House 235 to 199.

December 29—General Douglas MacArthur recommends that UN forces attack Communist China.

1951

January 1—Communist Chinese and North Korean troops drive UN forces out of Seoul.

January 1—Congress grants Truman power to freeze prices, in an attempt to stem inflation.

January 15—In *Feiner v. United States*, the Supreme Court holds that it is legal to arrest a speaker when he is presenting "a clear and present danger" of incitement to riot.

February 5—The Fulbright Committee issues a report stating that it has uncovered an influence ring with White House contacts.

February 8—A 12-day railroad strike that halted the nation's service ends with a temporary pay raise.

February 26—Truman signs the Twenty-second Amendment to the Constitution limiting the president to two terms or a maximum of 10 years.

February 26—In *Bus Employees v. Wisconsin Employment Relations Board*, the Supreme Court holds that state laws proscribing union activities protected under the National Labor Relations Act are invalid.

March 7—General Douglas MacArthur ridicules Truman's Korean policies in a statement to the press.

April 5—Julius and Ethel Rosenberg are sentenced to death after their espionage conviction for stealing atomic secrets.

April 11—Truman relieves MacArthur of his command in Korea and replaces him with General Matthew B. Ridgway.

April 19—Addressing a joint session of Congress, MacArthur urges an expanded war against the Communists in Asia.

April 30—In *Joint Anti-Fascist Refugee Committee v. McGrath*, the Supreme Court restricts the attorney general's right to place a group on his list of subversives without a hearing.

June 4—In *Dennis v. United States*, the Supreme Court upholds the constitutionality of the Smith Act.

June 4—In *Garner v. Los Angeles*, the Supreme Court holds that a state or municipality may require noncommunist affidavits from employment applicants.

July 7—Negotiations for a cease-fire in Korea begin in Kaesong between the UN, North Korea, and Communist China.

August 1—Truman cancels tariff concessions to all nations under Soviet domination.

September 8—The United States and 47 nations, excluding Russia and China, sign a peace treaty with Japan restoring that nation to full sovereignty. The same day Japan and the United States sign a security treaty permitting the United States to station troops in Japan.

October 19—The United States officially ends its state of war with Germany.

December 13—The State Department dismisses career employee John S. Service after charges of intentional and unauthorized disclosure of classified information are upheld by the Civil Service Loyalty Review Board.

1952

January 21—Truman submits a record peacetime budget of $85.4 billion for 1953.

January 22—Truman meets with Illinois Governor Adlai E. Stevenson to offer him the presidential nomination. Stevenson refuses.

January 23—Estes Kefauver announces his candidacy for the Democratic presidential nomination.

March 10—In *Harisiades v. Shaughnessey*, the Supreme Court rules that Congress may use past Communist Party membership as grounds for deportation.

March 24—In *Rutkin v. United States*, the Supreme Court opens the door to prosecuting organized crime through charges of tax evasion by ruling that income obtained by extortion is taxable.

March 29—Truman publicly reveals that he will not be a candidate in the 1952 presidential election.

April 3—In *Adler v. Board of Education*, the Supreme Court rules it permissible for a state to presume a member of a subversive organization is unfit for government employment.

April 3—Truman removes Attorney General J. Howard McGrath for refusing to cooperate in a campaign to clean up the government.

April 8—In order to block a scheduled steelworkers' strike, President Truman orders the government seizure of the nation's steel mills.

May 1—The State Department bans travel to the Soviet Union and its satellites.

May 26—In *Burstyn v. Wilson*, the Supreme Court extends First Amendment protection to movies.

May 29—Truman vetoes the tidelands oil bill, which would have given offshore oil rights to California, Texas, and Louisiana.

June 2—In *Youngstown Sheet & Tube Company v. Sawyer*, the Supreme Court rules that President Truman acted illegally in placing the steel mills under federal control to avoid a national strike. The following day 500,000 steelworkers strike.

June 27—Congress passes the McCarran-Walter immigration bill over Truman's veto.

July 11—The Republican National Convention nominates General Dwight D. Eisenhower for President over Senator Robert A. Taft by a vote of 595 to 500. The convention then nominates Senator Richard M. Nixon for vice president.

July 24—The steel strike is settled with the government permitting the industry to raise prices in return for increasing wages.

July 25—The Democratic National Convention meeting in Chicago nominates Adlai Stevenson for president on the third ballot. Senator John Sparkman is nominated for vice president the following day.

July 25—Puerto Rico becomes a U.S. commonwealth.

August 4—ANZUS (Pacific Council) is created by the mutual security pact between the U.S., Australia, and New Zealand.

November 1—Truman announces the explosion of the first hydrogen bomb.

November 4—Eisenhower and Nixon defeat Stevenson and Sparkman, 442 electoral votes to 89. The popular vote is 33.9 million for Eisenhower and 27.3 for Stevenson. Republicans win control of both houses of Congress by narrow margins.

November 21—George Meany succeeds the late William Green as head of the AFL.

December 4—Walter Reuther succeeds the late Philip Murray as head of the CIO.

PRINCIPAL U.S. GOVERNMENT OFFICIALS OF THE TRUMAN YEARS

SUPREME COURT

Harlan F. Stone, Chief Justice 1941–1946
Fred M. Vinson, Chief Justice 1946–1953
Hugo L. Black 1937–1971
Harold H. Burton 1945–1958
Tom C. Clark 1949–1967
Felix Frankfurter 1939–1962

Robert H. Jackson 1941–1954
Sherman Minton 1949–1956
Frank Murphy 1940–1949
Stanley F. Reed 1938–1957
Owen J. Roberts 1930–1945
Wiley B. Rutledge 1943–1949

EXECUTIVE DEPARTMENTS

Department of Agriculture

Secretary of Agriculture
Clinton P. Anderson, 1945–1948
Charles F. Brannan, 1948–1953
Undersecretary
John B. Hutson, 1945–1946
N. E. Dodd, 1946–1948
Albert J. Loveland, 1948–1950
C. J. McCormick, 1951–1953
Assistant Secretary
Charles F. Brannan, 1945–1948
Knox T. Hutchinson, 1950–1953
Administrator, Agricultural Research Administration
P. V. Cardon, 1945–1947
W. V. Lambert, 1947–1949
P. V. Cardon, 1949–1952
*Administrator, Commodity Exchange Authority**
Joseph M. Mehl, 1949–1953
*The position was created in 1949.

*Administrator, Farm Security Administration**
Frank Hancock, 1945–1946
Dillard B. Lasseter, 1946–1953
*The title was changed to Administrator, Farmers Home Administration in 1947.

Administrator, Production and Marketing Administration
John B. Hutson. 1945–1946
Robert H. Shields, 1946–1947
Jesse B. Gilmer, (acting) 1947–1948
Ralph S. Trigg, 1948–1951
Gus F. Geissler, 1951–1953

Department of Commerce

Secretary of Commerce
Henry A. Wallace, 1945–1947
W. Averell Harriman, 1947–1948
Charles Sawyer, 1948–1953

Undersecretary
  Alfred Schindler, 1945–1947
  William C. Foster, 1947–1948
  C. V. Whitney, 1949–1950
*Undersecretary for Transportation**
  Philip B. Fleming, (acting) 1950–1951
  Delos W. Rentzel, 1951–1952
*The position was created in 1950.

*Assistant Secretary**
  William A. M. Burden, 1945–1948
  John R. Alison, 1948–1949
  Thomas W. S. Davis, 1950–1952
*Reorganized in 1948 into Assistant Secretary for Aeronautics.

*Assistant Secretary for International Affairs**
  Thomas Blaisdell, Jr., 1950–1951
  R. C. Miller, (acting) 1951–1952
*The position was created in 1950.

Department of the Interior

Secretary of Interior
  Harold L. Ickes, 1933–1946
  Julius A. Krug, 1946–1950
  Oscar L. Chapman, 1950–1953
Undersecretary
  Abe Fortas, 1945–1946
  Oscar L. Chapman, 1946–1950
  Richard D. Searles, 1951–1953
Assistant Secretaries
  Michael W. Straus, 1945–1946
  Oscar L. Chapman, 1945—1946
  Warner W. Gardner, 1947–1948
  C. Girard Davidson, 1947–1951
  William E. Warne, 1948–1951
  Dale E. Doty, 1950–1951
  Robert R. Rose, Jr., 1952–1953
  Joel D. Wolfsohn, 1952–1953
  Robert M. McKinney, 1952–1953

Department of Justice

Attorney General
  Tom C. Clark, 1945–1950
  J. Howard McGrath, 1950–1952
  J. P. McGranery, 1952–1953
Solicitor General
  J. Howard McGrath, 1945–1947
  Philip B. Pearlman, 1948–1953
*The Assistant to the Attorney General**
  James P. McGranery, 1945–1947

  Douglas W. McGregor, 1947–1948
  Peyton Ford, 1948–1952
  A. Devitt Vanech, 1952–1953
*Reorganized in 1950 into Deputy Attorney General.

Assistant Attorney General/Antitrust Division
  Wendell Berge, 1945–1948
  Hebert A. Bergson, 1948–1951
  H. Graham Morison, 1951–1952
Assistant Attorney General/Tax Division
  Samuel O. Clark, Jr., 1945–1946
  Theron Lamar Caudle, 1948–1952
Assistant Attorney General/Claims Division
  Francis M. Shea, 1945–1946
  John F. Sonnett, 1946–1948
  H. Graham Morison, 1948–1951
  Holmes Baldridge, 1951–1953
Assistant Attorney General/Lands Division
  David L. Bazelon, 1947–1948
  A. Devitt Vanech, 1948–1952
  William A. Unerhill, 1952–1953
Assistant Attorney General/Criminal Division
  Theron Lamar Caudle, 1945–1948
  T. Vincent Quinn, 1948–1949
  Alexander M. Campbell, 1949–1950
  James M. McInerney, 1950–1953
*Assistant Attorney General/War Division**
  Herbert Wechsler, 1945–1946
*The position was eliminated in 1946.

Department of Labor

Secretary of Labor
  Lewis Schwellenbach, 1945–1948
  Lewis W. Gibson, (acting) 1948–1949
  Maurice J. Tobin, 1949–1953
*Undersecretary**
  Keen Johnson, 1947–1948
  David A. Morse, 1948–1949
  Michael J. Calvin, 1949–1953
*The position was created in 1946.

Assistant Secretaries of Labor
  D. W. Tracy, 1945–1946
  Edward C. Moran, Jr., 1945–1946
  John W. Gibson, 1946–1951
  Philip Hannah, 1947–1948
  David A. Morse, 1947–1948
  John T. Kmetz, 1948–1949
  Ralph Wright, 1949–1953
  Philip M. Kaiser, 1950–1953
  Robert T. Creasey, 1951–1953

*Administrative Assistant to the Secretary**
  James E. Dempsey, 1947–1949
  Stanley Wollaston, 1949–1950

*The position was created in 1947.

Director, Division of Labor Standards
  Verne A. Zimmer, 1945–1948
  William L. Connolly, 1948–1953
*Director, Office of International Labor Affairs**
  Philip M. Kaiser, 1949–1950
  Arnold L. Zernple, 1950–1953

*The position was created in 1949.

National Military Establishment*

*The agency was established by the National Security Act of 1947 and consisted of the Departments of the Army, Navy, and the Air Force. In 1950 it was reorganized by the National Security Act Amendment of 1949 as the Department of Defense.

Secretary of Defense
  James Forrestal, 1948–1949
  Louis A. Johnson, 1949–1951
  George C. Marshall, 1951–1952
  Robert A. Lovett, 1951–1953
*Undersecretary**
  Stephen T. Early, 1948–1951
  William C. Foster, 1951–1953

*The position was created in 1949 and reorganized in 1950 into Deputy Secretary of Defense.

Secretary of the Air Force
  W. Stuart Symington, 1948–1950
  Thomas K. Finletter, 1950–1953
Secretary of the Army
  Kenneth C. Royall, 1948–1949
  Gordon Gray, 1949–1950
  Frank Pace, Jr., 1950–1953
Secretary of the Navy
  John L. Sullivan, 1948–1949
  Francis P. Matthews, 1949–1952
  Dan Kimball, 1952–1953
*Assistant Secretary (Administrative and Public Affairs)**
  John H. Ohly, 1948–1950
  Paul H. Griffith, 1950–1951

*The title was originally Special Assistant to the Secretary of Defense (1948). In 1949 the title was changed to Special Assistant (Plans and Inter-Governmental Affairs), and in 1950 it was changed to the one listed above. The position was eliminated in 1951.

*Assistant Secretary (Comptroller)**
  Wilfred J. McNeil, 1948–1953

*The title was originally Special Assistant to the Secretary of Defense (1948). In 1949 the title was changed to Special Assistant, Financial Affairs, and in 1950 it was changed to the one listed above.

*Assistant Secretary (International Security Affairs)**
  James H. Burns, 1950–1952

*The position was created in 1950 as Assistant to the Secretary (Foreign Military Affairs and Military Assistance). The title was changed to the one listed in 1951, and in 1952 the position was eliminated.

*Assistant Secretary (Legal and Legislative Affairs)**
  Marx Leva, 1948–1951
  Daniel K. Edwards, 1951–1952
  Charles A. Coolidge, 1952–1953

*The title was originally Special Assistant to the Secretary of Defense (1948). In 1949 it was changed to Special Assistant (Legal and Legislative Affairs), and in 1950 it was changed to the one listed above.

*Assistant Secretary (Manpower and Personnel)**
  Anna M. Rosenberg, 1951–1953

*The position was created in 1951.

*Joint Chiefs of Staff Chief of Staff to the Commander in Chief of the Armed Forces**
  Fleet Admiral William Leahy, USN, 1948–1949

*The position was eliminated in 1949.

*Chairman**
  General Omar N. Bradley, USA, 1949–1953

*The position was created in 1949.

Chief of Staff, U.S. Army
  General Omar N. Bradley, 1948–1959
  General J. Lawton Collins, 1949–1953
Chief of Naval Operations
  Admiral Louis E. Denfeld, 1948–1950
  Admiral Forrest P. Sherman, 1950–1952
  Admiral William M. Fechteler, 1952–1953
Chief of Staff, U.S. Air Force
  General Hoyt S. Vandenberg, 1948–1953

Department of the Navy

Secretary of the Navy
  James Forrestal, 1945–1948
Undersecretary
  Artemus L. Gates, 1945–1946
  John L. Sullivan, 1947–1948
Assistant Secretary
  H. Struve Hensel, 1945–1946
  W. John Kenney, 1946–1948

Assistant Secretary for Air
John L. Sullivan, 1945–1947
John Nicholas Brown, 1947–1948
Commandant, U. S. Marine Corps*
General Alexander A. Vandegrift, 1945–1948

*Reorganized in 1948 as a Department under the jurisdiction of the National Military Establishment.

Post Office Department

Post Office Department Postmaster General
Robert E. Hannegan, 1945–1948
Jesse M. Donaldson, 1948–1953
Deputy Postmaster General*
Vincent C. Burke, 1950–1953

*The position was created in 1950.

Executive Assistant to the Postmaster General
Sidney Salomon, Jr., 1945–1946
Frank Pace, Jr., 1946–1948
Samuel R. Young, 1948–1949
Director of Budget and Administrative Planning*
Joseph F. Gartland, 1945–1949
Alfer B. Strom, 1950–1953

*The title was changed to Administrative Assistant to the Postmaster General in 1950.

First Assistant Postmaster General*
Jesse M. Donaldson, 1945–1948
Vincent C. Burke, 1948–1950
Joseph J. Lawler, 1950–1953

*Reorganized in 1950 as Assistant Postmaster General in Charge, Bureau of Post Office Operations.

Second Assistant Postmaster General*
Gael E. Sullivan, 1945–1948
Paul Aiken, 1948–1950
John M. Redding, 1950–1952

*Reorganized in 1950 as Assistant Postmaster General in Charge, Bureau of Transportation.

Third Assistant Postmaster General and Agent of the Board, Postal Savings System*
Joseph J. Lawler, 1945–1950
Osborne A. Pearson, 1950–1953

*Reorganized in 1950 as Assistant Postmaster General in Charge, Bureau of Finance.

Fourth Assistant Postmaster General*
Walter Myers, 1945–1953

*Reorganized in 1950 as Assistant Postmaster General in Charge, Bureau of Facilities.

Department of State

Secretary of State
Edward Stettinius, 1944–1945
James F. Byrnes, 1945–1948
George C. Marshall, 1948–1949
Dean G. Acheson, 1949–1953
Undersecretary
Dean G. Acheson, 1945–1948
Robert A. Lovett, 1948–1949
James E. Webb, 1949–1952
David K. E. Bruce, 1952–1953
Undersecretary for Economic Affairs*
William L. Clayton, 1947–1948

*The position was created in 1947 and eliminated in 1949.

Deputy Undersecretary*
Dean Rusk, 1949–1950
H. Freeman Matthews, 1950–1953

*The position was created in 1949.

Deputy Undersecretary for Administration*
John E. Peurifoy, 1949–1951
Carlisle H. Humelsine, 1951–1953

*The position was created in 1949.

Assistant Secretary for Congressional Relations
Donald S. Russell, 1945–1946
Ernest A. Gross, 1949–1950
Jack K. McFall, 1950–1953
Assistant Secretary for Economic Affairs
William L. Clayton, 1945–1947
Willard L. Thorp, 1948–1953
Assistant Secretary for Public and Cultural Relations*
William Benton, 1945–1948
George V. Allen, 1948–1950
Edward W. Barrett, 1950–1952
Rowland H. Sargeant, 1952–1953

*The title was changed in 1946 to Assistant Secretary for Public Affairs.

Assistant Secretary for American Republic Affairs
Spruille Braden, 1945–1948
Edward G. Miller, Jr., 1949–1950
Assistant Secretary for European, Far Eastern, Near Eastern, and African Affairs*
James C. Dunn, 1945–1947

*In 1949 this position was subdivided into the following three Offices:

Assistant Secretary for Near Eastern and African Affairs*
George C. McGhee, 1949–1952
Henry A. Byroade, 1952–1953

*The title was changed in 1950 to Assistant Secretary for Near Eastern, South Asian, and African Affairs

Assistant Secretary for European Affairs
George W. Perkins, 1949–1953
Assistant Secretary for Far Eastern Affairs
W. Walton Butterworth, (acting) 1949–1950
Dean Rusk, 1950–1952
John M. Allison, 1952–1953
Assistant Secretary for Occupied Areas*
John H. Hilldring, 1946–1948
Charles E. Saltzman, 1948–1949

*The position was created in 1946 and eliminated in 1949.

Assistant Secretary for Inter-American Affairs*
Edward G. Miller, Jr. 1950–1953

*The position was created in 1950.

Assistant Secretary for Administration
Frank McCarthy, 1945–1946
Donald S. Russell, 1946–1948
John E. Peurifoy, 1948–1949
Assistant Secretary for Political Affairs*
Norman Armour, 1948–1949

*The position was created in 1948 and eliminated in 1949.

Department of the Treasury
Secretary of the Treasury
Fred M. Vinson, 1945–1947
John W. Snyder, 1947–1953
Undersecretary
Daniel W. Bell, 1945–1946
O. Max Garner, 1946–1948
A. Lee M. Wiggins, 1948–1949
Edward H. Foley, Jr., 1949–1953
Assistant Secretaries
Herbert E. Gaston, 1945–1946
Harry D. White, 1945–1947

Edward H. Foley, Jr., 1946–1949
John S. Graham, 1949–1953
William McC. Martin, Jr., 1949–1951
Andrew N. Overby, 1952–1953
Fiscal Assistant Secretary
Edward F. Bartelt, 1945–1953
General Counsel
Joseph J. O'Connell, Jr., 1945–1948
Thomas J. Lynch, 1948–1953
Administrative Assistant to the Secretary*
Paul L. Kelley, 1945–1947
William W. Parsons, 1947–1953

*The title was changed in 1951 to Administrative Assistant Secretary.

War Department*
Secretary of War
Robert P. Patterson, 1945–1948

*Reorganized in 1948 into the National Military Establishment.

Undersecretary
Kenneth C. Royall, 1946–1948
Assistant Secretary
John J. McCloy, 1945–1946
Howard P. Peterson, 1946–1948
Assistant Secretary for Air
Robert A. Lovett, 1945–1946
W. Stuart Symington, 1946–1948
Administrative Assistant and Chief Clerk
John W. Martin, 1945–1948
Chief of Staff
General George C. Marshall, 1945–1946
General Dwight D. Eisenhower, 1946–1948

REGULATORY COMMISSIONS AND INDEPENDENT AGENCIES

Atomic Energy Commission
Robert F. Bacher, 1946–1949
Gordon E. Dean, 1949–1953, Chairman, 1950–1953
T. Keith Glennan, 1950–1952
David E. Lilienthal, Chairman, 1946–1950

Thomas E. Murray, 1950–1957
Sumner T. Pike, 1946–1951
Henry D. Smyth, 1949–1954
Lewis L. Strauss, 1946–1950; Chairman, 1953–1958
W. W. Waymack, 1946–1948
Eugene M. Zuckert, 1952–1954

Civil Aeronautics Board

Joseph P. Adams, 1951–1956
Russell B. Adams, 1948–1950
Harllee Branch, 1945–1948
Chan Gurney, 1951–1964; Chairman, 1954
Harold A. Jones, 1948–1951
James M. Landis, Chairman, 1946–1947
Josh Lee, 1945–1955
Donald W. Nyrop, Chairman, 1951–1952
Joseph J. O'Connell, Jr., Chairman, 1948–1950
L. Welch Pogue, Chairman, 1945–1946
Delos W. Rentzel, Chairman, 1950–1951
Oswail Ryan, 1945–1954; Chairman, 1953
Edward Warner, 1945
Clarence M. Young, 1946–1947

Federal Communications Commission

Robert T. Bartley, 1952–1972
Norman S. Case, 1945
Wayne Coy, Chairman, 1947–1952
Charles R. Denny, Jr., 1945–1947; Chairman, 1946–1947
Clifford J. Durr, 1945–1948
Frieda B. Hennock, 1948–1955
Rosel H. Hyde, 1946–1969; Chairman, 1953–1954
E. K. Jett, 1945–1947
Robert F. Jones, 1947–1952
Eugene H. Merrill, 1952–1953
Paul A. Porter, Chairman, 1945–1946
George E. Sterling, 1948–1954
Ray C. Wakefield, 1945–1947
Paul A. Walker, 1945–1953; Chairman, 1952–1953
Edward M. Webster, 1947–1956
William Henry Wills, 1945–1946

Federal Power Commission

Thomas C. Buchanan, 1948–1953; Chairman, 1952–1953
Dale E. Doty, 1952–1954
Claude L. Draper, 1945–1956
Basil Manly, Chairman, 1945
Leland Olds, 1945–1949; Chairman, 1945–1947
Richard Sachse, 1945–1947
John Q. Scott, 1945
Nelson Lee Smith, 1945–1955; Chairman, 1947–1950
Mon C. Wallgren, 1949–1951; Chairman, 1950–1951
Harrington Wimberly, 1945–1953

Federal Reserve Board

Lawrence Clayton, 1947–1949
Ernest G. Draper, 1945–1950
Marriner S. Eccles, 1945–1951; Chairman, 1945–1948
Rudolph M. Evans, 1945–1954
William McC. Martin, Jr., Chairman, 1951–1970
Thomas B. McCabe, Chairman, 1948–1951
John K. McKee, 1945–1946
A. L. Mills, Jr., 1952–1965
Edward L. Norton, 1950–1952
Oliver S. Powell, 1950–1952
Ronald Ransom, 1945–1947
J. L. Robertson, 1952–1973
M. S. Szymczak, 1945–1961
James K. Vardaman, Jr., 1946–1958

Federal Trade Commission

William A. Ayres, 1945–1952; Chairman, 1946
Albert A. Carretta, 1952–1954
John Carson, 1949–1953
Ewin L. Davis, 1945–1949; Chairman, 1945
Garland S. Ferguson, 1945–1949; Chairman, 1947
Robert E. Freer, 1945–1948; Chairman, 1948
Charles H. March, 1945
Lowell B. Mason, 1945–1956; Chairman, 1949–1950
James M. Mead, 1949–1955; Chairman, 1950–1953
Stephen J. Spingarn, 1950–1953

Securities and Exchange Commission

Clarence H. Adams, 1952–1956
James J. Caffrey, 1945–1947; Chairman, 1946–1947
Donald C. Cook, 1949–1953; Chairman, 1952–1953
Edmond M. Hanrahan, 1946–1949; Chairman, 1948–1949
Robert E. Healy, 1945–1946
Robert K. McConnaughey, 1945–1949
Edward T. McCormick, 1949–1951
Harry A. McDonald, 1947–1952; Chairman, 1949–1952
Richard B. McEntire, 1946–1953
Robert I. Millonzi, 1951–1952
Sumner T. Pike, 1945–1946
Ganson Purcell, Chairman, 1945–1946
Paul R. Rowen, 1948–1955

UNITED STATES HOUSE OF REPRESENTATIVES

Alabama

George W. Andrews (D) 1944–1971
Laurie C. Battle (D) 1947–1955
Frank W. Boykin (D) 1935–1963
Edward de Graffenried (D) 1949–1953
Carl Elliott (D) 1949–1965
George M. Grant (D) 1938–1965
Samuel Francis Hobbs (D) 1935–1951
Pete Jarman (D) 1937–1949
Robert E. Jones (D) 1947–1977
Carter Manasco (D) 1941–1949
Luther Patrick (D) 1937–1943; 1945–1947
Albert Rains (D) 1945–1965
Kenneth A. Roberts (D) 1951–1965
John J. Sparkman (D) 1937–1946

Arizona

Richard F. Harless (D) 1943–1949
John R. Murdock (D) 1937–1953
Harold A. Patten (D) 1949–1955

Arkansas

William Fadjo Cravens (D) 1939–1949
J. William Fulbright (D) 1943–1945
E. G. Gathings (D) 1939–1969
Oren Harris (D) 1941–1966
Brooks Hays (D) 1943–1959
Wilbur D. Mills (D) 1939–1974
W. F. Norrell (D) 1939–1961
Boyd Tackett (D) 1949–1953
James W. Trimble (D) 1945–1967

California

Helen Gahagan Douglas (D) 1945–1951
Clyde Doyle (D) 1945–1947; 1949–1963
Alfred J. Elliott (D) 1937–1949
Glair Engle (D) 1943–1959
Franck R. Havenner (D) 1945–1953
Ned R. Healy (D) 1945–1947
Chet Holifield (D) 1943–1975
Edoliard V. M. Izac (D) 1937–1947
Cecil R. King (D) 1942–1969
Clarence F. Lea (D) 1917–1949
Clinton D. McKinnon (D) 1949–1953
George P. Miller (D) 1945–1973
George E. Outland (D) 1943–1947
Ellis E. Patterson (D) 1945–1947

John F. Shelley (D) 1949–1964
Harry R. Sheppard (D) 1937–1965
John H. Tolan (D) 1935–1947
Jerry Voorhis (D) 1937–1947
Cecil F. White (D) 1949–1951
Samuel W. Yorty (D) 1951–1955
John J. Allen, Jr. (R) 1947–1959
Jack Z. Anderson (R) 1939–1953
Willis W. Bradley (R) 1947–1949
Ernest K. Bramblett (R) 1947–1955
Charles K. Fletcher (R) 1947–1949
Bertrand W. Gearhart (R) 1935–1949
Patrick J. Hillings (R) 1951–1959
Carl Hinshaw (R) 1939–1956
Allan Oakley Hunter (R) 1951–1955
Donald L. Jackson (R) 1947–1961
J. Leroy Johnson (R) 1943–1957
Gordon L. McDonough (R) 1945–1963
Richard M. Nixon (R) 1947–1950
John Phillips (R) 1943–1957
Norris Poulson (R) 1943–1945; 1947–1953
Hubert B. Scudder (R) 1949–1959
Richard J. Welch (R) 1926–1949
Thomas H. Werdel (R) 1949–1953

Colorado

Wayne N. Aspinall (D) 1949–1973
John A. Carroll (D) 1947–1951
John H. Marsalis (D) 1949–1951
Bryon G. Rogers (D) 1951–1971
J. Edgar Chenoweth (R) 1941–1949;
   1951–1965
Dean M. Gillespie (R) 1944–1947
William S. Hill (R) 1941–1959
Robert F. Rockwell (R) 1941–1949

Connecticut

James P. Geelan (D) 1945–1947
Herman P. Koppleman (D) 1941–1943;
   1945–1947
John A. McGuire (D) 1945–1953
Abraham A. Ribicoff (D) 1949–1953
Joseph F. Ryter (D) 1945–1947
Chase Going Woodhouse (D) 1945–1947;
   1949–1951
Ellsworth B. Foote (R) 1947–1949
John Davis Lodge (R) 1947–1951; 1951–1955

Clare Boothe Luce (R) 1943–1947
William J. Miller (R) 1939–1941; 1943–1945;
    1947–1949
Albert P. Morano (R) 1951–1959
James T. Patterson (R) 1947–1959
Antoni N. Sadlak (R) 1947–1959
Horace Seely-Brown, Jr. (R) 1947–1949;
    1951–1959; 1961–1963
Joseph E. Talbot (R) 1942–1947

Delaware

Philip A. Traynor (D) 1941–1943; 1945–1947
J. Caleb Boggs (R) 1947–1953

Florida

Charles E. Bennett (D) 1949–1993
Arthur Patrick Cannon (D) 1939–1947
Joe Hendricks (D) 1937–1949
A. Sydney Herlong, Jr. (D) 1949–1969
William C. Lantaff (D) 1951–1955
Chester B. McMullen (D) 1951–1953
J. Hardin Peterson (D) 1933–1951
Emory H. Price (D) 1943–1949
Dwight L. Rogers (D) 1945–1954
Robert L. F. Sikes (D) 1941–1944; 1945–1979
George A. Smathers (D) 1947–1951

Georgia

Paul Brown (D) 1933–1961
A. Sidney Camp (D) 1939–1954
E. E. Cox (D) 1925–1952
James C. Davis (D) 1947–1963
E. L. Forrester (D) 1951–1965
John S. Gibson (D) 1941–1947
Henderson Lanham (D) 1947–1957
Helen Douglas Mankin (D) 1946–1947
Stephen Pace (D) 1937–1951
Hugh Peterson (D) 1935–1947
Prince H. Preston, Jr. (D) 1947–1961
Malcolm C. Tarver (D) 1927–1947
Carl Vinson (D) 1914–1965
W. M. Wheeler (D) 1947–1955
John S. Wood (D) 1931–1935; 1945–1953

Idaho

Compton I. White (D) 1933–1947; 1949–1951
Hamer H. Budge (R) 1951–1961
Henry Dworshak (R) 1939–1946
Abe McGregor Goff (R) 1947–1949
John Sanborn (R) 1947–1951
John T. Wood (R) 1951–1953

Illinois

James V. Buckley (D) 1949–1951
Chester A. Cheshey (D) 1949–1951
William L. Dawson (D) 1943–1971
Emily Taft Doudlas (D) 1945–1947
Thomas S. Gordon (D) 1943–1959
Martin Gorski (D) 1943–1949
Edward Austin Kelly (D) 1931–1943;
    1945–1947
John C. Kluczynski (D) 1951–1971
Neil J. Linehan (D) 1949–1951
William W. Link (D) 1945–1947
Peter F. Mack, Jr. (D) 1949–1963
Thomas J. O'Brien (D) 1933–1937; 1943–1964
Barratt O'Hara (D) 1949–1951; 1953–1969
Charles Melvin Price (D) 1945–1988
Alexander J. Resa (D) 1945–1947
William A. Rowan (D) 1943–1947
Adolph J. Sabath (D) 1907–1952
Sidney R. Yates (D) 1949–1963; 1965–1999
Leo E. Allen (R) 1933–1961
Leslie C. Arends (R) 1935–1974
C. W. Bishop (R) 1941–1955
Fred E. Busby (R) 1943–1945; 1947–1949;
    1951–1955
Robert B. Chiperfield (R) 1939–1963
Marguerite Stitt Church (R) 1951–1963
Ralph E. Church (R) 1935–1941; 1943–1950
Roy Clippinger (R) 1945–1949
Everett McKinley Dirksen (R) 1933–1948
James V. Heidinger (R) 1941–1949
Richard W. Hoffman (R) 1949–1957
Evan Howell (R) 1941–1947
Edward H. Jenison (R) 1947–1949
Anton Joseph Johnson (R) 1939–1949
Edgar A. Jonas (R) 1949–1955
Noah M. Mason (R) 1937–1963
Rolla C. McMillen (R) 1943–1951
William E. McVey (R) 1951–1958
Thomas L. Owens (R) 1947–1948
Chauncey W. Reed (R) 1935–1956
Timothy P. Sheehan (R) 1951–1959
Sid Simpson (R) 1943–1958
William L. Springer (R) 1951–1973
William G. Stratton (R) 1941–1943;
    1947–1949
Jessie Sumner (R) 1939–1947
Robert J. Twyman (R) 1947–1949
Richard B. Vail (R) 1947–1949; 1951–1953
Harold H. Velde (R) 1949–1957
Charles W. Vursell (R) 1943–1959

Indiana

Thurman C. Crook (D) 1949–1951
Winfield K. Denton (D) 1949–1953
Andrew Jacobs, Sr. (D) 1949–1951
Edward H. Kruse, Jr. (D) 1949–1951
Louis L. Ludlow (D) 1929–1949
Ray J. Madden (D) 1943–1977
James E. Noland (D) 1949–1951
John R. Walsh (D) 1949–1951
E. Ross Adair (R) 1951–1971
John V. Beamer (R) 1951–1959
William G. Bray (R) 1951–1975
Charles B. Brownson (R) 1951–1959
Shepard J. Crumpacker, Jr. (R) 1951–1957
George W. Gillie (R) 1939–1949
Robert A. Grant (R) 1939–1949
Charles A. Halleck (R) 1935–1969
Cecil M. Harden (R) 1949–1959
Forest A. Harness (R) 1939–1949
Ralph Harvey (R) 1947–1959; 1961–1966
Noble J. Johnson (R) 1939–1948
Charles M. LaFollette (R) 1943–1947
Gerald W. Landus (R) 1939–1949
E. A. Mitchell (R) 1947–1949
Raymond S. Springer (R) 1939–1947
Earl Wilson (R) 1941–1959; 1961–1965

Iowa

Paul Cunningham (R) 1941–1959
James I. Dolliver (R) 1945–1957
H. R. Gross (R) 1949–1975
John W. Gwynne (R) 1935–1949
Charles B. Hoeven (R) 1943–1965
Ben F. Jensen (R) 1939–1965
Karl M. LeCompte (R) 1939–1959
Thomas E. Martin (R) 1939–1955
Henry O. Talle (R) 1939–1959

Kansas

Frank Carlson (R) 1935–1947
Albert M. Cole (R) 1945–1953
Myron V. George (R) 1950–1959
Clifford R. Hope (R) 1927–1957
Herbert A. Meyer (R) 1947–1950
Edward H. Rees (R) 1937–1961
Errett P. Scrivner (R) 1943–1959
Wint Smith (R) 1947–1961
Thomas Daniel Winter (R) 1939–1947

Kentucky

Joseph B. Bates (D) 1938–1953
Virgil M. Chapman (D) 1925–1929; 1931–1949

Frank Chelf (D) 1945–1967
Earle C. Clements (D) 1945–1948
Noble J. Gregory (D) 1937–1959
Andrew J. May (D) 1931–1947
Emmet O'Neal (D) 1935–1947
Carl D. Perkins (D) 1949–1984
Brent Spence (D) 1931–1963
Thomas R. Underwood (D) 1949–1951
John C. Watts (D) 1951–1971
John A. Whitaker (D) 1948–1951
Garrett L. Withers (D) 1952–1953
Chester Otto Carrier (R) 1943–1945
James S. Golden (R) 1949–1955
William Lewis (R) 1948–1949
W. Howes Meade (R) 1947–1949
Thruston B. Morton (R) 1947–1953
John M. Robsion (R) 1919–1930; 1935–1948

Louisiana

A. Leonard Allen (D) 1937–1953
Hale Boggs (D) 1941–1943; 1947–1973
Overton Brooks (D) 1937–1961
James Domengeaux (D) 1941–1944; 1944–1949
F. Edward Hébert (D) 1941–1977
Henry D. Larcade, Jr. (D) 1943–1953
Paul H. Maloney (D) 1931–1940; 1943–1947
Charles E. McKenzie (D) 1943–1947
James H. Morrison (D) 1943–1967
Otto E. Passman (D) 1947–1977
Edwin E. Willis (D) 1949–1969

Maine

Frank Fellows (R) 1941–1951
Robert Hale (R) 1943–1959
Clifford G. Mcintire (R) 1952–1965
Charles P. Nelson (R) 1949–1957
Margaret Chase Smith (R) 1940–1949

Maryland

H. Streett Baldwin (D) 1943–1947
William P. Bolton (D) 1949–1951
Thomas D'Alesandro, Jr. (D) 1939–1947
George H. Fallen (D) 1945–1971
Samuel N. Friedel (D) 1953–1971
Edward A. Garmatz (D) 1947–1973
Hugh A. Meade (D) 1947–1949
Dudley G. Roe (D) 1945–1947
Lansdale G. Sasscer (D) 1939–1953
J. Glenn Beall (R) 1943–1953

James P. S. Devereux (R) 1951–1959
Edward T. Miller (R) 1947–1959

Massachusetts

James M. Curley (D) 1943–1947
Harold D. Donohue (D) 1947–1975
Foster Furcolo (D) 1949–1952
John F. Kennedy (D) 1947–1953
Thomas J. Lane (D) 1941–1963
John W. McCormack (D) 1928–1971
Philip J. Philbin (D) 1943–1971
George J. Bates (R) 1937–1949
William H. Bates (R) 1950–1969
Charles R. Clason (R) 1937–1949
Charles L. Gifford (R) 1922–1947
Angier L. Goodwin (R) 1943–1955
Christian A. Herter (R) 1943–1953
John W. Heselton (R) 1945–1959
Pehr G. Holmes (R) 1931–1947
Joseph W. Martin, Jr. (R) 1925–1967
Donald W. Nicholson (R) 1947–1959
Edith Nourse Rogers (R) 1925–1960
Richard B. Wigglesworth (R) 1928–1959

Michigan

John D. Dingell (D) 1933–1955
Frank E. Hook (D) 1935–1947
John Lesinski (D) 1933–1950
John Lesinski, Jr. (D) 1951–1965
Thaddeus M. Machrowicz (D) 1951–1961
George D. O'Brien (D) 1937–1939;
    1941–1947; 1949–1955
Louis C. Rabaut (D) 1935–1947; 1949–1961
George G. Sadowski (D) 1933–1939;
    1943–1951
John B. Bennett (R) 1943–1945; 1947–1964
William W. Blackney (R) 1935–1937;
    1939–1953
Fred Bradley (R) 1939–1947
Howard A. Coffin (R) 1947–1949
Fred L. Crawford (R) 1935–1953
George A. Dondero (R) 1933–1957
Albert J. Engel (R) 1935–1951
Gerald R. Ford (R) 1949–1973
Clare E. Hoffman (R) 1935–1963
Bartel J. Jonkman (R) 1940–1949
George Meader (R) 1951–1965
Earl C. Michener (R) 1919–1933; 1935–1951
Charles E. Potter (R) 1947–1952
Paul W. Shafer (R) 1937–1954
Ruth Thompson (R) 1951–1957

Jesse P. Wolcott (R) 1931–1957
Roy O. Woodruff (R) 1913–1915; 1921–1953
Harold F. Youngblood (R) 1947–1949

Minnesota

John A. Blatnik (D) 1947–1975
William J. Gallagher (D) 1945–1946
Fred Marshall (D) 1949–1963
Eugene J. McCarthy (D) 1949–1959
Frank T. Starkev (D) 1945–1947
Roy W. Wier (D) 1949–1961
H. Carl Andresen (R) 1939–1963
August H. Andresen (R) 1925–1933; 1935–1958
Edward J. Devitt (R) 1947–1949
Harold C. Hagen (R) 1943–1955
Walter H. Judd (R) 1943–1963
Harold Knutson (R) 1917–1949
George MacKinnon (R) 1947–1949
Joseph P. O'Hara (R) 1941–1959
William A. Pittenger (R) 1929–1933;
    1935–1937; 1939–1947

Mississippi

Thomas G. Abernethy (D) 1943–1973
C. Jasper Bell (D) 1935–1949
William M. Colmer (D) 1933–1973
Dan R. McGehee (D) 1935–1947
John E. Rankin (D) 1921–1953
Frank E. Smith (D) 1951–1963
Jamie L. Whitten (D) 1941–1995
William M. Whittington (D) 1925–1951
John Bell Williams (D) 1947–1968
Arthur Winstead (D) 1943–1965

Missouri

Richard Bolling (D) 1949–1983
Clarence Cannon (D) 1923–1964
A. S. J. Carnahan (D) 1945–1947; 1949–1961
George H. Christopher (D) 1949–1951;
    1955–1959
John J. Cochran (D) 1926–1947
Leonard Irving (D) 1949–1953
Paul C. Jones (D) 1949–1969
Raymond W. Karst (D) 1949–1951
Frank M. Karsten (D) 1947–1969
Clare Magee (D) 1949–1953
Morgan M. Moulder (D) 1949–1963
Roger C. Slaughter (D) 1943–1947
John B. Sullivan (D) 1941–1943; 1945–1947;
    1949–1951

Phil J. Welch (D) 1949–1953
Orville Zimmerman (D) 1935–1948
O. K. Armstrong (R) 1951–1953
Samuel W. Arnold (R) 1943–1949
Claude I. Bakewell (R) 1947–1949; 1951–1953
Parke M. Banta (R) 1947–1949
Marion T. Bennett (R) 1943–1949
William C. Cole (R) 1943–1949; 1953–1955
Thomas B. Curtis (R) 1951–1969
Walter C. Ploeser (R) 1941–1949
Albert L. Reeves, Jr. (R) 1947–1949
Max Schwabe (R) 1943–1949
Dewey Short (R) 1929–1931; 1935–1957

Montana
Mike Mansfield (D) 1943–1953
James F. O'Connor (D) 1937–1945
Wesley H. D'Ewart (R) 1945–1955

Nebraska
Eugene D. O'Sullivan (D) 1949–1951
Howard H. Buffett (R) 1943–1949; 1951–1953
Carl T. Curtis (R) 1939–1954
Robert D. Harrison (R) 1951–1959
A. L. Miller (R) 1943–1959
Karl Stefan (R) 1935–1951

Nevada
Walter S. Baring (D) 1949–1953; 1957–1973
Berkeley L. Bunker (D) 1945–1947
Charles H. Russell (R) 1947–1949

New Hampshire
Sherman Adams (R) 1945–1947
Norris Cotton (R) 1947–1954
Chester E. Merrow (R) 1943–1963

New Jersey
Hugh J. Addonizio (D) 1949–1962
Edward J. Hart (D) 1935–1955
Charles R. Howell (D) 1949–1955
Mary T. Norton (D) 1925–1951
Peter W. Rodino, Jr. (D) 1949–1989
Alfred D. Sieminski (D) 1951–1959
James C. Auchincloss (R) 1943–1965
Gordon Canfield (R) 1941–1961
Clifford P. Case (R) 1945–1953
Charles A. Eaton (R) 1925–1953
T. Millet Hand (R) 1945–1956
Fred A. Hartley, Jr. (R) 1929–1949

Robert W. Kean (R) 1939–1959
Frank A. Mathews, Jr. (R) 1945–1949
Frank C. Osmer, Jr. (R) 1939–1943; 1951–1956
D. Lane Powers (R) 1943–1945
Frank L. Sundstrom (R) 1943–1949
J. Parnell Thomas (R) 1937–1950
William B. Widnall (R) 1950–1974
Charles A. Wolverton (R) 1927–1959

New Mexico
Clinton P. Anderson (D) 1941–1945
John J. Dempsey (D) 1935–1941; 1951–1958
Antonio M. Fernandez (D) 1943–1956
Georgia L. Lusk (D) 1947–1949
John E. Miles (D) 1949–1951

New York
Victor L. Anfuso (D) 1951–1953; 1955–1963
William B. Barry (D) 1935–1946
Sol Bloom (D) 1923–1949
Charles A. Buckley (D) 1935–1965
William T. Byrne (D) 1937–1952
Emanuel Celler (D) 1923–1973
L. Gary Clemente (D) 1949–1953
John C. Davies (D) 1949–1951
James J. Delaney (D) 1945–1947; 1949–1978
John Joseph Delaney (D) 1931–1948
Isidore Dollinger (D) 1949–1959
James G. Donovan (D) 1951–1957
Sidney A. Fine (D) 1951–1956
Chester C. Gorski (D) 1949–1951
Ernest Greenwood (D) 1951–1953
James Joseph Hefferman (D) 1941–1953
Louis B. Heller (D) 1949–1951; 1953–1954
Edna F. Kelly (D) 1949–1969
Eugene J. Keogh (D) 1937–1967
Arthur G. Klein (D) 1941–1945; 1946–1956
Walter A. Lynch (D) 1940–1951
Christopher C. McGrath (D) 1949–1953
Abraham J. Multer (D) 1947–1967
James J. Murphy (D) 1949–1953
Leo W. O'Brien (D) 1952–1967
Donald L. O'Toole (D) 1937–1953
Joseph Lawrence Pfeifer (D) 1935–1951
Adam G. Powell (D) 1945–1967; 1969–1971
Peter A. Quinn (D) 1945–1947
T. Vincent Quinn (D) 1949–1951
Benjamin J. Rabin (D) 1945–1947
Leo F. Rayfiel (D) 1945–1947
James A. Roe (D) 1945–1947

George F. Rogers (D) 1945–1947
John J. Rooney (D) 1944–1975
Franklin D. Roosevelt, Jr. (D) 1949–1955
Andrew L. Somers (D) 1925–1949
Anthony F. Tauriello (D) 1949–1951
James H. Torrens (D) 1944–1947
Walter G. Andrews (R) 1931–1949
Joseph Clark Baldwin (R) 1941–1947
Augustus W. Bennet (R) 1945–1947
Ellsworth B. Buck (R) 1944–1949
John C. Butler (R) 1941–1949; 1951–1953
W. Sterling Cole (R) 1935–1957
Frederic R. Coudert, Jr. (R) 1947–1959
Edward J. Elsaesser (R) 1945–1949
Hadwen C. Fuller (R) 1943–1949
Ralph A. Gamble (R) 1937–1957
Ralph W. Gwinn (R) 1945–1959
Edwin Arthur Hall (R) 1939–1953
Leonard W. Hall (R) 1939–1952
Clarence E. Hancock (R) 1927–1947
Jacob K. Javits (R) 1947–1954
Bernard W. Kearney (R) 1943–1959
Kenneth B. Keating (R) 1947–1959
Clarence E. Kilburn (R) 1940–1965
Henry J. Latham (R) 1945–1959
Jay LeFevre (R) 1943–1951
W. Kingsland Macy (R) 1947–1951
Gregory McMahon (R) 1947–1949
William E. Miller (R) 1951–1965
Robert Nodar, Jr. (R) 1947–1949
Harold C. Ostertag (R) 1951–1965
William L. Pfeiffer (R) 1949–1951
David M. Potts (R) 1947–1949
Edmund P. Radwan (R) 1951–1959
Daniel A. Reed (R) 1919–1959
R. Walter Riehiman (R) 1947–1965
Robert Tripp Ross (R) 1947–1949; 1952–1953
Edgar A. Sharp (R) 1945–1947
Katherine St. George (R) 1947–1965
John Taber (R) 1923–1963
Dean P. Taylor (R) 1943–1961
James W. Wadsworth, Jr. (R) 1933–1951
J. Ernest Wharton (R) 1951–1965
William R. Williams (R) 1951–1959
Leo Isacson (AL) 1948–1949
Vito Marcantonio (AL) 1939–1951

North Carolina

Graham A. Barden (D) 1935–1961
Herbert C. Bonner (D) 1940–1965
Alfred L. Bulwinkle (D) 1921–1929; 1931–1950

W. O. Burgin (D) 1939–1946
Frank Ertel Carlyle (D) 1949–1957
Richard Thurmond Chatham (D) 1949–1957
J. Bayard Clark (D) 1929–1949
Harold D. Cooley (D) 1934–1966
Charles B. Deane (D) 1947–1957
Robert L. Doughton (D) 1911–1953
Carl T. Durham (D) 1939–1961
Joe W. Ervin (D) 1945
Sam J. Ervin, Jr. (D) 1946
John H. Folger (D) 1945–1949
Hamilton C. Jones (D) 1947–1953
Woodrow W. Jones (D) 1950–1957
John H. Kerr (D) 1923–1953
Eliza Jane Pratt (D) 1946–1947
Monroe M. Redden (D) 1947–1953
Zebulon Weaver (D) 1919–1929; 1931–1947

North Dakota

Fred G. Aandahl (R) 1951–1953
Usher L. Burdick (R) 1935–1945
William Lemke (R) 1933–1950
Charles R. Robertson (R) 1941–1943;
    1945–1949

Ohio

Edward F. Breen (D) 1949–1951
Thomas H. Burke (D) 1949–1951
Henderson H. Carson (D) 1943–1945;
    1947–1949
Robert Grosser (D) 1913–1919; 1923–1955
Michael A. Feighan (D) 1943–1971
Edward J. Gardner (D) 1945–1947
Wayne L. Hays (D) 1949–1976
Walter B. Huber (D) 1945–1951
Michael J. Kirwan (D) 1937–1971
John McSweeney (D) 1949–1951
James G. Polk (D) 1931–1941; 1949–1959
Robert T. Secrest (D) 1949–1954; 1963–1966
William R. Thom (D) 1933–1939; 1941–1943;
    1945–1947
Earl T. Wagner (D) 1949–1951
Stephen M. Young (D) 1933–1937; 1941–1943;
    1949–1951
William H. Ayres (R) 1951–1971
George H. Bender (R) 1939–1949; 1951–1954
Jackson E. Betts (R) 1951–1973
Frances P. Bolton (R) 1940–1969
Frank T. Bow (R) 1951–1972
Walter E. Brehm (R) 1943–1953

Clarence J. Brown (R) 1939–1965
Raymond H. Burke (R) 1947–1949
Cliff Clevenger (R) 1939–1959
Charles H. Elston (R) 1939–1953
P. W. Griffiths (R) 1943–1949
William E. Hess (R) 1929–1937; 1939–1949;
    1951–1961
Thomas A. Jenkins (R) 1925–1959
Robert F. Jones (R) 1939–1947
Edward O. McCowen (R) 1943–1949
William M. McCulloch (R) 1947–1973
J. Harry McGregor (R) 1940–1958
Homer A. Ramey (R) 1943–1949
Paul F. Schenck (R) 1951–1965
Frederick C. Smith (R) 1939–1951
John M. Vorys (R) 1939–1959
Alvin F. Weichel (R) 1943–1955
Frazier Reams (Ind.) 1951–1955

Oklahoma

Carl Albert (D) 1947–1977
Lyle H. Boren (D) 1937–1947
Dixie Gilmer (D) 1949–1951
John Jarman (D) 1951–1975
Glen D. Johnson (D) 1947–1949
Jed Joseph Johnson (D) 1929–1947
A. S. Mike Monroney (D) 1939–1951
Preston E. Peden (D) 1947–1949
Tom Steed (D) 1949–1981
Paul Stewart (D) 1943–1947
William G. Stigler (D) 1944–1952
Victor Wickersham (D) 1941–1947;
    1949–1957; 1961–1965
George H. Wilson (D) 1949–1951
Page Belcher (R) 1941–1949
Ross Riziey (R) 1941–1949
George B. Schwabe (R) 1945–1949; 1951–1952

Oregon

Homer D. Angell (R) 1939–1955
Harris Ellsworth (R) 1943–1957
Walter A. Norblad (R) 1946–1964
Lowell Stockman (R) 1943–1953

Pennsylvania

William A. Barrett (D) 1945–1947; 1949–1976
Michael J. Bradley (D) 1937–1947
Frank Buchanan (D) 1946–1951
Vera Daerr Buchanan (D) 1951–1955
Anthony Cavalcante (D) 1949–1951

Earl Chudoff (D) 1949–1958
Robert L. Coffey, Jr. (D) 1949
Harry J. Davenport (D) 1949–1951
Herman Eberharter (D) 1937–1958
Daniel J. Flood (D) 1945–1947; 1949–1953
William T. Granahan (D) 1945–1947;
    1949–1956
William J. Green, Jr. 1945–1947; 1949–1963
Daniel K. Hoch (D) 1943–1947
Augustine B. Kelley (D) 1941–1957
James F. Lind (D) 1949–1953
Herbert J. McGlinchey (D) 1945–1947
Thomas E. Morgan (D) 1945–1977
John William Murphy (D) 1943–1946
Francis J. Myers (D) 1939–1945
Harry P. O'Neill (D) 1949–1953
George M. Rhodes (D) 1949–1969
John Edward Sheridan (D) 1939–1947
John B. Snyder (D) 1933–1946
Francis E. Walter (D) 1933–1963
Samuel A. Weiss (D) 1941–1946
D. Emmett Brumbaugh (R) 1943–1947
Alvin R. Bush (R) 1951–1959
Howard E. Campbell (R) 1945–1947
Joseph L. Carrigg (R) 1951–1959
E. Wallace Chadwick (R) 1947–1949
Robert J. Corbett (R) 1939–1941; 1945–1971
William J. Crow (R) 1947–1949
Paul B. Dague (R) 1947–1967
Harmar D. Denny, Jr. (R) 1951–1953
Ivor D. Fenton (R) 1939–1963
James G. Fulton (R) 1945–1971
James A. Gallagher (R) 1947–1949
Leon H. Gavin (R) 1943–1963
Charles L. Gerlach (R) 1939–1947
Wilson D. Gillette (R) 1941–1951
Louis E. Graham (R) 1939–1955
Chester H. Gross (R) 1943–1949
Carl Henry Hoffman (R) 1946–1947
Benjamin F. James (R) 1949–1959
Mitchell Jenkins (R) 1947–1949
Carroll D. Kearns (R) 1947–1963
Karl C. King (R) 1952–1957
J. Roland Kinzer (R) 1930–1947
John C. Kunkel (R) 1939–1951; 1961–1966
Franklin H. Lichtenwalter (R) 1947–1951
Franklin J. Maloney (R) 1947–1949
Samuel K. McConnell, Jr. (R) 1944–1957
John Ralph McDowell (R) 1939–1941;
    1947–1949
Robert N. McGarvey (R) 1947–1949

Frederick A. Muhlenberg (R) 1947–1949
Walter M. Mumma (R) 1951–1961
Robert F. Rich (R) 1930–1943; 1945–1951
Robert Lewis Rodgers (R) 1939–1947
George W. Sarbacher, Jr. (R) 1947–1949
John P. Saylor (R) 1949–1973
James Paul Scolick (R) 1946–1949
Hardie Scott (R) 1947–1953
Hugh D. Scott, Jr. (R) 1941–1945; 1947–1949
Richard M. Simpson (R) 1937–1960
Edward L. Sittler, Jr. (R) 1951–1953
Harve Tibbott (R) 1939–1949
James E. Van Zandt (R) 1939–1943; 1947–1963
Albert C. Vaughn (R) 1951
James Wolfenden (R) 1928–1947

Rhode Island

John E. Fogarty (D) 1941–1967
Aime J. Forand (D) 1941–1961

South Carolina

Joseph R. Bryson (D) 1939–1953
W. J. Bryan Dorn (D) 1947–1949; 1951–1975
Butler B. Hare (D) 1925–1933; 1939–1947
James B. Hare (D) 1949–1951
John L. McMillan (D) 1939–1973
James P. Richards (D) 1933–1957
John J. Riley (D) 1945–1949; 1951–1962
L. Mendel Rivers (D) 1941–1970
Hugo S. Sims, Jr. (D) 1949–1951

South Dakota

E. Y. Berry (R) 1951–1971
Francis H. Case (R) 1937–1951
Harold O. Lovre (R) 1949–1957
Karl E. Mundt (R) 1939–1948

Tennessee

Jere Cooper (D) 1929–1957
Wirt Courtney (D) 1939–1949
Clifford Davis (D) 1940–1965
Harold H. Earthman (D) 1945–1947
Joe L. Evins (D) 1947–
James B. Frazier, Jr. (D) 1949–1963
Albert Gore (D) 1939–1944; 1945–1953
Estes Kefauver (D) 1939–1949
Tom Murray (D) 1943–1966
J. Percy Priest (D) 1941–1956
Pat Sutton (D) 1949–1955
Howard H. Baker (R) 1951–1964

John Jennings, Jr. (R) 1939–1951
Dayton E. Phillips (R) 1947–1951
B. Carroll Reece (R) 1921–1931; 1935–1947;
    1951–1961

Texas

Lindley Beckworth (D) 1939–1953; 1957–1967
Lloyd M. Bentsen, Jr. (D) 1948–1955
Omar Burleson (D) 1947–1978
J. M. Combs (D) 1945–1953
Martin Dies, Jr. (D) 1931–1945; 1953–1959
John Dowdy (D) 1952–1973
O. C. Fisher (D) 1943–1975
Ed Gossett (D) 1939–1951
Frank lkard (D) 1951–1961
Luther A. Johnson (D) 1923–1946
Lyndon B. Johnson (D) 1937–1949
Paul J. Kilday (D) 1939–1961
Fritz G. Lanham (D) 1919–1947
Wingate H. Lucas (D) 1947–1955
John E. Lyle, Jr. (D) 1945–1955
George H. Mahon (D) 1935–1979
Joseph J. Mansfield (D) 1917–1947
Wright Patman (D) 1929–1976
Tom Pickett (D) 1945–1952
W. R. Poage (D) 1937–1978
Sam Rayburn (D) 1913–1961
Kenneth Regan (D) 1947–1955
Walter Rogers (D) 1951–1967
Sam M. Russell (D) 1941–1947
Olin E. Teague (D) 1946–1978
Albert Thomas (D) 1937–1966
R. Ewing Thomason (D) 1931–1947
Clark W. Thompson (D) 1947–1966
Homer Thornberry (D) 1949–1963
Hatton W. Sumners (D) 1913–1947
Milton H. West (D) 1933–1948
J. Franklin Wilson (D) 1947–1955
Eugene Worley (D) 1941–1950
Ben Hugh Guill (R) 1950–1951

Utah

Reva Beck Bosone (D) 1949–1953
Walter K. Granger (D) 1941–1953
Abe Murdoch (D) 1933–1941
J. W. Robinson (D) 1933–1947
William A. Dawson (R) 1947–1949: 1953–1959

Vermont

Charles A. Plumley (R) 1934–1951
Winston L. Prouty (R) 1951–1959

Virginia

Watkins M. Abbitt (D) 1948–1973
J. Lindsay Almond, Jr. (D) 1946–1948
Schyler Otis Bland (D) 1918–1950
Thomas G. Burch (D) 1931–1946
Clarence G. Burton (D) 1948–1953
Ralph H. Daughton (D) 1944–1947
Patrick H. Drewry (D) 1920–1947
John W. Flannagan, Jr. (D) 1931–1949
Tom B. Fugate (D) 1949–1953
J. Vaughan Gary (D) 1945–1965
Porter Hardy, Jr. (D) 1947–1969
Burr P. Harrison (D) 1946–1963
A. Willis Robertson (D) 1933–1946
Edward J. Robeson, Jr. (D) 1950–1959
David E. Satterfield, Jr. (D) 1937–1945
Howard W. Smith (D) 1931–1967
Thomas B. Stanley (D) 1946–1953
Clifton A. Woodrum (R) 1923–1945

Washington

John M. Coffee (D) 1937–1947
Hugh De Lacy (D) 1945–1947
Henry M. Jackson (D) 1941–1953
Warren G. Magnuson (D) 1937–1944
Hugh B. Mitchell (D) 1949–1953
Charles R. Savage (D) 1945–1947
Hal Holmes (R) 1943–1959
Walt Horan (R) 1943–1965
Homer R. Jones (R) 1947–1949
Russell V. Mack (R) 1947–1960
Fred Norman (R) 1943–1945; 1947
Thor C. Tollefson (R) 1947–1965

West Virginia

Cleveland M. Bailey (D) 1945–1947; 1949–1963
M. G. Burnside (D) 1949–1953; 1955–1957

E. H. Hedrick (D) 1945–1953
Elizabeth Kee (D) 1951–1965
John Kee (D) 1933–1951
Matthew M. Neely (D) 1913–1921; 1945–1947
Robert L. Ramsay (D) 1933–1939; 1941–1943; 1949–1953
Jennings Randolph (D) 1933–1947
Harley O. Staggers (D) 1949–1981
Hubert S. Ellis (R) 1943–1949
Francis J. Love (R) 1947–1949
Edward G. Rohrbough (R) 1943–1945; 1947–1949
Mervin C. Snyder (R) 1947–1949

Wisconsin

Andrew J. Biemiller (D) 1945–1947; 1949–1951
Thad F. Wasielewski (D) 1941–1947
Clement J. Zablocki (D) 1949–1983
John C. Brophy (R) 1947–1949
John W. Byrnes (R) 1945–1973
Glenn R. Davis (R) 1947–1957
Robert K. Henry (R) 1945–1946
Merlin Hull (R) 1929–1931; (P.) 1935–1947; (R) 1947–1953
Frank B. Keefe (R) 1938–1951
Charles J. Kersten (R) 1947–1949; 1951–1955
Reid F. Murray (R) 1939–1952
Alvin E. O'Konski (R) 1943–1973
Lawrence H. Smith (R) 1941–1958
William Henry Stevenson (R) 1941–1949
William K. Van Pelt (R) 1951–1965
Gardner R. Withrow (R) 1931–1939; 1949–1961

Wyoming

Frank A. Barrett (R) 1943–1950
William H. Harrison (R) 1951–1955; 1961–1965

UNITED STATES SENATE: 1945–1952

Alabama

John H. Bankhead II (D) 1931–1946
Lister Hill (D) 1938–1969
John J. Sparkman (D) 1946–1979
George R. Swift (D) 1946

Alaska

E. L. Bartlett (D) Delegate to Congress 1945–1950

Arizona

Carl T. Hayden (D) 1927–1969

Ernest W. McFarland (D) 1941–1953
Barry M. Goldwater (R) 1953–1965

Arkansas

J. William Fulbright (D) 1945–1975
John L. McClellan (D) 1943–1977

California

Sheridan Downey (D) 1939–1950
William F. Knowland (R) 1945–1959
Thomas H. Kuchel (R) 1953–1969
Richard M. Nixon (R) 1950–1953

Colorado

Edwin C. Johnson (D) 1937–1955
Eugene D. Millikin (R) 1941–1957

Connecticut

William Benton (D) 1949–1953
Brien McMahon (D) 1945–1952
Raymond E. Baldwin (R) 1946–1949
Thomas C. Hart (R) 1945–1946
William A. Purtell (R) 1952–1959

Delaware

J. Allen Frear, Jr. (D) 1949–1961
James M. Tunnell (D) 1941–1947
C. Douglass Buck (R) 1943–1949
John J. Williams (R) 1947–1971

Florida

Charles O. Andrews (D) 1937–1946
Spessard L. Holland (D) 1946–1971
Claude D. Pepper (D) 1936–1951

Georgia

Walter F. George (D) 1922–1957
Richard B. Russell, Jr. (D) 1933–1971

Hawaii

Joseph R. Farrington (R) Delegate to Congress
1943–1954

Idaho

Charles C. Gossett (D) 1945–1947
Bert H. Miller (D) 1949
Glen H. Taylor (D) 1945–1951
Henry C. Dworshak (R) 1949–1963
John Thomas (R) 1928–1933; 1940–1945
Herman Welker (R) 1951–1957

Illinois

Paul H. Douglas (D) 1949–1967
Scott W. Lucas (D) 1939–1951
C. Wayland Brooks (R) 1940–1949
Everett McKinley Dirksen (R) 1951–1969

Indiana

Homer E. Capehart (R) 1945–1963
William E. Jenner (R) 1944–1945; 1947–1959
Raymond E. Willis (R) 1941–1947

Iowa

Guy M. Gillette (D) 1936–1945; 1949–1955
Bourke B. Hickenlooper (R) 1945–1969
George A. Wilson (R) 1943–1949

Kansas

Frank Carlson (R) 1950–1969
Harry Darby (R) 1949–1950
George McGill (R) 1930–1949
Clyde M. Reed (R) 1939–1949
Andrew F. Schoeppel (R) 1949–1962

Kentucky

Alben W. Barkley (D) 1927–1949; 1955–1956
Albert B. Chandler (D) 1939–1945
Virgil M. Chapman (D) 1949–1951
Earle C. Clements (D) 1950–1957
Thomas R. Underwood (D) 1951–1952
Garrett L. Withers (D) 1949–1950
John Sherman Cooper (R) 1946–1949,
    1952–1955, 1956–1973
William A. Stanfill (R) 1945–1946

Louisiana

Allen J. Ellender (D) 1937–1973
William C. Feazel (D) 1948
Russell B. Long (D) 1948–1987
John H. Overton (D) 1933–1948

Maine

Owen Brewster (R) 1941–1952
Frederick G. Payne (R) 1952–1959
Margaret Chase Smith (R) 1949–1973
Wallace Humphrey White, Jr. (R) 1931–1949

Maryland

Herbert R. O'Conor (D) 1947–1953
George L. Radcliffe (D) 1935–1947

Millard E. Tydings (D) 1927–1951
John Marshall Butler (R) 1951–1963

Massachusetts
David L. Walsh (D) 1919–1925; 1926–1947
Henry Cabot Lodge, Jr. (R) 1937–1944;
   1947–1953
Leverett Saltonstall (R) 1945–1967

Michigan
Blair Moody (D) 1951–1952
Homer Ferguson (R) 1943–1955
Charles E. Potter (R) 1952–1959
Arthur H. Vandenberg (R) 1928–1951

Minnesota
Hubert H. Humphrey (D) 1949–1964;
   1971–1978
Joseph H. Ball (R) 1940–1942; 1943–1949
Henrik Shipstead (R) 1923–1947
Edward J. Thye (R) 1947–1959

Mississippi
Theodore G. Bilbo (D) 1935–1947
James O. Eastland (D) 1943–1979
John C. Stennis (D) 1947–1989

Missouri
Frank P. Briggs (D) 1945–1947
Thomas C. Hennings, Jr. (D) 1951–1960
Forrest C. Donnell (R) 1945–1951
James P. Kem (R) 1947–1953

Montana
James E. Murray (D) 1934–1961
Burton K. Wheeler (D) 1923–1947
Zales N. Ecton (R) 1947–1953

Nebraska
Hugh A. Butler (R) 1941–1954
Dwight P. Griswold (R) 1952–1954
Frederick A. Seaton (R) 1951–1952
Kenneth S. Wherry (R) 1943–1951

Nevada
E. P. Carville (D) 1945–1947
Pat McCarran (D) 1933–1954
George W. Malone (R) 1947–1959

New Hampshire
Styles Bridges (R) 1937–1962
Charles W. Tobey (R) 1939–1953

New Jersey
Albert W. Hawkes (R) 1943–1949
Robert C. Hendrickson (R) 1949–1955
H. Alexander Smith (R) 1944–1959

New Mexico
Clinton P. Anderson (D) 1949–1973
Dennis Chavez (D) 1935–1963
Carl A. Hatch (D) 1933–1949

New York
Herbert H. Lehman (D) 1949–1957
James M. Mead (D) 1939–1947
Robert F. Wagner (D) 1927–1949
John Foster Dulles (R) 1949
Irving M. Ives (R) 1947–1959

North Carolina
Josiah W. Bailey (D) 1931–1946
J. Melville Broughton (D) 1948–1949
Frank P. Graham (D) 1949–1950
Clyde R. Hoey (D) 1945–1954
Willis Smith (D) 1950–1953
William B. Umstead (D) 1946–1948

North Dakota
John Moses (D) 1945
William Langer (R) 1941–1959
Milton R. Young (R) 1945–1981

Ohio
John W. Bricker (R) 1947–1959
James W. Huffman (D) 1945–1946
Kingsley A. Taft (R) 1946–1947
Robert A. Taft (R) 1939–1953

Oklahoma
Robert S. Kerr (D) 1949–1963
A. S. Mike Monroney (D) 1951–1969
Elmer Thomas (D) 1927–1951
E. H. Moore (R) 1943–1949

Oregon
Guy Cordon (R) 1944–1955
Wayne Morse (R) 1945–1952; (Ind.)
   1952–1955; (D) 1955–1969

Pennsylvania

Joseph F. Guffey (D) 1935–1947
Francis J. Myers (D) 1945–1951
James H. Duff (R) 1951–1957
Edward Martin (R) 1947–1959

Rhode Island

Peter G. Gerry (D) 1917–1929; 1935–1947
Theodore Francis Green (D) 1937–1961
Edward Lawrence Leahy (D) 1949–1950
J. Howard McGrath (D) 1947–1949
John O. Pastore (D) 1950–1976

South Carolina

Olin D. Johnston (D) 1945–1965
Burnet R. Maybank (D) 1941–1954

South Dakota

Harlan J. Bushfield (R) 1943–1948
Vera C. Bushfield (R) 1948
Francis H. Case (R) 1951–1962
Chan Gurney (R) 1939–1951
Karl E. Mundt (R) 1948–1973

Tennessee

Estes Kefauver (D) 1949–1964
Kenneth D. McKellar (D) 1917–1953
A. Tom Stewart (D) 1939–1949

Virginia

Thomas G. Burch (D) 1946
Harry Flood Byrd (D) 1933–1965
Carter Glass (D) 1920–1946
A. Willis Robertson (D) 1946–1967

Washington

Warren G. Magnuson (D) 1944–1981
Hugh B. Mitchell (D) 1949–1953

Mon C. Wallgren (D) 1940–1945
Harry P. Cain (R) 1946–1953

Texas

Tom T. Connally (D) 1929–1953
Lyndon B. Johnson (D) 1949–1961
W. Lee O'Daniel (D) 1941–1949

Utah

Abe Murdock (D) 1941–1947
Elbert D. Thomas (D) 1933–1951
Wallace F. Bennett (R) 1951–1974
Arthur V. Watkins (R) 1947–1959

West Virginia

Harley Kilgore (D) 1941–1956
Matthew M. Neely (D) 1923–1929; 1931–1941;
    1949–1958
Chapman Revercomb (R) 1943–1949;
    1956–1959

Wisconsin

Robert M. La Follette, Jr. (R-P) 1925–1947
Joseph R. McCarthy (R) 1947–1957
Alexander Wiley (R) 1939–1963

Vermont

George D. Aiken (R) 1941–1975
Warren R. Austin (R) 1931–1946
Ralph E. Flanders (R) 1946–1959

Wyoming

Lester C. Hunt (D) 1949–1954
Joseph C. O'Mahoney (D) 1934–1953;
    1954–1961
Edward V. Robertson (R) 1943–1949

GOVERNORS

Alabama

Chauncey M. Sparks (D) 1943–1947
James Elisha Folsom (D) 1947–1951
Gordon Persons (D) 1951–1955

Arizona

Sidney P. Osborn (D) 1940–1948
Dan E. Garvey (D) 1948–1950
J. Howard Pyle (R) 1950–1954

Arkansas
Homer M. Adkins (D) 1941–1945
Benjamin T. Laney (D) 1945–1949
Sidney S. McMath (D) 1949–1953

California
Earl Warren (R) 1943–1953

Colorado
John C. Vivian (R) 1943–1947
William Lee Knous (D) 1947–1950
Walter Warren Johnson (D) 1950–1951
Dan Thornton (R) 1951–1955

Connecticut
Raymond Earl Baldwin (R) 1943–1946
Charles Wilbert Snow (D) 1946–1947
James Lukens McConaughy (R) 1947–1948
James Coughlin Shannon (R) 1948–1949
Chester Bowles (D) 1949–1951
John Davis Lodge (R) 1951–1955

Delaware
Walter W. Bacon (R) 1941–1949
Elbert N. Carvel (D) 1949–1953

Florida
Spessard L. Holland (D) 1941–1945
Millard F. Caldwell (D) 1945–1949
Fuller Warren (D) 1949–1953

Georgia
Ellis G. Arnall (D) 1943–1947
Melvin E. Thompson (D) 1947–1948
Herman E. Talmadge (D) 1948–1955

Idaho
C. A. Bottolfsen (R) 1943–1945
Charles C. Gossett (D) 1945
Arnold William (D) 1945–1947
Charles A. Robins (R) 1947–1951
Leonard B. Jordan (R) 1951–1955

Illinois
Dwight H. Green (R) 1941–1949
Adlai E. Stevenson (D) 1949–1953

Indiana
Henry F. Schricker (D) 1941–1945; 1949–1953
Ralph F. Gates (R) 1945–1949

Iowa
Bourke B. Hickenlooper (R) 1943–1945
Robert D. Blue (R) 1945–1949
William S. Beardsley (R) 1949–1954

Kansas
Andrew F. Schoeppel (R) 1943–1947
Frank Carlson (R) 1947–1950
Frank L. Hagaman (R) 1950–1951
Edward F. Am (R) 1951–1955

Kentucky
Simeon S. Willis (R) 1943–1947
Earle C. Clements (D) 1947–1950
Lawrence W. Wetherby (D) 1950–1955

Louisiana
Jimmie H. Davis (D) 1944–1948
Earl Kemp Long (D) 1948–1952
Robert F. Kennon (D) 1952–1956

Maine
Sumner Sewall (R) 1941–1945
Horace A. Hildreth (R) 1945–1949
Frederick G. Payne (R) 1949–1952
Burton M. Cross (R) 1952–1955

Maryland
Herbert R. O'Conor (D) 1939–1947
William Preston Lane, Jr. (D) 1947–1951
Theodore R. McKeldin (R) 1951–1959

Massachusetts
Leverett Saltonstall (R) 1939–1945
Maurice J. Tobin (D) 1945–1947
Robert F. Bradford (R) 1947–1949
Paul A. Dever (D) 1949–1953

Michigan
Harry F. Kelly (R) 1943–1947
Kirn Sigler (R) 1947–1949
G. Mennen Williams (D) 1949–1961

Minnesota
Edward J. Thye (R) 1943–1947
Luther W. Youngdahl (R) 1947–1951
C. Elmer Anderson (R) 1951–1955

Mississippi
Thomas L. Bailey (D) 1944–1946
Fielding L. Wright (D) 1946–1952
Hugh L. White (D) 1952–1956

Missouri

Forrest C. Donnell (R) 1941–1945
Phil M. Donnelly (D) 1945–1949
Forrest Smith (D) 1949–1953

Montana

Sam C. Ford (R) 1941–1949
John W. Bonner (D) 1949–1953

Nebraska

Dwight P. Griswold (R) 1941–1947
Val Peterson (R) 1947–1953

Nevada

Edward P. Carville (D) 1939–1946
Vail M. Pittman (D) 1946–1951
Charles H. Russell (R) 1951–1959

New Hampshire

Robert O. Blood (R) 1941–1945
Charles M. Dale (R) 1945–1949
Sherman Adams (R) 1949–1953

New Jersey

Charles Edison (D) 1941–1944
Walter E. Edge (R) 1944–1947
Alfred E. Driscoll (R) 1947–1950;
     1950–1954

New Mexico

John J. Dempsey (D) 1943–1945; 1945–1947
Thomas J. Mabry (D) 1947–1949; 1949–1951
Edwin L. Mechem (R) 1951–1953; 1953–1955

New York

Thomas E. Dewey (R) 1943–1955

North Carolina

Melville Broughton (D) 1941–1945
R. Gregg Cherry (D) 1945–1949
William Kerr Scott (D) 1949–1953

North Dakota

John Moses (D) 1939–1945
Fred G. Aandahl (R) 1945–1951
C. Norman Brunsdale (R) 1951–1957

Ohio

Frank J. Lausche (D) 1945–1947
Thomas J. Herbert (R) 1947–1949
Frank J. Lausche (D) 1949–1957

Oklahoma

Robert S. Kerr (D) 1943–1947
Roy J. Turner (D) 1947–1951
Johnston Murray (D) 1951–1955

Oregon

Earl Snell (R) 1943–1947
John H. Hall (R) 1947–1949
Douglas McKay (R) 1949–1951; 1951–1952
Paul L. Patterson (R) 1952–1956

Pennsylvania

Edward Martin (D) 1943–1947
James H. Duff (R) 1947–1951
John S. Fine (R) 1951–1955

Rhode Island

John O. Pastore (D) 1945–1950
John S. McKiernan (D) 1950–1951
Dennis J. Roberts (D) 1951–1953

South Carolina

Olin Dewitt Talmadge Johnston (D)
     1943–1945
Ransome Judson Williams (D) 1945–1947
J. Strom Thurmond (D) 1947–1951
James F. Byrnes (D) 1951–1955

South Dakota

M. Q. Sharpe (R) 1943–1947
George T. Mickelson (R) 1947–1951
Sigurd Anderson (R) 1951–1955

Tennessee

Jim Nance McCord (D) 1945–1949
Gordon Browning (D) 1949–1953

Texas

Coke R. Stevenson (D) 1941–1947
Beauford H. Jester (D) 1947–1949
Allan Shivers (D) 1949–1957

Utah

Herbert B. Maw (D) 1941–1949
J. Bracken Lee (R) 1949–1957

Vermont

William H. Willis (R) 1941–1945
Mortimer R. Proctor (R) 1945–1947
Ernest W. Gibson, Jr. (R) 1947–1950
Harold J. Arthur (R) 1950–1951
Lee E. Emerson (R) 1951–1955

Virginia

Colgate W. Darden, Jr. (D) 1942–1946
William Munford Tuck (D) 1946–1950
John Steward Battle (D) 1950–1954

Washington

Arthur B. Langlie (R) 1941–1945
Mon Wallgren (D) 1945–1949
Arthur B. Langlie (R) 1949–1957

West Virginia

Matthew Mansfield Neely (D) 1941–1945
Clarence W. Meadows (D) 1945–1949
Okey L. Patteson (D) 1949–1953

Wisconsin

Walter S. Goodland (R) 1943–1947
Oscar A. Rennebohm (R) 1947–1951
Walter J. Kohler, Jr. (R) 1951–1957

Wyoming

Lester C. Hunt (D) 1943–1949
Arthur G. Crane (R) 1949–1951
Frank A. Barrett (R) 1951–1953

SELECTED PRIMARY DOCUMENTS

1. Potsdam Declaration
July 26, 1945

British prime minister Winston Churchill, Soviet dictator Joseph Stalin, and U.S. president Harry S Truman met at Potsdam, Germany, after the end of the war in Europe. The British Labour Party triumphed over the Tories in a general election, and the new prime minister, Clement Atlee replaced Churchill at the conference. Atlee and Truman issued the following message laying out the surrender terms for the Japanese. It was also issued in the name of the president of the Republic of China, Chiang Kai-shek (Jiang Jieshi).

(1) We, the President of the United States, the President of the National Government of the Republic of China, and the Prime Minister of Great Britain, representing the hundreds of millions of our countrymen, have conferred and agree that Japan shall be given an opportunity to end this war.

(2) The prodigious land, sea and air forces of the United States, the British Empire and of China, many times reinforced by their armies and air fleets from the west, are poised to strike the final blows upon Japan. This military power is sustained and inspired by the determination of all the Allied Nations to prosecute the war against Japan until she ceases to resist.

(3) The result of the futile and senseless German resistance to the might of the aroused free peoples of the world stands forth in awful clarity as an example to the people of Japan. The might that now converges on Japan is immeasurably greater than that which, when applied to the resisting Nazis, necessarily laid waste to the lands, the industry and the method of life of the whole German people. The full application of our military power, backed by our resolve, will mean the inevitable and complete destruction of the Japanese armed forces and just as inevitably the utter devastation of the Japanese homeland.

(4) The time has come for Japan to decide whether she will continue to be controlled by those self-willed militaristic advisers whose unintelligent calculations have brought the Empire of Japan to the threshold of annihilation, or whether she will follow the path of reason.

(5) Following are our terms. We will not deviate from them. There are no alternatives. We shall brook no delay.

(6) There must be eliminated for all time the authority and influence of those who have deceived and misled the people of Japan into embarking on world conquest, for we insist that a new order of peace, security and justice will be impossible until irresponsible militarism is driven from the world.

(7) Until such a new order is established and until there is convincing proof that Japan's warmaking power is destroyed, points in Japanese territory to be designated by the Allies shall be occupied to secure the achievement of the basic objectives we are here setting forth.

(8) The terms of the Cairo Declaration shall be carried out and Japanese sovereignty shall be limited to the islands of Honshu, Hokkaido, Kyushu, Shikoku and such minor islands as we determine.

(9) The Japanese military forces, after being completely disarmed, shall be permitted to return to their homes with the opportunity to lead peaceful and productive lives.

(10) We do not intend that the Japanese shall be enslaved as a race or destroyed as a nation, but stern justice shall be meted out to all war criminals, including those who have visited cruelties upon our prisoners. The Japanese Government shall remove all obstacles to the revival and strengthening of democratic tendencies among the Japanese people. Freedom of speech, of religion, and of thought, as well as respect for the fundamental human rights shall be established.

(11) Japan shall be permitted to maintain such industries as will sustain her economy and permit the exaction of just reparations in kind, but not those which would enable her to re-arm for war. To this end, access to, as distinguished from control of, raw materials shall be permitted. Eventual Japanese, participation in world trade relations shall be permitted.

(12) The occupying forces of the Allies shall be withdrawn from Japan as soon as these objectives have been accomplished and there has been established in accordance with the freely expressed will of the Japanese people a peacefully inclined and responsible government.

(13) We call upon the government of Japan to proclaim now the unconditional surrender of all Japanese armed forces, and to provide proper and adequate assurances of their good faith in such action. The alternative for Japan is prompt and utter destruction.

UCLA Asia Institute, East Asian Studies Documents. Available online. URL: http://www.isop.ucla.edu/eas/documents/potsdam.htm. Accessed April 2005.

2. First Address to the Joint Session of Congress
April 16, 1945

"The Public Papers of the Presidents." The American Presidency Project at UC Santa Barbara. Available online. URL: http://www.presidency.ucsb.edu. Downloaded October 27, 2004.

Mr. Speaker, Mr. President, Members of the Congress:

It is with a heavy heart that I stand before you, my friends and colleagues, in the Congress of the United States.

Only yesterday, we laid to rest the mortal remains of our beloved President, Franklin Delano Roosevelt. At a time like this, words are inadequate. The most eloquent tribute would be a reverent silence.

Yet, in this decisive hour, when world events are moving so rapidly, our silence might be misunderstood and might give comfort to our enemies.

In His infinite wisdom, Almighty God has seen fit to take from us a great man who loved, and was beloved by, all humanity.

No man could possibly fill the tremendous void left by the passing of that noble soul. No words can ease the aching hearts of untold millions of every race, creed and color. The world knows it has lost a heroic champion of justice and freedom.

Tragic fate has thrust upon us grave responsibilities. We must carry on. Our departed leader never looked backward. He looked forward and moved forward. That is what he would want us to do. That is what America will do.

So much blood has already been shed for the ideals which we cherish, and for which Franklin Delano Roosevelt lived and died, that we dare not permit even a momentary pause in the hard fight for victory.

Today, the entire world is looking to America for enlightened leadership to peace and progress. Such a leadership requires vision, courage and tolerance. It can be provided only by a united nation deeply devoted to the highest ideals.

With great humility I call upon all Americans to help me keep our nation united in defense of those ideals which have been so eloquently proclaimed by Franklin Roosevelt.

I want in turn to assure my fellow Americans and all of those who love peace and liberty throughout the world that I will support and defend those ideals with all my strength and all my heart. That is my duty and I shall not shirk it.

So that there can be no possible misunderstanding, both Germany and Japan can be certain, beyond any shadow of a doubt, that America will continue the fight for freedom until no vestige of resistance remains!

We are deeply conscious of the fact that much hard fighting is still ahead of us. Having to pay such a heavy price to make complete victory certain, America will never become a party to any plan for partial victory!

To settle for merely another temporary respite would surely jeopardize the future security of all the world.

Our demand has been, and it remains—Unconditional Surrender!

We will not traffic with the breakers of the peace on the terms of the peace.

The responsibility for making of the peace—and it is a very grave responsibility—must rest with the defenders of the peace. We are not unconscious of the dictates of humanity. We do not wish to see unnecessary or unjustified suffering. But the laws of God and of man have been violated and the guilty must not go unpunished. Nothing shall shake our determination to punish the war criminals even though we must pursue them to the ends of the earth.

Lasting peace can never be secured if we permit our dangerous opponents to plot future wars with impunity at any mountain retreat—however distant.

In this shrinking world, it is futile to seek safety behind geographical barriers. Real security will be found only in law and in justice.

Here in America, we have labored long and hard to achieve a social order worthy of our great heritage. In our time, tremendous progress has been made toward a really democratic way of life. Let me assure the forward-looking people of America that there will be no relaxation in our efforts to improve the lot of the common people.

In the difficult days ahead, unquestionably we shall face problems of staggering proportions. However, with the faith of our fathers in our hearts, we do not fear the future.

On the battlefields, we have frequently faced overwhelming odds—and won! At home, Americans will not be less resolute!

We shall never cease our struggle to preserve and maintain our American way of life.

At this moment, America, along with her brave Allies, is paying again a heavy price for the defense of our freedom. With characteristic energy, we are assisting in the liberation of entire nations. Gradually, the shackles of slavery are being broken by the forces of freedom.

All of us are praying for a speedy victory. Every day peace is delayed costs a terrible toll.

The armies of liberation today are bringing to an end Hitler's ghastly threat to dominate the world. Tokyo rocks under the weight of our bombs.

The grand strategy of the United Nations' war has been determined—due in no small measure to the vision of our departed Commander in Chief. We are now carrying out our part of that strategy under the able direction of Admiral Leahy, General Marshall, Admiral King, General Arnold, General Eisenhower, Admiral Nimitz and General MacArthur.

I want the entire world to know that this direction must and will remain—unchanged and unhampered!

Our debt to the heroic men and valiant women in the service of our country can never be repaid. They have earned our undying gratitude. America will never forget their sacrifices. Because of these sacrifices, the dawn of justice and freedom throughout the world slowly casts its gleam across the horizon.

Our forefathers came to our rugged shores in search of religious tolerance, political freedom and economic opportunity. For those fundamental rights, they risked their lives. We well know today that such rights can be preserved only by constant vigilance, the eternal price of liberty!

Within an hour after I took the oath of office, I announced that the San Francisco Conference would proceed. We will face the problems of peace with the same courage that we have faced and mastered the problems of war.

In the memory of those who have made the supreme sacrifice—in the memory of our fallen President—we shall not fail!

It is not enough to yearn for peace. We must work, and if necessary, fight for it. The task of creating a sound international organization is complicated and difficult. Yet, without such organization, the rights of man on earth cannot be protected. Machinery for the just settlement of international differences must be found. Without such machinery, the entire world will have to remain an armed camp. The world will be doomed to deadly conflict, devoid of hope for real peace.

Fortunately, people have retained hope for a durable peace. Thoughtful people have always had faith that ultimately justice must triumph. Past experience surely indicates that, without justice, an enduring peace becomes impossible.

In bitter despair, some people have come to believe that wars are inevitable. With tragic fatalism, they insist that wars have always been, of necessity, and of necessity wars always will be. To such defeatism, men and women of good will must not and cannot yield. The outlook for humanity is not so hopeless.

During the dark hours of this horrible war, entire nations were kept going by something intangible—hope! When warned that abject submission offered the only salvation against overwhelming power, hope showed the way to victory.

Hope has become the secret weapon of the forces of liberation!

Aggressors could not dominate the human mind. As long as hope remains, the spirit of man will never be crushed.

But hope alone was not and is not sufficient to avert war. We must not only have hope but we must have faith enough to work with other peace-loving nations to maintain the peace. Hope was not enough to beat back the aggressors as long as the peace-loving nations were unwilling to come to each other's defense. The aggressors were beaten back only when the peace-loving nations united to defend themselves.

If wars in the future are to be prevented the nations must be united in their determination to keep the peace under law.

Nothing is more essential to the future peace of the world than continued cooperation of the nations which had to muster the force necessary to defeat the conspiracy of the Axis powers to dominate the world.

While these great states have a special responsibility to enforce the peace, their responsibility is based upon the obligations resting upon all states, large and small, not to use force in international relations except in the defense of law. The responsibility of the great states is to serve and not to dominate the world.

To build a foundation of enduring peace we must not only work in harmony with our friends abroad, but we must have the united support of our own people.

Even the most experienced pilot cannot bring a ship safely into harbor, unless he has the full cooperation of the crew. For the benefit of all, every individual must do his duty.

I appeal to every American, regardless of party, race, creed, or color, to support our efforts to build a strong and lasting United Nations Organization.

You, the Members of the Congress, surely know how I feel. Only with your help can I hope to complete one of the greatest tasks ever assigned to a public servant. With Divine guidance, and your help, we will find the new passage to a far better world, a kindly and friendly world, with just and lasting peace.

With confidence, I am depending upon all of you.

To destroy greedy tyrants with dreams of world domination, we cannot continue in successive generations to sacrifice our finest youth.

In the name of human decency and civilization, a more rational method of deciding national differences must and will be found!

America must assist suffering humanity back along the path of peaceful progress. This will require time and tolerance. We shall need also an abiding faith in the people, the kind of faith and courage which Franklin Delano Roosevelt always had!

Today, America has become one of the most powerful forces for good on earth. We must keep it so. We have achieved a world leadership which does not depend solely upon our military and naval might.

We have learned to fight with other nations in common defense of our freedom. We must now learn to live with other nations for our mutual good. We must learn to trade more with other nations so that there may be for our mutual advantage—increased production, increased employment and better standards of living throughout the world.

May we Americans all live up to our glorious heritage.

In that way, America may well lead the world to peace and prosperity.

At this moment, I have in my heart a prayer. As I have assumed my heavy duties, I humbly pray Almighty God, in the words of King Solomon:

"Give therefore thy servant an understanding heart to judge thy people, that I may discern between good and bad; for who is able to judge this thy so great a people?"

I ask only to be a good and faithful servant of my Lord and my people.

3. Statement by the President Announcing the Use of the A-Bomb at Hiroshima
August 6, 1945

Public Paper of the Presidents of the United States: Harry S. Truman, 1945. Washington, D.C.: U.S. Government Printing Press, 197–200.

SIXTEEN HOURS AGO an American airplane dropped one bomb on Hiroshima, an important Japanese Army base. That bomb had more power than 20,000 tons of T.N.T. It had more than two thousand times the blast power of the British "Grand Slam" which is the largest bomb ever yet used in the history of warfare.

The Japanese began the war from the air at Pearl Harbor. They have been repaid many fold. And the end is not yet. With this bomb we have now added a new and revolutionary increase in destruction to supplement the growing power of our armed forces. In their present form these bombs are now in production and even more powerful forms are in development.

It is an atomic bomb. It is a harnessing of the basic power of the universe. The force from which the sun draws its power has been loosed against those who brought war to the Far East.

Before 1939, it was the accepted belief of scientists that it was theoretically possible to release atomic energy. But no one knew any practical method of doing it. By 1942, however, we knew that the Germans were working feverishly to find a way to add atomic energy to the other engines of war with which they hoped to enslave the world. But they failed. We may be grateful to Providence that the Germans got the V-1's and V-2's late and in limited quantities and even more grateful that they did not get the atomic bomb at all.

The battle of the laboratories held fateful risks for us as well as the battles of the air, land and sea, and we have now won the battle of the laboratories as we have won the other battles.

Beginning in 1940, before Pearl Harbor, scientific knowledge useful in war was pooled between the United States and Great Britain, and many priceless helps to our victories have come from that arrangement. Under that general policy the research on the atomic bomb was begun. With American and British scientists working together we entered the race of discovery against the Germans.

The United States had available the large number of scientists of distinction in the many needed areas of knowledge. It had the tremendous industrial and financial resources necessary for the project and they could be devoted to it without undue impairment of other vital war work. In the United States the laboratory work and the production plants, on which a substantial start had already been made, would be out of reach of enemy bombing, while at that time Britain was exposed to constant air attack and was still threatened with the possibility of invasion. For these reasons Prime Minister Churchill and President Roosevelt agreed that it was wise to carry on the project here. We now have two great plants and many lesser works devoted to the production of atomic power. Employment during peak construction numbered 125,000 and over 65,000 individuals are even now engaged in operating the plants. Many have worked there for two and a half years. Few know what they have been producing. They see great quantities of material going in and they see nothing coming out of these plants, for the physical size of the explosive charge is exceedingly small. We have spent two billion dollars on the greatest scientific gamble in history—and won.

But the greatest marvel is not the size of the enterprise, its secrecy, nor its cost, but the achievement of scientific brains in putting together infinitely complex pieces of knowledge held by many men in different fields of science into a workable plan. And hardly less marvelous has been the capacity of industry to design, and of labor to operate, the machines and methods to do things never done before so that the brain child of many minds came forth in physical shape and performed as it was supposed to do. Both science and industry worked under the direction of the United States Army, which achieved a unique success in managing so diverse a problem in the advancement of knowledge in an amazingly short time. It is doubtful if such another combination could be got together in the world. What has been done is the greatest achievement of organized science in history. It was done under high pressure and without failure.

We are now prepared to obliterate more rapidly and completely every productive enterprise the Japanese have above ground in any city. We shall destroy their docks, their factories, and their communications. Let there be no mistake; we shall completely destroy Japan's power to make war.

It was to spare the Japanese people from utter destruction that the ultimatum of July 26 was issued at Potsdam. Their leaders promptly rejected that ultimatum. If they do not now accept our terms they may expect a rain of ruin from the air, the like of which has never been seen on this earth. Behind this air attack will follow sea and land forces in such numbers and power as they have not yet seen and with the fighting skill of which they are already well aware.

The Secretary of War, who has kept in personal touch with all phases of the project, will immediately make public a statement giving further details.

His statement will give facts concerning the sites at Oak Ridge near Knoxville, Tennessee, and at Richland near Pasco, Washington, and an installation near Santa Fe, New Mexico. Although the workers at the sites have been making materials to be used in producing the greatest destructive force in history they have not themselves been in danger beyond that of many other occupations, for the utmost care has been taken of their safety.

The fact that we can release atomic energy ushers in a new era in man's understanding of nature's forces. Atomic energy may in the future supplement the power that now comes from coal, oil, and falling water, but at present it cannot be produced on a basis to compete with them commercially. Before that comes there must be a long period of intensive research.

It has never been the habit of the scientists of this country or the policy of this Government to withhold from the world scientific knowledge. Normally, therefore, everything about the work with atomic energy would be made public.

But under present circumstances it is not intended to divulge the technical processes of production or all the military applications, pending further examination of possible methods of protecting us and the rest of the world from the danger of sudden destruction.

I shall recommend that the Congress of the United States consider promptly the establishment of an appropriate commission to control the production and use of atomic power within the United States. I shall give further consideration and make further recommendations to the Congress as to how atomic power can become a powerful and forceful influence towards the maintenance of world peace.

4. Special Message to the Congress Presenting a 21-Point Program for the Reconversion Period
September 6, 1945

Public Papers of the Presidents of the United States: Harry S. Truman, 1945. Washington, D.C.: U.S. Government Printing Office, 263–309.

To the Congress of the United States:

I regret that you have been compelled to cut short your recess period. I know, however, that you have been just as eager as any of us to meet the problems which naturally have crowded down upon us with the surrender of the Japanese.

You have cut short a well-merited vacation in order to do so. I hope that the American people realize as fully as I do, that from the very first days of the emergency, the Congress has most energetically and patriotically devoted its time, energies, and capabilities to the immediate problems of war and to the long-range problems of peace. The legislative branch of the Government is entitled to its full share of credit and glory for the victory of the Allied armies. I wish to take this opportunity on behalf of the Nation to congratulate you on the great victory which has been won—in which you played so important a part.

The Congress reconvenes at a time of great emergency. It is an emergency about which, however, we need have no undue fear if we exercise the same energy, foresight, and wisdom as we did in carrying on the war and winning this victory.

The sudden surrender of the Japanese has not caught us unawares. President Roosevelt, as early as the Fall of 1943, began to set up machinery which he foresaw would become necessary to meet the reconversion period. The Congress in its wisdom has adopted some of that machinery by statute, and has improved and added to it. As a result, Government agencies, for some time, have been able to plan for the immediate and long-range steps which now have to be taken.

As the Congress has undoubtedly noticed, many steps were taken immediately after the surrender of the Japanese. Many more have been taken since.

The process of reconversion will be a complicated and difficult one. The general line of approach to the problem is to achieve as full peacetime production and employment as possible in the most efficient and speedy manner. The following policies have been laid down and will be followed:

(1) Demobilize as soon as possible the armed forces no longer needed.

(2) Cancel and settle war contracts as quickly as possible.

(3) Clear the war plants so as to permit contractors to proceed with peacetime production.

(4) Hold the line on prices and rents until fair competition can operate to prevent inflation and undue hardship on consumers.

(5) Hold wages in line where their increase would cause inflationary price rises. Where price ceilings would not be endangered, collective bargaining should be restored.

(6) Remove all possible wartime government controls in order to speed and encourage reconversion and expansion.

(7) Keep only those controls which are necessary to help reconversion and expansion by preventing bottlenecks, shortages of material, and inflation.

(8) Prevent rapid decrease of wage incomes or purchasing power.

The major objective, of course, is to reestablish an expanded peacetime industry, trade, and agriculture, and to do it as quickly as possible.

Obviously during this process there will be a great deal of inevitable unemployment. What we must do is to assist industry to reconvert to peacetime production as quickly and effectively as possible so that the number of unemployed will be swiftly and substantially reduced as industry and business and agriculture get into high production.

The Government is now doing what it can to hurry this reconversion process.

Through contract termination procedures it is providing quick payment to contractors.

It has released controls on practically all materials which are necessary for peacetime production, reserving only those few in which there is still a critical shortage.

It has made arrangements for credit facilities for industry.

By plant and surplus property disposal, it is helping private enterprise to get started again.

In the consumer field the Government has released controls over articles which were needed for the war in such large quantities that civilians had to go without.

For the information of the Congress, I am submitting as an appendix to this message a report by the Director of War Mobilization and Reconversion showing what has already been done by the Federal Government in reconversion.[1]

There is much that the Congress can do to help this process and to tide over the period between now and the time when reconversion is completed and civilian jobs are plentiful in a stable economy that provides full production, full employment, and a high standard of living.

1. UNEMPLOYMENT COMPENSATION

The end of the war came more swiftly than most of us anticipated. Widespread cut-backs in war orders followed promptly. As a result, there has already been a considerable number of workers who are between jobs as war industries convert to peace. Other workers are returning to a 40-hour week and are faced with a corresponding reduction in take-home pay.

This has led to a natural feeling of uneasiness among the rank and file of our people. Let me emphasize that there will be no reason for undue timidity. A vast backlog of orders may soon make possible the greatest peacetime industrial activity that we have ever seen. But this can happen only if the Congress and the administration move vigorously and courageously to deal with the economic problems which peace has created. Then there need

be no reason to fear either the immediate future or the years that lie ahead of us.

Determined action now will create the atmosphere of confidence which is so vital to a rapid reconversion with a minimum of unemployment and hardship.

No matter how rapidly reconversion proceeds, however, no amount of effort or planning will be able immediately to provide a job for everyone displaced from war work. Obviously, displaced war workers cannot find jobs until industry has been regeared and made ready to produce peacetime goods. During this lag the Government should provide help. The cost of this transition from war to peace is as much a part of the cost of war as the transition from peace to war—and we should so consider it.

This course is recommended not only as a matter of justice and humanity, but also as a matter of sound business. Nothing would be more harmful to our economy than to have every displaced war worker stop buying consumer goods. And nothing would be more conducive to a large-scale cessation of buying than the feeling on the part of displaced war workers that all their income had stopped and that their remaining financial resources had to be hoarded.

For one group of those who may become unemployed in the near future—the demobilized veterans—the Congress has already made special provision. Any veteran who has satisfactorily completed 90 days of service is now entitled by law to a weekly unemployment allowance of $20 for as much as 52 weeks depending on the length of his service.

By contrast, there are more than 15,000,000 workers not protected under our present unemployment insurance laws. There are many millions more for whom protection is inadequate. Many of these have been unable to accumulate adequate savings.

On May 28, 1945, I recommended to the Congress that the Federal Government immediately supplement the unemployment insurance benefits now provided by the several States. That is the only feasible way to provide at least a subsistence payment in all parts of the United States during this coming unemployment period.

As I pointed out then, the existing State laws relative to unemployment insurance are inadequate in three respects:

(1) Only about 30,000,000 of our 43,000,000 nonagricultural workers are protected by unemploy-

---

[1]Mr. Snyder's report, dated September 4, 1945, and entitled "The Transition: Phase One," is printed with the message in House Document 282 (79th Cong., 1st sess.).

ment insurance. Federal Government employees, for example, such as Federal shipyard and arsenal workers, are not covered. Nor are employees of small businesses and small industrial establishments. Nor are the officers and men of the merchant marine who have braved enemy torpedoes and bombs to deliver supplies and the implements of war to our armed services and our allies.

(2) The weekly benefit payments under many of the State laws are now far too low to provide subsistence and purchasing power for the workers and their families. Almost half of the States have the clearly inadequate maximum of $15 to $18 a week.

(3) Many of the States pay benefits for too short a period. In more than one-third of the States, for example, 18 weeks is the maximum.

I recommended then, and I urgently renew my recommendation now, that the Congress take immediate action to make good these deficiencies for the present emergency period of reconversion.

Specifically, coverage should be extended to include Federal employees, maritime workers, and other workers not now insured. This additional compensation during the present emergency will have to be financed entirely by the Federal Government, but the benefits should appropriately be administered by the States.

I also recommended, and I now repeat that recommendation, that the Congress provide, through supplementary Federal emergency benefit payments, additional unemployment benefits so as to bring them up to adequate standards in all the States. All payments, however, should be made through the existing unemployment compensation machinery of the several States.

During this emergency every eligible worker should be entitled to 26 weeks of unemployment benefits in any one year. The maximum weekly payment for those workers whose previous earnings were high enough, should be not less than $25 per week.

If the Congress decides to take this very necessary step, it will also wish to reconsider and increase the unemployment allowance provided for veterans.

There has been so much misrepresentation about this temporary proposal that I think I should categorically state what the bill does not do.

It does not give everyone $25 a week. Under it, an applicant must be ready, willing, and able to work

and must have earned wages high enough so that the percentage rate will yield this maximum figure.

It does not federalize the unemployment compensation system. It leaves it with the States.

It is not intended to take the place of the permanent amendments to the unemployment compensation system which are now being studied by the Congress. It is an emergency measure designed to expand the present system without changing its principles. It is designed only to meet the immediate pressing human problems of reconversion.

This recommendation is not to be confused with the broader question of extending, expanding, and improving our entire social security program of which unemployment insurance is only a part. I expect to communicate with the Congress on this subject at a later date. But I sincerely urge that we do not wait for consideration of such a complex question before enacting this much needed emergency legislation.

2. FAIR LABOR STANDARDS ACT

In addition to those workers who will temporarily lose their jobs, there will be millions of others whose incomes will fall sharply with the end of war production. These will be added to the several million wage earners who even now have hourly earnings much below what is necessary for a decent standard of living.

The inadequacy of these wages, in many cases, has been temporarily concealed by wartime increases in take-home pay resulting from overtime work. As these props to income are removed, however, low wage earners will be hard pressed to feed, clothe, and house their families. This flies in the face of a sound public policy. Failure to correct this situation will slow down, if it will not actually stop, our drive toward an expanding market for business and agriculture. ˙

The foundations of a healthy national economy cannot be secure so long as any large section of our working people receive substandard wages. The existence of substandard wage levels sharply curtails the national purchasing power and narrows the market for the products of our farms and factories.

In the Fair Labor Standards Act of 1938, the Congress adopted a program intended to provide a minimum wage standard for a large number of American workers.

In that statute, the Congress declared it to be our national policy to eliminate, from interstate industry, wage levels detrimental to the maintenance of minimum standards of living. The establishment then of a minimum wage of 25 cents per hour represented a first step toward the realization of that policy. The goal of 40 cents per hour, which under the act was to be made effective by 1945, was actually made fully effective more than a year ago by the voluntary action of the industry committees.

I believed that the goal of a 40 cent minimum was inadequate when established. It has now become obsolete.

Increases in the cost of living since 1938 and changes in our national wage structure, require an immediate and substantial upward revision of this minimum. Only in that way can the objectives of the Fair Labor Standards Act be realized, the national purchasing power protected, and an economy of full production and abundance preserved and maintained for the American people.

The high prosperity which we seek in the postwar years will not be meaningful for all our people if any large proportion of our industrial wage earners receive wages as low as the minimum now sanctioned by the Fair Labor Standards Act.

I therefore recommend that the Congress amend the Fair Labor Standards Act by substantially increasing the minimum wage specified therein to a level which will eliminate substandards of living, and assure the maintenance of the health, efficiency, and general well-being of workers.

The scope of the Fair Labor Standards Act also should be clarified and extended. In view of changes which have occurred since 1938, I believe it is no longer necessary to exclude from the minimum wage program the large number of workers engaged in agricultural processing who are now excluded. There now exists a twilight zone in which some workers are covered, and others, doing similar work, are not. Extension of coverage would benefit both workers and employers by removing competitive inequities.

Our achievements in this field during the last seven years of establishing minimum wages have been gratifying; but we must continue to move forward, step by step.

I urge that the Congress act promptly. The wage structure on which businessmen may make future plans should be settled quickly.

3. WARTIME CONTROLS

One of the outstanding achievements of the war has been the success of the Government in holding the line against inflation. This is the first time in any major war that the United States has been able substantially to stabilize its economy.

That fact now permits us to enter into the difficult period of readjustment without the threat of a disastrous price collapse.

For this result much credit is due to the Congress, which in the face of great insistence from many interested pressure groups refused steadfastly to take the easy way.

Great credit is due to the Office of Economic Stabilization, the War Labor Board, the Office of Price Administration, the War Food Administration, the War Production Board, and the other stabilization agencies. Despite great pressure and often unjust abuse, they continued to hold the line for the benefit of the great mass of Americans.

And above all, great credit is due to the people of the United States, the great body of average citizens, who, for four difficult years and with only a few exceptions, subordinated their personal interest to the long-range interest of the Nation as a whole.

Many of the demands of the war for commodities have now decreased. They will decrease further during the initial period of unemployment which will come with the cancellation of war contracts. As a result, prices of some commodities are bound to soften. But if that happens in the next few months, we cannot allow ourselves to be misled. We must keep in mind the experience of the period immediately after the first World War. After a lull of a few months following the Armistice of 1918, prices turned upward, scrambling for inventories started, and prices soon got completely out of hand. We found ourselves in one of the worst inflations in our history, culminating in the crash of 1920 and the disastrous deflation of 1920 and 1921.

We must be sure this time not to repeat that bitter mistake. When reconversion really gets under way, and men go back to work, and payrolls increase, and the pent-up demands of the war years at home and abroad for peacetime products begin to make themselves felt, we shall face the same scramble for goods, the same speculative excesses that developed in 1919. We must be in a position to overcome that danger if we expect to achieve an orderly transition to peacetime levels of full production and full employment. However, we must not allow inflationary dangers to obscure our vision of the possibilities of lower incomes and widespread unemployment. Our policy must guard against both contingencies.

Immediately after the Japanese decision to surrender, the Office of Price Administration moved promptly to eliminate rationing on gasoline, fuel oil, stoves, and processed foods.

During the transition period the Price Administrator, of course, will eliminate rationing and price controls on one commodity after another just as soon as supply comes into balance with demand. At the same time he will make whatever price adjustments are required to facilitate rapid reconversion and reemployment.

However, it will be necessary for him to continue to resist unreasonable pressures for higher prices on some commodities, just as he has resisted them all through the war. In resisting these pressures and in carrying out his difficult responsibilities, I must state clearly that he has both my backing and my confidence.

It will similarly be necessary for the Government to resist pressures for increases in wage rates which would imperil price ceilings.

Without some general stabilization the consumer cannot be protected. Without stabilization, reconversion cannot proceed as rapidly as it should; for stability of cost is indispensable to sound business planning.

The price control and stabilization program has received the backing of the great majority of businessmen throughout the war period. With few exceptions, business groups have realized clearly their own personal stake and the stake of our basic economy in the success of the anti-inflation program.

During the months that lie ahead, however, some groups in business may be tempted to substitute for this long-range wartime thinking, a short-range policy designed to secure prices high enough to provide immediate profits over and above their temporarily high costs of production due to their initial low volume.

These pressures must be resisted. Prices must be held firmly on reconversion items as well as on cost of living items during the coming months.

The American people are entitled to a firm assurance not only on the part of the Administration, but from the Congress itself, that rents and the prices of clothing, food, and other essentials will be held in line. They are also entitled to buy washing machines, vacuum cleaners, automobiles and other products at prices based on our traditional system of high output and low unit costs.

The promise of good profits for businessmen must not be based on small initial volume. It must be based on the full all-out production which it is my belief that American industry will rapidly achieve.

Because of heavy wartime needs, it has been necessary to allocate available supplies of many foods among various claimants within this country, and among other countries. It has been necessary to set aside large blocks of specified commodities in order to make these commodities available for military and other essential needs. Rationing of food for consumers has been necessary in the interest of fair distribution.

Many of these controls have already been eliminated and all remaining allocations, set-asides, and rationing will be removed as rapidly as the supply situation will permit.

However, supplies of some of our principal foods will continue beyond the end of 1945 to be too small for the demand.

For example, the world will be short of requirements for fats and oils and sugar for some months, and allocations and rationing will probably have to be continued into 1946. We must not move so rapidly as to endanger the orderly distribution of goods on which we have based our living during the emergency.

Let me add that in no case should rationing controls be removed if by so doing we should jeopardize our relief shipments to Europe and other distressed war areas. We have a moral obligation to the people of these liberated areas. More than that, our own enlightened self-interest tells us that hungry people are rarely advocates of democracy. The rehabilitation of these countries, and indeed the removal of American occupational troops, may be unnecessarily delayed if we fail to meet these responsibilities during the next few months.

During the reconversion period and as long as shortages in certain materials other than food continue, the War Production Board will have to support the stabilization program as it has done during the past four years.

It must be in a position to take action where necessary, to increase scarce materials and facilities, break bottlenecks, channel production to meet essential needs, safeguard the opportunities for small business concerns, and, above all, to control inventories so as to prevent speculative hoarding and unbalanced distribution.

As the Congress knows, the War Production Board has already removed a great majority of the controls which were in force during the war, and many more will be removed during the next few months.

I trust that the Congress will agree, however, that the controls which still remain and which are still considered necessary by the agency charged with responsibility should not be removed until the need for them disappears. The need to control a few critical materials which the war has caused to be in short supply will continue for some time until adequate supplies are again available. Foremost among these materials are tin and crude rubber.

It will also be necessary for some period to prevent the hoarding of items now badly needed and in great demand for the civilian economy. Many critical shortages can be avoided by the extension of general inventory controls which would prevent the accumulation of unreasonably large stocks in the hands of a few. This will speed the reconversion program and will also greatly assist in avoiding inflation of the price structure.

The extension of one further type of control should have consideration at this time. In the national interest, this Government has made and should continue to make agreements for securing our fair share of materials from certain foreign sources and also agreements for supplying various materials and products abroad. The Government should have authority to assure the carrying out of such commitments.

These production and inventory controls, as well as the allocations of food, set-asides of commodities, and rationing among consumers have been set up under the Second War Powers Act.

Most of the provisions of this act expire on December 31, 1945.

I am convinced that an orderly transition to a peacetime economy will require the use of some of these controls after the first of the year.

I request the Congress, therefore, to extend the provisions of the Second War Powers Act, either in its present form or with appropriate limitations, preserving the powers necessary to achieve the objectives I have outlined.

The Congress has my definite assurance that none of these war powers will be exercised by the executive branch of the Government unless they are deemed essential to the attainment of the objective of an orderly stabilized reconversion. The Congress

should, of course, if it extends the statute, reserve the right to terminate it by legislation at any time it deems necessary.

I hope that the Congress will not delay the extension of this authority. Delay would retard reconversion by creating uncertainty on the part of business as to whether necessary controls will be retained or not. Businessmen, in planning for next year's activities, will be assisted greatly by knowing in advance whether or not the Government is going to keep a firm hand at the brakes to prevent inflation.

The termination of the wartime food subsidies, for which a total of $1,798,000,000 has been authorized for the current year, is one of the important problems in reconversion. Agencies dealing directly with this problem are now meeting jointly to determine in what order and at what time these food subsidies may be eliminated without an undue disturbance to farm income or living costs.

Subsidies for purposes other than food are also being reviewed by the agencies concerned, who are collecting the necessary data for an orderly liquidation at the earliest date compatible with the stabilization program.

Those subsidies which were designed originally to stimulate increased production should not be removed at a time or in a manner to incite inflation and upset our economy.

I have directed that early reports be made on this important problem.

4. WAR POWERS AND EXECUTIVE AGENCIES REORGANIZATION

I should like to bring to the attention of the Congress the legal difficulties that will arise unless care is taken in the drafting of legislation terminating wartime controls and wartime agencies.

I have asked the Attorney General to prepare a report on the principal statutes that confer wartime powers and on the various wartime agencies, with particular reference to the circumstances under which each terminates.

A copy of this memorandum[1] is attached for the information of the Congress. It is an able and comprehensive summary of the applicable laws.

Your attention is particularly called to the statement in the opinion of the Attorney General to the

---

[1]The report of the Attorney General to the President, in the form of a letter dated September 1, 1945, is printed with the message in House Document 282 (79th Cong., 1st sess.).

effect that the broad basis of governmental power on which the existing emergency and wartime statutes rest has not been terminated by the unconditional surrender of our enemies.

Certain of the wartime statutes which have been made effective "in time of war," "during the present war," or "for the duration of the war" continue to be effective until a formal state of peace has been restored, or until some earlier termination date is made applicable by appropriate governmental action. Another group of statutes which by their provisions terminate "upon the cessation of hostilities" or "upon termination of the war," will in fact and in law terminate only by a formal proclamation to that effect by the President or by appropriate congressional action.

From time to time action will be taken with respect to these agencies, with the general objective of streamlining the Government into a peacetime organization as quickly as possible.

The time has not yet arrived, however, for the proclamation of the cessation of hostilities, much less the termination of the war. Needless to say, such proclamations will be made as soon as circumstances permit.

It has been necessary during the course of the war to make numerous important redistributions of functions among executive agencies.

This has been accomplished by the President under the authority of title I of the First War Powers Act. This act expires six months after the termination of the war, or at such earlier time as may be designated by appropriate governmental action.

If the Congress or the President were formally to declare the present war terminated, it would automatically cause all the steps taken under the First War Powers Act with respect to the war agencies to expire, and would have the Government revert automatically to its preexisting status six months after the declaration.

If this were to occur, it would cause great confusion and chaos in the Government.

It is the policy of this administration not to exercise wartime powers beyond the point at which it is necessary to exercise them.

Similarly, the wartime agencies of the Government will not be allowed to continue to perform functions not required by present conditions.

Those functions of the wartime agencies which must be retained during part or all of the period of reconversion should be transferred as promptly as practicable to the permanent departments and agencies of the Government. The remaining functions, appropriate only to the crisis through which we have passed, should be terminated in an orderly, systematic fashion as soon as possible.

A program of winding up wartime agencies and distributing their functions on a peacetime basis is now being pursued under the powers vested in the President by title I of the First War Powers Act.

Therefore, I urge that the Congress do not yet adopt a resolution proclaiming the termination of the war or the termination of the emergency or the cessation of hostilities. Such a resolution would automatically cause the death of many war powers and wartime agencies before we are ready.

At the same time I recognize that the Congress may wish to repeal certain specific wartime statutes. If this is to be done, the repeal should be on a selective basis, through the adoption of specific statutes dealing with each wartime power which the Congress decides should be terminated.

In my message dated May 24, 1945, it was recommended that permanent legislation be enacted which would authorize the President to submit to the Congress, from time to time, plans providing for the reorganization of executive agencies, each such plan to become effective unless the Congress should reject it by concurrent resolution.

This type of joint action by the Congress and the President has produced, and will produce, far better results than can be achieved by the usual legislative process in the field of executive reorganization. If proper progress is to be made, it is necessary to permit the President to lay out the machinery for carrying out his responsibility for the conduct of the executive branch, subject to rejection by the two Houses of Congress. Executive initiative, subject to congressional veto, is an effective approach to governmental reorganization.

The responsibility of conducting the executive branch rests upon the President. It is fair and efficient to permit him to lay out the machinery for carrying out that responsibility.

The means for doing this should be generally along the lines of the Reorganization Act of 1939, which gives the initiative to the President, but reserves power to the Congress by a majority vote to nullify any action of the President which does not meet with its approval.

Considerable progress was made in efficiency of government under this Reorganization Act of

1939. I recommend that such powers be made of permanent duration and that the legislation be sufficiently flexible to permit any kind of adjustment for which necessity may arise.

It is clear to all of us that the Government has a difficult and important task in the years which lie ahead. Our Government belongs to the people and the people have a right to expect from their Government the greatest possible efficiency in carrying out its task.

Our Government has never been as efficient as we should like to see it. To some degree this may be charged to the size of some of the tasks assigned to it. To some extent, it is also due to the lack of trained Government personnel and the low salaries paid to Government officials.

There is no question that the war has taught us a great deal about Government administration. There is still, however, much room for improvement.

I have undertaken directly through the members of the Cabinet and also through the Directors of the Office of War Mobilization and Reconversion and the Bureau of the Budget to emphasize the need for more efficient operation in all the executive branches of the Government. I have requested them to examine administrative procedures, and to speed up and simplify their operations to the maximum practical degree.

I have also requested the Bureau of the Budget to examine closely with each department and agency head, the actual needs of his office following the surrender of Japan. They have been asked to reduce budgets promptly and fully wherever cuts are indicated. The Bureau of the Budget is now completing studies which will result in reductions of millions of dollars in the expense of operating our Government.

We must continue relentlessly this program for increased Government efficiency. The Congress can depend upon the Executive to push this program with the utmost vigor.

5. FULL EMPLOYMENT

I am confident that, with the cooperation of American industry, labor, and agriculture, we can bridge the gap between war and peace.

When we have reconverted our economy to a peacetime basis, however, we shall not be satisfied with merely our prewar economy. The American people have set high goals for their own future. They have set these goals high because they have

seen how great can be the productive capacity of our country.

The levels of production and income reached during the war years have given our citizens an appreciation of what a full production peacetime economy can be.

They are not interested in boom prosperity—for that only too often leads to panic and depression. But they are interested in providing opportunity for work and for ultimate security.

Government must do its part and assist industry and labor to get over the line from war to peace.

That is why I have asked for unemployment compensation legislation.

That is why I now ask for full-employment legislation.

The objectives for our domestic economy which we seek in our long-range plans were summarized by the late President Franklin D. Roosevelt over a year and a half ago in the form of an economic bill of rights. Let us make the attainment of those rights the essence of postwar American economic life.

I repeat the statement of President Roosevelt:

In our day these economic truths have become accepted as self-evident. We have accepted, so to speak, a second bill of rights under which a new basis of security and prosperity can be established for all—regardless of station, race, or creed.

Among these are:

The right to a useful and remunerative job in the industries, or shops or farms or mines of the Nation.

The right to earn enough to provide adequate food and clothing and recreation.

The right of every farmer to raise and sell his products at a return which will give him and his family a decent living.

The right of every businessman, large and small, to trade in an atmosphere of freedom from unfair competition and domination by monopolies at home or abroad.

The right of every family to a decent home.

The right to adequate medical care and the opportunity to achieve and enjoy good health.

The right to adequate protection from the economic fears of old age, sickness, accident, and unemployment.

The right to a good education.

All of these rights spell security. And after this war is won we must be prepared to move forward, in the implementation of these rights, to new goals of human happiness and well-being.

America's own rightful place in the world depends in large part upon how fully these and similar rights have been carried into practice for our citizens. For unless there is security here at home there cannot be lasting peace in the world.

I shall from time to time communicate with the Congress on some of the subjects included in this enumeration of economic rights.

Most of them, in the last analysis, depend upon full production and full employment at decent wages.

There has been much discussion about the necessity of continuing full employment after the war if we hope to continue in substantial degree the prosperity which came with the war years. The time has come for action along these lines.

To provide jobs we must look first and foremost to private enterprise—to industry, agriculture, and labor. Government must inspire enterprise with confidence. That confidence must come mainly through deeds, not words.

But it is clear that confidence will be promoted by certain assurances given by the Government:

Assurance that all the facts about full employment and opportunity will be gathered periodically for the use of all.

Assurance of stability and consistency in public policy, so that enterprise can plan better by knowing what the Government intends to do.

Assurance that every governmental policy and program will be pointed to promote maximum production and employment in private enterprise.

Assurance that priority will be given to doing those things first which stimulate normal employment most.

A national reassertion of the right to work for every American citizen able and willing to work—a declaration of the ultimate duty of Government to use its own resources if all other methods should fail to prevent prolonged unemployment—these will help to avert fear and establish full employment. The prompt and firm acceptance of this bedrock public responsibility will reduce the need for its exercise.

I ask that full employment legislation to provide these vital assurances be speedily enacted. Such legislation should also provide machinery for a continuous full-employment policy—to be developed and pursued in cooperation among industry, agriculture, and labor, between the Congress and the Chief Executive, between the people and their Government.

Full employment means full opportunity for all under the American economic system—nothing more and nothing less.

In human terms, full employment means opportunity to get a good peacetime job for every worker who is ready, able, and willing to take one. It does not mean made work, or making people work.

In economic terms, full employment means full production and the opportunity to sell goods—all the goods that industry and agriculture can produce.

In Government terms, full employment means opportunity to reduce the ratio of public spending to private investment without sacrificing essential services.

In world-wide terms, full employment in America means greater economic security and more opportunity for lasting peace throughout the world.

These goals and the machinery to carry them out are set forth in legislation now pending before the Congress on which extensive public hearings have been held. The country justifiably expects early action along these lines.

6. FAIR EMPLOYMENT PRACTICE COMMITTEE

During the years of war production we made substantial progress in overcoming many of the prejudices which had resulted in discriminations against minority groups.

Many of the injustices based upon considerations of race, religion, and color were removed. Many were prevented. Perfection was not reached, of course, but substantial progress was made.

In the reconversion period and thereafter, we should make every effort to continue this American ideal. It is one of the fundamentals of our political philosophy, and it should be an integral part of our economy.

The Fair Employment Practice Committee is continuing during the transition period. I have already requested that legislation be enacted placing the Fair Employment Practice Committee on a permanent basis. I repeat that recommendation.

7. LABOR DISPUTES AND WAGE STABILIZATION

Our national welfare requires that during the reconversion period production of civilian goods and services—as full production as possible—go forward without interruption, and that labor and industry cooperate to keep strikes and lock-outs at a minimum.

Those who have the responsibility of labor relations must recognize that responsibility. This is not the time for short-sighted management to seize upon the chance to reduce wages and try to injure labor unions. Equally it is not the time for labor leaders to shirk their responsibility and permit widespread industrial strife.

With this objective in view, I shall shortly convene a conference of representatives of organized labor and industry for the purpose of working out by agreement means to minimize labor disputes.

In the interim period, pending the convening of the conference, I have called upon the representatives of organized labor and industry to continue their adherence to the no-strike, no-lock-out policy. During this interim period, labor disputes which threaten a substantial interference with the transition to a peacetime economy should be submitted to the War Labor Board. They would there be handled by the Board under existing procedures. The country will expect parties to any such disputes to comply voluntarily with the determinations of the War Labor Board.

The threat of inflationary bidding-up of wage rates by competition in a short labor market has disappeared. Therefore the War Labor Board has removed the necessity of approving proposed voluntary wage increases, so long as they will not be used to obtain an increase in price ceilings.

I have conferred upon the War Labor Board adequate authority to correct maladjustments and inequities in wage rates arising in the reconversion period which will tend to interfere with the effective transition to a peacetime economy.

The Board should be terminated as soon after the conclusion of the forthcoming industry-labor conference as the orderly disposition of the work of the Board and the provisions of the War Labor Disputes Act permit, and after facilities have been provided to take care of the wage stabilization functions under the act of October 2, 1942.

Meanwhile, plans for strengthening the Department of Labor, and bringing under it functions properly belonging to it, are going forward. With the return to a peacetime economy and the elimination of the present temporary wartime agencies and procedures, we must look to collective bar-

gaining, aided and supplemented by a truly effective system of conciliation and voluntary arbitration, as the best and most democratic method of maintaining sound industrial relations.

8. UNITED STATES EMPLOYMENT SERVICE EXTENSION

Placing demobilized veterans and displaced war workers in new peacetime jobs is the major human problem of our country's reconversion to a peacetime economy. It is imperative that this work be done swiftly and efficiently, and that men and women lose a minimum amount of time between jobs.

The next few months are crucial. What we do now will affect our American way of life for decades to come.

The United States Employment Service has an important responsibility in the performance of this task.

At present, this agency operates as a national and centralized system with a free flow of information among its offices. Under the 1946 appropriation act, the offices are to be turned back to the 48 States within 90 days after the cessation of hostilities.

Shortly after the declaration of war, the Government realized that the manpower of the Nation could be mobilized more efficiently if the United States Employment Service were centralized under Federal control. Hundreds of thousands of workers had to be recruited from all parts of the country. Often, they were wanted in regions far from their homes. Certain areas had surpluses of labor; others were desperately in need of more workers. This situation could be met only through a centrally operated employment service that covered the entire Nation.

Now we are faced with this problem in reverse. Hundreds of thousands of men and women will want to seek jobs in towns and cities other than those in which they worked during the war. They may want to return home, or they may want to strike out in search of new opportunities in new surroundings. Millions of veterans also will be coming back in search of peacetime jobs. They will want to know where such jobs can be found, not only in their own areas, but also in other parts of the land.

The task of helping this vast army of job seekers to fit themselves into peacetime economy is fully as difficult as the mobilization of manpower for war.

To make any decided change in the machinery to handle this problem now would cause unnecessary hardship to workers and veterans. It would slow down the entire process of reconversion.

I urgently recommend that the Congress do not yet return the Employment Service to the States. Ultimately it should be so returned. However, it should be continued under Federal control at least until the expiration of the War Mobilization Act—June 30, 1947.

I also recommend that its appropriation be increased by $10,000,000 for the current fiscal year. Prompt action on this matter is especially important since personnel and facilities must be quickly enlarged to handle the rising tide of veterans and war workers who will be seeking jobs.

9. AGRICULTURE

One of the most magnificent production jobs in the war has been done by the farmers of the United States. They have met the unprecedented demands of the war, and, at the same time, have provided our civilian population with more food per capita than during the 1935–39 prewar period.

No other group in America labored longer or harder to meet the war demands put upon them. Food production last year reached a peak more than a third above the prewar years despite the fact that farm population has declined by about five million since 1940.

Fortunately, farmers were aided by better-than-average weather conditions over the country. We cannot, however, count on continuance of better-than-average weather. Therefore, because of the great demands for food that exist in this country and for relief abroad, the Department of Agriculture is planning for another year of full production. This does not mean the same volume of production for each individual crop, because the surrender of Japan has brought changes in the demand pattern. But the total acreage needed for next year will not be greatly different from this year.

The Government now must be prepared to carry out the Nation's responsibility to aid farmers in making their necessary readjustments from a wartime to a peacetime basis. The Congress already has provided postwar supports against price collapse for many farm products. This was a provision of wisdom and foresight.

After the First World War farm prices dropped more than 50 percent from the spring of 1920 to the spring of 1921. We do not intend to permit a repetition of the disaster that followed the First World War. The Secretary of Agriculture has assured me that he will use all means now authorized by the Congress to carry out the price-support commitments.

But there is need for additional measures to strengthen the machinery for carrying out price-support commitments, and for laying the basis for broader peacetime markets for agricultural products.

The Congress already has provided for one such postwar measure that needs now to be adapted to our changed situation. Recognizing that the lend-lease program required greatly increased production and that this increase could not be suddenly discontinued when the program stopped, the Congress wisely set aside $500,000,000 of lend-lease funds for price support of farm commodities. This money is now available for the purpose for which it was intended, but in order that it may be used most effectively whenever the need arises, I recommend early legislation which would make those funds available to the Commodity Credit Corporation on a continuing basis. Such action would reaffirm the specific intent of the Congress as to the use of this money in safeguarding farm prices.

Strengthening the machinery for carrying out price-support commitments is the one measure necessary to safeguard farm prices. Stimulation of the export of farm commodities is another. More food is needed in the war-ravaged areas of the world. In the process of meeting relief requirements abroad, we have the opportunity of developing export markets for the future.

The farmer has always faced certain specific problems which are peculiar to his occupation. His crops are at the mercy of the weather.

The factory owner and the worker at the machine have available to them insurance programs which protect them from losses. Our farmers have the right to the same kind of protection. Strengthening and further development of crop insurance for farmers, organized and backed by the Federal Government, can give them this protection. A well-rounded crop-insurance program, together with the assurance of reasonable and stable farm prices, will go a long way toward meeting basic problems which have plagued farmers in the past.

Much that has been accomplished during the war was made possible by the wise national program in support of scientific research in agriculture and forestry, and by the program for the conservation and improvement of our soil and forest resources. These policies have paid large dividends during the war. We ought to continue and strengthen them.

Within recent years the Congress has enacted various measures which have done much to improve the economic status of this country's farmers and to make rural living more attractive. In enacting individual pieces of legislation it has not been possible to make adjustments in existing measures in keeping with the changing pattern of needs. The Secretary of Agriculture is now reexamining existing agricultural programs in the light of peacetime needs in order that they make the fullest contribution to the welfare of farmers and the people as a whole. I hope that the Congress also, through its appropriate committees, will give careful consideration to this problem with a view to making such adjustments as are necessary to strengthen the effectiveness of these various measures.

10. SELECTIVE SERVICE

While the cruel lessons of war are fresh in every mind, it is fitting that we now undertake appropriate measures for the future security of the United States.

The times call for a broad and realistic appraisal of our military needs and obligations. This Nation, and the other members of the family of nations, are facing the hazardous transition to a peace economy in a world grown acutely sensitive to power.

We have charted the course to a stable world peace, but that course still remains to be sailed.

We must, of course, plan for the immediate needs of this year and the next. But we would break faith with those who won for us the victory, if we should fail at the same time to adopt an integrated and long-range program for the national security.

As a sovereign nation, we must continue to be ready to defend our national integrity by maintaining and manning adequate defense establishments within this continent, at the Panama Canal, and at all our bases overseas. As a member of the Security Council of the United Nations, we have an immediate obligation to bear a share, commensurate with our national standing, in safeguarding the future security of all peace-loving nations. As a victor in the greatest war of history, we are committed now to an armed occupation of the lands of our defeated enemies until it is assured that the principles for which we fought shall prevail in the reconstruction of those lands.

To meet these immediate obligations will require the maintenance for some time of a real measure of our present land, sea, and air power.

And in this first year after victory our people have another obligation, one which is felt in almost every American home. We owe it to those now in the armed forces that they be returned to civilian life with all possible speed.

To provide the personnel necessary to meet these immediate obligations we must obtain replacements for those veterans who have already rendered long and arduous service.

We shall make every effort to raise these replacements by recruiting volunteers. To that end I ask that the Congress consider ways and means to assure the maximum success of the recruiting campaigns which have already been authorized. I suggest that legislation be enacted to remove the present restriction on eligibility for voluntary enlistment and to allow the armed forces to enlist a larger number of volunteers than is now authorized. It is further recommended that, in order to enable the armed forces satisfactorily to compete in the procurement of personnel, the Congress provide suitable inducements for volunteer service in the Army and Navy.

However, in view of our extensive national commitments, I am certain, as are the War and Navy Departments, that we cannot rely on voluntary recruitment as the sole method of procuring the necessary replacements.

I, therefore, urge that the Congress continue inductions to assure replacements for these veterans, in such numbers as are not supplied by volunteers.

An unforgivable discrimination would result if, by suspending inductions now, we should favor those who have had no military service at the cost of requiring continued sacrifice from those who have already done their part.

Our first concern should be for those who have been in the armed forces for several years. They have been separated from their homes and from their loved ones. Many of them have been under constant fire and continuous danger for months and even years. We should try to avoid imposing further service upon them.

The only way that this can be done is to continue the induction of young men who as yet have not served a tour of active duty in the armed services. Only when we find that we are able to obtain a sufficient number of volunteers to fill the necessary quotas for our occupational needs, can we discontinue the Selective Service System.

Of course it is entirely up to the Congress to choose the means by which we will provide and maintain the necessary strength to meet our commitments. The alternatives presented are very simple. There are no offers. Either we retain men now in the service for a further indefinite period, or we provide replacements by further inductions.

As you know, I have already directed the Selective Service to cut down the number of inductions from 80,000 to 50,000 per month, and to limit them to the age group of 18 through 25.

It would seem reasonable to limit inductions hereafter to men between the ages of 18 and 25, inclusive, and fix their maximum term of service at two years.

Under the existing statute, inductees can be legally retained only for the duration of the war and a period of six months thereafter. I trust that, in any event, the Congress will not pass a resolution to the effect that the war has terminated for the purposes of this statute. To do so would give to all inducted men and temporary officers of the Army now on active duty the right to civilian status, and would create an impossible demobilization situation.

These are the military steps which it is apparent must be taken at once to meet the needs of the transition from war to peace. First things necessarily come first.

But the full needs of our national security run far beyond this immediate period of transition. We should make timely preparations for the Nation's long-range security, while we are still mindful of what it has cost us in this war to have been unprepared.

It is, therefore, my intention to communicate with the Congress from time to time during the current session with respect to a comprehensive and continuous program of national security, including a universal training program, unification of the armed services, and the use and control of atomic energy.

11. HOUSING

The largest single opportunity for the rapid postwar expansion of private investment and employment lies in the field of housing, both urban and rural. The present shortage of decent homes and the enforced widespread use of substandard housing indicate vital unfulfilled needs of the Nation. These needs will become more marked as veterans begin to come back and look for places to live.

There is wide agreement that, over the next ten years, there should be built in the United States an average of from a million to a million and a half homes a year.

Such a program would provide an opportunity for private capital to invest from six to seven billion dollars annually. Private enterprise in this field could provide employment for several million workers each year. A housing program of this realistic size would, in turn, stimulate a vast amount of business and employment in industries which make house furnishings and equipment of every kind, and in the industries which supply the materials for them. It would provide an impetus for new products, and would develop new markets for a variety of manufactured articles to be made by private enterprise.

Housing is high on the list of matters calling for decisive Congressional action. This is reflected in recommendations contained in reports recently issued by the postwar committees of the Senate and of the House of Representatives. While differing opinions may be held as to detail, these proposals for action already developed in the Congress appear to me sound and essential.

I urgently recommend that the Congress, at an early date, enact broad and comprehensive housing legislation.

The cardinal principle underlying such legislation should be that house construction and financing for the overwhelming majority of our citizens should be done by private enterprise.

We should retain and improve upon the present excellent Government facilities which permit the savings of the people to be channeled voluntarily into private house construction on financing terms that will serve the needs of home owners of moderate income.

The present principles of insurance of housing investment—now tested by years of experience—should be retained and extended, so as to encourage direct investment in housing by private financing institutions.

The Government, in addition to providing these facilities to help private enterprise and private capital build homes, should take effective measures to stimulate research in methods and materials of housing construction. In this way, better and cheaper methods may be developed to build homes.

In addition to this type of research, the Government might well undertake to assist communities in making recurrent community studies in matters relating to housing and real estate generally. Such a program would contribute in great degree to the progress of private initiative and private capital investment in housing.

We must go on. We must widen our horizon even further. We must consider the redevelopment of large areas of the blighted and slum sections of our cities so that in the truly American way they may be remade to accommodate families not only of low-income groups as heretofore, but of every income group. We must make it possible for private enterprise to do the major part of this job. In most cases, it is now impossible for private enterprise to contemplate rebuilding slum areas without public assistance. The land cost generally is too high.

The time has come for the Government to begin to undertake a program of Federal aid to stimulate and promote the redevelopment of these deteriorating areas. Such Federal aid should be extended only to those communities which are willing to bear a fair part of the cost of clearing their blighted city areas and preparing them for redevelopment and rebuilding.

The rebuilding of these areas should conform to broad city plans, provide adequately for displaced families and make maximum use of private capital. Here lies another road toward establishing a better standard of city living, toward increasing business activity and providing jobs.

This Nation has recognized the need of using public funds to clear slums and to provide homes for those families who could not otherwise enjoy adequate housing because of the difference between their present earning power and the cost or rental of a decent home. We cannot, and we will not, recede from these purposes.

For those low-income groups, representing but a small portion of the total housing need, our prewar program of Federal aid to communities for low-rent housing should be resumed. Only in that way can we make progress toward our ultimate goal laid down in the economic bill of rights of a decent home for every American family.

I recommend, also, that we quicken our rate of progress in rural housing. As a general rule, housing conditions on farms and in rural areas are relatively worse than in our cities. In housing, as well as in other benefits of the American system, farm families should enjoy equality with city dwellers.

A decent standard of housing for all is one of the irreducible obligations of modern civilization. The housing challenge is now squarely before us. The people of the United States, so far ahead in wealth and productive capacity, deserve to be the best housed people in the world. We must begin to meet that challenge at once.

12. RESEARCH

Progress in scientific research and development is an indispensable condition to the future welfare and security of the Nation. The events of the past few years are both proof and prophecy of what science can do.

Science in this war has worked through thousands of men and women who labored selflessly and, for the most part, anonymously in the laboratories, pilot plants, and proving grounds of the Nation.

Through them, science, always pushing forward the frontiers of knowledge, forged the new weapons that shortened the war.

Progress in science cannot depend alone upon brilliant inspiration or sudden flights of genius. We have recently had a dramatic demonstration of this truth. In peace and in war, progress comes slowly in small new bits, from the unremitting day-by-day labors of thousands of men and women.

No nation can maintain a position of leadership in the world of today unless it develops to the full its scientific and technological resources. No government adequately meets its responsibilities unless it generously and intelligently supports and encourages the work of science in university, industry, and in its own laboratories.

During the war we have learned much about the methods of organizing science, and about the ways of encouraging and supporting its activities.

The development of atomic energy is a clear-cut indication of what can be accomplished by our universities, industry, and Government working together. Vast scientific fields remain to be conquered in the same way.

In order to derive the full profit in the future from what we have learned, I urge upon the Congress the early adoption of legislation for the establishment of a single Federal research agency which would discharge the following functions:

1. Promote and support fundamental research and development projects in all matters pertaining to the defense and security of the Nation.
2. Promote and support research in the basic sciences and in the social sciences.
3. Promote and support research in medicine, public health, and allied fields.
4. Provide financial assistance in the form of scholarships and grants for young men and women of proved scientific ability.
5. Coordinate and control diverse scientific activities now conducted by the several departments and agencies of the Federal Government.
6. Make fully, freely, and publicly available to commerce, industry, agriculture, and academic institutions, the fruits of research financed by Federal funds.

Scientific knowledge and scientific research are a complex and interrelated structure. Technological advances in one field may have great significance for another apparently unrelated. Accordingly, I urge upon the Congress the desirability of centralizing these functions in a single agency.

Although science can be coordinated and encouraged, it cannot be dictated to or regimented. Science cannot progress unless founded on the free intelligence of the scientist. I stress the fact that the Federal research agency here proposed should in no way impair that freedom.

Even if the Congress promptly adopts the legislation I have recommended, some months must elapse before the newly established agency could commence its operations. To fill what I hope will be only a temporary gap, I have asked the Office of Scientific Research and Development and the Research Board for National Security to continue their work.

Our economic and industrial strength, the physical well-being of our people, the achievement of full employment and full production, the future of our security, and the preservation of our principles will be determined by the extent to which we give full and sincere support to the works of science.

It is with these works that we can build the highroads to the future.

13. TRANSITION TAX REVISION

Taxes will play a vital role in attaining a prosperous peace.

I recommend that a transitional tax bill be enacted as soon as possible to provide limited tax reductions for the calendar year 1946. Like the Tax Adjustment Act of 1945, the new bill should aim principally at removing barriers to speedy reconversion and to the expansion of our peacetime economy.

This matter has been under study jointly by congressional and Treasury tax staffs. I am assured that a program will be ready for early consideration by the Congress.

We must reconcile ourselves to the fact that room for tax reduction at this time is limited. A total war effort cannot be liquidated overnight.

It is estimated that war expenditures in the current fiscal year will drop 40 billion dollars below last year, but that they will still amount to 50 billion dollars out of total expenditures of 66 billion dollars. With current receipts estimated at 36 billion dollars, we face an estimated deficit of 30 billion dollars in the current fiscal year. Expenditures, although further reduced, will necessarily continue at high levels in the fiscal year 1947.

In considering tax reductions for 1946 we must not lose sight of the budgetary situation and our obligations to 85,000,000 bondholders.

After passage of the transitional bill, I hope that the Congress will give careful consideration to the modernization of the Federal tax structure. A major objective of this modernization should be the encouragement of business incentives and expansion, and of consumer purchasing power. In this connection consideration of further tax reductions should have due regard to the level of governmental expenditures and the health and stability of our economy.

14. SURPLUS-PROPERTY DISPOSAL

On July 17 I recommended that the Congress enact legislation creating a single Surplus Property Administrator in place of the board of three which was provided in the statute enacted last year.

I realize that this recommendation came too late to be dealt with prior to your recess, but I strongly urge that you act on it now.

A single administrator can do much to obviate the confusion which still exists in this field, and will be able to expedite the disposal of the many billions of dollars of surplus property.

The disposition of plants and equipment is of particular urgency. They should be disposed of promptly by sale or lease on a basis that is fair to the Government and to industry. Our objectives should be to provide early and continuous employment, and through private production, to supply hungry markets and check inflationary tendencies. Leases may often enable the Government and the operator to determine actual value by actual experience. The sooner we can put plants and equipment to work, the sooner we can discard our wartime controls in the transition from war to peace.

15. SMALL BUSINESS

During the war special attention was paid to small business. The American small business is the backbone of our free-enterprise system. The efforts of the Congress in protecting small business during the war paid high dividends, not only in protecting small business enterprise, but also in speeding victory. In spite of the fact, however, that many businesses were helped and saved, it is true that many thousands of them were obliged to close up because of lack of materials or manpower or inability to get into war production.

It is very important to the economy of the United States that these small businesses and many more of them be given opportunity to become a part of American trade and industry. To do this, assistance should be given to small businesses to enable them to obtain adequate materials, private financing, technological improvements, and surplus property.

While some special facilities for small business are required, the greatest help to it will come from the maintenance of general prosperity and full employment. It is much more difficult for small business to survive the hazards which come from trade recessions and widespread unemployment. What small business needs chiefly is a steady supply of customers with stable purchasing power.

I am sure that the Congress will see to it that in its legislation adequate protection and encouragement will be given to the small business of the Nation.

16. VETERANS

It has been a fundamental objective of the Congress and of the administration to make generous provision for those who have served the Nation in its armed forces, and for the dependents of those who have died in their country's cause.

Although a full list of what has been done toward this objective would be entirely too long to enumerate here, it might be well to list some of the major steps already taken:

(1) Adoption of a National Service Life Insurance Act under which about $17^1/_2$ million insurance applications have been approved, resulting in insurance coverage of more than $135,000,000,000.

(2) Provision of increased compensation or pension for disabled veterans.

(3) Extension and expansion of hospital benefits.

(4) Vocational education and training for veterans having a service-connected disability constituting a vocational handicap.

(5) Mustering-out pay ranging from $100 to $300 dependent upon length of service and rate of pay.

(6) Education or training for any veteran whose education or training was interrupted by entrance into the service.

(7) Guarantee of loans to veterans for the purchase of a home, a farm, or a business.

(8) Legislation to protect the veteran's right to reemployment in his preservice job, if desired.

(9) Provision of unemployment allowances for veterans who become unemployed at any time within two years after discharge, of $20 per week for not to exceed 52 weeks.

(10) Civil-service laws to insure preference to veterans in governmental service.

(11) There has also been instituted in each State pursuant to law an efficient system whereby the counseling and placement needs of veterans will be the responsibility of veterans appointed for that special work.

The transition of veterans from military to civilian activities cannot be accomplished satisfactorily by the Federal Government alone or the States alone, or, indeed, by both. Government can help chiefly through organization and over-all planning. But the real work must be done in each community, through cooperation of the industrial, labor, and civic organizations interested in the welfare of the community and of the veterans.

There have been established information centers in all the field activities of the Selective Service System, United States Employment Service, and Veterans Administration totaling more than 8,000. Veterans may there obtain information on any question of interest to them.

Also, the Retraining and Reemployment Administration in cooperation with the leadership of local communities has established approximately 1,450 community information centers. There are therefore 9,000 information centers of all types throughout the country available to veterans for information purposes. With respect to agricultural interests, use has been made of county committees.

Broad and generous as this legislation for veterans has been, there will be need of amendments and improvements. I recommend that the Congress give prompt consideration to the recommendations which have been made by the Veterans Administration for the purpose of clarifying and liberalizing the provisions relative to hospital and medical care, to vocational training under the Vocational Rehabilitation Act, and to education and training under the Servicemen's Readjustment Act. I also urge consideration of the suggestions made by the Veterans Administration with respect to the loan guarantee features of the latter Act, to amendments clarifying and liberalizing the National Service Life Insurance Act, and those which would increase the rates of compensation for specific injuries including multiple amputations.

I have recommended that the Selective Training and Service Act be continued; but if the Congress determines to the contrary, I urgently recommend that it clarify the provisions thereof which specifically deal with the right of reemployment.

Favorable consideration should be given by the Congress to Federal reclamation projects as outstanding opportunities for returning veterans. The great Columbia Basin project in the Northwest, the projects in the Missouri River Basin, and others of equal significance will bring into existence many thousands of new family-size farms upon which returning veterans can secure a livelihood for themselves and their families and create new wealth for the Nation. A number of farms can be made ready for veterans rapidly if legislation now pending is enacted without delay. This legislation would authorize necessary and proper assistance to veterans who seek to develop farm homes on irrigated lands in Federal reclamation project areas.

I also recommend that the Congress expedite legislation giving veterans social-security coverage credit for the period of their service in the armed services.

The latest available statistics in the Veterans' Administration shows that pension payments in varying amounts are now going forward each month to approximately 600,000 veterans of World War II and to the dependents of more than 100,000 deceased veterans of World War II.

Insurance claims under the National Service Life Insurance Act have been allowed in a total of 361,000 cases involving insurance of approximately $2\frac{1}{2}$ billion dollars.

More than 200,000 World War II veterans have already been afforded hospital care in Veterans Administration facilities.

At the time of Pearl Harbor, the Veterans Administration and the Federal Board of Hospitalization had under way a hospital-building program which by 1949, the estimated peak of needs for World War I veterans, would have provided a total of 100,000 beds for hospital and domiciliary care. Since Pearl Harbor the hospital-building program has been expedited.

The Veterans Administration now has approximately 82,000 hospital and 14,000 domiciliary beds. Thirteen thousand beds are now under construction, and funds are available for 15,000 more.

The Servicemen's Readjustment Act authorizes appropriations to the extent of $500,000,000 for the construction of veterans' hospitals and also the transfer to the Veterans Administration of suitable facilities of the Army and Navy after the end of the war, when surplus to their needs. The program of the Veterans Administration and the Federal Board of Hospitalization contemplates keeping abreast of developing needs through such transfers and additional construction. To this end a plan has just been approved for construction of 29,000 additional beds.

Since World War I there have been more than 3,000,000 hospital admissions in veterans' facilities—and most of them since 1925. Considering that the total number of veterans of World War I and all living veterans of prior wars did not exceed one-third the number of the veterans of World War II, it can readily be seen how important it is to provide hospital privilege. The subject is one which should receive the most careful consideration from the point of view of the extent and quality of facilities to be provided and maintained.

In the last analysis, if we can insure the proper economic conditions, we may be sure that the genius and initiative of Americans who met successfully all demands of the greatest war in history, both on the fighting front and on the production front, will make certain the reintegration of veterans into an expanding civilian economy. Anything less would not meet the country's obligations to its veterans.

17. PUBLIC WORKS AND NATIONAL RESOURCES

During the war years we have expended our resources—both human and natural—without stint. We have thrown into the battle for freedom everything we had.

Thousands of our finest young men—our best human resources—have given their lives. Additional thousands have been injured so that they may not be able to realize their full promise. The education of millions of young men and young women has been disrupted. At best, the Nation will be deprived of the full benefit of their services as scientists, doctors, technicians, lawyers, and educators for 3 to 5 years, or even longer, while they complete the preparation which the necessities of war interrupted.

The depletion of our natural resources is even more startling. We have torn from the earth copper, petroleum, iron ore, tungsten, and every other mineral required to fight a war, without regard to our future supplies. We have taken what we needed. We were not able to, and we did not, take account of tomorrow.

At the same time, our splendid prewar program to build up our national resources was sharply halted. The diligent and constant search for additional deposits of minerals was almost abandoned in favor of a frantic effort to discover and make possible the production of the materials of war.

The long-range programs to conserve the precious inches of topsoil which, in many parts of the country, lie between plenty and poverty were necessarily interrupted. We had neither the manpower nor the materials to spare for projects to prevent the ravages of floods which constantly despoil our land. We had neither the men nor the facilities to continue a large-scale program of reclaiming land and of bringing new land into cultivation.

With a few exceptions, we were forced to suspend the program to which this Nation is committed of harnessing the waters of our great rivers so that they may become vehicles of commerce, beneficent producers of cheap electric power, and servants of the Nation instead of instruments of destruction.

In brief, although during this war this Nation has reached the apex of its power—a peak of greatness and might which the world had never seen—our national capital account has greatly suffered. We must proceed with all possible diligence not merely to restore these depleted resources to their prewar standards but to make them greater and richer than ever before.

We must make a diligent effort to discover new deposits of the precious and indispensable minerals upon which our national life is rounded.

We must develop for the use of industry new technologies so that the vast deposits of low-grade ores that have not heretofore been considered usable may be put to work for the good of all of us.

We should build and improve our roads—the arteries of commerce; we must harness our streams for the general welfare; we must rebuild and reclaim our land; we must protect and restore our forests.

This is not only to provide men and women with work, it is to assure to the Nation the very basis of its life. It is to play the part of a good businessman who insists carefully on maintaining and rebuilding his plant and machinery.

We know that by the investment of Federal funds we can, within the limits of our own Nation, provide for our citizens new frontiers—new territories for the development of industry, agriculture, and commerce.

We have before us the example of the Tennessee Valley Authority, which has inspired regional resource development throughout the entire world.

We know that we have programs, carefully considered and extensively debated, for regional development of the Columbia River in the great Northwest, the Missouri River, the Central Valley of California, and the Arkansas River.

In the Columbia Valley the first major step has been completed for the reclamation of barren land and the production of enormous quantities of power. The waters of the Missouri and the Arkansas and the rivers of California can be put to work to serve the national interest in a similar fashion.

If these rivers remain scourges of our Nation, it is only because we do not have the prudence to harness them for the benefit of our people. If there are among us for any period of time farmers who do not farm because there is no suitable land available to them; workers who do not work because there is no labor for their hands, we have only ourselves to blame so long as we fail to make available to them the opportunities before our very eyes.

I hope that the Congress will proceed as rapidly as possible to authorize regional development of the natural resources of our great river valleys.

It should be unnecessary to say that the conservation and development of the national plant must proceed according to an intelligent and coordinated design. The watersheds of this Nation are not utterly independent, one of the other; our irreplaceable wealth of minerals, land, and timber is not composed of segments which can effectively be dealt with separately. Any program of public works must have as its unifying purpose the greatest possible contribution to the wealth of the Nation and to the wealth-producing capability of the Nation.

It is necessary that we proceed as speedily as possible to set up machinery to make an inventory of our national wealth and our basic resources, and to test the suitability of plans and proposals for public works in light of this purpose. An agency of this sort could provide us with consistent direction toward the goal of rehabilitation and improvement of our basic national resources.

Shortages of materials and manpower made it necessary in the interests of the war effort to suspend many public works which might otherwise have been undertaken. Now that materials and manpower will become more plentiful, we should be prepared to undertake a program of useful public works, not only to improve the physical plant of the United States but to provide employment to great masses of our citizens when private industry cannot do so. Only such public works should now be undertaken, however, as will not compete with the use of materials and manpower by private industry. Plans for other public works should be perfected and put in reserve.

In this connection I have several recommendations:

(1) During the war the construction of Federal public works has been restricted to those necessary for national defense and the prosecution of the war. Projects which normally would have been constructed were deferred, and a large backlog of needed construction has accumulated. Plans for some of these projects—specifically those relating to reclamation, rivers and harbors, flood control, and the conservation of our natural resources—are now ready, and their construction can go forward when funds are provided and materials and manpower are available without competing with private industry. Plans for other Federal projects are being prepared through the use of funds wisely appropriated by the Congress for advance preparation. Additional funds are needed for this purpose, and I urge that the Congress provide them.

(2) I recommend that the Congress enact legislation authorizing additional construction of certain Federal buildings. A portion of this program has already been authorized but has been held up by reason of cost limits imposed upon the buildings which cannot now be met because of increased needs and costs.

(3) I recommend that the Congress release the funds for the highway program authorized under the Federal Aid Highway Act of 1944 (Public Law 521, 78th Cong.). Under this act $500,000,000 has been authorized for the first year and $500,000,000 for each of the two succeeding years, making a total authorization of $1\frac{1}{2}$ billion. With the States' share of the cost included, this would provide a total highway construction program of $3,000,000,000 for a 3-year period.

(4) I recommend that the Congress appropriate $25,000,000 to continue the construction of the Inter-American Highway through the Central American Republics to the Canal Zone.

(5) I recommend that the Congress enact legislation to provide the necessary airports and airport facilities to serve the great needs of an expanded postwar air transportation and commerce. A well-planned airport program would improve transportation, amplify the usefulness of the airplane, and contribute to a healthy aircraft manufacturing industry.

The Congress now has before it a survey of the present and future needs for airports in the United States prepared by the Secretary of Commerce. This report indicates the necessity for approximately 3,000 new airports and for improvements to more than half of the existing 3,000 airports. The report recommends that the program be spread over a period of 10 years and that the cost be shared equally between Federal and non-Federal governmental agencies. I recommend passage of appropriate legislation to implement this program.

(6) States and local governments should be encouraged to construct useful public works of the types that must necessarily supplement and go along with the private construction of homes and industrial facilities. If private construction is to move forward at a rapid rate, it is vitally important that local governments promptly proceed with the construction of such facilities as streets, sewers, water supply, hospitals, airports, schools, and other necessary public facilities. Such projects should be undertaken at this time where they supplement and encourage private construction, not where they compete with it for manpower and materials.

The Congress has already authorized under title V of the War Mobilization and Reconversion Act of 1944 appropriations for advances of Federal funds to State and local governments to assist them in the preparation of detailed drawings and specifications for their public works. The appropriation thus far made is entirely inadequate and I shall request additional funds in order to speed up this important activity during the reconversion period.

The majority of State and local governments are awaiting a decision concerning Federal assistance. In order to get needed public facilities started promptly which do not compete with private construction, I recommend that the Congress give early consideration to grants for such public works under conditions that will insure that each level of government, Federal, State, and local, shall make its appropriate contribution.

(7) The Congress has also been giving consideration to legislation with respect to the construction of hospitals and health centers throughout the country. During the war the Government, through the Federal Works Agency and the Public Health Service, has assisted State and local governments and nonprofit organizations in the construction of such facilities. The beneficial results of this program are well known. The Federal Government must continue to recognize its obligation to maintain and improve the health of the Nation by providing Federal grants where necessary for the construction of hospital and health centers.

Programs of internal improvements of a public character—Federal, State, and local—must preserve competitive bidding, guarantee collective bargaining and good wages for labor, utilize the skills of our returned veterans to the fullest extent, and effectively prevent discrimination because of race, creed, or color.

18. LEND-LEASE AND POSTWAR RECONSTRUCTION

With the arrival of VJ-day lend-lease aid has practically come to an end. It was always understood that it would come to an end at that time. Immediately after Japan accepted the terms of unconditional surrender, I instructed the Foreign Economic Administrator to advise promptly all governments that deliveries of supplies under lend-lease would cease on VJ-day.

I also directed the Administrator in advance of the actual termination of lend-lease deliveries on VJ-day to enter into immediate negotiations with the receiving governments for the purchase of all goods in the pipe line or in storage. These negotiations are proceeding satisfactorily.

In due time we must consider the settlement of the lend-lease obligations which have been incurred during the course of the war. We must recognize that it will not be possible for our Allies to pay us dollars for the overwhelming portion of the lend-lease obligations which they have incurred. But this does not mean that all lend-lease obligations are to be canceled. We shall seek under the procedure prescribed in the Lend-Lease Act and in subsequent agreements with other governments to achieve settlements of our wartime lend-lease relations which will permit generally a sound world-wide economy and will contribute to international peace and our own national security.

We must turn from economic cooperation in war to economic cooperation in peace. We have taken steps to carry out the Bretton Woods proposals for an international monetary fund and an International Bank. We are preparing to extend the operations of the Export-Import Bank. Our objective is to enable the peace-loving nations of the world to become self-supporting in a world of expanding freedom and rising standards of living.

Further legislation is also necessary. If we are to avoid the maintenance of governmental monopoly of international credit, the Johnson Act must be repealed. Private loans on a sane basis are an essential adjunct to the operations of the Export-Import and International Bank operations.

I am directing the executive agencies to give full weight to foreign requirements in determining the need for maintaining domestic and export controls and priorities.

We have already solemnly stated that we will do all that is reasonably possible to help war-torn countries to get back on their feet. I am sure that the Congress will wish the Government to live up to that pledge.

Further legislative action is needed in connection with the United Nations Relief and Rehabilitation Administration. I recommend that the Congress fulfill the commitment already made by appropriating the remaining $550,000,000 granted by the Congress for United States participation.

The Council Meeting of the United Nations Relief and Rehabilitation Administration has just been brought to a successful conclusion. At that meeting our delegate found the need for an additional contribution from all participating countries, to enable the United Nations Relief and Rehabilitation Administration to complete its work in Europe and Asia. On his motion, the Council voted to recommend to member countries a further contribution. Our own share will amount to approximately $1,350,000,000. I am confident that you will find this request for an additional authorization and appropriation fully justified, and I ask for prompt examination and consideration of the request.

In meeting the needs of the United Nations Relief and Rehabilitation Administration, surplus military and lend-lease goods will be used to the fullest possible extent.

Finally, I foresee the need for additional interim lending power to insure a rapid and successful transition to peacetime world trade. Appropriate recommendations will be made to the Congress on this matter when we have completed the exploratory conversations already begun with our associates. We wish to maintain the flow of supplies without interruption. Accordingly, I have directed the executive agencies to complete their conversations and studies at the earliest possible moment. I ask the Congress for speedy consideration of the recommendations when they are made.

19. CONGRESSIONAL SALARIES

Now that restrictions on voluntary salary increases have been removed, I hope that the Congress will take action soon on the salaries of its Members.

My experience as a Member of the Senate has given me a very keen appreciation of the quantity and quality of the work of the Members of the Congress. They are called upon to carry great responsibility and make important decisions in a multitude of matters involving the welfare of the Nation and of the world. Their tasks continue day in and day out. They have increased in number and in importance year by year.

There is no doubt in the mind of any thinking American that Members of the Congress are grossly underpaid and have been for many years. I think that they are entitled—and have already so expressed myself—to a salary anywhere from fifteen to twenty-five thousand dollars a year. I recommend that the Congress enact legislation providing that the salaries of its Members be increased to twenty thousand dollars per year.

At the same time I recommend the repeal of the provision now applicable to the House of Representatives for an additional expense allowance. There should be a straight, out-and-out salary increase for all Members. We should make service in the Congress of the United States available without hardship to ordinary citizens who have to look to the salary for their sole support. I also recommend that an adequate retirement system should be provided for the Members of the Congress who have served for a long period of years.

This should be the first step in creating a decent salary scale for all Federal Government employees—executive, legislative, and judicial.

The most important impediment to obtaining efficient administrative officials in the Federal Government has been the pitiful wage scale. During the war many able and experienced men were obtained for Federal service on purely patriotic grounds. Some of these men who are unable to continue at the present salary scales would be willing to remain at adequate salaries.

In most of the various classifications of Federal employees, the wage scales, with few exceptions, are obsolete and inadequate. This is particularly true of the Federal judiciary.

I sincerely hope that the Congress will take early steps to provide decent wage scales for its Members and for the executive and judicial branches of the Government.

20. SALE OF SHIPS

Prompt resumption of the normal operation of our merchant marine to expedite the reestablishment of our foreign trade is a major part of general reconversion from a wartime to a peacetime economy. The Maritime Commission has already received numerous inquiries and applications from potential purchasers of ships at home and abroad for private ownership and operation.

It is recommended that suitable legislation to permit such sales be expedited so that the uncertainty about the disposal of our large surplus tonnage may be removed. In this way, American shipping companies may undertake commercial operation as rapidly as ships can be released from Government control, and the foreign market can also be used for selling those vessels which are in excess of the needs of our postwar American merchant marine and national defense.

21. STOCK PILING OF STRATEGIC MATERIAL

One of the costliest lessons of our unpreparedness for this war was the great danger involved in depending upon foreign sources for supplies of raw materials necessary in times of national emergency. The United States should never again permit itself to be placed in a position where its defense may be jeopardized by the fact that it has been cut off from the source of strategic raw materials.

I recommend that the Congress enact legislation to bring about the acquisition and retention of stock piles of materials in which we are naturally deficient but which are necessary to supply the needs of the Nation for its defense.

I shall shortly communicate with the Congress recommending a national health program to provide adequate medical care for all Americans and to protect them from financial loss and hardships resulting from illness and accident. I shall also communicate with the Congress with respect to expanding our social-security system, and improving our program of education for our citizens.

In this hour of victory over our enemies abroad, let us now resolve to use all our efforts and energies to build a better life here at home and a better world for generations to come.

The Congress has played its full part in shaping the domestic and foreign policies which have won this victory and started us on the road to lasting peace.

The Congress, I know, will continue to play its patriotic part in the difficult years ahead. We face the future together with confidence—that the job, the full job, can and will be done.

HARRY S. TRUMAN

5. "The Long Telegram": The Charge in the Soviet Union (Kennan) to the Secretary of State February 22, 1946

National Security Archive. George Washington University.

511. Answer to Dept's 284, Feb 3 [13] involves questions so intricate, so delicate, so strange to our form of thought, and so important to analysis of our international environment that I cannot compress answers into single brief message without yielding to what I feel would be dangerous degree of oversimplification. I hope, therefore, Dept will bear with me if I submit in answer to this question five parts, subjects of which will be roughly as follows:

(1) Basic features of post-war Soviet outlook.
(2) Background of this outlook
(3) Its projection in practical policy on official level.
(4) Its projection on unofficial level.
(5) Practical deductions from standpoint of US policy.

I apologize in advance for this burdening of telegraphic channel; but questions involved are of such urgent importance, particularly in view of recent events, that our answers to them, if they deserve attention at all, seem to me to deserve it at once. There follows

Part 1: Basic Features of Post War Soviet Outlook, as Put Forward by Official Propaganda Machine

Are as Follows:

(a) USSR still lives in antagonistic "capitalist encirclement" with which in the long run there can be no permanent peaceful coexistence. As stated by Stalin in 1927 to a delegation of American workers:

"In course of further development of international revolution there will emerge two centers of world significance: a socialist center, drawing to itself the countries which tend toward socialism, and a capitalist center, drawing to itself the countries that incline toward capitalism. Battle between these two centers for command of world economy will decide fate of capitalism and of communism in entire world."

(b) Capitalist world is beset with internal conflicts, inherent in nature of capitalist society. These conflicts are insoluble by means of peaceful compromise. Greatest of them is that between England and US.

(c) Internal conflicts of capitalism inevitably generate wars. Wars thus generated may be of two kinds: intra-capitalist wars between two capitalist states, and wars of intervention against socialist world. Smart capitalists, vainly seeking escape from inner conflicts of capitalism, incline toward latter.

(d) Intervention against USSR, while it would be disastrous to those who undertook it, would cause renewed delay in progress of Soviet socialism and must therefore be forestalled at all costs.

(e) Conflicts between capitalist states, though likewise fraught with danger for USSR, nevertheless hold out great possibilities for advancement of socialist cause, particularly if USSR remains militarily powerful, ideologically monolithic and faithful to its present brilliant leadership.

(f) It must be borne in mind that capitalist world is not all bad. In addition to hopelessly reactionary and bourgeois elements, it includes (1) certain wholly enlightened and positive elements united in acceptable communistic parties and (2) certain other elements (now described for tactical reasons as progressive or democratic) whose reactions, aspirations and activities happen to be "objectively" favorable to interests of USSR. These last must be encouraged and utilized for Soviet purposes.

(g) Among negative elements of bourgeois-capitalist society, most dangerous of all are those whom Lenin called false friends of the people, namely moderate-socialist or social-democratic leaders (in other words, non-Communist left-wing). These are more dangerous than out-and-out reactionaries, for latter at least march under their true colors, whereas moderate left-wing leaders confuse people by employing devices of socialism to serve interests of reactionary capital.

So much for premises. To what deductions do they lead from standpoint of Soviet policy? To following:

(a) Everything must be done to advance relative strength of USSR as factor in international society. Conversely, no opportunity most be missed to reduce strength and influence, collectively as well as individually, of capitalist powers.

(b) Soviet efforts, and those of Russia's friends abroad, must be directed toward deepening and

exploiting of differences and conflicts between capitalist powers. If these eventually deepen into an "imperialist" war, this war must be turned into revolutionary upheavals within the various capitalist countries.

(c) "Democratic-progressive" elements abroad are to be utilized to maximum to bring pressure to bear on capitalist governments along lines agreeable to Soviet interests.

(d) Relentless battle must be waged against socialist and social-democratic leaders abroad.

Part 2: Background of Outlook

Before examining ramifications of this party line in practice there are certain aspects of it to which I wish to draw attention.

First, it does not represent natural outlook of Russian people. Latter are, by and large, friendly to outside world, eager for experience of it, eager to measure against it talents they are conscious of possessing, eager above all to live in peace and enjoy fruits of their own labor. Party line only represents thesis which official propaganda machine puts forward with great skill and persistence to a public often remarkably resistant in the stronghold of its innermost thoughts. But party line is binding for outlook and conduct of people who make up apparatus of power—party, secret police and Government—and it is exclusively with these that we have to deal.

Second, please note that premises on which this party line is based are for most part simply not true. Experience has shown that peaceful and mutually profitable coexistence of capitalist and socialist states is entirely possible. Basic internal conflicts in advanced countries are no longer primarily those arising out of capitalist ownership of means of production, but are ones arising from advanced urbanism and industrialism as such, which Russia has thus far been spared not by socialism but only by her own backwardness. Internal rivalries of capitalism do not always generate wars; and not all wars are attributable to this cause. To speak of possibility of intervention against USSR today, after elimination of Germany and Japan and after example of recent war, is sheerest nonsense. If not provoked by forces of intolerance and subversion "capitalist" world of today is quite capable of living at peace with itself and with Russia. Finally, no sane person has reason to doubt sincerity of moderate socialist leaders in Western countries. Nor is it fair to deny success of their efforts to improve conditions for working population whenever, as in Scandinavia, they have been given chance to show what they could do.

Falseness of those premises, every one of which predates recent war, was amply demonstrated by that conflict itself. Anglo-American differences did not turn out to be major differences of Western World. Capitalist countries, other than those of Axis, showed no disposition to solve their differences by joining in crusade against USSR. Instead of imperialist war turning into civil wars and revolution, USSR found itself obliged to fight side by side with capitalist powers for an avowed community of aim.

Nevertheless, all these theses, however baseless and disproven, are being boldly put forward again today. What does this indicate? It indicates that Soviet party line is not based on any objective analysis of situation beyond Russia's borders; that it has, indeed, little to do with conditions outside of Russia; that it arises mainly from basic inner-Russian necessities which existed before recent war and exist today.

At bottom of Kremlin's neurotic view of world affairs is traditional and instinctive Russian sense of insecurity. Originally, this was insecurity of a peaceful agricultural people trying to live on vast exposed plain in neighborhood of fierce nomadic peoples. To this was added, as Russia came into contact with economically advanced West, fear of more competent, more powerful, more highly organized societies in that area. But this latter type of insecurity was one which afflicted rather Russian rulers than Russian people; for Russian rulers have invariably sensed that their rule was relatively archaic in form fragile and artificial in its psychological foundation, unable to stand comparison or contact with political systems of Western countries. For this reason they have always feared foreign penetration, feared direct contact between Western world and their own, feared what would happen if Russians learned truth about world without or if foreigners learned truth about world within. And they have learned to seek security only in patient but deadly struggle for total destruction of rival power, never in compacts and compromises with it.

It was no coincidence that Marxism, which had smoldered ineffectively for half a century in Western Europe, caught hold and blazed for first time in Russia. Only in this land which had never known a friendly neighbor or indeed any tolerant equilibrium of separate powers, either internal or international, could a doctrine thrive which viewed economic conflicts of society as insoluble by peaceful means. After establishment of Bolshevist regime, Marxist dogma, rendered even more truculent and intolerant by Lenin's interpretation, became a perfect vehicle for sense of insecurity with which Bolsheviks, even more than previous Russian rulers, were afflicted. In this dogma, with its basic altruism of purpose, they found justification for their instinctive fear of outside world, for the dictatorship without which they did not know how to rule, for cruelties they did not dare not to inflict, for sacrifice they felt bound to demand. In the name of Marxism they sacrificed every single ethical value in their methods and tactics. Today they cannot dispense with it. It is fig leaf of their moral and intellectual respectability. Without it they would stand before history, at best, as only the last of that long succession of cruel and wasteful Russian rulers who have relentlessly forced country on to ever new heights of military power in order to guarantee external security of their internally weak regimes. This is why Soviet purposes most always be solemnly clothed in trappings of Marxism, and why no one should underrate importance of dogma in Soviet affairs. Thus Soviet leaders are driven [by?] necessities of their own past and present position to put forward which [apparent omission] outside world as evil, hostile and menacing, but as bearing within itself germs of creeping disease and destined to be wracked with growing internal convulsions until it is given final Coup de grace by rising power of socialism and yields to new and better world. This thesis provides justification for that increase of military and police power of Russian state, for that isolation of Russian population from outside world, and for that fluid and constant pressure to extend limits of Russian police power which are together the natural and instinctive urges of Russian rulers. Basically this is only the steady advance of uneasy Russian nationalism, a centuries old movement in which conceptions of offense and defense are inextricably confused. But in new guise of international Marxism, with its honeyed promises to a desperate and war torn outside world, it is more dangerous and insidious than ever before.

It should not be thought from above that Soviet party line is necessarily disingenuous and insincere on part of all those who put it forward. Many of them are too ignorant of outside world and mentally too dependent to question [apparent omission] self-hypnotism, and who have no difficulty making themselves believe what they find it comforting and convenient to believe. Finally we have the unsolved mystery as to who, if anyone, in this great land actually receives accurate and unbiased information about outside world. In atmosphere of oriental secretiveness and conspiracy which pervades this Government, possibilities for distorting or poisoning sources and currents of information are infinite. The very disrespect of Russians for objective truth—indeed, their disbelief in its existence—leads them to view all stated facts as instruments for furtherance of one ulterior purpose or another. There is good reason to suspect that this Government is actually a conspiracy within a conspiracy; and I for one am reluctant to believe that Stalin himself receives anything like an objective picture of outside world. Here there is ample scope for the type of subtle intrigue at which Russians are past masters. Inability of foreign governments to place their case squarely before Russian policy makers—extent to which they are delivered up in their relations with Russia to good graces of obscure and unknown advisors whom they never see and cannot influence—this to my mind is most disquieting feature of diplomacy in Moscow, and one which Western statesmen would do well to keep in mind if they would understand nature of difficulties encountered here.

Part 3: Projection of Soviet Outlook in Practical Policy on Official Level

We have now seen nature and background of Soviet program. What may we expect by way of its practical implementation?

Soviet policy, as Department implies in its query under reference, is conducted on two planes: (1) official plane represented by actions undertaken officially in name of Soviet Government; and (2) subterranean plane of actions undertaken by agencies for which Soviet Government does not admit responsibility.

Policy promulgated on both planes will be calculated to serve basic policies (a) to (d) outlined in part 1. Actions taken on different planes will differ considerably, but will dovetail into each other in purpose, timing and effect.

On official plane we must look for following:

(a) Internal policy devoted to increasing in every way strength and prestige of Soviet state:

intensive military-industrialization; maximum development of armed forces; great displays to impress outsiders; continued secretiveness about internal matters, designed to conceal weaknesses and to keep opponents in dark.

(b) Wherever it is considered timely and promising, efforts will be made to advance official limits of Soviet power. For the moment, these efforts are restricted to certain neighboring points conceived of here as being of immediate strategic necessity, such as Northern Iran, Turkey, possibly Bornholm. However, other points may at any time come into question, if and as concealed Soviet political power is extended to new areas. Thus a friendly Persian Government might be asked to grant Russia a port on Persian Gulf. Should Spain fall under Communist control, question of Soviet base at Gibraltar Strait might be activated. But such claims will appear on official level only when unofficial preparation is complete.

(c) Russians will participate officially in international organizations where they see opportunity of extending Soviet power or of inhibiting or diluting power of others. Moscow sees in UNO not the mechanism for a permanent and stable world society founded on mutual interest and aims of all nations, but an arena in which aims just mentioned can be favorably pursued. As long as UNO is considered here to serve this purpose, Soviets will remain with it. But if at any time they come to conclusion that it is serving to embarrass or frustrate their aims for power expansion and if they see better prospects for pursuit of these aims along other lines, they will not hesitate to abandon UNO. This would imply, however, that they felt themselves strong enough to split unity of other nations by their withdrawal to render UNO ineffective as a threat to their aims or security, replace it with an international weapon more effective from their viewpoint. Thus Soviet attitude toward UNO will depend largely on loyalty of other nations to it, and on degree of vigor, decisiveness and cohesion with which those nations defend in UNO the peaceful and hopeful concept of international life, which that organization represents to our way of thinking. I reiterate, Moscow has no abstract devotion to UNO ideals. Its attitude to that organization will remain essentially pragmatic and tactical.

(d) Toward colonial areas and backward or dependent peoples, Soviet policy, even on official plane, will be directed toward weakening of power and influence and contacts of advanced Western nations, on theory that in so far as this policy is successful, there will be created a vacuum which will favor Communist-Soviet penetration. Soviet pressure for participation in trusteeship arrangements thus represents, in my opinion, a desire to be in a position to complicate and inhibit exertion of Western influence at such points rather than to provide major channel for exerting of Soviet power. Latter motive is not lacking, but for this Soviets prefer to rely on other channels than official trusteeship arrangements. Thus we may expect to find Soviets asking for admission everywhere to trusteeship or similar arrangements and using levers thus acquired to weaken Western influence among such peoples.

(e) Russians will strive energetically to develop Soviet representation in, and official ties with, countries in which they sense Strong possibilities of opposition to Western centers of power. This applies to such widely separated points as Germany, Argentina, Middle Eastern countries, etc.

(f) In international economic matters, Soviet policy will really be dominated by pursuit of autarchy for Soviet Union and Soviet-dominated adjacent areas taken together. That, however, will be underlying policy. As far as official line is concerned, position is not yet clear. Soviet Government has shown strange reticence since termination hostilities on subject foreign trade. If large scale long term credits should be forthcoming, I believe Soviet Government may eventually again do lip service, as it did in 1930's to desirability of building up international economic exchanges in general. Otherwise I think it possible Soviet foreign trade may be restricted largely to Soviet's own security sphere, including occupied areas in Germany, and that a cold official shoulder may be turned to principle of general economic collaboration among nations.

(g) With respect to cultural collaboration, lip service will likewise be rendered to desirability of deepening cultural contacts between peoples, but this will not in practice be interpreted in any way which could weaken security position of Soviet peoples. Actual manifestations of Soviet policy in this respect will be restricted to arid channels of closely shepherded official visits and functions, with superabundance of vodka and speeches and dearth of permanent effects.

(h) Beyond this, Soviet official relations will take what might be called "correct" course with individual foreign governments, with great stress being laid on prestige of Soviet Union and its representatives and with punctilious attention to protocol as distinct from good manners.

Part 4: Following May Be Said as to What We May Expect by Way of Implementation of Basic Soviet Policies on Unofficial, or Subterranean Plane, i.e. on Plane for Which Soviet Government Accepts no Responsibility

Agencies utilized for promulgation of policies on this plane are following:

1. Inner central core of Communist Parties in other countries. While many of persons who compose this category may also appear and act in unrelated public capacities, they are in reality working closely together as an underground operating directorate of world communism, a concealed Comintern tightly coordinated and directed by Moscow. It is important to remember that this inner core is actually working on underground lines, despite legality of parties with which it is associated.

2. Rank and file of Communist Parties. Note distinction is drawn between those and persons defined in paragraph 1. This distinction has become much sharper in recent years. Whereas formerly foreign Communist Parties represented a curious (and from Moscow's standpoint often inconvenient) mixture of conspiracy and legitimate activity, now the conspiratorial element has been neatly concentrated in inner circle and ordered underground, while rank and file—no longer even taken into confidence about realities of movement—are thrust forward as bona fide internal partisans of certain political tendencies within their respective countries, genuinely innocent of conspiratorial connection with foreign states. Only in certain countries where communists are numerically strong do they now regularly appear and act as a body. As a rule they are used to penetrate, and to influence or dominate, as case may be, other organizations less likely to be suspected of being tools of Soviet Government, with a view to accomplishing their purposes through [apparent omission] organizations, rather than by direct action as a separate political party.

3. A wide variety of national associations or bodies which can be dominated or influenced by such penetration. These include: labor unions, youth leagues, women's organizations, racial societies, religious societies, social organizations, cultural groups, liberal magazines, publishing houses, etc.

4. International organizations which can be similarly penetrated through influence over various national components. Labor, youth and women's organizations are prominent among them. Particular, almost vital importance is attached in this connection to international labor movement. In this, Moscow sees possibility of sidetracking western governments in world affairs and building up international lobby capable of compelling governments to take actions favorable to Soviet interests in various countries and of paralyzing actions disagreeable to USSR.

5. Russian Orthodox Church, with its foreign branches, and through it the Eastern Orthodox Church in general.

6. Pan-Slav movement and other movements (Azerbaijan, Armenian, Turcoman, etc.) based on racial groups within Soviet Union.

7. Governments or governing groups willing to lend themselves to Soviet purposes in one degree or another, such as present Bulgarian and Yugoslav Governments, North Persian regime, Chinese Communists, etc. Not only propaganda machines but actual policies of these regimes can be placed extensively at disposal of USSR.

It may be expected that component parts of this far-flung apparatus will be utilized in accordance with their individual suitability, as follows:

(a) To undermine general political and strategic potential of major western powers. Efforts will be made in such countries to disrupt national self confidence, to hamstring measures of national defense, to increase social and industrial unrest, to stimulate all forms of disunity. All persons with grievances, whether economic or racial, will be urged to spelt redress not in mediation and compromise, but in defiant violent struggle for destruction of other elements of society. Here poor will be set against rich, black against white, young against old, newcomers against established residents, etc.

(b) On unofficial plane particularly violent efforts will be made to weaken power and influence of Western Powers of [on] colonial backward, or dependent peoples. On this level, no holds will be barred. Mistakes and weaknesses of western colonial administration will be mercilessly exposed and exploited. Liberal opinion in Western countries will be mobilized to weaken colonial policies. Resentment among dependent peoples will be stimulated. And while latter are being encouraged to seek independence of Western Powers, Soviet dominated puppet political machines will be undergoing preparation to take over domestic power in respective colonial areas when independence is achieved.

(c) Where individual governments stand in path of Soviet purposes pressure will be brought for their removal from office. This can happen where governments directly oppose Soviet foreign policy aims (Turkey, Iran), where they seal their territories off against Communist penetration (Switzerland, Portugal), or where they compete too strongly, like Labor Government in England, for moral domination among elements which it is important for Communists to dominate. (Sometimes, two of these elements are present in a single case. Then Communist opposition becomes particularly shrill and savage. [)]

(d) In foreign countries Communists will, as a rule, work toward destruction of all forms of personal independence, economic, political or moral. Their system can handle only individuals who have been brought into complete dependence on higher power. Thus, persons who are financially independent—such as individual businessmen, estate owners, successful farmers, artisans and all those who exercise local leadership or have local prestige, such as popular local clergymen or political figures, are anathema. It is not by chance that even in USSR local officials are kept constantly on move from one job to another, to prevent their taking root.

(e) Everything possible will be done to set major Western Powers against each other. Anti-British talk will be plugged among Americans, anti-American talk among British. Continentals, including Germans, will be taught to abhor both Anglo-Saxon powers. Where suspicions exist, they will be fanned; where not, ignited. No effort will be spared to discredit and combat all efforts which threaten to lead to any sort of unity or cohesion among other [apparent omission] from which Russia might be excluded. Thus, all forms of international organization not amenable to Communist penetration and control, whether it be the Catholic [apparent omission] international economic concerns, or the international fraternity of royalty and aristocracy, must expect to find themselves under fire from many, and often [apparent omission].

(f) In general, all Soviet efforts on unofficial international plane will be negative and destructive in character, designed to tear down sources of strength beyond reach of Soviet control. This is only in line with basic Soviet instinct that there can be no compromise with rival power and that constructive work can start only when Communist power is dominant. But behind all this will be applied insistent, unceasing pressure for penetration and command of key positions in administration and especially in police apparatus of foreign countries. The Soviet regime is a police regime par excellence, reared in the dim half world of Tsarist police intrigue, accustomed to think primarily in terms of police power. This should never be lost sight of in ganging Soviet motives.

Part 5: [Practical Deductions From Standpoint of US Policy]

In summary, we have here a political force committed fanatically to the belief that with US there can be no permanent modus vivendi that it is desirable and necessary that the internal harmony of our society be disrupted, our traditional way of life be destroyed, the international authority of our state be broken, if Soviet power is to be secure. This political force has complete power of disposition over energies of one of world's greatest peoples and resources of world's richest national territory, and is borne along by deep and powerful currents of Russian nationalism. In addition, it has an elaborate and far flung apparatus for exertion of its influence in other countries, an apparatus of amazing flexibility and versatility, managed by people whose experience and skill in underground methods are presumably without parallel in history. Finally, it is seemingly inaccessible to considerations of reality in its basic reactions. For it, the vast fund of objective fact about human society is not, as with us, the measure against which outlook is constantly being tested and reformed, but a grab bag from which individual items are selected arbitrarily and tendentiously to bolster an outlook already preconceived. This is admittedly not a pleasant picture. Problem of how to cope with this force in [is] undoubtedly greatest task our diplomacy has ever faced and probably greatest it will ever have to face. It should be point of departure from which our political general staff work at present juncture should proceed. It should be approached with same thoroughness and care as solution of major strategic problem in war, and if necessary, with no smaller outlay in planning effort. I cannot attempt to suggest all answers here. But I would like to record my conviction that problem is within our power to solve—and that without recourse to any general military conflict. And in

support of this conviction there are certain observations of a more encouraging nature I should like to make:

(1) Soviet power, unlike that of Hitlerite Germany, is neither schematic nor adventuristic. It does not work by fixed plans. It does not take unnecessary risks. Impervious to logic of reason, and it is highly sensitive to logic of force. For this reason it can easily withdraw—and usually does when strong resistance is encountered at any point. Thus, if the adversary has sufficient force and makes clear his readiness to use it, he rarely has to do so. If situations are properly handled there need be no prestige-engaging showdowns.

(2) Gauged against Western World as a whole, Soviets are still by far the weaker force. Thus, their success will really depend on degree of cohesion, firmness and vigor which Western World can muster. And this is factor which it is within our power to influence.

(3) Success of Soviet system, as form of internal power, is not yet finally proven. It has yet to be demonstrated that it can survive supreme test of successive transfer of power from one individual or group to another. Lenin's death was first such transfer, and its effects wracked Soviet state for 15 years. After Stalin's death or retirement will be second. But even this will not be final test. Soviet internal system will now be subjected, by virtue of recent territorial expansions, to series of additional strains which once proved severe tax on Tsardom. We here are convinced that never since termination of civil war have mass of Russian people been emotionally farther removed from doctrines of Communist Party than they are today. In Russia, party has now become a great and—for the moment—highly successful apparatus of dictatorial administration, but it has ceased to be a source of emotional inspiration. Thus, internal soundness and permanence of movement need not yet be regarded as assured.

(4) All Soviet propaganda beyond Soviet security sphere is basically negative and destructive. It should therefore be relatively easy to combat it by any intelligent and really constructive program.

For those reasons I think we may approach calmly and with good heart problem of how to deal with Russia. As to how this approach should be made, I only wish to advance, by way of conclusion, following comments:

(1) Our first step must be to apprehend, and recognize for what it is, the nature of the movement

with which we are dealing. We must study it with same courage, detachment, objectivity, and same determination not to be emotionally provoked or unseated by it, with which doctor studies unruly and unreasonable individual.

(2) We must see that our public is educated to realities of Russian situation. I cannot over-emphasize importance of this. Press cannot do this alone. It must be done mainly by Government, which is necessarily more experienced and better informed on practical problems involved. In this we need not be deterred by [ugliness?] of picture. I am convinced that there would be far less hysterical anti-Sovietism in our country today if realities of this situation were better understood by our people. There is nothing as dangerous or as terrifying as the unknown. It may also be argued that to reveal more information on our difficulties with Russia would reflect unfavorably on Russian-American relations. I feel that if there is any real risk here involved, it is one which we should have courage to face, and sooner the better. But I cannot see what we would be risking. Our stake in this country, even coming on heels of tremendous demonstrations of our friendship for Russian people, is remarkably small. We have here no investments to guard, no actual trade to lose, virtually no citizens to protect, few cultural contacts to preserve. Our only stake lies in what we hope rather than what we have; and I am convinced we have better chance of realizing those hopes if our public is enlightened and if our dealings with Russians are placed entirely on realistic and matter-of-fact basis.

(3) Much depends on health and vigor of our own society. World communism is like malignant parasite which feeds only on diseased tissue. This is point at which domestic and foreign policies meets. Every courageous and incisive measure to solve internal problems of our own society, to improve self-confidence, discipline, morale and community spirit of our own people, is a diplomatic victory over Moscow worth a thousand diplomatic notes and joint communiqués. If we cannot abandon fatalism and indifference in face of deficiencies of our own society, Moscow will profit—Moscow cannot help profiting by them in its foreign policies.

(4) We must formulate and put forward for other nations a much more positive and constructive picture of sort of world we would like to see than we have put forward in past. It is not enough to urge people to develop political processes similar to our own. Many foreign peoples, in Europe at least, are tired and frightened by experiences of past, and are less interested in abstract freedom than in security. They are seeking guidance rather than responsibilities. We should be better able than Russians to give them this. And unless we do, Russians certainly will.

(5) Finally we must have courage and self-confidence to cling to our own methods and conceptions of human society. After Al, the greatest danger that can befall us in coping with this problem of Soviet communism, is that we shall allow ourselves to become like those with whom we are coping.

6. Special Message to the Congress Urging Legislation for Industrial Peace May 25, 1946

Public Papers of the Presidents of the United States: Harry S. Truman, 1946. Washington, D.C.: U.S. Government Printing Office, 277–280.

Mr. President, Mr. Speaker, Members of the Congress of the United States:

I desire to thank you for this privilege of appearing before you, in order to urge legislation which I deem essential to the welfare of our country. For the past two days the Nation has been in the grip of a railroad strike which threatens to paralyze all our industrial, agricultural, commercial, and social life.

Last night I tried to point out to the American people the bleak picture which we face at home and abroad if the strike is permitted to continue.

The disaster will spare no one. It will bear equally upon businessmen, workers, farmers and upon every citizen of the United States. Food, raw materials, fuel, shipping, housing, the public health, the public safety—all will be dangerously affected. Hundreds of thousands of liberated people of Europe and Asia will die who could be saved if the railroads were not now tied up.

As I stated last night, unless the railroads are manned by returning strikers, I shall immediately undertake to run them by the Army of the United States.

I assure you that I do not take this action lightly. But there is no alternative. This is no longer a dispute between labor and management. It has now become a strike against the Government of the United States itself. That kind of strike can never be tolerated. If allowed to continue, the Government will break down. Strikes against the Government must stop. I appear before you to request immediate legislation designed to help stop them.

I am sure that some of you may think that I should have taken this action earlier, and that I should have made this appearance here before today. The reason I did not do so, was that I was determined to make every possible human effort to avoid this strike against the Government and to make unnecessary the kind of legislation which I am about to request.

For months, publicly and privately, I have been supervising and directing negotiations between the railroad operators and the twenty different railroad unions. I have been doing the same with respect to the pending labor dispute in the coal mines. Time and again I have seen the leaders of the unions and the representatives of the operators. Many hours have been spent by me personally and many days have been spent by my representatives in attempting to negotiate settlements of these disputes.

I assure you that it was not easy to be patient. But until the very last moment I made every effort to avert this crisis. In fact my representatives were in conference with the two striking railroad unions up to 2 hours before I took my place at the microphone last night.

However, when the strike actually broke against the United States Government which was trying to run the railroads, the time for negotiation definitely had passed and the time for action had arrived. In that action you, the Congress of the United States, and I, the President of the United States, must work together—and we must work fast.

The action which I have already taken, and the action which I shall ask you to take are necessary for the preservation of our Government. That action is also necessary to save the great and mighty masses of working men and women from the dangerous effects of the ill-advised and misguided acts of some of their own leaders.

This particular crisis has been brought about by the obstinate arrogance of two men. They are Mr. Alvanley Johnston, President of the Brotherhood of Locomotive Engineers, and Mr. A. F. Whitney, President of the Brotherhood of Railway Trainmen. Eighteen other unions and all of the railroad companies of the Nation are ready to run the railroads, and these two men have tried to stop them.

I can well appreciate the attitude of those members of the Congress and those citizens of the United States outside of the Congress who would seek to take vengeance for the unpatriotic acts of these two men. However, I am sure that none of us wishes to take any action which will injure labor.

The contribution of labor to the growth of this country in peace and to victory in war, is at least as great as that of any other group in our population. Without Well-paid, well-housed, and well-nourished working men and women in this country, it would stagnate and decay. I am here not only to urge speedy action to meet the immediate crisis, but also deliberate and weighty consideration of any legislation which might affect the rights of labor.

The benefits which labor has gained in the last 13 years must be preserved. I voted for all these benefits while I was a member of the Congress. As President of the United States I have repeatedly urged not only their retention but their improvement. I shall continue to do so.

However, what we are dealing with here is not labor as a whole.

We are dealing with a handful of men who are striking against their own Government and against every one of their fellow citizens—and against themselves.

We are dealing with a handful of men who have it within their power to cripple the entire economy of the Nation.

I request temporary legislation to take care of this immediate crisis. I request permanent legislation leading to the formulation of a long-range labor policy designed to prevent the recurrence of such crises and generally to reduce stoppages of work in all industries for the future.

I request that the temporary legislation be effective only for a period of 6 months after the declaration by the President or by the Congress of the termination of hostilities. It should be applicable only to those few industries in which the President by proclamation declares that an emergency has arisen which affects the entire economy of the United States. It should be effective only in those situations where the President of the United States has taken over the operation of the industry. In such situations where the President has requested the men either to remain at work or to return to work and where such a request is ignored, the legislation should:

(a) authorize the institution of injunctive or mandatory proceedings against any union leader forbidding him from encouraging or inciting members of the union to leave their work or to refuse to return to work; subjecting him to contempt proceedings for failure to obey any order of the Court made in such proceedings;

(b) deprive workers of their seniority rights who, without good cause, persist in striking against the Government.

(c) provide criminal penalties against employers and union leaders who violate the provisions of the act.

The legislation should provide that after the Government has taken over an industry and has directed the men to remain at work or return to work, the wage scale be fixed either by negotiation or by arbitrators appointed by the President and when so fixed, it shall be retroactive.

This legislation must be used in a way that is fair to capital and to labor alike. The President will not permit either side-industry or workers—to use it to further their own selfish interest, or to foist upon the Government the carrying out of their selfish aims.

Net profits of Government operation, if any, should go to the Treasury of the United States.

As a part of this temporary emergency legislation, I request the Congress immediately to authorize the President to draft into the Armed Forces of the United States all workers who are on strike against their Government.

[At this point the President was handed a message by Leslie L. Biffle, Secretary of the Senate.]

Word has just been received that the railroad strike has been settled, on terms proposed by the President!

These measures may appear to you to be drastic. They are. I repeat that I recommend them only as temporary emergency expedients and only in cases where workers are striking against the Government.

I take this occasion again to request early action by the Congress to continue its price control and stabilization laws in an effective form. The stoppage of work in many industries has brought about a decline of production which has caused great pressure upon price levels. We must protect the workers whom we ask to remain on their jobs, as well as the millions of workers who have remained on their jobs and the many millions of other American citizens, against the extraordinary inflation which may come upon us. Delay by the Congress is daily increasing these pressures and I urge immediate action.

I have said that I am most anxious—as I am sure the majority of the Members of the Congress are—to do nothing which would injure labor or the cause of labor.

I believe that the time has come to adopt a comprehensive labor policy which will tend to reduce the number of stoppages of work and other acts which injure labor, capital, and the whole population.

The general right of workers to strike against private employers must be preserved. I am sure, however, that adequate study and consideration can produce permanent long-range legislation which will reduce the number of occasions where that ultimate remedy has to be adopted. The whole subject of labor relations should be studied afresh.

I recommend the immediate creation by the Congress of a joint committee to make that study. That committee should study the whole problem and, within a period of 6 months bring in recommendations for appropriate legislation which would be fair to labor and to industry and to the public at large.

I make these recommendations for temporary and long-range legislation with the same emphasis on each. They should both be part of one program designed to maintain our American system of private enterprise with fairness and justice to all the American citizens who contribute to it.

I thank you.

7. The Truman Doctrine
March 12, 1947

Public Papers of the Presidents of the United States: Harry S. Truman, 1947. Washington, D.C.: U.S. Government Printing Office, 176–180.

Mr. President, Mr. Speaker, Members of the Congress of the United States:

The gravity of the situation which confronts the world today necessitates my appearance before a joint session of the Congress.

The foreign policy and the national security of this country are involved.

One aspect of the present situation, which I present to you at this time for your consideration and decision, concerns Greece and Turkey.

The United States has received from the Greek Government an urgent appeal for financial and economic assistance. Preliminary reports from the American Economic Mission now in Greece and reports from the American Ambassador in Greece corroborate the statement of the Greek Government that assistance is imperative if Greece is to survive as a free nation.

I do not believe that the American people and the Congress wish to turn a deaf ear to the appeal of the Greek Government.

Greece is not a rich country. Lack of sufficient natural resources has always forced the Greek people to work hard to make both ends meet. Since 1940, this industrious, peace loving country has suffered invasion, four years of cruel enemy occupation, and bitter internal strife.

When forces of liberation entered Greece they found that the retreating Germans had destroyed virtually all the railways, roads, port facilities, communications, and merchant marine. More than a thousand villages had been burned. Eighty-five percent of the children were tubercular. Livestock, poultry, and draft animals had almost disappeared. Inflation had wiped out practically all savings.

As a result of these tragic conditions, a militant minority, exploiting human want and misery, was able to create political chaos which, until now, has made economic recovery impossible.

Greece is today without funds to finance the importation of those goods which are essential to bare subsistence. Under these circumstances the people of Greece cannot make progress in solving their problems of reconstruction. Greece is in desperate need of financial and economic assistance to enable it to resume purchases of food, clothing, fuel and seeds. These are indispensable for the subsistence of its people and are obtainable only from abroad. Greece must have help to import the goods necessary to restore internal order and security so essential for economic and political recovery.

The Greek Government has also asked for the assistance of experienced American administrators, economists and technicians to insure that the financial and other aid given to Greece shall be used effectively in creating a stable and self-sustaining economy and in improving its public administration.

The very existence of the Greek state is today threatened by the terrorist activities of several thousand armed men, led by Communists, who defy the government's authority at a number of points, particularly along the northern boundaries. A Commission appointed by the United Nations Security Council is at present investigating disturbed conditions in northern Greece and alleged border violations along the frontier between Greece on the one hand and Albania, Bulgaria, and Yugoslavia on the other.

Meanwhile, the Greek Government is unable to cope with the situation. The Greek army is small and poorly equipped. It needs supplies and equipment if it is to restore authority to the government throughout Greek territory.

Greece must have assistance if it is to become a self-supporting and self-respecting democracy.

The United States must supply this assistance. We have already extended to Greece certain types of relief and economic aid but these are inadequate.

There is no other country to which democratic Greece can turn.

No other nation is willing and able to provide the necessary support for a democratic Greek government.

The British Government, which has been helping Greece, can give no further financial or economic aid after March 31. Great Britain finds itself under the necessity of reducing or liquidating its commitments in several parts of the world, including Greece.

We have considered how the United Nations might assist in this crisis. But the situation is an urgent one requiring immediate action, and the United Nations and its related organizations are not in a position to extend help of the kind that is required.

It is important to note that the Greek Government has asked for our aid in utilizing effectively the financial and other assistance we may give to Greece, and in improving its public administration. It is of the utmost importance that we supervise the use of any funds made available to Greece, in such a manner that each dollar spent will count toward making Greece self-supporting, and will help to build an economy in which a healthy democracy can flourish.

No government is perfect. One of the chief virtues of a democracy, however, is that its defects are always visible and under democratic processes can be pointed out and corrected. The government of Greece is not perfect. Nevertheless it represents 85 percent of the members of the Greek Parliament who were chosen in an election last year. Foreign observers, including 692 Americans, considered this election to be a fair expression of the views of the Greek people.

The Greek Government has been operating in an atmosphere of chaos and extremism. It has made mistakes. The extension of aid by this country does not mean that the United States condones everything that the Greek Government has done or will do. We have condemned in the past, and we condemn now, extremist measures of the right or the left. We have in the past advised tolerance, and we advise tolerance now.

Greece's neighbor, Turkey, also deserves our attention.

The future of Turkey as an independent and economically sound state is clearly no less important to the freedom-loving peoples of the world than the future of Greece. The circumstances in which Turkey finds itself today are considerably different from those of Greece. Turkey has been spared the disasters that have beset Greece. And during the war, the United States and Great Britain furnished Turkey with material aid.

Nevertheless, Turkey now needs our support.

Since the war Turkey has sought additional financial assistance from Great Britain and the United States for the purpose of effecting that modernization necessary for the maintenance of its national integrity.

That integrity is essential to the preservation of order in the Middle East.

The British Government has informed us that, owing to its own difficulties, it can no longer extend financial or economic aid to Turkey.

As in the case of Greece, if Turkey is to have the assistance it needs, the United States must supply it. We are the only country able to provide that help.

I am fully aware of the broad implications involved if the United States extends assistance to Greece and Turkey, and I shall discuss these implications with you at this time.

One of the primary objectives of the foreign policy of the United States is the creation of conditions in which we and other nations will be able to work out a way of life free from coercion. This was fundamental issue in the war with Germany and Japan. Our victory was won over countries which sought to impose their will, and their way of life, upon other nations.

To ensure the peaceful development of nations, free from coercion, the United States has taken a leading part in establishing the United Nations. The United Nations is designed to make possible lasting freedom and independence for all its members. We shall not realize our objectives, however, unless we are willing to help free peoples to maintain their free institutions and their national integrity against aggressive movements that seek to impose upon them totalitarian regimes. This is no more than a frank recognition that totalitarian regimes imposed upon free peoples, by direct or indirect aggression, undermine the foundations of international peace and hence the security of the United States.

The peoples of a number of countries of the world have recently had totalitarian regimes forced upon them against their will. The Government of the United States has made frequent protests against coercion and intimidation, in violation of the Yalta agreement, in Poland, Rumania, and Bulgaria. I must also state that in a number of other countries there have been similar developments.

At the present moment in world history nearly every nation must choose between alternative ways of life. The choice is too often not a free one.

One way of life is based upon the will of the majority, and is distinguished by free institutions, representative government, free elections, guarantees of individual liberty, freedom of speech and religion, and freedom from political oppression.

The second way of life is based upon the will of a minority forcibly imposed upon the majority. It relies upon terror and oppression, a controlled press and radio, fixed elections, and the suppression of personal freedoms.

I believe that it must be the policy of the United States to support free peoples who are resisting attempted subjugation by armed minorities or by outside pressures.

I believe that we must assist free peoples to work out their own destinies in their own way.

I believe that our help should be primarily through economic and financial aid which is essential to economic stability and orderly political processes.

The world is not static, and the *status quo* is not sacred. But we cannot allow changes in the *status quo* in violation of the Charter of the United Nations by such methods as coercion, or by such subterfuges as political infiltration. In helping free and independent nations to maintain their freedom, the United States will be giving effect to the principles of the Charter of the United Nations.

It is necessary only to glance at a map to realize that the survival and integrity of the Greek nation are of grave importance in a much wider situation. If Greece should fall under the control of an armed minority, the effect upon its neighbor, Turkey, would be immediate and serious. Confusion and disorder might well spread throughout the entire Middle East.

Moreover, the disappearance of Greece as an independent state would have a profound effect upon those countries in Europe whose peoples are struggling against great difficulties to maintain their freedoms and their independence while they repair the damages of war.

It would be an unspeakable tragedy if these countries, which have struggled so long against overwhelming odds, should lose that victory for which they sacrificed so much. Collapse of free institutions and loss of independence would be disastrous not only for them but for the world. Discouragement and possibly failure would quickly be the lot of neighboring peoples striving to maintain their freedom and independence.

Should we fail to aid Greece and Turkey in this fateful hour, the effect will be far reaching to the West as well as to the East.

We must take immediate and resolute action.

I therefore ask the Congress to provide authority for assistance to Greece and Turkey in the amount of $400,000,000 for the period ending June 30, 1948. In requesting these funds, I have taken into consideration the maximum amount of relief assistance which would be furnished to Greece out of the $350,000,000 which I recently requested that the Congress authorize for the prevention of starvation and suffering in countries devastated by the war.

In addition to funds, I ask the Congress to authorize the detail of American civilian and military personnel to Greece and Turkey, at the request of those countries, to assist in the tasks of reconstruction, and for the purpose of supervising the use of such financial and material assistance as may be furnished. I recommend that authority also be provided for the instruction and training of selected Greek and Turkish personnel.

Finally, I ask that the Congress provide authority which will permit the speediest and most effective use, in terms of needed commodities, supplies, and equipment, of such funds as may be authorized.

If further funds, or further authority, should be needed for the purposes indicated in this message, I shall not hesitate to bring the situation before the Congress. On this subject the Executive and Legislative branches of the Government must work together.

This is a serious course upon which we embark.

I would not recommend it except that the alternative is much more serious.

The United States contributed $341,000,000,000 toward winning World War II. This is an investment in world freedom and world peace.

The assistance that I am recommending to Greece and Turkey amounts to little more than $1/10$ of 1 percent of this investment. It is only common sense that we should safeguard this investment and make sure that it was not in vain.

The seeds of totalitarian regimes are nurtured by misery and want. They spread and grow in the evil soil of poverty and strife. They reach their full growth when the hope of a people for a better life has died.

We must keep that hope alive.

The free peoples of the world look to us for support in maintaining their freedoms.

If we falter in our leadership, we may endanger the peace of the world—and we shall surely endanger the welfare of this Nation.

Great responsibilities have been placed upon us by the swift movement of events.

I am confident that the Congress will face these responsibilities squarely.

8. The Marshall Plan
June 5, 1947

Documents of American History. Boston: Harvard University Press, 531–532.

I need not tell you gentlemen that the world situation is very serious. That must be apparent to all intelligent people. I think one difficulty is that the problem is one of such enormous complexity that the very mass of facts presented to the public by press and radio make it exceedingly difficult for the man in the street to reach a clear appraisement of the situation. Furthermore, the people of this country are distant from the troubled areas of the earth and it is hard for them to comprehend the plight and consequent reactions of the long-suffering peoples, and the effect of those reactions on their governments in connection with our efforts to promote peace in the world.

In considering the requirements for the rehabilitation of Europe the physical loss of life, the visible destruction of cities, factories, mines, and railroads was correctly estimated, but it has become obvious during recent months that this visible destruction was probably less serious than the dislocation of the entire fabric of European economy. For the past 10 years conditions have been highly abnormal. The feverish preparation for war and the more feverish maintenance of the war effort engulfed all aspects of national economies. Machinery has fallen into disrepair or is entirely obsolete. Under the arbitrary and destructive Nazi rule, virtually every possible enterprise was geared into the German war machine. Long-standing commercial ties, private institutions, banks, insurance companies and shipping companies disappeared, through loss of capital, absorption through nationalization or by simple destruction. In many countries, confidence in the local currency has been severely shaken. The breakdown of the business structure of Europe during the war was complete. Recovery has been seriously retarded by the fact that 2 years after the close of hostilities a peace settlement with Germany and Austria has not been agreed upon. But even given a more prompt solution of these difficult problems, the rehabilitation of the economic structure of Europe quite evidently will require a much longer time and greater effort than had been foreseen.

There is a phase of this matter which is both interesting and serious. The farmer has always produced the foodstuffs to exchange with the city dweller for the other necessities of life. This division of labor is the basis of modern civilization. At the present time it is threatened with breakdown. The town and city industries are not producing adequate goods to exchange with the food-producing farmer. Raw materials and fuel are in short supply. Machinery is lacking or worn out. The farmer or the peasant cannot find the goods for sale which he desires to purchase. So the sale of his farm produce for money which he cannot use seems to him an unprofitable transaction. He, therefore, has withdrawn many fields from crop cultivation and is using them for grazing. He feeds more grain to stock and finds for himself and his family an ample supply of food, however short he may be on clothing and the

other ordinary gadgets of civilization. Meanwhile people in the cities are short of food and fuel. So the governments are forced to use their foreign money and credits to procure these necessities abroad. This process exhausts funds which are urgently needed for reconstruction. Thus a very serious situation is rapidly developing which bodes no good for the world. The modern system of the division of labor upon which the exchange of products is based is in danger of breaking down.

The truth of the matter is that Europe's requirements for the next 3 or 4 years of foreign food and other essential products—principally from America—are so much greater than her present ability to pay that she must have substantial additional help, or face economic, social, and political deterioration of a very grave character.

The remedy lies in breaking the vicious circle and restoring the confidence of the European people in the economic future of their own countries and of Europe as a whole. The manufacturer and the farmer throughout wide areas must be able and willing to exchange their products for currencies the continuing value of which is not open to question.

Aside from the demoralizing effect on the world at large and the responsibilities of disturbances arising as a result of the desperation of the people concerned, the consequences to the economy of the United States should be apparent to all. It is logical that the United States should do whatever it is able to do to assist in the return of normal economic health in the world, without which there can be no political stability and no assured peace. Our policy is directed not against any country or doctrine but against hunger, poverty, desperation, and chaos. Its purpose should be the revival of a working economy in the world so as to permit the emergence of political and social conditions in which free institutions can exist. Such assistance, I am convinced, must not be on a piecemeal basis as various crises develop. Any assistance that this Government may render in the future should provide a cure rather than a mere palliative. Any government that is willing to assist in the task of recovery will find full cooperation, I am sure, on the part of the United States Government. Any government which maneuvers to block the recovery of other countries cannot expect help from us. Furthermore, governments, political parties, or groups which seek to perpetuate human misery in order to profit therefrom politically or otherwise will encounter the opposition of the United States.

It is already evident that, before the United States Government can proceed much further in its efforts to alleviate the situation and help start the European world on its way to recovery, there must be some agreement among the countries of Europe as to the requirements of the situation and the part those countries themselves will take in order to give proper effect to whatever action might be undertaken by this Government. It would be neither fitting nor efficacious for this Government to undertake to draw up unilaterally a program designed to place Europe on its feet economically. This is the business of the Europeans. The initiative, I think, must come from Europe. The role of this country should consist of friendly aid in the drafting of a European program and of later support of such a program so far as it may be practical for us to do so. The program should be a joint one, agreed to by a number, if not all European nations.

An essential part of any successful action on the part of the United States is an understanding on the part of the people of America of the character of the problem and the remedies to be applied. Political passion and prejudice should have no part. With foresight, and a willingness on the part of our people to face up to the vast responsibility which history has clearly placed upon our country.

9. Special Message to the Congress on Civil Rights
February 2, 1948

Public Papers of the Presidents of the United States: Harry S. Truman, 1948. Washington, D.C.: U.S. Government Printing Office, 121–126.

To the Congress of the United States:

In the State of the Union Message on January 7, 1948, I spoke of five great goals toward which we should strive in our constant effort to strengthen our democracy and improve the welfare of our people. The first of these is to secure fully our essential human rights. I am now presenting to the Congress my recommendations for legislation to carry us forward toward that goal.

This Nation was founded by men and women who sought these shores that they might enjoy greater freedom and greater opportunity than they had known before. The founders of the United States proclaimed to the world the American belief that all men are created equal, and that governments are instituted to secure the inalienable rights with which all men are endowed. In the Declaration of Independence and the Constitution of the United States, they eloquently expressed the aspirations of all mankind for equality and freedom.

These ideals inspired the peoples of other lands, and their practical fulfillment made the United States the hope of the oppressed everywhere. Throughout our history men and women of all colors and creeds, of all races and religions, have come to this country to escape tyranny and discrimination. Millions strong, they have helped build this democratic Nation and have constantly reinforced our devotion to the great ideals of liberty and equality. With those who preceded them, they have helped to fashion and strengthen our American faith—a faith that can be simply stated:

We believe that all men are created equal and that they have the right to equal justice under law.

We believe that all men have the right to freedom of thought and of expression and the right to worship as they please.

We believe that all men are entitled to equal opportunities for jobs, for homes, for good health and for education.

We believe that all men should have a voice in their government and that government should protect, not usurp, the rights of the people.

These are the basic civil rights which are the source and the support of our democracy.

Today, the American people enjoy more freedom and opportunity than ever before. Never in our history has there been better reason to hope for the complete realization of the ideals of liberty and equality.

We shall not, however, finally achieve the ideals for which this Nation was founded so long as any American suffers discrimination as a result of his race, or religion, or color, or the land of origin of his forefathers.

Unfortunately, there still are examples—flagrant examples—of discrimination which are utterly contrary to our ideals. Not all groups of our population are free from the fear of violence. Not all groups are free to live and work where they please or to improve their conditions of life by their own efforts. Not all groups enjoy the full privileges of citizenship and participation in the government under which they live.

We cannot be satisfied until all our people have equal opportunities for jobs, for homes, for education, for health, and for political expression, and until all our people have equal protection under the law.

One year ago I appointed a committee of fifteen distinguished Americans and asked them to appraise the condition of our civil rights and to recommend appropriate action by Federal, state and local governments.

The committee's appraisal has resulted in a frank and revealing report. This report emphasizes that our basic human freedoms are better cared for and more vigilantly defended than ever before. But it also makes clear that there is a serious gap between our ideals and some of our practices. This gap must be closed.

This will take the strong efforts of each of us individually, and all of us acting together through voluntary organizations and our governments.

The protection of civil rights begins with the mutual respect for the rights of others which all of us should practice in our daily lives. Through organizations in every community—in all parts of the country—we must continue to develop practical, workable arrangements for achieving greater tolerance and brotherhood.

The protection of civil rights is the duty of every government which derives its powers from the consent of the people. This is equally true of local, state, and national governments. There is much that the states can and should do at this time to extend their protection of civil rights. Wherever the law enforcement measures of state and local governments are inadequate to discharge this primary function of government, these measures should be strengthened and improved.

The Federal Government has a clear duty to see that Constitutional guarantees of individual liberties and of equal protection under the laws are not denied or abridged anywhere in our Union. That duty is shared by all three branches of the Government, but it can be fulfilled only if the Congress enacts modern, comprehensive civil rights laws, adequate to the needs of the day, and demonstrating our continuing faith in the free way of life.

I recommend, therefore, that the Congress enact legislation at this session directed toward the following specific objectives:

1. Establishing a permanent Commission on Civil Rights, a Joint Congressional Committee on Civil Rights, and a Civil Rights Division in the Department of Justice.
2. Strengthening existing civil rights statutes.
3. Providing Federal protection against lynching.
4. Protecting more adequately the right to vote.
5. Establishing a Fair Employment Practice Commission to prevent unfair discrimination in employment.
6. Prohibiting discrimination in interstate transportation facilities.
7. Providing home-rule and suffrage in Presidential elections for the residents of the District of Columbia.
8. Providing Statehood for Hawaii and Alaska and a greater measure of self-government for our island possessions.
9. Equalizing the opportunities for residents of the United States to become naturalized citizens.
10. Settling the evacuation claims of Japanese-Americans.

Strengthening the Government Organization

As a first stop, we must strengthen the organization of the Federal Government in order to enforce civil rights legislation more adequately and to watch over the state of our traditional liberties.

I recommend that the Congress establish a permanent Commission on Civil Rights reporting to the President. The Commission should continuously review our civil rights policies and practices, study specific problems, and make recommendations to the President at frequent intervals. It should work with other agencies of the Federal Government, with state and local governments, and with private organizations.

I also suggest that the Congress establish a Joint Congressional Committee on Civil Rights. This Committee should make a continuing study of legislative matters relating to civil rights and should consider means of improving respect for and enforcement of those rights.

These two bodies together should keep all of us continuously aware of the condition of civil rights in the United States and keep us alert to opportunities to improve their protection.

To provide for better enforcement of Federal civil rights laws, there will be established a Division of Civil Rights in the Department of Justice. I recommend that the Congress provide for an additional Assistant Attorney General to supervise this Division.

Strengthening Existing Civil Rights Statutes

I recommend that the Congress amend and strengthen the existing provisions of Federal law which safeguard the right to vote and the right to safety and security of person and property. These provisions are the basis for our present civil rights enforcement program.

Section 51 of Title 18 of the United States Code, which now gives protection to citizens in the enjoyment of rights secured by the Constitution or Federal laws, needs to be strengthened in two respects. In its present form, this section protects persons only if they are citizens, and it affords protection only against conspiracies by two or more persons. This protection should be extended to all inhabitants of the United States, whether or not they are citizens, and should be afforded against infringement by persons acting individually as well as in conspiracy.

Section 52 of Title 18 of the United States Code, which now gives general protection to individuals against the deprivation of Federally secured rights by public officers, has proved to be inadequate in some cases because of the generality of its language. An enumeration of the principal rights protected under this section is needed to make more definite and certain the protection which the section affords.

Federal Protection Against Lynching

A specific Federal measure is needed to deal with the crime of lynching—against which I cannot speak too strongly. It is a principle of our democracy, written into our Constitution, that every person accused of an offense against the law shall have a fair, orderly trial in an impartial court. We have made great progress toward this end, but I regret to say that lynching has not yet finally disappeared from our land. So long as one person walks in fear of lynching, we shall not have achieved equal justice under law. I call upon the Congress to take decisive action against this crime.

Protecting the Right to Vote

Under the Constitution, the right of all properly qualified citizens to vote is beyond question. Yet the exercise of this right is still subject to interference.

Some individuals are prevented from voting by isolated acts of intimidation. Some whole groups are prevented by outmoded policies prevailing in certain states or communities.

We need stronger statutory protection of the right to vote. I urge the Congress to enact legislation forbidding interference by public officers or private persons with the right of qualified citizens to participate in primary, special and general elections in which Federal officers are to be chosen. This legislation should extend to elections for state as well as Federal officers insofar as interference with the right to vote results from discriminatory action by public officers based on race, color, or other unreasonable classification.

Requirements for the payment of poll taxes also interfere with the right to vote. There are still seven states which, by their constitutions, place this barrier between their citizens and the ballot box. The American people would welcome voluntary action on the part of these states to remove this barrier. Nevertheless, I believe the Congress should enact measures insuring that the right to vote in elections for Federal officers shall not be contingent upon the payment of taxes.

I wish to make it clear that the enactment of the measures I have recommended will in no sense result in Federal conduct of elections. They are designed to give qualified citizens Federal protection of their right to vote. The actual conduct of elections, as always, will remain the responsibility of State governments.

Fair Employment Practice Commission

We in the United States believe that all men are entitled to equality of opportunity. Racial, religious and other invidious forms of discrimination deprive the individual of an equal chance to develop and utilize his talents and to enjoy the rewards of his efforts.

Once more I repeat my request that the Congress enact fair employment practice legislation prohibiting discrimination in employment based on race, color, religion or national origin. The legislation should create a Fair Employment Practice Commission with authority to prevent discrimination by employers and labor unions, trade and professional associations, and government agencies and employment bureaus. The degree of effectiveness which the wartime Fair Employment Practice Committee attained shows that it is possible to equalize job opportunity by government action and thus to eliminate the influence of prejudice in employment.

Interstate Transportation
The channels of interstate commerce should be open to all Americans on a basis of complete equality. The Supreme Court has recently declared unconstitutional state laws requiring segregation on public carriers in interstate travel. Company regulations must not be allowed to replace unconstitutional state laws. I urge the Congress to prohibit discrimination and segregation, in the use of interstate transportation facilities, by both public officers and the employees of private companies.

The District of Columbia
I am in full accord with the principle of local self-government for residents of the District of Columbia. In addition, I believe that the Constitution should be amended to extend suffrage in Presidential elections to the residents of the District.

The District of Columbia should be a true symbol of American freedom and democracy for our own people, and for the people of the world. It is my earnest hope that the Congress will promptly give the citizens of the District of Columbia their own local, elective government. They themselves can then deal with the inequalities arising from segregation in the schools and other public facilities, and from racial barriers to places of public accommodation which now exist for one-third of the District's population.

The present inequalities in essential services are primarily a problem for the District itself, but they are also of great concern to the whole Nation. Failing local corrective action in the near future, the Congress should enact a model civil rights law for the Nation's Capital.

Our Territories and Possessions
The present political status of our Territories and possessions impairs the enjoyment of civil rights by their residents. I have in the past recommended legislation granting statehood to Alaska and Hawaii, and organic acts for Guam and American Samoa including a grant of citizenship to the people of these Pacific Islands. I repeat these recommendations.

Furthermore, the residents of the Virgin Islands should be granted an increasing measure of self-government, and the people of Puerto Rico should

be allowed to choose their form of government and their ultimate status with respect to the United States.

Equality in Naturalization
All properly qualified legal residents of the United States should be allowed to become citizens without regard to race, color, religion or national origin. The Congress has recently removed the bars which formerly prevented persons from China, India and the Philippines from becoming naturalized citizens. I urge the Congress to remove the remaining racial or nationality barriers which stand in the way of citizenship for some residents of our country.

Evacuation Claims of the Japanese-Americans
During the last war more than one hundred thousand Japanese-Americans were evacuated from their homes in the Pacific states solely because of their racial origin. Many of these people suffered property and business losses as a result of this forced evacuation and through no fault of their own. The Congress has before it legislation establishing a procedure by which claims based upon these losses can be promptly considered and settled. I trust that favorable action on this legislation will soon be taken.

The legislation I have recommended for enactment by the Congress at the present session is a minimum program if the Federal Government is to fulfill its obligation of insuring the Constitutional guarantees of individual liberties and of equal protection under the law.

Under the authority of existing law, the Executive branch is taking every possible action to improve the enforcement of the civil rights statutes and to eliminate discrimination in Federal employment, in providing Federal services and facilities, and in the armed forces.

I have already referred to the establishment of the Civil Rights Division of the Department of Justice. The Federal Bureau of Investigation will work closely with this new Division in the investigation of Federal civil rights cases. Specialized training is being given to the Bureau's agents so that they may render more effective service in this difficult field of law enforcement.

It is the settled policy of the United States Government that there shall be no discrimination in Federal employment or in providing Federal services and facilities. Steady progress has been made toward this objective in recent years. I shall shortly issue an Executive Order containing a comprehensive restatement of the Federal non-discrimination policy, together with appropriate measures to ensure compliance.

During the recent war and in the years since its close we have made much progress toward equality of opportunity in our armed services without regard to race, color, religion or national origin. I have instructed the Secretary of Defense to take steps to have the remaining instances of discrimination in the armed services eliminated as rapidly as possible. The personnel policies and practices of all the services in this regard will be made consistent.

I have instructed the Secretary of the Army to investigate the status of civil rights in the Panama Canal Zone with a view to eliminating such discrimination as may exist there. If legislation is necessary, I shall make appropriate recommendations to the Congress.

The position of the United States in the world today makes it especially urgent that we adopt these measures to secure for all our people their essential rights.

The peoples of the world are faced with the choice of freedom or enslavement, a choice between a form of government which harnesses the state in the service of the individual and a form of government which chains the individual to the needs of the state.

We in the United States are working in company with other nations who share our desire for enduring world peace and who believe with us that, above all else, men must be free. We are striving to build a world family of nations—a world where men may live under governments of their own choosing and under laws of their own making.

As a part of that endeavor, the Commission on Human Rights of the United Nations is now engaged in preparing an international bill of human rights by which the nations of the world may bind themselves. by international covenant to give effect to basic human rights and fundamental freedoms. We have played a leading role in this undertaking designed to create a world order of law and justice fully protective of the rights and the dignity of the individual.

To be effective in those efforts, we must protect our civil rights so that by providing all our people with the maximum enjoyment of personal freedom and personal opportunity we shall be a stronger nation—stronger in our leadership,

stronger in our moral position, stronger in the deeper satisfactions of a united citizenry.

We know that our democracy is not perfect. But we do know that it offers freer, happier life to our people than any totalitarian nation has ever offered.

If we wish to inspire the peoples of the world whose freedom is in jeopardy, if we wish to restore hope to those who have already lost their civil liberties, if we wish to fulfill the promise that is ours, we must correct the remaining imperfections in our practice of democracy.

We know the way. We need only the will.

HARRY S. TRUMAN

10. Address in Philadelphia upon Accepting the Nomination of the Democratic National Convention July 15, 1948

Public Papers of the Presidents of the United States: Harry S. Truman, 1948. Washington, D.C.: U.S. Government Printing Office, 406–410.

I AM SORRY that the microphones are in the way, but I must leave them the way they are because I have got to be able to see what I am doing—as I am always able to see what I am doing.

I can't tell you how very much I appreciate the honor which you have just conferred upon me. I shall continue to try to deserve it.

I accept the nomination.

And I want to thank this convention for its unanimous nomination of my good friend and colleague, Senator Barkley of Kentucky. He is a great man, and a great public servant. Senator Barkley and I will win this election and make these Republicans like it—don't you forget that!

We will do that because they are wrong and we are right, and I will prove it to you in just a few minutes.

This convention met to express the will and reaffirm the beliefs of the Democratic Party. There have been differences of opinion, and that is the democratic way. Those differences have been settled by a majority vote, as they should be.

Now it is time for us to get together and beat the common enemy. And that is up to you.

We have been working together for victory in a great cause. Victory has become a habit of our party. It has been elected four times in succession, and I am convinced it will be elected a fifth time next November.

The reason is that the people know that the Democratic Party is the people's party, and the Republican Party is the party of special interest, and it always has been and always will be.

The record of the Democratic Party is written in the accomplishments of the last 16 years. I don't need to repeat them. They have been very ably placed before this convention by the keynote speaker, the candidate for Vice President, and by the permanent chairman.

Confidence and security have been brought to the people by the Democratic Party. Farm income has increased from less than $2\frac{1}{2}$ billion in 1932 to more than $18 billion in 1947. Never in the world were the farmers of any republic or any kingdom or any other country as prosperous as the farmers of the United States; and if they don't do their duty by the Democratic Party, they are the most ungrateful people in the world!

Wages and salaries in this country have increased from 29 billion in 1933 to more than $128 billion in 1947. That's labor, and labor never had but one friend in politics, and that is the Democratic Party and Franklin D. Roosevelt.

And I say to labor what I have said to the farmers: they are the most ungrateful people in the world if they pass the Democratic Party by this year.

The total national income has increased from less than $40 billion in 1933 to $203 billion in 1947, the greatest in all the history of the world. These benefits have been spread to all the people, because it is the business of the Democratic Party to see that the people get a fair share of these things.

This last, worst 80th Congress proved just the opposite for the Republicans.

The record on foreign policy of the Democratic Party is that the United States has been turned away permanently from isolationism, and we have converted the greatest and best of the Republicans to our viewpoint on that subject.

The United States has to accept its full responsibility for leadership in international affairs. We have been the backers and the people who organized and started the United Nations, first started under that great Democratic President, Woodrow Wilson, as the League of Nations. The League was sabotaged by the Republicans in 1920. And we must see that the United Nations continues a strong and growing body, so we can have everlasting peace in the world.

We removed trade barriers in the world, which is the best asset we can have for peace. Those trade barriers must not be put back into operation again.

We have started the foreign aid program, which means the recovery of Europe and China, and the Far East. We instituted the program for Greece and Turkey, and I will say to you that all these things were done in a cooperative and bipartisan manner. The Foreign Relations Committees of the Senate and House were taken into the full confidence of the President in every one of these moves, and don't let anybody tell you anything else.

As I have said time and time again, foreign policy should be the policy of the whole Nation and not the policy of one party or the other. Partisanship should stop at the water's edge; and I shall continue to preach that through this whole campaign.

I would like to say a word or two now on what I think the Republican philosophy is; and I will speak from actions and from history and from experience.

The situation in 1932 was due to the policies of the Republican Party control of the Government of the United States. The Republican Party, as I said a while ago, favors the privileged few and not the common everyday man. Ever since its inception, that party has been under the control of special privilege; and they have completely proved it in the 80th Congress. They proved it by the things they did to the people, and not for them. They proved it by the things they failed to do.

Now, let's look at some of them—just a few.

Time and time again I recommended extension of price control before it expired June 30, 1946. I asked for that extension in September 1945, in November 1945, in a Message on the State of the Union in 1946; and that price control legislation did not come to my desk until June 30, 1946, on the day on which it was supposed to expire. And it was such a rotten bill that I couldn't sign it. And 30 days after that, they sent me one just as bad. I had to sign it, because they quit and went home.

They said, when OPA died, that prices would adjust themselves for the benefit of the country. They have been adjusting themselves all right! They have gone all the way off the chart in adjusting themselves, at the expense of the consumer and for the benefit of the people that hold the goods.

I called a special session of the Congress in November 1947—November 17, 1947—and I set out a 10-point program for the welfare and benefit of this country, among other things standby controls. I got nothing. Congress has still done nothing.

Way back 4¹/₂ years ago, while I was in the Senate, we passed a housing bill in the Senate known as the Wagner-Ellender-Taft bill. It was a bill to clear the slums in the big cities and to help to erect low-rent housing. That bill, as I said, passed the Senate 4 years ago. It died in the House. That bill was reintroduced in the 80th Congress as the Taft-Ellender-Wagner bill. The name was slightly changed, but it is practically the same bill. And it passed the Senate, but it was allowed to die in the House of Representatives; and they sat on that bill, and finally forced it out of the Banking and Currency Committee, and the Rules Committee took charge, and it still is in the Rules Committee.

But desperate pleas from Philadelphia in that convention that met here 3 weeks ago couldn't get that housing bill passed. They passed a bill they called a housing bill, which isn't worth the paper it's written on.

In the field of labor we needed moderate legislation to promote labor-management harmony, but Congress passed instead that so-called Taft-Hartley Act, which has disrupted labor-management relations and will cause strife and bitterness for years to come if it is not repealed, as the Democratic platform says it ought to be repealed.

On the Labor Department, the Republican platform of 1944 said, if they were in power, that they would build up a strong Labor Department. They have simply torn it up. Only one bureau is left that is functioning, and they cut the appropriation of that so it can hardly function.

I recommended an increase in the minimum wage. What did I get? Nothing. Absolutely nothing.

I suggested that the schools in this country are crowded, teachers underpaid, and that there is a shortage of teachers. One of our greatest national needs is more and better schools. I urged the Congress to provide $300 million to aid the States in the present educational crisis. Congress did nothing about it. Time and again I have recommended improvements in the social security law, including extending protection to those not now covered, and increasing the amount of benefits, to reduce the eligibility age of women from 65 to 60 years. Congress studied the matter for 2 years, but couldn't find the time to extend or increase the benefits. But they did find time to take social security benefits away from 750,000 people, and they passed that over my veto.

I have repeatedly asked the Congress to pass a health program. The Nation suffers from lack of medical care. That situation can be remedied any time the Congress wants to act upon it.

Everybody knows that I recommended to the Congress the civil rights program. I did that because I believed it to be my duty under the Constitution. Some of the members of my own party disagree with me violently on this matter. But they stand up and do it openly! People can tell where they stand. But the Republicans all professed to be for these measures. But Congress failed to act. They had enough men to do it, they could have had cloture, they didn't have to have a filibuster. They had enough people in that Congress that would vote for cloture.

Now everybody likes to have low taxes, but we must reduce the national debt in times of prosperity. And when tax relief can be given, it ought to go to those who need it most, and not those who need it least, as this Republican rich man's tax bill did when they passed it over my veto on the third try.

The first one of these was so rotten that they couldn't even stomach it themselves. They finally did send one that was somewhat improved, but it still helps the rich and sticks a knife into the back of the poor.

Now the Republicans came here a few weeks ago, and they wrote a platform. I hope you have all read that platform. They adopted the platform, and that platform had a lot of promises and statements of what the Republican Party is for, and what they would do if they were in power. They promised to do in that platform a lot of things I have been asking them to do that they have refused to do when they had the power.

The Republican platform cries about cruelly high prices. I have been trying to get them to do something about high prices ever since they met the first time.

Now listen! This is equally as bad, and as cynical. The Republican platform comes out for slum clearance and low-rental housing. I have been trying to get them to pass that housing bill ever since they met the first time, and it is still resting in the Rules Committee, that bill.

The Republican platform favors educational opportunity and promotion of education. I have been trying to get Congress to do something about that ever since they came there, and that bill is at rest in the House of Representatives.

The Republican platform is for extending and increasing social security benefits. Think of that! Increasing social security benefits! Yet when they had the opportunity, they took 750,000 off the social security rolls!

I wonder if they think they can fool the people of the United States with such poppycock as that!

There is a long list of these promises in that Republican platform. If it weren't so late, I would tell you all about them. I have discussed a number of these failures of the Republican 80th Congress. Every one of them is important. Two of them are of major concern to nearly every American family. They failed to do anything about high prices, they failed to do anything about housing.

My duty as President requires that I use every means within my power to get the laws the people need on matters of such importance and urgency.

I am therefore calling this Congress back into session July 26th.

On the 26th day of July, which out in Missouri we call "Turnip Day," I am going to call Congress back and ask them to pass laws to halt rising prices, to meet the housing crisis—which they are saying they are for in their platform.

At the same time I shall ask them to act upon other vitally needed measures such as aid to education, which they say they are for; a national health program; civil rights legislation, which they say they are for; an increase in the minimum wage, which I doubt very much they are for; extension of the social security coverage and increased benefits, which they say they are for; funds for projects needed in our program to provide public power and cheap electricity. By indirection, this 80th Congress has tried to sabotage the power policies the United States has pursued for 14 years. That power lobby is as bad as the real estate lobby, which is sitting on the housing bill.

I shall ask for adequate and decent laws for displaced persons in place of this anti-Semitic, anti-Catholic law which this 80th Congress passed.

Now, my friends, if there is any reality behind that Republican platform, we ought to get some action from a short session of the 80th Congress. They can do this job in 15 days, if they want to do it. They will still have time to go out and run for office.

They are going to try to dodge their responsibility. They are going to drag all the red herrings they can across this campaign, but I am here to say that Senator Barkley and I are not going to let them get away with it.

Now, what that worst 80th Congress does in this special session will be the test. The American people will not decide by listening to mere words, or by reading a mere platform. They will decide on the record, the record as it has been written. And in the record is the stark truth, that the battle lines of 1948 are the same as they were in 1932, when the Nation lay prostrate and helpless as a result of Republican misrule and inaction.

In 1932 we were attacking the citadel of special privilege and greed. We were fighting to drive the money changers from the temple. Today, in 1948, we are now the defenders of the stronghold of democracy and of equal opportunity, the haven of the ordinary people of this land and not of the favored classes or the powerful few. The battle cry is just the same now as it was in 1932, and I paraphrase the words of Franklin D. Roosevelt as he issued the challenge, in accepting nomination in Chicago: "This is more than a political call to arms. Give me your help, not to win votes alone, but to win in this new crusade to keep America secure and safe for its own people."

Now my friends, with the help of God and the wholehearted push which you can put behind this campaign, we can save this country from a continuation of the 80th Congress, and from misrule from now on.

I must have your help. You must get in and push, and win this election. The country can't afford another Republican Congress.

11. Annual Message to the Congress on the State of the Union January 5, 1949

Public Papers of the Presidents of the United States: Harry S. Truman, 1949. Washington, D.C.: U.S. Government Printing Office, 1–7.

Mr. President, Mr. Speaker, Members of the Congress:

I am happy to report to this 81st Congress that the state of the Union is good. Our Nation is better able than ever before to meet the needs of the American people, and to give them their fair chance in the pursuit of happiness. This great Republic is foremost among the nations of the world in the search for peace.

During the last 16 years, our people have been creating a society which offers new opportunities for every man to enjoy his share of the good things of life.

In this society, we are conservative about the values and principles which we cherish; but we are forward-looking in protecting those values and principles and in extending their benefits. We have rejected the discredited theory that the fortunes of the Nation should be in the hands of a privileged few. We have abandoned the "trickledown" concept of national prosperity. Instead, we believe that our economic system should rest on a democratic foundation and that wealth should be created for the benefit of all.

The recent election shows that the people of the United States are in favor of this kind of society and want to go on improving it.

The American people have decided that poverty is just as wasteful and just as unnecessary as preventable disease. We have pledged our common resources to help one another in the hazards and struggles of individual life. We believe that no unfair prejudice or artificial distinction should bar any citizen of the United States of America from an education, or from good health, or from a job that he is capable of performing.

The attainment of this kind of society demands the best efforts of every citizen in every walk of life, and it imposes increasing responsibilities on the Government.

The Government must work with industry, labor, and the farmers in keeping our economy running at full speed. The Government must see that every American has a chance to obtain his fair share of our increasing abundance. These responsibilities go hand in hand.

We cannot maintain prosperity unless we have a fair distribution of opportunity and a widespread consumption of the products of our factories and farms.

Our Government has undertaken to meet these responsibilities.

We have made tremendous public investments in highways, hydroelectric power projects, soil conservation, and reclamation. We have established a system of social security. We have enacted laws pro-

tecting the rights and the welfare of our working people and the income of our farmers. These Federal policies have paid for themselves many times over. They have strengthened the material foundations of our democratic ideals. Without them, our present prosperity would be impossible.

Reinforced by these policies, our private enterprise system has reached new heights of production. Since the boom year of 1929, while our population has increased by only 20 percent, our agricultural production has increased by 45 percent, and our industrial production has increased by 75 percent. We are turning out far more goods and more wealth per worker than we have ever done before.

This progress has confounded the gloomy prophets—at home and abroad who predicted the downfall of American capitalism. The people of the United States, going their own way, confident in their own powers, have achieved the greatest prosperity the world has even seen.

But, great as our progress has been, we still have a long way to go.

As we look around the country, many of our shortcomings stand out in bold relief.

We are suffering from excessively high prices.

Our production is still not large enough to satisfy our demands.

Our minimum wages are far too low.

Small business is losing ground to growing monopoly.

Our farmers still face an uncertain future. And too many of them lack the benefits of our modern civilization.

Some of our natural resources are still being wasted.

We are acutely short of electric power, although the means for developing such power are abundant.

Five million families are still living in slums and firetraps. Three million families share their homes with others.

Our health is far behind the progress of medical science. Proper medical care is so expensive that it is out of the reach of the great majority of our citizens.

Our schools, in many localities, are utterly inadequate.

Our democratic ideals are often thwarted by prejudice and intolerance.

Each of these shortcomings is also an opportunity—an opportunity for the Congress and the President to work for the good of the people.

Our first great opportunity is to protect our economy against the evils of "boom and bust."

This objective cannot be attained by government alone. Indeed, the greater part of the task must be performed by individual efforts under our system of free enterprise. We can keep our present prosperity, and increase it, only if free enterprise and free government work together to that end.

We cannot afford to float along ceaselessly on a postwar boom until it collapses. It is not enough merely to prepare to weather a recession if it comes. Instead, government and business must work together constantly to achieve more and more jobs and more and more production—which mean more and more prosperity for all the people.

The business cycle is man-made; and men of good will, working together, can smooth it out.

So far as business is concerned, it should plan for steady, vigorous expansion—seeking always to increase its output, lower its prices, and avoid the vices of monopoly and restriction. So long as business does this, it will be contributing to continued prosperity, and it will have the help and encouragement of the Government.

The Employment Act of 1946 pledges the Government to use all its resources to promote maximum employment, production, and purchasing power. This means that the Government is firmly committed to protect business and the people against the dangers of recession and against the evils of inflation. This means that the Government must adapt its plans and policies to meet changing circumstances.

At the present time, our prosperity is threatened by inflationary pressures at a number of critical points in our economy. And the Government must be in a position to take effective action at these danger spots. To that end, I recommend that the Congress enact legislation for the following purposes:

First, to continue the power to control consumer credit and enlarge the power to control bank credit.

Second, to grant authority to regulate speculation on the commodity exchanges.

Third, to continue export control authority and to provide adequate machinery for its enforcement.

Fourth, to continue the priorities and allocation authority in the field of transportation.

Fifth, to authorize priorities and allocations for key materials in short supply.

Sixth, to extend and strengthen rent control.

Seventh, to provide standby authority to impose price ceilings for scarce commodities which basically affect essential industrial production or the cost of living, and to limit unjustified wage adjustments which would force a break in an established price ceiling.

Eighth, to authorize an immediate study of the adequacy of production facilities for materials in critically short supply, such as steel; and, if found necessary, to authorize Government loans for the expansion of production facilities to relieve such shortages, and to authorize the construction of such facilities directly, if action by private industry fails to meet our needs.

The Economic Report, which I shall submit to the Congress shortly, will discuss in detail the economic background for these recommendations.

One of the most important factors in maintaining prosperity is the Government's fiscal policy. At this time, it is essential not only that the Federal budget be balanced, but also that there be a substantial surplus to reduce inflationary pressures, and to permit a sizable reduction in the national debt, which now stands at $252 billion. I recommend, therefore, that the Congress enact new tax legislation to bring in an additional $4 billion of Government revenue. This should come principally from additional corporate taxes. A portion should come from revised estate and gift taxes. Consideration should be given to raising personal income rates in the middle and upper brackets.

If we want to keep our economy running in high gear, we must be sure that every group has the incentive to make its full contribution to the national welfare. At present, the working men and women of the Nation are unfairly discriminated against by a statute that abridges their rights, curtails their constructive efforts, and hampers our system of free collective bargaining. That statute is the Labor-Management Relations Act of 1947, sometimes called the Taft-Hartley Act.

That act should be repealed!

The Wagner Act should be reenacted. However, certain improvements, which I recommended to the Congress 2 years ago, are needed. Jurisdictional strikes and unjustified secondary boycotts should be prohibited. The use of economic force to decide issues arising out of the interpretation of existing contracts should be prevented. Without endangering our democratic freedoms, means should be provided for setting up machinery for preventing strikes in vital industries which affect the public interest.

The Department of Labor should be rebuilt and strengthened and those units properly belonging within that department should be placed in it.

The health of our economy and its maintenance at high levels further require that the minimum wage fixed by law should be raised to at least 75 cents an hour.

If our free enterprise economy is to be strong and healthy, we must reinvigorate the forces of competition. We must assure small business the freedom and opportunity to grow and prosper. To this purpose, we should strengthen our antitrust laws by closing those loopholes that permit monopolistic mergers and consolidations.

Our national farm program should be improved—not only in the interest of the farmers, but for the lasting prosperity of the whole Nation. Our goals should be abundant farm production and parity income for agriculture. Standards of living on the farm should be just as good as anywhere else in the country.

Farm price supports are an essential part of our program to achieve these ends. Price supports should be used to prevent farm price declines which are out of line with general price levels, to facilitate adjustments in production to consumer demands, and to promote good land use. Our price support legislation must be adapted to these objectives. The authority of the Commodity Credit Corporation to provide adequate storage space for crops should be restored.

Our program for farm prosperity should also seek to expand the domestic market for agricultural products, particularly among low-income groups, and to increase and stabilize foreign markets.

We should give special attention to extending modern conveniences and services to our farms. Rural electrification should be pushed forward. And in considering legislation relating to housing, education, health, and social security, special attention should be given to rural problems.

Our growing population and the expansion of our economy depend upon the wise management of our land, water, forest, and mineral wealth. In our present dynamic economy, the task of conservation is not to lockup our resources but to develop and improve them. Failure, today, to make the investments which are necessary to support our progress in the future would be false economy.

We must push forward the development of our rivers for power, irrigation, navigation, and flood control. We should apply the lessons of our Tennessee Valley experience to our other great river basins.

I again recommend action be taken by the Congress to approve the St. Lawrence Seaway and Power project. This is about the fifth time I have recommended it.

We must adopt a program for the planned use of the petroleum reserves under the sea, which are—and must remain—vested in the Federal Government. We must extend our programs of soil conservation. We must place our forests on a sustained yield basis, and encourage the development of new sources of vital minerals.

In all this we must make sure that the benefits of these public undertakings are directly available to the people. Public power should be carried to consuming areas by public transmission lines where necessary to provide electricity at the lowest possible rates. Irrigation waters should serve family farms and not land speculators.

The Government has still other opportunities—to help raise the standard of living of our citizens. These opportunities lie in the fields of social security, health, education, housing, and civil rights.

The present coverage of the social security laws is altogether inadequate; the benefit payments are too low. One-third of our workers are not covered. Those who receive old-age and survivors insurance benefits receive an average payment of only $25 a month. Many others who cannot work because they are physically disabled are left to the mercy of charity. We should expand our social security program, both as to the size of the benefits and the extent of coverage, against the economic hazards due to unemployment, old age, sickness, and disability.

We must spare no effort to raise the general level of health in this country. In a nation as rich as ours, it is a shocking fact that tens of millions lack adequate medical care. We are short of doctors, hospitals, nurses. We must remedy these shortages. Moreover, we need—and we must have without further delay—a system of prepaid medical insurance which will enable every American to afford good medical care.

It is equally shocking that millions of our children are not receiving a good education. Millions of them are in overcrowded, obsolete buildings. We are short of teachers, because teachers' salaries are too low to attract new teachers, or to hold the ones we have. All these school problems will become much more acute as a result of the tremendous increase in the enrollment in our elementary schools in the next few years. I cannot repeat too strongly my desire for prompt Federal financial aid to the States to help them operate and maintain their school systems.

The governmental agency which now administers the programs of health, education, and social security should be given full departmental status.

The housing shortage continues to be acute. As an immediate step, the Congress should enact the provisions for low-rent public housing, slum clearance, farm housing, and housing research which I have repeatedly recommended. The number of lowrent public housing units provided for in the legislation should be increased to 1 million units in the next 7 years. Even this number of units will not begin to meet our need for new housing.

Most of the houses we need will have to be built by private enterprise, without public subsidy. By producing too few rental units and too large a proportion of high-priced houses, the building industry is rapidly pricing itself out of the market. Building costs must be lowered.

The Government is now engaged in a campaign to induce all segments of the building industry to concentrate on the production of lower priced housing. Additional legislation to encourage such housing will be submitted.

The authority which I have requested, to allocate materials in short supply and to impose price ceilings on such materials, could be used, if found necessary, to channel more materials into homes large enough for family life at prices which wage earners can afford.

The driving force behind our progress is our faith in our democratic institutions. That faith is embodied in the promise of equal rights and equal opportunities which the founders of our Republic proclaimed to their countrymen and to the whole world.

The fulfillment of this promise is among the highest purposes of government. The civil rights proposals I made to the 80th Congress, I now repeat to the 81st Congress. They should be enacted in order that the Federal Government may assume the leadership and discharge the obligations dearly placed upon it by the Constitution.

I stand squarely behind those proposals.

Our domestic programs are the foundation of our foreign policy. The world today looks to us for leadership because we have so largely realized, within our borders, those benefits of democratic government for which most of the peoples of the world are yearning.

We are following a foreign policy which is the outward expression of the democratic faith we profess. We are doing what we can to encourage free states and free peoples throughout the world, to aid the suffering and afflicted in foreign lands, and to strengthen democratic nations against aggression.

The heart of our foreign policy is peace. We are supporting a world organization to keep peace and a world economic policy to create prosperity for mankind. Our guiding star is the principle of international cooperation. To this concept we have made a national commitment as profound as anything in history.

To it we have pledged our resources and our honor.

Until a system of world security is established upon which we can safely rely, we cannot escape the burden of creating and maintaining armed forces sufficient to deter aggression. We have made great progress in the last year in the effective organization of our Armed Forces, but further improvements in our national security legislation are necessary. Universal training is essential to the security of the United States.

During the course of this session I shall have occasion to ask the Congress to consider several measures in the field of foreign policy. At this time, I recommend that we restore the Reciprocal Trade Agreements Act to full effectiveness, and extend it for 3 years. We should also open our doors to displaced persons without unfair discrimination.

It should be clear by now to all citizens that we are not seeking to freeze the status quo. We have no intention of preserving the injustices of the past. We welcome the constructive efforts being made by many nations to achieve a better life for their citizens. In the European recovery program, in our good-neighbor policy and in the United Nations, we have begun to batter down those national walls which block the economic growth and the social advancement of the peoples of the world.

We believe that if we hold resolutely to this course, the principle of international cooperation will eventually command the approval even of those nations which are now seeking to weaken or subvert it.

We stand at the opening of an era which can mean either great achievement or terrible catastrophe for ourselves and for all mankind.

The strength of our Nation must continue to be used in the interest of all our people rather than a privileged few. It must continue to be used unselfishly in the struggle for world peace and the betterment of mankind the world over.

This is the task before us.

It is not an easy one. It has many complications, and there will be strong opposition from selfish interests.

I hope for cooperation from farmers, from labor, and from business. Every segment of our population and every individual has a right to expect from our Government a fair deal.

In 1945, when I came down before the Congress for the first time on April 16, I quoted to you King Solomon's prayer that he wanted wisdom and the ability to govern his people as they should be governed. I explained to you at that time that the task before me was one of the greatest in the history of the world, and that it was necessary to have the complete cooperation of the Congress and the people of the United States.

Well now, we are taking a new start with the same situation. It is absolutely essential that your President have the complete cooperation of the Congress to carry out the great work that must be done to keep the peace in this world, and to keep this country prosperous.

The people of this great country have a right to expect that the Congress and the President will work in closest cooperation with one objective—the welfare of the people of this Nation as a whole.

In the months ahead I know that I shall be able to cooperate with this Congress.

Now, I am confident that the Divine Power which has guided us to this time of fateful responsibility and glorious opportunity will not desert us now.

With that help from Almighty God which we have humbly acknowledged at every turning point in our national life, we shall be able to perform the great tasks which He now sets before us.

12. Inaugural Address January 20, 1949

"The Public Papers of the Presidents of the United States: Harry S. Truman, 1949." The American Presidency Project at UC Santa Barbara. URL: http://www.presidency.ucsb.edu.

Mr. Vice President, Mr. Chief Justice, fellow citizens:

I accept with humility the honor which the American people have conferred upon me. I accept it with a resolve to do all that I can for the welfare of this Nation and for the peace of the world.

In performing the duties of my office, I need the help and the prayers of every one of you. I ask for your encouragement and for your support. The tasks we face are difficult. We can accomplish them only if we work together.

Each period of our national history has had its special challenges. Those that confront us now are as momentous as any in the past. Today marks the beginning not only of a new administration, but of a period that will be eventful, perhaps decisive, for us and for the world.

It may be our lot to experience, and in a large measure bring about, a major turning point in the long history of the human race. The first half of this century has been marked by unprecedented and brutal attacks on the rights of man, and by the two most frightful wars in history. The supreme need of our time is for men to learn to live together in peace and harmony.

The peoples of the earth face the future with grave uncertainty, composed almost equally of great hopes and great fears. In this time of doubt, they look to the United States as never before for good will, strength, and wise leadership.

It is fitting, therefore, that we take this occasion to proclaim to the world the essential principles of the faith by which we live, and to declare our aims to all peoples.

The American people stand firm in the faith which has inspired this Nation from the beginning. We believe that all men have a right to equal justice under law and equal opportunity to share in the common good. We believe that all men have a right to freedom of thought and expression. We believe that all men are created equal because they are created in the image of God.

From this faith we will not be moved.

The American people desire, and are determined to work for, a world in which all nations and all peoples are free to govern themselves as they see fit, and to achieve a decent and satisfying life. Above all else, our people desire, and are determined to work for, peace on earth—a just and lasting peace—based on genuine agreement freely arrived at by equals.

In the pursuit of these aims, the United States and other like-minded nations find themselves directly opposed by a regime with contrary aims and a totally different concept of life.

That regime adheres to a false philosophy which purports to offer freedom, security, and greater opportunity to mankind. Misled by that philosophy, many peoples have sacrificed their liberties only to learn to their sorrow that deceit and mockery, poverty and tyranny, are their reward.

That false philosophy is communism.

Communism is based on the belief that man is so weak and inadequate that he is able to govern himself, and therefore requires the rule of strong masters.

Democracy is based on the conviction that man has the moral and intellectual capacity, as well as the inalienable right, to govern himself with reason and justice.

Communism subjects the individual to arrest without lawful cause, punishment without trial, and forced labor as the chattel of the state. It decrees what information he shall receive, what art he shall produce, what leaders he shall follow, and what thoughts he shall think.

Democracy maintains that government is established for the benefit of the individual, and is charged with the responsibility of protecting the rights of the individual and his freedom in the exercise of those abilities of his.

Communism maintains that social wrongs can be corrected only by violence.

Democracy has proved that social justice can be achieved through peaceful change.

Communism holds that the world is so widely divided into opposing classes that war is inevitable.

Democracy holds that free nations can settle differences justly and maintain a lasting peace.

These differences between communism and democracy do not concern the United States alone. People everywhere are coming to realize that what is involved is material well-being, human dignity, and the right to believe in and worship God.

I state these differences, not to draw issues of belief as such, but because the actions resulting from the Communist philosophy are a threat to the efforts of free nations to bring about world recovery and lasting peace.

Since the end of hostilities, the United States has invested its substance and its energy in a great constructive effort to restore peace, stability, and freedom to the world.

We have sought no territory. We have imposed our will on none. We have asked for no privileges we would not extend to others.

We have constantly and vigorously supported the United Nations and related agencies as a means of applying democratic principles to international relations. We have consistently advocated and relied upon peaceful settlement of disputes among nations.

We have made every effort to secure agreement on effective international control of our most powerful weapon, and we have worked steadily for the limitation and control of all armaments.

We have encouraged, by precept and example, the expansion of world trade on a sound and fair basis.

Almost a year ago, in company with 16 free nations of Europe, we launched the greatest cooperative economic program in history. The purpose of that unprecedented effort is to invigorate and strengthen democracy in Europe, so that the free people of that continent can resume their rightful place in the forefront of civilization and can contribute once more to the security and welfare of the world.

Our efforts have brought new hope to all mankind. We have beaten back despair and defeatism. We have saved a number of countries from losing their liberty. Hundreds of millions of people all over the world now agree with us, that we need not have war—that we can have peace.

The initiative is ours.

We are moving on with other nations to build an even stronger structure of international order and justice. We shall have as our partners countries which, no longer solely concerned with the problem of national survival, are now working to improve the standards of living of all their people. We are ready to undertake new projects to strengthen a free world.

In the coming years, our program for peace and freedom will emphasize four major courses of action.

First, we will continue to give unfaltering support to the United Nations and related agencies, and we will continue to search for ways to strengthen their authority and increase their effectiveness. We believe that the United Nations will be strengthened by the new nations which are being formed in lands now advancing toward self-government under democratic principles.

Second, we will continue our programs for world economic recovery.

This means, first of all, that we must keep our full weight behind the European recovery program. We are confident of the success of this major venture in world recovery. We believe that our partners in this effort will achieve the status of self-supporting nations once again.

In addition, we must carry out our plans for reducing the barriers to world trade and increasing its volume. Economic recovery and peace itself depend on increased world trade.

Third, we will strengthen freedom-loving nations against the dangers of aggression.

We are now working out with a number of countries a joint agreement designed to strengthen the security of the North Atlantic area. Such an agreement would take the form of a collective defense arrangement within the terms of the United Nations Charter.

We have already established such a defense pact for the Western Hemisphere by the treaty of Rio de Janeiro.

The primary purpose of these agreements is to provide unmistakable proof of the joint determination of the free countries to resist armed attack from any quarter. Every country participating in these arrangements must contribute all it can to the common defense.

If we can make it sufficiently clear, in advance, that any armed attack affecting our national security would be met with overwhelming force, the armed attack might never occur.

I hope soon to send to the Senate a treaty respecting the North Atlantic security plan.

In addition, we will provide military advice and equipment to free nations which will cooperate with us in the maintenance of peace and security.

Fourth, we must embark on a bold new program for making the benefits of our scientific advances and industrial progress available for the improvement and growth of underdeveloped areas.

More than half the people of the world are living in conditions approaching misery. Their food is inadequate. They are victims of disease. Their economic life is primitive and stagnant. Their poverty is a handicap and a threat both to them and to more prosperous areas.

For the first time in history, humanity possesses the knowledge and skill to relieve suffering of these people.

The United States is pre-eminent among nations in the development of industrial and scientific techniques. The material resources which we can afford to use for assistance of other peoples are limited. But our imponderable resources in technical knowledge are constantly growing and are inexhaustible.

I believe that we should make available to peace-loving peoples the benefits of our store of technical knowledge in order to help them realize their aspirations for a better life. And, in cooperation with other nations, we should foster capital investment in areas needing development.

Our aim should be to help the free peoples of the world, through their own efforts, to produce more food, more clothing, more materials for housing, and more mechanical power to lighten their burdens.

We invite other countries to pool their technological resources in this undertaking. Their contributions will be warmly welcomed. This should be a cooperative enterprise in which all nations work together through the United Nations and its specialized agencies whenever practicable. It must be a worldwide effort for the achievement of peace, plenty, and freedom.

With the cooperation of business, private capital, agriculture, and labor in this country, this program can greatly increase the industrial activity in other nations and can raise substantially their standards of living.

Such new economic developments must be devised and controlled to the benefit of the peoples of the areas in which they are established. Guarantees to the investor must be balanced by guarantees in the interest of the people whose resources and whose labor go into these developments.

The old imperialism—exploitation for foreign profit—has no place in our plans. What we envisage is a program of development based on the concepts of democratic fair-dealing.

All countries, including our own, will greatly benefit from a constructive program for the better use of the world's human and natural resources. Experience shows that our commerce with other countries expands as they progress industrially and economically.

Greater production is the key to prosperity and peace. And the key to greater production is a wider and more vigorous application of modern scientific and technical knowledge.

Only by helping the least fortunate of its members to help themselves can the human family achieve the decent, satisfying life that is the right of all people.

Democracy alone can supply the vitalizing force to stir the peoples of the world into triumphant action, not only against their human oppressors, but also against their ancient enemies—hunger, misery, and despair.

On the basis of these four major courses of action we hope to help create the conditions that will lead eventually to personal freedom and happiness for all mankind.

If we are to be successful in carrying out these policies, it is clear that we must have continued prosperity in this country and we must keep ourselves strong.

Slowly but surely we are weaving a world fabric of international security and growing prosperity.

We are aided by all who wish to live in freedom from fear—even by those who live today in fear under their own governments.

We are aided by all who want relief from lies and propaganda—those who desire truth and sincerity.

We are aided by all who desire self-government and a voice in deciding their own affairs.

We are aided by all who long for economic security—for the security and abundance that men in free societies can enjoy.

We are aided by all who desire freedom of speech, freedom of religion, and freedom to live their own lives for useful ends.

Our allies are the millions who hunger and thirst after righteousness.

In due time, as our stability becomes manifest, as more and more nations come to know the benefits of democracy and to participate in growing abundance, I believe that those countries which now oppose us will abandon their delusions and join with the free nations of the world in a just settlement of international differences.

Events have brought our American democracy to new influence and new responsibilities. They will test our courage, our devotion to duty, and our concept of liberty.

But I say to all men, what we have achieved in liberty, we will surpass in greater liberty.

Steadfast in our faith in the Almighty, we will advance toward a world where man's freedom is secure.

To that end we will devote our strength, our resources, and our firmness of resolve. With God's help, the future of mankind will be assured in a world of justice, harmony, and peace.

13. NSC 68: United States Objectives and Programs for National Security April 14, 1950

Naval War College Review XXVII (May–June 1975): 51–108.

A Report to the President
Pursuant to the President's Directive
of January 31, 1950
TOP SECRET
[Washington,] April 7, 1950

Contents

Terms of Reference
Analysis
   I. Background of the Present World Crisis
  II. The Fundamental Purpose of the United States
  III. The Fundamental Design of the Kremlin
  IV. The Underlying Conflict in the Realm of Ideas and Values Between the U.S. Purpose and the Kremlin Design
     1. Nature of the Conflict
     2. Objectives
     3. Means
  V. Soviet Intentions and Capabilities—Actual and Potential
  VI. U.S. Intentions and Capabilities—Actual and Potential
 VII. Present Risks
VIII. Atomic Armaments
     A. Military Evaluation of U.S. and U.S.S.R. Atomic Capabilities
     B. Stockpiling and Use of Atomic Weapons
     C. International Control of Atomic Energy

IX. Possible Courses of Action
Introduction
The Role of Negotiation
A. The First Course—Continuation of Current Policies, with Current and Currently Projected Programs for Carrying Out These Projects
B. The Second Course—Isolation
C. The Third Course—War
D. The Remaining Course of Action—A Rapid Build-up of Political, Economic, and Military Strength in the Free World
Conclusions
Recommendations

TERMS OF REFERENCE

The following report is submitted in response to the President's directive of January 31 which reads:

That the President direct the Secretary of State and the Secretary of Defense to undertake a reexamination of our objectives in peace and war and of the effect of these objectives on our strategic plans, in the light of the probable fission bomb capability and possible thermonuclear bomb capability of the Soviet Union.

The document which recommended that such a directive be issued reads in part:

It must be considered whether a decision to proceed with a program directed toward determining feasibility prejudges the more fundamental decisions (a) as to whether, in the event that a test of a thermonuclear weapon proves successful, such weapons should be stockpiled, or (b) if stockpiled, the conditions under which they might be used in war. If a test of a thermonuclear weapon proves successful, the pressures to produce and stockpile such weapons to be held for the same purposes for which fission bombs are then being held will be greatly increased. The question of use policy can be adequately assessed only as a part of a general reexamination of this country's strategic plans and its objectives in peace and war. Such reexamination would need to consider national policy not only with respect to possible thermonuclear weapons, but also with respect to fission weapons—viewed in the light of the probable fission bomb capability and the possible thermonuclear bomb capability

of the Soviet Union. The moral, psychological, and political questions involved in this problem would need to be taken into account and be given due weight. The outcome of this reexamination would have a crucial bearing on the further question as to whether there should be a revision in the nature of the agreements, including the international control of atomic energy, which we have been seeking to reach with the U.S.S.R.

ANALYSIS

I. Background of the Present Crisis

Within the past thirty-five years the world has experienced two global wars of tremendous violence. It has witnessed two revolutions—the Russian and the Chinese—of extreme scope and intensity. It has also seen the collapse of five empires—the Ottoman, the Austro-Hungarian, German, Italian, and Japanese—and the drastic decline of two major imperial systems, the British and the French. During the span of one generation, the international distribution of power has been fundamentally altered. For several centuries it had proved impossible for any one nation to gain such preponderant strength that a coalition of other nations could not in time face it with greater strength. The international scene was marked by recurring periods of violence and war, but a system of sovereign and independent states was maintained, over which no state was able to achieve hegemony.

Two complex sets of factors have now basically altered this historic distribution of power. First, the defeat of Germany and Japan and the decline of the British and French Empires have interacted with the development of the United States and the Soviet Union in such a way that power increasingly gravitated to these two centers. Second, the Soviet Union, unlike previous aspirants to hegemony, is animated by a new fanatic faith, anti-thetical to our own, and seeks to impose its absolute authority over the rest of the world. Conflict has, therefore, become endemic and is waged, on the part of the Soviet Union, by violent or non-violent methods in accordance with the dictates of expediency. With the development of increasingly terrifying weapons of mass destruction, every individual faces the ever-present possibility of annihilation should the conflict enter the phase of total war.

On the one hand, the people of the world yearn for relief from the anxiety arising from the risk of atomic war. On the other hand, any substantial further extension of the area under the domination of the Kremlin would raise the possibility that no coalition adequate to confront the Kremlin with greater strength could be assembled. It is in this context that this Republic and its citizens in the ascendancy of their strength stand in their deepest peril.

The issues that face us are momentous, involving the fulfillment or destruction not only of this Republic but of civilization itself. They are issues which will not await our deliberations. With conscience and resolution this Government and the people it represents must now take new and fateful decisions.

II. Fundamental Purpose of the United States

The fundamental purpose of the United States is laid down in the Preamble to the Constitution: ". . . to form a more perfect Union, establish justice, insure domestic Tranquility, provide for the common defence, promote the general Welfare, and secure the Blessings of Liberty to ourselves and our Posterity." In essence, the fundamental purpose is to assure the integrity and vitality of our free society, which is founded upon the dignity and worth of the individual.

Three realities emerge as a consequence of this purpose: Our determination to maintain the essential elements of individual freedom, as set forth in the Constitution and Bill of Rights; our determination to create conditions under which our free and democratic system can live and prosper; and our determination to fight if necessary to defend our way of life, for which as in the Declaration of Independence, "with a firm reliance on the protection of Divine Providence, we mutually pledge to each other our lives, our Fortunes, and our sacred Honor."

III. Fundamental Design of the Kremlin

The fundamental design of those who control the Soviet Union and the international communist movement is to retain and solidify their absolute power, first in the Soviet Union and second in the areas now under their control. In the minds of the Soviet leaders, however, achievement of this design requires the dynamic extension of their authority and the ultimate elimination of any effective opposition to their authority.

The design, therefore, calls for the complete subversion or forcible destruction of the machinery of government and structure of society in the countries of the non-Soviet world and their replacement by an apparatus and structure subservient to and controlled from the Kremlin. To that end Soviet efforts are now directed toward the domination of the Eurasian land mass. The United States, as the principal center of power in the non-Soviet world and the bulwark of opposition to Soviet expansion, is the principal enemy whose integrity and vitality must be subverted or destroyed by one means or another if the Kremlin is to achieve its fundamental design.

IV. The Underlying Conflict in the Realm of Ideas and Values between the U.S. Purpose and the Kremlin Design

A. Nature of Conflict

The Kremlin regards the United States as the only major threat to the conflict between idea of slavery under the grim oligarchy of the Kremlin, which has come to a crisis with the polarization of power described in Section I, and the exclusive possession of atomic weapons by the two protagonists. The idea of freedom, moreover, is peculiarly and intolerably subversive of the idea of slavery. But the converse is not true. The implacable purpose of the slave state to eliminate the challenge of freedom has placed the two great powers at opposite poles. It is this fact which gives the present polarization of power the quality of crisis.

The free society values the individual as an end in himself, requiring of him only that measure of self-discipline and self-restraint which make the rights of each individual compatible with the rights of every other individual. The freedom of the individual has as its counterpart, therefore, the negative responsibility of the individual not to exercise his freedom in ways inconsistent with the freedom of other individuals and the positive responsibility to make constructive use of his freedom in the building of a just society.

From this idea of freedom with responsibility derives the marvelous diversity, the deep tolerance, the lawfulness of the free society. This is the explanation of the strength of free men. It constitutes the integrity and the vitality of a free and democratic system. The free society attempts to create and maintain an environment in which every individual has the opportunity to realize his creative powers. It also explains why the free society tolerates those within it who would use their freedom to destroy it. By the same token, in relations between nations, the prime reliance of the free society is on the strength and appeal of its idea, and it feels no compulsion sooner or later to bring all societies into conformity with it.

For the free society does not fear, it welcomes, diversity. It derives its strength from its hospitality even to antipathetic ideas. It is a market for free trade in ideas, secure in its faith that free men will take the best wares, and grow to a fuller and better realization of their powers in exercising their choice.

The idea of freedom is the most contagious idea in history, more contagious than the idea of submission to authority. For the breadth of freedom cannot be tolerated in a society which has come under the domination of an individual or group of individuals with a will to absolute power. Where the despot holds absolute power—the absolute power of the absolutely powerful will—all other wills must be subjugated in an act of willing submission, a degradation willed by the individual upon himself under the compulsion of a perverted faith. It is the first article of this faith that he finds and can only find the meaning of his existence in serving the ends of the system. The system becomes God, and submission to the will of God becomes submission to the will of the system. It is not enough to yield outwardly to the system—even Gandhian non-violence is not acceptable—for the spirit of resistance and the devotion to a higher authority might then remain, and the individual would not be wholly submissive.

The same compulsion which demands total power over all men within the Soviet state without a single exception, demands total power over all Communist Parties and all states under Soviet domination. Thus Stalin has said that the theory and tactics of Leninism as expounded by the Bolshevik party are mandatory for the proletarian parties of all countries. A true internationalist is defined as one who unhesitatingly upholds the position of the Soviet Union and in the satellite states true patriotism is love of the Soviet Union. By the same token the "peace policy" of the Soviet Union, described at a Party Congress as "a more advantageous form of fighting capitalism," is a device to divide and immobilize the non-Communist world, and the peace the Soviet Union seeks is the peace of total conformity to Soviet policy.

The antipathy of slavery to freedom explains the iron curtain, the isolation, the autarchy of the society whose end is absolute power. The existence and persistence of the idea of freedom is a permanent and continuous threat to the foundation of the slave society; and it therefore regards as intolerable the long continued existence of freedom in the world. What is new, what makes the continuing crisis, is the polarization of power which now inescapably confronts the slave society with the free.

The assault on free institutions is world-wide now, and in the context of the present polarization of power a defeat of free institutions anywhere is a defeat everywhere. The shock we sustained in the destruction of Czechoslovakia was not in the measure of Czechoslovakia's material importance to us. In a material sense, her capabilities were already at Soviet disposal. But when the integrity of Czechoslovak institutions was destroyed, it was in the intangible scale of values that we registered a loss more damaging than the material loss we had already suffered.

Thus unwillingly our free society finds itself mortally challenged by the Soviet system. No other value system is so wholly irreconcilable with ours, so implacable in its purpose to destroy ours, so capable of turning to its own uses the most dangerous and divisive trends in our own society, no other so skillfully and powerfully evokes the elements of irrationality in human nature everywhere, and no other has the support of a great and growing center of military power.

B. Objectives

The objectives of a free society are determined by its fundamental values and by the necessity for maintaining the material environment in which they flourish. Logically and in fact, therefore, the Kremlin's challenge to the United States is directed not only to our values but to our physical capacity to protect their environment. It is a challenge which encompasses both peace and war and our objectives in peace and war must take account of it.

1. Thus we must make ourselves strong, both in the way in which we affirm our values in the conduct of our national life, and in the development of our military and economic strength.
2. We must lead in building a successfully functioning political and economic system in the free world. It is only by practical affirmation, abroad

as well as at home, of our essential values, that we can preserve our own integrity, in which lies the real frustration of the Kremlin design.

3. But beyond thus affirming our values our policy and actions must be such as to foster a fundamental change in the nature of the Soviet system, a change toward which the frustration of the design is the first and perhaps the most important step. Clearly it will not only be less costly but more effective if this change occurs to a maximum extent as a result of internal forces in Soviet society.

In a shrinking world, which now faces the threat of atomic warfare, it is not an adequate objective merely to seek to check the Kremlin design, for the absence of order among nations is becoming less and less tolerable. This fact imposes on us, in our own interests, the responsibility of world leadership. It demands that we make the attempt, and accept the risks inherent in it, to bring about order and justice by means consistent with the principles of freedom and democracy. We should limit our requirement of the Soviet Union to its participation with other nations on the basis of equality and respect for the rights of others. Subject to this requirement, we must with our allies and the former subject peoples seek to create a world society based on the principle of consent. Its framework cannot be inflexible. It will consist of many national communities of great and varying abilities and resources, and hence of war potential. The seeds of conflicts will inevitably exist or will come into being. To acknowledge this is only to acknowledge the impossibility of a final solution. Not to acknowledge it can be fatally dangerous in a world in which there are no final solutions.

All these objectives of a free society are equally valid and necessary in peace and war. But every consideration of devotion to our fundamental values and to our national security demands that we seek to achieve them by the strategy of the cold war. It is only by developing the moral and material strength of the free world that the Soviet regime will become convinced of the falsity of its assumptions and that the pre-conditions for workable agreements can be created. By practically demonstrating the integrity and vitality of our system the free world widens the area of possible agreement and thus can hope gradually to bring about a Soviet acknowledgement of realities which in sum will eventually constitute a frustration of the Soviet design. Short of this, however, it might be possible to create a situation which will induce the Soviet Union to accommodate itself, with or without the conscious abandonment of its design, to coexistence on tolerable terms with the non-Soviet world. Such a development would be a triumph for the idea of freedom and democracy. It must be an immediate objective of United States policy. There is no reason, in the event of war, for us to alter our overall objectives. They do not include unconditional surrender, the subjugation of the Russian peoples or a Russia shorn of its economic potential. Such a course would irrevocably unite the Russian people behind the regime which enslaves them. Rather these objectives contemplate Soviet acceptance of the specific and limited conditions requisite to an international environment in which free institutions can flourish, and in which the Russian peoples will have a new chance to work out their own destiny. If we can make the Russian people our allies in the enterprise we will obviously have made our task easier and victory more certain.

The objectives outlined in NSC 20/4 (November 23, 1948) . . . are fully consistent with the objectives stated in this paper, and they remain valid. The growing intensity of the conflict which has been imposed upon us, however, requires the changes of emphasis and the additions that are apparent. Coupled with the probable fission bomb capability and possible thermonuclear bomb capability of the Soviet Union, the intensifying struggle requires us to face the fact that we can expect no lasting abatement of the crisis unless and until a change occurs in the nature of the Soviet system.

C. Means

The free society is limited in its choice of means to achieve its ends.

Compulsion is the negation of freedom, except when it is used to enforce the rights common to all. The resort to force, internally or externally, is therefore a last resort for a free society. The act is permissible only when one individual or groups of individuals within it threaten the basic rights of other individuals or when another society seeks to impose its will upon it. The free society cherishes and protects as fundamental the rights of the minority against the will of a majority, because these rights are the inalienable rights of each and every individual.

The resort to force, to compulsion, to the imposition of its will is therefore a difficult and dangerous act for a free society, which is warranted only in the face of even greater dangers. The necessity of the act must be clear and compelling; the act must commend itself to the overwhelming majority as an inescapable exception to the basic idea of freedom; or the regenerative capacity of free men after the act has been performed will be endangered.

The Kremlin is able to select whatever means are expedient in seeking to carry out its fundamental design. Thus it can make the best of several possible worlds, conducting the struggle on those levels where it considers it profitable and enjoying the benefits of a pseudo-peace on those levels where it is not ready for a contest. At the ideological or psychological level, in the struggle for men's minds, the conflict is worldwide. At the political and economic level, within states and in the relations between states, the struggle for power is being intensified. And at the military level, the Kremlin has thus far been careful not to commit a technical breach of the peace, although using its vast forces to intimidate its neighbors, and to support an aggressive foreign policy, and not hesitating through its agents to resort to arms in favorable circumstances. The attempt to carry out its fundamental design is being pressed, therefore, with all means which are believed expedient in the present situation, and the Kremlin has inextricably engaged us in the conflict between its design and our purpose.

We have no such freedom of choice, and least of all in the use of force. Resort to war is not only a last resort for a free society, but it is also an act which cannot definitively end the fundamental conflict in the realm of ideas. The idea of slavery can only be overcome by the timely and persistent demonstration of the superiority of the idea of freedom. Military victory alone would only partially and perhaps only temporarily affect the fundamental conflict, for although the ability of the Kremlin to threaten our security might be for a time destroyed, the resurgence of totalitarian forces and the re-establishment of the Soviet system or its equivalent would not be long delayed unless great progress were made in the fundamental conflict.

Practical and ideological considerations therefore both impel us to the conclusion that we have no choice but to demonstrate the superiority of the idea of freedom by its constructive application, and to attempt to change the world situation by means

short of war in such a way as to frustrate the Kremlin design and hasten the decay of the Soviet system.

For us the role of military power is to serve the national purpose by deterring an attack upon us while we seek by other means to create an environment in which our free society can flourish, and by fighting, if necessary, to defend the integrity and vitality of our free society and to defeat any aggressor. The Kremlin uses Soviet military power to back up and serve the Kremlin design. It does not hesitate to use military force aggressively if that course is expedient in the achievement of its design. The differences between our fundamental purpose and the Kremlin design, therefore, are reflected in our respective attitudes toward and use of military force.

Our free society, confronted by a threat to its basic values, naturally will take such action, including the use of military force, as may be required to protect those values. The integrity of our system will not be jeopardized by any measures, covert or overt, violent or non-violent, which serve the purposes of frustrating the Kremlin design, nor does the necessity for conducting ourselves so as to affirm our values in actions as well as words forbid such measures, provided only they are appropriately calculated to that end and are not so excessive or misdirected as to make us enemies of the people instead of the evil men who have enslaved them.

But if war comes, what is the role of force? Unless we so use it that the Russian people can perceive that our effort is directed against the regime and its power for aggression, and not against their own interests, we will unite the regime and the people in the kind of last ditch fight in which no underlying problems are solved, new ones are created, and where our basic principles are obscured and compromised. If we do not in the application of force demonstrate the nature of our objectives we will, in fact, have compromised from the outset our fundamental purpose. In the words of the Federalist (No. 28) "The means to be employed must be proportioned to the extent of the mischief." The mischief may be a global war or it may be a Soviet campaign for limited objectives. In either case we should take no avoidable initiative which would cause it to become a war of annihilation, and if we have the forces to defeat a Soviet drive for limited objectives it may well be to our interest not to let it become a global war. Our aim in applying force must be to compel the acceptance of terms consistent with our objectives, and our capabilities for the application of force should, therefore, within the limits of what we can sustain over the long pull, be congruent to the range of tasks which we may encounter.

V. Soviet Intentions and Capabilities

A. Political and Psychological

The Kremlin's design for world domination begins at home. The first concern of a despotic oligarchy is that the local base of its power and authority be secure. The massive fact of the iron curtain isolating the Soviet peoples from the outside world, the repeated political purges within the USSR and the institutionalized crimes of the MVD [the Soviet Ministry of Internal Affairs] are evidence that the Kremlin does not feel secure at home and that "the entire coercive force of the socialist state" is more than ever one of seeking to impose its absolute authority over "the economy, manner of life, and consciousness of people" (Vyshinski, *The Law of the Soviet State*, p. 74). Similar evidence in the satellite states of Eastern Europe leads to the conclusion that this same policy, in less advanced phases, is being applied to the Kremlin's colonial areas.

Being a totalitarian dictatorship, the Kremlin's objectives in these policies is the total subjective submission of the peoples now under its control. The concentration camp is the prototype of the society which these policies are designed to achieve, a society in which the personality of the individual is so broken and perverted that he participates affirmatively in his own degradation.

The Kremlin's policy toward areas not under its control is the elimination of resistance to its will and the extension of its influence and control. It is driven to follow this policy because it cannot, for the reasons set forth in Chapter IV, tolerate the existence of free societies; to the Kremlin the most mild and inoffensive free society is an affront, a challenge and a subversive influence. Given the nature of the Kremlin, and the evidence at hand, it seems clear that the ends toward which this policy is directed are the same as those where its control has already been established.

The means employed by the Kremlin in pursuit of this policy are limited only by considerations of expediency. Doctrine is not a limiting factor; rather it dictates the employment of violence, subversion, and deceit, and rejects moral considerations. In any event, the Kremlin's conviction of its own infallibility has made its devotion to theory so subjective that past or present pronouncements as to doctrine offer no reliable guide to future actions. The only apparent restraints on resort to war are, therefore, calculations of practicality.

With particular reference to the United States, the Kremlin's strategic and tactical policy is affected by its estimate that we are not only the greatest immediate obstacle which stands between it and world domination, we are also the only power which could release forces in the free and Soviet worlds which could destroy it. The Kremlin's policy toward us is consequently animated by a peculiarly virulent blend of hatred and fear. Its strategy has been one of attempting to undermine the complex of forces, in this country and in the rest of the free world, on which our power is based. In this it has both adhered to doctrine and followed the sound principle of seeking maximum results with minimum risks and commitments. The present application of this strategy is a new form of expression for traditional Russian caution. However, there is no justification in Soviet theory or practice for predicting that, should the Kremlin become convinced that it could cause our downfall by one conclusive blow, it would not seek that solution.

In considering the capabilities of the Soviet world, it is of prime importance to remember that, in contrast to ours, they are being drawn upon close to the maximum possible extent. Also in contrast to us, the Soviet world can do more with less—it has a lower standard of living, its economy requires less to keep it functioning, and its military machine operates effectively with less elaborate equipment and organization.

The capabilities of the Soviet world are being exploited to the full because the Kremlin is inescapably militant. It is inescapably militant because it possesses and is possessed by a world-wide revolutionary movement, because it is the inheritor of Russian imperialism, and because it is a totalitarian dictatorship. Persistent crisis, conflict, and expansion are the essence of the Kremlin's militancy. This dynamism serves to intensify all Soviet capabilities.

Two enormous organizations, the Communist Party and the secret police, are an outstanding source of strength to the Kremlin. In the Party, it has an apparatus designed to impose at home an ideological uniformity among its people and to act abroad as an instrument of propaganda, subversion and espionage. In its police apparatus, it has a domestic repressive instrument guaranteeing under present circumstances the continued security of the Kremlin. The demonstrated capabilities of these two basic organizations, operating openly or in disguise, in mass or through single agents, is unparalleled in history. The party, the police and the conspicuous might of the Soviet military machine together tend to create an overall impression of irresistible Soviet power among many peoples of the free world.

The ideological pretensions of the Kremlin are another great source of strength. Its identification of the Soviet system with communism, its peace campaigns and its championing of colonial peoples may be viewed with apathy, if not cynicism, by the oppressed totalitariat of the Soviet world, but in the free world these ideas find favorable responses in vulnerable segments of society. They have found a particularly receptive audience in Asia, especially as the Asiatics have been impressed by what has been plausibly portrayed to them as the rapid advance of the USSR from a backward society to a position of great world power. Thus, in its pretensions to being (a) the source of a new universal faith and (b) the model "scientific" society, the Kremlin cynically identifies itself with the genuine aspirations of large numbers of people, and places itself at the head of an international crusade with all of the benefits which derive therefrom.

Finally, there is a category of capabilities, strictly speaking neither institutional nor ideological, which should be taken into consideration. The extraordinary flexibility of Soviet tactics is certainly a strength. It derives from the utterly amoral and opportunistic conduct of Soviet policy. Combining this quality with the elements of secrecy, the Kremlin possesses a formidable capacity to act with the widest tactical latitude, with stealth, and with speed.

The greatest vulnerability of the Kremlin lies in the basic nature of its relations with the Soviet people.

That relationship is characterized by universal suspicion, fear, and denunciation. It is a relationship in which the Kremlin relies, not only for its power but its very survival, on intricately devised mechanisms of coercion. The Soviet monolith is held together by the iron curtain around it and the iron bars within it, not by any force of natural cohesion. These artificial mechanisms of unity have never been intelligently challenged by a strong outside force. The full measure of their vulnerability is therefore not yet evident.

The Kremlin's relations with its satellites and their peoples is likewise a vulnerability. Nationalism still remains the most potent emotional-political force. The well-known ills of colonialism are compounded, however, by the excessive demands of the Kremlin that its satellites accept not only the imperial authority of Moscow but that they believe in and proclaim the ideological primacy and infallibility of the Kremlin. These excessive requirements can be made good only through extreme coercion. The result is that if a satellite feels able to effect its independence of the Kremlin, as Tito was able to do, it is likely to break away.

In short, Soviet ideas and practices run counter to the best and potentially the strongest instincts of men, and deny their most fundamental aspirations. Against an adversary which effectively affirmed the constructive and hopeful instincts of men and was capable of fulfilling their fundamental aspirations, the Soviet system might prove to be fatally weak.

The problem of succession to Stalin is also a Kremlin vulnerability. In a system where supreme power is acquired and held through violence and intimidation, the transfer of that power may well produce a period of instability.

In a very real sense, the Kremlin is a victim of its own dynamism. This dynamism can become a weakness if it is frustrated, if in its forward thrusts it encounters a superior force which halts the expansion and exerts a superior counterpressure. Yet the Kremlin cannot relax the condition of crisis and mobilization, for to do so would be to lose its dynamism, whereas the seeds of decay within the Soviet system would begin to flourish and fructify.

The Kremlin is, of course, aware of these weaknesses. It must know that in the present world situation they are of secondary significance. So long as the Kremlin retains the initiative, so long as it can keep on the offensive unchallenged by clearly superior counter-force—spiritual as well as material—its vulnerabilities are largely inoperative and even concealed by its successes. The Kremlin has not yet been given real reason to fear and be diverted by the rot within its system.

B. Economic

The Kremlin has no economic intentions unrelated to its overall policies. Economics in the Soviet world is not an end in itself. The Kremlin's policy, in so far as it has to do with economics, is to utilize economic processes to contribute to the overall strength, particularly the war-making capacity of the Soviet system. The material welfare of the totalitariat is severely subordinated to the interest of the system.

As for capabilities, even granting optimistic Soviet reports of production, the total economic strength of the U.S.S.R. compares with that of the U.S. as roughly one to four. This is reflected not only in gross national product (1949: USSR $65 billion; U.S. $250 billion), but in production of key commodities in 1949:

	U.S.	USSR	USSR and European Orbit Combined
Ingot Steel (million met. tons)	80.4	21.5	28.0
Primary aluminum (thousand met. tons)	617.6	130–135	140–145
Electric power (billion kwh)	410	72	112
Crude oil (million met. tons)	276.5	33.0	38.9

Assuming the maintenance of present policies, while a large U.S. advantage is likely to remain, the Soviet Union will be steadily reducing the discrepancy between its overall economic strength and that of the U.S. by continuing to devote proportionately more to capital investment than the U.S.

But a full-scale effort by the U.S. would be capable of precipitately altering this trend. The USSR today is on a near maximum production basis. No matter what efforts Moscow might make, only a relatively slight change in the rate of increase in overall production could be brought about. In the U.S., on the other hand, a very rapid absolute expansion could be realized. The fact remains, however, that so long as the Soviet Union is virtually mobilized, and the United States has scarcely begun to summon up its forces, the greater capabilities of the U.S. are to that extent inoperative in the struggle for power. Moreover, as the Soviet attainment of an atomic capability has demonstrated, the totalitarian state, at least in time of peace, can focus its efforts on any given project far more readily than the democratic state.

In other fields—general technological competence, skilled labor resources, productivity of labor force, etc.—the gap between the USSR and the U.S. roughly corresponds to the gap in production. In the field of scientific research, however, the margin of United States superiority is unclear, especially if the Kremlin can utilize European talents.

C. Military

The Soviet Union is developing the military capacity to support its design for world domination. The Soviet Union actually possesses armed forces far in excess of those necessary to defend its national territory. These armed forces are probably not yet considered by the Soviet Union to be sufficient to initiate a war which would involve the United States. This excessive strength, coupled now with an atomic capability, provides the Soviet Union with great coercive power for use in time of peace in furtherance of its objectives and serves as a deterrent to the victims of its aggression from taking any action in opposition to its tactics which would risk war.

Should a major war occur in 1950 the Soviet Union and its satellites are considered by the Joint Chiefs of Staff to be in a sufficiently advanced state of preparation immediately to undertake and carry out the following campaigns.

a. To overrun Western Europe, with the possible exception of the Iberian and Scandinavian Peninsulas; to drive toward the oil-bearing areas of the Near and Middle East; and to consolidate Communist gains in the Far East;

b. To launch air attacks against the British Isles and air and sea attacks against the lines of communications of the Western Powers in the Atlantic and the Pacific;

c. To attack selected targets with atomic weapons, now including the likelihood of such attacks against targets in Alaska, Canada, and the United States. Alternatively, this capability, coupled with other actions open to the Soviet Union, might deny the United Kingdom as an effective base of operations for allied forces. It also should be possible for the Soviet Union to prevent any allied "Normandy" type amphibious operations intended to force a reentry into the continent of Europe.

After the Soviet Union completed its initial campaigns and consolidated its positions in the

Western European area, it could simultaneously conduct:

a. Full-scale air and limited sea operations against the British Isles;
b. Invasions of the Iberian and Scandinavian Peninsulas;
c. Further operations in the Near and Middle East, continued air operations against the North American continent, and air and sea operations against Atlantic and Pacific lines of communication; and
d. Diversionary attacks in other areas.

During the course of the offensive operations listed in the second and third paragraphs above, the Soviet Union will have an air defense capability with respect to the vital areas of its own and its satellites' territories which can oppose but cannot prevent allied air operations against these areas.

It is not known whether the Soviet Union possesses war reserves and arsenal capabilities sufficient to supply its satellite armies or even its own forces throughout a long war. It might not be in the interest of the Soviet Union to equip fully its satellite armies, since the possibility of defections would exist.

It is not possible at this time to assess accurately the finite disadvantages to the Soviet Union which may accrue through the implementation of the Economic Cooperation Act of 1948, as amended, and the Mutual Defense Assistance Act of 1949. It should be expected that, as this implementation progresses, the internal security situation of the recipient nations should improve concurrently. In addition, a strong United States military position, plus increases in the armaments of the nations of Western Europe, should strengthen the determination of the recipient nations to counter Soviet moves and in event of war could be considered as likely to delay operations and increase the time required for the Soviet Union to overrun Western Europe. In all probability, although United States backing will stiffen their determination, the armaments increase under the present aid programs will not be of any major consequence prior to 1952. Unless the military strength of the Western European nations is increased on a much larger scale than under current programs and at an accelerated rate, it is more than likely that those nations will not be able to oppose even by 1960 the Soviet armed forces in war with

any degree of effectiveness. Considering the Soviet Union military capability, the long-range allied military objective in Western Europe must envisage an increased military strength in that area sufficient possibly to deter the Soviet Union from a major war or, in any event, to delay materially the overrunning of Western Europe and, if feasible, to hold a bridgehead on the continent against Soviet Union offensives.

We do not know accurately what the Soviet atomic capability is but the Central Intelligence Agency intelligence estimates, concurred in by State, Army, Navy, Air Force, and Atomic Energy Commission, assign to the Soviet Union a production capability giving it a fission bomb stockpile within the following ranges:

By mid-1950	10–20
By mid-1951	25–45
By mid-1952	45–90
By mid-1953	70–135
By mid-1954	200

This estimate is admittedly based on incomplete coverage of Soviet activities and represents the production capabilities of known or deducible Soviet plants. If others exist, as is possible, this estimate could lead us into a feeling of superiority in our atomic stockpile that might be dangerously misleading, particularly with regard to the timing of a possible Soviet offensive. On the other hand, if the Soviet Union experiences operating difficulties, this estimate would be reduced. There is some evidence that the Soviet Union is acquiring certain materials essential to research on and development of thermonuclear weapons.

The Soviet Union now has aircraft able to deliver the atomic bomb. Our Intelligence estimates assign to the Soviet Union an atomic bomber capability already in excess of that needed to deliver available bombs. We have at present no evaluated estimate regarding the Soviet accuracy of delivery on target. It is believed that the Soviets cannot deliver their bombs on target with a degree of accuracy comparable to ours, but a planning estimate might well place it at 40–60 percent of bombs sorted. For planning purposes, therefore, the date the Soviets possess an atomic stockpile of 200 bombs would be a critical date for the United States, for the delivery of 100 atomic bombs on targets in the United States would seriously damage this country.

At the time the Soviet Union has a substantial atomic stockpile and if it is assumed that it will strike a strong surprise blow and if it is assumed further that its atomic attacks will be met with no more effective defense opposition than the United States and its allies have programmed, results of those attacks could include:

a. Laying waste to the British Isles and thus depriving the Western Powers of their use as a base;
b. Destruction of the vital centers and of the communications of Western Europe, thus precluding effective defense by the Western Powers; and
c. Delivering devastating attacks on certain vital centers of the United States and Canada.

The possession by the Soviet Union of a thermonuclear capability in addition to this substantial atomic stockpile would result in tremendously increased damage. During this decade, the defensive capabilities of the Soviet Union will probably be strengthened, particularly by the development and use of modern aircraft, aircraft warning and communications devices, and defensive guided missiles.

VI. U.S. Intentions and Capabilities—Actual and Potential

A. Political and Psychological

Our overall policy at the present time may be described as one designed to foster a world environment in which the American system can survive and flourish. It therefore rejects the concept of isolation and affirms the necessity of our positive participation in the world community.

This broad intention embraces two subsidiary policies. One is a policy which we would probably pursue even if there were no Soviet threat. It is a policy of attempting to develop a healthy international community. The other is the policy of "containing" the Soviet system. These two policies are closely interrelated and interact on one another. Nevertheless, the distinction between them is basically valid and contributes to a clearer understanding of what we are trying to do.

The policy of striving to develop a healthy international community is the long-term constructive effort which we are engaged in. It was this policy which gave rise to our vigorous sponsorship of the United Nations. It is of course the principal reason for our long continuing endeavors to create and now develop the Inter-American system. It, as much as containment, underlay our efforts to rehabilitate Western Europe. Most of our international economic activities can likewise be explained in terms of this policy.

In a world of polarized power, the policies designed to develop a healthy international community are more than ever necessary to our own strength.

As for the policy of "containment," it is one which seeks by all means short of war to (1) block further expansion of Soviet power, (2) expose the falsities of Soviet pretensions, (3) induce a retraction of the Kremlin's control and influence, and (4) in general, so foster the seeds of destruction within the Soviet system that the Kremlin is brought at least to the point of modifying its behavior to conform to generally accepted international standards.

It was and continues to be cardinal in this policy that we possess superior overall power in ourselves or in dependable combination with other likeminded nations. One of the most important ingredients of power is military strength. In the concept of "containment," the maintenance of a strong military posture is deemed to be essential for two reasons: (1) as an ultimate guarantee of our national security and (2) as an indispensable backdrop to the conduct of the policy of "containment." Without superior aggregate military strength, in being and readily mobilizable, a policy of "containment"—which is in effect a policy of calculated and gradual coercion—is no more than a policy of bluff.

At the same time, it is essential to the successful conduct of a policy of "containment" that we always leave open the possibility of negotiation with the USSR. A diplomatic freeze—and we are in one now—tends to defeat the very purposes of "containment" because it raises tensions at the same time that it makes Soviet retractions and adjustments in the direction of moderated behavior more difficult. It also tends to inhibit our initiative and deprives us of opportunities for maintaining a moral ascendancy in our struggle with the Soviet system.

In "containment" it is desirable to exert pressure in a fashion which will avoid so far as possible directly challenging Soviet prestige, to keep open the possibility for the USSR to retreat before pressure with a minimum loss of face and to secure political advantage from the failure of the Kremlin to yield or take advantage of the openings we leave it.

We have failed to implement adequately these two fundamental aspects of "containment." In the face of obviously mounting Soviet military strength ours has declined relatively. Partly as a byproduct of this, but also for other reasons, we now find ourselves at a diplomatic impasse with the Soviet Union, with the Kremlin growing bolder, with both of us holding on grimly to what we have, and with ourselves facing difficult decisions.

In examining our capabilities it is relevant to ask at the outset—capabilities for what? The answer cannot be stated solely in the negative terms of resisting the Kremlin design. It includes also our capabilities to attain the fundamental purpose of the United States, and to foster a world environment in which our free society can survive and flourish.

Potentially we have these capabilities. We know we have them in the economic and military fields. Potentially we also have them in the political and psychological fields. The vast majority of Americans are confident that the system of values which animates our society—the principles of freedom, tolerance, the importance of the individual, and the supremacy of reason over will—are valid and more vital than the ideology which is the fuel of Soviet dynamism. Translated into terms relevant to the lives of other peoples—our system of values can become perhaps a powerful appeal to millions who now seek or find in authoritarianism a refuge from anxieties, bafflement, and insecurity.

Essentially, our democracy also possesses a unique degree of unity. Our society is fundamentally more cohesive than the Soviet system, the solidarity of which is artificially created through force, fear, and favor. This means that expressions of national consensus in our society are soundly and solidly based. It means that the possibility of revolution in this country is fundamentally less than that in the Soviet system.

These capabilities within us constitute a great potential force in our international relations. The potential within us of bearing witness to the values by which we live holds promise for a dynamic manifestation to the rest of the world of the vitality of our system. The essential tolerance of our world outlook, our generous and constructive impulses, and the absence of covetousness in our international relations are assets of potentially enormous influence.

These then are our potential capabilities. Between them and our capabilities currently being utilized is a wide gap of unactualized power. In sharp contrast is the situation of the Soviet world. Its capabilities are inferior to those of our allies and to our own. But they are mobilized close to the maximum possible extent.

The full power which resides within the American people will be evoked only through the traditional democratic process: This process requires, firstly, that sufficient information regarding the basic political, economic, and military elements of the present situation be made publicly available so that an intelligent popular opinion may be formed. Having achieved a comprehension of the issues now confronting this Republic, it will then be possible for the American people and the American Government to arrive at a consensus. Out of this common view will develop a determination of the national will and a solid resolute expression of that will. The initiative in this process lies with the Government.

The democratic way is harder than the authoritarian way because, in seeking to protect and fulfill the individual, it demands of him understanding, judgment, and positive participation in the increasingly complex and exacting problems of the modern world. It demands that he exercise discrimination: that while pursuing through free inquiry the search for truth he knows when he should commit an act of faith; that he distinguish between the necessity for tolerance and the necessity for just suppression. A free society is vulnerable in that it is easy for people to lapse into excesses—the excesses of a permanently open mind wishfully waiting for evidence that evil design may become noble purpose, the excess of faith becoming prejudice, the excess of tolerance degenerating into indulgence of conspiracy and the excess of resorting to suppression when more moderate measures are not only more appropriate but more effective.

In coping with dictatorial governments acting in secrecy and with speed, we are also vulnerable in that the democratic process necessarily operates in the open and at a deliberate tempo. Weaknesses in our situation are readily apparent and subject to immediate exploitation. This Government therefore cannot afford in the face of the totalitarian challenge to operate on a narrow margin of strength. A democracy can compensate for its natural vulnerability only if it maintains clearly superior overall power in its most inclusive sense.

The very virtues of our system likewise handicap us in certain respects in our relations with our allies. While it is a general source of strength to us that our relations with our allies are conducted on a basis of persuasion and consent rather than compulsion and capitulation, it is also evident that dissent among us can become a vulnerability. Sometimes the dissent has its principal roots abroad in situations about which we can do nothing. Sometimes it arises largely out of certain weaknesses within ourselves, about which we can do something—our native impetuosity and a tendency to expect too much from people widely divergent from us.

The full capabilities of the rest of the free world are a potential increment to our own capabilities. It may even be said that the capabilities of the Soviet world, specifically the capabilities of the masses who have nothing to lose but their Soviet chains, are a potential which can be enlisted on our side.

Like our own capabilities, those of the rest of the free world exceed the capabilities of the Soviet system. Like our own they are far from being effectively mobilized and employed in the struggle against the Kremlin design. This is so because the rest of the free world lacks a sense of unity, confidence, and common purpose. This is true in even the most homogeneous and advanced segment of the free world—Western Europe.

As we ourselves demonstrate power, confidence, and a sense of moral and political direction, so those same qualities will be evoked in Western Europe. In such a situation, we may also anticipate a general improvement in the political tone in Latin America, Asia, and Africa and the real beginnings of awakening among the Soviet totalitariat.

In the absence of affirmative decision on our part, the rest of the free world is almost certain to become demoralized. Our friends will become more than a liability to us; they can eventually become a positive increment to Soviet power.

In sum, the capabilities of our allies are, in an important sense, a function of our own. An affirmative decision to summon up the potential within ourselves would evoke the potential strength within others and add it to our own.

B. Economic

1. Capabilities. In contrast to the war economy of the Soviet world (cf. Ch. V-B), the American economy (and the economy of the free world as a whole) is at present directed to the provision of rising standards of living. The military budget of the United States represents 6 to 7 percent of its gross national product (as against 13.8 percent for the Soviet Union). Our North Atlantic Treaty [NAT] allies devoted 4.8 percent of their national product to military purposes in 1949.

This difference in emphasis between the two economies means that the readiness of the free world to support a war effort is tending to decline relative to that of the Soviet Union. There is little direct investment in production facilities for military end-products and in dispersal. There are relatively few men receiving military training and a relatively low rate of production of weapons. However, given time to convert to a war effort, the capabilities of the United States economy and also of the Western European economy would be tremendous. In the light of Soviet military capabilities, a question which may be of decisive importance in the event of war is the question whether there will be time to mobilize our superior human and material resources for a war effort (cf. Chs. VIII and IX).

The capability of the American economy to support a build-up of economic and military strength at home and to assist a build-up abroad is limited not, as in the case of the Soviet Union, so much by the ability to produce as by the decision on the proper allocation of resources to this and other purposes. Even Western Europe could afford to assign a substantially larger proportion of its resources to defense, if the necessary foundation in public understanding and will could be laid, and if the assistance needed to meet its dollar deficit were provided.

A few statistics will help to clarify this point [Table 1].

The Soviet Union is now allocating nearly 40 percent of its gross available resources to military purposes and investment, much of which is in war-supporting industries. It is estimated that even in an emergency the Soviet Union could not increase this proportion to much more than 50 percent, or by one-fourth. The United States, on the other hand, is allocating only about 20 percent of its resources to defense and investment (or 22 percent including foreign assistance), and little of its investment outlays are directed to war-supporting industries. In an emergency the United States could allocate more than 50 percent of its resources to military purposes and foreign assistance, or five to six times as much as at present.

The same point can be brought out by statistics on the use of important products. The Soviet Union

Table 1. Percentage of Gross Available Resources Allocated to Investment, National Defense, and Consumption in East and West, 1949 (in percent of total)

Country	Gross Investment	Defense	Consumption
USSR	25.4	13.8	60.8
Soviet Orbit	22.0(a)	4.0(b)	74.0(a)
U.S.	13.6	6.5	79.9
European NAT countries	20.4	4.8	74.8

(a) crude estimate.

(b) Includes Soviet Zone of Germany; otherwise 5 percent.

is using 14 percent of its ingot steel, 47 percent of its primary aluminum, and 18.5 percent of its crude oil for military purposes, while the corresponding percentages for the United States are 1.7, 8.6, and 5.6. Despite the tremendously larger production of these goods in the United States than the Soviet Union, the latter is actually using, for military purposes, nearly twice as much steel as the United States and 8 to 26 percent more aluminum.

Perhaps the most impressive indication of the economic superiority of the free world over the Soviet world which can be made on the basis of available data is provided in comparisons (based mainly on the Economic Survey of Europe, 1948) [Table 2].

It should be noted that these comparisons understate the relative position of the NAT countries for several reasons: (1) Canada is excluded because comparable data were not available; (2) the data for the USSR are the 1950 targets (as stated in the fourth five-year plan) rather than actual rates of production and are believed to exceed in many cases the production actually achieved; (3) the data for the European NAT countries are actual data for 1948, and production has generally increased since that time.

Furthermore, the United States could achieve a substantial absolute increase in output and could thereby increase the allocation of resources to a build-up of the economic and military strength of itself and its allies without suffering a decline in its

Table 2. Comparative Statistics on Economic Capabilities of East and West

	U.S. 1948–49	European Nat Countries	Total	USSR (1950 Plan)	Satellites 1948–49	Total
Population (millions)	149	173	322	198(a)	75	273
Employment in non-agricultural establishments (millions)	45	–	–	31(a)	–	–
Gross National Production (billion dollars)	250	84	334	65(a)	21	86
National income per capita (current dollars)	1700	480	1040	330	280	315
Production data(b):						
Coal (million tons)	582	306	888	250	88	338
Electric power (billion kwh)	356	124	480	82	15	97
Crude petroleum (million tons)	277	1	278	35	5	40
Pig iron (million tons)	55	24	79	19.5	3.2	22.7
Steel (million tons)	80	32	112	25	6	31
Cement (million tons)	35	21	56	10.5	2.1	12.6
Motor vehicles (thousands)	5273	580	5853	500	25	525

(a) 1949 data. [Footnote in the source text.]

(b) for the European NAT countries and for the satellites, the data include output by major producers. [Footnote in the source text.]

real standard of living. Industrial production declined by 10 percent between the first quarter of 1948 and the last quarter of 1949, and by approximately one-fourth between 1944 and 1949. In March 1950 there were approximately 4,750,000 unemployed, as compared to 1,070,000 in 1943 and 670,000 in 1944. The gross national product declined slowly in 1949 from the peak reached in 1948 ($262 billion in 1948 to an annual rate of $256 billion in the last six months of 1949), and in terms of constant prices declined by about 20 percent between 1944 and 1948.

With a high level of economic activity, the United States could soon attain a gross national product of $300 billion per year, as was pointed out in the President's Economic Report (January 1950). Progress in this direction would permit, and might itself be aided by, a build-up of the economic and military strength of the United States and the free world; furthermore, if a dynamic expansion of the economy were achieved, the necessary build-up could be accomplished without a decrease in the national standard of living because the required resources could be obtained by siphoning off a part of the annual increment in the gross national product. These are facts of fundamental importance in considering the courses of action open to the United States (cf. Ch. IX).

2. Intentions. Foreign economic policy is a major instrument in the conduct of United States foreign relations. It is an instrument which can powerfully influence the world environment in ways favorable to the security and welfare of this country. It is also an instrument which, if unwisely formulated and employed, can do actual harm to our national interests. It is an instrument uniquely suited to our capabilities, provided we have the tenacity of purpose and the understanding requisite to a realization of its potentials. Finally, it is an instrument peculiarly appropriate to the cold war.

The preceding analysis has indicated that an essential element in a program to frustrate the Kremlin design is the development of a successfully functioning system among the free nations. It is clear that economic conditions are among the fundamental determinants of the will and the strength to resist subversion and aggression.

United States foreign economic policy has been designed to assist in the building of such a system and such conditions in the free world. The principal features of this policy can be summarized as follows:

1. assistance to Western Europe in recovery and the creation of a viable economy (the European Recovery Program);

2. assistance to other countries because of their special needs arising out of the war or the cold war and our special interests in or responsibility for meeting them (grant assistance to Japan, the Philippines, and Korea, loans and credits by the Export-Import Bank, the International Monetary Fund, and the International Bank to Indonesia, Yugoslavia, Iran, etc.);

3. assistance in the development of underdeveloped areas (the Point IV program and loans and credits to various countries, overlapping to some extent with those mentioned under 2);

4. military assistance to the North Atlantic Treaty countries, Greece, Turkey, etc.;

5. restriction of East-West trade in items of military importance to the East;

6. purchase and stockpiling of strategic materials; and

7. efforts to reestablish an international economy based on multilateral trade, declining trade barriers, and convertible currencies (the GATT-ITO program, the Reciprocal Trade Agreements program, the IMF-IBRD program, and the program now being developed to solve the problem of the United States balance of payments).

In both their short and long term aspects, these policies and programs are directed to the strengthening of the free world and therefore to the frustration of the Kremlin design. Despite certain inadequacies and inconsistencies, which are now being studied in connection with the problem of the United States balance of payments, the United States has generally pursued a foreign economic policy which has powerfully supported its overall objectives. The question must nevertheless be asked whether current and currently projected programs will adequately support this policy in the future, in terms both of need and urgency.

The last year has been indecisive in the economic field. The Soviet Union has made considerable progress in integrating the satellite economies of Eastern Europe into the Soviet economy, but still faces very large problems, especially with China. The free nations have important accomplishments to record, but also have tremendous problems still ahead. On balance, neither side can claim any great advantage in this field over its relative position a year ago. The important question therefore becomes: what are the trends?

Several conclusions seem to emerge. First, the Soviet Union is widening the gap between its preparedness for war and the unpreparedness of the free world for war. It is devoting a far greater proportion of its resources to military purposes than are the free nations and, in significant components of military power, a greater absolute quantity of resources. Second, the Communist success in China, taken with the politico-economic situation in the rest of South and South-East Asia, provides a springboard for a further incursion in this troubled area. Although Communist China faces serious economic problems which may impose some strains on the Soviet economy, it is probable that the social and economic problems faced by the free nations in this area present more than offsetting opportunities for Communist expansion. Third, the Soviet Union holds positions in Europe which, if it maneuvers skillfully, could be used to do great damage to the Western European economy and to the maintenance of the Western orientation of certain countries, particularly Germany and Austria. Fourth, despite (and in part because of) the Titoist' defection, the Soviet Union has accelerated its efforts to integrate satellite economy with its own and to increase the degree of autarchy within the areas under its control.

Fifth, meanwhile, Western Europe, with American (and Canadian) assistance, has achieved a record level of production. However, it faces the prospect of a rapid tapering off of American assistance without the possibility of achieving, by its own efforts, a satisfactory equilibrium with the dollar area. It has also made very little progress toward "economic integration," which would in the long run tend to improve its productivity and to provide an economic environment conducive to political stability. In particular, the movement toward economic integration does not appear to be rapid enough to provide Western Germany with adequate economic opportunities in the West. The United Kingdom still faces economic problems which may require a moderate but politically difficult decline in the British standard of living or more American assistance than is contemplated. At the same time, a strengthening of the British position is needed if the stability of the Commonwealth is not to be impaired and if it is to be a focus of resistance to Communist expansion in South and South-East Asia. Improve-

ment of the British position is also vital in building up the defensive capabilities of Western Europe.

Sixth, throughout Asia the stability of the present moderate governments, which are more in sympathy with our purposes than any probable successor regimes would be, is doubtful. The problem is only in part an economic one. Assistance in economic development is important as a means of holding out to the peoples of Asia some prospect of improvement in standards of living under their present governments. But probably more important are a strengthening of central institutions, an improvement in administration, and generally a development of an economic and social structure within which the peoples of Asia can make more effective use of their great human and material resources.

Seventh, and perhaps most important, there are indications of a let-down of United States efforts under the pressure of the domestic budgetary situation, disillusion resulting from excessively optimistic expectations about the duration and results of our assistance programs, and doubts about the wisdom of continuing to strengthen the free nations as against preparedness measures in light of the intensity of the cold war.

Eighth, there are grounds for predicting that the United States and other free nations will within a period of a few years at most experience a decline in economic activity of serious proportions unless more positive governmental programs are developed than are now available.

In short, as we look into the future, the programs now planned will not meet the requirements of the free nations. The difficulty does not lie so much in the inadequacy or misdirection of policy as in the inadequacy of planned programs, in terms of timing or impact, to achieve our objectives. The risks inherent in this situation are set forth in the following chapter and a course of action designed to reinvigorate our efforts in order to reverse the present trends and to achieve our fundamental purpose is outlined in Chapter IX.

C. Military

The United States now possesses the greatest military potential of any single nation in the world. The military weaknesses of the United States vis-à-vis the Soviet Union, however, include its numerical inferiority in forces in being and in total manpower. Coupled with the inferiority of forces in being, the United States also lacks tenable positions from which to employ its forces in event of war and munitions power in being and readily available.

It is true that the United States armed forces are now stronger than ever before in other times of apparent peace; it is also true that there exists a sharp disparity between our actual military strength and our commitments. The relationship of our strength to our present commitments, however, is not alone the governing factor. The world situation, as well as commitments, should govern; hence, our military strength more properly should be related to the world situation confronting us. When our military strength is related to the world situation and balanced against the likely exigencies of such a situation, it is clear that our military strength is becoming dangerously inadequate.

If war should begin in 1950, the United States and its allies will have the military capability of conducting defensive operations to provide a reasonable measure of protection to the Western Hemisphere, bases in the Western Pacific, and essential military lines of communication; and an inadequate measure of protection to vital military bases in the United Kingdom and in the Near and Middle East. We will have the capability of conducting powerful offensive air operations against vital elements of the Soviet war-making capacity.

The scale of the operations listed in the preceding paragraph is limited by the effective forces and material in being of the United States and its allies vis-à-vis the Soviet Union. Consistent with the aggressive threat facing us and in consonance with overall strategic plans, the United States must provide to its allies on a continuing basis as large amounts of military assistance as possible without serious detriment to the United States operational requirements.

If the potential military capabilities of the United States and its allies were rapidly and effectively developed, sufficient forces could be produced probably to deter war, or if the Soviet Union chooses war, to withstand the initial Soviet attacks, to stabilize supporting attacks, and to retaliate in turn with even greater impact on the Soviet capabilities. From the military point of view alone, however, this would require not only the generation of the necessary military forces but also the development and stockpiling of improved weapons of all types.

Under existing peacetime conditions, a period of from two to three years is required to produce a material increase in military power. Such increased power could be provided in a somewhat shorter period in a declared period of emergency or in wartime through a full-out national effort. Any increase in military power in peacetime, however, should be related both to its probable military role in war, to the implementation of immediate and long-term United States foreign policy vis-à-vis the Soviet Union, and to the realities of the existing situation. If such a course of increasing our military power is adopted now, the United States would have the capability of eliminating the disparity between its military strength and the exigencies of the situation we face; eventually of gaining the initiative in the "cold" war and of materially delaying if not stopping the Soviet offensives in war itself.

VII. Present Risks

A. General

It is apparent from the preceding sections that the integrity and vitality of our system is in greater jeopardy than ever before in our history. Even if there were no Soviet Union we would face the great problem of the free society, accentuated many fold in this industrial age, of reconciling order, security, the need for participation, with the requirement of freedom. We would face the fact that in a shrinking world the absence of order among nations is becoming less and less tolerable. The Kremlin design seeks to impose order among nations by means which would destroy our free and democratic system. The Kremlin's possession of atomic weapons puts new power behind its design, and increases the jeopardy to our system. It adds new strains to the uneasy equilibrium-without-order which exists in the world and raises new doubts in men's minds whether the world will long tolerate this tension without moving toward some kind of order, on somebody's terms.

The risks we face are of a new order of magnitude, commensurate with the total struggle in which we are engaged. For a free society there is never total victory, since freedom and democracy are never wholly attained, are always in the process of being attained. But defeat at the hands of the totalitarian is total defeat. These risks crowd in on us, in a shrinking world of polarized power, so as to give us no choice, ultimately, between meeting them effectively or being overcome by them.

B. Specific

It is quite clear from Soviet theory and practice that the Kremlin seeks to bring the free world under its dominion by the methods of the cold war. The preferred technique is to subvert by infiltration and intimidation. Every institution of our society is an instrument which it is sought to stultify and turn against our purposes. Those that touch most closely our material and moral strength are obviously the prime targets, labor unions, civic enterprises, schools, churches, and all media for influencing opinion. The effort is not so much to make them serve obvious Soviet ends as to prevent them from serving our ends, and thus to make them sources of confusion in our economy, our culture, and our body politic. The doubts and diversities that in terms of our values are part of the merit of a free system, the weaknesses and the problems that are peculiar to it, the rights and privileges that free men enjoy, and the disorganization and destruction left in the wake of the last attack on our freedoms, all are but opportunities for the Kremlin to do its evil work. Every advantage is taken of the fact that our means of prevention and retaliation are limited by those principles and scruples which are precisely the ones that give our freedom and democracy its meaning for us. None of our scruples deter those whose only code is "morality is that which serves the revolution."

Since everything that gives us or others respect for our institutions is a suitable object for attack, it also fits the Kremlin's design that where, with impunity, we can be insulted and made to suffer indignity the opportunity shall not be missed, particularly in any context which can be used to cast dishonor on our country, our system, our motives, or our methods. Thus the means by which we sought to restore our own economic health in the '30's, and now seek to restore that of the free world, come equally under attack. The military aid by which we sought to help the free world was frantically denounced by the Communists in the early days of the last war, and of course our present efforts to develop adequate military strength for ourselves and our allies are equally denounced.

At the same time the Soviet Union is seeking to create overwhelming military force, in order to back up infiltration with intimidation. In the only terms in which it understands strength, it is seeking to demonstrate to the free world that force and the will to use it are on the side of the Kremlin, that those who lack it are decadent and doomed. In local incidents it threatens and encroaches both for the sake of local gains and to increase anxiety and defeatism in all the free world.

The possession of atomic weapons at each of the opposite poles of power, and the inability (for different reasons) of either side to place any trust in the other, puts a premium on a surprise attack against us. It equally puts a premium on a more violent and ruthless prosecution of its design by cold war, especially if the Kremlin is sufficiently objective to realize the improbability of our prosecuting a preventive war. It also puts a premium on piecemeal aggression against others, counting on our unwillingness to engage in atomic war unless we are directly attacked. We run all these risks and the added risk of being confused and immobilized by our inability to weigh and choose, and pursue a firm course based on a rational assessment of each.

The risk that we may thereby be prevented or too long delayed in taking all needful measures to maintain the integrity and vitality of our system is great. The risk that our allies will lose their determination is greater. And the risk that in this manner a descending spiral of too little and too late, of doubt and recrimination, may present us with ever narrower and more desperate alternatives, is the greatest risk of all. For example, it is clear that our present weakness would prevent us from offering effective resistance at any of several vital pressure points. The only deterrent we can present to the Kremlin is the evidence we give that we may make any of the critical points which we cannot hold the occasion for a global war of annihilation.

The risk of having no better choice than to capitulate or precipitate a global war at any of a number of pressure points is bad enough in itself, but it is multiplied by the weakness it imparts to our position in the cold war. Instead of appearing strong and resolute we are continually at the verge of appearing and being alternately irresolute and desperate; yet it is the cold war which we must win, because both the Kremlin design, and our fundamental purpose give it the first priority.

The frustration of the Kremlin design, however, cannot be accomplished by us alone, as will appear from the analysis in Chapter IX, B. Strength at the center, in the United States, is only the first of two essential elements. The second is that our allies and potential allies do not as a result of a sense of frustration or of Soviet intimidation drift into a course of neutrality eventually leading to Soviet domination. If this were to happen in Germany the effect upon Western Europe and eventually upon us might be catastrophic.

But there are risks in making ourselves strong. A large measure of sacrifice and discipline will be demanded of the American people. They will be asked to give up some of the benefits which they have come to associate with their freedoms. Nothing could be more important than that they fully understand the reasons for this. The risks of a superficial understanding or of an inadequate appreciation of the issues are obvious and might lead to the adoption of measures which in themselves would jeopardize the integrity of our system. At any point in the process of demonstrating our will to make good our fundamental purpose, the Kremlin may decide to precipitate a general war, or in testing us, may go too far. These are risks we will invite by making ourselves strong, but they are lesser risks than those we seek to avoid. Our fundamental purpose is more likely to be defeated from lack of the will to maintain it, than from any mistakes we may make or assault we may undergo because of asserting that will. No people in history have preserved their freedom who thought that by not being strong enough to protect themselves they might prove inoffensive to their enemies.

VIII. Atomic Armaments

A. Military Evaluation of U.S. and USSR Atomic Capabilities

1. The United States now has an atomic capability, including both numbers and deliverability, estimated to be adequate, if effectively utilized, to deliver a serious blow against the war-making capacity of the USSR. It is doubted whether such a blow, even if it resulted in the complete destruction of the contemplated target systems, would cause the USSR to sue for terms or prevent Soviet forces from occupying Western Europe against such ground resistance as could presently be mobilized. A very serious initial blow could, however, so reduce the capabilities of the USSR to supply and equip its military organization and its civilian population as to give the United States the prospect of developing a general military superiority in a war of long duration.

2. As the atomic capability of the USSR increases, it will have an increased ability to hit at our atomic bases and installations and thus seriously hamper the ability of the United States to carry out an attack such as that outlined above. It is quite possible that in the near future the USSR will have a sufficient number of atomic bombs and a sufficient deliverability to raise a question whether Britain with its present inadequate air defense could be relied upon as an advance base from which a major portion of the U.S. attack could be launched.

It is estimated that, within the next four years, the USSR will attain the capability of seriously damaging vital centers of the United States, provided it strikes a surprise blow and provided further that the blow is opposed by no more effective opposition than we now have programmed. Such a blow could so seriously damage the United States as to greatly reduce its superiority in economic potential.

Effective opposition to this Soviet capability will require among other measures greatly increased air warning systems, air defenses, and vigorous development and implementation of a civilian defense program which has been thoroughly integrated with the military defense systems.

In time the atomic capability of the USSR can be expected to grow to a point where, given surprise and no more effective opposition than we now have programmed, the possibility of a decisive initial attack cannot be excluded.

3. In the initial phases of an atomic war, the advantages of initiative and surprise would be very great. A police state living behind an iron curtain has an enormous advantage in maintaining the necessary security and centralization of decision required to capitalize on this advantage.

4. For the moment our atomic retaliatory capability is probably adequate to deter the Kremlin from a deliberate direct military attack against ourselves or other free peoples. However, when it calculates that it has a sufficient atomic capability to make a surprise attack on us, nullifying our atomic superiority and creating a military situation decisively in its favor, the Kremlin might be tempted to strike swiftly and with stealth. The existence of two large atomic capabilities in such a relationship might well act, therefore, not as a deterrent, but as an incitement to war.

5. A further increase in the number and power of our atomic weapons is necessary in order to assure the effectiveness of any U.S. retaliatory blow, but would not of itself seem to change the basic logic of the above points. Greatly increased general air, ground, and sea strength, and increased air

defense and civilian defense programs would also be necessary to provide reasonable assurance that the free world could survive an initial surprise atomic attack of the weight which it is estimated the USSR will be capable of delivering by 1954 and still permit the free world to go on to the eventual attainment of its objectives. Furthermore, such a build-up of strength could safeguard and increase our retaliatory power, and thus might put off for some time the date when the Soviet Union could calculate that a surprise blow would be advantageous. This would provide additional time for the effects of our policies to produce a modification of the Soviet system.

6. If the USSR develops a thermonuclear weapon ahead of the U.S., the risks of greatly increased Soviet pressure against all the free world, or an attack against the U.S., will be greatly increased.

7. If the U.S. develops a thermonuclear weapon ahead of the USSR, the U.S. should for the time being be able to bring increased pressure on the USSR.

B. Stockpiling and Use of Atomic Weapons

1. From the foregoing analysis it appears that it would be to the long-term advantage of the United States if atomic weapons were to be effectively eliminated from national peacetime armaments; the additional objectives which must be secured if there is to be a reasonable prospect of such effective elimination of atomic weapons are discussed in Chapter IX. In the absence of such elimination and the securing of these objectives, it would appear that we have no alternative but to increase our atomic capability as rapidly as other considerations make appropriate. In either case, it appears to be imperative to increase as rapidly as possible our general air, ground, and sea strength and that of our allies to a point where we are militarily not so heavily dependent on atomic weapons.

2. As is indicated in Chapter IV, it is important that the United States employ military force only if the necessity for its use is clear and compelling and commends itself to the overwhelming majority of our people. The United States cannot therefore engage in war except as a reaction to aggression of so clear and compelling a nature as to bring the overwhelming majority of our people to accept the use of military force. In the event war comes, our use of force must be to compel the acceptance of our objectives and must be congruent to the range of tasks which we may encounter.

In the event of a general war with the USSR, it must be anticipated that atomic weapons will be used by each side in the manner it deems best suited to accomplish its objectives. In view of our vulnerability to Soviet atomic attack, it has been argued that we might wish to hold our atomic weapons only for retaliation against prior use by the USSR. To be able to do so and still have hope of achieving our objectives, the non-atomic military capabilities of ourselves and our allies would have to be fully developed and the political weaknesses of the Soviet Union fully exploited. In the event of war, however, we could not be sure that we could move toward the attainment of these objectives without the USSR's resorting sooner or later to the use of its atomic weapons. Only if we had overwhelming atomic superiority and obtained command of the air might the USSR be deterred from employing its atomic weapons as we progressed toward the attainment of our objectives.

In the event the USSR develops by 1954 the atomic capability which we now anticipate, it is hardly conceivable that, if war comes, the Soviet leaders would refrain from the use of atomic weapons unless they felt fully confident of attaining their objectives by other means.

In the event we use atomic weapons either in retaliation for their prior use by the USSR or because there is no alternative method by which we can attain our objectives, it is imperative that the strategic and tactical targets against which they are used be appropriate and the manner in which they are used be consistent with those objectives.

It appears to follow from the above that we should produce and stockpile thermonuclear weapons in the event they prove feasible and would add significantly to our net capability. Not enough is yet known of their potentialities to warrant a judgment at this time regarding their use in war to attain our objectives.

3. It has been suggested that we announce that we will not use atomic weapons except in retaliation against the prior use of such weapons by an aggressor. It has been argued that such a declaration would decrease the danger of an atomic attack against the United States and its allies.

In our present situation of relative unpreparedness in conventional weapons, such a declaration would be interpreted by the USSR as an admission of great weakness and by our allies as a clear indication that we intended to abandon them. Furthermore, it is doubtful whether such a declaration would be taken sufficiently seriously by the Kremlin to constitute an important factor in determining whether or not to attack the United States. It is to be anticipated that the Kremlin would weigh the facts of our capability far more heavily than a declaration of what we proposed to do with that capability.

Unless we are prepared to abandon our objectives, we cannot make such a declaration in good faith until we are confident that we will be in a position to attain our objectives without war, or, in the event of war, without recourse to the use of atomic weapons for strategic or tactical purposes.

C. International Control of Atomic Energy

1. A discussion of certain of the basic considerations involved in securing effective international control is necessary to make clear why the additional objectives discussed in Chapter IX must be secured.

2. No system of international control could prevent the production and use of atomic weapons in the event of a prolonged war. Even the most effective system of international control could, of itself, only provide (a) assurance that atomic weapons had been eliminated from national peacetime armaments and (b) immediate notice of a violation. In essence, an effective international control system would be expected to assure a certain amount of time after notice of violation before atomic weapons could be used in war.

3. The time period between notice of violation and possible use of atomic weapons in war which a control system could be expected to assure depends upon a number of factors.

The dismantling of existing stockpiles of bombs and the destruction of casings and firing mechanisms could by themselves give little assurance of securing time. Casings and firing mechanisms are presumably easy to produce, even surreptitiously, and the assembly of weapons does not take much time.

If existing stocks of fissionable materials were in some way eliminated and the future production of fissionable materials effectively controlled, war could not start with a surprise atomic attack.

In order to assure an appreciable time lag between notice of violation and the time when atomic weapons might be available in quantity, it would be necessary to destroy all plants capable of making large amounts of fissionable material. Such action would, however, require a moratorium on those possible peacetime uses which call for large quantities of fissionable materials.

Effective control over the production and stockpiling of raw materials might further extend the time period which effective international control would assure. Now that the Russians have learned the technique of producing atomic weapons, the time between violation of an international control agreement and production of atomic weapons will be shorter than was estimated in 1946, except possibly in the field of thermonuclear or other new types of weapons.

4. The certainty of notice of violation also depends upon a number of factors. In the absence of good faith, it is to be doubted whether any system can be designed which will give certainty of notice of violation. International ownership of raw materials and fissionable materials and international ownership and operation of dangerous facilities, coupled with inspection based on continuous unlimited freedom of access to all parts of the Soviet Union (as well as to all parts of the territory of other signatories to the control agreement) appear to be necessary to give the requisite degree of assurance against secret violations. As the Soviet stockpile of fissionable materials grows, the amount which the USSR might secretly withhold and not declare to the inspection agency grows. In this sense, the earlier an agreement is consummated the greater the security it would offer. The possibility of successful secret production operations also increases with developments which may reduce the size and power consumption of individual reactors. The development of a thermonuclear bomb would increase many fold the damage a given amount of fissionable material could do and would, therefore, vastly increase the danger that a decisive advantage could be gained through secret operations.

5. The relative sacrifices which would be involved in international control need also to be considered. If it were possible to negotiate an effective system of international control the United States would presumably sacrifice a much larger stockpile of atomic weapons and a much larger production capacity than would the USSR. The opening up of national territory to international inspection involved in an adequate control and inspection system would have a far greater

impact on the USSR than on the United States. If the control system involves the destruction of all large reactors and thus a moratorium on certain possible peacetime uses, the USSR can be expected to argue that it, because of greater need for new sources of energy, would be making a greater sacrifice in this regard than the United States.

6. The United States and the peoples of the world as a whole desire a respite from the dangers of atomic warfare. The chief difficulty lies in the danger that the respite would be short and that we might not have adequate notice of its pending termination. For such an arrangement to be in the interest of the United States, it is essential that the agreement be entered into in good faith by both sides and the probability against its violation high.

7. The most substantial contribution to security of an effective international control system would, of course, be the opening up of the Soviet Union, as required under the UN plan. Such opening up is not, however, compatible with the maintenance of the Soviet system in its present rigor. This is a major reason for the Soviet refusal to accept the UN plan.

The studies which began with the Acheson-Lilienthal committee and culminated in the present UN plan made it clear that inspection of atomic facilities would not alone give the assurance of control; but that ownership and operation by an international authority of the world's atomic energy activities from the mine to the last use of fissionable materials was also essential. The delegation of sovereignty which this implies is necessary for effective control and, therefore, is as necessary for the United States and the rest of the free world as it is presently unacceptable to the Soviet Union.

It is also clear that a control authority not susceptible directly or indirectly to Soviet domination is equally essential. As the Soviet Union would regard any country not under its domination as under the potential if not the actual domination of the United States, it is clear that what the United States and the non-Soviet world must insist on, the Soviet Union at present rejects.

The principal immediate benefit of international control would be to make a surprise atomic attack impossible, assuming the elimination of large reactors and the effective disposal of stockpiles of fissionable materials. But it is almost certain that the Soviet Union would not agree to the elimination of large reactors, unless the impracticability of producing atomic power for peaceful purposes had been demonstrated beyond a doubt. By the same token, it would not now agree to elimination of its stockpile of fissionable materials.

Finally, the absence of good faith on the part of the USSR must be assumed until there is concrete evidence that there has been a decisive change in Soviet policies. It is to be doubted whether such a change can take place without a change in the nature of the Soviet system itself.

The above considerations make it clear that at least a major change in the relative power positions of the United States and the Soviet Union would have to take place before an effective system of international control could be negotiated. The Soviet Union would have had to have moved a substantial distance down the path of accommodation and compromise before such an arrangement would be conceivable. This conclusion is supported by the Third Report of the United Nations Atomic Energy Commission to the Security Council, May 17, 1948, in which it is stated that ". . . the majority of the Commission has been unable to secure . . . their acceptance of the nature and extent of participation in the world community required of all nations in this field. . . . As a result, the Commission has been forced to recognize that agreement on effective measures for the control of atomic energy is itself dependent on cooperation in broader fields of policy."

In short, it is impossible to hope than an effective plan for international control can be negotiated unless and until the Kremlin design has been frustrated to a point at which a genuine and drastic change in Soviet policies has taken place.

IX. Possible Courses of Action
Introduction. Four possible courses of action by the United States in the present situation can be distinguished. They are:

a. Continuation of current policies, with current and currently projected programs for carrying out these policies;
b. Isolation;
c. War; and
d. A more rapid building up of the political, economic, and military strength of the free world than provided under a, with the purpose of reaching, if possible, a tolerable state of order

among nations without war and of preparing to defend ourselves in the event that the free world is attacked.

The role of negotiation. Negotiation must be considered in relation to these courses of action. A negotiator always attempts to achieve an agreement which is somewhat better than the realities of his fundamental position would justify and which is, in any case, not worse than his fundamental position requires. This is as true in relations among sovereign states as in relations between individuals. The Soviet Union possesses several advantages over the free world in negotiations on any issue:

a. It can and does enforce secrecy on all significant facts about conditions within the Soviet Union, so that it can be expected to know more about the realities of the free world's position than the free world knows about its position;
b. It does not have to be responsive in any important sense to public opinion;
c. It does not have to consult and agree with any other countries on the terms it will offer and accept; and
d. It can influence public opinion in other countries while insulating the peoples under its control.

These are important advantages. Together with the unfavorable trend of our power position, they militate, as is shown in Section A below, against successful negotiation of a general settlement at this time. For although the United States probably now possesses, principally in atomic weapons, a force adequate to deliver a powerful blow upon the Soviet Union and to open the road to victory in a long war, it is not sufficient by itself to advance the position of the United States in the cold war.

The problem is to create such political and economic conditions in the free world, backed by force sufficient to inhibit Soviet attack, that the Kremlin will accommodate itself to these conditions, gradually withdraw, and eventually change its policies drastically. It has been shown in Chapter VIII that truly effective control of atomic energy would require such an opening up of the Soviet Union and such evidence in other ways of its good faith and its intent to co-exist in peace as to reflect or at least initiate a change in the Soviet system.

Clearly under present circumstances we will not be able to negotiate a settlement which calls for

a change in the Soviet system. What, then, is the role of negotiation?

In the first place, the public in the United States and in other free countries will require, as a condition to firm policies and adequate programs directed to the frustration of the Kremlin design, that the free world be continuously prepared to negotiate agreements with the Soviet Union on equitable terms. It is still argued by many people here and abroad that equitable agreements with the Soviet Union are possible, and this view will gain force if the Soviet Union begins to show signs of accommodation, even on unimportant issues.

The free countries must always, therefore, be prepared to negotiate and must be ready to take the initiative at times in seeking negotiation. They must develop a negotiating position which defines the issues and the terms on which they would be prepared—and at what stages—to accept agreements with the Soviet Union. The terms must be fair in the view of popular opinion in the free world. This means that they must be consistent with a positive program for peace—in harmony with the United Nations' Charter and providing, at a minimum, for the effective control of all armaments by the United Nations or a successor organization. The terms must not require more of the Soviet Union than such behavior and such participation in a world organization. The fact that such conduct by the Soviet Union is impossible without such a radical change in Soviet policies as to constitute a change in the Soviet system would then emerge as a result of the Kremlin's unwillingness to accept such terms or of its bad faith in observing them.

A sound negotiating position is, therefore, an essential element in the ideological conflict. For some time after a decision to build up strength, any offer of, or attempt at, negotiation of a general settlement along the lines of the Berkeley speech by the Secretary of State could be only a tactic. Nevertheless, concurrently with a decision and a start on building up the strength of the free world, it may be desirable to pursue this tactic both to gain public support for the program and to minimize the immediate risks of war. It is urgently necessary for the United States to determine its negotiating position and to obtain agreement with its major allies on the purposes and terms of negotiation.

In the second place, assuming that the United States in cooperation with other free countries decides and acts to increase the strength of the free world and assuming that the Kremlin chooses the path of accommodation, it will from time to time be necessary and desirable to negotiate on various specific issues with the Kremlin as the area of possible agreement widens.

The Kremlin will have three major objectives in negotiations with the United States. The first is to eliminate the atomic capabilities of the United States; the second is to prevent the effective mobilization of the superior potential of the free world in human and material resources; and the third is to secure a withdrawal of United States forces from, and commitments to, Europe and Japan. Depending on its evaluation of its own strengths and weaknesses as against the West's (particularly the ability and will of the West to sustain its efforts), it will or will not be prepared to make important concessions to achieve these major objectives. It is unlikely that the Kremlin's evaluation is such that it would now be prepared to make significant concessions.

The objectives of the United States and other free countries in negotiations with the Soviet Union (apart from the ideological objectives discussed above) are to record, in a formal fashion which will facilitate the consolidation and further advance of our position, the process of Soviet accommodation to the new political, psychological, and economic conditions in the world which will result from adoption of the fourth course of action and which will be supported by the increasing military strength developed as an integral part of that course of action. In short, our objectives are to record, where desirable, the gradual withdrawal of the Soviet Union and to facilitate that process by making negotiation, if possible, always more expedient than resort to force.

It must be presumed that for some time the Kremlin will accept agreements only if it is convinced that by acting in bad faith whenever and wherever there is an opportunity to do so with impunity, it can derive greater advantage from the agreements than the free world. For this reason, we must take care that any agreements are enforceable or that they are not susceptible of violation without detection and the possibility of effective countermeasures.

This further suggests that we will have to consider carefully the order in which agreements can be concluded. Agreement on the control of atomic energy would result in a relatively greater disarmament of the United States than of the Soviet Union,

even assuming considerable progress in building up the strength of the free world in conventional forces and weapons. It might be accepted by the Soviet Union as part of a deliberate design to move against Western Europe and other areas of strategic importance with conventional forces and weapons. In this event, the United States would find itself at war, having previously disarmed itself in its most important weapon, and would be engaged in a race to redevelop atomic weapons.

This seems to indicate that for the time being the United States and other free countries would have to insist on concurrent agreement on the control of nonatomic forces and weapons and perhaps on the other elements of a general settlement, notably peace treaties with Germany, Austria, and Japan and the withdrawal of Soviet influence from the satellites. If, contrary to our expectations, the Soviet Union should accept agreements promising effective control of atomic energy and conventional armaments, without any other changes in Soviet policies, we would have to consider very carefully whether we could accept such agreements. It is unlikely that this problem will arise.

To the extent that the United States and the rest of the free world succeed in so building up their strength in conventional forces and weapons that a Soviet attack with similar forces could be thwarted or held, we will gain increased flexibility and can seek agreements on the various issues in any order, as they become negotiable.

In the third place, negotiation will play a part in the building up of the strength of the free world, apart from the ideological strength discussed above. This is most evident in the problems of Germany, Austria, and Japan. In the process of building up strength, it may be desirable for the free nations, without the Soviet Union, to conclude separate arrangements with Japan, Western Germany, and Austria which would enlist the energies and resources of these countries in support of the free world. This will be difficult unless it has been demonstrated by attempted negotiation with the Soviet Union that the Soviet Union is not prepared to accept treaties of peace which would leave these countries free, under adequate safeguards, to participate in the United Nations and in regional or broader associations of states consistent with the United Nations' Charter and providing security and adequate opportunities for the peaceful development of their political and economic life.

This demonstrates the importance, from the point of view of negotiation as well as for its relationship to the building up of the strength of the free world (see Section D below), of the problem of closer association—on a regional or a broader basis—among the free countries.

In conclusion, negotiation is not a possible separate course of action but rather a means of gaining support for a program of building strength, of recording, where necessary and desirable, progress in the cold war, and of facilitating further progress while helping to minimize the risks of war. Ultimately, it is our objective to negotiate a settlement with the Soviet Union (or a successor state or states) on which the world can place reliance as an enforceable instrument of peace. But it is important to emphasize that such a settlement can only record the progress which the free world will have made in creating a political and economic system in the world so successful that the frustration of the Kremlin's design for world domination will be complete. The analysis in the following sections indicates that the building of such a system requires expanded and accelerated programs for the carrying out of current policies.

A. The First Course—Continuation of Current Policies, with Current and Currently Projected Programs for Carrying Out These Policies

1. Military aspects. On the basis of current programs, the United States has a large potential military capability but an actual capability which, though improving, is declining relative to the USSR, particularly in light of its probable fission bomb capability and possible thermonuclear bomb capability. The same holds true for the free world as a whole relative to the Soviet world as a whole. If war breaks out in 1950 or in the next few years, the United States and its allies, apart from a powerful atomic blow, will be compelled to conduct delaying actions, while building up their strength for a general offensive. A frank evaluation of the requirements, to defend the United States and its vital interests and to support a vigorous initiative in the cold war, on the one hand, and of present capabilities, on the other, indicates that there is a sharp and growing disparity between them.

A review of Soviet policy shows that the military capabilities, actual and potential, of the United States and the rest of the free world, together with the apparent determination of the free world to resist further Soviet expansion, have not induced the Kremlin to relax its pressures generally or to give up the initiative in the cold war. On the contrary, the Soviet Union has consistently pursued a bold foreign policy, modified only when its probing revealed a determination and an ability of the free world to resist encroachment upon it. The relative military capabilities of the free world are declining, with the result that its determination to resist may also decline and that the security of the United States and the free world as a whole will be jeopardized.

From the military point of view, the actual and potential capabilities of the United States, given a continuation of current and projected programs, will become less and less effective as a war deterrent. Improvement of the state of readiness will become more and more important not only to inhibit the launching of war by the Soviet Union but also to support a national policy designed to reverse the present ominous trends in international relations. A building up of the military capabilities of the United States and the free world is a precondition to the achievement of the objectives outlined in this report and to the protection of the United States against disaster.

Fortunately, the United States military establishment has been developed into a unified and effective force as a result of the policies laid down by the Congress and the vigorous carrying out of these policies by the Administration in the fields of both organization and economy. It is, therefore, a base upon which increased strength can be rapidly built with maximum efficiency and economy.

2. Political aspects. The Soviet Union is pursuing the initiative in the conflict with the free world. Its atomic capabilities, together with its successes in the Far East, have led to an increasing confidence on its part and to an increasing nervousness in Western Europe and the rest of the free world. We cannot be sure, of course, how vigorously the Soviet Union will pursue its initiative, nor can we be sure of the strength or weakness of the other free countries in reacting to it. There are, however, ominous signs of further deterioration in the Far East. There are also some indications that a decline in morale and confidence in Western Europe may be expected. In particular, the situation in Germany is unsettled. Should the belief or suspicion spread that the free nations are not now able to prevent the Soviet Union from taking, if it chooses, the military actions

outlined in Chapter V, the determination of the free countries to resist probably would lessen and there would be an increasing temptation for them to seek a position of neutrality.

Politically, recognition of the military implications of a continuation of present trends will mean that the United States and especially other free countries will tend to shift to the defensive, or to follow a dangerous policy of bluff, because the maintenance of a firm initiative in the cold war is closely related to aggregate strength in being and readily available.

This is largely a problem of the incongruity of the current actual capabilities of the free world and the threat to it, for the free world has an economic and military potential far superior to the potential of the Soviet Union and its satellites. The shadow of Soviet force falls darkly on Western Europe and Asia and supports a policy of encroachment. The free world lacks adequate means—in the form of forces in being—to thwart such expansion locally. The United States will therefore be confronted more frequently with the dilemma of reacting totally to a limited extension of Soviet control or of not reacting at all (except with ineffectual protests and half measures). Continuation of present trends is likely to lead, therefore, to a gradual withdrawal under the direct or indirect pressure of the Soviet Union, until we discover one day that we have sacrificed positions of vital interest. In other words, the United States would have chosen, by lack of the necessary decisions and actions, to fall back to isolation in the Western Hemisphere. This course would at best result in only a relatively brief truce and would be ended either by our capitulation or by a defensive war—on unfavorable terms from unfavorable positions—against a Soviet Empire compromising all or most of Eurasia. (See Section B.)

3. Economic and social aspects. As was pointed out in Chapter VI, the present foreign economic policies and programs of the United States will not produce a solution to the problem of international economic equilibrium, notably the problem of the dollar gap, and will not create an economic base conducive to political stability in many important free countries.

The European Recovery Program has been successful in assisting the restoration and expansion of production in Western Europe and has been a major factor in checking the dry rot of Communism in Western Europe. However, little progress has been made toward the resumption by Western Europe of a position of influence in world affairs commensurate with its potential strength. Progress in this direction will require integrated political, economic, and military policies and programs, which are supported by the United States and the Western European countries and which will probably require a deeper participation by the United States than has been contemplated.

The Point IV Program and other assistance programs will not adequately supplement, as now projected, the efforts of other important countries to develop effective institutions, to improve the administration of their affairs, and to achieve a sufficient measure of economic development. The moderate regimes now in power in many countries, like India, Indonesia, Pakistan, and the Philippines, will probably be unable to restore or retain their popular support and authority unless they are assisted in bringing about a more rapid improvement of the economic and social structure than present programs will make possible.

The Executive Branch is now undertaking a study of the problem of the United States balance of payments and of the measures which might be taken by the United States to assist in establishing international economic equilibrium. This is a very important project and work on it should have a high priority. However, unless such an economic program is matched and supplemented by an equally far-sighted and vigorous political and military program, we will not be successful in checking and rolling back the Kremlin's drive.

4. Negotiation. In short, by continuing along its present course the free world will not succeed in making effective use of its vastly superior political, economic, and military potential to build a tolerable state of order among nations. On the contrary, the political, economic, and military situation of the free world is already unsatisfactory and will become less favorable unless we act to reverse present trends.

This situation is one which militates against successful negotiations with the Kremlin—for the terms of agreements on important pending issues would reflect present realities and would therefore be unacceptable, if not disastrous, to the United States and the rest of the free world. Unless a decision had been made and action undertaken to build up the strength, in the broadest sense, of the United States and the free world, an attempt to negotiate a general settlement on terms acceptable to us would be ineffective and probably long drawn out, and might thereby seriously delay the necessary measures to build up our strength.

This is true despite the fact that the United States now has the capability of delivering a powerful blow against the Soviet Union in the event of war, for one of the present realities is that the United States is not prepared to threaten the use of our present atomic superiority to coerce the Soviet Union into acceptable agreements. In light of present trends, the Soviet Union will not withdraw and the only conceivable basis for a general settlement would be spheres of influence and of no influenced "settlement" which the Kremlin could readily exploit to its great advantage. The idea that Germany or Japan or other important areas can exist as islands of neutrality in a divided world is unreal, given the Kremlin design for world domination.

B. The Second Course—Isolation

Continuation of present trends, it has been shown above, will lead progressively to the withdrawal of the United States from most of its present commitments in Europe and Asia and to our isolation in the Western Hemisphere and its approaches. This would result not from a conscious decision but from a failure to take the actions necessary to bring our capabilities into line with our commitments and thus to a withdrawal under pressure. This pressure might come from our present Allies, who will tend to seek other "solutions" unless they have confidence in our determination to accelerate our efforts to build a successfully functioning political and economic system in the free world.

There are some who advocate a deliberate decision to isolate ourselves. Superficially, this has some attractiveness as a course of action, for it appears to bring our commitments and capabilities into harmony by reducing the former and by concentrating our present, or perhaps even reduced, military expenditures on the defense of the United States.

This argument overlooks the relativity of capabilities. With the United States in an isolated position, we would have to face the probability that the Soviet Union would quickly dominate most of Eurasia, probably without meeting armed resistance. It would thus acquire a potential far superior to our own, and would promptly proceed to develop this potential with the purpose of eliminating our power, which would, even in isolation, remain as a challenge to it and as an obstacle to the imposition of its

kind of order in the world. There is no way to make ourselves inoffensive to the Kremlin except by complete submission to its will. Therefore isolation would in the end condemn us to capitulate or to fight alone and on the defensive, with drastically limited offensive and retaliatory capabilities in comparison with the Soviet Union. (These are the only possibilities, unless we are prepared to risk the future on the hazard that the Soviet Empire, because of over-extension or other reasons, will spontaneously destroy itself from within.)

The argument also overlooks the imponderable, but nevertheless drastic, effects on our belief in ourselves and in our way of life of a deliberate decision to isolate ourselves. As the Soviet Union came to dominate free countries, it is clear that many Americans would feel a deep sense of responsibility and guilt for having abandoned their former friends and allies. As the Soviet Union mobilized the resources of Eurasia, increased its relative military capabilities, and heightened its threat to our security, some would be tempted to accept "peace" on its terms, while many would seek to defend the United States by creating a regimented system which would permit the assignment of a tremendous part of our resources to defense. Under such a state of affairs our national morale would be corrupted and the integrity and vitality of our system subverted.

Under this course of action, there would be no negotiation, unless on the Kremlin's terms, for we would have given up everything of importance.

It is possible that at some point in the course of isolation, many Americans would come to favor a surprise attack on the Soviet Union and the area under its control, in a desperate attempt to alter decisively the balance of power by an overwhelming blow with modern weapons of mass destruction. It appears unlikely that the Soviet Union would wait for such an attack before launching one of its own. But even if it did and even if our attack were successful, it is clear that the United States would face appalling tasks in establishing a tolerable state of order among nations after such a war and after Soviet occupation of all or most of Eurasia for some years. These tasks appear so enormous and success so unlikely that reason dictates an attempt to achieve our objectives by other means.

C. The Third Course—War

Some Americans favor a deliberate decision to go to war against the Soviet Union in the near future. It goes without saying that the idea of "preventive" war—in the sense of a military attack not provoked by a military attack upon us or our allies—is generally unacceptable to Americans. Its supporters argue that since the Soviet Union is in fact at war with the free world now and that since the failure of the Soviet Union to use all-out military force is explainable on grounds of expediency, we are at war and should conduct ourselves accordingly. Some further argue that the free world is probably unable, except under the crisis of war, to mobilize and direct its resources to the checking and rolling back of the Kremlin's drive for world dominion. This is a powerful argument in the light of history, but the considerations against war are so compelling that the free world must demonstrate that this argument is wrong. The case for war is premised on the assumption that the United States could launch and sustain an attack of sufficient impact to gain a decisive advantage for the free world in a long war and perhaps to win an early decision.

The ability of the United States to launch effective offensive operations is now limited to attack with atomic weapons. A powerful blow could be delivered upon the Soviet Union, but it is estimated that these operations alone would not force or induce the Kremlin to capitulate and that the Kremlin would still be able to use the forces under its control to dominate most or all of Eurasia. This would probably mean a long and difficult struggle during which the free institutions of Western Europe and many freedom-loving people would be destroyed and the regenerative capacity of Western Europe dealt a crippling blow.

Apart from this, however, a surprise attack upon the Soviet Union, despite the provocativeness of recent Soviet behavior, would be repugnant to many Americans. Although the American people would probably rally in support of the war effort, the shock of responsibility for a surprise attack would be morally corrosive. Many would doubt that it was a "just war" and that all reasonable possibilities for a peaceful settlement had been explored in good faith. Many more, proportionately, would hold such views in other countries, particularly in Western Europe and particularly after Soviet occupation, if only because the Soviet Union would liquidate articulate opponents. It would, therefore, be difficult after such a war to create a satisfactory international order among nations. Victory in such a war would

have brought us little if at all closer to victory in the fundamental ideological conflict.

These considerations are no less weighty because they are imponderable, and they rule out an attack unless it is demonstrably in the nature of a counter-attack to a blow which is on its way or about to be delivered. (The military advantages of landing the first blow become increasingly important with modern weapons, and this is a fact which requires us to be on the alert in order to strike with our full weight as soon as we are attacked, and, if possible, before the Soviet blow is actually delivered.) If the argument of Chapter IV is accepted, it follows that there is no "easy" solution and that the only sure victory lies in the frustration of the Kremlin design by the steady development of the moral and material strength of the free world and its projection into the Soviet world in such a way as to bring about an internal change in the Soviet system.

D. The Remaining Course of Action—A Rapid Build-Up of Political, Economic, and Military Strength in the Free World

A more rapid build-up of political, economic, and military strength and thereby of confidence in the free world than is now contemplated is the only course which is consistent with progress toward achieving our fundamental purpose. The frustration of the Kremlin design requires the free world to develop a successfully functioning political and economic system and a vigorous political offensive against the Soviet Union. These, in turn, require an adequate military shield under which they can develop. It is necessary to have the military power to deter, if possible, Soviet expansion, and to defeat, if necessary, aggressive Soviet or Soviet-directed actions of a limited or total character. The potential strength of the free world is great; its ability to develop these military capabilities and its will to resist Soviet expansion will be determined by the wisdom and will with which it undertakes to meet its political and economic problems.

1. Military aspects. It has been indicated in Chapter VI that U.S. military capabilities are strategically more defensive in nature than offensive and are more potential than actual. It is evident, from an analysis of the past and of the trend of weapon development, that there is now and will be in the future no absolute defense. The history of war also indicates that a favorable decision can only be achieved through offensive action. Even a defensive

strategy, if it is to be successful, calls not only for defensive forces to hold vital positions while mobilizing and preparing for the offensive, but also for offensive forces to attack the enemy and keep him off balance.

The two fundamental requirements which must be met by forces in being or readily available are support of foreign policy and protection against disaster. To meet the second requirement, the forces in being or readily available must be able, at a minimum, to perform certain basic tasks:

a. To defend the Western Hemisphere and essential allied areas in order that their war-making capabilities can be developed;
b. To provide and protect a mobilization base while the offensive forces required for victory are being built up;
c. To conduct offensive operations to destroy vital elements of the Soviet war-making capacity, and to keep the enemy off balance until the full offensive strength of the United States and its allies can be brought to bear;
d. To defend and maintain the lines of communication and base areas necessary to the execution of the above tasks; and
e. To provide such aid to allies as is essential to the execution of their role in the above tasks.

In the broadest terms, the ability to perform these tasks requires a build-up of military strength by the United States and its allies to a point at which the combined strength will be superior for at least these tasks, both initially and throughout a war, to the forces that can be brought to bear by the Soviet Union and its satellites. In specific terms, it is not essential to match item for item with the Soviet Union, but to provide an adequate defense against air attack on the United States and Canada and an adequate defense against air and surface attack on the United Kingdom and Western Europe, Alaska, the Western Pacific, Africa, and the Near and Middle East, and on the long lines of communication to these areas. Furthermore, it is mandatory that in building up our strength, we enlarge upon our technical superiority by an accelerated exploitation of the scientific potential of the United States and our allies.

Forces of this size and character are necessary not only for protection against disaster but also to support our foreign policy. In fact, it can be argued that larger forces in being and readily available are necessary to inhibit a would-be aggressor than to provide the nucleus of strength and the mobilization base on which the tremendous forces required for victory can be built. For example, in both World Wars I and II the ultimate victors had the strength, in the end, to win though they had not had the strength in being or readily available to prevent the outbreak of war. In part, at least, this was because they had not had the military strength on which to base a strong foreign policy. At any rate, it is clear that a substantial and rapid building up of strength in the free world is necessary to support a firm policy intended to check and to roll back the Kremlin's drive for world domination.

Moreover, the United States and the other free countries do not now have the forces in being and readily available to defeat local Soviet moves with local action, but must accept reverses or make these local moves the occasion for war—for which we are not prepared. This situation makes for great uneasiness among our allies, particularly in Western Europe, for whom total war means, initially, Soviet occupation. Thus, unless our combined strength is rapidly increased, our allies will tend to become increasingly reluctant to support a firm foreign policy on our part and increasingly anxious to seek other solutions, even though they are aware that appeasement means defeat. An important advantage in adopting the fourth course of action lies in its psychological impact—the revival of confidence and hope in the future. It is recognized, of course, that any announcement of the recommended course of action could be exploited by the Soviet Union in its peace campaign and would have adverse psychological effects in certain parts of the free world until the necessary increase in strength has been achieved. Therefore, in any announcement of policy and in the character of the measures adopted, emphasis should be given to the essentially defensive character and care should be taken to minimize, so far as possible, unfavorable domestic and foreign reactions.

2. Political and economic aspects. The immediate objectives—to the achievement of which such a build-up of strength is a necessary though not a sufficient condition—are a renewed initiative in the cold war and a situation to which the Kremlin would find it expedient to accommodate itself, first by relaxing tensions and pressures and then by gradual withdrawal. The United States cannot alone pro-

vide the resources required for such a build-up of strength. The other free countries must carry their part of the burden, but their ability and determination to do it will depend on the action the United States takes to develop its own strength and on the adequacy of its foreign political and economic policies. Improvement in political and economic conditions in the free world, as has been emphasized above, is necessary as a basis for building up the will and the means to resist and for dynamically affirming the integrity and vitality of our free and democratic way of life on which our ultimate victory depends.

At the same time, we should take dynamic steps to reduce the power and influence of the Kremlin inside the Soviet Union and other areas under its control. The objective would be the establishment of friendly regimes not under Kremlin domination. Such action is essential to engage the Kremlin's attention, keep it off balance, and force an increased expenditure of Soviet resources in counteraction. In other words, it would be the current Soviet cold war technique used against the Soviet Union.

A program for rapidly building up strength and improving political and economic conditions will place heavy demands on our courage and intelligence; it will be costly; it will be dangerous. But half-measures will be more costly and more dangerous, for they will be inadequate to prevent and may actually invite war. Budgetary considerations will need to be subordinated to the stark fact that our very independence as a nation may be at stake.

A comprehensive and decisive program to win the peace and frustrate the Kremlin design should be so designed that it can be sustained for as long as necessary to achieve our national objectives. It would probably involve:

1. The development of an adequate political and economic framework for the achievement of our long-range objectives.
2. A substantial increase in expenditures for military purposes adequate to meet the requirements for the tasks listed in Section D-1.
3. A substantial increase in military assistance programs, designed to foster cooperative efforts, which will adequately and efficiently meet the requirements of our allies for the tasks referred to in Section D-l-e.
4. Some increase in economic assistance programs and recognition of the need to continue these programs until their purposes have been accomplished.
5. A concerted attack on the problem of the United States balance of payments, along the lines already approved by the President.
6. Development of programs designed to build and maintain confidence among other peoples in our strength and resolution, and to wage overt psychological warfare calculated to encourage mass defections from Soviet allegiance and to frustrate the Kremlin design in other ways.
7. Intensification of affirmative and timely measures and operations by covert means in the fields of economic warfare and political and psychological warfare with a view to fomenting and supporting unrest and revolt in selected strategic satellite countries.
8. Development of internal security and civilian defense programs.
9. Improvement and intensification of intelligence activities.
10. Reduction of Federal expenditures for purposes other than defense and foreign assistance, if necessary by the deferment of certain desirable programs.
11. Increased taxes.

Essential as prerequisites to the success of this program would be (a) consultations with Congressional leaders designed to make the program the object of non-partisan legislative support, and (b) a presentation to the public of a full explanation of the facts and implications of present international trends.

The program will be costly, but it is relevant to recall the disproportion between the potential capabilities of the Soviet and non-Soviet worlds (cf. Chapters V and VI). The Soviet Union is currently devoting about 40 percent of available resources (gross national product plus reparations, equal in 1949 to about $65 billion) to military expenditures (14 percent) and to investment (26 percent), much of which is in war-supporting industries. In an emergency the Soviet Union could increase the allocation of resources to these purposes to about 50 percent, or by one-fourth.

The United States is currently devoting about 22 percent of its gross national product ($255 billion in 1949) to military expenditures (6 percent), foreign assistance (2 percent), and investment (14 percent), little of which is in war-supporting industries. (As was pointed out in Chapter V, the "fighting value" obtained per dollar of expenditure by the Soviet Union considerably exceeds that obtained by the United States, primarily because of the extremely low military and civilian living standards in the Soviet Union.) In an emergency the United States could devote upward of 50 percent of its gross national product to these purposes (as it did during the last war), an increase of several times present expenditures for direct and indirect military purposes and foreign assistance. From the point of view of the economy as a whole, the program might not result in a real decrease in the standard of living, for the economic effects of the program might be to increase the gross national product by more than the amount being absorbed for additional military and foreign assistance purposes. One of the most significant lessons of our World War II experience was that the American economy, when it operates at a level approaching full efficiency, can provide enormous resources for purposes other than civilian consumption while simultaneously providing a high standard of living. After allowing for price changes, personal consumption expenditures rose by about one-fifth between 1939 and 1944, even though the economy had in the meantime increased the amount of resources going into Government use by $60–$65 billion (in 1939 prices).

This comparison between the potentials of the Soviet Union and the United States also holds true for the Soviet world and the free world and is of fundamental importance in considering the courses of action open to the United States.

The comparison gives renewed emphasis to the fact that the problems faced by the free countries in their efforts to build a successfully functioning system lie not so much in the field of economics as in the field of politics. The building of such a system may require more rapid progress toward the closer association of the free countries in harmony with the concept of the United Nations. It is clear that our long-range objectives require a strengthened United Nations, or a successor organization, to which the world can look for the maintenance of peace and order in a system based on freedom and justice. It also seems clear that a unifying ideal of this kind might awaken and arouse the latent spiritual energies of free men everywhere and obtain their enthusiastic support for a positive program for peace going far beyond the frustration of the Kremlin design and opening vistas to the future that would outweigh short-run sacrifices.

The threat to the free world involved in the development of the Soviet Union's atomic and other capabilities will rise steadily and rather rapidly. For the time being, the United States possesses a marked atomic superiority over the Soviet Union which, together with the potential capabilities of the United States and other free countries in other forces and weapons, inhibits aggressive Soviet action. This provides an opportunity for the United States, in cooperation with other free countries, to launch a build-up of strength which will support a firm policy directed to the frustration of the Kremlin design. The immediate goal of our efforts to build a successfully functioning political and economic system in the free world backed by adequate military strength is to postpone and avert the disastrous situation which, in light of the Soviet Union's probable fission bomb capability and possible thermonuclear bomb capability, might arise in 1954 on a continuation of our present programs. By acting promptly and vigorously in such a way that this date is, so to speak, pushed into the future, we would permit time for the process of accommodation, withdrawal and frustration to produce the necessary changes in the Soviet system. Time is short, however, and the risks of war attendant upon a decision to build up strength will steadily increase the longer we defer it.

CONCLUSIONS AND RECOMMENDATIONS

Conclusions

The foregoing analysis indicates that the probable fission bomb capability and possible thermonuclear bomb capability of the Soviet Union have greatly intensified the Soviet threat to the security of the United States. This threat is of the same character as that described in NSC 20/4 (approved by the President on November 24, 1948) but is more immediate than had previously been estimated. In particular, the United States now faces the contingency that within the next four or five years the Soviet Union will possess the military capability of delivering a surprise atomic attack of such weight that the United States must have substantially increased general air, ground, and sea strength, atomic capabilities, and air and civilian defenses to deter war and to provide reasonable assurance, in the event of war, that it could survive the initial blow and go on to the eventual attainment of its objectives. In return, this contingency requires the intensification of our efforts in the fields of intelligence and research and development.

Allowing for the immediacy of the danger, the following statement of Soviet threats, contained in NSC 20/4, remains valid:

14. The gravest threat to the security of the United States within the foreseeable future stems from the hostile designs and formidable power of the USSR, and from the nature of the Soviet system.
15. The political, economic, and psychological warfare which the USSR is now waging has dangerous potentialities for weakening the relative world position of the United States and disrupting its traditional institutions by means short of war, unless sufficient resistance is encountered in the policies of this and other non-communist countries.
16. The risk of war with the USSR is sufficient to warrant, in common prudence, timely and adequate preparation by the United States.
    a. Even though present estimates indicate that the Soviet leaders probably do not intend deliberate armed action involving the United States at this time, the possibility of such deliberate resort to war cannot be ruled out.
    b. Now and for the foreseeable future there is a continuing danger that war will arise either through Soviet miscalculation of the determination of the United States to use all the means at its command to safeguard its security, through Soviet misinterpretation of our intentions, or through U.S. miscalculation of Soviet reactions to measures which we might take.
17. Soviet domination of the potential power of Eurasia, whether achieved by armed aggression or by political and subversive means, would be strategically and politically unacceptable to the United States.
18. The capability of the United States either in peace or in the event of war to cope with threats to its security or to gain its objectives would be severely weakened by internal development, important among which are:
    a. Serious espionage, subversion and sabotage, particularly by concerted and well-directed communist activity.
    b. Prolonged or exaggerated economic instability.
    c. Internal political and social disunity.
    d. Inadequate or excessive armament or foreign aid expenditures.
    e. An excessive or wasteful usage of our resources in time of peace.
    f. Lessening of U.S. prestige and influence through vacillation of appeasement or lack of skill and imagination in the conduct of its foreign policy or by shirking world responsibilities.
    g. Development of a false sense of security through a deceptive change in Soviet tactics.

Although such developments as those indicated in paragraph 18 above would severely weaken the capability of the United States and its allies to cope with the Soviet threat to their security, considerable progress has been made since 1948 in laying the foundation upon which adequate strength can now be rapidly built.

The analysis also confirms that our objectives with respect to the Soviet Union, in time of peace as well as in time of war, as stated in NSC 20/4 (para. 19), are still valid, as are the aims and measures stated therein (paras. 20 and 21). Our current security programs and strategic plans are based upon these objectives, aims, and measures:

19.
    a. To reduce the power and influence of the USSR to limits which no longer constitute a threat to the peace, national independence, and stability of the world family of nations.
    b. To bring about a basic change in the conduct of international relations by the government in power in Russia, to conform with the purposes and principles set forth in the UN Charter.

In pursuing these objectives, due care must be taken to avoid permanently impairing our economy and the fundamental values and institutions inherent in our way of life.

20. We should endeavor to achieve our general objectives by methods short of war through the pursuit of the following aims:
    a. To encourage and promote the gradual retraction of undue Russian power and influence from the present perimeter areas around traditional Russian boundaries and the emergence of the satellite countries as entities independent of the USSR.

b. To encourage the development among the Russian peoples of attitudes which may help to modify current Soviet behavior and permit a revival of the national life of groups evidencing the ability and determination to achieve and maintain national independence.

c. To eradicate the myth by which people remote from Soviet military influence are held in a position of subservience to Moscow and to cause the world at large to see and understand the true nature of the USSR and the Soviet-directed world communist party, and to adopt a logical and realistic attitude toward them.

d. To create situations which will compel the Soviet Government to recognize the practical undesirability of acting on the basis of its present concepts and the necessity of behaving in accordance with precepts of international conduct, as set forth in the purposes and principles of the UN Charter.

21. Attainment of these aims requires that the United States:

a. Develop a level of military readiness which can be maintained as long as necessary as a deterrent to Soviet aggression, as indispensable support to our political attitude toward the USSR, as a source of encouragement to nations resisting Soviet political aggression, and as an adequate basis for immediate military commitments and for rapid mobilization should war prove unavoidable.

b. Assure the internal security of the United States against dangers of sabotage, subversion, and espionage.

c. Maximize our economic potential, including the strengthening of our peacetime economy and the establishment of essential reserves readily available in the event of war.

d. Strengthen the orientation toward the United States of the non-Soviet nations; and help such of those nations as are able and willing to make an important contribution to U.S. security, to increase their economic and political stability and their military capability.

e. Place the maximum strain on the Soviet structure of power and particularly on the relationships between Moscow and the satellite countries.

f. Keep the U.S. public fully informed and cognizant of the threats to our national security

so that it will be prepared to support the measures which we must accordingly adopt.

In the light of present and prospective Soviet atomic capabilities, the action which can be taken under present programs and plans, however, becomes dangerously inadequate, in both timing and scope, to accomplish the rapid progress toward the attainment of the United States political, economic, and military objectives which is now imperative.

A continuation of present trends would result in a serious decline in the strength of the free world relative to the Soviet Union and its satellites. This unfavorable trend arises from the inadequacy of current programs and plans rather than from any error in our objectives and aims. These trends lead in the direction of isolation, not by deliberate decision but by lack of the necessary basis for a vigorous initiative in the conflict with the Soviet Union.

Our position as the center of power in the free world places a heavy responsibility upon the United States for leadership. We must organize and enlist the energies and resources of the free world in a positive program for peace which will frustrate the Kremlin design for world domination by creating a situation in the free world to which the Kremlin will be compelled to adjust. Without such a cooperative effort, led by the United States, we will have to make gradual withdrawals under pressure until we discover one day that we have sacrificed positions of vital interest.

It is imperative that this trend be reversed by a much more rapid and concerted build-up of the actual strength of both the United States and the other nations of the free world. The analysis shows that this will be costly and will involve significant domestic financial and economic adjustments.

The execution of such a build-up, however, requires that the United States have an affirmative program beyond the solely defensive one of countering the threat posed by the Soviet Union. This program must light the path to peace and order among nations in a system based on freedom and justice, as contemplated in the Charter of the United Nations. Further, it must envisage the political and economic measures with which and the military shield behind which the free world can work to frustrate the Kremlin design by the strategy of the cold war; for every consideration of devotion to our fundamental values and to our national security demands that we achieve our objectives by the strategy of the cold war, building up our military strength in order that it may not have to be used. The only sure victory lies in the frustration of the Kremlin design by the steady development of the moral and material strength of the free world and its projection into the Soviet world in such a way as to bring about an internal change in the Soviet system. Such a positive program—harmonious with our fundamental national purpose and our objectives—is necessary if we are to regain and retain the initiative and to win and hold the necessary popular support and cooperation in the United States and the rest of the free world.

This program should include a plan for negotiation with the Soviet Union, developed and agreed with our allies and which is consonant with our objectives. The United States and its allies, particularly the United Kingdom and France, should always be ready to negotiate with the Soviet Union on terms consistent with our objectives. The present world situation, however, is one which militates against successful negotiations with the Kremlin—for the terms of agreements on important pending issues would reflect present realities and would therefore be unacceptable, if not disastrous, to the United States and the rest of the free world. After a decision and a start on building up the strength of the free world has been made, it might then be desirable for the United States to take an initiative in seeking negotiations in the hope that it might facilitate the process of accommodation by the Kremlin to the new situation. Failing that, the unwillingness of the Kremlin to accept equitable terms or its bad faith in observing them would assist in consolidating popular opinion in the free world in support of the measures necessary to sustain the build-up.

In summary, we must, by means of a rapid and sustained build-up of the political, economic, and military strength of the free world, and by means of an affirmative program intended to wrest the initiative from the Soviet Union, confront it with convincing evidence of the determination and ability of the free world to frustrate the Kremlin design of a world dominated by its will. Such evidence is the only means short of war which eventually may force the Kremlin to abandon its present course of action and to negotiate acceptable agreements on issues of major importance.

The whole success of the proposed program hangs ultimately on recognition by this Government, the American people, and all free peoples, that the cold war is in fact a real war in which the survival of the free world is at stake. Essential prerequisites to success are consultations with Congressional leaders designed to make the program the object of non-partisan legislative support, and a presentation to the public of a full explanation of the facts and implications of the present international situation. The prosecution of the program will require of us all the ingenuity, sacrifice, and unity demanded by the vital importance of the issue and the tenacity to persevere until our national objectives have been attained.

Recommendations

That the President:

a. Approve the foregoing Conclusions.
b. Direct the National Security Council, under the continuing direction of the President, and with the participation of other Departments and Agencies as appropriate, to coordinate and insure the implementation of the Conclusions herein on an urgent and continuing basis for as long as necessary to achieve our objectives. For this purpose, representatives of the member Departments and Agencies, the Joint Chiefs of Staff or their deputies, and other Departments and Agencies as required should be constituted as a revised and strengthened staff organization under the National Security Council to develop coordinated programs for consideration by the National Security Council.

NOTES

1. Marshal Tito, the Communist leader of Yugoslavia, broke away from the Soviet bloc in 1948.
2. The Secretary of State listed seven areas in which the Soviet Union could modify its behavior in such a way as to permit co-existence in reasonable security. These were:
   1. Treaties of peace with Austria, Germany, Japan and relaxation of pressures in the Far East;
   2. Withdrawal of Soviet forces and influence from satellite area;
   3. Cooperation in the United Nations;
   4. Control of atomic energy and of conventional armaments;

5. Abandonment of indirect aggression;
6. Proper treatment of official representatives of the U.S.;
7. Increased access to the Soviet Union of persons and ideas from other countries.

[Footnote in the source text. For the text of the address delivered by Secretary Acheson at the University of California, Berkeley, on March 16, 1950, concerning United States—Soviet relations, see Department of State Bulletin, March 27, 1950, pp. 473–478.]

14. The President's News Conference June 29, 1950

Public Papers of the Presidents of the United States: Harry S. Truman, 1950. Washington, D.C.: U.S. Government Printing Office, 502–506.

THE PRESIDENT. [1.] I have an announcement to make.

We have appointed an economic survey mission to go to the Philippines as soon as it can make the arrangements.

It is headed by the Honorable Daniel W. Bell, president of the American Security and Trust Co. of Washington and former Under Secretary of the Treasury; and by Gen. Richard I. Marshall, president of the Virginia Military Institute.

And as soon as the appointment of the mission is completed, why they will leave for the Philippines as promptly as possible.

This mission was appointed at the request of the Philippine President. He made that request of me when he was here on his visit.

And we have had some difficulty in finding the people to head the mission, and in ironing out some differences between the various departments of the Government. Everything has been ironed out now, and that mission will go to work. That's all the announcements I have to make.

[2.] Q. Mr. President, just to set the record straight, is there or has there been any differences among members of your Cabinet on your policy statement of Tuesday[1] regarding the—

THE PRESIDENT. Never was any differences. Never has been.

[3.] Q. Mr. President, did you have a call from the Ambassador of Australia this afternoon?

THE PRESIDENT. No, I did not.

[4.] Q. Mr. President, I have been requested to ask you this question. Was there on the high seas, at the time that South Korea was attacked, was there a shipment of heavy artillery and antitank weapons on its way to the South Korean Government?

THE PRESIDENT. Can't answer that question, for I don't know.

I intended to tell you that there will be a statement on this Philippine situation which will be handed to you when you go out.[2]

I can't answer your question, because I don't know.

[5.] Q. Mr. President, since issuing your statement, have you had any indication as to the effect that it may have on peace ?

THE PRESIDENT. My idea in issuing the statement and the orders preliminary to the issuance of the statement was that it is a move in favor of peace. If I hadn't thought that, I would have taken other steps.

Q. Have you, sir—have you had any indication as to whether it is being universally accepted as that?

THE PRESIDENT. Well, only that most of the members of the United Nations are in full accord with what we are doing.

Q. Mr. President, everybody is asking in this country, are we or are we not at war?

THE PRESIDENT. We are not at war.

Q. Mr. President, another question that is being asked is, are we going to use ground troops in Korea?

THE PRESIDENT. No comment on that.

Q. Mr. President, in that connection it has been asked whether there might be any possibility of having to use the atomic bomb?

[1] See Item 173.
[2] See Item 180.

THE PRESIDENT. No comment.

[6.] Q. Mr. President, the Alaska and Hawaii statehood bills are being filed in the Senate this afternoon. Do you think that there will be time for the Senate to act on those bills at this session?

THE PRESIDENT. Why not? It wouldn't take 10 minutes to do what they have got to do and vote yes and no.

Q. Do you expect to use your good offices—

THE PRESIDENT. Certainly do.

Q.—to act strongly for the admission of those two states? Thank you.

[7.] Q. Mr. President, have you had any report on Russian reaction through any official channels?

THE PRESIDENT. No, I have not.

[8.] Q. Mr. President, James Roosevelt had a press conference this morning. Can you tell us whether you support him as strongly as he indicated?

THE PRESIDENT. Yes, I am. I want to see a Democrat Governor in California, and I told him I hoped he would be elected, and that I would do anything I could to help him get elected.

[9.] Q. Another question, Mr. President. Are you going to call in Ed Pauley on this Korean situation?

THE PRESIDENT. Ask that question again. I didn't hear you.

Q. Are you going to call in Ed Pauley on this Korean situation as an adviser—

THE PRESIDENT. I haven't talked to Mr. Pauley, if that is what you asked me.

[10.] Q. Mr. President, the Joint Atomic Energy Committee this morning pulled a sleeper and voted not to approve the nomination of Mr. Sumner Pike, who is acting as Chairman of the Atomic Energy Commission. I wonder whether you would comment on that, sir?

THE PRESIDENT. I can't understand it, because Mr. Pike has been one of the ablest members of that Commission, and one of its most faithful members. I think the Atomic Energy Committee should take another look at it, and another vote.

[11.] Q. Mr. President, could you elaborate on this statement that—I believe the direct quote was, "We are not at war." And could we use that quote in quotes?

THE PRESIDENT. Yes, I will allow you to use that. We are not at war.

Q. Could you elaborate sir, a little more on the reason for this move, and the peace angle on it?

THE PRESIDENT. The Republic of Korea was set up with the United Nations help. It is a recognized government by the members of the United Nations. It was unlawfully attacked by a bunch of bandits which are neighbors of North Korea. The United Nations Security Council held a meeting and passed on the situation and asked the members to go to the relief of the Korean Republic.

And the members of the United Nations are going to the relief of the Korean Republic to suppress a bandit raid on the Republic of Korea.

Q. Mr. President, would it be correct, against your explanation, to call this a police action under the United Nations?

THE PRESIDENT. Yes. That is exactly what it amounts to.

[12.] Q. Mr. President, in a speech in the Senate yesterday, Senator Taft suggested that Mr. Acheson ought to resign.[3] Would you comment on that, please?

THE PRESIDENT. I think that the political statement of Mr. Taft at this time is entirely uncalled for.

Q. Can we put that in quotes?

THE PRESIDENT. Yes.

Q. Mr. President, that quote was, "I think the political statement of Mr. Taft at this time is entirely uncalled for"?

THE PRESIDENT. Uncalled for. That is correct.

---

[3] The text of Senator Robert A. Taft's remarks is printed in the Congressional Record (vol. 96, p. 9319).

Q. Mr. President, Senator Taft also said that you have reversed Secretary Acheson.

THE PRESIDENT. Not a word of truth in that, and you can put that in quotes, too. [Laughter] Ask the question again, and I will give you the answer.

Q. Senator Taft also said that you had reversed Secretary Acheson. Would you comment on that, sir?

THE PRESIDENT. I say there isn't a word of truth in that. [More laughter]

[13.] Q. Mr. President, were you disappointed in the results of the North Carolina senatorial race?

THE PRESIDENT. I was very friendly to Doctor Graham.[4]

Q. Mr. President, if you were in North Carolina, would you vote the straight Democratic ticket?

THE PRESIDENT. Surely I would. I would vote the Democratic ticket no matter where I should happen to be.

[14.] Q. Mr. President, the Export-Import Bank Directors called on you last week about the Mexican loan. Is there anything you could comment on that?

THE PRESIDENT. No comment. They discussed several things besides the Mexican loan, and I have no comment on the visit. It was a friendly visit, at my request. Which Tony had the floor?[5] [Laughter]

Q. I miss so many questions. I am getting old—I didn't catch them all. I get all your answers.

THE PRESIDENT. The question was what was the cause of the visit of the Export-Import Bank Directors to the President, and was the Mexican loan discussed. A great many subjects were discussed. It was a friendly visit by the Directors on the President, at his request. No pressure was being put on them for anything.

[15.] Q. Mr. President, when you referred to police action, do I understand you mean United Nations police action?

THE PRESIDENT. I beg your pardon?

Q. When you refer to police action on behalf of Korea, you mean United Nations?

THE PRESIDENT. That is correct. That is correct.

Q. Mr. President, a minute ago you said South Korea was attacked by a bunch of bandits, then made this reference to them being neighbors. Do I understand you told us neighbors of Korea, or neighbors in Korea?

THE PRESIDENT. They are neighbors of South Korea.

[16.] Q. Do you have any comment on India's decision to support the United Nations?

THE PRESIDENT. I am very happy, of course. I was sure that India would do that.

[17.] Q. Mr. President, since you have been so very gracious with some of the other direct quotes, may we quote "bandits" directly, too?

THE PRESIDENT. Yes.

[18.] Q. The Argentine Chamber of Deputies overwhelmingly voted approval of ratification of the hemispheric defense treaty adopted at Rio de Janeiro. Would you comment on that?

THE PRESIDENT. I am very happy about that. I knew about it yesterday, and I am very happy that it took place.

[19.] Q. Mr. President, as a result of the action in Korea, are we apt to expedite the Japanese peace treaty?

THE PRESIDENT. I can't comment on that.

Q. Mr. President, in view of the pressed conditions in the situation in Korea, do you now feel that it is necessary to increase the speed with which we are ordering munitions?

THE PRESIDENT. I can't comment on that.

[20.] Q. Mr. President, any comment on the fact that the Russians are cutting off power in West Berlin?

[4] On June 24 Willis Smith defeated Senator Frank P. Graham in a special primary election for North Carolina's Democratic senatorial nomination.
[5] Ernest B. (Tony) Vaccaro of the Associated Press responded. Anthony H. Leviero of the *New York Times* was also present.

THE PRESIDENT. NO comment. I have not been officially notified of it. I heard about it, but I have not been officially notified of it.

[21.] Q. Mr. President, in spite of the apparent reverses in South Korea, do you have any doubt that we will enable South Korea to remain an independent republic?

THE PRESIDENT. Sure—that's what the program is for.

[22.] Q. Mr. President, the Council of Organization of American States yesterday adopted a resolution reasserting the solidarity of the American Republics. Has that come to your attention, and do you wish to comment?

THE PRESIDENT. That has not come to my attention, but I am glad they did that.

[23.] Q. Mr. President, the Senate Appropriations Committee has just cut off another quarter of a billion dollars from the Marshall plan bills. Any comment about that?

THE PRESIDENT. I don't believe that bill is ready for comment yet. When it comes to me, then I will comment on it.

[24.] Q. Mr. President, just to clear the record, Mr. Bourgholtzer[6] asked you if you had a doubt, and you said certainly—

THE PRESIDENT. Certainly—certainly not.

Q. No doubt—

THE PRESIDENT. Tony,[7] you're getting so you can't hear. [Laughter]

Q. Tony was right. That's what you said, Mr. President.

Q. I believe you said surely, sir. You didn't say certainly, you said sure.

THE PRESIDENT. There is no doubt that the program will be to maintain the Korean Republic. The Republic of Korea I think is the proper name.

[25.] Q. Mr. President, you had a conference with Stuart Symington.[8] Does that mean that the NSRB program will be speeded up?

THE PRESIDENT. Well, it has been speeded up all the time. It will be carried on in the same expeditious manner in which it has always been carried on.

Q. Did the Korean thing have anything

THE PRESIDENT. What's that?

Q. Did the Korean.—

THE PRESIDENT. Not a thing in the world. Symington has a session with me twice a week, for 30 minutes each time, as did Doctor Steelman when he was running the same organization.

[26.] Q. Mr. President, your "no comment" on the atomic bomb might be subject to misinterpretation. Has there been any change—

THE PRESIDENT. No comment will be made on any matter of strategy. I don't expect to comment on any matter of strategy.

Reporter: Thank you, Mr. President.

THE PRESIDENT. You're welcome.

15. The President's News Conference November 30, 1950

Public Papers of the Presidents of the United States: Harry S. Truman, 1950. Washington, D.C.: U.S. Government Printing Office, 724–728.

THE PRESIDENT. Good morning, everybody. Sit down.

[1.] I have got a statement I want to read to you. There will be copies available when you get ready to leave here. I will take it as slowly as I can.

[Reading] "Recent developments in Korea confront the world with a serious crisis. The Chinese Communist leaders have sent their troops from Manchuria to launch a strong and well-

---

[6] Frank Bourgholtzer of the National Broadcasting Company.
[7] Ernest B. Vaccaro of the Associated Press.
[8] W. Stuart Symington, Chairman of the National Security Resources Board.

organized attack against the United Nations forces in North Korea. This has been done despite prolonged and earnest efforts to bring home to the Communist leaders of China the plain fact that neither the United Nations nor the United States has any aggressive intentions toward China. Because of the historic friendship between the people of the United States and China, it is particularly shocking to us to think that Chinese are being forced into battle against our troops in the United Nations command.

"The Chinese attack was made in great force, and it still continues. It has resulted in the forced withdrawal of large parts of the United Nations command. The battlefield situation is uncertain at this time. We may suffer reverses as we have suffered them before. But the forces of the United Nations have no intention of abandoning their mission in Korea."

[The following sentence is in the statement as released by the White House but was not read by the President.]

"The forces of the United Nations are in Korea to put down an aggression that threatens not only the whole fabric of the United Nations, but all human hopes of peace and justice."

[Reading] "If the United Nations yields to the forces of aggression, no nation will be safe or secure. If aggression is successful in Korea, we can expect it to spread throughout Asia and Europe to this hemisphere. We are fighting in Korea for our own national security and survival.

"We have committed ourselves to the cause of a just and peaceful world order through the United Nations. We stand by that commitment.

"We shall meet the new situation in three ways.

"We shall continue to work in the United Nations for concerted action to halt this aggression in Korea.

"We shall intensify our efforts to help other free nations strengthen their defenses in order to meet the threat of aggression elsewhere.

"We shall rapidly increase our own military strength.

"In the United Nations, the first step is action by the Security Council to halt this aggression. And Ambassador Warren Austin is pressing for such action. We shall exert every effort to help bring the full influence of the United Nations to bear on the situation in Korea.

"Some had hoped that the normal peaceful process of discussion and negotiation, which is provided through the United Nations, could be successfully entered into with the present Chinese Communist delegation at Lake Success. There is, however, no indication that the representatives of Communist China are willing to engage in this process. Instead of discussing the real issues, they have been making violent and wholly false statements of the type which have often been used by the Soviet representatives in an effort to prevent the Security Council from acting.

"We hope that the Chinese people will not continue to be forced or deceived into serving the ends of Russian colonial policy in Asia.

"I am certain that, if the Chinese people now under the control of the Communists were free to speak for themselves, they would denounce this aggression against the United Nations.

"Because this new act of aggression in Korea is only a part of a worldwide pattern of danger to all the free nations of the world, it is more necessary than ever before for us to increase at a very rapid rate the combined military strength of the free nations. It is more necessary than ever that integrated forces in Europe under a supreme command be established at once.

"With respect to our own defense, I shall submit a supplemental request for appropriations needed immediately to increase the size and effectiveness of our Armed Forces. The request will include a substantial amount for the Atomic Energy Commission in addition to large amounts for the Army, the Navy, and the Air Force.[1]

"I expect to confer tomorrow with congressional leaders and ask them to give urgent consideration to these new appropriations.

"This is a time for all our citizens to lay aside differences and unite in firmness and mutual determination to do what is best for our country and the cause of freedom throughout the world. This country is the keystone of the hopes of mankind for peace and justice. We must show that we are guided by a common purpose and a common faith."

All right. Ask any questions now.

---

[1] See Item 296.

[2.] Q. Mr. President, do you think, in view of this situation, that we should delay any further general mobilization and control of materials and prices and supports and—

THE PRESIDENT. That matter is being constantly considered. I do not intend to answer the question.

[3.] Q. Mr. President, are you about to name a supreme commander then?

THE PRESIDENT. I have been ready to name a supreme commander for a long time.

Q. You are waiting on European—

THE PRESIDENT. I am waiting on agreement with our European allies.

[4.] Q. Mr. President, in what detail were you informed about these MacArthur moves?[2]

THE PRESIDENT. Every detail.

Q. Did you or the State Department raise the question of whether this offensive would affect the chances of a negotiated settlement with the Peiping government?

THE PRESIDENT. The whole matter was clearly discussed with General MacArthur every day.

Q. Mr. President, there has been some criticism of General MacArthur in the European press—

THE PRESIDENT. Some in the American press, too, if I'm not mistaken.

Q.—particularly in the British press—

THE PRESIDENT. They are always for a man when he is winning, but when he is in a little trouble, they all jump on him with what ought to be done, which they didn't tell him before. He has done a good job, and he is continuing to do a good job. Go ahead with your question.

Q. The particular criticism is that he exceeded his authority and went beyond the point he was supposed to go?

THE PRESIDENT. He did nothing of the kind.
[Slight pause]
Well, what's the matter with you?

[5.] Q. Mr. President, a few months ago this Government declined the offer of Chinese Nationalist troops. Has that been up for reconsideration, in view—

THE PRESIDENT. The offer of Nationalist Chinese troops was refused for the reason that we hoped not to be involved in a world war. That situation still continues.

[6.] Q. Along the same line then, our Formosa policy of neutralization—

THE PRESIDENT. Still continues.

[7.] Q. Mr. President, since the Chinese delegation has shown no inclination to resolve the difficulties, what can be done then?

THE PRESIDENT. We are still working on the thing from every angle. The best thing that can be done is to increase our defenses to a point where we can talk—as we should always talk—with authority.

Q. Mr. President, how wide an increase do you expect to authorize in mobilization of the military—

THE PRESIDENT. I will answer that question when I send up the request for the appropriation.

Q. Can you say how large that appropriation will be, sir?

THE PRESIDENT. No. I will give it to you when I send it up, which will be in a day or two.

Q. Is it to go up tomorrow?

THE PRESIDENT. Well, I don't think it will be ready. I hope it will be, but I don't think it will be.

[8.] Q. Mr. President, what congressional leaders will you see?

THE PRESIDENT. The usual ones.

Q. Will that include Republicans—

THE PRESIDENT. They will come in the White House. It's the usual conference that I have—with the usual agenda.

---

[2] On November 23 General MacArthur had launched an assault on the Communist forces in Korea in an attempt to end the war. On November 28 he issued a special communiqué stating that the United Nations forces faced an "entirely new war" with an enemy force of 200,000 men, including a major segment of the Communist Chinese army.

Q. Will it include Republicans?

THE PRESIDENT. It always does. Of course it will. Don't you remember? Remember back, there have been 9 or 10 of these conferences. If you will look back and edit them, you will find that your question will be answered.

Q. My editor tells me not to take anything for granted. [Laughter]

THE PRESIDENT. That's too bad. Of course, that is one of the things that's the matter with the country. It just exactly states—you have answered a national question when you said that. Confidence in your Government is the first thing to keep it running as it should.

[9.] Q. Mr. President, will the United Nations troops be allowed to bomb across the Manchurian border?

THE PRESIDENT. I can't answer that question this morning.

[10.] Q. Mr. President, in increasing our military strength, do you consider using the Japanese manpower?

THE PRESIDENT. Using what?

Q. The Japanese manpower, in increasing our military strength—speaking of the United Nations?

THE PRESIDENT. We will cross that bridge when we come to it.

[11.] Q. Mr. President, will attacks in Manchuria depend on action in the United Nations?

THE PRESIDENT. Yes, entirely.

Q. In other words, if the United Nations resolution should authorize General MacArthur to go further than he has, he will—

THE PRESIDENT. We will take whatever steps are necessary to meet the military situation, just as we always have.

[12.] Q. Will that include the atomic bomb?

THE PRESIDENT. That includes every weapon that we have.

Q. Mr. President, you said "every weapon that we have." Does that mean that there is active consideration of the use of the atomic bomb?

THE PRESIDENT. There has always been active consideration of its use. I don't want to see it used. It is a terrible weapon, and it should not be used on innocent men, women, and children who have nothing whatever to do with this military aggression. That happens when it is used.[3]

"The President wants to make it certain that there is no misinterpretation of his answers to questions at his press conference today about the use of the atom bomb. Naturally, there has been consideration of this subject since the outbreak of the hostilities in Korea, just as there is consideration of the use of all military weapons whenever our forces are in combat.

"Consideration of the use of any weapon is always implicit in the very possession of that weapon.

"However, it should be emphasized, that, by law, only the President can authorize the use of the atom bomb, and no such authorization has been given. If and when such authorization should be given, the military commander in the field would have charge of the tactical delivery of the weapon.

"In brief, the replies to the questions at today's press conference do not represent any change in this situation."

[13.] Q. Mr. President, Senator Byrd[4] says not a single dollar for Yugoslavia, and he backed it up this morning with the Southern bloc. Have you any comment? [Laughter]

THE PRESIDENT. No comment. We would expect that from Senator Byrd, however.

[14.] Q. Mr. President, I wonder if we could retrace that reference to the atom bomb? Did we understand you clearly that the use of the atomic bomb is under active consideration?

THE PRESIDENT. Always has been. It is one of our weapons.

Q. Does that mean, Mr. President, use against military objectives, or civilian—

---

[3] Later the same day the White House issued the following press release:

[4] Senator Harry F. Byrd of Virginia.

THE PRESIDENT. It's a matter that the military people will have to decide. I'm not a military authority that passes on those things.

Q. Mr. President, perhaps it would be better if we are allowed to quote your remarks on that directly?

THE PRESIDENT. I don't think—I don't think that is necessary.

Q. Mr. President, you said this depends on United Nations action. Does that mean that we wouldn't use the atomic bomb except on a United Nations authorization?

THE PRESIDENT. No, it doesn't mean that at all. The action against Communist China depends on the action of the United Nations. The military commander in the field will have charge of the use of the weapons, as he always has.

[15.] Q. Mr. President, how close are we to all-out mobilization.

THE PRESIDENT. Depends on how this matter we are faced with now works out.

[16.] Q. Mr. President, will the United Nations decide whether the Manchurian border is crossed, either with bombing planes or—

THE PRESIDENT. The resolution that is now pending before the United Nations will answer that question.

Q. Or with troops?

THE PRESIDENT. That question will be answered by this resolution.[5]

[17.] Q. Mr. President, do you have to ask any congressional action to proceed further in this situation in Asia?

THE PRESIDENT. Money. Always have to ask them for money.

Q. Is it going beyond police action at this time?

THE PRESIDENT. I Can't answer that question. That is what we are examining. We have exerted every effort possible to prevent a third world war. Every maneuver that has been made since June

[5] On December 14, 1950, the United Nations General Assembly adopted a resolution listing its conditions for a cease-fire in Korea (see the *Department of State Bulletin*, vol. 24, p. 113).

25th has had in mind not to create a situation which would cause another terrible war. We are still trying to prevent that war from happening, and I hope we may be able to prevent it.

All these attacks and speculations and lies that have been told on the members of this Government have not helped that situation one little bit. There's a big one on the front page of the paper this morning, about Acheson having interfered with the command in the Far East. There isn't one word of truth in that, and never has been. Acheson has attended strictly to his business as Secretary of State, and he has done a good job.

I am getting tired of all this foolishment and I'm going to "bust loose" on you one of these days. [Laughter]

[18.] Q. You said we are going to—in your statement—intensify our military efforts. Do you mean to step it up more than you had planned to step it up, before the events of the—

THE PRESIDENT. Yes, it will. The end will be attained sooner than we had anticipated would be necessary—that is what it means.

Q. Same size program?

THE PRESIDENT. Probably—probably. Gotten together more rapidly.

[19.] Q. Mr. President, in intensifying our efforts to build up strong free nations, you refer particularly to the North Atlantic pact countries?

THE PRESIDENT. That's correct. Reporter: Thank you, Mr. President.

16. Address at the Jefferson-Jackson Day Dinner
March 29, 1952

Public Papers of the Presidents of the United States: Harry S. Truman, 1952. Washington, D.C.: U.S. Government Printing Office, 220–226.

Mr. Chairman, Mr. Vice President, Mr. Speaker, Mr. Chairman of the Democratic Committee, distinguished guests and fellow Democrats:

I am very happy to be here tonight. This makes seven Jefferson-Jackson dinners that I have spoken to in the city of Washington. I hope to attend several more, in one capacity or another.

They have all been wonderful dinners. One of the things I like about the dinners is the fact that they are political meetings. I like political meetings, and I like politics.

Politics—good politics—is public service. There is no life or occupation in which a man can find a greater opportunity to serve his community or his country.

I have been in politics more than 30 years, and I know that nothing else could have given me greater satisfaction. I have had a career from precinct to President, and I am a little bit proud of that career.

I am sure all of you here tonight are very much interested in the presidential election this year.

In view of that fact, I thought I would give you a little analysis of the political situation as I see it.

The political situation in this country may look complicated, but you can find the key to it in a simple thing: The Republicans have been out of office for 20 long years—and they are desperate to get back in office so they can control the country again.

For 20 years the Republicans have been wandering in a political desert—like camels looking for an oasis. They don't drink the same thing that camels do, though. And if they don't find it pretty soon, the Republican Party may die out, altogether.

And you know, I would just hate to see that happen. I would like to help keep the Republican Party alive, if that is at all possible. So I am going to offer them a little advice about the error of their ways.

There are some very good reasons why the Republicans have been out of office so long and haven't been able to get back in control.

The first reason is that they were voted out in 1932 because they had brought the country to the brink of ruin.

In the 1920's the Republican administrations drew back in petrified isolation from our world responsibilities. They spent all their time trying to help the rich get richer, and paid no attention to the welfare of the workers and the farmers. All in all, they paved the way for the biggest economic smashup this country has ever seen.

That is the reason the Republicans were thrown out of office in 1932 and one of the very good reasons why they have been kept out ever since. People don't want any more "Great Depressions."

The second reason why the Republicans have been out of office for 20 years is that the Demo-

cratic Party has been giving the country good government. Instead of trying to build up the prosperity of the favored few, and letting some of it trickle down to the rest, we have been working to raise the incomes of the vast majority of the people. And we have been steadily expanding the base for prosperity and freedom in this country. The people have kept right on reelecting Democrats because we have been serving them well and they know it.

The third reason the Republicans have been kept out of power for 20 years is because they have never been able to agree on a sensible program to put before the country. They have been on almost every side of every question, but they have seldom or never been on the right side.

In 1936 they said the New Deal was terrible and they were against it and all its works. And in the election that fall they just lost by a landslide.

In 1940 they admitted there might be some good in some parts of the New Deal, but they said you needed a Republican to run it. And they were overwhelmingly beaten again.

In 1944 the Republicans said the New Deal might have been good in its day, but it had gotten old and tired and it was no good any more. But the people didn't agree, and the Republicans were snowed under once more.

Now in 1948 they said—well, as a matter of fact, by 1948 they were so sure of winning that they really didn't bother to take a position on anything. And they got just exactly what they deserved—they got another good licking.

And by now the Republicans can't figure out what to do. Every day you hear a new Republican theory of how to win the election of 1952.

One theory they have is that they ought to come right out and say they are against all advances the country has made since 1932.

This is the kind of dinosaur school of Republican strategy. They want to go back to prehistoric times. Republicans of this school say: "Let's stop beating about the bush—and let's say what we really believe. Let's say we're against social security—and we're against the labor unions and good wages—and we're opposed to price supports for farmers—that we're against the Government doing anything for anybody except big business."

Now, I have a lot of sympathy for these Republicans. They have been hushed up for a long time. They would certainly be happier if they could tell the truth for once and campaign for what they really believe. It would be good for their souls. But it wouldn't be good for their party, or for the country either. This dinosaur school of Republican strategy would only get the dinosaur vote—and there are not many of them left, except over at the Smithsonian.

Next, there is the Republican theory that the Republicans can win if they oppose the foreign policy of the United States. They can't agree among themselves as to how they want to oppose it, but most of them want to oppose it somehow.

Some Republicans seem to think it would be popular to pull out of Korea, and to abandon Europe, and to let the United Nations go to smash. They reason this way: "The American people aren't very bright. Let's tell them they don't have to build up defenses, or serve in the Army, or strengthen our allies overseas. If they fall for that, then we Republicans will be in—and that's all that matters."

The trouble with the Republican theory is that the American people are a lot smarter than the Republicans who thought it up. The American people have learned a lot from two world wars and from the last 7 years of working to keep the peace. They know that as long as communism is loose in the world we must have allies and we must resist aggression. The American people are living in the atomic age, and they know that the ideas of the stone age won't work any more—if they ever did work.

And there is another group of Republicans who attack our foreign policy by advocating the "all-out" or "let's get it over with" theory. These are the Republicans who say they want to expand the fighting in Korea, and start dropping atomic bombs, and invite a new world war. They figure it's good politics to talk that way. They don't stop to count the cost. They think people don't understand that the hardest and bravest thing in the world is to work for peace—and not for war. But if war comes—and God forbid that it comes—if the showdown comes, these loud talkers would be the first people to run for the bomb shelters. And the voters know it.

None of these Republican theories of how to win the election holds much promise of success this year. All they show is that the platform that the Republicans write in Chicago in July will have to be a fearful and wonderful thing to cover all these different theories. It will have to be a bigger tent than the Ringling Brothers circus—and it will have to cover just about as many freaks. It has even become fashionable for the Republican candidates to saw

themselves in half and put part on each side of the fence. That would fit under the tent, too.

The real Republican campaign is not going to be fought on the issues. The Republicans are going to wage a campaign of phony propaganda. They are going to try what we might call the "white is black" and the "black is white" strategy. The reasoning behind it is this: The Republicans know that the Nation is strong and prosperous, that we are building up defenses against communism, that the Democratic administration has worked for the good of the people. The only chance for the Republicans, therefore, is to make the people think the facts aren't so. The job for the Republicans is to make people believe that white is black and black is white.

This is a pretty difficult way to win an election. It wouldn't appeal to anybody but very desperate Republican politicians. But the Republicans have some reason for thinking it might succeed. They will have the support of most of the press, and most of the radio commentators. And they may have the professional poll-takers with them again—as they were in 1948. The Republicans, as always, will have a lot of money. They have slick advertising experts. And they don't have too many scruples about how they use them. Remember that carpetbagger from Chicago who got convicted for the way he elected a Republican Senator in Maryland in 1950? They will try that all over the country.

The Republicans are all set to try this "white is black" technique. And this is the way it will work. First of all, they will try to make people believe that everything the Government has done for the country is socialism. They will go to the people and say: "Did you see that social security check you received the other day—you thought that was good for you, didn't you? That's just too bad! That's nothing in the world but socialism. Did you see that new flood control dam the Government is building over there for the protection of your property? Sorry—that's awful socialism! That new hospital that they are building is socialism. Price supports, more socialism for the farmers! Minimum wage laws? Socialism for labor! Socialism is bad for you, my friend. Everybody knows that. And here you are, with your new car, and your home, and better opportunities for the kids, and a television set—you are just surrounded by socialism!"

Now the Republicans say, "That's a terrible thing, my friend, and the only way out of this sinkhole of socialism is to vote for the Republican ticket."

And if you do that, you will probably have a garage and no car, a crystal radio set and no television—and probably not even a garage to live in, but a secondhand tent out on the lawn. I don't believe people are going to be fooled into that condition, because they went through it once before.

Now, do you think they can sell that bill of goods? This country today has more freedom for all its people than any country in the history of the world. And all the efforts of all the Republican politicians can't convince the people that this is socialism.

The next part of this "white is black" campaign is to try to make people believe that the Democratic Party is in favor of communism. That is an even tougher job than selling the socialism nonsense, but the Republicans are desperate, so they are going to try it.

Of course, we have spent billions of dollars to build up our defenses against communism; we have created an alliance of the free nations against communism; we are helping them to arm against communism; we have met and halted communism in Greece and Turkey, in Berlin and Austria, in Italy and Iran, and the most important of all, in Korea. We have fought communism abroad. We have fought communism at home. We have an FBI and a Central Intelligence Agency defending us against spies and saboteurs. The Federal loyalty program keeps Communists out of Government.

That's the record, and how do the Republicans propose to get around it? Here's what they will try to do. They will go to the voters and say, "Did you know the Government was full of Communists?" And the voters say, "No. What makes you say that?" And then the Republicans explain that somebody named Joe Doakes works for the Government, and he has a cousin who sells shoelaces, or a ribbon clerk in a department store, and this cousin has a wife who wrote an article, before Joe married her, that was printed in a magazine that also printed an article in favor of Chinese Communists—and they will continue that ad lib. This may sound very silly, and it is. But some political fakers spend all their time trying to pull the wool over the people's eyes with this sort of nonsense.

The real test of anti-communism is whether we are willing to devote our resources and our strength to stopping Communist aggression and saving free people from its horrible tyranny. This kind of anti-communism takes money and courage—and not just a lot of talk. The next time you hear some of this loud anti-Communist talk from our Republican friends, ask them how they voted—ask them how they voted on aid to Greece, ask them how they voted on the Marshall plan, ask them how they voted on the mutual security program. The chances are they voted to cut or cripple these all-important measures against communism.

I say to you in all seriousness, beware of those who pretend to be so violently anti-Communist in this country, and at the same time vote to appease communism abroad. In my book, that is talking out of both sides of the mouth at once; and I don't think the American people are going to be taken in by it.

The next part of the Republican "white is black" campaign is to try to fool the voters into thinking that the Democratic Party is dishonest—that the Government is full of grafters and thieves and all kinds of assorted crooks. To hear them talk you wouldn't think that there was an honest man in Washington. And that includes some of them, too, maybe.

Now, I want to say something very important to you about this issue of morality in government.

I stand for honest government. I have worked for it. I have probably done more for it than any other President. I have done more than any other President to reorganize the Government on an efficient basis, and to extend the civil service merit system. I hate corruption not only because it is bad in itself, but also because it is the deadly enemy of all things the Democratic Party has been doing all these years.

I hate corruption everywhere, but I hate it most of all in a Democratic officeholder, because that is a betrayal of all that the Democratic Party stands for.

Here is the reason. To me, morality in government means more than a mere absence of wrongdoing. It means a government that is fair to all. I think it is just as immoral for the Congress to enact special tax favors into law as it is for a tax official to connive in a crooked tax return. It is just as immoral to use the lawmaking power of: the Government to enrich the few at the expense of the many, as it is to steal money from the public treasury. That is stealing money from the public treasury.

All of us know, of course, about the scandals and corruption of the Republican officeholders in the 1920's. But to my mind the Veterans' Administration scandals, in those days, and the Teapot Dome steal, were no worse—no more immoral—than the tax laws of Andrew Mellon, or the attempt to sell Muscle Shoals to private owners. Legislation that favored the greed of monopoly and the trickery of Wall Street was a form of corruption that did the country four times as much harm as Teapot Dome ever did.

Private selfish interests are always trying to corrupt the Government in this way. Powerful financial groups are always trying to get favors for themselves.

Now, the Democratic administration has been fighting against these efforts to corrupt the powers of Government. We haven't always won, but we have never surrendered, and we never will.

For all these years, we have been fighting to use our natural resources for the benefit of the public, to develop our forests and our public oil reserves and our water power for the benefit of all, to raise the incomes of all our citizens, to protect the farmer and the worker against the power of monopoly.

And where have the Republicans been in this fight for morality in Government? Do they come out and vote with us to keep the special interests from robbing the public? Not at all. Most of them are on the other side.

It's the same thing when you come to the question of the conduct of Government officials. The Republicans make a great whoop and holier about the honesty of Federal employees, but they are usually the first to show up in a Government office asking for special favors for private interests, and in raising cain if they don't get them. These Republican gentlemen can't have it both ways—they can't be for morality on Tuesday and Thursday, and then be for special privileges for their clients on Monday, Wednesday, and Friday.

The press recently—for a wonder—has been giving some facts on this subject that have been very hard to get at.

I'm disgusted with these efforts to discredit and blacken the character and reputation of the whole Federal service. We have a higher percentage of Federal employees under civil service than ever before, and on the whole they are a finer, better type of men and women than we have ever had in the service before. It is just as much our duty to protect the innocent as it is to punish the guilty. If a man is accused, he ought to have his day in court, and I don't mean a kangaroo court, either.

I hate injustice just as much as I hate corruption.

Of course, we must always work to keep our Government clean. Our Democratic Senators and Congressmen have been working and I have been working to clean up bad conditions where they exist, and to devise procedures and systems to prevent them in the future. And I would like to have help in this fight from everybody, Democrats and Republicans alike. I have just got one reorganization plan through the Congress, and I am going to send up some more plans to the Congress soon—to put more of our Federal officials under civil service and out of politics. I would like to see how many of the Republicans vote for them.

I don't think the "black is white" campaign of the Republican Party is going to succeed. I think the voters are going to see through this holier-than-thou disguise that our Republican friends are putting on.

All the tricks of Republican propaganda cannot make the people forget that the Democratic Party has been working for their welfare.

We are working for the welfare of the farmer. We hold to the ideal that goes back to Jefferson, that a farmer should have the opportunity to own his farm, to share in the benefits of scientific progress, and to secure a fair income for his efforts.

The Democratic Party is working for the success of our free enterprise system. We have worked to prevent monopoly, to give the small businessman a fair chance, and to develop our natural resources for all the people, and not just for the favored few.

The Democratic Party is working for the welfare of labor. We have worked for good wages and hour legislation, for unemployment compensation, and for fair labor relations laws.

The Democratic Party is dedicated to the ideal that every family is entitled to fair opportunities for decent living conditions, to a chance to educate their children, to have good medical services, and reasonable provision for retirement. That is why we have worked for good social security laws, for better education and health services, for good housing, and for equal rights and opportunities for all our people, regardless of color, religion, or national origin.

Above all, the Democratic Party is working for peace on earth and goodwill among men. We believe that war is not inevitable, that peace can be won, that free men of all lands can find the way to live together in the world as good neighbors. That is why we have been willing to sacrifice to stop aggression, willing to send our money and our goods to help men in other countries stand up against tyranny, willing to fight in Korea to stop World War III before it begins. For if the bloody harvest of world war were to begin anew, most of us would never see a peaceful world again.

This is the record of the Democratic Party. It is a proud record, and an honorable record. It is a record of progress, of actions that are right because they are solidly founded on American ideals.

Whoever the Democrats nominate for President this year, he will have this record to run upon.

I shall not be a candidate for reelection. I have served my country long, and I think efficiently and honestly. I shall not accept a renomination. I do not feel that it is my duty to spend another 4 years in the White House.

We must always remember the things the Democratic Party has done, and the high ideals that have made it great. We must be true to its principles and keep it foremost in service of the people.

If we do that, we can be sure that there will be a Democratic President in the White House for the next 4 years.

SELECTED BIBLIOGRAPHY

Abramson, Rudy. *Spanning the Century: The Life of W. Averell Harriman, 1891–1986*. New York: Morrow, 1992.

Acheson, Dean. *Present at the Creation: My Years in the State Department*. New York: W. W. Norton, 1969.

Allen, Thomas B., and Norman Polmar. *Code-Name Downfall: The Secret Plan to Invade Japan and Why Truman Dropped the Bomb*. New York: Simon & Schuster, 1995.

Allen, Oliver E. The Tiger: *The Rise and Fall of Tammany Hall*. Reading, Mass.: Addison-Wesley, 1993.

Alperovitz, Gar. *The Decision to Use the Atomic Bomb and the Architecture of an American Myth*. New York: Knopf, 1995.

Ambrose, Stephen E. *Soldier, General of the Army, President-Elect, 1890–1952*. Vol. 1 of *Eisenhower*. New York: Simon & Schuster, 1983.

Baker, Leonard. *Brandeis and Frankfurter: A Dual Biography*. New York: Harper & Row, 1984.

Barlow, Jeffrey G. *Revolt of the Admirals: The Fight for Naval Aviation, 1945–1950*. Washington, D.C.: Naval Historical Center, 1994.

Bass, Jack Solomon. "A Biography of Strom Thurmond." Ph.D. diss., Emory University, 1998.

Biles, Roger. *Crusading Liberal: Paul H. Douglas of Illinois*. DeKalb: Northern Illinois University Press, 2002.

Billingsley, Lloyd. *Hollywood Party: How Communism Seduced the American Film Industry in the 1930s and 1940s*. Rocklin, Calif.: Forum, 1998.

Bird, Kai. *The Chairman: John J. McCloy, the Making of the American Establishment*. New York: Simon & Schuster, 1992.

Blair, Clay. *The Forgotten War: America in Korea, 1950–1953*. New York: Times Books, 1987.

Brill, Steven. *The Teamsters*. New York: Simon & Schuster, 1978.

Broadwater, Jeff. *Adlai Stevenson and American Politics: The Odyssey of a Cold War Liberal*. New York: Twayne, 1994.

Caro, Robert A. *Master of the Senate*. Vol. 3 of *The Years of Lyndon Johnson*. New York: Knopf 2002.

———. *Means of Ascent*. Vol. 3 of *The Years of Lyndon Johnson*. New York: Knopf, 1990.

Caute, David. *The Great Fear*. New York: Simon & Schuster, 1978.

Chace, James. *Acheson: The Secretary of State Who Created the American World*. New York: Simon & Schuster, 1998.

Chambers, Whittaker. *Witness*. New York: Random House, 1952.

Clifford, Clark, with Richard Holbrooke. *Counsel to the President: A Memoir*. New York: Random House, 1991.

Cohen, Michael J. *Truman and Israel*. Berkeley: University of California Press, 1990.

Condit, Doris M. *The Test of War, 1950–1953*. Vol. 2 of *History of the Office of the Secretary of Defense*, edited by Alfred Goldberg. Washington, D.C.: Historical Office, Office of the Secretary of Defense, 1988.

Cook, James F. *Carl Vinson: Patriarch of the Armed Forces*. Macon, Ga.: Mercer University Press, 2004.

Craig, R. Bruce. *Treasonable Doubt: The Harry Dexter White Spy Case*. Lawrence: University Press of Kansas, 2004.

Cray, Ed. *Chief Justice: A Biography of Earl Warren*. New York: Simon & Schuster, 1997.

Culver, John C., and John Hyde. *American Dreamer: The Life and Times of Henry A. Wallace*. New York: Norton, 2000.

Cumings, Bruce. *Liberation and the Emergence of Separate Regimes, 1945–1947*. Vol. 1 of *The Origins of the Korean War*. Princeton, N.J.: Princeton University Press, 1981.

———. *The Roaring of the Cataract, 1947–1950*. Vol. 2 of *The Origins of the Korean War*. Princeton, N.J.: Princeton University Press, 1990.

Danese, Tracy E. *Claude Pepper and Ed Ball: Politics, Purpose, and Power*. Gainesville: University Press of Florida, 2000.

Davies, Richard O. *Defender of the Old Guard: John Bricker and American Politics*. Columbus: Ohio State University Press, 1993.

Davis, Polly Ann. *Alben W. Barkley: Senate Majority Leader and Vice President*. New York: Garland, 1979.

Dierenfield, Bruce J. *Keeper of the Rules: Congressman Howard W. Smith of Virginia*. Charlottesville: University Press of Virginia, 1987.

Diggins, John Patrick. *The Proud Decades: America in War and Peace, 1941–1960*. New York: W. W. Norton, 1988.

Donovan, Robert J. *Conflict and Crisis*. Vol. 1 of *The Presidency of Harry S Truman, 1945–1948*. New York: W. W. Norton, 1977.

———. *Tumultuous Years*. Vol. 2 of *The Presidency of Harry S Truman 1949–1953*. New York: W. W. Norton, 1982.

Duberman, Martin B. *Paul Robeson*. New York: Knopf, 1989.

Dubofsky, Melvyn, and Warren Van Tine. *John L. Lewis*. New York: Quadrangle/New York Times Book Co., 1977.

Dunar, Andrew J. *The Truman Scandals and the Politics of Morality.* Columbia: University of Missouri Press, 1984.

Edwards, Jerome E. *Pat McCarran, Political Boss of Nevada.* Reno: University of Nevada Press, 1982.

Ferrell, Robert H. *Harry S. Truman: A Life.* Columbia: University of Missouri Press, 1994.

———. *Choosing Truman: The Democratic Convention of 1944.* Columbia: University of Missouri Press, 1994.

Fine, Sidney. *The Washington Years.* Vol. 3 of *Frank Murphy.* Ann Arbor: University of Michigan Press, 1984.

Fite, Gilbert Courtland. *Richard B. Russell, Jr., Senator from Georgia.* Chapel Hill: University of North Carolina Press, 1991.

Fossedal, Gregory A. *Our Finest Hour: Will Clayton, the Marshall Plan, and the Triumph of Democracy.* Stanford, Calif.: Hoover Institution Press, 1993.

Fredickson, Kari. *The Dixiecrat Revolt and the End of the Solid South, 1932–1968.* Chapel Hill: University of North Carolina Press, 2001.

Fried, Richard M. *Nightmare in Red: The McCarthy Era in Perspective.* New York: Oxford University Press, 1990.

Friedman, Leon, and Fred L. Israel. *The Justices of the United States Supreme Court: Their Lives and Major Opinions.* New York: Chelsea House Publishers, 1969.

Gabler, Neal. *Winchell: Gossip, Power and the Culture of Celebrity.* New York: Knopf, 1994.

Gaddis, John Lewis. *The United States and the Origins of the Cold War, 1941–1947.* New York: Columbia University Press, 1972.

———. *We Now Know: Rethinking Cold War History.* New York: Oxford University Press, 1997.

Garrettson, Charles Lloyd. *Hubert H. Humphrey: The Politics of Joy.* New Brunswick, N.J.: Transaction Publishers, 1993.

Gellman, Irwin F. *The Contender: Richard Nixon: The Congress Years, 1946–1952.* New York: Free Press, 1999.

Gullan, Harold I. *The Upset That Wasn't: Harry S. Truman and the Crucial Election of 1948.* Chicago: Ivan R. Dee, 1998.

Hamby, Alonzo L. *A Man of the People: A Life of Harry S. Truman.* New York: Oxford University Press, 1995.

———. *Beyond the New Deal: Truman and American Liberalism.* New York: Columbia University Press, 1973.

Harbutt, Fraser J. *The Iron Curtain: Churchill, America, and the Origins of the Cold War.* New York: Oxford University Press, 1986.

Hardeman, D. B., and Donald C. Bacon. *Rayburn: A Biography.* Austin: Texas Monthly Press, 1987.

Haynes, John Earl, and Harvey Klehr. *Venona: Decoding Soviet Espionage in America.* New Haven, Conn.: Yale University Press, 1999.

Heinemann, Ronald L. *Harry Byrd of Virginia.* Charlottesville: University Press of Virginia, 1996.

Herken, Gregg. *Brotherhood of the Bomb: The Tangled Lives and Loyalties of Robert Oppenheimer, Ernest Lawrence, and Edward Teller.* New York: Henry Holt, 2002.

Herman, Arthur. *Joseph McCarthy: Reexamining the Life and Legacy of America's Most Hated Senator.* New York: Free Press, 2000.

Hoff Wilson, Joan. *Herbert Hoover: Forgotten Progressive.* Boston: Little, Brown, 1975.

Hogan, Michael J. *A Cross of Iron: Harry S. Truman and the Origins of the National Security State, 1945–1954.* Cambridge: Cambridge University Press, 1998.

———. *The Marshall Plan: America, Britain, and the Reconstruction of Western Europe, 1947–1952.* Cambridge: Cambridge University Press, 1987.

Hoopes, Townsend, and Douglas Brinkley. *Driven Patriot: The Life and Times of James Forrestal.* New York: Knopf, 1992.

Howard, J. Woodford, Jr. *Mr. Justice Murphy: A Political Biography.* Princeton, N.J.: Princeton University Press, 1968.

Isaacson, Walter, and Evan Thomas. *The Wise Men: Six Friends and the World They Made: Acheson, Bohlen, Harriman, Kennan, Lovett, McCloy.* Simon & Schuster, 1986.

James, D. Clayton, with Anne Sharp Wells. *Refighting the Last War: Command and Crisis in Korea, 1950–1953.* New York: Free Press, 1993.

James, D. Clayton. *Triumph and Disaster, 1945–1964.* Vol. 3 of *The Years of MacArthur.* Boston: Houghton Mifflin, 1985.

Janken, Kenneth Robert. *White: The Biography of Walter White, Mr. NAACP.* New York: New Press, 2003.

Jensen, Kenneth M., ed. *The Origins of the Cold War: The Novikov, Kennan, and Roberts Long Telegrams of 1946.* Rev. ed. Washington, D.C.: United States Institute of Peace Press, 1993.

Jensen, Vernon H. *Strife on the Waterfront: The Port of New York since 1945.* Ithaca, N.Y.: Cornell University Press, 1974.

Jerome, Fred. *The Einstein File: J. Edgar Hoover's Secret War against the World's Most Famous Scientist.* New York: St. Martin's Griffin, 2002.

Jones, Howard. *"A New Kind of War": America's Global Strategy and the Truman Doctrine in Greece.* New York: Oxford University Press, 1989.

Kaplan, Lawrence S. *The United States and NATO: The Formative Years.* Lexington: University Press of Kentucky, 1984.

Karabell, Zachary. *Architects of Intervention: The United States, the Third World, and the Cold War, 1946–1962.* Baton Rouge: Louisiana State University Press, 1999.

Kennan, George F. *Memoirs.* 2 vols. Boston: Little, Brown, 1967, 1972.

Kepley, David R. *The Collapse of the Middle Way: Senate Republicans and the Bipartisan Foreign Policy, 1948–1952.* New York: Greenwood Press, 1988.

Kettl, Donald F. *Leadership at the Fed.* New Haven, Conn.: Yale University Press, 1986.

Kirby, Alexander B. "Childe Harold's Pilgrimage: A Political Biography of Harold Stassen." Ph.D. diss., George Washington University, 1992.

Klehr, Harvey, and Ronald Radosh. *The Amerasia Spy Case: Prelude to McCarthyism.* Chapel Hill: University of North Carolina Press, 1996.

Kuniholm, Bruce Robellet. *The Origins of the Cold War in the Near East: Great Power Conflict and Diplomacy in Iran, Turkey, and Greece.* Princeton, N.J.: Princeton University Press, 1980.

Leffler, Melvyn P. *A Preponderance of Power: National Security, the Truman Administration, and the Cold War.* Stanford, Calif.: Stanford University Press 1991.

———. *The Specter of Communism: The United States and the Origins of the Cold War, 1917–1953.* New York: Hill and Wang, 1994.

Levering, Ralph B., et. al. *Debating the Origins of the Cold War: American and Russian Perspectives.* Lanham, Md.: Rowman & Littlefield Publishers, 2002.

Lichtenstein, Nelson. *Walter Reuther: The Most Dangerous Man in Detroit.* Urbana: University of Illinois Press, 1995.

Malsberger, John W. *From Obstruction to Moderation: The Transformation of Senate Conservatism, 1938–1952.* Cranbury, N.J.: Susquehanna University Press, 2000.

Marcus, Maeva. *Truman and the Steel Seizure Case.* New York: Columbia University Press, 1977.

Matusow, Allen J. *Farm Policies and Politics in the Truman Administration.* Cambridge, Mass.: Harvard University Press, 1967.

May, Ernest, ed. *American Cold War Strategy: Interpreting NSC 68.* Boston: Bedford Books of St. Martin's Press, 1993.

May, Gary. *China Scapegoat: The Diplomatic Ordeal of John Carter Vincent.* Washington, D.C.: New Republic Books, 1979.

McClure, Arthur F. *The Truman Administration and the Problems of Postwar Labor, 1945–1948.* Rutherford, N.J.: Fairleigh Dickinson University Press, 1969.

McCoy, Donald R. *The Presidency of Harry S. Truman.* Lawrence: University Press of Kansas, 1984.

McCoy, Donald R., and Richard Ruetten. *Quest and Response: Minority Rights in the Truman Administration.* Lawrence: University Press of Kansas, 1973.

McCullough, David. *Truman.* New York: Simon & Schuster, 1992.

McLellan, David S. *Dean Acheson: The State Department Years.* New York: Dodd, Mead, 1976.

Meyer, Gerald. *Vito Marcantonio: Radical Politician, 1902–1954.* Albany: State University of New York Press, 1989.

Meyers, Jeffrey. *Edmund Wilson: A Biography.* Boston: Houghton Mifflin, 1995.

Miscamble, Wilson D. *George F. Kennan and the Making of American Foreign Policy, 1947–1950.* Princeton, N.J.: Princeton University Press, 1992.

Montague, Ludwell Lee. *General Walter Bedell Smith as Director of Central Intelligence, October 1950–February 1953.* University Park: Pennsylvania State University Press, 1992.

Morris, Roger. *Richard Milhous Nixon: The Rise of an American Politician.* New York: Henry Holt, 1990.

Murphy, Bruce Allen. *Wild Bill: The Legend and Life of William O. Douglas.* New York: Random House, 2003.

Namorato, Michael V. *Rexford G. Tugwell: A Biography.* New York: Praeger, 1988.

Newman, Roger K. *Hugo Black: A Biography.* New York: Pantheon, 1994.

Nitze, Paul H., with Ann M. Smith and Steven L. Rearden. *From Hiroshima to Glasnost: at the Center of Decision: A Memoir.* New York: Weidenfeld, 1989.

Offner, Arnold A. *Another Such Victory: President Truman and the Cold War, 1945–1953.* Stanford, Calif.: Stanford University Press, 2002.

Olmsted, Kathryn S. *Red Spy Queen: A Biography of Elizabeth Bentley.* Chapel Hill: University of North Carolina Press, 2002.

Paterson, Thomas G. *The Origins of the Cold War.* 3rd ed. Lexington, Mass.: D. C. Heath and Co., 1991.

Patterson, James T. *Grand Expectations: The United States, 1945–1974.* New York: Oxford University Press, 1996.

———. *Mr. Republican.* Boston: Houghton Mifflin, 1972.

Pierpaoli, Paul G. *Truman and Korea: The Political Culture of the Early Cold War.* Columbia: University of Missouri Press, 1999.

Poder, Michael Paul. "The Senatorial Career of William E. Jenner." Ph.D. diss., University of Notre Dame, 1976.

Pogue, Forrest C. *George C. Marshall: Statesman, 1945–1959.* New York: Viking, 1987.

Radosh, Ronald, and Joyce Milton Radosh. *The Rosenberg File.* 2nd ed. New Haven, Conn.: Yale University Press, 1997.

Rampersad, Arnold. *Jackie Robinson: A Biography.* New York: Knopf, 1997.

Ranelagh, John. *The Agency: The Rise and Decline of the CIA.* New York: Simon & Schuster, 1986.

Rearden, Steven L. *The Formative Years, 1947–1950.* Vol. 2 of *History of the Office of the Secretary of Defense,* edited by Alfred Goldberg. Washington, D.C.: Historical Office, Office of the Secretary of Defense, 1984.

Reeves, Thomas C. *The Life and Times of Joe McCarthy: A Biography.* New York: Stein and Day, 1982.

Reich, Cary. *The Life of Nelson A. Rockefeller, 1908–1958: Worlds to Conquer.* New York: Doubleday, 1996.

Reichard, Gary W. *Politics As Usual: The Age of Truman and Eisenhower.* 2nd ed. Arlington Heights, Ill.: Harlan Davidson 2004.

Rhodes, Richard. *Dark Sun: The Making of the Hydrogen Bomb.* New York: Simon & Schuster, 1995.

———. *The Making of the Atomic Bomb.* New York: Simon & Schuster, 1986.

Robertson, David. *Sly and Able: A Political Biography of James F. Byrnes.* New York: W. W. Norton, 1994.

Romerstein, Herbert, and Eric Breindel. *The Venona Secrets: Exposing Soviet Espionage and America's Traitors.* Washington, D.C.: Regnery Pub., 2000.

Rose, Lisle Abbott. *The Cold War Comes to Main Street: America in 1950.* Lawrence: University Press of Kansas, 1999.

Savage, Sean J. *Truman and the Democratic Party.* Lexington: University Press of Kentucky, 1997.

Schaller, Michael. *Douglas MacArthur: The Far Eastern General.* New York: Oxford University Press, 1989.

———. *The American Occupation of Japan: The Origins of the Cold War in Asia.* New York: Oxford University Press, 1985.

Schrecker, Ellen. *Many Are the Crimes: McCarthyism in America.* Boston: Little, Brown, 1998.

Schwartzberg, Steven. *Democracy and U.S. Policy in Latin America during the Truman Years.* Gainesville: University Press of Florida, 2003.

Sherman, Janann. *No Place for a Woman: A Life of Senator Margaret Chase Smith*. New Brunswick, N.J.: Rutgers University Press, 2000.

Sherrill, Robert. *Gothic Politics in the Deep South*. New York: Grossman Publishers, 1968.

Simon, James F. *Independent Journey: The Life of William O. Douglas*. New York: Harper & Row, 1980.

Smith, Jean Edward. *Lucius D. Clay: An American Life*. New York: Holt, 1990.

Smith, Richard Norton. *Thomas E. Dewey and His Times*. New York: Simon & Schuster, 1982.

Spritzer, Donald E. *Senator James E. Murray and the Limits of Post-war Liberalism*. New York: Garland, 1985.

St. Clair, James, and Linda Gugin. *Chief Justice Fred M. Vinson of Kentucky: A Political Biography*. Lexington: University Press of Kentucky, 2002.

Steel, Ronald. *Walter Lippmann and the American Century*. Boston: Little, Brown, 1980.

Stein, Herbert. *The Fiscal Revolution in America*. Chicago: University of Chicago Press, 1969.

Stromer, Marvin E. *The Making of a Political Leader: Kenneth S. Wherry and the United States Senate*. Lincoln: University of Nebraska Press, 1969.

Stueck, William. *Rethinking the Korean War: A New Diplomatic and Strategic History*. Princeton, N.J.: Princeton University Press, 2002.

———. *The Korean War: An International History*. Princeton, N.J.: Princeton University Press, 1995.

Swanberg, W.A. *Norman Thomas: The Last Idealist*. New York: Scribner, 1976.

Tanenhaus, Sam. *Whittaker Chambers: A Biography*. New York: Random House, 1997.

Theoharis, Athan G., and John Stuart Cox. *The Boss: J. Edgar Hoover and the Great American Inquisition*. Philadelphia: Temple University Press, 1988.

Thornton, Richard C. *Odd Man Out: Truman, Stalin, Mao, and the Origins of the Korean War*. Washington, D.C.: Brassey's, 2000.

Truman, Harry S. *Memoirs by Harry S. Truman*. 2 vols. Garden City, N.Y.: Doubleday, 1955–1956.

Truman, Margaret. *Bess W. Truman*. New York: Macmillan, 1986.

Tusa, Ann, and John Tusa. *The Berlin Airlift*. New York: Atheneum, 1988.

Tushnet, Mark V. *Making Civil Rights Law: Thurgood Marshall and the Supreme Court, 1936–1961*. New York: Oxford University Press, 1994.

Tygiel, Jules. *Baseball's Great Experiment: Jackie Robinson and His Legacy*. New York: Oxford University Press, 1983.

Weinstein, Allen. *Perjury: The Hiss-Chambers Case*. New York: Knopf, 1978.

Weinstein, Allen, and Alexander Vassiliev. *The Haunted Wood: Soviet Espionage in America—The Stalin Era*. New York: Random House, 1999.

Whitfield, Stephen J. *The Culture of the Cold War*. Baltimore: Johns Hopkins University Press, 1991.

Woods, Randall B., and Howard Jones. *Dawning of the Cold War: The United States' Quest for Order*. Athens: University of Georgia Press, 1991.

Ybarra, Michael J. *Washington Gone Crazy: Senator Pat McCarran and the Great American Communist Hunt*. Hanover, N.H.: Steerforth Press, 2004.

Yergin, Daniel. *Shattered Peace: The Origins of the Cold War and the National Security State*. Boston: Houghton Mifflin, 1977.

Young, Nancy Beck. *Wright Patman: Populism, Liberalism, and the American Dream*. Dallas, Tex.: Southern Methodist University Press, 2000.

Youngs, J. William T. *Eleanor Roosevelt: A Personal and Public Life*. Boston: Little, Brown, 1985.

Zelizer, Julian E. *Taxing America: Wilbur D. Mills, Congress, and the State, 1945–1975*. Cambridge: Cambridge University Press, 1998.

Zieger, Robert H. *The CIO: 1935–1955*. Chapel Hill: University of North Carolina Press, 1995.

INDEX

Boldface page numbers indicate primary discussions. *Italic* page numbers indicate illustrations.